Statistics Canada

Profile of Census Divisions and Subdivisions in Ontario

Volume 1 of 3

Statistique Canada

Profil des divisions et subdivisions de recensement de l'Ontario

Volume 1 de 3

Published by authority of the Minister responsible for Statistics Canada

April 2009

Catalogue no. 95-550-XPB

Frequency: occasional

ISBN 978-0-660-63523-1

Ottawa

Note of appreciation

Canada owes the success of its statistical system to a long-standing partnership between Statistics Canada, the citizens of Canada, its businesses, governments and other institutions. Accurate and timely statistical information could not be produced without their continued cooperation and goodwill.

Publication autorisée par le ministre responsable de Statistique Canada

Avril 2009

N° 95-550-XPB au catalogue

Périodicité : hors série

ISBN 978-0-660-63523-1

Ottawa

Note de reconnaissance

Le succès du système statistique du Canada repose sur un partenariat bien établi entre Statistique Canada et la population, les entreprises, les administrations canadiennes et les autres organismes. Sans cette collaboration et cette bonne volonté, il serait impossible de produire des statistiques précises et actuelles.

Library and Archives Canada Cataloguing in Publication Data

Profile of census divisions and subdivisions in Ontario = Profil des divisions et subdivisions de recensement de l'Ontario

Complete in 3 v.
Text in English and French.
ISBN 978-0-660-63523-1
CS95-550-XPB

1. Census districts - Ontario - Statistics. 2. Ontario - Population - Statistics. 3. Canada - Census, 2006. I. Statistics Canada.
II. Title: Profil des divisions et subdivisions de recensement de l'Ontario.

HA741.5.2006 304.609713'021
C2008-988049-8E

Données de catalogage avant publication de la Bibliothèque et Archives Canada

Profile of census divisions and subdivisions in Ontario = Profil des divisions et subdivisions de recensement de l'Ontario

Complet en 3 v.
Texte en anglais et en français.
ISBN 978-0-660-63523-1
CS95-550-XPB

1. Districts de recensement - Ontario - Statistiques. 2. Ontario - Statistiques démographiques. 3. Canada - Recensement, 2006. I. Statistique Canada. II. Titre : Profil des divisions et subdivisions de recensement de l'Ontario.

HA741.5.2006 304.609713'021
C2008-988049-8F

Source: Statistics Canada, 2006 Census of Population.

How to cite:

Statistics Canada. 2009. *Profile of Census Divisions and Subdivisions in Ontario*. Vol. 1 of 3. 2006 Census. Statistics Canada Catalogue no. 95-550-XPB. Ottawa.

The paper used in this publication meets the minimum requirements of American National Standard for Information Sciences – Permanence of Paper for Printed Library Materials, ANSI Z39.48 – 1984.

∞

Source : STATISTIQUE CANADA, Recensement de la population de 2006.

Comment citer :

STATISTIQUE CANADA. 2009. *Profil des divisions et subdivisions de recensement de l'Ontario,* vol. 1 de 3, Recensement de 2006, produit no 95-550-XPB au catalogue de Statistique Canada, Ottawa.

Le papier utilisé dans la présente publication répond aux exigences minimales de l'« American National Standard for Information Sciences » – « Permanence of Paper for Printed Library Materials », ANSI Z39.48 – 1984.

∞

Table of contents

Table des matières

Introduction

The 2006 Census divisions and subdivisions profiles are designed to provide a statistical overview, or profile, for lower levels of geography. Each publication in this series provides a profile of census divisions and census subdivisions in a province or territory. The census divisions and census subdivisions profiles are based on data collected by the 2006 Census of Canada from all households.

The 2006 Census divisions and subdivisions profiles contain population counts for characteristics from both 100% data and 20% sample data, in each publication. New for 2006 is data on location of study. This series also contains incidence reporting for single- or multiple-response variables. Incidence reporting will display specific categories based on the most frequently reported responses in a province or territory. The variables affected by incidence reporting are mother tongue, language spoken most often at home, knowledge of non-official languages, language used most often at work and ethnic origin.

Each publication in this series consists of a single table displaying the data for geographic areas in a columnar format. The data variables, also referred to as "stubs", are displayed in English on the left side of the table and in French on the right side. With the combination of variables from the 100% and 20% databases, the stubset covers 24 pages. Characteristics of the data have been grouped into blocks by theme, or universe (i.e. population, dwelling and household, family and income). Within each theme, the data are displayed showing different characteristics such as marital status, ethnic origin and census family structure. Unless otherwise indicated, 'number' is the unit of measure used in the table.

The geographic headings run across the top of the page. The census divisions are presented in alphabetical order for each province or territory. For each census division, the census subdivisions are again listed alphabetically. Columns containing the data for Canada and the province or territory are also shown. The user is advised to refer to the Geographic index of census divisions and census subdivisions at the beginning of each publication. It includes a reference to the page number for the corresponding data.

Definitions of the geographic areas and variables displayed in each publication can be found in the Reference material section. Also provided at the end of each publication are data quality notes and special notes.

Introduction

Les Profils des divisions et subdivisions du Recensement de 2006 sont conçus de façon à fournir un aperçu statistique, ou profil, de petites régions géographiques. Chaque publication de cette série fournit un profil des divisions de recensement et des subdivisions de recensement d'une province ou d'un territoire. Les Profils des divisions et subdivisions du recensement sont fondés sur les données du Recensement du Canada de 2006 pour tous les ménages.

Les Profils des divisions et subdivisions de Recensement de 2006 contiennent les chiffres de la population selon des caractéristiques des données intégrales (100 %) et des données-échantillon (20 %), réunies dans chaque publication. Du nouveau pour 2006 : il y a des données portant sur le lieu des études. Cette série comprend également des fréquences de déclaration pour les variables à réponses uniques et à réponses multiples. La fréquence de déclaration verra certaines catégories présentées selon les réponses le plus souvent déclarées dans une province ou un territoire. Les variables touchées par la fréquence de déclaration sont la langue maternelle, la langue parlée le plus souvent à la maison, la connaissance des langues non officielles, la langue utilisée le plus souvent au travail et l'origine ethnique.

Chaque publication de cette série consiste en un seul tableau auquel figurent, sous forme de colonnes, les données pour les régions géographiques. Les variables de données, ou « titres », sont affichées en anglais du côté gauche du tableau et en français du côté droit. L'ensemble de titres résultant de la combinaison des variables provenant de la base de données intégrales (100 %) et de la base de données-échantillon (20 %) compte 24 pages. Les caractéristiques des données ont été regroupées en blocs, selon des thèmes ou univers (c'est-à-dire la population, les logements et les ménages, les familles et le revenu). À partir de chacun de ces thèmes, les données sont affichées de façon à souligner les diverses caractéristiques telles l'état matrimonial, l'origine ethnique et la structure de la famille de recensement. À moins d'indication contraire, « nombre » est l'unité de mesure utilisée dans le tableau.

Les en-têtes géographiques figurent d'un côté à l'autre du haut de la page. Les divisions de recensement sont présentées selon l'ordre alphabétique pour la province ou le territoire dont il est question. Pour chacune des divisions de recensement, les subdivisions sont, une fois de plus, listées selon l'ordre alphabétique. Les colonnes contenant les données pour le Canada et la province ou le territoire sont également présentes. Les utilisateurs sont priés de consulter l'Index géographique des divisions de recensement et subdivisions de recensement au début de chaque publication. L'index comporte un renvoi à la page dans laquelle figurent les données correspondantes.

Les définitions des régions géographiques et des variables comprises dans chaque publication apparaissent dans la section sur les Documents de référence. On retrouve aussi les notes sur la qualité des données et les notes spéciales à la fin de chaque publication.

Symbols

The following symbols are found in this publication.

... not applicable.

0 true zero or a value rounded to zero.

x suppressed to meet the confidentiality requirements of the *Statistics Act*.

E use with caution.

Care should be exercised in comparing the Northwest Territories 2006 Census population counts with counts from the 2001 Census. In 2001, the net undercount for the Northwest Territories was estimated at 8.11%, substantially higher than the national level of 2.99%, and almost double its 1996 level. The increase in the population between 2001 and 2006 is likely overstated due to improvements in coverage of the Northwest Territories in 2006.

F too unreliable to be published.

A adjusted figure due to boundary change.

¶ Incompletely enumerated Indian reserve or Indian settlement (suppressed).

† excludes census data for one or more incompletely enumerated Indian reserves or Indian settlements.

◆ data quality index showing, for the short census questionnaire (100% data), a global non-response rate higher than or equal to 5% but lower than 10%.

◆◆ data quality index showing, for the short census questionnaire (100% data), a global non-response rate higher than or equal to 10% but lower than 25%.

◆◆◆ data quality index showing, for the short census questionnaire (100% data), a global non-response rate higher than or equal to 25% (suppressed).

◇ data quality index showing, for the long census questionnaire (20% sample data), a global non-response rate higher than or equal to 5% but lower than 10%.

◇◇ data quality index showing, for the long census questionnaire (20% sample data), a global non-response rate higher than or equal to 10% but lower than 25%.

Symboles

Les symboles suivants sont retrouvés dans cette publication.

... n'ayant pas lieu de figurer.

0 zéro absolu ou valeur arrondie à zéro.

x confidentiel en vertu des dispositions de la *Loi sur la statistique*.

E à utiliser avec prudence.

Il importe de faire preuve de circonspection lorsqu'on compare les chiffres de population des Territoires du Nord-Ouest du Recensement de 2006 avec ceux du Recensement de 2001. En effet, en 2001, le sous-dénombrement net pour les Territoires du Nord-Ouest a été estimé à 8,11 %, ce qui est beaucoup plus élevé que le taux national de 2,99 %, et représente presque le double du sous-dénombrement estimé en 1996. L'accroissement de la population entre 2001 et 2006 est probablement surévalué en raison de l'amélioration de la couverture dans les Territoires du Nord-Ouest en 2006.

F trop peu fiable pour être publié.

A chiffre ajusté à cause de changement de limite.

¶ Réserve indienne ou établissement indien partiellement dénombré (supprimées).

† ne comprend pas les données du recensement pour une ou plusieurs réserves indiennes ou établissements indiens partiellement dénombrés.

◆ indice de la qualité des données indiquant, pour le questionnaire de recensement abrégé (données intégrales [100 %]), un taux global de non-réponse supérieur ou égal à 5 %, mais inférieur à 10 %.

◆◆ indice de la qualité des données indiquant, pour le questionnaire de recensement abrégé (données intégrales [100 %]), un taux global de non-réponse supérieur ou égal à 10 %, mais inférieur à 25 %.

◆◆◆ indice de la qualité des données indiquant, pour le questionnaire de recensement abrégé (données intégrales [100 %]), un taux global de non-réponse supérieur ou égal à 25 % (supprimées).

◇ indice de la qualité des données indiquant, pour le questionnaire de recensement complet (données-échantillon [20 %]), un taux global de non-réponse supérieur ou égal à 5 %, mais inférieur à 10 %.

◇◇ indice de la qualité des données indiquant, pour le questionnaire de recensement complet (données-échantillon [20 %]), un taux global de non-réponse supérieur ou égal à 10 %, mais inférieur à 25 %.

Symbols (continued)

◇◇◇ data quality index showing, for the long census questionnaire (20% sample data), a global non-response rate higher than or equal to 25% (suppressed).

■ An error exists in the 2006 population and dwelling counts for this area. For further information, refer to the 'Special notes' section.

■■ In 2001, the population and/or dwelling counts for this census subdivision were found to be incorrect. Since it is not possible to make changes to the 2001 Census data presented in these tables, the 2001 data should be used with caution. For further information, refer to the 'Special notes' section.

■■■ Both the 2006 and 2001 population and/or dwelling counts for this area were found to be incorrect. Since it is not possible to make changes to the census data presented in these tables, these counts should be used with caution. For further information, refer to the 'Special notes' section.

• part of a census tract.

Symboles (suite)

◇◇◇ indice de la qualité des données indiquant, pour le questionnaire de recensement complet (données-échantillon [20 %]), un taux global de non-réponse supérieur ou égal à 25 % (supprimées).

■ Il y a une erreur dans les chiffres de population et des logements de 2006 pour cette région. Pour de plus amples renseignements, veuillez consulter la section « Notes spéciales ».

■■ En 2001, les chiffres de population et/ou des logements sont erronés pour cette subdivision de recensement. Étant donné qu'il n'est pas possible d'apporter des changements aux données de 2001 présentées dans ces tableaux, les données de 2001 doivent être utilisées avec prudence. Pour de plus amples renseignements, veuillez consulter la section « Notes spéciales ».

■■■ Les chiffres de population et/ou des logements de 2006 et de 2001 pour cette région sont erronés. Étant donné qu'il n'est pas possible d'apporter des changements aux données du recensement présentées dans ces tableaux, ces données doivent être utilisées avec prudence. Pour de plus amples renseignements, veuillez consulter la section « Notes spéciales ».

• partie de secteur de recensement.

Abbreviations

CA	census agglomeration
CD	census division
CMA	census metropolitan area
CSD	census subdivision
CT	census tract
NAICS 2002	North American Industry Classification System 2002
n.i.e.	not included elsewhere
No.	number
NOC-S 2006	National Occupational Classification for Statistics 2006
n.o.s.	not otherwise specified

Abréviations

AR	agglomération de recensement
DR	division de recensement
RMR	région métropolitaine de recensement
SDR	subdivision de recensement
SD	secteur de recensement
SCIAN 2002	Système de classification des industries de l'Amérique du Nord de 2002
n.i.a.	non inclus ailleurs
N^{o}	numéro
CNP-S 2006	Classification nationale des professions pour statistiques de 2006
n.d.a.	non déclaré ailleurs

Census subdivision types – Genres de subdivision de recensement

C	City / Cité
CC	Chartered community
CÉ	Cité
CG	Community government
CM	County (municipality)
CN	Crown colony / Colonie de la couronne
COM	Community
CT	Canton (municipalité de)
CU	Cantons unis (municipalité de)
CY	City
DM	District municipality
HAM	Hamlet
ID	Improvement district
IGD	Indian government district
IM	Island municipality
IRI	Indian reserve / Réserve indienne
LGD	Local government district
LOT	Township and royalty
M	Municipality / Municipalité
MD	Municipal district
MÉ	Municipalité
MU	Municipality
NH	Northern hamlet
NL	Nisga'a land
NO	Unorganized / Non organisé
NV	Northern village
NVL	Nisga'a village
P	Parish / Paroisse (municipalité de)
PE	Paroisse (municipalité de)
RCR	Rural community / Communauté rurale
RDA	Regional district electoral area
RG	Region
RGM	Regional municipality
RM	Rural municipality
RV	Resort village
S-É	Indian settlement / Établissement indien
SA	Special area
SC	Subdivision of county municipality / Subdivision municipalité de comté
SÉ	Settlement / Établissement
SET	Settlement
SM	Specialized municipality
SNO	Subdivision of unorganized / Subdivision non organisée
SV	Summer village
T	Town
TC	Terres réservées aux Cris
TI	Terre inuite
TK	Terres réservées aux Naskapis
TL	Teslin land
TP	Township
TV	Town / Ville
V	Ville
VC	Village cri
VK	Village naskapi
VL	Village
VN	Village nordique

Geographic index – Index géographique

Census divisions and census subdivisions – Divisions de recensement et subdivisions de recensement

Volume 1:	Canada	to – à	Kenora CD/DR	Pages:	12	to – à 395
Volume 2:	Kenora CD/DR (continued/suite)	to – à	Perth CD/DR	Pages:	462	to – à 845
Volume 3:	Perth CD/DR (continued/suite)	to – à	York CD/DR	Pages:	912	to – à 1319

Census divisions (CD)
Divisions de recensement (DR)

Census subdivisions (CSD) Subdivisions de recensement (SDR)	Corresponding Census Division Division de recensement correspondante	

A

Note: See symbols and abbreviations in the introductory material and see reference material at the end of the publication. – Nota : Voir les symboles et les abréviations dans les documents d'introduction et voir les documents de référence à la fin de la publication.

Note: See symbols and abbreviations in the introductory material and see reference material at the end of the publication. – Nota : Voir les symboles et les abréviations dans les documents d'introduction et voir les documents de référence à la fin de la publication.

Geographic index (continued) – Index géographique (suite)

Census divisions and census subdivisions – Divisions de recensement et subdivisions de recensement

Page

Note: See symbols and abbreviations in the introductory material and see reference material at the end of the publication. – Nota : Voir les symboles et les abréviations dans les documents d'introduction et voir les documents de référence à la fin de la publication.

Page

Note: See symbols and abbreviations in the introductory material and see reference material at the end of the publication. – Nota : Voir les symboles et les abréviations dans les documents d'introduction et voir les documents de référence à la fin de la publication.

Note: See symbols and abbreviations in the introductory material and see reference material at the end of the publication. – Nota : Voir les symboles et les abréviations dans les documents d'introduction et voir les documents de référence à la fin de la publication.

Table
–
Tableau

Selected characteristics for census divisions and census subdivisions – 100% data and 20% sample data, Ontario, 2006 Census

No.	Characteristics	Canada †	Ontario PROVINCE †◊	Algoma CD/DR ◆◊	Algoma, Unorganized, North Part, NO ◆◆◊◊	Blind River, T ◊	Bruce Mines, T ◆◊◊
	Population characteristics						
1	**Population, 2001[1]**	**30,007,094**	**11,410,046**	**118,567**	**6,114**	**3,969**	**627**
2	**Population, 2006[2]**	**31,612,897**	**12,160,282**	**117,461**	**5,717**	**3,780**	**584**
3	Population percentage change, 2001 to 2006	5.4	6.6	-0.9	-6.5	-4.8	-6.9
4	Land area in square kilometres, 2006	9,017,698.92	907,573.82	48,734.66	44,096.97	520.59	6.13
5	**Total population – 100% data[3]**	**31,612,895**	**12,160,285**	**117,460**	**5,715**	**3,780**	**585**
	Sex and age groups						
6	Male	15,475,970	5,930,700	57,190	2,980	1,815	290
7	0 to 4 years	864,600	343,475	2,470	100	80	15
8	5 to 9 years	926,860	369,675	2,965	135	95	15
9	10 to 14 years	1,065,860	420,700	3,820	215	115	20
10	15 to 19 years	1,095,285	427,185	4,140	195	135	25
11	20 to 24 years	1,047,945	400,445	3,330	135	110	10
12	25 to 29 years	975,945	360,525	2,545	95	55	5
13	30 to 34 years	987,715	382,030	2,545	105	65	5
14	35 to 39 years	1,083,495	430,215	3,165	160	80	20
15	40 to 44 years	1,285,535	507,135	4,195	220	140	10
16	45 to 49 years	1,290,130	486,385	4,850	270	160	25
17	50 to 54 years	1,158,970	423,345	4,810	270	175	15
18	55 to 59 years	1,026,395	378,530	4,450	280	155	25
19	60 to 64 years	780,140	283,540	3,620	270	140	20
20	65 to 69 years	593,805	222,640	3,295	225	105	15
21	70 to 74 years	493,465	187,505	2,850	140	90	25
22	75 to 79 years	386,485	149,585	2,235	110	55	20
23	80 to 84 years	251,420	97,240	1,235	40	30	10
24	85 years and over	161,925	60,550	665	25	15	10
25	Female	16,136,930	6,229,580	60,275	2,740	1,970	295
26	0 to 4 years	825,940	327,290	2,410	85	70	10
27	5 to 9 years	882,515	351,920	2,715	125	85	15
28	10 to 14 years	1,014,065	397,740	3,450	145	100	15
29	15 to 19 years	1,045,205	405,925	3,895	200	145	15
30	20 to 24 years	1,032,440	396,815	3,380	95	115	10
31	25 to 29 years	1,009,635	383,170	2,860	100	75	0
32	30 to 34 years	1,032,510	409,930	2,890	130	80	15
33	35 to 39 years	1,124,775	453,770	3,385	155	110	20
34	40 to 44 years	1,324,925	525,280	4,600	220	150	25
35	45 to 49 years	1,330,470	505,585	5,350	275	205	25
36	50 to 54 years	1,198,335	446,060	4,875	280	160	25
37	55 to 59 years	1,058,230	395,995	4,535	280	165	20
38	60 to 64 years	809,730	298,440	3,915	230	130	20
39	65 to 69 years	640,770	243,600	3,355	160	120	25
40	70 to 74 years	560,320	214,440	2,985	110	100	10
41	75 to 79 years	493,090	189,330	2,470	90	60	20
42	80 to 84 years	395,285	153,035	1,760	40	55	5
43	85 years and over	358,685	131,260	1,450	25	35	15
44	**Total population 15 years and over[3]**	**26,033,060**	**9,949,485**	**99,635**	**4,920**	**3,240**	**500**
	Legal marital status						
45	Never legally married (single)	9,087,030	3,143,960	28,980	1,230	995	105
46	Legally married (and not separated)[4,5]	12,470,395	5,168,655	50,615	2,855	1,650	285
47	Separated, but still legally married	775,420	345,075	3,875	160	105	25
48	Divorced	2,087,385	679,990	8,020	400	215	40
49	Widowed	1,612,820	611,800	8,140	270	275	50
	Common-law status						
50	Not in a common-law relationship	23,301,425	9,257,725	90,995	4,420	2,935	470
51	In a common-law relationship	2,731,635	691,755	8,645	495	305	30
52	**Total population – 20% sample data[6]**	**31,241,030**	**12,028,895**	**116,075**	**5,725**	**3,720**	**560**
	Mother tongue						
53	Single responses	30,848,270	11,853,565	115,010	5,655	3,635	560
54	English	17,882,775	8,230,705	95,265	4,945	2,785	550
55	French	6,817,655	488,815	8,010	260	715	10
56	Non-official languages[7]	6,147,840	3,134,045	11,735	455	140	10
57	Italian	455,040	282,750	5,075	60	15	0
58	Chinese, n.o.s.[61]	456,710	215,345	125	0	10	0
59	Cantonese	361,450	181,825	200	65	0	0
60	Spanish	345,345	160,280	235	0	0	0
61	German	450,570	158,005	1,410	85	30	0
62	Other languages[8]	4,078,725	2,135,845	4,685	240	90	10

Note: See symbols and abbreviations in the introductory material and see reference material at the end of the publication.

Certaines caractéristiques des divisions de recensement et des subdivisions de recensement – Données intégrales et données-échantillon (20 %), Ontario, Recensement de 2006

Dubreuilville, TP ◆◇	Elliot Lake, CY ◆◇	Garden River 14, IRI ◆	Goulais Bay 15A, IRI ◆◆◇◇	Gros Cap 49, IRI	Hilton, TP ◆◇◇	Caractéristiques	N°
						Caractéristiques de la population	
967	**11,956**	**859**	**X**	**61**	**258**	**Population, 2001[1]**	1
773	**11,549**	**985**	**82**	**54**	**243**	**Population, 2006[2]**	2
-20.1	-3.4	14.7	X	-11.5	-5.8	Variation en pourcentage de la population, 2001 à 2006	3
89.57	698.12	163.14	6.42	34.57	115.78	Superficie des terres en kilomètres carrés, 2006	4
775	**11,550**	**985**	**85**	**55**	**245**	**Population totale – Données intégrales[3]**	5
						Sexe et groupes d'âge	
420	5,555	470	40	25	120	Sexe masculin	6
25	155	35	0	5	5	0 à 4 ans	7
30	200	45	0	0	5	5 à 9 ans	8
20	285	45	5	5	10	10 à 14 ans	9
25	340	35	5	0	5	15 à 19 ans	10
30	210	35	0	0	5	20 à 24 ans	11
35	140	25	0	0	5	25 à 29 ans	12
35	165	30	5	0	5	30 à 34 ans	13
50	185	25	0	0	5	35 à 39 ans	14
40	310	40	5	5	5	40 à 44 ans	15
20	400	35	0	0	5	45 à 49 ans	16
40	415	35	5	5	10	50 à 54 ans	17
30	435	30	0	0	20	55 à 59 ans	18
20	505	15	5	5	15	60 à 64 ans	19
10	630	25	0	0	15	65 à 69 ans	20
10	555	5	0	0	5	70 à 74 ans	21
0	395	5	0	0	0	75 à 79 ans	22
0	180	0	0	0	0	80 à 84 ans	23
0	60	0	0	0	0	85 ans et plus	24
350	5,990	510	45	30	125	Sexe féminin	25
25	155	40	5	0	0	0 à 4 ans	26
30	175	45	5	0	5	5 à 9 ans	27
30	265	65	5	0	10	10 à 14 ans	28
20	330	45	5	0	5	15 à 19 ans	29
30	210	35	5	0	5	20 à 24 ans	30
25	180	40	0	0	5	25 à 29 ans	31
30	175	35	0	5	0	30 à 34 ans	32
30	225	35	5	5	5	35 à 39 ans	33
35	350	40	10	0	10	40 à 44 ans	34
25	475	45	0	10	5	45 à 49 ans	35
25	470	25	0	0	10	50 à 54 ans	36
25	525	20	5	0	20	55 à 59 ans	37
15	615	15	5	0	20	60 à 64 ans	38
5	630	10	0	0	5	65 à 69 ans	39
0	525	5	0	0	5	70 à 74 ans	40
0	360	5	0	0	5	75 à 79 ans	41
0	230	0	0	0	5	80 à 84 ans	42
5	100	0	0	0	0	85 ans et plus	43
615	**10,305**	**715**	**65**	**50**	**215**	**Population totale de 15 ans et plus[3]**	44
						État matrimonial légal	
255	2,240	365	35	30	40	Jamais légalement marié(e) (célibataire)	45
265	5,375	250	20	15	140	Légalement marié(e) (et non séparé[e])[4,5]	46
35	540	20	5	0	5	Séparé(e), mais toujours légalement marié(e)	47
35	1,055	50	5	0	15	Divorcé(e)	48
25	1,090	25	5	5	15	Veuf(ve)	49
						Union libre	
455	9,300	610	45	35	195	Ne vivant pas en union libre	50
165	1,005	110	15	10	15	Vivant en union libre	51
765	**11,435**	**985**	**85**	**50**	**240**	**Population totale – Données-échantillon (20 %)[6]**	52
						Langue maternelle	
750	11,295	985	85	55	235	Réponses uniques	53
115	8,415	940	70	55	220	Anglais	54
630	1,860	10	0	0	0	Français	55
10	1,015	35	10	0	10	Langues non officielles[7]	56
0	140	0	0	0	0	Italien	57
0	10	0	0	0	0	Chinois, n.d.a.[61]	58
0	0	0	0	0	0	Cantonais	59
0	45	0	0	0	0	Espagnol	60
0	315	0	0	0	0	Allemand	61
10	500	35	10	0	10	Autres langues[8]	62

Nota : Voir les symboles et les abréviations dans les documents d'introduction et voir les documents de référence à la fin de la publication.

Selected characteristics for census divisions and census subdivisions – 100% data and 20% sample data, Ontario, 2006 Census (continued)

No.	Characteristics	Canada †	Ontario PROVINCE †◊	Algoma CD/DR ◆◊	Algoma, Unorganized, North Part, NO ◆◆◊◊	Blind River, T ◊	Bruce Mines, T ◆◊◊
	Population characteristics						
	Mother tongue (continued)						
63	Multiple responses	392,760	175,335	1,070	70	80	0
64	English and French	98,625	32,685	580	30	70	0
65	English and non-official language	240,005	131,290	470	40	0	0
66	French and non-official language	43,335	7,790	15	0	0	0
67	English, French and non-official language	10,790	3,565	10	0	10	0
	Language spoken most often at home[9]						
68	Single responses	30,665,025	11,756,485	115,215	5,685	3,665	565
69	English	20,584,775	9,655,830	107,895	5,510	3,350	565
70	French	6,608,125	289,035	3,450	50	295	0
71	Non-official languages[7]	3,472,130	1,811,620	3,870	125	30	0
72	Chinese, n.o.s.[61]	341,480	161,810	90	0	0	0
73	Cantonese	300,595	154,310	60	0	0	0
74	Panjabi (Punjabi)	278,500	117,445	0	0	0	0
75	Italian	170,330	107,175	1,870	15	10	0
76	Spanish	209,955	97,895	125	0	0	0
77	Other languages[8]	2,171,270	1,172,980	1,710	105	20	0
78	Multiple responses	576,005	272,410	860	40	50	0
79	English and French	94,060	26,045	440	15	40	0
80	English and non-official language	406,455	239,895	405	30	10	0
81	French and non-official language	58,885	3,065	0	0	0	0
82	English, French and non-official language	16,600	3,405	10	0	0	0
	Knowledge of official languages[10]						
83	English only	21,129,945	10,335,700	99,625	5,115	2,285	530
84	French only	4,141,850	49,205	770	0	55	0
85	English and French	5,448,850	1,377,325	15,210	585	1,380	30
86	Neither English nor French	520,385	266,655	470	20	0	0
	Knowledge of non-official languages[7,11]						
87	Italian	660,945	396,955	6,490	80	20	0
88	Spanish	758,280	280,395	540	0	0	0
89	German	622,645	230,330	1,710	100	20	10
90	Chinese, n.o.s.[61]	472,080	220,490	135	0	0	0
91	Cantonese	434,715	218,525	130	0	0	0
92	Panjabi (Punjabi)	456,085	201,720	15	0	0	0
93	Portuguese	274,670	189,920	405	10	15	0
	First official language spoken[10]						
94	English	23,197,090	11,189,935	107,775	5,460	3,015	555
95	French	7,204,390	497,155	7,695	235	695	10
96	English and French	331,925	80,890	145	10	0	0
97	Neither English nor French	507,620	260,920	460	20	0	0
98	Official language minority - (number)[12]	7,370,350	537,595	7,765	240	700	0
99	Official language minority - (percentage)[12]	23.6	4.5	6.7	4.2	18.8	0.0
	Ethnic origin[13]						
100	English	6,570,015	2,971,365	34,665	2,085	865	240
101	Canadian	10,066,290	2,768,870	33,825	1,645	1,755	175
102	Scottish	4,719,850	2,101,100	25,800	1,260	705	275
103	Irish	4,354,155	1,988,940	24,275	1,350	730	165
104	French	4,941,215	1,351,600	29,540	1,490	1,580	160
105	German	3,179,425	1,144,560	10,980	615	255	55
106	Italian	1,445,330	867,980	19,140	285	150	0
107	Chinese	1,346,515	644,460	620	0	20	0
108	East Indian	962,670	573,250	150	15	10	0
109	Dutch (Netherlands)	1,035,965	490,995	3,655	220	165	10
110	Polish	984,565	465,565	3,840	225	100	10
111	Ukrainian	1,209,090	336,355	4,925	325	75	10
112	North American Indian	1,253,615	317,890	11,015	500	265	35
113	Portuguese	410,850	282,870	515	20	10	0
114	Filipino	436,195	215,750	245	75	0	0
	Aboriginal and non-Aboriginal identity						
115	Total Aboriginal identity population[14]	1,172,785	242,490	12,925	585	375	95
116	Total non-Aboriginal identity population	30,068,240	11,786,405	103,150	5,140	3,345	465

Note: See symbols and abbreviations in the introductory material and see reference material at the end of the publication.

Certaines caractéristiques des divisions de recensement et des subdivisions de recensement – Données intégrales et données-échantillon (20 %), Ontario, Recensement de 2006 (suite)

Dubreuilville, TP ◆◊	Elliot Lake, CY ◆◊	Garden River 14, IRI ◆	Goulais Bay 15A, IRI ◆◆◊◊	Gros Cap 49, IRI	Hilton, TP ◆◊◊	Caractéristiques	N°
						Caractéristiques de la population	
						Langue maternelle (suite)	
10	145	0	0	0	0	Réponses multiples	63
0	105	0	0	0	0	Anglais et français	64
0	40	0	0	0	0	Anglais et langue non officielle	65
0	0	0	0	0	0	Français et langue non officielle	66
0	0	0	0	0	0	Anglais, français et langue non officielle	67
						Langue parlée le plus souvent à la maison[9]	
740	11,275	985	80	55	235	Réponses uniques	68
110	10,040	975	80	55	240	Anglais	69
630	990	0	0	0	0	Français	70
0	245	10	0	0	0	Langues non officielles[7]	71
0	0	0	0	0	0	Chinois, n.d.a.[61]	72
0	0	0	0	0	0	Cantonais	73
0	0	0	0	0	0	Pendjabi	74
0	30	0	0	0	0	Italien	75
0	10	0	0	0	0	Espagnol	76
0	200	10	0	0	0	Autres langues[8]	77
25	160	0	0	0	0	Réponses multiples	78
25	95	0	0	0	0	Anglais et français	79
0	65	0	0	0	0	Anglais et langue non officielle	80
0	0	0	0	0	0	Français et langue non officielle	81
0	0	0	0	0	0	Anglais, français et langue non officielle	82
						Connaissance des langues officielles[10]	
70	8,155	945	75	50	220	Anglais seulement	83
295	230	0	0	0	0	Français seulement	84
395	3,045	40	0	0	15	Anglais et français	85
0	10	0	0	0	0	Ni l'anglais ni le français	86
						Connaissance des langues non officielles[7,11]	
0	150	10	0	0	0	Italien	87
0	125	0	0	0	0	Espagnol	88
0	390	10	0	0	0	Allemand	89
0	10	0	0	0	0	Chinois, n.d.a.[61]	90
0	0	0	0	0	0	Cantonais	91
0	10	0	0	0	0	Pendjabi	92
0	90	0	0	0	0	Portugais	93
						Première langue officielle parlée[10]	
125	9,565	980	80	55	230	Anglais	94
635	1,825	0	0	0	0	Français	95
0	45	0	0	0	0	Anglais et français	96
0	0	10	0	0	0	Ni l'anglais ni le français	97
635	1,845	0	0	0	10	Minorité de langue officielle - (nombre)[12]	98
83.6	16.1	0.0	0.0	0.0	4.3	Minorité de langue officielle - (pourcentage)[12]	99
						Origine ethnique[13]	
30	3,535	40	0	0	80	Anglais	100
585	4,255	25	0	0	105	Canadien	101
15	2,230	15	0	0	55	Écossais	102
10	2,320	20	0	0	30	Irlandais	103
280	3,430	60	15	0	25	Français	104
15	1,310	10	0	0	35	Allemand	105
10	365	15	0	0	0	Italien	106
0	105	0	0	0	0	Chinois	107
0	20	0	0	0	0	Indien de l'Inde	108
0	375	0	0	0	0	Hollandais (Néerlandais)	109
0	315	10	0	0	10	Polonais	110
0	265	0	0	10	10	Ukrainien	111
50	715	920	75	50	10	Indien de l'Amérique du Nord	112
0	90	0	0	0	0	Portugais	113
0	60	0	0	0	0	Philippin	114
						Population ayant une identité autochtone et population n'ayant pas d'identité autochtone	
60	815	925	75	45	0	Total de la population ayant une identité autochtone[14]	115
700	10,625	55	0	10	240	Total de la population n'ayant pas d'identité autochtone	116

Nota : Voir les symboles et les abréviations dans les documents d'introduction et voir les documents de référence à la fin de la publication.

Selected characteristics for census divisions and census subdivisions – 100% data and 20% sample data, Ontario, 2006 Census (continued)

No.	Characteristics	Canada †	Ontario PROVINCE †◊	Algoma CD/DR ◆◊	Algoma, Unorganized, North Part, NO ◆◆◊◊	Blind River, T ◊	Bruce Mines, T ◆◊◊
	Population characteristics						
	Aboriginal and non-Aboriginal ancestry						
117	Total Aboriginal ancestry population[15]	1,678,235	403,795	15,440	745	465	100
118	Total non-Aboriginal ancestry population	29,562,795	11,625,105	100,635	4,980	3,255	465
	Registered Indian status						
119	Registered Indian[16]	623,780	123,595	6,990	255	135	25
120	Not a Registered Indian	30,617,250	11,905,300	109,080	5,465	3,580	540
	Visible minority groups						
121	Total visible minority population[17]	5,068,090	2,745,205	1,525	95	35	10
122	Chinese	1,216,565	576,975	405	0	20	0
123	South Asian[18]	1,262,865	794,170	190	0	10	0
124	Black	783,800	473,765	285	0	10	0
125	Filipino	410,695	203,220	205	75	0	0
126	Latin American	304,250	147,135	155	0	0	0
127	Southeast Asian[19]	239,935	110,045	10	0	0	0
128	Arab	265,550	111,405	35	0	0	0
129	West Asian[20]	156,700	96,615	0	0	0	0
130	Korean	141,890	69,540	25	0	0	0
131	Japanese	81,305	28,080	70	0	0	0
132	Visible minority, n.i.e.[21]	71,420	56,845	30	0	0	0
133	Multiple visible minority[22]	133,120	77,405	105	0	0	0
	Citizenship[23]						
134	Canadian citizens[24]	29,480,160	11,131,465	114,005	5,510	3,685	555
135	Not Canadian citizens[25]	1,760,865	897,430	2,070	215	35	10
	Immigrant status and place of birth[26]						
136	Non-immigrants[27]	24,788,720	8,512,020	104,445	5,255	3,520	530
137	Born in province of residence	20,933,115	7,482,530	95,455	4,875	3,110	495
138	Immigrants[28]	6,186,950	3,398,725	11,230	365	185	30
139	United States of America	250,540	106,410	1,095	80	35	0
140	Central and South America	381,165	216,645	215	0	0	0
141	Caribbean and Bermuda	317,765	211,380	115	10	0	0
142	United Kingdom	579,620	321,650	1,930	80	30	25
143	Other Europe	1,698,725	986,240	7,300	185	95	10
144	Africa	374,565	164,795	60	0	10	0
145	Asia and the Middle East	2,525,155	1,376,590	455	10	10	0
146	Oceania and other[29]	59,410	15,025	60	0	0	0
147	Non-permanent residents[30]	265,355	118,150	395	105	10	0
148	**Total immigrant population[28]**	**6,186,950**	**3,398,725**	**11,230**	**370**	**185**	**30**
	Period of immigration						
149	Before 1961	791,225	442,695	5,710	190	90	25
150	1961 to 1970	710,285	405,180	2,685	85	30	0
151	1971 to 1980	903,705	478,340	1,370	30	25	10
152	1981 to 1990	1,003,205	558,225	665	50	0	0
153	1991 to 2000	1,668,555	933,550	555	10	30	0
154	1991 to 1995	823,925	462,075	260	0	0	0
155	1996 to 2000	844,625	471,470	295	0	25	0
156	2001 to 2006[31]	1,109,980	580,740	240	0	10	0
	Age at immigration						
157	Under 5 years	543,395	289,465	1,275	60	15	0
158	5 to 19 years	1,661,010	929,835	3,505	120	65	20
159	20 years and over	3,982,545	2,179,430	6,450	185	100	10
160	**Total population 15 years and over**	**25,664,225**	**9,819,420**	**98,255**	**4,935**	**3,175**	**485**
	Generation status						
161	1st generation[32]	6,124,560	3,340,210	11,455	425	195	35
162	2nd generation[33]	4,006,420	1,912,460	16,975	775	350	20
163	3rd generation or more[34]	15,533,245	4,566,750	69,830	3,730	2,630	430

Note: See symbols and abbreviations in the introductory material and see reference material at the end of the publication.

Certaines caractéristiques des divisions de recensement et des subdivisions de recensement – Données intégrales et données-échantillon (20 %), Ontario, Recensement de 2006 (suite)

Dubreuilville, TP ◆◊	Elliot Lake, CY ◆◊	Garden River 14, IRI ◆	Goulais Bay 15A, IRI ◆◆◊◊	Gros Cap 49, IRI	Hilton, TP ◆◊◊	Caractéristiques	N°
						Caractéristiques de la population	
						Population ayant une ascendance autochtone et population n'ayant pas d'ascendance autochtone	
80	1,110	920	75	50	10	Total de la population ayant une ascendance autochtone[15]	117
685	10,325	65	10	0	225	Total de la population n'ayant pas d'ascendance autochtone	118
						Statut d'Indien inscrit	
15	305	875	70	45	0	Indien inscrit[16]	119
750	11,130	105	15	10	240	Pas un Indien inscrit	120
						Groupes de minorités visibles	
0	240	10	0	0	0	Total de la population des minorités visibles[17]	121
0	35	0	0	0	0	Chinois	122
0	35	0	0	0	0	Sud-Asiatique[18]	123
0	30	10	0	0	0	Noir	124
0	30	0	0	0	0	Philippin	125
0	65	0	0	0	0	Latino-Américain	126
0	0	0	0	0	0	Asiatique du Sud-Est[19]	127
0	0	0	0	0	0	Arabe	128
0	0	0	0	0	0	Asiatique occidental[20]	129
0	0	0	0	0	0	Coréen	130
0	0	0	0	0	0	Japonais	131
0	0	0	0	0	0	Minorité visible, n.i.a.[21]	132
0	50	0	0	0	0	Minorités visibles multiples[22]	133
						Citoyenneté[23]	
760	11,170	X	X	X	230	Citoyens canadiens[24]	134
0	270	X	X	X	10	Ne sont pas des citoyens canadiens[25]	135
						Statut d'immigrant et le lieu de naissance[26]	
755	9,880	X	X	X	205	Non-immigrants[27]	136
435	7,725	X	X	X	190	Né dans la province de résidence	137
10	1,500	X	X	X	30	Immigrants[28]	138
0	75	X	X	X	0	États-Unis d'Amérique	139
0	55	X	X	X	0	Amérique centrale et Amérique du Sud	140
0	15	X	X	X	0	Antilles et Bermudes	141
0	565	X	X	X	20	Royaume-Uni	142
10	710	X	X	X	10	Autre Europe	143
0	20	X	X	X	0	Afrique	144
0	45	X	X	X	0	Asie et Moyen-Orient	145
0	10	X	X	X	0	Océanie et autres[29]	146
0	55	X	X	X	0	Résidents non permanents[30]	147
10	**1,505**	**X**	**X**	**X**	**30**	**Population totale des immigrants[28]**	148
						Période d'immigration	
0	765	X	X	X	10	Avant 1961	149
0	405	X	X	X	15	1961 à 1970	150
0	195	X	X	X	0	1971 à 1980	151
0	60	X	X	X	0	1981 à 1990	152
10	60	X	X	X	0	1991 à 2000	153
10	20	X	X	X	0	1991 à 1995	154
0	40	X	X	X	0	1996 à 2000	155
0	10	X	X	X	0	2001 à 2006[31]	156
						Âge à l'immigration	
0	95	X	X	X	0	Moins de 5 ans	157
10	360	X	X	X	0	5 à 19 ans	158
0	1,050	X	X	X	25	20 ans et plus	159
630	**10,200**	**715**	**65**	**50**	**200**	**Population totale de 15 ans et plus**	160
						Statut des générations	
10	1,540	15	0	0	30	1re génération[32]	161
25	1,540	40	0	10	10	2e génération[33]	162
595	7,120	660	65	40	160	3e génération ou plus[34]	163

Nota : Voir les symboles et les abréviations dans les documents d'introduction et voir les documents de référence à la fin de la publication.

Selected characteristics for census divisions and census subdivisions – 100% data and 20% sample data, Ontario, 2006 Census (continued)

No.	Characteristics	Canada †	Ontario PROVINCE †◊	Algoma CD/DR ◆◊	Algoma, Unorganized, North Part, NO ◆◆◊◊	Blind River, T ◊	Bruce Mines, T ◆◊◊
	Population characteristics						
164	**Total population 1 year and over[35]**	**30,897,210**	**11,893,180**	**115,030**	**5,710**	**3,680**	**560**
	Place of residence 1 year ago (mobility)						
165	Non-movers	26,534,115	10,299,250	101,045	5,355	3,205	485
166	Movers	4,363,095	1,593,925	13,980	355	470	75
167	Non-migrants	2,554,260	951,995	9,580	135	270	25
168	Migrants	1,808,830	641,930	4,405	225	195	45
169	Internal migrants	1,511,305	510,300	4,190	225	195	45
170	Intraprovincial migrants	1,221,560	453,460	3,810	220	180	45
171	Interprovincial migrants	289,745	56,840	380	0	15	0
172	External migrants	297,530	131,630	215	0	0	0
173	**Total population 5 years and over[36]**	**29,544,485**	**11,354,360**	**111,135**	**5,525**	**3,535**	**545**
	Place of residence 5 years ago (mobility)						
174	Non-movers	17,457,165	6,660,315	74,555	4,175	2,355	380
175	Movers	12,087,315	4,694,045	36,585	1,345	1,180	160
176	Non-migrants	6,507,905	2,542,885	23,160	700	690	50
177	Migrants	5,579,410	2,151,160	13,420	650	490	105
178	Internal migrants	4,419,370	1,584,450	12,695	535	485	110
179	Intraprovincial migrants	3,566,795	1,398,665	11,365	500	405	110
180	Interprovincial migrants	852,580	185,785	1,330	35	75	0
181	External migrants	1,160,035	566,715	730	110	0	0
182	**Total population 15 years and over**	**25,664,220**	**9,819,420**	**98,260**	**4,935**	**3,175**	**485**
	Highest certificate, diploma or degree[37]						
183	No certificate, diploma or degree	6,098,330	2,183,625	27,025	1,500	905	115
184	Certificate, diploma or degree	19,565,900	7,635,790	71,230	3,440	2,265	370
185	High school certificate or equivalent[38]	6,553,420	2,628,570	26,925	1,240	920	210
186	Apprenticeship or trades certificate or diploma	2,785,420	785,115	10,650	815	375	45
187	College, CEGEP or other non-university certificate or diploma[39]	4,435,135	1,804,775	19,250	835	560	45
188	University certificate or diploma below bachelor level[40]	1,136,150	405,270	2,685	170	45	10
189	University certificate or degree[41]	4,655,765	2,012,055	11,725	380	360	60
190	Bachelor's degree	2,981,465	1,243,730	7,710	270	235	30
191	University certificate or diploma above bachelor level	493,540	245,150	1,915	40	55	10
192	Degree in medicine, dentistry, veterinary medicine or optometry	136,845	57,685	305	10	20	0
193	Master's degree	866,980	391,700	1,535	60	35	15
194	Earned doctorate	176,945	73,790	255	15	10	10
195	**Total population 15 years and over with postsecondary qualifications**	**13,012,470**	**5,007,225**	**44,305**	**2,195**	**1,345**	**160**
	Major field of study - Classification of Instructional Programs, 2000[42]						
196	Education	994,665	335,715	3,615	125	180	10
197	Visual and performing arts, and communications technologies	481,190	193,795	825	20	0	0
198	Humanities	717,125	292,845	1,790	75	50	40
199	Social and behavioural sciences and law	1,275,105	576,100	3,750	145	85	0
200	Business, management and public administration	2,801,720	1,061,210	7,855	280	150	15
201	Physical and life sciences and technologies	451,960	181,250	1,060	95	65	0
202	Mathematics, computer and information sciences	568,755	254,440	1,405	40	30	10
203	Architecture, engineering, and related technologies	2,922,080	1,089,310	11,915	755	365	30
204	Agriculture, natural resources and conservation	291,510	91,965	1,380	70	105	0
205	Health, parks, recreation and fitness	1,728,890	665,490	7,205	370	215	40
206	Personal, protective and transportation services	777,370	264,620	3,515	225	100	0
207	Other fields of study[43]	2,100	480	0	0	0	0
	Location of study[44]						
208	Inside Canada	10,948,470	3,928,515	39,965	1,935	1,280	150
209	Outside Canada	2,064,000	1,078,710	4,340	260	65	10
210	**Total population 15 years and over**	**25,664,220**	**9,819,420**	**98,260**	**4,935**	**3,175**	**485**
	Unpaid work						
211	Males 15 years and over	12,470,785	4,744,710	47,505	2,555	1,500	235
212	Reported unpaid work[45]	11,164,005	4,259,925	42,555	2,245	1,390	220
213	Housework and child care and care or assistance to seniors	971,775	388,570	4,025	190	155	15
214	Housework and child care only	3,133,020	1,208,200	9,975	450	290	35

Note: See symbols and abbreviations in the introductory material and see reference material at the end of the publication.

Certaines caractéristiques des divisions de recensement et des subdivisions de recensement – Données intégrales et données-échantillon (20 %), Ontario, Recensement de 2006 (suite)

Dubreuilville, TP ◆◇	Elliot Lake, CY ◆◇	Garden River 14, IRI ◆	Goulais Bay 15A, IRI ◆◆◇◇	Gros Cap 49, IRI	Hilton, TP ◆◇◇	Caractéristiques	Nº
						Caractéristiques de la population	
765	**11,335**	**970**	**85**	**55**	**240**	**Population totale de 1 an et plus[35]**	164
						Lieu de résidence 1 an auparavant (mobilité)	
640	9,755	880	85	45	225	Personnes n'ayant pas déménagé	165
120	1,580	90	0	10	10	Personnes ayant déménagé	166
70	895	45	0	0	0	Non-migrants	167
50	680	45	0	10	10	Migrants	168
50	665	40	0	0	10	Migrants internes	169
0	645	45	0	0	10	Migrants infraprovinciaux	170
50	20	0	0	0	0	Migrants interprovinciaux	171
0	20	0	0	0	0	Migrants externes	172
715	**11,100**	**915**	**80**	**50**	**230**	**Population totale de 5 ans et plus[36]**	173
						Lieu de résidence 5 ans auparavant (mobilité)	
490	6,605	670	65	35	190	Personnes n'ayant pas déménagé	174
225	4,495	245	20	20	40	Personnes ayant déménagé	175
165	2,010	100	0	0	10	Non-migrants	176
55	2,485	145	10	15	30	Migrants	177
60	2,395	145	15	20	35	Migrants internes	178
15	2,240	135	15	15	25	Migrants infraprovinciaux	179
45	150	0	0	0	0	Migrants interprovinciaux	180
0	90	0	0	0	0	Migrants externes	181
625	**10,200**	**715**	**70**	**45**	**205**	**Population totale de 15 ans et plus**	182
						Plus haut certificat, diplôme ou grade[37]	
260	3,270	270	35	15	35	Aucun certificat, diplôme ou grade	183
365	6,930	445	35	30	165	Certificat, diplôme ou grade	184
120	2,485	170	10	10	55	Diplôme d'études secondaires ou l'équivalent[38]	185
130	1,495	60	15	10	20	Certificat ou diplôme d'apprenti ou d'une école de métiers	186
105	1,925	150	10	10	55	Certificat ou diplôme d'un collège, d'un cégep ou d'un autre établissement d'enseignement non universitaire[39]	187
0	200	10	0	0	10	Certificat ou diplôme universitaire inférieur au baccalauréat[40]	188
0	825	50	0	0	30	Certificat ou grade universitaire[41]	189
0	475	40	0	0	25	Baccalauréat	190
0	155	10	0	0	0	Certificat ou diplôme universitaire supérieur au baccalauréat	191
0	15	0	0	0	0	Diplôme en médecine, en art dentaire, en médecine vétérinaire ou en optométrie	192
10	160	10	0	0	0	Maîtrise	193
0	25	0	0	0	0	Doctorat acquis	194
245	**4,450**	**270**	**25**	**25**	**110**	**Population totale de 15 ans et plus avec titres du niveau postsecondaire**	195
						Principal domaine d'études - Classification des programmes d'enseignement, 2000[42]	
0	310	0	0	0	15	Éducation	196
0	105	0	0	0	0	Arts visuels et d'interprétation, et technologie des communications	197
0	195	10	0	10	0	Sciences humaines	198
10	225	55	0	0	15	Sciences sociales et de comportements, et droit	199
30	865	45	10	0	30	Commerce, gestion et administration publique	200
0	80	10	0	0	0	Sciences physiques et de la vie, et technologies	201
10	130	10	0	0	0	Mathématiques, informatique et sciences de l'information	202
80	1,260	65	10	10	30	Architecture, génie et services connexes	203
25	80	20	10	0	0	Agriculture, ressources naturelles et conservation	204
30	795	30	10	0	15	Santé, parcs, récréation et conditionnement physique	205
50	400	20	0	0	0	Services personnels, de protection et de transport	206
0	0	0	0	0	0	Autres domaines d'études[43]	207
						Lieu des études[44]	
245	3,915	260	25	20	90	À l'intérieur du Canada	208
0	535	10	0	0	20	À l'extérieur du Canada	209
625	**10,200**	**715**	**70**	**45**	**205**	**Population totale de 15 ans et plus**	210
						Travail non rémunéré	
325	4,880	350	35	20	105	Hommes de 15 ans et plus	211
265	4,235	320	25	15	85	Travail non rémunéré déclaré[45]	212
25	190	50	0	0	10	Travaux ménagers et soins aux enfants et soins ou aide aux personnes âgées	213
85	805	100	10	10	20	Travaux ménagers et soins aux enfants seulement	214

Nota : Voir les symboles et les abréviations dans les documents d'introduction et voir les documents de référence à la fin de la publication.

Selected characteristics for census divisions and census subdivisions – 100% data and 20% sample data, Ontario, 2006 Census (continued)

No.	Characteristics	Canada †	Ontario PROVINCE †◊	Algoma CD/DR ◆◊	Algoma, Unorganized, North Part, NO ◆◆◊◊	Blind River, T ◊	Bruce Mines, T ◆◊◊
	Population characteristics						
	Unpaid work (continued)						
215	Housework and care or assistance to seniors only	919,075	357,735	4,535	190	190	25
216	Child care and care or assistance to seniors only	18,735	6,990	20	0	10	0
217	Housework only	5,940,490	2,232,225	23,450	1,390	740	140
218	Child care only	128,450	46,080	230	15	0	0
219	Care or assistance to seniors only	52,450	20,135	315	10	10	0
220	Females 15 years and over	13,193,440	5,074,710	50,755	2,375	1,675	250
221	Reported unpaid work[45]	12,332,920	4,731,085	47,725	2,270	1,590	250
222	Housework and child care and care or assistance to seniors	1,497,805	585,490	6,035	330	220	25
223	Housework and child care only	3,794,530	1,467,905	12,715	525	385	65
224	Housework and care or assistance to seniors only	1,214,760	459,905	6,120	245	200	40
225	Child care and care or assistance to seniors only	12,155	4,940	15	0	0	0
226	Housework only	5,706,925	2,169,035	22,380	1,145	755	125
227	Child care only	69,175	28,735	235	10	15	0
228	Care or assistance to seniors only	37,560	15,075	215	0	10	0
	Labour force activity						
229	Males 15 years and over	12,470,785	4,744,710	47,500	2,560	1,495	230
230	In the labour force	9,020,595	3,437,675	28,990	1,555	1,010	140
231	Employed	8,431,530	3,230,050	26,260	1,365	875	125
232	Unemployed	589,065	207,625	2,730	195	140	15
233	Not in the labour force	3,450,190	1,307,035	18,515	995	485	95
234	Participation rate	72.3	72.5	61.0	60.7	67.6	60.9
235	Employment rate	67.6	68.1	55.3	53.3	58.5	54.3
236	Unemployment rate	6.5	6.0	9.4	12.5	13.9	10.7
237	Females 15 years and over	13,193,435	5,074,710	50,755	2,380	1,675	250
238	In the labour force	8,125,540	3,149,905	27,390	1,165	885	140
239	Employed	7,589,645	2,934,195	25,125	1,055	850	135
240	Unemployed	535,895	215,710	2,260	105	35	10
241	Not in the labour force	5,067,900	1,924,805	23,365	1,210	790	110
242	Participation rate	61.6	62.1	54.0	48.9	52.8	56.0
243	Employment rate	57.5	57.8	49.5	44.3	50.7	54.0
244	Unemployment rate	6.6	6.8	8.3	9.0	4.0	7.1
245	Both sexes - Participation rate	66.8	67.1	57.4	55.2	59.7	59.4
246	15 to 24 years	65.5	65.2	66.6	61.3	67.0	66.7
247	25 years and over	67.1	67.5	55.8	54.4	58.3	57.6
248	Both sexes - Employment rate	62.4	62.8	52.3	49.1	54.3	53.1
249	15 to 24 years	57.2	55.7	53.4	49.6	55.0	50.0
250	25 years and over	63.5	64.2	52.1	48.8	54.0	52.9
251	Both sexes - Unemployment rate	6.6	6.4	8.9	11.0	8.9	8.9
252	15 to 24 years	12.8	14.5	19.7	17.8	16.4	0.0
253	25 years and over	5.4	4.9	6.6	10.0	7.5	8.3
254	**Total labour force 15 years and over**	**17,146,135**	**6,587,575**	**56,380**	**2,725**	**1,900**	**280**
	Industry - North American Industry Classification System 2002						
255	Industry - Not applicable[46]	284,950	113,845	1,170	70	20	10
256	All industries[47]	16,861,185	6,473,730	55,210	2,655	1,875	275
257	11 Agriculture, forestry, fishing and hunting	523,650	114,345	1,345	215	65	10
258	21 Mining and oil and gas extraction	238,815	25,440	445	25	25	10
259	22 Utilities	132,950	50,215	360	25	10	0
260	23 Construction	1,069,095	384,780	3,045	245	130	25
261	31-33 Manufacturing	2,005,985	899,670	6,745	240	235	35
262	41 Wholesale trade	739,305	307,465	910	60	40	10
263	44-45 Retail trade	1,917,170	720,235	6,850	285	205	60
264	48-49 Transportation and warehousing	820,195	307,475	2,695	205	120	10
265	51 Information and cultural industries	417,325	172,795	795	30	30	0
266	52 Finance and insurance	689,210	316,170	1,090	60	15	15
267	53 Real estate and rental and leasing	303,510	126,440	825	50	30	0
268	54 Professional, scientific and technical services	1,122,445	471,625	1,765	50	15	10
269	55 Management of companies and enterprises	20,530	8,440	35	0	0	0
270	56 Administrative and support, waste management and remediation services	722,695	314,005	3,675	120	55	0
271	61 Educational services	1,150,535	433,485	4,275	125	185	15
272	62 Health care and social assistance	1,716,255	611,745	6,900	230	250	25

Note: See symbols and abbreviations in the introductory material and see reference material at the end of the publication.

Certaines caractéristiques des divisions de recensement et des subdivisions de recensement – Données intégrales et données-échantillon (20 %), Ontario, Recensement de 2006 (suite)

Dubreuilville, TP ◆◊	Elliot Lake, CY ◆◊	Garden River 14, IRI ◆	Goulais Bay 15A, IRI ◆◆◊◊	Gros Cap 49, IRI	Hilton, TP ◆◊◊	Caractéristiques	N°
						Caractéristiques de la population	
						Travail non rémunéré (suite)	
10	460	40	0	0	0	Travaux ménagers et soins ou aide aux personnes âgées seulement	215
0	0	0	0	0	0	Soins aux enfants et soins ou aide aux personnes âgées seulement	216
140	2,715	120	10	10	60	Travaux ménagers seulement	217
0	25	10	0	0	0	Soins aux enfants seulement	218
0	35	0	0	0	0	Soins ou aide aux personnes âgées seulement	219
300	5,320	365	35	25	100	Femmes de 15 ans et plus	220
295	4,925	340	30	25	85	Travail non rémunéré déclaré[45]	221
30	325	70	0	0	15	Travaux ménagers et soins aux enfants et soins ou aide aux personnes âgées	222
120	965	135	10	10	25	Travaux ménagers et soins aux enfants seulement	223
25	710	25	0	10	10	Travaux ménagers et soins ou aide aux personnes âgées seulement	224
0	0	0	0	0	0	Soins aux enfants et soins ou aide aux personnes âgées seulement	225
115	2,900	100	10	10	35	Travaux ménagers seulement	226
0	10	0	0	10	0	Soins aux enfants seulement	227
0	10	0	0	0	0	Soins ou aide aux personnes âgées seulement	228
						Activité	
325	4,880	355	30	20	100	Hommes de 15 ans et plus	229
265	1,915	235	25	15	35	Population active	230
245	1,645	200	20	10	35	Personnes occupées	231
20	265	35	10	0	0	Chômeurs	232
60	2,965	110	10	0	70	Inactifs	233
81.5	39.2	66.2	83.3	75.0	35.0	Taux d'activité	234
75.4	33.7	56.3	66.7	50.0	35.0	Taux d'emploi	235
7.5	13.8	14.9	40.0	0.0	0.0	Taux de chômage	236
305	5,320	365	30	25	100	Femmes de 15 ans et plus	237
185	1,980	230	15	10	25	Population active	238
165	1,735	210	15	0	20	Personnes occupées	239
20	245	15	0	0	0	Chômeuses	240
115	3,335	130	15	15	75	Inactives	241
60.7	37.2	63.0	50.0	40.0	25.0	Taux d'activité	242
54.1	32.6	57.5	50.0	0.0	20.0	Taux d'emploi	243
10.8	12.4	6.5	0.0	0.0	0.0	Taux de chômage	244
72.0	38.2	65.7	61.5	50.0	30.0	Les deux sexes - Taux d'activité	245
69.2	59.6	70.0	100.0	0.0	0.0	15 à 24 ans	246
72.7	35.6	64.9	54.5	62.5	31.6	25 ans et plus	247
65.6	33.2	57.3	42.9	40.0	30.0	Les deux sexes - Taux d'emploi	248
53.8	41.7	60.0	66.7	0.0	0.0	15 à 24 ans	249
67.7	32.2	56.6	45.5	50.0	28.2	25 ans et plus	250
8.9	13.2	12.8	25.0	40.0	0.0	Les deux sexes - Taux de chômage	251
16.7	30.5	15.0	0.0	0.0	0.0	15 à 24 ans	252
6.9	9.7	12.2	28.6	0.0	0.0	25 ans et plus	253
450	**3,900**	**470**	**40**	**25**	**55**	**Population active totale de 15 ans et plus**	254
						Industrie - Système de classification des industries de l'Amérique du Nord de 2002	
0	135	20	0	0	0	Industrie - Sans objet[46]	255
450	3,760	450	35	20	60	Toutes les industries[47]	256
85	100	20	10	0	0	11 Agriculture, foresterie, pêche et chasse	257
0	170	0	0	0	0	21 Extraction minière et extraction de pétrole et de gaz	258
0	25	0	0	0	0	22 Services publics	259
0	245	65	10	0	0	23 Construction	260
190	135	25	0	0	15	31-33 Fabrication	261
0	80	0	0	0	0	41 Commerce de gros	262
20	600	25	0	0	0	44-45 Commerce de détail	263
35	185	20	0	0	0	48-49 Transport et entreposage	264
0	75	0	0	0	0	51 Industrie de l'information et industrie culturelle	265
0	50	0	0	0	0	52 Finance et assurances	266
0	90	10	0	0	10	53 Services immobiliers et services de location et de location à bail	267
0	115	0	0	0	10	54 Services professionnels, scientifiques et techniques	268
0	0	0	0	0	0	55 Gestion de sociétés et d'entreprises	269
0	135	25	0	0	0	56 Services administratifs, services de soutien, services de gestion des déchets et services d'assainissement	270
10	280	15	0	0	0	61 Services d'enseignement	271
15	650	60	0	0	0	62 Soins de santé et assistance sociale	272

Nota : Voir les symboles et les abréviations dans les documents d'introduction et voir les documents de référence à la fin de la publication.

Selected characteristics for census divisions and census subdivisions – 100% data and 20% sample data, Ontario, 2006 Census (continued)

No.	Characteristics	Canada †	Ontario PROVINCE †◊	Algoma CD/DR ♦◊	Algoma, Unorganized, North Part, NO ♦♦◊◊	Blind River, T ◊	Bruce Mines, T ♦◊◊
	Population characteristics						
	Industry - North American Industry Classification System 2002 (continued)						
273	71 Arts, entertainment and recreation	346,315	140,830	1,705	55	25	30
274	72 Accommodation and food services	1,126,695	414,975	4,550	360	205	0
275	81 Other services (except public administration)	819,885	303,515	3,210	145	110	10
276	91 Public administration	978,615	350,075	3,985	120	125	15
	Class of worker						
277	Class of worker - Not applicable[46]	284,950	113,845	1,170	70	20	0
278	All classes of worker[47]	16,861,185	6,473,735	55,210	2,655	1,880	275
279	Paid workers	15,535,410	5,966,775	51,820	2,310	1,685	245
280	Employees	14,816,200	5,719,805	50,765	2,220	1,625	240
281	Self-employed (incorporated)	719,210	246,975	1,060	90	55	0
282	Self-employed (unincorporated)	1,274,505	487,950	3,270	325	175	35
283	Unpaid family workers	51,265	19,010	120	15	15	0
	Occupation - National Occupational Classification for Statistics 2006						
284	Male labour force 15 years and over	9,020,595	3,437,670	28,990	1,560	1,015	140
285	Occupation - Not applicable[46]	135,790	51,790	590	40	0	0
286	All occupations[47]	8,884,810	3,385,885	28,400	1,515	1,005	135
287	A Management occupations	1,032,940	418,355	2,645	190	105	30
288	B Business, finance and administrative occupations	863,420	360,230	2,065	50	50	10
289	C Natural and applied sciences and related occupations	865,825	349,305	2,620	130	60	10
290	D Health occupations	188,850	66,945	580	10	35	0
291	E Occupations in social science, education, government service and religion	451,145	174,765	1,270	50	45	0
292	F Occupations in art, culture, recreation and sport	225,340	90,590	425	10	0	10
293	G Sales and service occupations	1,716,465	657,605	5,965	170	200	15
294	H Trades, transport and equipment operators and related occupations	2,374,600	845,600	9,035	670	335	35
295	I Occupations unique to primary industry	503,790	125,655	1,580	170	60	15
296	J Occupations unique to processing, manufacturing and utilities	662,430	296,825	2,215	70	100	25
297	Female labour force 15 years and over	8,125,540	3,149,905	27,390	1,165	885	145
298	Occupation - Not applicable[46]	149,165	62,060	580	30	15	0
299	All occupations[47]	7,976,370	3,087,850	26,810	1,135	870	140
300	A Management occupations	598,790	248,125	1,785	120	20	15
301	B Business, finance and administrative occupations	2,162,005	844,260	6,165	290	205	35
302	C Natural and applied sciences and related occupations	242,225	102,625	720	20	20	0
303	D Health occupations	761,515	273,740	3,175	165	75	15
304	E Occupations in social science, education, government service and religion	963,180	371,620	3,615	35	190	25
305	F Occupations in art, culture, recreation and sport	276,850	110,385	690	10	10	0
306	G Sales and service occupations	2,321,255	865,215	9,665	405	310	40
307	H Trades, transport and equipment operators and related occupations	175,695	65,655	475	45	25	0
308	I Occupations unique to primary industry	144,525	39,425	185	15	0	0
309	J Occupations unique to processing, manufacturing and utilities	330,335	166,780	325	20	0	10
310	**Total employed labour force 15 years and over**	**16,021,180**	**6,164,250**	**51,390**	**2,420**	**1,725**	**260**
	Place of work status						
311	Males	8,431,530	3,230,050	26,260	1,365	875	125
312	Usual place of work	6,494,825	2,539,870	21,450	905	695	80
313	At home	623,290	220,340	1,205	165	50	10
314	Outside Canada	52,480	24,215	190	0	0	0
315	No fixed workplace address	1,260,940	445,625	3,415	290	135	25
316	Females	7,589,645	2,934,195	25,125	1,055	850	135
317	Usual place of work	6,575,070	2,554,780	22,945	855	735	110
318	At home	607,060	216,040	1,175	130	80	10
319	Outside Canada	24,090	12,695	190	0	0	0
320	No fixed workplace address	383,425	150,680	820	75	35	10

Note: See symbols and abbreviations in the introductory material and see reference material at the end of the publication.

Certaines caractéristiques des divisions de recensement et des subdivisions de recensement – Données intégrales et données-échantillon (20 %), Ontario, Recensement de 2006 (suite)

Dubreuilville, TP ◆◇	Elliot Lake, CY ◆◇	Garden River 14, IRI ◆	Goulais Bay 15A, IRI ◆◆◇◇	Gros Cap 49, IRI	Hilton, TP ◆◇◇	Caractéristiques	N°
						Caractéristiques de la population	
						Industrie - Système de classification des industries de l'Amérique du Nord de 2002 (suite)	
25	95	35	0	0	10	71 Arts, spectacles et loisirs	273
30	280	20	0	0	0	72 Hébergement et services de restauration	274
10	235	20	0	0	0	81 Autres services (sauf les administrations publiques)	275
10	195	95	10	10	10	91 Administrations publiques	276
						Catégorie de travailleurs	
0	140	20	10	0	0	Catégorie de travailleurs - Sans objet[46]	277
450	3,760	450	40	20	60	Toutes les catégories de travailleurs[47]	278
450	3,445	430	30	25	55	Travailleurs rémunérés	279
440	3,355	430	30	20	55	Employés	280
0	85	0	10	0	0	Travailleurs autonomes (entreprise constituée en société)	281
10	300	15	10	0	10	Travailleurs autonomes (entreprise non constituée en société)	282
0	15	0	0	0	0	Travailleurs familiaux non rémunérés	283
						Profession - Classification nationale des professions pour statistiques de 2006	
265	1,915	240	20	10	35	Hommes actifs de 15 ans et plus	284
0	70	10	0	0	0	Profession - Sans objet[46]	285
260	1,845	230	25	15	35	Toutes les professions[47]	286
10	170	25	10	0	0	A Gestion	287
0	125	10	0	0	0	B Affaires, finance et administration	288
10	65	10	0	0	0	C Sciences naturelles et appliquées et professions apparentées	289
0	70	0	0	0	0	D Secteur de la santé	290
0	85	0	0	0	0	E Sciences sociales, enseignement, administration publique et religion	291
0	55	0	0	0	0	F Arts, culture, sports et loisirs	292
15	415	30	0	0	10	G Ventes et services	293
110	560	95	10	10	0	H Métiers, transport et machinerie	294
45	240	40	0	0	0	I Professions propres au secteur primaire	295
65	60	10	0	0	0	J Transformation, fabrication et services d'utilité publique	296
185	1,985	230	15	10	25	Femmes actives de 15 ans et plus	297
0	65	10	0	10	0	Profession - Sans objet[46]	298
185	1,915	225	20	10	25	Toutes les professions[47]	299
10	180	10	0	0	0	A Gestion	300
40	330	50	0	0	10	B Affaires, finance et administration	301
10	0	0	0	0	10	C Sciences naturelles et appliquées et professions apparentées	302
0	315	15	10	0	0	D Secteur de la santé	303
15	230	50	0	10	10	E Sciences sociales, enseignement, administration publique et religion	304
0	80	15	0	0	0	F Arts, culture, sports et loisirs	305
75	710	80	0	0	0	G Ventes et services	306
10	35	10	0	0	0	H Métiers, transport et machinerie	307
0	10	0	0	0	0	I Professions propres au secteur primaire	308
35	15	0	0	10	10	J Transformation, fabrication et services d'utilité publique	309
410	**3,385**	**415**	**30**	**20**	**55**	**Population active occupée totale de 15 ans et plus**	310
						Catégorie de lieu de travail	
245	1,645	200	20	10	35	Hommes	311
225	1,270	130	10	0	35	Lieu habituel de travail	312
10	95	0	0	10	0	À domicile	313
0	20	0	0	0	0	En dehors du Canada	314
15	255	60	10	10	0	Sans adresse de travail fixe	315
165	1,735	210	15	10	25	Femmes	316
160	1,620	195	10	10	20	Lieu habituel de travail	317
0	70	0	0	0	0	À domicile	318
0	0	10	0	0	0	En dehors du Canada	319
10	50	10	0	0	10	Sans adresse de travail fixe	320

Nota : Voir les symboles et les abréviations dans les documents d'introduction et voir les documents de référence à la fin de la publication.

Selected characteristics for census divisions and census subdivisions – 100% data and 20% sample data, Ontario, 2006 Census (continued)

No.	Characteristics	Canada †	Ontario PROVINCE †◊	Algoma CD/DR ◆◊	Algoma, Unorganized, North Part, NO ◆◆◊◊	Blind River, T ◊	Bruce Mines, T ◆◊◊
	Population characteristics						
321	**Total employed labour force 15 years and over with usual place of work or no fixed workplace address**	**14,714,260**	**5,690,960**	**48,630**	**2,130**	**1,595**	**230**
	Mode of transportation						
322	Males	7,755,765	2,985,495	24,865	1,200	825	110
323	Car, truck, van, as driver	5,961,465	2,274,805	19,580	1,095	645	85
324	Car, truck, van, as passenger	468,570	191,695	2,060	55	70	15
325	Public transit	670,350	299,915	695	10	0	0
326	Walked	413,990	141,330	1,790	15	60	10
327	All other modes	241,380	77,750	740	25	50	0
328	Females	6,958,490	2,705,465	23,765	930	770	120
329	Car, truck, van, as driver	4,682,860	1,763,230	17,560	745	530	80
330	Car, truck, van, as passenger	664,575	278,715	2,755	120	50	10
331	Public transit	952,370	436,140	855	0	10	0
332	Walked	525,295	178,745	2,190	25	140	30
333	All other modes	133,385	48,640	410	40	35	0
334	**Total population 15 years and over who worked since January 1, 2005**	**18,418,100**	**7,054,270**	**61,170**	**3,065**	**2,015**	**305**
	Language used most often at work						
335	Single responses	18,062,905	6,964,135	60,730	3,045	1,935	305
336	English	14,064,105	6,754,040	59,515	3,015	1,835	305
337	French	3,724,970	97,970	1,040	35	100	0
338	Non-official languages[7]	273,830	112,125	175	0	0	0
339	Chinese, n.o.s.[61]	51,055	22,905	0	0	0	0
340	Cantonese	39,245	18,855	0	0	0	0
341	Other languages[8]	183,530	70,365	160	0	0	0
342	Multiple responses	355,195	90,135	440	15	75	0
343	English and French	252,300	42,945	395	0	75	0
344	English and non-official language	86,820	45,400	40	10	0	0
345	French and non-official language	5,055	230	0	0	0	0
346	English, French and non-official language	11,020	1,560	0	0	0	0
	Dwelling and household characteristics						
347	**Total number of occupied private dwellings**	**12,437,465**	**4,555,030**	**50,005**	**2,415**	**1,610**	**245**
	Housing tenure						
348	Owned	8,509,785	3,235,495	35,610	2,220	1,155	230
349	Rented	3,878,500	1,312,295	13,990	195	455	20
350	Band housing	49,185	7,240	410	0	0	0
	Structural type of dwelling						
351	Single-detached house	6,871,315	2,551,760	34,255	2,225	1,330	230
352	Semi-detached house	591,590	260,170	3,175	45	45	5
353	Row house	690,490	358,495	1,570	5	0	0
354	Apartment, duplex	676,290	158,755	1,780	10	30	0
355	Apartment, building that has five or more storeys	1,114,925	710,785	2,610	0	0	0
356	Apartment, building that has fewer than five storeys	2,289,390	490,355	6,320	5	205	10
357	Other single-attached house	37,995	11,725	165	10	0	0
358	Movable dwelling[48]	163,520	12,200	175	115	0	0
	Condition of dwelling						
359	Regular maintenance only	8,168,615	3,092,900	31,545	1,215	940	135
360	Minor repairs	3,339,840	1,162,105	14,310	920	500	95
361	Major repairs	929,020	300,020	4,150	280	175	25
	Period of construction						
362	Before 1946	1,595,320	677,875	6,525	170	205	75
363	1946 to 1960	1,812,520	690,155	11,495	350	415	15
364	1961 to 1970	1,753,170	640,660	8,940	440	215	25
365	1971 to 1980	2,421,395	776,745	11,450	700	385	40
366	1981 to 1985	1,028,180	338,575	4,000	145	180	25
367	1986 to 1990	1,055,955	410,160	2,780	195	100	15
368	1991 to 1995	894,855	291,480	2,160	170	45	20
369	1996 to 2000	820,370	312,215	1,515	110	45	10
370	2001 to 2006[49]	1,055,690	417,165	1,130	130	20	20

Note: See symbols and abbreviations in the introductory material and see reference material at the end of the publication.

Certaines caractéristiques des divisions de recensement et des subdivisions de recensement – Données intégrales et données-échantillon (20 %), Ontario, Recensement de 2006 (suite)

Dubreuilville, TP ◆◇	Elliot Lake, CY ◆◇	Garden River 14, IRI ◆	Goulais Bay 15A, IRI ◆◆◇◇	Gros Cap 49, IRI	Hilton, TP ◆◇◇	Caractéristiques	N°
						Caractéristiques de la population	
405	**3,195**	**400**	**30**	**20**	**60**	**Population active occupée totale de 15 ans et plus ayant un lieu habituel de travail ou sans adresse de travail fixe**	321
						Mode de transport	
240	1,525	190	20	15	35	Hommes	322
180	1,050	135	15	10	35	Automobile, camion ou fourgonnette, en tant que conducteur	323
15	165	40	0	0	0	Automobile, camion ou fourgonnette, en tant que passager	324
0	30	0	0	0	0	Transport en commun	325
35	205	10	10	10	0	À pied	326
10	75	10	0	10	0	Tous les autres modes	327
165	1,665	210	10	0	20	Femmes	328
110	1,145	155	10	10	20	Automobile, camion ou fourgonnette, en tant que conductrice	329
10	210	35	0	0	0	Automobile, camion ou fourgonnette, en tant que passagère	330
0	30	0	0	0	0	Transport en commun	331
45	245	20	0	0	0	À pied	332
0	30	0	0	0	0	Tous les autres modes	333
500	**4,330**	**475**	**40**	**25**	**60**	**Population totale de 15 ans et plus ayant travaillé depuis le 1er janvier 2005**	334
						Langue utilisée le plus souvent au travail	
485	4,230	475	40	25	60	Réponses uniques	335
95	4,080	475	45	25	65	Anglais	336
390	130	0	0	0	0	Français	337
0	20	0	0	0	0	Langues non officielles[7]	338
0	0	0	0	0	0	Chinois, n.d.a.[61]	339
0	0	0	0	0	0	Cantonais	340
0	20	0	0	0	0	Autres langues[8]	341
10	100	0	0	0	0	Réponses multiples	342
10	100	0	0	0	0	Anglais et français	343
0	0	0	0	0	0	Anglais et langue non officielle	344
0	0	0	0	0	0	Français et langue non officielle	345
0	0	0	0	0	0	Anglais, français et langue non officielle	346
						Caractéristiques des logements et des ménages	
285	**5,650**	**350**	**30**	**30**	**105**	**Nombre total de logements privés occupés**	347
						Mode d'occupation	
245	3,440	245	30	10	95	Possédé	348
40	2,205	50	0	0	10	Loué	349
0	0	55	0	10	0	Logement de bande	350
						Type de construction résidentielle	
225	2,530	345	30	20	105	Maison individuelle non attenante	351
45	1,030	0	0	0	0	Maison jumelée	352
0	585	0	0	5	0	Maison en rangée	353
0	130	0	0	0	0	Appartement, duplex	354
0	570	0	0	0	0	Appartement, immeuble de cinq étages ou plus	355
15	790	0	0	0	0	Appartement, immeuble de moins de cinq étages	356
0	0	0	0	0	0	Autre maison individuelle attenante	357
0	10	5	0	0	0	Logement mobile[48]	358
						État du logement	
145	3,765	150	10	10	70	Entretien régulier seulement	359
105	1,430	120	10	10	25	Réparations mineures	360
35	455	85	10	10	10	Réparations majeures	361
						Période de construction	
10	100	0	0	0	0	Avant 1946	362
25	1,860	10	0	0	0	1946 à 1960	363
35	665	35	0	0	20	1961 à 1970	364
120	1,955	75	0	10	25	1971 à 1980	365
20	925	30	0	0	10	1981 à 1985	366
45	85	30	0	0	15	1986 à 1990	367
15	35	35	0	10	10	1991 à 1995	368
15	10	65	0	10	15	1996 à 2000	369
0	10	70	0	0	0	2001 à 2006[49]	370

Nota : Voir les symboles et les abréviations dans les documents d'introduction et voir les documents de référence à la fin de la publication.

Selected characteristics for census divisions and census subdivisions – 100% data and 20% sample data, Ontario, 2006 Census (continued)

No.	Characteristics	Canada †	Ontario PROVINCE †◊	Algoma CD/DR ◆◊	Algoma, Unorganized, North Part, NO ◆◆◊◊	Blind River, T ◊	Bruce Mines, T ◆◊◊
	Dwelling and household characteristics						
371	Average number of rooms per dwelling	6.4	6.6	6.5	6.4	6.6	6.7
372	Average number of bedrooms per dwelling	2.7	2.7	2.7	2.7	2.7	2.9
373	Average value of dwelling $	263,369	297,479	123,912	141,011	122,854	113,055
374	**Total number of private households**	**12,435,520**	**4,554,250**	**50,045**	**2,410**	**1,620**	**250**
	Household size						
375	1 person	3,328,370	1,105,075	14,330	570	460	65
376	2 persons	4,176,930	1,449,975	18,940	1,065	635	110
377	3 persons	1,982,305	755,060	7,380	315	240	35
378	4 to 5 persons	2,590,725	1,082,905	8,720	425	265	35
379	6 or more persons	357,185	161,245	675	35	15	5
	Household type						
380	One-family households[50]	8,421,050	3,187,935	34,130	1,770	1,100	180
381	Multiple-family households	230,285	113,190	405	45	10	0
382	Non-family households	3,786,135	1,253,900	15,475	600	510	65
383	Number of persons in private households	31,072,420	11,980,410	115,785	5,695	3,710	560
384	Average number of persons in private households	2.5	2.6	2.3	2.4	2.3	2.2
385	Tenant-occupied private non-farm, non-reserve dwellings[51]	3,861,155	1,308,760	13,775	195	455	15
386	Average gross rent $[51]	728	834	572	534	454	0
387	Tenant-occupied households spending 30% or more of household income on gross rent[52]	1,546,980	580,270	5,520	50	135	10
388	Tenant-occupied households spending from 30% to 99% of household income on gross rent[52]	1,311,810	487,775	4,975	50	130	10
389	Owner-occupied private non-farm, non-reserve dwellings[53]	8,381,125	3,204,400	34,815	2,195	1,155	230
390	Average owner's major payments $[53]	998	1,167	707	578	676	736
391	Owner households spending 30% or more of household income on owner's major payments[52]	1,491,265	665,170	4,040	320	110	50
392	Owner households spending from 30% to 99% of household income on owner's major payments[52]	1,279,730	574,625	3,370	245	80	50
	Census family characteristics						
393	**Total number of census families in private households**	**8,896,845**	**3,422,320**	**34,945**	**1,855**	**1,110**	**180**
	Family structure and number of children						
394	Total couple families	7,482,780	2,881,605	29,245	1,670	960	155
395	Total families of married couples	6,105,910	2,530,560	24,910	1,430	790	145
396	Without children at home	2,662,135	1,008,545	13,225	820	430	95
397	With children at home	3,443,780	1,522,010	11,685	605	360	55
398	1 child	1,267,620	542,650	4,620	255	120	20
399	2 children	1,497,750	675,125	5,020	250	160	30
400	3 or more children	678,400	304,240	2,045	95	75	0
401	Total families of common-law couples	1,376,865	351,040	4,335	240	175	10
402	Without children at home	758,715	209,300	2,285	130	100	10
403	With children at home	618,150	141,745	2,045	110	80	10
404	1 child	291,255	69,395	940	40	45	10
405	2 children	234,755	50,755	750	50	35	0
406	3 or more children	92,140	21,595	355	15	10	0
407	Total lone-parent families	1,414,060	540,715	5,700	185	145	20
408	Female parent	1,132,290	441,105	4,585	120	120	20
409	1 child	682,025	260,195	2,865	95	80	10
410	2 children	327,665	130,650	1,275	15	45	0
411	3 or more children	122,600	50,265	445	10	0	10
412	Male parent	281,770	99,605	1,115	70	20	10
413	1 child	188,790	66,340	810	60	15	0
414	2 children	72,665	26,005	245	0	10	0
415	3 or more children	20,320	7,270	50	0	0	0

Note: See symbols and abbreviations in the introductory material and see reference material at the end of the publication.

Certaines caractéristiques des divisions de recensement et des subdivisions de recensement – Données intégrales et données-échantillon (20 %), Ontario, Recensement de 2006 (suite)

Dubreuilville, TP ◆◊	Elliot Lake, CY ◆◊	Garden River 14, IRI ◆	Goulais Bay 15A, IRI ◆◆◊◊	Gros Cap 49, IRI	Hilton, TP ◆◊◊	Caractéristiques	N°
						Caractéristiques des logements et des ménages	
6.8	5.9	6.2	4.7	6.6	6.7	Nombre moyen de pièces par logement	371
3.1	2.6	2.8	2.3	2.8	2.9	Nombre moyen de chambres à coucher par logement	372
79,242	78,057	0	0	0	161,155	Valeur moyenne du logement $	373
285	**5,645**	**350**	**30**	**30**	**105**	**Nombre total de ménages privés**	374
						Taille du ménage	
50	1,915	75	5	10	25	1 personne	375
95	2,560	100	15	10	55	2 personnes	376
55	555	65	5	5	10	3 personnes	377
75	575	100	5	0	15	4 à 5 personnes	378
5	45	10	0	0	5	6 personnes ou plus	379
						Genre de ménage	
220	3,565	250	25	15	75	Ménages unifamiliaux[50]	380
10	0	0	0	0	0	Ménages multifamiliaux	381
55	2,080	90	10	10	30	Ménages non familiaux	382
770	11,435	985	80	50	245	Nombre de personnes dans les ménages privés	383
2.7	2.0	2.8	2.3	2.2	2.3	Nombre moyen de personnes dans les ménages privés	384
40	2,200	0	0	0	10	Ménages locataires dans les logements privés non agricoles hors réserve[51]	385
534	555	0	0	0	0	Loyer brut moyen $[51]	386
0	885	0	0	0	0	Ménages locataires consacrant 30 % ou plus du revenu du ménage au loyer brut[52]	387
0	800	0	0	0	0	Ménages locataires consacrant de 30 % à 99 % du revenu du ménage au loyer brut[52]	388
245	3,440	0	0	0	95	Ménages propriétaires dans les logements privés non agricoles hors réserve[53]	389
664	585	0	0	0	528	Principales dépenses de propriété moyennes $[53]	390
20	430	0	0	0	0	Ménages propriétaires consacrant 30 % ou plus du revenu du ménage aux principales dépenses de propriété[52]	391
15	360	0	0	0	0	Ménages propriétaires consacrant de 30 % à 99 % du revenu du ménage aux principales dépenses de propriété[52]	392
						Caractéristiques des familles de recensement	
235	**3,570**	**265**	**30**	**15**	**80**	**Nombre total de familles de recensement dans les ménages privés**	393
						Structure de la famille et le nombre d'enfants	
210	3,160	180	20	15	80	Total des familles avec conjoints	394
125	2,660	125	10	10	65	Total des familles avec couples mariés	395
55	1,960	30	10	10	45	Sans enfants à la maison	396
70	700	95	0	0	20	Avec enfants à la maison	397
25	295	30	0	0	15	1 enfant	398
25	260	30	0	0	0	2 enfants	399
15	145	35	0	0	0	3 enfants ou plus	400
85	500	55	10	0	15	Total des familles avec couples en union libre	401
35	295	15	0	0	15	Sans enfants à la maison	402
45	205	40	0	0	0	Avec enfants à la maison	403
20	75	15	0	0	0	1 enfant	404
20	95	10	0	0	0	2 enfants	405
0	35	10	0	0	0	3 enfants ou plus	406
25	415	90	10	0	10	Total des familles monoparentales	407
25	305	70	10	0	0	Parent de sexe féminin	408
20	180	40	0	0	0	1 enfant	409
10	110	20	10	0	10	2 enfants	410
0	15	10	0	0	0	3 enfants ou plus	411
0	105	15	0	0	0	Parent de sexe masculin	412
0	80	15	0	0	0	1 enfant	413
0	15	0	0	0	0	2 enfants	414
0	10	0	0	0	0	3 enfants ou plus	415

Nota : Voir les symboles et les abréviations dans les documents d'introduction et voir les documents de référence à la fin de la publication.

Selected characteristics for census divisions and census subdivisions – 100% data and 20% sample data, Ontario, 2006 Census (continued)

No.	Characteristics	Canada †	Ontario PROVINCE †◊	Algoma CD/DR ◆◊	Algoma, Unorganized, North Part, NO ◆◆◊◊	Blind River, T ◊	Bruce Mines, T ◆◊◊
	Census family characteristics						
416	**Total number of children at home**	**9,733,770**	**3,977,005**	**33,190**	**1,500**	**985**	**140**
	Age group						
417	Under 6 years	2,013,065	800,660	5,740	230	190	15
418	6 to 14 years	3,501,480	1,390,905	11,890	550	340	60
419	15 to 17 years	1,270,255	493,590	4,740	240	135	25
420	18 to 24 years	1,934,225	828,155	7,170	295	235	25
421	25 years and over	1,014,740	463,690	3,640	180	90	10
422	Average number of children at home per census family[54]	1.1	1.2	0.9	0.8	0.9	0.8
423	**Total number of persons in private households**	**31,074,405**	**11,981,235**	**115,715**	**5,710**	**3,695**	**560**
	Census family status and living arrangements						
424	Number of persons not in census families	4,961,015	1,700,305	18,340	680	635	85
425	Living with relatives[55]	644,015	258,915	1,835	10	65	0
426	Living with non-relatives only	989,950	336,520	2,185	125	125	20
427	Living alone	3,327,045	1,104,870	14,320	545	445	55
428	Number of census family persons	26,113,390	10,280,925	97,380	5,025	3,060	480
429	Average number of persons per census family	2.9	3.0	2.8	2.7	2.8	2.7
430	**Total number of persons aged 65 years and over**	**4,011,910**	**1,536,475**	**20,985**	**955**	**600**	**130**
431	Number of persons not in census families aged 65 years and over	1,406,915	513,470	7,240	270	220	35
432	Living with relatives[55]	209,205	94,535	565	0	30	10
433	Living with non-relatives only	69,045	23,715	335	35	25	10
434	Living alone	1,128,665	395,220	6,345	230	165	25
435	Number of census family persons aged 65 years and over	2,604,995	1,023,005	13,740	685	375	95
	Economic family characteristics						
436	**Total number of economic families in private households**	**8,782,350**	**3,347,610**	**34,905**	**1,815**	**1,120**	**180**
	Size of family						
437	2 persons	4,002,680	1,401,145	18,415	1,045	615	105
438	3 persons	1,907,675	733,455	7,290	305	240	35
439	4 persons	1,835,335	756,415	6,310	330	185	35
440	5 or more persons	1,036,660	456,590	2,890	130	80	10
441	Total number of persons in economic families	26,757,400	10,539,845	99,215	5,040	3,125	485
442	Average number of persons per economic family	3.0	3.0	3.0	3.0	3.0	3.0
443	Total number of persons not in economic families	4,317,000	1,441,385	16,505	670	570	75
	2005 income characteristics						
444	**Population 15 years and over**	**25,664,220**	**9,819,420**	**98,260**	**4,935**	**3,170**	**485**
	Sex and total income groups in 2005						
445	Without income	1,241,065	479,400	4,195	280	190	10
446	With income	24,423,165	9,340,020	94,065	4,655	2,985	470
447	Under $1,000[56]	963,270	405,540	3,395	275	90	0
448	$1,000 to $2,999	819,530	332,410	3,285	155	105	10
449	$3,000 to $4,999	792,565	310,580	3,075	165	90	35
450	$5,000 to $6,999	896,425	332,820	3,625	205	150	45
451	$7,000 to $9,999	1,514,745	536,680	5,480	350	175	10
452	$10,000 to $11,999	1,037,220	387,130	4,630	175	220	40
453	$12,000 to $14,999	1,581,205	558,640	5,880	300	190	10
454	$15,000 to $19,999	2,430,720	832,550	10,815	605	330	45
455	$20,000 to $24,999	1,935,750	684,095	7,775	330	180	30
456	$25,000 to $29,999	1,745,745	613,670	7,040	290	205	55
457	$30,000 to $34,999	1,716,180	618,315	6,910	340	165	40
458	$35,000 to $39,999	1,473,270	559,150	5,645	230	200	30
459	$40,000 to $44,999	1,255,425	490,075	4,435	210	165	15
460	$45,000 to $49,999	1,038,085	412,215	3,745	205	95	25
461	$50,000 to $59,999	1,587,765	649,410	5,630	255	225	20
462	$60,000 and over	3,635,265	1,616,730	12,695	565	385	40
463	Median income $[57]	25,615	27,258	24,427	21,953	23,949	25,204
464	Average income $[57]	35,498	38,099	31,858	28,905	34,144	28,817
465	Standard error of average income $[57]	30	56	247	697	1,427	2,201

Note: See symbols and abbreviations in the introductory material and see reference material at the end of the publication.

Certaines caractéristiques des divisions de recensement et des subdivisions de recensement – Données intégrales et données-échantillon (20 %), Ontario, Recensement de 2006 (suite)

Dubreuilville, TP ♦◊	Elliot Lake, CY ♦◊	Garden River 14, IRI ♦	Goulais Bay 15A, IRI ♦♦◊◊	Gros Cap 49, IRI	Hilton, TP ♦◊◊	Caractéristiques	N°
						Caractéristiques des familles de recensement	
230	**2,225**	**405**	**30**	**10**	**35**	**Nombre total d'enfants à la maison**	416
						Groupes d'âge	
65	380	80	0	0	10	Moins de 6 ans	417
65	830	185	10	0	10	6 à 14 ans	418
40	410	35	0	10	10	15 à 17 ans	419
25	440	75	10	0	10	18 à 24 ans	420
25	160	25	0	0	10	25 ans et plus	421
1.0	0.6	1.5	1.0	0.5	0.4	Nombre moyen d'enfants à la maison par famille de recensement[54]	422
760	**11,440**	**985**	**80**	**50**	**235**	**Nombre total de personnes dans les ménages privés**	423
						Situation des particuliers dans la famille de recensement et des particuliers dans le ménage	
85	2,480	135	10	10	45	Nombre de personnes hors famille de recensement	424
20	190	40	0	0	20	Vivant avec des personnes apparentées[55]	425
15	375	20	0	0	0	Vivant avec des personnes non apparentées seulement	426
55	1,915	80	0	10	25	Vivant seules	427
675	8,955	850	75	40	195	Nombre de membres d'une famille de recensement	428
2.9	2.5	3.2	2.5	2.0	2.2	Nombre moyen de personnes par famille de recensement	429
30	**3,615**	**65**	**10**	**0**	**65**	**Nombre total de personnes âgées de 65 ans et plus**	430
10	1,275	30	0	0	20	Nombre de personnes hors famille de recensement âgées de 65 ans et plus	431
10	75	10	0	0	0	Vivant avec des personnes apparentées[55]	432
0	130	0	0	0	0	Vivant avec des personnes non apparentées seulement	433
0	1,075	15	0	0	20	Vivant seules	434
20	2,340	40	10	0	45	Nombre de membres d'une famille de recensement âgés de 65 ans et plus	435
						Caractéristiques des familles économiques	
225	**3,595**	**265**	**25**	**20**	**80**	**Nombre total de familles économiques dans les ménages privés**	436
						Taille de la famille	
90	2,450	95	10	10	55	2 personnes	437
60	560	65	10	0	10	3 personnes	438
60	390	60	0	0	0	4 personnes	439
15	200	55	0	0	10	5 personnes ou plus	440
695	9,145	890	80	45	210	Nombre total de personnes dans les familles économiques	441
3.0	3.0	3.0	3.0	3.0	3.0	Nombre moyen de personnes par famille économique	442
65	2,290	95	0	10	30	Nombre total de personnes hors famille économique	443
						Caractéristiques du revenu de 2005	
630	**10,200**	**715**	**X**	**X**	**X**	**Population de 15 ans et plus**	444
						Sexe et groupes de revenu total en 2005	
30	390	50	X	X	X	Sans revenu	445
600	9,815	665	X	X	X	Avec un revenu	446
30	380	60	X	X	X	Moins de 1 000 $[56]	447
10	365	40	X	X	X	1 000 $ à 2 999 $	448
20	265	35	X	X	X	3 000 $ à 4 999 $	449
30	400	40	X	X	X	5 000 $ à 6 999 $	450
25	595	60	X	X	X	7 000 $ à 9 999 $	451
10	555	45	X	X	X	10 000 $ à 11 999 $	452
25	735	55	X	X	X	12 000 $ à 14 999 $	453
40	1,585	65	X	X	X	15 000 $ à 19 999 $	454
40	895	55	X	X	X	20 000 $ à 24 999 $	455
30	870	55	X	X	X	25 000 $ à 29 999 $	456
15	735	30	X	X	X	30 000 $ à 34 999 $	457
30	565	35	X	X	X	35 000 $ à 39 999 $	458
30	385	30	X	X	X	40 000 $ à 44 999 $	459
35	280	15	X	X	X	45 000 $ à 49 999$	460
105	415	15	X	X	X	50 000 $ à 59 999$	461
115	770	15	X	X	X	60 000 $ et plus	462
39,947	20,111	14,912	X	X	X	Revenu médian $[57]	463
39,881	26,406	19,564	X	X	X	Revenu moyen $[57]	464
3,110	497	0	X	X	X	Erreur type de revenu moyen $[57]	465

Nota : Voir les symboles et les abréviations dans les documents d'introduction et voir les documents de référence à la fin de la publication.

Selected characteristics for census divisions and census subdivisions – 100% data and 20% sample data, Ontario, 2006 Census (continued)

No.	Characteristics	Canada †	Ontario PROVINCE †◊	Algoma CD/DR ◆◊	Algoma, Unorganized, North Part, NO ◆◆◊◊	Blind River, T ◊	Bruce Mines, T ◆◊◊
	2005 income characteristics						
	Sex and total income groups in 2005 (continued)						
466	Total - Males	12,470,785	4,744,710	47,500	2,560	1,500	235
467	Without income	518,630	203,815	1,680	105	65	10
468	With income	11,952,160	4,540,895	45,825	2,455	1,430	220
469	Under $1,000[56]	518,615	219,110	1,685	145	50	0
470	$1,000 to $2,999	323,030	125,450	1,365	55	50	0
471	$3,000 to $4,999	294,645	115,660	1,050	50	25	10
472	$5,000 to $6,999	327,550	119,495	1,185	60	55	15
473	$7,000 to $9,999	554,785	200,580	1,935	85	60	0
474	$10,000 to $11,999	397,875	147,945	1,725	80	75	15
475	$12,000 to $14,999	568,160	200,165	1,860	85	70	0
476	$15,000 to $19,999	937,015	314,955	3,735	255	110	15
477	$20,000 to $24,999	837,305	288,360	3,250	150	85	15
478	$25,000 to $29,999	810,605	274,580	3,485	190	105	30
479	$30,000 to $34,999	838,090	292,450	3,790	245	85	10
480	$35,000 to $39,999	751,425	273,870	2,980	120	80	20
481	$40,000 to $44,999	681,735	257,430	2,630	170	105	15
482	$45,000 to $49,999	597,145	229,090	2,185	150	60	15
483	$50,000 to $59,999	972,070	386,575	3,630	180	130	15
484	$60,000 and over	2,542,100	1,095,175	9,330	420	280	35
485	Median income $[57]	32,224	34,454	31,986	32,010	32,035	29,694
486	Average income $[57]	43,684	46,962	39,259	35,663	41,674	35,418
487	Standard error of average income $[57]	56	107	457	1,056	2,310	3,527
488	Total - Females	13,193,440	5,074,710	50,755	2,380	1,675	250
489	Without income	722,435	275,585	2,520	175	120	0
490	With income	12,471,000	4,799,125	48,240	2,205	1,555	250
491	Under $1,000[56]	444,650	186,425	1,710	130	35	10
492	$1,000 to $2,999	496,500	206,960	1,920	100	55	0
493	$3,000 to $4,999	497,920	194,915	2,025	110	70	25
494	$5,000 to $6,999	568,875	213,325	2,440	145	95	25
495	$7,000 to $9,999	959,965	336,100	3,545	260	120	0
496	$10,000 to $11,999	639,345	239,190	2,900	95	140	30
497	$12,000 to $14,999	1,013,040	358,480	4,015	215	120	10
498	$15,000 to $19,999	1,493,705	517,595	7,075	355	220	30
499	$20,000 to $24,999	1,098,445	395,735	4,525	175	90	20
500	$25,000 to $29,999	935,140	339,090	3,550	100	100	20
501	$30,000 to $34,999	878,085	325,860	3,120	95	80	30
502	$35,000 to $39,999	721,840	285,275	2,665	100	120	10
503	$40,000 to $44,999	573,680	232,645	1,810	45	60	0
504	$45,000 to $49,999	440,935	183,130	1,565	55	40	10
505	$50,000 to $59,999	615,695	262,835	2,000	75	95	0
506	$60,000 and over	1,093,160	521,555	3,365	140	105	10
507	Median income $[57]	20,460	21,669	18,716	15,791	17,624	18,641
508	Average income $[57]	27,653	29,712	24,827	21,381	27,218	23,025
509	Standard error of average income $[57]	21	41	194	801	1,634	2,408
	Composition of total income						
510	Composition of total income in 2005 %	100.0	100.0	100.0	100.0	100.0	100.0
511	Employment income %	76.2	77.4	66.6	64.3	68.5	62.8
512	Government transfer payments %	11.1	9.8	16.9	19.4	17.4	20.0
513	Other %	12.7	12.9	16.5	16.3	14.1	17.6
514	**Population 15 years and over with employment income in 2005**	**18,201,265**	**6,991,675**	**63,680**	**3,095**	**1,995**	**325**
	Sex and work activity						
515	Median employment income in 2005 $	26,850	29,335	22,738	18,310	25,210	23,466
516	Average employment income in 2005 $	36,301	39,386	31,360	27,947	35,010	26,169
517	Standard error of average employment income $	34	63	271	983	1,887	2,990
518	Worked full year, full time[59]	9,275,765	3,690,670	29,445	1,375	865	155
519	Median employment income in 2005 $	41,401	44,748	43,279	42,359	44,140	38,983
520	Average employment income in 2005 $	51,221	55,626	49,076	44,046	55,185	40,674
521	Standard error of average employment income $	52	95	435	1,690	3,448	3,477
522	Worked part year or part time[60]	7,766,075	2,839,180	27,440	1,450	995	140
523	Median employment income in 2005 $	13,072	12,810	10,826	11,086	11,463	6,189
524	Average employment income in 2005 $	22,398	22,895	18,861	17,602	20,476	14,853
525	Standard error of average employment income $	41	83	293	900	1,571	4,380
526	Males 15 years and over with employment income[58]	9,480,555	3,621,765	33,755	1,795	1,050	170
527	Median employment income in 2005 $	32,874	35,702	29,244	24,039	32,704	23,489
528	Average employment income in 2005 $	43,869	47,513	36,806	32,158	42,493	26,818
529	Standard error of average employment income $	60	113	447	1,434	2,883	4,682

Note: See symbols and abbreviations in the introductory material and see reference material at the end of the publication.

Certaines caractéristiques des divisions de recensement et des subdivisions de recensement – Données intégrales et données-échantillon (20 %), Ontario, Recensement de 2006 (suite)

Dubreuilville, TP ◆◇	Elliot Lake, CY ◆◇	Garden River 14, IRI ◆	Goulais Bay 15A, IRI ◆◆◇◇	Gros Cap 49, IRI	Hilton, TP ◆◇◇	Caractéristiques	N°
						Caractéristiques du revenu de 2005	
						Sexe et groupes de revenu total en 2005 (suite)	
325	4,885	355	X	X	X	Total - Hommes	466
10	145	20	X	X	X	Sans revenu	467
320	4,735	330	X	X	X	Avec un revenu	468
30	170	40	X	X	X	Moins de 1 000 $[56]	469
0	170	20	X	X	X	1 000 $ à 2 999 $	470
0	55	10	X	X	X	3 000 $ à 4 999 $	471
10	125	15	X	X	X	5 000 $ à 6 999 $	472
0	190	30	X	X	X	7 000 $ à 9 999 $	473
0	185	20	X	X	X	10 000 $ à 11 999 $	474
0	230	25	X	X	X	12 000 $ à 14 999 $	475
0	740	35	X	X	X	15 000 $ à 19 999 $	476
10	430	35	X	X	X	20 000 $ à 24 999 $	477
25	450	25	X	X	X	25 000 $ à 29 999 $	478
10	410	20	X	X	X	30 000 $ à 34 999 $	479
0	365	20	X	X	X	35 000 $ à 39 999 $	480
20	225	15	X	X	X	40 000 $ à $44 999 $	481
25	150	10	X	X	X	45 000 $ à $49 999 $	482
85	315	10	X	X	X	50 000 $ à $59 999 $	483
100	515	10	X	X	X	60 000 $ et plus	484
54,272	25,809	16,064	X	X	X	Revenu médian $[57]	485
50,288	31,626	20,153	X	X	X	Revenu moyen $[57]	486
3,486	846	0	X	X	X	Erreur type de revenu moyen $[57]	487
300	5,320	365	X	X	X	Total - Femmes	488
25	245	30	X	X	X	Sans revenu	489
280	5,075	335	X	X	X	Avec un revenu	490
10	215	20	X	X	X	Moins de 1 000 $[56]	491
10	195	30	X	X	X	1 000$ à 2 999 $	492
20	210	25	X	X	X	3 000 $ à 4 999 $	493
20	275	25	X	X	X	5 000 $ à 6 999 $	494
25	410	35	X	X	X	7 000 $ à 9 999 $	495
15	375	25	X	X	X	10 000 $ à 11 999 $	496
20	510	25	X	X	X	12 000 $ à 14 999 $	497
40	840	30	X	X	X	15 000 $ à 19 999 $	498
30	465	20	X	X	X	20 000 $ à 24 999 $	499
0	420	30	X	X	X	25 000 $ à 29 999 $	500
10	325	10	X	X	X	30 000 $ à 34 999 $	501
30	200	20	X	X	X	35 000 $ à 39 999 $	502
15	155	15	X	X	X	40 000 $ à 44 999 $	503
10	130	10	X	X	X	45 000 $ à 49 999 $	504
20	105	10	X	X	X	50 000 $ à 59 999 $	505
15	255	10	X	X	X	60 000 $ et plus	506
19,623	16,735	14,400	X	X	X	Revenu médian $[57]	507
27,983	21,538	18,978	X	X	X	Revenu moyen $[57]	508
4,951	506	0	X	X	X	Erreur type de revenu moyen $[57]	509
						Composition du revenu total	
100.0	100.0	100.0	X	X	X	Composition du revenu total en 2005 %	510
86.8	46.3	70.8	X	X	X	Revenu d'emploi %	511
8.3	30.2	24.6	X	X	X	Transferts gouvernementaux %	512
4.0	23.5	5.3	X	X	X	Autres %	513
480	**4,630**	**430**	**X**	**X**	**X**	**Population de 15 ans et plus avec un revenu d'emploi en 2005**	514
						Sexe et travail	
46,035	16,288	17,088	X	X	X	Revenu médian d'emploi en 2005 $	515
43,278	25,880	21,250	X	X	X	Revenu moyen d'emploi en 2005 $	516
3,359	919	0	X	X	X	Erreur type de revenu moyen d'emploi $	517
285	1,835	205	X	X	X	A travaillé toute l'année à plein temps[59]	518
49,984	38,256	30,037	X	X	X	Revenu médian d'emploi en 2005 $	519
49,072	43,238	31,874	X	X	X	Revenu moyen d'emploi en 2005 $	520
4,219	1,311	0	X	X	X	Erreur type de revenu moyen d'emploi $	521
160	2,170	175	X	X	X	A travaillé une partie de l'année ou à temps partiel[60]	522
25,461	8,564	9,088	X	X	X	Revenu médian d'emploi en 2005 $	523
40,332	17,183	12,739	X	X	X	Revenu moyen d'emploi en 2005 $	524
6,093	1,285	0	X	X	X	Erreur type de revenu moyen d'emploi $	525
265	2,395	205	X	X	X	Hommes de 15 ans et plus avec un revenu d'emploi[58]	526
56,076	18,467	17,728	X	X	X	Revenu médian d'emploi en 2005 $	527
56,219	29,354	21,959	X	X	X	Revenu moyen d'emploi en 2005 $	528
3,417	1,529	0	X	X	X	Erreur type de revenu moyen d'emploi $	529

Nota : Voir les symboles et les abréviations dans les documents d'introduction et voir les documents de référence à la fin de la publication.

Selected characteristics for census divisions and census subdivisions – 100% data and 20% sample data, Ontario, 2006 Census (continued)

No.	Characteristics	Canada †	Ontario PROVINCE †◊	Algoma CD/DR ◆◊	Algoma, Unorganized, North Part, NO ◆◆◊◊	Blind River, T ◊	Bruce Mines, T ◆◊◊
	2005 income characteristics						
	Sex and work activity (continued)						
530	Worked full year, full time[59]	5,332,045	2,116,730	16,705	870	490	75
531	Median employment income in 2005 $	46,778	50,057	51,486	49,290	51,536	38,899
532	Average employment income in 2005 $	58,537	63,446	56,231	49,247	62,518	39,254
533	Standard error of average employment income $	86	157	677	2,189	4,771	5,607
534	Worked part year or part time[60]	3,575,985	1,274,490	12,390	720	500	65
535	Median employment income in 2005 $	15,047	14,302	12,002	12,724	17,986	6,183
536	Average employment income in 2005 $	27,304	27,619	22,993	20,144	26,040	22,993
537	Standard error of average employment income $	82	168	554	1,425	2,826	8,730
538	Females 15 years and over with employment income[58]	8,720,715	3,369,915	29,920	1,300	945	155
539	Median employment income in 2005 $	21,543	23,755	18,906	15,009	18,040	21,865
540	Average employment income in 2005 $	28,073	30,653	25,217	22,148	26,690	25,456
541	Standard error of average employment income $	24	47	270	1,208	2,217	3,490
542	Worked full year, full time[59]	3,943,725	1,573,940	12,740	500	370	80
543	Median employment income in 2005 $	35,830	38,914	35,822	31,525	35,100	39,761
544	Average employment income in 2005 $	41,331	45,109	39,695	34,971	45,443	42,023
545	Standard error of average employment income $	37	69	440	2,440	4,659	4,044
546	Worked part year or part time[60]	4,190,095	1,564,685	15,050	735	490	75
547	Median employment income in 2005 $	11,840	11,952	10,019	10,014	9,889	6,280
548	Average employment income in 2005 $	18,211	19,048	15,460	15,114	14,816	7,923
549	Standard error of average employment income $	29	60	259	1,084	1,194	1,419
550	**Total number of economic families in private households**	**8,782,350**	**3,347,610**	**34,905**	**1,815**	**1,125**	**180**
	Family income groups in 2005						
551	Under $10,000	210,915	81,820	720	65	25	0
552	$10,000 to $19,999	391,775	132,405	1,840	100	60	0
553	$20,000 to $29,999	719,910	228,360	2,960	185	100	15
554	$30,000 to $39,999	863,010	288,085	4,235	215	160	45
555	$40,000 to $49,999	867,165	294,340	3,905	185	150	15
556	$50,000 to $59,999	831,100	288,750	3,255	140	95	25
557	$60,000 to $69,999	786,305	283,825	3,265	200	95	20
558	$70,000 to $79,999	715,905	269,270	2,870	160	90	30
559	$80,000 to $89,999	628,425	246,270	2,395	165	85	15
560	$90,000 to $99,999	531,025	214,415	1,965	105	55	0
561	$100,000 and over	2,236,805	1,020,065	7,500	290	220	15
562	Median family income $	66,343	72,734	61,547	61,283	58,521	59,089
563	Average family income $	82,325	90,526	71,961	64,592	71,320	58,778
564	Standard error of average family income $	83	159	673	1,778	3,211	4,162
	Family after-tax income groups in 2005						
565	Under $10,000	217,720	84,330	730	65	20	0
566	$10,000 to $19,999	404,475	136,530	1,905	105	65	10
567	$20,000 to $29,999	805,650	255,635	3,365	205	130	20
568	$30,000 to $39,999	1,102,730	365,265	5,355	265	210	40
569	$40,000 to $49,999	1,106,915	378,700	4,615	225	145	25
570	$50,000 to $59,999	1,035,660	369,600	4,030	260	120	25
571	$60,000 to $69,999	919,945	349,905	3,770	165	100	45
572	$70,000 to $79,999	768,590	307,525	3,045	215	105	10
573	$80,000 to $89,999	605,465	250,365	2,115	105	40	0
574	$90,000 to $99,999	462,865	203,270	1,645	45	50	0
575	$100,000 and over	1,352,335	646,475	4,325	150	145	10
576	Median after-tax family income $	57,178	62,288	53,601	52,865	49,781	49,617
577	Average after-tax family income $	67,567	73,454	60,707	54,802	60,784	51,524
578	Standard error of average after-tax family income $	54	102	480	1,363	2,509	3,181
	Income status in 2005						
579	Total population in private households for income status	30,628,935	11,926,140	112,270	5,700	3,695	565
580	Below low income cut-off before tax in 2005	4,701,020	1,749,965	14,840	585	465	40
581	Prevalence of low income before tax in 2005 %	15.3	14.7	13.2	10.3	12.4	7.1
582	Below low income cut-off after tax in 2005	3,484,625	1,324,485	10,070	420	280	0
583	Prevalence of low income after tax in 2005 %	11.4	11.1	9.0	7.5	7.7	0.0

Note: See symbols and abbreviations in the introductory material and see reference material at the end of the publication.

Certaines caractéristiques des divisions de recensement et des subdivisions de recensement – Données intégrales et données-échantillon (20 %), Ontario, Recensement de 2006 (suite)

Dubreuilville, TP ◆◇	Elliot Lake, CY ◆◇	Garden River 14, IRI ◆	Goulais Bay 15A, IRI ◆◆◇◇	Gros Cap 49, IRI	Hilton, TP ◆◇◇	Caractéristiques	N°
						Caractéristiques du revenu de 2005	
						Sexe et travail (suite)	
170	965	90	X	X	X	A travaillé toute l'année à plein temps[59]	530
56,085	43,207	30,720	X	X	X	Revenu médian d'emploi en 2005 $	531
56,836	48,028	32,849	X	X	X	Revenu moyen d'emploi en 2005 $	532
2,807	2,052	0	X	X	X	Erreur type de revenu moyen d'emploi $	533
85	1,025	95	X	X	X	A travaillé une partie de l'année ou à temps partiel[60]	534
60,522	8,855	11,008	X	X	X	Revenu médian d'emploi en 2005 $	535
57,826	21,706	14,833	X	X	X	Revenu moyen d'emploi en 2005 $	536
7,644	2,444	0	X	X	X	Erreur type de revenu moyen d'emploi $	537
220	2,240	220	X	X	X	Femmes de 15 ans et plus avec un revenu d'emploi[58]	538
18,212	15,725	16,576	X	X	X	Revenu médian d'emploi en 2005 $	539
27,733	22,163	20,592	X	X	X	Revenu moyen d'emploi en 2005 $	540
5,396	933	0	X	X	X	Erreur type de revenu moyen d'emploi $	541
110	865	110	X	X	X	A travaillé toute l'année à plein temps[59]	542
39,379	33,158	29,568	X	X	X	Revenu médian d'emploi en 2005 $	543
37,090	37,889	31,073	X	X	X	Revenu moyen d'emploi en 2005 $	544
9,262	1,497	0	X	X	X	Erreur type de revenu moyen d'emploi $	545
75	1,145	85	X	X	X	A travaillé une partie de l'année ou à temps partiel[60]	546
6,458	8,535	6,640	X	X	X	Revenu médian d'emploi en 2005 $	547
20,883	13,128	10,446	X	X	X	Revenu moyen d'emploi en 2005 $	548
7,005	882	0	X	X	X	Erreur type de revenu moyen d'emploi $	549
230	**3,595**	**265**	**X**	**X**	**X**	**Nombre total des familles économiques dans les ménages privés**	550
						Revenu de la famille économique en 2005	
10	50	25	X	X	X	Moins de 10 000 $	551
10	265	25	X	X	X	10 000 $ à 19 999 $	552
0	465	50	X	X	X	20 000 $ à 29 999 $	553
15	620	45	X	X	X	30 000 $ à 39 999 $	554
10	550	40	X	X	X	40 000 $ à 49 999 $	555
0	305	35	X	X	X	50 000 $ à 59 999 $	556
15	400	15	X	X	X	60 000 $ à 69 999 $	557
30	260	15	X	X	X	70 000 $ à 79 999 $	558
20	205	10	X	X	X	80 000 $ à 89 999 $	559
25	135	0	X	X	X	90 000 $ à 99 999 $	560
80	340	10	X	X	X	100 000 $ et plus	561
86,098	47,283	38,315	X	X	X	Revenu médian des familles $	562
87,677	56,829	42,258	X	X	X	Revenu moyen des familles $	563
6,772	1,345	0	X	X	X	Erreur type de revenu moyen des familles $	564
						Revenu après impôt de la famille économique en 2005	
10	50	25	X	X	X	Moins de 10 000 $	565
10	280	25	X	X	X	10 000 $ à 19 999 $	566
0	495	50	X	X	X	20 000 $ à 29 999 $	567
30	790	50	X	X	X	30 000 $ à 39 999 $	568
0	615	35	X	X	X	40 000 $ à 49 999 $	569
15	415	35	X	X	X	50 000 $ à 59 999 $	570
50	315	15	X	X	X	60 000 $ à 69 999 $	571
25	215	15	X	X	X	70 000 $ à 79 999 $	572
10	115	0	X	X	X	80 000 $ à 89 999 $	573
25	75	0	X	X	X	90 000 $ à 99 999 $	574
50	225	10	X	X	X	100 000 $ et plus	575
69,920	42,315	36,608	X	X	X	Revenu médian après impôt des familles $	576
71,861	49,451	40,959	X	X	X	Revenu moyen après impôt des familles $	577
5,080	994	0	X	X	X	Erreur type de revenu moyen après impôt des familles $	578
						Catégorie de revenu en 2005	
760	11,435	0	X	X	X	Population totale dans les ménages privés pour la catégorie de revenu	579
35	1,775	0	X	X	X	Au-dessous du seuil de faible revenu avant impôt en 2005	580
4.6	15.5	0.0	X	X	X	Fréquence du faible revenu avant impôt en 2005 %	581
35	1,185	0	X	X	X	Au-dessous du seuil de faible revenu après impôt en 2005	582
4.6	10.4	0.0	X	X	X	Fréquence du faible revenu après impôt en 2005 %	583

Nota : Voir les symboles et les abréviations dans les documents d'introduction et voir les documents de référence à la fin de la publication.

Selected characteristics for census divisions and census subdivisions – 100% data and 20% sample data, Ontario, 2006 Census (continued)

No.	Characteristics	Canada †	Ontario PROVINCE †◊	Algoma CD/DR ♦◊	Algoma, Unorganized, North Part, NO ♦♦◊◊	Blind River, T ◊	Bruce Mines, T ♦◊◊
	2005 income characteristics						
584	**Total number of private households**	**12,437,470**	**4,555,025**	**50,010**	**2,415**	**1,615**	**245**
	Household income groups in 2005						
585	Under $10,000	628,745	198,235	2,310	135	90	0
586	$10,000 to $19,999	1,270,335	398,830	6,705	320	210	25
587	$20,000 to $29,999	1,301,045	408,130	5,655	305	145	25
588	$30,000 to $39,999	1,364,975	447,475	6,155	275	225	50
589	$40,000 to $49,999	1,234,765	419,525	5,335	240	185	25
590	$50,000 to $59,999	1,094,520	385,555	4,055	160	140	30
591	$60,000 to $69,999	982,730	356,990	3,910	230	95	30
592	$70,000 to $79,999	848,285	324,835	3,330	170	105	30
593	$80,000 to $89,999	715,080	282,910	2,665	170	100	15
594	$90,000 to $99,999	588,560	238,720	2,075	105	55	0
595	$100,000 and over	2,408,415	1,093,810	7,815	300	265	25
596	Median household income $	53,634	60,455	47,567	47,422	46,713	50,024
597	Average household income $	69,548	77,967	59,829	55,624	63,072	55,002
598	Standard error of average household income $	63	123	517	1,535	2,899	4,195
	Household after-tax income groups in 2005						
599	Under $10,000	643,685	203,380	2,355	140	95	0
600	$10,000 to $19,999	1,376,140	430,210	7,295	330	220	25
601	$20,000 to $29,999	1,558,365	482,430	6,380	330	195	40
602	$30,000 to $39,999	1,655,270	552,230	7,495	345	260	40
603	$40,000 to $49,999	1,460,320	509,315	5,865	255	200	30
604	$50,000 to $59,999	1,259,265	457,855	4,855	295	145	30
605	$60,000 to $69,999	1,053,420	408,185	4,170	180	105	45
606	$70,000 to $79,999	846,405	340,580	3,235	220	120	10
607	$80,000 to $89,999	653,235	270,450	2,185	105	40	0
608	$90,000 to $99,999	494,335	216,760	1,685	55	60	0
609	$100,000 and over	1,437,025	683,630	4,485	155	175	15
610	Median after-tax household income $	46,584	52,117	42,113	41,126	40,944	44,392
611	Average after-tax household income $	57,217	63,441	50,670	47,415	53,466	47,994
612	Standard error of average after-tax household income $	42	80	377	1,193	2,212	3,187

Note: See symbols and abbreviations in the introductory material and see reference material at the end of the publication.

Certaines caractéristiques des divisions de recensement et des subdivisions de recensement – Données intégrales et données-échantillon (20 %), Ontario, Recensement de 2006 (suite)

Dubreuilville, TP ◆◇	Elliot Lake, CY ◆◇	Garden River 14, IRI ◆	Goulais Bay 15A, IRI ◆◆◇◇	Gros Cap 49, IRI	Hilton, TP ◆◇◇	Caractéristiques	N°
						Caractéristiques du revenu de 2005	
285	**5,645**	**350**	**X**	**X**	**X**	**Nombre total des ménages privés**	584
						Tranches de revenu des ménages en 2005	
10	245	50	X	X	X	Moins de 10 000 $	585
0	1,020	50	X	X	X	10 000 $ à 19 999 $	586
10	900	65	X	X	X	20 000 $ à 29 999 $	587
15	955	55	X	X	X	30 000 $ à 39 999 $	588
40	700	40	X	X	X	40 000 $ à 49 999 $	589
10	370	35	X	X	X	50 000 $ à 59 999 $	590
25	445	15	X	X	X	60 000 $ à 69 999 $	591
35	285	20	X	X	X	70 000 $ à 79 999 $	592
20	220	10	X	X	X	80 000 $ à 89 999 $	593
25	145	10	X	X	X	90 000 $ à 99 999 $	594
90	350	10	X	X	X	100 000 $ et plus	595
77,805	36,366	32,064	X	X	X	Revenu médian des ménages $	596
83,625	45,891	36,793	X	X	X	Revenu moyen des ménages $	597
6,568	982	0	X	X	X	Erreur type de revenu moyen des ménages $	598
						Tranches du revenu après impôt des ménages en 2005	
15	250	50	X	X	X	Moins de 10 000 $	599
0	1,080	55	X	X	X	10 000 $ à 19 999 $	600
10	1,020	70	X	X	X	20 000 $ à 29 999 $	601
45	1,115	55	X	X	X	30 000 $ à 39 999 $	602
15	720	40	X	X	X	40 000 $ à 49 999 $	603
15	470	35	X	X	X	50 000 $ à 59 999 $	604
55	335	20	X	X	X	60 000 $ à 69 999 $	605
20	230	15	X	X	X	70 000 $ à 79 999 $	606
10	120	10	X	X	X	80 000 $ à 89 999 $	607
25	75	10	X	X	X	90 000 $ à 99 999 $	608
55	230	10	X	X	X	100 000 $ et plus	609
62,650	33,872	30,912	X	X	X	Revenu médian après impôt des ménages $	610
67,756	40,209	35,542	X	X	X	Revenu moyen après impôt des ménages $	611
4,561	749	0	X	X	X	Erreur type de revenu moyen après impôt des ménages $	612

Nota : Voir les symboles et les abréviations dans les documents d'introduction et voir les documents de référence à la fin de la publication.

Selected characteristics for census divisions and census subdivisions – 100% data and 20% sample data, Ontario, 2006 Census (continued)

No.	Characteristics	Hilton Beach, VL	Hornepayne, TP ◆◊	Huron Shores, MU ◆	Jocelyn, TP ◆◊	Johnson, TP ◆	Laird, TP ◆◊
	Population characteristics						
1	**Population, 2001[1]**	**174**	**1,362**	**1,794**	**298**	**658**	**1,021**
2	**Population, 2006[2]**	**172**	**1,209**	**1,696**	**277**	**701**	**1,078**
3	Population percentage change, 2001 to 2006	-1.1	-11.2	-5.5	-7.0	6.5	5.6
4	Land area in square kilometres, 2006	2.46	204.52	455.33	131.37	119.67	101.77
5	**Total population – 100% data[3]**	**170**	**1,210**	**1,695**	**280**	**700**	**1,075**
	Sex and age groups						
6	Male	85	625	885	140	345	565
7	0 to 4 years	5	30	25	0	25	20
8	5 to 9 years	5	50	45	0	25	30
9	10 to 14 years	5	50	45	10	25	35
10	15 to 19 years	5	45	75	5	25	40
11	20 to 24 years	0	30	25	0	15	30
12	25 to 29 years	0	20	15	5	10	15
13	30 to 34 years	5	35	30	5	15	15
14	35 to 39 years	0	55	40	0	20	30
15	40 to 44 years	0	55	70	5	15	40
16	45 to 49 years	10	65	75	10	40	50
17	50 to 54 years	5	70	85	20	25	70
18	55 to 59 years	5	45	85	15	30	55
19	60 to 64 years	10	20	65	15	20	50
20	65 to 69 years	5	15	80	10	20	30
21	70 to 74 years	0	15	50	15	15	25
22	75 to 79 years	5	10	45	5	20	15
23	80 to 84 years	0	10	20	5	5	5
24	85 years and over	0	5	10	0	5	5
25	Female	90	580	810	135	355	515
26	0 to 4 years	5	35	25	5	25	20
27	5 to 9 years	0	40	35	0	25	20
28	10 to 14 years	0	40	45	10	20	35
29	15 to 19 years	0	50	45	10	25	40
30	20 to 24 years	0	35	35	5	15	30
31	25 to 29 years	0	30	20	10	10	20
32	30 to 34 years	0	35	25	0	20	30
33	35 to 39 years	5	45	45	5	15	30
34	40 to 44 years	5	55	70	10	25	30
35	45 to 49 years	5	60	75	10	30	65
36	50 to 54 years	15	45	80	10	25	60
37	55 to 59 years	10	30	80	25	15	50
38	60 to 64 years	10	30	65	10	30	40
39	65 to 69 years	10	20	55	10	20	20
40	70 to 74 years	5	10	45	5	25	20
41	75 to 79 years	0	10	25	5	15	10
42	80 to 84 years	5	5	20	5	10	0
43	85 years and over	0	5	5	5	10	0
44	**Total population 15 years and over[3]**	**150**	**960**	**1,470**	**250**	**560**	**920**
	Legal marital status						
45	Never legally married (single)	40	355	310	40	135	205
46	Legally married (and not separated)[4,5]	75	445	920	170	350	580
47	Separated, but still legally married	5	50	45	0	15	35
48	Divorced	10	55	115	25	30	60
49	Widowed	15	60	85	10	35	35
	Common-law status						
50	Not in a common-law relationship	130	820	1,335	225	525	855
51	In a common-law relationship	15	145	135	25	35	60
52	**Total population – 20% sample data[6]**	**175**	**1,205**	**1,695**	**275**	**700**	**1,075**
	Mother tongue						
53	Single responses	175	1,190	1,690	280	695	1,080
54	English	170	945	1,590	240	510	1,000
55	French	0	195	35	30	15	25
56	Non-official languages[7]	0	55	65	0	170	50
57	Italian	0	10	0	0	0	10
58	Chinese, n.o.s.[61]	0	0	20	0	0	0
59	Cantonese	0	0	0	0	0	0
60	Spanish	0	0	0	0	0	0
61	German	0	10	10	0	155	15
62	Other languages[8]	0	35	35	10	15	25

Note: See symbols and abbreviations in the introductory material and see reference material at the end of the publication.

Certaines caractéristiques des divisions de recensement et des subdivisions de recensement – Données intégrales et données-échantillon (20 %), Ontario, Recensement de 2006 (suite)

Macdonald, Meredith and Aberdeen Additional, TP ◆◇	Michipicoten, TP ◇	Mississagi River 8, IRI	North Shore, TP	Plummer Additional, TP ◆	Prince, TP ◆◇	Caractéristiques	N°
						Caractéristiques de la population	
1,452	**3,668**	**360**	**544**	**671**	**1,010**	**Population, 2001[1]**	1
1,550	**3,204**	**414**	**549**	**625**	**971**	**Population, 2006[2]**	2
6.7	-12.6	15.0	0.9	-6.9	-3.9	Variation en pourcentage de la population, 2001 à 2006	3
161.73	417.78	18.26	230.79	221.31	84.28	Superficie des terres en kilomètres carrés, 2006	4
1,550	**3,200**	**415**	**550**	**625**	**970**	**Population totale – Données intégrales[3]**	5
						Sexe et groupes d'âge	
800	1,635	210	280	325	490	Sexe masculin	6
30	85	15	5	10	15	0 à 4 ans	7
50	95	30	5	20	30	5 à 9 ans	8
50	125	20	5	20	25	10 à 14 ans	9
85	130	20	15	20	30	15 à 19 ans	10
35	90	10	10	10	35	20 à 24 ans	11
35	70	10	5	10	15	25 à 29 ans	12
35	95	10	5	10	20	30 à 34 ans	13
45	125	25	10	10	25	35 à 39 ans	14
75	150	15	15	20	45	40 à 44 ans	15
75	130	15	30	30	45	45 à 49 ans	16
75	140	20	30	30	50	50 à 54 ans	17
70	115	15	40	40	45	55 à 59 ans	18
35	85	5	30	25	35	60 à 64 ans	19
30	55	0	35	25	25	65 à 69 ans	20
35	50	5	25	10	25	70 à 74 ans	21
20	45	0	10	10	10	75 à 79 ans	22
10	20	0	5	5	5	80 à 84 ans	23
0	15	0	0	5	0	85 ans et plus	24
750	1,570	205	265	305	480	Sexe féminin	25
35	75	15	5	15	15	0 à 4 ans	26
30	90	20	10	10	30	5 à 9 ans	27
60	115	15	15	15	30	10 à 14 ans	28
70	105	20	10	15	35	15 à 19 ans	29
35	80	15	10	15	20	20 à 24 ans	30
35	95	10	5	10	20	25 à 29 ans	31
35	85	15	10	10	20	30 à 34 ans	32
55	115	15	5	15	40	35 à 39 ans	33
65	135	25	25	20	35	40 à 44 ans	34
75	130	20	30	35	50	45 à 49 ans	35
80	130	15	35	40	50	50 à 54 ans	36
60	120	10	30	25	55	55 à 59 ans	37
35	90	5	30	30	30	60 à 64 ans	38
30	50	5	25	15	20	65 à 69 ans	39
30	60	0	10	15	15	70 à 74 ans	40
10	50	5	10	10	10	75 à 79 ans	41
5	30	0	5	5	10	80 à 84 ans	42
5	20	0	0	5	0	85 ans et plus	43
1,295	**2,620**	**305**	**500**	**530**	**825**	**Population totale de 15 ans et plus[3]**	44
						État matrimonial légal	
355	855	180	100	100	200	Jamais légalement marié(e) (célibataire)	45
755	1,310	80	310	335	525	Légalement marié(e) (et non séparé[e])[4,5]	46
50	80	10	20	15	20	Séparé(e), mais toujours légalement marié(e)	47
80	195	25	45	40	50	Divorcé(e)	48
50	180	10	35	30	35	Veuf(ve)	49
						Union libre	
1,210	2,255	245	450	490	765	Ne vivant pas en union libre	50
85	360	60	50	35	60	Vivant en union libre	51
1,550	**3,185**	**415**	**550**	**625**	**970**	**Population totale – Données-échantillon (20 %)[6]**	52
						Langue maternelle	
1,550	3,095	415	525	625	955	Réponses uniques	53
1,410	2,225	365	390	515	865	Anglais	54
15	590	15	120	15	25	Français	55
125	275	25	25	90	60	Langues non officielles[7]	56
25	40	0	0	0	25	Italien	57
0	0	0	0	0	0	Chinois, n.d.a.[61]	58
0	0	0	0	0	0	Cantonais	59
0	0	0	0	0	0	Espagnol	60
35	40	0	0	50	15	Allemand	61
60	200	30	15	45	20	Autres langues[8]	62

Nota : Voir les symboles et les abréviations dans les documents d'introduction et voir les documents de référence à la fin de la publication.

Selected characteristics for census divisions and census subdivisions – 100% data and 20% sample data, Ontario, 2006 Census (continued)

No.	Characteristics	Hilton Beach, VL	Hornepayne, TP ◆◇	Huron Shores, MU ◆	Jocelyn, TP ◆◇	Johnson, TP ◆	Laird, TP ◆◇
	Population characteristics						
	Mother tongue (continued)						
63	Multiple responses	0	10	0	0	10	0
64	English and French	0	0	0	0	10	0
65	English and non-official language	0	15	0	0	0	0
66	French and non-official language	0	0	0	0	0	0
67	English, French and non-official language	0	0	0	0	0	0
	Language spoken most often at home[9]						
68	Single responses	180	1,190	1,695	275	700	1,075
69	English	175	1,060	1,670	275	550	1,075
70	French	0	120	0	0	0	0
71	Non-official languages[7]	0	0	25	0	150	0
72	Chinese, n.o.s.[61]	0	0	20	0	0	0
73	Cantonese	0	0	0	0	0	0
74	Panjabi (Punjabi)	0	0	0	0	0	0
75	Italian	0	0	0	0	0	0
76	Spanish	0	0	0	0	0	0
77	Other languages[8]	0	10	0	0	150	0
78	Multiple responses	0	10	0	0	0	0
79	English and French	0	0	0	0	0	0
80	English and non-official language	0	0	0	0	0	0
81	French and non-official language	0	0	0	0	0	0
82	English, French and non-official language	0	0	0	0	0	0
	Knowledge of official languages[10]						
83	English only	170	935	1,615	240	655	995
84	French only	0	0	0	0	0	0
85	English and French	10	265	85	30	45	85
86	Neither English nor French	0	0	0	0	10	0
	Knowledge of non-official languages[7,11]						
87	Italian	0	15	0	0	0	10
88	Spanish	0	10	0	0	0	0
89	German	0	10	15	0	145	15
90	Chinese, n.o.s.[61]	0	0	20	0	0	0
91	Cantonese	0	0	0	0	0	0
92	Panjabi (Punjabi)	0	0	0	0	0	0
93	Portuguese	0	0	0	0	0	0
	First official language spoken[10]						
94	English	175	1,010	1,655	255	685	1,055
95	French	0	190	40	20	15	25
96	English and French	0	0	0	0	0	0
97	Neither English nor French	0	0	0	0	0	0
98	Official language minority - (number)[12]	10	190	40	20	15	25
99	Official language minority - (percentage)[12]	5.6	15.8	2.4	7.1	2.1	2.3
	Ethnic origin[13]						
100	English	65	370	665	80	195	440
101	Canadian	55	300	530	100	230	255
102	Scottish	65	295	460	40	205	365
103	Irish	65	355	475	45	105	410
104	French	55	290	320	65	110	255
105	German	50	135	335	25	50	125
106	Italian	0	80	70	20	0	65
107	Chinese	0	0	20	0	0	0
108	East Indian	0	0	0	0	0	0
109	Dutch (Netherlands)	10	140	55	40	140	60
110	Polish	10	70	10	0	10	10
111	Ukrainian	0	65	10	0	115	25
112	North American Indian	45	170	70	10	60	70
113	Portuguese	0	0	0	0	0	0
114	Filipino	0	0	0	0	0	0
	Aboriginal and non-Aboriginal identity						
115	Total Aboriginal identity population[14]	45	135	110	0	40	110
116	Total non-Aboriginal identity population	130	1,065	1,585	275	660	970

Note: See symbols and abbreviations in the introductory material and see reference material at the end of the publication.

Certaines caractéristiques des divisions de recensement et des subdivisions de recensement – Données intégrales et données-échantillon (20 %), Ontario, Recensement de 2006 (suite)

Macdonald, Meredith and Aberdeen Additional, TP ◆◇	Michipicoten, TP ◇	Mississagi River 8, IRI	North Shore, TP	Plummer Additional, TP ◆	Prince, TP ◆◇	Caractéristiques	Nº
						Caractéristiques de la population	
						Langue maternelle (suite)	
0	90	10	20	0	15	Réponses multiples	63
0	80	0	15	0	0	Anglais et français	64
0	10	0	0	0	10	Anglais et langue non officielle	65
0	0	0	0	0	0	Français et langue non officielle	66
0	0	0	0	0	0	Anglais, français et langue non officielle	67
						Langue parlée le plus souvent à la maison[9]	
1,550	3,160	415	545	615	965	Réponses uniques	68
1,475	2,710	410	485	600	965	Anglais	69
0	390	0	55	0	0	Français	70
70	55	0	10	15	0	Langues non officielles[7]	71
0	0	0	0	0	0	Chinois, n.d.a.[61]	72
0	0	0	0	0	0	Cantonais	73
0	0	0	0	0	0	Pendjabi	74
0	0	0	0	0	0	Italien	75
0	0	0	0	0	0	Espagnol	76
65	55	0	0	15	0	Autres langues[8]	77
0	25	0	0	10	0	Réponses multiples	78
0	20	0	0	0	0	Anglais et français	79
0	10	0	0	10	0	Anglais et langue non officielle	80
0	0	0	0	0	0	Français et langue non officielle	81
0	0	0	0	0	0	Anglais, français et langue non officielle	82
						Connaissance des langues officielles[10]	
1,495	2,235	380	375	600	875	Anglais seulement	83
0	45	0	15	0	0	Français seulement	84
35	890	35	155	25	95	Anglais et français	85
15	10	0	0	0	0	Ni l'anglais ni le français	86
						Connaissance des langues non officielles[7,11]	
25	60	0	0	0	45	Italien	87
0	20	0	0	0	15	Espagnol	88
35	60	10	15	60	20	Allemand	89
0	0	0	0	0	0	Chinois, n.d.a.[61]	90
0	0	0	0	0	0	Cantonais	91
0	0	0	0	0	0	Pendjabi	92
0	0	0	0	0	0	Portugais	93
						Première langue officielle parlée[10]	
1,520	2,565	395	435	610	945	Anglais	94
15	585	15	110	15	30	Français	95
0	20	0	0	0	0	Anglais et français	96
15	10	0	0	0	0	Ni l'anglais ni le français	97
15	600	15	110	15	30	Minorité de langue officielle - (nombre)[12]	98
1.0	18.8	3.6	20.0	2.4	3.1	Minorité de langue officielle - (pourcentage)[12]	99
						Origine ethnique[13]	
605	775	25	175	135	335	Anglais	100
680	1,195	10	205	155	330	Canadien	101
650	510	10	70	130	145	Écossais	102
590	685	15	115	135	135	Irlandais	103
280	1,005	70	195	115	145	Français	104
125	245	0	45	180	90	Allemand	105
45	205	0	30	10	110	Italien	106
15	0	0	0	0	0	Chinois	107
0	0	0	0	0	0	Indien de l'Inde	108
55	125	0	15	60	15	Hollandais (Néerlandais)	109
15	130	10	15	20	35	Polonais	110
15	240	0	10	15	25	Ukrainien	111
135	260	375	30	70	60	Indien de l'Amérique du Nord	112
0	0	0	0	0	0	Portugais	113
0	15	0	0	0	0	Philippin	114
						Population ayant une identité autochtone et population n'ayant pas d'identité autochtone	
175	275	375	60	45	40	Total de la population ayant une identité autochtone[14]	115
1,375	2,915	40	490	580	930	Total de la population n'ayant pas d'identité autochtone	116

Nota : Voir les symboles et les abréviations dans les documents d'introduction et voir les documents de référence à la fin de la publication.

Selected characteristics for census divisions and census subdivisions – 100% data and 20% sample data, Ontario, 2006 Census (continued)

No.	Characteristics	Hilton Beach, VL	Hornepayne, TP ◆◇	Huron Shores, MU ◆	Jocelyn, TP ◆◇	Johnson, TP ◆	Laird, TP ◆◇
	Population characteristics						
	Aboriginal and non-Aboriginal ancestry						
117	Total Aboriginal ancestry population[15]	50	170	105	10	80	130
118	Total non-Aboriginal ancestry population	125	1,035	1,590	270	620	945
	Registered Indian status						
119	Registered Indian[16]	0	125	25	0	10	20
120	Not a Registered Indian	180	1,080	1,670	275	695	1,060
	Visible minority groups						
121	Total visible minority population[17]	0	80	25	0	0	0
122	Chinese	0	0	25	0	0	0
123	South Asian[18]	0	20	10	0	0	0
124	Black	0	0	0	0	0	0
125	Filipino	0	0	0	0	0	0
126	Latin American	0	0	0	0	0	0
127	Southeast Asian[19]	0	0	0	0	0	0
128	Arab	0	0	0	0	0	0
129	West Asian[20]	0	0	0	0	0	0
130	Korean	0	0	0	0	0	0
131	Japanese	0	60	0	0	0	0
132	Visible minority, n.i.e.[21]	0	0	0	0	0	0
133	Multiple visible minority[22]	0	0	0	0	0	0
	Citizenship[23]						
134	Canadian citizens[24]	180	1,190	1,655	275	675	1,075
135	Not Canadian citizens[25]	0	10	40	0	25	0
	Immigrant status and place of birth[26]						
136	Non-immigrants[27]	175	1,160	1,555	270	635	1,030
137	Born in province of residence	165	1,070	1,435	220	605	1,000
138	Immigrants[28]	0	35	140	0	65	45
139	United States of America	0	10	30	0	15	10
140	Central and South America	0	0	0	0	10	0
141	Caribbean and Bermuda	0	0	0	0	0	0
142	United Kingdom	0	0	40	0	15	0
143	Other Europe	10	20	40	0	15	30
144	Africa	0	0	0	0	0	0
145	Asia and the Middle East	0	0	25	0	0	0
146	Oceania and other[29]	0	0	10	0	10	0
147	Non-permanent residents[30]	0	10	0	0	0	0
148	**Total immigrant population[28]**	**0**	**35**	**140**	**10**	**70**	**45**
	Period of immigration						
149	Before 1961	10	10	70	0	20	30
150	1961 to 1970	0	20	20	0	15	0
151	1971 to 1980	0	0	10	0	10	0
152	1981 to 1990	0	0	20	0	0	10
153	1991 to 2000	0	0	20	0	20	0
154	1991 to 1995	0	0	0	0	15	0
155	1996 to 2000	0	0	15	0	0	0
156	2001 to 2006[31]	0	0	0	0	0	0
	Age at immigration						
157	Under 5 years	0	0	15	0	0	20
158	5 to 19 years	10	20	45	0	0	15
159	20 years and over	0	15	80	0	65	10
160	**Total population 15 years and over**	**155**	**950**	**1,465**	**245**	**530**	**925**
	Generation status						
161	1st generation[32]	10	45	135	10	65	45
162	2nd generation[33]	20	110	145	40	55	135
163	3rd generation or more[34]	130	790	1,180	200	405	745

Note: See symbols and abbreviations in the introductory material and see reference material at the end of the publication.

Certaines caractéristiques des divisions de recensement et des subdivisions de recensement – Données intégrales et données-échantillon (20 %), Ontario, Recensement de 2006 (suite)

Macdonald, Meredith and Aberdeen Additional, TP ◆◇	Michipicoten, TP ◇	Mississagi River 8, IRI	North Shore, TP	Plummer Additional, TP ◆	Prince, TP ◆◇	Caractéristiques	N°
						Caractéristiques de la population	
						Population ayant une ascendance autochtone et population n'ayant pas d'ascendance autochtone	
235	340	375	80	85	80	Total de la population ayant une ascendance autochtone[15]	117
1,315	2,845	35	470	535	890	Total de la population n'ayant pas d'ascendance autochtone	118
						Statut d'Indien inscrit	
60	165	365	25	25	25	Indien inscrit[16]	119
1,490	3,020	50	520	595	945	Pas un Indien inscrit	120
						Groupes de minorités visibles	
0	45	0	0	0	10	Total de la population des minorités visibles[17]	121
0	10	0	0	0	10	Chinois	122
0	0	0	0	0	0	Sud-Asiatique[18]	123
0	10	0	0	0	0	Noir	124
0	15	0	0	0	0	Philippin	125
0	0	0	0	0	0	Latino-Américain	126
0	0	0	0	0	0	Asiatique du Sud-Est[19]	127
0	0	0	0	0	0	Arabe	128
0	0	0	0	0	0	Asiatique occidental[20]	129
0	0	0	0	0	0	Coréen	130
0	0	0	0	0	0	Japonais	131
0	0	0	0	0	0	Minorité visible, n.i.a.[21]	132
0	0	0	0	0	0	Minorités visibles multiples[22]	133
						Citoyenneté[23]	
1,515	3,155	X	545	610	970	Citoyens canadiens[24]	134
35	30	X	0	15	10	Ne sont pas des citoyens canadiens[25]	135
						Statut d'immigrant et le lieu de naissance[26]	
1,485	2,860	X	525	530	920	Non-immigrants[27]	136
1,420	2,445	X	440	515	840	Né dans la province de résidence	137
60	325	X	25	95	50	Immigrants[28]	138
10	25	X	0	10	10	États-Unis d'Amérique	139
0	0	X	0	0	0	Amérique centrale et Amérique du Sud	140
0	10	X	0	0	0	Antilles et Bermudes	141
0	50	X	0	0	10	Royaume-Uni	142
50	225	X	20	80	40	Autre Europe	143
0	0	X	0	0	0	Afrique	144
0	20	X	0	0	0	Asie et Moyen-Orient	145
0	0	X	0	0	0	Océanie et autres[29]	146
0	0	X	0	0	0	Résidents non permanents[30]	147
65	**330**	**X**	**25**	**95**	**50**	**Population totale des immigrants[28]**	148
						Période d'immigration	
25	210	X	15	15	30	Avant 1961	149
0	35	X	10	20	0	1961 à 1970	150
15	20	X	0	10	15	1971 à 1980	151
15	25	X	10	0	0	1981 à 1990	152
10	30	X	0	50	10	1991 à 2000	153
10	10	X	0	35	10	1991 à 1995	154
0	20	X	0	15	0	1996 à 2000	155
0	10	X	0	0	0	2001 à 2006[31]	156
						Âge à l'immigration	
15	60	X	0	0	10	Moins de 5 ans	157
0	90	X	0	0	20	5 à 19 ans	158
45	175	X	25	95	20	20 ans et plus	159
1,320	**2,600**	**300**	**500**	**510**	**850**	**Population totale de 15 ans et plus**	160
						Statut des générations	
65	325	0	30	95	50	1re génération[32]	161
185	380	10	70	85	175	2e génération[33]	162
1,080	1,900	295	400	325	625	3e génération ou plus[34]	163

Nota : Voir les symboles et les abréviations dans les documents d'introduction et voir les documents de référence à la fin de la publication.

Selected characteristics for census divisions and census subdivisions – 100% data and 20% sample data, Ontario, 2006 Census (continued)

No.	Characteristics	Hilton Beach, VL	Hornepayne, TP ◆◇	Huron Shores, MU ◆	Jocelyn, TP ◆◇	Johnson, TP ◆	Laird, TP ◆◇
	Population characteristics						
164	**Total population 1 year and over[35]**	**175**	**1,190**	**1,695**	**280**	**680**	**1,070**
	Place of residence 1 year ago (mobility)						
165	Non-movers	155	990	1,610	245	675	1,010
166	Movers	20	200	90	30	10	65
167	Non-migrants	20	130	10	0	0	10
168	Migrants	0	75	75	30	0	55
169	Internal migrants	0	70	70	30	0	45
170	Intraprovincial migrants	0	65	60	30	0	45
171	Interprovincial migrants	0	10	10	0	0	0
172	External migrants	0	10	0	0	0	10
173	**Total population 5 years and over[36]**	**180**	**1,145**	**1,645**	**260**	**655**	**1,035**
	Place of residence 5 years ago (mobility)						
174	Non-movers	135	830	1,245	195	445	800
175	Movers	40	315	395	65	210	235
176	Non-migrants	20	205	160	0	10	40
177	Migrants	20	110	235	65	200	195
178	Internal migrants	20	105	230	65	200	195
179	Intraprovincial migrants	20	100	170	60	200	200
180	Interprovincial migrants	0	10	60	0	0	0
181	External migrants	0	0	0	0	0	0
182	**Total population 15 years and over**	**155**	**945**	**1,465**	**240**	**525**	**925**
	Highest certificate, diploma or degree[37]						
183	No certificate, diploma or degree	65	315	500	50	215	190
184	Certificate, diploma or degree	95	635	965	190	315	735
185	High school certificate or equivalent[38]	30	320	350	70	125	330
186	Apprenticeship or trades certificate or diploma	20	70	220	50	50	145
187	College, CEGEP or other non-university certificate or diploma[39]	25	145	245	55	80	120
188	University certificate or diploma below bachelor level[40]	0	25	10	0	0	40
189	University certificate or degree[41]	15	70	140	15	50	95
190	Bachelor's degree	0	35	100	0	45	85
191	University certificate or diploma above bachelor level	0	35	30	0	0	10
192	Degree in medicine, dentistry, veterinary medicine or optometry	0	0	10	0	0	0
193	Master's degree	0	0	10	0	0	0
194	Earned doctorate	0	0	0	0	10	0
195	**Total population 15 years and over with postsecondary qualifications**	**60**	**315**	**610**	**120**	**185**	**400**
	Major field of study - Classification of Instructional Programs, 2000[42]						
196	Education	10	35	30	0	10	30
197	Visual and performing arts, and communications technologies	0	0	15	0	10	0
198	Humanities	0	30	15	0	0	10
199	Social and behavioural sciences and law	0	40	55	10	10	15
200	Business, management and public administration	0	25	110	15	45	50
201	Physical and life sciences and technologies	0	0	25	10	0	30
202	Mathematics, computer and information sciences	0	10	0	0	0	15
203	Architecture, engineering, and related technologies	15	70	225	65	70	140
204	Agriculture, natural resources and conservation	0	0	25	0	0	25
205	Health, parks, recreation and fitness	20	55	65	25	35	40
206	Personal, protective and transportation services	0	45	40	0	10	30
207	Other fields of study[43]	0	0	0	0	0	0
	Location of study[44]						
208	Inside Canada	55	310	570	120	150	370
209	Outside Canada	10	10	40	0	35	30
210	**Total population 15 years and over**	**155**	**945**	**1,465**	**240**	**525**	**925**
	Unpaid work						
211	Males 15 years and over	65	500	750	135	240	485
212	Reported unpaid work[45]	45	450	705	115	220	455
213	Housework and child care and care or assistance to seniors	30	45	75	15	20	25
214	Housework and child care only	10	130	150	10	65	140

Note: See symbols and abbreviations in the introductory material and see reference material at the end of the publication.

Certaines caractéristiques des divisions de recensement et des subdivisions de recensement – Données intégrales et données-échantillon (20 %), Ontario, Recensement de 2006 (suite)

Macdonald, Meredith and Aberdeen Additional, TP ◆◊	Michipicoten, TP ◊	Mississagi River 8, IRI	North Shore, TP	Plummer Additional, TP ◆	Prince, TP ◆◊	Caractéristiques	N°
						Caractéristiques de la population	
1,530	**3,155**	**410**	**540**	**615**	**960**	**Population totale de 1 an et plus**[35]	164
						Lieu de résidence 1 an auparavant (mobilité)	
1,375	2,665	360	495	550	900	Personnes n'ayant pas déménagé	165
155	490	45	50	65	60	Personnes ayant déménagé	166
75	290	15	0	20	40	Non-migrants	167
75	200	30	50	50	25	Migrants	168
75	200	35	50	50	15	Migrants internes	169
75	175	30	50	45	15	Migrants infraprovinciaux	170
0	30	10	0	0	0	Migrants interprovinciaux	171
0	0	0	0	0	10	Migrants externes	172
1,485	**3,025**	**390**	**530**	**580**	**955**	**Population totale de 5 ans et plus**[36]	173
						Lieu de résidence 5 ans auparavant (mobilité)	
1,045	1,910	220	415	440	615	Personnes n'ayant pas déménagé	174
435	1,115	170	120	135	340	Personnes ayant déménagé	175
215	645	75	20	35	300	Non-migrants	176
225	470	95	100	100	40	Migrants	177
225	460	95	105	105	35	Migrants internes	178
225	410	90	90	105	40	Migrants infraprovinciaux	179
0	50	0	0	0	0	Migrants interprovinciaux	180
0	10	0	0	0	0	Migrants externes	181
1,325	**2,600**	**300**	**500**	**505**	**850**	**Population totale de 15 ans et plus**	182
						Plus haut certificat, diplôme ou grade[37]	
375	705	110	155	130	200	Aucun certificat, diplôme ou grade	183
945	1,895	195	345	375	650	Certificat, diplôme ou grade	184
360	570	55	145	115	280	Diplôme d'études secondaires ou l'équivalent[38]	185
185	310	30	60	95	70	Certificat ou diplôme d'apprenti ou d'une école de métiers	186
285	585	85	120	75	145	Certificat ou diplôme d'un collège, d'un cégep ou d'un autre établissement d'enseignement non universitaire[39]	187
30	45	10	0	0	40	Certificat ou diplôme universitaire inférieur au baccalauréat[40]	188
85	385	10	20	85	115	Certificat ou grade universitaire[41]	189
60	255	0	20	35	70	Baccalauréat	190
15	70	0	0	35	25	Certificat ou diplôme universitaire supérieur au baccalauréat	191
0	0	0	0	0	0	Diplôme en médecine, en art dentaire, en médecine vétérinaire ou en optométrie	192
10	60	0	0	10	10	Maîtrise	193
0	0	0	0	10	0	Doctorat acquis	194
585	**1,325**	**135**	**200**	**260**	**370**	**Population totale de 15 ans et plus avec titres du niveau postsecondaire**	195
						Principal domaine d'études - Classification des programmes d'enseignement, 2000[42]	
15	110	0	15	45	55	Éducation	196
10	0	0	10	0	25	Arts visuels et d'interprétation, et technologie des communications	197
10	40	0	0	0	15	Sciences humaines	198
25	135	20	10	10	20	Sciences sociales et de comportements, et droit	199
50	235	25	30	55	70	Commerce, gestion et administration publique	200
0	50	0	15	0	10	Sciences physiques et de la vie, et technologies	201
10	15	10	0	0	10	Mathématiques, informatique et sciences de l'information	202
220	340	40	45	70	100	Architecture, génie et services connexes	203
65	90	10	10	20	10	Agriculture, ressources naturelles et conservation	204
90	155	25	40	35	30	Santé, parcs, récréation et conditionnement physique	205
80	140	10	25	20	25	Services personnels, de protection et de transport	206
0	0	0	0	0	0	Autres domaines d'études[43]	207
						Lieu des études[44]	
560	1,275	135	200	195	325	À l'intérieur du Canada	208
30	50	0	0	60	40	À l'extérieur du Canada	209
1,325	**2,600**	**300**	**500**	**505**	**850**	**Population totale de 15 ans et plus**	210
						Travail non rémunéré	
695	1,320	150	255	240	430	Hommes de 15 ans et plus	211
605	1,230	125	225	235	385	Travail non rémunéré déclaré[45]	212
45	100	25	15	35	80	Travaux ménagers et soins aux enfants et soins ou aide aux personnes âgées	213
145	345	35	20	45	60	Travaux ménagers et soins aux enfants seulement	214

Nota : Voir les symboles et les abréviations dans les documents d'introduction et voir les documents de référence à la fin de la publication.

Selected characteristics for census divisions and census subdivisions – 100% data and 20% sample data, Ontario, 2006 Census (continued)

No.	Characteristics	Hilton Beach, VL	Hornepayne, TP ◆◊	Huron Shores, MU ◆	Jocelyn, TP ◆◊	Johnson, TP ◆	Laird, TP ◆◊
	Population characteristics						
	Unpaid work (continued)						
215	Housework and care or assistance to seniors only	0	25	40	20	20	35
216	Child care and care or assistance to seniors only	0	0	10	0	0	0
217	Housework only	15	255	430	55	110	255
218	Child care only	0	0	0	0	0	0
219	Care or assistance to seniors only	0	0	0	0	0	0
220	Females 15 years and over	90	450	710	105	285	435
221	Reported unpaid work[45]	85	425	685	110	280	425
222	Housework and child care and care or assistance to seniors	30	65	45	10	45	85
223	Housework and child care only	10	145	190	20	80	125
224	Housework and care or assistance to seniors only	20	15	95	0	30	35
225	Child care and care or assistance to seniors only	0	0	0	10	0	0
226	Housework only	30	195	350	70	115	175
227	Child care only	0	10	0	0	10	0
228	Care or assistance to seniors only	0	0	0	0	0	0
	Labour force activity						
229	Males 15 years and over	65	495	750	135	245	485
230	In the labour force	25	365	465	55	145	360
231	Employed	30	335	420	50	140	320
232	Unemployed	0	25	50	0	10	35
233	Not in the labour force	35	135	285	85	90	125
234	Participation rate	38.5	73.7	62.0	40.7	59.2	74.2
235	Employment rate	46.2	67.7	56.0	37.0	57.1	66.0
236	Unemployment rate	0.0	6.8	10.8	0.0	6.9	9.7
237	Females 15 years and over	85	450	710	105	285	435
238	In the labour force	45	325	355	35	105	270
239	Employed	40	315	335	30	85	250
240	Unemployed	10	0	20	0	20	15
241	Not in the labour force	40	125	355	65	180	165
242	Participation rate	52.9	72.2	50.0	33.3	36.8	62.1
243	Employment rate	47.1	70.0	47.2	28.6	29.8	57.5
244	Unemployment rate	22.2	0.0	5.6	0.0	19.0	5.6
245	Both sexes - Participation rate	48.4	72.6	56.0	36.7	48.6	68.1
246	15 to 24 years	0.0	73.5	82.8	0.0	69.2	59.4
247	25 years and over	50.0	72.0	53.6	34.8	46.7	70.4
248	Both sexes - Employment rate	41.9	68.9	51.5	35.4	42.5	62.7
249	15 to 24 years	40.0	69.7	69.0	0.0	53.8	51.5
250	25 years and over	44.0	69.9	49.6	31.9	40.9	64.5
251	Both sexes - Unemployment rate	13.3	5.1	8.5	0.0	11.8	7.9
252	15 to 24 years	0.0	8.0	12.5	0.0	0.0	10.5
253	25 years and over	0.0	4.4	7.1	11.8	11.9	8.4
254	**Total labour force 15 years and over**	**75**	**690**	**825**	**90**	**255**	**630**
	Industry - North American Industry Classification System 2002						
255	Industry - Not applicable[46]	10	0	20	0	0	0
256	All industries[47]	65	690	805	90	250	630
257	11 Agriculture, forestry, fishing and hunting	0	15	80	0	60	15
258	21 Mining and oil and gas extraction	0	0	10	0	10	0
259	22 Utilities	0	0	10	0	0	0
260	23 Construction	10	20	70	0	20	50
261	31-33 Manufacturing	0	115	105	10	25	85
262	41 Wholesale trade	0	0	0	0	0	10
263	44-45 Retail trade	0	65	95	10	10	20
264	48-49 Transportation and warehousing	15	150	75	10	20	60
265	51 Information and cultural industries	0	10	0	10	0	0
266	52 Finance and insurance	0	10	20	0	0	0
267	53 Real estate and rental and leasing	0	0	20	10	0	15
268	54 Professional, scientific and technical services	0	0	35	0	10	10
269	55 Management of companies and enterprises	0	0	0	0	0	0
270	56 Administrative and support, waste management and remediation services	0	15	45	0	20	45
271	61 Educational services	10	70	60	0	25	65
272	62 Health care and social assistance	10	100	60	15	25	60

Note: See symbols and abbreviations in the introductory material and see reference material at the end of the publication.

Certaines caractéristiques des divisions de recensement et des subdivisions de recensement – Données intégrales et données-échantillon (20 %), Ontario, Recensement de 2006 (suite)

Macdonald, Meredith and Aberdeen Additional, TP ◆◊	Michipicoten, TP ◊	Mississagi River 8, IRI	North Shore, TP	Plummer Additional, TP ◆	Prince, TP ◆◊	Caractéristiques	N°
						Caractéristiques de la population	
						Travail non rémunéré (suite)	
90	105	10	45	30	40	Travaux ménagers et soins ou aide aux personnes âgées seulement	215
0	0	0	0	0	0	Soins aux enfants et soins ou aide aux personnes âgées seulement	216
320	660	65	145	120	190	Travaux ménagers seulement	217
0	0	0	0	0	0	Soins aux enfants seulement	218
10	20	0	0	0	20	Soins ou aide aux personnes âgées seulement	219
630	1,280	155	240	265	415	Femmes de 15 ans et plus	220
585	1,220	145	230	260	390	Travail non rémunéré déclaré[45]	221
80	115	25	15	45	65	Travaux ménagers et soins aux enfants et soins ou aide aux personnes âgées	222
185	375	60	45	60	65	Travaux ménagers et soins aux enfants seulement	223
70	100	0	40	40	80	Travaux ménagers et soins ou aide aux personnes âgées seulement	224
0	0	0	0	0	0	Soins aux enfants et soins ou aide aux personnes âgées seulement	225
250	615	55	125	115	165	Travaux ménagers seulement	226
0	10	0	0	0	0	Soins aux enfants seulement	227
0	10	0	0	0	20	Soins ou aide aux personnes âgées seulement	228
						Activité	
690	1,320	150	255	245	430	Hommes de 15 ans et plus	229
495	920	100	145	140	335	Population active	230
430	865	75	125	130	325	Personnes occupées	231
65	50	30	25	15	15	Chômeurs	232
200	400	45	115	105	95	Inactifs	233
71.7	69.7	66.7	56.9	57.1	77.9	Taux d'activité	234
62.3	65.5	50.0	49.0	53.1	75.6	Taux d'emploi	235
13.1	5.4	30.0	17.2	10.7	4.5	Taux de chômage	236
630	1,280	155	245	265	420	Femmes de 15 ans et plus	237
370	760	115	120	140	275	Population active	238
355	700	95	115	135	260	Personnes occupées	239
15	55	20	10	10	10	Chômeuses	240
265	520	45	120	125	140	Inactives	241
58.7	59.4	74.2	49.0	52.8	65.5	Taux d'activité	242
56.3	54.7	61.3	46.9	50.9	61.9	Taux d'emploi	243
4.1	7.2	17.4	8.3	7.1	3.6	Taux de chômage	244
64.8	64.4	70.5	53.0	55.4	72.4	Les deux sexes - Taux d'activité	245
56.2	58.8	50.0	66.7	33.3	86.2	15 à 24 ans	246
67.4	65.7	75.5	51.6	56.2	69.0	25 ans et plus	247
59.1	60.5	55.7	48.0	51.5	68.8	Les deux sexes - Taux d'emploi	248
42.9	50.0	16.7	44.4	33.3	85.7	15 à 24 ans	249
62.5	62.3	63.3	48.4	54.7	66.0	25 ans et plus	250
9.3	6.5	22.7	9.4	7.1	4.1	Les deux sexes - Taux de chômage	251
25.9	14.9	66.7	33.3	100.0	0.0	15 à 24 ans	252
6.2	5.2	16.2	8.5	5.6	4.1	25 ans et plus	253
860	**1,680**	**220**	**270**	**280**	**615**	**Population active totale de 15 ans et plus**	254
						Industrie - Système de classification des industries de l'Amérique du Nord de 2002	
25	10	15	0	0	0	Industrie - Sans objet[46]	255
830	1,665	205	265	275	610	Toutes les industries[47]	256
60	70	0	20	35	25	11 Agriculture, foresterie, pêche et chasse	257
0	55	0	15	0	15	21 Extraction minière et extraction de pétrole et de gaz	258
10	15	0	10	0	0	22 Services publics	259
115	90	15	10	25	40	23 Construction	260
140	230	15	25	25	70	31-33 Fabrication	261
10	15	0	10	0	25	41 Commerce de gros	262
85	185	20	35	30	50	44-45 Commerce de détail	263
40	40	0	10	10	35	48-49 Transport et entreposage	264
10	10	0	0	0	10	51 Industrie de l'information et industrie culturelle	265
20	40	0	20	0	10	52 Finance et assurances	266
10	40	0	0	0	25	53 Services immobiliers et services de location et de location à bail	267
10	20	10	20	0	30	54 Services professionnels, scientifiques et techniques	268
0	0	0	0	0	0	55 Gestion de sociétés et d'entreprises	269
20	30	10	0	10	20	56 Services administratifs, services de soutien, services de gestion des déchets et services d'assainissement	270
35	145	0	15	15	70	61 Services d'enseignement	271
80	195	40	20	20	50	62 Soins de santé et assistance sociale	272

Nota : Voir les symboles et les abréviations dans les documents d'introduction et voir les documents de référence à la fin de la publication.

Selected characteristics for census divisions and census subdivisions – 100% data and 20% sample data, Ontario, 2006 Census (continued)

No.	Characteristics	Hilton Beach, VL	Hornepayne, TP ◆◊	Huron Shores, MU ◆	Jocelyn, TP ◆◊	Johnson, TP ◆	Laird, TP ◆◊
	Population characteristics						
	Industry - North American Industry Classification System 2002 (continued)						
273	71 Arts, entertainment and recreation	10	0	15	0	10	20
274	72 Accommodation and food services	0	55	40	10	0	25
275	81 Other services (except public administration)	0	20	30	10	10	65
276	91 Public administration	0	30	25	15	10	60
	Class of worker						
277	Class of worker - Not applicable[46]	10	0	20	0	0	0
278	All classes of worker[47]	65	690	800	90	250	630
279	Paid workers	65	660	670	75	200	595
280	Employees	65	655	670	80	195	585
281	Self-employed (incorporated)	0	0	0	0	10	10
282	Self-employed (unincorporated)	0	30	125	15	50	35
283	Unpaid family workers	0	0	0	0	10	0
	Occupation - National Occupational Classification for Statistics 2006						
284	Male labour force 15 years and over	25	365	465	50	150	360
285	Occupation - Not applicable[46]	0	0	15	0	0	0
286	All occupations[47]	30	360	455	50	150	360
287	A Management occupations	0	20	15	0	0	40
288	B Business, finance and administrative occupations	0	15	10	10	0	25
289	C Natural and applied sciences and related occupations	0	0	10	10	0	15
290	D Health occupations	0	0	0	0	0	0
291	E Occupations in social science, education, government service and religion	0	15	10	0	0	30
292	F Occupations in art, culture, recreation and sport	0	10	15	0	0	0
293	G Sales and service occupations	10	50	65	10	10	40
294	H Trades, transport and equipment operators and related occupations	10	190	240	15	65	175
295	I Occupations unique to primary industry	0	0	55	0	55	10
296	J Occupations unique to processing, manufacturing and utilities	0	50	35	0	0	35
297	Female labour force 15 years and over	45	325	360	35	105	270
298	Occupation - Not applicable[46]	10	0	0	0	0	0
299	All occupations[47]	40	325	350	35	105	270
300	A Management occupations	0	35	0	0	15	0
301	B Business, finance and administrative occupations	10	35	75	15	20	70
302	C Natural and applied sciences and related occupations	0	0	20	10	0	0
303	D Health occupations	0	50	35	0	10	25
304	E Occupations in social science, education, government service and religion	15	50	20	0	10	50
305	F Occupations in art, culture, recreation and sport	0	0	0	0	0	0
306	G Sales and service occupations	10	105	155	10	35	105
307	H Trades, transport and equipment operators and related occupations	10	25	10	0	0	15
308	I Occupations unique to primary industry	0	10	0	0	10	0
309	J Occupations unique to processing, manufacturing and utilities	0	0	15	0	0	0
310	**Total employed labour force 15 years and over**	**65**	**655**	**755**	**80**	**225**	**575**
	Place of work status						
311	Males	30	335	420	50	140	320
312	Usual place of work	20	280	275	40	65	225
313	At home	10	0	40	0	45	30
314	Outside Canada	0	0	0	0	0	0
315	No fixed workplace address	0	55	105	10	30	65
316	Females	40	320	340	35	90	255
317	Usual place of work	30	265	270	15	70	205
318	At home	0	20	45	15	15	25
319	Outside Canada	0	0	0	0	0	0
320	No fixed workplace address	0	30	20	0	0	25

Note: See symbols and abbreviations in the introductory material and see reference material at the end of the publication.

Certaines caractéristiques des divisions de recensement et des subdivisions de recensement – Données intégrales et données-échantillon (20 %), Ontario, Recensement de 2006 (suite)

Macdonald, Meredith and Aberdeen Additional, TP ◆◇	Michipicoten, TP ◇	Mississagi River 8, IRI	North Shore, TP	Plummer Additional, TP ◆	Prince, TP ◆◇	Caractéristiques	N°
						Caractéristiques de la population	
						Industrie - Système de classification des industries de l'Amérique du Nord de 2002 (suite)	
25	20	10	0	0	15	71 Arts, spectacles et loisirs	273
40	140	10	25	60	80	72 Hébergement et services de restauration	274
25	115	0	15	20	15	81 Autres services (sauf les administrations publiques)	275
95	190	65	15	15	30	91 Administrations publiques	276
						Catégorie de travailleurs	
25	10	15	10	0	0	Catégorie de travailleurs - Sans objet[46]	277
830	1,665	205	265	275	615	Toutes les catégories de travailleurs[47]	278
790	1,575	195	245	205	540	Travailleurs rémunérés	279
775	1,545	195	225	160	530	Employés	280
20	35	0	20	45	10	Travailleurs autonomes (entreprise constituée en société)	281
40	80	0	15	55	70	Travailleurs autonomes (entreprise non constituée en société)	282
0	15	0	0	10	0	Travailleurs familiaux non rémunérés	283
						Profession - Classification nationale des professions pour statistiques de 2006	
495	920	105	145	140	335	Hommes actifs de 15 ans et plus	284
25	0	10	0	0	0	Profession - Sans objet[46]	285
470	920	95	140	135	335	Toutes les professions[47]	286
15	120	10	20	30	30	A Gestion	287
20	35	10	10	0	15	B Affaires, finance et administration	288
30	65	10	0	0	35	C Sciences naturelles et appliquées et professions apparentées	289
0	15	0	0	0	0	D Secteur de la santé	290
10	55	0	0	0	15	E Sciences sociales, enseignement, administration publique et religion	291
0	0	0	0	0	0	F Arts, culture, sports et loisirs	292
80	165	20	25	10	90	G Ventes et services	293
270	320	30	50	70	110	H Métiers, transport et machinerie	294
20	75	15	25	15	10	I Professions propres au secteur primaire	295
10	60	15	10	10	30	J Transformation, fabrication et services d'utilité publique	296
365	760	115	120	140	275	Femmes actives de 15 ans et plus	297
0	10	10	0	0	0	Profession - Sans objet[46]	298
360	745	110	120	140	275	Toutes les professions[47]	299
10	60	15	20	40	15	A Gestion	300
100	150	20	40	10	50	B Affaires, finance et administration	301
15	15	0	0	0	15	C Sciences naturelles et appliquées et professions apparentées	302
60	75	0	15	0	20	D Secteur de la santé	303
25	145	35	0	15	80	E Sciences sociales, enseignement, administration publique et religion	304
0	25	0	10	0	20	F Arts, culture, sports et loisirs	305
135	245	30	25	45	60	G Ventes et services	306
10	10	0	0	0	0	H Métiers, transport et machinerie	307
0	10	0	0	15	15	I Professions propres au secteur primaire	308
10	20	0	0	10	0	J Transformation, fabrication et services d'utilité publique	309
780	**1,565**	**170**	**240**	**260**	**590**	**Population active occupée totale de 15 ans et plus**	310
						Catégorie de lieu de travail	
430	865	70	125	125	320	Hommes	311
335	730	45	80	55	245	Lieu habituel de travail	312
30	50	10	20	30	15	À domicile	313
0	0	0	10	0	0	En dehors du Canada	314
65	85	25	15	35	65	Sans adresse de travail fixe	315
350	700	95	115	130	265	Femmes	316
280	665	85	90	85	225	Lieu habituel de travail	317
35	40	0	20	35	30	À domicile	318
0	0	0	0	0	0	En dehors du Canada	319
40	0	10	0	15	10	Sans adresse de travail fixe	320

Nota : Voir les symboles et les abréviations dans les documents d'introduction et voir les documents de référence à la fin de la publication.

Selected characteristics for census divisions and census subdivisions – 100% data and 20% sample data, Ontario, 2006 Census (continued)

No.	Characteristics	Hilton Beach, VL	Hornepayne, TP ◆◊	Huron Shores, MU ◆	Jocelyn, TP ◆◊	Johnson, TP ◆	Laird, TP ◆◊
	Population characteristics						
321	**Total employed labour force 15 years and over with usual place of work or no fixed workplace address**	**55**	**635**	**670**	**70**	**170**	**515**
	Mode of transportation						
322	Males	25	335	380	50	95	290
323	Car, truck, van, as driver	25	175	295	40	80	235
324	Car, truck, van, as passenger	0	55	50	10	0	40
325	Public transit	0	10	0	0	0	0
326	Walked	0	85	10	0	10	15
327	All other modes	0	10	25	10	0	0
328	Females	35	295	290	20	70	225
329	Car, truck, van, as driver	25	150	235	20	50	185
330	Car, truck, van, as passenger	10	35	30	0	0	25
331	Public transit	0	0	0	0	0	0
332	Walked	0	105	20	0	15	10
333	All other modes	0	10	0	0	10	0
334	**Total population 15 years and over who worked since January 1, 2005**	**80**	**745**	**910**	**125**	**310**	**745**
	Language used most often at work						
335	Single responses	80	730	910	120	310	745
336	English	85	725	910	120	285	740
337	French	0	10	0	0	0	0
338	Non-official languages[7]	0	0	0	0	30	10
339	Chinese, n.o.s.[61]	0	0	0	0	0	0
340	Cantonese	0	0	0	0	0	0
341	Other languages[8]	0	0	0	0	25	10
342	Multiple responses	0	15	0	0	0	0
343	English and French	0	15	0	0	0	0
344	English and non-official language	0	0	0	0	0	0
345	French and non-official language	0	0	0	0	0	0
346	English, French and non-official language	0	0	0	0	0	0
	Dwelling and household characteristics						
347	**Total number of occupied private dwellings**	**80**	**480**	**695**	**125**	**260**	**430**
	Housing tenure						
348	Owned	55	385	630	120	210	405
349	Rented	25	90	60	0	50	25
350	Band housing	0	0	10	0	0	0
	Structural type of dwelling						
351	Single-detached house	70	420	685	120	250	435
352	Semi-detached house	0	5	0	0	0	0
353	Row house	0	0	0	0	0	0
354	Apartment, duplex	0	5	10	0	0	0
355	Apartment, building that has five or more storeys	0	30	0	0	0	0
356	Apartment, building that has fewer than five storeys	10	25	10	0	5	0
357	Other single-attached house	0	0	0	0	0	0
358	Movable dwelling[48]	0	0	10	0	0	0
	Condition of dwelling						
359	Regular maintenance only	45	230	365	70	150	270
360	Minor repairs	20	220	280	45	75	140
361	Major repairs	15	25	50	10	35	20
	Period of construction						
362	Before 1946	25	80	80	15	70	30
363	1946 to 1960	10	120	130	0	45	75
364	1961 to 1970	15	70	140	10	35	60
365	1971 to 1980	20	130	125	15	60	75
366	1981 to 1985	0	0	95	30	0	35
367	1986 to 1990	0	20	55	10	10	25
368	1991 to 1995	10	15	10	25	25	40
369	1996 to 2000	10	25	35	0	15	60
370	2001 to 2006[49]	0	20	15	15	0	35

Note: See symbols and abbreviations in the introductory material and see reference material at the end of the publication.

Certaines caractéristiques des divisions de recensement et des subdivisions de recensement – Données intégrales et données-échantillon (20 %), Ontario, Recensement de 2006 (suite)

Macdonald, Meredith and Aberdeen Additional, TP ◆◇	Michipicoten, TP ◇	Mississagi River 8, IRI	North Shore, TP	Plummer Additional, TP ◆	Prince, TP ◆◇	Caractéristiques	N°
						Caractéristiques de la population	
715	**1,475**	**165**	**190**	**190**	**540**	**Population active occupée totale de 15 ans et plus ayant un lieu habituel de travail ou sans adresse de travail fixe**	321
						Mode de transport	
405	815	70	100	95	305	Hommes	322
375	530	45	90	80	265	Automobile, camion ou fourgonnette, en tant que conducteur	323
20	155	20	0	0	30	Automobile, camion ou fourgonnette, en tant que passager	324
0	10	0	0	0	0	Transport en commun	325
0	90	10	0	10	0	À pied	326
0	35	0	0	10	0	Tous les autres modes	327
315	665	95	90	95	235	Femmes	328
285	460	60	70	85	205	Automobile, camion ou fourgonnette, en tant que conductrice	329
15	75	10	15	10	20	Automobile, camion ou fourgonnette, en tant que passagère	330
0	0	0	0	0	10	Transport en commun	331
10	115	15	10	0	0	À pied	332
0	10	0	0	0	0	Tous les autres modes	333
900	**1,930**	**225**	**290**	**305**	**665**	**Population totale de 15 ans et plus ayant travaillé depuis le 1er janvier 2005**	334
						Langue utilisée le plus souvent au travail	
905	1,920	225	295	305	665	Réponses uniques	335
905	1,810	225	280	295	660	Anglais	336
0	110	10	10	10	0	Français	337
0	0	0	0	0	0	Langues non officielles[7]	338
0	0	0	0	0	0	Chinois, n.d.a.[61]	339
0	0	0	0	0	0	Cantonais	340
0	10	0	0	0	0	Autres langues[8]	341
0	10	0	0	0	0	Réponses multiples	342
0	10	0	0	0	0	Anglais et français	343
0	0	0	0	0	0	Anglais et langue non officielle	344
0	0	0	0	0	0	Français et langue non officielle	345
0	0	0	0	0	0	Anglais, français et langue non officielle	346
						Caractéristiques des logements et des ménages	
605	**1,295**	**160**	**250**	**255**	**365**	**Nombre total de logements privés occupés**	347
						Mode d'occupation	
510	995	25	210	235	360	Possédé	348
90	305	20	40	20	0	Loué	349
0	0	115	0	0	0	Logement de bande	350
						Type de construction résidentielle	
565	1,045	140	240	255	270	Maison individuelle non attenante	351
0	5	5	0	5	75	Maison jumelée	352
0	45	0	0	0	10	Maison en rangée	353
10	30	0	0	5	5	Appartement, duplex	354
0	0	0	0	0	0	Appartement, immeuble de cinq étages ou plus	355
25	165	10	0	0	0	Appartement, immeuble de moins de cinq étages	356
0	15	0	0	0	5	Autre maison individuelle attenante	357
0	0	0	0	0	0	Logement mobile[48]	358
						État du logement	
355	680	95	150	95	270	Entretien régulier seulement	359
145	450	35	80	150	80	Réparations mineures	360
105	160	30	15	15	20	Réparations majeures	361
						Période de construction	
125	130	0	0	95	30	Avant 1946	362
100	530	0	80	30	45	1946 à 1960	363
95	230	10	30	10	35	1961 à 1970	364
105	195	20	30	45	90	1971 à 1980	365
40	65	10	40	20	65	1981 à 1985	366
50	50	20	15	0	70	1986 à 1990	367
45	50	25	30	35	0	1991 à 1995	368
20	35	40	10	15	15	1996 à 2000	369
25	0	35	20	10	15	2001 à 2006[49]	370

Nota : Voir les symboles et les abréviations dans les documents d'introduction et voir les documents de référence à la fin de la publication.

Selected characteristics for census divisions and census subdivisions – 100% data and 20% sample data, Ontario, 2006 Census (continued)

No.	Characteristics	Hilton Beach, VL	Hornepayne, TP ◆◊	Huron Shores, MU ◆	Jocelyn, TP ◆◊	Johnson, TP ◆	Laird, TP ◆◊
	Dwelling and household characteristics						
371	Average number of rooms per dwelling	5.9	6.6	7.1	6.0	7.0	6.9
372	Average number of bedrooms per dwelling	2.6	2.9	2.9	2.8	3.2	2.9
373	Average value of dwelling $	131,882	64,345	121,889	138,805	97,742	145,385
374	**Total number of private households**	**85**	**480**	**720**	**125**	**265**	**430**
	Household size						
375	1 person	25	135	160	25	55	75
376	2 persons	35	145	340	80	110	195
377	3 persons	5	80	80	5	35	70
378	4 to 5 persons	10	115	120	15	45	80
379	6 or more persons	5	10	10	0	15	5
	Household type						
380	One-family households[50]	50	320	500	105	185	330
381	Multiple-family households	0	0	10	0	0	0
382	Non-family households	30	155	180	20	70	100
383	Number of persons in private households	175	1,190	1,680	275	700	1,080
384	Average number of persons in private households	2.2	2.5	2.3	2.2	2.6	2.5
385	Tenant-occupied private non-farm, non-reserve dwellings[51]	25	95	60	0	50	25
386	Average gross rent $[51]	0	595	379	0	481	725
387	Tenant-occupied households spending 30% or more of household income on gross rent[52]	0	0	35	0	25	0
388	Tenant-occupied households spending from 30% to 99% of household income on gross rent[52]	0	0	25	0	15	10
389	Owner-occupied private non-farm, non-reserve dwellings[53]	55	385	605	120	195	400
390	Average owner's major payments $[53]	876	777	567	578	595	747
391	Owner households spending 30% or more of household income on owner's major payments[52]	0	55	60	25	40	45
392	Owner households spending from 30% to 99% of household income on owner's major payments[52]	0	50	40	25	25	40
	Census family characteristics						
393	**Total number of census families in private households**	**50**	**325**	**520**	**105**	**195**	**330**
	Family structure and number of children						
394	Total couple families	40	280	480	100	160	325
395	Total families of married couples	30	200	435	85	150	300
396	Without children at home	15	80	275	60	80	135
397	With children at home	15	115	165	25	70	165
398	1 child	10	25	60	10	30	65
399	2 children	0	50	70	10	15	65
400	3 or more children	0	40	30	0	20	30
401	Total families of common-law couples	10	80	45	15	10	25
402	Without children at home	0	35	20	15	0	25
403	With children at home	10	50	25	0	10	0
404	1 child	0	30	10	0	10	0
405	2 children	0	10	10	0	0	0
406	3 or more children	10	10	10	0	0	0
407	Total lone-parent families	10	40	35	10	35	0
408	Female parent	10	25	25	10	25	10
409	1 child	10	10	20	0	20	10
410	2 children	0	10	0	0	0	0
411	3 or more children	0	10	0	0	10	0
412	Male parent	0	15	10	0	10	0
413	1 child	0	15	10	0	10	0
414	2 children	0	0	0	0	0	0
415	3 or more children	0	0	0	0	0	0

Note: See symbols and abbreviations in the introductory material and see reference material at the end of the publication.

Certaines caractéristiques des divisions de recensement et des subdivisions de recensement – Données intégrales et données-échantillon (20 %), Ontario, Recensement de 2006 (suite)

Macdonald, Meredith and Aberdeen Additional, TP ◆◇	Michipicoten, TP ◇	Mississagi River 8, IRI	North Shore, TP	Plummer Additional, TP ◆	Prince, TP ◆◇	Caractéristiques	N°
						Caractéristiques des logements et des ménages	
6.4	6.5	5.8	6.8	6.2	7.2	Nombre moyen de pièces par logement	371
2.6	2.8	2.8	2.6	2.7	3.1	Nombre moyen de chambres à coucher par logement	372
116,235	92,826	0	176,434	123,675	154,496	Valeur moyenne du logement $	373
605	**1,295**	**155**	**250**	**265**	**365**	**Nombre total de ménages privés**	374
						Taille du ménage	
110	335	45	55	65	50	1 personne	375
250	470	45	140	125	160	2 personnes	376
95	195	20	25	30	65	3 personnes	377
140	275	35	25	40	85	4 à 5 personnes	378
10	20	10	5	5	10	6 personnes ou plus	379
						Genre de ménage	
490	900	105	185	195	300	Ménages unifamiliaux[50]	380
0	20	0	0	0	0	Ménages multifamiliaux	381
110	375	55	65	65	70	Ménages non familiaux	382
1,550	3,165	415	545	620	975	Nombre de personnes dans les ménages privés	383
2.6	2.4	2.6	2.2	2.4	2.7	Nombre moyen de personnes dans les ménages privés	384
90	305	0	35	20	10	Ménages locataires dans les logements privés non agricoles hors réserve[51]	385
526	591	0	609	714	0	Loyer brut moyen $[51]	386
20	120	0	25	0	0	Ménages locataires consacrant 30 % ou plus du revenu du ménage au loyer brut[52]	387
20	120	0	30	10	0	Ménages locataires consacrant de 30 % à 99 % du revenu du ménage au loyer brut[52]	388
505	995	0	215	225	355	Ménages propriétaires dans les logements privés non agricoles hors réserve[53]	389
823	680	0	567	727	953	Principales dépenses de propriété moyennes $[53]	390
70	90	0	20	55	70	Ménages propriétaires consacrant 30 % ou plus du revenu du ménage aux principales dépenses de propriété[52]	391
40	70	0	20	45	65	Ménages propriétaires consacrant de 30 % à 99 % du revenu du ménage aux principales dépenses de propriété[52]	392
						Caractéristiques des familles de recensement	
495	**940**	**105**	**190**	**190**	**295**	**Nombre total de familles de recensement dans les ménages privés**	393
						Structure de la famille et le nombre d'enfants	
430	815	70	175	180	275	Total des familles avec conjoints	394
385	635	40	160	160	245	Total des familles avec couples mariés	395
200	320	15	110	95	125	Sans enfants à la maison	396
185	310	25	50	65	120	Avec enfants à la maison	397
50	130	10	30	35	40	1 enfant	398
95	130	10	20	25	50	2 enfants	399
35	50	10	0	15	35	3 enfants ou plus	400
45	185	30	15	20	35	Total des familles avec couples en union libre	401
45	95	10	15	20	25	Sans enfants à la maison	402
0	90	15	0	0	10	Avec enfants à la maison	403
0	20	0	0	0	0	1 enfant	404
0	45	10	0	0	10	2 enfants	405
0	25	0	0	0	0	3 enfants ou plus	406
65	125	35	20	15	20	Total des familles monoparentales	407
50	65	25	15	10	15	Parent de sexe féminin	408
25	40	20	10	0	0	1 enfant	409
10	20	10	0	0	15	2 enfants	410
15	0	0	10	0	0	3 enfants ou plus	411
15	55	0	0	0	10	Parent de sexe masculin	412
0	35	0	0	0	10	1 enfant	413
15	10	0	0	0	10	2 enfants	414
0	10	0	0	0	0	3 enfants ou plus	415

Nota : Voir les symboles et les abréviations dans les documents d'introduction et voir les documents de référence à la fin de la publication.

Selected characteristics for census divisions and census subdivisions – 100% data and 20% sample data, Ontario, 2006 Census (continued)

No.	Characteristics	Hilton Beach, VL	Hornepayne, TP ◆◊	Huron Shores, MU ◆	Jocelyn, TP ◆◊	Johnson, TP ◆	Laird, TP ◆◊
	Census family characteristics						
416	**Total number of children at home**	**55**	**420**	**400**	**55**	**270**	**305**
	Age group						
417	Under 6 years	0	80	65	15	70	55
418	6 to 14 years	25	175	165	20	100	95
419	15 to 17 years	25	75	35	10	25	40
420	18 to 24 years	0	65	75	0	35	105
421	25 years and over	0	20	50	0	35	0
422	Average number of children at home per census family[54]	1.1	1.3	0.8	0.5	1.4	0.9
423	**Total number of persons in private households**	**175**	**1,195**	**1,635**	**275**	**700**	**1,075**
	Census family status and living arrangements						
424	Number of persons not in census families	30	170	235	20	75	115
425	Living with relatives[55]	0	0	10	0	0	20
426	Living with non-relatives only	0	20	65	0	0	0
427	Living alone	30	150	155	20	70	95
428	Number of census family persons	145	1,025	1,400	260	625	965
429	Average number of persons per census family	2.9	3.1	2.7	2.4	3.2	2.9
430	**Total number of persons aged 65 years and over**	**40**	**90**	**320**	**55**	**140**	**125**
431	Number of persons not in census families aged 65 years and over	15	60	95	10	35	30
432	Living with relatives[55]	0	0	0	0	0	10
433	Living with non-relatives only	0	0	10	0	0	0
434	Living alone	15	60	80	10	30	25
435	Number of census family persons aged 65 years and over	25	30	230	50	105	95
	Economic family characteristics						
436	**Total number of economic families in private households**	**50**	**320**	**510**	**110**	**190**	**340**
	Size of family						
437	2 persons	25	140	305	80	95	175
438	3 persons	10	65	85	10	50	65
439	4 persons	0	70	80	15	15	65
440	5 or more persons	10	50	40	0	25	35
441	Total number of persons in economic families	145	1,020	1,410	260	630	985
442	Average number of persons per economic family	3.0	3.0	3.0	3.0	3.0	3.0
443	Total number of persons not in economic families	30	170	225	20	70	90
	2005 income characteristics						
444	**Population 15 years and over**	**X**	**950**	**1,465**	**240**	**525**	**925**
	Sex and total income groups in 2005						
445	Without income	X	40	135	0	10	20
446	With income	X	910	1,330	230	520	900
447	Under $1,000[56]	X	20	50	10	25	25
448	$1,000 to $2,999	X	40	45	10	25	70
449	$3,000 to $4,999	X	10	70	0	45	25
450	$5,000 to $6,999	X	30	55	15	20	30
451	$7,000 to $9,999	X	75	50	10	15	40
452	$10,000 to $11,999	X	30	80	15	25	10
453	$12,000 to $14,999	X	25	115	10	40	80
454	$15,000 to $19,999	X	55	155	30	70	75
455	$20,000 to $24,999	X	50	120	40	35	45
456	$25,000 to $29,999	X	55	110	10	20	70
457	$30,000 to $34,999	X	60	100	10	50	60
458	$35,000 to $39,999	X	40	90	0	30	30
459	$40,000 to $44,999	X	30	50	35	30	60
460	$45,000 to $49,999	X	65	30	0	20	40
461	$50,000 to $59,999	X	80	90	10	35	35
462	$60,000 and over	X	240	110	40	25	190
463	Median income $[57]	X	34,872	21,509	21,977	18,357	29,355
464	Average income $[57]	X	41,682	27,789	35,269	24,722	35,933
465	Standard error of average income $[57]	X	2,125	1,412	3,850	1,699	2,337

Note: See symbols and abbreviations in the introductory material and see reference material at the end of the publication.

Certaines caractéristiques des divisions de recensement et des subdivisions de recensement – Données intégrales et données-échantillon (20 %), Ontario, Recensement de 2006 (suite)

Macdonald, Meredith and Aberdeen Additional, TP ◆◇	Michipicoten, TP ◇	Mississagi River 8, IRI	North Shore, TP	Plummer Additional, TP ◆	Prince, TP ◆◇	Caractéristiques	N°
						Caractéristiques des familles de recensement	
490	**940**	**160**	**105**	**140**	**300**	**Nombre total d'enfants à la maison**	416
						Groupes d'âge	
80	180	35	20	45	15	Moins de 6 ans	417
150	400	75	30	70	105	6 à 14 ans	418
95	140	20	20	10	25	15 à 17 ans	419
130	165	15	15	15	110	18 à 24 ans	420
35	50	10	20	0	45	25 ans et plus	421
1.0	1.0	1.5	0.6	0.7	1.0	Nombre moyen d'enfants à la maison par famille de recensement[54]	422
1,550	**3,160**	**415**	**550**	**610**	**970**	**Nombre total de personnes dans les ménages privés**	423
						Situation des particuliers dans la famille de recensement et des particuliers dans le ménage	
135	465	80	80	95	95	Nombre de personnes hors famille de recensement	424
10	70	20	0	20	25	Vivant avec des personnes apparentées[55]	425
30	55	10	15	10	10	Vivant avec des personnes non apparentées seulement	426
100	335	45	55	60	65	Vivant seules	427
1,415	2,690	335	470	515	875	Nombre de membres d'une famille de recensement	428
2.9	2.9	3.2	2.5	2.7	2.9	Nombre moyen de personnes par famille de recensement	429
160	**385**	**20**	**125**	**120**	**125**	**Nombre total de personnes âgées de 65 ans et plus**	430
20	120	0	40	45	55	Nombre de personnes hors famille de recensement âgées de 65 ans et plus	431
0	10	0	0	20	20	Vivant avec des personnes apparentées[55]	432
0	0	0	0	0	0	Vivant avec des personnes non apparentées seulement	433
15	115	0	30	20	30	Vivant seules	434
140	260	10	85	70	70	Nombre de membres d'une famille de recensement âgés de 65 ans et plus	435
						Caractéristiques des familles économiques	
495	**945**	**105**	**190**	**195**	**295**	**Nombre total de familles économiques dans les ménages privés**	436
						Taille de la famille	
265	480	45	130	115	150	2 personnes	437
80	180	20	25	30	55	3 personnes	438
105	195	25	25	15	55	4 personnes	439
40	95	15	0	30	40	5 personnes ou plus	440
1,420	2,765	355	475	535	900	Nombre total de personnes dans les familles économiques	441
3.0	3.0	3.0	3.0	3.0	3.0	Nombre moyen de personnes par famille économique	442
130	395	60	70	70	75	Nombre total de personnes hors famille économique	443
						Caractéristiques du revenu de 2005	
1,325	**2,600**	**305**	**500**	**510**	**850**	**Population de 15 ans et plus**	444
						Sexe et groupes de revenu total en 2005	
125	85	15	25	40	15	Sans revenu	445
1,195	2,510	290	475	470	835	Avec un revenu	446
90	80	35	0	20	40	Moins de 1 000 $[56]	447
40	55	10	10	20	15	1 000 $ à 2 999 $	448
40	110	25	20	35	10	3 000 $ à 4 999 $	449
30	110	10	15	10	35	5 000 $ à 6 999 $	450
65	165	30	15	10	45	7 000 $ à 9 999 $	451
60	75	15	25	10	50	10 000 $ à 11 999 $	452
60	155	25	25	20	15	12 000 $ à 14 999 $	453
110	250	25	75	100	75	15 000 $ à 19 999 $	454
75	175	30	65	40	50	20 000 $ à 24 999 $	455
135	125	25	35	35	60	25 000 $ à 29 999 $	456
65	170	20	35	20	70	30 000 $ à 34 999 $	457
50	115	15	25	25	55	35 000 $ à 39 999 $	458
50	70	10	15	30	20	40 000 $ à 44 999 $	459
60	155	10	10	35	50	45 000 $ à 49 999$	460
70	130	10	35	25	75	50 000 $ à 59 999$	461
180	565	10	60	30	175	60 000 $ et plus	462
26,032	28,715	14,672	23,985	22,161	32,404	Revenu médian $[57]	463
30,499	35,371	19,336	34,625	28,033	37,012	Revenu moyen $[57]	464
1,420	1,176	0	2,999	2,370	1,981	Erreur type de revenu moyen $[57]	465

Nota : Voir les symboles et les abréviations dans les documents d'introduction et voir les documents de référence à la fin de la publication.

Selected characteristics for census divisions and census subdivisions – 100% data and 20% sample data, Ontario, 2006 Census (continued)

No.	Characteristics	Hilton Beach, VL	Hornepayne, TP ◆◊	Huron Shores, MU ◆	Jocelyn, TP ◆◊	Johnson, TP ◆	Laird, TP ◆◊
	2005 income characteristics						
	Sex and total income groups in 2005 (continued)						
466	Total - Males	X	500	750	135	240	490
467	Without income	X	20	65	0	0	15
468	With income	X	480	690	135	245	470
469	Under $1,000[56]	X	0	20	0	20	0
470	$1,000 to $2,999	X	10	15	0	10	0
471	$3,000 to $4,999	X	0	15	0	20	10
472	$5,000 to $6,999	X	10	20	0	0	10
473	$7,000 to $9,999	X	20	20	0	15	15
474	$10,000 to $11,999	X	10	25	10	0	10
475	$12,000 to $14,999	X	0	40	0	0	35
476	$15,000 to $19,999	X	0	60	10	35	25
477	$20,000 to $24,999	X	15	65	20	15	20
478	$25,000 to $29,999	X	20	55	15	15	35
479	$30,000 to $34,999	X	40	70	0	20	40
480	$35,000 to $39,999	X	20	60	0	10	25
481	$40,000 to $44,999	X	20	30	25	10	40
482	$45,000 to $49,999	X	55	20	0	10	25
483	$50,000 to $59,999	X	50	75	10	35	30
484	$60,000 and over	X	190	90	25	15	160
485	Median income $[57]	X	50,045	30,773	29,792	23,194	42,924
486	Average income $[57]	X	55,141	35,783	38,562	28,517	49,399
487	Standard error of average income $[57]	X	3,050	2,248	4,866	2,477	3,502
488	Total - Females	X	445	715	105	285	440
489	Without income	X	20	70	0	10	10
490	With income	X	425	640	100	275	430
491	Under $1,000[56]	X	15	35	0	10	25
492	$1,000 to $2,999	X	40	30	0	15	70
493	$3,000 to $4,999	X	0	55	0	25	15
494	$5,000 to $6,999	X	20	35	15	25	25
495	$7,000 to $9,999	X	55	30	0	0	20
496	$10,000 to $11,999	X	20	55	0	20	10
497	$12,000 to $14,999	X	20	75	0	30	45
498	$15,000 to $19,999	X	50	90	20	35	50
499	$20,000 to $24,999	X	35	55	15	20	25
500	$25,000 to $29,999	X	30	55	0	10	35
501	$30,000 to $34,999	X	15	25	10	35	20
502	$35,000 to $39,999	X	25	30	0	20	0
503	$40,000 to $44,999	X	0	20	0	20	20
504	$45,000 to $49,999	X	10	10	0	0	20
505	$50,000 to $59,999	X	25	15	0	0	10
506	$60,000 and over	X	50	20	20	0	30
507	Median income $[57]	X	19,376	15,152	19,065	15,862	14,094
508	Average income $[57]	X	26,621	19,203	30,938	21,384	21,012
509	Standard error of average income $[57]	X	2,252	1,308	6,106	2,252	2,149
	Composition of total income						
510	Composition of total income in 2005 %	X	100.0	100.0	100.0	100.0	100.0
511	Employment income %	X	83.3	60.1	70.2	53.0	77.0
512	Government transfer payments %	X	8.4	21.3	16.2	30.4	8.9
513	Other %	X	8.5	18.7	15.1	16.8	13.6
514	**Population 15 years and over with employment income in 2005**	**X**	**760**	**890**	**150**	**315**	**740**
	Sex and work activity						
515	Median employment income in 2005 $	X	33,841	18,827	28,585	12,077	25,321
516	Average employment income in 2005 $	X	41,597	24,833	37,960	21,650	33,855
517	Standard error of average employment income $	X	2,417	2,066	6,128	2,476	2,486
518	Worked full year, full time[59]	X	365	320	70	115	300
519	Median employment income in 2005 $	X	51,166	33,795	75,167	31,286	48,730
520	Average employment income in 2005 $	X	57,615	44,502	66,784	35,857	56,161
521	Standard error of average employment income $	X	3,344	4,093	7,971	4,541	3,868
522	Worked part year or part time[60]	X	340	480	50	155	405
523	Median employment income in 2005 $	X	17,994	11,354	6,319	7,151	12,690
524	Average employment income in 2005 $	X	28,479	15,599	11,191	15,366	19,714
525	Standard error of average employment income $	X	2,815	1,624	2,756	2,632	2,288
526	Males 15 years and over with employment income[58]	X	395	530	95	175	415
527	Median employment income in 2005 $	X	51,070	21,533	24,308	12,077	42,463
528	Average employment income in 2005 $	X	55,274	30,286	36,424	22,304	45,042
529	Standard error of average employment income $	X	3,635	3,117	7,365	3,220	3,542

Note: See symbols and abbreviations in the introductory material and see reference material at the end of the publication.

Certaines caractéristiques des divisions de recensement et des subdivisions de recensement – Données intégrales et données-échantillon (20 %), Ontario, Recensement de 2006 (suite)

Macdonald, Meredith and Aberdeen Additional, TP ◆◇	Michipicoten, TP ◇	Mississagi River 8, IRI	North Shore, TP	Plummer Additional, TP ◆	Prince, TP ◆◇	Caractéristiques	N°
						Caractéristiques du revenu de 2005	
						Sexe et groupes de revenu total en 2005 (suite)	
690	1,320	150	260	240	430	Total - Hommes	466
35	40	10	10	15	10	Sans revenu	467
655	1,285	140	245	230	420	Avec un revenu	468
50	30	15	0	10	10	Moins de 1 000 $[56]	469
20	15	10	0	15	0	1 000 $ à 2 999 $	470
15	40	15	0	20	10	3 000 $ à 4 999 $	471
15	60	0	0	0	0	5 000 $ à 6 999 $	472
25	60	15	0	0	30	7 000 $ à 9 999 $	473
25	30	10	10	10	35	10 000 $ à 11 999 $	474
15	65	10	0	10	10	12 000 $ à 14 999 $	475
40	50	10	40	30	30	15 000 $ à 19 999 $	476
50	85	10	40	20	20	20 000 $ à 24 999 $	477
65	75	15	20	10	40	25 000 $ à 29 999 $	478
35	125	0	20	20	30	30 000 $ à 34 999 $	479
20	60	0	10	20	30	35 000 $ à 39 999 $	480
30	45	0	10	15	15	40 000 $ à $44 999 $	481
50	80	0	10	30	15	45 000 $ à $49 999 $	482
45	85	0	25	0	25	50 000 $ à $59 999 $	483
150	380	10	45	15	135	60 000 $ et plus	484
30,118	35,497	11,296	28,909	25,008	38,452	Revenu médian $[57]	485
36,554	41,989	17,557	44,260	29,066	44,129	Revenu moyen $[57]	486
2,152	1,722	0	5,236	3,002	3,004	Erreur type de revenu moyen $[57]	487
630	1,280	155	240	265	420	Total - Femmes	488
90	45	0	15	20	0	Sans revenu	489
540	1,225	150	225	240	415	Avec un revenu	490
40	50	15	10	10	35	Moins de 1 000 $[56]	491
15	40	10	10	0	10	1 000$ à 2 999 $	492
25	70	0	15	20	0	3 000 $ à 4 999 $	493
15	50	10	10	10	30	5 000 $ à 6 999 $	494
40	105	15	10	0	15	7 000 $ à 9 999 $	495
35	45	10	15	0	15	10 000 $ à 11 999 $	496
45	95	10	25	15	10	12 000 $ à 14 999 $	497
75	200	15	35	70	50	15 000 $ à 19 999 $	498
25	95	15	20	20	30	20 000 $ à 24 999 $	499
70	55	10	15	30	20	25 000 $ à 29 999 $	500
35	45	10	10	10	40	30 000 $ à 34 999 $	501
30	50	15	10	0	25	35 000 $ à 39 999 $	502
20	20	10	0	10	10	40 000 $ à 44 999 $	503
10	70	10	0	0	40	45 000 $ à 49 999 $	504
25	45	0	15	15	50	50 000 $ à 59 999 $	505
30	180	0	10	15	35	60 000 $ et plus	506
16,696	18,428	19,392	18,582	19,726	27,063	Revenu médian $[57]	507
23,147	28,456	21,030	24,081	27,060	29,783	Revenu moyen $[57]	508
1,542	1,487	0	2,144	3,605	2,297	Erreur type de revenu moyen $[57]	509
						Composition du revenu total	
100.0	100.0	100.0	100.0	100.0	100.0	Composition du revenu total en 2005 %	510
74.6	78.1	78.8	67.3	51.4	74.6	Revenu d'emploi %	511
13.8	11.6	20.6	21.7	21.3	8.9	Transferts gouvernementaux %	512
11.7	10.1	1.9	11.4	27.0	15.8	Autres %	513
930	**2,010**	**205**	**280**	**275**	**695**	**Population de 15 ans et plus avec un revenu d'emploi en 2005**	514
						Sexe et travail	
24,962	28,151	18,992	28,226	14,697	28,777	Revenu médian d'emploi en 2005 $	515
29,233	34,583	21,565	39,087	24,605	33,611	Revenu moyen d'emploi en 2005 $	516
1,699	1,402	0	4,740	3,757	2,200	Erreur type de revenu moyen d'emploi $	517
445	950	90	105	135	365	A travaillé toute l'année à plein temps[59]	518
44,630	51,167	28,256	42,529	16,887	47,590	Revenu médian d'emploi en 2005 $	519
46,972	52,284	30,961	48,546	33,720	51,995	Revenu moyen d'emploi en 2005 $	520
2,257	1,963	0	5,373	6,608	2,575	Erreur type de revenu moyen d'emploi $	521
425	905	95	165	125	255	A travaillé une partie de l'année ou à temps partiel[60]	522
9,100	11,574	10,000	20,928	6,012	10,839	Revenu médian d'emploi en 2005 $	523
14,489	21,242	15,033	35,591	16,876	15,440	Revenu moyen d'emploi en 2005 $	524
1,628	1,490	0	7,142	3,435	1,858	Erreur type de revenu moyen d'emploi $	525
545	1,095	95	155	135	365	Hommes de 15 ans et plus avec un revenu d'emploi[58]	526
27,128	33,872	13,008	32,411	33,284	34,057	Revenu médian d'emploi en 2005 $	527
34,513	39,434	19,974	48,142	25,611	40,199	Revenu moyen d'emploi en 2005 $	528
2,510	2,046	0	8,045	4,490	3,194	Erreur type de revenu moyen d'emploi $	529

Nota : Voir les symboles et les abréviations dans les documents d'introduction et voir les documents de référence à la fin de la publication.

Selected characteristics for census divisions and census subdivisions – 100% data and 20% sample data, Ontario, 2006 Census (continued)

No.	Characteristics	Hilton Beach, VL	Hornepayne, TP ◆◇	Huron Shores, MU ◆	Jocelyn, TP ◆◇	Johnson, TP ◆	Laird, TP ◆◇
	2005 income characteristics						
	Sex and work activity (continued)						
530	Worked full year, full time[59]	x	255	225	40	65	195
531	Median employment income in 2005 $	x	53,159	37,832	74,937	31,183	69,306
532	Average employment income in 2005 $	x	63,816	49,109	66,507	35,651	67,489
533	Standard error of average employment income $	x	4,079	5,479	9,722	5,022	4,651
534	Worked part year or part time[60]	x	115	225	30	105	210
535	Median employment income in 2005 $	x	35,060	12,027	10,236	4,175	20,090
536	Average employment income in 2005 $	x	42,648	20,069	12,695	15,318	27,939
537	Standard error of average employment income $	x	6,147	2,659	3,459	3,712	3,623
538	Females 15 years and over with employment income[58]	x	365	365	55	140	325
539	Median employment income in 2005 $	x	18,002	12,812	28,596	11,584	12,353
540	Average employment income in 2005 $	x	26,739	16,962	40,632	20,824	19,310
541	Standard error of average employment income $	x	2,457	2,037	10,866	3,869	2,436
542	Worked full year, full time[59]	x	110	95	25	50	110
543	Median employment income in 2005 $	x	44,196	31,047	90,702	31,328	30,708
544	Average employment income in 2005 $	x	43,228	33,710	67,181	36,144	35,526
545	Standard error of average employment income $	x	4,953	4,410	13,544	8,630	4,756
546	Worked part year or part time[60]	x	225	255	20	55	200
547	Median employment income in 2005 $	x	15,226	5,624	5,172	10,912	7,983
548	Average employment income in 2005 $	x	21,248	11,582	9,012	15,456	11,116
549	Standard error of average employment income $	x	2,497	1,762	4,377	2,919	1,747
550	**Total number of economic families in private households**	**x**	**325**	**510**	**105**	**190**	**340**
	Family income groups in 2005						
551	Under $10,000	x	0	0	0	10	0
552	$10,000 to $19,999	x	0	40	0	10	0
553	$20,000 to $29,999	x	0	55	10	20	15
554	$30,000 to $39,999	x	10	40	15	20	40
555	$40,000 to $49,999	x	20	90	25	10	35
556	$50,000 to $59,999	x	35	85	0	40	20
557	$60,000 to $69,999	x	45	50	10	25	50
558	$70,000 to $79,999	x	40	30	15	20	35
559	$80,000 to $89,999	x	20	25	0	20	45
560	$90,000 to $99,999	x	20	0	0	20	0
561	$100,000 and over	x	115	90	15	15	85
562	Median family income $	x	80,971	52,564	48,196	57,357	72,783
563	Average family income $	x	90,605	62,660	70,400	59,942	80,539
564	Standard error of average family income $	x	4,815	3,558	11,022	3,870	5,612
	Family after-tax income groups in 2005						
565	Under $10,000	x	0	0	0	0	0
566	$10,000 to $19,999	x	0	40	10	0	0
567	$20,000 to $29,999	x	10	70	20	20	30
568	$30,000 to $39,999	x	15	75	10	25	40
569	$40,000 to $49,999	x	30	110	20	30	35
570	$50,000 to $59,999	x	55	60	10	40	65
571	$60,000 to $69,999	x	55	45	10	15	65
572	$70,000 to $79,999	x	20	20	10	25	10
573	$80,000 to $89,999	x	35	35	0	15	45
574	$90,000 to $99,999	x	25	10	0	0	20
575	$100,000 and over	x	70	45	15	0	30
576	Median after-tax family income $	x	68,670	46,339	42,347	51,798	59,880
577	Average after-tax family income $	x	76,455	53,654	58,424	51,993	66,692
578	Standard error of average after-tax family income $	x	3,853	2,705	7,672	3,016	4,170
	Income status in 2005						
579	Total population in private households for income status	x	1,190	1,630	280	700	1,075
580	Below low income cut-off before tax in 2005	x	15	140	0	75	15
581	Prevalence of low income before tax in 2005 %	x	1.3	8.3	0.0	10.7	0.0
582	Below low income cut-off after tax in 2005	x	15	75	0	65	10
583	Prevalence of low income after tax in 2005 %	x	1.3	4.6	0.0	10.0	0.0

Note: See symbols and abbreviations in the introductory material and see reference material at the end of the publication.

Certaines caractéristiques des divisions de recensement et des subdivisions de recensement – Données intégrales et données-échantillon (20 %), Ontario, Recensement de 2006 (suite)

Macdonald, Meredith and Aberdeen Additional, TP ◆◇	Michipicoten, TP ◇	Mississagi River 8, IRI	North Shore, TP	Plummer Additional, TP ◆	Prince, TP ◆◇	Caractéristiques	N°
						Caractéristiques du revenu de 2005	
						Sexe et travail (suite)	
290	530	35	60	55	210	A travaillé toute l'année à plein temps[59]	530
51,298	60,606	26,176	40,687	43,175	62,724	Revenu médian d'emploi en 2005 $	531
53,160	58,673	33,731	55,968	34,503	58,671	Revenu moyen d'emploi en 2005 $	532
2,849	2,731	0	8,193	7,569	3,450	Erreur type de revenu moyen d'emploi $	533
205	445	55	80	70	130	A travaillé une partie de l'année ou à temps partiel[60]	534
8,023	14,707	9,632	24,594	23,466	10,860	Revenu médian d'emploi en 2005 $	535
15,665	25,605	14,594	48,735	20,414	16,351	Revenu moyen d'emploi en 2005 $	536
2,729	2,292	0	13,513	5,008	2,836	Erreur type de revenu moyen d'emploi $	537
390	910	105	125	140	330	Femmes de 15 ans et plus avec un revenu d'emploi[58]	538
19,020	21,029	23,104	24,001	14,043	19,735	Revenu médian d'emploi en 2005 $	539
21,827	28,739	23,049	28,059	23,648	26,251	Revenu moyen d'emploi en 2005 $	540
1,862	1,767	0	3,241	5,928	2,717	Erreur type de revenu moyen d'emploi $	541
150	415	60	45	80	155	A travaillé toute l'année à plein temps[59]	542
31,075	45,091	29,024	42,538	15,368	43,794	Revenu médian d'emploi en 2005 $	543
35,148	44,081	29,406	38,442	33,150	43,015	Revenu moyen d'emploi en 2005 $	544
2,957	2,518	0	4,944	10,079	3,293	Erreur type de revenu moyen d'emploi $	545
220	455	40	80	55	130	A travaillé une partie de l'année ou à temps partiel[60]	546
9,131	9,366	10,032	17,992	5,987	8,244	Revenu médian d'emploi en 2005 $	547
13,390	16,993	15,601	22,530	12,140	14,527	Revenu moyen d'emploi en 2005 $	548
1,777	1,823	0	3,818	4,165	2,411	Erreur type de revenu moyen d'emploi $	549
495	**950**	**110**	**190**	**195**	**300**	**Nombre total des familles économiques dans les ménages privés**	550
						Revenu de la famille économique en 2005	
20	10	10	0	10	0	Moins de 10 000 $	551
15	45	10	20	15	15	10 000 $ à 19 999 $	552
40	55	15	20	10	10	20 000 $ à 29 999 $	553
75	75	30	10	25	0	30 000 $ à 39 999 $	554
55	60	10	35	15	30	40 000 $ à 49 999 $	555
65	110	15	35	35	15	50 000 $ à 59 999 $	556
30	55	10	10	30	65	60 000 $ à 69 999 $	557
35	75	10	0	10	25	70 000 $ à 79 999 $	558
35	95	10	10	15	10	80 000 $ à 89 999 $	559
15	70	0	10	0	15	90 000 $ à 99 999 $	560
105	295	10	50	15	110	100 000 $ et plus	561
52,379	76,985	36,480	53,207	56,070	75,643	Revenu médian des familles $	562
64,132	81,882	43,740	76,324	56,897	93,676	Revenu moyen des familles $	563
3,394	3,110	0	8,205	4,672	6,248	Erreur type de revenu moyen des familles $	564
						Revenu après impôt de la famille économique en 2005	
20	10	10	0	10	0	Moins de 10 000 $	565
15	45	0	20	15	20	10 000 $ à 19 999 $	566
60	60	20	20	10	0	20 000 $ à 29 999 $	567
80	75	30	25	30	10	30 000 $ à 39 999 $	568
90	105	10	35	40	30	40 000 $ à 49 999 $	569
35	130	10	25	30	55	50 000 $ à 59 999 $	570
50	95	0	0	20	45	60 000 $ à 69 999 $	571
35	110	10	15	15	20	70 000 $ à 79 999 $	572
20	70	0	10	10	20	80 000 $ à 89 999 $	573
40	65	10	10	0	20	90 000 $ à 99 999 $	574
40	170	0	30	10	75	100 000 $ et plus	575
47,754	65,480	34,688	47,387	48,662	66,144	Revenu médian après impôt des familles $	576
54,651	68,155	41,868	63,920	48,772	77,576	Revenu moyen après impôt des familles $	577
2,621	2,319	0	6,076	3,468	4,874	Erreur type de revenu moyen après impôt des familles $	578
						Catégorie de revenu en 2005	
1,550	3,155	0	550	610	970	Population totale dans les ménages privés pour la catégorie de revenu	579
155	410	0	75	75	65	Au-dessous du seuil de faible revenu avant impôt en 2005	580
10.0	13.0	0.0	13.8	12.3	6.2	Fréquence du faible revenu avant impôt en 2005 %	581
120	275	0	40	30	65	Au-dessous du seuil de faible revenu après impôt en 2005	582
7.7	8.9	0.0	7.3	4.9	6.7	Fréquence du faible revenu après impôt en 2005 %	583

Nota : Voir les symboles et les abréviations dans les documents d'introduction et voir les documents de référence à la fin de la publication.

Selected characteristics for census divisions and census subdivisions – 100% data and 20% sample data, Ontario, 2006 Census (continued)

No.	Characteristics	Hilton Beach, VL	Hornepayne, TP ◆◊	Huron Shores, MU ◆	Jocelyn, TP ◆◊	Johnson, TP ◆	Laird, TP ◆◊
	2005 income characteristics						
584	**Total number of private households**	**X**	**480**	**695**	**125**	**260**	**430**
	Household income groups in 2005						
585	Under $10,000	X	0	25	0	35	0
586	$10,000 to $19,999	X	10	110	10	25	10
587	$20,000 to $29,999	X	40	80	20	25	15
588	$30,000 to $39,999	X	35	75	10	30	50
589	$40,000 to $49,999	X	45	100	30	20	55
590	$50,000 to $59,999	X	50	85	0	40	20
591	$60,000 to $69,999	X	60	60	10	25	55
592	$70,000 to $79,999	X	50	30	20	20	65
593	$80,000 to $89,999	X	35	25	10	15	45
594	$90,000 to $99,999	X	25	10	0	15	10
595	$100,000 and over	X	125	90	15	15	95
596	Median household income $	X	68,217	44,422	44,081	48,771	69,862
597	Average household income $	X	77,759	53,088	65,633	48,801	74,778
598	Standard error of average household income $	X	4,168	2,942	9,498	3,859	4,894
	Household after-tax income groups in 2005						
599	Under $10,000	X	10	25	0	30	0
600	$10,000 to $19,999	X	20	110	10	25	10
601	$20,000 to $29,999	X	40	100	25	35	40
602	$30,000 to $39,999	X	50	110	15	35	65
603	$40,000 to $49,999	X	50	115	20	30	35
604	$50,000 to $59,999	X	70	70	15	40	90
605	$60,000 to $69,999	X	60	45	10	15	75
606	$70,000 to $79,999	X	20	25	10	25	10
607	$80,000 to $89,999	X	45	35	0	15	55
608	$90,000 to $99,999	X	25	10	0	0	15
609	$100,000 and over	X	75	45	15	10	30
610	Median after-tax household income $	X	57,580	40,207	40,240	45,682	58,383
611	Average after-tax household income $	X	65,295	45,875	54,615	42,515	61,459
612	Standard error of average after-tax household income $	X	3,378	2,277	6,675	3,119	3,653

Note: See symbols and abbreviations in the introductory material and see reference material at the end of the publication.

Certaines caractéristiques des divisions de recensement et des subdivisions de recensement – Données intégrales et données-échantillon (20 %), Ontario, Recensement de 2006 (suite)

Macdonald, Meredith and Aberdeen Additional, TP ◆◇	Michipicoten, TP ◇	Mississagi River 8, IRI	North Shore, TP	Plummer Additional, TP ◆	Prince, TP ◆◇	Caractéristiques	Nº
						Caractéristiques du revenu de 2005	
605	**1,295**	**160**	**250**	**255**	**365**	**Nombre total des ménages privés**	584
						Tranches de revenu des ménages en 2005	
40	55	30	10	15	0	Moins de 10 000 $	585
15	155	25	40	35	20	10 000 $ à 19 999 $	586
60	115	25	30	15	25	20 000 $ à 29 999 $	587
70	115	35	15	35	10	30 000 $ à 39 999 $	588
80	110	10	40	20	30	40 000 $ à 49 999 $	589
85	105	15	30	45	15	50 000 $ à 59 999 $	590
45	60	10	10	35	90	60 000 $ à 69 999 $	591
30	90	10	10	15	25	70 000 $ à 79 999 $	592
45	105	0	10	20	10	80 000 $ à 89 999 $	593
15	75	0	10	10	15	90 000 $ à 99 999 $	594
100	305	0	55	15	115	100 000 $ et plus	595
52,189	58,771	30,464	45,809	52,582	68,834	Revenu médian des ménages $	596
60,374	68,396	35,367	65,400	50,899	84,442	Revenu moyen des ménages $	597
3,070	2,714	0	6,761	3,850	5,461	Erreur type de revenu moyen des ménages $	598
						Tranches du revenu après impôt des ménages en 2005	
40	60	30	10	10	10	Moins de 10 000 $	599
20	170	25	40	35	30	10 000 $ à 19 999 $	600
80	115	20	35	20	25	20 000 $ à 29 999 $	601
105	140	35	30	45	10	30 000 $ à 39 999 $	602
110	130	10	40	50	40	40 000 $ à 49 999 $	603
50	125	10	25	35	75	50 000 $ à 59 999 $	604
60	115	10	0	25	45	60 000 $ à 69 999 $	605
40	130	10	10	15	20	70 000 $ à 79 999 $	606
20	70	0	10	10	25	80 000 $ à 89 999 $	607
45	60	0	10	0	20	90 000 $ à 99 999 $	608
40	185	0	35	10	75	100 000 $ et plus	609
45,669	50,887	30,144	43,079	46,359	59,861	Revenu médian après impôt des ménages $	610
51,031	57,279	33,870	55,255	43,849	69,923	Revenu moyen après impôt des ménages $	611
2,388	2,069	0	5,078	2,924	4,265	Erreur type de revenu moyen après impôt des ménages $	612

Nota : Voir les symboles et les abréviations dans les documents d'introduction et voir les documents de référence à la fin de la publication.

Selected characteristics for census divisions and census subdivisions – 100% data and 20% sample data, Ontario, 2006 Census (continued)

No.	Characteristics	Rankin Location 15D, IRI ◆◆◇◇	Sagamok, IRI	Sault Ste. Marie, CY ◆◇	Serpent River 7, IRI ◇	Spanish, T ◆◇	St. Joseph, TP
	Population characteristics						
1	**Population, 2001[1]**	**X**	**870**	**74,566**	**323**	**816**	**1,201**
2	**Population, 2006[2]**	**566**	**884**	**74,948**	**340**	**728**	**1,129**
3	Population percentage change, 2001 to 2006	X	1.6	0.5	5.3	-10.8	-6.0
4	Land area in square kilometres, 2006	15.51	97.65	221.71	75.75	106.02	129.18
5	**Total population – 100% data[3]**	**565**	**880**	**74,950**	**340**	**725**	**1,130**
	Sex and age groups						
6	Male	280	450	35,925	170	370	570
7	0 to 4 years	20	30	1,625	10	20	15
8	5 to 9 years	35	35	1,860	10	20	30
9	10 to 14 years	30	45	2,420	20	35	30
10	15 to 19 years	25	45	2,625	20	30	40
11	20 to 24 years	20	35	2,320	5	15	30
12	25 to 29 years	15	15	1,850	10	5	10
13	30 to 34 years	15	25	1,730	5	15	10
14	35 to 39 years	15	30	2,065	0	15	20
15	40 to 44 years	25	35	2,680	10	25	25
16	45 to 49 years	20	30	3,060	20	35	45
17	50 to 54 years	20	20	2,960	10	40	55
18	55 to 59 years	20	35	2,650	10	35	70
19	60 to 64 years	10	30	2,050	10	20	50
20	65 to 69 years	5	15	1,765	10	20	45
21	70 to 74 years	0	5	1,615	5	15	55
22	75 to 79 years	0	5	1,350	5	15	25
23	80 to 84 years	5	5	825	5	10	10
24	85 years and over	5	0	475	0	0	5
25	Female	290	435	39,020	170	360	560
26	0 to 4 years	15	30	1,610	15	10	15
27	5 to 9 years	20	40	1,740	15	15	20
28	10 to 14 years	30	50	2,180	5	40	30
29	15 to 19 years	30	50	2,485	10	20	30
30	20 to 24 years	20	25	2,430	10	20	30
31	25 to 29 years	20	10	2,050	10	20	10
32	30 to 34 years	25	30	1,965	10	15	25
33	35 to 39 years	35	45	2,205	5	20	25
34	40 to 44 years	20	35	3,030	15	30	35
35	45 to 49 years	25	20	3,420	20	40	40
36	50 to 54 years	20	35	3,050	5	25	60
37	55 to 59 years	15	25	2,740	5	25	60
38	60 to 64 years	10	20	2,270	15	20	50
39	65 to 69 years	5	10	1,955	15	20	55
40	70 to 74 years	0	5	1,835	5	20	35
41	75 to 79 years	0	10	1,655	5	20	25
42	80 to 84 years	0	5	1,250	0	15	15
43	85 years and over	0	0	1,150	5	0	15
44	**Total population 15 years and over[3]**	**415**	**645**	**63,520**	**255**	**590**	**990**
	Legal marital status						
45	Never legally married (single)	235	330	19,150	110	155	175
46	Legally married (and not separated)[4,5]	115	235	31,365	100	285	670
47	Separated, but still legally married	20	35	2,430	10	35	25
48	Divorced	20	25	5,175	15	55	55
49	Widowed	25	30	5,395	15	60	65
	Common-law status						
50	Not in a common-law relationship	355	560	58,620	220	515	935
51	In a common-law relationship	65	85	4,900	35	75	55
52	**Total population – 20% sample data[6]**	**560**	**885**	**73,895**	**340**	**725**	**1,130**
	Mother tongue						
53	Single responses	560	885	73,325	335	695	1,125
54	English	530	620	61,695	310	475	1,050
55	French	15	10	3,005	0	185	25
56	Non-official languages[7]	20	260	8,620	30	30	55
57	Italian	0	0	4,715	0	0	0
58	Chinese, n.o.s.[61]	0	0	90	0	0	0
59	Cantonese	0	0	135	0	0	0
60	Spanish	0	0	175	0	0	0
61	German	0	0	625	0	0	10
62	Other languages[8]	15	260	2,880	30	25	45

Note: See symbols and abbreviations in the introductory material and see reference material at the end of the publication.

Certaines caractéristiques des divisions de recensement et des subdivisions de recensement – Données intégrales et données-échantillon (20 %), Ontario, Recensement de 2006 (suite)

Tarbutt and Tarbutt Additional, TP ◆◇	Thessalon, T ◆	Thessalon 12, IRI ◆◇	White River, TP ◆	**Brant CD/DR** †	Brant, CY	**Caractéristiques**	N°
						Caractéristiques de la population	
466	**1,386**	**123**	**993**	**118,485**	**31,669**	**Population, 2001[1]**	1
388	**1,312**	**112**	**841**	**125,099**	**34,415**	**Population, 2006[2]**	2
-16.7	-5.3	-8.9	-15.3	5.6	8.7	Variation en pourcentage de la population, 2001 à 2006	3
52.82	4.37	9.79	96.94	1,092.95	843.10	Superficie des terres en kilomètres carrés, 2006	4
385	**1,310**	**110**	**840**	**125,100**	**34,415**	**Population totale – Données intégrales[3]**	5
						Sexe et groupes d'âge	
205	620	55	450	60,730	17,180	Sexe masculin	6
10	30	0	20	3,530	925	0 à 4 ans	7
15	30	5	20	3,940	1,095	5 à 9 ans	8
15	45	10	25	4,390	1,270	10 à 14 ans	9
10	40	5	35	4,430	1,330	15 à 19 ans	10
5	40	5	35	3,990	1,070	20 à 24 ans	11
5	20	0	25	3,560	795	25 à 29 ans	12
10	20	0	20	3,730	935	30 à 34 ans	13
15	40	5	35	4,035	1,105	35 à 39 ans	14
10	50	5	35	4,960	1,425	40 à 44 ans	15
20	55	0	70	4,860	1,405	45 à 49 ans	16
15	45	10	45	4,440	1,345	50 à 54 ans	17
15	45	5	30	4,130	1,250	55 à 59 ans	18
15	30	5	20	3,010	930	60 à 64 ans	19
10	40	5	15	2,360	725	65 à 69 ans	20
5	35	0	10	1,930	600	70 à 74 ans	21
10	25	5	10	1,565	440	75 à 79 ans	22
5	20	0	5	1,180	330	80 à 84 ans	23
0	25	0	5	695	190	85 ans et plus	24
185	690	55	385	64,370	17,240	Sexe féminin	25
20	30	5	20	3,525	870	0 à 4 ans	26
15	30	10	10	3,770	1,030	5 à 9 ans	27
10	30	5	25	4,325	1,250	10 à 14 ans	28
10	40	5	35	4,360	1,250	15 à 19 ans	29
10	35	0	25	3,945	940	20 à 24 ans	30
10	20	5	25	3,670	775	25 à 29 ans	31
15	30	5	20	3,860	905	30 à 34 ans	32
15	40	5	25	4,150	1,125	35 à 39 ans	33
10	40	5	35	5,105	1,465	40 à 44 ans	34
15	60	5	40	5,045	1,410	45 à 49 ans	35
15	35	5	40	4,855	1,395	50 à 54 ans	36
15	50	0	25	4,165	1,190	55 à 59 ans	37
10	40	5	25	3,120	935	60 à 64 ans	38
0	35	0	10	2,505	695	65 à 69 ans	39
10	45	0	10	2,320	635	70 à 74 ans	40
5	45	0	5	2,165	535	75 à 79 ans	41
0	30	0	10	1,820	435	80 à 84 ans	42
0	50	0	0	1,665	385	85 ans et plus	43
300	**1,115**	**75**	**725**	**101,630**	**27,975**	**Population totale de 15 ans et plus[3]**	44
						État matrimonial légal	
65	280	40	270	30,705	7,320	Jamais légalement marié(e) (célibataire)	45
195	580	20	340	51,515	16,575	Légalement marié(e) (et non séparé[e])[4,5]	46
10	30	5	25	4,495	855	Séparé(e), mais toujours légalement marié(e)	47
15	70	10	60	7,700	1,515	Divorcé(e)	48
20	160	5	30	7,215	1,710	Veuf(ve)	49
						Union libre	
285	1,040	55	625	92,625	26,140	Ne vivant pas en union libre	50
15	75	20	100	9,010	1,835	Vivant en union libre	51
385	**1,205**	**115**	**840**	**123,315**	**33,980**	**Population totale – Données-échantillon (20 %)[6]**	52
						Langue maternelle	
390	1,205	110	835	122,605	33,895	Réponses uniques	53
340	1,140	105	665	108,185	31,120	Anglais	54
10	55	0	130	1,310	235	Français	55
40	0	0	40	13,115	2,535	Langues non officielles[7]	56
0	0	0	20	1,680	160	Italien	57
0	0	0	0	260	10	Chinois, n.d.a.[61]	58
0	0	0	0	70	15	Cantonais	59
0	0	0	0	370	25	Espagnol	60
0	0	0	0	930	385	Allemand	61
40	0	0	20	9,795	1,945	Autres langues[8]	62

Nota : Voir les symboles et les abréviations dans les documents d'introduction et voir les documents de référence à la fin de la publication.

Selected characteristics for census divisions and census subdivisions – 100% data and 20% sample data, Ontario, 2006 Census (continued)

No.	Characteristics	Rankin Location 15D, IRI ◆◆◇◇	Sagamok, IRI	Sault Ste. Marie, CY ◆◇	Serpent River 7, IRI ◇	Spanish, T ◆◇	St. Joseph, TP
	Population characteristics						
	Mother tongue (continued)						
63	Multiple responses	0	0	565	0	35	0
64	English and French	0	0	225	0	25	0
65	English and non-official language	0	0	335	0	10	0
66	French and non-official language	0	0	15	0	0	0
67	English, French and non-official language	0	0	0	0	0	0
	Language spoken most often at home[9]						
68	Single responses	555	880	73,390	340	720	1,130
69	English	555	750	69,790	330	545	1,120
70	French	0	0	680	0	150	0
71	Non-official languages[7]	0	135	2,915	10	30	10
72	Chinese, n.o.s.[61]	0	0	70	0	0	0
73	Cantonese	0	0	65	0	0	0
74	Panjabi (Punjabi)	0	0	0	0	0	0
75	Italian	0	0	1,805	0	0	0
76	Spanish	0	0	100	0	10	0
77	Other languages[8]	0	130	870	10	20	0
78	Multiple responses	10	10	505	0	10	0
79	English and French	10	0	220	0	10	0
80	English and non-official language	0	0	270	0	0	0
81	French and non-official language	0	0	0	0	0	0
82	English, French and non-official language	0	0	15	0	0	0
	Knowledge of official languages[10]						
83	English only	535	875	65,990	330	495	1,095
84	French only	0	0	100	0	15	0
85	English and French	25	10	7,390	10	210	30
86	Neither English nor French	0	0	415	0	0	0
	Knowledge of non-official languages[7,11]						
87	Italian	0	0	6,035	0	0	0
88	Spanish	0	0	330	0	10	0
89	German	0	0	760	0	0	10
90	Chinese, n.o.s.[61]	0	0	95	0	0	0
91	Cantonese	0	0	130	0	0	0
92	Panjabi (Punjabi)	0	0	0	0	0	0
93	Portuguese	0	0	295	0	0	0
	First official language spoken[10]						
94	English	550	880	70,625	340	535	1,110
95	French	10	10	2,815	0	185	15
96	English and French	0	0	45	0	10	0
97	Neither English nor French	0	0	405	0	0	0
98	Official language minority - (number)[12]	10	0	2,840	0	195	15
99	Official language minority - (percentage)[12]	1.8	0.0	3.8	0.0	26.7	1.3
	Ethnic origin[13]						
100	English	30	10	22,340	10	150	630
101	Canadian	10	0	19,765	10	265	305
102	Scottish	20	0	17,100	20	120	410
103	Irish	20	10	15,650	20	85	335
104	French	60	30	18,080	35	380	220
105	German	0	10	6,840	10	25	140
106	Italian	10	0	17,480	0	10	25
107	Chinese	0	0	430	0	0	10
108	East Indian	0	0	105	0	0	0
109	Dutch (Netherlands)	0	10	1,940	0	0	175
110	Polish	0	0	2,805	0	10	10
111	Ukrainian	0	0	3,525	0	20	0
112	North American Indian	520	870	4,800	315	70	15
113	Portuguese	0	0	380	0	0	0
114	Filipino	0	0	90	0	0	0
	Aboriginal and non-Aboriginal identity						
115	Total Aboriginal identity population[14]	530	875	5,980	320	200	25
116	Total non-Aboriginal identity population	30	10	67,915	20	525	1,105

Note: See symbols and abbreviations in the introductory material and see reference material at the end of the publication.

Certaines caractéristiques des divisions de recensement et des subdivisions de recensement – Données intégrales et données-échantillon (20 %), Ontario, Recensement de 2006 (suite)

Tarbutt and Tarbutt Additional, TP ◆◊	Thessalon, T ◆	Thessalon 12, IRI ◆◊	White River, TP ◆	**Brant CD/DR** †	Brant, CY	**Caractéristiques**	N°
						Caractéristiques de la population	
						Langue maternelle (suite)	
0	0	0	0	710	85	Réponses multiples	63
0	0	0	0	105	10	Anglais et français	64
0	0	0	0	570	75	Anglais et langue non officielle	65
0	0	0	0	15	0	Français et langue non officielle	66
0	0	0	0	15	0	Anglais, français et langue non officielle	67
						Langue parlée le plus souvent à la maison[9]	
380	1,205	110	840	122,420	33,810	Réponses uniques	68
380	1,185	115	740	116,840	33,115	Anglais	69
0	10	0	75	360	55	Français	70
0	0	0	20	5,215	640	Langues non officielles[7]	71
0	0	0	0	175	10	Chinois, n.d.a.[61]	72
0	0	0	0	60	15	Cantonais	73
0	0	0	0	570	20	Pendjabi	74
0	0	0	0	455	25	Italien	75
0	10	0	0	165	0	Espagnol	76
0	0	0	20	3,795	565	Autres langues[8]	77
10	0	0	0	895	175	Réponses multiples	78
0	0	0	0	55	0	Anglais et français	79
10	0	0	0	840	170	Anglais et langue non officielle	80
0	0	0	0	0	0	Français et langue non officielle	81
0	0	0	0	0	0	Anglais, français et langue non officielle	82
						Connaissance des langues officielles[10]	
380	1,120	105	660	116,890	32,570	Anglais seulement	83
0	0	0	10	65	0	Français seulement	84
10	90	10	170	5,820	1,345	Anglais et français	85
0	0	0	10	545	60	Ni l'anglais ni le français	86
						Connaissance des langues non officielles[7,11]	
0	0	0	20	2,055	190	Italien	87
0	10	0	0	980	195	Espagnol	88
10	0	0	15	1,420	490	Allemand	89
0	0	0	0	290	15	Chinois, n.d.a.[61]	90
0	0	0	0	100	20	Cantonais	91
0	0	0	0	890	60	Pendjabi	92
0	0	0	0	940	320	Portugais	93
						Première langue officielle parlée[10]	
380	1,165	110	705	121,320	33,715	Anglais	94
10	45	0	135	1,310	205	Français	95
0	0	0	0	175	15	Anglais et français	96
0	0	0	0	515	50	Ni l'anglais ni le français	97
0	45	10	135	1,395	210	Minorité de langue officielle - (nombre)[12]	98
0.0	3.7	9.1	16.1	1.1	0.6	Minorité de langue officielle - (pourcentage)[12]	99
						Origine ethnique[13]	
130	475	0	135	46,455	14,325	Anglais	100
95	505	10	270	36,440	10,505	Canadien	101
155	350	0	100	29,300	9,035	Écossais	102
45	265	0	60	23,430	6,570	Irlandais	103
115	300	15	355	11,420	2,935	Français	104
70	110	0	65	15,270	4,890	Allemand	105
20	40	0	95	6,710	1,040	Italien	106
0	0	0	0	1,120	75	Chinois	107
0	0	0	0	1,540	195	Indien de l'Inde	108
10	10	0	10	9,025	3,755	Hollandais (Néerlandais)	109
0	0	0	0	6,845	1,675	Polonais	110
30	45	0	90	4,765	1,085	Ukrainien	111
30	105	100	215	5,660	730	Indien de l'Amérique du Nord	112
0	0	0	0	1,880	510	Portugais	113
0	0	0	0	755	45	Philippin	114
						Population ayant une identité autochtone et population n'ayant pas d'identité autochtone	
45	120	100	320	4,310	425	Total de la population ayant une identité autochtone[14]	115
345	1,085	15	515	119,010	33,555	Total de la population n'ayant pas d'identité autochtone	116

Nota : Voir les symboles et les abréviations dans les documents d'introduction et voir les documents de référence à la fin de la publication.

Selected characteristics for census divisions and census subdivisions – 100% data and 20% sample data, Ontario, 2006 Census (continued)

No.	Characteristics	Rankin Location 15D, IRI ◆◆◇◇	Sagamok, IRI	Sault Ste. Marie, CY ◆◇	Serpent River 7, IRI ◇	Spanish, T ◆◇	St. Joseph, TP
	Population characteristics						
	Aboriginal and non-Aboriginal ancestry						
117	Total Aboriginal ancestry population[15]	525	875	7,535	315	190	40
118	Total non-Aboriginal ancestry population	35	10	66,360	25	535	1,090
	Registered Indian status						
119	Registered Indian[16]	500	850	2,455	310	55	20
120	Not a Registered Indian	60	35	71,440	30	665	1,110
	Visible minority groups						
121	Total visible minority population[17]	0	0	940	0	30	10
122	Chinese	0	0	295	0	10	10
123	South Asian[18]	0	0	95	0	25	0
124	Black	0	0	230	0	0	0
125	Filipino	0	0	85	0	0	0
126	Latin American	0	0	90	0	0	0
127	Southeast Asian[19]	0	0	0	0	0	0
128	Arab	0	0	25	0	0	0
129	West Asian[20]	0	0	0	0	0	0
130	Korean	0	0	25	0	0	0
131	Japanese	0	0	0	0	0	0
132	Visible minority, n.i.e.[21]	0	0	30	0	0	0
133	Multiple visible minority[22]	0	0	55	0	0	0
	Citizenship[23]						
134	Canadian citizens[24]	X	X	72,580	X	720	1,115
135	Not Canadian citizens[25]	X	X	1,315	X	0	15
	Immigrant status and place of birth[26]						
136	Non-immigrants[27]	X	X	65,620	X	695	1,040
137	Born in province of residence	X	X	61,405	X	610	960
138	Immigrants[28]	X	X	8,050	X	35	85
139	United States of America	X	X	745	X	0	0
140	Central and South America	X	X	145	X	0	0
141	Caribbean and Bermuda	X	X	75	X	0	0
142	United Kingdom	X	X	1,040	X	0	25
143	Other Europe	X	X	5,655	X	10	55
144	Africa	X	X	35	X	0	0
145	Asia and the Middle East	X	X	320	X	25	10
146	Oceania and other[29]	X	X	30	X	0	0
147	Non-permanent residents[30]	X	X	225	X	0	0
148	**Total immigrant population[28]**	**X**	**X**	**8,050**	**X**	**35**	**85**
	Period of immigration						
149	Before 1961	X	X	4,105	X	10	60
150	1961 to 1970	X	X	1,980	X	0	15
151	1971 to 1980	X	X	1,020	X	0	0
152	1981 to 1990	X	X	465	X	0	0
153	1991 to 2000	X	X	295	X	0	0
154	1991 to 1995	X	X	135	X	0	0
155	1996 to 2000	X	X	160	X	0	0
156	2001 to 2006[31]	X	X	175	X	25	0
	Age at immigration						
157	Under 5 years	X	X	955	X	0	0
158	5 to 19 years	X	X	2,630	X	10	60
159	20 years and over	X	X	4,465	X	20	20
160	**Total population 15 years and over**	**410**	**645**	**62,455**	**260**	**600**	**995**
	Generation status						
161	1st generation[32]	0	0	8,150	0	20	95
162	2nd generation[33]	15	10	12,325	0	40	165
163	3rd generation or more[34]	395	630	41,980	245	535	730

Note: See symbols and abbreviations in the introductory material and see reference material at the end of the publication.

Certaines caractéristiques des divisions de recensement et des subdivisions de recensement – Données intégrales et données-échantillon (20 %), Ontario, Recensement de 2006 (suite)

Tarbutt and Tarbutt Additional, TP ◆◇	Thessalon, T ◆	Thessalon 12, IRI ◆◇	White River, TP ◆	**Brant CD/DR †**	Brant, CY	**Caractéristiques**	Nº
						Caractéristiques de la population	
						Population ayant une ascendance autochtone et population n'ayant pas d'ascendance autochtone	
50	190	100	325	6,330	920	Total de la population ayant une ascendance autochtone[15]	117
335	1,015	15	515	116,985	33,060	Total de la population n'ayant pas d'ascendance autochtone	118
						Statut d'Indien inscrit	
10	30	100	90	3,010	270	Indien inscrit[16]	119
380	1,175	15	750	120,305	33,710	Pas un Indien inscrit	120
						Groupes de minorités visibles	
0	0	0	0	6,715	510	Total de la population des minorités visibles[17]	121
0	0	0	0	700	45	Chinois	122
0	0	0	0	1,785	125	Sud-Asiatique[18]	123
0	0	0	0	1,695	120	Noir	124
0	0	0	0	655	30	Philippin	125
0	0	0	0	390	30	Latino-Américain	126
0	0	0	0	585	10	Asiatique du Sud-Est[19]	127
0	0	0	0	240	50	Arabe	128
0	0	0	0	30	0	Asiatique occidental[20]	129
0	0	0	0	250	50	Coréen	130
0	0	0	0	95	0	Japonais	131
0	0	0	0	70	20	Minorité visible, n.i.a.[21]	132
0	0	0	0	210	20	Minorités visibles multiples[22]	133
						Citoyenneté[23]	
380	1,205	X	835	120,060	33,385	Citoyens canadiens[24]	134
10	0	X	10	3,260	595	Ne sont pas des citoyens canadiens[25]	135
						Statut d'immigrant et le lieu de naissance[26]	
355	1,200	X	835	106,980	30,510	Non-immigrants[27]	136
335	1,145	X	675	97,845	28,385	Né dans la province de résidence	137
30	0	X	10	15,960	3,425	Immigrants[28]	138
0	0	X	0	1,010	255	États-Unis d'Amérique	139
0	0	X	0	520	140	Amérique centrale et Amérique du Sud	140
0	0	X	0	560	40	Antilles et Bermudes	141
0	10	X	10	3,840	945	Royaume-Uni	142
25	0	X	0	6,980	1,750	Autre Europe	143
0	0	X	0	365	75	Afrique	144
0	0	X	0	2,625	190	Asie et Moyen-Orient	145
0	0	X	0	50	25	Océanie et autres[29]	146
0	0	X	0	375	45	Résidents non permanents[30]	147
30	**0**	**X**	**10**	**15,960**	**3,425**	**Population totale des immigrants[28]**	148
						Période d'immigration	
10	10	X	10	4,460	1,245	Avant 1961	149
20	0	X	0	2,910	655	1961 à 1970	150
0	0	X	0	2,565	600	1971 à 1980	151
0	0	X	0	2,220	435	1981 à 1990	152
0	0	X	0	2,600	330	1991 à 2000	153
0	0	X	0	1,490	115	1991 à 1995	154
0	0	X	0	1,105	215	1996 à 2000	155
0	0	X	0	1,205	165	2001 à 2006[31]	156
						Âge à l'immigration	
0	0	X	0	1,845	480	Moins de 5 ans	157
0	0	X	10	4,595	1,180	5 à 19 ans	158
30	10	X	0	9,525	1,765	20 ans et plus	159
310	**1,015**	**80**	**695**	**99,860**	**27,540**	**Population totale de 15 ans et plus**	160
						Statut des générations	
35	10	0	10	16,000	3,365	1re génération[32]	161
75	45	0	105	20,020	5,575	2e génération[33]	162
200	955	80	585	63,835	18,600	3e génération ou plus[34]	163

Nota : Voir les symboles et les abréviations dans les documents d'introduction et voir les documents de référence à la fin de la publication.

Selected characteristics for census divisions and census subdivisions – 100% data and 20% sample data, Ontario, 2006 Census (continued)

No.	Characteristics	Rankin Location 15D, IRI ◆◆◇◇	Sagamok, IRI	Sault Ste. Marie, CY ◆◇	Serpent River 7, IRI ◇	Spanish, T ◆◇	St. Joseph, TP
	Population characteristics						
164	**Total population 1 year and over[35]**	**555**	**870**	**73,185**	**335**	**715**	**1,125**
	Place of residence 1 year ago (mobility)						
165	Non-movers	525	825	63,700	315	590	1,095
166	Movers	25	40	9,485	20	125	35
167	Non-migrants	10	25	7,260	0	110	10
168	Migrants	15	15	2,230	20	20	30
169	Internal migrants	15	20	2,070	20	20	25
170	Intraprovincial migrants	15	15	1,835	20	20	30
171	Interprovincial migrants	0	0	235	0	0	0
172	External migrants	0	0	155	0	0	0
173	**Total population 5 years and over[36]**	**530**	**820**	**70,645**	**315**	**700**	**1,105**
	Place of residence 5 years ago (mobility)						
174	Non-movers	330	615	47,105	225	470	860
175	Movers	195	205	23,540	85	230	250
176	Non-migrants	95	105	16,815	50	145	125
177	Migrants	105	100	6,725	40	85	120
178	Internal migrants	100	100	6,240	45	80	120
179	Intraprovincial migrants	100	90	5,435	40	80	120
180	Interprovincial migrants	0	0	805	0	0	0
181	External migrants	0	0	485	0	10	0
182	**Total population 15 years and over**	**410**	**645**	**62,455**	**255**	**595**	**995**
	Highest certificate, diploma or degree[37]						
183	No certificate, diploma or degree	160	285	15,840	100	295	255
184	Certificate, diploma or degree	250	360	46,615	150	300	740
185	High school certificate or equivalent[38]	90	110	17,720	45	140	220
186	Apprenticeship or trades certificate or diploma	45	80	5,810	40	35	110
187	College, CEGEP or other non-university certificate or diploma[39]	75	120	12,595	55	100	220
188	University certificate or diploma below bachelor level[40]	0	20	1,895	0	10	65
189	University certificate or degree[41]	30	30	8,585	10	20	125
190	Bachelor's degree	30	10	5,690	10	10	80
191	University certificate or diploma above bachelor level	10	0	1,370	0	0	20
192	Degree in medicine, dentistry, veterinary medicine or optometry	0	0	260	0	0	0
193	Master's degree	0	0	1,100	10	10	20
194	Earned doctorate	0	0	160	0	0	0
195	**Total population 15 years and over with postsecondary qualifications**	**160**	**250**	**28,890**	**110**	**160**	**520**
	Major field of study - Classification of Instructional Programs, 2000[42]						
196	Education	10	25	2,430	0	15	40
197	Visual and performing arts, and communications technologies	10	0	560	0	15	10
198	Humanities	0	10	1,210	0	10	40
199	Social and behavioural sciences and law	30	25	2,620	15	30	60
200	Business, management and public administration	30	45	5,405	30	10	75
201	Physical and life sciences and technologies	0	0	625	0	0	0
202	Mathematics, computer and information sciences	0	0	1,090	0	0	0
203	Architecture, engineering, and related technologies	40	45	7,335	30	40	160
204	Agriculture, natural resources and conservation	10	35	705	0	0	15
205	Health, parks, recreation and fitness	25	30	4,795	15	15	70
206	Personal, protective and transportation services	10	35	2,105	10	15	50
207	Other fields of study[43]	0	0	0	0	0	0
	Location of study[44]						
208	Inside Canada	150	250	25,855	110	140	480
209	Outside Canada	10	0	3,035	0	15	40
210	**Total population 15 years and over**	**410**	**645**	**62,455**	**255**	**595**	**995**
	Unpaid work						
211	Males 15 years and over	195	335	29,680	125	305	490
212	Reported unpaid work[45]	155	310	26,685	115	275	435
213	Housework and child care and care or assistance to seniors	20	50	2,630	15	10	65
214	Housework and child care only	50	85	6,515	40	55	55

Note: See symbols and abbreviations in the introductory material and see reference material at the end of the publication.

Certaines caractéristiques des divisions de recensement et des subdivisions de recensement – Données intégrales et données-échantillon (20 %), Ontario, Recensement de 2006 (suite)

Tarbutt and Tarbutt Additional, TP ◆◊	Thessalon, T ◆	Thessalon 12, IRI ◆◊	White River, TP ◆	**Brant CD/DR †**	Brant, CY	Caractéristiques	N°
						Caractéristiques de la population	
385	**1,195**	**110**	**840**	**122,050**	**33,670**	**Population totale de 1 an et plus[35]**	164
						Lieu de résidence 1 an auparavant (mobilité)	
360	1,065	110	750	105,630	30,590	Personnes n'ayant pas déménagé	165
25	130	10	95	16,415	3,080	Personnes ayant déménagé	166
0	55	0	50	10,195	1,130	Non-migrants	167
25	75	10	40	6,220	1,950	Migrants	168
25	75	0	35	5,715	1,890	Migrants internes	169
25	70	10	30	5,275	1,790	Migrants infraprovinciaux	170
0	0	0	0	435	95	Migrants interprovinciaux	171
0	0	0	10	505	60	Migrants externes	172
365	**1,155**	**110**	**810**	**116,240**	**32,185**	**Population totale de 5 ans et plus[36]**	173
						Lieu de résidence 5 ans auparavant (mobilité)	
305	710	90	580	69,770	22,185	Personnes n'ayant pas déménagé	174
55	445	20	235	46,470	9,995	Personnes ayant déménagé	175
0	190	10	165	26,925	3,780	Non-migrants	176
60	255	10	70	19,550	6,215	Migrants	177
60	255	10	70	18,160	6,010	Migrants internes	178
55	200	0	65	16,905	5,655	Migrants infraprovinciaux	179
0	50	0	0	1,255	355	Migrants interprovinciaux	180
0	0	0	0	1,390	205	Migrants externes	181
315	**1,015**	**80**	**695**	**99,860**	**27,540**	**Population totale de 15 ans et plus**	182
						Plus haut certificat, diplôme ou grade[37]	
50	345	45	230	28,500	7,175	Aucun certificat, diplôme ou grade	183
260	670	30	460	71,360	20,365	Certificat, diplôme ou grade	184
100	290	10	220	28,370	7,580	Diplôme d'études secondaires ou l'équivalent[38]	185
35	135	0	65	9,600	2,985	Certificat ou diplôme d'apprenti ou d'une école de métiers	186
80	170	15	140	19,585	5,835	Certificat ou diplôme d'un collège, d'un cégep ou d'un autre établissement d'enseignement non universitaire[39]	187
25	15	0	10	2,790	835	Certificat ou diplôme universitaire inférieur au baccalauréat[40]	188
20	60	0	30	11,010	3,130	Certificat ou grade universitaire[41]	189
15	35	0	20	7,235	2,025	Baccalauréat	190
0	20	0	0	1,500	450	Certificat ou diplôme universitaire supérieur au baccalauréat	191
0	0	0	0	355	115	Diplôme en médecine, en art dentaire, en médecine vétérinaire ou en optométrie	192
0	0	0	10	1,645	470	Maîtrise	193
0	0	0	0	275	70	Doctorat acquis	194
160	**380**	**25**	**245**	**42,985**	**12,785**	**Population totale de 15 ans et plus avec titres du niveau postsecondaire**	195
						Principal domaine d'études - Classification des programmes d'enseignement, 2000[42]	
25	20	10	20	3,135	970	Éducation	196
0	10	0	0	1,600	470	Arts visuels et d'interprétation, et technologie des communications	197
0	0	0	20	2,155	640	Sciences humaines	198
10	35	0	35	3,940	1,035	Sciences sociales et de comportements, et droit	199
20	25	10	55	7,690	2,120	Commerce, gestion et administration publique	200
0	10	0	0	1,030	255	Sciences physiques et de la vie, et technologies	201
15	10	0	0	1,195	335	Mathématiques, informatique et sciences de l'information	202
65	140	10	50	10,505	3,230	Architecture, génie et services connexes	203
10	20	0	10	1,105	575	Agriculture, ressources naturelles et conservation	204
10	75	10	30	7,205	2,115	Santé, parcs, récréation et conditionnement physique	205
10	40	10	15	3,330	1,015	Services personnels, de protection et de transport	206
0	0	0	0	85	25	Autres domaines d'études[43]	207
						Lieu des études[44]	
150	365	25	240	38,500	11,905	À l'intérieur du Canada	208
10	10	0	0	4,490	880	À l'extérieur du Canada	209
315	**1,015**	**80**	**695**	**99,860**	**27,540**	**Population totale de 15 ans et plus**	210
						Travail non rémunéré	
160	505	40	385	48,250	13,745	Hommes de 15 ans et plus	211
155	450	35	320	43,920	12,550	Travail non rémunéré déclaré[45]	212
10	60	10	0	3,925	1,180	Travaux ménagers et soins aux enfants et soins ou aide aux personnes âgées	213
35	95	10	85	12,520	3,645	Travaux ménagers et soins aux enfants seulement	214

Nota : Voir les symboles et les abréviations dans les documents d'introduction et voir les documents de référence à la fin de la publication.

Selected characteristics for census divisions and census subdivisions – 100% data and 20% sample data, Ontario, 2006 Census (continued)

No.	Characteristics	Rankin Location 15D, IRI ◆◆◊◊	Sagamok, IRI	Sault Ste. Marie, CY ◆◊	Serpent River 7, IRI ◊	Spanish, T ◆◊	St. Joseph, TP
	Population characteristics						
	Unpaid work (continued)						
215	Housework and care or assistance to seniors only	0	40	2,915	10	20	65
216	Child care and care or assistance to seniors only	0	0	0	0	0	10
217	Housework only	75	110	14,305	40	185	235
218	Child care only	10	10	140	10	0	0
219	Care or assistance to seniors only	0	15	180	0	0	0
220	Females 15 years and over	215	310	32,775	130	285	500
221	Reported unpaid work[45]	200	290	30,780	120	270	475
222	Housework and child care and care or assistance to seniors	30	70	4,050	25	0	80
223	Housework and child care only	100	85	8,440	60	100	80
224	Housework and care or assistance to seniors only	10	45	4,035	10	25	90
225	Child care and care or assistance to seniors only	0	0	10	0	0	0
226	Housework only	65	75	13,955	35	150	220
227	Child care only	10	10	150	0	0	0
228	Care or assistance to seniors only	0	0	140	0	0	0
	Labour force activity						
229	Males 15 years and over	195	335	29,675	125	310	490
230	In the labour force	120	185	18,680	70	115	280
231	Employed	105	130	17,140	45	85	265
232	Unemployed	15	55	1,545	25	35	15
233	Not in the labour force	70	155	11,000	60	190	210
234	Participation rate	61.5	55.2	62.9	56.0	37.1	57.1
235	Employment rate	53.8	38.8	57.8	36.0	27.4	54.1
236	Unemployment rate	12.5	29.7	8.3	35.7	30.4	5.4
237	Females 15 years and over	215	310	32,775	135	290	500
238	In the labour force	145	170	18,450	75	110	270
239	Employed	125	130	17,000	60	95	255
240	Unemployed	20	40	1,450	15	20	10
241	Not in the labour force	75	140	14,325	55	175	235
242	Participation rate	67.4	54.8	56.3	55.6	37.9	54.0
243	Employment rate	58.1	41.9	51.9	44.4	32.8	51.0
244	Unemployment rate	13.8	23.5	7.9	20.0	18.2	3.7
245	Both sexes - Participation rate	64.6	54.3	59.5	53.8	37.5	54.8
246	15 to 24 years	55.6	34.4	69.7	37.5	38.9	46.4
247	25 years and over	67.2	60.8	57.6	55.8	38.2	56.5
248	Both sexes - Employment rate	54.9	39.5	54.7	41.2	30.0	52.5
249	15 to 24 years	38.9	19.4	56.2	25.0	16.7	32.1
250	25 years and over	59.4	45.9	54.4	41.9	32.7	55.6
251	Both sexes - Unemployment rate	15.1	27.1	8.1	25.0	21.7	4.6
252	15 to 24 years	22.2	45.5	19.3	50.0	66.7	33.3
253	25 years and over	14.0	23.3	5.5	29.2	15.4	2.1
254	**Total labour force 15 years and over**	**265**	**355**	**37,130**	**140**	**225**	**545**
	Industry - North American Industry Classification System 2002						
255	Industry - Not applicable[46]	20	30	715	10	15	10
256	All industries[47]	245	325	36,420	135	215	535
257	11 Agriculture, forestry, fishing and hunting	10	45	225	0	20	50
258	21 Mining and oil and gas extraction	0	10	85	0	10	0
259	22 Utilities	0	0	240	0	0	0
260	23 Construction	25	20	1,630	10	15	60
261	31-33 Manufacturing	20	0	4,565	10	20	95
262	41 Wholesale trade	0	10	620	0	0	0
263	44-45 Retail trade	15	15	4,810	15	25	25
264	48-49 Transportation and warehousing	10	0	1,515	0	10	25
265	51 Information and cultural industries	0	0	585	0	10	0
266	52 Finance and insurance	0	0	740	0	25	15
267	53 Real estate and rental and leasing	0	0	495	0	0	15
268	54 Professional, scientific and technical services	0	15	1,345	10	0	15
269	55 Management of companies and enterprises	0	0	30	0	0	0
270	56 Administrative and support, waste management and remediation services	30	10	3,015	10	0	0
271	61 Educational services	20	30	2,875	0	10	80
272	62 Health care and social assistance	25	80	4,665	25	10	45

Note: See symbols and abbreviations in the introductory material and see reference material at the end of the publication.

Certaines caractéristiques des divisions de recensement et des subdivisions de recensement – Données intégrales et données-échantillon (20 %), Ontario, Recensement de 2006 (suite)

Tarbutt and Tarbutt Additional, TP ◆◇	Thessalon, T ◆	Thessalon 12, IRI ◆◇	White River, TP ◆	**Brant CD/DR †**	Brant, CY	**Caractéristiques**	N°
						Caractéristiques de la population	
						Travail non rémunéré (suite)	
10	45	10	50	3,990	1,155	Travaux ménagers et soins ou aide aux personnes âgées seulement	215
0	0	0	0	70	35	Soins aux enfants et soins ou aide aux personnes âgées seulement	216
100	235	10	180	22,635	6,365	Travaux ménagers seulement	217
0	0	0	0	460	105	Soins aux enfants seulement	218
0	0	0	0	310	60	Soins ou aide aux personnes âgées seulement	219
155	510	40	315	51,610	13,795	Femmes de 15 ans et plus	220
145	450	35	295	48,610	13,075	Travail non rémunéré déclaré[45]	221
15	75	10	35	6,645	2,010	Travaux ménagers et soins aux enfants et soins ou aide aux personnes âgées	222
45	105	10	95	14,875	3,780	Travaux ménagers et soins aux enfants seulement	223
10	55	10	45	5,005	1,430	Travaux ménagers et soins ou aide aux personnes âgées seulement	224
0	0	0	0	35	0	Soins aux enfants et soins ou aide aux personnes âgées seulement	225
80	205	10	120	21,720	5,790	Travaux ménagers seulement	226
0	10	0	0	220	50	Soins aux enfants seulement	227
0	0	0	0	105	10	Soins ou aide aux personnes âgées seulement	228
						Activité	
160	500	40	385	48,250	13,745	Hommes de 15 ans et plus	229
85	305	30	355	35,290	10,525	Population active	230
80	290	20	350	33,375	10,180	Personnes occupées	231
0	15	10	0	1,910	345	Chômeurs	232
75	195	10	25	12,960	3,215	Inactifs	233
53.1	61.0	75.0	92.2	73.1	76.6	Taux d'activité	234
50.0	58.0	50.0	90.9	69.2	74.1	Taux d'emploi	235
0.0	4.9	33.3	0.0	5.4	3.3	Taux de chômage	236
150	515	40	310	51,610	13,795	Femmes de 15 ans et plus	237
90	265	25	230	32,420	9,180	Population active	238
90	235	15	190	30,245	8,660	Personnes occupées	239
0	30	10	35	2,170	520	Chômeuses	240
60	245	20	80	19,190	4,615	Inactives	241
60.0	51.5	62.5	74.2	62.8	66.5	Taux d'activité	242
60.0	45.6	37.5	61.3	58.6	62.8	Taux d'emploi	243
0.0	11.3	40.0	15.2	6.7	5.7	Taux de chômage	244
55.6	56.7	62.5	84.9	67.8	71.6	Les deux sexes - Taux d'activité	245
0.0	46.9	0.0	89.5	72.0	74.2	15 à 24 ans	246
57.6	58.5	69.2	84.2	67.0	71.0	25 ans et plus	247
54.8	51.7	43.8	77.7	63.7	68.4	Les deux sexes - Taux d'emploi	248
40.0	29.0	0.0	78.9	62.4	65.9	15 à 24 ans	249
56.9	56.1	50.0	78.3	64.0	68.9	25 ans et plus	250
5.9	8.7	30.0	7.6	6.0	4.4	Les deux sexes - Taux de chômage	251
0.0	35.7	100.0	11.8	13.3	11.2	15 à 24 ans	252
5.9	4.0	22.2	7.9	4.5	3.0	25 ans et plus	253
170	**575**	**50**	**590**	**67,710**	**19,710**	**Population active totale de 15 ans et plus**	254
						Industrie - Système de classification des industries de l'Amérique du Nord de 2002	
0	10	0	10	880	150	Industrie - Sans objet[46]	255
175	565	50	585	66,830	19,555	Toutes les industries[47]	256
10	25	0	40	1,800	1,415	11 Agriculture, foresterie, pêche et chasse	257
0	0	0	15	105	55	21 Extraction minière et extraction de pétrole et de gaz	258
0	0	0	10	405	150	22 Services publics	259
15	40	10	30	4,085	1,310	23 Construction	260
25	85	0	200	14,225	3,670	31-33 Fabrication	261
0	10	0	0	3,585	1,115	41 Commerce de gros	262
10	30	0	90	6,975	1,785	44-45 Commerce de détail	263
15	30	0	15	3,245	1,080	48-49 Transport et entreposage	264
0	0	0	0	825	250	51 Industrie de l'information et industrie culturelle	265
0	25	0	0	1,485	415	52 Finance et assurances	266
0	0	0	0	980	235	53 Services immobiliers et services de location et de location à bail	267
15	30	0	0	2,660	980	54 Services professionnels, scientifiques et techniques	268
0	0	0	0	70	0	55 Gestion de sociétés et d'entreprises	269
0	20	0	20	4,160	855	56 Services administratifs, services de soutien, services de gestion des déchets et services d'assainissement	270
20	30	0	55	4,055	1,120	61 Services d'enseignement	271
20	90	0	0	6,805	1,775	62 Soins de santé et assistance sociale	272

Nota : Voir les symboles et les abréviations dans les documents d'introduction et voir les documents de référence à la fin de la publication.

Selected characteristics for census divisions and census subdivisions – 100% data and 20% sample data, Ontario, 2006 Census (continued)

No.	Characteristics	Rankin Location 15D, IRI ◆◆◇◇	Sagamok, IRI	Sault Ste. Marie, CY ◆◇	Serpent River 7, IRI ◇	Spanish, T ◆◇	St. Joseph, TP
	Population characteristics						
	Industry - North American Industry Classification System 2002 (continued)						
273	71 Arts, entertainment and recreation	30	0	1,265	0	0	10
274	72 Accommodation and food services	10	10	2,955	0	20	50
275	81 Other services (except public administration)	10	10	2,215	0	0	30
276	91 Public administration	40	65	2,540	40	20	20
	Class of worker						
277	Class of worker - Not applicable[46]	20	35	710	10	15	10
278	All classes of worker[47]	245	320	36,420	130	215	540
279	Paid workers	235	305	34,690	125	195	455
280	Employees	230	300	34,105	125	200	430
281	Self-employed (incorporated)	0	10	585	10	0	20
282	Self-employed (unincorporated)	10	15	1,700	10	15	85
283	Unpaid family workers	0	0	30	0	0	0
	Occupation - National Occupational Classification for Statistics 2006						
284	Male labour force 15 years and over	125	185	18,685	65	120	280
285	Occupation - Not applicable[46]	10	20	340	10	15	10
286	All occupations[47]	110	165	18,340	60	100	270
287	A Management occupations	10	10	1,650	10	0	30
288	B Business, finance and administrative occupations	0	10	1,620	10	0	10
289	C Natural and applied sciences and related occupations	0	0	2,055	0	0	30
290	D Health occupations	0	0	440	10	0	0
291	E Occupations in social science, education, government service and religion	0	10	880	10	0	0
292	F Occupations in art, culture, recreation and sport	10	0	300	0	0	0
293	G Sales and service occupations	20	30	4,330	10	10	25
294	H Trades, transport and equipment operators and related occupations	40	55	5,120	25	50	90
295	I Occupations unique to primary industry	15	50	495	0	25	35
296	J Occupations unique to processing, manufacturing and utilities	10	0	1,435	0	0	40
297	Female labour force 15 years and over	145	170	18,450	75	110	265
298	Occupation - Not applicable[46]	0	10	370	10	0	0
299	All occupations[47]	135	155	18,075	75	110	265
300	A Management occupations	10	15	1,105	10	10	20
301	B Business, finance and administrative occupations	20	30	4,320	20	25	55
302	C Natural and applied sciences and related occupations	0	0	565	0	10	0
303	D Health occupations	0	15	2,180	10	10	25
304	E Occupations in social science, education, government service and religion	30	50	2,385	20	15	30
305	F Occupations in art, culture, recreation and sport	0	0	475	0	0	0
306	G Sales and service occupations	60	30	6,630	20	40	115
307	H Trades, transport and equipment operators and related occupations	0	0	225	0	0	10
308	I Occupations unique to primary industry	0	10	45	0	0	15
309	J Occupations unique to processing, manufacturing and utilities	0	10	140	0	0	0
310	**Total employed labour force 15 years and over**	**230**	**260**	**34,140**	**105**	**180**	**520**
	Place of work status						
311	Males	105	125	17,140	45	85	265
312	Usual place of work	80	70	14,675	25	60	160
313	At home	0	0	515	0	0	45
314	Outside Canada	0	0	150	0	0	0
315	No fixed workplace address	15	60	1,800	15	30	50
316	Females	120	130	16,995	60	90	255
317	Usual place of work	110	115	15,870	55	85	200
318	At home	0	0	485	0	0	60
319	Outside Canada	0	0	175	0	0	0
320	No fixed workplace address	0	10	460	0	0	0

Note: See symbols and abbreviations in the introductory material and see reference material at the end of the publication.

Certaines caractéristiques des divisions de recensement et des subdivisions de recensement – Données intégrales et données-échantillon (20 %), Ontario, Recensement de 2006 (suite)

Tarbutt and Tarbutt Additional, TP ◆◇	Thessalon, T ◆	Thessalon 12, IRI ◆◇	White River, TP ◆	**Brant CD/DR †**	Brant, CY	**Caractéristiques**	N°
						Caractéristiques de la population	
						Industrie - Système de classification des industries de l'Amérique du Nord de 2002 (suite)	
0	0	0	0	1,745	420	71 Arts, spectacles et loisirs	273
10	50	0	40	4,250	990	72 Hébergement et services de restauration	274
20	30	0	30	3,185	1,105	81 Autres services (sauf les administrations publiques)	275
15	60	15	10	2,190	815	91 Administrations publiques	276
						Catégorie de travailleurs	
0	10	0	10	880	150	Catégorie de travailleurs - Sans objet[46]	277
170	565	50	580	66,830	19,555	Toutes les catégories de travailleurs[47]	278
150	540	40	575	62,115	17,535	Travailleurs rémunérés	279
140	540	40	555	60,235	16,650	Employés	280
10	0	0	15	1,880	890	Travailleurs autonomes (entreprise constituée en société)	281
20	25	0	10	4,570	1,920	Travailleurs autonomes (entreprise non constituée en société)	282
0	0	0	10	145	95	Travailleurs familiaux non rémunérés	283
						Profession - Classification nationale des professions pour statistiques de 2006	
85	305	30	360	35,290	10,530	Hommes actifs de 15 ans et plus	284
0	0	0	0	340	75	Profession - Sans objet[46]	285
85	305	30	360	34,950	10,450	Toutes les professions[47]	286
10	45	0	20	3,440	1,145	A Gestion	287
0	20	0	10	3,080	750	B Affaires, finance et administration	288
10	30	0	15	2,080	675	C Sciences naturelles et appliquées et professions apparentées	289
0	0	0	0	565	160	D Secteur de la santé	290
10	0	0	15	1,355	465	E Sciences sociales, enseignement, administration publique et religion	291
0	0	0	0	545	125	F Arts, culture, sports et loisirs	292
10	60	0	35	6,205	1,415	G Ventes et services	293
35	90	15	145	10,885	3,415	H Métiers, transport et machinerie	294
10	25	0	45	1,675	1,095	I Professions propres au secteur primaire	295
0	30	0	80	5,115	1,215	J Transformation, fabrication et services d'utilité publique	296
90	270	20	235	32,420	9,180	Femmes actives de 15 ans et plus	297
0	10	0	10	540	80	Profession - Sans objet[46]	298
90	255	20	225	31,875	9,100	Toutes les professions[47]	299
0	40	0	15	2,200	715	A Gestion	300
35	35	10	70	7,770	2,350	B Affaires, finance et administration	301
0	0	0	0	590	210	C Sciences naturelles et appliquées et professions apparentées	302
0	50	0	0	3,340	840	D Secteur de la santé	303
20	25	0	35	3,270	925	E Sciences sociales, enseignement, administration publique et religion	304
0	10	0	0	645	275	F Arts, culture, sports et loisirs	305
20	85	0	65	9,930	2,530	G Ventes et services	306
0	0	0	15	1,020	255	H Métiers, transport et machinerie	307
0	0	0	0	685	480	I Professions propres au secteur primaire	308
0	0	0	30	2,420	520	J Transformation, fabrication et services d'utilité publique	309
170	**525**	**35**	**545**	**63,630**	**18,840**	**Population active occupée totale de 15 ans et plus**	310
						Catégorie de lieu de travail	
80	290	20	350	33,380	10,180	Hommes	311
60	250	15	300	26,900	7,570	Lieu habituel de travail	312
10	0	0	10	2,155	1,220	À domicile	313
0	0	0	10	180	70	En dehors du Canada	314
10	30	10	30	4,135	1,320	Sans adresse de travail fixe	315
90	240	20	195	30,250	8,655	Femmes	316
75	235	15	175	26,655	7,210	Lieu habituel de travail	317
10	0	0	10	2,090	990	À domicile	318
0	0	0	0	30	10	En dehors du Canada	319
0	0	10	0	1,475	445	Sans adresse de travail fixe	320

Nota : Voir les symboles et les abréviations dans les documents d'introduction et voir les documents de référence à la fin de la publication.

Selected characteristics for census divisions and census subdivisions – 100% data and 20% sample data, Ontario, 2006 Census (continued)

No.	Characteristics	Rankin Location 15D, IRI ◆◆◇◇	Sagamok, IRI	Sault Ste. Marie, CY ◆◇	Serpent River 7, IRI ◇	Spanish, T ◆◇	St. Joseph, TP
	Population characteristics						
321	**Total employed labour force 15 years and over with usual place of work or no fixed workplace address**	**215**	**250**	**32,805**	**95**	**170**	**415**
	Mode of transportation						
322	Males	95	125	16,475	40	85	215
323	Car, truck, van, as driver	60	80	13,135	25	65	190
324	Car, truck, van, as passenger	25	25	1,185	10	15	20
325	Public transit	0	0	625	0	0	0
326	Walked	10	15	1,105	10	0	0
327	All other modes	10	10	425	0	0	10
328	Females	120	130	16,335	60	85	200
329	Car, truck, van, as driver	90	95	12,065	45	60	185
330	Car, truck, van, as passenger	10	20	1,980	10	10	10
331	Public transit	10	0	755	0	10	0
332	Walked	20	10	1,265	0	15	0
333	All other modes	0	0	265	0	0	0
334	**Total population 15 years and over who worked since January 1, 2005**	**265**	**370**	**39,945**	**155**	**230**	**635**
	Language used most often at work						
335	Single responses	260	370	39,765	155	225	635
336	English	260	345	39,450	155	225	635
337	French	0	0	235	0	0	0
338	Non-official languages[7]	0	25	80	0	0	0
339	Chinese, n.o.s.[61]	0	0	10	0	0	0
340	Cantonese	0	0	0	0	0	0
341	Other languages[8]	0	25	70	0	0	0
342	Multiple responses	0	0	180	0	10	0
343	English and French	10	0	145	0	10	0
344	English and non-official language	0	0	30	0	0	0
345	French and non-official language	0	0	0	0	0	0
346	English, French and non-official language	0	0	0	0	0	0
	Dwelling and household characteristics						
347	**Total number of occupied private dwellings**	**205**	**290**	**31,760**	**135**	**320**	**485**
	Housing tenure						
348	Owned	125	150	22,020	40	220	425
349	Rented	60	35	9,740	35	100	60
350	Band housing	15	110	0	65	10	0
	Structural type of dwelling						
351	Single-detached house	205	270	20,465	125	285	460
352	Semi-detached house	0	5	1,825	10	0	0
353	Row house	0	10	895	0	0	10
354	Apartment, duplex	0	0	1,500	0	0	0
355	Apartment, building that has five or more storeys	0	0	2,010	0	0	0
356	Apartment, building that has fewer than five storeys	0	10	4,950	0	30	10
357	Other single-attached house	0	0	105	0	0	5
358	Movable dwelling[48]	0	0	5	0	5	0
	Condition of dwelling						
359	Regular maintenance only	80	110	21,035	50	160	310
360	Minor repairs	65	95	8,585	50	85	130
361	Major repairs	60	85	2,140	35	75	45
	Period of construction						
362	Before 1946	0	10	4,865	0	40	60
363	1946 to 1960	10	10	7,335	15	105	35
364	1961 to 1970	15	30	6,450	0	55	45
365	1971 to 1980	75	50	6,705	15	55	145
366	1981 to 1985	25	35	2,045	15	20	35
367	1986 to 1990	10	45	1,765	15	10	55
368	1991 to 1995	20	35	1,280	25	15	60
369	1996 to 2000	20	80	765	25	10	30
370	2001 to 2006[49]	40	10	540	15	10	15

Note: See symbols and abbreviations in the introductory material and see reference material at the end of the publication.

Certaines caractéristiques des divisions de recensement et des subdivisions de recensement – Données intégrales et données-échantillon (20 %), Ontario, Recensement de 2006 (suite)

Tarbutt and Tarbutt Additional, TP ◆◇	Thessalon, T ◆	Thessalon 12, IRI ◆◇	White River, TP ◆	**Brant CD/DR †**	Brant, CY	Caractéristiques	N°
						Caractéristiques de la population	
145	**520**	**35**	**510**	**59,170**	**16,555**	**Population active occupée totale de 15 ans et plus ayant un lieu habituel de travail ou sans adresse de travail fixe**	321
						Mode de transport	
70	285	20	330	31,040	8,890	Hommes	322
60	220	15	255	25,590	7,820	Automobile, camion ou fourgonnette, en tant que conducteur	323
10	10	0	20	2,650	545	Automobile, camion ou fourgonnette, en tant que passager	324
0	0	0	0	730	35	Transport en commun	325
0	35	10	40	1,175	360	À pied	326
0	25	0	15	895	130	Tous les autres modes	327
75	240	15	180	28,130	7,660	Femmes	328
70	170	10	120	21,895	6,540	Automobile, camion ou fourgonnette, en tant que conductrice	329
0	15	0	20	2,980	565	Automobile, camion ou fourgonnette, en tant que passagère	330
0	10	0	10	1,110	55	Transport en commun	331
0	40	10	30	1,680	405	À pied	332
0	0	0	0	470	100	Tous les autres modes	333
200	**665**	**55**	**590**	**72,115**	**21,095**	**Population totale de 15 ans et plus ayant travaillé depuis le 1er janvier 2005**	334
						Langue utilisée le plus souvent au travail	
200	665	55	570	71,870	21,045	Réponses uniques	335
200	660	55	560	71,475	20,990	Anglais	336
0	10	0	0	165	20	Français	337
0	0	0	0	235	40	Langues non officielles[7]	338
0	0	0	0	70	0	Chinois, n.d.a.[61]	339
0	0	0	0	10	10	Cantonais	340
0	0	0	0	155	25	Autres langues[8]	341
0	0	0	20	250	50	Réponses multiples	342
0	0	0	20	70	10	Anglais et français	343
0	0	0	0	165	25	Anglais et langue non officielle	344
0	0	0	0	0	0	Français et langue non officielle	345
0	0	0	0	15	10	Anglais, français et langue non officielle	346
						Caractéristiques des logements et des ménages	
145	**525**	**45**	**360**	**48,020**	**12,235**	**Nombre total de logements privés occupés**	347
						Mode d'occupation	
130	400	15	255	35,430	10,735	Possédé	348
15	120	0	95	12,590	1,505	Loué	349
0	0	25	0	0	0	Logement de bande	350
						Type de construction résidentielle	
145	455	45	250	32,270	10,340	Maison individuelle non attenante	351
0	20	0	50	2,765	805	Maison jumelée	352
0	10	0	0	3,345	385	Maison en rangée	353
0	35	0	0	1,580	150	Appartement, duplex	354
0	0	0	0	3,730	50	Appartement, immeuble de cinq étages ou plus	355
0	5	0	45	4,105	455	Appartement, immeuble de moins de cinq étages	356
0	0	0	0	170	40	Autre maison individuelle attenante	357
0	0	0	5	50	10	Logement mobile[48]	358
						État du logement	
85	280	20	195	32,880	8,435	Entretien régulier seulement	359
40	165	20	145	11,925	2,970	Réparations mineures	360
15	75	10	20	3,215	830	Réparations majeures	361
						Période de construction	
35	145	0	90	11,660	3,445	Avant 1946	362
30	85	0	35	7,910	1,650	1946 à 1960	363
10	90	10	50	5,990	1,285	1961 à 1970	364
15	95	0	95	7,850	1,455	1971 à 1980	365
10	35	10	15	2,470	565	1981 à 1985	366
10	15	0	30	3,475	870	1986 à 1990	367
10	20	10	35	2,880	680	1991 à 1995	368
10	20	15	0	2,390	1,000	1996 à 2000	369
10	20	20	0	3,390	1,295	2001 à 2006[49]	370

Nota : Voir les symboles et les abréviations dans les documents d'introduction et voir les documents de référence à la fin de la publication.

Selected characteristics for census divisions and census subdivisions – 100% data and 20% sample data, Ontario, 2006 Census (continued)

No.	Characteristics	Rankin Location 15D, IRI ◆◆◇◇	Sagamok, IRI	Sault Ste. Marie, CY ◆◇	Serpent River 7, IRI ◇	Spanish, T ◆◇	St. Joseph, TP
	Dwelling and household characteristics						
371	Average number of rooms per dwelling	5.6	5.6	6.6	5.9	5.8	7.1
372	Average number of bedrooms per dwelling	2.8	2.7	2.7	3.0	2.5	2.7
373	Average value of dwelling $	0	0	132,035	0	70,246	144,742
374	**Total number of private households**	**205**	**295**	**31,765**	**135**	**320**	**485**
	Household size						
375	1 person	40	70	9,375	35	105	100
376	2 persons	65	70	11,260	50	120	245
377	3 persons	40	50	4,995	20	45	55
378	4 to 5 persons	40	80	5,750	25	50	70
379	6 or more persons	10	25	380	10	10	10
	Household type						
380	One-family households[50]	160	210	21,445	90	195	375
381	Multiple-family households	0	10	270	0	10	0
382	Non-family households	45	75	10,045	40	120	110
383	Number of persons in private households	560	885	73,700	340	725	1,125
384	Average number of persons in private households	2.7	3.0	2.3	2.5	2.2	2.3
385	Tenant-occupied private non-farm, non-reserve dwellings[51]	0	0	9,735	0	95	60
386	Average gross rent $[51]	0	0	587	0	527	392
387	Tenant-occupied households spending 30% or more of household income on gross rent[52]	0	0	4,065	0	25	30
388	Tenant-occupied households spending from 30% to 99% of household income on gross rent[52]	0	0	3,645	0	20	30
389	Owner-occupied private non-farm, non-reserve dwellings[53]	0	0	22,010	0	220	385
390	Average owner's major payments $[53]	0	0	746	0	497	730
391	Owner households spending 30% or more of household income on owner's major payments[52]	0	0	2,415	0	30	45
392	Owner households spending from 30% to 99% of household income on owner's major payments[52]	0	0	2,070	0	25	35
	Census family characteristics						
393	**Total number of census families in private households**	**165**	**230**	**21,985**	**95**	**215**	**375**
	Family structure and number of children						
394	Total couple families	90	160	17,955	65	175	350
395	Total families of married couples	60	115	15,475	45	145	325
396	Without children at home	30	40	7,575	25	90	210
397	With children at home	30	75	7,900	25	60	120
398	1 child	10	20	3,150	0	30	35
399	2 children	10	20	3,505	10	0	45
400	3 or more children	0	35	1,245	0	25	30
401	Total families of common-law couples	30	45	2,475	15	30	25
402	Without children at home	0	10	1,290	10	25	15
403	With children at home	35	35	1,190	10	10	10
404	1 child	10	10	620	10	0	0
405	2 children	10	0	385	0	0	0
406	3 or more children	10	10	185	0	10	0
407	Total lone-parent families	70	65	4,035	30	40	25
408	Female parent	60	50	3,315	30	40	30
409	1 child	35	30	2,080	20	25	10
410	2 children	25	10	925	10	0	10
411	3 or more children	10	15	310	10	15	10
412	Male parent	15	15	715	0	0	0
413	1 child	0	10	525	0	0	0
414	2 children	0	10	160	0	0	0
415	3 or more children	0	0	35	0	0	0

Note: See symbols and abbreviations in the introductory material and see reference material at the end of the publication.

Certaines caractéristiques des divisions de recensement et des subdivisions de recensement – Données intégrales et données-échantillon (20 %), Ontario, Recensement de 2006 (suite)

Tarbutt and Tarbutt Additional, TP ◆◇	Thessalon, T ◆	Thessalon 12, IRI ◆◇	White River, TP ◆	**Brant CD/DR †**	Brant, CY	**Caractéristiques**	Nº
						Caractéristiques des logements et des ménages	
6.9	6.5	6.0	6.4	7.0	7.7	Nombre moyen de pièces par logement	371
2.8	2.7	2.8	2.8	2.8	3.1	Nombre moyen de chambres à coucher par logement	372
147,335	111,411	0	82,921	225,084	283,774	Valeur moyenne du logement $	373
145	**525**	**50**	**355**	**48,015**	**12,240**	**Nombre total de ménages privés**	374
						Taille du ménage	
25	155	15	90	11,670	2,095	1 personne	375
65	200	15	125	16,290	4,460	2 personnes	376
25	70	5	75	7,870	1,950	3 personnes	377
30	95	10	60	10,835	3,255	4 à 5 personnes	378
5	10	0	5	1,345	470	6 personnes ou plus	379
						Genre de ménage	
125	360	30	255	34,265	9,710	Ménages unifamiliaux[50]	380
0	10	0	0	760	200	Ménages multifamiliaux	381
25	160	15	100	12,990	2,325	Ménages non familiaux	382
385	1,205	110	835	123,045	33,925	Nombre de personnes dans les ménages privés	383
2.7	2.3	2.6	2.4	2.6	2.8	Nombre moyen de personnes dans les ménages privés	384
10	125	0	95	12,565	1,495	Ménages locataires dans les logements privés non agricoles hors réserve[51]	385
0	507	0	519	717	760	Loyer brut moyen $[51]	386
0	30	0	30	5,320	560	Ménages locataires consacrant 30 % ou plus du revenu du ménage au loyer brut[52]	387
0	35	0	25	4,675	490	Ménages locataires consacrant de 30 % à 99 % du revenu du ménage au loyer brut[52]	388
130	400	0	255	34,890	10,355	Ménages propriétaires dans les logements privés non agricoles hors réserve[53]	389
592	598	0	694	983	1,011	Principales dépenses de propriété moyennes $[53]	390
0	25	0	25	5,765	1,470	Ménages propriétaires consacrant 30 % ou plus du revenu du ménage aux principales dépenses de propriété[52]	391
0	10	0	15	5,100	1,345	Ménages propriétaires consacrant de 30 % à 99 % du revenu du ménage aux principales dépenses de propriété[52]	392
						Caractéristiques des familles de recensement	
125	**370**	**35**	**255**	**35,825**	**10,115**	**Nombre total de familles de recensement dans les ménages privés**	393
						Structure de la famille et le nombre d'enfants	
120	300	25	215	29,885	9,135	Total des familles avec conjoints	394
105	260	10	170	25,410	8,205	Total des familles avec couples mariés	395
65	145	0	80	11,125	3,575	Sans enfants à la maison	396
40	115	10	90	14,285	4,625	Avec enfants à la maison	397
10	40	0	60	5,055	1,480	1 enfant	398
20	60	0	30	6,280	2,095	2 enfants	399
10	15	10	0	2,950	1,045	3 enfants ou plus	400
10	40	10	45	4,475	935	Total des familles avec couples en union libre	401
0	10	0	15	2,270	515	Sans enfants à la maison	402
10	25	0	30	2,200	415	Avec enfants à la maison	403
0	0	0	0	1,080	200	1 enfant	404
10	20	0	10	790	155	2 enfants	405
0	10	0	15	335	60	3 enfants ou plus	406
10	70	15	35	5,940	975	Total des familles monoparentales	407
0	50	0	35	4,770	720	Parent de sexe féminin	408
10	35	0	20	2,870	470	1 enfant	409
0	10	10	10	1,320	150	2 enfants	410
0	0	0	0	580	100	3 enfants ou plus	411
0	20	0	0	1,175	255	Parent de sexe masculin	412
0	0	10	0	775	145	1 enfant	413
0	10	0	0	305	80	2 enfants	414
0	0	0	0	90	30	3 enfants ou plus	415

Nota : Voir les symboles et les abréviations dans les documents d'introduction et voir les documents de référence à la fin de la publication.

Selected characteristics for census divisions and census subdivisions – 100% data and 20% sample data, Ontario, 2006 Census (continued)

No.	Characteristics	Rankin Location 15D, IRI ◆◆◊◊	Sagamok, IRI	Sault Ste. Marie, CY ◆◊	Serpent River 7, IRI ◊	Spanish, T ◆◊	St. Joseph, TP
	Census family characteristics						
416	**Total number of children at home**	**245**	**390**	**21,965**	**120**	**200**	**290**
	Age group						
417	Under 6 years	50	80	3,765	35	30	25
418	6 to 14 years	100	160	7,570	45	100	115
419	15 to 17 years	25	60	3,010	10	25	60
420	18 to 24 years	50	60	4,920	15	35	75
421	25 years and over	20	35	2,690	15	10	15
422	Average number of children at home per census family[54]	1.5	1.7	1.0	1.2	1.0	0.8
423	**Total number of persons in private households**	**560**	**885**	**73,700**	**340**	**725**	**1,130**
	Census family status and living arrangements						
424	Number of persons not in census families	65	100	11,795	60	130	110
425	Living with relatives[55]	20	25	1,195	15	15	0
426	Living with non-relatives only	0	10	1,255	10	0	0
427	Living alone	40	65	9,350	35	115	100
428	Number of census family persons	495	785	61,905	285	595	1,015
429	Average number of persons per census family	3.1	3.5	2.8	2.9	2.8	2.7
430	**Total number of persons aged 65 years and over**	**20**	**55**	**12,920**	**45**	**140**	**270**
431	Number of persons not in census families aged 65 years and over	10	15	4,580	15	65	50
432	Living with relatives[55]	0	0	340	0	0	0
433	Living with non-relatives only	0	0	115	0	0	0
434	Living alone	10	10	4,125	10	60	55
435	Number of census family persons aged 65 years and over	10	40	8,340	30	85	220
	Economic family characteristics						
436	**Total number of economic families in private households**	**165**	**220**	**21,970**	**100**	**205**	**380**
	Size of family						
437	2 persons	65	70	11,005	50	105	240
438	3 persons	45	45	4,950	20	40	50
439	4 persons	30	40	4,230	15	25	50
440	5 or more persons	25	60	1,785	15	30	30
441	Total number of persons in economic families	520	810	63,095	300	610	1,015
442	Average number of persons per economic family	3.0	4.0	3.0	3.0	3.0	3.0
443	Total number of persons not in economic families	45	70	10,600	40	115	110
	2005 income characteristics						
444	**Population 15 years and over**	**410**	**645**	**62,450**	**255**	**595**	**995**
	Sex and total income groups in 2005						
445	Without income	35	75	2,430	0	40	30
446	With income	375	565	60,025	245	555	960
447	Under $1,000[56]	45	70	1,865	15	15	35
448	$1,000 to $2,999	30	50	1,995	15	10	45
449	$3,000 to $4,999	15	35	1,850	15	40	25
450	$5,000 to $6,999	10	35	2,190	15	10	25
451	$7,000 to $9,999	30	50	3,485	20	20	60
452	$10,000 to $11,999	30	45	2,880	25	65	30
453	$12,000 to $14,999	30	55	3,590	25	55	90
454	$15,000 to $19,999	30	55	6,575	25	115	80
455	$20,000 to $24,999	40	50	5,025	20	50	95
456	$25,000 to $29,999	35	35	4,445	20	40	75
457	$30,000 to $34,999	25	30	4,550	15	10	85
458	$35,000 to $39,999	20	25	3,790	10	40	40
459	$40,000 to $44,999	0	15	2,975	10	10	45
460	$45,000 to $49,999	10	0	2,400	10	10	30
461	$50,000 to $59,999	10	10	3,695	10	30	50
462	$60,000 and over	10	10	8,690	10	40	155
463	Median income $[57]	14,944	12,032	25,545	14,069	17,650	25,232
464	Average income $[57]	19,178	15,577	33,159	19,451	23,719	32,935
465	Standard error of average income $[57]	0	0	378	0	1,668	1,854

Note: See symbols and abbreviations in the introductory material and see reference material at the end of the publication.

Certaines caractéristiques des divisions de recensement et des subdivisions de recensement – Données intégrales et données-échantillon (20 %), Ontario, Recensement de 2006 (suite)

Tarbutt and Tarbutt Additional, TP ◆◊	Thessalon, T ◆	Thessalon 12, IRI ◆◊	White River, TP ◆	**Brant CD/DR †**	Brant, CY	**Caractéristiques**	N°
						Caractéristiques des familles de recensement	
105	**370**	**45**	**260**	**40,310**	**11,525**	**Nombre total d'enfants à la maison**	416
						Groupes d'âge	
25	60	0	30	8,525	2,220	Moins de 6 ans	417
50	130	30	115	14,600	4,130	6 à 14 ans	418
10	65	0	35	4,895	1,500	15 à 17 ans	419
10	90	10	50	8,220	2,555	18 à 24 ans	420
15	30	0	30	4,065	1,115	25 ans et plus	421
0.9	1.0	1.5	1.0	1.1	1.1	Nombre moyen d'enfants à la maison par famille de recensement[54]	422
385	**1,205**	**110**	**840**	**123,055**	**33,925**	**Nombre total de personnes dans les ménages privés**	423
						Situation des particuliers dans la famille de recensement et des particuliers dans le ménage	
35	165	20	105	17,030	3,145	Nombre de personnes hors famille de recensement	424
20	0	0	10	2,380	510	Vivant avec des personnes apparentées[55]	425
0	0	0	0	2,990	545	Vivant avec des personnes non apparentées seulement	426
15	160	15	100	11,665	2,090	Vivant seules	427
350	1,040	95	735	106,025	30,775	Nombre de membres d'une famille de recensement	428
2.8	2.8	3.2	2.9	3.0	3.0	Nombre moyen de personnes par famille de recensement	429
60	**230**	**10**	**40**	**16,820**	**4,650**	**Nombre total de personnes âgées de 65 ans et plus**	430
15	85	0	0	5,780	1,260	Nombre de personnes hors famille de recensement âgées de 65 ans et plus	431
0	0	0	0	790	200	Vivant avec des personnes apparentées[55]	432
0	0	0	0	230	35	Vivant avec des personnes non apparentées seulement	433
10	80	0	10	4,760	1,015	Vivant seules	434
40	150	10	30	11,040	3,395	Nombre de membres d'une famille de recensement âgés de 65 ans et plus	435
						Caractéristiques des familles économiques	
135	**360**	**30**	**255**	**35,430**	**10,025**	**Nombre total de familles économiques dans les ménages privés**	436
						Taille de la famille	
70	185	15	120	15,860	4,465	2 personnes	437
20	65	10	80	7,685	1,890	3 personnes	438
30	90	10	45	7,595	2,310	4 personnes	439
10	25	10	15	4,290	1,355	5 personnes ou plus	440
370	1,045	95	740	108,405	31,285	Nombre total de personnes dans les familles économiques	441
3.0	3.0	3.0	3.0	3.0	3.0	Nombre moyen de personnes par famille économique	442
15	160	15	100	14,650	2,635	Nombre total de personnes hors famille économique	443
						Caractéristiques du revenu de 2005	
315	**1,015**	**X**	**695**	**99,860**	**27,540**	**Population de 15 ans et plus**	444
						Sexe et groupes de revenu total en 2005	
25	20	X	25	4,010	945	Sans revenu	445
285	995	X	665	95,850	26,595	Avec un revenu	446
0	45	X	35	2,690	880	Moins de 1 000 $[56]	447
15	50	X	45	3,080	930	1 000 $ à 2 999 $	448
0	45	X	15	3,190	885	3 000 $ à 4 999 $	449
10	65	X	10	3,425	925	5 000 $ à 6 999 $	450
15	25	X	15	5,195	1,400	7 000 $ à 9 999 $	451
15	25	X	20	4,220	1,080	10 000 $ à 11 999 $	452
15	70	X	0	5,805	1,350	12 000 $ à 14 999 $	453
10	120	X	60	9,695	2,405	15 000 $ à 19 999 $	454
35	85	X	65	8,105	2,025	20 000 $ à 24 999 $	455
40	90	X	25	7,035	1,810	25 000 $ à 29 999 $	456
25	90	X	20	7,120	1,790	30 000 $ à 34 999 $	457
10	50	X	50	6,260	1,605	35 000 $ à 39 999 $	458
30	35	X	40	5,205	1,285	40 000 $ à 44 999 $	459
0	55	X	65	4,585	1,470	45 000 $ à 49 999$	460
30	45	X	95	6,735	2,145	50 000 $ à 59 999$	461
25	100	X	90	13,510	4,610	60 000 $ et plus	462
26,875	21,431	X	36,209	26,693	28,842	Revenu médian $[57]	463
32,777	28,402	X	35,154	33,938	36,826	Revenu moyen $[57]	464
2,647	1,671	X	2,191	244	552	Erreur type de revenu moyen $[57]	465

Nota : Voir les symboles et les abréviations dans les documents d'introduction et voir les documents de référence à la fin de la publication.

Selected characteristics for census divisions and census subdivisions – 100% data and 20% sample data, Ontario, 2006 Census (continued)

No.	Characteristics	Rankin Location 15D, IRI ◆◆◇◇	Sagamok, IRI	Sault Ste. Marie, CY ◆◇	Serpent River 7, IRI ◇	Spanish, T ◆◇	St. Joseph, TP
	2005 income characteristics						
	Sex and total income groups in 2005 (continued)						
466	Total - Males	195	335	29,675	125	305	490
467	Without income	25	40	990	10	25	10
468	With income	170	295	28,690	120	280	480
469	Under $1,000[56]	35	40	920	15	15	15
470	$1,000 to $2,999	15	30	810	10	10	30
471	$3,000 to $4,999	10	25	635	0	15	10
472	$5,000 to $6,999	0	20	700	10	10	10
473	$7,000 to $9,999	10	30	1,275	10	0	10
474	$10,000 to $11,999	10	20	1,075	0	20	10
475	$12,000 to $14,999	15	25	1,135	10	10	20
476	$15,000 to $19,999	10	25	2,035	15	70	15
477	$20,000 to $24,999	20	30	1,935	10	20	50
478	$25,000 to $29,999	15	15	2,105	10	20	40
479	$30,000 to $34,999	15	20	2,390	0	15	50
480	$35,000 to $39,999	10	10	1,965	10	20	20
481	$40,000 to $44,999	0	10	1,720	10	10	20
482	$45,000 to $49,999	0	10	1,340	0	0	15
483	$50,000 to $59,999	0	0	2,295	0	25	35
484	$60,000 and over	10	0	6,345	0	35	130
485	Median income $[57]	14,816	10,592	33,355	14,432	20,644	34,600
486	Average income $[57]	19,229	14,177	41,214	19,341	28,484	42,260
487	Standard error of average income $[57]	0	0	730	0	2,588	2,920
488	Total - Females	215	310	32,775	130	285	495
489	Without income	15	40	1,445	0	15	20
490	With income	205	270	31,330	130	275	475
491	Under $1,000[56]	10	25	945	0	0	15
492	$1,000 to $2,999	15	20	1,185	10	0	20
493	$3,000 to $4,999	10	10	1,215	10	30	15
494	$5,000 to $6,999	15	15	1,485	0	0	10
495	$7,000 to $9,999	15	25	2,210	10	20	45
496	$10,000 to $11,999	20	20	1,805	15	50	25
497	$12,000 to $14,999	20	30	2,455	15	45	70
498	$15,000 to $19,999	20	30	4,540	10	45	65
499	$20,000 to $24,999	20	20	3,085	10	25	40
500	$25,000 to $29,999	20	20	2,340	10	20	35
501	$30,000 to $34,999	10	15	2,165	10	0	35
502	$35,000 to $39,999	10	15	1,830	0	20	20
503	$40,000 to $44,999	10	10	1,255	0	0	20
504	$45,000 to $49,999	0	0	1,060	0	10	15
505	$50,000 to $59,999	0	0	1,395	10	10	10
506	$60,000 and over	10	0	2,340	0	10	30
507	Median income $[57]	15,456	13,504	19,758	14,037	14,155	16,884
508	Average income $[57]	19,135	17,112	25,782	19,551	18,800	23,484
509	Standard error of average income $[57]	0	0	260	0	1,769	1,872
	Composition of total income						
510	Composition of total income in 2005 %	100.0	100.0	100.0	100.0	100.0	100.0
511	Employment income %	72.3	63.2	68.2	63.9	52.0	64.6
512	Government transfer payments %	25.9	32.5	15.3	31.0	35.0	15.1
513	Other %	3.4	3.8	16.6	6.9	13.4	20.4
514	**Population 15 years and over with employment income in 2005**	**245**	**340**	**42,030**	**150**	**245**	**680**
	Sex and work activity						
515	Median employment income in 2005 $	16,512	12,128	23,649	14,976	19,659	16,320
516	Average employment income in 2005 $	20,800	16,366	32,277	20,307	27,370	30,037
517	Standard error of average employment income $	0	0	377	0	3,101	2,523
518	Worked full year, full time[59]	110	115	19,980	50	105	260
519	Median employment income in 2005 $	28,992	29,376	43,798	26,624	38,233	50,603
520	Average employment income in 2005 $	32,810	28,886	50,260	32,807	38,370	55,768
521	Standard error of average employment income $	0	0	597	0	4,190	4,179
522	Worked part year or part time[60]	110	170	17,420	80	115	320
523	Median employment income in 2005 $	7,984	7,472	10,982	10,464	10,400	11,790
524	Average employment income in 2005 $	11,973	10,768	19,001	15,964	21,149	17,705
525	Standard error of average employment income $	0	0	406	0	4,050	2,296
526	Males 15 years and over with employment income[58]	105	170	22,050	70	120	355
527	Median employment income in 2005 $	20,928	11,104	29,985	13,952	28,639	31,846
528	Average employment income in 2005 $	22,882	15,044	37,814	19,621	37,022	37,745
529	Standard error of average employment income $	0	0	635	0	4,928	3,892

Note: See symbols and abbreviations in the introductory material and see reference material at the end of the publication.

Certaines caractéristiques des divisions de recensement et des subdivisions de recensement – Données intégrales et données-échantillon (20 %), Ontario, Recensement de 2006 (suite)

Tarbutt and Tarbutt Additional, TP ◆◇	Thessalon, T ◆	Thessalon 12, IRI ◆◇	White River, TP ◆	**Brant CD/DR** †	Brant, CY	**Caractéristiques**	N°
						Caractéristiques du revenu de 2005	
						Sexe et groupes de revenu total en 2005 (suite)	
160	505	X	385	48,250	13,745	Total - Hommes	466
0	0	X	0	1,800	395	Sans revenu	467
160	500	X	385	46,445	13,345	Avec un revenu	468
0	20	X	20	1,470	475	Moins de 1 000 $[56]	469
10	30	X	30	1,095	295	1 000 $ à 2 999 $	470
0	30	X	0	1,160	320	3 000 $ à 4 999 $	471
0	25	X	0	1,130	325	5 000 $ à 6 999 $	472
15	10	X	0	1,745	455	7 000 $ à 9 999 $	473
10	15	X	10	1,495	350	10 000 $ à 11 999 $	474
0	10	X	0	1,925	515	12 000 $ à 14 999 $	475
0	50	X	15	3,570	880	15 000 $ à 19 999 $	476
0	15	X	45	3,440	940	20 000 $ à 24 999 $	477
25	45	X	0	2,995	840	25 000 $ à 29 999 $	478
25	45	X	15	3,135	760	30 000 $ à 34 999 $	479
0	35	X	30	3,080	800	35 000 $ à 39 999 $	480
15	35	X	15	3,005	705	40 000 $ à $44 999 $	481
0	30	X	50	2,935	905	45 000 $ à $49 999 $	482
25	40	X	70	4,405	1,360	50 000 $ à $59 999 $	483
25	75	X	90	9,855	3,425	60 000 $ et plus	484
32,458	32,023	X	45,550	35,089	38,461	Revenu médian $[57]	485
40,481	34,061	X	43,293	41,634	45,452	Revenu moyen $[57]	486
4,065	2,717	X	3,228	421	932	Erreur type de revenu moyen $[57]	487
155	510	X	310	51,610	13,795	Total - Femmes	488
25	20	X	30	2,205	550	Sans revenu	489
125	495	X	280	49,405	13,250	Avec un revenu	490
0	30	X	15	1,215	405	Moins de 1 000 $[56]	491
10	25	X	20	1,990	630	1 000$ à 2 999 $	492
0	10	X	15	2,030	565	3 000 $ à 4 999 $	493
0	40	X	15	2,295	605	5 000 $ à 6 999 $	494
0	10	X	15	3,445	945	7 000 $ à 9 999 $	495
15	15	X	15	2,720	730	10 000 $ à 11 999 $	496
15	60	X	10	3,880	835	12 000 $ à 14 999 $	497
0	70	X	40	6,125	1,525	15 000 $ à 19 999 $	498
30	75	X	20	4,665	1,085	20 000 $ à 24 999 $	499
15	45	X	20	4,050	965	25 000 $ à 29 999 $	500
0	45	X	0	3,980	1,030	30 000 $ à 34 999 $	501
0	10	X	25	3,175	805	35 000 $ à 39 999 $	502
15	0	X	30	2,200	575	40 000 $ à 44 999 $	503
0	25	X	15	1,650	565	45 000 $ à 49 999 $	504
0	10	X	30	2,330	785	50 000 $ à 59 999 $	505
0	30	X	0	3,655	1,180	60 000 $ et plus	506
21,916	18,803	X	19,829	20,938	21,783	Revenu médian $[57]	507
22,977	22,697	X	24,086	26,703	28,134	Revenu moyen $[57]	508
2,289	1,833	X	2,194	245	552	Erreur type de revenu moyen $[57]	509
						Composition du revenu total	
100.0	100.0	X	100.0	100.0	100.0	Composition du revenu total en 2005 %	510
68.9	63.4	X	84.9	76.1	77.8	Revenu d'emploi %	511
13.1	18.6	X	8.0	12.6	10.0	Transferts gouvernementaux %	512
18.3	18.3	X	6.1	11.3	12.3	Autres %	513
210	**710**	**X**	**560**	**71,755**	**21,070**	**Population de 15 ans et plus avec un revenu d'emploi en 2005**	514
						Sexe et travail	
23,160	14,378	X	38,593	28,319	29,499	Revenu médian d'emploi en 2005 $	515
30,646	25,106	X	36,044	34,504	36,154	Revenu moyen d'emploi en 2005 $	516
3,434	2,245	X	2,410	293	614	Erreur type de revenu moyen d'emploi $	517
100	295	X	345	39,570	11,585	A travaillé toute l'année à plein temps[59]	518
43,439	39,412	X	45,685	41,706	45,055	Revenu médian d'emploi en 2005 $	519
45,399	42,002	X	44,202	47,788	50,723	Revenu moyen d'emploi en 2005 $	520
4,661	3,971	X	2,675	434	937	Erreur type de revenu moyen d'emploi $	521
90	315	X	200	28,105	8,240	A travaillé une partie de l'année ou à temps partiel[60]	522
12,857	7,175	X	14,373	11,643	10,581	Revenu médian d'emploi en 2005 $	523
20,146	13,457	X	24,732	19,449	19,737	Revenu moyen d'emploi en 2005 $	524
3,771	1,725	X	3,883	316	609	Erreur type de revenu moyen d'emploi $	525
120	405	X	340	37,145	11,205	Hommes de 15 ans et plus avec un revenu d'emploi[58]	526
43,328	19,535	X	46,695	37,343	39,931	Revenu médian d'emploi en 2005 $	527
37,509	27,217	X	43,823	41,877	43,797	Revenu moyen d'emploi en 2005 $	528
5,558	3,182	X	3,285	482	974	Erreur type de revenu moyen d'emploi $	529

Nota : Voir les symboles et les abréviations dans les documents d'introduction et voir les documents de référence à la fin de la publication.

Selected characteristics for census divisions and census subdivisions – 100% data and 20% sample data, Ontario, 2006 Census (continued)

No.	Characteristics	Rankin Location 15D, IRI ◆◆◊◊	Sagamok, IRI	Sault Ste. Marie, CY ◆◊	Serpent River 7, IRI ◊	Spanish, T ◆◊	St. Joseph, TP
	2005 income characteristics						
	Sex and work activity (continued)						
530	Worked full year, full time[59]	45	40	11,215	20	50	175
531	Median employment income in 2005 $	27,968	26,432	52,822	24,832	46,874	64,886
532	Average employment income in 2005 $	35,290	27,493	58,008	30,255	46,280	63,125
533	Standard error of average employment income $	0	0	946	0	6,650	4,931
534	Worked part year or part time[60]	50	105	7,500	40	55	110
535	Median employment income in 2005 $	11,808	8,576	11,972	9,376	28,600	12,868
536	Average employment income in 2005 $	15,774	11,582	22,891	18,053	31,750	20,803
537	Standard error of average employment income $	0	0	815	0	7,020	4,264
538	Females 15 years and over with employment income[58]	140	175	19,980	75	130	320
539	Median employment income in 2005 $	15,584	13,000	20,151	14,976	13,831	14,087
540	Average employment income in 2005 $	19,250	17,635	26,166	20,923	18,493	21,344
541	Standard error of average employment income $	0	0	356	0	2,984	2,641
542	Worked full year, full time[59]	65	75	8,770	30	55	80
543	Median employment income in 2005 $	30,528	29,760	36,169	28,352	27,980	25,050
544	Average employment income in 2005 $	31,194	29,676	40,349	34,508	31,575	39,597
545	Standard error of average employment income $	0	0	559	0	4,219	6,294
546	Worked part year or part time[60]	60	65	9,920	40	55	205
547	Median employment income in 2005 $	7,120	6,704	10,395	11,040	9,372	10,978
548	Average employment income in 2005 $	8,933	9,528	16,060	13,768	10,299	16,034
549	Standard error of average employment income $	0	0	349	0	1,989	2,608
550	**Total number of economic families in private households**	**165**	**225**	**21,970**	**100**	**205**	**380**
	Family income groups in 2005						
551	Under $10,000	15	30	390	0	0	10
552	$10,000 to $19,999	30	40	1,055	15	25	15
553	$20,000 to $29,999	15	35	1,675	20	20	35
554	$30,000 to $39,999	25	40	2,515	10	30	40
555	$40,000 to $49,999	20	25	2,355	10	30	45
556	$50,000 to $59,999	20	25	1,985	15	25	20
557	$60,000 to $69,999	15	15	1,955	10	15	35
558	$70,000 to $79,999	10	10	1,800	0	20	35
559	$80,000 to $89,999	15	10	1,465	0	10	45
560	$90,000 to $99,999	0	0	1,355	10	10	15
561	$100,000 and over	0	0	5,415	0	10	85
562	Median family income $	36,448	31,936	64,938	40,064	43,657	69,823
563	Average family income $	40,760	35,182	76,151	43,361	50,015	75,435
564	Standard error of average family income $	0	0	1,054	0	4,098	4,923
	Family after-tax income groups in 2005						
565	Under $10,000	20	35	405	0	10	0
566	$10,000 to $19,999	30	40	1,085	15	25	10
567	$20,000 to $29,999	20	35	1,905	20	25	45
568	$30,000 to $39,999	25	45	3,225	15	45	50
569	$40,000 to $49,999	25	20	2,750	10	30	60
570	$50,000 to $59,999	15	25	2,425	15	30	10
571	$60,000 to $69,999	15	10	2,390	10	15	80
572	$70,000 to $79,999	10	10	2,000	10	15	25
573	$80,000 to $89,999	0	10	1,470	0	10	35
574	$90,000 to $99,999	0	0	1,180	0	10	20
575	$100,000 and over	0	0	3,130	0	0	40
576	Median after-tax family income $	35,712	31,936	56,647	38,656	43,657	60,316
577	Average after-tax family income $	38,725	34,583	63,742	40,469	45,365	62,601
578	Standard error of average after-tax family income $	0	0	741	0	3,422	3,585
	Income status in 2005						
579	Total population in private households for income status	0	0	73,690	0	725	1,130
580	Below low income cut-off before tax in 2005	0	0	10,485	0	145	65
581	Prevalence of low income before tax in 2005 %	0.0	0.0	14.2	0.0	19.3	6.2
582	Below low income cut-off after tax in 2005	0	0	7,180	0	75	50
583	Prevalence of low income after tax in 2005 %	0.0	0.0	9.7	0.0	11.0	4.4

Note: See symbols and abbreviations in the introductory material and see reference material at the end of the publication.

Certaines caractéristiques des divisions de recensement et des subdivisions de recensement – Données intégrales et données-échantillon (20 %), Ontario, Recensement de 2006 (suite)

Tarbutt and Tarbutt Additional, TP ◆◊	Thessalon, T ◆	Thessalon 12, IRI ◆◊	White River, TP ◆	**Brant CD/DR †**	Brant, CY	**Caractéristiques**	N°
						Caractéristiques du revenu de 2005	
						Sexe et travail (suite)	
70	180	X	215	23,405	7,140	A travaillé toute l'année à plein temps[59]	530
53,292	42,757	X	49,128	47,927	50,956	Revenu médian d'emploi en 2005 $	531
53,622	44,831	X	50,772	53,957	56,416	Revenu moyen d'emploi en 2005 $	532
5,856	5,237	X	3,471	647	1,297	Erreur type de revenu moyen d'emploi $	533
30	160	X	120	11,785	3,470	A travaillé une partie de l'année ou à temps partiel[60]	534
24,833	6,712	X	39,350	13,491	11,376	Revenu médian d'emploi en 2005 $	535
23,782	15,791	X	33,527	23,195	23,875	Revenu moyen d'emploi en 2005 $	536
8,790	2,990	X	5,925	590	1,265	Erreur type de revenu moyen d'emploi $	537
95	305	X	220	34,610	9,865	Femmes de 15 ans et plus avec un revenu d'emploi[58]	538
21,695	14,337	X	21,593	21,880	21,907	Revenu médian d'emploi en 2005 $	539
22,206	22,266	X	23,969	26,590	27,470	Revenu moyen d'emploi en 2005 $	540
2,772	3,041	X	2,572	298	664	Erreur type de revenu moyen d'emploi $	541
35	115	X	125	16,165	4,445	A travaillé toute l'année à plein temps[59]	542
22,127	33,735	X	35,165	34,040	36,234	Revenu médian d'emploi en 2005 $	543
28,814	37,647	X	33,281	38,854	41,574	Revenu moyen d'emploi en 2005 $	544
3,293	5,985	X	2,970	463	1,227	Erreur type de revenu moyen d'emploi $	545
60	155	X	80	16,320	4,770	A travaillé une partie de l'année ou à temps partiel[60]	546
12,857	7,183	X	8,025	10,747	10,233	Revenu médian d'emploi en 2005 $	547
18,494	11,118	X	11,630	16,743	16,722	Revenu moyen d'emploi en 2005 $	548
3,569	1,473	X	2,421	335	499	Erreur type de revenu moyen d'emploi $	549
130	**365**	**X**	**260**	**35,430**	**10,025**	**Nombre total des familles économiques dans les ménages privés**	550
						Revenu de la famille économique en 2005	
0	0	X	10	640	125	Moins de 10 000 $	551
0	10	X	10	1,475	225	10 000 $ à 19 999 $	552
10	50	X	20	2,585	635	20 000 $ à 29 999 $	553
30	55	X	15	3,310	665	30 000 $ à 39 999 $	554
20	20	X	25	3,460	770	40 000 $ à 49 999 $	555
10	40	X	25	3,395	1,010	50 000 $ à 59 999 $	556
10	40	X	20	3,120	870	60 000 $ à 69 999 $	557
15	60	X	10	3,325	935	70 000 $ à 79 999 $	558
15	30	X	25	2,945	910	80 000 $ à 89 999 $	559
0	20	X	30	2,455	750	90 000 $ à 99 999 $	560
20	40	X	60	8,715	3,130	100 000 $ et plus	561
62,034	61,489	X	74,289	69,235	77,735	Revenu médian des familles $	562
66,207	63,724	X	75,147	78,600	88,715	Revenu moyen des familles $	563
5,338	4,364	X	6,150	693	1,600	Erreur type de revenu moyen des familles $	564
						Revenu après impôt de la famille économique en 2005	
0	10	X	10	670	135	Moins de 10 000 $	565
0	10	X	10	1,505	230	10 000 $ à 19 999 $	566
20	50	X	25	2,825	685	20 000 $ à 29 999 $	567
30	60	X	20	4,360	880	30 000 $ à 39 999 $	568
15	50	X	35	4,480	1,170	40 000 $ à 49 999 $	569
10	50	X	25	4,255	1,245	50 000 $ à 59 999 $	570
15	60	X	25	4,125	1,155	60 000 $ à 69 999 $	571
15	40	X	30	3,525	1,130	70 000 $ à 79 999 $	572
0	20	X	30	2,790	930	80 000 $ à 89 999 $	573
15	0	X	15	1,960	580	90 000 $ à 99 999 $	574
0	15	X	30	4,920	1,870	100 000 $ et plus	575
52,818	53,809	X	62,233	59,039	65,609	Revenu médian après impôt des familles $	576
56,547	55,080	X	62,381	65,510	72,896	Revenu moyen après impôt des familles $	577
4,025	3,412	X	4,997	474	1,056	Erreur type de revenu moyen après impôt des familles $	578
						Catégorie de revenu en 2005	
385	1,205	X	840	122,490	33,905	Population totale dans les ménages privés pour la catégorie de revenu	579
0	155	X	55	14,270	2,040	Au-dessous du seuil de faible revenu avant impôt en 2005	580
0.0	12.9	X	6.5	11.6	6.0	Fréquence du faible revenu avant impôt en 2005 %	581
0	105	X	35	10,340	1,440	Au-dessous du seuil de faible revenu après impôt en 2005	582
0.0	8.3	X	4.1	8.4	4.2	Fréquence du faible revenu après impôt en 2005 %	583

Nota : Voir les symboles et les abréviations dans les documents d'introduction et voir les documents de référence à la fin de la publication.

Selected characteristics for census divisions and census subdivisions – 100% data and 20% sample data, Ontario, 2006 Census (continued)

No.	Characteristics	Rankin Location 15D, IRI ◆◆◇◇	Sagamok, IRI	Sault Ste. Marie, CY ◆◇	Serpent River 7, IRI ◇	Spanish, T ◆◇	St. Joseph, TP
	2005 income characteristics						
584	**Total number of private households**	**205**	**295**	**31,760**	**135**	**325**	**485**
	Household income groups in 2005						
585	Under $10,000	35	70	1,335	10	20	10
586	$10,000 to $19,999	40	60	4,215	35	85	55
587	$20,000 to $29,999	25	40	3,410	25	40	55
588	$30,000 to $39,999	30	40	3,700	10	50	60
589	$40,000 to $49,999	20	30	3,315	15	30	45
590	$50,000 to $59,999	20	25	2,560	15	25	25
591	$60,000 to $69,999	15	15	2,405	10	20	40
592	$70,000 to $79,999	10	10	2,115	10	20	50
593	$80,000 to $89,999	10	10	1,640	10	10	40
594	$90,000 to $99,999	10	0	1,450	0	10	15
595	$100,000 and over	0	10	5,595	0	10	85
596	Median household income $	30,848	26,048	49,590	28,672	34,417	53,177
597	Average household income $	35,097	30,091	62,568	35,327	40,602	65,023
598	Standard error of average household income $	0	0	789	0	3,217	4,153
	Household after-tax income groups in 2005						
599	Under $10,000	40	65	1,375	15	15	10
600	$10,000 to $19,999	40	55	4,660	40	85	60
601	$20,000 to $29,999	20	40	3,775	25	45	70
602	$30,000 to $39,999	30	45	4,595	15	65	60
603	$40,000 to $49,999	25	25	3,635	15	30	65
604	$50,000 to $59,999	20	25	2,985	15	30	20
605	$60,000 to $69,999	15	15	2,665	10	25	80
606	$70,000 to $79,999	10	10	2,140	10	10	25
607	$80,000 to $89,999	10	10	1,510	0	0	35
608	$90,000 to $99,999	0	0	1,200	0	10	15
609	$100,000 and over	0	0	3,215	0	0	40
610	Median after-tax household income $	30,848	25,152	43,515	28,416	32,400	46,294
611	Average after-tax household income $	33,459	29,454	52,615	33,218	36,842	54,185
612	Standard error of average after-tax household income $	0	0	567	0	2,707	3,092

Note: See symbols and abbreviations in the introductory material and see reference material at the end of the publication.

Certaines caractéristiques des divisions de recensement et des subdivisions de recensement – Données intégrales et données-échantillon (20 %), Ontario, Recensement de 2006 (suite)

Tarbutt and Tarbutt Additional, TP ◆◊	Thessalon, T ◆	Thessalon 12, IRI ◆◊	White River, TP ◆	**Brant CD/DR †**	Brant, CY	**Caractéristiques**	N°
						Caractéristiques du revenu de 2005	
145	**525**	**X**	**355**	**48,020**	**12,240**	**Nombre total des ménages privés**	584
						Tranches de revenu des ménages en 2005	
0	25	X	20	1,585	260	Moins de 10 000 $	585
0	60	X	15	4,660	725	10 000 $ à 19 999 $	586
0	75	X	40	4,835	1,060	20 000 $ à 29 999 $	587
35	80	X	25	5,290	930	30 000 $ à 39 999 $	588
20	30	X	45	4,775	1,015	40 000 $ à 49 999 $	589
10	40	X	35	4,345	1,255	50 000 $ à 59 999 $	590
15	45	X	35	3,780	940	60 000 $ à 69 999 $	591
15	65	X	10	3,835	1,055	70 000 $ à 79 999 $	592
10	30	X	30	3,165	965	80 000 $ à 89 999 $	593
0	15	X	35	2,615	765	90 000 $ à 99 999 $	594
25	50	X	60	9,135	3,260	100 000 $ et plus	595
55,009	48,768	X	57,297	56,607	69,146	Revenu médian des ménages $	596
64,020	53,876	X	65,830	67,651	79,916	Revenu moyen des ménages $	597
5,025	3,586	X	4,861	562	1,373	Erreur type de revenu moyen des ménages $	598
						Tranches du revenu après impôt des ménages en 2005	
0	30	X	15	1,645	280	Moins de 10 000 $	599
10	60	X	30	5,020	765	10 000 $ à 19 999 $	600
20	95	X	35	5,750	1,230	20 000 $ à 29 999 $	601
30	65	X	40	6,395	1,205	30 000 $ à 39 999 $	602
20	50	X	55	5,805	1,440	40 000 $ à 49 999 $	603
15	55	X	40	5,025	1,370	50 000 $ à 59 999 $	604
15	75	X	35	4,565	1,260	60 000 $ à 69 999 $	605
15	40	X	25	3,730	1,175	70 000 $ à 79 999 $	606
0	25	X	30	2,940	970	80 000 $ à 89 999 $	607
20	0	X	15	2,020	595	90 000 $ à 99 999 $	608
0	15	X	30	5,125	1,945	100 000 $ et plus	609
47,329	42,067	X	47,600	49,000	58,536	Revenu médian après impôt des ménages $	610
54,759	46,291	X	54,870	56,548	65,885	Revenu moyen après impôt des ménages $	611
3,812	2,829	X	3,920	393	924	Erreur type de revenu moyen après impôt des ménages $	612

Nota : Voir les symboles et les abréviations dans les documents d'introduction et voir les documents de référence à la fin de la publication.

Selected characteristics for census divisions and census subdivisions – 100% data and 20% sample data, Ontario, 2006 Census (continued)

No.	Characteristics	Brantford, CY	Bruce CD/DR ◆◇	Arran-Elderslie, MU	Brockton, MU	Huron-Kinloss, TP ◆◇	Kincardine, MU
	Population characteristics						
1	**Population, 2001[1]**	**86,417**	**63,892**	**6,577**	**9,658**	**6,224**	**11,029**
2	**Population, 2006[2]**	**90,192**	**65,349**	**6,747**	**9,641**	**6,515**	**11,173**
3	Population percentage change, 2001 to 2006	4.4	2.3	2.6	-0.2	4.7	1.3
4	Land area in square kilometres, 2006	72.47	4,079.17	460.13	565.07	440.59	537.65
5	**Total population – 100% data[3]**	**90,195**	**65,345**	**6,750**	**9,640**	**6,515**	**11,175**
	Sex and age groups						
6	Male	43,295	32,445	3,330	4,795	3,270	5,490
7	0 to 4 years	2,580	1,475	180	255	160	200
8	5 to 9 years	2,815	1,680	180	265	195	250
9	10 to 14 years	3,080	2,235	245	360	235	350
10	15 to 19 years	3,090	2,425	275	360	265	425
11	20 to 24 years	2,915	2,025	200	335	220	360
12	25 to 29 years	2,750	1,470	200	220	160	250
13	30 to 34 years	2,770	1,380	195	225	125	225
14	35 to 39 years	2,925	1,530	165	260	145	240
15	40 to 44 years	3,490	2,240	250	400	205	360
16	45 to 49 years	3,440	2,640	245	385	255	505
17	50 to 54 years	3,080	2,715	245	370	275	530
18	55 to 59 years	2,875	2,745	270	370	275	505
19	60 to 64 years	2,055	2,300	210	285	235	405
20	65 to 69 years	1,625	1,840	150	225	165	305
21	70 to 74 years	1,320	1,525	110	190	140	240
22	75 to 79 years	1,120	1,115	90	135	115	180
23	80 to 84 years	855	660	60	95	60	105
24	85 years and over	505	450	50	65	45	70
25	Female	46,895	32,905	3,415	4,845	3,245	5,680
26	0 to 4 years	2,620	1,400	185	220	165	235
27	5 to 9 years	2,725	1,595	195	265	170	240
28	10 to 14 years	3,050	2,070	265	325	215	365
29	15 to 19 years	3,095	2,360	250	375	255	405
30	20 to 24 years	2,995	1,855	200	300	180	330
31	25 to 29 years	2,880	1,370	180	210	130	225
32	30 to 34 years	2,940	1,350	160	210	125	230
33	35 to 39 years	3,005	1,685	195	265	150	275
34	40 to 44 years	3,610	2,405	250	395	220	415
35	45 to 49 years	3,630	2,620	260	370	240	530
36	50 to 54 years	3,440	2,865	280	395	295	530
37	55 to 59 years	2,965	2,670	240	345	260	470
38	60 to 64 years	2,180	2,245	190	305	210	390
39	65 to 69 years	1,805	1,775	160	200	170	300
40	70 to 74 years	1,685	1,545	130	220	145	230
41	75 to 79 years	1,615	1,270	105	155	130	210
42	80 to 84 years	1,385	920	90	130	90	150
43	85 years and over	1,275	890	85	155	105	145
44	**Total population 15 years and over[3]**	**73,320**	**54,890**	**5,495**	**7,945**	**5,380**	**9,530**
	Legal marital status						
45	Never legally married (single)	23,230	14,245	1,500	2,200	1,395	2,410
46	Legally married (and not separated)[4,5]	34,835	31,275	3,085	4,410	3,205	5,485
47	Separated, but still legally married	3,630	1,790	190	270	115	340
48	Divorced	6,150	3,555	360	450	285	645
49	Widowed	5,475	4,020	365	615	380	645
	Common-law status						
50	Not in a common-law relationship	66,215	50,805	5,035	7,405	5,035	8,845
51	In a common-law relationship	7,105	4,090	460	540	345	685
52	**Total population – 20% sample data[6]**	**88,845**	**64,555**	**6,655**	**9,480**	**6,445**	**11,065**
	Mother tongue						
53	Single responses	88,220	64,365	6,610	9,475	6,440	11,015
54	English	76,600	59,450	6,275	9,020	5,540	10,060
55	French	1,075	540	25	20	40	190
56	Non-official languages[7]	10,545	4,370	305	430	860	765
57	Italian	1,520	85	0	10	10	45
58	Chinese, n.o.s.[61]	250	65	0	0	0	15
59	Cantonese	60	25	0	0	0	10
60	Spanish	340	35	0	10	0	0
61	German	550	2,135	220	175	625	220
62	Other languages[8]	7,820	2,020	80	230	235	475

Note: See symbols and abbreviations in the introductory material and see reference material at the end of the publication.

Certaines caractéristiques des divisions de recensement et des subdivisions de recensement – Données intégrales et données-échantillon (20 %), Ontario, Recensement de 2006 (suite)

Neyaas-hiinigmiing 27, IRI ◆◆◇◇	Northern Bruce Peninsula, MU ◆◇	Saugeen 29, IRI ◆◆◇◇	Saugeen Shores, T ◆◇	South Bruce, MU	South Bruce Peninsula, T ◆◇	Caractéristiques	N°
						Caractéristiques de la population	
587	**3,599**	**677**	**11,388**	**6,063**	**8,090**	**Population, 2001[1]**	1
591	**3,850**	**758**	**11,720**	**5,939**	**8,415**	**Population, 2006[2]**	2
0.7	7.0	12.0	2.9	-2.0	4.0	Variation en pourcentage de la population, 2001 à 2006	3
63.78	781.51	40.78	170.58	487.17	531.90	Superficie des terres en kilomètres carrés, 2006	4
590	**3,850**	**760**	**11,720**	**5,935**	**8,415**	**Population totale – Données intégrales[3]**	5
						Sexe et groupes d'âge	
300	1,915	395	5,740	3,020	4,180	Sexe masculin	6
20	45	30	225	175	175	0 à 4 ans	7
25	75	40	265	200	185	5 à 9 ans	8
35	90	50	365	250	260	10 à 14 ans	9
25	110	25	405	265	260	15 à 19 ans	10
15	80	25	370	220	205	20 à 24 ans	11
10	40	25	235	165	170	25 à 29 ans	12
20	75	25	215	145	145	30 à 34 ans	13
20	70	30	245	165	190	35 à 39 ans	14
20	120	30	360	215	280	40 à 44 ans	15
35	130	30	505	250	305	45 à 49 ans	16
15	150	30	545	230	320	50 à 54 ans	17
10	180	10	535	200	375	55 à 59 ans	18
10	210	25	425	145	345	60 à 64 ans	19
10	190	10	350	130	320	65 à 69 ans	20
10	150	5	295	115	265	70 à 74 ans	21
5	95	0	210	70	210	75 à 79 ans	22
0	55	0	130	45	100	80 à 84 ans	23
5	35	0	70	35	75	85 ans et plus	24
290	1,930	360	5,975	2,920	4,235	Sexe féminin	25
20	40	25	190	180	140	0 à 4 ans	26
20	65	30	235	180	190	5 à 9 ans	27
15	100	35	330	240	190	10 à 14 ans	28
20	100	35	415	250	250	15 à 19 ans	29
5	75	20	355	195	195	20 à 24 ans	30
20	55	25	230	155	135	25 à 29 ans	31
25	55	30	210	145	165	30 à 34 ans	32
15	75	15	280	170	230	35 à 39 ans	33
30	125	35	440	220	280	40 à 44 ans	34
20	135	25	510	245	285	45 à 49 ans	35
20	160	25	585	205	370	50 à 54 ans	36
30	185	20	545	185	400	55 à 59 ans	37
10	215	5	440	125	350	60 à 64 ans	38
15	170	5	340	120	295	65 à 69 ans	39
15	140	15	290	120	250	70 à 74 ans	40
10	110	0	245	80	220	75 à 79 ans	41
5	70	0	195	50	140	80 à 84 ans	42
0	50	0	155	40	150	85 ans et plus	43
455	**3,430**	**540**	**10,120**	**4,715**	**7,280**	**Population totale de 15 ans et plus[3]**	44
						État matrimonial légal	
200	685	300	2,535	1,380	1,635	Jamais légalement marié(e) (célibataire)	45
150	2,080	145	5,775	2,740	4,195	Légalement marié(e) (et non séparé[e])[4,5]	46
30	105	30	330	130	250	Séparé(e), mais toujours légalement marié(e)	47
50	255	30	705	210	570	Divorcé(e)	48
25	300	35	775	250	630	Veuf(ve)	49
						Union libre	
380	3,150	440	9,430	4,395	6,700	Ne vivant pas en union libre	50
80	280	105	690	325	580	Vivant en union libre	51
595	**3,805**	**755**	**11,555**	**5,930**	**8,275**	**Population totale – Données-échantillon (20 %)[6]**	52
						Langue maternelle	
590	3,805	745	11,535	5,920	8,220	Réponses uniques	53
515	3,460	595	10,600	5,535	7,850	Anglais	54
10	30	0	185	10	25	Français	55
70	310	150	750	385	340	Langues non officielles[7]	56
0	10	0	10	0	10	Italien	57
0	0	0	30	0	10	Chinois, n.d.a.[61]	58
0	0	0	0	0	15	Cantonais	59
0	0	0	10	0	0	Espagnol	60
0	225	0	230	270	170	Allemand	61
70	75	145	465	110	140	Autres langues[8]	62

Nota : Voir les symboles et les abréviations dans les documents d'introduction et voir les documents de référence à la fin de la publication.

Selected characteristics for census divisions and census subdivisions – 100% data and 20% sample data, Ontario, 2006 Census (continued)

No.	Characteristics	Brantford, CY	**Bruce CD/DR** ◆◇	Arran-Elderslie, MU	Brockton, MU	Huron-Kinloss, TP ◆◇	Kincardine, MU
	Population characteristics						
	Mother tongue (continued)						
63	Multiple responses	620	195	45	10	0	50
64	English and French	95	55	10	0	0	25
65	English and non-official language	495	130	40	0	0	25
66	French and non-official language	15	0	0	0	0	0
67	English, French and non-official language	10	0	0	0	0	0
	Language spoken most often at home[9]						
68	Single responses	88,120	64,415	6,655	9,475	6,435	11,050
69	English	83,240	62,675	6,500	9,365	5,840	10,740
70	French	315	80	0	0	0	20
71	Non-official languages[7]	4,560	1,660	160	115	590	285
72	Chinese, n.o.s.[61]	165	25	0	0	0	0
73	Cantonese	50	10	0	0	0	10
74	Panjabi (Punjabi)	545	15	0	0	0	0
75	Italian	430	0	0	0	0	0
76	Spanish	155	15	0	10	0	0
77	Other languages[8]	3,220	1,595	165	110	585	280
78	Multiple responses	725	140	0	0	10	15
79	English and French	55	30	0	0	0	0
80	English and non-official language	670	110	0	0	0	10
81	French and non-official language	0	0	0	0	0	0
82	English, French and non-official language	0	0	0	0	0	0
	Knowledge of official languages[10]						
83	English only	83,830	61,265	6,355	9,095	6,145	10,320
84	French only	55	0	0	0	0	0
85	English and French	4,470	3,050	260	380	170	725
86	Neither English nor French	485	235	40	0	125	20
	Knowledge of non-official languages[7,11]						
87	Italian	1,865	130	10	10	10	65
88	Spanish	785	290	50	20	0	65
89	German	930	2,420	275	180	655	330
90	Chinese, n.o.s.[61]	270	55	0	0	0	20
91	Cantonese	75	35	0	0	0	15
92	Panjabi (Punjabi)	830	25	0	0	0	0
93	Portuguese	620	120	0	40	25	15
	First official language spoken[10]						
94	English	87,115	63,810	6,590	9,465	6,290	10,860
95	French	1,105	490	25	15	25	180
96	English and French	160	25	0	0	0	10
97	Neither English nor French	465	235	40	0	125	20
98	Official language minority - (number)[12]	1,185	495	30	15	30	180
99	Official language minority - (percentage)[12]	1.3	0.8	0.5	0.2	0.5	1.6
	Ethnic origin[13]						
100	English	32,095	23,270	2,445	2,910	2,320	4,285
101	Canadian	25,935	18,760	2,535	2,545	1,930	2,920
102	Scottish	20,255	20,045	2,080	2,600	2,245	3,985
103	Irish	16,855	17,485	1,815	2,740	1,830	3,225
104	French	8,475	5,620	600	880	425	1,175
105	German	10,385	18,050	1,590	4,710	1,420	2,220
106	Italian	5,655	985	95	130	90	240
107	Chinese	1,050	300	0	40	0	30
108	East Indian	1,345	140	0	0	0	85
109	Dutch (Netherlands)	5,265	3,855	490	665	565	730
110	Polish	5,165	1,285	210	155	95	315
111	Ukrainian	3,675	780	80	40	60	195
112	North American Indian	4,480	2,500	65	155	120	205
113	Portuguese	1,365	205	15	50	20	25
114	Filipino	705	135	0	10	25	35
	Aboriginal and non-Aboriginal identity						
115	Total Aboriginal identity population[14]	3,440	2,180	85	85	40	100
116	Total non-Aboriginal identity population	85,405	62,370	6,575	9,395	6,405	10,965

Note: See symbols and abbreviations in the introductory material and see reference material at the end of the publication.

Certaines caractéristiques des divisions de recensement et des subdivisions de recensement – Données intégrales et données-échantillon (20 %), Ontario, Recensement de 2006 (suite)

Neyaas-hiinigmiing 27, IRI ◆◆◇◇	Northern Bruce Peninsula, MU ◆◇	Saugeen 29, IRI ◆◆◇◇	Saugeen Shores, T ◆◇	South Bruce, MU	South Bruce Peninsula, T ◆◇	Caractéristiques	N°
						Caractéristiques de la population	
						Langue maternelle (suite)	
0	0	10	20	10	50	Réponses multiples	63
0	0	0	10	0	0	Anglais et français	64
0	10	10	10	10	45	Anglais et langue non officielle	65
0	0	0	0	0	0	Français et langue non officielle	66
0	0	0	0	0	0	Anglais, français et langue non officielle	67
						Langue parlée le plus souvent à la maison[9]	
590	3,800	750	11,505	5,915	8,240	Réponses uniques	68
580	3,765	720	11,200	5,740	8,220	Anglais	69
0	0	0	55	0	0	Français	70
10	30	35	245	175	20	Langues non officielles[7]	71
0	0	0	25	0	0	Chinois, n.d.a.[61]	72
0	0	0	0	0	0	Cantonais	73
0	0	0	15	0	0	Pendjabi	74
0	0	0	0	0	0	Italien	75
0	0	0	10	0	0	Espagnol	76
10	35	30	200	170	20	Autres langues[8]	77
0	10	0	50	10	30	Réponses multiples	78
0	0	0	25	0	0	Anglais et français	79
0	10	0	30	10	30	Anglais et langue non officielle	80
0	0	0	0	0	0	Français et langue non officielle	81
0	0	0	0	0	0	Anglais, français et langue non officielle	82
						Connaissance des langues officielles[10]	
565	3,645	735	10,740	5,690	7,960	Anglais seulement	83
0	0	0	0	0	0	Français seulement	84
25	165	10	795	205	310	Anglais et français	85
0	0	0	15	30	0	Ni l'anglais ni le français	86
						Connaissance des langues non officielles[7,11]	
0	15	0	0	0	10	Italien	87
0	45	0	70	0	25	Espagnol	88
0	250	0	275	255	185	Allemand	89
0	0	0	30	0	10	Chinois, n.d.a.[61]	90
0	0	0	0	0	15	Cantonais	91
0	0	0	25	0	0	Pendjabi	92
0	20	0	15	0	10	Portugais	93
						Première langue officielle parlée[10]	
585	3,775	745	11,370	5,890	8,240	Anglais	94
10	35	10	155	10	25	Français	95
0	0	0	15	0	0	Anglais et français	96
0	0	0	15	30	0	Ni l'anglais ni le français	97
10	30	0	160	0	30	Minorité de langue officielle - (nombre)[12]	98
1.7	0.8	0.0	1.4	0.0	0.4	Minorité de langue officielle - (pourcentage)[12]	99
						Origine ethnique[13]	
15	1,610	25	4,950	1,070	3,630	Anglais	100
10	1,090	15	3,680	1,260	2,780	Canadien	101
15	1,060	25	3,505	1,495	3,035	Écossais	102
10	940	10	3,150	1,385	2,390	Irlandais	103
30	220	20	1,180	505	575	Français	104
10	715	10	2,290	3,595	1,490	Allemand	105
0	60	0	235	25	95	Italien	106
0	10	0	110	25	80	Chinois	107
0	0	0	45	0	0	Indien de l'Inde	108
0	100	0	630	355	325	Hollandais (Néerlandais)	109
0	120	0	150	80	170	Polonais	110
0	45	0	195	30	130	Ukrainien	111
535	115	705	325	10	260	Indien de l'Amérique du Nord	112
0	25	0	45	0	25	Portugais	113
0	0	0	60	0	0	Philippin	114
						Population ayant une identité autochtone et population n'ayant pas d'identité autochtone	
550	95	720	310	35	170	Total de la population ayant une identité autochtone[14]	115
40	3,710	35	11,245	5,895	8,100	Total de la population n'ayant pas d'identité autochtone	116

Nota : Voir les symboles et les abréviations dans les documents d'introduction et voir les documents de référence à la fin de la publication.

Selected characteristics for census divisions and census subdivisions – 100% data and 20% sample data, Ontario, 2006 Census (continued)

No.	Characteristics	Brantford, CY	**Bruce CD/DR** ◆◊	Arran-Elderslie, MU	Brockton, MU	Huron-Kinloss, TP ◆◊	Kincardine, MU
	Population characteristics						
	Aboriginal and non-Aboriginal ancestry						
117	Total Aboriginal ancestry population[15]	4,960	2,960	155	190	125	255
118	Total non-Aboriginal ancestry population	83,880	61,595	6,500	9,285	6,315	10,810
	Registered Indian status						
119	Registered Indian[16]	2,305	1,625	0	0	30	60
120	Not a Registered Indian	86,540	62,930	6,655	9,480	6,415	11,005
	Visible minority groups						
121	Total visible minority population[17]	6,200	965	20	110	30	230
122	Chinese	650	260	0	35	0	35
123	South Asian[18]	1,660	185	0	10	10	75
124	Black	1,580	140	10	10	0	35
125	Filipino	625	125	0	35	10	35
126	Latin American	360	45	0	10	0	0
127	Southeast Asian[19]	570	40	0	10	0	0
128	Arab	190	20	10	0	0	0
129	West Asian[20]	30	40	0	0	0	0
130	Korean	200	45	0	0	10	35
131	Japanese	90	30	0	0	10	0
132	Visible minority, n.i.e.[21]	50	25	0	10	0	0
133	Multiple visible minority[22]	185	10	0	0	0	0
	Citizenship[23]						
134	Canadian citizens[24]	86,210	63,410	6,580	9,415	6,375	10,785
135	Not Canadian citizens[25]	2,630	1,150	75	70	70	275
	Immigrant status and place of birth[26]						
136	Non-immigrants[27]	76,005	59,180	6,400	8,995	5,985	9,690
137	Born in province of residence	69,005	55,405	6,075	8,635	5,635	8,930
138	Immigrants[28]	12,505	5,270	260	485	455	1,310
139	United States of America	730	490	45	45	45	95
140	Central and South America	380	55	10	10	0	10
141	Caribbean and Bermuda	520	90	10	10	0	10
142	United Kingdom	2,895	2,115	100	130	150	615
143	Other Europe	5,220	1,985	95	255	230	390
144	Africa	290	75	0	10	10	25
145	Asia and the Middle East	2,435	405	0	30	20	170
146	Oceania and other[29]	30	65	0	10	0	0
147	Non-permanent residents[30]	330	110	0	0	10	65
148	**Total immigrant population[28]**	**12,505**	**5,270**	**260**	**485**	**455**	**1,310**
	Period of immigration						
149	Before 1961	3,215	1,775	100	150	200	325
150	1961 to 1970	2,255	1,285	60	120	110	420
151	1971 to 1980	1,965	755	50	55	65	215
152	1981 to 1990	1,780	465	20	95	30	65
153	1991 to 2000	2,260	605	15	50	40	160
154	1991 to 1995	1,375	170	15	25	0	20
155	1996 to 2000	890	435	0	20	40	135
156	2001 to 2006[31]	1,030	385	15	10	0	130
	Age at immigration						
157	Under 5 years	1,360	710	50	60	40	195
158	5 to 19 years	3,400	1,520	95	145	170	370
159	20 years and over	7,745	3,030	120	280	240	750
160	**Total population 15 years and over**	**71,985**	**54,065**	**5,400**	**7,785**	**5,305**	**9,400**
	Generation status						
161	1st generation[32]	12,605	5,170	260	475	455	1,290
162	2nd generation[33]	14,420	6,710	570	600	705	1,430
163	3rd generation or more[34]	44,960	42,175	4,575	6,705	4,145	6,680

Note: See symbols and abbreviations in the introductory material and see reference material at the end of the publication.

Certaines caractéristiques des divisions de recensement et des subdivisions de recensement – Données intégrales et données-échantillon (20 %), Ontario, Recensement de 2006 (suite)

Neyaas-hiinigmiing 27, IRI ◆◆◇◇	Northern Bruce Peninsula, MU ◆◇	Saugeen 29, IRI ◆◆◇◇	Saugeen Shores, T ◆◇	South Bruce, MU	South Bruce Peninsula, T ◆◇	Caractéristiques	N°
						Caractéristiques de la population	
						Population ayant une ascendance autochtone et population n'ayant pas d'ascendance autochtone	
535	200	710	475	30	285	Total de la population ayant une ascendance autochtone[15]	117
50	3,605	45	11,080	5,900	7,990	Total de la population n'ayant pas d'ascendance autochtone	118
						Statut d'Indien inscrit	
535	15	705	140	10	125	Indien inscrit[16]	119
55	3,790	45	11,415	5,920	8,150	Pas un Indien inscrit	120
						Groupes de minorités visibles	
0	25	0	425	15	115	Total de la population des minorités visibles[17]	121
0	0	0	100	10	80	Chinois	122
0	0	0	95	0	0	Sud-Asiatique[18]	123
0	15	0	35	0	30	Noir	124
0	0	0	50	0	0	Philippin	125
0	0	0	25	0	0	Latino-Américain	126
0	0	0	30	0	0	Asiatique du Sud-Est[19]	127
0	0	0	10	0	0	Arabe	128
0	0	0	30	0	0	Asiatique occidental[20]	129
0	0	0	0	0	0	Coréen	130
0	0	0	15	0	0	Japonais	131
0	0	0	20	0	0	Minorité visible, n.i.a.[21]	132
0	0	0	10	0	0	Minorités visibles multiples[22]	133
						Citoyenneté[23]	
X	3,655	X	11,290	5,850	8,145	Citoyens canadiens[24]	134
X	155	X	265	80	125	Ne sont pas des citoyens canadiens[25]	135
						Statut d'immigrant et le lieu de naissance[26]	
X	3,240	X	10,190	5,725	7,645	Non-immigrants[27]	136
X	2,945	X	9,110	5,600	7,195	Né dans la province de résidence	137
X	570	X	1,335	200	620	Immigrants[28]	138
X	70	X	90	25	50	États-Unis d'Amérique	139
X	10	X	25	0	0	Amérique centrale et Amérique du Sud	140
X	20	X	40	0	0	Antilles et Bermudes	141
X	175	X	570	55	310	Royaume-Uni	142
X	275	X	415	105	215	Autre Europe	143
X	10	X	15	0	0	Afrique	144
X	10	X	130	10	35	Asie et Moyen-Orient	145
X	0	X	40	10	0	Océanie et autres[29]	146
X	0	X	30	0	0	Résidents non permanents[30]	147
X	**570**	**X**	**1,335**	**200**	**620**	**Population totale des immigrants[28]**	148
						Période d'immigration	
X	210	X	440	20	335	Avant 1961	149
X	80	X	290	65	125	1961 à 1970	150
X	100	X	155	35	70	1971 à 1980	151
X	20	X	155	25	50	1981 à 1990	152
X	130	X	175	20	20	1991 à 2000	153
X	0	X	65	15	15	1991 à 1995	154
X	120	X	105	10	0	1996 à 2000	155
X	25	X	120	35	20	2001 à 2006[31]	156
						Âge à l'immigration	
X	65	X	200	25	75	Moins de 5 ans	157
X	185	X	320	25	200	5 à 19 ans	158
X	320	X	815	150	345	20 ans et plus	159
455	**3,385**	**535**	**9,955**	**4,700**	**7,130**	**Population totale de 15 ans et plus**	160
						Statut des générations	
25	515	10	1,350	180	620	1re génération[32]	161
15	365	15	1,760	310	930	2e génération[33]	162
415	2,505	515	6,845	4,210	5,580	3e génération ou plus[34]	163

Nota : Voir les symboles et les abréviations dans les documents d'introduction et voir les documents de référence à la fin de la publication.

Selected characteristics for census divisions and census subdivisions – 100% data and 20% sample data, Ontario, 2006 Census (continued)

No.	Characteristics	Brantford, CY	Bruce CD/DR ◆◊	Arran-Elderslie, MU	Brockton, MU	Huron-Kinloss, TP ◆◊	Kincardine, MU
	Population characteristics						
164	**Total population 1 year and over[35]**	**87,900**	**64,000**	**6,570**	**9,385**	**6,400**	**10,970**
	Place of residence 1 year ago (mobility)						
165	Non-movers	74,580	57,635	6,070	8,415	5,795	9,830
166	Movers	13,320	6,360	495	965	600	1,140
167	Non-migrants	9,055	2,760	160	505	200	560
168	Migrants	4,260	3,600	335	465	400	580
169	Internal migrants	3,820	3,490	320	455	395	545
170	Intraprovincial migrants	3,480	3,330	310	455	395	495
171	Interprovincial migrants	340	155	10	0	0	55
172	External migrants	445	110	15	10	10	35
173	**Total population 5 years and over[36]**	**83,625**	**61,675**	**6,290**	**9,005**	**6,115**	**10,625**
	Place of residence 5 years ago (mobility)						
174	Non-movers	47,295	42,645	4,345	6,095	4,340	7,235
175	Movers	36,330	19,030	1,945	2,915	1,780	3,390
176	Non-migrants	23,025	7,535	745	1,295	655	1,340
177	Migrants	13,305	11,495	1,200	1,620	1,125	2,050
178	Internal migrants	12,125	11,020	1,160	1,595	1,120	1,855
179	Intraprovincial migrants	11,225	10,425	1,095	1,585	1,080	1,745
180	Interprovincial migrants	900	595	60	15	40	110
181	External migrants	1,185	475	35	20	0	195
182	**Total population 15 years and over**	**71,985**	**54,065**	**5,405**	**7,790**	**5,310**	**9,400**
	Highest certificate, diploma or degree[37]						
183	No certificate, diploma or degree	21,190	14,895	1,805	2,545	1,675	2,035
184	Certificate, diploma or degree	50,795	39,170	3,595	5,245	3,630	7,370
185	High school certificate or equivalent[38]	20,735	14,055	1,330	2,115	1,170	2,550
186	Apprenticeship or trades certificate or diploma	6,585	6,180	615	785	610	1,100
187	College, CEGEP or other non-university certificate or diploma[39]	13,660	11,415	1,105	1,510	1,080	2,230
188	University certificate or diploma below bachelor level[40]	1,935	1,505	120	175	155	295
189	University certificate or degree[41]	7,875	6,005	425	665	615	1,190
190	Bachelor's degree	5,210	3,890	295	410	395	825
191	University certificate or diploma above bachelor level	1,050	1,045	80	100	130	180
192	Degree in medicine, dentistry, veterinary medicine or optometry	240	160	10	10	15	40
193	Master's degree	1,170	805	30	120	55	145
194	Earned doctorate	210	100	0	15	20	0
195	**Total population 15 years and over with postsecondary qualifications**	**30,060**	**25,110**	**2,270**	**3,130**	**2,460**	**4,820**
	Major field of study - Classification of Instructional Programs, 2000[42]						
196	Education	2,140	2,265	235	265	315	365
197	Visual and performing arts, and communications technologies	1,125	605	55	55	45	90
198	Humanities	1,515	815	95	100	70	105
199	Social and behavioural sciences and law	2,895	1,800	145	245	195	310
200	Business, management and public administration	5,545	3,695	300	515	330	715
201	Physical and life sciences and technologies	770	785	50	65	70	230
202	Mathematics, computer and information sciences	860	535	35	80	40	85
203	Architecture, engineering, and related technologies	7,240	7,160	585	710	630	1,685
204	Agriculture, natural resources and conservation	530	1,135	190	210	100	110
205	Health, parks, recreation and fitness	5,070	4,355	390	555	460	800
206	Personal, protective and transportation services	2,300	1,945	190	325	195	325
207	Other fields of study[43]	65	0	0	0	0	0
	Location of study[44]						
208	Inside Canada	26,455	23,005	2,145	2,940	2,295	4,315
209	Outside Canada	3,605	2,105	125	195	160	505
210	**Total population 15 years and over**	**71,985**	**54,065**	**5,405**	**7,790**	**5,310**	**9,400**
	Unpaid work						
211	Males 15 years and over	34,335	26,755	2,675	3,860	2,655	4,640
212	Reported unpaid work[45]	31,210	24,670	2,530	3,540	2,390	4,285
213	Housework and child care and care or assistance to seniors	2,715	2,190	240	415	170	280
214	Housework and child care only	8,850	5,985	610	875	685	1,105

Note: See symbols and abbreviations in the introductory material and see reference material at the end of the publication.

Certaines caractéristiques des divisions de recensement et des subdivisions de recensement – Données intégrales et données-échantillon (20 %), Ontario, Recensement de 2006 (suite)

Neyaas-hiinigmiing 27, IRI ◆◆◇◇	Northern Bruce Peninsula, MU ◆◇	Saugeen 29, IRI ◆◆◇◇	Saugeen Shores, T ◆◇	South Bruce, MU	South Bruce Peninsula, T ◆◇	Caractéristiques	N°
						Caractéristiques de la population	
580	**3,805**	**740**	**11,475**	**5,870**	**8,200**	**Population totale de 1 an et plus[35]**	164
						Lieu de résidence 1 an auparavant (mobilité)	
535	3,305	680	10,190	5,350	7,470	Personnes n'ayant pas déménagé	165
45	500	65	1,290	520	735	Personnes ayant déménagé	166
20	115	35	690	125	355	Non-migrants	167
25	385	25	600	395	375	Migrants	168
25	390	20	570	390	370	Migrants internes	169
25	385	25	485	395	355	Migrants infraprovinciaux	170
0	0	0	80	0	10	Migrants interprovinciaux	171
0	0	0	25	0	10	Migrants externes	172
550	**3,725**	**690**	**11,145**	**5,575**	**7,950**	**Population totale de 5 ans et plus[36]**	173
						Lieu de résidence 5 ans auparavant (mobilité)	
400	2,560	520	7,350	4,325	5,470	Personnes n'ayant pas déménagé	174
150	1,165	175	3,790	1,245	2,475	Personnes ayant déménagé	175
80	255	115	1,575	475	1,000	Non-migrants	176
65	905	60	2,215	770	1,480	Migrants	177
65	885	60	2,085	735	1,445	Migrants internes	178
70	770	60	1,900	725	1,395	Migrants infraprovinciaux	179
0	115	10	185	10	45	Migrants interprovinciaux	180
0	20	0	130	35	30	Migrants externes	181
455	**3,390**	**540**	**9,955**	**4,700**	**7,130**	**Population totale de 15 ans et plus**	182
						Plus haut certificat, diplôme ou grade[37]	
170	905	215	1,990	1,670	1,900	Aucun certificat, diplôme ou grade	183
285	2,480	325	7,970	3,035	5,230	Certificat, diplôme ou grade	184
80	930	95	2,545	1,345	1,900	Diplôme d'études secondaires ou l'équivalent[38]	185
50	410	65	1,040	530	965	Certificat ou diplôme d'apprenti ou d'une école de métiers	186
105	625	130	2,365	800	1,465	Certificat ou diplôme d'un collège, d'un cégep ou d'un autre établissement d'enseignement non universitaire[39]	187
15	105	20	355	70	200	Certificat ou diplôme universitaire inférieur au baccalauréat[40]	188
40	420	10	1,660	285	695	Certificat ou grade universitaire[41]	189
25	270	10	1,080	225	355	Baccalauréat	190
10	70	0	275	30	165	Certificat ou diplôme universitaire supérieur au baccalauréat	191
0	0	0	70	0	0	Diplôme en médecine, en art dentaire, en médecine vétérinaire ou en optométrie	192
0	45	0	205	35	160	Maîtrise	193
0	30	0	30	0	10	Doctorat acquis	194
200	**1,555**	**230**	**5,420**	**1,690**	**3,330**	**Population totale de 15 ans et plus avec titres du niveau postsecondaire**	195
						Principal domaine d'études - Classification des programmes d'enseignement, 2000[42]	
15	185	15	440	115	310	Éducation	196
0	45	10	120	35	150	Arts visuels et d'interprétation, et technologie des communications	197
15	80	10	190	50	105	Sciences humaines	198
35	120	25	370	75	280	Sciences sociales et de comportements, et droit	199
35	190	20	820	310	455	Commerce, gestion et administration publique	200
0	55	0	270	10	35	Sciences physiques et de la vie, et technologies	201
10	25	10	170	40	55	Mathématiques, informatique et sciences de l'information	202
55	390	75	1,595	500	935	Architecture, génie et services connexes	203
0	60	0	175	140	145	Agriculture, ressources naturelles et conservation	204
25	290	45	865	295	625	Santé, parcs, récréation et conditionnement physique	205
20	110	30	400	120	240	Services personnels, de protection et de transport	206
0	0	0	0	0	0	Autres domaines d'études[43]	207
						Lieu des études[44]	
205	1,310	225	4,895	1,600	3,080	À l'intérieur du Canada	208
0	245	0	525	90	245	À l'extérieur du Canada	209
455	**3,390**	**540**	**9,955**	**4,700**	**7,130**	**Population totale de 15 ans et plus**	210
						Travail non rémunéré	
215	1,685	275	4,845	2,390	3,505	Hommes de 15 ans et plus	211
200	1,525	260	4,475	2,215	3,250	Travail non rémunéré déclaré[45]	212
25	125	60	315	215	340	Travaux ménagers et soins aux enfants et soins ou aide aux personnes âgées	213
75	225	60	1,060	675	620	Travaux ménagers et soins aux enfants seulement	214

Nota : Voir les symboles et les abréviations dans les documents d'introduction et voir les documents de référence à la fin de la publication.

Selected characteristics for census divisions and census subdivisions – 100% data and 20% sample data, Ontario, 2006 Census (continued)

No.	Characteristics	Brantford, CY	**Bruce CD/DR** ◆◇	Arran-Elderslie, MU	Brockton, MU	Huron-Kinloss, TP ◆◇	Kincardine, MU
	Population characteristics						
	Unpaid work (continued)						
215	Housework and care or assistance to seniors only	2,800	2,630	280	420	225	380
216	Child care and care or assistance to seniors only	30	35	0	15	0	0
217	Housework only	16,210	13,605	1,375	1,800	1,235	2,485
218	Child care only	355	170	15	10	50	35
219	Care or assistance to seniors only	250	50	10	10	20	0
220	Females 15 years and over	37,650	27,310	2,725	3,925	2,655	4,760
221	Reported unpaid work[45]	35,375	25,955	2,580	3,770	2,535	4,540
222	Housework and child care and care or assistance to seniors	4,575	3,470	420	670	275	550
223	Housework and child care only	11,040	6,575	660	995	755	1,175
224	Housework and care or assistance to seniors only	3,560	3,265	325	485	345	490
225	Child care and care or assistance to seniors only	30	10	0	0	0	0
226	Housework only	15,905	12,520	1,170	1,615	1,135	2,305
227	Child care only	170	70	10	0	10	10
228	Care or assistance to seniors only	100	45	0	0	15	10
	Labour force activity						
229	Males 15 years and over	34,335	26,755	2,680	3,860	2,655	4,640
230	In the labour force	24,680	18,690	1,900	2,855	1,885	3,260
231	Employed	23,130	17,760	1,810	2,740	1,840	3,085
232	Unemployed	1,550	930	90	110	45	170
233	Not in the labour force	9,655	8,065	780	1,005	765	1,380
234	Participation rate	71.9	69.9	70.9	74.0	71.0	70.3
235	Employment rate	67.4	66.4	67.5	71.0	69.3	66.5
236	Unemployment rate	6.3	5.0	4.7	3.9	2.4	5.2
237	Females 15 years and over	37,650	27,310	2,725	3,925	2,655	4,760
238	In the labour force	23,150	15,935	1,625	2,475	1,515	2,760
239	Employed	21,505	15,035	1,540	2,365	1,440	2,635
240	Unemployed	1,645	905	85	110	75	125
241	Not in the labour force	14,505	11,375	1,105	1,450	1,140	2,000
242	Participation rate	61.5	58.3	59.6	63.1	57.1	58.0
243	Employment rate	57.1	55.1	56.5	60.3	54.2	55.4
244	Unemployment rate	7.1	5.7	5.2	4.4	5.0	4.5
245	Both sexes - Participation rate	66.4	64.0	65.1	68.5	64.1	64.0
246	15 to 24 years	71.2	76.4	72.3	74.5	79.9	76.3
247	25 years and over	65.5	61.7	63.7	67.2	60.8	61.6
248	Both sexes - Employment rate	62.0	60.7	62.0	65.6	61.9	60.9
249	15 to 24 years	61.2	67.2	66.3	67.9	72.8	65.8
250	25 years and over	62.2	59.4	61.2	65.2	59.6	59.9
251	Both sexes - Unemployment rate	6.7	5.3	4.8	4.2	3.5	4.9
252	15 to 24 years	14.1	12.0	8.3	9.3	8.8	13.8
253	25 years and over	5.0	3.7	4.0	3.0	1.9	2.8
254	**Total labour force 15 years and over**	**47,825**	**34,625**	**3,520**	**5,335**	**3,400**	**6,020**
	Industry - North American Industry Classification System 2002						
255	Industry - Not applicable[46]	720	355	30	30	15	85
256	All industries[47]	47,100	34,265	3,490	5,300	3,385	5,935
257	11 Agriculture, forestry, fishing and hunting	385	3,095	515	580	540	450
258	21 Mining and oil and gas extraction	45	280	10	0	10	10
259	22 Utilities	255	4,340	270	305	425	1,500
260	23 Construction	2,745	2,545	365	445	235	225
261	31-33 Manufacturing	10,540	3,115	360	740	310	265
262	41 Wholesale trade	2,460	920	85	260	60	125
263	44-45 Retail trade	5,175	4,145	385	620	375	725
264	48-49 Transportation and warehousing	2,145	1,185	150	190	150	155
265	51 Information and cultural industries	570	400	15	45	30	130
266	52 Finance and insurance	1,070	550	65	95	40	70
267	53 Real estate and rental and leasing	740	395	15	60	20	60
268	54 Professional, scientific and technical services	1,665	1,320	105	200	100	280
269	55 Management of companies and enterprises	60	15	0	0	0	10
270	56 Administrative and support, waste management and remediation services	3,290	770	75	100	60	120
271	61 Educational services	2,925	1,980	210	330	205	250
272	62 Health care and social assistance	5,005	3,100	320	520	275	445

Note: See symbols and abbreviations in the introductory material and see reference material at the end of the publication.

Certaines caractéristiques des divisions de recensement et des subdivisions de recensement – Données intégrales et données-échantillon (20 %), Ontario, Recensement de 2006 (suite)

Neyaas-hiinigmiing 27, IRI ◆◆◇◇	Northern Bruce Peninsula, MU ◆◇	Saugeen 29, IRI ◆◆◇◇	Saugeen Shores, T ◆◇	South Bruce, MU	South Bruce Peninsula, T ◆◇	Caractéristiques	Nº
						Caractéristiques de la population	
						Travail non rémunéré (suite)	
35	255	50	460	185	340	Travaux ménagers et soins ou aide aux personnes âgées seulement	215
0	0	0	0	0	20	Soins aux enfants et soins ou aide aux personnes âgées seulement	216
65	920	80	2,610	1,120	1,905	Travaux ménagers seulement	217
0	10	10	10	25	20	Soins aux enfants seulement	218
0	0	10	15	0	0	Soins ou aide aux personnes âgées seulement	219
235	1,705	265	5,105	2,310	3,625	Femmes de 15 ans et plus	220
225	1,630	255	4,795	2,190	3,425	Travail non rémunéré déclaré[45]	221
45	195	80	465	305	465	Travaux ménagers et soins aux enfants et soins ou aide aux personnes âgées	222
95	235	85	1,090	745	735	Travaux ménagers et soins aux enfants seulement	223
20	305	35	560	225	475	Travaux ménagers et soins ou aide aux personnes âgées seulement	224
0	0	0	0	0	0	Soins aux enfants et soins ou aide aux personnes âgées seulement	225
65	880	45	2,660	910	1,725	Travaux ménagers seulement	226
0	10	0	10	0	10	Soins aux enfants seulement	227
10	0	0	10	0	10	Soins ou aide aux personnes âgées seulement	228
						Activité	
220	1,685	275	4,845	2,390	3,505	Hommes de 15 ans et plus	229
140	915	200	3,365	1,945	2,215	Population active	230
105	850	165	3,135	1,890	2,125	Personnes occupées	231
35	60	35	235	55	90	Chômeurs	232
80	775	75	1,475	440	1,285	Inactifs	233
63.6	54.3	72.7	69.5	81.4	63.2	Taux d'activité	234
47.7	50.4	60.0	64.7	79.1	60.6	Taux d'emploi	235
25.0	6.6	17.5	7.0	2.8	4.1	Taux de chômage	236
235	1,700	260	5,105	2,315	3,620	Femmes de 15 ans et plus	237
135	840	175	2,870	1,635	1,905	Population active	238
120	750	135	2,690	1,580	1,780	Personnes occupées	239
15	95	40	180	50	130	Chômeuses	240
105	860	85	2,235	675	1,715	Inactives	241
57.4	49.4	67.3	56.2	70.6	52.6	Taux d'activité	242
51.1	44.1	51.9	52.7	68.3	49.2	Taux d'emploi	243
11.1	11.3	22.9	6.3	3.1	6.8	Taux de chômage	244
60.4	51.6	71.0	62.6	76.3	57.9	Les deux sexes - Taux d'activité	245
71.4	64.4	60.0	78.7	83.9	76.4	15 à 24 ans	246
59.7	50.2	74.7	59.8	74.5	55.1	25 ans et plus	247
49.5	47.1	55.6	58.5	73.9	54.8	Les deux sexes - Taux d'emploi	248
57.1	49.3	45.0	64.6	75.9	70.7	15 à 24 ans	249
48.7	46.9	59.8	57.4	73.5	52.5	25 ans et plus	250
18.2	8.9	21.1	6.7	2.9	5.3	Les deux sexes - Taux de chômage	251
0.0	21.3	27.3	17.9	9.0	7.9	15 à 24 ans	252
20.0	6.9	20.0	4.0	1.2	4.8	25 ans et plus	253
275	**1,750**	**380**	**6,235**	**3,585**	**4,130**	**Population active totale de 15 ans et plus**	254
						Industrie - Système de classification des industries de l'Amérique du Nord de 2002	
10	25	15	85	0	50	Industrie - Sans objet[46]	255
260	1,725	360	6,150	3,580	4,075	Toutes les industries[47]	256
20	90	10	125	620	150	11 Agriculture, foresterie, pêche et chasse	257
0	80	15	10	15	135	21 Extraction minière et extraction de pétrole et de gaz	258
10	15	20	1,600	90	105	22 Services publics	259
25	135	35	395	355	330	23 Construction	260
10	160	0	150	650	455	31-33 Fabrication	261
0	45	10	80	170	80	41 Commerce de gros	262
10	220	20	795	360	635	44-45 Commerce de détail	263
0	70	10	220	130	100	48-49 Transport et entreposage	264
0	15	10	75	40	50	51 Industrie de l'information et industrie culturelle	265
0	10	0	65	95	105	52 Finance et assurances	266
0	30	0	110	15	75	53 Services immobiliers et services de location et de location à bail	267
10	85	10	310	55	175	54 Services professionnels, scientifiques et techniques	268
0	0	0	0	0	0	55 Gestion de sociétés et d'entreprises	269
10	45	25	95	85	150	56 Services administratifs, services de soutien, services de gestion des déchets et services d'assainissement	270
15	125	25	400	190	225	61 Services d'enseignement	271
40	145	60	590	265	425	62 Soins de santé et assistance sociale	272

Nota : Voir les symboles et les abréviations dans les documents d'introduction et voir les documents de référence à la fin de la publication.

Selected characteristics for census divisions and census subdivisions – 100% data and 20% sample data, Ontario, 2006 Census (continued)

No.	Characteristics	Brantford, CY	**Bruce CD/DR** ◆◊	Arran-Elderslie, MU	Brockton, MU	Huron-Kinloss, TP ◆◊	Kincardine, MU
	Population characteristics						
	Industry - North American Industry Classification System 2002 (continued)						
273	71 Arts, entertainment and recreation	1,315	785	100	100	90	90
274	72 Accommodation and food services	3,260	2,620	175	240	240	525
275	81 Other services (except public administration)	2,065	1,600	170	290	115	285
276	91 Public administration	1,355	1,110	105	170	85	190
	Class of worker						
277	Class of worker - Not applicable[46]	725	355	30	30	15	85
278	All classes of worker[47]	47,100	34,265	3,490	5,295	3,385	5,935
279	Paid workers	44,410	29,610	2,885	4,695	2,755	5,240
280	Employees	43,425	28,410	2,765	4,530	2,665	5,025
281	Self-employed (incorporated)	985	1,200	120	160	90	215
282	Self-employed (unincorporated)	2,635	4,350	565	550	540	625
283	Unpaid family workers	55	310	35	55	90	65
	Occupation - National Occupational Classification for Statistics 2006						
284	Male labour force 15 years and over	24,680	18,690	1,900	2,855	1,885	3,265
285	Occupation - Not applicable[46]	260	140	10	15	0	35
286	All occupations[47]	24,415	18,555	1,885	2,840	1,880	3,225
287	A Management occupations	2,280	1,735	135	240	160	380
288	B Business, finance and administrative occupations	2,325	825	60	120	95	170
289	C Natural and applied sciences and related occupations	1,400	1,510	65	140	140	430
290	D Health occupations	405	235	25	45	25	15
291	E Occupations in social science, education, government service and religion	895	585	30	70	30	125
292	F Occupations in art, culture, recreation and sport	420	260	20	10	25	35
293	G Sales and service occupations	4,785	2,750	205	445	220	480
294	H Trades, transport and equipment operators and related occupations	7,425	6,555	750	1,015	620	1,075
295	I Occupations unique to primary industry	575	2,620	455	440	430	355
296	J Occupations unique to processing, manufacturing and utilities	3,900	1,470	130	315	140	160
297	Female labour force 15 years and over	23,145	15,935	1,620	2,475	1,510	2,760
298	Occupation - Not applicable[46]	460	220	20	15	10	50
299	All occupations[47]	22,685	15,715	1,605	2,455	1,505	2,705
300	A Management occupations	1,480	1,010	50	130	90	200
301	B Business, finance and administrative occupations	5,410	3,280	415	515	280	625
302	C Natural and applied sciences and related occupations	375	340	25	55	45	65
303	D Health occupations	2,490	1,750	150	275	170	305
304	E Occupations in social science, education, government service and religion	2,320	1,625	155	245	135	205
305	F Occupations in art, culture, recreation and sport	370	445	30	40	45	110
306	G Sales and service occupations	7,375	5,335	545	785	580	875
307	H Trades, transport and equipment operators and related occupations	765	460	40	45	30	125
308	I Occupations unique to primary industry	205	780	100	155	85	110
309	J Occupations unique to processing, manufacturing and utilities	1,895	695	90	215	45	80
310	**Total employed labour force 15 years and over**	**44,630**	**32,790**	**3,345**	**5,110**	**3,280**	**5,720**
	Place of work status						
311	Males	23,130	17,760	1,810	2,740	1,845	3,090
312	Usual place of work	19,270	12,745	1,045	1,980	1,270	2,325
313	At home	935	2,540	425	400	400	385
314	Outside Canada	110	65	0	15	0	15
315	No fixed workplace address	2,810	2,415	340	345	175	365
316	Females	21,505	15,035	1,540	2,365	1,440	2,635
317	Usual place of work	19,370	12,530	1,300	1,930	1,195	2,185
318	At home	1,085	1,780	200	285	225	280
319	Outside Canada	25	30	0	0	0	20
320	No fixed workplace address	1,025	690	30	150	20	155

Note: See symbols and abbreviations in the introductory material and see reference material at the end of the publication.

Certaines caractéristiques des divisions de recensement et des subdivisions de recensement – Données intégrales et données-échantillon (20 %), Ontario, Recensement de 2006 (suite)

Neyaas-hiinigmiing 27, IRI ◆◆◇◇	Northern Bruce Peninsula, MU ◆◇	Saugeen 29, IRI ◆◆◇◇	Saugeen Shores, T ◆◇	South Bruce, MU	South Bruce Peninsula, T ◆◇	Caractéristiques	Nº
						Caractéristiques de la population	
						Industrie - Système de classification des industries de l'Amérique du Nord de 2002 (suite)	
15	105	20	130	40	95	71 Arts, spectacles et loisirs	273
20	240	15	530	230	390	72 Hébergement et services de restauration	274
0	75	10	285	125	235	81 Autres services (sauf les administrations publiques)	275
75	20	85	160	40	170	91 Administrations publiques	276
						Catégorie de travailleurs	
15	25	15	85	0	50	Catégorie de travailleurs - Sans objet[46]	277
260	1,725	365	6,150	3,580	4,075	Toutes les catégories de travailleurs[47]	278
225	1,315	345	5,560	3,140	3,445	Travailleurs rémunérés	279
230	1,235	340	5,425	2,915	3,280	Employés	280
0	80	0	135	225	160	Travailleurs autonomes (entreprise constituée en société)	281
35	385	20	585	410	620	Travailleurs autonomes (entreprise non constituée en société)	282
0	25	0	0	25	15	Travailleurs familiaux non rémunérés	283
						Profession - Classification nationale des professions pour statistiques de 2006	
140	915	205	3,365	1,945	2,215	Hommes actifs de 15 ans et plus	284
10	0	0	35	0	25	Profession - Sans objet[46]	285
130	910	195	3,330	1,950	2,190	Toutes les professions[47]	286
10	140	10	375	90	200	A Gestion	287
10	20	10	155	75	110	B Affaires, finance et administration	288
0	25	15	475	45	170	C Sciences naturelles et appliquées et professions apparentées	289
0	20	0	70	15	15	D Secteur de la santé	290
10	35	10	120	35	115	E Sciences sociales, enseignement, administration publique et religion	291
0	50	0	60	15	50	F Arts, culture, sports et loisirs	292
15	120	35	610	250	370	G Ventes et services	293
55	365	75	1,105	695	790	H Métiers, transport et machinerie	294
25	100	35	170	440	175	I Professions propres au secteur primaire	295
0	30	15	195	290	185	J Transformation, fabrication et services d'utilité publique	296
130	840	180	2,870	1,635	1,905	Femmes actives de 15 ans et plus	297
10	20	15	50	10	25	Profession - Sans objet[46]	298
130	815	170	2,820	1,630	1,885	Toutes les professions[47]	299
10	95	0	180	80	165	A Gestion	300
20	125	25	640	285	350	B Affaires, finance et administration	301
0	25	0	85	0	25	C Sciences naturelles et appliquées et professions apparentées	302
10	95	20	385	140	205	D Secteur de la santé	303
25	80	45	380	120	230	E Sciences sociales, enseignement, administration publique et religion	304
10	15	0	105	30	50	F Arts, culture, sports et loisirs	305
35	280	55	930	555	700	G Ventes et services	306
10	30	10	70	60	50	H Métiers, transport et machinerie	307
0	40	0	40	215	30	I Professions propres au secteur primaire	308
10	35	0	10	135	75	J Transformation, fabrication et services d'utilité publique	309
225	**1,595**	**300**	**5,820**	**3,475**	**3,905**	**Population active occupée totale de 15 ans et plus**	310
						Catégorie de lieu de travail	
110	845	160	3,130	1,895	2,125	Hommes	311
80	515	115	2,630	1,260	1,515	Lieu habituel de travail	312
10	160	15	145	365	245	À domicile	313
0	10	0	20	10	0	En dehors du Canada	314
20	170	35	335	265	365	Sans adresse de travail fixe	315
120	745	135	2,685	1,580	1,780	Femmes	316
105	585	130	2,440	1,245	1,425	Lieu habituel de travail	317
10	125	0	190	250	210	À domicile	318
0	0	0	0	0	10	En dehors du Canada	319
10	35	0	60	85	140	Sans adresse de travail fixe	320

Nota : Voir les symboles et les abréviations dans les documents d'introduction et voir les documents de référence à la fin de la publication.

Selected characteristics for census divisions and census subdivisions – 100% data and 20% sample data, Ontario, 2006 Census (continued)

No.	Characteristics	Brantford, CY	**Bruce CD/DR** ◆◇	Arran-Elderslie, MU	Brockton, MU	Huron-Kinloss, TP ◆◇	Kincardine, MU
	Population characteristics						
321	**Total employed labour force 15 years and over with usual place of work or no fixed workplace address**	**42,475**	**28,375**	**2,720**	**4,410**	**2,660**	**5,030**
	Mode of transportation						
322	Males	22,085	15,155	1,385	2,330	1,445	2,690
323	Car, truck, van, as driver	17,720	12,595	1,235	2,045	1,220	2,230
324	Car, truck, van, as passenger	2,090	1,105	90	120	135	190
325	Public transit	695	200	0	0	15	70
326	Walked	810	795	50	115	45	130
327	All other modes	765	460	10	45	30	75
328	Females	20,390	13,225	1,335	2,080	1,215	2,340
329	Car, truck, van, as driver	15,285	10,145	1,015	1,685	995	1,770
330	Car, truck, van, as passenger	2,410	1,240	125	180	70	230
331	Public transit	1,055	150	15	15	10	25
332	Walked	1,270	1,385	170	160	110	240
333	All other modes	370	305	10	40	25	65
334	**Total population 15 years and over who worked since January 1, 2005**	**50,810**	**37,790**	**3,880**	**5,865**	**3,675**	**6,575**
	Language used most often at work						
335	Single responses	50,610	37,695	3,875	5,860	3,665	6,565
336	English	50,275	37,340	3,795	5,845	3,515	6,530
337	French	140	50	10	0	0	10
338	Non-official languages[7]	190	310	65	15	150	35
339	Chinese, n.o.s.[61]	70	0	0	0	0	0
340	Cantonese	0	0	0	0	0	0
341	Other languages[8]	120	310	65	10	150	35
342	Multiple responses	200	95	10	0	15	10
343	English and French	60	20	0	0	0	0
344	English and non-official language	135	70	0	0	10	10
345	French and non-official language	0	0	0	0	10	0
346	English, French and non-official language	10	0	0	0	0	0
	Dwelling and household characteristics						
347	**Total number of occupied private dwellings**	**35,615**	**26,320**	**2,615**	**3,735**	**2,465**	**4,605**
	Housing tenure						
348	Owned	24,545	21,765	2,160	3,020	2,100	3,765
349	Rented	11,070	4,555	450	715	365	835
350	Band housing	0	0	0	0	0	0
	Structural type of dwelling						
351	Single-detached house	21,790	22,275	2,075	3,050	2,245	3,755
352	Semi-detached house	1,960	510	70	75	10	110
353	Row house	2,955	635	15	95	0	230
354	Apartment, duplex	1,425	205	5	45	40	50
355	Apartment, building that has five or more storeys	3,680	15	0	0	0	0
356	Apartment, building that has fewer than five storeys	3,650	2,320	405	410	120	370
357	Other single-attached house	135	280	35	50	45	60
358	Movable dwelling[48]	20	90	10	10	15	5
	Condition of dwelling						
359	Regular maintenance only	24,395	16,520	1,540	2,295	1,490	3,120
360	Minor repairs	8,885	7,730	775	1,150	805	1,210
361	Major repairs	2,330	2,075	300	285	175	275
	Period of construction						
362	Before 1946	8,205	8,140	1,345	1,355	925	1,210
363	1946 to 1960	6,255	1,940	165	435	95	275
364	1961 to 1970	4,685	2,485	175	360	165	345
365	1971 to 1980	6,375	5,700	360	605	570	1,545
366	1981 to 1985	1,900	1,605	85	230	110	315
367	1986 to 1990	2,580	2,185	100	260	120	350
368	1991 to 1995	2,185	1,800	180	215	190	290
369	1996 to 2000	1,365	835	90	100	115	80
370	2001 to 2006[49]	2,065	1,630	105	165	175	190

Note: See symbols and abbreviations in the introductory material and see reference material at the end of the publication.

Certaines caractéristiques des divisions de recensement et des subdivisions de recensement – Données intégrales et données-échantillon (20 %), Ontario, Recensement de 2006 (suite)

Neyaashiinigmiing 27, IRI ◆◆◇◇	Northern Bruce Peninsula, MU ◆◇	Saugeen 29, IRI ◆◆◇◇	Saugeen Shores, T ◆◇	South Bruce, MU	South Bruce Peninsula, T ◆◇	Caractéristiques	N°
						Caractéristiques de la population	
205	**1,305**	**285**	**5,460**	**2,860**	**3,445**	**Population active occupée totale de 15 ans et plus ayant un lieu habituel de travail ou sans adresse de travail fixe**	321
						Mode de transport	
95	685	150	2,965	1,525	1,880	Hommes	322
60	550	90	2,395	1,230	1,545	Automobile, camion ou fourgonnette, en tant que conducteur	323
15	35	40	160	160	150	Automobile, camion ou fourgonnette, en tant que passager	324
0	0	0	60	35	20	Transport en commun	325
0	65	10	205	55	105	À pied	326
15	35	10	140	35	55	Tous les autres modes	327
105	620	135	2,495	1,330	1,565	Femmes	328
75	415	85	1,730	1,155	1,210	Automobile, camion ou fourgonnette, en tant que conductrice	329
15	50	25	310	65	165	Automobile, camion ou fourgonnette, en tant que passagère	330
0	0	0	60	10	0	Transport en commun	331
10	130	15	315	65	170	À pied	332
10	25	0	80	35	15	Tous les autres modes	333
290	**2,025**	**395**	**6,765**	**3,760**	**4,565**	**Population totale de 15 ans et plus ayant travaillé depuis le 1er janvier 2005**	334
						Langue utilisée le plus souvent au travail	
285	2,020	390	6,760	3,735	4,530	Réponses uniques	335
285	2,015	385	6,745	3,690	4,535	Anglais	336
0	0	0	15	0	0	Français	337
0	0	10	0	35	0	Langues non officielles[7]	338
0	0	0	0	0	0	Chinois, n.d.a.[61]	339
0	0	0	0	0	0	Cantonais	340
0	0	0	0	35	0	Autres langues[8]	341
0	0	0	0	30	30	Réponses multiples	342
0	0	0	0	15	0	Anglais et français	343
0	0	0	0	15	30	Anglais et langue non officielle	344
0	0	0	0	0	0	Français et langue non officielle	345
0	0	0	0	0	0	Anglais, français et langue non officielle	346
						Caractéristiques des logements et des ménages	
240	**1,730**	**280**	**4,920**	**2,155**	**3,580**	**Nombre total de logements privés occupés**	347
						Mode d'occupation	
185	1,535	235	4,035	1,775	2,945	Possédé	348
60	195	40	885	380	630	Loué	349
0	0	0	0	0	0	Logement de bande	350
						Type de construction résidentielle	
230	1,655	270	3,865	1,935	3,200	Maison individuelle non attenante	351
0	5	0	200	15	20	Maison jumelée	352
0	15	0	235	35	20	Maison en rangée	353
0	10	0	15	10	30	Appartement, duplex	354
0	0	0	15	0	0	Appartement, immeuble de cinq étages ou plus	355
15	45	10	535	140	265	Appartement, immeuble de moins de cinq étages	356
0	0	0	50	10	40	Autre maison individuelle attenante	357
0	15	0	10	10	10	Logement mobile[48]	358
						État du logement	
125	1,095	90	3,285	1,325	2,155	Entretien régulier seulement	359
50	510	75	1,350	670	1,125	Réparations mineures	360
65	130	110	280	165	295	Réparations majeures	361
						Période de construction	
10	300	10	840	1,135	1,020	Avant 1946	362
10	190	10	335	110	305	1946 à 1960	363
25	185	25	615	120	465	1961 à 1970	364
45	305	55	1,415	255	550	1971 à 1980	365
25	110	30	300	100	285	1981 à 1985	366
25	270	40	505	155	360	1986 à 1990	367
40	135	40	360	90	260	1991 à 1995	368
30	110	20	100	85	105	1996 à 2000	369
40	125	40	450	100	230	2001 à 2006[49]	370

Nota : Voir les symboles et les abréviations dans les documents d'introduction et voir les documents de référence à la fin de la publication.

Selected characteristics for census divisions and census subdivisions – 100% data and 20% sample data, Ontario, 2006 Census (continued)

No.	Characteristics	Brantford, CY	**Bruce CD/DR** ◆◇	Arran-Elderslie, MU	Brockton, MU	Huron-Kinloss, TP ◆◇	Kincardine, MU
	Dwelling and household characteristics						
371	Average number of rooms per dwelling	6.8	7.3	7.1	7.4	7.6	7.6
372	Average number of bedrooms per dwelling	2.7	3.0	3.0	3.0	3.2	3.1
373	Average value of dwelling $	200,319	220,969	183,033	194,452	222,247	239,221
374	**Total number of private households**	**35,605**	**26,325**	**2,610**	**3,740**	**2,470**	**4,585**
	Household size						
375	1 person	9,550	6,540	605	925	560	1,160
376	2 persons	11,770	10,625	985	1,360	1,015	1,870
377	3 persons	5,885	3,510	410	540	305	615
378	4 to 5 persons	7,545	4,975	515	830	485	850
379	6 or more persons	860	675	95	90	110	95
	Household type						
380	One-family households[50]	24,425	19,085	1,945	2,705	1,860	3,295
381	Multiple-family households	555	135	0	30	0	25
382	Non-family households	10,635	7,100	660	995	600	1,280
383	Number of persons in private households	88,630	64,185	6,655	9,420	6,365	10,990
384	Average number of persons in private households	2.5	2.4	2.5	2.5	2.6	2.4
385	Tenant-occupied private non-farm, non-reserve dwellings[51]	11,070	4,405	445	705	350	830
386	Average gross rent $[51]	712	605	549	558	554	734
387	Tenant-occupied households spending 30% or more of household income on gross rent[52]	4,760	1,815	185	335	155	300
388	Tenant-occupied households spending from 30% to 99% of household income on gross rent[52]	4,185	1,640	150	305	150	280
389	Owner-occupied private non-farm, non-reserve dwellings[53]	24,535	20,290	1,990	2,820	1,915	3,630
390	Average owner's major payments $[53]	972	805	845	828	810	809
391	Owner households spending 30% or more of household income on owner's major payments[52]	4,290	2,975	455	395	315	430
392	Owner households spending from 30% to 99% of household income on owner's major payments[52]	3,760	2,500	395	315	265	345
	Census family characteristics						
393	**Total number of census families in private households**	**25,570**	**19,360**	**1,955**	**2,765**	**1,870**	**3,350**
	Family structure and number of children						
394	Total couple families	20,665	17,425	1,760	2,460	1,730	3,035
395	Total families of married couples	17,155	15,375	1,525	2,185	1,560	2,705
396	Without children at home	7,525	8,225	715	1,040	780	1,500
397	With children at home	9,630	7,145	810	1,145	775	1,205
398	1 child	3,565	2,380	295	365	235	380
399	2 children	4,170	3,005	305	470	310	565
400	3 or more children	1,895	1,765	210	310	230	250
401	Total families of common-law couples	3,505	2,050	235	280	170	335
402	Without children at home	1,745	1,205	155	145	125	185
403	With children at home	1,760	845	80	130	50	155
404	1 child	870	395	30	70	30	105
405	2 children	630	290	35	50	15	25
406	3 or more children	265	155	20	10	10	20
407	Total lone-parent families	4,900	1,940	200	300	140	315
408	Female parent	4,005	1,460	140	235	95	250
409	1 child	2,385	885	75	155	70	165
410	2 children	1,145	410	45	50	15	65
411	3 or more children	475	155	15	35	10	20
412	Male parent	895	475	60	65	40	70
413	1 child	605	310	40	30	25	50
414	2 children	230	135	15	25	10	20
415	3 or more children	60	25	0	0	0	0

Note: See symbols and abbreviations in the introductory material and see reference material at the end of the publication.

Certaines caractéristiques des divisions de recensement et des subdivisions de recensement – Données intégrales et données-échantillon (20 %), Ontario, Recensement de 2006 (suite)

Neyaas-hiinigmiing 27, IRI ◆◆◊◊	Northern Bruce Peninsula, MU ◆◊	Saugeen 29, IRI ◆◆◊◊	Saugeen Shores, T ◆◊	South Bruce, MU	South Bruce Peninsula, T ◆◊	Caractéristiques	N°
						Caractéristiques des logements et des ménages	
5.5	6.5	5.7	7.4	7.6	6.8	Nombre moyen de pièces par logement	371
2.7	2.7	2.7	3.0	3.2	2.8	Nombre moyen de chambres à coucher par logement	372
0	222,223	0	252,482	220,822	205,174	Valeur moyenne du logement $	373
245	**1,735**	**280**	**4,925**	**2,155**	**3,585**	**Nombre total de ménages privés**	374
						Taille du ménage	
85	470	75	1,285	450	935	1 personne	375
65	860	80	2,035	755	1,605	2 personnes	376
50	165	35	655	300	425	3 personnes	377
35	225	60	885	545	555	4 à 5 personnes	378
15	20	20	70	105	65	6 personnes ou plus	379
						Genre de ménage	
155	1,195	180	3,530	1,650	2,570	Ménages unifamiliaux[50]	380
10	0	10	20	10	30	Ménages multifamiliaux	381
90	535	85	1,370	500	980	Ménages non familiaux	382
590	3,765	750	11,505	5,930	8,215	Nombre de personnes dans les ménages privés	383
2.5	2.2	2.7	2.3	2.8	2.3	Nombre moyen de personnes dans les ménages privés	384
0	195	0	880	365	630	Ménages locataires dans les logements privés non agricoles hors réserve[51]	385
0	599	0	609	489	621	Loyer brut moyen $[51]	386
0	70	0	390	120	260	Ménages locataires consacrant 30 % ou plus du revenu du ménage au loyer brut[52]	387
0	70	0	350	115	215	Ménages locataires consacrant de 30 % à 99 % du revenu du ménage au loyer brut[52]	388
0	1,500	0	3,990	1,550	2,885	Ménages propriétaires dans les logements privés non agricoles hors réserve[53]	389
0	689	0	891	765	709	Principales dépenses de propriété moyennes $[53]	390
0	255	0	425	250	445	Ménages propriétaires consacrant 30 % ou plus du revenu du ménage aux principales dépenses de propriété[52]	391
0	190	0	380	225	380	Ménages propriétaires consacrant de 30 % à 99 % du revenu du ménage aux principales dépenses de propriété[52]	392
						Caractéristiques des familles de recensement	
155	**1,195**	**205**	**3,575**	**1,660**	**2,630**	**Nombre total de familles de recensement dans les ménages privés**	393
						Structure de la famille et le nombre d'enfants	
115	1,145	120	3,180	1,530	2,340	Total des familles avec conjoints	394
70	1,000	70	2,845	1,370	2,050	Total des familles avec couples mariés	395
35	705	30	1,585	575	1,265	Sans enfants à la maison	396
40	290	40	1,260	800	785	Avec enfants à la maison	397
20	70	15	445	235	310	1 enfant	398
0	150	10	575	270	335	2 enfants	399
15	65	15	240	290	140	3 enfants ou plus	400
40	145	55	335	160	290	Total des familles avec couples en union libre	401
10	105	20	200	95	155	Sans enfants à la maison	402
25	35	35	130	70	135	Avec enfants à la maison	403
15	10	10	50	20	55	1 enfant	404
10	15	10	65	40	30	2 enfants	405
0	0	15	20	0	45	3 enfants ou plus	406
45	50	80	390	130	285	Total des familles monoparentales	407
35	40	65	285	85	235	Parent de sexe féminin	408
20	10	30	185	40	140	1 enfant	409
10	20	20	90	30	70	2 enfants	410
10	10	10	10	15	25	3 enfants ou plus	411
10	10	20	110	40	45	Parent de sexe masculin	412
10	10	15	75	15	40	1 enfant	413
0	0	10	30	15	10	2 enfants	414
0	0	0	10	10	0	3 enfants ou plus	415

Nota : Voir les symboles et les abréviations dans les documents d'introduction et voir les documents de référence à la fin de la publication.

Selected characteristics for census divisions and census subdivisions – 100% data and 20% sample data, Ontario, 2006 Census (continued)

No.	Characteristics	Brantford, CY	Bruce CD/DR ◆◇	Arran-Elderslie, MU	Brockton, MU	Huron-Kinloss, TP ◆◇	Kincardine, MU
	Census family characteristics						
416	**Total number of children at home**	**28,560**	**19,010**	**2,150**	**3,035**	**2,020**	**3,025**
	Age group						
417	Under 6 years	6,235	3,395	420	585	380	535
418	6 to 14 years	10,380	7,015	825	1,110	740	1,100
419	15 to 17 years	3,380	2,645	285	440	285	415
420	18 to 24 years	5,645	4,520	455	680	475	810
421	25 years and over	2,915	1,435	160	220	145	170
422	Average number of children at home per census family[54]	1.1	1.0	1.1	1.1	1.1	0.9
423	**Total number of persons in private households**	**88,640**	**64,155**	**6,655**	**9,415**	**6,350**	**11,005**
	Census family status and living arrangements						
424	Number of persons not in census families	13,845	8,365	790	1,150	735	1,590
425	Living with relatives[55]	1,865	755	85	70	50	115
426	Living with non-relatives only	2,440	1,020	100	165	115	300
427	Living alone	9,545	6,585	605	915	565	1,170
428	Number of census family persons	74,795	55,795	5,870	8,260	5,620	9,415
429	Average number of persons per census family	2.9	2.9	3.0	3.0	3.0	2.8
430	**Total number of persons aged 65 years and over**	**12,135**	**11,080**	**960**	**1,375**	**1,030**	**1,805**
431	Number of persons not in census families aged 65 years and over	4,510	3,375	335	445	300	510
432	Living with relatives[55]	585	280	20	30	10	30
433	Living with non-relatives only	195	115	15	0	0	15
434	Living alone	3,725	2,985	295	405	285	460
435	Number of census family persons aged 65 years and over	7,625	7,700	630	935	725	1,290
	Economic family characteristics						
436	**Total number of economic families in private households**	**25,265**	**19,360**	**1,965**	**2,750**	**1,870**	**3,325**
	Size of family						
437	2 persons	11,335	10,335	960	1,310	985	1,805
438	3 persons	5,755	3,420	405	530	305	600
439	4 persons	5,260	3,450	355	565	330	605
440	5 or more persons	2,915	2,155	250	345	250	315
441	Total number of persons in economic families	76,660	56,550	5,950	8,330	5,670	9,535
442	Average number of persons per economic family	3.0	3.0	3.0	3.0	3.0	3.0
443	Total number of persons not in economic families	11,980	7,605	710	1,085	680	1,470
	2005 income characteristics						
444	**Population 15 years and over**	**71,985**	**54,060**	**5,405**	**7,785**	**5,310**	**9,400**
	Sex and total income groups in 2005						
445	Without income	3,040	1,870	175	275	265	325
446	With income	68,945	52,190	5,230	7,505	5,045	9,075
447	Under $1,000[56]	1,800	2,170	285	315	150	450
448	$1,000 to $2,999	2,135	1,995	160	270	195	345
449	$3,000 to $4,999	2,295	2,090	190	240	285	335
450	$5,000 to $6,999	2,495	2,420	245	375	255	415
451	$7,000 to $9,999	3,750	3,330	375	410	325	605
452	$10,000 to $11,999	3,125	2,355	335	385	215	410
453	$12,000 to $14,999	4,435	3,080	300	420	295	460
454	$15,000 to $19,999	7,255	5,400	690	775	515	750
455	$20,000 to $24,999	6,060	3,885	375	475	355	595
456	$25,000 to $29,999	5,210	3,730	435	625	430	505
457	$30,000 to $34,999	5,290	3,240	385	580	315	395
458	$35,000 to $39,999	4,635	2,890	285	550	205	390
459	$40,000 to $44,999	3,920	2,330	220	405	215	300
460	$45,000 to $49,999	3,090	1,850	115	310	165	345
461	$50,000 to $59,999	4,585	2,855	245	395	315	515
462	$60,000 and over	8,855	8,550	570	975	810	2,240
463	Median income $[57]	26,073	24,142	20,489	25,570	24,080	26,213
464	Average income $[57]	32,842	34,590	28,266	31,901	33,722	40,827
465	Standard error of average income $[57]	266	379	754	710	915	897

Note: See symbols and abbreviations in the introductory material and see reference material at the end of the publication.

Certaines caractéristiques des divisions de recensement et des subdivisions de recensement – Données intégrales et données-échantillon (20 %), Ontario, Recensement de 2006 (suite)

Neyaas-hiinigmiing 27, IRI ◆◆◇◇	Northern Bruce Peninsula, MU ◆◇	Saugeen 29, IRI ◆◆◇◇	Saugeen Shores, T ◆◇	South Bruce, MU	South Bruce Peninsula, T ◆◇	Caractéristiques	Nº
						Caractéristiques des familles de recensement	
205	**790**	**315**	**3,165**	**2,150**	**2,150**	**Nombre total d'enfants à la maison**	416
						Groupes d'âge	
50	105	70	450	410	395	Moins de 6 ans	417
90	315	140	1,150	800	750	6 à 14 ans	418
30	130	30	440	310	280	15 à 17 ans	419
25	165	40	880	515	465	18 à 24 ans	420
20	70	25	245	120	265	25 ans et plus	421
1.3	0.7	1.5	0.9	1.3	0.8	Nombre moyen d'enfants à la maison par famille de recensement[54]	422
590	**3,750**	**750**	**11,495**	**5,930**	**8,215**	**Nombre total de personnes dans les ménages privés**	423
						Situation des particuliers dans la famille de recensement et des particuliers dans le ménage	
115	620	115	1,575	585	1,090	Nombre de personnes hors famille de recensement	424
25	95	30	135	75	70	Vivant avec des personnes apparentées[55]	425
10	30	0	150	55	85	Vivant avec des personnes non apparentées seulement	426
80	500	75	1,290	450	935	Vivant seules	427
475	3,130	635	9,915	5,345	7,125	Nombre de membres d'une famille de recensement	428
3.1	2.6	3.2	2.8	3.2	2.7	Nombre moyen de personnes par famille de recensement	429
70	**990**	**40**	**2,115**	**810**	**1,890**	**Nombre total de personnes âgées de 65 ans et plus**	430
25	290	10	695	265	500	Nombre de personnes hors famille de recensement âgées de 65 ans et plus	431
0	35	0	70	25	50	Vivant avec des personnes apparentées[55]	432
0	15	0	25	20	10	Vivant avec des personnes non apparentées seulement	433
20	240	10	590	220	445	Vivant seules	434
45	695	25	1,420	545	1,385	Nombre de membres d'une famille de recensement âgés de 65 ans et plus	435
						Caractéristiques des familles économiques	
160	**1,225**	**200**	**3,575**	**1,680**	**2,615**	**Nombre total de familles économiques dans les ménages privés**	436
						Taille de la famille	
60	840	80	1,980	730	1,580	2 personnes	437
50	130	40	640	310	425	3 personnes	438
25	170	35	665	335	370	4 personnes	439
25	90	40	295	305	245	5 personnes ou plus	440
500	3,220	665	10,055	5,420	7,190	Nombre total de personnes dans les familles économiques	441
3.0	3.0	3.0	3.0	3.0	3.0	Nombre moyen de personnes par famille économique	442
85	525	80	1,440	505	1,020	Nombre total de personnes hors famille économique	443
						Caractéristiques du revenu de 2005	
450	**3,390**	**535**	**9,950**	**4,700**	**7,130**	**Population de 15 ans et plus**	444
						Sexe et groupes de revenu total en 2005	
30	130	30	275	135	225	Sans revenu	445
420	3,260	505	9,675	4,560	6,910	Avec un revenu	446
50	105	40	380	180	210	Moins de 1 000 $[56]	447
45	105	55	470	150	205	1 000 $ à 2 999 $	448
25	75	25	525	135	260	3 000 $ à 4 999 $	449
25	165	40	355	220	325	5 000 $ à 6 999 $	450
50	245	50	495	330	440	7 000 $ à 9 999 $	451
45	190	35	280	175	280	10 000 $ à 11 999 $	452
45	190	50	500	360	455	12 000 $ à 14 999 $	453
40	365	50	840	450	920	15 000 $ à 19 999 $	454
20	340	40	665	405	610	20 000 $ à 24 999 $	455
15	295	40	430	355	600	25 000 $ à 29 999 $	456
20	220	20	445	355	495	30 000 $ à 34 999 $	457
20	180	15	370	370	505	35 000 $ à 39 999 $	458
0	170	15	475	220	300	40 000 $ à 44 999 $	459
0	140	10	290	140	335	45 000 $ à 49 999$	460
10	160	15	490	310	400	50 000 $ à 59 999$	461
10	305	10	2,660	415	560	60 000 $ et plus	462
10,704	21,819	12,512	28,461	23,856	22,422	Revenu médian $[57]	463
14,526	27,760	16,605	45,747	28,995	28,565	Revenu moyen $[57]	464
0	819	0	1,627	796	596	Erreur type de revenu moyen $[57]	465

Nota : Voir les symboles et les abréviations dans les documents d'introduction et voir les documents de référence à la fin de la publication.

Selected characteristics for census divisions and census subdivisions – 100% data and 20% sample data, Ontario, 2006 Census (continued)

No.	Characteristics	Brantford, CY	**Bruce CD/DR** ◆◊	Arran-Elderslie, MU	Brockton, MU	Huron-Kinloss, TP ◆◊	Kincardine, MU
	2005 income characteristics						
	Sex and total income groups in 2005 (continued)						
466	Total - Males	34,335	26,755	2,680	3,860	2,655	4,640
467	Without income	1,395	670	50	105	75	100
468	With income	32,940	26,080	2,630	3,755	2,580	4,535
469	Under $1,000[56]	995	995	165	155	85	175
470	$1,000 to $2,999	795	690	55	75	70	95
471	$3,000 to $4,999	835	730	70	70	95	100
472	$5,000 to $6,999	810	825	65	175	80	110
473	$7,000 to $9,999	1,260	1,330	180	160	100	260
474	$10,000 to $11,999	1,145	905	170	150	105	115
475	$12,000 to $14,999	1,405	1,110	100	130	120	115
476	$15,000 to $19,999	2,680	2,040	280	315	215	255
477	$20,000 to $24,999	2,490	1,625	145	200	145	255
478	$25,000 to $29,999	2,135	1,770	215	300	225	235
479	$30,000 to $34,999	2,370	1,690	205	300	170	220
480	$35,000 to $39,999	2,275	1,580	165	335	75	180
481	$40,000 to $44,999	2,295	1,410	125	240	145	150
482	$45,000 to $49,999	2,015	1,255	90	220	105	225
483	$50,000 to $59,999	3,040	1,810	170	270	215	325
484	$60,000 and over	6,390	6,300	420	655	630	1,720
485	Median income $[57]	33,992	33,019	27,057	32,673	30,974	45,454
486	Average income $[57]	40,112	44,223	34,321	38,472	42,653	54,998
487	Standard error of average income $[57]	460	680	1,258	1,153	1,469	1,447
488	Total - Females	37,650	27,310	2,725	3,925	2,650	4,760
489	Without income	1,645	1,205	130	175	185	225
490	With income	36,005	26,110	2,600	3,750	2,465	4,540
491	Under $1,000[56]	810	1,175	120	155	65	280
492	$1,000 to $2,999	1,340	1,310	105	195	120	245
493	$3,000 to $4,999	1,460	1,360	120	165	185	230
494	$5,000 to $6,999	1,685	1,595	180	195	175	310
495	$7,000 to $9,999	2,490	2,000	195	250	225	345
496	$10,000 to $11,999	1,980	1,455	160	235	110	300
497	$12,000 to $14,999	3,030	1,970	200	295	175	350
498	$15,000 to $19,999	4,575	3,360	415	455	300	495
499	$20,000 to $24,999	3,570	2,255	230	275	210	340
500	$25,000 to $29,999	3,075	1,960	225	325	205	275
501	$30,000 to $34,999	2,925	1,545	180	280	145	180
502	$35,000 to $39,999	2,355	1,315	115	215	130	210
503	$40,000 to $44,999	1,625	925	90	170	70	150
504	$45,000 to $49,999	1,075	595	20	85	60	120
505	$50,000 to $59,999	1,540	1,040	75	125	95	185
506	$60,000 and over	2,465	2,255	155	320	175	520
507	Median income $[57]	20,752	18,184	17,023	19,173	17,713	16,940
508	Average income $[57]	26,190	24,966	22,139	25,321	24,372	26,661
509	Standard error of average income $[57]	269	293	754	765	966	879
	Composition of total income						
510	Composition of total income in 2005 %	100.0	100.0	100.0	100.0	100.0	100.0
511	Employment income %	75.4	71.0	71.6	74.9	72.0	73.5
512	Government transfer payments %	13.6	12.2	15.1	12.1	12.3	9.1
513	Other %	11.0	16.9	13.4	13.1	15.7	17.4
514	**Population 15 years and over with employment income in 2005**	**50,490**	**38,060**	**3,810**	**5,860**	**3,660**	**6,780**
	Sex and work activity						
515	Median employment income in 2005 $	27,977	21,825	20,254	25,204	20,643	21,591
516	Average employment income in 2005 $	33,804	33,664	27,746	30,584	33,456	40,169
517	Standard error of average employment income $	330	493	938	856	1,201	1,117
518	Worked full year, full time[59]	27,865	18,560	2,085	3,080	1,830	3,235
519	Median employment income in 2005 $	40,479	40,054	32,099	37,973	40,807	59,279
520	Average employment income in 2005 $	46,565	51,279	37,425	44,691	49,586	64,345
521	Standard error of average employment income $	479	873	1,401	1,252	1,845	1,622
522	Worked part year or part time[60]	19,795	16,340	1,485	2,405	1,550	2,865
523	Median employment income in 2005 $	12,002	9,897	10,711	10,361	9,274	8,690
524	Average employment income in 2005 $	19,321	19,129	17,965	17,246	19,612	20,100
525	Standard error of average employment income $	372	410	1,044	797	1,323	1,241
526	Males 15 years and over with employment income[58]	25,840	20,650	2,080	3,135	2,045	3,720
527	Median employment income in 2005 $	36,513	29,766	25,447	32,614	30,055	41,736
528	Average employment income in 2005 $	41,022	42,016	32,573	36,625	41,988	51,631
529	Standard error of average employment income $	552	835	1,464	1,344	1,832	1,722

Note: See symbols and abbreviations in the introductory material and see reference material at the end of the publication.

Certaines caractéristiques des divisions de recensement et des subdivisions de recensement – Données intégrales et données-échantillon (20 %), Ontario, Recensement de 2006 (suite)

Neyaas-hiinigmiing 27, IRI ◆◆◇◇	Northern Bruce Peninsula, MU ◆◇	Saugeen 29, IRI ◆◆◇◇	Saugeen Shores, T ◆◇	South Bruce, MU	South Bruce Peninsula, T ◆◇	Caractéristiques	N°
						Caractéristiques du revenu de 2005	
						Sexe et groupes de revenu total en 2005 (suite)	
220	1,685	275	4,840	2,390	3,505	Total - Hommes	466
20	45	20	110	55	95	Sans revenu	467
200	1,645	260	4,730	2,335	3,415	Avec un revenu	468
25	70	25	130	75	90	Moins de 1 000 $[56]	469
25	55	40	170	55	50	1 000 $ à 2 999 $	470
10	30	15	155	55	125	3 000 $ à 4 999 $	471
10	55	20	110	90	115	5 000 $ à 6 999 $	472
25	125	20	155	120	175	7 000 $ à 9 999 $	473
20	75	15	90	80	85	10 000 $ à 11 999 $	474
25	80	15	135	185	195	12 000 $ à 14 999 $	475
10	140	20	230	220	350	15 000 $ à 19 999 $	476
10	115	30	280	180	275	20 000 $ à 24 999 $	477
10	145	20	150	165	320	25 000 $ à 29 999 $	478
10	120	10	205	175	285	30 000 $ à 34 999 $	479
10	95	10	210	220	280	35 000 $ à 39 999 $	480
0	115	10	280	140	205	40 000 $ à $44 999 $	481
0	90	10	200	105	210	45 000 $ à $49 999 $	482
0	100	10	330	145	240	50 000 $ à $59 999 $	483
10	230	0	1,900	325	405	60 000 $ et plus	484
10,288	27,498	10,768	46,166	28,776	28,351	Revenu médian $[57]	485
14,617	32,518	16,249	64,065	34,123	33,930	Revenu moyen $[57]	486
0	1,308	0	3,102	1,331	957	Erreur type de revenu moyen $[57]	487
235	1,705	265	5,110	2,310	3,625	Total - Femmes	488
15	85	15	165	85	130	Sans revenu	489
220	1,615	250	4,945	2,230	3,495	Avec un revenu	490
20	40	15	250	105	125	Moins de 1 000 $[56]	491
25	50	20	300	95	155	1 000$ à 2 999 $	492
10	45	15	370	80	130	3 000 $ à 4 999 $	493
20	110	15	245	130	210	5 000 $ à 6 999 $	494
20	120	30	345	210	265	7 000 $ à 9 999 $	495
25	120	15	185	95	195	10 000 $ à 11 999 $	496
20	110	35	365	175	260	12 000 $ à 14 999 $	497
25	225	35	610	230	570	15 000 $ à 19 999 $	498
15	225	15	385	220	330	20 000 $ à 24 999 $	499
10	150	15	285	195	285	25 000 $ à 29 999 $	500
10	100	15	240	180	210	30 000 $ à 34 999 $	501
10	85	15	160	150	220	35 000 $ à 39 999 $	502
10	55	10	195	80	100	40 000 $ à 44 999 $	503
0	50	0	90	35	125	45 000 $ à 49 999 $	504
0	60	0	160	170	155	50 000 $ à 59 999 $	505
10	75	0	760	90	155	60 000 $ et plus	506
11,040	18,959	13,760	18,322	20,124	18,640	Revenu médian $[57]	507
14,443	22,922	16,975	28,228	23,619	23,328	Revenu moyen $[57]	508
0	899	0	870	787	669	Erreur type de revenu moyen $[57]	509
						Composition du revenu total	
100.0	100.0	100.0	100.0	100.0	100.0	Composition du revenu total en 2005 %	510
57.7	51.3	71.0	73.3	76.7	60.4	Revenu d'emploi %	511
35.5	19.5	26.1	8.5	12.3	19.1	Transferts gouvernementaux %	512
7.3	29.2	2.4	18.1	10.9	20.4	Autres %	513
195	**2,090**	**325**	**7,050**	**3,685**	**4,610**	**Population de 15 ans et plus avec un revenu d'emploi en 2005**	514
						Sexe et travail	
13,056	14,567	13,792	25,543	23,434	20,062	Revenu médian d'emploi en 2005 $	515
18,278	22,179	18,316	46,088	27,561	25,886	Revenu moyen d'emploi en 2005 $	516
0	1,081	0	2,133	898	775	Erreur type de revenu moyen d'emploi $	517
100	750	140	3,240	2,055	2,055	A travaillé toute l'année à plein temps[59]	518
27,328	32,835	27,072	65,346	34,680	34,127	Revenu médian d'emploi en 2005 $	519
26,853	36,275	28,718	76,582	37,356	38,379	Revenu moyen d'emploi en 2005 $	520
0	2,054	0	4,248	1,321	1,140	Erreur type de revenu moyen d'emploi $	521
75	1,090	175	3,115	1,435	2,135	A travaillé une partie de l'année ou à temps partiel[60]	522
4,859	10,615	7,040	9,604	11,145	11,970	Revenu médian d'emploi en 2005 $	523
8,090	16,760	10,911	23,797	16,112	17,892	Revenu moyen d'emploi en 2005 $	524
0	1,162	0	1,354	853	936	Erreur type de revenu moyen d'emploi $	525
85	1,110	180	3,825	1,985	2,480	Hommes de 15 ans et plus avec un revenu d'emploi[58]	526
10,896	16,482	11,320	40,781	28,008	24,753	Revenu médian d'emploi en 2005 $	527
19,101	26,524	18,358	61,402	32,134	29,854	Revenu moyen d'emploi en 2005 $	528
0	1,714	0	3,723	1,423	1,186	Erreur type de revenu moyen d'emploi $	529

Nota : Voir les symboles et les abréviations dans les documents d'introduction et voir les documents de référence à la fin de la publication.

Selected characteristics for census divisions and census subdivisions – 100% data and 20% sample data, Ontario, 2006 Census (continued)

No.	Characteristics	Brantford, CY	**Bruce CD/DR** ◆◊	Arran-Elderslie, MU	Brockton, MU	Huron-Kinloss, TP ◆◊	Kincardine, MU
	2005 income characteristics						
	Sex and work activity (continued)						
530	Worked full year, full time[59]	16,190	11,665	1,310	1,920	1,200	2,040
531	Median employment income in 2005 $	46,564	46,263	35,520	40,198	50,037	75,261
532	Average employment income in 2005 $	52,858	58,690	40,971	49,554	56,698	74,751
533	Standard error of average employment income $	746	1,322	1,996	1,746	2,381	2,201
534	Worked part year or part time[60]	8,290	7,270	670	1,040	675	1,245
535	Median employment income in 2005 $	14,365	11,437	11,123	10,076	12,894	9,277
536	Average employment income in 2005 $	22,915	23,868	20,840	19,572	24,882	27,673
537	Standard error of average employment income $	651	765	1,723	1,425	2,544	2,363
538	Females 15 years and over with employment income[58]	24,650	17,415	1,725	2,720	1,620	3,055
539	Median employment income in 2005 $	21,850	16,004	16,434	18,128	13,871	13,864
540	Average employment income in 2005 $	26,238	23,759	21,921	23,623	22,667	26,232
541	Standard error of average employment income $	326	383	1,020	910	1,296	1,143
542	Worked full year, full time[59]	11,675	6,895	770	1,155	625	1,195
543	Median employment income in 2005 $	33,487	33,200	29,054	32,038	31,306	39,452
544	Average employment income in 2005 $	37,839	38,742	31,393	36,617	35,894	46,587
545	Standard error of average employment income $	436	658	1,579	1,493	2,546	1,889
546	Worked part year or part time[60]	11,510	9,070	820	1,365	875	1,620
547	Median employment income in 2005 $	11,007	9,415	10,160	10,442	8,031	8,141
548	Average employment income in 2005 $	16,731	15,330	15,620	15,470	15,543	14,257
549	Standard error of average employment income $	431	389	1,253	877	1,275	1,151
550	**Total number of economic families in private households**	**25,265**	**19,365**	**1,965**	**2,750**	**1,870**	**3,325**
	Family income groups in 2005						
551	Under $10,000	510	440	80	105	10	50
552	$10,000 to $19,999	1,250	730	90	80	105	60
553	$20,000 to $29,999	1,930	1,550	230	155	165	245
554	$30,000 to $39,999	2,620	2,100	235	320	230	220
555	$40,000 to $49,999	2,675	1,905	230	260	135	245
556	$50,000 to $59,999	2,370	1,875	180	260	175	345
557	$60,000 to $69,999	2,245	1,735	185	315	165	210
558	$70,000 to $79,999	2,355	1,515	195	225	145	205
559	$80,000 to $89,999	2,025	1,155	85	225	140	200
560	$90,000 to $99,999	1,710	1,150	110	150	115	275
561	$100,000 and over	5,560	5,210	345	645	485	1,270
562	Median family income $	65,892	66,164	55,858	64,475	67,913	83,165
563	Average family income $	74,679	79,471	65,645	74,306	78,287	92,462
564	Standard error of average family income $	740	982	2,003	1,858	2,339	2,023
	Family after-tax income groups in 2005						
565	Under $10,000	530	485	90	110	25	50
566	$10,000 to $19,999	1,270	740	85	80	100	70
567	$20,000 to $29,999	2,130	1,825	255	195	195	280
568	$30,000 to $39,999	3,460	2,585	290	380	275	295
569	$40,000 to $49,999	3,290	2,450	270	315	180	370
570	$50,000 to $59,999	2,995	2,230	230	415	215	295
571	$60,000 to $69,999	2,935	1,915	220	290	170	315
572	$70,000 to $79,999	2,395	1,605	140	255	220	330
573	$80,000 to $89,999	1,850	1,325	65	190	100	335
574	$90,000 to $99,999	1,365	1,125	85	130	110	260
575	$100,000 and over	3,045	3,070	230	375	285	725
576	Median after-tax family income $	56,887	56,865	49,829	56,921	57,721	69,685
577	Average after-tax family income $	62,631	65,282	56,040	62,245	64,654	74,294
578	Standard error of average after-tax family income $	517	678	1,542	1,352	1,751	1,460
	Income status in 2005						
579	Total population in private households for income status	88,585	62,810	6,655	9,410	6,355	11,005
580	Below low income cut-off before tax in 2005	12,225	5,440	790	905	695	855
581	Prevalence of low income before tax in 2005 %	13.8	8.7	11.9	9.6	10.9	7.8
582	Below low income cut-off after tax in 2005	8,905	3,415	475	575	420	525
583	Prevalence of low income after tax in 2005 %	10.1	5.4	7.1	6.1	6.6	4.8

Note: See symbols and abbreviations in the introductory material and see reference material at the end of the publication.

Certaines caractéristiques des divisions de recensement et des subdivisions de recensement – Données intégrales et données-échantillon (20 %), Ontario, Recensement de 2006 (suite)

Neyaas-hiinigmiing 27, IRI ◆◆◇◇	Northern Bruce Peninsula, MU ◆◇	Saugeen 29, IRI ◆◆◇◇	Saugeen Shores, T ◆◇	South Bruce, MU	South Bruce Peninsula, T ◆◇	Caractéristiques	N°
						Caractéristiques du revenu de 2005	
						Sexe et travail (suite)	
45	480	75	2,075	1,280	1,225	A travaillé toute l'année à plein temps[59]	530
27,968	35,764	25,451	82,118	37,042	36,749	Revenu médian d'emploi en 2005 $	531
29,491	39,020	30,498	91,040	40,167	42,319	Revenu moyen d'emploi en 2005 $	532
0	2,803	0	6,438	1,905	1,651	Erreur type de revenu moyen d'emploi $	533
40	490	95	1,345	645	1,020	A travaillé une partie de l'année ou à temps partiel[60]	534
4,837	11,694	4,768	10,035	12,572	14,892	Revenu médian d'emploi en 2005 $	535
6,954	20,176	9,196	32,448	17,971	21,125	Revenu moyen d'emploi en 2005 $	536
0	2,116	0	2,665	1,437	1,655	Erreur type de revenu moyen d'emploi $	537
100	980	150	3,225	1,700	2,130	Femmes de 15 ans et plus avec un revenu d'emploi[58]	538
14,816	12,024	14,432	16,268	19,383	17,192	Revenu médian d'emploi en 2005 $	539
17,566	17,270	18,265	27,937	22,215	21,278	Revenu moyen d'emploi en 2005 $	540
0	1,152	0	1,143	946	908	Erreur type de revenu moyen d'emploi $	541
55	265	65	1,160	775	825	A travaillé toute l'année à plein temps[59]	542
27,008	26,776	27,584	49,271	30,640	31,816	Revenu médian d'emploi en 2005 $	543
24,687	31,269	26,507	50,687	32,715	32,554	Revenu moyen d'emploi en 2005 $	544
0	2,486	0	2,042	1,428	1,347	Erreur type de revenu moyen d'emploi $	545
35	605	75	1,770	795	1,110	A travaillé une partie de l'année ou à temps partiel[60]	546
5,936	9,917	9,824	9,415	9,908	9,878	Revenu médian d'emploi en 2005 $	547
9,320	13,963	13,022	17,231	14,606	14,921	Revenu moyen d'emploi en 2005 $	548
0	1,162	0	1,117	1,007	891	Erreur type de revenu moyen d'emploi $	549
160	**1,220**	**200**	**3,575**	**1,680**	**2,615**	**Nombre total des familles économiques dans les ménages privés**	550
						Revenu de la famille économique en 2005	
20	35	20	20	30	55	Moins de 10 000 $	551
40	40	35	115	65	100	10 000 $ à 19 999 $	552
30	130	35	170	120	275	20 000 $ à 29 999 $	553
20	165	30	255	235	385	30 000 $ à 39 999 $	554
15	200	35	215	220	335	40 000 $ à 49 999 $	555
10	125	20	330	125	305	50 000 $ à 59 999 $	556
0	100	10	305	175	270	60 000 $ à 69 999 $	557
0	95	0	215	170	255	70 000 $ à 79 999 $	558
0	95	0	185	105	110	80 000 $ à 89 999 $	559
10	100	0	220	70	110	90 000 $ à 99 999 $	560
0	145	10	1,535	370	405	100 000 $ et plus	561
25,408	51,915	31,840	86,412	61,873	54,438	Revenu médian des familles $	562
30,332	61,920	36,565	106,464	69,227	63,797	Revenu moyen des familles $	563
0	2,153	0	4,284	2,077	1,582	Erreur type de revenu moyen des familles $	564
						Revenu après impôt de la famille économique en 2005	
25	35	25	25	35	70	Moins de 10 000 $	565
40	45	35	120	60	90	10 000 $ à 19 999 $	566
35	140	35	195	130	355	20 000 $ à 29 999 $	567
20	200	30	330	315	440	30 000 $ à 39 999 $	568
20	255	35	370	215	415	40 000 $ à 49 999 $	569
10	115	15	390	190	350	50 000 $ à 59 999 $	570
10	115	15	310	195	285	60 000 $ à 69 999 $	571
0	125	0	290	115	115	70 000 $ à 79 999 $	572
0	70	10	270	110	170	80 000 $ à 89 999 $	573
0	40	0	225	155	115	90 000 $ à 99 999 $	574
0	75	0	1,030	160	195	100 000 $ et plus	575
24,928	46,226	31,680	71,260	54,095	47,535	Revenu médian après impôt des familles $	576
29,320	53,286	35,134	82,421	59,621	54,730	Revenu moyen après impôt des familles $	577
0	1,659	0	2,811	1,598	1,225	Erreur type de revenu moyen après impôt des familles $	578
						Catégorie de revenu en 2005	
0	3,750	0	11,490	5,925	8,210	Population totale dans les ménages privés pour la catégorie de revenu	579
0	380	0	765	355	685	Au-dessous du seuil de faible revenu avant impôt en 2005	580
0.0	10.1	0.0	6.7	6.0	8.3	Fréquence du faible revenu avant impôt en 2005 %	581
0	195	0	425	280	515	Au-dessous du seuil de faible revenu après impôt en 2005	582
0.0	5.2	0.0	3.7	4.8	6.3	Fréquence du faible revenu après impôt en 2005 %	583

Nota : Voir les symboles et les abréviations dans les documents d'introduction et voir les documents de référence à la fin de la publication.

Selected characteristics for census divisions and census subdivisions – 100% data and 20% sample data, Ontario, 2006 Census (continued)

No.	Characteristics	Brantford, CY	**Bruce CD/DR** ◆◇	Arran-Elderslie, MU	Brockton, MU	Huron-Kinloss, TP ◆◇	Kincardine, MU
	2005 income characteristics						
584	**Total number of private households**	**35,610**	**26,320**	**2,615**	**3,735**	**2,470**	**4,605**
	Household income groups in 2005						
585	Under $10,000	1,315	980	115	160	55	170
586	$10,000 to $19,999	3,915	2,900	365	440	270	360
587	$20,000 to $29,999	3,745	2,675	360	250	260	445
588	$30,000 to $39,999	4,340	3,015	315	475	320	350
589	$40,000 to $49,999	3,745	2,455	270	360	165	325
590	$50,000 to $59,999	3,070	2,245	215	330	225	420
591	$60,000 to $69,999	2,825	2,075	195	365	210	280
592	$70,000 to $79,999	2,750	1,775	200	260	190	270
593	$80,000 to $89,999	2,190	1,310	100	230	145	245
594	$90,000 to $99,999	1,850	1,300	115	175	120	335
595	$100,000 and over	5,855	5,585	355	685	500	1,405
596	Median household income $	52,330	54,403	43,803	55,232	58,504	68,217
597	Average household income $	63,495	68,464	56,547	64,093	68,355	80,399
598	Standard error of average household income $	592	789	1,677	1,585	2,046	1,766
	Household after-tax income groups in 2005						
599	Under $10,000	1,355	1,035	125	165	75	170
600	$10,000 to $19,999	4,230	3,050	380	455	280	380
601	$20,000 to $29,999	4,500	3,250	410	365	340	535
602	$30,000 to $39,999	5,160	3,490	355	525	310	415
603	$40,000 to $49,999	4,350	2,970	310	405	250	480
604	$50,000 to $59,999	3,630	2,640	265	490	255	360
605	$60,000 to $69,999	3,270	2,210	220	315	205	400
606	$70,000 to $79,999	2,550	1,835	160	270	235	415
607	$80,000 to $89,999	1,965	1,445	70	230	105	370
608	$90,000 to $99,999	1,420	1,170	90	125	110	280
609	$100,000 and over	3,175	3,210	225	380	290	785
610	Median after-tax household income $	45,687	47,499	40,795	48,796	48,437	58,270
611	Average after-tax household income $	53,369	56,461	48,473	53,813	56,641	64,742
612	Standard error of average after-tax household income $	423	556	1,306	1,177	1,545	1,298

Note: See symbols and abbreviations in the introductory material and see reference material at the end of the publication.

Certaines caractéristiques des divisions de recensement et des subdivisions de recensement – Données intégrales et données-échantillon (20 %), Ontario, Recensement de 2006 (suite)

Neyaas-hiinigmiing 27, IRI ◆◆◇◇	Northern Bruce Peninsula, MU ◆◇	Saugeen 29, IRI ◆◆◇◇	Saugeen Shores, T ◆◇	South Bruce, MU	South Bruce Peninsula, T ◆◇	Caractéristiques	N°
						Caractéristiques du revenu de 2005	
245	**1,735**	**280**	**4,915**	**2,155**	**3,575**	**Nombre total des ménages privés**	584
						Tranches de revenu des ménages en 2005	
55	70	55	75	70	145	Moins de 10 000 $	585
75	190	60	495	230	410	10 000 $ à 19 999 $	586
40	260	40	375	205	445	20 000 $ à 29 999 $	587
30	235	35	415	305	550	30 000 $ à 39 999 $	588
20	260	40	355	240	430	40 000 $ à 49 999 $	589
15	165	20	365	135	355	50 000 $ à 59 999 $	590
10	105	15	410	200	290	60 000 $ à 69 999 $	591
10	115	0	265	175	290	70 000 $ à 79 999 $	592
0	95	0	225	125	140	80 000 $ à 89 999 $	593
0	95	10	255	85	110	90 000 $ à 99 999 $	594
0	140	10	1,680	380	415	100 000 $ et plus	595
17,216	44,607	25,472	68,867	50,952	45,577	Revenu médian des ménages $	596
25,286	52,128	30,383	89,915	61,379	55,009	Revenu moyen des ménages $	597
0	1,789	0	3,268	1,871	1,316	Erreur type de revenu moyen des ménages $	598
						Tranches du revenu après impôt des ménages en 2005	
55	70	55	80	75	155	Moins de 10 000 $	599
75	220	60	535	240	425	10 000 $ à 19 999 $	600
40	270	45	435	235	575	20 000 $ à 29 999 $	601
25	295	35	550	375	600	30 000 $ à 39 999 $	602
25	305	40	440	230	485	40 000 $ à 49 999 $	603
10	120	20	525	210	385	50 000 $ à 59 999 $	604
0	135	15	360	220	335	60 000 $ à 69 999 $	605
10	130	0	355	135	120	70 000 $ à 79 999 $	606
0	70	10	310	110	165	80 000 $ à 89 999 $	607
0	45	0	250	155	120	90 000 $ à 99 999 $	608
0	70	0	1,080	165	200	100 000 $ et plus	609
17,216	40,192	24,960	57,905	45,173	40,352	Revenu médian après impôt des ménages $	610
24,308	45,045	29,250	70,197	52,900	47,358	Revenu moyen après impôt des ménages $	611
0	1,403	0	2,173	1,472	1,037	Erreur type de revenu moyen après impôt des ménages $	612

Nota : Voir les symboles et les abréviations dans les documents d'introduction et voir les documents de référence à la fin de la publication.

Selected characteristics for census divisions and census subdivisions – 100% data and 20% sample data, Ontario, 2006 Census (continued)

No.	Characteristics	**Chatham-Kent CD/DR** ◆◇	Chatham-Kent, MU ◆◇	Moravian 47, IRI ◆◆◇◇	**Cochrane CD/DR** †◆◇	Abitibi 70, IRI ◇	Black River-Matheson, TP ◆A
	Population characteristics						
1	**Population, 2001**[1]	**107,709**	**107,341**	**368**	**85,247**	**127**	**2,886**
2	**Population, 2006**[2]	**108,589**	**108,177**	**412**	**82,503**	**114**	**2,619**
3	Population percentage change, 2001 to 2006	0.8	0.8	12.0	-3.2	-10.2	-9.3
4	Land area in square kilometres, 2006	2,470.66	2,458.06	12.61	141,247.30	78.70	1,161.67
5	**Total population – 100% data**[3]	**108,590**	**108,175**	**410**	**82,500**	**110**	**2,620**
	Sex and age groups						
6	Male	52,855	52,675	180	40,985	65	1,300
7	0 to 4 years	3,025	3,010	15	2,200	5	60
8	5 to 9 years	3,260	3,240	25	2,535	5	85
9	10 to 14 years	3,705	3,690	15	2,920	10	75
10	15 to 19 years	3,965	3,950	15	3,110	0	95
11	20 to 24 years	3,525	3,515	10	2,470	5	70
12	25 to 29 years	2,835	2,820	10	2,110	10	40
13	30 to 34 years	2,795	2,785	10	2,340	5	60
14	35 to 39 years	3,285	3,270	20	2,645	5	80
15	40 to 44 years	4,140	4,130	15	3,475	5	115
16	45 to 49 years	4,465	4,455	10	3,765	5	105
17	50 to 54 years	4,055	4,045	10	3,395	5	115
18	55 to 59 years	3,660	3,650	10	2,855	0	115
19	60 to 64 years	2,840	2,840	5	2,180	0	90
20	65 to 69 years	2,330	2,320	10	1,585	0	75
21	70 to 74 years	1,880	1,865	10	1,420	0	55
22	75 to 79 years	1,540	1,545	0	1,050	0	50
23	80 to 84 years	995	995	0	590	0	20
24	85 years and over	550	555	0	345	0	10
25	Female	55,735	55,500	235	41,520	50	1,320
26	0 to 4 years	2,880	2,860	15	2,115	0	55
27	5 to 9 years	3,190	3,160	30	2,385	5	70
28	10 to 14 years	3,745	3,735	15	2,845	5	90
29	15 to 19 years	3,815	3,795	20	2,970	10	90
30	20 to 24 years	3,465	3,450	15	2,400	5	45
31	25 to 29 years	2,745	2,725	20	2,260	5	60
32	30 to 34 years	2,985	2,970	15	2,375	0	55
33	35 to 39 years	3,295	3,280	15	2,770	5	90
34	40 to 44 years	4,390	4,375	10	3,465	5	95
35	45 to 49 years	4,585	4,570	20	3,690	5	135
36	50 to 54 years	3,955	3,950	10	3,165	0	110
37	55 to 59 years	3,670	3,655	10	2,760	5	105
38	60 to 64 years	3,045	3,035	10	2,010	0	70
39	65 to 69 years	2,480	2,470	10	1,760	0	75
40	70 to 74 years	2,180	2,180	0	1,520	0	60
41	75 to 79 years	2,005	1,995	5	1,330	0	45
42	80 to 84 years	1,765	1,765	5	945	0	40
43	85 years and over	1,535	1,535	0	765	0	25
44	**Total population 15 years and over**[3]	**88,785**	**88,485**	**295**	**67,505**	**85**	**2,185**
	Legal marital status						
45	Never legally married (single)	25,470	25,315	150	21,630	50	555
46	Legally married (and not separated)[4,5]	46,255	46,180	75	33,250	25	1,205
47	Separated, but still legally married	3,400	3,385	15	3,025	5	90
48	Divorced	6,755	6,730	25	4,455	0	145
49	Widowed	6,910	6,880	30	5,140	5	195
	Common-law status						
50	Not in a common-law relationship	81,430	81,190	245	59,125	65	1,950
51	In a common-law relationship	7,350	7,300	55	8,385	15	235
52	**Total population – 20% sample data**[6]	**107,150**	**106,740**	**410**	**81,460**	**115**	**2,600**
	Mother tongue						
53	Single responses	106,335	105,920	410	80,010	115	2,555
54	English	92,955	92,565	385	36,345	80	1,535
55	French	2,860	2,860	10	38,105	10	955
56	Non-official languages[7]	10,515	10,495	20	5,560	25	70
57	Italian	555	555	0	820	0	0
58	Chinese, n.o.s.[61]	90	90	0	75	0	0
59	Cantonese	35	35	0	55	0	0
60	Spanish	260	265	0	105	0	0
61	German	3,075	3,075	0	305	0	15
62	Other languages[8]	6,500	6,480	20	4,200	25	45

Note: See symbols and abbreviations in the introductory material and see reference material at the end of the publication.

Certaines caractéristiques des divisions de recensement et des subdivisions de recensement – Données intégrales et données-échantillon (20 %), Ontario, Recensement de 2006 (suite)

Cochrane, T	Cochrane, Unorganized, North Part, NO ◆■■A	Constance Lake 92, IRI	Fauquier-Strickland, TP ◆	Hearst, T ◆	Iroquois Falls, T	Caractéristiques	N°
						Caractéristiques de la population	
5,690	**2,975**	**723**	**678**	**5,825**	**5,217**	**Population, 2001[1]**	1
5,487	**2,447**	**702**	**568**	**5,620**	**4,729**	**Population, 2006[2]**	2
-3.6	X	-2.9	-16.2	-3.5	-9.4	Variation en pourcentage de la population, 2001 à 2006	3
538.76	131,706.99	26.20	1,013.54	98.67	599.43	Superficie des terres en kilomètres carrés, 2006	4
5,485	**2,450**	**705**	**570**	**5,620**	**4,730**	**Population totale – Données intégrales[3]**	5
						Sexe et groupes d'âge	
2,735	1,275	365	300	2,815	2,345	Sexe masculin	6
145	50	35	10	120	90	0 à 4 ans	7
160	55	35	10	165	125	5 à 9 ans	8
190	80	35	15	185	165	10 à 14 ans	9
210	90	35	25	185	155	15 à 19 ans	10
160	60	30	15	175	120	20 à 24 ans	11
135	55	30	10	175	70	25 à 29 ans	12
170	60	25	10	185	105	30 à 34 ans	13
170	90	30	15	185	125	35 à 39 ans	14
240	125	30	20	240	185	40 à 44 ans	15
255	125	20	25	275	245	45 à 49 ans	16
210	130	15	30	220	235	50 à 54 ans	17
190	90	10	15	215	185	55 à 59 ans	18
150	75	5	25	165	145	60 à 64 ans	19
115	70	5	20	105	105	65 à 69 ans	20
110	65	15	20	90	110	70 à 74 ans	21
75	30	5	15	85	105	75 à 79 ans	22
40	15	0	10	35	55	80 à 84 ans	23
10	10	5	0	25	20	85 ans et plus	24
2,750	1,170	335	270	2,800	2,380	Sexe féminin	25
150	45	35	10	140	75	0 à 4 ans	26
140	55	35	10	135	105	5 à 9 ans	27
205	80	25	10	190	125	10 à 14 ans	28
200	110	30	10	205	165	15 à 19 ans	29
140	55	40	10	160	105	20 à 24 ans	30
165	65	25	5	160	80	25 à 29 ans	31
145	55	20	10	145	120	30 à 34 ans	32
170	90	20	15	185	145	35 à 39 ans	33
225	100	20	20	245	195	40 à 44 ans	34
225	110	25	30	260	200	45 à 49 ans	35
210	110	20	20	205	210	50 à 54 ans	36
195	75	15	25	205	200	55 à 59 ans	37
150	60	5	30	150	130	60 à 64 ans	38
110	65	15	35	110	125	65 à 69 ans	39
115	35	10	10	110	115	70 à 74 ans	40
90	30	0	10	75	135	75 à 79 ans	41
60	10	0	0	70	85	80 à 84 ans	42
50	5	5	10	50	65	85 ans et plus	43
4,490	**2,080**	**505**	**510**	**4,675**	**4,030**	**Population totale de 15 ans et plus[3]**	44
						État matrimonial légal	
1,420	625	290	120	1,665	1,015	Jamais légalement marié(e) (célibataire)	45
2,315	1,170	140	315	2,140	2,230	Légalement marié(e) (et non séparé[e])[4,5]	46
155	65	25	20	250	145	Séparé(e), mais toujours légalement marié(e)	47
265	110	15	15	280	265	Divorcé(e)	48
330	105	35	40	340	370	Veuf(ve)	49
						Union libre	
3,985	1,815	400	460	3,915	3,690	Ne vivant pas en union libre	50
505	265	105	50	760	340	Vivant en union libre	51
5,430	**2,435**	**690**	**565**	**5,510**	**4,645**	**Population totale – Données-échantillon (20 %)[6]**	52
						Langue maternelle	
5,290	2,415	690	565	5,440	4,580	Réponses uniques	53
2,745	785	525	95	415	2,395	Anglais	54
2,375	1,570	0	445	4,905	2,030	Français	55
165	65	160	25	120	160	Langues non officielles[7]	56
20	0	0	0	0	30	Italien	57
10	0	0	0	0	0	Chinois, n.d.a.[61]	58
0	0	0	0	0	0	Cantonais	59
15	0	0	10	0	10	Espagnol	60
20	10	0	0	0	0	Allemand	61
100	50	160	10	115	115	Autres langues[8]	62

Nota : Voir les symboles et les abréviations dans les documents d'introduction et voir les documents de référence à la fin de la publication.

Selected characteristics for census divisions and census subdivisions – 100% data and 20% sample data, Ontario, 2006 Census (continued)

No.	Characteristics	Chatham-Kent CD/DR ◆◊	Chatham-Kent, MU ◆◊	Moravian 47, IRI ◆◆◊◊	Cochrane CD/DR †◆◊	Abitibi 70, IRI ◊	Black River-Matheson, TP ◆A
	Population characteristics						
	Mother tongue (continued)						
63	Multiple responses	810	815	0	1,450	0	45
64	English and French	340	340	0	1,110	0	45
65	English and non-official language	445	445	0	310	0	0
66	French and non-official language	20	20	0	10	0	0
67	English, French and non-official language	0	0	0	20	0	0
	Language spoken most often at home[9]						
68	Single responses	106,410	106,000	410	79,685	115	2,595
69	English	100,930	100,525	405	47,625	105	1,880
70	French	730	730	0	29,520	10	715
71	Non-official languages[7]	4,750	4,740	10	2,535	0	0
72	Chinese, n.o.s.[61]	75	75	0	25	0	0
73	Cantonese	25	20	0	30	0	0
74	Panjabi (Punjabi)	70	70	0	0	0	0
75	Italian	215	215	0	270	0	0
76	Spanish	185	185	0	15	0	0
77	Other languages[8]	4,180	4,170	10	2,190	10	0
78	Multiple responses	740	740	0	1,780	0	0
79	English and French	160	160	0	1,345	0	0
80	English and non-official language	575	575	0	430	0	0
81	French and non-official language	0	0	0	0	0	0
82	English, French and non-official language	0	0	0	0	0	0
	Knowledge of official languages[10]						
83	English only	98,810	98,410	400	32,310	90	1,330
84	French only	75	75	0	5,695	0	105
85	English and French	7,685	7,675	10	43,230	25	1,165
86	Neither English nor French	580	575	0	230	0	0
	Knowledge of non-official languages[7,11]						
87	Italian	735	735	0	1,055	0	10
88	Spanish	850	845	0	485	0	0
89	German	3,535	3,530	0	410	0	10
90	Chinese, n.o.s.[61]	100	100	0	80	0	10
91	Cantonese	50	50	0	55	0	0
92	Panjabi (Punjabi)	165	165	0	0	0	0
93	Portuguese	975	975	0	110	0	0
	First official language spoken[10]						
94	English	103,850	103,440	410	42,625	100	1,650
95	French	2,575	2,570	0	38,210	10	955
96	English and French	155	155	0	400	0	0
97	Neither English nor French	570	565	0	230	0	0
98	Official language minority - (number)[12]	2,650	2,645	0	38,410	15	955
99	Official language minority - (percentage)[12]	2.5	2.5	0.0	47.1	13.0	36.7
	Ethnic origin[13]						
100	English	35,170	35,160	10	14,400	0	845
101	Canadian	37,075	37,070	0	41,690	0	1,170
102	Scottish	21,580	21,565	15	8,800	10	375
103	Irish	20,425	20,415	15	10,550	10	485
104	French	23,405	23,400	0	33,940	10	1,110
105	German	13,065	13,060	10	4,110	0	215
106	Italian	2,225	2,220	0	3,720	0	30
107	Chinese	290	295	0	310	0	30
108	East Indian	650	650	0	50	0	0
109	Dutch (Netherlands)	11,880	11,880	0	1,370	0	90
110	Polish	2,205	2,200	10	2,170	0	55
111	Ukrainian	2,185	2,185	0	1,810	0	10
112	North American Indian	3,755	3,360	395	8,695	110	110
113	Portuguese	1,245	1,245	0	245	0	0
114	Filipino	180	185	0	150	0	0
	Aboriginal and non-Aboriginal identity						
115	Total Aboriginal identity population[14]	2,715	2,325	395	9,665	110	75
116	Total non-Aboriginal identity population	104,430	104,410	20	71,800	10	2,525

Note: See symbols and abbreviations in the introductory material and see reference material at the end of the publication.

Certaines caractéristiques des divisions de recensement et des subdivisions de recensement – Données intégrales et données-échantillon (20 %), Ontario, Recensement de 2006 (suite)

Cochrane, T	Cochrane, Unorganized, North Part, NO ◆■■A	Constance Lake 92, IRI	Fauquier-Strickland, TP ◆	Hearst, T ◆	Iroquois Falls, T	Caractéristiques	N°
						Caractéristiques de la population	
						Langue maternelle (suite)	
140	20	0	0	75	65	Réponses multiples	63
80	20	0	0	70	60	Anglais et français	64
45	0	0	0	0	10	Anglais et langue non officielle	65
0	0	0	0	0	0	Français et langue non officielle	66
15	0	0	0	0	0	Anglais, français et langue non officielle	67
						Langue parlée le plus souvent à la maison[9]	
5,305	2,395	690	565	5,425	4,575	Réponses uniques	68
3,405	950	585	150	535	3,145	Anglais	69
1,875	1,425	0	415	4,850	1,410	Français	70
25	15	105	0	35	20	Langues non officielles[7]	71
0	0	0	0	0	0	Chinois, n.d.a.[61]	72
0	0	0	0	0	0	Cantonais	73
0	0	0	0	0	0	Pendjabi	74
10	0	0	0	0	0	Italien	75
0	0	0	0	0	0	Espagnol	76
15	15	105	0	35	20	Autres langues[8]	77
130	40	0	0	90	75	Réponses multiples	78
120	30	0	0	75	70	Anglais et français	79
0	15	0	0	15	0	Anglais et langue non officielle	80
0	0	0	0	0	0	Français et langue non officielle	81
0	0	0	0	0	0	Anglais, français et langue non officielle	82
						Connaissance des langues officielles[10]	
2,115	720	680	50	250	1,790	Anglais seulement	83
320	375	0	105	1,525	105	Français seulement	84
3,000	1,345	0	410	3,740	2,755	Anglais et français	85
0	0	10	0	0	0	Ni l'anglais ni le français	86
						Connaissance des langues non officielles[7,11]	
40	10	0	0	10	20	Italien	87
65	10	0	10	15	35	Espagnol	88
25	15	10	0	10	25	Allemand	89
15	0	0	0	0	0	Chinois, n.d.a.[61]	90
0	0	0	0	0	0	Cantonais	91
0	0	0	0	0	0	Pendjabi	92
10	0	0	0	40	0	Portugais	93
						Première langue officielle parlée[10]	
3,005	850	680	125	520	2,570	Anglais	94
2,375	1,570	0	445	4,980	2,070	Français	95
50	15	0	0	15	10	Anglais et français	96
0	0	10	0	0	0	Ni l'anglais ni le français	97
2,400	1,575	0	445	4,985	2,070	Minorité de langue officielle - (nombre)[12]	98
44.2	64.5	0.0	78.8	90.5	44.5	Minorité de langue officielle - (pourcentage)[12]	99
						Origine ethnique[13]	
1,235	460	10	55	275	1,230	Anglais	100
2,915	1,395	0	470	4,125	2,455	Canadien	101
600	220	10	20	125	475	Écossais	102
590	265	15	25	240	960	Irlandais	103
2,230	955	15	305	2,560	1,900	Français	104
320	120	0	0	125	280	Allemand	105
245	20	0	10	15	175	Italien	106
15	0	0	0	10	10	Chinois	107
15	0	0	0	0	10	Indien de l'Inde	108
170	10	0	0	20	50	Hollandais (Néerlandais)	109
90	40	0	0	45	130	Polonais	110
50	55	0	0	15	65	Ukrainien	111
385	105	685	15	150	220	Indien de l'Amérique du Nord	112
20	10	0	0	40	0	Portugais	113
10	0	0	0	0	0	Philippin	114
						Population ayant une identité autochtone et population n'ayant pas d'identité autochtone	
660	95	685	95	175	375	Total de la population ayant une identité autochtone[14]	115
4,770	2,345	10	470	5,335	4,270	Total de la population n'ayant pas d'identité autochtone	116

Nota : Voir les symboles et les abréviations dans les documents d'introduction et voir les documents de référence à la fin de la publication.

Selected characteristics for census divisions and census subdivisions – 100% data and 20% sample data, Ontario, 2006 Census (continued)

No.	Characteristics	Chatham-Kent CD/DR ◆◇	Chatham-Kent, MU ◆◇	Moravian 47, IRI ◆◆◇◇	Cochrane CD/DR †◆◇	Abitibi 70, IRI ◇	Black River-Matheson, TP ◆A
	Population characteristics						
	Aboriginal and non-Aboriginal ancestry						
117	Total Aboriginal ancestry population[15]	5,010	4,615	395	11,920	110	170
118	Total non-Aboriginal ancestry population	102,135	102,120	15	69,545	0	2,430
	Registered Indian status						
119	Registered Indian[16]	1,270	880	385	6,320	110	15
120	Not a Registered Indian	105,875	105,850	20	75,145	10	2,585
	Visible minority groups						
121	Total visible minority population[17]	4,555	4,555	0	880	0	30
122	Chinese	220	220	0	245	0	20
123	South Asian[18]	615	610	0	20	0	0
124	Black	2,190	2,195	0	250	0	10
125	Filipino	185	185	0	130	0	0
126	Latin American	235	235	0	80	0	0
127	Southeast Asian[19]	365	365	0	50	0	0
128	Arab	130	125	0	15	0	0
129	West Asian[20]	45	45	0	10	0	0
130	Korean	260	265	0	15	0	0
131	Japanese	125	125	0	35	0	0
132	Visible minority, n.i.e.[21]	65	65	0	0	0	0
133	Multiple visible minority[22]	110	115	0	35	0	0
	Citizenship[23]						
134	Canadian citizens[24]	104,850	104,465	X	80,880	X	2,575
135	Not Canadian citizens[25]	2,295	2,275	X	585	X	25
	Immigrant status and place of birth[26]						
136	Non-immigrants[27]	95,900	95,510	X	78,780	X	2,510
137	Born in province of residence	91,160	90,770	X	69,215	X	2,170
138	Immigrants[28]	10,830	10,810	X	2,610	X	90
139	United States of America	1,030	1,015	X	190	X	30
140	Central and South America	1,855	1,855	X	30	X	0
141	Caribbean and Bermuda	110	110	X	85	X	10
142	United Kingdom	1,425	1,425	X	405	X	15
143	Other Europe	4,940	4,935	X	1,595	X	30
144	Africa	185	190	X	55	X	0
145	Asia and the Middle East	1,260	1,255	X	235	X	0
146	Oceania and other[29]	20	20	X	15	X	0
147	Non-permanent residents[30]	415	420	X	70	X	0
148	**Total immigrant population[28]**	**10,830**	**10,805**	**X**	**2,610**	**X**	**90**
	Period of immigration						
149	Before 1961	3,690	3,690	X	1,220	X	35
150	1961 to 1970	1,395	1,390	X	475	X	15
151	1971 to 1980	1,505	1,500	X	350	X	15
152	1981 to 1990	1,460	1,460	X	245	X	20
153	1991 to 2000	1,745	1,740	X	215	X	0
154	1991 to 1995	760	760	X	130	X	0
155	1996 to 2000	985	980	X	85	X	0
156	2001 to 2006[31]	1,035	1,030	X	105	X	0
	Age at immigration						
157	Under 5 years	1,730	1,725	X	380	X	15
158	5 to 19 years	3,645	3,645	X	785	X	25
159	20 years and over	5,450	5,440	X	1,440	X	50
160	**Total population 15 years and over**	**87,325**	**87,025**	**300**	**66,460**	**80**	**2,165**
	Generation status						
161	1st generation[32]	10,615	10,595	20	2,660	0	95
162	2nd generation[33]	14,130	14,120	10	5,760	0	215
163	3rd generation or more[34]	62,580	62,310	270	58,040	80	1,855

Note: See symbols and abbreviations in the introductory material and see reference material at the end of the publication.

Certaines caractéristiques des divisions de recensement et des subdivisions de recensement – Données intégrales et données-échantillon (20 %), Ontario, Recensement de 2006 (suite)

Cochrane, T	Cochrane, Unorganized, North Part, NO ◆■■A	Constance Lake 92, IRI	Fauquier-Strickland, TP ◆	Hearst, T ◆	Iroquois Falls, T	Caractéristiques	N°
						Caractéristiques de la population	
						Population ayant une ascendance autochtone et population n'ayant pas d'ascendance autochtone	
675	195	685	60	245	520	Total de la population ayant une ascendance autochtone[15]	117
4,755	2,240	10	505	5,265	4,125	Total de la population n'ayant pas d'ascendance autochtone	118
						Statut d'Indien inscrit	
265	50	680	10	100	100	Indien inscrit[16]	119
5,165	2,390	10	560	5,415	4,545	Pas un Indien inscrit	120
						Groupes de minorités visibles	
110	10	0	20	30	25	Total de la population des minorités visibles[17]	121
15	0	0	0	0	20	Chinois	122
15	0	0	0	0	0	Sud-Asiatique[18]	123
15	0	0	0	15	0	Noir	124
10	0	0	0	0	0	Philippin	125
20	0	0	10	0	0	Latino-Américain	126
0	0	0	0	0	0	Asiatique du Sud-Est[19]	127
0	0	0	0	0	0	Arabe	128
0	0	0	0	0	0	Asiatique occidental[20]	129
10	0	0	0	0	0	Coréen	130
0	0	0	10	0	0	Japonais	131
0	0	0	0	0	0	Minorité visible, n.i.a.[21]	132
35	0	0	0	0	0	Minorités visibles multiples[22]	133
						Citoyenneté[23]	
5,365	2,425	X	565	5,480	4,640	Citoyens canadiens[24]	134
60	15	X	0	30	10	Ne sont pas des citoyens canadiens[25]	135
						Statut d'immigrant et le lieu de naissance[26]	
5,225	2,390	X	550	5,430	4,570	Non-immigrants[27]	136
4,620	2,050	X	465	4,405	4,045	Né dans la province de résidence	137
180	50	X	15	75	85	Immigrants[28]	138
30	15	X	0	10	0	États-Unis d'Amérique	139
0	0	X	10	0	0	Amérique centrale et Amérique du Sud	140
20	0	X	0	0	0	Antilles et Bermudes	141
25	10	X	0	0	30	Royaume-Uni	142
90	25	X	0	70	50	Autre Europe	143
0	0	X	0	0	0	Afrique	144
20	0	X	10	0	0	Asie et Moyen-Orient	145
0	0	X	0	0	0	Océanie et autres[29]	146
20	10	X	0	0	0	Résidents non permanents[30]	147
180	**50**	**X**	**15**	**75**	**80**	**Population totale des immigrants[28]**	148
						Période d'immigration	
70	25	X	0	30	30	Avant 1961	149
20	0	X	0	15	10	1961 à 1970	150
25	10	X	15	15	10	1971 à 1980	151
10	10	X	0	10	25	1981 à 1990	152
45	10	X	0	0	0	1991 à 2000	153
20	0	X	0	0	0	1991 à 1995	154
25	10	X	0	0	0	1996 à 2000	155
10	0	X	0	10	10	2001 à 2006[31]	156
						Âge à l'immigration	
20	0	X	0	0	10	Moins de 5 ans	157
95	15	X	10	30	20	5 à 19 ans	158
65	25	X	10	45	55	20 ans et plus	159
4,425	**2,060**	**495**	**500**	**4,565**	**3,950**	**Population totale de 15 ans et plus**	160
						Statut des générations	
200	60	10	15	80	85	1re génération[32]	161
350	150	0	20	135	425	2e génération[33]	162
3,880	1,855	485	460	4,350	3,445	3e génération ou plus[34]	163

Nota : Voir les symboles et les abréviations dans les documents d'introduction et voir les documents de référence à la fin de la publication.

Selected characteristics for census divisions and census subdivisions – 100% data and 20% sample data, Ontario, 2006 Census (continued)

No.	Characteristics	Chatham-Kent CD/DR ♦◊	Chatham-Kent, MU ♦◊	Moravian 47, IRI ♦♦◊◊	Cochrane CD/DR †♦◊	Abitibi 70, IRI ◊	Black River-Matheson, TP ♦A
	Population characteristics						
164	**Total population 1 year and over[35]**	**106,090**	**105,675**	**410**	**80,600**	**115**	**2,585**
	Place of residence 1 year ago (mobility)						
165	Non-movers	93,870	93,510	360	70,355	110	2,265
166	Movers	12,215	12,165	50	10,245	0	320
167	Non-migrants	8,805	8,785	20	7,145	0	120
168	Migrants	3,410	3,380	25	3,100	0	195
169	Internal migrants	2,885	2,855	25	3,055	0	195
170	Intraprovincial migrants	2,690	2,660	25	2,705	0	175
171	Interprovincial migrants	190	190	0	350	0	20
172	External migrants	530	530	0	45	0	0
173	**Total population 5 years and over[36]**	**101,220**	**100,840**	**385**	**77,230**	**105**	**2,490**
	Place of residence 5 years ago (mobility)						
174	Non-movers	68,825	68,595	230	50,835	60	1,900
175	Movers	32,400	32,245	155	26,395	45	590
176	Non-migrants	23,795	23,710	85	17,785	25	285
177	Migrants	8,605	8,535	70	8,610	15	305
178	Internal migrants	7,515	7,450	65	8,380	15	305
179	Intraprovincial migrants	6,950	6,890	60	7,180	15	280
180	Interprovincial migrants	570	565	0	1,205	0	30
181	External migrants	1,090	1,085	0	230	0	0
182	**Total population 15 years and over**	**87,325**	**87,030**	**300**	**66,460**	**80**	**2,165**
	Highest certificate, diploma or degree[37]						
183	No certificate, diploma or degree	26,805	26,695	115	22,770	30	820
184	Certificate, diploma or degree	60,520	60,335	185	43,685	50	1,345
185	High school certificate or equivalent[38]	25,515	25,455	60	15,600	15	435
186	Apprenticeship or trades certificate or diploma	7,570	7,540	30	8,110	20	305
187	College, CEGEP or other non-university certificate or diploma[39]	17,790	17,720	70	13,390	15	445
188	University certificate or diploma below bachelor level[40]	1,920	1,910	10	1,230	0	30
189	University certificate or degree[41]	7,720	7,705	15	5,355	0	120
190	Bachelor's degree	4,900	4,890	10	3,575	0	60
191	University certificate or diploma above bachelor level	1,310	1,310	0	980	0	30
192	Degree in medicine, dentistry, veterinary medicine or optometry	170	165	0	155	0	0
193	Master's degree	1,195	1,195	0	615	0	30
194	Earned doctorate	145	145	0	35	0	0
195	**Total population 15 years and over with postsecondary qualifications**	**35,005**	**34,880**	**130**	**28,080**	**35**	**910**
	Major field of study - Classification of Instructional Programs, 2000[42]						
196	Education	2,625	2,620	10	2,460	10	75
197	Visual and performing arts, and communications technologies	680	675	0	420	0	10
198	Humanities	1,205	1,200	10	595	0	35
199	Social and behavioural sciences and law	2,645	2,625	25	1,755	0	50
200	Business, management and public administration	7,515	7,490	25	5,650	0	155
201	Physical and life sciences and technologies	600	595	0	510	0	20
202	Mathematics, computer and information sciences	1,090	1,085	10	540	0	25
203	Architecture, engineering, and related technologies	8,410	8,395	20	8,450	0	305
204	Agriculture, natural resources and conservation	1,865	1,865	0	915	10	50
205	Health, parks, recreation and fitness	5,965	5,940	25	4,270	10	105
206	Personal, protective and transportation services	2,400	2,390	15	2,515	10	85
207	Other fields of study[43]	0	0	0	0	0	0
	Location of study[44]						
208	Inside Canada	32,620	32,500	120	27,250	40	875
209	Outside Canada	2,380	2,380	0	830	0	30
210	**Total population 15 years and over**	**87,325**	**87,030**	**300**	**66,460**	**80**	**2,165**
	Unpaid work						
211	Males 15 years and over	42,325	42,200	125	32,940	45	1,060
212	Reported unpaid work[45]	38,530	38,405	120	29,730	35	975
213	Housework and child care and care or assistance to seniors	3,805	3,785	20	2,835	0	105
214	Housework and child care only	10,680	10,645	40	8,610	15	205

Note: See symbols and abbreviations in the introductory material and see reference material at the end of the publication.

Certaines caractéristiques des divisions de recensement et des subdivisions de recensement – Données intégrales et données-échantillon (20 %), Ontario, Recensement de 2006 (suite)

Cochrane, T	Cochrane, Unorganized, North Part, NO ◆■■A	Constance Lake 92, IRI	Fauquier-Strickland, TP ◆	Hearst, T ◆	Iroquois Falls, T	Caractéristiques	N°
						Caractéristiques de la population	
5,375	**2,405**	**670**	**565**	**5,465**	**4,615**	**Population totale de 1 an et plus[35]**	164
						Lieu de résidence 1 an auparavant (mobilité)	
4,660	2,155	595	560	4,835	4,100	Personnes n'ayant pas déménagé	165
720	245	75	10	630	510	Personnes ayant déménagé	166
460	120	45	0	445	320	Non-migrants	167
260	125	25	10	185	190	Migrants	168
240	125	20	10	185	190	Migrants internes	169
235	120	15	10	175	180	Migrants infraprovinciaux	170
0	0	0	0	0	10	Migrants interprovinciaux	171
20	0	0	0	10	0	Migrants externes	172
5,130	**2,315**	**620**	**540**	**5,250**	**4,480**	**Population totale de 5 ans et plus[36]**	173
						Lieu de résidence 5 ans auparavant (mobilité)	
3,410	1,755	405	515	3,440	3,195	Personnes n'ayant pas déménagé	174
1,725	560	215	20	1,810	1,280	Personnes ayant déménagé	175
1,155	285	140	0	1,135	680	Non-migrants	176
570	270	70	20	670	605	Migrants	177
555	270	70	20	650	595	Migrants internes	178
420	260	65	25	540	485	Migrants infraprovinciaux	179
130	10	0	0	105	110	Migrants interprovinciaux	180
10	10	0	0	25	0	Migrants externes	181
4,425	**2,060**	**490**	**500**	**4,565**	**3,950**	**Population totale de 15 ans et plus**	182
						Plus haut certificat, diplôme ou grade[37]	
1,555	865	305	250	1,685	1,215	Aucun certificat, diplôme ou grade	183
2,875	1,195	185	245	2,885	2,735	Certificat, diplôme ou grade	184
1,155	465	45	100	1,155	895	Diplôme d'études secondaires ou l'équivalent[38]	185
495	240	80	55	460	600	Certificat ou diplôme d'apprenti ou d'une école de métiers	186
830	355	35	60	770	850	Certificat ou diplôme d'un collège, d'un cégep ou d'un autre établissement d'enseignement non universitaire[39]	187
60	40	15	10	75	60	Certificat ou diplôme universitaire inférieur au baccalauréat[40]	188
330	90	10	25	420	330	Certificat ou grade universitaire[41]	189
260	60	10	10	315	220	Baccalauréat	190
50	25	0	0	40	85	Certificat ou diplôme universitaire supérieur au baccalauréat	191
0	0	0	10	10	0	Diplôme en médecine, en art dentaire, en médecine vétérinaire ou en optométrie	192
0	0	0	10	45	20	Maîtrise	193
0	0	0	0	10	0	Doctorat acquis	194
1,715	**730**	**145**	**150**	**1,725**	**1,840**	**Population totale de 15 ans et plus avec titres du niveau postsecondaire**	195
						Principal domaine d'études - Classification des programmes d'enseignement, 2000[42]	
135	40	15	25	135	190	Éducation	196
50	10	0	0	10	10	Arts visuels et d'interprétation, et technologie des communications	197
20	0	0	0	45	20	Sciences humaines	198
155	60	10	0	130	85	Sciences sociales et de comportements, et droit	199
380	100	10	35	380	330	Commerce, gestion et administration publique	200
0	0	0	0	10	30	Sciences physiques et de la vie, et technologies	201
35	10	0	10	25	30	Mathématiques, informatique et sciences de l'information	202
385	265	20	55	460	645	Architecture, génie et services connexes	203
130	25	0	0	45	40	Agriculture, ressources naturelles et conservation	204
240	110	15	15	260	310	Santé, parcs, récréation et conditionnement physique	205
175	95	60	10	220	150	Services personnels, de protection et de transport	206
0	0	0	0	0	0	Autres domaines d'études[43]	207
						Lieu des études[44]	
1,620	725	140	145	1,705	1,780	À l'intérieur du Canada	208
95	0	0	10	25	55	À l'extérieur du Canada	209
4,425	**2,060**	**490**	**500**	**4,565**	**3,950**	**Population totale de 15 ans et plus**	210
						Travail non rémunéré	
2,215	1,085	255	250	2,300	1,925	Hommes de 15 ans et plus	211
2,040	975	225	235	2,075	1,790	Travail non rémunéré déclaré[45]	212
190	80	10	10	265	240	Travaux ménagers et soins aux enfants et soins ou aide aux personnes âgées	213
560	280	95	75	540	420	Travaux ménagers et soins aux enfants seulement	214

Nota : Voir les symboles et les abréviations dans les documents d'introduction et voir les documents de référence à la fin de la publication.

Selected characteristics for census divisions and census subdivisions – 100% data and 20% sample data, Ontario, 2006 Census (continued)

No.	Characteristics	Chatham-Kent CD/DR ◆◊	Chatham-Kent, MU ◆◊	Moravian 47, IRI ◆◆◊◊	Cochrane CD/DR †◆◊	Abitibi 70, IRI ◊	Black River-Matheson, TP ◆A
	Population characteristics						
	Unpaid work (continued)						
215	Housework and care or assistance to seniors only	3,450	3,435	15	2,805	10	85
216	Child care and care or assistance to seniors only	50	50	0	35	0	0
217	Housework only	20,055	20,015	35	15,050	10	555
218	Child care only	260	255	0	265	0	10
219	Care or assistance to seniors only	225	225	0	135	0	10
220	Females 15 years and over	45,000	44,825	170	33,515	35	1,100
221	Reported unpaid work[45]	42,070	41,910	165	31,295	35	1,050
222	Housework and child care and care or assistance to seniors	5,855	5,825	35	4,395	0	135
223	Housework and child care only	12,400	12,340	60	9,900	15	310
224	Housework and care or assistance to seniors only	4,575	4,565	10	3,210	0	120
225	Child care and care or assistance to seniors only	10	10	0	35	0	0
226	Housework only	18,950	18,900	50	13,495	10	485
227	Child care only	165	160	0	175	0	0
228	Care or assistance to seniors only	110	110	0	95	0	0
	Labour force activity						
229	Males 15 years and over	42,325	42,200	130	32,940	50	1,065
230	In the labour force	30,300	30,225	80	22,440	35	670
231	Employed	28,130	28,075	65	20,415	25	600
232	Unemployed	2,165	2,150	20	2,025	10	65
233	Not in the labour force	12,025	11,975	45	10,495	10	395
234	Participation rate	71.6	71.6	61.5	68.1	70.0	62.9
235	Employment rate	66.5	66.5	50.0	62.0	50.0	56.3
236	Unemployment rate	7.1	7.1	25.0	9.0	28.6	9.7
237	Females 15 years and over	45,000	44,825	170	33,515	35	1,100
238	In the labour force	27,130	27,020	110	18,925	25	530
239	Employed	25,160	25,070	90	17,370	25	465
240	Unemployed	1,965	1,950	15	1,555	10	65
241	Not in the labour force	17,875	17,810	65	14,590	0	570
242	Participation rate	60.3	60.3	64.7	56.5	71.4	48.2
243	Employment rate	55.9	55.9	52.9	51.8	71.4	42.3
244	Unemployment rate	7.2	7.2	13.6	8.2	40.0	12.3
245	Both sexes - Participation rate	65.8	65.8	61.7	62.2	76.5	55.4
246	15 to 24 years	71.4	71.5	45.5	65.2	75.0	50.0
247	25 years and over	64.6	64.6	67.3	61.7	76.9	56.5
248	Both sexes - Employment rate	61.0	61.1	50.0	56.9	52.9	49.8
249	15 to 24 years	58.8	58.9	18.2	52.5	0.0	37.7
250	25 years and over	61.5	61.5	57.1	57.7	61.5	51.5
251	Both sexes - Unemployment rate	7.2	7.2	16.2	8.6	30.8	10.4
252	15 to 24 years	17.7	17.6	40.0	19.4	100.0	24.1
253	25 years and over	4.8	4.8	15.6	6.4	18.2	8.6
254	**Total labour force 15 years and over**	**57,425**	**57,245**	**185**	**41,365**	**65**	**1,205**
	Industry - North American Industry Classification System 2002						
255	Industry - Not applicable[46]	705	705	10	830	10	30
256	All industries[47]	56,720	56,540	180	40,535	55	1,170
257	11 Agriculture, forestry, fishing and hunting	4,015	4,010	0	1,625	10	70
258	21 Mining and oil and gas extraction	130	130	0	2,830	0	145
259	22 Utilities	925	920	0	630	0	15
260	23 Construction	2,775	2,760	15	2,615	0	70
261	31-33 Manufacturing	11,780	11,770	15	4,075	0	55
262	41 Wholesale trade	2,245	2,240	0	980	0	0
263	44-45 Retail trade	6,625	6,610	15	5,315	0	95
264	48-49 Transportation and warehousing	2,970	2,965	0	2,490	0	85
265	51 Information and cultural industries	620	620	0	515	0	0
266	52 Finance and insurance	1,315	1,315	0	835	0	25
267	53 Real estate and rental and leasing	700	695	10	405	0	15
268	54 Professional, scientific and technical services	1,375	1,370	0	1,070	0	15
269	55 Management of companies and enterprises	30	30	0	10	0	0
270	56 Administrative and support, waste management and remediation services	3,305	3,295	10	1,765	0	60
271	61 Educational services	2,880	2,870	10	3,125	10	80
272	62 Health care and social assistance	5,350	5,315	40	4,840	0	145

Note: See symbols and abbreviations in the introductory material and see reference material at the end of the publication.

Certaines caractéristiques des divisions de recensement et des subdivisions de recensement – Données intégrales et données-échantillon (20 %), Ontario, Recensement de 2006 (suite)

Cochrane, T	Cochrane, Unorganized, North Part, NO ◆■■A	Constance Lake 92, IRI	Fauquier-Strickland, TP ◆	Hearst, T ◆	Iroquois Falls, T	Caractéristiques	N°
						Caractéristiques de la population	
						Travail non rémunéré (suite)	
180	100	10	10	250	155	Travaux ménagers et soins ou aide aux personnes âgées seulement	215
0	0	0	0	0	0	Soins aux enfants et soins ou aide aux personnes âgées seulement	216
1,050	490	90	135	955	960	Travaux ménagers seulement	217
30	0	15	0	35	0	Soins aux enfants seulement	218
15	10	0	0	15	15	Soins ou aide aux personnes âgées seulement	219
2,210	975	235	245	2,270	2,025	Femmes de 15 ans et plus	220
2,025	945	225	245	2,140	1,870	Travail non rémunéré déclaré[45]	221
255	120	20	15	420	320	Travaux ménagers et soins aux enfants et soins ou aide aux personnes âgées	222
680	285	115	85	590	455	Travaux ménagers et soins aux enfants seulement	223
225	90	10	30	255	225	Travaux ménagers et soins ou aide aux personnes âgées seulement	224
0	0	0	0	0	0	Soins aux enfants et soins ou aide aux personnes âgées seulement	225
815	440	65	110	840	855	Travaux ménagers seulement	226
35	0	10	0	25	0	Soins aux enfants seulement	227
10	0	0	0	0	10	Soins ou aide aux personnes âgées seulement	228
						Activité	
2,215	1,085	255	250	2,300	1,925	Hommes de 15 ans et plus	229
1,540	700	145	150	1,720	1,165	Population active	230
1,425	600	110	140	1,515	1,060	Personnes occupées	231
110	100	35	15	205	100	Chômeurs	232
675	385	110	95	580	760	Inactifs	233
69.5	64.5	56.9	60.0	74.8	60.5	Taux d'activité	234
64.3	55.3	43.1	56.0	65.9	55.1	Taux d'emploi	235
7.1	14.3	24.1	10.0	11.9	8.6	Taux de chômage	236
2,210	980	235	250	2,270	2,030	Femmes de 15 ans et plus	237
1,275	555	95	140	1,330	915	Population active	238
1,215	495	70	145	1,225	845	Personnes occupées	239
60	60	25	0	100	75	Chômeuses	240
940	420	140	105	945	1,110	Inactives	241
57.7	56.6	40.4	56.0	58.6	45.1	Taux d'activité	242
55.0	50.5	29.8	58.0	54.0	41.6	Taux d'emploi	243
4.7	10.8	26.3	0.0	7.5	8.2	Taux de chômage	244
63.5	60.8	48.5	59.0	66.7	52.6	Les deux sexes - Taux d'activité	245
67.1	67.9	28.6	100.0	69.5	52.8	15 à 24 ans	246
63.0	59.9	57.7	52.3	66.2	52.7	25 ans et plus	247
59.7	53.2	35.4	56.6	60.0	48.2	Les deux sexes - Taux d'emploi	248
60.0	51.9	11.1	92.3	55.3	44.0	15 à 24 ans	249
59.6	53.5	45.1	49.4	61.0	48.8	25 ans et plus	250
6.2	12.7	25.0	5.1	10.0	8.4	Les deux sexes - Taux de chômage	251
9.7	22.9	50.0	0.0	20.2	17.5	15 à 24 ans	252
5.3	11.6	19.5	4.3	7.8	7.2	25 ans et plus	253
2,810	**1,255**	**240**	**290**	**3,045**	**2,080**	**Population active totale de 15 ans et plus**	254
						Industrie - Système de classification des industries de l'Amérique du Nord de 2002	
60	30	20	0	25	30	Industrie - Sans objet[46]	255
2,755	1,225	220	295	3,015	2,045	Toutes les industries[47]	256
145	165	30	30	230	55	11 Agriculture, foresterie, pêche et chasse	257
25	10	0	0	0	100	21 Extraction minière et extraction de pétrole et de gaz	258
30	30	0	10	10	35	22 Services publics	259
180	95	10	35	210	60	23 Construction	260
440	180	40	40	580	475	31-33 Fabrication	261
35	0	0	0	65	10	41 Commerce de gros	262
365	150	10	45	400	185	44-45 Commerce de détail	263
270	105	10	20	200	80	48-49 Transport et entreposage	264
35	15	0	0	35	30	51 Industrie de l'information et industrie culturelle	265
25	20	0	0	95	15	52 Finance et assurances	266
20	25	0	0	15	20	53 Services immobiliers et services de location et de location à bail	267
85	10	0	0	45	10	54 Services professionnels, scientifiques et techniques	268
0	0	0	0	0	0	55 Gestion de sociétés et d'entreprises	269
65	30	10	0	45	95	56 Services administratifs, services de soutien, services de gestion des déchets et services d'assainissement	270
185	70	35	30	220	205	61 Services d'enseignement	271
300	120	25	20	280	255	62 Soins de santé et assistance sociale	272

Nota : Voir les symboles et les abréviations dans les documents d'introduction et voir les documents de référence à la fin de la publication.

Selected characteristics for census divisions and census subdivisions – 100% data and 20% sample data, Ontario, 2006 Census (continued)

No.	Characteristics	**Chatham-Kent CD/DR** ◆◇	Chatham-Kent, MU ◆◇	Moravian 47, IRI ◆◆◇◇	**Cochrane CD/DR** †◆◇	Abitibi 70, IRI ◇	Black River-Matheson, TP ◆A
	Population characteristics						
	Industry - North American Industry Classification System 2002 (continued)						
273	71 Arts, entertainment and recreation	1,035	1,035	0	430	0	10
274	72 Accommodation and food services	3,535	3,530	0	2,690	0	20
275	81 Other services (except public administration)	3,070	3,060	10	1,930	0	135
276	91 Public administration	2,030	1,985	45	2,350	30	115
	Class of worker						
277	Class of worker - Not applicable[46]	705	705	10	830	10	30
278	All classes of worker[47]	56,720	56,535	180	40,535	60	1,170
279	Paid workers	51,775	51,610	170	38,510	55	1,135
280	Employees	49,860	49,690	165	37,400	55	1,070
281	Self-employed (incorporated)	1,915	1,915	0	1,110	0	65
282	Self-employed (unincorporated)	4,690	4,680	10	1,960	0	35
283	Unpaid family workers	250	250	0	65	0	0
	Occupation - National Occupational Classification for Statistics 2006						
284	Male labour force 15 years and over	30,300	30,220	80	22,440	35	670
285	Occupation - Not applicable[46]	375	370	10	455	0	20
286	All occupations[47]	29,925	29,850	75	21,980	30	645
287	A Management occupations	2,665	2,655	0	1,835	10	30
288	B Business, finance and administrative occupations	2,120	2,120	0	1,405	0	30
289	C Natural and applied sciences and related occupations	1,740	1,740	10	1,500	0	45
290	D Health occupations	385	380	0	365	0	10
291	E Occupations in social science, education, government service and religion	1,015	1,015	10	925	0	20
292	F Occupations in art, culture, recreation and sport	260	260	0	195	0	0
293	G Sales and service occupations	4,835	4,815	20	3,640	0	75
294	H Trades, transport and equipment operators and related occupations	8,845	8,820	25	7,895	10	290
295	I Occupations unique to primary industry	3,235	3,230	10	2,220	10	110
296	J Occupations unique to processing, manufacturing and utilities	4,820	4,805	15	2,005	0	35
297	Female labour force 15 years and over	27,125	27,020	110	18,925	30	530
298	Occupation - Not applicable[46]	335	330	0	370	0	10
299	All occupations[47]	26,795	26,690	110	18,555	25	520
300	A Management occupations	1,555	1,550	10	1,175	0	10
301	B Business, finance and administrative occupations	6,640	6,615	25	4,840	10	125
302	C Natural and applied sciences and related occupations	370	365	0	250	0	10
303	D Health occupations	2,660	2,660	0	1,955	0	65
304	E Occupations in social science, education, government service and religion	2,585	2,550	35	2,530	10	65
305	F Occupations in art, culture, recreation and sport	585	575	0	345	0	20
306	G Sales and service occupations	8,060	8,030	25	6,450	0	175
307	H Trades, transport and equipment operators and related occupations	630	625	0	510	0	25
308	I Occupations unique to primary industry	955	950	0	240	0	20
309	J Occupations unique to processing, manufacturing and utilities	2,750	2,745	10	255	0	0
310	**Total employed labour force 15 years and over**	**53,295**	**53,145**	**150**	**37,785**	**45**	**1,075**
	Place of work status						
311	Males	28,135	28,075	60	20,420	20	605
312	Usual place of work	22,585	22,535	45	17,195	15	450
313	At home	2,340	2,335	10	740	0	70
314	Outside Canada	170	175	0	25	0	0
315	No fixed workplace address	3,035	3,025	10	2,455	10	85
316	Females	25,165	25,070	95	17,365	20	470
317	Usual place of work	22,335	22,255	80	15,850	20	405
318	At home	1,760	1,755	10	735	0	40
319	Outside Canada	85	90	0	0	0	0
320	No fixed workplace address	980	980	0	780	0	25

Note: See symbols and abbreviations in the introductory material and see reference material at the end of the publication.

Certaines caractéristiques des divisions de recensement et des subdivisions de recensement – Données intégrales et données-échantillon (20 %), Ontario, Recensement de 2006 (suite)

Cochrane, T	Cochrane, Unorganized, North Part, NO ◆■■A	Constance Lake 92, IRI	Fauquier-Strickland, TP ◆	Hearst, T ◆	Iroquois Falls, T	Caractéristiques	N°
						Caractéristiques de la population	
						Industrie - Système de classification des industries de l'Amérique du Nord de 2002 (suite)	
50	10	0	0	30	35	71 Arts, spectacles et loisirs	273
155	80	10	45	255	95	72 Hébergement et services de restauration	274
90	50	0	10	195	105	81 Autres services (sauf les administrations publiques)	275
240	65	35	10	110	170	91 Administrations publiques	276
						Catégorie de travailleurs	
60	25	20	0	30	30	Catégorie de travailleurs - Sans objet[46]	277
2,755	1,225	220	295	3,020	2,045	Toutes les catégories de travailleurs[47]	278
2,580	1,110	215	285	2,810	1,940	Travailleurs rémunérés	279
2,515	1,060	210	280	2,645	1,910	Employés	280
70	45	0	10	165	35	Travailleurs autonomes (entreprise constituée en société)	281
160	105	10	0	205	90	Travailleurs autonomes (entreprise non constituée en société)	282
10	10	0	10	10	10	Travailleurs familiaux non rémunérés	283
						Profession - Classification nationale des professions pour statistiques de 2006	
1,540	700	145	155	1,720	1,165	Hommes actifs de 15 ans et plus	284
35	15	10	0	0	20	Profession - Sans objet[46]	285
1,500	685	140	150	1,710	1,145	Toutes les professions[47]	286
130	40	10	0	135	80	A Gestion	287
95	20	0	0	85	40	B Affaires, finance et administration	288
100	55	0	0	100	80	C Sciences naturelles et appliquées et professions apparentées	289
15	0	0	10	15	20	D Secteur de la santé	290
55	35	10	10	45	40	E Sciences sociales, enseignement, administration publique et religion	291
10	10	0	0	10	0	F Arts, culture, sports et loisirs	292
220	60	10	20	220	205	G Ventes et services	293
495	265	35	75	625	410	H Métiers, transport et machinerie	294
90	90	30	15	175	60	I Professions propres au secteur primaire	295
280	100	35	20	295	195	J Transformation, fabrication et services d'utilité publique	296
1,275	555	95	140	1,325	915	Femmes actives de 15 ans et plus	297
20	10	10	0	20	10	Profession - Sans objet[46]	298
1,255	540	85	140	1,305	905	Toutes les professions[47]	299
70	50	10	10	115	50	A Gestion	300
375	100	15	10	245	205	B Affaires, finance et administration	301
0	0	10	0	10	0	C Sciences naturelles et appliquées et professions apparentées	302
75	65	0	0	150	110	D Secteur de la santé	303
190	55	25	15	175	150	E Sciences sociales, enseignement, administration publique et religion	304
20	0	0	10	35	25	F Arts, culture, sports et loisirs	305
440	195	15	95	500	320	G Ventes et services	306
25	15	0	10	20	15	H Métiers, transport et machinerie	307
10	25	0	0	15	10	I Professions propres au secteur primaire	308
55	25	0	0	50	15	J Transformation, fabrication et services d'utilité publique	309
2,640	**1,100**	**180**	**275**	**2,740**	**1,905**	**Population active occupée totale de 15 ans et plus**	310
						Catégorie de lieu de travail	
1,430	605	110	140	1,515	1,060	Hommes	311
1,160	410	75	100	1,295	945	Lieu habituel de travail	312
60	45	0	0	65	20	À domicile	313
0	0	0	0	0	0	En dehors du Canada	314
205	140	30	35	145	100	Sans adresse de travail fixe	315
1,215	495	70	140	1,225	840	Femmes	316
1,120	450	60	120	1,145	765	Lieu habituel de travail	317
45	35	0	0	30	50	À domicile	318
0	0	0	0	0	0	En dehors du Canada	319
45	10	10	15	50	25	Sans adresse de travail fixe	320

Nota : Voir les symboles et les abréviations dans les documents d'introduction et voir les documents de référence à la fin de la publication.

Selected characteristics for census divisions and census subdivisions – 100% data and 20% sample data, Ontario, 2006 Census (continued)

No.	Characteristics	Chatham-Kent CD/DR ◆◇	Chatham-Kent, MU ◆◇	Moravian 47, IRI ◆◆◇◇	Cochrane CD/DR †◆◇	Abitibi 70, IRI ◇	Black River-Matheson, TP ◆A
	Population characteristics						
321	**Total employed labour force 15 years and over with usual place of work or no fixed workplace address**	**48,935**	**48,790**	**145**	**36,285**	**45**	**965**
	Mode of transportation						
322	Males	25,620	25,560	60	19,650	20	535
323	Car, truck, van, as driver	21,325	21,285	45	14,745	10	465
324	Car, truck, van, as passenger	2,050	2,045	10	2,060	10	25
325	Public transit	135	135	0	390	0	0
326	Walked	1,300	1,300	10	1,590	10	30
327	All other modes	805	805	10	865	0	20
328	Females	23,315	23,230	85	16,635	20	430
329	Car, truck, van, as driver	18,645	18,575	65	11,310	10	320
330	Car, truck, van, as passenger	2,475	2,465	10	1,940	0	20
331	Public transit	300	300	0	595	0	0
332	Walked	1,510	1,505	0	2,410	0	70
333	All other modes	385	380	0	380	0	15
334	**Total population 15 years and over who worked since January 1, 2005**	**62,200**	**61,995**	**210**	**44,335**	**60**	**1,320**
	Language used most often at work						
335	Single responses	61,970	61,755	215	41,545	65	1,240
336	English	61,570	61,355	210	31,335	65	1,095
337	French	220	215	0	10,070	0	145
338	Non-official languages[7]	180	180	0	140	0	0
339	Chinese, n.o.s.[61]	0	0	0	10	0	0
340	Cantonese	0	0	0	15	0	0
341	Other languages[8]	180	180	0	115	0	0
342	Multiple responses	235	235	0	2,790	0	80
343	English and French	170	170	0	2,620	0	80
344	English and non-official language	60	60	0	150	0	0
345	French and non-official language	0	0	0	10	0	0
346	English, French and non-official language	0	0	0	20	0	0
	Dwelling and household characteristics						
347	**Total number of occupied private dwellings**	**43,670**	**43,525**	**145**	**33,335**	**40**	**1,075**
	Housing tenure						
348	Owned	31,905	31,780	125	23,255	10	910
349	Rented	11,750	11,740	15	9,805	0	165
350	Band housing	10	0	10	275	25	0
	Structural type of dwelling						
351	Single-detached house	33,240	33,090	145	22,465	35	960
352	Semi-detached house	1,265	1,265	0	1,945	0	15
353	Row house	1,480	1,480	0	890	0	10
354	Apartment, duplex	780	780	0	1,850	0	5
355	Apartment, building that has five or more storeys	1,530	1,530	0	540	0	0
356	Apartment, building that has fewer than five storeys	5,180	5,175	0	4,670	0	75
357	Other single-attached house	105	110	0	315	0	15
358	Movable dwelling[48]	130	130	0	655	0	5
	Condition of dwelling						
359	Regular maintenance only	29,290	29,240	45	20,345	10	540
360	Minor repairs	11,075	11,035	40	9,865	15	405
361	Major repairs	3,305	3,250	55	3,125	15	130
	Period of construction						
362	Before 1946	10,800	10,790	10	6,685	0	190
363	1946 to 1960	8,720	8,710	10	6,670	0	295
364	1961 to 1970	6,070	6,035	30	4,765	0	145
365	1971 to 1980	8,095	8,070	25	7,340	0	185
366	1981 to 1985	2,390	2,375	20	2,625	10	60
367	1986 to 1990	2,335	2,315	15	2,195	10	80
368	1991 to 1995	1,845	1,835	10	1,530	0	60
369	1996 to 2000	2,225	2,215	15	885	10	40
370	2001 to 2006[49]	1,190	1,175	15	645	0	20

Note: See symbols and abbreviations in the introductory material and see reference material at the end of the publication.

Certaines caractéristiques des divisions de recensement et des subdivisions de recensement – Données intégrales et données-échantillon (20 %), Ontario, Recensement de 2006 (suite)

Cochrane, T	Cochrane, Unorganized, North Part, NO ◆■■A	Constance Lake 92, IRI	Fauquier-Strickland, TP ◆	Hearst, T ◆	Iroquois Falls, T	Caractéristiques	N°
						Caractéristiques de la population	
2,535	**1,010**	**170**	**280**	**2,635**	**1,835**	**Population active occupée totale de 15 ans et plus ayant un lieu habituel de travail ou sans adresse de travail fixe**	321
						Mode de transport	
1,370	555	105	135	1,445	1,045	Hommes	322
1,085	485	45	140	1,035	815	Automobile, camion ou fourgonnette, en tant que conducteur	323
60	30	40	0	100	50	Automobile, camion ou fourgonnette, en tant que passager	324
0	10	0	0	10	10	Transport en commun	325
115	10	15	0	180	150	À pied	326
105	25	0	0	120	20	Tous les autres modes	327
1,165	460	70	140	1,195	790	Femmes	328
840	385	40	75	865	555	Automobile, camion ou fourgonnette, en tant que conductrice	329
160	50	10	10	70	80	Automobile, camion ou fourgonnette, en tant que passagère	330
10	10	0	15	0	0	Transport en commun	331
140	10	20	30	235	130	À pied	332
15	0	0	0	15	15	Tous les autres modes	333
2,955	**1,330**	**270**	**310**	**3,325**	**2,290**	**Population totale de 15 ans et plus ayant travaillé depuis le 1er janvier 2005**	334
						Langue utilisée le plus souvent au travail	
2,795	1,245	265	305	3,165	2,120	Réponses uniques	335
2,295	525	265	90	395	1,880	Anglais	336
495	720	0	210	2,770	245	Français	337
0	0	0	0	0	0	Langues non officielles[7]	338
0	0	0	0	0	0	Chinois, n.d.a.[61]	339
0	0	0	0	0	0	Cantonais	340
10	0	0	0	10	0	Autres langues[8]	341
165	85	0	10	155	165	Réponses multiples	342
155	80	0	0	155	160	Anglais et français	343
10	0	10	0	0	0	Anglais et langue non officielle	344
0	0	0	0	0	0	Français et langue non officielle	345
0	0	0	0	0	0	Anglais, français et langue non officielle	346
						Caractéristiques des logements et des ménages	
2,280	**975**	**195**	**255**	**2,405**	**2,020**	**Nombre total de logements privés occupés**	347
						Mode d'occupation	
1,625	885	50	220	1,440	1,610	Possédé	348
660	85	45	35	960	410	Loué	349
0	0	95	0	0	0	Logement de bande	350
						Type de construction résidentielle	
1,505	915	170	225	1,195	1,520	Maison individuelle non attenante	351
165	15	10	0	65	125	Maison jumelée	352
30	0	10	0	40	50	Maison en rangée	353
150	10	0	5	170	85	Appartement, duplex	354
0	0	0	0	0	5	Appartement, immeuble de cinq étages ou plus	355
295	20	0	20	740	210	Appartement, immeuble de moins de cinq étages	356
10	0	0	0	50	15	Autre maison individuelle attenante	357
120	25	0	5	150	20	Logement mobile[48]	358
						État du logement	
1,440	530	60	160	1,635	1,150	Entretien régulier seulement	359
645	335	40	100	625	685	Réparations mineures	360
195	105	90	0	140	180	Réparations majeures	361
						Période de construction	
445	85	0	70	205	590	Avant 1946	362
510	170	0	55	385	495	1946 à 1960	363
235	150	15	15	385	340	1961 à 1970	364
535	205	35	65	790	285	1971 à 1980	365
220	100	25	20	145	70	1981 à 1985	366
135	110	20	15	165	90	1986 à 1990	367
115	60	15	10	130	110	1991 à 1995	368
60	55	45	0	65	20	1996 à 2000	369
30	45	35	0	120	25	2001 à 2006[49]	370

Nota : Voir les symboles et les abréviations dans les documents d'introduction et voir les documents de référence à la fin de la publication.

Selected characteristics for census divisions and census subdivisions – 100% data and 20% sample data, Ontario, 2006 Census (continued)

No.	Characteristics	**Chatham-Kent CD/DR** ◆◊	Chatham-Kent, MU ◆◊	Moravian 47, IRI ◆◆◊◊	**Cochrane CD/DR** †◆◊	Abitibi 70, IRI ◊	Black River-Matheson, TP ◆A
	Dwelling and household characteristics						
371	Average number of rooms per dwelling	7.0	7.0	5.9	6.2	5.1	6.4
372	Average number of bedrooms per dwelling	2.8	2.8	2.8	2.7	3.0	3.0
373	Average value of dwelling $	156,809	156,809	0	116,880	0	82,056
374	**Total number of private households**	**43,710**	**43,560**	**145**	**33,330**	**35**	**1,080**
	Household size						
375	1 person	11,860	11,825	35	8,910	5	275
376	2 persons	15,780	15,745	35	11,805	10	425
377	3 persons	6,455	6,425	25	5,185	5	150
378	4 to 5 persons	8,530	8,490	40	6,765	15	205
379	6 or more persons	1,080	1,075	10	670	5	15
	Household type						
380	One-family households[50]	30,575	30,480	100	23,410	25	780
381	Multiple-family households	335	330	10	340	0	10
382	Non-family households	12,755	12,715	40	9,585	10	290
383	Number of persons in private households	106,485	106,070	410	81,245	110	2,590
384	Average number of persons in private households	2.4	2.4	2.7	2.4	3.3	2.4
385	Tenant-occupied private non-farm, non-reserve dwellings[51]	11,695	11,695	0	9,695	0	170
386	Average gross rent $[51]	625	625	0	568	0	465
387	Tenant-occupied households spending 30% or more of household income on gross rent[52]	4,910	4,905	0	3,585	0	40
388	Tenant-occupied households spending from 30% to 99% of household income on gross rent[52]	4,400	4,400	0	3,325	0	40
389	Owner-occupied private non-farm, non-reserve dwellings[53]	30,910	30,915	0	22,970	0	880
390	Average owner's major payments $[53]	854	854	0	809	0	602
391	Owner households spending 30% or more of household income on owner's major payments[52]	4,585	4,590	0	2,840	0	105
392	Owner households spending from 30% to 99% of household income on owner's major payments[52]	3,935	3,935	0	2,340	0	75
	Census family characteristics						
393	**Total number of census families in private households**	**31,260**	**31,145**	**115**	**24,120**	**30**	**790**
	Family structure and number of children						
394	Total couple families	26,525	26,465	60	20,625	20	720
395	Total families of married couples	22,760	22,725	35	16,435	15	610
396	Without children at home	11,065	11,050	15	8,100	10	370
397	With children at home	11,695	11,675	25	8,335	10	240
398	1 child	4,105	4,100	0	2,945	0	75
399	2 children	4,925	4,915	10	3,870	0	95
400	3 or more children	2,670	2,660	0	1,525	0	65
401	Total families of common-law couples	3,760	3,735	25	4,185	10	110
402	Without children at home	1,885	1,880	10	1,945	0	30
403	With children at home	1,875	1,860	15	2,240	10	75
404	1 child	860	860	10	975	0	15
405	2 children	670	665	10	945	0	45
406	3 or more children	340	335	0	320	10	15
407	Total lone-parent families	4,735	4,680	50	3,500	10	70
408	Female parent	3,790	3,740	45	2,640	0	45
409	1 child	2,190	2,165	25	1,515	0	25
410	2 children	1,110	1,095	15	815	0	25
411	3 or more children	490	485	10	310	0	0
412	Male parent	945	940	0	860	10	20
413	1 child	690	685	0	570	10	10
414	2 children	220	220	0	215	0	10
415	3 or more children	40	35	0	75	0	0

Note: See symbols and abbreviations in the introductory material and see reference material at the end of the publication.

Certaines caractéristiques des divisions de recensement et des subdivisions de recensement – Données intégrales et données-échantillon (20 %), Ontario, Recensement de 2006 (suite)

Cochrane, T	Cochrane, Unorganized, North Part, NO ◆■■A	Constance Lake 92, IRI	Fauquier-Strickland, TP ◆	Hearst, T ◆	Iroquois Falls, T	Caractéristiques	N°
						Caractéristiques des logements et des ménages	
6.3	6.5	6.2	6.5	6.1	6.6	Nombre moyen de pièces par logement	371
2.7	2.9	3.1	2.9	2.6	2.9	Nombre moyen de chambres à coucher par logement	372
109,393	109,552	0	67,357	146,402	83,792	Valeur moyenne du logement $	373
2,285	**980**	**195**	**255**	**2,400**	**2,020**	**Nombre total de ménages privés**	374
						Taille du ménage	
635	210	30	70	735	545	1 personne	375
825	400	35	115	835	840	2 personnes	376
335	145	45	35	360	245	3 personnes	377
465	205	50	40	455	375	4 à 5 personnes	378
25	20	35	0	20	20	6 personnes ou plus	379
						Genre de ménage	
1,590	730	125	170	1,615	1,425	Ménages unifamiliaux[50]	380
0	10	30	0	10	0	Ménages multifamiliaux	381
690	245	35	85	780	585	Ménages non familiaux	382
5,425	2,440	690	570	5,505	4,650	Nombre de personnes dans les ménages privés	383
2.4	2.5	3.6	2.2	2.3	2.3	Nombre moyen de personnes dans les ménages privés	384
655	85	0	40	960	410	Ménages locataires dans les logements privés non agricoles hors réserve[51]	385
501	692	0	387	562	581	Loyer brut moyen $[51]	386
235	25	0	15	325	170	Ménages locataires consacrant 30 % ou plus du revenu du ménage au loyer brut[52]	387
210	15	0	15	280	160	Ménages locataires consacrant de 30 % à 99 % du revenu du ménage au loyer brut[52]	388
1,605	885	0	220	1,440	1,610	Ménages propriétaires dans les logements privés non agricoles hors réserve[53]	389
832	648	0	862	893	623	Principales dépenses de propriété moyennes $[53]	390
300	100	0	35	180	110	Ménages propriétaires consacrant 30 % ou plus du revenu du ménage aux principales dépenses de propriété[52]	391
210	70	0	10	145	90	Ménages propriétaires consacrant de 30 % à 99 % du revenu du ménage aux principales dépenses de propriété[52]	392
						Caractéristiques des familles de recensement	
1,595	**735**	**190**	**170**	**1,635**	**1,445**	**Nombre total de familles de recensement dans les ménages privés**	393
						Structure de la famille et le nombre d'enfants	
1,400	705	115	170	1,445	1,270	Total des familles avec conjoints	394
1,145	600	65	150	1,060	1,095	Total des familles avec couples mariés	395
530	325	20	90	530	650	Sans enfants à la maison	396
620	275	50	60	525	450	Avec enfants à la maison	397
225	85	20	30	195	145	1 enfant	398
255	150	10	25	250	235	2 enfants	399
130	35	20	10	85	70	3 enfants ou plus	400
255	110	50	20	385	175	Total des familles avec couples en union libre	401
155	35	20	0	195	90	Sans enfants à la maison	402
95	75	30	20	190	80	Avec enfants à la maison	403
20	35	15	0	80	50	1 enfant	404
45	35	10	20	105	25	2 enfants	405
20	0	10	0	10	0	3 enfants ou plus	406
200	25	70	10	185	175	Total des familles monoparentales	407
150	20	50	0	155	115	Parent de sexe féminin	408
95	20	30	10	65	65	1 enfant	409
30	10	10	0	80	10	2 enfants	410
25	0	10	0	15	40	3 enfants ou plus	411
50	0	25	0	30	60	Parent de sexe masculin	412
25	10	15	0	25	35	1 enfant	413
20	0	10	0	10	25	2 enfants	414
0	0	0	0	0	0	3 enfants ou plus	415

Nota : Voir les symboles et les abréviations dans les documents d'introduction et voir les documents de référence à la fin de la publication.

Selected characteristics for census divisions and census subdivisions – 100% data and 20% sample data, Ontario, 2006 Census (continued)

No.	Characteristics	Chatham-Kent CD/DR ◆◊	Chatham-Kent, MU ◆◊	Moravian 47, IRI ◆◆◊◊	Cochrane CD/DR †◆◊	Abitibi 70, IRI ◊	Black River-Matheson, TP ◆A
	Census family characteristics						
416	**Total number of children at home**	**33,775**	**33,600**	**175**	**25,150**	**50**	**755**
	Age group						
417	Under 6 years	7,050	7,010	40	5,075	10	140
418	6 to 14 years	12,595	12,525	70	9,825	20	300
419	15 to 17 years	4,615	4,600	15	3,690	0	160
420	18 to 24 years	7,125	7,100	25	4,660	10	110
421	25 years and over	2,390	2,365	20	1,900	0	45
422	Average number of children at home per census family[54]	1.1	1.1	1.5	1.0	1.7	1.0
423	**Total number of persons in private households**	**106,415**	**106,005**	**410**	**81,260**	**115**	**2,600**
	Census family status and living arrangements						
424	Number of persons not in census families	14,855	14,795	60	11,365	15	340
425	Living with relatives[55]	1,445	1,420	20	1,210	10	20
426	Living with non-relatives only	1,545	1,545	0	1,235	0	45
427	Living alone	11,860	11,830	35	8,915	10	270
428	Number of census family persons	91,560	91,210	350	69,895	100	2,265
429	Average number of persons per census family	2.9	2.9	3.0	2.9	3.3	2.9
430	**Total number of persons aged 65 years and over**	**15,730**	**15,690**	**40**	**10,385**	**10**	**460**
431	Number of persons not in census families aged 65 years and over	5,465	5,440	25	3,895	0	170
432	Living with relatives[55]	465	455	10	410	0	10
433	Living with non-relatives only	200	200	0	125	0	10
434	Living alone	4,795	4,780	10	3,360	0	145
435	Number of census family persons aged 65 years and over	10,265	10,245	20	6,490	10	290
	Economic family characteristics						
436	**Total number of economic families in private households**	**31,245**	**31,130**	**110**	**24,025**	**30**	**785**
	Size of family						
437	2 persons	15,380	15,335	35	11,640	10	420
438	3 persons	6,350	6,325	25	5,010	0	140
439	4 persons	6,065	6,035	25	5,150	10	150
440	5 or more persons	3,450	3,430	20	2,225	10	80
441	Total number of persons in economic families	93,005	92,630	375	71,105	100	2,285
442	Average number of persons per economic family	3.0	3.0	4.0	3.0	4.0	3.0
443	Total number of persons not in economic families	13,410	13,375	35	10,155	10	315
	2005 income characteristics						
444	**Population 15 years and over**	**87,325**	**87,030**	**300**	**66,460**	**X**	**2,165**
	Sex and total income groups in 2005						
445	Without income	3,165	3,145	20	3,135	X	145
446	With income	84,160	83,880	280	63,320	X	2,015
447	Under $1,000[56]	3,075	3,045	25	2,435	X	100
448	$1,000 to $2,999	2,690	2,670	20	2,070	X	105
449	$3,000 to $4,999	2,715	2,695	20	2,130	X	50
450	$5,000 to $6,999	3,075	3,060	20	2,410	X	60
451	$7,000 to $9,999	5,195	5,170	25	3,920	X	135
452	$10,000 to $11,999	3,870	3,865	10	2,770	X	105
453	$12,000 to $14,999	4,930	4,905	25	3,960	X	105
454	$15,000 to $19,999	8,610	8,575	35	6,705	X	235
455	$20,000 to $24,999	6,900	6,875	25	4,900	X	190
456	$25,000 to $29,999	6,460	6,445	20	4,225	X	90
457	$30,000 to $34,999	6,035	6,015	15	3,710	X	85
458	$35,000 to $39,999	5,385	5,375	10	3,485	X	95
459	$40,000 to $44,999	4,530	4,520	10	3,135	X	140
460	$45,000 to $49,999	4,100	4,095	10	3,025	X	75
461	$50,000 to $59,999	5,955	5,945	10	4,410	X	160
462	$60,000 and over	10,635	10,625	10	10,020	X	280
463	Median income $[57]	25,753	25,797	14,864	25,417	X	23,102
464	Average income $[57]	32,335	32,375	20,159	33,553	X	30,134
465	Standard error of average income $[57]	258	261	0	246	X	1,087

Note: See symbols and abbreviations in the introductory material and see reference material at the end of the publication.

Certaines caractéristiques des divisions de recensement et des subdivisions de recensement – Données intégrales et données-échantillon (20 %), Ontario, Recensement de 2006 (suite)

Cochrane, T	Cochrane, Unorganized, North Part, NO ◆■■A	Constance Lake 92, IRI	Fauquier-Strickland, TP ◆	Hearst, T ◆	Iroquois Falls, T	Caractéristiques	N°
						Caractéristiques des familles de recensement	
1,645	**660**	**295**	**140**	**1,565**	**1,270**	**Nombre total d'enfants à la maison**	416
						Groupes d'âge	
355	145	85	35	330	220	Moins de 6 ans	417
640	230	105	35	615	475	6 à 14 ans	418
230	85	40	25	225	210	15 à 17 ans	419
310	145	45	30	285	260	18 à 24 ans	420
105	50	25	20	115	100	25 ans et plus	421
1.0	0.9	1.6	0.8	1.0	0.9	Nombre moyen d'enfants à la maison par famille de recensement[54]	422
5,430	**2,425**	**690**	**565**	**5,510**	**4,650**	**Nombre total de personnes dans les ménages privés**	423
						Situation des particuliers dans la famille de recensement et des particuliers dans le ménage	
790	325	85	85	860	670	Nombre de personnes hors famille de recensement	424
75	25	40	0	75	50	Vivant avec des personnes apparentées[55]	425
80	105	15	0	50	75	Vivant avec des personnes non apparentées seulement	426
635	195	30	80	735	545	Vivant seules	427
4,640	2,100	605	480	4,645	3,980	Nombre de membres d'une famille de recensement	428
2.9	2.9	3.2	2.9	2.8	2.8	Nombre moyen de personnes par famille de recensement	429
735	**365**	**40**	**105**	**665**	**840**	**Nombre total de personnes âgées de 65 ans et plus**	430
255	70	15	20	300	310	Nombre de personnes hors famille de recensement âgées de 65 ans et plus	431
10	10	10	0	45	40	Vivant avec des personnes apparentées[55]	432
10	10	0	0	0	0	Vivant avec des personnes non apparentées seulement	433
235	50	10	20	260	265	Vivant seules	434
485	295	25	85	365	530	Nombre de membres d'une famille de recensement âgés de 65 ans et plus	435
						Caractéristiques des familles économiques	
1,610	**730**	**160**	**175**	**1,655**	**1,445**	**Nombre total de familles économiques dans les ménages privés**	436
						Taille de la famille	
805	375	35	90	820	810	2 personnes	437
305	125	45	30	365	250	3 personnes	438
340	165	25	45	370	285	4 personnes	439
160	65	60	10	100	100	5 personnes ou plus	440
4,715	2,125	650	480	4,725	4,030	Nombre total de personnes dans les familles économiques	441
3.0	3.0	4.0	3.0	3.0	3.0	Nombre moyen de personnes par famille économique	442
710	300	40	80	785	615	Nombre total de personnes hors famille économique	443
						Caractéristiques du revenu de 2005	
4,430	**2,065**	**495**	**500**	**4,570**	**3,955**	**Population de 15 ans et plus**	444
						Sexe et groupes de revenu total en 2005	
235	105	50	25	185	245	Sans revenu	445
4,195	1,955	445	470	4,385	3,705	Avec un revenu	446
165	60	30	10	160	185	Moins de 1 000 $[56]	447
145	100	40	20	110	95	1 000 $ à 2 999 $	448
195	40	45	25	175	100	3 000 $ à 4 999 $	449
120	90	30	25	105	115	5 000 $ à 6 999 $	450
340	130	45	15	230	205	7 000 $ à 9 999 $	451
220	125	25	10	220	115	10 000 $ à 11 999 $	452
290	110	50	60	235	185	12 000 $ à 14 999 $	453
445	190	35	45	495	460	15 000 $ à 19 999 $	454
295	175	25	15	235	250	20 000 $ à 24 999 $	455
225	95	15	35	270	215	25 000 $ à 29 999 $	456
215	135	15	20	215	250	30 000 $ à 34 999 $	457
290	85	15	25	230	255	35 000 $ à 39 999 $	458
165	100	15	15	285	185	40 000 $ à 44 999 $	459
245	120	15	25	295	150	45 000 $ à 49 999$	460
295	165	25	30	355	270	50 000 $ à 59 999$	461
545	235	25	95	760	660	60 000 $ et plus	462
22,541	24,128	12,896	28,075	28,975	28,357	Revenu médian $[57]	463
30,933	31,169	19,484	35,501	35,210	34,763	Revenu moyen $[57]	464
898	1,056	0	3,014	886	1,073	Erreur type de revenu moyen $[57]	465

Nota : Voir les symboles et les abréviations dans les documents d'introduction et voir les documents de référence à la fin de la publication.

Selected characteristics for census divisions and census subdivisions – 100% data and 20% sample data, Ontario, 2006 Census (continued)

No.	Characteristics	Chatham-Kent CD/DR ◆◇	Chatham-Kent, MU ◆◇	Moravian 47, IRI ◆◆◇◇	Cochrane CD/DR †◆◇	Abitibi 70, IRI ◇	Black River-Matheson, TP ◆A
	2005 income characteristics						
	Sex and total income groups in 2005 (continued)						
466	Total - Males	42,325	42,200	125	32,940	X	1,060
467	Without income	1,200	1,195	10	1,365	X	50
468	With income	41,125	41,005	120	31,575	X	1,010
469	Under $1,000[56]	1,650	1,640	10	1,190	X	55
470	$1,000 to $2,999	1,070	1,065	0	660	X	20
471	$3,000 to $4,999	1,005	1,000	0	735	X	15
472	$5,000 to $6,999	1,130	1,115	10	795	X	15
473	$7,000 to $9,999	1,870	1,855	15	1,215	X	30
474	$10,000 to $11,999	1,450	1,445	10	930	X	15
475	$12,000 to $14,999	1,535	1,520	10	1,325	X	35
476	$15,000 to $19,999	3,180	3,165	15	2,215	X	85
477	$20,000 to $24,999	2,885	2,875	10	2,285	X	105
478	$25,000 to $29,999	2,840	2,835	10	1,995	X	50
479	$30,000 to $34,999	2,970	2,965	10	1,730	X	50
480	$35,000 to $39,999	2,885	2,885	10	1,955	X	50
481	$40,000 to $44,999	2,720	2,710	0	1,775	X	55
482	$45,000 to $49,999	2,425	2,420	0	1,925	X	60
483	$50,000 to $59,999	3,885	3,885	0	3,225	X	135
484	$60,000 and over	7,620	7,615	0	7,605	X	230
485	Median income $[57]	33,175	33,225	13,856	36,889	X	37,831
486	Average income $[57]	38,922	38,976	20,019	42,271	X	39,222
487	Standard error of average income $[57]	451	455	0	409	X	1,652
488	Total - Females	44,995	44,825	170	33,515	X	1,100
489	Without income	1,965	1,950	15	1,765	X	100
490	With income	43,035	42,875	160	31,750	X	1,005
491	Under $1,000[56]	1,420	1,410	10	1,250	X	45
492	$1,000 to $2,999	1,615	1,605	10	1,405	X	85
493	$3,000 to $4,999	1,705	1,690	10	1,395	X	35
494	$5,000 to $6,999	1,950	1,935	10	1,615	X	50
495	$7,000 to $9,999	3,330	3,315	10	2,710	X	105
496	$10,000 to $11,999	2,425	2,420	10	1,840	X	90
497	$12,000 to $14,999	3,400	3,380	20	2,635	X	70
498	$15,000 to $19,999	5,430	5,405	20	4,490	X	150
499	$20,000 to $24,999	4,010	4,000	10	2,615	X	85
500	$25,000 to $29,999	3,620	3,605	15	2,230	X	35
501	$30,000 to $34,999	3,055	3,045	10	1,980	X	35
502	$35,000 to $39,999	2,500	2,490	10	1,530	X	45
503	$40,000 to $44,999	1,810	1,810	10	1,360	X	85
504	$45,000 to $49,999	1,680	1,670	10	1,100	X	15
505	$50,000 to $59,999	2,065	2,060	10	1,185	X	25
506	$60,000 and over	3,015	3,010	10	2,420	X	50
507	Median income $[57]	20,276	20,297	15,040	18,285	X	15,374
508	Average income $[57]	26,041	26,062	20,264	24,883	X	20,978
509	Standard error of average income $[57]	246	249	0	240	X	1,180
	Composition of total income						
510	Composition of total income in 2005 %	100.0	100.0	100.0	100.0	X	100.0
511	Employment income %	72.1	72.0	71.0	75.0	X	70.4
512	Government transfer payments %	13.9	13.9	22.9	14.0	X	18.2
513	Other %	14.0	14.1	4.8	11.0	X	11.4
514	**Population 15 years and over with employment income in 2005**	**62,885**	**62,700**	**185**	**45,400**	**X**	**1,350**
	Sex and work activity						
515	Median employment income in 2005 $	24,922	24,963	14,944	28,202	X	26,426
516	Average employment income in 2005 $	31,179	31,207	21,667	35,098	X	31,663
517	Standard error of average employment income $	298	301	0	318	X	1,454
518	Worked full year, full time[59]	32,260	32,180	80	22,400	X	620
519	Median employment income in 2005 $	40,888	40,920	32,448	45,902	X	47,957
520	Average employment income in 2005 $	45,545	45,567	36,891	50,570	X	48,862
521	Standard error of average employment income $	480	484	0	481	X	1,920
522	Worked part year or part time[60]	25,615	25,515	95	19,070	X	595
523	Median employment income in 2005 $	10,548	10,570	5,232	13,053	X	14,425
524	Average employment income in 2005 $	17,687	17,715	10,096	22,557	X	19,903
525	Standard error of average employment income $	282	286	0	377	X	1,590
526	Males 15 years and over with employment income[58]	33,130	33,050	80	24,525	X	740
527	Median employment income in 2005 $	31,998	32,015	15,968	40,012	X	42,062
528	Average employment income in 2005 $	36,992	37,025	23,438	42,911	X	40,238
529	Standard error of average employment income $	501	505	0	503	X	2,070

Note: See symbols and abbreviations in the introductory material and see reference material at the end of the publication.

Certaines caractéristiques des divisions de recensement et des subdivisions de recensement – Données intégrales et données-échantillon (20 %), Ontario, Recensement de 2006 (suite)

Cochrane, T	Cochrane, Unorganized, North Part, NO ◆■■A	Constance Lake 92, IRI	Fauquier-Strickland, TP ◆	Hearst, T ◆	Iroquois Falls, T	Caractéristiques	N°
						Caractéristiques du revenu de 2005	
						Sexe et groupes de revenu total en 2005 (suite)	
2,215	1,085	250	245	2,300	1,925	Total - Hommes	466
145	30	20	0	45	60	Sans revenu	467
2,070	1,060	230	250	2,250	1,865	Avec un revenu	468
115	35	20	0	65	80	Moins de 1 000 $[56]	469
45	20	25	0	50	30	1 000 $ à 2 999 $	470
60	10	25	0	45	15	3 000 $ à 4 999 $	471
45	30	0	10	20	40	5 000 $ à 6 999 $	472
70	50	20	0	60	70	7 000 $ à 9 999 $	473
45	55	10	0	80	40	10 000 $ à 11 999 $	474
130	50	20	10	45	20	12 000 $ à 14 999 $	475
165	55	20	10	200	95	15 000 $ à 19 999 $	476
105	95	10	15	130	135	20 000 $ à 24 999 $	477
95	35	10	25	115	85	25 000 $ à 29 999 $	478
105	65	10	20	70	150	30 000 $ à 34 999 $	479
185	55	10	15	130	175	35 000 $ à 39 999 $	480
80	65	10	0	175	110	40 000 $ à $44 999 $	481
195	90	10	20	210	85	45 000 $ à $49 999 $	482
220	145	15	15	270	205	50 000 $ à $59 999 $	483
405	195	15	95	585	530	60 000 $ et plus	484
36,346	38,959	13,483	45,992	43,852	40,002	Revenu médian $[57]	485
38,788	39,193	22,158	50,720	44,387	45,052	Revenu moyen $[57]	486
1,427	1,587	0	4,553	1,350	1,553	Erreur type de revenu moyen $[57]	487
2,215	975	240	245	2,270	2,025	Total - Femmes	488
90	80	25	25	135	185	Sans revenu	489
2,125	900	210	225	2,130	1,840	Avec un revenu	490
50	25	10	0	95	105	Moins de 1 000 $[56]	491
95	80	15	15	60	60	1 000$ à 2 999 $	492
130	25	25	25	130	90	3 000 $ à 4 999 $	493
70	55	20	10	90	75	5 000 $ à 6 999 $	494
265	90	20	20	165	140	7 000 $ à 9 999 $	495
170	65	15	0	140	75	10 000 $ à 11 999 $	496
165	60	30	55	190	170	12 000 $ à 14 999 $	497
280	135	20	35	295	365	15 000 $ à 19 999 $	498
190	80	15	0	100	115	20 000 $ à 24 999 $	499
125	55	10	10	150	130	25 000 $ à 29 999 $	500
110	75	0	0	145	100	30 000 $ à 34 999 $	501
100	30	10	10	100	85	35 000 $ à 39 999 $	502
90	30	0	10	110	70	40 000 $ à 44 999 $	503
50	35	10	0	90	65	45 000 $ à 49 999 $	504
70	20	10	15	85	65	50 000 $ à 59 999 $	505
140	45	10	10	175	130	60 000 $ et plus	506
16,631	16,795	11,232	14,739	18,265	18,192	Revenu médian $[57]	507
23,283	21,720	16,504	18,486	25,526	24,343	Revenu moyen $[57]	508
987	1,088	0	2,183	982	1,303	Erreur type de revenu moyen $[57]	509
						Composition du revenu total	
100.0	100.0	100.0	100.0	100.0	100.0	Composition du revenu total en 2005 %	510
75.6	72.4	78.5	72.0	75.9	68.5	Revenu d'emploi %	511
15.0	15.9	20.4	12.9	11.7	15.8	Transferts gouvernementaux %	512
9.4	11.5	2.1	15.7	12.4	15.8	Autres %	513
2,850	**1,350**	**290**	**330**	**3,335**	**2,390**	**Population de 15 ans et plus avec un revenu d'emploi en 2005**	514
						Sexe et travail	
30,580	27,542	14,272	37,810	31,935	28,448	Revenu médian d'emploi en 2005 $	515
34,427	32,793	23,210	36,416	35,182	36,857	Revenu moyen d'emploi en 2005 $	516
1,212	1,348	0	3,769	979	1,465	Erreur type de revenu moyen d'emploi $	517
1,490	605	105	160	1,490	1,110	A travaillé toute l'année à plein temps[59]	518
46,420	47,041	40,768	48,266	46,524	53,459	Revenu médian d'emploi en 2005 $	519
47,516	48,550	40,724	51,571	49,609	54,234	Revenu moyen d'emploi en 2005 $	520
1,417	1,994	0	5,417	1,399	2,071	Erreur type de revenu moyen d'emploi $	521
1,150	620	120	125	1,630	1,040	A travaillé une partie de l'année ou à temps partiel[60]	522
11,614	15,090	10,528	14,485	17,937	15,802	Revenu médian d'emploi en 2005 $	523
22,426	22,954	15,259	27,998	25,316	25,861	Revenu moyen d'emploi en 2005 $	524
1,947	1,537	0	4,817	1,126	1,927	Erreur type de revenu moyen d'emploi $	525
1,515	770	170	185	1,840	1,355	Hommes de 15 ans et plus avec un revenu d'emploi[58]	526
40,304	43,130	20,160	48,541	43,876	41,698	Revenu médian d'emploi en 2005 $	527
42,279	40,600	26,160	48,001	42,728	45,094	Revenu moyen d'emploi en 2005 $	528
1,796	1,957	0	5,401	1,353	1,956	Erreur type de revenu moyen d'emploi $	529

Nota : Voir les symboles et les abréviations dans les documents d'introduction et voir les documents de référence à la fin de la publication.

Selected characteristics for census divisions and census subdivisions – 100% data and 20% sample data, Ontario, 2006 Census (continued)

No.	Characteristics	**Chatham-Kent CD/DR** ◆◊	Chatham-Kent, MU ◆◊	Moravian 47, IRI ◆◆◊◊	**Cochrane CD/DR** †◆◊	Abitibi 70, IRI ◊	Black River-Matheson, TP ◆A
	2005 income characteristics						
	Sex and work activity (continued)						
530	Worked full year, full time[59]	18,940	18,910	30	13,450	X	425
531	Median employment income in 2005 $	45,887	45,898	40,832	53,991	X	51,341
532	Average employment income in 2005 $	51,158	51,176	40,302	58,199	X	52,525
533	Standard error of average employment income $	752	756	0	710	X	2,230
534	Worked part year or part time[60]	11,660	11,615	40	8,800	X	255
535	Median employment income in 2005 $	11,935	11,948	6,672	18,484	X	21,920
536	Average employment income in 2005 $	20,561	20,587	13,245	29,036	X	27,624
537	Standard error of average employment income $	506	512	0	674	X	3,131
538	Females 15 years and over with employment income[58]	29,755	29,650	110	20,875	X	610
539	Median employment income in 2005 $	19,340	19,356	13,136	19,786	X	15,019
540	Average employment income in 2005 $	24,706	24,722	20,343	25,917	X	21,298
541	Standard error of average employment income $	270	273	0	324	X	1,705
542	Worked full year, full time[59]	13,320	13,270	50	8,950	X	190
543	Median employment income in 2005 $	34,468	34,499	28,160	35,064	X	40,085
544	Average employment income in 2005 $	37,565	37,575	34,776	39,105	X	40,714
545	Standard error of average employment income $	411	415	0	486	X	3,432
546	Worked part year or part time[60]	13,955	13,905	50	10,265	X	345
547	Median employment income in 2005 $	9,764	9,802	4,720	10,630	X	10,661
548	Average employment income in 2005 $	15,286	15,316	7,601	17,001	X	14,133
549	Standard error of average employment income $	290	293	0	360	X	1,292
550	**Total number of economic families in private households**	**31,245**	**31,130**	**115**	**24,025**	**X**	**785**
	Family income groups in 2005						
551	Under $10,000	610	600	10	530	X	30
552	$10,000 to $19,999	1,505	1,480	20	1,090	X	45
553	$20,000 to $29,999	2,470	2,455	15	2,145	X	75
554	$30,000 to $39,999	3,240	3,225	15	2,255	X	75
555	$40,000 to $49,999	3,495	3,485	15	2,090	X	65
556	$50,000 to $59,999	2,945	2,935	10	2,100	X	65
557	$60,000 to $69,999	3,255	3,245	10	2,210	X	125
558	$70,000 to $79,999	2,575	2,570	0	2,260	X	90
559	$80,000 to $89,999	2,445	2,445	0	2,005	X	50
560	$90,000 to $99,999	1,975	1,970	0	1,630	X	40
561	$100,000 and over	6,715	6,715	0	5,710	X	135
562	Median family income $	64,055	64,172	34,688	68,266	X	61,377
563	Average family income $	73,732	73,842	42,813	75,300	X	65,161
564	Standard error of average family income $	760	769	0	649	X	2,603
	Family after-tax income groups in 2005						
565	Under $10,000	625	615	10	540	X	30
566	$10,000 to $19,999	1,550	1,530	20	1,145	X	45
567	$20,000 to $29,999	2,785	2,770	20	2,320	X	90
568	$30,000 to $39,999	4,320	4,305	20	2,815	X	70
569	$40,000 to $49,999	4,145	4,135	20	2,850	X	105
570	$50,000 to $59,999	4,010	4,005	10	3,050	X	155
571	$60,000 to $69,999	3,520	3,515	10	2,580	X	60
572	$70,000 to $79,999	2,885	2,885	10	2,565	X	95
573	$80,000 to $89,999	2,075	2,070	10	1,800	X	40
574	$90,000 to $99,999	1,735	1,730	0	1,505	X	25
575	$100,000 and over	3,580	3,570	10	2,860	X	65
576	Median after-tax family income $	55,410	55,473	34,432	57,832	X	52,436
577	Average after-tax family income $	62,213	62,289	40,951	62,812	X	55,531
578	Standard error of average after-tax family income $	593	600	0	455	X	2,038
	Income status in 2005						
579	Total population in private households for income status	105,945	105,945	0	78,535	X	2,600
580	Below low income cut-off before tax in 2005	12,655	12,655	0	9,610	X	220
581	Prevalence of low income before tax in 2005 %	11.9	11.9	0.0	12.2	X	8.5
582	Below low income cut-off after tax in 2005	8,330	8,330	0	6,385	X	165
583	Prevalence of low income after tax in 2005 %	7.9	7.9	0.0	8.1	X	6.3

Note: See symbols and abbreviations in the introductory material and see reference material at the end of the publication.

Certaines caractéristiques des divisions de recensement et des subdivisions de recensement – Données intégrales et données-échantillon (20 %), Ontario, Recensement de 2006 (suite)

Cochrane, T	Cochrane, Unorganized, North Part, NO ◆■■A	Constance Lake 92, IRI	Fauquier-Strickland, TP ◆	Hearst, T ◆	Iroquois Falls, T	Caractéristiques	N°
						Caractéristiques du revenu de 2005	
						Sexe et travail (suite)	
875	400	65	105	910	700	A travaillé toute l'année à plein temps[59]	530
52,132	51,322	46,976	56,025	53,806	62,304	Revenu médian d'emploi en 2005 $	531
53,769	54,676	43,182	60,720	55,877	61,305	Revenu moyen d'emploi en 2005 $	532
1,777	2,659	0	6,857	1,753	1,931	Erreur type de revenu moyen d'emploi $	533
515	285	70	50	840	490	A travaillé une partie de l'année ou à temps partiel[60]	534
21,446	26,404	10,800	48,552	25,594	20,560	Revenu médian d'emploi en 2005 $	535
30,314	31,184	17,290	47,006	32,511	35,424	Revenu moyen d'emploi en 2005 $	536
3,722	2,477	0	7,036	1,740	3,479	Erreur type de revenu moyen d'emploi $	537
1,335	580	120	145	1,490	1,040	Femmes de 15 ans et plus avec un revenu d'emploi[58]	538
18,275	16,112	11,360	13,483	19,398	18,373	Revenu médian d'emploi en 2005 $	539
25,493	22,436	19,138	21,584	25,872	26,140	Revenu moyen d'emploi en 2005 $	540
1,438	1,429	0	3,407	1,262	2,029	Erreur type de revenu moyen d'emploi $	541
610	200	45	55	580	410	A travaillé toute l'année à plein temps[59]	542
35,810	33,433	35,968	37,753	32,113	35,854	Revenu médian d'emploi en 2005 $	543
38,554	36,354	36,887	33,804	39,733	42,148	Revenu moyen d'emploi en 2005 $	544
2,110	2,240	0	5,096	2,070	4,232	Erreur type de revenu moyen d'emploi $	545
635	335	50	75	790	550	A travaillé une partie de l'année ou à temps partiel[60]	546
8,834	10,796	9,280	11,299	11,140	12,579	Revenu médian d'emploi en 2005 $	547
16,050	16,008	12,376	15,736	17,705	17,419	Revenu moyen d'emploi en 2005 $	548
1,733	1,568	0	3,991	1,211	1,505	Erreur type de revenu moyen d'emploi $	549
1,615	**735**	**160**	**170**	**1,655**	**1,445**	**Nombre total des familles économiques dans les ménages privés**	550
						Revenu de la famille économique en 2005	
65	10	10	0	45	20	Moins de 10 000 $	551
90	0	20	0	35	50	10 000 $ à 19 999 $	552
145	95	30	20	125	65	20 000 $ à 29 999 $	553
190	55	15	25	100	150	30 000 $ à 39 999 $	554
125	70	20	15	150	125	40 000 $ à 49 999 $	555
155	70	0	10	135	135	50 000 $ à 59 999 $	556
155	95	15	10	170	180	60 000 $ à 69 999 $	557
155	80	10	35	145	155	70 000 $ à 79 999 $	558
145	40	10	10	180	90	80 000 $ à 89 999 $	559
110	50	10	0	120	105	90 000 $ à 99 999 $	560
270	165	15	50	445	355	100 000 $ et plus	561
61,613	65,671	40,405	73,239	73,672	69,009	Revenu médian des familles $	562
66,631	73,684	49,338	71,278	79,868	76,108	Revenu moyen des familles $	563
2,136	2,773	0	5,737	2,309	2,666	Erreur type de revenu moyen des familles $	564
						Revenu après impôt de la famille économique en 2005	
70	10	10	0	40	25	Moins de 10 000 $	565
100	0	20	0	45	50	10 000 $ à 19 999 $	566
155	100	30	20	130	75	20 000 $ à 29 999 $	567
215	65	15	30	140	195	30 000 $ à 39 999 $	568
200	110	20	15	200	170	40 000 $ à 49 999 $	569
200	125	10	15	220	250	50 000 $ à 59 999 $	570
190	65	20	40	215	195	60 000 $ à 69 999 $	571
175	60	10	0	175	125	70 000 $ à 79 999 $	572
70	65	10	10	150	125	80 000 $ à 89 999 $	573
100	35	0	35	120	110	90 000 $ à 99 999 $	574
135	80	15	0	220	140	100 000 $ et plus	575
54,098	56,069	40,405	61,959	61,413	58,012	Revenu médian après impôt des familles $	576
56,294	62,271	48,565	60,534	66,346	63,367	Revenu moyen après impôt des familles $	577
1,627	2,082	0	4,236	1,731	1,853	Erreur type de revenu moyen après impôt des familles $	578
						Catégorie de revenu en 2005	
5,425	2,430	0	570	5,505	4,650	Population totale dans les ménages privés pour la catégorie de revenu	579
910	225	0	10	605	440	Au-dessous du seuil de faible revenu avant impôt en 2005	580
16.8	9.3	0.0	0.0	10.9	9.6	Fréquence du faible revenu avant impôt en 2005 %	581
650	105	0	10	415	360	Au-dessous du seuil de faible revenu après impôt en 2005	582
12.0	4.3	0.0	0.0	7.5	7.7	Fréquence du faible revenu après impôt en 2005 %	583

Nota : Voir les symboles et les abréviations dans les documents d'introduction et voir les documents de référence à la fin de la publication.

Selected characteristics for census divisions and census subdivisions – 100% data and 20% sample data, Ontario, 2006 Census (continued)

No.	Characteristics	**Chatham-Kent CD/DR ◆◊**	Chatham-Kent, MU ◆◊	Moravian 47, IRI ◆◆◊◊	**Cochrane CD/DR †◆◊**	Abitibi 70, IRI ◊	Black River-Matheson, TP ◆A
	2005 income characteristics						
584	**Total number of private households**	**43,670**	**43,525**	**145**	**33,340**	**X**	**1,075**
	Household income groups in 2005						
585	Under $10,000	1,750	1,730	15	1,365	X	45
586	$10,000 to $19,999	4,970	4,940	35	4,415	X	170
587	$20,000 to $29,999	4,815	4,790	25	3,540	X	100
588	$30,000 to $39,999	5,035	5,015	20	3,240	X	105
589	$40,000 to $49,999	4,850	4,835	15	3,075	X	80
590	$50,000 to $59,999	3,880	3,875	10	2,630	X	90
591	$60,000 to $69,999	3,735	3,725	10	2,600	X	145
592	$70,000 to $79,999	2,885	2,880	10	2,555	X	105
593	$80,000 to $89,999	2,635	2,630	0	2,165	X	50
594	$90,000 to $99,999	2,075	2,070	10	1,745	X	40
595	$100,000 and over	7,030	7,025	0	6,010	X	145
596	Median household income $	51,002	51,081	29,760	53,691	X	54,794
597	Average household income $	62,169	62,248	38,524	63,642	X	56,496
598	Standard error of average household income $	588	594	0	543	X	2,304
	Household after-tax income groups in 2005						
599	Under $10,000	1,805	1,785	15	1,370	X	45
600	$10,000 to $19,999	5,400	5,370	30	4,790	X	170
601	$20,000 to $29,999	5,605	5,585	20	3,905	X	125
602	$30,000 to $39,999	6,325	6,300	20	4,030	X	105
603	$40,000 to $49,999	5,440	5,425	15	3,725	X	140
604	$50,000 to $59,999	4,540	4,530	10	3,435	X	175
605	$60,000 to $69,999	3,815	3,810	0	2,880	X	75
606	$70,000 to $79,999	3,070	3,065	0	2,735	X	95
607	$80,000 to $89,999	2,185	2,180	10	1,930	X	50
608	$90,000 to $99,999	1,790	1,790	0	1,570	X	25
609	$100,000 and over	3,685	3,675	10	2,960	X	65
610	Median after-tax household income $	44,501	44,568	29,120	46,834	X	46,477
611	Average after-tax household income $	52,563	52,617	36,664	53,270	X	48,215
612	Standard error of average after-tax household income $	461	466	0	390	X	1,821

Note: See symbols and abbreviations in the introductory material and see reference material at the end of the publication.

Certaines caractéristiques des divisions de recensement et des subdivisions de recensement – Données intégrales et données-échantillon (20 %), Ontario, Recensement de 2006 (suite)

Cochrane, T	Cochrane, Unorganized, North Part, NO ◆■■A	Constance Lake 92, IRI	Fauquier-Strickland, TP ◆	Hearst, T ◆	Iroquois Falls, T	Caractéristiques	N°
						Caractéristiques du revenu de 2005	
2,280	**975**	**195**	**260**	**2,405**	**2,020**	**Nombre total des ménages privés**	584
						Tranches de revenu des ménages en 2005	
145	50	25	10	125	55	Moins de 10 000 $	585
325	75	30	25	325	300	10 000 $ à 19 999 $	586
245	140	35	20	225	115	20 000 $ à 29 999 $	587
270	65	20	30	155	225	30 000 $ à 39 999 $	588
185	105	20	20	225	180	40 000 $ à 49 999 $	589
185	80	10	15	200	170	50 000 $ à 59 999 $	590
175	100	20	20	195	210	60 000 $ à 69 999 $	591
180	100	10	40	170	170	70 000 $ à 79 999 $	592
155	40	0	20	185	95	80 000 $ à 89 999 $	593
120	50	10	0	135	120	90 000 $ à 99 999 $	594
285	165	15	60	455	370	100 000 $ et plus	595
48,286	54,986	36,147	64,926	56,897	56,160	Revenu médian des ménages $	596
56,854	62,474	45,056	65,168	64,244	63,757	Revenu moyen des ménages $	597
1,849	2,399	0	4,834	1,948	2,199	Erreur type de revenu moyen des ménages $	598
						Tranches du revenu après impôt des ménages en 2005	
145	55	20	10	130	55	Moins de 10 000 $	599
345	80	30	25	345	325	10 000 $ à 19 999 $	600
285	140	30	25	240	140	20 000 $ à 29 999 $	601
310	85	20	40	230	275	30 000 $ à 39 999 $	602
245	145	25	25	295	220	40 000 $ à 49 999 $	603
225	145	10	35	235	260	50 000 $ à 59 999 $	604
215	65	25	45	235	215	60 000 $ à 69 999 $	605
175	65	10	0	190	140	70 000 $ à 79 999 $	606
85	65	0	10	155	125	80 000 $ à 89 999 $	607
100	35	10	35	125	120	90 000 $ à 99 999 $	608
140	85	15	15	220	140	100 000 $ et plus	609
41,822	48,863	35,968	51,644	48,098	49,765	Revenu médian après impôt des ménages $	610
48,068	53,135	44,384	53,840	53,720	53,355	Revenu moyen après impôt des ménages $	611
1,388	1,842	0	3,686	1,494	1,585	Erreur type de revenu moyen après impôt des ménages $	612

Nota : Voir les symboles et les abréviations dans les documents d'introduction et voir les documents de référence à la fin de la publication.

Selected characteristics for census divisions and census subdivisions – 100% data and 20% sample data, Ontario, 2006 Census (continued)

No.	Characteristics	Kapuskasing, T	Mattice-Val Côté, TP ◆	Moonbeam, TP ◆◆◇	New Post 69A, IRI ◆◆◇◇	Opasatika, TP ◆	Smooth Rock Falls, T ◇
	Population characteristics						
1	**Population, 2001[1]**	**9,238**	**891**	**1,201**	**105**	**325**	**1,830**
2	**Population, 2006[2]**	**8,509**	**772**	**1,298**	**73**	**280**	**1,473**
3	Population percentage change, 2001 to 2006	-7.9	-13.4	8.1	-30.5	-13.8	-19.5
4	Land area in square kilometres, 2006	83.98	414.64	235.17	1.22	329.98	199.79
5	**Total population – 100% data[3]**	**8,505**	**770**	**1,295**	**70**	**280**	**1,470**
	Sex and age groups						
6	Male	4,215	380	675	45	140	740
7	0 to 4 years	180	25	30	0	5	20
8	5 to 9 years	230	20	30	0	5	40
9	10 to 14 years	265	20	40	5	5	40
10	15 to 19 years	300	25	40	5	10	50
11	20 to 24 years	230	20	25	5	15	30
12	25 to 29 years	175	30	30	0	5	25
13	30 to 34 years	205	20	25	0	5	35
14	35 to 39 years	225	20	30	10	10	50
15	40 to 44 years	365	40	45	5	10	55
16	45 to 49 years	430	35	65	0	15	75
17	50 to 54 years	365	30	70	0	15	90
18	55 to 59 years	330	20	55	5	10	50
19	60 to 64 years	275	25	60	5	10	55
20	65 to 69 years	165	25	40	0	10	35
21	70 to 74 years	190	15	45	0	10	30
22	75 to 79 years	130	10	25	0	10	40
23	80 to 84 years	90	5	10	0	0	15
24	85 years and over	55	0	5	0	0	5
25	Female	4,290	390	625	25	140	735
26	0 to 4 years	175	20	25	0	0	20
27	5 to 9 years	170	20	20	0	10	35
28	10 to 14 years	255	25	35	5	5	45
29	15 to 19 years	290	35	50	10	15	45
30	20 to 24 years	235	20	25	0	5	35
31	25 to 29 years	160	25	20	0	0	25
32	30 to 34 years	200	20	30	0	5	40
33	35 to 39 years	270	25	40	5	10	40
34	40 to 44 years	360	35	50	5	15	55
35	45 to 49 years	435	30	70	0	15	70
36	50 to 54 years	345	20	40	0	10	75
37	55 to 59 years	305	35	55	5	10	60
38	60 to 64 years	240	25	55	0	10	35
39	65 to 69 years	205	25	45	0	10	40
40	70 to 74 years	210	15	35	0	10	45
41	75 to 79 years	200	5	15	0	5	35
42	80 to 84 years	140	5	5	0	5	25
43	85 years and over	90	5	10	5	0	20
44	**Total population 15 years and over[3]**	**7,225**	**635**	**1,115**	**60**	**245**	**1,270**
	Legal marital status						
45	Never legally married (single)	2,040	215	290	30	65	340
46	Legally married (and not separated)[4,5]	3,740	310	645	15	135	720
47	Separated, but still legally married	350	30	40	0	10	45
48	Divorced	430	25	75	5	15	50
49	Widowed	670	50	65	5	20	115
	Common-law status						
50	Not in a common-law relationship	6,445	535	960	50	210	1,145
51	In a common-law relationship	780	105	150	15	35	125
52	**Total population – 20% sample data[6]**	**8,355**	**775**	**1,290**	**75**	**280**	**1,440**
	Mother tongue						
53	Single responses	8,205	755	1,260	75	280	1,425
54	English	2,280	90	165	55	35	405
55	French	5,610	645	1,070	0	235	1,010
56	Non-official languages[7]	320	25	20	20	10	10
57	Italian	20	0	0	0	0	0
58	Chinese, n.o.s.[61]	25	0	0	0	0	0
59	Cantonese	35	0	0	0	0	0
60	Spanish	0	20	0	0	0	0
61	German	30	0	0	0	10	0
62	Other languages[8]	200	10	20	20	0	10

Note: See symbols and abbreviations in the introductory material and see reference material at the end of the publication.

Certaines caractéristiques des divisions de recensement et des subdivisions de recensement – Données intégrales et données-échantillon (20 %), Ontario, Recensement de 2006 (suite)

Timmins, CY ◆◊	Val Rita-Harty, TP	**Dufferin CD/DR A**	Amaranth, TP **A**	East Garafraxa, TP	East Luther Grand Valley, TP ◆◊	**Caractéristiques**	N°
						Caractéristiques de la population	
43,686	**1,022**	**51,003**	**3,736**	**2,214**	**2,842**	**Population, 2001**[1]	1
42,997	**939**	**54,436**	**3,845**	**2,389**	**2,844**	**Population, 2006**[2]	2
-1.6	-8.1	6.7	2.9	7.9	0.1	Variation en pourcentage de la population, 2001 à 2006	3
2,961.58	382.64	1,485.58	264.35	165.72	158.20	Superficie des terres en kilomètres carrés, 2006	4
42,995	**940**	**54,435**	**3,845**	**2,385**	**2,845**	**Population totale – Données intégrales**[3]	5
						Sexe et groupes d'âge	
21,165	480	27,130	2,030	1,240	1,500	Sexe masculin	6
1,140	25	1,595	105	70	95	0 à 4 ans	7
1,345	30	2,020	160	95	120	5 à 9 ans	8
1,535	35	2,340	185	95	135	10 à 14 ans	9
1,645	40	2,245	165	100	140	15 à 19 ans	10
1,300	35	1,650	125	80	85	20 à 24 ans	11
1,150	20	1,335	65	40	50	25 à 29 ans	12
1,300	20	1,600	80	45	80	30 à 34 ans	13
1,470	35	2,055	135	85	110	35 à 39 ans	14
1,825	35	2,560	200	110	170	40 à 44 ans	15
1,935	40	2,280	180	100	145	45 à 49 ans	16
1,725	40	1,920	165	110	90	50 à 54 ans	17
1,455	35	1,625	135	95	85	55 à 59 ans	18
1,015	35	1,245	120	75	70	60 à 64 ans	19
760	15	915	90	50	45	65 à 69 ans	20
640	25	720	50	30	25	70 à 74 ans	21
460	10	510	40	30	30	75 à 79 ans	22
280	0	330	20	15	10	80 à 84 ans	23
175	0	200	15	5	0	85 ans et plus	24
21,830	465	27,305	1,815	1,150	1,340	Sexe féminin	25
1,085	20	1,600	80	50	70	0 à 4 ans	26
1,275	35	1,800	115	70	90	5 à 9 ans	27
1,475	35	2,205	150	110	125	10 à 14 ans	28
1,505	20	2,160	170	95	125	15 à 19 ans	29
1,320	30	1,395	90	45	75	20 à 24 ans	30
1,305	25	1,330	60	40	65	25 à 29 ans	31
1,380	30	1,690	90	60	80	30 à 34 ans	32
1,485	35	2,180	125	85	105	35 à 39 ans	33
1,895	45	2,645	200	100	165	40 à 44 ans	34
1,910	40	2,310	185	115	120	45 à 49 ans	35
1,675	30	1,850	155	95	70	50 à 54 ans	36
1,380	40	1,670	130	95	75	55 à 59 ans	37
1,000	25	1,225	90	60	65	60 à 64 ans	38
840	20	890	70	40	35	65 à 69 ans	39
720	10	690	30	30	30	70 à 74 ans	40
650	5	640	35	20	25	75 à 79 ans	41
490	5	495	20	15	20	80 à 84 ans	42
430	5	525	15	15	15	85 ans et plus	43
35,135	**760**	**42,875**	**3,045**	**1,900**	**2,210**	**Population totale de 15 ans et plus**[3]	44
						État matrimonial légal	
11,340	215	12,385	845	490	665	Jamais légalement marié(e) (célibataire)	45
16,865	445	23,370	1,835	1,170	1,225	Légalement marié(e) (et non séparé[e])[4,5]	46
1,665	25	1,685	90	50	100	Séparé(e), mais toujours légalement marié(e)	47
2,635	30	3,110	165	110	150	Divorcé(e)	48
2,625	40	2,330	110	80	75	Veuf(ve)	49
						Union libre	
30,725	670	38,995	2,805	1,770	2,000	Ne vivant pas en union libre	50
4,410	90	3,875	240	130	210	Vivant en union libre	51
42,455	**940**	**53,925**	**3,845**	**2,390**	**2,840**	**Population totale – Données-échantillon (20 %)**[6]	52
						Langue maternelle	
41,685	940	53,640	3,840	2,385	2,840	Réponses uniques	53
22,900	145	49,170	3,345	2,125	2,625	Anglais	54
16,400	795	595	40	15	30	Français	55
2,380	0	3,885	455	235	180	Langues non officielles[7]	56
745	0	365	55	15	15	Italien	57
25	0	0	0	0	0	Chinois, n.d.a.[61]	58
20	0	10	0	0	0	Cantonais	59
50	0	220	15	10	0	Espagnol	60
195	0	950	110	45	80	Allemand	61
1,340	0	2,335	275	165	85	Autres langues[8]	62

Nota : Voir les symboles et les abréviations dans les documents d'introduction et voir les documents de référence à la fin de la publication.

Selected characteristics for census divisions and census subdivisions – 100% data and 20% sample data, Ontario, 2006 Census (continued)

No.	Characteristics	Kapuskasing, T	Mattice-Val Côté, TP ◆	Moonbeam, TP ◆◆◇	New Post 69A, IRI ◆◆◇◇	Opasatika, TP ◆	Smooth Rock Falls, T ◇
	Population characteristics						
	Mother tongue (continued)						
63	Multiple responses	145	15	30	0	0	15
64	English and French	125	10	20	0	0	15
65	English and non-official language	15	0	10	0	0	0
66	French and non-official language	0	0	0	0	0	0
67	English, French and non-official language	0	0	0	0	0	0
	Language spoken most often at home[9]						
68	Single responses	8,210	770	1,280	75	280	1,440
69	English	3,015	45	265	65	35	510
70	French	5,060	705	1,015	0	220	930
71	Non-official languages[7]	130	15	0	10	25	0
72	Chinese, n.o.s.[61]	30	0	0	0	0	0
73	Cantonese	20	0	0	0	0	0
74	Panjabi (Punjabi)	0	0	0	0	0	0
75	Italian	0	0	0	0	0	0
76	Spanish	0	15	0	0	0	0
77	Other languages[8]	75	0	0	10	25	0
78	Multiple responses	140	0	0	0	0	0
79	English and French	125	0	10	0	0	0
80	English and non-official language	15	0	0	0	0	0
81	French and non-official language	0	0	0	0	0	0
82	English, French and non-official language	0	0	0	0	0	0
	Knowledge of official languages[10]						
83	English only	1,660	20	130	70	15	240
84	French only	655	290	290	0	55	180
85	English and French	6,015	440	870	0	205	1,015
86	Neither English nor French	20	15	0	0	0	0
	Knowledge of non-official languages[7,11]						
87	Italian	30	0	0	0	0	10
88	Spanish	10	25	15	0	0	10
89	German	35	0	0	0	25	0
90	Chinese, n.o.s.[61]	25	0	0	0	0	0
91	Cantonese	35	0	0	0	0	0
92	Panjabi (Punjabi)	0	0	0	0	0	0
93	Portuguese	10	0	0	0	0	0
	First official language spoken[10]						
94	English	2,625	95	205	75	35	430
95	French	5,660	655	1,075	0	230	1,015
96	English and French	45	0	10	0	15	0
97	Neither English nor French	15	20	0	10	0	0
98	Official language minority - (number)[12]	5,680	655	1,075	0	240	1,015
99	Official language minority - (percentage)[12]	68.0	85.1	83.7	0.0	85.7	70.5
	Ethnic origin[13]						
100	English	960	15	65	0	40	165
101	Canadian	4,905	590	840	0	235	935
102	Scottish	785	15	75	10	15	75
103	Irish	830	25	50	0	30	190
104	French	3,955	270	570	0	90	735
105	German	280	0	15	0	20	35
106	Italian	235	0	45	0	0	10
107	Chinese	60	0	0	0	0	0
108	East Indian	0	0	0	0	0	10
109	Dutch (Netherlands)	170	0	10	0	0	35
110	Polish	320	0	10	0	0	25
111	Ukrainian	245	0	10	0	0	35
112	North American Indian	365	55	20	70	10	80
113	Portuguese	20	0	15	0	0	0
114	Filipino	0	0	0	0	0	0
	Aboriginal and non-Aboriginal identity						
115	Total Aboriginal identity population[14]	360	10	35	70	10	55
116	Total non-Aboriginal identity population	7,990	760	1,255	0	265	1,385

Note: See symbols and abbreviations in the introductory material and see reference material at the end of the publication.

Certaines caractéristiques des divisions de recensement et des subdivisions de recensement – Données intégrales et données-échantillon (20 %), Ontario, Recensement de 2006 (suite)

Timmins, CY ◆◊	Val Rita-Harty, TP	**Dufferin CD/DR A**	Amaranth, TP A	East Garafraxa, TP	East Luther Grand Valley, TP ◆◊	**Caractéristiques**	N°
						Caractéristiques de la population	
						Langue maternelle (suite)	
770	0	280	10	0	10	Réponses multiples	63
650	0	90	0	0	0	Anglais et français	64
110	0	195	10	0	10	Anglais et langue non officielle	65
10	0	0	0	0	0	Français et langue non officielle	66
0	0	0	0	0	0	Anglais, français et langue non officielle	67
						Langue parlée le plus souvent à la maison[9]	
41,400	930	53,695	3,835	2,380	2,840	Réponses uniques	68
30,615	180	52,555	3,665	2,325	2,765	Anglais	69
10,120	750	80	10	0	0	Français	70
660	0	1,060	165	60	65	Langues non officielles[7]	71
0	0	0	0	0	0	Chinois, n.d.a.[61]	72
10	0	10	0	0	0	Cantonais	73
0	0	105	0	20	0	Pendjabi	74
255	0	60	25	0	0	Italien	75
0	0	70	0	0	0	Espagnol	76
400	0	815	140	35	70	Autres langues[8]	77
1,055	10	235	10	10	10	Réponses multiples	78
905	10	0	0	0	0	Anglais et français	79
145	0	225	10	10	10	Anglais et langue non officielle	80
0	0	0	0	0	0	Français et langue non officielle	81
0	0	0	0	0	0	Anglais, français et langue non officielle	82
						Connaissance des langues officielles[10]	
19,420	115	50,875	3,610	2,195	2,750	Anglais seulement	83
1,525	165	0	0	0	0	Français seulement	84
21,460	655	2,940	225	175	80	Anglais et français	85
45	0	105	10	15	15	Ni l'anglais ni le français	86
						Connaissance des langues non officielles[7,11]	
940	0	530	70	35	20	Italien	87
285	0	545	40	10	10	Espagnol	88
260	0	1,170	170	80	90	Allemand	89
35	0	0	0	0	0	Chinois, n.d.a.[61]	90
25	0	10	0	0	0	Cantonais	91
0	0	225	0	30	0	Pendjabi	92
50	0	490	40	15	10	Portugais	93
						Première langue officielle parlée[10]	
25,860	145	53,200	3,800	2,355	2,805	Anglais	94
16,330	795	550	40	20	20	Français	95
220	0	65	0	0	0	Anglais et français	96
45	0	105	10	15	15	Ni l'anglais ni le français	97
16,440	795	585	40	20	25	Minorité de langue officielle - (nombre)[12]	98
38.7	85.0	1.1	1.0	0.8	0.9	Minorité de langue officielle - (pourcentage)[12]	99
						Origine ethnique[13]	
8,730	65	21,805	1,290	905	1,095	Anglais	100
20,870	660	17,710	1,340	595	1,065	Canadien	101
5,685	75	15,135	895	720	760	Écossais	102
6,650	70	13,740	920	615	690	Irlandais	103
18,645	425	5,085	405	170	185	Français	104
2,635	0	6,240	450	355	345	Allemand	105
2,915	10	2,515	190	150	105	Italien	106
170	0	220	15	30	0	Chinois	107
25	0	550	55	25	0	Indien de l'Inde	108
785	10	3,655	500	160	415	Hollandais (Néerlandais)	109
1,435	10	1,590	185	55	75	Polonais	110
1,295	20	1,325	85	55	0	Ukrainien	111
2,795	15	1,075	90	20	110	Indien de l'Amérique du Nord	112
135	10	1,075	130	30	50	Portugais	113
135	0	135	0	10	0	Philippin	114
						Population ayant une identité autochtone et population n'ayant pas d'identité autochtone	
3,275	50	525	25	30	25	Total de la population ayant une identité autochtone[14]	115
39,175	890	53,400	3,815	2,360	2,820	Total de la population n'ayant pas d'identité autochtone	116

Nota : Voir les symboles et les abréviations dans les documents d'introduction et voir les documents de référence à la fin de la publication.

Selected characteristics for census divisions and census subdivisions – 100% data and 20% sample data, Ontario, 2006 Census (continued)

No.	Characteristics	Kapuskasing, T	Mattice-Val Côté, TP ◆	Moonbeam, TP ◆◆◊	New Post 69A, IRI ◆◆◊◊	Opasatika, TP ◆	Smooth Rock Falls, T ◊
	Population characteristics						
	Aboriginal and non-Aboriginal ancestry						
117	Total Aboriginal ancestry population[15]	565	55	35	70	15	130
118	Total non-Aboriginal ancestry population	7,785	715	1,250	10	265	1,310
	Registered Indian status						
119	Registered Indian[16]	200	10	15	70	10	15
120	Not a Registered Indian	8,155	760	1,270	0	270	1,420
	Visible minority groups						
121	Total visible minority population[17]	140	0	0	0	0	0
122	Chinese	55	0	0	0	0	0
123	South Asian[18]	0	0	0	0	0	0
124	Black	60	0	0	0	0	0
125	Filipino	0	0	0	0	0	0
126	Latin American	0	0	0	0	0	0
127	Southeast Asian[19]	0	0	0	0	0	0
128	Arab	0	0	0	0	0	0
129	West Asian[20]	0	0	0	0	0	0
130	Korean	0	0	0	0	0	0
131	Japanese	15	0	0	0	0	0
132	Visible minority, n.i.e.[21]	0	0	0	0	0	0
133	Multiple visible minority[22]	0	0	0	0	0	0
	Citizenship[23]						
134	Canadian citizens[24]	8,330	760	1,290	X	280	1,440
135	Not Canadian citizens[25]	25	10	0	X	0	0
	Immigrant status and place of birth[26]						
136	Non-immigrants[27]	8,145	735	1,255	X	255	1,425
137	Born in province of residence	7,200	640	1,100	X	250	1,200
138	Immigrants[28]	205	35	30	X	20	15
139	United States of America	10	0	0	X	0	0
140	Central and South America	0	0	0	X	0	0
141	Caribbean and Bermuda	0	0	0	X	0	0
142	United Kingdom	10	0	0	X	0	0
143	Other Europe	140	25	30	X	20	10
144	Africa	35	0	0	X	0	0
145	Asia and the Middle East	15	0	0	X	0	0
146	Oceania and other[29]	10	0	0	X	0	0
147	Non-permanent residents[30]	10	0	0	X	0	0
148	**Total immigrant population[28]**	**205**	**30**	**30**	**X**	**25**	**15**
	Period of immigration						
149	Before 1961	105	10	15	X	0	10
150	1961 to 1970	30	0	0	X	10	0
151	1971 to 1980	10	15	15	X	10	0
152	1981 to 1990	55	10	0	X	0	0
153	1991 to 2000	0	0	0	X	0	0
154	1991 to 1995	0	0	0	X	0	0
155	1996 to 2000	0	0	0	X	0	0
156	2001 to 2006[31]	10	0	0	X	0	0
	Age at immigration						
157	Under 5 years	40	10	0	X	0	0
158	5 to 19 years	50	10	15	X	0	0
159	20 years and over	120	20	15	X	20	10
160	**Total population 15 years and over**	**7,070**	**635**	**1,090**	**60**	**230**	**1,265**
	Generation status						
161	1st generation[32]	200	35	30	0	25	15
162	2nd generation[33]	620	10	90	0	0	75
163	3rd generation or more[34]	6,250	590	970	60	210	1,175

Note: See symbols and abbreviations in the introductory material and see reference material at the end of the publication.

Certaines caractéristiques des divisions de recensement et des subdivisions de recensement – Données intégrales et données-échantillon (20 %), Ontario, Recensement de 2006 (suite)

Timmins, CY ◆◇	Val Rita-Harty, TP	**Dufferin CD/DR A**	Amaranth, TP A	East Garafraxa, TP	East Luther Grand Valley, TP ◆◇	**Caractéristiques**	N°
						Caractéristiques de la population	
						Population ayant une ascendance autochtone et population n'ayant pas d'ascendance autochtone	
4,810	35	1,390	135	30	125	Total de la population ayant une ascendance autochtone[15]	117
37,645	905	52,530	3,710	2,360	2,720	Total de la population n'ayant pas d'ascendance autochtone	118
						Statut d'Indien inscrit	
1,300	10	135	30	0	20	Indien inscrit[16]	119
41,155	925	53,790	3,815	2,385	2,825	Pas un Indien inscrit	120
						Groupes de minorités visibles	
510	0	2,065	75	125	30	Total de la population des minorités visibles[17]	121
125	0	180	0	40	0	Chinois	122
10	0	575	25	55	0	Sud-Asiatique[18]	123
140	0	660	20	0	0	Noir	124
115	0	120	0	20	0	Philippin	125
40	0	160	10	0	0	Latino-Américain	126
50	0	45	0	0	20	Asiatique du Sud-Est[19]	127
15	0	20	0	0	0	Arabe	128
10	0	70	0	0	0	Asiatique occidental[20]	129
10	0	30	0	0	0	Coréen	130
0	0	90	0	15	0	Japonais	131
0	0	40	0	0	0	Minorité visible, n.i.a.[21]	132
0	0	70	20	0	0	Minorités visibles multiples[22]	133
						Citoyenneté[23]	
42,050	940	51,895	3,665	2,325	2,680	Citoyens canadiens[24]	134
405	0	2,030	180	65	165	Ne sont pas des citoyens canadiens[25]	135
						Statut d'immigrant et le lieu de naissance[26]	
40,645	930	46,840	3,235	2,105	2,510	Non-immigrants[27]	136
35,795	705	42,415	2,940	1,950	2,315	Né dans la province de résidence	137
1,770	0	6,930	585	280	335	Immigrants[28]	138
95	0	385	25	10	20	États-Unis d'Amérique	139
15	0	245	20	0	10	Amérique centrale et Amérique du Sud	140
60	0	310	30	0	10	Antilles et Bermudes	141
300	10	2,775	145	55	140	Royaume-Uni	142
1,090	0	2,510	350	145	155	Autre Europe	143
20	0	140	0	0	0	Afrique	144
180	0	515	10	55	10	Asie et Moyen-Orient	145
0	0	50	0	10	0	Océanie et autres[29]	146
35	0	160	20	0	0	Résidents non permanents[30]	147
1,765	**0**	**6,925**	**585**	**280**	**335**	**Population totale des immigrants[28]**	148
						Période d'immigration	
870	0	1,710	215	95	50	Avant 1961	149
360	0	1,660	145	40	120	1961 à 1970	150
210	0	1,230	75	50	65	1971 à 1980	151
95	0	865	55	30	30	1981 à 1990	152
155	0	790	40	55	0	1991 à 2000	153
110	0	390	40	45	0	1991 à 1995	154
45	0	400	0	10	0	1996 à 2000	155
75	0	660	65	10	60	2001 à 2006[31]	156
						Âge à l'immigration	
265	0	910	60	60	35	Moins de 5 ans	157
505	0	2,245	215	90	115	5 à 19 ans	158
995	0	3,770	310	130	185	20 ans et plus	159
34,580	**780**	**42,365**	**3,045**	**1,930**	**2,180**	**Population totale de 15 ans et plus**	160
						Statut des générations	
1,785	0	6,885	585	285	340	1re génération[32]	161
3,570	45	8,460	535	385	360	2e génération[33]	162
29,225	730	27,020	1,925	1,255	1,480	3e génération ou plus[34]	163

Nota : Voir les symboles et les abréviations dans les documents d'introduction et voir les documents de référence à la fin de la publication.

Selected characteristics for census divisions and census subdivisions – 100% data and 20% sample data, Ontario, 2006 Census (continued)

No.	Characteristics	Kapuskasing, T	Mattice-Val Côté, TP ◆	Moonbeam, TP ◆◆◊	New Post 69A, IRI ◆◆◊◊	Opasatika, TP ◆	Smooth Rock Falls, T ◊
	Population characteristics						
164	**Total population 1 year and over[35]**	**8,270**	**765**	**1,275**	**70**	**275**	**1,435**
	Place of residence 1 year ago (mobility)						
165	Non-movers	7,390	720	1,200	65	215	1,355
166	Movers	880	45	75	10	60	80
167	Non-migrants	610	25	45	0	15	35
168	Migrants	270	15	30	10	40	40
169	Internal migrants	270	20	30	0	40	40
170	Intraprovincial migrants	250	10	30	10	35	30
171	Interprovincial migrants	20	10	0	0	0	0
172	External migrants	0	0	0	0	0	10
173	**Total population 5 years and over[36]**	**7,990**	**740**	**1,250**	**70**	**260**	**1,390**
	Place of residence 5 years ago (mobility)						
174	Non-movers	5,785	540	965	55	215	1,130
175	Movers	2,210	205	285	20	50	255
176	Non-migrants	1,400	115	110	0	20	170
177	Migrants	805	85	170	10	25	90
178	Internal migrants	805	85	170	15	25	90
179	Intraprovincial migrants	730	85	165	15	25	60
180	Interprovincial migrants	75	0	0	0	0	30
181	External migrants	0	0	0	0	0	0
182	**Total population 15 years and over**	**7,070**	**640**	**1,085**	**60**	**230**	**1,265**
	Highest certificate, diploma or degree[37]						
183	No certificate, diploma or degree	2,270	260	315	30	70	395
184	Certificate, diploma or degree	4,800	375	775	30	165	870
185	High school certificate or equivalent[38]	1,645	145	245	0	40	250
186	Apprenticeship or trades certificate or diploma	1,045	100	225	15	50	215
187	College, CEGEP or other non-university certificate or diploma[39]	1,400	75	175	10	65	290
188	University certificate or diploma below bachelor level[40]	120	0	15	10	0	30
189	University certificate or degree[41]	585	45	110	0	0	80
190	Bachelor's degree	425	40	75	0	0	35
191	University certificate or diploma above bachelor level	60	0	35	0	0	30
192	Degree in medicine, dentistry, veterinary medicine or optometry	0	0	0	0	0	0
193	Master's degree	90	0	0	0	0	10
194	Earned doctorate	0	0	0	0	0	10
195	**Total population 15 years and over with postsecondary qualifications**	**3,155**	**230**	**525**	**30**	**125**	**620**
	Major field of study - Classification of Instructional Programs, 2000[42]						
196	Education	245	30	35	10	15	55
197	Visual and performing arts, and communications technologies	35	0	0	0	0	0
198	Humanities	75	0	20	0	0	10
199	Social and behavioural sciences and law	190	10	40	0	0	0
200	Business, management and public administration	630	40	105	10	25	65
201	Physical and life sciences and technologies	50	0	0	0	0	10
202	Mathematics, computer and information sciences	55	0	0	0	0	10
203	Architecture, engineering, and related technologies	975	70	215	10	50	325
204	Agriculture, natural resources and conservation	125	25	10	10	0	10
205	Health, parks, recreation and fitness	440	15	55	0	15	85
206	Personal, protective and transportation services	330	35	50	10	15	50
207	Other fields of study[43]	0	0	0	0	0	0
	Location of study[44]						
208	Inside Canada	3,125	230	510	25	100	620
209	Outside Canada	30	0	20	0	20	0
210	**Total population 15 years and over**	**7,070**	**640**	**1,085**	**60**	**230**	**1,265**
	Unpaid work						
211	Males 15 years and over	3,490	325	575	35	110	660
212	Reported unpaid work[45]	3,140	260	510	30	110	610
213	Housework and child care and care or assistance to seniors	295	40	80	0	30	35
214	Housework and child care only	825	65	130	10	25	140

Note: See symbols and abbreviations in the introductory material and see reference material at the end of the publication.

Certaines caractéristiques des divisions de recensement et des subdivisions de recensement – Données intégrales et données-échantillon (20 %), Ontario, Recensement de 2006 (suite)

Timmins, CY ◆◇	Val Rita-Harty, TP	**Dufferin CD/DR A**	Amaranth, TP **A**	East Garafraxa, TP	East Luther Grand Valley, TP ◆◇	**Caractéristiques**	N°
						Caractéristiques de la population	
42,010	**935**	**53,415**	**3,805**	**2,380**	**2,820**	**Population totale de 1 an et plus[35]**	164
						Lieu de résidence 1 an auparavant (mobilité)	
36,005	820	47,225	3,400	2,085	2,515	Personnes n'ayant pas déménagé	165
6,005	120	6,195	410	295	300	Personnes ayant déménagé	166
4,610	0	2,570	115	115	140	Non-migrants	167
1,390	115	3,625	295	180	155	Migrants	168
1,380	120	3,450	295	180	160	Migrants internes	169
1,145	105	3,345	295	180	155	Migrants infraprovinciaux	170
235	10	110	0	0	0	Migrants interprovinciaux	171
15	0	170	0	0	0	Migrants externes	172
40,300	**910**	**50,700**	**3,655**	**2,295**	**2,655**	**Population totale de 5 ans et plus[36]**	173
						Lieu de résidence 5 ans auparavant (mobilité)	
24,375	695	30,460	2,645	1,405	1,630	Personnes n'ayant pas déménagé	174
15,925	215	20,240	1,010	890	1,025	Personnes ayant déménagé	175
11,515	95	7,455	150	315	350	Non-migrants	176
4,410	120	12,785	855	575	675	Migrants	177
4,235	120	11,995	735	540	620	Migrants internes	178
3,580	105	11,395	710	540	620	Migrants infraprovinciaux	179
655	10	595	30	0	0	Migrants interprovinciaux	180
175	0	790	120	35	50	Migrants externes	181
34,580	**775**	**42,365**	**3,045**	**1,930**	**2,180**	**Population totale de 15 ans et plus**	182
						Plus haut certificat, diplôme ou grade[37]	
10,925	275	10,150	670	450	570	Aucun certificat, diplôme ou grade	183
23,655	500	32,220	2,375	1,485	1,610	Certificat, diplôme ou grade	184
8,500	180	13,670	1,060	575	765	Diplôme d'études secondaires ou l'équivalent[38]	185
3,895	100	3,835	360	305	295	Certificat ou diplôme d'apprenti ou d'une école de métiers	186
7,515	155	8,955	620	335	410	Certificat ou diplôme d'un collège, d'un cégep ou d'un autre établissement d'enseignement non universitaire[39]	187
710	0	985	45	50	35	Certificat ou diplôme universitaire inférieur au baccalauréat[40]	188
3,035	70	4,770	285	220	110	Certificat ou grade universitaire[41]	189
1,940	55	3,005	150	150	85	Baccalauréat	190
600	0	855	65	20	15	Certificat ou diplôme universitaire supérieur au baccalauréat	191
110	0	120	10	15	0	Diplôme en médecine, en art dentaire, en médecine vétérinaire ou en optométrie	192
360	15	690	60	25	10	Maîtrise	193
15	0	95	0	10	10	Doctorat acquis	194
15,155	**320**	**18,545**	**1,315**	**910**	**845**	**Population totale de 15 ans et plus avec titres du niveau postsecondaire**	195
						Principal domaine d'études - Classification des programmes d'enseignement, 2000[42]	
1,315	25	1,575	115	65	50	Éducation	196
275	0	665	20	15	30	Arts visuels et d'interprétation, et technologie des communications	197
315	0	745	25	35	30	Sciences humaines	198
950	30	1,775	90	80	65	Sciences sociales et de comportements, et droit	199
3,170	50	3,725	285	165	145	Commerce, gestion et administration publique	200
325	35	475	35	35	25	Sciences physiques et de la vie, et technologies	201
340	0	495	15	30	20	Mathématiques, informatique et sciences de l'information	202
4,455	65	4,640	365	285	240	Architecture, génie et services connexes	203
435	15	505	80	40	30	Agriculture, ressources naturelles et conservation	204
2,485	35	2,610	170	100	95	Santé, parcs, récréation et conditionnement physique	205
1,085	60	1,320	100	55	125	Services personnels, de protection et de transport	206
0	0	0	0	0	0	Autres domaines d'études[43]	207
						Lieu des études[44]	
14,620	325	16,445	1,130	820	735	À l'intérieur du Canada	208
530	0	2,095	185	90	115	À l'extérieur du Canada	209
34,580	**775**	**42,365**	**3,045**	**1,930**	**2,180**	**Population totale de 15 ans et plus**	210
						Travail non rémunéré	
16,940	385	21,025	1,595	1,020	1,110	Hommes de 15 ans et plus	211
15,205	355	19,315	1,475	945	1,070	Travail non rémunéré déclaré[45]	212
1,235	35	1,645	120	95	75	Travaux ménagers et soins aux enfants et soins ou aide aux personnes âgées	213
4,605	70	6,390	400	235	410	Travaux ménagers et soins aux enfants seulement	214

Nota : Voir les symboles et les abréviations dans les documents d'introduction et voir les documents de référence à la fin de la publication.

Selected characteristics for census divisions and census subdivisions – 100% data and 20% sample data, Ontario, 2006 Census (continued)

No.	Characteristics	Kapuskasing, T	Mattice-Val Côté, TP ◆	Moonbeam, TP ◆◆◊	New Post 69A, IRI ◆◆◊◊	Opasatika, TP ◆	Smooth Rock Falls, T ◊
	Population characteristics						
	Unpaid work (continued)						
215	Housework and care or assistance to seniors only	245	40	45	0	15	90
216	Child care and care or assistance to seniors only	0	0	0	0	0	0
217	Housework only	1,745	85	260	20	35	340
218	Child care only	30	15	0	0	0	0
219	Care or assistance to seniors only	10	10	0	0	0	0
220	Females 15 years and over	3,580	315	515	25	120	600
221	Reported unpaid work[45]	3,350	280	490	25	120	550
222	Housework and child care and care or assistance to seniors	475	65	125	0	30	75
223	Housework and child care only	940	70	100	10	20	125
224	Housework and care or assistance to seniors only	390	50	40	0	20	60
225	Child care and care or assistance to seniors only	0	0	0	0	0	0
226	Housework only	1,530	90	220	10	50	280
227	Child care only	15	10	0	0	0	10
228	Care or assistance to seniors only	0	0	0	0	0	0
	Labour force activity						
229	Males 15 years and over	3,490	325	575	30	110	665
230	In the labour force	2,225	225	350	25	75	385
231	Employed	2,015	205	275	25	60	355
232	Unemployed	205	20	75	0	10	30
233	Not in the labour force	1,265	100	220	0	35	280
234	Participation rate	63.8	69.2	60.9	83.3	68.2	57.9
235	Employment rate	57.7	63.1	47.8	83.3	54.5	53.4
236	Unemployment rate	9.2	8.9	21.4	0.0	13.3	7.8
237	Females 15 years and over	3,580	315	515	25	125	605
238	In the labour force	1,860	150	290	15	70	285
239	Employed	1,735	150	215	15	60	265
240	Unemployed	125	0	75	0	10	20
241	Not in the labour force	1,720	165	220	10	50	320
242	Participation rate	52.0	47.6	56.3	60.0	56.0	47.1
243	Employment rate	48.5	47.6	41.7	60.0	48.0	43.8
244	Unemployment rate	6.7	0.0	25.9	0.0	14.3	7.0
245	Both sexes - Participation rate	57.8	59.1	59.4	75.0	61.7	52.6
246	15 to 24 years	67.6	55.0	73.3	40.0	22.2	60.7
247	25 years and over	55.9	59.3	56.4	85.7	68.4	51.6
248	Both sexes - Employment rate	53.0	55.9	45.4	66.7	48.9	49.0
249	15 to 24 years	54.7	52.6	30.0	40.0	22.2	57.1
250	25 years and over	52.7	57.4	47.3	62.5	56.8	48.0
251	Both sexes - Unemployment rate	8.2	5.3	24.0	25.0	17.9	6.8
252	15 to 24 years	19.4	18.2	56.5	0.0	0.0	11.8
253	25 years and over	5.8	4.7	16.0	28.6	18.5	6.9
254	**Total labour force 15 years and over**	**4,085**	**375**	**645**	**45**	**145**	**665**
	Industry - North American Industry Classification System 2002						
255	Industry - Not applicable[46]	75	0	20	0	0	0
256	All industries[47]	4,010	375	630	40	140	660
257	11 Agriculture, forestry, fishing and hunting	130	50	50	10	25	0
258	21 Mining and oil and gas extraction	170	0	20	0	10	0
259	22 Utilities	155	0	15	10	0	10
260	23 Construction	210	10	40	0	0	55
261	31-33 Manufacturing	625	90	135	10	10	200
262	41 Wholesale trade	105	0	0	0	0	0
263	44-45 Retail trade	560	30	65	10	25	40
264	48-49 Transportation and warehousing	215	55	25	10	25	30
265	51 Information and cultural industries	10	0	10	0	0	15
266	52 Finance and insurance	115	10	10	0	10	20
267	53 Real estate and rental and leasing	15	10	0	0	0	10
268	54 Professional, scientific and technical services	80	0	25	0	0	15
269	55 Management of companies and enterprises	0	0	0	0	0	0
270	56 Administrative and support, waste management and remediation services	80	0	10	0	0	25
271	61 Educational services	255	35	80	0	10	55
272	62 Health care and social assistance	565	20	35	10	10	90

Note: See symbols and abbreviations in the introductory material and see reference material at the end of the publication.

Certaines caractéristiques des divisions de recensement et des subdivisions de recensement – Données intégrales et données-échantillon (20 %), Ontario, Recensement de 2006 (suite)

Timmins, CY ◆◊	Val Rita-Harty, TP	**Dufferin CD/DR A**	Amaranth, TP A	East Garafraxa, TP	East Luther Grand Valley, TP ◆◊	**Caractéristiques**	N°
						Caractéristiques de la population	
						Travail non rémunéré (suite)	
1,505	35	1,225	145	100	95	Travaux ménagers et soins ou aide aux personnes âgées seulement	215
10	0	15	0	0	0	Soins aux enfants et soins ou aide aux personnes âgées seulement	216
7,700	200	9,725	795	485	450	Travaux ménagers seulement	217
90	0	215	10	20	20	Soins aux enfants seulement	218
45	10	100	0	0	20	Soins ou aide aux personnes âgées seulement	219
17,640	390	21,340	1,445	915	1,070	Femmes de 15 ans et plus	220
16,420	365	20,115	1,380	885	1,010	Travail non rémunéré déclaré[45]	221
2,065	40	2,660	180	155	175	Travaux ménagers et soins aux enfants et soins ou aide aux personnes âgées	222
5,345	135	7,090	460	230	375	Travaux ménagers et soins aux enfants seulement	223
1,620	30	1,765	140	80	125	Travaux ménagers et soins ou aide aux personnes âgées seulement	224
10	0	10	0	0	0	Soins aux enfants et soins ou aide aux personnes âgées seulement	225
7,250	160	8,505	590	410	330	Travaux ménagers seulement	226
65	0	65	0	0	0	Soins aux enfants seulement	227
65	0	25	0	0	10	Soins ou aide aux personnes âgées seulement	228
						Activité	
16,935	390	21,025	1,595	1,020	1,110	Hommes de 15 ans et plus	229
12,080	255	16,700	1,270	830	900	Population active	230
11,285	225	16,020	1,230	815	870	Personnes occupées	231
795	30	675	40	15	30	Chômeurs	232
4,855	130	4,325	325	185	210	Inactifs	233
71.3	65.4	79.4	79.6	81.4	81.1	Taux d'activité	234
66.6	57.7	76.2	77.1	79.9	78.4	Taux d'emploi	235
6.6	11.8	4.0	3.1	1.8	3.3	Taux de chômage	236
17,640	390	21,340	1,450	915	1,070	Femmes de 15 ans et plus	237
10,575	195	14,430	970	640	775	Population active	238
9,770	190	13,705	950	600	725	Personnes occupées	239
800	10	725	20	40	55	Chômeuses	240
7,065	200	6,910	475	270	290	Inactives	241
59.9	50.0	67.6	66.9	69.9	72.4	Taux d'activité	242
55.4	48.7	64.2	65.5	65.6	67.8	Taux d'emploi	243
7.6	5.1	5.0	2.1	6.2	7.1	Taux de chômage	244
65.5	57.7	73.5	73.7	76.4	77.1	Les deux sexes - Taux d'activité	245
70.8	81.8	68.6	62.4	74.3	60.5	15 à 24 ans	246
64.5	51.6	74.5	76.0	76.9	80.3	25 ans et plus	247
60.9	52.6	70.2	71.6	73.3	73.2	Les deux sexes - Taux d'emploi	248
57.7	75.8	60.1	53.6	68.9	53.2	15 à 24 ans	249
61.5	46.7	72.3	75.8	74.7	77.4	25 ans et plus	250
7.1	7.8	4.5	2.7	3.7	4.8	Les deux sexes - Taux de chômage	251
18.5	0.0	12.5	13.2	7.3	10.9	15 à 24 ans	252
4.6	7.9	2.9	0.8	3.3	3.8	25 ans et plus	253
22,660	**450**	**31,130**	**2,245**	**1,475**	**1,675**	**Population active totale de 15 ans et plus**	254
						Industrie - Système de classification des industries de l'Amérique du Nord de 2002	
325	0	205	15	10	15	Industrie - Sans objet[46]	255
22,330	450	30,925	2,230	1,465	1,660	Toutes les industries[47]	256
560	50	920	145	195	90	11 Agriculture, foresterie, pêche et chasse	257
2,340	0	85	0	10	15	21 Extraction minière et extraction de pétrole et de gaz	258
305	0	240	15	0	10	22 Services publics	259
1,560	10	2,405	275	210	195	23 Construction	260
1,145	55	5,620	340	195	270	31-33 Fabrication	261
735	0	1,855	175	85	100	41 Commerce de gros	262
3,130	55	3,490	185	190	185	44-45 Commerce de détail	263
1,180	50	2,040	125	75	175	48-49 Transport et entreposage	264
325	0	515	25	20	25	51 Industrie de l'information et industrie culturelle	265
475	0	715	60	40	45	52 Finance et assurances	266
275	0	530	65	15	15	53 Services immobiliers et services de location et de location à bail	267
760	10	1,415	140	45	70	54 Services professionnels, scientifiques et techniques	268
0	0	15	0	0	0	55 Gestion de sociétés et d'entreprises	269
1,305	30	1,465	110	25	65	56 Services administratifs, services de soutien, services de gestion des déchets et services d'assainissement	270
1,650	60	1,800	140	65	35	61 Services d'enseignement	271
2,610	55	2,490	140	55	120	62 Soins de santé et assistance sociale	272

Nota : Voir les symboles et les abréviations dans les documents d'introduction et voir les documents de référence à la fin de la publication.

Selected characteristics for census divisions and census subdivisions – 100% data and 20% sample data, Ontario, 2006 Census (continued)

No.	Characteristics	Kapuskasing, T	Mattice-Val Côté, TP ◆	Moonbeam, TP ◆◆◇	New Post 69A, IRI ◆◆◇◇	Opasatika, TP ◆	Smooth Rock Falls, T ◇
	Population characteristics						
	Industry - North American Industry Classification System 2002 (continued)						
273	71 Arts, entertainment and recreation	35	0	15	0	10	10
274	72 Accommodation and food services	320	15	45	0	0	35
275	81 Other services (except public administration)	185	15	20	10	10	45
276	91 Public administration	180	20	20	10	10	10
	Class of worker						
277	Class of worker - Not applicable[46]	70	0	20	0	0	10
278	All classes of worker[47]	4,010	375	630	45	140	660
279	Paid workers	3,750	320	610	45	135	635
280	Employees	3,675	315	590	40	120	635
281	Self-employed (incorporated)	75	0	20	10	10	0
282	Self-employed (unincorporated)	255	60	20	0	10	25
283	Unpaid family workers	10	0	0	0	0	0
	Occupation - National Occupational Classification for Statistics 2006						
284	Male labour force 15 years and over	2,225	225	350	25	70	385
285	Occupation - Not applicable[46]	40	0	0	0	0	10
286	All occupations[47]	2,185	225	350	25	70	380
287	A Management occupations	135	10	10	0	0	25
288	B Business, finance and administrative occupations	135	30	0	0	0	15
289	C Natural and applied sciences and related occupations	145	0	10	0	15	25
290	D Health occupations	50	0	0	0	0	10
291	E Occupations in social science, education, government service and religion	60	0	25	0	0	10
292	F Occupations in art, culture, recreation and sport	25	0	15	0	0	0
293	G Sales and service occupations	315	25	55	0	0	25
294	H Trades, transport and equipment operators and related occupations	880	105	155	0	35	195
295	I Occupations unique to primary industry	145	40	35	10	20	0
296	J Occupations unique to processing, manufacturing and utilities	290	20	50	0	0	60
297	Female labour force 15 years and over	1,855	150	290	15	70	280
298	Occupation - Not applicable[46]	30	0	15	0	0	0
299	All occupations[47]	1,830	155	275	15	70	280
300	A Management occupations	135	0	20	0	0	0
301	B Business, finance and administrative occupations	370	40	85	0	20	45
302	C Natural and applied sciences and related occupations	20	0	0	0	0	10
303	D Health occupations	195	15	10	0	10	35
304	E Occupations in social science, education, government service and religion	265	35	45	0	10	50
305	F Occupations in art, culture, recreation and sport	50	0	0	0	0	0
306	G Sales and service occupations	725	40	75	10	15	120
307	H Trades, transport and equipment operators and related occupations	35	0	15	0	0	10
308	I Occupations unique to primary industry	20	0	0	0	0	0
309	J Occupations unique to processing, manufacturing and utilities	0	15	25	0	0	0
310	**Total employed labour force 15 years and over**	**3,750**	**355**	**490**	**35**	**120**	**615**
	Place of work status						
311	Males	2,015	205	275	25	60	360
312	Usual place of work	1,715	160	230	10	55	280
313	At home	45	0	25	0	0	25
314	Outside Canada	0	0	0	0	0	0
315	No fixed workplace address	260	45	30	10	0	50
316	Females	1,735	150	215	15	60	260
317	Usual place of work	1,590	135	200	10	35	235
318	At home	70	10	15	0	15	20
319	Outside Canada	0	0	0	0	0	0
320	No fixed workplace address	70	10	0	10	0	10

Note: See symbols and abbreviations in the introductory material and see reference material at the end of the publication.

Certaines caractéristiques des divisions de recensement et des subdivisions de recensement – Données intégrales et données-échantillon (20 %), Ontario, Recensement de 2006 (suite)

Timmins, CY ◆◊	Val Rita-Harty, TP	**Dufferin CD/DR A**	Amaranth, TP A	East Garafraxa, TP	East Luther Grand Valley, TP ◆◊	**Caractéristiques**	N°
						Caractéristiques de la population	
						Industrie - Système de classification des industries de l'Amérique du Nord de 2002 (suite)	
225	0	615	45	45	15	71 Arts, spectacles et loisirs	273
1,520	30	1,885	75	75	110	72 Hébergement et services de restauration	274
1,020	10	1,495	110	75	90	81 Autres services (sauf les administrations publiques)	275
1,215	30	1,320	60	40	25	91 Administrations publiques	276
						Catégorie de travailleurs	
320	0	205	15	10	10	Catégorie de travailleurs - Sans objet[46]	277
22,330	450	30,920	2,225	1,465	1,665	Toutes les catégories de travailleurs[47]	278
21,405	425	27,890	1,900	1,205	1,395	Travailleurs rémunérés	279
20,840	410	26,425	1,735	1,065	1,285	Employés	280
565	20	1,465	165	140	105	Travailleurs autonomes (entreprise constituée en société)	281
925	15	2,880	305	230	245	Travailleurs autonomes (entreprise non constituée en société)	282
10	10	155	20	30	30	Travailleurs familiaux non rémunérés	283
						Profession - Classification nationale des professions pour statistiques de 2006	
12,085	255	16,700	1,275	835	900	Hommes actifs de 15 ans et plus	284
170	0	105	15	10	0	Profession - Sans objet[46]	285
11,915	255	16,595	1,260	830	895	Toutes les professions[47]	286
1,130	10	2,145	140	150	110	A Gestion	287
895	20	1,185	70	50	70	B Affaires, finance et administration	288
895	0	1,060	55	40	30	C Sciences naturelles et appliquées et professions apparentées	289
210	0	180	10	10	10	D Secteur de la santé	290
510	45	585	45	15	25	E Sciences sociales, enseignement, administration publique et religion	291
95	10	310	15	0	10	F Arts, culture, sports et loisirs	292
2,215	25	3,030	190	160	110	G Ventes et services	293
4,025	110	5,500	485	280	400	H Métiers, transport et machinerie	294
1,330	45	940	115	110	60	I Professions propres au secteur primaire	295
595	10	1,660	130	15	75	J Transformation, fabrication et services d'utilité publique	296
10,575	195	14,430	975	640	780	Femmes actives de 15 ans et plus	297
155	0	105	0	0	10	Profession - Sans objet[46]	298
10,420	190	14,325	970	635	765	Toutes les professions[47]	299
620	15	1,105	45	45	55	A Gestion	300
3,055	35	3,700	300	215	225	B Affaires, finance et administration	301
190	0	270	15	30	0	C Sciences naturelles et appliquées et professions apparentées	302
1,115	30	1,110	65	30	60	D Secteur de la santé	303
1,250	30	1,540	105	45	40	E Sciences sociales, enseignement, administration publique et religion	304
185	0	395	30	10	25	F Arts, culture, sports et loisirs	305
3,505	50	4,390	270	185	215	G Ventes et services	306
305	20	505	25	30	30	H Métiers, transport et machinerie	307
125	10	265	65	25	25	I Professions propres au secteur primaire	308
60	0	1,040	40	15	70	J Transformation, fabrication et services d'utilité publique	309
21,055	**415**	**29,720**	**2,185**	**1,415**	**1,595**	**Population active occupée totale de 15 ans et plus**	310
						Catégorie de lieu de travail	
11,285	225	16,020	1,230	815	870	Hommes	311
9,710	145	11,865	875	455	535	Lieu habituel de travail	312
345	10	1,385	150	185	70	À domicile	313
15	0	90	10	10	10	En dehors du Canada	314
1,210	70	2,675	200	165	250	Sans adresse de travail fixe	315
9,770	190	13,700	950	600	725	Femmes	316
8,955	150	11,505	785	415	595	Lieu habituel de travail	317
345	10	1,410	135	140	70	À domicile	318
0	0	15	0	10	0	En dehors du Canada	319
475	25	770	25	40	50	Sans adresse de travail fixe	320

Nota : Voir les symboles et les abréviations dans les documents d'introduction et voir les documents de référence à la fin de la publication.

Selected characteristics for census divisions and census subdivisions – 100% data and 20% sample data, Ontario, 2006 Census (continued)

No.	Characteristics	Kapuskasing, T	Mattice-Val Côté, TP ◆	Moonbeam, TP ◆◆◇	New Post 69A, IRI ◆◆◇◇	Opasatika, TP ◆	Smooth Rock Falls, T ◇
	Population characteristics						
321	**Total employed labour force 15 years and over with usual place of work or no fixed workplace address**	**3,630**	**345**	**450**	**35**	**95**	**575**
	Mode of transportation						
322	Males	1,970	205	250	20	55	335
323	Car, truck, van, as driver	1,440	155	185	10	45	205
324	Car, truck, van, as passenger	200	30	55	10	0	20
325	Public transit	45	0	10	0	0	0
326	Walked	175	10	0	0	0	90
327	All other modes	110	0	10	0	0	10
328	Females	1,660	140	200	15	40	245
329	Car, truck, van, as driver	1,265	70	170	10	30	175
330	Car, truck, van, as passenger	140	25	10	0	0	15
331	Public transit	0	0	0	0	0	0
332	Walked	225	40	15	0	10	40
333	All other modes	30	0	0	0	0	15
334	**Total population 15 years and over who worked since January 1, 2005**	**4,395**	**420**	**680**	**45**	**170**	**755**
	Language used most often at work						
335	Single responses	3,890	400	645	50	170	690
336	English	2,250	10	205	45	25	375
337	French	1,620	395	440	0	140	305
338	Non-official languages[7]	20	0	0	10	0	0
339	Chinese, n.o.s.[61]	10	0	0	0	0	0
340	Cantonese	10	0	0	0	0	0
341	Other languages[8]	0	0	0	10	0	0
342	Multiple responses	505	15	30	0	10	60
343	English and French	505	15	30	0	0	65
344	English and non-official language	0	0	0	0	0	0
345	French and non-official language	0	0	0	0	0	0
346	English, French and non-official language	10	0	0	0	0	0
	Dwelling and household characteristics						
347	**Total number of occupied private dwellings**	**3,745**	**315**	**540**	**25**	**110**	**655**
	Housing tenure						
348	Owned	2,505	280	470	0	105	570
349	Rented	1,240	35	75	10	0	90
350	Band housing	0	0	0	15	0	0
	Structural type of dwelling						
351	Single-detached house	2,345	275	470	20	100	535
352	Semi-detached house	160	10	5	0	10	45
353	Row house	85	0	0	0	0	0
354	Apartment, duplex	215	0	10	0	5	15
355	Apartment, building that has five or more storeys	80	0	0	0	0	0
356	Apartment, building that has fewer than five storeys	825	20	50	0	0	45
357	Other single-attached house	20	10	5	0	0	5
358	Movable dwelling[48]	0	0	5	0	0	15
	Condition of dwelling						
359	Regular maintenance only	2,510	185	325	10	45	380
360	Minor repairs	905	105	205	10	50	190
361	Major repairs	325	25	15	10	10	80
	Period of construction						
362	Before 1946	775	30	50	0	25	135
363	1946 to 1960	930	85	130	0	20	205
364	1961 to 1970	870	40	105	0	20	90
365	1971 to 1980	760	85	105	0	25	170
366	1981 to 1985	170	20	55	0	10	30
367	1986 to 1990	110	20	25	10	10	25
368	1991 to 1995	55	25	30	0	0	0
369	1996 to 2000	50	0	25	0	0	0
370	2001 to 2006[49]	20	10	25	0	10	0

Note: See symbols and abbreviations in the introductory material and see reference material at the end of the publication.

Certaines caractéristiques des divisions de recensement et des subdivisions de recensement – Données intégrales et données-échantillon (20 %), Ontario, Recensement de 2006 (suite)

Timmins, CY ◆◇	Val Rita-Harty, TP	**Dufferin CD/DR A**	Amaranth, TP A	East Garafraxa, TP	East Luther Grand Valley, TP ◆◇	Caractéristiques	N°
						Caractéristiques de la population	
20,350	**390**	**26,820**	**1,890**	**1,075**	**1,435**	**Population active occupée totale de 15 ans et plus ayant un lieu habituel de travail ou sans adresse de travail fixe**	321
						Mode de transport	
10,920	215	14,545	1,075	625	785	Hommes	322
8,285	190	12,540	950	530	695	Automobile, camion ou fourgonnette, en tant que conducteur	323
1,365	20	1,075	55	65	45	Automobile, camion ou fourgonnette, en tant que passager	324
295	0	35	0	10	0	Transport en commun	325
595	0	645	35	15	45	À pied	326
380	0	255	35	10	0	Tous les autres modes	327
9,425	175	12,275	815	455	650	Femmes	328
6,240	135	9,935	705	385	570	Automobile, camion ou fourgonnette, en tant que conductrice	329
1,310	10	1,195	60	55	35	Automobile, camion ou fourgonnette, en tant que passagère	330
540	0	185	0	10	0	Transport en commun	331
1,145	35	760	35	10	45	À pied	332
190	0	200	0	0	0	Tous les autres modes	333
24,280	**495**	**33,285**	**2,500**	**1,570**	**1,760**	**Population totale de 15 ans et plus ayant travaillé depuis le 1er janvier 2005**	334
						Langue utilisée le plus souvent au travail	
22,895	465	33,215	2,495	1,570	1,755	Réponses uniques	335
20,540	220	33,070	2,495	1,570	1,725	Anglais	336
2,335	240	70	0	0	0	Français	337
20	0	80	0	0	25	Langues non officielles[7]	338
0	0	0	0	0	0	Chinois, n.d.a.[61]	339
10	0	10	0	0	0	Cantonais	340
15	0	75	0	0	30	Autres langues[8]	341
1,385	30	70	10	0	0	Réponses multiples	342
1,330	30	35	0	0	0	Anglais et français	343
35	0	35	0	0	0	Anglais et langue non officielle	344
0	0	0	0	0	0	Français et langue non officielle	345
15	0	0	0	0	0	Anglais, français et langue non officielle	346
						Caractéristiques des logements et des ménages	
17,390	**355**	**18,765**	**1,240**	**775**	**945**	**Nombre total de logements privés occupés**	347
						Mode d'occupation	
11,930	305	15,925	1,145	735	790	Possédé	348
5,465	55	2,835	95	40	155	Loué	349
0	0	0	0	0	0	Logement de bande	350
						Type de construction résidentielle	
11,160	330	13,975	1,185	760	835	Maison individuelle non attenante	351
1,230	0	1,375	15	5	0	Maison jumelée	352
625	0	1,060	0	0	15	Maison en rangée	353
1,140	0	310	20	5	5	Appartement, duplex	354
460	0	570	0	0	0	Appartement, immeuble de cinq étages ou plus	355
2,320	25	1,390	5	0	90	Appartement, immeuble de moins de cinq étages	356
165	0	70	0	0	5	Autre maison individuelle attenante	357
285	5	45	10	0	15	Logement mobile[48]	358
						État du logement	
10,860	150	12,245	720	530	485	Entretien régulier seulement	359
5,150	165	5,305	420	200	350	Réparations mineures	360
1,375	35	1,210	105	45	110	Réparations majeures	361
						Période de construction	
4,040	30	2,920	300	235	340	Avant 1946	362
3,320	30	1,180	85	25	60	1946 à 1960	363
2,090	80	1,980	75	15	80	1961 à 1970	364
3,815	90	3,820	280	130	165	1971 à 1980	365
1,420	65	1,195	80	35	50	1981 à 1985	366
1,260	30	2,190	145	95	105	1986 à 1990	367
790	10	1,700	100	60	65	1991 à 1995	368
445	0	1,780	85	20	25	1996 à 2000	369
210	0	1,995	90	155	50	2001 à 2006[49]	370

Nota : Voir les symboles et les abréviations dans les documents d'introduction et voir les documents de référence à la fin de la publication.

Selected characteristics for census divisions and census subdivisions – 100% data and 20% sample data, Ontario, 2006 Census (continued)

No.	Characteristics	Kapuskasing, T	Mattice-Val Côté, TP ◆	Moonbeam, TP ◆◆◊	New Post 69A, IRI ◆◆◊◊	Opasatika, TP ◆	Smooth Rock Falls, T ◊
	Dwelling and household characteristics						
371	Average number of rooms per dwelling	6.3	6.9	6.4	5.8	8.3	7.0
372	Average number of bedrooms per dwelling	2.8	3.0	2.8	3.8	3.2	3.2
373	Average value of dwelling $	97,422	67,938	167,692	0	42,326	54,618
374	**Total number of private households**	**3,740**	**310**	**540**	**25**	**115**	**650**
	Household size						
375	1 person	1,190	75	110	5	25	195
376	2 persons	1,375	115	260	0	55	265
377	3 persons	500	55	80	5	20	75
378	4 to 5 persons	655	65	95	5	25	110
379	6 or more persons	30	5	10	5	0	5
	Household type						
380	One-family households[50]	2,510	230	425	15	90	475
381	Multiple-family households	10	0	0	0	0	0
382	Non-family households	1,225	85	120	10	20	180
383	Number of persons in private households	8,345	770	1,290	75	280	1,445
384	Average number of persons in private households	2.2	2.5	2.4	2.8	2.4	2.2
385	Tenant-occupied private non-farm, non-reserve dwellings[51]	1,245	35	75	0	10	85
386	Average gross rent $[51]	536	452	730	0	0	480
387	Tenant-occupied households spending 30% or more of household income on gross rent[52]	570	15	30	0	0	15
388	Tenant-occupied households spending from 30% to 99% of household income on gross rent[52]	540	15	20	0	0	15
389	Owner-occupied private non-farm, non-reserve dwellings[53]	2,500	275	465	0	105	570
390	Average owner's major payments $[53]	781	574	770	0	479	623
391	Owner households spending 30% or more of household income on owner's major payments[52]	295	30	60	0	10	40
392	Owner households spending from 30% to 99% of household income on owner's major payments[52]	250	25	60	0	0	25
	Census family characteristics						
393	**Total number of census families in private households**	**2,530**	**230**	**425**	**20**	**90**	**475**
	Family structure and number of children						
394	Total couple families	2,235	195	390	15	80	430
395	Total families of married couples	1,840	145	320	10	65	345
396	Without children at home	985	60	195	0	25	245
397	With children at home	855	90	130	10	45	105
398	1 child	310	40	40	0	30	35
399	2 children	420	45	65	0	10	60
400	3 or more children	130	0	25	10	10	10
401	Total families of common-law couples	390	50	70	0	15	85
402	Without children at home	220	15	35	0	0	45
403	With children at home	170	35	35	10	10	40
404	1 child	75	10	15	10	0	20
405	2 children	85	10	15	0	10	10
406	3 or more children	0	10	0	0	10	15
407	Total lone-parent families	305	30	30	0	0	40
408	Female parent	210	20	25	0	0	25
409	1 child	155	10	25	10	0	10
410	2 children	40	0	0	0	0	20
411	3 or more children	10	0	0	0	0	0
412	Male parent	95	10	0	10	0	15
413	1 child	60	0	10	0	0	15
414	2 children	15	10	0	0	0	0
415	3 or more children	15	0	0	0	0	0

Note: See symbols and abbreviations in the introductory material and see reference material at the end of the publication.

Certaines caractéristiques des divisions de recensement et des subdivisions de recensement – Données intégrales et données-échantillon (20 %), Ontario, Recensement de 2006 (suite)

Timmins, CY ◆◊	Val Rita-Harty, TP	**Dufferin CD/DR A**	Amaranth, TP A	East Garafraxa, TP	East Luther Grand Valley, TP ◆◊	Caractéristiques	N°
						Caractéristiques des logements et des ménages	
6.1	6.9	7.3	7.9	8.2	7.2	Nombre moyen de pièces par logement	371
2.7	2.9	3.1	3.4	3.5	3.0	Nombre moyen de chambres à coucher par logement	372
130,761	68,315	314,637	340,389	491,675	250,072	Valeur moyenne du logement $	373
17,385	**355**	**18,800**	**1,240**	**775**	**965**	**Nombre total de ménages privés**	374
						Taille du ménage	
4,620	55	3,275	145	75	170	1 personne	375
5,940	150	5,960	405	250	300	2 personnes	376
2,925	65	3,265	220	155	160	3 personnes	377
3,655	80	5,555	385	245	290	4 à 5 personnes	378
245	10	750	85	40	50	6 personnes ou plus	379
						Genre de ménage	
12,230	285	14,685	1,060	655	790	Ménages unifamiliaux[50]	380
145	0	485	40	10	10	Ménages multifamiliaux	381
5,010	70	3,595	145	100	145	Ménages non familiaux	382
42,260	940	53,690	3,845	2,390	2,820	Nombre de personnes dans les ménages privés	383
2.4	2.6	2.9	3.1	3.1	2.9	Nombre moyen de personnes dans les ménages privés	384
5,460	50	2,830	95	40	155	Ménages locataires dans les logements privés non agricoles hors réserve[51]	385
589	474	856	841	1,368	674	Loyer brut moyen $[51]	386
2,065	15	1,250	45	20	40	Ménages locataires consacrant 30 % ou plus du revenu du ménage au loyer brut[52]	387
1,930	0	1,120	40	20	40	Ménages locataires consacrant de 30 % à 99 % du revenu du ménage au loyer brut[52]	388
11,920	295	15,570	1,075	640	765	Ménages propriétaires dans les logements privés non agricoles hors réserve[53]	389
875	642	1,350	1,394	1,525	1,260	Principales dépenses de propriété moyennes $[53]	390
1,490	40	3,795	285	195	190	Ménages propriétaires consacrant 30 % ou plus du revenu du ménage aux principales dépenses de propriété[52]	391
1,310	30	3,235	245	190	170	Ménages propriétaires consacrant de 30 % à 99 % du revenu du ménage aux principales dépenses de propriété[52]	392
						Caractéristiques des familles de recensement	
12,525	**290**	**15,665**	**1,135**	**680**	**810**	**Nombre total de familles de recensement dans les ménages privés**	393
						Structure de la famille et le nombre d'enfants	
10,580	235	13,485	1,025	635	710	Total des familles avec conjoints	394
8,350	205	11,550	905	595	580	Total des familles avec couples mariés	395
3,830	140	4,365	305	220	195	Sans enfants à la maison	396
4,520	65	7,180	600	380	385	Avec enfants à la maison	397
1,640	10	2,250	175	120	120	1 enfant	398
2,120	35	3,325	280	140	170	2 enfants	399
760	20	1,600	140	115	95	3 enfants ou plus	400
2,225	30	1,930	120	35	130	Total des familles avec couples en union libre	401
1,010	20	970	90	25	60	Sans enfants à la maison	402
1,220	10	965	30	10	75	Avec enfants à la maison	403
580	10	355	30	0	20	1 enfant	404
480	10	420	0	10	45	2 enfants	405
155	0	195	0	0	10	3 enfants ou plus	406
1,940	55	2,180	115	45	105	Total des familles monoparentales	407
1,550	40	1,605	65	30	70	Parent de sexe féminin	408
920	0	875	35	20	50	1 enfant	409
505	0	540	30	10	15	2 enfants	410
125	25	190	10	0	0	3 enfants ou plus	411
395	15	575	45	15	30	Parent de sexe masculin	412
285	10	385	45	0	20	1 enfant	413
70	0	125	0	10	10	2 enfants	414
35	0	65	0	0	0	3 enfants ou plus	415

Nota : Voir les symboles et les abréviations dans les documents d'introduction et voir les documents de référence à la fin de la publication.

Selected characteristics for census divisions and census subdivisions – 100% data and 20% sample data, Ontario, 2006 Census (continued)

No.	Characteristics	Kapuskasing, T	Mattice-Val Côté, TP ◆	Moonbeam, TP ◆◆◇	New Post 69A, IRI ◆◆◇◇	Opasatika, TP ◆	Smooth Rock Falls, T ◇
	Census family characteristics						
416	**Total number of children at home**	**2,240**	**250**	**345**	**30**	**90**	**320**
	Age group						
417	Under 6 years	405	40	60	0	25	65
418	6 to 14 years	870	95	140	10	20	110
419	15 to 17 years	360	35	65	10	10	45
420	18 to 24 years	480	35	70	0	20	95
421	25 years and over	130	40	15	0	10	15
422	Average number of children at home per census family[54]	0.9	1.1	0.8	1.8	1.0	0.7
423	**Total number of persons in private households**	**8,350**	**770**	**1,285**	**75**	**280**	**1,440**
	Census family status and living arrangements						
424	Number of persons not in census families	1,345	90	125	10	20	205
425	Living with relatives[55]	85	0	10	0	0	30
426	Living with non-relatives only	75	10	0	0	0	0
427	Living alone	1,190	80	120	0	20	175
428	Number of census family persons	7,005	680	1,165	65	260	1,235
429	Average number of persons per census family	2.8	3.0	2.7	3.2	3.1	2.6
430	**Total number of persons aged 65 years and over**	**1,340**	**85**	**205**	**0**	**30**	**275**
431	Number of persons not in census families aged 65 years and over	575	60	55	0	10	95
432	Living with relatives[55]	55	0	10	0	0	15
433	Living with non-relatives only	20	0	0	0	0	0
434	Living alone	495	55	50	0	10	80
435	Number of census family persons aged 65 years and over	765	25	150	0	20	180
	Economic family characteristics						
436	**Total number of economic families in private households**	**2,535**	**225**	**425**	**15**	**90**	**475**
	Size of family						
437	2 persons	1,370	95	255	0	40	295
438	3 persons	490	60	60	10	25	95
439	4 persons	540	60	80	0	15	70
440	5 or more persons	140	10	30	10	10	20
441	Total number of persons in economic families	7,085	680	1,165	65	260	1,260
442	Average number of persons per economic family	3.0	3.0	3.0	4.0	3.0	3.0
443	Total number of persons not in economic families	1,260	90	120	10	20	180
	2005 income characteristics						
444	**Population 15 years and over**	**7,070**	**635**	**1,090**	**x**	**230**	**1,265**
	Sex and total income groups in 2005						
445	Without income	285	40	45	x	15	30
446	With income	6,785	600	1,040	x	215	1,240
447	Under $1,000[56]	285	20	15	x	20	75
448	$1,000 to $2,999	165	20	50	x	15	35
449	$3,000 to $4,999	240	30	65	x	10	25
450	$5,000 to $6,999	295	30	25	x	0	35
451	$7,000 to $9,999	355	50	75	x	0	85
452	$10,000 to $11,999	285	10	70	x	0	50
453	$12,000 to $14,999	500	40	35	x	0	60
454	$15,000 to $19,999	775	40	85	x	20	115
455	$20,000 to $24,999	535	55	55	x	25	70
456	$25,000 to $29,999	495	65	70	x	40	85
457	$30,000 to $34,999	435	25	85	x	15	80
458	$35,000 to $39,999	270	20	50	x	0	45
459	$40,000 to $44,999	300	20	60	x	10	65
460	$45,000 to $49,999	280	45	65	x	10	50
461	$50,000 to $59,999	555	70	45	x	25	100
462	$60,000 and over	1,035	55	190	x	20	255
463	Median income $[57]	24,818	25,751	27,730	x	27,069	29,703
464	Average income $[57]	33,164	28,695	33,477	x	29,216	35,081
465	Standard error of average income $[57]	770	1,782	1,774	x	2,921	1,552

Note: See symbols and abbreviations in the introductory material and see reference material at the end of the publication.

Certaines caractéristiques des divisions de recensement et des subdivisions de recensement – Données intégrales et données-échantillon (20 %), Ontario, Recensement de 2006 (suite)

Timmins, CY ◆◇	Val Rita-Harty, TP	**Dufferin CD/DR A**	Amaranth, TP **A**	East Garafraxa, TP	East Luther Grand Valley, TP ◆◇	**Caractéristiques**	Nº
						Caractéristiques des familles de recensement	
13,260	**280**	**19,465**	**1,435**	**890**	**1,065**	**Nombre total d'enfants à la maison**	416
						Groupes d'âge	
2,565	35	3,970	255	115	225	Moins de 6 ans	417
5,280	130	7,500	530	335	440	6 à 14 ans	418
1,915	65	2,690	180	155	170	15 à 17 ans	419
2,425	50	3,835	320	205	165	18 à 24 ans	420
1,070	0	1,465	145	75	65	25 ans et plus	421
1.1	1.0	1.2	1.3	1.3	1.3	Nombre moyen d'enfants à la maison par famille de recensement[54]	422
42,275	**940**	**53,640**	**3,845**	**2,390**	**2,790**	**Nombre total de personnes dans les ménages privés**	423
						Situation des particuliers dans la famille de recensement et des particuliers dans le ménage	
5,905	140	5,035	245	185	200	Nombre de personnes hors famille de recensement	424
625	10	860	65	45	40	Vivant avec des personnes apparentées[55]	425
650	70	940	40	45	25	Vivant avec des personnes non apparentées seulement	426
4,630	60	3,235	140	95	135	Vivant seules	427
36,370	800	48,605	3,595	2,205	2,590	Nombre de membres d'une famille de recensement	428
2.9	2.8	3.1	3.2	3.2	3.2	Nombre moyen de personnes par famille de recensement	429
4,935	**100**	**5,275**	**380**	**265**	**155**	**Nombre total de personnes âgées de 65 ans et plus**	430
1,880	25	1,615	85	95	70	Nombre de personnes hors famille de recensement âgées de 65 ans et plus	431
180	10	405	55	30	25	Vivant avec des personnes apparentées[55]	432
65	0	35	0	15	0	Vivant avec des personnes non apparentées seulement	433
1,630	20	1,180	30	55	45	Vivant seules	434
3,055	75	3,655	295	170	80	Nombre de membres d'une famille de recensement âgés de 65 ans et plus	435
						Caractéristiques des familles économiques	
12,545	**285**	**15,275**	**1,100**	**670**	**800**	**Nombre total de familles économiques dans les ménages privés**	436
						Taille de la famille	
5,865	170	5,890	415	225	305	2 personnes	437
2,815	30	3,130	205	155	155	3 personnes	438
2,780	50	3,895	275	160	215	4 personnes	439
1,080	35	2,365	200	125	130	5 personnes ou plus	440
36,995	805	49,465	3,665	2,250	2,630	Nombre total de personnes dans les familles économiques	441
3.0	3.0	3.0	3.0	3.0	3.0	Nombre moyen de personnes par famille économique	442
5,280	130	4,175	180	140	160	Nombre total de personnes hors famille économique	443
						Caractéristiques du revenu de 2005	
34,580	**780**	**42,365**	**3,045**	**1,930**	**2,180**	**Population de 15 ans et plus**	444
						Sexe et groupes de revenu total en 2005	
1,475	35	2,205	185	85	180	Sans revenu	445
33,100	745	40,160	2,865	1,845	2,005	Avec un revenu	446
915	65	1,555	135	80	90	Moins de 1 000 $[56]	447
975	35	1,415	90	55	60	1 000 $ à 2 999 $	448
980	25	1,285	75	85	45	3 000 $ à 4 999 $	449
1,290	35	1,365	90	85	75	5 000 $ à 6 999 $	450
2,005	90	2,335	185	145	85	7 000 $ à 9 999 $	451
1,355	15	1,525	155	50	95	10 000 $ à 11 999 $	452
2,050	30	2,075	125	100	110	12 000 $ à 14 999 $	453
3,485	65	3,360	210	150	180	15 000 $ à 19 999 $	454
2,795	45	2,760	250	100	185	20 000 $ à 24 999 $	455
2,395	35	2,505	185	95	150	25 000 $ à 29 999 $	456
1,920	60	2,525	150	115	150	30 000 $ à 34 999 $	457
1,955	40	2,475	170	110	150	35 000 $ à 39 999 $	458
1,635	35	2,110	125	85	80	40 000 $ à 44 999 $	459
1,540	30	1,875	110	70	105	45 000 $ à 49 999$	460
2,195	45	3,295	255	125	205	50 000 $ à 59 999$	461
5,620	90	7,690	540	405	235	60 000 $ et plus	462
26,364	21,731	29,795	27,771	29,264	26,528	Revenu médian $[57]	463
35,238	27,648	37,565	36,667	39,912	31,141	Revenu moyen $[57]	464
426	1,822	408	1,329	1,956	1,021	Erreur type de revenu moyen $[57]	465

Nota : Voir les symboles et les abréviations dans les documents d'introduction et voir les documents de référence à la fin de la publication.

Selected characteristics for census divisions and census subdivisions – 100% data and 20% sample data, Ontario, 2006 Census (continued)

No.	Characteristics	Kapuskasing, T	Mattice-Val Côté, TP ◆	Moonbeam, TP ◆◆◊	New Post 69A, IRI ◆◆◊◊	Opasatika, TP ◆	Smooth Rock Falls, T ◊
	2005 income characteristics						
	Sex and total income groups in 2005 (continued)						
466	Total - Males	3,490	320	575	X	110	660
467	Without income	60	10	10	X	0	0
468	With income	3,430	315	560	X	110	660
469	Under $1,000[56]	130	15	10	X	15	40
470	$1,000 to $2,999	35	0	15	X	0	0
471	$3,000 to $4,999	95	0	30	X	0	0
472	$5,000 to $6,999	90	10	10	X	0	15
473	$7,000 to $9,999	95	30	20	X	0	15
474	$10,000 to $11,999	120	0	20	X	0	20
475	$12,000 to $14,999	175	0	15	X	0	15
476	$15,000 to $19,999	230	10	30	X	10	20
477	$20,000 to $24,999	260	40	25	X	0	35
478	$25,000 to $29,999	265	25	55	X	30	65
479	$30,000 to $34,999	210	20	25	X	0	25
480	$35,000 to $39,999	160	10	20	X	0	20
481	$40,000 to $44,999	175	25	35	X	0	45
482	$45,000 to $49,999	185	40	50	X	10	40
483	$50,000 to $59,999	425	35	40	X	15	80
484	$60,000 and over	775	50	155	X	15	205
485	Median income $[57]	35,461	36,476	40,010	X	27,642	45,008
486	Average income $[57]	42,192	36,297	42,332	X	34,810	45,268
487	Standard error of average income $[57]	1,263	2,490	2,692	X	4,291	2,170
488	Total - Females	3,580	315	515	X	120	600
489	Without income	220	30	35	X	15	20
490	With income	3,360	285	480	X	105	580
491	Under $1,000[56]	150	0	0	X	0	35
492	$1,000 to $2,999	130	20	35	X	15	30
493	$3,000 to $4,999	145	30	35	X	0	20
494	$5,000 to $6,999	200	15	15	X	10	20
495	$7,000 to $9,999	260	25	50	X	0	65
496	$10,000 to $11,999	165	10	45	X	0	30
497	$12,000 to $14,999	320	40	20	X	0	50
498	$15,000 to $19,999	540	30	55	X	15	100
499	$20,000 to $24,999	270	15	30	X	25	35
500	$25,000 to $29,999	230	40	15	X	10	15
501	$30,000 to $34,999	220	0	60	X	10	55
502	$35,000 to $39,999	110	0	30	X	0	20
503	$40,000 to $44,999	125	0	25	X	10	20
504	$45,000 to $49,999	90	10	15	X	0	10
505	$50,000 to $59,999	135	35	10	X	10	20
506	$60,000 and over	260	0	30	X	10	45
507	Median income $[57]	17,598	14,367	18,178	X	22,018	15,869
508	Average income $[57]	23,951	20,292	23,110	X	23,440	23,523
509	Standard error of average income $[57]	733	2,081	1,801	X	3,578	1,802
	Composition of total income						
510	Composition of total income in 2005 %	100.0	100.0	100.0	X	100.0	100.0
511	Employment income %	72.7	74.8	67.5	X	76.4	66.8
512	Government transfer payments %	15.4	15.8	16.3	X	14.0	14.8
513	Other %	11.8	9.8	16.4	X	9.6	18.3
514	**Population 15 years and over with employment income in 2005**	**4,725**	**425**	**730**	**X**	**160**	**755**
	Sex and work activity						
515	Median employment income in 2005 $	27,524	26,994	27,523	X	27,003	33,960
516	Average employment income in 2005 $	34,660	30,060	32,184	X	30,691	38,460
517	Standard error of average employment income $	1,045	2,128	2,248	X	3,438	2,300
518	Worked full year, full time[59]	2,240	185	270	X	55	335
519	Median employment income in 2005 $	49,472	46,726	49,436	X	38,623	65,743
520	Average employment income in 2005 $	51,316	44,844	50,162	X	42,236	58,321
521	Standard error of average employment income $	1,457	2,615	3,156	X	4,490	2,852
522	Worked part year or part time[60]	1,910	215	375	X	100	395
523	Median employment income in 2005 $	14,596	20,371	14,839	X	18,390	12,070
524	Average employment income in 2005 $	24,196	19,866	25,488	X	24,777	23,638
525	Standard error of average employment income $	1,498	2,154	2,878	X	4,533	2,599
526	Males 15 years and over with employment income[58]	2,685	250	410	X	75	440
527	Median employment income in 2005 $	37,881	33,079	39,963	X	44,389	53,821
528	Average employment income in 2005 $	41,702	34,365	37,659	X	41,024	45,982
529	Standard error of average employment income $	1,603	2,874	3,458	X	4,777	3,158

Note: See symbols and abbreviations in the introductory material and see reference material at the end of the publication.

Certaines caractéristiques des divisions de recensement et des subdivisions de recensement – Données intégrales et données-échantillon (20 %), Ontario, Recensement de 2006 (suite)

Timmins, CY ◆◇	Val Rita-Harty, TP	**Dufferin CD/DR A**	Amaranth, TP **A**	East Garafraxa, TP	East Luther Grand Valley, TP ◆◇	**Caractéristiques**	Nº
						Caractéristiques du revenu de 2005	
						Sexe et groupes de revenu total en 2005 (suite)	
16,940	390	21,025	1,595	1,015	1,110	Total - Hommes	466
775	10	910	85	20	95	Sans revenu	467
16,160	375	20,110	1,510	995	1,010	Avec un revenu	468
375	25	890	95	65	45	Moins de 1 000 $[56]	469
315	20	500	45	25	10	1 000 $ à 2 999 $	470
355	10	480	25	25	20	3 000 $ à 4 999 $	471
410	10	395	10	20	20	5 000 $ à 6 999 $	472
645	20	810	65	100	25	7 000 $ à 9 999 $	473
425	0	540	55	25	60	10 000 $ à 11 999 $	474
705	0	695	30	45	45	12 000 $ à 14 999 $	475
1,165	25	1,190	90	55	65	15 000 $ à 19 999 $	476
1,255	15	1,090	135	50	75	20 000 $ à 24 999 $	477
1,065	25	1,105	100	40	60	25 000 $ à 29 999 $	478
875	30	1,095	65	35	40	30 000 $ à 34 999 $	479
1,065	10	1,200	95	60	45	35 000 $ à 39 999 $	480
910	30	1,145	65	45	50	40 000 $ à $44 999 $	481
870	25	1,060	75	20	85	45 000 $ à $49 999 $	482
1,535	35	2,085	155	75	145	50 000 $ à $59 999 $	483
4,180	70	5,835	405	315	205	60 000 $ et plus	484
37,240	31,192	40,209	36,910	35,935	37,768	Revenu médian $[57]	485
44,496	34,717	47,103	44,429	48,766	37,906	Revenu moyen $[57]	486
741	2,614	709	2,078	3,205	1,643	Erreur type de revenu moyen $[57]	487
17,645	390	21,340	1,450	910	1,070	Total - Femmes	488
700	25	1,295	100	60	75	Sans revenu	489
16,945	365	20,050	1,350	850	995	Avec un revenu	490
540	40	660	40	15	45	Moins de 1 000 $[56]	491
660	15	920	45	30	50	1 000$ à 2 999 $	492
625	15	800	50	60	25	3 000 $ à 4 999 $	493
875	20	970	80	65	55	5 000 $ à 6 999 $	494
1,360	65	1,525	115	50	55	7 000 $ à 9 999 $	495
925	15	985	95	25	35	10 000 $ à 11 999 $	496
1,340	20	1,375	100	55	65	12 000 $ à 14 999 $	497
2,320	40	2,175	125	95	110	15 000 $ à 19 999 $	498
1,540	25	1,675	120	45	105	20 000 $ à 24 999 $	499
1,325	10	1,400	80	55	90	25 000 $ à 29 999 $	500
1,045	30	1,435	80	80	105	30 000 $ à 34 999 $	501
890	30	1,275	75	50	100	35 000 $ à 39 999 $	502
720	10	970	60	35	30	40 000 $ à 44 999 $	503
670	10	815	40	45	25	45 000 $ à 49 999 $	504
655	10	1,210	100	50	60	50 000 $ à 59 999 $	505
1,440	20	1,855	135	95	30	60 000 $ et plus	506
19,389	12,859	21,917	21,888	21,236	22,040	Revenu médian $[57]	507
26,405	20,351	27,994	27,970	29,505	24,242	Revenu moyen $[57]	508
387	2,252	360	1,455	1,851	1,072	Erreur type de revenu moyen $[57]	509
						Composition du revenu total	
100.0	100.0	100.0	100.0	100.0	100.0	Composition du revenu total en 2005 %	510
77.1	67.2	81.2	82.6	80.1	86.9	Revenu d'emploi %	511
12.9	16.6	8.4	8.9	6.9	8.4	Transferts gouvernementaux %	512
10.0	16.3	10.3	8.6	13.2	4.5	Autres %	513
24,775	**510**	**32,645**	**2,415**	**1,580**	**1,750**	**Population de 15 ans et plus avec un revenu d'emploi en 2005**	514
						Sexe et travail	
28,428	19,136	30,489	27,941	25,830	28,328	Revenu médian d'emploi en 2005 $	515
36,304	26,973	37,541	35,868	37,315	30,991	Revenu moyen d'emploi en 2005 $	516
527	2,341	455	1,513	2,110	1,154	Erreur type de revenu moyen d'emploi $	517
12,920	155	18,515	1,295	810	1,070	A travaillé toute l'année à plein temps[59]	518
44,818	50,800	45,543	47,435	45,017	37,046	Revenu médian d'emploi en 2005 $	519
51,252	49,753	51,122	52,735	56,552	36,951	Revenu moyen d'emploi en 2005 $	520
792	4,302	548	2,144	3,260	1,481	Erreur type de revenu moyen d'emploi $	521
9,985	295	12,440	955	700	615	A travaillé une partie de l'année ou à temps partiel[60]	522
12,138	12,754	11,993	10,022	12,008	15,304	Revenu médian d'emploi en 2005 $	523
21,978	18,673	20,989	18,046	18,070	21,910	Revenu moyen d'emploi en 2005 $	524
584	2,112	726	1,482	1,635	1,672	Erreur type de revenu moyen d'emploi $	525
13,055	285	17,335	1,320	885	940	Hommes de 15 ans et plus avec un revenu d'emploi[58]	526
40,013	24,400	41,197	34,978	28,681	39,651	Revenu médian d'emploi en 2005 $	527
44,879	31,595	46,180	43,351	44,007	37,140	Revenu moyen d'emploi en 2005 $	528
868	3,252	756	2,329	3,435	1,809	Erreur type de revenu moyen d'emploi $	529

Nota : Voir les symboles et les abréviations dans les documents d'introduction et voir les documents de référence à la fin de la publication.

Selected characteristics for census divisions and census subdivisions – 100% data and 20% sample data, Ontario, 2006 Census (continued)

No.	Characteristics	Kapuskasing, T	Mattice-Val Côté, TP ◆	Moonbeam, TP ◆◆◇	New Post 69A, IRI ◆◆◇◇	Opasatika, TP ◆	Smooth Rock Falls, T ◇
	2005 income characteristics						
	Sex and work activity (continued)						
530	Worked full year, full time[59]	1,370	125	150	X	35	235
531	Median employment income in 2005 $	56,444	46,884	60,563	X	57,442	67,467
532	Average employment income in 2005 $	59,972	48,781	60,966	X	49,168	62,665
533	Standard error of average employment income $	2,000	2,676	4,119	X	4,952	3,417
534	Worked part year or part time[60]	915	120	210	X	40	185
535	Median employment income in 2005 $	19,297	20,661	22,542	X	43,193	28,162
536	Average employment income in 2005 $	31,242	22,955	30,138	X	33,514	29,398
537	Standard error of average employment income $	2,792	3,402	4,589	X	7,431	4,302
538	Females 15 years and over with employment income[58]	2,040	170	320	X	80	320
539	Median employment income in 2005 $	19,706	20,376	20,051	X	19,976	22,034
540	Average employment income in 2005 $	25,386	23,786	25,173	X	20,883	28,072
541	Standard error of average employment income $	1,032	2,895	2,428	X	3,794	2,944
542	Worked full year, full time[59]	875	65	120	X	20	105
543	Median employment income in 2005 $	33,458	44,896	36,368	X	20,060	48,939
544	Average employment income in 2005 $	37,816	37,696	36,835	X	26,113	48,447
545	Standard error of average employment income $	1,648	5,161	3,566	X	4,013	4,630
546	Worked part year or part time[60]	995	95	165	X	60	210
547	Median employment income in 2005 $	11,478	12,805	14,803	X	8,109	9,524
548	Average employment income in 2005 $	17,738	16,011	19,584	X	18,885	18,572
549	Standard error of average employment income $	1,131	2,409	3,050	X	5,119	2,946
550	**Total number of economic families in private households**	**2,535**	**225**	**425**	**X**	**85**	**480**
	Family income groups in 2005						
551	Under $10,000	40	0	0	X	0	10
552	$10,000 to $19,999	130	15	15	X	0	10
553	$20,000 to $29,999	280	30	40	X	10	20
554	$30,000 to $39,999	235	15	70	X	10	40
555	$40,000 to $49,999	160	30	25	X	0	95
556	$50,000 to $59,999	285	15	40	X	15	35
557	$60,000 to $69,999	175	30	30	X	10	40
558	$70,000 to $79,999	260	25	40	X	10	30
559	$80,000 to $89,999	215	20	35	X	15	45
560	$90,000 to $99,999	150	15	35	X	0	45
561	$100,000 and over	605	35	90	X	20	115
562	Median family income $	66,030	63,248	62,681	X	62,137	69,936
563	Average family income $	73,482	64,253	72,086	X	67,479	76,624
564	Standard error of average family income $	1,901	4,276	4,059	X	7,153	3,601
	Family after-tax income groups in 2005						
565	Under $10,000	40	0	10	X	0	0
566	$10,000 to $19,999	125	10	10	X	0	10
567	$20,000 to $29,999	295	30	50	X	10	25
568	$30,000 to $39,999	280	30	85	X	10	85
569	$40,000 to $49,999	340	30	35	X	15	75
570	$50,000 to $59,999	290	15	50	X	10	50
571	$60,000 to $69,999	265	50	40	X	15	45
572	$70,000 to $79,999	260	20	45	X	10	55
573	$80,000 to $89,999	190	0	25	X	10	45
574	$90,000 to $99,999	140	25	35	X	10	20
575	$100,000 and over	305	0	50	X	0	60
576	Median after-tax family income $	56,603	51,451	54,916	X	53,433	58,341
577	Average after-tax family income $	61,413	55,455	60,244	X	57,500	64,763
578	Standard error of average after-tax family income $	1,422	3,383	3,011	X	5,608	2,830
	Income status in 2005						
579	Total population in private households for income status	8,350	765	1,290	X	280	1,440
580	Below low income cut-off before tax in 2005	965	75	85	X	20	65
581	Prevalence of low income before tax in 2005 %	11.6	10.4	6.6	X	5.4	4.5
582	Below low income cut-off after tax in 2005	565	50	45	X	15	40
583	Prevalence of low income after tax in 2005 %	6.8	7.2	3.5	X	5.4	2.8

Note: See symbols and abbreviations in the introductory material and see reference material at the end of the publication.

Certaines caractéristiques des divisions de recensement et des subdivisions de recensement – Données intégrales et données-échantillon (20 %), Ontario, Recensement de 2006 (suite)

Timmins, CY ◆◇	Val Rita-Harty, TP	**Dufferin CD/DR A**	Amaranth, TP A	East Garafraxa, TP	East Luther Grand Valley, TP ◆◇	Caractéristiques	N°
						Caractéristiques du revenu de 2005	
						Sexe et travail (suite)	
7,620	85	11,115	840	530	620	A travaillé toute l'année à plein temps[59]	530
53,698	58,626	53,059	52,209	52,285	47,039	Revenu médian d'emploi en 2005 $	531
59,689	56,913	58,403	57,682	62,250	43,470	Revenu moyen d'emploi en 2005 $	532
1,220	5,143	784	2,908	4,636	2,075	Erreur type de revenu moyen d'emploi $	533
4,425	155	5,415	405	335	295	A travaillé une partie de l'année ou à temps partiel[60]	534
16,646	16,232	13,472	10,696	9,882	17,576	Revenu médian d'emploi en 2005 $	535
28,029	24,210	26,547	22,423	18,052	25,730	Revenu moyen d'emploi en 2005 $	536
1,078	3,154	1,608	2,824	2,954	3,149	Erreur type de revenu moyen d'emploi $	537
11,715	225	15,310	1,095	695	815	Femmes de 15 ans et plus avec un revenu d'emploi[58]	538
20,636	16,292	22,173	19,539	24,674	22,091	Revenu médian d'emploi en 2005 $	539
26,745	21,102	27,761	26,797	28,737	23,913	Revenu moyen d'emploi en 2005 $	540
489	3,118	407	1,636	1,975	1,230	Erreur type de revenu moyen d'emploi $	541
5,300	70	7,400	460	275	450	A travaillé toute l'année à plein temps[59]	542
34,858	32,980	36,150	38,358	39,487	28,505	Revenu médian d'emploi en 2005 $	543
39,111	40,824	40,184	43,723	45,761	28,023	Revenu moyen d'emploi en 2005 $	544
664	6,703	611	2,662	3,332	1,661	Erreur type de revenu moyen d'emploi $	545
5,555	145	7,025	555	365	320	A travaillé une partie de l'année ou à temps partiel[60]	546
10,458	8,129	11,007	9,890	12,935	11,828	Revenu médian d'emploi en 2005 $	547
17,160	12,780	16,706	14,867	18,086	18,406	Revenu moyen d'emploi en 2005 $	548
567	2,307	406	1,504	1,766	1,702	Erreur type de revenu moyen d'emploi $	549
12,545	**285**	**15,275**	**1,100**	**670**	**800**	**Nombre total des familles économiques dans les ménages privés**	550
						Revenu de la famille économique en 2005	
240	10	255	30	10	15	Moins de 10 000 $	551
530	25	400	35	40	15	10 000 $ à 19 999 $	552
1,075	0	805	60	25	60	20 000 $ à 29 999 $	553
1,100	50	1,060	60	55	70	30 000 $ à 39 999 $	554
1,090	25	1,055	65	40	95	40 000 $ à 49 999 $	555
1,030	0	1,345	85	50	50	50 000 $ à 59 999 $	556
1,075	45	1,445	105	40	85	60 000 $ à 69 999 $	557
1,150	35	1,490	115	55	110	70 000 $ à 79 999 $	558
1,075	30	1,360	110	40	85	80 000 $ à 89 999 $	559
895	30	1,200	70	0	60	90 000 $ à 99 999 $	560
3,275	25	4,865	370	300	160	100 000 $ et plus	561
70,853	64,367	78,404	79,980	84,502	72,766	Revenu médian des familles $	562
79,459	61,544	88,596	89,630	100,396	72,067	Revenu moyen des familles $	563
1,148	3,813	1,057	3,664	5,638	2,610	Erreur type de revenu moyen des familles $	564
						Revenu après impôt de la famille économique en 2005	
250	10	280	30	20	15	Moins de 10 000 $	565
570	25	405	40	40	15	10 000 $ à 19 999 $	566
1,160	10	935	70	30	70	20 000 $ à 29 999 $	567
1,410	70	1,360	80	40	85	30 000 $ à 39 999 $	568
1,400	10	1,605	95	70	115	40 000 $ à 49 999 $	569
1,515	50	1,795	115	70	90	50 000 $ à 59 999 $	570
1,310	30	2,125	195	60	125	60 000 $ à 69 999 $	571
1,435	40	1,530	100	30	95	70 000 $ à 79 999 $	572
985	20	1,370	105	45	75	80 000 $ à 89 999 $	573
785	15	1,005	70	50	30	90 000 $ à 99 999 $	574
1,715	0	2,865	205	205	85	100 000 $ et plus	575
59,790	52,878	65,883	67,733	70,823	60,957	Revenu médian après impôt des familles $	576
65,521	52,804	72,479	72,918	79,995	61,589	Revenu moyen après impôt des familles $	577
776	3,079	736	2,587	4,206	2,127	Erreur type de revenu moyen après impôt des familles $	578
						Catégorie de revenu en 2005	
42,270	940	53,625	3,845	2,385	2,790	Population totale dans les ménages privés pour la catégorie de revenu	579
5,370	120	3,525	195	140	165	Au-dessous du seuil de faible revenu avant impôt en 2005	580
12.7	12.8	6.6	5.1	5.6	5.9	Fréquence du faible revenu avant impôt en 2005 %	581
3,535	90	2,520	170	115	95	Au-dessous du seuil de faible revenu après impôt en 2005	582
8.4	9.1	4.7	4.4	5.0	3.2	Fréquence du faible revenu après impôt en 2005 %	583

Nota : Voir les symboles et les abréviations dans les documents d'introduction et voir les documents de référence à la fin de la publication.

Selected characteristics for census divisions and census subdivisions – 100% data and 20% sample data, Ontario, 2006 Census (continued)

No.	Characteristics	Kapuskasing, T	Mattice-Val Côté, TP ◆	Moonbeam, TP ◆◆◇	New Post 69A, IRI ◆◆◇◇	Opasatika, TP ◆	Smooth Rock Falls, T ◇
	2005 income characteristics						
584	**Total number of private households**	**3,745**	**315**	**540**	**X**	**105**	**655**
	Household income groups in 2005						
585	Under $10,000	165	10	10	X	10	20
586	$10,000 to $19,999	615	45	60	X	0	40
587	$20,000 to $29,999	425	45	45	X	20	45
588	$30,000 to $39,999	370	25	75	X	10	55
589	$40,000 to $49,999	310	30	60	X	0	140
590	$50,000 to $59,999	345	30	40	X	15	40
591	$60,000 to $69,999	210	30	40	X	15	50
592	$70,000 to $79,999	285	30	35	X	10	40
593	$80,000 to $89,999	230	20	45	X	15	45
594	$90,000 to $99,999	160	15	35	X	0	60
595	$100,000 and over	635	35	100	X	20	120
596	Median household income $	48,857	51,703	55,093	X	60,967	56,844
597	Average household income $	60,091	54,446	64,155	X	58,811	66,336
598	Standard error of average household income $	1,629	4,032	3,678	X	6,846	3,130
	Household after-tax income groups in 2005						
599	Under $10,000	165	10	15	X	10	20
600	$10,000 to $19,999	660	45	55	X	0	40
601	$20,000 to $29,999	480	45	70	X	10	60
602	$30,000 to $39,999	455	30	90	X	10	140
603	$40,000 to $49,999	435	50	60	X	20	95
604	$50,000 to $59,999	320	10	50	X	10	60
605	$60,000 to $69,999	300	50	40	X	20	45
606	$70,000 to $79,999	260	30	50	X	0	65
607	$80,000 to $89,999	200	10	20	X	10	50
608	$90,000 to $99,999	140	30	30	X	10	25
609	$100,000 and over	325	0	55	X	0	65
610	Median after-tax household income $	42,648	43,698	45,769	X	48,423	47,119
611	Average after-tax household income $	50,244	47,013	53,628	X	50,148	56,039
612	Standard error of average after-tax household income $	1,221	3,261	2,786	X	5,491	2,491

Note: See symbols and abbreviations in the introductory material and see reference material at the end of the publication.

Certaines caractéristiques des divisions de recensement et des subdivisions de recensement – Données intégrales et données-échantillon (20 %), Ontario, Recensement de 2006 (suite)

Timmins, CY ◆◊	Val Rita-Harty, TP	**Dufferin CD/DR A**	Amaranth, TP A	East Garafraxa, TP	East Luther Grand Valley, TP ◆◊	Caractéristiques	N°
						Caractéristiques du revenu de 2005	
17,390	**355**	**18,760**	**1,240**	**775**	**945**	**Nombre total des ménages privés**	584
						Tranches de revenu des ménages en 2005	
595	20	565	55	15	20	Moins de 10 000 $	585
2,185	40	1,120	45	55	55	10 000 $ à 19 999 $	586
1,925	15	1,260	95	30	95	20 000 $ à 29 999 $	587
1,665	50	1,540	70	65	95	30 000 $ à 39 999 $	588
1,565	40	1,450	80	50	110	40 000 $ à 49 999 $	589
1,285	15	1,620	100	65	50	50 000 $ à 59 999 $	590
1,280	50	1,685	105	45	85	60 000 $ à 69 999 $	591
1,300	35	1,655	125	50	105	70 000 $ à 79 999 $	592
1,175	30	1,475	115	55	90	80 000 $ à 89 999 $	593
940	25	1,280	75	20	75	90 000 $ à 99 999 $	594
3,470	25	5,120	380	310	160	100 000 $ et plus	595
55,623	53,125	70,688	77,082	81,035	66,763	Revenu médian des ménages $	596
66,926	57,832	80,278	84,580	95,359	66,006	Revenu moyen des ménages $	597
931	3,902	933	3,500	5,043	2,472	Erreur type de revenu moyen des ménages $	598
						Tranches du revenu après impôt des ménages en 2005	
600	20	595	55	25	20	Moins de 10 000 $	599
2,440	45	1,220	60	55	65	10 000 $ à 19 999 $	600
2,085	20	1,585	100	35	125	20 000 $ à 29 999 $	601
2,025	85	1,905	95	55	105	30 000 $ à 39 999 $	602
1,830	15	1,985	115	85	125	40 000 $ à 49 999 $	603
1,745	50	2,100	125	85	90	50 000 $ à 59 999 $	604
1,470	35	2,240	200	75	130	60 000 $ à 69 999 $	605
1,540	40	1,655	100	30	100	70 000 $ à 79 999 $	606
1,070	20	1,415	85	45	80	80 000 $ à 89 999 $	607
830	15	1,055	65	40	35	90 000 $ à 99 999 $	608
1,760	0	3,000	235	225	85	100 000 $ et plus	609
48,526	42,942	60,045	64,322	67,193	55,756	Revenu médian après impôt des ménages $	610
55,468	49,710	65,755	69,016	75,887	56,423	Revenu moyen après impôt des ménages $	611
648	3,261	663	2,529	3,779	2,023	Erreur type de revenu moyen après impôt des ménages $	612

Nota : Voir les symboles et les abréviations dans les documents d'introduction et voir les documents de référence à la fin de la publication.

Selected characteristics for census divisions and census subdivisions – 100% data and 20% sample data, Ontario, 2006 Census (continued)

No.	Characteristics	Melancthon, TP A	Mono, T A	Mulmur, TP ◆◇	Orangeville, T	Shelburne, T A	**Durham CD/DR**
	Population characteristics						
1	**Population, 2001**[1]	**2,739**	**6,912**	**3,099**	**25,248**	**4,213**	**506,901**
2	**Population, 2006**[2]	**2,895**	**7,071**	**3,318**	**26,925**	**5,149**	**561,258**
3	Population percentage change, 2001 to 2006	5.7	2.3	7.1	6.6	22.2	10.7
4	Land area in square kilometres, 2006	310.88	277.67	286.73	15.57	6.44	2,523.15
5	**Total population – 100% data**[3]	**2,895**	**7,070**	**3,320**	**26,925**	**5,150**	**561,255**
	Sex and age groups						
6	Male	1,550	3,580	1,705	13,065	2,465	274,535
7	0 to 4 years	75	110	65	895	180	16,760
8	5 to 9 years	100	235	105	1,000	200	19,120
9	10 to 14 years	125	305	145	1,135	205	23,090
10	15 to 19 years	145	330	135	1,060	165	22,185
11	20 to 24 years	105	195	105	800	165	17,915
12	25 to 29 years	60	105	45	830	150	14,980
13	30 to 34 years	70	115	60	955	195	16,540
14	35 to 39 years	115	225	120	1,075	190	19,705
15	40 to 44 years	150	340	160	1,215	210	25,730
16	45 to 49 years	135	325	150	1,070	180	24,485
17	50 to 54 years	115	330	160	805	135	19,730
18	55 to 59 years	120	290	125	655	120	16,680
19	60 to 64 years	75	235	105	485	80	11,570
20	65 to 69 years	50	175	85	335	80	8,265
21	70 to 74 years	50	125	70	300	70	7,025
22	75 to 79 years	30	80	45	200	55	5,425
23	80 to 84 years	15	45	25	150	50	3,375
24	85 years and over	10	20	10	100	35	1,950
25	Female	1,345	3,490	1,615	13,860	2,685	286,720
26	0 to 4 years	65	165	85	915	175	15,655
27	5 to 9 years	80	225	90	965	165	18,555
28	10 to 14 years	115	280	125	1,115	195	21,955
29	15 to 19 years	120	300	125	1,055	170	21,285
30	20 to 24 years	65	190	65	740	125	17,270
31	25 to 29 years	55	80	45	805	175	15,635
32	30 to 34 years	70	125	75	1,020	170	18,155
33	35 to 39 years	125	230	130	1,160	220	22,040
34	40 to 44 years	140	335	160	1,325	215	27,570
35	45 to 49 years	125	360	140	1,070	190	25,060
36	50 to 54 years	105	320	140	830	140	20,455
37	55 to 59 years	90	300	145	710	125	17,150
38	60 to 64 years	70	190	105	530	115	11,840
39	65 to 69 years	45	145	70	405	80	9,165
40	70 to 74 years	35	90	55	345	80	8,160
41	75 to 79 years	20	65	35	330	105	7,060
42	80 to 84 years	15	55	15	265	95	5,505
43	85 years and over	10	25	10	285	150	4,210
44	**Total population 15 years and over**[3]	**2,330**	**5,750**	**2,710**	**20,905**	**4,030**	**446,125**
	Legal marital status						
45	Never legally married (single)	705	1,520	720	6,325	1,110	137,150
46	Legally married (and not separated)[4,5]	1,265	3,530	1,595	10,775	1,970	237,770
47	Separated, but still legally married	90	140	90	925	215	16,820
48	Divorced	175	350	190	1,640	325	31,430
49	Widowed	95	205	110	1,245	410	22,965
	Common-law status						
50	Not in a common-law relationship	2,045	5,390	2,445	19,015	3,520	412,510
51	In a common-law relationship	280	360	260	1,890	505	33,615
52	**Total population – 20% sample data**[6]	**2,895**	**7,050**	**3,300**	**26,695**	**4,905**	**557,330**
	Mother tongue						
53	Single responses	2,880	7,005	3,285	26,505	4,905	552,205
54	English	2,620	6,235	2,970	24,595	4,645	472,285
55	French	10	110	50	315	25	9,790
56	Non-official languages[7]	255	650	270	1,595	235	70,130
57	Italian	15	35	0	210	15	6,825
58	Chinese, n.o.s.[61]	0	0	0	0	0	2,295
59	Cantonese	0	0	0	0	10	1,630
60	Spanish	0	20	0	145	30	3,610
61	German	70	215	165	245	15	5,020
62	Other languages[8]	170	375	100	995	165	50,750

Note: See symbols and abbreviations in the introductory material and see reference material at the end of the publication.

Certaines caractéristiques des divisions de recensement et des subdivisions de recensement – Données intégrales et données-échantillon (20 %), Ontario, Recensement de 2006 (suite)

Ajax, T	Brock, TP	Clarington, MU	Mississaugas of Scugog Island, IRI	Oshawa, CY	Pickering, CY	Caractéristiques	N°
						Caractéristiques de la population	
73,753	**12,110**	**69,834**	**51**	**139,051**	**87,139**	**Population, 2001[1]**	1
90,167	**11,979**	**77,820**	**72**	**141,590**	**87,838**	**Population, 2006[2]**	2
22.3	-1.1	11.4	41.2	1.8	0.8	Variation en pourcentage de la population, 2001 à 2006	3
67.09	423.31	611.10	2.58	145.67	231.59	Superficie des terres en kilomètres carrés, 2006	4
90,165	**11,980**	**77,820**	**70**	**141,590**	**87,835**	**Population totale – Données intégrales[3]**	5
						Sexe et groupes d'âge	
43,805	5,850	38,485	40	69,025	42,745	Sexe masculin	6
2,935	310	2,425	5	3,865	2,290	0 à 4 ans	7
3,340	335	2,895	5	4,090	3,000	5 à 9 ans	8
4,060	465	3,525	5	5,020	3,660	10 à 14 ans	9
3,750	435	3,175	0	5,115	3,660	15 à 19 ans	10
2,940	340	2,060	5	4,715	3,160	20 à 24 ans	11
2,345	280	2,020	5	4,270	2,305	25 à 29 ans	12
2,780	255	2,465	0	4,360	2,180	30 à 34 ans	13
3,360	345	2,830	5	4,765	2,860	35 à 39 ans	14
4,310	500	3,855	5	6,100	3,920	40 à 44 ans	15
4,075	525	3,355	5	6,080	3,825	45 à 49 ans	16
3,030	450	2,540	5	4,990	3,405	50 à 54 ans	17
2,395	400	2,095	0	4,290	3,005	55 à 59 ans	18
1,505	330	1,605	5	3,155	1,900	60 à 64 ans	19
1,000	260	1,130	0	2,520	1,225	65 à 69 ans	20
845	215	1,000	5	2,115	990	70 à 74 ans	21
625	190	765	0	1,750	720	75 à 79 ans	22
335	130	475	0	1,165	420	80 à 84 ans	23
180	95	275	0	650	230	85 ans et plus	24
46,365	6,125	39,335	30	72,565	45,090	Sexe féminin	25
2,815	305	2,235	5	3,590	2,160	0 à 4 ans	26
3,275	335	2,855	0	4,090	2,860	5 à 9 ans	27
3,930	435	3,355	0	4,815	3,425	10 à 14 ans	28
3,710	455	2,850	0	4,880	3,640	15 à 19 ans	29
2,815	315	2,105	5	4,600	3,015	20 à 24 ans	30
2,605	250	2,100	0	4,415	2,285	25 à 29 ans	31
3,240	290	2,595	0	4,580	2,410	30 à 34 ans	32
3,895	370	3,245	0	4,965	3,370	35 à 39 ans	33
4,720	530	4,045	5	6,345	4,480	40 à 44 ans	34
4,280	540	3,190	5	6,020	4,250	45 à 49 ans	35
3,075	425	2,510	5	5,270	3,695	50 à 54 ans	36
2,415	450	2,125	5	4,615	2,945	55 à 59 ans	37
1,535	305	1,650	0	3,420	1,875	60 à 64 ans	38
1,165	260	1,255	5	2,760	1,355	65 à 69 ans	39
1,040	240	1,035	0	2,560	1,205	70 à 74 ans	40
850	235	940	0	2,335	920	75 à 79 ans	41
605	200	690	0	1,900	710	80 à 84 ans	42
395	195	555	0	1,400	505	85 ans et plus	43
69,815	**9,795**	**60,530**	**55**	**116,110**	**70,450**	**Population totale de 15 ans et plus[3]**	44
						État matrimonial légal	
22,095	2,685	17,075	25	38,405	22,630	Jamais légalement marié(e) (célibataire)	45
38,340	5,280	34,385	15	53,900	37,780	Légalement marié(e) (et non séparé[e])[4,5]	46
2,380	375	2,250	0	5,660	2,305	Séparé(e), mais toujours légalement marié(e)	47
4,235	735	3,960	5	10,585	4,475	Divorcé(e)	48
2,765	725	2,850	5	7,565	3,255	Veuf(ve)	49
						Union libre	
65,280	8,880	55,455	40	105,055	66,470	Ne vivant pas en union libre	50
4,540	910	5,075	10	11,050	3,980	Vivant en union libre	51
89,835	**11,755**	**77,370**	**70**	**140,240**	**87,360**	**Population totale – Données-échantillon (20 %)[6]**	52
						Langue maternelle	
88,740	11,710	76,990	75	139,210	86,110	Réponses uniques	53
71,195	11,110	70,180	70	120,610	69,130	Anglais	54
1,370	50	1,405	0	3,245	1,125	Français	55
16,170	555	5,400	0	15,350	15,855	Langues non officielles[7]	56
890	30	780	0	1,745	1,625	Italien	57
570	10	45	0	595	310	Chinois, n.d.a.[61]	58
495	15	50	0	160	425	Cantonais	59
835	20	190	0	785	815	Espagnol	60
585	160	620	0	1,110	1,105	Allemand	61
12,795	325	3,720	10	10,950	11,570	Autres langues[8]	62

Nota : Voir les symboles et les abréviations dans les documents d'introduction et voir les documents de référence à la fin de la publication.

Selected characteristics for census divisions and census subdivisions – 100% data and 20% sample data, Ontario, 2006 Census (continued)

No.	Characteristics	Melancthon, TP A	Mono, T A	Mulmur, TP ◆◇	Orangeville, T	Shelburne, T A	**Durham CD/DR**
	Population characteristics						
	Mother tongue (continued)						
63	Multiple responses	15	45	10	190	0	5,120
64	English and French	15	25	10	40	0	995
65	English and non-official language	0	20	10	145	0	3,795
66	French and non-official language	0	0	0	0	0	245
67	English, French and non-official language	0	0	0	0	0	80
	Language spoken most often at home[9]						
68	Single responses	2,895	6,950	3,295	26,590	4,905	550,535
69	English	2,775	6,840	3,205	26,165	4,805	519,150
70	French	0	20	0	50	0	4,220
71	Non-official languages[7]	115	95	80	370	100	27,160
72	Chinese, n.o.s.[61]	0	0	0	0	0	1,265
73	Cantonese	0	0	0	0	0	1,180
74	Panjabi (Punjabi)	20	0	0	45	20	805
75	Italian	0	10	0	30	0	1,680
76	Spanish	0	0	0	35	30	1,595
77	Other languages[8]	95	85	80	265	45	20,640
78	Multiple responses	0	100	10	105	0	6,795
79	English and French	0	0	0	0	0	710
80	English and non-official language	0	100	10	100	0	5,950
81	French and non-official language	0	0	0	0	0	70
82	English, French and non-official language	0	0	0	0	0	60
	Knowledge of official languages[10]						
83	English only	2,755	6,405	3,145	25,280	4,725	513,415
84	French only	0	0	0	0	0	555
85	English and French	135	645	150	1,365	160	40,590
86	Neither English nor French	10	0	0	50	10	2,765
	Knowledge of non-official languages[7,11]						
87	Italian	25	60	20	280	25	9,245
88	Spanish	0	130	35	280	35	6,885
89	German	70	235	130	370	20	7,305
90	Chinese, n.o.s.[61]	0	0	0	0	0	2,435
91	Cantonese	0	10	0	0	10	2,165
92	Panjabi (Punjabi)	30	30	0	115	20	2,515
93	Portuguese	65	55	20	195	95	3,775
	First official language spoken[10]						
94	English	2,880	6,930	3,240	26,330	4,855	543,575
95	French	10	105	50	300	15	9,775
96	English and French	10	15	10	20	15	1,320
97	Neither English nor French	0	0	0	45	15	2,660
98	Official language minority - (number)[12]	0	110	55	310	25	10,435
99	Official language minority - (percentage)[12]	0.0	1.6	1.7	1.2	0.5	1.9
	Ethnic origin[13]						
100	English	1,320	2,860	1,460	10,965	1,905	186,100
101	Canadian	865	1,940	950	8,915	2,035	158,005
102	Scottish	895	2,045	1,005	7,325	1,495	126,855
103	Irish	680	1,910	960	6,680	1,275	119,155
104	French	190	630	265	2,685	550	54,715
105	German	345	860	410	2,980	495	47,440
106	Italian	60	330	130	1,380	165	31,200
107	Chinese	10	35	0	130	10	11,215
108	East Indian	35	70	0	335	30	20,770
109	Dutch (Netherlands)	140	460	175	1,625	175	26,320
110	Polish	130	220	65	750	110	19,540
111	Ukrainian	90	160	130	670	130	17,340
112	North American Indian	25	65	85	555	120	13,180
113	Portuguese	80	75	0	590	110	12,045
114	Filipino	10	15	0	100	0	8,160
	Aboriginal and non-Aboriginal identity						
115	Total Aboriginal identity population[14]	55	35	65	275	15	6,565
116	Total non-Aboriginal identity population	2,840	7,015	3,235	26,420	4,890	550,765

Note: See symbols and abbreviations in the introductory material and see reference material at the end of the publication.

Certaines caractéristiques des divisions de recensement et des subdivisions de recensement – Données intégrales et données-échantillon (20 %), Ontario, Recensement de 2006 (suite)

Ajax, T	Brock, TP	Clarington, MU	Mississaugas of Scugog Island, IRI	Oshawa, CY	Pickering, CY	Caractéristiques	N°
						Caractéristiques de la population	
						Langue maternelle (suite)	
1,095	50	385	0	1,030	1,250	Réponses multiples	63
210	20	90	0	270	170	Anglais et français	64
790	20	265	0	735	995	Anglais et langue non officielle	65
90	0	30	0	20	50	Français et langue non officielle	66
0	0	0	0	0	25	Anglais, français et langue non officielle	67
						Langue parlée le plus souvent à la maison[9]	
87,770	11,750	76,970	70	138,900	85,675	Réponses uniques	68
80,060	11,600	75,165	70	131,475	78,630	Anglais	69
705	0	430	0	1,265	630	Français	70
7,005	140	1,375	0	6,160	6,425	Langues non officielles[7]	71
325	0	20	0	305	140	Chinois, n.d.a.[61]	72
385	0	40	0	130	275	Cantonais	73
405	0	0	0	35	260	Pendjabi	74
150	10	265	0	595	315	Italien	75
350	20	35	0	365	375	Espagnol	76
5,380	115	1,010	0	4,720	5,050	Autres langues[8]	77
2,065	0	405	0	1,345	1,680	Réponses multiples	78
155	10	85	0	150	140	Anglais et français	79
1,850	0	315	0	1,185	1,500	Anglais et langue non officielle	80
40	0	10	0	0	25	Français et langue non officielle	81
20	0	10	0	10	10	Anglais, français et langue non officielle	82
						Connaissance des langues officielles[10]	
82,470	11,210	71,545	65	129,870	80,500	Anglais seulement	83
55	0	65	0	155	95	Français seulement	84
6,600	535	5,700	10	9,545	6,210	Anglais et français	85
710	15	65	0	665	555	Ni l'anglais ni le français	86
						Connaissance des langues non officielles[7,11]	
1,285	30	1,005	0	2,315	2,110	Italien	87
1,390	55	540	0	1,635	1,375	Espagnol	88
960	230	810	0	1,670	1,495	Allemand	89
565	0	55	0	605	425	Chinois, n.d.a.[61]	90
635	0	60	0	315	545	Cantonais	91
1,145	0	30	0	140	755	Pendjabi	92
765	15	455	0	1,185	455	Portugais	93
						Première langue officielle parlée[10]	
87,430	11,695	75,840	75	136,245	85,265	Anglais	94
1,410	50	1,420	0	3,100	1,210	Français	95
295	0	50	0	270	355	Anglais et français	96
700	15	65	0	625	530	Ni l'anglais ni le français	97
1,555	50	1,445	0	3,235	1,385	Minorité de langue officielle - (nombre)[12]	98
1.7	0.4	1.9	0.0	2.3	1.6	Minorité de langue officielle - (pourcentage)[12]	99
						Origine ethnique[13]	
23,025	5,620	30,785	0	47,650	23,755	Anglais	100
19,920	3,860	25,810	10	46,445	18,725	Canadien	101
17,060	3,505	19,885	10	32,245	16,885	Écossais	102
14,955	3,440	18,850	15	32,295	15,460	Irlandais	103
6,885	1,135	9,000	10	17,270	6,670	Français	104
6,065	1,230	7,120	0	11,965	6,525	Allemand	105
4,805	300	3,850	0	6,850	6,100	Italien	106
3,025	15	420	0	1,865	2,795	Chinois	107
8,100	30	655	0	1,510	6,780	Indien de l'Inde	108
2,895	755	5,830	0	6,615	2,665	Hollandais (Néerlandais)	109
2,280	335	3,085	0	6,380	2,370	Polonais	110
1,680	190	2,935	0	6,235	1,895	Ukrainien	111
1,535	330	2,190	50	4,630	1,510	Indien de l'Amérique du Nord	112
2,690	60	1,360	0	2,625	2,470	Portugais	113
2,910	40	250	0	760	2,885	Philippin	114
						Population ayant une identité autochtone et population n'ayant pas d'identité autochtone	
705	120	1,095	55	2,510	600	Total de la population ayant une identité autochtone[14]	115
89,125	11,635	76,275	15	137,730	86,760	Total de la population n'ayant pas d'identité autochtone	116

Nota : Voir les symboles et les abréviations dans les documents d'introduction et voir les documents de référence à la fin de la publication.

Selected characteristics for census divisions and census subdivisions – 100% data and 20% sample data, Ontario, 2006 Census (continued)

No.	Characteristics	Melancthon, TP A	Mono, T A	Mulmur, TP ◆◇	Orangeville, T	Shelburne, T A	**Durham CD/DR**
	Population characteristics						
	Aboriginal and non-Aboriginal ancestry						
117	Total Aboriginal ancestry population[15]	60	90	125	695	130	16,185
118	Total non-Aboriginal ancestry population	2,835	6,960	3,175	26,000	4,775	541,145
	Registered Indian status						
119	Registered Indian[16]	0	0	0	70	0	2,020
120	Not a Registered Indian	2,895	7,045	3,300	26,625	4,900	555,310
	Visible minority groups						
121	Total visible minority population[17]	65	225	15	1,400	135	93,420
122	Chinese	0	10	0	120	0	7,560
123	South Asian[18]	35	75	0	350	35	24,110
124	Black	0	60	10	475	85	33,300
125	Filipino	0	0	0	85	0	7,655
126	Latin American	0	30	0	125	10	3,105
127	Southeast Asian[19]	0	10	0	15	0	1,405
128	Arab	0	0	0	20	0	3,050
129	West Asian[20]	0	0	0	65	0	2,605
130	Korean	0	10	10	20	0	1,165
131	Japanese	0	20	0	60	0	1,535
132	Visible minority, n.i.e.[21]	0	10	0	35	0	3,425
133	Multiple visible minority[22]	15	0	0	25	0	4,505
	Citizenship[23]						
134	Canadian citizens[24]	2,805	6,750	3,180	25,700	4,790	535,915
135	Not Canadian citizens[25]	90	300	120	995	120	21,420
	Immigrant status and place of birth[26]						
136	Non-immigrants[27]	2,550	5,905	2,925	23,200	4,415	442,080
137	Born in province of residence	2,390	5,355	2,660	20,745	4,060	394,380
138	Immigrants[28]	340	1,105	365	3,435	480	113,395
139	United States of America	0	50	45	190	35	3,685
140	Central and South America	20	30	0	145	25	9,270
141	Caribbean and Bermuda	0	35	0	210	20	17,500
142	United Kingdom	170	395	125	1,520	225	23,765
143	Other Europe	130	500	190	920	130	28,945
144	Africa	0	15	0	110	10	4,425
145	Asia and the Middle East	15	75	10	310	30	25,140
146	Oceania and other[29]	0	10	0	35	0	650
147	Non-permanent residents[30]	10	40	15	60	10	1,855
148	**Total immigrant population[28]**	**340**	**1,110**	**360**	**3,435**	**480**	**113,390**
	Period of immigration						
149	Before 1961	70	280	150	710	135	18,665
150	1961 to 1970	105	240	65	880	60	19,200
151	1971 to 1980	90	260	35	570	85	23,445
152	1981 to 1990	25	140	50	470	70	19,850
153	1991 to 2000	25	140	15	450	65	22,335
154	1991 to 1995	10	75	10	180	35	12,710
155	1996 to 2000	20	65	0	270	35	9,625
156	2001 to 2006[31]	20	40	45	365	60	9,890
	Age at immigration						
157	Under 5 years	35	130	25	470	90	11,695
158	5 to 19 years	95	330	115	1,125	165	34,400
159	20 years and over	205	650	220	1,845	220	67,295
160	**Total population 15 years and over**	**2,365**	**5,735**	**2,655**	**20,670**	**3,780**	**442,285**
	Generation status						
161	1st generation[32]	330	1,125	365	3,400	460	111,565
162	2nd generation[33]	390	1,280	505	4,455	545	99,825
163	3rd generation or more[34]	1,645	3,330	1,790	12,815	2,775	230,900

Note: See symbols and abbreviations in the introductory material and see reference material at the end of the publication.

Certaines caractéristiques des divisions de recensement et des subdivisions de recensement – Données intégrales et données-échantillon (20 %), Ontario, Recensement de 2006 (suite)

Ajax, T	Brock, TP	Clarington, MU	Mississaugas of Scugog Island, IRI	Oshawa, CY	Pickering, CY	Caractéristiques	N°
						Caractéristiques de la population	
						Population ayant une ascendance autochtone et population n'ayant pas d'ascendance autochtone	
1,915	440	2,770	50	5,740	1,750	Total de la population ayant une ascendance autochtone[15]	117
87,920	11,315	74,600	25	134,500	85,610	Total de la population n'ayant pas d'ascendance autochtone	118
						Statut d'Indien inscrit	
265	10	325	50	750	160	Indien inscrit[16]	119
89,570	11,750	77,045	25	139,490	87,200	Pas un Indien inscrit	120
						Groupes de minorités visibles	
32,010	190	3,600	0	11,370	26,685	Total de la population des minorités visibles[17]	121
1,870	10	255	0	1,325	1,800	Chinois	122
9,735	55	610	0	1,910	7,940	Sud-Asiatique[18]	123
11,680	25	1,640	0	4,265	8,850	Noir	124
2,690	45	220	0	750	2,715	Philippin	125
705	15	170	0	715	655	Latino-Américain	126
420	0	40	0	280	310	Asiatique du Sud-Est[19]	127
1,280	0	165	0	255	610	Arabe	128
575	20	40	0	505	800	Asiatique occidental[20]	129
270	0	125	0	215	310	Coréen	130
285	0	60	0	200	375	Japonais	131
1,000	0	100	0	425	1,040	Minorité visible, n.i.a.[21]	132
1,495	0	160	0	520	1,275	Minorités visibles multiples[22]	133
						Citoyenneté[23]	
84,400	11,535	75,485	X	136,000	83,070	Citoyens canadiens[24]	134
5,435	220	1,890	X	4,245	4,295	Ne sont pas des citoyens canadiens[25]	135
						Statut d'immigrant et le lieu de naissance[26]	
61,760	10,695	67,825	X	118,000	60,730	Non-immigrants[27]	136
55,230	10,005	61,225	X	103,300	54,700	Né dans la province de résidence	137
27,550	1,060	9,370	X	21,925	26,375	Immigrants[28]	138
530	85	495	X	740	585	États-Unis d'Amérique	139
2,985	15	420	X	1,175	2,725	Amérique centrale et Amérique du Sud	140
6,155	25	605	X	2,025	5,055	Antilles et Bermudes	141
3,720	515	3,260	X	5,745	3,855	Royaume-Uni	142
4,065	325	3,475	X	8,505	5,250	Autre Europe	143
1,465	20	215	X	520	1,080	Afrique	144
8,500	60	815	X	3,005	7,715	Asie et Moyen-Orient	145
125	0	85	X	210	100	Océanie et autres[29]	146
525	0	175	X	315	255	Résidents non permanents[30]	147
27,550	**1,060**	**9,370**	**X**	**21,925**	**26,375**	**Population totale des immigrants[28]**	148
						Période d'immigration	
2,200	405	2,570	X	5,355	3,090	Avant 1961	149
3,455	245	2,000	X	4,475	4,175	1961 à 1970	150
5,875	175	1,875	X	4,315	5,935	1971 à 1980	151
5,795	110	1,235	X	3,225	5,090	1981 à 1990	152
7,060	90	1,135	X	3,030	5,815	1991 à 2000	153
4,070	40	725	X	1,635	3,245	1991 à 1995	154
2,990	55	415	X	1,395	2,565	1996 à 2000	155
3,170	30	550	X	1,530	2,270	2001 à 2006[31]	156
						Âge à l'immigration	
2,430	120	1,345	X	2,580	2,145	Moins de 5 ans	157
8,350	310	3,035	X	6,210	8,005	5 à 19 ans	158
16,770	625	4,995	X	13,130	16,230	20 ans et plus	159
69,470	**9,585**	**60,085**	**55**	**114,785**	**70,010**	**Population totale de 15 ans et plus**	160
						Statut des générations	
26,940	1,065	9,265	0	21,835	25,720	1re génération[32]	161
16,200	1,605	12,535	0	23,340	17,950	2e génération[33]	162
26,335	6,910	38,280	45	69,610	26,340	3e génération ou plus[34]	163

Nota : Voir les symboles et les abréviations dans les documents d'introduction et voir les documents de référence à la fin de la publication.

Selected characteristics for census divisions and census subdivisions – 100% data and 20% sample data, Ontario, 2006 Census (continued)

No.	Characteristics	Melancthon, TP A	Mono, T A	Mulmur, TP ◆◊	Orangeville, T	Shelburne, T A	Durham CD/DR
	Population characteristics						
164	**Total population 1 year and over[35]**	**2,875**	**7,030**	**3,270**	**26,400**	**4,835**	**550,840**
	Place of residence 1 year ago (mobility)						
165	Non-movers	2,555	6,325	3,100	23,310	3,930	484,785
166	Movers	315	700	170	3,090	905	66,055
167	Non-migrants	85	220	10	1,545	335	29,775
168	Migrants	230	480	165	1,545	570	36,280
169	Internal migrants	230	405	160	1,480	545	33,795
170	Intraprovincial migrants	205	380	160	1,425	545	32,240
171	Interprovincial migrants	25	20	0	55	0	1,560
172	External migrants	0	80	10	65	25	2,485
173	**Total population 5 years and over[36]**	**2,745**	**6,780**	**3,165**	**24,865**	**4,545**	**524,635**
	Place of residence 5 years ago (mobility)						
174	Non-movers	1,700	4,715	2,220	13,935	2,205	315,030
175	Movers	1,045	2,065	940	10,925	2,335	209,600
176	Non-migrants	190	610	140	5,020	675	87,005
177	Migrants	855	1,450	805	5,905	1,665	122,600
178	Internal migrants	850	1,375	745	5,515	1,600	112,660
179	Intraprovincial migrants	805	1,325	710	5,140	1,540	106,825
180	Interprovincial migrants	45	55	40	370	60	5,840
181	External migrants	0	75	55	395	65	9,930
182	**Total population 15 years and over**	**2,365**	**5,730**	**2,660**	**20,670**	**3,780**	**442,285**
	Highest certificate, diploma or degree[37]						
183	No certificate, diploma or degree	750	1,075	610	4,830	1,190	93,490
184	Certificate, diploma or degree	1,610	4,655	2,050	15,840	2,590	348,795
185	High school certificate or equivalent[38]	675	1,635	680	6,985	1,295	128,885
186	Apprenticeship or trades certificate or diploma	260	480	270	1,495	360	38,730
187	College, CEGEP or other non-university certificate or diploma[39]	480	1,235	535	4,690	650	99,255
188	University certificate or diploma below bachelor level[40]	55	240	65	445	40	16,435
189	University certificate or degree[41]	140	1,060	490	2,225	240	65,495
190	Bachelor's degree	85	590	305	1,505	130	44,680
191	University certificate or diploma above bachelor level	40	200	80	370	55	9,155
192	Degree in medicine, dentistry, veterinary medicine or optometry	0	40	0	40	20	1,300
193	Master's degree	10	180	100	275	35	9,095
194	Earned doctorate	0	50	0	35	0	1,260
195	**Total population 15 years and over with postsecondary qualifications**	**935**	**3,020**	**1,365**	**8,855**	**1,295**	**219,910**
	Major field of study - Classification of Instructional Programs, 2000[42]						
196	Education	40	365	160	670	105	14,080
197	Visual and performing arts, and communications technologies	25	155	45	315	55	8,605
198	Humanities	0	145	70	410	25	10,095
199	Social and behavioural sciences and law	60	260	115	1,005	95	24,485
200	Business, management and public administration	210	615	240	1,815	250	48,965
201	Physical and life sciences and technologies	15	75	45	240	10	6,105
202	Mathematics, computer and information sciences	20	60	50	260	35	10,845
203	Architecture, engineering, and related technologies	280	770	280	2,105	305	50,550
204	Agriculture, natural resources and conservation	50	75	60	150	20	3,230
205	Health, parks, recreation and fitness	160	380	200	1,245	255	29,590
206	Personal, protective and transportation services	60	110	85	640	135	13,355
207	Other fields of study[43]	0	0	0	0	0	0
	Location of study[44]						
208	Inside Canada	840	2,570	1,200	7,960	1,180	188,305
209	Outside Canada	90	445	160	895	110	31,605
210	**Total population 15 years and over**	**2,365**	**5,730**	**2,660**	**20,670**	**3,780**	**442,285**
	Unpaid work						
211	Males 15 years and over	1,290	2,915	1,325	9,960	1,815	214,090
212	Reported unpaid work[45]	1,215	2,680	1,195	9,105	1,625	194,975
213	Housework and child care and care or assistance to seniors	85	310	85	730	145	18,885
214	Housework and child care only	305	785	300	3,305	650	63,485

Note: See symbols and abbreviations in the introductory material and see reference material at the end of the publication.

Certaines caractéristiques des divisions de recensement et des subdivisions de recensement – Données intégrales et données-échantillon (20 %), Ontario, Recensement de 2006 (suite)

Ajax, T	Brock, TP	Clarington, MU	Mississaugas of Scugog Island, IRI	Oshawa, CY	Pickering, CY	Caractéristiques	N°
						Caractéristiques de la population	
88,640	**11,640**	**76,495**	**75**	**138,680**	**86,545**	**Population totale de 1 an et plus[35]**	164
						Lieu de résidence 1 an auparavant (mobilité)	
76,870	10,455	67,720	60	118,700	78,575	Personnes n'ayant pas déménagé	165
11,775	1,185	8,775	10	19,975	7,970	Personnes ayant déménagé	166
3,895	380	3,825	0	12,300	3,010	Non-migrants	167
7,885	800	4,955	0	7,670	4,960	Migrants	168
7,185	785	4,685	0	7,270	4,600	Migrants internes	169
7,025	730	4,475	0	6,715	4,485	Migrants infraprovinciaux	170
160	50	210	0	555	105	Migrants interprovinciaux	171
695	20	265	0	400	360	Migrants externes	172
84,040	**11,145**	**72,700**	**70**	**132,705**	**82,825**	**Population totale de 5 ans et plus[36]**	173
						Lieu de résidence 5 ans auparavant (mobilité)	
47,195	7,920	44,375	30	77,815	55,795	Personnes n'ayant pas déménagé	174
36,840	3,225	28,320	30	54,890	27,030	Personnes ayant déménagé	175
13,275	1,065	11,600	25	30,395	10,435	Non-migrants	176
23,565	2,165	16,725	10	24,500	16,595	Migrants	177
20,690	2,095	15,910	10	22,825	14,790	Migrants internes	178
19,975	1,965	15,085	10	21,045	14,390	Migrants infraprovinciaux	179
710	130	820	0	1,780	400	Migrants interprovinciaux	180
2,875	65	815	0	1,670	1,805	Migrants externes	181
69,470	**9,585**	**60,085**	**55**	**114,785**	**70,010**	**Population totale de 15 ans et plus**	182
						Plus haut certificat, diplôme ou grade[37]	
12,750	2,775	13,715	20	30,525	11,830	Aucun certificat, diplôme ou grade	183
56,720	6,805	46,370	30	84,260	58,175	Certificat, diplôme ou grade	184
19,695	2,860	17,895	15	34,585	20,380	Diplôme d'études secondaires ou l'équivalent[38]	185
5,615	1,095	5,560	0	10,880	6,025	Certificat ou diplôme d'apprenti ou d'une école de métiers	186
15,750	1,820	14,880	10	24,800	14,970	Certificat ou diplôme d'un collège, d'un cégep ou d'un autre établissement d'enseignement non universitaire[39]	187
3,480	205	1,440	0	2,895	3,700	Certificat ou diplôme universitaire inférieur au baccalauréat[40]	188
12,180	825	6,585	0	11,095	13,100	Certificat ou grade universitaire[41]	189
8,540	520	4,575	10	7,235	9,125	Baccalauréat	190
1,520	190	965	0	1,660	1,760	Certificat ou diplôme universitaire supérieur au baccalauréat	191
240	30	210	0	185	215	Diplôme en médecine, en art dentaire, en médecine vétérinaire ou en optométrie	192
1,705	60	695	0	1,735	1,745	Maîtrise	193
175	25	135	0	280	250	Doctorat acquis	194
37,020	**3,945**	**28,475**	**15**	**49,675**	**37,795**	**Population totale de 15 ans et plus avec titres du niveau postsecondaire**	195
						Principal domaine d'études - Classification des programmes d'enseignement, 2000[42]	
1,920	225	2,020	0	3,285	1,975	Éducation	196
1,530	225	840	0	2,005	1,595	Arts visuels et d'interprétation, et technologie des communications	197
1,835	170	1,000	0	2,130	2,070	Sciences humaines	198
4,180	450	2,755	0	5,045	4,605	Sciences sociales et de comportements, et droit	199
9,205	540	5,370	0	10,325	9,500	Commerce, gestion et administration publique	200
1,150	55	660	0	1,065	1,235	Sciences physiques et de la vie, et technologies	201
2,420	100	935	0	2,100	2,285	Mathématiques, informatique et sciences de l'information	202
8,070	955	7,520	0	11,820	8,245	Architecture, génie et services connexes	203
425	190	465	0	680	365	Agriculture, ressources naturelles et conservation	204
4,405	635	4,590	0	7,415	4,350	Santé, parcs, récréation et conditionnement physique	205
1,885	395	2,310	0	3,790	1,570	Services personnels, de protection et de transport	206
0	0	0	0	0	0	Autres domaines d'études[43]	207
						Lieu des études[44]	
29,320	3,680	25,825	15	44,060	30,275	À l'intérieur du Canada	208
7,700	265	2,650	0	5,610	7,520	À l'extérieur du Canada	209
69,470	**9,585**	**60,085**	**55**	**114,785**	**70,010**	**Population totale de 15 ans et plus**	210
						Travail non rémunéré	
33,305	4,675	29,505	25	55,560	33,590	Hommes de 15 ans et plus	211
29,910	4,345	27,135	25	50,300	30,395	Travail non rémunéré déclaré[45]	212
3,305	395	2,550	10	4,105	3,130	Travaux ménagers et soins aux enfants et soins ou aide aux personnes âgées	213
10,480	1,120	9,410	0	14,485	9,670	Travaux ménagers et soins aux enfants seulement	214

Nota : Voir les symboles et les abréviations dans les documents d'introduction et voir les documents de référence à la fin de la publication.

Selected characteristics for census divisions and census subdivisions – 100% data and 20% sample data, Ontario, 2006 Census (continued)

No.	Characteristics	Melancthon, TP A	Mono, T A	Mulmur, TP ◆◇	Orangeville, T	Shelburne, T A	Durham CD/DR
	Population characteristics						
	Unpaid work (continued)						
215	Housework and care or assistance to seniors only	60	175	85	490	80	14,500
216	Child care and care or assistance to seniors only	0	10	0	0	0	210
217	Housework only	755	1,355	710	4,455	710	95,335
218	Child care only	10	20	10	90	30	1,795
219	Care or assistance to seniors only	0	30	0	35	0	770
220	Females 15 years and over	1,075	2,815	1,335	10,715	1,965	228,190
221	Reported unpaid work[45]	1,030	2,645	1,270	10,005	1,885	213,955
222	Housework and child care and care or assistance to seniors	100	455	140	1,205	245	28,165
223	Housework and child care only	365	835	375	3,795	650	74,895
224	Housework and care or assistance to seniors only	95	260	165	735	165	18,570
225	Child care and care or assistance to seniors only	0	0	10	0	10	165
226	Housework only	465	1,070	580	4,230	820	90,515
227	Child care only	0	10	10	40	0	1,100
228	Care or assistance to seniors only	0	0	0	0	0	540
	Labour force activity						
229	Males 15 years and over	1,290	2,915	1,325	9,960	1,810	214,090
230	In the labour force	1,045	2,275	975	7,980	1,420	163,215
231	Employed	990	2,150	945	7,640	1,375	153,815
232	Unemployed	55	130	25	340	40	9,400
233	Not in the labour force	245	635	350	1,980	395	50,880
234	Participation rate	81.0	78.0	73.6	80.1	78.5	76.2
235	Employment rate	76.7	73.8	71.3	76.7	76.0	71.8
236	Unemployment rate	5.3	5.7	2.6	4.3	2.8	5.8
237	Females 15 years and over	1,075	2,815	1,335	10,715	1,970	228,190
238	In the labour force	720	1,860	850	7,370	1,230	150,655
239	Employed	685	1,775	825	6,980	1,155	140,340
240	Unemployed	35	85	25	390	75	10,310
241	Not in the labour force	355	955	480	3,340	735	77,535
242	Participation rate	67.0	66.1	63.7	68.8	62.4	66.0
243	Employment rate	63.7	63.1	61.8	65.1	58.6	61.5
244	Unemployment rate	4.9	4.6	2.9	5.3	6.1	6.8
245	Both sexes - Participation rate	74.4	72.3	68.9	74.3	70.1	71.0
246	15 to 24 years	65.6	63.7	53.1	72.4	73.6	67.0
247	25 years and over	76.8	74.1	71.8	74.6	69.4	71.8
248	Both sexes - Employment rate	71.0	68.5	66.9	70.7	66.9	66.5
249	15 to 24 years	57.8	52.7	44.4	63.0	69.8	56.3
250	25 years and over	74.2	71.8	70.7	72.4	66.3	68.7
251	Both sexes - Unemployment rate	4.8	5.2	3.0	4.8	4.3	6.3
252	15 to 24 years	13.6	17.2	14.3	13.1	4.3	15.9
253	25 years and over	3.1	3.0	1.2	3.1	4.3	4.3
254	**Total labour force 15 years and over**	**1,760**	**4,140**	**1,830**	**15,350**	**2,650**	**313,865**
	Industry - North American Industry Classification System 2002						
255	Industry - Not applicable[46]	15	25	0	95	25	4,975
256	All industries[47]	1,750	4,115	1,820	15,250	2,625	308,895
257	11 Agriculture, forestry, fishing and hunting	175	115	95	55	45	2,950
258	21 Mining and oil and gas extraction	0	10	10	45	10	445
259	22 Utilities	0	45	15	125	25	7,485
260	23 Construction	165	265	170	885	230	20,755
261	31-33 Manufacturing	320	610	330	2,985	575	40,535
262	41 Wholesale trade	130	175	70	985	140	16,045
263	44-45 Retail trade	130	410	165	1,955	275	36,605
264	48-49 Transportation and warehousing	80	250	120	1,035	190	13,870
265	51 Information and cultural industries	40	70	40	280	20	9,360
266	52 Finance and insurance	20	120	25	355	45	18,345
267	53 Real estate and rental and leasing	35	130	20	230	30	6,325
268	54 Professional, scientific and technical services	105	395	110	495	55	19,855
269	55 Management of companies and enterprises	0	0	0	20	0	375
270	56 Administrative and support, waste management and remediation services	115	220	100	680	140	15,485
271	61 Educational services	45	270	115	995	125	20,335
272	62 Health care and social assistance	105	275	120	1,295	360	27,980

Note: See symbols and abbreviations in the introductory material and see reference material at the end of the publication.

Certaines caractéristiques des divisions de recensement et des subdivisions de recensement – Données intégrales et données-échantillon (20 %), Ontario, Recensement de 2006 (suite)

Ajax, T	Brock, TP	Clarington, MU	Mississaugas of Scugog Island, IRI	Oshawa, CY	Pickering, CY	Caractéristiques	N°
						Caractéristiques de la population	
						Travail non rémunéré (suite)	
1,785	390	1,900	0	4,075	2,335	Travaux ménagers et soins ou aide aux personnes âgées seulement	215
30	10	10	0	65	40	Soins aux enfants et soins ou aide aux personnes âgées seulement	216
13,925	2,385	12,935	10	26,905	14,660	Travaux ménagers seulement	217
290	25	230	0	455	440	Soins aux enfants seulement	218
90	20	110	0	205	120	Soins ou aide aux personnes âgées seulement	219
36,165	4,910	30,580	25	59,225	36,420	Femmes de 15 ans et plus	220
33,730	4,615	29,080	25	55,425	33,870	Travail non rémunéré déclaré[45]	221
4,700	595	3,890	0	6,630	4,745	Travaux ménagers et soins aux enfants et soins ou aide aux personnes âgées	222
12,645	1,360	10,570	10	18,205	11,660	Travaux ménagers et soins aux enfants seulement	223
2,515	470	2,315	0	5,115	3,055	Travaux ménagers et soins ou aide aux personnes âgées seulement	224
10	0	20	0	35	50	Soins aux enfants et soins ou aide aux personnes âgées seulement	225
13,600	2,175	12,150	10	25,015	14,015	Travaux ménagers seulement	226
200	10	90	0	255	195	Soins aux enfants seulement	227
50	10	40	0	170	145	Soins ou aide aux personnes âgées seulement	228
						Activité	
33,310	4,670	29,505	30	55,560	33,585	Hommes de 15 ans et plus	229
26,430	3,450	22,395	25	40,120	26,095	Population active	230
24,990	3,295	21,310	20	37,120	24,425	Personnes occupées	231
1,435	160	1,090	0	3,000	1,670	Chômeurs	232
6,880	1,220	7,110	0	15,435	7,495	Inactifs	233
79.3	73.9	75.9	83.3	72.2	77.7	Taux d'activité	234
75.0	70.6	72.2	66.7	66.8	72.7	Taux d'emploi	235
5.4	4.6	4.9	0.0	7.5	6.4	Taux de chômage	236
36,160	4,910	30,580	25	59,225	36,425	Femmes de 15 ans et plus	237
25,270	2,940	19,990	15	36,225	24,920	Population active	238
23,410	2,815	18,805	15	33,405	23,245	Personnes occupées	239
1,860	125	1,185	10	2,820	1,675	Chômeuses	240
10,890	1,970	10,585	10	23,000	11,500	Inactives	241
69.9	59.9	65.4	60.0	61.2	68.4	Taux d'activité	242
64.7	57.3	61.5	60.0	56.4	63.8	Taux d'emploi	243
7.4	4.3	5.9	66.7	7.8	6.7	Taux de chômage	244
74.4	66.7	70.6	72.7	66.5	72.9	Les deux sexes - Taux d'activité	245
65.7	72.6	66.6	100.0	66.3	64.9	15 à 24 ans	246
76.5	65.5	71.4	77.8	66.6	74.7	25 ans et plus	247
69.7	63.8	66.8	63.6	61.4	68.1	Les deux sexes - Taux d'emploi	248
55.2	62.9	57.1	0.0	54.0	54.0	15 à 24 ans	249
73.1	64.0	68.7	66.7	62.9	71.4	25 ans et plus	250
6.4	4.5	5.4	0.0	7.6	6.6	Les deux sexes - Taux de chômage	251
16.0	13.7	14.1	0.0	18.4	16.9	15 à 24 ans	252
4.4	2.4	3.7	0.0	5.5	4.4	25 ans et plus	253
51,700	**6,390**	**42,385**	**40**	**76,350**	**51,015**	**Population active totale de 15 ans et plus**	254
						Industrie - Système de classification des industries de l'Amérique du Nord de 2002	
955	75	485	0	1,350	945	Industrie - Sans objet[46]	255
50,740	6,315	41,905	40	75,000	50,070	Toutes les industries[47]	256
110	365	725	0	280	145	11 Agriculture, foresterie, pêche et chasse	257
85	30	10	0	25	120	21 Extraction minière et extraction de pétrole et de gaz	258
1,065	65	1,805	0	1,450	845	22 Services publics	259
2,895	655	3,125	0	5,100	3,315	23 Construction	260
5,860	710	7,120	0	12,765	5,100	31-33 Fabrication	261
2,920	260	1,865	0	3,175	3,010	41 Commerce de gros	262
6,730	740	4,640	0	9,200	5,915	44-45 Commerce de détail	263
2,400	510	2,015	0	3,550	2,025	48-49 Transport et entreposage	264
2,005	60	755	0	1,725	2,125	51 Industrie de l'information et industrie culturelle	265
4,410	235	1,310	0	2,455	4,600	52 Finance et assurances	266
1,030	130	665	0	1,395	1,180	53 Services immobiliers et services de location et de location à bail	267
3,420	265	2,010	0	3,395	4,310	54 Services professionnels, scientifiques et techniques	268
70	0	20	0	60	90	55 Gestion de sociétés et d'entreprises	269
2,610	295	1,850	10	4,890	2,340	56 Services administratifs, services de soutien, services de gestion des déchets et services d'assainissement	270
2,870	330	2,665	0	4,960	3,005	61 Services d'enseignement	271
4,315	500	4,225	10	7,175	4,255	62 Soins de santé et assistance sociale	272

Nota : Voir les symboles et les abréviations dans les documents d'introduction et voir les documents de référence à la fin de la publication.

Selected characteristics for census divisions and census subdivisions – 100% data and 20% sample data, Ontario, 2006 Census (continued)

No.	Characteristics	Melancthon, TP A	Mono, T A	Mulmur, TP ◆◇	Orangeville, T	Shelburne, T A	Durham CD/DR
	Population characteristics						
	Industry - North American Industry Classification System 2002 (continued)						
273	71 Arts, entertainment and recreation	30	120	80	270	15	6,085
274	72 Accommodation and food services	90	305	95	1,005	125	16,390
275	81 Other services (except public administration)	120	155	70	745	115	13,465
276	91 Public administration	40	175	50	815	110	16,185
	Class of worker						
277	Class of worker - Not applicable[46]	15	30	10	95	25	4,975
278	All classes of worker[47]	1,750	4,115	1,820	15,255	2,620	308,890
279	Paid workers	1,490	3,585	1,555	14,340	2,415	288,015
280	Employees	1,365	3,215	1,430	13,975	2,350	278,630
281	Self-employed (incorporated)	120	375	130	365	60	9,385
282	Self-employed (unincorporated)	245	505	255	890	210	20,260
283	Unpaid family workers	15	20	0	25	0	620
	Occupation - National Occupational Classification for Statistics 2006						
284	Male labour force 15 years and over	1,045	2,280	975	7,980	1,415	163,215
285	Occupation - Not applicable[46]	10	15	0	55	0	2,135
286	All occupations[47]	1,035	2,265	975	7,925	1,410	161,080
287	A Management occupations	100	420	120	960	150	21,160
288	B Business, finance and administrative occupations	55	190	75	590	85	17,180
289	C Natural and applied sciences and related occupations	10	245	70	560	45	15,030
290	D Health occupations	20	25	10	90	10	2,160
291	E Occupations in social science, education, government service and religion	35	95	30	295	45	6,640
292	F Occupations in art, culture, recreation and sport	10	110	25	130	0	3,755
293	G Sales and service occupations	125	385	120	1,660	270	31,500
294	H Trades, transport and equipment operators and related occupations	425	515	355	2,540	505	44,485
295	I Occupations unique to primary industry	155	145	95	200	65	4,315
296	J Occupations unique to processing, manufacturing and utilities	95	135	80	890	240	14,855
297	Female labour force 15 years and over	720	1,865	855	7,370	1,230	150,650
298	Occupation - Not applicable[46]	0	15	0	40	20	2,840
299	All occupations[47]	715	1,850	845	7,330	1,210	147,810
300	A Management occupations	45	235	85	510	80	12,370
301	B Business, finance and administrative occupations	135	505	185	1,830	300	45,150
302	C Natural and applied sciences and related occupations	15	45	30	110	20	4,595
303	D Health occupations	85	130	45	530	160	12,955
304	E Occupations in social science, education, government service and religion	55	195	125	815	150	17,540
305	F Occupations in art, culture, recreation and sport	15	115	45	145	10	4,460
306	G Sales and service occupations	205	495	235	2,470	315	40,545
307	H Trades, transport and equipment operators and related occupations	45	45	40	250	45	3,355
308	I Occupations unique to primary industry	35	30	25	40	10	1,515
309	J Occupations unique to processing, manufacturing and utilities	80	50	40	630	115	5,325
310	**Total employed labour force 15 years and over**	**1,680**	**3,930**	**1,775**	**14,615**	**2,530**	**294,155**
	Place of work status						
311	Males	990	2,155	950	7,635	1,375	153,815
312	Usual place of work	640	1,555	605	6,110	1,085	122,720
313	At home	170	315	160	295	40	8,525
314	Outside Canada	0	25	0	30	10	520
315	No fixed workplace address	175	260	180	1,200	245	22,050
316	Females	690	1,775	825	6,980	1,155	140,340
317	Usual place of work	560	1,370	640	6,155	985	123,380
318	At home	100	335	105	440	80	9,950
319	Outside Canada	0	10	0	0	0	320
320	No fixed workplace address	30	65	80	385	80	6,690

Note: See symbols and abbreviations in the introductory material and see reference material at the end of the publication.

Certaines caractéristiques des divisions de recensement et des subdivisions de recensement – Données intégrales et données-échantillon (20 %), Ontario, Recensement de 2006 (suite)

Ajax, T	Brock, TP	Clarington, MU	Mississaugas of Scugog Island, IRI	Oshawa, CY	Pickering, CY	Caractéristiques	N°
						Caractéristiques de la population	
						Industrie - Système de classification des industries de l'Amérique du Nord de 2002 (suite)	
750	205	630	10	1,245	1,035	71 Arts, spectacles et loisirs	273
2,480	355	2,300	0	4,425	2,275	72 Hébergement et services de restauration	274
2,190	265	1,860	0	3,635	2,105	81 Autres services (sauf les administrations publiques)	275
2,530	320	2,315	10	4,080	2,270	91 Administrations publiques	276
						Catégorie de travailleurs	
955	75	485	0	1,350	945	Catégorie de travailleurs - Sans objet[46]	277
50,740	6,315	41,905	40	75,000	50,070	Toutes les catégories de travailleurs[47]	278
47,625	5,640	38,925	35	70,620	46,895	Travailleurs rémunérés	279
46,335	5,325	37,605	35	69,035	45,100	Employés	280
1,295	315	1,315	0	1,585	1,790	Travailleurs autonomes (entreprise constituée en société)	281
3,055	640	2,870	0	4,310	3,060	Travailleurs autonomes (entreprise non constituée en société)	282
65	35	105	0	70	120	Travailleurs familiaux non rémunérés	283
						Profession - Classification nationale des professions pour statistiques de 2006	
26,430	3,450	22,395	25	40,125	26,095	Hommes actifs de 15 ans et plus	284
390	45	200	0	625	425	Profession - Sans objet[46]	285
26,035	3,405	22,200	25	39,500	25,665	Toutes les professions[47]	286
3,665	375	2,430	0	3,600	3,980	A Gestion	287
3,460	185	1,675	0	3,840	3,640	B Affaires, finance et administration	288
2,955	180	1,760	0	2,540	2,915	C Sciences naturelles et appliquées et professions apparentées	289
350	10	310	0	410	370	D Secteur de la santé	290
1,000	135	725	0	1,640	1,025	E Sciences sociales, enseignement, administration publique et religion	291
595	45	390	0	890	720	F Arts, culture, sports et loisirs	292
5,255	600	4,005	10	7,615	5,110	G Ventes et services	293
6,485	1,285	7,215	10	12,510	6,045	H Métiers, transport et machinerie	294
365	360	750	10	850	390	I Professions propres au secteur primaire	295
1,895	225	2,940	10	5,590	1,465	J Transformation, fabrication et services d'utilité publique	296
25,275	2,940	19,995	15	36,225	24,920	Femmes actives de 15 ans et plus	297
565	30	285	0	730	520	Profession - Sans objet[46]	298
24,705	2,905	19,700	15	35,500	24,405	Toutes les professions[47]	299
2,010	195	1,500	0	2,460	2,490	A Gestion	300
8,595	700	5,615	10	9,525	8,220	B Affaires, finance et administration	301
840	25	595	0	875	820	C Sciences naturelles et appliquées et professions apparentées	302
1,955	295	2,020	0	3,145	1,980	D Secteur de la santé	303
2,885	325	2,325	0	3,950	2,825	E Sciences sociales, enseignement, administration publique et religion	304
555	95	495	10	1,050	875	F Arts, culture, sports et loisirs	305
6,485	920	5,310	10	11,250	6,190	G Ventes et services	306
490	145	485	0	1,010	420	H Métiers, transport et machinerie	307
95	130	330	0	210	125	I Professions propres au secteur primaire	308
790	80	1,025	0	2,020	455	J Transformation, fabrication et services d'utilité publique	309
48,400	**6,110**	**40,115**	**35**	**70,525**	**47,665**	**Population active occupée totale de 15 ans et plus**	310
						Catégorie de lieu de travail	
24,995	3,295	21,305	20	37,120	24,420	Hommes	311
20,485	2,170	17,475	10	30,010	19,245	Lieu habituel de travail	312
1,100	410	1,000	0	1,455	1,455	À domicile	313
110	0	55	0	100	110	En dehors du Canada	314
3,295	705	2,775	0	5,550	3,610	Sans adresse de travail fixe	315
23,405	2,815	18,805	15	33,410	23,245	Femmes	316
20,880	2,285	16,505	15	29,760	20,515	Lieu habituel de travail	317
1,485	345	1,445	0	1,850	1,555	À domicile	318
65	10	25	0	60	55	En dehors du Canada	319
975	170	830	0	1,730	1,115	Sans adresse de travail fixe	320

Nota : Voir les symboles et les abréviations dans les documents d'introduction et voir les documents de référence à la fin de la publication.

Selected characteristics for census divisions and census subdivisions – 100% data and 20% sample data, Ontario, 2006 Census (continued)

No.	Characteristics	Melancthon, TP A	Mono, T A	Mulmur, TP ◆◇	Orangeville, T	Shelburne, T A	**Durham CD/DR**
	Population characteristics						
321	**Total employed labour force 15 years and over with usual place of work or no fixed workplace address**	**1,405**	**3,245**	**1,505**	**13,850**	**2,405**	**274,845**
	Mode of transportation						
322	Males	815	1,815	780	7,310	1,330	144,775
323	Car, truck, van, as driver	710	1,560	715	6,185	1,185	119,975
324	Car, truck, van, as passenger	70	175	50	555	60	9,670
325	Public transit	0	0	10	20	0	9,710
326	Walked	15	65	0	395	65	3,755
327	All other modes	25	10	10	150	15	1,660
328	Females	590	1,430	720	6,540	1,070	130,070
329	Car, truck, van, as driver	515	1,235	635	5,065	815	94,020
330	Car, truck, van, as passenger	50	130	50	715	105	14,020
331	Public transit	0	10	15	135	0	15,260
332	Walked	10	45	15	470	140	5,385
333	All other modes	10	15	0	150	15	1,385
334	**Total population 15 years and over who worked since January 1, 2005**	**1,885**	**4,540**	**1,970**	**16,275**	**2,780**	**334,705**
	Language used most often at work						
335	Single responses	1,880	4,530	1,970	16,235	2,780	333,330
336	English	1,870	4,505	1,945	16,180	2,780	331,215
337	French	10	25	10	30	0	1,255
338	Non-official languages[7]	10	0	10	25	0	855
339	Chinese, n.o.s.[61]	0	0	0	0	0	120
340	Cantonese	0	0	0	0	0	120
341	Other languages[8]	10	10	10	25	0	605
342	Multiple responses	0	0	10	45	0	1,375
343	English and French	0	10	10	20	0	750
344	English and non-official language	0	10	0	25	0	585
345	French and non-official language	0	0	0	0	0	0
346	English, French and non-official language	0	0	0	0	0	30
	Dwelling and household characteristics						
347	**Total number of occupied private dwellings**	**1,005**	**2,340**	**1,190**	**9,420**	**1,850**	**194,670**
	Housing tenure						
348	Owned	915	2,225	1,120	7,535	1,460	159,880
349	Rented	85	115	65	1,885	390	34,785
350	Band housing	0	0	0	0	0	0
	Structural type of dwelling						
351	Single-detached house	915	2,275	1,105	5,620	1,280	131,345
352	Semi-detached house	40	15	45	1,180	75	11,345
353	Row house	15	0	10	935	80	17,860
354	Apartment, duplex	25	20	0	155	70	7,085
355	Apartment, building that has five or more storeys	0	0	0	570	0	13,420
356	Apartment, building that has fewer than five storeys	0	10	15	955	310	13,150
357	Other single-attached house	5	10	10	15	30	300
358	Movable dwelling[48]	0	5	5	0	0	165
	Condition of dwelling						
359	Regular maintenance only	545	1,505	680	6,460	1,315	137,090
360	Minor repairs	355	670	425	2,465	415	47,850
361	Major repairs	100	155	85	495	120	9,730
	Period of construction						
362	Before 1946	405	300	220	775	340	16,005
363	1946 to 1960	65	170	90	575	105	20,155
364	1961 to 1970	70	210	120	1,215	195	20,765
365	1971 to 1980	145	480	255	1,945	425	30,965
366	1981 to 1985	40	195	75	645	75	17,520
367	1986 to 1990	95	490	205	960	95	27,735
368	1991 to 1995	60	190	90	995	140	16,855
369	1996 to 2000	45	125	55	1,325	90	18,600
370	2001 to 2006[49]	80	175	85	980	380	26,070

Note: See symbols and abbreviations in the introductory material and see reference material at the end of the publication.

Certaines caractéristiques des divisions de recensement et des subdivisions de recensement – Données intégrales et données-échantillon (20 %), Ontario, Recensement de 2006 (suite)

Ajax, T	Brock, TP	Clarington, MU	Mississaugas of Scugog Island, IRI	Oshawa, CY	Pickering, CY	Caractéristiques	N°
						Caractéristiques de la population	
45,640	**5,335**	**37,590**	**35**	**67,060**	**44,480**	**Population active occupée totale de 15 ans et plus ayant un lieu habituel de travail ou sans adresse de travail fixe**	321
						Mode de transport	
23,780	2,880	20,255	20	35,560	22,850	Hommes	322
19,290	2,390	17,870	15	28,780	18,730	Automobile, camion ou fourgonnette, en tant que conducteur	323
1,415	280	1,405	0	2,690	1,325	Automobile, camion ou fourgonnette, en tant que passager	324
2,250	15	440	0	2,310	2,155	Transport en commun	325
570	160	375	0	1,215	445	À pied	326
255	35	160	0	575	200	Tous les autres modes	327
21,860	2,455	17,330	15	31,495	21,630	Femmes	328
14,540	2,000	14,065	10	22,500	14,630	Automobile, camion ou fourgonnette, en tant que conductrice	329
2,445	220	1,660	0	3,480	2,405	Automobile, camion ou fourgonnette, en tant que passagère	330
3,865	10	905	0	3,280	3,635	Transport en commun	331
735	210	555	0	1,855	740	À pied	332
270	15	150	0	375	215	Tous les autres modes	333
54,630	**7,010**	**45,475**	**45**	**81,430**	**54,200**	**Population totale de 15 ans et plus ayant travaillé depuis le 1er janvier 2005**	334
						Langue utilisée le plus souvent au travail	
54,325	7,005	45,370	45	81,045	53,930	Réponses uniques	335
53,940	6,995	45,140	45	80,535	53,610	Anglais	336
205	10	175	0	310	140	Français	337
180	0	55	0	205	180	Langues non officielles[7]	338
25	0	0	0	40	15	Chinois, n.d.a.[61]	339
40	0	0	0	15	30	Cantonais	340
115	0	55	0	135	140	Autres langues[8]	341
310	0	105	0	385	265	Réponses multiples	342
105	0	70	0	230	145	Anglais et français	343
175	0	35	0	155	115	Anglais et langue non officielle	344
10	0	0	0	0	0	Français et langue non officielle	345
25	0	0	0	0	10	Anglais, français et langue non officielle	346
						Caractéristiques des logements et des ménages	
28,615	**4,420**	**26,850**	**30**	**54,925**	**28,220**	**Nombre total de logements privés occupés**	347
						Mode d'occupation	
25,000	3,700	23,845	20	38,395	25,140	Possédé	348
3,615	725	3,000	0	16,530	3,085	Loué	349
0	0	0	0	0	0	Logement de bande	350
						Type de construction résidentielle	
19,600	3,810	21,435	30	29,530	18,025	Maison individuelle non attenante	351
1,365	55	980	0	5,180	2,230	Maison jumelée	352
3,245	125	2,020	5	4,750	3,370	Maison en rangée	353
1,045	35	665	0	2,955	1,485	Appartement, duplex	354
2,010	0	240	0	6,630	2,150	Appartement, immeuble de cinq étages ou plus	355
1,325	355	1,440	0	5,745	935	Appartement, immeuble de moins de cinq étages	356
15	40	40	0	130	10	Autre maison individuelle attenante	357
5	5	45	0	10	10	Logement mobile[48]	358
						État du logement	
21,410	2,600	19,065	25	36,300	19,870	Entretien régulier seulement	359
6,210	1,415	6,550	10	14,765	7,230	Réparations mineures	360
995	405	1,230	10	3,855	1,125	Réparations majeures	361
						Période de construction	
740	1,460	2,785	0	6,065	985	Avant 1946	362
1,710	490	2,090	0	10,380	1,525	1946 à 1960	363
2,060	440	1,835	0	9,870	2,935	1961 à 1970	364
3,670	750	2,755	0	12,140	4,550	1971 à 1980	365
3,655	290	1,520	0	3,925	3,820	1981 à 1985	366
5,855	420	4,845	0	4,310	5,900	1986 à 1990	367
2,265	195	3,420	10	2,370	3,410	1991 à 1995	368
2,925	235	3,485	10	2,465	3,390	1996 à 2000	369
5,735	135	4,120	10	3,390	1,705	2001 à 2006[49]	370

Nota : Voir les symboles et les abréviations dans les documents d'introduction et voir les documents de référence à la fin de la publication.

Selected characteristics for census divisions and census subdivisions – 100% data and 20% sample data, Ontario, 2006 Census (continued)

No.	Characteristics	Melancthon, TP A	Mono, T A	Mulmur, TP ◆◊	Orangeville, T	Shelburne, T A	**Durham CD/DR**
	Dwelling and household characteristics						
371	Average number of rooms per dwelling	7.5	8.2	7.9	6.9	6.9	7.2
372	Average number of bedrooms per dwelling	3.2	3.3	3.2	3.0	2.9	3.1
373	Average value of dwelling $	336,899	470,977	378,787	263,056	225,280	291,844
374	**Total number of private households**	**1,005**	**2,340**	**1,195**	**9,430**	**1,850**	**194,670**
	Household size						
375	1 person	145	265	190	1,850	435	35,100
376	2 persons	360	840	475	2,755	575	58,040
377	3 persons	165	380	175	1,715	300	35,745
378	4 to 5 persons	290	745	310	2,790	490	58,555
379	6 or more persons	45	105	45	325	50	7,230
	Household type						
380	One-family households[50]	815	1,950	970	7,090	1,360	149,705
381	Multiple-family households	30	95	15	270	15	5,250
382	Non-family households	165	295	205	2,065	475	39,715
383	Number of persons in private households	2,895	7,020	3,295	26,525	4,905	556,080
384	Average number of persons in private households	2.9	3.0	2.8	2.8	2.7	2.9
385	Tenant-occupied private non-farm, non-reserve dwellings[51]	80	115	70	1,885	385	34,745
386	Average gross rent $[51]	911	837	648	892	735	874
387	Tenant-occupied households spending 30% or more of household income on gross rent[52]	35	35	10	920	150	15,600
388	Tenant-occupied households spending from 30% to 99% of household income on gross rent[52]	35	25	0	840	125	13,390
389	Owner-occupied private non-farm, non-reserve dwellings[53]	840	2,175	1,080	7,535	1,460	159,160
390	Average owner's major payments $[53]	1,222	1,567	1,136	1,350	1,202	1,343
391	Owner households spending 30% or more of household income on owner's major payments[52]	215	505	220	1,835	335	34,510
392	Owner households spending from 30% to 99% of household income on owner's major payments[52]	160	380	190	1,595	295	30,720
	Census family characteristics						
393	**Total number of census families in private households**	**870**	**2,135**	**1,000**	**7,630**	**1,390**	**160,410**
	Family structure and number of children						
394	Total couple families	785	1,935	905	6,300	1,185	134,690
395	Total families of married couples	615	1,760	805	5,340	950	117,620
396	Without children at home	280	765	400	1,845	355	40,645
397	With children at home	325	990	405	3,500	595	76,975
398	1 child	135	335	115	1,070	185	24,830
399	2 children	120	425	180	1,715	290	36,425
400	3 or more children	70	230	115	710	120	15,715
401	Total families of common-law couples	175	170	105	960	235	17,065
402	Without children at home	45	75	55	495	125	9,210
403	With children at home	125	95	45	470	115	7,860
404	1 child	45	25	10	190	45	3,510
405	2 children	45	50	20	195	45	2,970
406	3 or more children	35	20	20	80	25	1,385
407	Total lone-parent families	85	210	90	1,330	200	25,720
408	Female parent	55	140	65	1,010	165	20,680
409	1 child	25	90	45	540	75	11,625
410	2 children	15	30	15	360	60	6,695
411	3 or more children	15	20	0	110	35	2,360
412	Male parent	35	65	25	325	35	5,040
413	1 child	30	40	0	200	35	3,280
414	2 children	0	15	10	75	0	1,400
415	3 or more children	0	10	10	40	0	360

Note: See symbols and abbreviations in the introductory material and see reference material at the end of the publication.

Certaines caractéristiques des divisions de recensement et des subdivisions de recensement – Données intégrales et données-échantillon (20 %), Ontario, Recensement de 2006 (suite)

Ajax, T	Brock, TP	Clarington, MU	Mississaugas of Scugog Island, IRI	Oshawa, CY	Pickering, CY	Caractéristiques	N°
						Caractéristiques des logements et des ménages	
7.4	7.1	7.4	6.6	6.7	7.6	Nombre moyen de pièces par logement	371
3.2	2.9	3.1	2.9	2.8	3.3	Nombre moyen de chambres à coucher par logement	372
307,305	256,417	274,598	0	231,151	329,200	Valeur moyenne du logement $	373
28,615	**4,420**	**26,865**	**35**	**54,925**	**28,210**	**Nombre total de ménages privés**	374
						Taille du ménage	
3,910	910	4,410	15	13,505	3,985	1 personne	375
7,205	1,610	8,330	10	18,215	7,390	2 personnes	376
5,605	660	4,800	5	9,670	5,525	3 personnes	377
10,335	1,105	8,475	5	12,110	9,885	4 à 5 personnes	378
1,565	140	845	0	1,415	1,430	6 personnes ou plus	379
						Genre de ménage	
22,965	3,370	21,505	20	38,440	22,490	Ménages unifamiliaux[50]	380
1,125	80	545	0	1,085	1,170	Ménages multifamiliaux	381
4,530	970	4,805	15	15,395	4,560	Ménages non familiaux	382
89,780	11,735	77,120	70	139,715	87,245	Nombre de personnes dans les ménages privés	383
3.1	2.7	2.9	2.3	2.5	3.1	Nombre moyen de personnes dans les ménages privés	384
3,615	715	3,005	0	16,525	3,080	Ménages locataires dans les logements privés non agricoles hors réserve[51]	385
925	729	914	0	810	1,019	Loyer brut moyen $[51]	386
1,720	315	1,250	0	7,375	1,315	Ménages locataires consacrant 30 % ou plus du revenu du ménage au loyer brut[52]	387
1,445	255	1,025	0	6,405	1,100	Ménages locataires consacrant de 30 % à 99 % du revenu du ménage au loyer brut[52]	388
24,995	3,540	23,665	0	38,385	25,125	Ménages propriétaires dans les logements privés non agricoles hors réserve[53]	389
1,526	1,106	1,257	0	1,163	1,436	Principales dépenses de propriété moyennes $[53]	390
6,590	960	4,560	0	7,530	6,070	Ménages propriétaires consacrant 30 % ou plus du revenu du ménage aux principales dépenses de propriété[52]	391
5,875	870	4,105	0	6,645	5,390	Ménages propriétaires consacrant de 30 % à 99 % du revenu du ménage aux principales dépenses de propriété[52]	392
						Caractéristiques des familles de recensement	
25,280	**3,535**	**22,590**	**20**	**40,635**	**24,895**	**Nombre total de familles de recensement dans les ménages privés**	393
						Structure de la famille et le nombre d'enfants	
21,245	3,065	19,620	15	32,265	20,725	Total des familles avec conjoints	394
18,940	2,600	17,065	10	26,655	18,665	Total des familles avec couples mariés	395
5,220	1,295	6,250	10	11,125	5,545	Sans enfants à la maison	396
13,720	1,305	10,815	0	15,530	13,120	Avec enfants à la maison	397
4,065	365	3,245	10	5,865	4,065	1 enfant	398
6,690	625	5,300	0	6,870	6,305	2 enfants	399
2,960	310	2,270	0	2,795	2,750	3 enfants ou plus	400
2,310	465	2,550	0	5,610	2,060	Total des familles avec couples en union libre	401
1,190	225	1,390	0	3,090	1,030	Sans enfants à la maison	402
1,115	240	1,160	10	2,520	1,030	Avec enfants à la maison	403
420	120	495	0	1,215	475	1 enfant	404
450	80	460	0	895	380	2 enfants	405
240	45	200	10	410	170	3 enfants ou plus	406
4,035	465	2,975	10	8,370	4,170	Total des familles monoparentales	407
3,345	375	2,350	0	6,790	3,335	Parent de sexe féminin	408
1,820	160	1,215	0	4,020	1,920	1 enfant	409
1,100	155	840	0	2,105	1,025	2 enfants	410
430	60	290	0	670	390	3 enfants ou plus	411
685	90	625	0	1,580	835	Parent de sexe masculin	412
445	50	340	0	1,080	595	1 enfant	413
185	20	220	0	420	175	2 enfants	414
55	20	70	0	75	60	3 enfants ou plus	415

Nota : Voir les symboles et les abréviations dans les documents d'introduction et voir les documents de référence à la fin de la publication.

Selected characteristics for census divisions and census subdivisions – 100% data and 20% sample data, Ontario, 2006 Census (continued)

No.	Characteristics	Melancthon, TP A	Mono, T A	Mulmur, TP ◆◇	Orangeville, T	Shelburne, T A	**Durham CD/DR**
	Census family characteristics						
416	**Total number of children at home**	**1,030**	**2,445**	**1,105**	**9,815**	**1,680**	**202,945**
	Age group						
417	Under 6 years	195	330	170	2,235	435	39,175
418	6 to 14 years	330	965	465	3,755	675	75,035
419	15 to 17 years	170	335	155	1,340	180	26,840
420	18 to 24 years	255	575	230	1,750	325	42,040
421	25 years and over	85	230	80	735	55	19,850
422	Average number of children at home per census family[54]	1.2	1.1	1.1	1.3	1.2	1.3
423	**Total number of persons in private households**	**2,895**	**7,020**	**3,285**	**26,515**	**4,905**	**556,095**
	Census family status and living arrangements						
424	Number of persons not in census families	210	505	270	2,770	650	58,050
425	Living with relatives[55]	35	130	50	385	105	11,665
426	Living with non-relatives only	30	110	25	550	115	11,255
427	Living alone	150	260	190	1,830	430	35,135
428	Number of census family persons	2,685	6,515	3,010	23,745	4,255	498,045
429	Average number of persons per census family	3.1	3.1	3.0	3.1	3.1	3.1
430	**Total number of persons aged 65 years and over**	**220**	**825**	**475**	**2,395**	**555**	**57,040**
431	Number of persons not in census families aged 65 years and over	40	140	90	855	240	18,705
432	Living with relatives[55]	10	60	20	150	50	4,615
433	Living with non-relatives only	0	10	0	0	10	840
434	Living alone	35	70	65	700	185	13,250
435	Number of census family persons aged 65 years and over	180	690	390	1,540	310	38,335
	Economic family characteristics						
436	**Total number of economic families in private households**	**860**	**2,050**	**985**	**7,425**	**1,390**	**156,470**
	Size of family						
437	2 persons	355	835	475	2,710	575	57,020
438	3 persons	205	370	135	1,635	270	35,090
439	4 persons	180	495	220	1,985	365	41,255
440	5 or more persons	120	355	155	1,090	180	23,100
441	Total number of persons in economic families	2,720	6,645	3,065	24,130	4,360	509,710
442	Average number of persons per economic family	3.0	3.0	3.0	3.0	3.0	3.0
443	Total number of persons not in economic families	175	375	220	2,385	545	46,385
	2005 income characteristics						
444	**Population 15 years and over**	**2,365**	**5,735**	**2,660**	**20,670**	**3,780**	**442,285**
	Sex and total income groups in 2005						
445	Without income	150	235	160	1,035	175	23,450
446	With income	2,210	5,500	2,495	19,635	3,600	418,835
447	Under $1,000[56]	105	245	70	705	115	16,680
448	$1,000 to $2,999	95	195	110	675	140	15,650
449	$3,000 to $4,999	95	175	75	595	130	13,060
450	$5,000 to $6,999	60	215	100	620	115	14,165
451	$7,000 to $9,999	145	305	110	1,160	190	21,855
452	$10,000 to $11,999	80	230	65	715	135	14,275
453	$12,000 to $14,999	140	245	155	950	245	20,770
454	$15,000 to $19,999	220	420	205	1,645	330	31,060
455	$20,000 to $24,999	110	305	205	1,365	240	25,570
456	$25,000 to $29,999	110	385	135	1,225	220	24,755
457	$30,000 to $34,999	125	255	140	1,365	230	26,825
458	$35,000 to $39,999	135	275	175	1,250	210	25,100
459	$40,000 to $44,999	105	245	160	1,070	245	23,920
460	$45,000 to $49,999	115	220	90	985	175	20,395
461	$50,000 to $59,999	150	385	150	1,750	280	34,005
462	$60,000 and over	405	1,400	555	3,560	590	90,750
463	Median income $[57]	25,804	30,623	31,023	30,373	28,729	32,005
464	Average income $[57]	35,632	46,346	41,554	36,049	33,926	40,202
465	Standard error of average income $[57]	1,674	1,877	2,093	438	917	153

Note: See symbols and abbreviations in the introductory material and see reference material at the end of the publication.

Certaines caractéristiques des divisions de recensement et des subdivisions de recensement – Données intégrales et données-échantillon (20 %), Ontario, Recensement de 2006 (suite)

Ajax, T	Brock, TP	Clarington, MU	Mississaugas of Scugog Island, IRI	Oshawa, CY	Pickering, CY	Caractéristiques	N°
						Caractéristiques des familles de recensement	
35,615	**3,875**	**28,200**	**25**	**45,710**	**33,975**	**Nombre total d'enfants à la maison**	416
						Groupes d'âge	
7,000	715	5,645	10	8,935	5,545	Moins de 6 ans	417
13,265	1,455	11,575	10	16,295	11,640	6 à 14 ans	418
4,540	530	3,900	10	5,810	4,520	15 à 17 ans	419
7,395	820	5,100	0	9,350	7,855	18 à 24 ans	420
3,420	350	1,980	0	5,325	4,410	25 ans et plus	421
1.4	1.1	1.2	1.7	1.1	1.4	Nombre moyen d'enfants à la maison par famille de recensement[54]	422
89,780	**11,740**	**77,110**	**70**	**139,720**	**87,260**	**Nombre total de personnes dans les ménages privés**	423
						Situation des particuliers dans la famille de recensement et des particuliers dans le ménage	
7,640	1,270	6,695	20	21,105	7,670	Nombre de personnes hors famille de recensement	424
2,195	210	1,195	10	3,010	2,265	Vivant avec des personnes apparentées[55]	425
1,525	150	1,105	0	4,590	1,390	Vivant avec des personnes non apparentées seulement	426
3,920	915	4,395	10	13,500	4,015	Vivant seules	427
82,145	10,475	70,415	55	118,610	79,595	Nombre de membres d'une famille de recensement	428
3.2	3.0	3.1	3.0	2.9	3.2	Nombre moyen de personnes par famille de recensement	429
6,800	**1,795**	**7,770**	**10**	**18,095**	**7,870**	**Nombre total de personnes âgées de 65 ans et plus**	430
2,315	615	2,135	10	6,295	2,560	Nombre de personnes hors famille de recensement âgées de 65 ans et plus	431
900	80	475	0	955	960	Vivant avec des personnes apparentées[55]	432
130	25	60	0	295	120	Vivant avec des personnes non apparentées seulement	433
1,280	510	1,600	0	5,040	1,475	Vivant seules	434
4,485	1,175	5,635	10	11,795	5,315	Nombre de membres d'une famille de recensement âgés de 65 ans et plus	435
						Caractéristiques des familles économiques	
24,320	**3,475**	**22,165**	**20**	**40,020**	**23,955**	**Nombre total de familles économiques dans les ménages privés**	436
						Taille de la famille	
7,140	1,605	8,250	10	17,615	7,445	2 personnes	437
5,475	650	4,735	0	9,380	5,440	3 personnes	438
7,160	750	6,075	10	8,585	6,925	4 personnes	439
4,555	470	3,100	10	4,440	4,145	5 personnes ou plus	440
84,335	10,680	71,605	60	121,625	81,855	Nombre total de personnes dans les familles économiques	441
4.0	3.0	3.0	3.0	3.0	3.0	Nombre moyen de personnes par famille économique	442
5,440	1,065	5,500	15	18,090	5,405	Nombre total de personnes hors famille économique	443
						Caractéristiques du revenu de 2005	
69,470	**9,580**	**60,085**	**X**	**114,790**	**70,015**	**Population de 15 ans et plus**	444
						Sexe et groupes de revenu total en 2005	
4,275	440	2,980	X	6,050	3,950	Sans revenu	445
65,195	9,140	57,105	X	108,735	66,060	Avec un revenu	446
2,775	395	2,010	X	3,810	3,270	Moins de 1 000 $[56]	447
2,510	395	2,215	X	3,460	2,685	1 000 $ à 2 999 $	448
2,070	285	1,590	X	3,315	2,070	3 000 $ à 4 999 $	449
2,495	325	1,870	X	3,545	2,220	5 000 $ à 6 999 $	450
3,465	505	2,985	X	5,780	3,300	7 000 $ à 9 999 $	451
2,180	440	1,870	X	4,270	2,050	10 000 $ à 11 999 $	452
3,020	490	2,730	X	6,020	3,350	12 000 $ à 14 999 $	453
4,395	955	4,050	X	9,330	4,735	15 000 $ à 19 999 $	454
3,775	670	3,360	X	7,730	3,645	20 000 $ à 24 999 $	455
3,620	545	3,310	X	7,455	3,605	25 000 $ à 29 999 $	456
3,980	690	3,475	X	8,045	3,915	30 000 $ à 34 999 $	457
3,805	525	3,540	X	7,160	3,940	35 000 $ à 39 999 $	458
3,820	600	3,225	X	6,345	3,700	40 000 $ à 44 999 $	459
3,395	430	2,655	X	5,410	3,160	45 000 $ à 49 999$	460
5,655	640	4,780	X	7,855	5,735	50 000 $ à 59 999$	461
14,230	1,265	13,435	X	19,190	14,680	60 000 $ et plus	462
33,026	25,821	33,515	X	29,788	32,530	Revenu médian $[57]	463
40,414	32,454	40,649	X	35,899	41,882	Revenu moyen $[57]	464
374	657	343	X	199	404	Erreur type de revenu moyen $[57]	465

Nota : Voir les symboles et les abréviations dans les documents d'introduction et voir les documents de référence à la fin de la publication.

Selected characteristics for census divisions and census subdivisions – 100% data and 20% sample data, Ontario, 2006 Census (continued)

No.	Characteristics	Melancthon, TP A	Mono, T A	Mulmur, TP ♦◊	Orangeville, T	Shelburne, T A	Durham CD/DR
	2005 income characteristics						
	Sex and total income groups in 2005 (continued)						
466	Total - Males	1,285	2,915	1,325	9,955	1,810	214,095
467	Without income	75	90	75	385	80	9,830
468	With income	1,215	2,820	1,255	9,570	1,730	204,255
469	Under $1,000[56]	75	160	30	350	70	8,775
470	$1,000 to $2,999	35	65	55	215	40	5,380
471	$3,000 to $4,999	45	85	10	225	35	4,655
472	$5,000 to $6,999	25	50	30	210	30	4,950
473	$7,000 to $9,999	70	105	35	365	45	7,930
474	$10,000 to $11,999	30	105	25	180	50	5,110
475	$12,000 to $14,999	70	85	25	325	70	6,670
476	$15,000 to $19,999	120	150	85	500	125	10,910
477	$20,000 to $24,999	45	140	95	470	80	9,860
478	$25,000 to $29,999	50	210	45	505	90	10,270
479	$30,000 to $34,999	30	130	75	630	75	12,215
480	$35,000 to $39,999	65	105	110	600	115	11,490
481	$40,000 to $44,999	70	125	65	595	135	11,670
482	$45,000 to $49,999	60	105	65	535	110	10,910
483	$50,000 to $59,999	115	205	85	1,110	200	19,490
484	$60,000 and over	290	995	410	2,745	470	63,970
485	Median income $[57]	34,931	40,284	39,998	41,583	42,011	41,452
486	Average income $[57]	41,890	59,449	52,766	45,272	43,397	49,862
487	Standard error of average income $[57]	2,748	3,413	3,580	703	1,496	272
488	Total - Females	1,075	2,820	1,335	10,710	1,970	228,195
489	Without income	80	140	90	650	90	13,615
490	With income	1,000	2,675	1,245	10,060	1,875	214,580
491	Under $1,000[56]	25	85	40	350	50	7,905
492	$1,000 to $2,999	55	130	50	460	100	10,270
493	$3,000 to $4,999	50	90	60	370	100	8,405
494	$5,000 to $6,999	40	165	65	410	85	9,215
495	$7,000 to $9,999	80	205	70	795	145	13,920
496	$10,000 to $11,999	50	120	40	530	80	9,170
497	$12,000 to $14,999	70	165	125	630	175	14,100
498	$15,000 to $19,999	100	270	120	1,140	215	20,145
499	$20,000 to $24,999	60	165	110	900	165	15,710
500	$25,000 to $29,999	65	170	85	720	130	14,485
501	$30,000 to $34,999	90	120	70	730	160	14,610
502	$35,000 to $39,999	70	165	65	650	95	13,610
503	$40,000 to $44,999	30	120	85	480	115	12,245
504	$45,000 to $49,999	50	115	30	450	65	9,495
505	$50,000 to $59,999	35	180	60	640	80	14,510
506	$60,000 and over	115	405	145	810	125	26,780
507	Median income $[57]	21,602	22,979	20,935	22,170	19,797	24,444
508	Average income $[57]	28,017	32,527	30,248	27,275	25,196	31,007
509	Standard error of average income $[57]	1,494	1,231	1,951	467	944	138
	Composition of total income						
510	Composition of total income in 2005 %	100.0	100.0	100.0	100.0	100.0	100.0
511	Employment income %	81.2	79.2	71.6	83.2	79.5	81.9
512	Government transfer payments %	8.0	6.6	8.1	8.8	11.1	8.0
513	Other %	10.8	14.3	20.2	8.0	9.6	10.1
514	**Population 15 years and over with employment income in 2005**	**1,835**	**4,395**	**1,955**	**16,015**	**2,700**	**334,130**
	Sex and work activity						
515	Median employment income in 2005 $	28,925	28,909	27,209	32,045	31,911	34,063
516	Average employment income in 2005 $	34,855	45,936	38,071	36,752	35,877	41,296
517	Standard error of average employment income $	1,549	2,204	2,007	493	1,101	177
518	Worked full year, full time[59]	1,055	2,250	1,045	9,505	1,490	185,650
519	Median employment income in 2005 $	43,003	53,027	43,508	46,034	45,862	49,823
520	Average employment income in 2005 $	44,506	65,228	51,998	49,816	48,091	57,230
521	Standard error of average employment income $	1,987	2,488	2,650	615	1,481	261
522	Worked part year or part time[60]	720	1,865	785	5,700	1,100	127,510
523	Median employment income in 2005 $	13,416	10,570	12,895	11,236	16,234	12,867
524	Average employment income in 2005 $	23,236	26,968	24,387	18,761	22,397	23,214
525	Standard error of average employment income $	2,272	3,911	3,054	568	1,248	195
526	Males 15 years and over with employment income[58]	1,055	2,350	1,055	8,275	1,460	173,465
527	Median employment income in 2005 $	37,550	39,628	35,884	43,366	43,644	42,775
528	Average employment income in 2005 $	40,029	58,445	45,186	45,653	44,276	49,967
529	Standard error of average employment income $	2,317	3,897	3,098	766	1,675	301

Note: See symbols and abbreviations in the introductory material and see reference material at the end of the publication.

Certaines caractéristiques des divisions de recensement et des subdivisions de recensement – Données intégrales et données-échantillon (20 %), Ontario, Recensement de 2006 (suite)

Ajax, T	Brock, TP	Clarington, MU	Mississaugas of Scugog Island, IRI	Oshawa, CY	Pickering, CY	Caractéristiques	N°
						Caractéristiques du revenu de 2005	
						Sexe et groupes de revenu total en 2005 (suite)	
33,310	4,670	29,505	X	55,565	33,590	Total - Hommes	466
1,840	145	1,265	X	2,630	1,590	Sans revenu	467
31,470	4,525	28,245	X	52,930	32,000	Avec un revenu	468
1,530	210	935	X	2,120	1,720	Moins de 1 000 $[56]	469
765	130	730	X	1,245	1,055	1 000 $ à 2 999 $	470
780	75	535	X	1,125	735	3 000 $ à 4 999 $	471
850	150	665	X	1,175	760	5 000 $ à 6 999 $	472
1,315	215	1,035	X	1,895	1,270	7 000 $ à 9 999 $	473
780	180	575	X	1,585	800	10 000 $ à 11 999 $	474
1,070	130	850	X	1,770	1,200	12 000 $ à 14 999 $	475
1,590	390	1,350	X	3,050	1,850	15 000 $ à 19 999 $	476
1,500	260	1,265	X	2,885	1,505	20 000 $ à 24 999 $	477
1,625	175	1,275	X	3,050	1,595	25 000 $ à 29 999 $	478
1,770	325	1,535	X	3,865	1,775	30 000 $ à 34 999 $	479
1,750	310	1,670	X	3,470	1,685	35 000 $ à 39 999 $	480
1,710	325	1,625	X	3,355	1,615	40 000 $ à $44 999 $	481
1,685	245	1,405	X	3,215	1,575	45 000 $ à $49 999 $	482
2,950	460	2,950	X	4,895	3,295	50 000 $ à $59 999 $	483
9,810	940	9,840	X	14,225	9,535	60 000 $ et plus	484
40,879	35,092	45,143	X	38,768	40,020	Revenu médian $[57]	485
49,022	39,598	51,337	X	44,409	51,114	Revenu moyen $[57]	486
629	1,101	574	X	332	720	Erreur type de revenu moyen $[57]	487
36,165	4,910	30,580	X	59,225	36,425	Total - Femmes	488
2,440	295	1,715	X	3,420	2,360	Sans revenu	489
33,725	4,615	28,860	X	55,810	34,065	Avec un revenu	490
1,250	185	1,075	X	1,685	1,555	Moins de 1 000 $[56]	491
1,745	265	1,485	X	2,220	1,625	1 000$ à 2 999 $	492
1,290	205	1,055	X	2,190	1,340	3 000 $ à 4 999 $	493
1,645	175	1,200	X	2,375	1,455	5 000 $ à 6 999 $	494
2,155	285	1,945	X	3,885	2,025	7 000 $ à 9 999 $	495
1,400	255	1,295	X	2,690	1,245	10 000 $ à 11 999 $	496
1,945	360	1,885	X	4,250	2,150	12 000 $ à 14 999 $	497
2,805	570	2,705	X	6,280	2,885	15 000 $ à 19 999 $	498
2,280	405	2,095	X	4,845	2,140	20 000 $ à 24 999 $	499
1,995	365	2,040	X	4,410	2,000	25 000 $ à 29 999 $	500
2,210	360	1,940	X	4,180	2,140	30 000 $ à 34 999 $	501
2,055	210	1,870	X	3,690	2,250	35 000 $ à 39 999 $	502
2,105	275	1,600	X	2,990	2,080	40 000 $ à 44 999 $	503
1,705	180	1,240	X	2,190	1,580	45 000 $ à 49 999 $	504
2,705	180	1,835	X	2,960	2,440	50 000 $ à 59 999 $	505
4,415	325	3,595	X	4,970	5,140	60 000 $ et plus	506
25,637	20,053	24,053	X	22,269	26,473	Revenu médian $[57]	507
32,382	25,451	30,191	X	27,830	33,208	Revenu moyen $[57]	508
403	651	336	X	202	372	Erreur type de revenu moyen $[57]	509
						Composition du revenu total	
100.0	100.0	100.0	X	100.0	100.0	Composition du revenu total en 2005 %	510
86.3	73.0	81.9	X	76.8	84.5	Revenu d'emploi %	511
6.7	12.8	7.7	X	11.1	6.6	Transferts gouvernementaux %	512
7.0	14.2	10.4	X	12.0	8.9	Autres %	513
53,715	**6,795**	**46,075**	**X**	**82,630**	**53,500**	**Population de 15 ans et plus avec un revenu d'emploi en 2005**	514
						Sexe et travail	
35,701	25,264	34,892	X	30,393	35,369	Revenu médian d'emploi en 2005 $	515
42,354	31,871	41,256	X	36,304	43,713	Revenu moyen d'emploi en 2005 $	516
413	827	397	X	238	461	Erreur type de revenu moyen d'emploi $	517
31,030	3,425	25,265	X	44,395	30,355	A travaillé toute l'année à plein temps[59]	518
49,860	42,093	51,164	X	45,373	50,278	Revenu médian d'emploi en 2005 $	519
57,114	46,240	57,007	X	50,617	59,868	Revenu moyen d'emploi en 2005 $	520
585	1,059	554	X	316	629	Erreur type de revenu moyen d'emploi $	521
20,130	2,870	17,535	X	31,780	20,220	A travaillé une partie de l'année ou à temps partiel[60]	522
12,998	10,496	13,733	X	12,954	12,947	Revenu médian d'emploi en 2005 $	523
23,285	18,987	24,394	X	22,073	24,017	Revenu moyen d'emploi en 2005 $	524
443	1,211	470	X	302	621	Erreur type de revenu moyen d'emploi $	525
27,220	3,615	24,370	X	43,565	27,090	Hommes de 15 ans et plus avec un revenu d'emploi[58]	526
43,383	33,233	46,553	X	39,253	42,307	Revenu médian d'emploi en 2005 $	527
50,355	37,632	50,594	X	43,672	52,402	Revenu moyen d'emploi en 2005 $	528
651	1,308	633	X	375	796	Erreur type de revenu moyen d'emploi $	529

Nota : Voir les symboles et les abréviations dans les documents d'introduction et voir les documents de référence à la fin de la publication.

Selected characteristics for census divisions and census subdivisions – 100% data and 20% sample data, Ontario, 2006 Census (continued)

No.	Characteristics	Melancthon, TP A	Mono, T A	Mulmur, TP ◆◇	Orangeville, T	Shelburne, T A	**Durham CD/DR**
	2005 income characteristics						
	Sex and work activity (continued)						
530	Worked full year, full time[59]	695	1,330	620	5,585	900	107,335
531	Median employment income in 2005 $	45,842	65,379	52,755	53,213	54,416	56,522
532	Average employment income in 2005 $	47,615	77,295	57,332	57,128	56,113	64,986
533	Standard error of average employment income $	2,621	3,759	3,462	863	1,949	413
534	Worked part year or part time[60]	310	915	365	2,305	485	55,205
535	Median employment income in 2005 $	15,891	11,784	15,794	13,420	21,183	14,743
536	Average employment income in 2005 $	29,104	35,601	32,593	23,426	27,792	28,769
537	Standard error of average employment income $	4,655	8,025	6,215	1,123	2,340	385
538	Females 15 years and over with employment income[58]	780	2,045	900	7,740	1,245	160,670
539	Median employment income in 2005 $	21,023	23,528	20,932	22,891	21,066	26,766
540	Average employment income in 2005 $	27,874	31,577	29,735	27,237	26,072	31,935
541	Standard error of average employment income $	1,748	1,361	2,277	526	1,179	158
542	Worked full year, full time[59]	360	915	425	3,920	590	78,315
543	Median employment income in 2005 $	33,376	44,354	36,570	36,214	34,694	42,124
544	Average employment income in 2005 $	38,541	47,697	44,235	39,387	35,805	46,599
545	Standard error of average employment income $	2,716	2,153	4,000	716	1,856	232
546	Worked part year or part time[60]	410	945	420	3,390	620	72,310
547	Median employment income in 2005 $	12,347	10,019	12,164	10,191	13,966	11,879
548	Average employment income in 2005 $	18,792	18,592	17,264	15,587	18,139	18,974
549	Standard error of average employment income $	1,925	1,305	1,633	548	1,229	169
550	**Total number of economic families in private households**	**860**	**2,050**	**985**	**7,425**	**1,390**	**156,470**
	Family income groups in 2005						
551	Under $10,000	10	40	15	130	20	2,845
552	$10,000 to $19,999	30	45	15	165	50	4,235
553	$20,000 to $29,999	60	65	45	420	70	6,575
554	$30,000 to $39,999	65	100	45	550	110	9,805
555	$40,000 to $49,999	40	110	90	490	130	11,230
556	$50,000 to $59,999	110	160	85	660	155	12,000
557	$60,000 to $69,999	85	170	120	710	125	12,260
558	$70,000 to $79,999	85	140	110	690	190	12,835
559	$80,000 to $89,999	70	135	90	670	145	12,405
560	$90,000 to $99,999	70	115	65	695	110	12,120
561	$100,000 and over	225	970	305	2,245	280	60,150
562	Median family income $	73,567	93,458	78,457	78,310	71,894	85,121
563	Average family income $	84,735	116,298	94,846	83,586	75,468	95,873
564	Standard error of average family income $	4,539	4,940	5,109	1,069	2,222	406
	Family after-tax income groups in 2005						
565	Under $10,000	10	50	10	130	20	2,970
566	$10,000 to $19,999	35	45	20	165	50	4,340
567	$20,000 to $29,999	70	70	50	490	80	7,610
568	$30,000 to $39,999	75	150	95	660	175	13,175
569	$40,000 to $49,999	75	175	105	800	170	15,310
570	$50,000 to $59,999	145	190	130	890	165	16,095
571	$60,000 to $69,999	110	195	150	1,005	275	16,715
572	$70,000 to $79,999	90	185	85	820	125	16,385
573	$80,000 to $89,999	65	120	95	755	95	14,750
574	$90,000 to $99,999	35	180	70	480	85	12,080
575	$100,000 and over	145	690	170	1,225	135	37,035
576	Median after-tax family income $	60,916	78,176	65,773	65,245	62,297	71,186
577	Average after-tax family income $	69,999	91,183	76,482	69,291	62,916	77,778
578	Standard error of average after-tax family income $	3,240	3,208	3,464	796	1,646	272
	Income status in 2005						
579	Total population in private households for income status	2,895	7,015	3,280	26,515	4,890	555,870
580	Below low income cut-off before tax in 2005	160	390	150	1,910	415	52,200
581	Prevalence of low income before tax in 2005 %	5.7	5.6	4.6	7.2	8.5	9.4
582	Below low income cut-off after tax in 2005	120	310	100	1,330	280	38,390
583	Prevalence of low income after tax in 2005 %	4.1	4.3	3.0	5.0	5.6	6.9

Note: See symbols and abbreviations in the introductory material and see reference material at the end of the publication.

Certaines caractéristiques des divisions de recensement et des subdivisions de recensement – Données intégrales et données-échantillon (20 %), Ontario, Recensement de 2006 (suite)

Ajax, T	Brock, TP	Clarington, MU	Mississaugas of Scugog Island, IRI	Oshawa, CY	Pickering, CY	Caractéristiques	Nº
						Caractéristiques du revenu de 2005	
						Sexe et travail (suite)	
17,555	2,080	14,970	X	25,590	17,005	A travaillé toute l'année à plein temps[59]	530
55,568	47,335	60,457	X	52,169	55,198	Revenu médian d'emploi en 2005 $	531
63,372	50,452	65,452	X	57,596	67,591	Revenu moyen d'emploi en 2005 $	532
856	1,472	808	X	463	1,012	Erreur type de revenu moyen d'emploi $	533
8,605	1,275	7,590	X	14,150	8,770	A travaillé une partie de l'année ou à temps partiel[60]	534
14,760	10,963	16,672	X	17,321	13,655	Revenu médian d'emploi en 2005 $	535
28,432	22,990	30,957	X	28,491	28,996	Revenu moyen d'emploi en 2005 $	536
829	2,424	897	X	567	1,261	Erreur type de revenu moyen d'emploi $	537
26,490	3,175	21,705	X	39,065	26,405	Femmes de 15 ans et plus avec un revenu d'emploi[58]	538
29,798	19,857	25,556	X	23,488	29,738	Revenu médian d'emploi en 2005 $	539
34,132	25,307	30,771	X	28,088	34,799	Revenu moyen d'emploi en 2005 $	540
482	872	407	X	253	424	Erreur type de revenu moyen d'emploi $	541
13,475	1,350	10,290	X	18,805	13,350	A travaillé toute l'année à plein temps[59]	542
44,131	36,318	41,000	X	37,977	44,622	Revenu médian d'emploi en 2005 $	543
48,961	39,742	44,723	X	41,118	50,031	Revenu moyen d'emploi en 2005 $	544
734	1,350	615	X	352	583	Erreur type de revenu moyen d'emploi $	545
11,525	1,590	9,950	X	17,630	11,450	A travaillé une partie de l'année ou à temps partiel[60]	546
11,972	10,390	12,707	X	11,086	12,550	Revenu médian d'emploi en 2005 $	547
19,443	15,785	19,385	X	16,923	20,202	Revenu moyen d'emploi en 2005 $	548
451	903	443	X	268	505	Erreur type de revenu moyen d'emploi $	549
24,320	**3,475**	**22,165**	**X**	**40,020**	**23,960**	**Nombre total des familles économiques dans les ménages privés**	550
						Revenu de la famille économique en 2005	
480	85	355	X	815	445	Moins de 10 000 $	551
445	115	355	X	1,890	505	10 000 $ à 19 999 $	552
970	250	740	X	2,325	800	20 000 $ à 29 999 $	553
1,515	280	1,470	X	2,895	1,295	30 000 $ à 39 999 $	554
1,460	345	1,665	X	3,725	1,520	40 000 $ à 49 999 $	555
1,735	335	1,765	X	3,715	1,630	50 000 $ à 59 999 $	556
1,995	380	1,785	X	3,370	1,700	60 000 $ à 69 999 $	557
1,825	305	1,920	X	3,550	1,790	70 000 $ à 79 999 $	558
1,895	270	1,740	X	3,255	1,780	80 000 $ à 89 999 $	559
1,965	300	1,845	X	2,875	1,920	90 000 $ à 99 999 $	560
10,025	805	8,515	X	11,600	10,560	100 000 $ et plus	561
89,069	68,269	85,847	X	73,591	92,023	Revenu médian des familles $	562
98,995	75,888	94,093	X	81,455	105,650	Revenu moyen des familles $	563
1,018	1,725	856	X	550	1,078	Erreur type de revenu moyen des familles $	564
						Revenu après impôt de la famille économique en 2005	
495	90	375	X	830	455	Moins de 10 000 $	565
470	120	360	X	1,935	515	10 000 $ à 19 999 $	566
1,095	290	880	X	2,665	915	20 000 $ à 29 999 $	567
1,910	385	1,990	X	4,100	1,760	30 000 $ à 39 999 $	568
2,035	455	2,360	X	4,900	2,120	40 000 $ à 49 999 $	569
2,560	485	2,230	X	4,585	2,160	50 000 $ à 59 999 $	570
2,475	395	2,520	X	4,395	2,345	60 000 $ à 69 999 $	571
2,495	340	2,445	X	4,225	2,360	70 000 $ à 79 999 $	572
2,495	275	2,355	X	3,445	2,280	80 000 $ à 89 999 $	573
2,225	220	1,635	X	2,410	1,920	90 000 $ à 99 999 $	574
6,065	420	5,005	X	6,530	7,115	100 000 $ et plus	575
74,732	58,170	71,320	X	62,302	77,274	Revenu médian après impôt des familles $	576
80,457	64,070	76,454	X	67,569	85,018	Revenu moyen après impôt des familles $	577
687	1,405	596	X	404	721	Erreur type de revenu moyen après impôt des familles $	578
						Catégorie de revenu en 2005	
89,760	11,740	77,105	X	139,675	87,235	Population totale dans les ménages privés pour la catégorie de revenu	579
9,770	1,030	4,515	X	18,065	8,640	Au-dessous du seuil de faible revenu avant impôt en 2005	580
10.9	8.8	5.9	X	12.9	9.9	Fréquence du faible revenu avant impôt en 2005 %	581
7,290	635	3,510	X	13,250	6,280	Au-dessous du seuil de faible revenu après impôt en 2005	582
8.1	5.4	4.6	X	9.5	7.2	Fréquence du faible revenu après impôt en 2005 %	583

Nota : Voir les symboles et les abréviations dans les documents d'introduction et voir les documents de référence à la fin de la publication.

Selected characteristics for census divisions and census subdivisions – 100% data and 20% sample data, Ontario, 2006 Census (continued)

No.	Characteristics	Melancthon, TP A	Mono, T A	Mulmur, TP ◆◇	Orangeville, T	Shelburne, T A	Durham CD/DR
	2005 income characteristics						
584	**Total number of private households**	**1,000**	**2,340**	**1,190**	**9,420**	**1,850**	**194,670**
	Household income groups in 2005						
585	Under $10,000	40	90	20	260	60	5,200
586	$10,000 to $19,999	60	75	50	635	135	11,310
587	$20,000 to $29,999	70	110	70	630	150	12,110
588	$30,000 to $39,999	65	150	80	830	180	14,785
589	$40,000 to $49,999	60	125	110	715	200	15,475
590	$50,000 to $59,999	120	185	95	835	170	15,355
591	$60,000 to $69,999	90	195	130	865	165	14,905
592	$70,000 to $79,999	105	145	135	780	210	15,310
593	$80,000 to $89,999	60	135	95	760	155	14,020
594	$90,000 to $99,999	70	125	70	725	115	13,205
595	$100,000 and over	250	1,010	330	2,380	295	62,990
596	Median household income $	66,670	88,757	73,597	69,154	61,643	75,397
597	Average household income $	78,500	108,692	87,083	74,962	66,097	86,391
598	Standard error of average household income $	4,152	4,579	4,514	965	1,918	350
	Household after-tax income groups in 2005						
599	Under $10,000	45	100	25	265	60	5,415
600	$10,000 to $19,999	60	85	70	670	155	12,215
601	$20,000 to $29,999	85	140	65	850	185	14,505
602	$30,000 to $39,999	95	175	140	975	260	19,585
603	$40,000 to $49,999	85	190	110	1,055	220	19,770
604	$50,000 to $59,999	170	230	175	1,040	180	19,660
605	$60,000 to $69,999	110	195	155	1,060	315	19,190
606	$70,000 to $79,999	90	200	85	915	140	17,660
607	$80,000 to $89,999	65	125	110	800	100	15,620
608	$90,000 to $99,999	35	185	70	530	85	12,555
609	$100,000 and over	165	710	175	1,260	140	38,490
610	Median after-tax household income $	57,127	71,953	61,473	58,786	50,948	63,175
611	Average after-tax household income $	64,802	85,346	70,063	62,168	55,331	70,222
612	Standard error of average after-tax household income $	3,012	3,018	3,101	733	1,455	239

Note: See symbols and abbreviations in the introductory material and see reference material at the end of the publication.

Certaines caractéristiques des divisions de recensement et des subdivisions de recensement – Données intégrales et données-échantillon (20 %), Ontario, Recensement de 2006 (suite)

Ajax, T	Brock, TP	Clarington, MU	Mississaugas of Scugog Island, IRI	Oshawa, CY	Pickering, CY	Caractéristiques	N°
						Caractéristiques du revenu de 2005	
28,615	**4,425**	**26,850**	**X**	**54,920**	**28,220**	**Nombre total des ménages privés**	584
						Tranches de revenu des ménages en 2005	
700	155	580	X	1,920	645	Moins de 10 000 $	585
1,170	370	1,160	X	4,760	1,200	10 000 $ à 19 999 $	586
1,605	450	1,365	X	4,655	1,385	20 000 $ à 29 999 $	587
1,970	385	2,115	X	5,115	1,830	30 000 $ à 39 999 $	588
1,835	460	2,190	X	5,480	1,970	40 000 $ à 49 999 $	589
2,220	390	2,180	X	4,845	2,015	50 000 $ à 59 999 $	590
2,255	445	2,200	X	4,260	1,995	60 000 $ à 69 999 $	591
2,090	345	2,270	X	4,475	2,045	70 000 $ à 79 999 $	592
2,100	280	1,920	X	3,800	2,105	80 000 $ à 89 999 $	593
2,250	300	1,955	X	3,155	2,080	90 000 $ à 99 999 $	594
10,425	830	8,920	X	12,455	10,950	100 000 $ et plus	595
81,940	59,608	77,627	X	61,514	84,595	Revenu médian des ménages $	596
92,000	67,002	86,337	X	70,916	97,967	Revenu moyen des ménages $	597
904	1,508	759	X	454	986	Erreur type de revenu moyen des ménages $	598
						Tranches du revenu après impôt des ménages en 2005	
725	165	610	X	1,975	660	Moins de 10 000 $	599
1,260	400	1,280	X	5,115	1,330	10 000 $ à 19 999 $	600
1,840	540	1,660	X	5,690	1,640	20 000 $ à 29 999 $	601
2,485	500	2,790	X	6,800	2,455	30 000 $ à 39 999 $	602
2,580	540	2,975	X	6,430	2,600	40 000 $ à 49 999 $	603
3,000	575	2,765	X	5,805	2,505	50 000 $ à 59 999 $	604
2,795	420	2,800	X	5,255	2,740	60 000 $ à 69 999 $	605
2,685	340	2,590	X	4,655	2,545	70 000 $ à 79 999 $	606
2,650	280	2,450	X	3,690	2,390	80 000 $ à 89 999 $	607
2,285	230	1,715	X	2,585	1,960	90 000 $ à 99 999 $	608
6,305	435	5,210	X	6,900	7,390	100 000 $ et plus	609
68,527	51,787	64,782	X	52,482	70,819	Revenu médian après impôt des ménages $	610
74,822	56,688	70,196	X	58,879	78,929	Revenu moyen après impôt des ménages $	611
620	1,229	538	X	340	666	Erreur type de revenu moyen après impôt des ménages $	612

Nota : Voir les symboles et les abréviations dans les documents d'introduction et voir les documents de référence à la fin de la publication.

Selected characteristics for census divisions and census subdivisions – 100% data and 20% sample data, Ontario, 2006 Census (continued)

No.	Characteristics	Scugog, TP	Uxbridge, TP	Whitby, T	**Elgin CD/DR**	Aylmer, T A	Bayham, MU
	Population characteristics						
1	**Population, 2001[1]**	**20,173**	**17,377**	**87,413**	**81,553**	**7,158**	**6,375**
2	**Population, 2006[2]**	**21,439**	**19,169**	**111,184**	**85,351**	**7,069**	**6,727**
3	Population percentage change, 2001 to 2006	6.3	10.3	27.2	4.7	-1.2	5.5
4	Land area in square kilometres, 2006	474.63	420.65	146.52	1,880.84	6.22	244.99
5	**Total population – 100% data[3]**	**21,440**	**19,170**	**111,180**	**85,350**	**7,070**	**6,725**
	Sex and age groups						
6	Male	10,620	9,520	54,445	42,015	3,355	3,450
7	0 to 4 years	510	510	3,905	2,595	235	275
8	5 to 9 years	660	705	4,090	2,870	225	265
9	10 to 14 years	765	820	4,765	3,115	275	305
10	15 to 19 years	835	800	4,405	3,220	260	325
11	20 to 24 years	650	565	3,480	2,575	250	235
12	25 to 29 years	455	370	2,925	2,220	205	165
13	30 to 34 years	450	385	3,660	2,640	190	190
14	35 to 39 years	615	580	4,345	2,860	200	215
15	40 to 44 years	875	885	5,285	3,460	245	250
16	45 to 49 years	990	930	4,705	3,320	245	265
17	50 to 54 years	920	735	3,660	2,945	205	230
18	55 to 59 years	875	605	3,020	2,755	195	195
19	60 to 64 years	600	460	2,020	2,260	155	165
20	65 to 69 years	450	350	1,340	1,750	125	130
21	70 to 74 years	400	315	1,145	1,265	95	90
22	75 to 79 years	275	250	860	1,045	125	80
23	80 to 84 years	180	155	530	670	70	30
24	85 years and over	125	95	305	445	50	25
25	Female	10,820	9,650	56,740	43,340	3,715	3,275
26	0 to 4 years	430	445	3,675	2,505	255	230
27	5 to 9 years	605	590	3,950	2,665	220	275
28	10 to 14 years	715	770	4,495	3,165	235	280
29	15 to 19 years	830	745	4,175	3,130	280	280
30	20 to 24 years	655	510	3,260	2,415	275	215
31	25 to 29 years	440	320	3,225	2,220	195	140
32	30 to 34 years	450	450	4,135	2,645	190	195
33	35 to 39 years	640	715	4,855	2,900	200	210
34	40 to 44 years	960	955	5,530	3,435	260	255
35	45 to 49 years	1,055	935	4,785	3,300	265	230
36	50 to 54 years	895	745	3,840	3,050	220	230
37	55 to 59 years	860	590	3,140	2,900	225	185
38	60 to 64 years	565	475	2,015	2,245	165	175
39	65 to 69 years	445	395	1,520	1,775	160	125
40	70 to 74 years	410	315	1,360	1,450	140	95
41	75 to 79 years	335	305	1,135	1,330	175	75
42	80 to 84 years	285	220	885	1,140	130	40
43	85 years and over	245	165	755	1,065	130	35
44	**Total population 15 years and over[3]**	**17,750**	**15,330**	**86,290**	**68,430**	**5,625**	**5,095**
	Legal marital status						
45	Never legally married (single)	4,735	4,150	25,345	18,800	1,470	1,460
46	Legally married (and not separated)[4,5]	10,210	8,925	48,940	37,290	3,115	2,945
47	Separated, but still legally married	545	475	2,830	2,765	190	155
48	Divorced	1,225	940	5,260	4,995	345	270
49	Widowed	1,035	845	3,915	4,580	510	260
	Common-law status						
50	Not in a common-law relationship	16,370	14,310	80,650	62,715	5,255	4,665
51	In a common-law relationship	1,385	1,025	5,640	5,715	370	425
52	**Total population – 20% sample data[6]**	**21,155**	**19,075**	**110,455**	**84,255**	**7,000**	**6,725**
	Mother tongue						
53	Single responses	21,065	19,000	109,310	83,785	6,985	6,680
54	English	19,585	17,720	92,680	71,265	5,045	4,760
55	French	285	145	2,165	790	40	55
56	Non-official languages[7]	1,190	1,130	14,465	11,730	1,900	1,865
57	Italian	100	170	1,490	265	40	0
58	Chinese, n.o.s.[61]	10	30	735	70	0	15
59	Cantonese	15	20	445	15	0	0
60	Spanish	50	45	865	270	75	20
61	German	395	245	790	6,680	1,465	1,700
62	Other languages[8]	615	630	10,135	4,430	325	135

Note: See symbols and abbreviations in the introductory material and see reference material at the end of the publication.

Certaines caractéristiques des divisions de recensement et des subdivisions de recensement – Données intégrales et données-échantillon (20 %), Ontario, Recensement de 2006 (suite)

Central Elgin, MU A	Dutton/ Dunwich, MU	Malahide, TP A	Southwold, TP	St. Thomas, CY A	West Elgin, MU	Caractéristiques	N°
						Caractéristiques de la population	
12,293	**3,696**	**8,777**	**4,487**	**33,303**	**5,464**	**Population, 2001[1]**	1
12,723	**3,821**	**8,828**	**4,724**	**36,110**	**5,349**	**Population, 2006[2]**	2
3.5	3.4	0.6	5.3	8.4	-2.1	Variation en pourcentage de la population, 2001 à 2006	3
280.22	294.63	395.07	301.71	35.48	322.52	Superficie des terres en kilomètres carrés, 2006	4
12,725	**3,820**	**8,825**	**4,720**	**36,110**	**5,350**	**Population totale – Données intégrales[3]**	5
						Sexe et groupes d'âge	
6,340	1,875	4,455	2,425	17,460	2,650	Sexe masculin	6
305	110	320	125	1,110	125	0 à 4 ans	7
380	145	415	140	1,155	150	5 à 9 ans	8
430	165	375	195	1,190	175	10 à 14 ans	9
460	165	390	200	1,220	205	15 à 19 ans	10
335	75	305	135	1,065	175	20 à 24 ans	11
235	80	240	100	1,080	115	25 à 29 ans	12
340	95	255	160	1,290	125	30 à 34 ans	13
400	130	290	185	1,275	155	35 à 39 ans	14
595	180	370	220	1,375	225	40 à 44 ans	15
560	160	310	210	1,340	225	45 à 49 ans	16
540	130	315	170	1,160	195	50 à 54 ans	17
525	115	260	150	1,090	225	55 à 59 ans	18
410	90	190	155	925	170	60 à 64 ans	19
305	85	180	90	695	130	65 à 69 ans	20
205	60	105	70	535	100	70 à 74 ans	21
155	40	65	65	440	65	75 à 79 ans	22
90	30	45	40	300	65	80 à 84 ans	23
55	25	30	25	210	25	85 ans et plus	24
6,380	1,940	4,375	2,295	18,650	2,705	Sexe féminin	25
290	80	350	135	1,040	130	0 à 4 ans	26
360	145	355	140	1,030	140	5 à 9 ans	27
475	180	415	190	1,205	185	10 à 14 ans	28
480	140	375	165	1,200	200	15 à 19 ans	29
305	85	255	105	1,055	125	20 à 24 ans	30
240	75	220	100	1,135	110	25 à 29 ans	31
295	125	255	150	1,300	135	30 à 34 ans	32
465	125	305	150	1,280	160	35 à 39 ans	33
560	165	340	195	1,435	225	40 à 44 ans	34
545	145	315	195	1,410	190	45 à 49 ans	35
555	125	275	175	1,240	235	50 à 54 ans	36
520	135	260	165	1,200	210	55 à 59 ans	37
375	95	180	120	975	165	60 à 64 ans	38
300	85	145	90	755	115	65 à 69 ans	39
215	80	95	70	645	115	70 à 74 ans	40
160	55	75	55	635	100	75 à 79 ans	41
145	45	60	65	565	90	80 à 84 ans	42
95	65	100	40	550	60	85 ans et plus	43
10,480	**3,005**	**6,600**	**3,805**	**29,385**	**4,440**	**Population totale de 15 ans et plus[3]**	44
						État matrimonial légal	
2,515	735	1,810	970	8,695	1,150	Jamais légalement marié(e) (célibataire)	45
6,375	1,720	3,980	2,320	14,380	2,460	Légalement marié(e) (et non séparé[e])[4,5]	46
325	105	185	120	1,500	190	Séparé(e), mais toujours légalement marié(e)	47
715	210	310	195	2,680	280	Divorcé(e)	48
550	240	325	200	2,135	360	Veuf(ve)	49
						Union libre	
9,690	2,790	6,225	3,530	26,490	4,070	Ne vivant pas en union libre	50
785	220	380	270	2,895	365	Vivant en union libre	51
12,605	**3,750**	**8,705**	**4,635**	**35,525**	**5,315**	**Population totale – Données-échantillon (20 %)[6]**	52
						Langue maternelle	
12,585	3,750	8,690	4,625	35,205	5,270	Réponses uniques	53
11,340	3,510	5,705	4,275	32,170	4,460	Anglais	54
120	45	30	25	395	70	Français	55
1,125	190	2,955	315	2,635	740	Langues non officielles[7]	56
55	0	10	10	150	0	Italien	57
10	0	0	0	45	0	Chinois, n.d.a.[61]	58
0	0	0	0	15	0	Cantonais	59
20	15	0	0	140	0	Espagnol	60
405	25	2,410	70	440	165	Allemand	61
630	145	530	240	1,845	575	Autres langues[8]	62

Nota : Voir les symboles et les abréviations dans les documents d'introduction et voir les documents de référence à la fin de la publication.

Selected characteristics for census divisions and census subdivisions – 100% data and 20% sample data, Ontario, 2006 Census (continued)

No.	Characteristics	Scugog, TP	Uxbridge, TP	Whitby, T	**Elgin CD/DR**	Aylmer, T A	Bayham, MU
	Population characteristics						
	Mother tongue (continued)						
63	Multiple responses	90	80	1,140	470	15	40
64	English and French	35	15	175	85	0	10
65	English and non-official language	55	60	875	370	10	25
66	French and non-official language	0	0	45	15	0	10
67	English, French and non-official language	0	0	35	0	0	0
	Language spoken most often at home[9]						
68	Single responses	21,115	19,035	109,245	83,810	6,985	6,670
69	English	20,770	18,740	102,640	78,885	6,165	5,640
70	French	90	30	1,060	125	0	10
71	Non-official languages[7]	245	265	5,545	4,795	825	1,025
72	Chinese, n.o.s.[61]	0	20	440	55	0	10
73	Cantonese	15	20	305	10	0	0
74	Panjabi (Punjabi)	20	0	80	60	0	0
75	Italian	20	20	305	50	0	0
76	Spanish	15	0	425	130	35	10
77	Other languages[8]	165	200	3,990	4,495	785	1,005
78	Multiple responses	45	40	1,205	450	10	55
79	English and French	0	0	170	40	0	0
80	English and non-official language	45	40	1,010	405	10	55
81	French and non-official language	0	0	0	0	0	0
82	English, French and non-official language	0	0	20	0	0	0
	Knowledge of official languages[10]						
83	English only	19,740	17,505	100,510	79,960	6,625	6,360
84	French only	15	0	165	15	0	0
85	English and French	1,375	1,525	9,090	3,525	210	140
86	Neither English nor French	20	40	690	755	165	220
	Knowledge of non-official languages[7,11]						
87	Italian	120	265	2,105	310	20	10
88	Spanish	135	160	1,600	1,135	325	165
89	German	475	360	1,300	7,110	1,495	1,775
90	Chinese, n.o.s.[61]	10	50	725	80	0	15
91	Cantonese	15	20	570	15	0	0
92	Panjabi (Punjabi)	30	0	400	100	0	0
93	Portuguese	20	50	815	380	0	15
	First official language spoken[10]						
94	English	20,885	18,900	107,250	82,725	6,800	6,450
95	French	255	120	2,210	745	35	55
96	English and French	0	15	335	40	0	0
97	Neither English nor French	15	40	660	750	160	220
98	Official language minority - (number)[12]	260	125	2,380	760	35	55
99	Official language minority - (percentage)[12]	1.2	0.7	2.2	0.9	0.5	0.8
	Ethnic origin[13]						
100	English	9,020	8,665	37,580	31,405	2,195	1,705
101	Canadian	6,885	6,215	30,130	26,650	2,195	2,090
102	Scottish	6,125	5,290	25,850	19,550	1,410	885
103	Irish	4,845	4,885	24,410	15,755	1,050	875
104	French	1,740	1,670	10,340	7,760	450	435
105	German	2,560	2,460	9,510	15,950	2,055	2,635
106	Italian	675	1,100	7,515	1,925	115	35
107	Chinese	80	130	2,880	285	20	10
108	East Indian	65	115	3,505	245	0	10
109	Dutch (Netherlands)	1,530	1,180	4,845	9,560	1,080	590
110	Polish	660	475	3,960	2,045	65	110
111	Ukrainian	570	440	3,380	1,475	65	135
112	North American Indian	400	375	2,155	1,850	120	120
113	Portuguese	135	160	2,540	835	0	80
114	Filipino	25	30	1,265	180	0	0
	Aboriginal and non-Aboriginal identity						
115	Total Aboriginal identity population[14]	175	120	1,175	910	45	45
116	Total non-Aboriginal identity population	20,980	18,950	109,275	83,345	6,955	6,675

Note: See symbols and abbreviations in the introductory material and see reference material at the end of the publication.

Certaines caractéristiques des divisions de recensement et des subdivisions de recensement – Données intégrales et données-échantillon (20 %), Ontario, Recensement de 2006 (suite)

Central Elgin, MU **A**	Dutton/ Dunwich, MU	Malahide, TP **A**	Southwold, TP	St. Thomas, CY **A**	West Elgin, MU	Caractéristiques	N°
						Caractéristiques de la population	
						Langue maternelle (suite)	
20	0	15	10	320	45	Réponses multiples	63
0	0	0	0	65	10	Anglais et français	64
20	0	15	10	245	40	Anglais et langue non officielle	65
0	0	0	0	10	0	Français et langue non officielle	66
0	0	0	0	0	0	Anglais, français et langue non officielle	67
						Langue parlée le plus souvent à la maison[9]	
12,570	3,745	8,625	4,630	35,295	5,280	Réponses uniques	68
12,250	3,720	7,335	4,530	34,230	5,015	Anglais	69
0	0	0	15	85	10	Français	70
315	25	1,285	90	975	255	Langues non officielles[7]	71
10	0	0	0	35	0	Chinois, n.d.a.[61]	72
0	0	0	0	10	0	Cantonais	73
0	0	0	0	65	0	Pendjabi	74
10	0	0	0	40	0	Italien	75
10	10	0	0	80	0	Espagnol	76
295	20	1,285	90	755	250	Autres langues[8]	77
30	0	80	10	230	30	Réponses multiples	78
0	0	0	0	40	0	Anglais et français	79
35	0	80	0	195	35	Anglais et langue non officielle	80
0	0	0	0	0	0	Français et langue non officielle	81
0	0	0	0	0	0	Anglais, français et langue non officielle	82
						Connaissance des langues officielles[10]	
12,100	3,535	8,285	4,435	33,610	5,000	Anglais seulement	83
0	0	0	0	15	0	Français seulement	84
480	210	240	165	1,815	255	Anglais et français	85
15	10	170	30	85	55	Ni l'anglais ni le français	86
						Connaissance des langues non officielles[7,11]	
80	0	15	0	185	0	Italien	87
85	30	205	25	295	10	Espagnol	88
450	55	2,485	105	590	150	Allemand	89
20	0	0	0	50	0	Chinois, n.d.a.[61]	90
0	0	0	0	15	0	Cantonais	91
0	0	0	0	95	0	Pendjabi	92
20	10	30	30	90	185	Portugais	93
						Première langue officielle parlée[10]	
12,485	3,695	8,505	4,575	35,015	5,200	Anglais	94
105	50	30	25	385	60	Français	95
0	0	0	0	35	0	Anglais et français	96
20	0	170	35	85	55	Ni l'anglais ni le français	97
105	45	30	25	405	60	Minorité de langue officielle - (nombre)[12]	98
0.8	1.2	0.3	0.5	1.1	1.1	Minorité de langue officielle - (pourcentage)[12]	99
						Origine ethnique[13]	
6,000	1,420	2,100	1,855	14,495	1,635	Anglais	100
3,715	1,375	2,250	1,720	11,770	1,530	Canadien	101
3,250	1,225	1,245	1,255	9,005	1,260	Écossais	102
2,550	800	865	1,065	7,515	1,035	Irlandais	103
1,125	340	330	330	4,150	585	Français	104
1,900	575	2,915	490	4,570	815	Allemand	105
320	100	60	145	1,090	65	Italien	106
45	10	0	30	150	15	Chinois	107
10	35	0	0	180	10	Indien de l'Inde	108
1,330	550	1,625	625	3,070	690	Hollandais (Néerlandais)	109
355	115	95	60	1,065	180	Polonais	110
125	95	135	90	695	120	Ukrainien	111
170	75	85	40	990	235	Indien de l'Amérique du Nord	112
85	40	25	115	280	205	Portugais	113
0	0	15	0	170	0	Philippin	114
						Population ayant une identité autochtone et population n'ayant pas d'identité autochtone	
105	25	35	30	555	60	Total de la population ayant une identité autochtone[14]	115
12,500	3,725	8,670	4,600	34,965	5,250	Total de la population n'ayant pas d'identité autochtone	116

Nota : Voir les symboles et les abréviations dans les documents d'introduction et voir les documents de référence à la fin de la publication.

Selected characteristics for census divisions and census subdivisions – 100% data and 20% sample data, Ontario, 2006 Census (continued)

No.	Characteristics	Scugog, TP	Uxbridge, TP	Whitby, T	**Elgin CD/DR**	Aylmer, T A	Bayham, MU
	Population characteristics						
	Aboriginal and non-Aboriginal ancestry						
117	Total Aboriginal ancestry population[15]	450	410	2,655	2,385	135	140
118	Total non-Aboriginal ancestry population	20,710	18,665	107,800	81,870	6,865	6,585
	Registered Indian status						
119	Registered Indian[16]	25	75	365	410	20	25
120	Not a Registered Indian	21,135	19,000	110,090	83,855	6,980	6,695
	Visible minority groups						
121	Total visible minority population[17]	390	440	18,735	2,015	145	105
122	Chinese	75	115	2,110	160	0	10
123	South Asian[18]	75	110	3,680	215	0	10
124	Black	70	75	6,695	500	45	40
125	Filipino	25	20	1,180	155	0	0
126	Latin American	15	40	780	275	85	30
127	Southeast Asian[19]	0	0	345	345	0	0
128	Arab	0	20	715	30	0	0
129	West Asian[20]	10	0	645	15	0	0
130	Korean	40	0	205	100	0	0
131	Japanese	45	30	540	60	0	0
132	Visible minority, n.i.e.[21]	35	15	800	70	0	20
133	Multiple visible minority[22]	10	20	1,030	85	15	0
	Citizenship[23]						
134	Canadian citizens[24]	20,565	18,560	106,230	81,935	6,820	6,295
135	Not Canadian citizens[25]	590	515	4,225	2,325	175	430
	Immigrant status and place of birth[26]						
136	Non-immigrants[27]	18,840	16,820	87,340	72,605	5,495	5,240
137	Born in province of residence	17,335	15,390	77,120	67,455	5,105	4,970
138	Immigrants[28]	2,260	2,220	22,625	11,155	1,500	1,285
139	United States of America	300	155	790	695	50	55
140	Central and South America	55	75	1,815	3,695	975	1,015
141	Caribbean and Bermuda	50	45	3,530	145	10	0
142	United Kingdom	860	945	4,860	1,700	60	65
143	Other Europe	780	810	5,725	4,035	370	130
144	Africa	55	15	1,055	105	25	0
145	Asia and the Middle East	130	150	4,765	705	0	15
146	Oceania and other[29]	25	20	80	70	0	0
147	Non-permanent residents[30]	55	35	490	495	0	195
148	**Total immigrant population[28]**	**2,260**	**2,225**	**22,625**	**11,155**	**1,505**	**1,285**
	Period of immigration						
149	Before 1961	865	810	3,370	3,065	370	125
150	1961 to 1970	505	485	3,865	1,760	185	150
151	1971 to 1980	300	340	4,635	1,735	210	185
152	1981 to 1990	185	185	4,025	1,815	375	290
153	1991 to 2000	290	255	4,660	1,460	155	320
154	1991 to 1995	150	150	2,700	825	95	245
155	1996 to 2000	135	105	1,955	635	65	80
156	2001 to 2006[31]	120	150	2,075	1,320	210	205
	Age at immigration						
157	Under 5 years	345	320	2,410	1,675	275	290
158	5 to 19 years	580	725	7,185	4,310	590	590
159	20 years and over	1,330	1,180	13,035	5,165	640	400
160	**Total population 15 years and over**	**17,490**	**15,215**	**85,585**	**67,315**	**5,550**	**5,085**
	Generation status						
161	1st generation[32]	2,290	2,230	22,215	11,085	1,435	1,260
162	2nd generation[33]	3,615	3,440	21,130	13,040	1,170	1,070
163	3rd generation or more[34]	11,585	9,540	42,240	43,190	2,945	2,755

Note: See symbols and abbreviations in the introductory material and see reference material at the end of the publication.

Certaines caractéristiques des divisions de recensement et des subdivisions de recensement – Données intégrales et données-échantillon (20 %), Ontario, Recensement de 2006 (suite)

Central Elgin, MU **A**	Dutton/ Dunwich, MU	Malahide, TP **A**	Southwold, TP	St. Thomas, CY **A**	West Elgin, MU	Caractéristiques	N°
						Caractéristiques de la population	
						Population ayant une ascendance autochtone et population n'ayant pas d'ascendance autochtone	
275	85	80	120	1,305	245	Total de la population ayant une ascendance autochtone[15]	117
12,335	3,665	8,620	4,515	34,215	5,070	Total de la population n'ayant pas d'ascendance autochtone	118
						Statut d'Indien inscrit	
35	10	0	15	275	25	Indien inscrit[16]	119
12,570	3,740	8,705	4,620	35,245	5,290	Pas un Indien inscrit	120
						Groupes de minorités visibles	
200	40	40	110	1,310	60	Total de la population des minorités visibles[17]	121
25	0	0	15	90	15	Chinois	122
0	10	0	0	195	0	Sud-Asiatique[18]	123
75	10	10	95	210	15	Noir	124
0	0	15	0	140	0	Philippin	125
10	20	0	0	125	0	Latino-Américain	126
30	0	0	0	310	0	Asiatique du Sud-Est[19]	127
20	0	0	0	10	0	Arabe	128
0	0	0	0	20	0	Asiatique occidental[20]	129
10	0	0	0	95	0	Coréen	130
10	0	10	0	35	0	Japonais	131
0	0	0	0	35	20	Minorité visible, n.i.a.[21]	132
35	0	0	0	40	0	Minorités visibles multiples[22]	133
						Citoyenneté[23]	
12,315	3,675	8,360	4,465	34,855	5,140	Citoyens canadiens[24]	134
290	70	345	165	675	175	Ne sont pas des citoyens canadiens[25]	135
						Statut d'immigrant et le lieu de naissance[26]	
11,210	3,475	6,745	4,225	31,760	4,450	Non-immigrants[27]	136
10,430	3,275	6,365	3,990	29,090	4,230	Né dans la province de résidence	137
1,370	260	1,895	325	3,675	845	Immigrants[28]	138
95	40	80	40	265	65	États-Unis d'Amérique	139
85	10	1,275	25	275	15	Amérique centrale et Amérique du Sud	140
20	0	0	0	115	10	Antilles et Bermudes	141
405	50	70	80	850	120	Royaume-Uni	142
675	125	465	160	1,495	620	Autre Europe	143
20	0	0	0	40	0	Afrique	144
55	15	10	10	600	0	Asie et Moyen-Orient	145
0	10	0	15	35	10	Océanie et autres[29]	146
30	15	60	85	90	15	Résidents non permanents[30]	147
1,370	**260**	**1,895**	**320**	**3,675**	**850**	**Population totale des immigrants[28]**	148
						Période d'immigration	
480	100	325	125	1,195	345	Avant 1961	149
290	50	200	95	670	120	1961 à 1970	150
280	25	350	20	510	150	1971 à 1980	151
160	30	365	25	445	115	1981 à 1990	152
95	35	340	10	445	60	1991 à 2000	153
55	20	210	0	160	35	1991 à 1995	154
40	10	125	10	285	20	1996 à 2000	155
65	25	320	45	400	55	2001 à 2006[31]	156
						Âge à l'immigration	
170	30	330	50	410	115	Moins de 5 ans	157
515	55	890	110	1,310	250	5 à 19 ans	158
680	175	680	160	1,950	480	20 ans et plus	159
10,360	**2,935**	**6,470**	**3,715**	**28,795**	**4,405**	**Population totale de 15 ans et plus**	160
						Statut des générations	
1,385	285	1,825	395	3,655	845	1re génération[32]	161
2,025	530	1,550	665	5,180	850	2e génération[33]	162
6,955	2,125	3,095	2,650	19,955	2,705	3e génération ou plus[34]	163

Nota : Voir les symboles et les abréviations dans les documents d'introduction et voir les documents de référence à la fin de la publication.

Selected characteristics for census divisions and census subdivisions – 100% data and 20% sample data, Ontario, 2006 Census (continued)

No.	Characteristics	Scugog, TP	Uxbridge, TP	Whitby, T	**Elgin CD/DR**	Aylmer, T A	Bayham, MU
	Population characteristics						
164	**Total population 1 year and over[35]**	**20,985**	**18,905**	**108,875**	**83,175**	**6,890**	**6,635**
	Place of residence 1 year ago (mobility)						
165	Non-movers	18,845	17,075	96,480	72,140	5,895	6,080
166	Movers	2,140	1,825	12,400	11,035	990	555
167	Non-migrants	935	685	4,730	5,755	515	125
168	Migrants	1,205	1,140	7,670	5,275	475	430
169	Internal migrants	1,165	1,005	7,095	4,785	345	325
170	Intraprovincial migrants	1,120	960	6,715	4,560	340	300
171	Interprovincial migrants	45	40	375	225	0	25
172	External migrants	40	135	570	490	130	105
173	**Total population 5 years and over[36]**	**20,225**	**18,120**	**102,810**	**79,145**	**6,505**	**6,225**
	Place of residence 5 years ago (mobility)						
174	Non-movers	13,135	11,660	57,110	48,255	3,740	4,220
175	Movers	7,090	6,460	45,700	30,885	2,765	2,010
176	Non-migrants	2,335	2,380	15,495	15,515	1,295	570
177	Migrants	4,755	4,080	30,205	15,370	1,470	1,440
178	Internal migrants	4,645	3,890	27,805	13,955	1,140	1,235
179	Intraprovincial migrants	4,430	3,720	26,200	13,000	1,110	1,125
180	Interprovincial migrants	215	170	1,610	955	35	110
181	External migrants	110	190	2,400	1,420	325	200
182	**Total population 15 years and over**	**17,490**	**15,215**	**85,590**	**67,320**	**5,555**	**5,085**
	Highest certificate, diploma or degree[37]						
183	No certificate, diploma or degree	3,810	2,990	15,060	20,050	2,230	2,370
184	Certificate, diploma or degree	13,680	12,225	70,530	47,265	3,325	2,715
185	High school certificate or equivalent[38]	5,370	4,575	23,505	19,265	1,350	1,255
186	Apprenticeship or trades certificate or diploma	1,795	1,230	6,525	6,760	415	460
187	College, CEGEP or other non-university certificate or diploma[39]	3,585	3,000	20,435	13,865	875	775
188	University certificate or diploma below bachelor level[40]	555	620	3,540	1,525	225	30
189	University certificate or degree[41]	2,375	2,805	16,520	5,845	455	200
190	Bachelor's degree	1,450	1,935	11,290	3,690	295	130
191	University certificate or diploma above bachelor level	410	375	2,260	1,095	75	20
192	Degree in medicine, dentistry, veterinary medicine or optometry	55	50	320	135	15	0
193	Master's degree	375	390	2,400	785	70	45
194	Earned doctorate	80	60	255	145	0	10
195	**Total population 15 years and over with postsecondary qualifications**	**8,310**	**7,650**	**47,025**	**28,000**	**1,975**	**1,460**
	Major field of study - Classification of Instructional Programs, 2000[42]						
196	Education	705	680	3,255	1,850	195	60
197	Visual and performing arts, and communications technologies	380	290	1,730	735	40	20
198	Humanities	455	390	2,035	1,030	80	95
199	Social and behavioural sciences and law	840	910	5,700	2,195	130	85
200	Business, management and public administration	1,560	1,385	11,080	5,260	320	220
201	Physical and life sciences and technologies	210	245	1,490	415	10	30
202	Mathematics, computer and information sciences	295	265	2,440	690	35	30
203	Architecture, engineering, and related technologies	2,095	1,865	9,975	6,935	440	475
204	Agriculture, natural resources and conservation	285	215	600	1,140	95	75
205	Health, parks, recreation and fitness	1,065	960	6,165	5,735	470	240
206	Personal, protective and transportation services	420	440	2,540	2,000	145	115
207	Other fields of study[43]	0	0	0	0	0	0
	Location of study[44]						
208	Inside Canada	7,535	6,840	40,760	25,920	1,870	1,360
209	Outside Canada	775	815	6,265	2,080	105	95
210	**Total population 15 years and over**	**17,490**	**15,215**	**85,590**	**67,320**	**5,555**	**5,085**
	Unpaid work						
211	Males 15 years and over	8,590	7,445	41,390	33,050	2,600	2,595
212	Reported unpaid work[45]	7,920	6,860	38,085	30,410	2,325	2,405
213	Housework and child care and care or assistance to seniors	625	610	4,170	2,720	270	230
214	Housework and child care only	2,290	2,145	13,865	9,075	660	655

Note: See symbols and abbreviations in the introductory material and see reference material at the end of the publication.

Certaines caractéristiques des divisions de recensement et des subdivisions de recensement – Données intégrales et données-échantillon (20 %), Ontario, Recensement de 2006 (suite)

Central Elgin, MU A	Dutton/ Dunwich, MU	Malahide, TP A	Southwold, TP	St. Thomas, CY A	West Elgin, MU	Caractéristiques	N°
						Caractéristiques de la population	
12,480	**3,715**	**8,540**	**4,600**	**35,040**	**5,270**	**Population totale de 1 an et plus[35]**	164
						Lieu de résidence 1 an auparavant (mobilité)	
11,275	3,330	7,530	4,290	28,900	4,835	Personnes n'ayant pas déménagé	165
1,205	390	1,010	310	6,135	435	Personnes ayant déménagé	166
420	85	490	55	3,870	190	Non-migrants	167
780	300	520	260	2,265	245	Migrants	168
720	290	465	235	2,165	245	Migrants internes	169
700	285	465	235	1,995	245	Migrants infraprovinciaux	170
25	10	0	0	170	0	Migrants interprovinciaux	171
60	10	55	25	100	0	Migrants externes	172
12,010	**3,565**	**8,035**	**4,370**	**33,375**	**5,055**	**Population totale de 5 ans et plus[36]**	173
						Lieu de résidence 5 ans auparavant (mobilité)	
8,435	2,570	5,595	3,120	16,960	3,625	Personnes n'ayant pas déménagé	174
3,580	995	2,440	1,245	16,415	1,430	Personnes ayant déménagé	175
1,310	305	1,200	470	9,875	490	Non-migrants	176
2,270	690	1,240	780	6,535	940	Migrants	177
2,145	670	1,025	700	6,125	910	Migrants internes	178
2,045	635	990	685	5,555	850	Migrants infraprovinciaux	179
105	30	35	10	570	55	Migrants interprovinciaux	180
125	20	215	85	410	35	Migrants externes	181
10,360	**2,935**	**6,475**	**3,715**	**28,790**	**4,405**	**Population totale de 15 ans et plus**	182
						Plus haut certificat, diplôme ou grade[37]	
2,210	780	2,565	835	7,435	1,635	Aucun certificat, diplôme ou grade	183
8,150	2,155	3,910	2,880	21,355	2,765	Certificat, diplôme ou grade	184
2,970	885	1,675	1,145	8,735	1,245	Diplôme d'études secondaires ou l'équivalent[38]	185
970	335	660	445	2,985	490	Certificat ou diplôme d'apprenti ou d'une école de métiers	186
2,490	645	1,130	825	6,395	735	Certificat ou diplôme d'un collège, d'un cégep ou d'un autre établissement d'enseignement non universitaire[39]	187
280	90	150	60	640	60	Certificat ou diplôme universitaire inférieur au baccalauréat[40]	188
1,445	205	305	405	2,600	230	Certificat ou grade universitaire[41]	189
860	155	185	280	1,630	155	Baccalauréat	190
310	25	75	65	475	45	Certificat ou diplôme universitaire supérieur au baccalauréat	191
35	0	15	0	60	10	Diplôme en médecine, en art dentaire, en médecine vétérinaire ou en optométrie	192
210	15	20	45	350	20	Maîtrise	193
40	0	10	10	85	0	Doctorat acquis	194
5,180	**1,275**	**2,240**	**1,730**	**12,620**	**1,520**	**Population totale de 15 ans et plus avec titres du niveau postsecondaire**	195
						Principal domaine d'études - Classification des programmes d'enseignement, 2000[42]	
370	100	110	120	785	105	Éducation	196
185	55	15	65	310	45	Arts visuels et d'interprétation, et technologie des communications	197
245	45	50	65	400	45	Sciences humaines	198
505	85	125	140	1,025	100	Sciences sociales et de comportements, et droit	199
915	210	395	345	2,610	245	Commerce, gestion et administration publique	200
110	15	35	15	150	40	Sciences physiques et de la vie, et technologies	201
85	20	35	55	405	25	Mathématiques, informatique et sciences de l'information	202
1,195	335	740	455	2,870	415	Architecture, génie et services connexes	203
270	90	165	75	265	105	Agriculture, ressources naturelles et conservation	204
1,015	225	375	300	2,845	265	Santé, parcs, récréation et conditionnement physique	205
295	85	190	80	945	140	Services personnels, de protection et de transport	206
0	0	0	0	0	0	Autres domaines d'études[43]	207
						Lieu des études[44]	
4,815	1,190	2,110	1,650	11,570	1,360	À l'intérieur du Canada	208
365	80	130	80	1,055	155	À l'extérieur du Canada	209
10,360	**2,935**	**6,475**	**3,715**	**28,790**	**4,405**	**Population totale de 15 ans et plus**	210
						Travail non rémunéré	
5,175	1,445	3,325	1,935	13,785	2,185	Hommes de 15 ans et plus	211
4,840	1,350	3,045	1,845	12,585	2,015	Travail non rémunéré déclaré[45]	212
505	130	310	220	895	160	Travaux ménagers et soins aux enfants et soins ou aide aux personnes âgées	213
1,440	475	925	500	3,860	560	Travaux ménagers et soins aux enfants seulement	214

Nota : Voir les symboles et les abréviations dans les documents d'introduction et voir les documents de référence à la fin de la publication.

Selected characteristics for census divisions and census subdivisions – 100% data and 20% sample data, Ontario, 2006 Census (continued)

No.	Characteristics	Scugog, TP	Uxbridge, TP	Whitby, T	**Elgin CD/DR**	Aylmer, T A	Bayham, MU
	Population characteristics						
	Unpaid work (continued)						
215	Housework and care or assistance to seniors only	620	550	2,840	2,735	185	280
216	Child care and care or assistance to seniors only	10	0	45	50	0	10
217	Housework only	4,310	3,495	16,710	15,455	1,150	1,200
218	Child care only	50	45	250	280	55	20
219	Care or assistance to seniors only	15	15	195	95	0	20
220	Females 15 years and over	8,900	7,770	44,195	34,270	2,950	2,490
221	Reported unpaid work[45]	8,430	7,375	41,400	32,405	2,775	2,380
222	Housework and child care and care or assistance to seniors	985	1,030	5,580	4,320	440	335
223	Housework and child care only	2,505	2,310	15,635	10,395	855	725
224	Housework and care or assistance to seniors only	820	805	3,465	3,265	230	275
225	Child care and care or assistance to seniors only	10	10	35	10	0	0
226	Housework only	4,070	3,175	16,305	14,200	1,225	1,010
227	Child care only	35	35	275	130	15	15
228	Care or assistance to seniors only	10	0	100	80	15	0
	Labour force activity						
229	Males 15 years and over	8,590	7,440	41,390	33,045	2,600	2,595
230	In the labour force	6,340	5,795	32,560	24,740	1,835	1,920
231	Employed	5,985	5,650	31,015	23,515	1,735	1,820
232	Unemployed	350	145	1,545	1,220	100	100
233	Not in the labour force	2,250	1,645	8,830	8,310	770	675
234	Participation rate	73.8	77.9	78.7	74.9	70.6	74.0
235	Employment rate	69.7	75.9	74.9	71.2	66.7	70.1
236	Unemployment rate	5.5	2.5	4.7	4.9	5.4	5.2
237	Females 15 years and over	8,900	7,770	44,195	34,270	2,955	2,490
238	In the labour force	5,865	5,100	30,320	20,960	1,605	1,375
239	Employed	5,465	4,815	28,360	19,680	1,510	1,235
240	Unemployed	395	285	1,960	1,275	95	135
241	Not in the labour force	3,030	2,675	13,880	13,310	1,345	1,115
242	Participation rate	65.9	65.6	68.6	61.2	54.3	55.2
243	Employment rate	61.4	62.0	64.2	57.4	51.1	49.6
244	Unemployment rate	6.7	5.6	6.5	6.1	5.9	9.8
245	Both sexes - Participation rate	69.8	71.6	73.5	67.9	62.1	64.8
246	15 to 24 years	77.6	69.1	68.1	70.7	71.2	64.8
247	25 years and over	68.2	72.1	74.6	67.3	59.8	64.8
248	Both sexes - Employment rate	65.5	68.8	69.4	64.2	58.5	60.2
249	15 to 24 years	66.7	64.8	57.6	61.1	64.2	52.6
250	25 years and over	65.3	69.6	71.9	64.8	57.2	62.2
251	Both sexes - Unemployment rate	6.1	3.9	5.6	5.5	5.5	7.1
252	15 to 24 years	14.1	6.4	15.4	13.7	9.3	19.1
253	25 years and over	4.3	3.4	3.6	3.7	4.5	4.0
254	**Total labour force 15 years and over**	**12,205**	**10,895**	**62,880**	**45,695**	**3,440**	**3,295**
	Industry - North American Industry Classification System 2002						
255	Industry - Not applicable[46]	150	120	890	555	50	20
256	All industries[47]	12,060	10,775	61,990	45,140	3,390	3,270
257	11 Agriculture, forestry, fishing and hunting	575	455	290	3,180	155	530
258	21 Mining and oil and gas extraction	15	40	120	65	10	15
259	22 Utilities	185	125	1,945	150	45	0
260	23 Construction	995	1,170	3,490	2,505	175	255
261	31-33 Manufacturing	1,550	895	6,540	10,855	785	920
262	41 Wholesale trade	550	710	3,555	1,655	115	65
263	44-45 Retail trade	1,445	1,010	6,930	4,430	340	265
264	48-49 Transportation and warehousing	550	465	2,355	2,945	205	240
265	51 Information and cultural industries	230	195	2,250	575	40	30
266	52 Finance and insurance	415	420	4,505	845	85	45
267	53 Real estate and rental and leasing	240	280	1,400	425	15	35
268	54 Professional, scientific and technical services	660	990	4,810	1,595	110	90
269	55 Management of companies and enterprises	10	20	90	10	0	0
270	56 Administrative and support, waste management and remediation services	490	535	2,470	2,005	145	120
271	61 Educational services	1,000	885	4,610	2,055	190	85
272	62 Health care and social assistance	985	785	5,745	4,880	345	165

Note: See symbols and abbreviations in the introductory material and see reference material at the end of the publication.

Certaines caractéristiques des divisions de recensement et des subdivisions de recensement – Données intégrales et données-échantillon (20 %), Ontario, Recensement de 2006 (suite)

Central Elgin, MU A	Dutton/ Dunwich, MU	Malahide, TP A	Southwold, TP	St. Thomas, CY A	West Elgin, MU	Caractéristiques	N°
						Caractéristiques de la population	
						Travail non rémunéré (suite)	
500	130	335	150	960	195	Travaux ménagers et soins ou aide aux personnes âgées seulement	215
10	0	15	0	15	10	Soins aux enfants et soins ou aide aux personnes âgées seulement	216
2,340	605	1,415	960	6,710	1,080	Travaux ménagers seulement	217
35	10	30	10	105	10	Soins aux enfants seulement	218
10	10	10	0	50	0	Soins ou aide aux personnes âgées seulement	219
5,185	1,490	3,150	1,775	15,010	2,215	Femmes de 15 ans et plus	220
4,910	1,445	2,990	1,710	14,055	2,130	Travail non rémunéré déclaré[45]	221
705	210	505	310	1,450	355	Travaux ménagers et soins aux enfants et soins ou aide aux personnes âgées	222
1,605	485	1,045	495	4,615	570	Travaux ménagers et soins aux enfants seulement	223
495	135	350	165	1,380	230	Travaux ménagers et soins ou aide aux personnes âgées seulement	224
0	10	0	0	10	0	Soins aux enfants et soins ou aide aux personnes âgées seulement	225
2,105	585	1,085	725	6,505	955	Travaux ménagers seulement	226
0	10	10	0	65	10	Soins aux enfants seulement	227
0	10	0	0	30	15	Soins ou aide aux personnes âgées seulement	228
						Activité	
5,170	1,445	3,325	1,935	13,785	2,185	Hommes de 15 ans et plus	229
4,070	1,110	2,745	1,580	9,895	1,580	Population active	230
3,865	1,070	2,675	1,545	9,290	1,515	Personnes occupées	231
205	40	70	35	605	65	Chômeurs	232
1,105	335	580	355	3,885	605	Inactifs	233
78.7	76.8	82.6	81.7	71.8	72.3	Taux d'activité	234
74.8	74.0	80.5	79.8	67.4	69.3	Taux d'emploi	235
5.0	3.6	2.6	2.2	6.1	4.1	Taux de chômage	236
5,185	1,490	3,145	1,780	15,010	2,215	Femmes de 15 ans et plus	237
3,465	990	1,910	1,310	9,135	1,170	Population active	238
3,285	955	1,765	1,265	8,540	1,115	Personnes occupées	239
175	35	145	40	595	50	Chômeuses	240
1,720	500	1,235	470	5,880	1,045	Inactives	241
66.8	66.4	60.7	73.6	60.9	52.8	Taux d'activité	242
63.4	64.1	56.1	71.1	56.9	50.3	Taux d'emploi	243
5.1	3.5	7.6	3.1	6.5	4.3	Taux de chômage	244
72.7	71.4	71.9	77.9	66.1	62.5	Les deux sexes - Taux d'activité	245
72.7	64.9	70.6	80.0	73.1	56.3	15 à 24 ans	246
72.7	72.8	72.3	77.7	64.8	63.8	25 ans et plus	247
69.0	69.0	68.6	75.9	61.9	59.8	Les deux sexes - Taux d'emploi	248
64.0	59.1	63.4	75.2	60.8	49.3	15 à 24 ans	249
70.0	71.0	70.0	75.7	62.1	61.9	25 ans et plus	250
5.1	3.8	4.5	2.8	6.3	4.4	Les deux sexes - Taux de chômage	251
12.0	9.8	10.3	4.2	16.8	12.5	15 à 24 ans	252
3.8	2.5	3.2	2.3	4.1	2.8	25 ans et plus	253
7,530	**2,100**	**4,655**	**2,890**	**19,025**	**2,750**	**Population active totale de 15 ans et plus**	254
						Industrie - Système de classification des industries de l'Amérique du Nord de 2002	
80	10	15	0	325	50	Industrie - Sans objet[46]	255
7,455	2,090	4,640	2,890	18,705	2,695	Toutes les industries[47]	256
495	255	890	405	105	335	11 Agriculture, foresterie, pêche et chasse	257
15	0	10	0	20	0	21 Extraction minière et extraction de pétrole et de gaz	258
30	0	30	10	30	10	22 Services publics	259
445	135	370	200	755	180	23 Construction	260
1,265	465	910	555	5,305	645	31-33 Fabrication	261
335	95	175	135	645	80	41 Commerce de gros	262
815	215	355	265	1,935	245	44-45 Commerce de détail	263
475	115	470	155	1,100	180	48-49 Transport et entreposage	264
75	40	75	15	265	20	51 Industrie de l'information et industrie culturelle	265
155	75	35	45	330	75	52 Finance et assurances	266
85	0	15	35	200	25	53 Services immobiliers et services de location et de location à bail	267
300	75	150	135	650	75	54 Services professionnels, scientifiques et techniques	268
0	0	0	0	10	0	55 Gestion de sociétés et d'entreprises	269
360	85	115	80	975	110	56 Services administratifs, services de soutien, services de gestion des déchets et services d'assainissement	270
460	55	145	190	830	100	61 Services d'enseignement	271
990	210	340	310	2,360	160	62 Soins de santé et assistance sociale	272

Nota : Voir les symboles et les abréviations dans les documents d'introduction et voir les documents de référence à la fin de la publication.

Selected characteristics for census divisions and census subdivisions – 100% data and 20% sample data, Ontario, 2006 Census (continued)

No.	Characteristics	Scugog, TP	Uxbridge, TP	Whitby, T	**Elgin CD/DR**	Aylmer, T A	Bayham, MU
	Population characteristics						
	Industry - North American Industry Classification System 2002 (continued)						
273	71 Arts, entertainment and recreation	480	430	1,295	685	55	50
274	72 Accommodation and food services	690	470	3,385	2,640	245	110
275	81 Other services (except public administration)	625	405	2,375	2,315	195	210
276	91 Public administration	360	485	3,815	1,315	115	55
	Class of worker						
277	Class of worker - Not applicable[46]	150	120	890	555	50	20
278	All classes of worker[47]	12,055	10,775	61,995	45,135	3,390	3,275
279	Paid workers	10,710	9,400	58,160	40,990	3,165	2,815
280	Employees	10,100	8,690	56,395	39,645	3,115	2,695
281	Self-employed (incorporated)	610	710	1,770	1,345	50	120
282	Self-employed (unincorporated)	1,315	1,330	3,670	3,935	230	395
283	Unpaid family workers	35	40	160	215	0	60
	Occupation - National Occupational Classification for Statistics 2006						
284	Male labour force 15 years and over	6,340	5,795	32,560	24,740	1,835	1,920
285	Occupation - Not applicable[46]	80	40	335	270	20	10
286	All occupations[47]	6,260	5,760	32,225	24,470	1,815	1,910
287	A Management occupations	810	990	5,300	1,870	185	125
288	B Business, finance and administrative occupations	365	350	3,650	1,705	120	75
289	C Natural and applied sciences and related occupations	395	435	3,845	1,095	70	40
290	D Health occupations	95	75	530	350	10	0
291	E Occupations in social science, education, government service and religion	280	255	1,580	725	65	60
292	F Occupations in art, culture, recreation and sport	120	160	825	200	20	0
293	G Sales and service occupations	1,160	1,150	6,590	3,330	280	125
294	H Trades, transport and equipment operators and related occupations	1,990	1,635	7,310	8,180	600	755
295	I Occupations unique to primary industry	520	495	580	2,245	130	300
296	J Occupations unique to processing, manufacturing and utilities	510	210	2,010	4,765	325	415
297	Female labour force 15 years and over	5,865	5,100	30,320	20,955	1,605	1,370
298	Occupation - Not applicable[46]	65	85	555	290	25	10
299	All occupations[47]	5,800	5,015	29,765	20,670	1,580	1,360
300	A Management occupations	475	420	2,810	1,180	95	65
301	B Business, finance and administrative occupations	1,405	1,470	9,610	4,575	300	260
302	C Natural and applied sciences and related occupations	210	150	1,075	410	20	10
303	D Health occupations	495	440	2,620	2,340	195	90
304	E Occupations in social science, education, government service and religion	625	625	3,975	1,875	170	80
305	F Occupations in art, culture, recreation and sport	245	180	960	480	40	10
306	G Sales and service occupations	1,780	1,285	7,315	5,945	480	375
307	H Trades, transport and equipment operators and related occupations	195	150	465	695	65	80
308	I Occupations unique to primary industry	205	230	195	1,000	35	190
309	J Occupations unique to processing, manufacturing and utilities	155	55	735	2,160	160	195
310	**Total employed labour force 15 years and over**	**11,455**	**10,465**	**59,380**	**43,200**	**3,250**	**3,060**
	Place of work status						
311	Males	5,985	5,650	31,020	23,520	1,735	1,820
312	Usual place of work	4,420	3,700	25,190	18,340	1,450	1,180
313	At home	620	710	1,765	2,060	55	320
314	Outside Canada	15	10	115	170	0	10
315	No fixed workplace address	930	1,230	3,945	2,945	220	310
316	Females	5,465	4,815	28,365	19,680	1,510	1,240
317	Usual place of work	4,595	3,925	24,895	17,110	1,375	975
318	At home	590	625	2,045	1,680	70	180
319	Outside Canada	10	0	80	30	0	0
320	No fixed workplace address	275	255	1,335	865	75	85

Note: See symbols and abbreviations in the introductory material and see reference material at the end of the publication.

Central Elgin, MU A	Dutton/ Dunwich, MU	Malahide, TP A	Southwold, TP	St. Thomas, CY A	West Elgin, MU	Caractéristiques	N°
						Caractéristiques de la population	
						Industrie - Système de classification des industries de l'Amérique du Nord de 2002 (suite)	
160	40	25	20	290	35	71 Arts, spectacles et loisirs	273
370	100	135	110	1,425	145	72 Hébergement et services de restauration	274
330	75	285	135	910	170	81 Autres services (sauf les administrations publiques)	275
275	35	90	90	560	85	91 Administrations publiques	276
						Catégorie de travailleurs	
80	10	20	0	325	55	Catégorie de travailleurs - Sans objet[46]	277
7,450	2,090	4,640	2,890	18,705	2,700	Toutes les catégories de travailleurs[47]	278
6,675	1,790	3,965	2,610	17,715	2,255	Travailleurs rémunérés	279
6,370	1,705	3,680	2,490	17,475	2,115	Employés	280
305	80	285	115	245	140	Travailleurs autonomes (entreprise constituée en société)	281
730	290	630	245	975	440	Travailleurs autonomes (entreprise non constituée en société)	282
50	10	45	40	15	0	Travailleurs familiaux non rémunérés	283
						Profession - Classification nationale des professions pour statistiques de 2006	
4,070	1,110	2,745	1,580	9,895	1,580	Hommes actifs de 15 ans et plus	284
50	0	0	0	145	40	Profession - Sans objet[46]	285
4,020	1,110	2,740	1,580	9,750	1,545	Toutes les professions[47]	286
445	75	145	95	725	80	A Gestion	287
290	65	110	125	850	60	B Affaires, finance et administration	288
230	35	115	60	480	65	C Sciences naturelles et appliquées et professions apparentées	289
90	0	20	20	190	0	D Secteur de la santé	290
180	15	15	50	305	25	E Sciences sociales, enseignement, administration publique et religion	291
60	0	20	10	80	0	F Arts, culture, sports et loisirs	292
625	80	235	185	1,650	145	G Ventes et services	293
1,290	440	1,150	480	2,840	620	H Métiers, transport et machinerie	294
315	210	550	315	185	235	I Professions propres au secteur primaire	295
500	175	370	240	2,435	305	J Transformation, fabrication et services d'utilité publique	296
3,465	990	1,910	1,310	9,130	1,170	Femmes actives de 15 ans et plus	297
35	10	10	0	180	15	Profession - Sans objet[46]	298
3,430	980	1,900	1,310	8,955	1,155	Toutes les professions[47]	299
320	60	110	55	395	75	A Gestion	300
890	220	420	320	1,895	270	B Affaires, finance et administration	301
60	15	30	35	205	30	C Sciences naturelles et appliquées et professions apparentées	302
490	100	220	145	1,030	65	D Secteur de la santé	303
370	85	100	120	890	60	E Sciences sociales, enseignement, administration publique et religion	304
90	20	50	40	210	10	F Arts, culture, sports et loisirs	305
800	330	385	400	2,855	315	G Ventes et services	306
105	15	95	25	265	45	H Métiers, transport et machinerie	307
135	45	295	70	105	115	I Professions propres au secteur primaire	308
165	80	200	90	1,095	160	J Transformation, fabrication et services d'utilité publique	309
7,150	**2,025**	**4,440**	**2,815**	**17,830**	**2,635**	**Population active occupée totale de 15 ans et plus**	310
						Catégorie de lieu de travail	
3,865	1,065	2,680	1,545	9,290	1,515	Hommes	311
2,985	770	1,710	1,180	8,065	1,005	Lieu habituel de travail	312
350	150	460	215	250	255	À domicile	313
45	10	10	0	70	15	En dehors du Canada	314
480	135	495	155	910	235	Sans adresse de travail fixe	315
3,290	955	1,765	1,265	8,535	1,120	Femmes	316
2,795	810	1,390	1,045	7,840	875	Lieu habituel de travail	317
340	95	265	155	390	185	À domicile	318
10	0	0	10	10	0	En dehors du Canada	319
140	50	110	55	300	50	Sans adresse de travail fixe	320

Nota : Voir les symboles et les abréviations dans les documents d'introduction et voir les documents de référence à la fin de la publication.

Selected characteristics for census divisions and census subdivisions – 100% data and 20% sample data, Ontario, 2006 Census (continued)

No.	Characteristics	Scugog, TP	Uxbridge, TP	Whitby, T	**Elgin CD/DR**	Aylmer, T A	Bayham, MU
	Population characteristics						
321	**Total employed labour force 15 years and over with usual place of work or no fixed workplace address**	**10,225**	**9,115**	**55,365**	**39,260**	**3,115**	**2,550**
	Mode of transportation						
322	Males	5,350	4,930	29,135	21,285	1,670	1,490
323	Car, truck, van, as driver	4,565	4,180	24,150	17,745	1,375	1,310
324	Car, truck, van, as passenger	440	400	1,715	1,895	180	120
325	Public transit	55	105	2,385	60	0	0
326	Walked	220	165	605	1,005	105	50
327	All other modes	80	85	275	575	10	10
328	Females	4,875	4,180	26,230	17,970	1,445	1,055
329	Car, truck, van, as driver	4,000	3,300	18,960	14,365	1,060	885
330	Car, truck, van, as passenger	485	455	2,860	1,800	180	70
331	Public transit	100	120	3,345	180	0	10
332	Walked	235	225	830	1,415	190	75
333	All other modes	50	75	240	220	10	15
334	**Total population 15 years and over who worked since January 1, 2005**	**13,025**	**11,775**	**67,110**	**48,915**	**3,790**	**3,640**
	Language used most often at work						
335	Single responses	13,010	11,765	66,840	48,790	3,770	3,605
336	English	12,985	11,695	66,275	48,235	3,700	3,395
337	French	15	20	380	40	0	0
338	Non-official languages[7]	10	45	180	510	70	215
339	Chinese, n.o.s.[61]	0	15	25	0	0	0
340	Cantonese	0	10	20	0	0	0
341	Other languages[8]	10	20	130	510	70	215
342	Multiple responses	15	15	270	130	15	35
343	English and French	10	10	175	10	0	0
344	English and non-official language	0	10	90	120	20	35
345	French and non-official language	0	0	0	0	0	0
346	English, French and non-official language	0	0	0	0	0	0
	Dwelling and household characteristics						
347	**Total number of occupied private dwellings**	**7,705**	**6,655**	**37,240**	**32,205**	**2,695**	**2,195**
	Housing tenure						
348	Owned	6,755	5,735	31,290	24,615	1,930	1,775
349	Rented	945	920	5,955	7,585	765	420
350	Band housing	0	0	0	0	0	0
	Structural type of dwelling						
351	Single-detached house	6,960	5,555	26,410	24,750	1,875	1,940
352	Semi-detached house	140	105	1,295	1,195	125	25
353	Row house	90	270	4,000	925	175	60
354	Apartment, duplex	45	105	750	785	60	10
355	Apartment, building that has five or more storeys	0	10	2,375	745	0	0
356	Apartment, building that has fewer than five storeys	435	610	2,305	3,355	375	55
357	Other single-attached house	15	10	25	155	60	5
358	Movable dwelling[48]	10	5	75	295	15	100
	Condition of dwelling						
359	Regular maintenance only	5,010	4,515	28,290	21,235	1,740	1,480
360	Minor repairs	2,195	1,825	7,655	8,525	785	535
361	Major repairs	500	315	1,295	2,445	165	180
	Period of construction						
362	Before 1946	1,465	1,155	1,335	9,600	615	550
363	1946 to 1960	745	510	2,705	4,310	455	355
364	1961 to 1970	750	715	2,160	3,535	295	230
365	1971 to 1980	1,290	865	4,935	4,705	365	330
366	1981 to 1985	635	505	3,175	1,615	175	100
367	1986 to 1990	875	720	4,815	1,870	280	180
368	1991 to 1995	445	540	4,200	2,085	285	145
369	1996 to 2000	690	655	4,745	1,890	110	155
370	2001 to 2006[49]	810	995	9,165	2,590	110	140

Note: See symbols and abbreviations in the introductory material and see reference material at the end of the publication.

Certaines caractéristiques des divisions de recensement et des subdivisions de recensement – Données intégrales et données-échantillon (20 %), Ontario, Recensement de 2006 (suite)

Central Elgin, MU A	Dutton/ Dunwich, MU	Malahide, TP A	Southwold, TP	St. Thomas, CY A	West Elgin, MU	Caractéristiques	N°
						Caractéristiques de la population	
6,400	**1,765**	**3,700**	**2,435**	**17,115**	**2,175**	**Population active occupée totale de 15 ans et plus ayant un lieu habituel de travail ou sans adresse de travail fixe**	321
						Mode de transport	
3,470	905	2,200	1,330	8,970	1,240	Hommes	322
2,965	765	1,880	1,165	7,300	995	Automobile, camion ou fourgonnette, en tant que conducteur	323
295	60	180	70	845	135	Automobile, camion ou fourgonnette, en tant que passager	324
10	0	0	20	20	10	Transport en commun	325
130	45	110	45	455	65	À pied	326
70	35	35	35	345	35	Tous les autres modes	327
2,935	860	1,495	1,105	8,140	930	Femmes	328
2,600	725	1,305	975	6,055	755	Automobile, camion ou fourgonnette, en tant que conductrice	329
160	50	100	95	1,085	60	Automobile, camion ou fourgonnette, en tant que passagère	330
10	0	0	15	135	0	Transport en commun	331
120	65	85	10	775	100	À pied	332
45	20	10	10	100	15	Tous les autres modes	333
7,965	**2,195**	**5,080**	**3,025**	**20,230**	**2,980**	**Population totale de 15 ans et plus ayant travaillé depuis le 1er janvier 2005**	334
						Langue utilisée le plus souvent au travail	
7,960	2,195	5,040	3,025	20,220	2,960	Réponses uniques	335
7,945	2,190	4,880	3,015	20,190	2,920	Anglais	336
10	0	0	10	15	0	Français	337
0	0	160	0	15	35	Langues non officielles[7]	338
0	0	0	0	0	0	Chinois, n.d.a.[61]	339
0	0	0	0	0	0	Cantonais	340
10	0	160	0	10	35	Autres langues[8]	341
0	0	40	0	10	25	Réponses multiples	342
0	0	0	0	0	10	Anglais et français	343
0	0	35	0	10	20	Anglais et langue non officielle	344
0	0	0	0	0	0	Français et langue non officielle	345
0	0	0	0	0	0	Anglais, français et langue non officielle	346
						Caractéristiques des logements et des ménages	
4,775	**1,390**	**2,730**	**1,605**	**14,735**	**2,075**	**Nombre total de logements privés occupés**	347
						Mode d'occupation	
4,240	1,190	2,275	1,425	10,045	1,730	Possédé	348
535	200	455	175	4,690	345	Loué	349
0	0	0	0	0	0	Logement de bande	350
						Type de construction résidentielle	
4,395	1,285	2,525	1,575	9,280	1,880	Maison individuelle non attenante	351
35	15	25	10	945	15	Maison jumelée	352
110	30	0	0	540	5	Maison en rangée	353
60	10	15	5	610	20	Appartement, duplex	354
0	0	0	0	745	0	Appartement, immeuble de cinq étages ou plus	355
145	40	15	10	2,590	125	Appartement, immeuble de moins de cinq étages	356
30	15	10	0	25	5	Autre maison individuelle attenante	357
10	0	145	0	0	25	Logement mobile[48]	358
						État du logement	
3,220	915	1,630	1,000	10,045	1,195	Entretien régulier seulement	359
1,255	380	960	475	3,445	675	Réparations mineures	360
295	100	135	125	1,240	200	Réparations majeures	361
						Période de construction	
1,360	605	700	610	4,350	805	Avant 1946	362
760	115	325	80	1,835	380	1946 à 1960	363
550	70	315	160	1,755	160	1961 à 1970	364
515	160	510	190	2,380	250	1971 à 1980	365
180	75	180	95	755	45	1981 à 1985	366
340	75	205	90	520	175	1986 à 1990	367
325	85	195	75	825	145	1991 à 1995	368
285	110	95	115	940	80	1996 à 2000	369
450	100	210	170	1,370	40	2001 à 2006[49]	370

Nota : Voir les symboles et les abréviations dans les documents d'introduction et voir les documents de référence à la fin de la publication.

Selected characteristics for census divisions and census subdivisions – 100% data and 20% sample data, Ontario, 2006 Census (continued)

No.	Characteristics	Scugog, TP	Uxbridge, TP	Whitby, T	**Elgin CD/DR**	Aylmer, T A	Bayham, MU
	Dwelling and household characteristics						
371	Average number of rooms per dwelling	7.5	7.7	7.4	7.2	7.1	7.3
372	Average number of bedrooms per dwelling	3.1	3.1	3.2	2.9	2.8	3.0
373	Average value of dwelling $	326,302	400,647	314,350	196,257	200,206	180,828
374	**Total number of private households**	**7,705**	**6,660**	**37,240**	**32,200**	**2,695**	**2,190**
	Household size						
375	1 person	1,290	1,105	5,975	7,405	675	365
376	2 persons	2,820	2,160	10,300	11,515	915	795
377	3 persons	1,275	1,130	7,080	5,085	425	340
378	4 to 5 persons	2,130	2,000	12,515	7,050	575	500
379	6 or more persons	195	265	1,370	1,145	110	200
	Household type						
380	One-family households[50]	6,130	5,265	29,525	23,765	1,975	1,705
381	Multiple-family households	185	170	895	445	20	75
382	Non-family households	1,385	1,220	6,825	7,995	700	410
383	Number of persons in private households	21,130	19,065	110,210	83,795	6,990	6,685
384	Average number of persons in private households	2.7	2.9	3.0	2.6	2.6	3.1
385	Tenant-occupied private non-farm, non-reserve dwellings[51]	940	915	5,955	7,535	765	410
386	Average gross rent $[51]	848	881	946	668	625	623
387	Tenant-occupied households spending 30% or more of household income on gross rent[52]	420	410	2,790	2,945	290	120
388	Tenant-occupied households spending from 30% to 99% of household income on gross rent[52]	340	360	2,460	2,610	275	90
389	Owner-occupied private non-farm, non-reserve dwellings[53]	6,585	5,585	31,270	24,035	1,930	1,710
390	Average owner's major payments $[53]	1,211	1,382	1,457	989	929	940
391	Owner households spending 30% or more of household income on owner's major payments[52]	1,260	1,165	6,375	4,055	320	395
392	Owner households spending from 30% to 99% of household income on owner's major payments[52]	1,090	1,010	5,720	3,605	305	330
	Census family characteristics						
393	**Total number of census families in private households**	**6,505**	**5,600**	**31,350**	**24,675**	**2,020**	**1,855**
	Family structure and number of children						
394	Total couple families	5,710	4,930	27,105	21,255	1,710	1,660
395	Total families of married couples	5,020	4,420	24,250	18,390	1,525	1,445
396	Without children at home	2,310	1,725	7,170	8,400	645	620
397	With children at home	2,705	2,695	17,080	9,990	875	825
398	1 child	945	805	5,470	3,440	270	280
399	2 children	1,200	1,250	8,185	4,125	370	250
400	3 or more children	555	645	3,430	2,425	240	300
401	Total families of common-law couples	695	510	2,860	2,865	180	215
402	Without children at home	385	300	1,590	1,580	105	110
403	With children at home	310	210	1,270	1,280	75	100
404	1 child	150	90	540	640	35	45
405	2 children	95	90	510	395	20	35
406	3 or more children	70	25	220	250	15	25
407	Total lone-parent families	790	670	4,235	3,415	305	195
408	Female parent	575	525	3,375	2,665	255	165
409	1 child	315	280	1,890	1,565	155	90
410	2 children	215	180	1,080	845	90	50
411	3 or more children	45	65	405	255	15	20
412	Male parent	215	145	860	750	55	30
413	1 child	140	85	540	500	35	20
414	2 children	60	55	265	210	15	15
415	3 or more children	20	10	55	40	0	0

Note: See symbols and abbreviations in the introductory material and see reference material at the end of the publication.

Certaines caractéristiques des divisions de recensement et des subdivisions de recensement – Données intégrales et données-échantillon (20 %), Ontario, Recensement de 2006 (suite)

Central Elgin, MU A	Dutton/ Dunwich, MU	Malahide, TP A	Southwold, TP	St. Thomas, CY A	West Elgin, MU	Caractéristiques	N°
						Caractéristiques des logements et des ménages	
7.7	7.9	7.6	8.1	6.8	7.4	Nombre moyen de pièces par logement	371
3.0	3.1	3.1	3.3	2.7	2.9	Nombre moyen de chambres à coucher par logement	372
241,016	211,608	245,802	226,172	168,400	165,197	Valeur moyenne du logement $	373
4,780	**1,390**	**2,725**	**1,605**	**14,730**	**2,075**	**Nombre total de ménages privés**	374
						Taille du ménage	
865	300	375	230	4,110	485	1 personne	375
1,885	470	895	600	5,170	790	2 personnes	376
760	215	450	265	2,350	290	3 personnes	377
1,170	345	730	450	2,820	455	4 à 5 personnes	378
100	55	275	60	280	60	6 personnes ou plus	379
						Genre de ménage	
3,785	1,050	2,275	1,325	10,095	1,550	Ménages unifamiliaux[50]	380
85	20	35	30	170	10	Ménages multifamiliaux	381
905	315	420	250	4,470	515	Ménages non familiaux	382
12,560	3,740	8,675	4,560	35,300	5,295	Nombre de personnes dans les ménages privés	383
2.6	2.7	3.2	2.8	2.4	2.5	Nombre moyen de personnes dans les ménages privés	384
535	190	425	180	4,695	340	Ménages locataires dans les logements privés non agricoles hors réserve[51]	385
788	609	616	719	669	684	Loyer brut moyen $[51]	386
205	60	75	25	2,025	140	Ménages locataires consacrant 30 % ou plus du revenu du ménage au loyer brut[52]	387
165	55	65	20	1,825	105	Ménages locataires consacrant de 30 % à 99 % du revenu du ménage au loyer brut[52]	388
4,145	1,130	2,130	1,335	10,040	1,610	Ménages propriétaires dans les logements privés non agricoles hors réserve[53]	389
1,075	974	1,010	1,011	983	889	Principales dépenses de propriété moyennes $[53]	390
590	180	400	260	1,545	365	Ménages propriétaires consacrant 30 % ou plus du revenu du ménage aux principales dépenses de propriété[52]	391
510	160	350	225	1,390	330	Ménages propriétaires consacrant de 30 % à 99 % du revenu du ménage aux principales dépenses de propriété[52]	392
						Caractéristiques des familles de recensement	
3,950	**1,090**	**2,350**	**1,390**	**10,450**	**1,565**	**Nombre total de familles de recensement dans les ménages privés**	393
						Structure de la famille et le nombre d'enfants	
3,540	960	2,170	1,260	8,570	1,380	Total des familles avec conjoints	394
3,140	850	1,975	1,140	7,090	1,220	Total des familles avec couples mariés	395
1,445	365	680	485	3,495	655	Sans enfants à la maison	396
1,690	480	1,295	655	3,600	565	Avec enfants à la maison	397
630	155	375	210	1,370	160	1 enfant	398
715	215	435	270	1,605	260	2 enfants	399
340	115	480	180	625	140	3 enfants ou plus	400
400	110	190	125	1,475	160	Total des familles avec couples en union libre	401
285	75	125	100	730	55	Sans enfants à la maison	402
120	35	70	30	740	105	Avec enfants à la maison	403
50	15	40	20	375	45	1 enfant	404
55	0	15	0	215	35	2 enfants	405
10	10	10	0	145	25	3 enfants ou plus	406
415	130	180	125	1,885	180	Total des familles monoparentales	407
295	115	105	100	1,490	135	Parent de sexe féminin	408
205	55	85	45	860	60	1 enfant	409
65	50	10	45	480	60	2 enfants	410
20	10	15	15	150	10	3 enfants ou plus	411
115	15	70	20	390	50	Parent de sexe masculin	412
85	0	65	10	260	25	1 enfant	413
30	10	10	0	120	15	2 enfants	414
10	0	0	10	15	10	3 enfants ou plus	415

Nota : Voir les symboles et les abréviations dans les documents d'introduction et voir les documents de référence à la fin de la publication.

Selected characteristics for census divisions and census subdivisions – 100% data and 20% sample data, Ontario, 2006 Census (continued)

No.	Characteristics	Scugog, TP	Uxbridge, TP	Whitby, T	**Elgin CD/DR**	Aylmer, T A	Bayham, MU
	Census family characteristics						
416	**Total number of children at home**	**6,925**	**6,845**	**41,765**	**28,030**	**2,450**	**2,625**
	Age group						
417	Under 6 years	1,110	1,175	9,040	6,200	630	605
418	6 to 14 years	2,530	2,665	15,590	10,620	815	1,030
419	15 to 17 years	1,060	960	5,515	3,905	340	390
420	18 to 24 years	1,625	1,485	8,405	5,110	460	430
421	25 years and over	595	555	3,215	2,195	200	180
422	Average number of children at home per census family[54]	1.1	1.2	1.3	1.1	1.2	1.4
423	**Total number of persons in private households**	**21,130**	**19,065**	**110,210**	**83,795**	**6,985**	**6,685**
	Census family status and living arrangements						
424	Number of persons not in census families	1,985	1,685	9,990	9,835	805	535
425	Living with relatives[55]	395	345	2,050	1,020	75	105
426	Living with non-relatives only	305	225	1,955	1,420	65	70
427	Living alone	1,280	1,110	5,980	7,395	670	360
428	Number of census family persons	19,145	17,385	100,220	73,960	6,180	6,150
429	Average number of persons per census family	2.9	3.1	3.2	3.0	3.1	3.3
430	**Total number of persons aged 65 years and over**	**2,905**	**2,500**	**9,295**	**10,870**	**1,130**	**690**
431	Number of persons not in census families aged 65 years and over	800	780	3,205	3,665	470	180
432	Living with relatives[55]	185	195	855	400	40	25
433	Living with non-relatives only	35	25	150	120	10	20
434	Living alone	585	560	2,200	3,135	420	135
435	Number of census family persons aged 65 years and over	2,105	1,720	6,090	7,205	660	510
	Economic family characteristics						
436	**Total number of economic families in private households**	**6,370**	**5,480**	**30,655**	**24,380**	**2,005**	**1,800**
	Size of family						
437	2 persons	2,855	2,150	9,950	11,335	915	765
438	3 persons	1,270	1,105	7,025	5,050	410	335
439	4 persons	1,465	1,380	8,915	4,850	400	300
440	5 or more persons	785	845	4,760	3,150	285	400
441	Total number of persons in economic families	19,540	17,730	102,270	74,980	6,250	6,250
442	Average number of persons per economic family	3.0	3.0	3.0	3.0	3.0	4.0
443	Total number of persons not in economic families	1,590	1,340	7,940	8,815	735	430
	2005 income characteristics						
444	**Population 15 years and over**	**17,485**	**15,215**	**85,585**	**67,320**	**5,555**	**5,085**
	Sex and total income groups in 2005						
445	Without income	790	690	4,270	3,030	245	215
446	With income	16,700	14,520	81,320	64,285	5,310	4,865
447	Under $1,000[56]	570	530	3,310	2,125	195	160
448	$1,000 to $2,999	570	665	3,155	2,035	220	140
449	$3,000 to $4,999	515	480	2,725	2,100	120	250
450	$5,000 to $6,999	705	445	2,555	2,390	245	295
451	$7,000 to $9,999	920	805	4,090	3,615	300	265
452	$10,000 to $11,999	585	490	2,390	2,405	125	265
453	$12,000 to $14,999	835	740	3,575	3,990	380	415
454	$15,000 to $19,999	1,430	1,050	5,105	6,095	695	580
455	$20,000 to $24,999	1,015	950	4,410	5,220	380	400
456	$25,000 to $29,999	1,035	725	4,460	4,800	465	395
457	$30,000 to $34,999	1,035	885	4,790	4,675	400	330
458	$35,000 to $39,999	945	810	4,380	4,230	250	300
459	$40,000 to $44,999	965	790	4,470	3,545	260	245
460	$45,000 to $49,999	640	580	4,130	3,085	275	210
461	$50,000 to $59,999	1,160	1,050	7,115	4,725	355	290
462	$60,000 and over	3,770	3,530	20,650	9,250	630	325
463	Median income $[57]	30,820	32,122	35,063	27,172	24,608	20,593
464	Average income $[57]	41,221	44,856	43,946	33,346	30,138	26,547
465	Standard error of average income $[57]	871	1,560	422	270	660	693

Note: See symbols and abbreviations in the introductory material and see reference material at the end of the publication.

Certaines caractéristiques des divisions de recensement et des subdivisions de recensement – Données intégrales et données-échantillon (20 %), Ontario, Recensement de 2006 (suite)

Central Elgin, MU A	Dutton/ Dunwich, MU	Malahide, TP A	Southwold, TP	St. Thomas, CY A	West Elgin, MU	Caractéristiques	N°
						Caractéristiques des familles de recensement	
3,955	**1,295**	**3,615**	**1,595**	**10,800**	**1,680**	**Nombre total d'enfants à la maison**	416
						Groupes d'âge	
755	245	835	305	2,545	280	Moins de 6 ans	417
1,475	555	1,385	620	4,130	610	6 à 14 ans	418
605	205	460	235	1,390	275	15 à 17 ans	419
800	205	660	325	1,895	330	18 à 24 ans	420
310	80	270	120	840	190	25 ans et plus	421
1.0	1.2	1.5	1.1	1.0	1.1	Nombre moyen d'enfants à la maison par famille de recensement[54]	422
12,540	**3,740**	**8,680**	**4,555**	**35,315**	**5,285**	**Nombre total de personnes dans les ménages privés**	423
						Situation des particuliers dans la famille de recensement et des particuliers dans le ménage	
1,100	390	545	305	5,490	660	Nombre de personnes hors famille de recensement	424
115	35	80	25	480	110	Vivant avec des personnes apparentées[55]	425
120	50	85	50	905	65	Vivant avec des personnes non apparentées seulement	426
860	300	380	230	4,105	485	Vivant seules	427
11,445	3,350	8,135	4,250	29,820	4,630	Nombre de membres d'une famille de recensement	428
2.9	3.1	3.5	3.1	2.9	3.0	Nombre moyen de personnes par famille de recensement	429
1,640	**510**	**795**	**450**	**4,835**	**810**	**Nombre total de personnes âgées de 65 ans et plus**	430
480	205	205	85	1,765	275	Nombre de personnes hors famille de recensement âgées de 65 ans et plus	431
40	15	20	10	180	70	Vivant avec des personnes apparentées[55]	432
25	0	10	15	40	0	Vivant avec des personnes non apparentées seulement	433
415	185	175	60	1,545	195	Vivant seules	434
1,165	305	590	370	3,070	540	Nombre de membres d'une famille de recensement âgés de 65 ans et plus	435
						Caractéristiques des familles économiques	
3,885	**1,080**	**2,325**	**1,360**	**10,345**	**1,580**	**Nombre total de familles économiques dans les ménages privés**	436
						Taille de la famille	
1,875	470	895	585	5,035	785	2 personnes	437
770	220	430	270	2,320	285	3 personnes	438
815	230	465	300	2,010	315	4 personnes	439
420	150	530	200	975	185	5 personnes ou plus	440
11,560	3,385	8,215	4,280	30,305	4,740	Nombre total de personnes dans les familles économiques	441
3.0	3.0	4.0	3.0	3.0	3.0	Nombre moyen de personnes par famille économique	442
980	355	465	280	5,010	550	Nombre total de personnes hors famille économique	443
						Caractéristiques du revenu de 2005	
10,360	**2,940**	**6,470**	**3,715**	**28,790**	**4,400**	**Population de 15 ans et plus**	444
						Sexe et groupes de revenu total en 2005	
460	185	220	165	1,315	215	Sans revenu	445
9,900	2,750	6,250	3,545	27,480	4,185	Avec un revenu	446
255	115	230	155	780	245	Moins de 1 000 $[56]	447
285	70	200	100	855	160	1 000 $ à 2 999 $	448
300	45	245	120	930	100	3 000 $ à 4 999 $	449
290	60	280	105	930	185	5 000 $ à 6 999 $	450
555	190	355	155	1,495	295	7 000 $ à 9 999 $	451
340	45	290	70	1,055	210	10 000 $ à 11 999 $	452
570	190	430	185	1,600	220	12 000 $ à 14 999 $	453
690	240	615	360	2,475	440	15 000 $ à 19 999 $	454
785	215	485	275	2,370	305	20 000 $ à 24 999 $	455
600	270	535	255	1,965	300	25 000 $ à 29 999 $	456
580	195	445	225	2,125	385	30 000 $ à 34 999 $	457
675	245	380	235	1,890	245	35 000 $ à 39 999 $	458
545	205	320	155	1,605	215	40 000 $ à 44 999 $	459
485	80	185	250	1,390	215	45 000 $ à 49 999$	460
910	225	400	255	2,055	230	50 000 $ à 59 999$	461
2,040	360	850	650	3,960	425	60 000 $ et plus	462
32,394	28,511	24,781	29,948	27,982	24,184	Revenu médian $[57]	463
40,213	33,294	31,374	37,235	33,325	28,890	Revenu moyen $[57]	464
1,104	1,062	756	1,192	355	788	Erreur type de revenu moyen $[57]	465

Nota : Voir les symboles et les abréviations dans les documents d'introduction et voir les documents de référence à la fin de la publication.

Selected characteristics for census divisions and census subdivisions – 100% data and 20% sample data, Ontario, 2006 Census (continued)

No.	Characteristics	Scugog, TP	Uxbridge, TP	Whitby, T	**Elgin CD/DR**	Aylmer, T A	Bayham, MU
	2005 income characteristics						
	Sex and total income groups in 2005 (continued)						
466	Total - Males	8,590	7,445	41,390	33,050	2,600	2,595
467	Without income	330	250	1,775	1,235	105	70
468	With income	8,255	7,190	39,615	31,810	2,500	2,530
469	Under $1,000[56]	310	280	1,660	1,130	90	105
470	$1,000 to $2,999	220	240	1,000	775	70	55
471	$3,000 to $4,999	190	195	1,015	800	45	90
472	$5,000 to $6,999	230	210	900	795	75	95
473	$7,000 to $9,999	350	345	1,505	1,165	105	115
474	$10,000 to $11,999	210	150	830	900	25	120
475	$12,000 to $14,999	220	225	1,195	1,365	120	190
476	$15,000 to $19,999	520	425	1,740	2,235	285	265
477	$20,000 to $24,999	400	340	1,700	2,115	150	195
478	$25,000 to $29,999	475	300	1,775	2,050	175	175
479	$30,000 to $34,999	500	390	2,045	2,215	230	165
480	$35,000 to $39,999	395	405	1,810	2,030	140	190
481	$40,000 to $44,999	505	420	2,110	2,040	130	130
482	$45,000 to $49,999	365	320	2,080	2,010	175	155
483	$50,000 to $59,999	705	560	3,675	3,200	235	190
484	$60,000 and over	2,660	2,385	14,570	6,980	450	270
485	Median income $[57]	41,030	40,522	46,001	35,870	32,107	25,518
486	Average income $[57]	50,341	56,392	55,661	40,633	36,830	31,439
487	Standard error of average income $[57]	1,217	3,011	794	427	1,098	1,106
488	Total - Females	8,900	7,770	44,200	34,270	2,950	2,490
489	Without income	460	440	2,490	1,795	145	150
490	With income	8,445	7,335	41,705	32,475	2,810	2,340
491	Under $1,000[56]	265	250	1,650	1,005	105	55
492	$1,000 to $2,999	350	430	2,150	1,255	155	85
493	$3,000 to $4,999	325	280	1,715	1,305	70	165
494	$5,000 to $6,999	470	240	1,655	1,595	175	195
495	$7,000 to $9,999	570	460	2,585	2,445	195	150
496	$10,000 to $11,999	380	340	1,560	1,505	105	140
497	$12,000 to $14,999	610	515	2,380	2,630	260	225
498	$15,000 to $19,999	915	620	3,365	3,865	410	315
499	$20,000 to $24,999	615	610	2,715	3,100	230	200
500	$25,000 to $29,999	560	425	2,685	2,745	295	220
501	$30,000 to $34,999	535	495	2,750	2,460	170	160
502	$35,000 to $39,999	550	405	2,570	2,195	115	105
503	$40,000 to $44,999	460	370	2,360	1,505	125	115
504	$45,000 to $49,999	275	265	2,050	1,075	95	55
505	$50,000 to $59,999	460	485	3,440	1,520	125	95
506	$60,000 and over	1,105	1,140	6,075	2,265	185	60
507	Median income $[57]	22,732	24,201	26,869	20,797	19,362	16,890
508	Average income $[57]	32,303	33,542	32,819	26,207	24,190	21,261
509	Standard error of average income $[57]	1,214	853	293	312	712	699
	Composition of total income						
510	Composition of total income in 2005 %	100.0	100.0	100.0	100.0	100.0	100.0
511	Employment income %	74.4	79.1	85.1	75.1	71.2	73.5
512	Government transfer payments %	8.6	7.3	6.3	12.5	15.7	17.0
513	Other %	17.0	13.7	8.6	12.3	13.1	9.5
514	**Population 15 years and over with employment income in 2005**	**12,995**	**11,550**	**66,830**	**49,210**	**3,870**	**3,660**
	Sex and work activity						
515	Median employment income in 2005 $	29,071	30,699	37,940	27,128	24,674	20,284
516	Average employment income in 2005 $	39,408	44,586	45,477	32,730	29,434	25,948
517	Standard error of average employment income $	844	1,913	474	300	799	853
518	Worked full year, full time[59]	6,835	6,135	38,190	26,225	2,075	1,740
519	Median employment income in 2005 $	50,704	52,231	53,581	41,077	39,663	34,346
520	Average employment income in 2005 $	57,365	67,351	62,408	45,422	41,434	36,742
521	Standard error of average employment income $	1,255	3,401	705	402	1,045	1,326
522	Worked part year or part time[60]	5,280	4,685	24,990	19,640	1,485	1,745
523	Median employment income in 2005 $	10,810	10,759	13,240	11,662	10,850	10,996
524	Average employment income in 2005 $	21,277	20,121	24,613	19,945	16,087	16,577
525	Standard error of average employment income $	930	763	518	413	931	961
526	Males 15 years and over with employment income[58]	6,905	6,090	34,580	26,245	1,990	2,100
527	Median employment income in 2005 $	38,456	39,640	47,945	35,648	33,066	25,739
528	Average employment income in 2005 $	47,519	55,547	56,056	39,048	35,292	30,400
529	Standard error of average employment income $	1,401	3,488	846	461	1,245	1,271

Note: See symbols and abbreviations in the introductory material and see reference material at the end of the publication.

Central Elgin, MU A	Dutton/ Dunwich, MU	Malahide, TP A	Southwold, TP	St. Thomas, CY A	West Elgin, MU	Caractéristiques	N°
						Caractéristiques du revenu de 2005	
						Sexe et groupes de revenu total en 2005 (suite)	
5,175	1,445	3,325	1,940	13,785	2,185	Total - Hommes	466
175	105	75	65	565	85	Sans revenu	467
5,000	1,340	3,255	1,870	13,220	2,100	Avec un revenu	468
130	35	115	110	415	125	Moins de 1 000 $[56]	469
130	30	60	45	345	35	1 000 $ à 2 999 $	470
165	10	75	55	330	30	3 000 $ à 4 999 $	471
110	20	110	35	305	40	5 000 $ à 6 999 $	472
205	75	85	20	445	115	7 000 $ à 9 999 $	473
140	10	110	20	380	105	10 000 $ à 11 999 $	474
195	60	175	85	435	95	12 000 $ à 14 999 $	475
200	70	290	145	820	155	15 000 $ à 19 999 $	476
335	115	205	125	865	125	20 000 $ à 24 999 $	477
215	130	340	135	735	140	25 000 $ à 29 999 $	478
260	55	255	90	945	205	30 000 $ à 34 999 $	479
295	105	190	80	880	150	35 000 $ à 39 999 $	480
305	110	185	70	960	140	40 000 $ à $44 999 $	481
290	60	135	175	845	170	45 000 $ à $49 999 $	482
560	155	285	175	1,450	145	50 000 $ à $59 999 $	483
1,455	295	625	510	3,045	325	60 000 $ et plus	484
42,949	38,750	31,148	39,431	38,583	32,550	Revenu médian $[57]	485
47,886	41,672	36,968	44,466	41,504	35,068	Revenu moyen $[57]	486
1,618	1,793	1,031	1,810	611	1,203	Erreur type de revenu moyen $[57]	487
5,185	1,490	3,150	1,775	15,005	2,215	Total - Femmes	488
285	80	150	105	745	130	Sans revenu	489
4,900	1,410	2,995	1,670	14,260	2,080	Avec un revenu	490
125	70	120	45	360	120	Moins de 1 000 $[56]	491
155	45	140	50	505	125	1 000$ à 2 999 $	492
140	35	170	60	600	65	3 000 $ à 4 999 $	493
180	40	165	65	625	150	5 000 $ à 6 999 $	494
350	110	275	135	1,050	175	7 000 $ à 9 999 $	495
200	45	185	45	680	105	10 000 $ à 11 999 $	496
370	125	250	100	1,160	130	12 000 $ à 14 999 $	497
490	170	325	215	1,655	290	15 000 $ à 19 999 $	498
455	100	280	150	1,505	180	20 000 $ à 24 999 $	499
385	140	195	125	1,225	160	25 000 $ à 29 999 $	500
315	140	185	135	1,175	180	30 000 $ à 34 999 $	501
380	140	190	150	1,010	95	35 000 $ à 39 999 $	502
235	95	130	85	640	80	40 000 $ à 44 999 $	503
195	10	55	80	550	45	45 000 $ à 49 999 $	504
350	70	115	80	605	80	50 000 $ à 59 999 $	505
580	65	220	135	915	100	60 000 $ et plus	506
24,776	21,334	17,681	24,016	21,339	17,785	Revenu médian $[57]	507
32,383	25,336	25,306	29,126	25,744	22,659	Revenu moyen $[57]	508
1,463	998	1,063	1,358	337	946	Erreur type de revenu moyen $[57]	509
						Composition du revenu total	
100.0	100.0	100.0	100.0	100.0	100.0	Composition du revenu total en 2005 %	510
76.2	77.3	78.7	79.6	74.7	69.1	Revenu d'emploi %	511
9.0	10.8	11.8	8.6	13.3	16.2	Transferts gouvernementaux %	512
14.8	11.8	9.4	11.8	12.0	14.6	Autres %	513
8,075	**2,215**	**5,245**	**2,985**	**20,245**	**2,915**	**Population de 15 ans et plus avec un revenu d'emploi en 2005**	514
						Sexe et travail	
29,872	27,843	22,178	27,954	29,814	24,583	Revenu médian d'emploi en 2005 $	515
37,562	31,955	29,492	35,183	33,798	28,705	Revenu moyen d'emploi en 2005 $	516
979	1,287	865	1,278	445	1,045	Erreur type de revenu moyen d'emploi $	517
4,285	1,320	2,505	1,610	11,130	1,555	A travaillé toute l'année à plein temps[59]	518
47,763	39,156	36,728	46,318	42,074	35,979	Revenu médian d'emploi en 2005 $	519
52,341	43,266	42,381	49,275	45,943	40,381	Revenu moyen d'emploi en 2005 $	520
1,125	1,774	1,241	1,842	609	1,514	Erreur type de revenu moyen d'emploi $	521
3,240	740	2,340	1,185	7,745	1,150	A travaillé une partie de l'année ou à temps partiel[60]	522
11,836	11,670	10,179	13,522	12,264	10,784	Revenu médian d'emploi en 2005 $	523
23,575	17,607	19,687	19,846	20,703	16,829	Revenu moyen d'emploi en 2005 $	524
1,702	1,327	1,136	1,533	561	1,111	Erreur type de revenu moyen d'emploi $	525
4,340	1,200	2,880	1,660	10,450	1,625	Hommes de 15 ans et plus avec un revenu d'emploi[58]	526
38,460	36,448	29,288	38,827	39,951	32,299	Revenu médian d'emploi en 2005 $	527
43,518	38,116	34,661	41,455	41,438	33,512	Revenu moyen d'emploi en 2005 $	528
1,439	2,092	1,129	1,926	734	1,498	Erreur type de revenu moyen d'emploi $	529

Nota : Voir les symboles et les abréviations dans les documents d'introduction et voir les documents de référence à la fin de la publication.

Selected characteristics for census divisions and census subdivisions – 100% data and 20% sample data, Ontario, 2006 Census (continued)

No.	Characteristics	Scugog, TP	Uxbridge, TP	Whitby, T	**Elgin CD/DR**	Aylmer, T A	Bayham, MU
	2005 income characteristics						
	Sex and work activity (continued)						
530	Worked full year, full time[59]	4,050	3,725	22,350	15,795	1,230	1,170
531	Median employment income in 2005 $	58,686	59,128	61,601	46,862	45,169	36,542
532	Average employment income in 2005 $	65,594	77,020	71,670	50,505	46,269	39,912
533	Standard error of average employment income $	1,916	5,475	1,146	574	1,434	1,825
534	Worked part year or part time[60]	2,265	2,075	10,455	8,865	645	840
535	Median employment income in 2005 $	11,463	11,313	14,005	13,280	12,003	12,927
536	Average employment income in 2005 $	25,587	22,440	30,312	24,156	19,306	18,807
537	Standard error of average employment income $	1,847	1,365	1,098	718	1,763	1,566
538	Females 15 years and over with employment income[58]	6,095	5,460	32,255	22,960	1,880	1,560
539	Median employment income in 2005 $	23,379	23,688	29,789	20,681	18,228	14,582
540	Average employment income in 2005 $	30,219	32,358	34,135	25,509	23,229	19,955
541	Standard error of average employment income $	773	1,016	338	341	905	891
542	Worked full year, full time[59]	2,790	2,410	15,835	10,425	845	570
543	Median employment income in 2005 $	40,247	44,346	45,570	34,484	29,711	28,671
544	Average employment income in 2005 $	45,424	52,417	49,330	37,720	34,406	30,239
545	Standard error of average employment income $	1,151	1,751	458	475	1,363	1,381
546	Worked part year or part time[60]	3,010	2,610	14,530	10,780	840	900
547	Median employment income in 2005 $	10,033	10,300	12,748	10,723	9,736	9,973
548	Average employment income in 2005 $	18,036	18,279	20,511	16,483	13,636	14,494
549	Standard error of average employment income $	833	830	397	449	883	1,025
550	**Total number of economic families in private households**	**6,370**	**5,480**	**30,655**	**24,380**	**2,005**	**1,805**
	Family income groups in 2005						
551	Under $10,000	100	100	465	390	25	25
552	$10,000 to $19,999	185	75	665	840	100	70
553	$20,000 to $29,999	295	230	960	1,730	175	170
554	$30,000 to $39,999	520	335	1,490	2,145	205	220
555	$40,000 to $49,999	425	410	1,665	2,625	215	250
556	$50,000 to $59,999	460	400	1,955	2,445	195	180
557	$60,000 to $69,999	475	365	2,180	2,520	240	150
558	$70,000 to $79,999	530	350	2,560	2,125	155	195
559	$80,000 to $89,999	505	505	2,445	2,120	150	175
560	$90,000 to $99,999	455	410	2,345	1,610	130	105
561	$100,000 and over	2,415	2,300	13,920	5,835	420	265
562	Median family income $	84,096	89,417	94,289	68,065	62,628	59,328
563	Average family income $	96,684	108,831	105,664	75,903	69,254	65,334
564	Standard error of average family income $	2,056	4,152	1,098	773	1,809	1,846
	Family after-tax income groups in 2005						
565	Under $10,000	110	100	505	410	40	30
566	$10,000 to $19,999	200	85	660	890	95	70
567	$20,000 to $29,999	350	240	1,160	1,920	180	200
568	$30,000 to $39,999	585	505	1,935	2,820	305	265
569	$40,000 to $49,999	635	510	2,295	3,450	280	280
570	$50,000 to $59,999	590	490	3,000	3,205	250	205
571	$60,000 to $69,999	680	540	3,360	2,830	210	280
572	$70,000 to $79,999	695	555	3,265	2,460	190	175
573	$80,000 to $89,999	545	515	2,835	1,895	130	100
574	$90,000 to $99,999	530	420	2,710	1,570	135	65
575	$100,000 and over	1,445	1,515	8,930	2,930	180	135
576	Median after-tax family income $	70,693	74,359	77,342	58,387	53,602	52,700
577	Average after-tax family income $	77,812	85,596	84,440	63,698	57,838	56,860
578	Standard error of average after-tax family income $	1,399	2,463	711	541	1,530	1,403
	Income status in 2005						
579	Total population in private households for income status	21,125	19,070	110,155	83,770	6,990	6,685
580	Below low income cut-off before tax in 2005	1,260	1,190	7,730	7,690	785	555
581	Prevalence of low income before tax in 2005 %	5.9	6.2	7.0	9.2	11.2	8.4
582	Below low income cut-off after tax in 2005	750	755	5,915	5,185	515	330
583	Prevalence of low income after tax in 2005 %	3.5	4.0	5.4	6.2	7.4	4.9

Note: See symbols and abbreviations in the introductory material and see reference material at the end of the publication.

Certaines caractéristiques des divisions de recensement et des subdivisions de recensement – Données intégrales et données-échantillon (20 %), Ontario, Recensement de 2006 (suite)

Central Elgin, MU A	Dutton/ Dunwich, MU	Malahide, TP A	Southwold, TP	St. Thomas, CY A	West Elgin, MU	Caractéristiques	N°
						Caractéristiques du revenu de 2005	
						Sexe et travail (suite)	
2,500	775	1,725	1,010	6,400	985	A travaillé toute l'année à plein temps[59]	530
53,995	46,643	40,377	51,542	48,547	41,006	Revenu médian d'emploi en 2005 $	531
58,429	49,690	43,398	55,022	52,511	43,634	Revenu moyen d'emploi en 2005 $	532
1,583	2,728	1,419	2,526	933	1,909	Erreur type de revenu moyen d'emploi $	533
1,545	330	1,075	545	3,360	525	A travaillé une partie de l'année ou à temps partiel[60]	534
11,801	12,078	14,176	13,286	15,063	13,082	Revenu médian d'emploi en 2005 $	535
26,647	20,135	23,272	22,297	26,834	20,497	Revenu moyen d'emploi en 2005 $	536
2,729	2,329	1,640	2,713	1,102	2,056	Erreur type de revenu moyen d'emploi $	537
3,735	1,025	2,360	1,320	9,795	1,285	Femmes de 15 ans et plus avec un revenu d'emploi[58]	538
23,815	23,745	12,392	22,913	21,971	16,547	Revenu médian d'emploi en 2005 $	539
30,639	24,744	23,176	27,308	25,650	22,643	Revenu moyen d'emploi en 2005 $	540
1,256	1,199	1,288	1,360	425	1,351	Erreur type de revenu moyen d'emploi $	541
1,785	545	780	600	4,730	570	A travaillé toute l'année à plein temps[59]	542
38,872	33,228	32,259	35,666	34,650	29,258	Revenu médian d'emploi en 2005 $	543
43,800	34,124	40,127	39,598	37,055	34,793	Revenu moyen d'emploi en 2005 $	544
1,428	1,531	2,445	2,285	585	2,413	Erreur type de revenu moyen d'emploi $	545
1,695	410	1,270	640	4,390	625	A travaillé une partie de l'année ou à temps partiel[60]	546
12,026	11,043	8,712	13,921	11,109	10,146	Revenu médian d'emploi en 2005 $	547
20,783	15,585	16,661	17,763	16,013	13,725	Revenu moyen d'emploi en 2005 $	548
2,095	1,453	1,553	1,240	472	1,075	Erreur type de revenu moyen d'emploi $	549
3,885	**1,075**	**2,325**	**1,360**	**10,350**	**1,580**	**Nombre total des familles économiques dans les ménages privés**	550
						Revenu de la famille économique en 2005	
60	25	30	15	180	30	Moins de 10 000 $	551
55	10	65	20	455	55	10 000 $ à 19 999 $	552
170	70	155	80	755	150	20 000 $ à 29 999 $	553
230	70	190	120	945	155	30 000 $ à 39 999 $	554
310	115	315	105	1,060	245	40 000 $ à 49 999 $	555
295	115	280	95	1,110	180	50 000 $ à 59 999 $	556
385	90	200	135	1,150	165	60 000 $ à 69 999 $	557
325	125	185	90	945	105	70 000 $ à 79 999 $	558
415	120	185	165	800	110	80 000 $ à 89 999 $	559
280	85	145	85	685	90	90 000 $ à 99 999 $	560
1,355	230	570	440	2,265	295	100 000 $ et plus	561
82,477	71,182	67,000	80,370	66,173	58,334	Revenu médian des familles $	562
93,216	74,851	75,896	89,167	72,248	67,087	Revenu moyen des familles $	563
3,492	2,535	1,963	3,564	838	2,228	Erreur type de revenu moyen des familles $	564
						Revenu après impôt de la famille économique en 2005	
60	25	25	15	180	30	Moins de 10 000 $	565
60	15	65	35	475	70	10 000 $ à 19 999 $	566
200	70	175	80	860	150	20 000 $ à 29 999 $	567
295	100	225	150	1,230	250	30 000 $ à 39 999 $	568
445	165	415	140	1,475	250	40 000 $ à 49 999 $	569
495	135	285	150	1,480	200	50 000 $ à 59 999 $	570
410	200	270	150	1,120	185	60 000 $ à 69 999 $	571
465	95	205	150	1,045	130	70 000 $ à 79 999 $	572
325	115	200	110	805	110	80 000 $ à 89 999 $	573
310	55	140	145	620	95	90 000 $ à 99 999 $	574
815	95	305	220	1,060	120	100 000 $ et plus	575
69,193	61,132	57,551	67,351	56,709	51,363	Revenu médian après impôt des familles $	576
75,738	62,885	64,968	73,817	60,964	57,222	Revenu moyen après impôt des familles $	577
2,247	1,870	1,523	2,551	630	1,664	Erreur type de revenu moyen après impôt des familles $	578
						Catégorie de revenu en 2005	
12,540	3,725	8,680	4,560	35,300	5,285	Population totale dans les ménages privés pour la catégorie de revenu	579
670	230	340	215	4,390	505	Au-dessous du seuil de faible revenu avant impôt en 2005	580
5.3	6.2	3.9	4.7	12.4	9.6	Fréquence du faible revenu avant impôt en 2005 %	581
520	115	200	175	3,005	325	Au-dessous du seuil de faible revenu après impôt en 2005	582
4.1	3.2	2.3	3.8	8.5	6.1	Fréquence du faible revenu après impôt en 2005 %	583

Nota : Voir les symboles et les abréviations dans les documents d'introduction et voir les documents de référence à la fin de la publication.

Selected characteristics for census divisions and census subdivisions – 100% data and 20% sample data, Ontario, 2006 Census (continued)

No.	Characteristics	Scugog, TP	Uxbridge, TP	Whitby, T	**Elgin CD/DR**	Aylmer, T A	Bayham, MU
	2005 income characteristics						
584	**Total number of private households**	**7,705**	**6,655**	**37,245**	**32,205**	**2,695**	**2,195**
	Household income groups in 2005						
585	Under $10,000	180	155	855	950	65	65
586	$10,000 to $19,999	455	365	1,825	2,965	350	220
587	$20,000 to $29,999	500	370	1,770	3,070	305	240
588	$30,000 to $39,999	660	535	2,175	3,250	295	255
589	$40,000 to $49,999	605	545	2,380	3,415	285	285
590	$50,000 to $59,999	575	480	2,650	3,075	250	205
591	$60,000 to $69,999	570	425	2,755	3,050	265	165
592	$70,000 to $79,999	640	425	3,015	2,370	150	210
593	$80,000 to $89,999	535	535	2,750	2,270	155	175
594	$90,000 to $99,999	480	415	2,570	1,720	140	100
595	$100,000 and over	2,510	2,410	14,490	6,060	425	270
596	Median household income $	74,737	80,455	84,219	57,839	50,957	51,191
597	Average household income $	89,271	97,813	95,874	66,442	59,266	58,674
598	Standard error of average household income $	1,981	3,441	949	646	1,520	1,663
	Household after-tax income groups in 2005						
599	Under $10,000	200	165	920	980	80	60
600	$10,000 to $19,999	465	405	1,950	3,230	365	230
601	$20,000 to $29,999	605	420	2,105	3,600	360	275
602	$30,000 to $39,999	795	765	2,985	4,030	395	330
603	$40,000 to $49,999	830	600	3,215	4,405	360	305
604	$50,000 to $59,999	750	580	3,670	3,670	270	225
605	$60,000 to $69,999	720	595	3,855	3,035	210	285
606	$70,000 to $79,999	735	590	3,515	2,610	205	180
607	$80,000 to $89,999	575	535	3,045	2,005	140	100
608	$90,000 to $99,999	545	430	2,805	1,600	135	65
609	$100,000 and over	1,490	1,570	9,180	3,040	180	135
610	Median after-tax household income $	62,822	67,110	69,774	49,711	43,992	46,069
611	Average after-tax household income $	72,148	77,211	76,824	55,838	49,874	51,088
612	Standard error of average after-tax household income $	1,478	2,070	626	462	1,267	1,291

Note: See symbols and abbreviations in the introductory material and see reference material at the end of the publication.

Certaines caractéristiques des divisions de recensement et des subdivisions de recensement – Données intégrales et données-échantillon (20 %), Ontario, Recensement de 2006 (suite)

Central Elgin, MU **A**	Dutton/ Dunwich, MU	Malahide, TP **A**	Southwold, TP	St. Thomas, CY **A**	West Elgin, MU	**Caractéristiques**	N°
						Caractéristiques du revenu de 2005	
4,775	**1,390**	**2,730**	**1,605**	**14,735**	**2,075**	**Nombre total des ménages privés**	584
						Tranches de revenu des ménages en 2005	
115	35	55	45	495	70	Moins de 10 000 $	585
240	115	200	50	1,545	240	10 000 $ à 19 999 $	586
320	140	210	115	1,510	225	20 000 $ à 29 999 $	587
375	115	235	160	1,570	235	30 000 $ à 39 999 $	588
405	130	335	140	1,545	290	40 000 $ à 49 999 $	589
375	155	290	105	1,475	220	50 000 $ à 59 999 $	590
475	120	210	170	1,470	175	60 000 $ à 69 999 $	591
355	135	185	115	1,100	115	70 000 $ à 79 999 $	592
430	120	210	165	900	110	80 000 $ à 89 999 $	593
285	100	180	95	720	95	90 000 $ à 99 999 $	594
1,395	235	605	440	2,395	300	100 000 $ et plus	595
71,300	60,226	61,530	71,189	54,876	49,415	Revenu médian des ménages $	596
83,368	65,715	71,638	81,537	62,064	58,088	Revenu moyen des ménages $	597
2,912	2,241	1,878	3,189	746	1,861	Erreur type de revenu moyen des ménages $	598
						Tranches du revenu après impôt des ménages en 2005	
115	35	60	55	500	75	Moins de 10 000 $	599
250	115	215	70	1,725	260	10 000 $ à 19 999 $	600
410	160	235	130	1,800	240	20 000 $ à 29 999 $	601
450	140	270	185	1,900	360	30 000 $ à 39 999 $	602
560	210	445	200	2,045	280	40 000 $ à 49 999 $	603
585	150	290	160	1,765	220	50 000 $ à 59 999 $	604
425	210	295	170	1,245	185	60 000 $ à 69 999 $	605
480	105	220	160	1,140	125	70 000 $ à 79 999 $	606
345	115	230	110	845	120	80 000 $ à 89 999 $	607
310	60	155	140	645	95	90 000 $ à 99 999 $	608
840	90	315	225	1,125	125	100 000 $ et plus	609
60,403	52,873	53,900	60,479	47,276	42,323	Revenu médian après impôt des ménages $	610
67,919	55,371	60,907	67,479	52,425	49,682	Revenu moyen après impôt des ménages $	611
1,900	1,689	1,444	2,320	566	1,426	Erreur type de revenu moyen après impôt des ménages $	612

Nota : Voir les symboles et les abréviations dans les documents d'introduction et voir les documents de référence à la fin de la publication.

Selected characteristics for census divisions and census subdivisions – 100% data and 20% sample data, Ontario, 2006 Census (continued)

No.	Characteristics	Essex CD/DR	Amherstburg, T	Essex, T ◊	Kingsville, T ◊	Lakeshore, T	LaSalle, T
	Population characteristics						
1	**Population, 2001[1]**	**374,975**	**20,339**	**20,085**	**19,619**	**28,746**	**25,285**
2	**Population, 2006[2]**	**393,402**	**21,748**	**20,032**	**20,908**	**33,245**	**27,652**
3	Population percentage change, 2001 to 2006	4.9	6.9	-0.3	6.6	15.7	9.4
4	Land area in square kilometres, 2006	1,851.34	185.65	277.95	246.84	530.32	65.25
5	**Total population – 100% data[3]**	**393,400**	**21,750**	**20,030**	**20,910**	**33,245**	**27,655**
	Sex and age groups						
6	Male	193,925	10,765	9,960	10,535	16,805	13,660
7	0 to 4 years	11,925	615	540	570	1,125	925
8	5 to 9 years	12,830	790	630	640	1,260	1,025
9	10 to 14 years	13,790	790	740	765	1,320	1,160
10	15 to 19 years	13,970	835	795	745	1,280	1,050
11	20 to 24 years	13,165	630	590	645	955	825
12	25 to 29 years	12,020	630	490	580	850	615
13	30 to 34 years	13,185	620	575	715	1,020	830
14	35 to 39 years	14,440	755	635	790	1,315	1,070
15	40 to 44 years	16,285	955	865	830	1,510	1,265
16	45 to 49 years	15,430	945	840	875	1,415	1,205
17	50 to 54 years	13,275	755	725	770	1,265	990
18	55 to 59 years	11,945	765	735	695	1,120	825
19	60 to 64 years	9,115	550	545	565	825	610
20	65 to 69 years	6,900	375	400	405	535	460
21	70 to 74 years	5,875	280	325	360	420	375
22	75 to 79 years	4,835	245	255	290	320	235
23	80 to 84 years	3,135	145	170	165	170	140
24	85 years and over	1,815	70	100	130	95	65
25	Female	199,475	10,985	10,070	10,375	16,440	13,990
26	0 to 4 years	11,275	590	505	560	1,035	850
27	5 to 9 years	11,980	695	580	595	1,175	955
28	10 to 14 years	13,145	820	690	710	1,235	1,125
29	15 to 19 years	13,120	780	670	705	1,165	1,020
30	20 to 24 years	13,215	645	560	610	860	790
31	25 to 29 years	12,365	600	470	505	860	680
32	30 to 34 years	13,680	685	610	630	1,195	935
33	35 to 39 years	14,380	820	665	720	1,295	1,200
34	40 to 44 years	16,090	930	865	795	1,515	1,355
35	45 to 49 years	15,085	920	820	810	1,345	1,225
36	50 to 54 years	13,640	820	785	775	1,240	970
37	55 to 59 years	12,305	720	680	710	1,060	885
38	60 to 64 years	9,300	510	555	530	790	580
39	65 to 69 years	7,710	375	415	460	525	475
40	70 to 74 years	6,690	320	360	355	420	345
41	75 to 79 years	6,140	305	320	315	285	295
42	80 to 84 years	5,185	240	295	280	260	210
43	85 years and over	4,175	215	225	315	190	110
44	**Total population 15 years and over[3]**	**318,450**	**17,440**	**16,345**	**17,060**	**26,105**	**21,615**
	Legal marital status						
45	Never legally married (single)	97,995	4,725	4,435	4,340	6,750	5,700
46	Legally married (and not separated)[4,5]	167,895	10,180	9,160	10,160	16,190	13,415
47	Separated, but still legally married	9,375	445	455	445	570	480
48	Divorced	23,070	1,130	1,220	990	1,465	1,125
49	Widowed	20,120	960	1,075	1,130	1,125	900
	Common-law status						
50	Not in a common-law relationship	299,120	16,370	15,265	16,095	24,550	20,695
51	In a common-law relationship	19,340	1,070	1,075	970	1,555	920
52	**Total population – 20% sample data[6]**	**389,585**	**21,600**	**19,820**	**20,500**	**33,110**	**27,565**
	Mother tongue						
53	Single responses	383,975	21,370	19,665	20,390	32,665	27,215
54	English	282,150	18,945	17,425	16,650	26,480	22,250
55	French	12,380	570	535	275	2,875	615
56	Non-official languages[7]	89,445	1,855	1,705	3,455	3,315	4,355
57	Italian	12,090	855	135	340	630	1,070
58	Chinese, n.o.s.[61]	4,800	35	10	10	80	245
59	Cantonese	1,155	0	10	10	0	100
60	Spanish	4,970	30	50	390	35	85
61	German	10,040	185	360	1,500	330	285
62	Other languages[8]	56,390	750	1,140	1,205	2,230	2,570

Note: See symbols and abbreviations in the introductory material and see reference material at the end of the publication.

Certaines caractéristiques des divisions de recensement et des subdivisions de recensement – Données intégrales et données-échantillon (20 %), Ontario, Recensement de 2006 (suite)

Leamington, MU ◊	Pelee, TP ◆◊	Tecumseh, T **A**	Windsor, CY ◊**A**	**Frontenac CD/DR** ◆◊	Central Frontenac, TP ◆◊	**Caractéristiques**	N°
						Caractéristiques de la population	
27,138	**256**	**24,289**	**209,218**	**138,606**	**4,557**	**Population, 2001**[1]	1
28,833	**287**	**24,224**	**216,473**	**143,865**	**4,665**	**Population, 2006**[2]	2
6.2	12.1	-0.3	3.5	3.8	2.4	Variation en pourcentage de la population, 2001 à 2006	3
261.92	41.79	94.71	146.91	3,672.49	970.07	Superficie des terres en kilomètres carrés, 2006	4
28,830	**290**	**24,225**	**216,475**	**143,865**	**4,665**	**Population totale – Données intégrales**[3]	5
						Sexe et groupes d'âge	
14,570	165	11,905	105,560	69,935	2,360	Sexe masculin	6
1,010	0	570	6,565	3,530	90	0 à 4 ans	7
995	5	790	6,695	3,785	160	5 à 9 ans	8
1,005	10	940	7,060	4,530	165	10 à 14 ans	9
1,130	15	1,035	7,090	4,870	155	15 à 19 ans	10
1,005	5	845	7,675	5,290	115	20 à 24 ans	11
975	15	515	7,350	4,595	90	25 à 29 ans	12
980	15	585	7,840	4,190	105	30 à 34 ans	13
1,060	5	765	8,040	4,650	105	35 à 39 ans	14
1,235	20	950	8,650	5,695	175	40 à 44 ans	15
1,100	25	1,130	7,900	5,440	175	45 à 49 ans	16
885	15	990	6,880	5,100	195	50 à 54 ans	17
750	10	915	6,120	4,725	190	55 à 59 ans	18
625	10	680	4,705	3,800	205	60 à 64 ans	19
465	5	435	3,820	3,030	155	65 à 69 ans	20
490	5	335	3,295	2,520	130	70 à 74 ans	21
405	5	240	2,830	2,015	85	75 à 79 ans	22
265	5	125	1,940	1,340	50	80 à 84 ans	23
190	0	55	1,105	845	30	85 ans et plus	24
14,260	120	12,315	110,915	73,930	2,305	Sexe féminin	25
930	0	575	6,230	3,300	100	0 à 4 ans	26
925	5	765	6,285	3,580	115	5 à 9 ans	27
995	5	925	6,640	4,305	135	10 à 14 ans	28
1,045	10	965	6,770	4,685	150	15 à 19 ans	29
950	5	840	7,955	5,485	100	20 à 24 ans	30
880	10	505	7,860	4,640	85	25 à 29 ans	31
820	5	680	8,125	4,120	115	30 à 34 ans	32
890	5	865	7,920	4,695	125	35 à 39 ans	33
1,000	15	1,140	8,480	5,790	170	40 à 44 ans	34
970	15	1,150	7,840	5,975	200	45 à 49 ans	35
840	15	1,020	7,175	5,435	180	50 à 54 ans	36
745	10	965	6,540	5,135	200	55 à 59 ans	37
660	5	605	5,065	4,050	175	60 à 64 ans	38
585	5	430	4,440	3,195	145	65 à 69 ans	39
565	5	330	3,985	2,995	135	70 à 74 ans	40
565	0	270	3,780	2,580	75	75 à 79 ans	41
465	5	185	3,250	2,170	50	80 à 84 ans	42
440	0	105	2,575	1,795	45	85 ans et plus	43
22,980	**255**	**19,660**	**177,005**	**120,835**	**3,905**	**Population totale de 15 ans et plus**[3]	44
						État matrimonial légal	
6,190	55	5,590	60,210	39,985	990	Jamais légalement marié(e) (célibataire)	45
13,150	170	11,680	83,795	58,650	2,195	Légalement marié(e) (et non séparé[e])[4,5]	46
665	0	440	5,875	4,350	130	Séparé(e), mais toujours légalement marié(e)	47
1,260	10	1,105	14,770	9,830	320	Divorcé(e)	48
1,720	20	850	12,350	8,025	270	Veuf(ve)	49
						Union libre	
21,715	240	18,855	165,330	109,980	3,520	Ne vivant pas en union libre	50
1,260	15	810	11,670	10,855	385	Vivant en union libre	51
28,280	**265**	**24,200**	**214,260**	**140,655**	**4,625**	**Population totale – Données-échantillon (20 %)**[6]	52
						Langue maternelle	
27,880	265	23,920	210,600	139,645	4,620	Réponses uniques	53
16,920	230	18,940	144,310	122,335	4,315	Anglais	54
470	0	1,115	5,930	4,070	55	Français	55
10,490	35	3,870	60,365	13,240	250	Langues non officielles[7]	56
605	0	1,055	7,400	700	0	Italien	57
85	0	40	4,300	1,180	10	Chinois, n.d.a.[61]	58
10	0	25	1,000	350	0	Cantonais	59
1,600	30	130	2,605	745	15	Espagnol	60
5,180	0	225	1,975	1,335	75	Allemand	61
3,015	0	2,395	43,080	8,930	145	Autres langues[8]	62

Nota : Voir les symboles et les abréviations dans les documents d'introduction et voir les documents de référence à la fin de la publication.

Selected characteristics for census divisions and census subdivisions – 100% data and 20% sample data, Ontario, 2006 Census (continued)

No.	Characteristics	Essex CD/DR	Amherstburg, T	Essex, T ◊	Kingsville, T ◊	Lakeshore, T	LaSalle, T
	Population characteristics						
	Mother tongue (continued)						
63	Multiple responses	5,610	225	155	105	440	350
64	English and French	1,230	100	40	25	205	60
65	English and non-official language	3,950	95	115	75	205	265
66	French and non-official language	345	20	0	0	20	25
67	English, French and non-official language	85	15	0	0	0	0
	Language spoken most often at home[9]						
68	Single responses	382,080	21,465	19,745	20,305	32,650	27,275
69	English	332,025	20,830	19,120	18,925	30,820	25,540
70	French	3,125	130	25	45	830	85
71	Non-official languages[7]	46,935	510	595	1,340	1,000	1,655
72	Chinese, n.o.s.[61]	3,735	35	10	10	45	215
73	Cantonese	810	0	0	10	25	45
74	Panjabi (Punjabi)	1,845	25	0	0	130	65
75	Italian	4,195	230	10	110	70	295
76	Spanish	3,390	0	30	365	20	15
77	Other languages[8]	32,955	220	545	845	715	1,010
78	Multiple responses	7,505	135	75	190	455	295
79	English and French	760	35	15	35	210	10
80	English and non-official language	6,460	90	60	155	245	280
81	French and non-official language	70	0	0	0	0	0
82	English, French and non-official language	210	0	0	0	0	0
	Knowledge of official languages[10]						
83	English only	344,965	19,310	18,390	18,800	26,865	24,450
84	French only	420	20	0	10	45	10
85	English and French	37,740	2,210	1,330	1,220	6,110	2,990
86	Neither English nor French	6,465	60	100	460	85	115
	Knowledge of non-official languages[7,11]						
87	Italian	16,255	1,035	170	455	910	1,560
88	Spanish	8,105	95	125	655	230	235
89	German	11,720	215	420	1,540	440	420
90	Chinese, n.o.s.[61]	5,050	40	0	10	105	280
91	Cantonese	1,345	0	15	10	35	110
92	Panjabi (Punjabi)	3,330	20	0	0	240	105
93	Portuguese	3,640	75	595	450	80	85
	First official language spoken[10]						
94	English	369,120	20,985	19,295	19,755	30,170	26,800
95	French	11,765	505	420	255	2,790	595
96	English and French	2,430	50	0	25	65	70
97	Neither English nor French	6,265	55	95	460	85	105
98	Official language minority - (number)[12]	12,980	530	425	270	2,820	625
99	Official language minority - (percentage)[12]	3.3	2.5	2.1	1.3	8.5	2.3
	Ethnic origin[13]						
100	English	90,150	6,530	6,635	6,670	8,515	6,225
101	Canadian	103,955	7,885	6,945	5,590	11,550	8,005
102	Scottish	56,115	3,040	3,780	3,945	4,895	4,250
103	Irish	60,025	4,435	3,905	3,405	6,590	4,475
104	French	94,935	7,370	5,980	4,240	12,815	7,810
105	German	47,365	2,460	3,385	4,460	4,075	3,290
106	Italian	37,955	2,745	830	1,565	2,645	4,310
107	Chinese	9,065	90	30	45	185	535
108	East Indian	7,380	60	15	45	500	440
109	Dutch (Netherlands)	12,590	745	1,085	1,405	1,190	990
110	Polish	14,990	850	645	535	1,310	1,210
111	Ukrainian	11,640	635	470	550	1,035	930
112	North American Indian	11,405	775	855	405	1,100	715
113	Portuguese	5,510	135	880	670	135	120
114	Filipino	3,460	60	10	20	80	230
	Aboriginal and non-Aboriginal identity						
115	Total Aboriginal identity population[14]	6,380	410	305	180	595	280
116	Total non-Aboriginal identity population	383,205	21,185	19,515	20,315	32,505	27,285

Note: See symbols and abbreviations in the introductory material and see reference material at the end of the publication.

Certaines caractéristiques des divisions de recensement et des subdivisions de recensement – Données intégrales et données-échantillon (20 %), Ontario, Recensement de 2006 (suite)

Leamington, MU ◊	Pelee, TP ♦◊	Tecumseh, T **A**	Windsor, CY ◊**A**	**Frontenac CD/DR** ♦◊	Central Frontenac, TP ♦◊	**Caractéristiques**	N°
						Caractéristiques de la population	
						Langue maternelle (suite)	
395	0	275	3,660	1,005	0	Réponses multiples	63
45	0	105	650	350	0	Anglais et français	64
340	0	160	2,685	620	0	Anglais et langue non officielle	65
0	0	10	255	20	0	Français et langue non officielle	66
0	0	0	60	15	0	Anglais, français et langue non officielle	67
						Langue parlée le plus souvent à la maison[9]	
27,895	265	23,895	208,590	139,460	4,630	Réponses uniques	68
21,880	230	22,100	172,580	131,960	4,430	Anglais	69
100	0	330	1,575	2,005	0	Français	70
5,915	35	1,460	34,430	5,490	200	Langues non officielles[7]	71
65	0	40	3,320	750	0	Chinois, n.d.a.[61]	72
0	0	0	730	295	0	Cantonais	73
0	0	105	1,520	190	95	Pendjabi	74
245	0	330	2,905	120	0	Italien	75
1,485	35	80	1,360	470	10	Espagnol	76
4,110	0	900	24,605	3,660	90	Autres langues[8]	77
380	0	305	5,665	1,195	0	Réponses multiples	78
0	0	75	375	265	0	Anglais et français	79
365	0	215	5,045	895	0	Anglais et langue non officielle	80
0	0	15	45	25	0	Français et langue non officielle	81
0	0	0	205	10	0	Anglais, français et langue non officielle	82
						Connaissance des langues officielles[10]	
25,020	225	20,705	191,195	121,490	4,320	Anglais seulement	83
10	0	35	285	450	0	Français seulement	84
1,610	10	3,360	18,905	18,160	310	Anglais et français	85
1,635	35	100	3,875	550	0	Ni l'anglais ni le français	86
						Connaissance des langues non officielles[7,11]	
825	0	1,455	9,845	1,095	10	Italien	87
2,415	35	280	4,040	2,200	40	Espagnol	88
5,490	0	275	2,905	2,690	125	Allemand	89
85	0	50	4,465	1,145	0	Chinois, n.d.a.[61]	90
15	0	30	1,130	445	0	Cantonais	91
0	0	230	2,730	325	100	Pendjabi	92
1,450	0	55	850	2,245	0	Portugais	93
						Première langue officielle parlée[10]	
26,100	230	22,940	202,845	135,200	4,515	Anglais	94
435	0	1,050	5,715	4,170	50	Français	95
125	0	115	1,970	755	65	Anglais et français	96
1,615	30	90	3,720	530	0	Ni l'anglais ni le français	97
500	0	1,105	6,705	4,545	80	Minorité de langue officielle - (nombre)[12]	98
1.8	0.0	4.6	3.1	3.2	1.7	Minorité de langue officielle - (pourcentage)[12]	99
						Origine ethnique[13]	
5,825	100	6,030	43,620	49,080	1,475	Anglais	100
6,205	45	6,700	51,025	48,760	1,875	Canadien	101
3,160	50	3,715	29,270	37,210	1,410	Écossais	102
3,015	25	4,290	29,870	39,265	1,420	Irlandais	103
3,450	35	7,580	45,660	21,125	520	Français	104
7,800	115	2,690	19,080	14,235	590	Allemand	105
1,830	0	3,540	20,485	3,790	55	Italien	106
160	0	265	7,755	2,540	0	Chinois	107
60	0	425	5,835	1,600	105	Indien de l'Inde	108
1,515	10	715	4,935	8,645	305	Hollandais (Néerlandais)	109
390	0	970	9,090	3,575	60	Polonais	110
895	0	845	6,270	2,625	105	Ukrainien	111
430	30	440	6,650	5,260	395	Indien de l'Amérique du Nord	112
1,975	0	200	1,395	3,315	20	Portugais	113
25	0	245	2,790	530	0	Philippin	114
						Population ayant une identité autochtone et population n'ayant pas d'identité autochtone	
305	0	335	3,960	3,360	375	Total de la population ayant une identité autochtone[14]	115
27,970	265	23,865	210,295	137,290	4,255	Total de la population n'ayant pas d'identité autochtone	116

Nota : Voir les symboles et les abréviations dans les documents d'introduction et voir les documents de référence à la fin de la publication.

Selected characteristics for census divisions and census subdivisions – 100% data and 20% sample data, Ontario, 2006 Census (continued)

No.	Characteristics	Essex CD/DR	Amherstburg, T	Essex, T ◊	Kingsville, T ◊	Lakeshore, T	LaSalle, T
	Population characteristics						
	Aboriginal and non-Aboriginal ancestry						
117	Total Aboriginal ancestry population[15]	14,015	980	965	485	1,470	795
118	Total non-Aboriginal ancestry population	375,570	20,625	18,850	20,010	31,635	26,770
	Registered Indian status						
119	Registered Indian[16]	1,795	50	110	55	135	85
120	Not a Registered Indian	387,790	21,550	19,710	20,445	32,970	27,480
	Visible minority groups						
121	Total visible minority population[17]	55,240	725	355	745	1,490	2,530
122	Chinese	8,035	45	35	25	155	460
123	South Asian[18]	10,350	25	10	0	495	525
124	Black	10,115	400	190	190	260	310
125	Filipino	3,200	60	10	20	65	185
126	Latin American	4,770	20	40	395	30	105
127	Southeast Asian[19]	3,230	70	0	15	115	10
128	Arab	10,700	20	65	75	230	540
129	West Asian[20]	1,860	15	0	0	80	10
130	Korean	605	10	0	0	15	210
131	Japanese	195	35	0	0	0	10
132	Visible minority, n.i.e.[21]	1,075	15	0	0	15	0
133	Multiple visible minority[22]	1,095	15	0	10	30	155
	Citizenship[23]						
134	Canadian citizens[24]	364,370	21,015	19,270	19,340	32,060	26,480
135	Not Canadian citizens[25]	25,220	585	545	1,160	1,045	1,085
	Immigrant status and place of birth[26]						
136	Non-immigrants[27]	296,670	19,105	17,820	16,860	29,355	22,795
137	Born in province of residence	278,465	18,240	17,000	16,000	27,960	21,845
138	Immigrants[28]	87,170	2,440	1,925	2,955	3,605	4,710
139	United States of America	7,635	510	310	310	605	720
140	Central and South America	7,035	55	110	725	155	110
141	Caribbean and Bermuda	1,160	30	35	10	15	25
142	United Kingdom	6,390	520	365	400	525	420
143	Other Europe	33,425	1,115	1,015	1,395	1,515	1,925
144	Africa	3,465	50	10	0	95	185
145	Asia and the Middle East	27,750	145	70	110	675	1,305
146	Oceania and other[29]	305	10	0	10	20	10
147	Non-permanent residents[30]	5,745	55	75	680	145	65
148	**Total immigrant population[28]**	**87,170**	**2,440**	**1,925**	**2,955**	**3,605**	**4,705**
	Period of immigration						
149	Before 1961	13,960	765	605	915	580	720
150	1961 to 1970	12,390	630	425	530	660	930
151	1971 to 1980	11,635	455	375	515	680	915
152	1981 to 1990	11,410	165	210	335	580	625
153	1991 to 2000	22,605	230	180	380	685	970
154	1991 to 1995	10,155	70	95	275	310	470
155	1996 to 2000	12,445	160	85	105	375	495
156	2001 to 2006[31]	15,165	200	125	275	410	550
	Age at immigration						
157	Under 5 years	9,810	440	235	435	515	550
158	5 to 19 years	25,540	855	635	1,165	1,200	1,365
159	20 years and over	51,820	1,145	1,055	1,365	1,890	2,795
160	**Total population 15 years and over**	**314,630**	**17,270**	**16,145**	**16,630**	**25,970**	**21,500**
	Generation status						
161	1st generation[32]	86,385	2,330	1,960	3,450	3,485	4,445
162	2nd generation[33]	62,915	3,110	2,825	3,465	4,770	5,010
163	3rd generation or more[34]	165,325	11,835	11,360	9,715	17,715	12,040

Note: See symbols and abbreviations in the introductory material and see reference material at the end of the publication.

Certaines caractéristiques des divisions de recensement et des subdivisions de recensement – Données intégrales et données-échantillon (20 %), Ontario, Recensement de 2006 (suite)

Leamington, MU ◊	Pelee, TP ♦◊	Tecumseh, T **A**	Windsor, CY ◊**A**	**Frontenac CD/DR** ♦◊	Central Frontenac, TP ♦◊	**Caractéristiques**	N°
						Caractéristiques de la population	
						Population ayant une ascendance autochtone et population n'ayant pas d'ascendance autochtone	
535	30	580	8,180	6,585	530	Total de la population ayant une ascendance autochtone[15]	117
27,740	230	23,620	206,080	134,065	4,100	Total de la population n'ayant pas d'ascendance autochtone	118
						Statut d'Indien inscrit	
110	0	80	1,175	1,025	160	Indien inscrit[16]	119
28,165	265	24,120	213,085	139,625	4,470	Pas un Indien inscrit	120
						Groupes de minorités visibles	
2,915	35	1,395	45,060	8,540	105	Total de la population des minorités visibles[17]	121
150	0	200	6,965	2,440	0	Chinois	122
80	0	455	8,765	1,865	95	Sud-Asiatique[18]	123
245	0	120	8,395	1,115	0	Noir	124
25	0	215	2,630	455	0	Philippin	125
1,390	35	105	2,645	735	10	Latino-Américain	126
275	0	30	2,730	325	0	Asiatique du Sud-Est[19]	127
585	0	195	8,990	365	0	Arabe	128
25	0	15	1,710	280	0	Asiatique occidental[20]	129
0	0	20	350	310	0	Coréen	130
40	0	0	95	255	0	Japonais	131
80	0	30	930	170	0	Minorité visible, n.i.a.[21]	132
25	0	0	850	210	0	Minorités visibles multiples[22]	133
						Citoyenneté[23]	
25,655	195	23,570	196,780	136,370	4,550	Citoyens canadiens[24]	134
2,620	65	625	17,475	4,280	80	Ne sont pas des citoyens canadiens[25]	135
						Statut d'immigrant et le lieu de naissance[26]	
19,365	175	19,900	151,295	121,670	4,305	Non-immigrants[27]	136
17,940	175	18,930	140,365	101,055	3,990	Né dans la province de résidence	137
7,485	35	4,155	59,855	17,940	305	Immigrants[28]	138
350	35	475	4,320	1,540	75	États-Unis d'Amérique	139
3,425	0	140	2,310	700	15	Amérique centrale et Amérique du Sud	140
40	0	30	970	365	0	Antilles et Bermudes	141
320	0	485	3,355	4,250	45	Royaume-Uni	142
2,370	0	2,160	21,925	6,465	100	Autre Europe	143
0	0	50	3,055	705	0	Afrique	144
960	0	790	23,690	3,755	65	Asie et Moyen-Orient	145
10	0	25	225	150	0	Océanie et autres[29]	146
1,430	50	140	3,105	1,045	20	Résidents non permanents[30]	147
7,480	**35**	**4,160**	**59,855**	**17,935**	**305**	**Population totale des immigrants[28]**	148
						Période d'immigration	
1,320	20	760	8,265	4,810	100	Avant 1961	149
1,180	15	915	7,105	3,580	65	1961 à 1970	150
1,175	0	985	6,535	2,485	75	1971 à 1980	151
1,335	0	585	7,580	2,310	40	1981 à 1990	152
1,540	0	530	18,090	2,655	20	1991 à 2000	153
705	0	275	7,955	1,235	0	1991 à 1995	154
835	0	250	10,140	1,420	15	1996 à 2000	155
935	0	385	12,280	2,100	0	2001 à 2006[31]	156
						Âge à l'immigration	
970	0	625	6,040	2,155	55	Moins de 5 ans	157
2,820	15	1,025	16,465	4,935	60	5 à 19 ans	158
3,695	20	2,505	37,345	10,850	190	20 ans et plus	159
22,390	**250**	**19,630**	**174,835**	**117,615**	**3,865**	**Population totale de 15 ans et plus**	160
						Statut des générations	
8,465	85	4,030	58,130	18,715	325	1re génération[32]	161
5,080	40	4,345	34,265	20,220	365	2e génération[33]	162
8,840	120	11,250	82,440	78,680	3,165	3e génération ou plus[34]	163

Nota : Voir les symboles et les abréviations dans les documents d'introduction et voir les documents de référence à la fin de la publication.

Selected characteristics for census divisions and census subdivisions – 100% data and 20% sample data, Ontario, 2006 Census (continued)

No.	Characteristics	Essex CD/DR	Amherstburg, T	Essex, T ◊	Kingsville, T ◊	Lakeshore, T	LaSalle, T
	Population characteristics						
164	**Total population 1 year and over[35]**	**384,985**	**21,370**	**19,665**	**20,270**	**32,765**	**27,310**
	Place of residence 1 year ago (mobility)						
165	Non-movers	338,895	19,450	17,485	18,415	30,210	25,030
166	Movers	46,095	1,920	2,180	1,855	2,555	2,275
167	Non-migrants	29,470	935	970	680	860	1,165
168	Migrants	16,620	990	1,210	1,170	1,690	1,110
169	Internal migrants	12,970	935	1,130	860	1,530	995
170	Intraprovincial migrants	11,930	895	1,080	815	1,450	960
171	Interprovincial migrants	1,035	45	50	45	80	35
172	External migrants	3,650	50	80	310	160	115
173	**Total population 5 years and over[36]**	**366,220**	**20,375**	**18,795**	**19,350**	**30,945**	**25,785**
	Place of residence 5 years ago (mobility)						
174	Non-movers	227,695	13,580	13,290	13,475	20,885	18,155
175	Movers	138,525	6,795	5,500	5,875	10,060	7,625
176	Non-migrants	83,960	3,435	2,675	2,435	4,275	4,300
177	Migrants	54,560	3,360	2,825	3,435	5,780	3,325
178	Internal migrants	38,355	3,155	2,635	2,640	5,340	2,855
179	Intraprovincial migrants	34,530	3,040	2,540	2,450	5,195	2,740
180	Interprovincial migrants	3,825	115	100	190	145	115
181	External migrants	16,210	205	185	790	445	470
182	**Total population 15 years and over**	**314,630**	**17,270**	**16,150**	**16,635**	**25,970**	**21,500**
	Highest certificate, diploma or degree[37]						
183	No certificate, diploma or degree	76,115	3,980	4,405	4,645	5,395	3,760
184	Certificate, diploma or degree	238,520	13,295	11,745	11,985	20,575	17,735
185	High school certificate or equivalent[38]	94,490	5,395	5,285	4,680	8,080	6,055
186	Apprenticeship or trades certificate or diploma	26,165	1,755	1,795	1,520	2,480	1,835
187	College, CEGEP or other non-university certificate or diploma[39]	56,875	3,625	3,055	3,185	5,550	4,555
188	University certificate or diploma below bachelor level[40]	9,745	450	380	455	585	710
189	University certificate or degree[41]	51,240	2,065	1,235	2,150	3,880	4,585
190	Bachelor's degree	30,840	1,340	760	1,275	2,260	2,750
191	University certificate or diploma above bachelor level	7,330	340	180	520	670	665
192	Degree in medicine, dentistry, veterinary medicine or optometry	1,735	60	65	55	220	135
193	Master's degree	9,320	270	175	245	645	790
194	Earned doctorate	2,010	55	45	50	75	240
195	**Total population 15 years and over with postsecondary qualifications**	**144,025**	**7,900**	**6,465**	**7,310**	**12,495**	**11,685**
	Major field of study - Classification of Instructional Programs, 2000[42]						
196	Education	10,260	515	355	635	815	830
197	Visual and performing arts, and communications technologies	3,045	145	125	125	225	200
198	Humanities	6,060	320	185	375	330	450
199	Social and behavioural sciences and law	14,795	655	560	705	1,280	1,185
200	Business, management and public administration	27,145	1,285	1,095	1,275	2,410	2,275
201	Physical and life sciences and technologies	3,975	175	110	155	270	350
202	Mathematics, computer and information sciences	5,740	170	225	155	450	445
203	Architecture, engineering, and related technologies	38,390	2,490	1,970	1,830	3,600	3,175
204	Agriculture, natural resources and conservation	1,910	115	145	275	150	100
205	Health, parks, recreation and fitness	23,190	1,415	1,140	1,220	2,055	2,000
206	Personal, protective and transportation services	9,495	610	555	560	910	675
207	Other fields of study[43]	20	0	0	0	0	0
	Location of study[44]						
208	Inside Canada	116,455	7,190	5,980	6,615	11,155	9,805
209	Outside Canada	27,575	705	480	695	1,340	1,885
210	**Total population 15 years and over**	**314,630**	**17,270**	**16,150**	**16,635**	**25,970**	**21,500**
	Unpaid work						
211	Males 15 years and over	153,910	8,500	7,975	8,400	13,090	10,500
212	Reported unpaid work[45]	138,415	7,805	7,205	7,460	12,160	9,705
213	Housework and child care and care or assistance to seniors	12,980	750	770	750	1,145	1,145
214	Housework and child care only	39,780	2,470	2,040	2,070	3,960	3,100

Note: See symbols and abbreviations in the introductory material and see reference material at the end of the publication.

Certaines caractéristiques des divisions de recensement et des subdivisions de recensement – Données intégrales et données-échantillon (20 %), Ontario, Recensement de 2006 (suite)

Leamington, MU ◊	Pelee, TP ♦◊	Tecumseh, T A	Windsor, CY ◊A	**Frontenac CD/DR ♦◊**	Central Frontenac, TP ♦◊	Caractéristiques	N°
						Caractéristiques de la population	
27,965	**265**	**24,020**	**211,355**	**139,365**	**4,580**	**Population totale de 1 an et plus[35]**	164
						Lieu de résidence 1 an auparavant (mobilité)	
23,680	245	22,360	182,010	117,700	4,235	Personnes n'ayant pas déménagé	165
4,285	20	1,660	29,345	21,660	345	Personnes ayant déménagé	166
2,525	10	830	21,495	12,585	60	Non-migrants	167
1,760	15	830	7,850	9,075	285	Migrants	168
1,205	0	730	5,575	7,985	255	Migrants internes	169
1,125	0	695	4,915	6,025	240	Migrants infraprovinciaux	170
80	0	35	660	1,960	10	Migrants interprovinciaux	171
555	0	100	2,275	1,090	30	Migrants externes	172
26,375	**265**	**23,055**	**201,285**	**133,760**	**4,405**	**Population totale de 5 ans et plus[36]**	173
						Lieu de résidence 5 ans auparavant (mobilité)	
14,780	205	17,280	116,035	76,065	3,180	Personnes n'ayant pas déménagé	174
11,595	60	5,770	85,240	57,695	1,225	Personnes ayant déménagé	175
6,400	30	3,535	56,860	29,365	365	Non-migrants	176
5,195	25	2,235	28,385	28,330	855	Migrants	177
3,330	0	1,880	16,515	24,680	800	Migrants internes	178
2,985	10	1,830	13,755	19,050	760	Migrants infraprovinciaux	179
345	10	55	2,755	5,635	45	Migrants interprovinciaux	180
1,860	20	355	11,875	3,645	50	Migrants externes	181
22,395	**250**	**19,630**	**174,835**	**117,615**	**3,860**	**Population totale de 15 ans et plus**	182
						Plus haut certificat, diplôme ou grade[37]	
9,940	85	3,605	40,295	22,430	1,215	Aucun certificat, diplôme ou grade	183
12,450	160	16,020	134,535	95,185	2,650	Certificat, diplôme ou grade	184
5,995	90	5,630	53,280	31,575	1,130	Diplôme d'études secondaires ou l'équivalent[38]	185
1,465	10	1,610	13,690	9,390	345	Certificat ou diplôme d'apprenti ou d'une école de métiers	186
3,000	20	3,955	29,935	24,465	625	Certificat ou diplôme d'un collège, d'un cégep ou d'un autre établissement d'enseignement non universitaire[39]	187
395	20	830	5,925	3,660	130	Certificat ou diplôme universitaire inférieur au baccalauréat[40]	188
1,600	30	3,995	31,705	26,085	420	Certificat ou grade universitaire[41]	189
950	20	2,350	19,135	14,060	215	Baccalauréat	190
260	0	735	3,960	2,840	80	Certificat ou diplôme universitaire supérieur au baccalauréat	191
70	0	185	935	1,280	0	Diplôme en médecine, en art dentaire, en médecine vétérinaire ou en optométrie	192
270	10	665	6,245	5,405	110	Maîtrise	193
45	0	70	1,425	2,510	10	Doctorat acquis	194
6,460	**70**	**10,390**	**81,260**	**63,610**	**1,520**	**Population totale de 15 ans et plus avec titres du niveau postsecondaire**	195
						Principal domaine d'études - Classification des programmes d'enseignement, 2000[42]	
535	15	1,090	5,470	5,030	185	Éducation	196
95	0	195	1,930	1,860	35	Arts visuels et d'interprétation, et technologie des communications	197
280	10	445	3,670	4,185	70	Sciences humaines	198
450	0	1,055	8,905	7,740	140	Sciences sociales et de comportements, et droit	199
1,300	10	2,030	15,470	10,720	260	Commerce, gestion et administration publique	200
130	0	270	2,510	3,065	65	Sciences physiques et de la vie, et technologies	201
190	0	305	3,800	2,480	25	Mathématiques, informatique et sciences de l'information	202
1,575	30	2,470	21,255	11,800	330	Architecture, génie et services connexes	203
275	0	120	725	815	30	Agriculture, ressources naturelles et conservation	204
1,095	0	1,810	12,445	11,930	270	Santé, parcs, récréation et conditionnement physique	205
525	0	605	5,055	3,970	95	Services personnels, de protection et de transport	206
10	0	0	10	0	0	Autres domaines d'études[43]	207
						Lieu des études[44]	
5,590	35	8,675	61,405	56,765	1,400	À l'intérieur du Canada	208
865	35	1,710	19,855	6,840	120	À l'extérieur du Canada	209
22,395	**250**	**19,630**	**174,835**	**117,615**	**3,860**	**Population totale de 15 ans et plus**	210
						Travail non rémunéré	
11,395	165	9,570	84,310	55,955	1,945	Hommes de 15 ans et plus	211
9,990	130	8,775	75,200	50,670	1,770	Travail non rémunéré déclaré[45]	212
770	0	1,235	6,410	4,045	145	Travaux ménagers et soins aux enfants et soins ou aide aux personnes âgées	213
3,165	15	2,575	20,380	13,395	375	Travaux ménagers et soins aux enfants seulement	214

Nota : Voir les symboles et les abréviations dans les documents d'introduction et voir les documents de référence à la fin de la publication.

Selected characteristics for census divisions and census subdivisions – 100% data and 20% sample data, Ontario, 2006 Census (continued)

No.	Characteristics	Essex CD/DR	Amherstburg, T	Essex, T ◊	Kingsville, T ◊	Lakeshore, T	LaSalle, T
	Population characteristics						
	Unpaid work (continued)						
215	Housework and care or assistance to seniors only	11,375	680	640	655	990	855
216	Child care and care or assistance to seniors only	175	15	0	10	15	0
217	Housework only	72,050	3,800	3,700	3,960	5,855	4,470
218	Child care only	1,435	55	35	10	125	75
219	Care or assistance to seniors only	620	30	10	10	70	55
220	Females 15 years and over	160,725	8,770	8,170	8,235	12,885	11,000
221	Reported unpaid work[45]	150,075	8,240	7,655	7,740	12,305	10,405
222	Housework and child care and care or assistance to seniors	19,830	1,200	1,025	1,135	1,925	1,715
223	Housework and child care only	48,505	2,785	2,380	2,245	4,515	3,535
224	Housework and care or assistance to seniors only	14,000	740	935	805	1,105	885
225	Child care and care or assistance to seniors only	215	10	0	15	20	10
226	Housework only	66,165	3,450	3,280	3,495	4,655	4,175
227	Child care only	985	45	20	15	35	60
228	Care or assistance to seniors only	370	10	15	15	40	35
	Labour force activity						
229	Males 15 years and over	153,905	8,505	7,970	8,400	13,085	10,500
230	In the labour force	108,485	6,030	5,740	6,260	10,005	7,860
231	Employed	100,350	5,670	5,430	5,950	9,520	7,425
232	Unemployed	8,125	355	310	305	485	435
233	Not in the labour force	45,425	2,475	2,230	2,140	3,085	2,635
234	Participation rate	70.5	70.9	72.0	74.5	76.5	74.9
235	Employment rate	65.2	66.7	68.1	70.8	72.8	70.7
236	Unemployment rate	7.5	5.9	5.4	4.9	4.8	5.5
237	Females 15 years and over	160,720	8,770	8,175	8,235	12,880	11,000
238	In the labour force	95,290	5,340	4,945	5,080	8,425	7,285
239	Employed	87,320	4,925	4,665	4,750	7,885	6,930
240	Unemployed	7,970	415	285	330	545	355
241	Not in the labour force	65,435	3,430	3,225	3,155	4,455	3,715
242	Participation rate	59.3	60.9	60.5	61.7	65.4	66.2
243	Employment rate	54.3	56.2	57.1	57.7	61.2	63.0
244	Unemployment rate	8.4	7.8	5.8	6.5	6.5	4.9
245	Both sexes - Participation rate	64.8	65.8	66.2	68.2	71.0	70.5
246	15 to 24 years	67.3	71.4	73.4	75.5	72.2	69.5
247	25 years and over	64.2	64.6	64.8	66.8	70.7	70.7
248	Both sexes - Employment rate	59.6	61.3	62.5	64.3	67.0	66.8
249	15 to 24 years	56.5	58.5	64.1	66.9	63.9	61.0
250	25 years and over	60.3	61.9	62.2	63.8	67.6	68.0
251	Both sexes - Unemployment rate	7.9	6.8	5.5	5.6	5.6	5.2
252	15 to 24 years	16.1	18.2	12.5	11.4	11.5	12.1
253	25 years and over	6.1	4.3	4.0	4.4	4.4	3.8
254	**Total labour force 15 years and over**	**203,770**	**11,365**	**10,685**	**11,335**	**18,435**	**15,145**
	Industry - North American Industry Classification System 2002						
255	Industry - Not applicable[46]	4,725	245	95	100	320	225
256	All industries[47]	199,045	11,115	10,590	11,235	18,115	14,920
257	11 Agriculture, forestry, fishing and hunting	7,095	245	495	1,575	405	60
258	21 Mining and oil and gas extraction	365	55	20	25	35	80
259	22 Utilities	890	65	75	60	165	100
260	23 Construction	9,800	650	635	650	1,295	770
261	31-33 Manufacturing	47,480	2,815	2,710	2,200	5,035	3,440
262	41 Wholesale trade	5,900	265	385	340	565	460
263	44-45 Retail trade	21,960	1,155	1,135	985	1,800	1,560
264	48-49 Transportation and warehousing	8,800	425	805	515	860	485
265	51 Information and cultural industries	2,640	120	130	130	195	200
266	52 Finance and insurance	5,315	305	245	275	690	530
267	53 Real estate and rental and leasing	2,695	140	105	140	235	195
268	54 Professional, scientific and technical services	8,695	445	365	385	885	865
269	55 Management of companies and enterprises	150	0	0	0	25	10
270	56 Administrative and support, waste management and remediation services	6,470	285	295	365	425	480
271	61 Educational services	13,085	755	405	690	1,060	1,165
272	62 Health care and social assistance	19,540	1,265	1,090	1,100	1,665	1,570

Note: See symbols and abbreviations in the introductory material and see reference material at the end of the publication.

Certaines caractéristiques des divisions de recensement et des subdivisions de recensement – Données intégrales et données-échantillon (20 %), Ontario, Recensement de 2006 (suite)

Leamington, MU ◊	Pelee, TP ♦◊	Tecumseh, T A	Windsor, CY ◊A	**Frontenac CD/DR** ♦◊	Central Frontenac, TP ♦◊	**Caractéristiques**	Nº
						Caractéristiques de la population	
						Travail non rémunéré (suite)	
740	35	745	6,025	4,395	165	Travaux ménagers et soins ou aide aux personnes âgées seulement	215
30	0	15	90	60	0	Soins aux enfants et soins ou aide aux personnes âgées seulement	216
5,135	75	4,090	40,970	28,285	1,060	Travaux ménagers seulement	217
110	0	85	935	290	20	Soins aux enfants seulement	218
35	0	25	385	200	0	Soins ou aide aux personnes âgées seulement	219
10,990	80	10,060	90,530	61,660	1,920	Femmes de 15 ans et plus	220
10,245	80	9,510	83,895	57,615	1,810	Travail non rémunéré déclaré[45]	221
1,250	15	1,820	9,735	5,875	250	Travaux ménagers et soins aux enfants et soins ou aide aux personnes âgées	222
3,710	15	2,780	26,540	16,450	375	Travaux ménagers et soins aux enfants seulement	223
940	20	995	7,565	6,080	175	Travaux ménagers et soins ou aide aux personnes âgées seulement	224
10	0	20	130	25	10	Soins aux enfants et soins ou aide aux personnes âgées seulement	225
4,255	25	3,805	39,025	28,775	985	Travaux ménagers seulement	226
40	0	80	685	225	0	Soins aux enfants seulement	227
30	0	0	220	190	15	Soins ou aide aux personnes âgées seulement	228
						Activité	
11,400	165	9,570	84,305	55,960	1,940	Hommes de 15 ans et plus	229
8,420	125	7,095	56,945	37,925	1,015	Population active	230
7,920	120	6,690	51,615	35,315	950	Personnes occupées	231
500	0	405	5,330	2,615	70	Chômeurs	232
2,975	45	2,470	27,360	18,025	925	Inactifs	233
73.9	75.8	74.1	67.5	67.8	52.3	Taux d'activité	234
69.5	72.7	69.9	61.2	63.1	49.0	Taux d'emploi	235
5.9	0.0	5.7	9.4	6.9	6.9	Taux de chômage	236
10,995	80	10,065	90,525	61,660	1,920	Femmes de 15 ans et plus	237
6,265	40	6,610	51,295	37,275	845	Population active	238
5,800	40	6,230	46,095	34,840	820	Personnes occupées	239
465	0	375	5,200	2,430	25	Chômeuses	240
4,730	35	3,450	39,230	24,380	1,075	Inactives	241
57.0	50.0	65.7	56.7	60.5	44.0	Taux d'activité	242
52.8	50.0	61.9	50.9	56.5	42.7	Taux d'emploi	243
7.4	0.0	5.7	10.1	6.5	3.0	Taux de chômage	244
65.6	66.0	69.8	61.9	63.9	48.3	Les deux sexes - Taux d'activité	245
73.5	100.0	70.2	63.4	68.2	52.8	15 à 24 ans	246
63.8	61.4	69.7	61.6	63.1	47.7	25 ans et plus	247
61.3	67.3	65.8	55.9	59.6	45.7	Les deux sexes - Taux d'emploi	248
65.8	100.0	61.2	51.1	57.8	46.6	15 à 24 ans	249
60.3	60.5	66.9	56.8	60.0	45.6	25 ans et plus	250
6.6	6.1	5.7	9.7	6.7	5.1	Les deux sexes - Taux de chômage	251
10.4	0.0	12.8	19.4	15.3	12.8	15 à 24 ans	252
5.6	0.0	4.0	7.7	4.8	4.0	25 ans et plus	253
14,685	**165**	**13,710**	**108,240**	**75,205**	**1,860**	**Population active totale de 15 ans et plus**	254
						Industrie - Système de classification des industries de l'Amérique du Nord de 2002	
225	0	190	3,315	1,060	10	Industrie - Sans objet[46]	255
14,460	165	13,515	104,925	74,140	1,850	Toutes les industries[47]	256
3,440	25	120	730	750	45	11 Agriculture, foresterie, pêche et chasse	257
15	0	20	115	110	0	21 Extraction minière et extraction de pétrole et de gaz	258
25	0	50	340	410	15	22 Services publics	259
720	10	610	4,455	4,500	195	23 Construction	260
3,015	45	3,160	25,060	3,930	175	31-33 Fabrication	261
600	10	335	2,945	1,715	50	41 Commerce de gros	262
1,265	15	1,555	12,485	8,905	235	44-45 Commerce de détail	263
815	10	475	4,395	2,315	120	48-49 Transport et entreposage	264
110	0	225	1,530	1,265	35	51 Industrie de l'information et industrie culturelle	265
280	0	550	2,440	2,125	40	52 Finance et assurances	266
130	10	335	1,410	1,490	30	53 Services immobiliers et services de location et de location à bail	267
245	0	475	5,020	3,360	55	54 Services professionnels, scientifiques et techniques	268
0	0	0	110	60	0	55 Gestion de sociétés et d'entreprises	269
420	10	275	3,915	3,610	100	56 Services administratifs, services de soutien, services de gestion des déchets et services d'assainissement	270
535	0	1,140	7,325	9,550	160	61 Services d'enseignement	271
940	0	1,585	10,325	10,480	195	62 Soins de santé et assistance sociale	272

Nota : Voir les symboles et les abréviations dans les documents d'introduction et voir les documents de référence à la fin de la publication.

Selected characteristics for census divisions and census subdivisions – 100% data and 20% sample data, Ontario, 2006 Census (continued)

No.	Characteristics	Essex CD/DR	Amherstburg, T	Essex, T ◊	Kingsville, T ◊	Lakeshore, T	LaSalle, T
	Population characteristics						
	Industry - North American Industry Classification System 2002 (continued)						
273	71 Arts, entertainment and recreation	7,190	510	245	240	440	605
274	72 Accommodation and food services	15,415	685	615	730	880	1,075
275	81 Other services (except public administration)	8,825	510	555	495	725	585
276	91 Public administration	6,735	400	275	315	715	685
	Class of worker						
277	Class of worker - Not applicable[46]	4,725	245	95	100	320	225
278	All classes of worker[47]	199,045	11,120	10,595	11,235	18,115	14,920
279	Paid workers	187,600	10,465	9,855	10,315	16,895	14,165
280	Employees	181,685	10,120	9,570	9,880	16,030	13,700
281	Self-employed (incorporated)	5,920	345	285	435	865	465
282	Self-employed (unincorporated)	10,960	605	695	875	1,135	735
283	Unpaid family workers	485	45	40	45	80	20
	Occupation - National Occupational Classification for Statistics 2006						
284	Male labour force 15 years and over	108,480	6,025	5,740	6,255	10,005	7,865
285	Occupation - Not applicable[46]	2,105	100	40	40	135	130
286	All occupations[47]	106,370	5,930	5,700	6,220	9,870	7,735
287	A Management occupations	9,595	655	355	480	1,170	905
288	B Business, finance and administrative occupations	7,010	355	425	335	555	590
289	C Natural and applied sciences and related occupations	8,350	360	270	240	690	845
290	D Health occupations	2,155	130	65	95	210	215
291	E Occupations in social science, education, government service and religion	4,580	205	135	235	290	385
292	F Occupations in art, culture, recreation and sport	1,525	65	65	70	100	80
293	G Sales and service occupations	20,025	1,020	860	1,020	1,515	1,350
294	H Trades, transport and equipment operators and related occupations	29,515	1,945	2,230	1,915	3,305	2,015
295	I Occupations unique to primary industry	6,015	290	395	1,120	440	245
296	J Occupations unique to processing, manufacturing and utilities	17,590	900	905	710	1,595	1,095
297	Female labour force 15 years and over	95,285	5,335	4,945	5,075	8,425	7,285
298	Occupation - Not applicable[46]	2,615	150	55	65	190	100
299	All occupations[47]	92,675	5,190	4,890	5,015	8,245	7,190
300	A Management occupations	5,820	300	330	360	595	540
301	B Business, finance and administrative occupations	20,470	1,210	1,160	1,170	2,115	1,755
302	C Natural and applied sciences and related occupations	2,080	85	125	50	195	240
303	D Health occupations	10,220	670	580	650	865	915
304	E Occupations in social science, education, government service and religion	10,065	575	365	520	945	935
305	F Occupations in art, culture, recreation and sport	1,985	75	95	50	165	155
306	G Sales and service occupations	30,045	1,760	1,465	1,365	2,200	2,080
307	H Trades, transport and equipment operators and related occupations	2,045	150	160	60	260	95
308	I Occupations unique to primary industry	1,945	50	175	350	90	40
309	J Occupations unique to processing, manufacturing and utilities	8,000	320	435	435	805	425
310	**Total employed labour force 15 years and over**	**187,670**	**10,595**	**10,095**	**10,700**	**17,405**	**14,355**
	Place of work status						
311	Males	100,350	5,675	5,430	5,950	9,520	7,425
312	Usual place of work	80,405	4,670	4,425	4,650	7,495	5,955
313	At home	5,405	255	355	540	625	225
314	Outside Canada	4,365	145	130	80	255	615
315	No fixed workplace address	10,175	605	520	675	1,145	625
316	Females	87,315	4,920	4,665	4,745	7,885	6,930
317	Usual place of work	75,675	4,365	4,065	4,065	6,685	5,835
318	At home	4,610	250	295	445	540	360
319	Outside Canada	3,285	140	80	60	270	475
320	No fixed workplace address	3,750	170	220	175	385	260

Note: See symbols and abbreviations in the introductory material and see reference material at the end of the publication.

Certaines caractéristiques des divisions de recensement et des subdivisions de recensement – Données intégrales et données-échantillon (20 %), Ontario, Recensement de 2006 (suite)

Leamington, MU ◊	Pelee, TP ◆◊	Tecumseh, T A	Windsor, CY ◊A	**Frontenac CD/DR** ◆◊	Central Frontenac, TP ◆◊	Caractéristiques	N°
						Caractéristiques de la population	
						Industrie - Système de classification des industries de l'Amérique du Nord de 2002 (suite)	
160	10	415	4,565	1,465	60	71 Arts, spectacles et loisirs	273
905	25	985	9,515	6,050	130	72 Hébergement et services de restauration	274
565	0	610	4,765	3,205	85	81 Autres services (sauf les administrations publiques)	275
270	10	585	3,475	8,850	110	91 Administrations publiques	276
						Catégorie de travailleurs	
220	0	190	3,320	1,060	10	Catégorie de travailleurs - Sans objet[46]	277
14,460	165	13,515	104,925	74,140	1,850	Toutes les catégories de travailleurs[47]	278
13,280	140	12,855	99,630	68,540	1,630	Travailleurs rémunérés	279
12,775	140	12,235	97,235	66,640	1,530	Employés	280
505	0	615	2,395	1,895	100	Travailleurs autonomes (entreprise constituée en société)	281
1,100	25	650	5,135	5,510	210	Travailleurs autonomes (entreprise non constituée en société)	282
80	0	15	155	95	10	Travailleurs familiaux non rémunérés	283
						Profession - Classification nationale des professions pour statistiques de 2006	
8,420	125	7,095	56,945	37,930	1,015	Hommes actifs de 15 ans et plus	284
100	0	80	1,480	555	0	Profession - Sans objet[46]	285
8,320	120	7,010	55,460	37,375	1,015	Toutes les professions[47]	286
505	0	970	4,545	4,215	130	A Gestion	287
295	0	505	3,940	3,225	40	B Affaires, finance et administration	288
265	0	555	5,120	3,525	15	C Sciences naturelles et appliquées et professions apparentées	289
95	0	250	1,105	1,345	10	D Secteur de la santé	290
170	0	280	2,880	3,905	65	E Sciences sociales, enseignement, administration publique et religion	291
40	0	95	1,000	885	15	F Arts, culture, sports et loisirs	292
1,085	20	1,445	11,720	9,445	130	G Ventes et services	293
2,395	25	1,715	13,965	8,365	415	H Métiers, transport et machinerie	294
2,310	70	170	970	1,070	80	I Professions propres au secteur primaire	295
1,150	0	1,015	10,220	1,395	105	J Transformation, fabrication et services d'utilité publique	296
6,265	40	6,610	51,295	37,275	845	Femmes actives de 15 ans et plus	297
125	0	105	1,835	510	0	Profession - Sans objet[46]	298
6,140	45	6,505	49,460	36,770	840	Toutes les professions[47]	299
380	15	425	2,870	2,600	60	A Gestion	300
1,195	10	1,720	10,135	9,320	145	B Affaires, finance et administration	301
105	0	125	1,150	885	15	C Sciences naturelles et appliquées et professions apparentées	302
470	0	795	5,265	4,595	70	D Secteur de la santé	303
425	0	905	5,390	5,585	70	E Sciences sociales, enseignement, administration publique et religion	304
95	0	115	1,230	1,470	65	F Arts, culture, sports et loisirs	305
1,855	15	1,825	17,490	11,105	345	G Ventes et services	306
180	0	110	1,020	480	35	H Métiers, transport et machinerie	307
800	0	50	375	330	15	I Professions propres au secteur primaire	308
630	0	435	4,510	395	20	J Transformation, fabrication et services d'utilité publique	309
13,720	**165**	**12,925**	**97,710**	**70,150**	**1,770**	**Population active occupée totale de 15 ans et plus**	310
						Catégorie de lieu de travail	
7,920	120	6,690	51,615	35,315	945	Hommes	311
5,740	90	5,510	41,870	27,825	590	Lieu habituel de travail	312
1,125	25	385	1,865	2,420	90	À domicile	313
70	0	270	2,795	230	0	En dehors du Canada	314
985	0	520	5,075	4,840	265	Sans adresse de travail fixe	315
5,795	40	6,230	46,095	34,840	820	Femmes	316
5,080	20	5,290	40,270	30,700	620	Lieu habituel de travail	317
470	10	330	1,895	2,415	105	À domicile	318
25	0	315	1,910	95	0	En dehors du Canada	319
220	10	290	2,015	1,630	90	Sans adresse de travail fixe	320

Nota : Voir les symboles et les abréviations dans les documents d'introduction et voir les documents de référence à la fin de la publication.

Selected characteristics for census divisions and census subdivisions – 100% data and 20% sample data, Ontario, 2006 Census (continued)

No.	Characteristics	Essex CD/DR	Amherstburg, T	Essex, T ◊	Kingsville, T ◊	Lakeshore, T	LaSalle, T
	Population characteristics						
321	**Total employed labour force 15 years and over with usual place of work or no fixed workplace address**	**170,005**	**9,810**	**9,230**	**9,570**	**15,710**	**12,680**
	Mode of transportation						
322	Males	90,580	5,280	4,945	5,325	8,640	6,580
323	Car, truck, van, as driver	76,780	4,785	4,335	4,355	7,920	6,005
324	Car, truck, van, as passenger	5,750	245	350	350	435	380
325	Public transit	1,390	10	10	0	25	35
326	Walked	4,240	165	180	525	160	60
327	All other modes	2,420	75	65	95	95	105
328	Females	79,425	4,530	4,285	4,245	7,070	6,095
329	Car, truck, van, as driver	63,955	3,955	3,730	3,575	6,245	5,400
330	Car, truck, van, as passenger	7,665	360	305	365	600	500
331	Public transit	2,675	0	0	15	25	25
332	Walked	3,885	165	215	245	155	105
333	All other modes	1,235	50	35	45	45	65
334	**Total population 15 years and over who worked since January 1, 2005**	**216,180**	**12,170**	**11,440**	**12,155**	**19,585**	**16,075**
	Language used most often at work						
335	Single responses	214,925	12,155	11,420	12,080	19,480	15,985
336	English	210,740	12,060	11,380	11,600	19,140	15,845
337	French	1,235	85	0	35	310	105
338	Non-official languages[7]	2,950	10	35	440	30	35
339	Chinese, n.o.s.[61]	285	0	0	0	0	0
340	Cantonese	75	0	0	0	0	0
341	Other languages[8]	2,590	10	30	445	30	25
342	Multiple responses	1,260	15	15	75	100	95
343	English and French	400	10	0	10	80	35
344	English and non-official language	820	10	20	65	20	50
345	French and non-official language	0	0	0	0	0	0
346	English, French and non-official language	35	0	0	10	0	10
	Dwelling and household characteristics						
347	**Total number of occupied private dwellings**	**150,845**	**7,930**	**7,640**	**7,450**	**11,630**	**9,315**
	Housing tenure						
348	Owned	113,825	6,800	6,535	6,510	10,690	8,780
349	Rented	37,015	1,130	1,105	940	940	535
350	Band housing	0	0	0	0	0	0
	Structural type of dwelling						
351	Single-detached house	106,555	6,725	6,950	6,395	10,955	8,135
352	Semi-detached house	6,225	90	70	185	175	540
353	Row house	7,560	310	200	350	175	110
354	Apartment, duplex	4,350	80	55	80	60	40
355	Apartment, building that has five or more storeys	13,015	305	0	5	0	100
356	Apartment, building that has fewer than five storeys	12,790	395	350	420	215	395
357	Other single-attached house	290	20	10	15	20	15
358	Movable dwelling[48]	75	5	5	5	25	0
	Condition of dwelling						
359	Regular maintenance only	109,805	5,955	5,285	5,485	8,475	7,415
360	Minor repairs	32,205	1,515	1,855	1,585	2,585	1,545
361	Major repairs	8,830	465	500	380	575	360
	Period of construction						
362	Before 1946	27,575	1,330	1,460	1,685	1,370	505
363	1946 to 1960	29,670	1,060	1,280	1,215	1,355	885
364	1961 to 1970	19,405	870	830	785	1,330	1,135
365	1971 to 1980	22,935	1,540	1,670	1,385	1,675	1,080
366	1981 to 1985	6,715	360	335	235	475	285
367	1986 to 1990	8,730	640	560	325	950	945
368	1991 to 1995	9,145	680	455	435	945	1,315
369	1996 to 2000	13,420	690	615	655	1,390	1,850
370	2001 to 2006[49]	13,245	760	440	725	2,145	1,305

Note: See symbols and abbreviations in the introductory material and see reference material at the end of the publication.

Leamington, MU ◊	Pelee, TP ♦◊	Tecumseh, T **A**	Windsor, CY ◊**A**	**Frontenac CD/DR** ♦◊	Central Frontenac, TP ♦◊	**Caractéristiques**	Nº
						Caractéristiques de la population	
12,025	**125**	**11,620**	**89,235**	**64,995**	**1,570**	**Population active occupée totale de 15 ans et plus ayant un lieu habituel de travail ou sans adresse de travail fixe**	321
						Mode de transport	
6,725	95	6,035	46,950	32,665	855	Hommes	322
5,130	50	5,470	38,725	24,510	680	Automobile, camion ou fourgonnette, en tant que conducteur	323
645	40	280	3,020	2,265	80	Automobile, camion ou fourgonnette, en tant que passager	324
10	0	20	1,275	1,055	0	Transport en commun	325
720	0	165	2,265	3,240	65	À pied	326
220	10	100	1,660	1,590	25	Tous les autres modes	327
5,300	30	5,585	42,285	32,330	710	Femmes	328
4,015	30	4,945	32,055	22,285	540	Automobile, camion ou fourgonnette, en tant que conductrice	329
860	0	435	4,235	3,835	40	Automobile, camion ou fourgonnette, en tant que passagère	330
15	0	15	2,590	1,715	15	Transport en commun	331
330	0	145	2,530	3,395	85	À pied	332
75	0	40	875	1,095	35	Tous les autres modes	333
15,650	**180**	**14,840**	**114,090**	**82,015**	**2,085**	**Population totale de 15 ans et plus ayant travaillé depuis le 1er janvier 2005**	334
						Langue utilisée le plus souvent au travail	
15,495	180	14,770	113,360	81,560	2,085	Réponses uniques	335
14,210	145	14,550	111,805	80,460	2,080	Anglais	336
55	0	175	460	740	0	Français	337
1,225	35	45	1,095	360	0	Langues non officielles[7]	338
0	0	0	280	50	0	Chinois, n.d.a.[61]	339
0	0	0	75	30	0	Cantonais	340
1,225	35	40	745	275	0	Autres langues[8]	341
160	0	70	730	455	0	Réponses multiples	342
20	0	25	215	375	0	Anglais et français	343
135	0	40	490	75	10	Anglais et langue non officielle	344
0	0	0	0	0	0	Français et langue non officielle	345
0	0	0	25	0	0	Anglais, français et langue non officielle	346
						Caractéristiques des logements et des ménages	
9,815	**95**	**8,495**	**88,465**	**59,190**	**1,840**	**Nombre total de logements privés occupés**	347
						Mode d'occupation	
7,190	90	7,810	59,420	39,750	1,605	Possédé	348
2,620	10	685	29,045	19,440	235	Loué	349
0	0	0	0	0	0	Logement de bande	350
						Type de construction résidentielle	
6,540	95	7,040	53,735	33,515	1,755	Maison individuelle non attenante	351
830	0	420	3,925	4,245	20	Maison jumelée	352
665	0	445	5,305	3,205	5	Maison en rangée	353
295	5	75	3,665	1,945	5	Appartement, duplex	354
525	0	350	11,735	7,125	0	Appartement, immeuble de cinq étages ou plus	355
920	0	170	9,925	8,580	35	Appartement, immeuble de moins de cinq étages	356
35	0	5	165	215	10	Autre maison individuelle attenante	357
15	0	0	20	315	15	Logement mobile[48]	358
						État du logement	
7,170	65	6,645	63,310	38,680	1,025	Entretien régulier seulement	359
2,115	20	1,520	19,460	16,350	620	Réparations mineures	360
530	10	330	5,690	4,160	200	Réparations majeures	361
						Période de construction	
2,060	45	725	18,405	8,285	545	Avant 1946	362
1,800	15	935	21,135	8,795	195	1946 à 1960	363
1,245	10	740	12,465	8,635	210	1961 à 1970	364
1,295	0	1,180	13,095	10,780	305	1971 à 1980	365
595	10	645	3,770	5,320	120	1981 à 1985	366
645	0	1,445	3,230	6,080	130	1986 à 1990	367
635	0	1,130	3,540	3,900	130	1991 à 1995	368
795	20	1,135	6,270	3,270	150	1996 à 2000	369
745	10	550	6,565	4,120	60	2001 à 2006[49]	370

Nota : Voir les symboles et les abréviations dans les documents d'introduction et voir les documents de référence à la fin de la publication.

Selected characteristics for census divisions and census subdivisions – 100% data and 20% sample data, Ontario, 2006 Census (continued)

No.	Characteristics	Essex CD/DR	Amherstburg, T	Essex, T ◊	Kingsville, T ◊	Lakeshore, T	LaSalle, T
	Dwelling and household characteristics						
371	Average number of rooms per dwelling	6.9	7.6	7.3	7.6	7.8	8.1
372	Average number of bedrooms per dwelling	2.7	2.9	2.8	2.9	3.1	3.2
373	Average value of dwelling $	204,678	233,520	204,608	235,165	270,371	247,661
374	**Total number of private households**	**150,860**	**7,925**	**7,640**	**7,455**	**11,630**	**9,325**
	Household size						
375	1 person	39,390	1,590	1,800	1,510	1,920	1,390
376	2 persons	48,080	2,615	2,685	2,700	3,855	2,790
377	3 persons	24,150	1,315	1,160	1,145	1,965	1,730
378	4 to 5 persons	34,525	2,215	1,775	1,865	3,480	3,065
379	6 or more persons	4,720	200	220	235	405	355
	Household type						
380	One-family households[50]	105,010	6,135	5,620	5,810	9,410	7,655
381	Multiple-family households	2,345	100	80	65	160	150
382	Non-family households	43,490	1,695	1,945	1,580	2,060	1,510
383	Number of persons in private households	386,965	21,545	19,695	19,890	33,085	27,550
384	Average number of persons in private households	2.6	2.7	2.6	2.7	2.8	3.0
385	Tenant-occupied private non-farm, non-reserve dwellings[51]	37,005	1,130	1,105	930	940	535
386	Average gross rent $[51]	706	754	713	681	806	758
387	Tenant-occupied households spending 30% or more of household income on gross rent[52]	16,920	580	430	290	390	175
388	Tenant-occupied households spending from 30% to 99% of household income on gross rent[52]	13,995	505	365	250	325	145
389	Owner-occupied private non-farm, non-reserve dwellings[53]	113,155	6,725	6,450	6,380	10,510	8,780
390	Average owner's major payments $[53]	1,026	1,107	989	957	1,188	1,165
391	Owner households spending 30% or more of household income on owner's major payments[52]	18,600	960	965	860	1,520	1,190
392	Owner households spending from 30% to 99% of household income on owner's major payments[52]	15,860	775	845	725	1,255	1,040
	Census family characteristics						
393	**Total number of census families in private households**	**109,775**	**6,335**	**5,785**	**5,935**	**9,725**	**7,965**
	Family structure and number of children						
394	Total couple families	91,820	5,580	5,080	5,340	8,830	7,125
395	Total families of married couples	81,825	5,040	4,525	4,840	8,045	6,635
396	Without children at home	33,040	2,030	1,990	2,165	3,145	2,350
397	With children at home	48,785	3,010	2,535	2,670	4,895	4,290
398	1 child	16,615	975	795	855	1,540	1,255
399	2 children	20,970	1,330	1,125	1,190	2,160	2,065
400	3 or more children	11,205	705	615	625	1,200	970
401	Total families of common-law couples	9,995	545	550	500	785	485
402	Without children at home	5,610	290	345	230	410	225
403	With children at home	4,380	255	205	270	375	260
404	1 child	2,130	120	125	105	145	110
405	2 children	1,615	90	50	105	165	65
406	3 or more children	635	45	30	60	60	85
407	Total lone-parent families	17,955	750	710	595	895	840
408	Female parent	14,630	625	600	450	680	660
409	1 child	8,715	310	340	265	420	320
410	2 children	4,190	220	175	165	170	255
411	3 or more children	1,725	95	90	15	90	80
412	Male parent	3,325	125	105	145	215	180
413	1 child	2,310	100	65	100	125	95
414	2 children	835	20	35	35	85	80
415	3 or more children	180	10	10	15	0	10

Note: See symbols and abbreviations in the introductory material and see reference material at the end of the publication.

Certaines caractéristiques des divisions de recensement et des subdivisions de recensement – Données intégrales et données-échantillon (20 %), Ontario, Recensement de 2006 (suite)

Leamington, MU ◊	Pelee, TP ◆◊	Tecumseh, T A	Windsor, CY ◊A	**Frontenac CD/DR** ◆◊	Central Frontenac, TP ◆◊	Caractéristiques	N°
						Caractéristiques des logements et des ménages	
6.9	7.4	8.0	6.3	6.6	6.8	Nombre moyen de pièces par logement	371
2.7	3.0	3.2	2.6	2.7	2.8	Nombre moyen de chambres à coucher par logement	372
197,360	217,925	262,911	173,392	239,826	147,574	Valeur moyenne du logement $	373
9,820	**95**	**8,500**	**88,465**	**59,130**	**1,855**	**Nombre total de ménages privés**	374
						Taille du ménage	
2,210	25	1,425	27,515	16,720	375	1 personne	375
3,225	35	2,705	27,475	21,575	835	2 personnes	376
1,490	15	1,480	13,865	8,860	255	3 personnes	377
2,330	20	2,630	17,135	10,985	340	4 à 5 personnes	378
565	0	255	2,480	990	50	6 personnes ou plus	379
						Genre de ménage	
7,265	60	6,875	56,185	39,140	1,375	Ménages unifamiliaux[50]	380
185	0	105	1,495	635	30	Ménages multifamiliaux	381
2,360	35	1,515	30,780	19,415	435	Ménages non familiaux	382
27,045	235	24,195	213,715	139,500	4,570	Nombre de personnes dans les ménages privés	383
2.8	2.5	2.8	2.4	2.4	2.5	Nombre moyen de personnes dans les ménages privés	384
2,620	0	690	29,045	19,425	235	Ménages locataires dans les logements privés non agricoles hors réserve[51]	385
700	0	842	698	773	611	Loyer brut moyen $[51]	386
1,055	0	265	13,725	9,325	95	Ménages locataires consacrant 30 % ou plus du revenu du ménage au loyer brut[52]	387
955	0	260	11,180	7,840	75	Ménages locataires consacrant de 30 % à 99 % du revenu du ménage au loyer brut[52]	388
7,010	85	7,785	59,420	39,550	1,585	Ménages propriétaires dans les logements privés non agricoles hors réserve[53]	389
941	715	1,075	983	990	697	Principales dépenses de propriété moyennes $[53]	390
1,260	0	790	11,045	6,655	380	Ménages propriétaires consacrant 30 % ou plus du revenu du ménage aux principales dépenses de propriété[52]	391
1,110	10	635	9,465	5,780	315	Ménages propriétaires consacrant de 30 % à 99 % du revenu du ménage aux principales dépenses de propriété[52]	392
						Caractéristiques des familles de recensement	
7,640	**60**	**7,095**	**59,230**	**40,420**	**1,435**	**Nombre total de familles de recensement dans les ménages privés**	393
						Structure de la famille et le nombre d'enfants	
6,650	60	6,235	46,915	34,290	1,255	Total des familles avec conjoints	394
5,990	55	5,825	40,865	28,770	1,075	Total des familles avec couples mariés	395
2,460	35	2,060	16,800	13,655	640	Sans enfants à la maison	396
3,535	20	3,765	24,065	15,115	440	Avec enfants à la maison	397
1,050	0	1,160	8,960	5,635	145	1 enfant	398
1,410	15	1,690	9,990	6,780	200	2 enfants	399
1,070	0	910	5,110	2,690	90	3 enfants ou plus	400
655	10	410	6,050	5,520	180	Total des familles avec couples en union libre	401
355	0	265	3,500	3,530	125	Sans enfants à la maison	402
305	0	145	2,555	1,990	60	Avec enfants à la maison	403
150	0	95	1,280	975	40	1 enfant	404
125	10	45	965	710	10	2 enfants	405
30	0	10	315	310	0	3 enfants ou plus	406
990	0	860	12,315	6,125	180	Total des familles monoparentales	407
820	0	685	10,110	4,940	160	Parent de sexe féminin	408
500	0	375	6,185	3,125	70	1 enfant	409
195	0	250	2,755	1,445	60	2 enfants	410
125	0	60	1,170	375	35	3 enfants ou plus	411
170	0	175	2,200	1,185	20	Parent de sexe masculin	412
120	0	130	1,575	875	20	1 enfant	413
45	0	30	510	260	0	2 enfants	414
10	0	15	120	50	0	3 enfants ou plus	415

Nota : Voir les symboles et les abréviations dans les documents d'introduction et voir les documents de référence à la fin de la publication.

Selected characteristics for census divisions and census subdivisions – 100% data and 20% sample data, Ontario, 2006 Census (continued)

No.	Characteristics	Essex CD/DR	Amherstburg, T	Essex, T ◊	Kingsville, T ◊	Lakeshore, T	LaSalle, T
	Census family characteristics						
416	**Total number of children at home**	**131,215**	**7,570**	**6,525**	**6,755**	**11,910**	**10,495**
	Age group						
417	Under 6 years	27,815	1,530	1,185	1,380	2,620	2,130
418	6 to 14 years	46,635	2,775	2,450	2,470	4,470	3,920
419	15 to 17 years	15,850	1,035	825	855	1,565	1,420
420	18 to 24 years	27,210	1,565	1,485	1,475	2,295	2,130
421	25 years and over	13,700	665	580	575	955	895
422	Average number of children at home per census family[54]	1.2	1.2	1.1	1.1	1.2	1.3
423	**Total number of persons in private households**	**386,930**	**21,555**	**19,700**	**19,885**	**33,085**	**27,530**
	Census family status and living arrangements						
424	Number of persons not in census families	54,115	2,060	2,305	1,850	2,620	1,950
425	Living with relatives[55]	6,920	285	265	225	465	340
426	Living with non-relatives only	7,845	195	235	125	235	220
427	Living alone	39,355	1,580	1,800	1,500	1,920	1,385
428	Number of census family persons	332,810	19,490	17,390	18,030	30,470	25,580
429	Average number of persons per census family	3.0	3.1	3.0	3.0	3.1	3.2
430	**Total number of persons aged 65 years and over**	**49,290**	**2,440**	**2,655**	**2,665**	**3,150**	**2,570**
431	Number of persons not in census families aged 65 years and over	16,940	760	935	655	870	660
432	Living with relatives[55]	2,100	95	120	60	175	160
433	Living with non-relatives only	610	10	35	30	10	40
434	Living alone	14,225	655	780	560	685	465
435	Number of census family persons aged 65 years and over	32,355	1,680	1,720	2,015	2,280	1,910
	Economic family characteristics						
436	**Total number of economic families in private households**	**108,835**	**6,285**	**5,760**	**5,910**	**9,680**	**7,865**
	Size of family						
437	2 persons	46,685	2,575	2,640	2,680	3,900	2,760
438	3 persons	23,355	1,305	1,135	1,130	1,945	1,700
439	4 persons	24,155	1,565	1,220	1,320	2,445	2,185
440	5 or more persons	14,640	840	760	775	1,390	1,215
441	Total number of persons in economic families	339,730	19,770	17,660	18,260	30,930	25,925
442	Average number of persons per economic family	3.0	3.0	3.0	3.0	3.0	3.0
443	Total number of persons not in economic families	47,200	1,780	2,035	1,625	2,155	1,610
	2005 income characteristics						
444	**Population 15 years and over**	**314,630**	**17,275**	**16,145**	**16,630**	**25,970**	**21,500**
	Sex and total income groups in 2005						
445	Without income	15,760	900	685	660	1,100	1,135
446	With income	298,875	16,370	15,465	15,975	24,865	20,365
447	Under $1,000[56]	13,070	570	525	645	1,035	730
448	$1,000 to $2,999	10,335	540	610	500	915	670
449	$3,000 to $4,999	9,825	595	485	405	625	650
450	$5,000 to $6,999	10,890	410	545	570	675	640
451	$7,000 to $9,999	17,800	1,015	770	915	1,265	1,045
452	$10,000 to $11,999	12,180	470	635	575	815	705
453	$12,000 to $14,999	16,505	715	810	845	1,160	765
454	$15,000 to $19,999	26,135	1,255	1,315	1,555	1,735	1,295
455	$20,000 to $24,999	21,830	1,100	1,155	1,170	1,445	1,160
456	$25,000 to $29,999	18,420	910	1,080	1,010	1,430	1,070
457	$30,000 to $34,999	19,090	1,055	1,005	1,080	1,700	1,185
458	$35,000 to $39,999	17,680	1,050	1,095	980	1,275	1,040
459	$40,000 to $44,999	15,835	955	895	840	1,340	1,060
460	$45,000 to $49,999	13,090	745	675	720	1,095	945
461	$50,000 to $59,999	20,365	1,260	1,075	1,270	1,905	1,740
462	$60,000 and over	55,825	3,715	2,770	2,890	6,450	5,655
463	Median income $[57]	27,852	32,509	28,999	29,035	33,811	35,993
464	Average income $[57]	36,830	41,971	36,378	37,008	43,555	45,519
465	Standard error of average income $[57]	168	1,035	538	658	612	793

Note: See symbols and abbreviations in the introductory material and see reference material at the end of the publication.

Certaines caractéristiques des divisions de recensement et des subdivisions de recensement – Données intégrales et données-échantillon (20 %), Ontario, Recensement de 2006 (suite)

Leamington, MU ◊	Pelee, TP ◆◊	Tecumseh, T A	Windsor, CY ◊A	**Frontenac CD/DR** ◆◊	Central Frontenac, TP ◆◊	Caractéristiques	N°
						Caractéristiques des familles de recensement	
9,870	**45**	**9,025**	**69,005**	**40,035**	**1,275**	**Nombre total d'enfants à la maison**	416
						Groupes d'âge	
2,255	0	1,355	15,360	8,120	255	Moins de 6 ans	417
3,590	15	3,170	23,775	14,720	490	6 à 14 ans	418
1,230	20	1,305	7,595	5,305	140	15 à 17 ans	419
1,995	10	2,265	13,985	8,145	215	18 à 24 ans	420
805	0	930	8,285	3,750	165	25 ans et plus	421
1.3	0.8	1.3	1.2	1.0	0.9	Nombre moyen d'enfants à la maison par famille de recensement[54]	422
27,055	**215**	**24,195**	**213,710**	**139,590**	**4,560**	**Nombre total de personnes dans les ménages privés**	423
						Situation des particuliers dans la famille de recensement et des particuliers dans le ménage	
2,885	40	1,840	38,555	24,845	595	Nombre de personnes hors famille de recensement	424
355	15	220	4,735	2,145	130	Vivant avec des personnes apparentées[55]	425
345	0	195	6,300	5,950	90	Vivant avec des personnes non apparentées seulement	426
2,190	30	1,420	27,520	16,755	375	Vivant seules	427
24,165	175	22,360	175,155	114,740	3,970	Nombre de membres d'une famille de recensement	428
3.2	2.6	3.2	3.0	2.8	2.8	Nombre moyen de personnes par famille de recensement	429
3,765	**100**	**2,500**	**29,445**	**20,910**	**890**	**Nombre total de personnes âgées de 65 ans et plus**	430
1,120	30	690	11,215	7,055	200	Nombre de personnes hors famille de recensement âgées de 65 ans et plus	431
120	15	75	1,275	725	85	Vivant avec des personnes apparentées[55]	432
45	0	45	400	430	0	Vivant avec des personnes non apparentées seulement	433
955	15	570	9,540	5,895	110	Vivant seules	434
2,645	70	1,810	18,230	13,855	695	Nombre de membres d'une famille de recensement âgés de 65 ans et plus	435
						Caractéristiques des familles économiques	
7,510	**70**	**7,010**	**58,750**	**40,240**	**1,440**	**Nombre total de familles économiques dans les ménages privés**	436
						Taille de la famille	
3,160	40	2,665	26,260	20,215	815	2 personnes	437
1,380	10	1,480	13,265	8,400	250	3 personnes	438
1,655	20	1,810	11,930	7,955	235	4 personnes	439
1,315	0	1,050	7,290	3,665	140	5 personnes ou plus	440
24,520	185	22,580	179,890	116,880	4,095	Nombre total de personnes dans les familles économiques	441
3.0	3.0	3.0	3.0	3.0	3.0	Nombre moyen de personnes par famille économique	442
2,535	30	1,615	33,815	22,710	465	Nombre total de personnes hors famille économique	443
						Caractéristiques du revenu de 2005	
22,390	**245**	**19,630**	**174,830**	**117,615**	**3,860**	**Population de 15 ans et plus**	444
						Sexe et groupes de revenu total en 2005	
925	0	915	9,435	5,010	220	Sans revenu	445
21,460	245	18,720	165,400	112,605	3,645	Avec un revenu	446
925	15	620	8,000	3,725	215	Moins de 1 000 $[56]	447
720	10	730	5,635	4,135	170	1 000 $ à 2 999 $	448
785	0	620	5,650	3,445	95	3 000 $ à 4 999 $	449
755	10	640	6,650	4,125	125	5 000 $ à 6 999 $	450
1,520	0	920	10,340	6,520	275	7 000 $ à 9 999 $	451
955	15	530	7,470	4,940	240	10 000 $ à 11 999 $	452
1,215	0	745	10,235	6,430	320	12 000 $ à 14 999 $	453
2,640	60	1,175	15,090	11,105	410	15 000 $ à 19 999 $	454
1,975	30	1,140	12,645	8,395	300	20 000 $ à 24 999 $	455
1,480	30	960	10,450	7,650	250	25 000 $ à 29 999 $	456
1,320	20	1,035	10,690	7,530	175	30 000 $ à 34 999 $	457
1,350	15	1,120	9,750	7,140	205	35 000 $ à 39 999 $	458
1,130	0	950	8,655	6,320	135	40 000 $ à 44 999 $	459
885	15	845	7,165	4,835	165	45 000 $ à 49 999$	460
1,355	0	1,440	10,320	8,110	235	50 000 $ à 59 999$	461
2,460	15	5,235	26,640	18,190	315	60 000 $ et plus	462
22,459	19,961	35,987	25,443	27,012	19,534	Revenu médian $[57]	463
31,425	25,193	46,354	33,905	35,789	26,820	Revenu moyen $[57]	464
481	1,738	1,003	200	241	835	Erreur type de revenu moyen $[57]	465

Nota : Voir les symboles et les abréviations dans les documents d'introduction et voir les documents de référence à la fin de la publication.

Selected characteristics for census divisions and census subdivisions – 100% data and 20% sample data, Ontario, 2006 Census (continued)

No.	Characteristics	Essex CD/DR	Amherstburg, T	Essex, T ◊	Kingsville, T ◊	Lakeshore, T	LaSalle, T
	2005 income characteristics						
	Sex and total income groups in 2005 (continued)						
466	Total - Males	153,905	8,500	7,970	8,400	13,085	10,500
467	Without income	6,490	375	315	225	440	380
468	With income	147,415	8,125	7,660	8,175	12,645	10,120
469	Under $1,000[56]	7,095	265	265	345	450	350
470	$1,000 to $2,999	3,370	145	205	155	260	255
471	$3,000 to $4,999	3,555	225	170	105	205	290
472	$5,000 to $6,999	3,685	115	140	155	250	205
473	$7,000 to $9,999	6,250	305	255	375	330	300
474	$10,000 to $11,999	4,210	145	185	215	265	275
475	$12,000 to $14,999	5,620	190	225	315	455	240
476	$15,000 to $19,999	9,780	435	505	635	560	415
477	$20,000 to $24,999	8,600	415	355	495	590	405
478	$25,000 to $29,999	7,900	440	505	435	560	470
479	$30,000 to $34,999	8,920	500	430	495	835	500
480	$35,000 to $39,999	9,060	570	610	515	660	475
481	$40,000 to $44,999	8,620	510	520	460	720	500
482	$45,000 to $49,999	7,260	395	445	450	560	455
483	$50,000 to $59,999	12,260	780	700	860	1,050	920
484	$60,000 and over	41,235	2,685	2,140	2,165	4,890	4,060
485	Median income $[57]	37,408	42,835	39,938	38,779	46,644	49,216
486	Average income $[57]	46,177	54,359	45,946	46,091	55,802	56,788
487	Standard error of average income $[57]	284	1,958	839	1,071	940	1,076
488	Total - Females	160,720	8,770	8,175	8,235	12,880	11,000
489	Without income	9,265	525	365	430	660	755
490	With income	151,455	8,240	7,805	7,800	12,225	10,245
491	Under $1,000[56]	5,980	305	265	295	585	380
492	$1,000 to $2,999	6,960	395	405	345	650	415
493	$3,000 to $4,999	6,265	375	315	310	425	360
494	$5,000 to $6,999	7,200	290	405	410	420	435
495	$7,000 to $9,999	11,550	710	515	540	935	745
496	$10,000 to $11,999	7,965	325	450	360	550	430
497	$12,000 to $14,999	10,880	525	590	525	705	530
498	$15,000 to $19,999	16,355	820	815	920	1,175	885
499	$20,000 to $24,999	13,235	690	805	675	855	755
500	$25,000 to $29,999	10,520	465	575	575	870	600
501	$30,000 to $34,999	10,165	555	570	585	865	685
502	$35,000 to $39,999	8,625	480	485	470	620	560
503	$40,000 to $44,999	7,215	445	375	375	620	560
504	$45,000 to $49,999	5,835	350	235	270	530	495
505	$50,000 to $59,999	8,105	475	370	415	850	820
506	$60,000 and over	14,590	1,025	630	725	1,560	1,590
507	Median income $[57]	20,822	22,518	21,079	21,322	23,551	26,192
508	Average income $[57]	27,732	29,756	26,989	27,493	30,886	34,389
509	Standard error of average income $[57]	166	611	605	605	708	1,118
	Composition of total income						
510	Composition of total income in 2005 %	100.0	100.0	100.0	100.0	100.0	100.0
511	Employment income %	76.3	78.9	76.0	75.3	81.6	82.5
512	Government transfer payments %	11.1	9.6	11.8	10.6	7.4	6.9
513	Other %	12.6	11.6	12.2	14.1	11.1	10.6
514	**Population 15 years and over with employment income in 2005**	**220,485**	**12,340**	**11,745**	**12,360**	**20,110**	**16,340**
	Sex and work activity						
515	Median employment income in 2005 $	29,245	34,894	29,340	26,388	34,936	37,275
516	Average employment income in 2005 $	38,075	43,909	36,404	36,027	43,932	46,768
517	Standard error of average employment income $	211	1,315	653	785	670	953
518	Worked full year, full time[59]	111,070	6,720	5,865	6,010	10,520	8,695
519	Median employment income in 2005 $	47,328	52,130	45,217	46,544	55,593	57,946
520	Average employment income in 2005 $	55,296	61,711	51,327	53,213	62,675	65,649
521	Standard error of average employment income $	355	2,204	900	1,478	999	1,459
522	Worked part year or part time[60]	90,230	4,750	4,905	5,385	7,935	6,545
523	Median employment income in 2005 $	13,066	12,328	13,346	13,945	15,090	13,937
524	Average employment income in 2005 $	23,221	25,183	24,462	21,596	26,866	27,967
525	Standard error of average employment income $	204	1,040	891	626	755	1,099
526	Males 15 years and over with employment income[58]	117,670	6,535	6,400	6,795	10,935	8,480
527	Median employment income in 2005 $	38,617	45,987	39,082	34,541	48,892	52,567
528	Average employment income in 2005 $	46,306	55,564	43,470	43,441	54,402	57,127
529	Standard error of average employment income $	335	2,351	963	1,208	1,017	1,229

Note: See symbols and abbreviations in the introductory material and see reference material at the end of the publication.

Certaines caractéristiques des divisions de recensement et des subdivisions de recensement – Données intégrales et données-échantillon (20 %), Ontario, Recensement de 2006 (suite)

Leamington, MU ◊	Pelee, TP ◆◊	Tecumseh, T A	Windsor, CY ◊A	**Frontenac CD/DR** ◆◊	Central Frontenac, TP ◆◊	Caractéristiques	N°
						Caractéristiques du revenu de 2005	
						Sexe et groupes de revenu total en 2005 (suite)	
11,400	170	9,565	84,305	55,955	1,945	Total - Hommes	466
410	0	410	3,930	2,415	125	Sans revenu	467
10,985	170	9,160	80,380	53,540	1,820	Avec un revenu	468
610	10	300	4,495	2,085	150	Moins de 1 000 $[56]	469
160	10	265	1,905	1,635	30	1 000 $ à 2 999 $	470
255	0	230	2,080	1,115	55	3 000 $ à 4 999 $	471
300	10	195	2,305	1,530	15	5 000 $ à 6 999 $	472
550	0	290	3,850	2,355	85	7 000 $ à 9 999 $	473
325	0	195	2,600	2,000	85	10 000 $ à 11 999 $	474
425	0	210	3,555	2,360	95	12 000 $ à 14 999 $	475
1,335	50	375	5,475	4,275	195	15 000 $ à 19 999 $	476
780	15	465	5,090	3,515	120	20 000 $ à 24 999 $	477
660	0	330	4,490	3,380	150	25 000 $ à 29 999 $	478
690	15	425	5,030	3,420	90	30 000 $ à 34 999 $	479
690	10	490	5,025	3,470	140	35 000 $ à 39 999 $	480
750	0	485	4,660	3,065	80	40 000 $ à $44 999 $	481
530	15	385	4,025	2,490	130	45 000 $ à $49 999 $	482
960	0	760	6,225	4,775	145	50 000 $ à $59 999 $	483
1,975	10	3,745	19,560	12,060	245	60 000 $ et plus	484
30,662	21,200	48,747	34,176	33,659	28,128	Revenu médian $[57]	485
39,049	27,486	60,239	41,941	43,041	32,840	Revenu moyen $[57]	486
761	2,084	1,915	343	427	1,329	Erreur type de revenu moyen $[57]	487
10,995	80	10,065	90,525	61,660	1,920	Total - Femmes	488
515	0	505	5,505	2,600	95	Sans revenu	489
10,475	80	9,555	85,025	59,065	1,825	Avec un revenu	490
315	0	315	3,505	1,640	70	Moins de 1 000 $[56]	491
555	0	460	3,730	2,500	135	1 000$ à 2 999 $	492
530	0	385	3,575	2,325	45	3 000 $ à 4 999 $	493
450	10	445	4,345	2,595	105	5 000 $ à 6 999 $	494
970	0	635	6,490	4,160	195	7 000 $ à 9 999 $	495
635	15	335	4,865	2,935	150	10 000 $ à 11 999 $	496
785	0	535	6,680	4,070	225	12 000 $ à 14 999 $	497
1,310	15	795	9,620	6,835	215	15 000 $ à 19 999 $	498
1,195	10	680	7,560	4,885	180	20 000 $ à 24 999 $	499
820	25	635	5,955	4,270	95	25 000 $ à 29 999 $	500
635	0	615	5,660	4,105	85	30 000 $ à 34 999 $	501
660	0	630	4,720	3,670	65	35 000 $ à 39 999 $	502
380	0	460	3,995	3,255	55	40 000 $ à 44 999 $	503
355	0	460	3,140	2,345	40	45 000 $ à 49 999 $	504
395	0	675	4,100	3,335	90	50 000 $ à 59 999 $	505
480	10	1,490	7,080	6,130	75	60 000 $ et plus	506
18,689	19,034	26,296	19,830	22,215	14,705	Revenu médian $[57]	507
23,427	20,394	33,048	26,309	29,215	20,818	Revenu moyen $[57]	508
437	2,771	619	202	232	932	Erreur type de revenu moyen $[57]	509
						Composition du revenu total	
100.0	100.0	100.0	100.0	100.0	100.0	Composition du revenu total en 2005 %	510
72.9	42.9	80.4	73.8	70.5	55.5	Revenu d'emploi %	511
13.9	30.0	6.5	13.0	11.6	22.5	Transferts gouvernementaux %	512
13.1	27.1	13.1	13.1	17.9	22.0	Autres %	513
15,885	**160**	**15,175**	**116,365**	**82,015**	**2,095**	**Population de 15 ans et plus avec un revenu d'emploi en 2005**	514
						Sexe et travail	
20,914	15,015	35,791	27,543	25,864	20,073	Revenu médian d'emploi en 2005 $	515
30,970	16,538	45,979	35,578	34,650	25,874	Revenu moyen d'emploi en 2005 $	516
602	1,541	1,137	263	279	1,135	Erreur type de revenu moyen d'emploi $	517
7,230	45	7,790	58,190	40,670	975	A travaillé toute l'année à plein temps[59]	518
39,103	22,757	57,976	44,863	43,648	35,863	Revenu médian d'emploi en 2005 $	519
46,593	28,814	66,831	51,846	50,469	36,124	Revenu moyen d'emploi en 2005 $	520
1,263	4,643	1,962	429	397	1,674	Erreur type de revenu moyen d'emploi $	521
7,155	105	6,185	47,270	35,185	910	A travaillé une partie de l'année ou à temps partiel[60]	522
13,147	11,332	13,492	12,525	11,977	13,076	Revenu médian d'emploi en 2005 $	523
19,189	11,587	27,013	21,951	21,032	19,922	Revenu moyen d'emploi en 2005 $	524
435	1,203	933	271	367	1,526	Erreur type de revenu moyen d'emploi $	525
8,925	130	7,860	61,610	41,415	1,120	Hommes de 15 ans et plus avec un revenu d'emploi[58]	526
28,294	17,334	50,436	35,721	30,709	27,630	Revenu médian d'emploi en 2005 $	527
37,644	16,833	58,388	42,782	40,406	30,060	Revenu moyen d'emploi en 2005 $	528
892	1,808	2,061	420	467	1,716	Erreur type de revenu moyen d'emploi $	529

Nota : Voir les symboles et les abréviations dans les documents d'introduction et voir les documents de référence à la fin de la publication.

Selected characteristics for census divisions and census subdivisions – 100% data and 20% sample data, Ontario, 2006 Census (continued)

No.	Characteristics	Essex CD/DR	Amherstburg, T	Essex, T ◊	Kingsville, T ◊	Lakeshore, T	LaSalle, T
	2005 income characteristics						
	Sex and work activity (continued)						
530	Worked full year, full time[59]	65,890	4,125	3,570	3,750	6,560	4,960
531	Median employment income in 2005 $	55,988	59,908	54,500	52,176	66,135	68,918
532	Average employment income in 2005 $	63,583	71,128	59,124	60,569	72,333	74,850
533	Standard error of average employment income $	520	3,491	1,255	2,149	1,319	1,400
534	Worked part year or part time[60]	41,145	1,900	2,225	2,490	3,520	2,875
535	Median employment income in 2005 $	15,501	17,039	16,521	15,352	16,437	16,513
536	Average employment income in 2005 $	28,807	34,411	28,572	25,824	32,899	37,675
537	Standard error of average employment income $	364	2,184	1,345	1,001	1,418	2,267
538	Females 15 years and over with employment income[58]	102,815	5,800	5,345	5,570	9,170	7,860
539	Median employment income in 2005 $	21,996	23,918	21,451	21,108	25,276	27,680
540	Average employment income in 2005 $	28,655	30,786	27,938	26,989	31,447	35,594
541	Standard error of average employment income $	219	785	794	776	752	1,429
542	Worked full year, full time[59]	45,175	2,595	2,290	2,260	3,965	3,735
543	Median employment income in 2005 $	38,450	41,448	34,413	35,955	42,118	45,734
544	Average employment income in 2005 $	43,208	46,724	39,159	41,004	46,699	53,439
545	Standard error of average employment income $	403	1,158	1,023	1,502	1,371	2,814
546	Worked part year or part time[60]	49,090	2,850	2,680	2,890	4,410	3,665
547	Median employment income in 2005 $	11,641	10,410	12,446	12,199	14,444	12,350
548	Average employment income in 2005 $	18,539	19,033	21,055	17,949	22,048	20,353
549	Standard error of average employment income $	195	867	1,172	655	716	766
550	**Total number of economic families in private households**	**108,835**	**6,285**	**5,755**	**5,910**	**9,680**	**7,865**
	Family income groups in 2005						
551	Under $10,000	2,840	135	100	110	165	115
552	$10,000 to $19,999	4,480	160	175	90	170	110
553	$20,000 to $29,999	7,005	280	290	360	270	245
554	$30,000 to $39,999	8,795	395	430	400	645	400
555	$40,000 to $49,999	9,275	400	560	565	620	375
556	$50,000 to $59,999	9,410	485	565	535	800	465
557	$60,000 to $69,999	9,170	485	535	495	630	495
558	$70,000 to $79,999	8,570	500	400	545	660	585
559	$80,000 to $89,999	8,240	540	580	450	810	660
560	$90,000 to $99,999	7,065	530	375	425	705	685
561	$100,000 and over	33,985	2,370	1,750	1,925	4,190	3,735
562	Median family income $	74,013	85,604	76,387	77,361	90,808	97,206
563	Average family income $	85,706	98,251	84,228	87,920	102,262	107,876
564	Standard error of average family income $	490	2,673	1,425	1,928	1,522	1,990
	Family after-tax income groups in 2005						
565	Under $10,000	2,910	140	100	125	175	120
566	$10,000 to $19,999	4,560	170	180	100	180	105
567	$20,000 to $29,999	7,910	340	340	370	320	260
568	$30,000 to $39,999	11,170	480	580	565	840	500
569	$40,000 to $49,999	12,325	580	695	755	905	555
570	$50,000 to $59,999	11,975	655	730	650	980	650
571	$60,000 to $69,999	11,670	665	610	735	965	825
572	$70,000 to $79,999	10,125	740	670	590	995	835
573	$80,000 to $89,999	8,240	565	425	515	820	790
574	$90,000 to $99,999	6,715	520	410	410	720	690
575	$100,000 and over	21,225	1,430	1,005	1,090	2,775	2,520
576	Median after-tax family income $	62,907	71,910	64,009	65,354	75,003	81,031
577	Average after-tax family income $	71,054	79,739	69,903	72,466	83,105	88,312
578	Standard error of average after-tax family income $	330	1,684	1,050	1,322	1,086	1,339
	Income status in 2005						
579	Total population in private households for income status	386,880	21,550	19,695	19,885	33,090	27,535
580	Below low income cut-off before tax in 2005	50,695	1,390	1,275	1,160	1,875	1,565
581	Prevalence of low income before tax in 2005 %	13.1	6.5	6.5	5.9	5.7	5.7
582	Below low income cut-off after tax in 2005	38,260	970	745	910	1,280	1,165
583	Prevalence of low income after tax in 2005 %	9.9	4.5	3.8	4.6	3.9	4.2

Note: See symbols and abbreviations in the introductory material and see reference material at the end of the publication.

Certaines caractéristiques des divisions de recensement et des subdivisions de recensement – Données intégrales et données-échantillon (20 %), Ontario, Recensement de 2006 (suite)

Leamington, MU ◊	Pelee, TP ♦◊	Tecumseh, T A	Windsor, CY ◊A	**Frontenac CD/DR** ♦◊	Central Frontenac, TP ♦◊	Caractéristiques	N°
						Caractéristiques du revenu de 2005	
						Sexe et travail (suite)	
4,495	20	4,640	33,760	22,345	560	A travaillé toute l'année à plein temps[59]	530
45,927	32,986	69,332	52,657	48,486	40,049	Revenu médian d'emploi en 2005 $	531
54,384	41,057	77,619	59,424	56,308	39,567	Revenu moyen d'emploi en 2005 $	532
1,887	7,103	3,189	631	615	2,327	Erreur type de revenu moyen d'emploi $	533
3,660	100	2,580	21,785	15,615	415	A travaillé une partie de l'année ou à temps partiel[60]	534
16,262	11,481	16,400	14,916	12,442	19,859	Revenu médian d'emploi en 2005 $	535
22,398	12,087	36,770	27,062	24,878	26,508	Revenu moyen d'emploi en 2005 $	536
575	1,275	1,934	496	717	2,724	Erreur type de revenu moyen d'emploi $	537
6,960	30	7,315	54,755	40,600	975	Femmes de 15 ans et plus avec un revenu d'emploi[58]	538
17,082	14,991	26,019	21,320	22,568	16,075	Revenu médian d'emploi en 2005 $	539
22,409	15,364	32,647	27,472	28,778	21,072	Revenu moyen d'emploi en 2005 $	540
569	2,452	717	280	287	1,382	Erreur type de revenu moyen d'emploi $	541
2,730	20	3,150	24,430	18,320	415	A travaillé toute l'année à plein temps[59]	542
29,694	14,995	45,217	37,315	39,043	28,738	Revenu médian d'emploi en 2005 $	543
33,757	17,597	50,932	41,373	43,348	31,495	Revenu moyen d'emploi en 2005 $	544
1,004	3,120	1,097	498	434	2,301	Erreur type de revenu moyen d'emploi $	545
3,495	0	3,600	25,485	19,565	495	A travaillé une partie de l'année ou à temps partiel[60]	546
10,605	0	12,256	11,042	11,432	8,748	Revenu médian d'emploi en 2005 $	547
15,825	0	20,022	17,584	17,961	14,464	Revenu moyen d'emploi en 2005 $	548
623	0	717	255	320	1,488	Erreur type de revenu moyen d'emploi $	549
7,510	**70**	**7,010**	**58,750**	**40,240**	**1,440**	**Nombre total des familles économiques dans les ménages privés**	550
						Revenu de la famille économique en 2005	
160	0	100	1,950	845	55	Moins de 10 000 $	551
245	0	80	3,450	1,720	110	10 000 $ à 19 999 $	552
610	10	205	4,735	2,745	165	20 000 $ à 29 999 $	553
810	10	300	5,400	3,525	165	30 000 $ à 39 999 $	554
690	0	385	5,685	3,890	175	40 000 $ à 49 999 $	555
860	20	440	5,235	4,210	190	50 000 $ à 59 999 $	556
835	0	440	5,255	3,245	130	60 000 $ à 69 999 $	557
645	15	475	4,740	3,425	120	70 000 $ à 79 999 $	558
655	0	515	4,035	3,125	60	80 000 $ à 89 999 $	559
455	0	510	3,385	2,750	110	90 000 $ à 99 999 $	560
1,555	10	3,560	14,890	10,760	150	100 000 $ et plus	561
64,411	52,296	101,470	65,404	69,631	52,085	Revenu médian des familles $	562
76,751	62,047	111,926	76,634	81,648	58,734	Revenu moyen des familles $	563
1,657	8,784	2,621	624	674	2,108	Erreur type de revenu moyen des familles $	564
						Revenu après impôt de la famille économique en 2005	
160	0	105	1,980	870	65	Moins de 10 000 $	565
265	0	85	3,480	1,760	100	10 000 $ à 19 999 $	566
700	10	240	5,330	3,160	195	20 000 $ à 29 999 $	567
970	0	460	6,760	4,485	195	30 000 $ à 39 999 $	568
1,025	10	565	7,230	5,345	235	40 000 $ à 49 999 $	569
1,010	10	505	6,780	4,585	220	50 000 $ à 59 999 $	570
920	15	700	6,240	4,505	130	60 000 $ à 69 999 $	571
710	0	705	4,870	3,945	95	70 000 $ à 79 999 $	572
460	0	710	3,955	3,015	95	80 000 $ à 89 999 $	573
320	0	685	2,960	2,300	40	90 000 $ à 99 999 $	574
975	10	2,260	9,160	6,260	65	100 000 $ et plus	575
55,946	51,260	81,941	56,635	59,794	46,190	Revenu médian après impôt des familles $	576
64,467	56,817	89,972	64,400	67,345	50,484	Revenu moyen après impôt des familles $	577
1,169	7,602	1,702	417	468	1,607	Erreur type de revenu moyen après impôt des familles $	578
						Catégorie de revenu en 2005	
27,055	220	24,195	213,665	139,560	4,560	Population totale dans les ménages privés pour la catégorie de revenu	579
3,255	0	1,270	38,890	19,300	650	Au-dessous du seuil de faible revenu avant impôt en 2005	580
12.0	0.0	5.2	18.2	13.8	14.2	Fréquence du faible revenu avant impôt en 2005 %	581
1,870	0	915	30,400	13,825	445	Au-dessous du seuil de faible revenu après impôt en 2005	582
6.9	0.0	3.8	14.2	9.9	9.8	Fréquence du faible revenu après impôt en 2005 %	583

Nota : Voir les symboles et les abréviations dans les documents d'introduction et voir les documents de référence à la fin de la publication.

Selected characteristics for census divisions and census subdivisions – 100% data and 20% sample data, Ontario, 2006 Census (continued)

No.	Characteristics	Essex CD/DR	Amherstburg, T	Essex, T ◊	Kingsville, T ◊	Lakeshore, T	LaSalle, T
	2005 income characteristics						
584	**Total number of private households**	**150,845**	**7,930**	**7,640**	**7,450**	**11,635**	**9,315**
	Household income groups in 2005						
585	Under $10,000	7,310	265	210	210	265	205
586	$10,000 to $19,999	13,625	520	545	385	580	300
587	$20,000 to $29,999	13,695	535	660	625	560	435
588	$30,000 to $39,999	14,640	645	710	645	860	600
589	$40,000 to $49,999	13,710	565	820	745	855	505
590	$50,000 to $59,999	12,720	630	710	705	950	625
591	$60,000 to $69,999	11,635	585	620	590	810	615
592	$70,000 to $79,999	10,525	620	505	595	780	705
593	$80,000 to $89,999	9,450	575	630	505	915	705
594	$90,000 to $99,999	7,780	555	395	455	740	735
595	$100,000 and over	35,745	2,440	1,830	1,980	4,315	3,885
596	Median household income $	59,752	73,653	62,743	66,319	81,556	89,269
597	Average household income $	72,700	86,519	73,371	78,229	93,085	99,451
598	Standard error of average household income $	385	2,251	1,224	1,646	1,399	1,754
	Household after-tax income groups in 2005						
599	Under $10,000	7,450	280	210	235	275	215
600	$10,000 to $19,999	14,560	565	575	405	630	325
601	$20,000 to $29,999	16,475	625	810	720	705	515
602	$30,000 to $39,999	18,100	805	945	885	1,135	735
603	$40,000 to $49,999	16,790	725	920	955	1,140	770
604	$50,000 to $59,999	14,890	795	845	745	1,145	810
605	$60,000 to $69,999	13,585	755	690	815	1,110	915
606	$70,000 to $79,999	11,075	790	725	630	1,060	895
607	$80,000 to $89,999	8,800	590	460	530	865	800
608	$90,000 to $99,999	7,065	525	410	415	740	715
609	$100,000 and over	22,050	1,460	1,040	1,110	2,830	2,620
610	Median after-tax household income $	51,330	62,125	54,086	57,428	66,751	74,437
611	Average after-tax household income $	60,390	70,370	61,051	64,552	75,662	81,432
612	Standard error of average after-tax household income $	266	1,442	916	1,148	1,002	1,201

Note: See symbols and abbreviations in the introductory material and see reference material at the end of the publication.

Certaines caractéristiques des divisions de recensement et des subdivisions de recensement – Données intégrales et données-échantillon (20 %), Ontario, Recensement de 2006 (suite)

Leamington, MU ◊	Pelee, TP ◆◊	Tecumseh, T **A**	Windsor, CY ◊**A**	**Frontenac CD/DR** ◆◊	Central Frontenac, TP ◆◊	**Caractéristiques**	N°
						Caractéristiques du revenu de 2005	
9,815	**95**	**8,495**	**88,465**	**59,190**	**1,845**	**Nombre total des ménages privés**	584
						Tranches de revenu des ménages en 2005	
335	0	170	5,650	2,880	115	Moins de 10 000 $	585
815	10	250	10,220	6,080	250	10 000 $ à 19 999 $	586
1,125	15	410	9,315	5,875	210	20 000 $ à 29 999 $	587
1,180	20	520	9,460	6,325	200	30 000 $ à 39 999 $	588
860	0	560	8,800	6,025	240	40 000 $ à 49 999 $	589
1,055	20	575	7,445	5,450	205	50 000 $ à 59 999 $	590
945	0	590	6,880	4,155	145	60 000 $ à 69 999 $	591
690	20	585	6,020	4,180	120	70 000 $ à 79 999 $	592
710	0	560	4,845	3,555	70	80 000 $ à 89 999 $	593
500	0	555	3,855	3,005	115	90 000 $ à 99 999 $	594
1,595	10	3,715	15,965	11,645	165	100 000 $ et plus	595
54,940	52,030	90,206	50,884	54,275	45,826	Revenu médian des ménages $	596
66,918	55,885	102,103	63,276	67,762	52,755	Revenu moyen des ménages $	597
1,347	6,171	2,276	454	522	1,878	Erreur type de revenu moyen des ménages $	598
						Tranches du revenu après impôt des ménages en 2005	
335	0	175	5,725	2,940	125	Moins de 10 000 $	599
955	0	295	10,800	6,535	250	10 000 $ à 19 999 $	600
1,270	15	480	11,330	7,075	240	20 000 $ à 29 999 $	601
1,320	20	750	11,500	7,805	290	30 000 $ à 39 999 $	602
1,250	10	795	10,215	7,080	250	40 000 $ à 49 999 $	603
1,115	15	635	8,780	5,750	245	50 000 $ à 59 999 $	604
1,035	15	800	7,450	5,250	130	60 000 $ à 69 999 $	605
725	0	780	5,455	4,355	100	70 000 $ à 79 999 $	606
465	0	735	4,350	3,270	110	80 000 $ à 89 999 $	607
320	0	715	3,225	2,470	35	90 000 $ à 99 999 $	608
1,015	10	2,330	9,625	6,660	75	100 000 $ et plus	609
48,176	48,315	74,052	44,388	47,395	40,768	Revenu médian après impôt des ménages $	610
56,301	50,294	82,049	53,249	56,084	45,245	Revenu moyen après impôt des ménages $	611
964	5,320	1,498	314	371	1,451	Erreur type de revenu moyen après impôt des ménages $	612

Nota : Voir les symboles et les abréviations dans les documents d'introduction et voir les documents de référence à la fin de la publication.

Selected characteristics for census divisions and census subdivisions – 100% data and 20% sample data, Ontario, 2006 Census (continued)

No.	Characteristics	Frontenac Islands, TP ◆◊	Kingston, CY ◆◊	North Frontenac, TP ◆◊◊	South Frontenac, TP ◆◊	**Greater Sudbury / Grand Sudbury CD/DR** ◊	Greater Sudbury / Grand Sudbury, C ◊
	Population characteristics						
1	**Population, 2001**[1]	**1,638**	**114,195**	**1,801**	**16,415**	**155,268**	**155,219**
2	**Population, 2006**[2]	**1,862**	**117,207**	**1,904**	**18,227**	**157,909**	**157,857**
3	Population percentage change, 2001 to 2006	13.7	2.6	5.7	11.0	1.7	1.7
4	Land area in square kilometres, 2006	174.99	450.39	1,135.75	941.28	3,211.19	3,200.56
5	**Total population – 100% data**[3]	**1,865**	**117,210**	**1,905**	**18,225**	**157,910**	**157,860**
	Sex and age groups						
6	Male	940	56,525	960	9,150	76,715	76,685
7	0 to 4 years	40	2,895	35	475	3,900	3,900
8	5 to 9 years	45	2,995	35	555	4,465	4,465
9	10 to 14 years	55	3,575	40	690	5,225	5,220
10	15 to 19 years	45	3,930	50	690	5,300	5,300
11	20 to 24 years	35	4,650	30	455	5,140	5,145
12	25 to 29 years	40	4,095	20	350	4,525	4,520
13	30 to 34 years	40	3,540	30	475	4,645	4,645
14	35 to 39 years	45	3,795	55	650	4,995	5,000
15	40 to 44 years	70	4,615	60	780	6,490	6,485
16	45 to 49 years	75	4,315	65	805	6,370	6,365
17	50 to 54 years	90	3,955	70	790	5,710	5,710
18	55 to 59 years	95	3,560	90	785	5,545	5,540
19	60 to 64 years	75	2,820	115	585	4,185	4,185
20	65 to 69 years	90	2,275	95	420	3,200	3,195
21	70 to 74 years	45	1,975	85	280	2,720	2,720
22	75 to 79 years	40	1,640	45	210	2,195	2,195
23	80 to 84 years	10	1,155	15	105	1,355	1,355
24	85 years and over	5	745	10	55	745	745
25	Female	925	60,685	940	9,080	81,195	81,175
26	0 to 4 years	40	2,710	35	415	3,740	3,740
27	5 to 9 years	35	2,875	20	535	4,225	4,220
28	10 to 14 years	40	3,435	35	665	5,025	5,025
29	15 to 19 years	50	3,855	35	595	5,320	5,320
30	20 to 24 years	45	4,860	40	440	5,250	5,245
31	25 to 29 years	40	4,120	15	380	4,610	4,605
32	30 to 34 years	45	3,420	45	495	4,780	4,775
33	35 to 39 years	40	3,825	40	665	5,240	5,235
34	40 to 44 years	65	4,645	50	860	6,765	6,765
35	45 to 49 years	80	4,755	65	875	6,920	6,915
36	50 to 54 years	90	4,295	75	795	6,300	6,295
37	55 to 59 years	100	3,985	110	735	5,465	5,465
38	60 to 64 years	80	3,160	105	525	4,300	4,300
39	65 to 69 years	50	2,505	95	400	3,575	3,575
40	70 to 74 years	45	2,460	70	285	3,285	3,285
41	75 to 79 years	45	2,220	50	185	2,790	2,785
42	80 to 84 years	15	1,945	30	130	2,080	2,080
43	85 years and over	20	1,615	25	90	1,535	1,535
44	**Total population 15 years and over**[3]	**1,615**	**98,725**	**1,705**	**14,890**	**131,325**	**131,285**
	Legal marital status						
45	Never legally married (single)	380	34,700	325	3,585	41,100	41,080
46	Legally married (and not separated)[4,5]	985	45,295	1,040	9,140	65,085	65,065
47	Separated, but still legally married	30	3,710	50	430	5,825	5,820
48	Divorced	115	8,265	130	995	9,640	9,635
49	Widowed	100	6,760	155	735	9,680	9,675
	Common-law status						
50	Not in a common-law relationship	1,460	89,765	1,580	13,650	118,445	118,410
51	In a common-law relationship	150	8,960	130	1,240	12,890	12,875
52	**Total population – 20% sample data**[6]	**1,870**	**114,045**	**1,895**	**18,210**	**156,045**	**155,995**
	Mother tongue						
53	Single responses	1,865	113,115	1,895	18,145	153,820	153,765
54	English	1,745	97,255	1,805	17,215	99,130	99,085
55	French	15	3,715	10	275	42,945	42,940
56	Non-official languages[7]	110	12,150	80	650	11,750	11,745
57	Italian	10	655	0	35	3,325	3,325
58	Chinese, n.o.s.[61]	10	1,145	0	20	295	300
59	Cantonese	20	325	0	10	55	60
60	Spanish	0	715	0	20	185	185
61	German	15	1,065	45	135	1,000	995
62	Other languages[8]	65	8,250	35	435	6,885	6,885

Note: See symbols and abbreviations in the introductory material and see reference material at the end of the publication.

Certaines caractéristiques des divisions de recensement et des subdivisions de recensement – Données intégrales et données-échantillon (20 %), Ontario, Recensement de 2006 (suite)

Wahnapitei 11, IRI	**Grey CD/DR** ◆	Blue Mountains, T ◆◆◊	Chatsworth, TP	Georgian Bluffs, TP ◊**A**	Grey Highlands, MU ◆◊	**Caractéristiques**	N°
						Caractéristiques de la population	
49	**89,073**	**6,116**	**6,280**	**10,127**	**9,196**	**Population, 2001**[1]	1
52	**92,411**	**6,825**	**6,392**	**10,506**	**9,480**	**Population, 2006**[2]	2
6.1	3.7	11.6	1.8	3.7	3.1	Variation en pourcentage de la population, 2001 à 2006	3
10.63	4,508.12	286.78	595.35	603.58	880.60	Superficie des terres en kilomètres carrés, 2006	4
50	**92,410**	**6,825**	**6,390**	**10,505**	**9,480**	**Population totale – Données intégrales**[3]	5
						Sexe et groupes d'âge	
30	45,450	3,380	3,235	5,320	4,760	Sexe masculin	6
0	2,270	120	180	210	240	0 à 4 ans	7
5	2,610	155	205	260	270	5 à 9 ans	8
0	3,035	200	200	360	335	10 à 14 ans	9
0	3,405	195	235	420	375	15 à 19 ans	10
5	2,685	170	190	295	265	20 à 24 ans	11
0	2,010	110	145	200	215	25 à 29 ans	12
0	2,060	130	150	190	205	30 à 34 ans	13
0	2,445	150	170	270	265	35 à 39 ans	14
5	3,305	195	240	400	345	40 à 44 ans	15
5	3,665	255	265	490	390	45 à 49 ans	16
0	3,585	255	255	495	335	50 à 54 ans	17
0	3,535	295	300	505	340	55 à 59 ans	18
5	2,945	315	215	415	325	60 à 64 ans	19
0	2,435	260	165	295	290	65 à 69 ans	20
5	2,085	230	140	230	235	70 à 74 ans	21
0	1,705	185	100	160	170	75 à 79 ans	22
0	930	90	50	90	85	80 à 84 ans	23
0	750	60	30	45	80	85 ans et plus	24
25	46,960	3,445	3,160	5,185	4,715	Sexe féminin	25
0	1,985	115	165	190	220	0 à 4 ans	26
0	2,385	135	205	275	255	5 à 9 ans	27
0	2,930	165	250	345	320	10 à 14 ans	28
0	3,190	200	210	365	325	15 à 19 ans	29
0	2,460	160	130	255	250	20 à 24 ans	30
0	2,060	125	135	195	200	25 à 29 ans	31
5	2,140	130	150	220	210	30 à 34 ans	32
5	2,635	145	185	295	260	35 à 39 ans	33
0	3,390	210	220	420	355	40 à 44 ans	34
5	3,965	295	285	495	380	45 à 49 ans	35
5	3,705	270	265	510	350	50 à 54 ans	36
0	3,665	330	275	480	370	55 à 59 ans	37
0	3,055	305	190	395	355	60 à 64 ans	38
0	2,485	290	160	280	250	65 à 69 ans	39
0	2,175	215	120	180	235	70 à 74 ans	40
0	1,910	165	100	130	150	75 à 79 ans	41
0	1,410	100	60	110	125	80 à 84 ans	42
0	1,415	100	50	50	105	85 ans et plus	43
45	**77,200**	**5,935**	**5,180**	**8,870**	**7,830**	**Population totale de 15 ans et plus**[3]	44
						État matrimonial légal	
15	20,435	1,405	1,310	2,085	2,085	Jamais légalement marié(e) (célibataire)	45
20	42,270	3,445	3,050	5,590	4,385	Légalement marié(e) (et non séparé[e])[4,5]	46
5	2,750	175	160	230	270	Séparé(e), mais toujours légalement marié(e)	47
0	5,740	470	375	530	540	Divorcé(e)	48
0	6,010	445	285	430	550	Veuf(ve)	49
						Union libre	
30	70,790	5,530	4,765	8,220	7,115	Ne vivant pas en union libre	50
10	6,415	405	420	655	715	Vivant en union libre	51
55	**90,905**	**6,745**	**6,325**	**10,485**	**9,410**	**Population totale – Données-échantillon (20 %)**[6]	52
						Langue maternelle	
50	90,510	6,735	6,315	10,475	9,320	Réponses uniques	53
40	83,580	6,005	5,520	9,935	8,380	Anglais	54
10	775	80	55	35	160	Français	55
0	6,150	650	740	495	785	Langues non officielles[7]	56
0	280	40	0	35	45	Italien	57
0	165	0	0	10	0	Chinois, n.d.a.[61]	58
0	20	10	0	0	0	Cantonais	59
0	80	0	0	0	15	Espagnol	60
0	2,790	265	575	145	340	Allemand	61
0	2,815	340	160	305	375	Autres langues[8]	62

Nota : Voir les symboles et les abréviations dans les documents d'introduction et voir les documents de référence à la fin de la publication.

Selected characteristics for census divisions and census subdivisions – 100% data and 20% sample data, Ontario, 2006 Census (continued)

No.	Characteristics	Frontenac Islands, TP ◆◊	Kingston, CY ◆◊	North Frontenac, TP ◆◊◊	South Frontenac, TP ◆◊	**Greater Sudbury / Grand Sudbury CD/DR** ◊	Greater Sudbury / Grand Sudbury, C ◊
	Population characteristics						
	Mother tongue (continued)						
63	Multiple responses	0	930	0	65	2,230	2,225
64	English and French	0	325	0	20	1,675	1,675
65	English and non-official language	0	575	0	40	495	490
66	French and non-official language	0	25	0	0	40	40
67	English, French and non-official language	0	0	0	10	15	15
	Language spoken most often at home[9]						
68	Single responses	1,860	112,895	1,890	18,185	154,015	153,965
69	English	1,810	105,885	1,890	17,950	124,950	124,900
70	French	0	1,910	0	90	25,495	25,500
71	Non-official languages[7]	50	5,100	0	140	3,570	3,565
72	Chinese, n.o.s.[61]	0	745	0	10	190	190
73	Cantonese	15	275	0	0	40	40
74	Panjabi (Punjabi)	0	95	0	0	10	0
75	Italian	0	120	0	0	1,310	1,305
76	Spanish	0	450	0	10	45	45
77	Other languages[8]	35	3,410	0	115	1,980	1,975
78	Multiple responses	10	1,155	10	25	2,030	2,030
79	English and French	0	250	0	10	1,405	1,405
80	English and non-official language	0	865	0	15	595	595
81	French and non-official language	0	25	0	0	10	10
82	English, French and non-official language	0	10	0	0	20	20
	Knowledge of official languages[10]						
83	English only	1,705	97,035	1,780	16,640	92,525	92,480
84	French only	0	450	0	10	2,550	2,550
85	English and French	160	16,015	115	1,565	60,685	60,675
86	Neither English nor French	0	550	0	0	290	290
	Knowledge of non-official languages[7,11]						
87	Italian	10	1,005	15	55	4,550	4,545
88	Spanish	35	1,905	0	215	1,195	1,195
89	German	30	2,210	40	285	1,365	1,365
90	Chinese, n.o.s.[61]	10	1,130	0	10	295	295
91	Cantonese	20	415	0	10	90	90
92	Panjabi (Punjabi)	0	230	0	0	80	80
93	Portuguese	0	2,090	10	150	210	210
	First official language spoken[10]						
94	English	1,850	109,035	1,885	17,920	112,530	112,485
95	French	10	3,825	10	270	42,735	42,730
96	English and French	0	655	0	25	510	515
97	Neither English nor French	0	530	0	0	270	270
98	Official language minority - (number)[12]	15	4,155	10	280	42,990	42,985
99	Official language minority - (percentage)[12]	0.8	3.6	0.5	1.5	27.5	27.6
	Ethnic origin[13]						
100	English	585	39,440	675	6,910	35,720	35,715
101	Canadian	680	37,530	795	7,875	64,345	64,340
102	Scottish	415	29,620	590	5,175	26,575	26,570
103	Irish	685	31,090	630	5,440	30,415	30,415
104	French	360	17,430	220	2,585	62,465	62,465
105	German	145	11,215	460	1,820	12,140	12,135
106	Italian	35	3,385	55	270	13,410	13,410
107	Chinese	40	2,435	10	55	750	750
108	East Indian	0	1,400	0	90	590	590
109	Dutch (Netherlands)	195	6,650	95	1,400	2,890	2,890
110	Polish	80	2,925	70	440	4,750	4,750
111	Ukrainian	10	2,255	0	255	7,585	7,585
112	North American Indian	55	3,790	40	980	8,200	8,165
113	Portuguese	0	3,085	15	190	460	460
114	Filipino	0	525	0	0	230	235
	Aboriginal and non-Aboriginal identity						
115	Total Aboriginal identity population[14]	20	2,360	55	545	9,635	9,590
116	Total non-Aboriginal identity population	1,845	111,685	1,840	17,660	146,410	146,400

Note: See symbols and abbreviations in the introductory material and see reference material at the end of the publication.

Certaines caractéristiques des divisions de recensement et des subdivisions de recensement – Données intégrales et données-échantillon (20 %), Ontario, Recensement de 2006 (suite)

Wahnapitei 11, IRI	**Grey CD/DR** ◆	Blue Mountains, T ◆◆◇	Chatsworth, TP	Georgian Bluffs, TP ◇**A**	Grey Highlands, MU ◆◇	**Caractéristiques**	N°
						Caractéristiques de la population	
						Langue maternelle (suite)	
0	390	10	10	10	95	Réponses multiples	63
0	165	0	0	10	45	Anglais et français	64
0	205	10	10	0	45	Anglais et langue non officielle	65
0	15	0	0	0	10	Français et langue non officielle	66
0	0	0	0	0	0	Anglais, français et langue non officielle	67
						Langue parlée le plus souvent à la maison[9]	
50	90,665	6,735	6,270	10,460	9,380	Réponses uniques	68
50	88,380	6,640	5,795	10,350	9,055	Anglais	69
0	150	0	20	10	20	Français	70
0	2,135	85	455	110	305	Langues non officielles[7]	71
0	105	0	0	0	0	Chinois, n.d.a.[61]	72
0	0	0	0	0	0	Cantonais	73
0	0	0	0	0	0	Pendjabi	74
0	35	0	0	15	0	Italien	75
0	20	0	0	0	0	Espagnol	76
0	1,975	85	450	95	305	Autres langues[8]	77
0	235	10	55	20	30	Réponses multiples	78
0	80	0	0	10	15	Anglais et français	79
0	155	10	55	15	15	Anglais et langue non officielle	80
0	0	0	0	0	0	Français et langue non officielle	81
0	0	0	0	0	0	Anglais, français et langue non officielle	82
						Connaissance des langues officielles[10]	
45	85,360	6,135	6,040	9,920	8,700	Anglais seulement	83
0	30	0	0	0	0	Français seulement	84
10	5,260	610	260	540	615	Anglais et français	85
0	250	0	20	15	95	Ni l'anglais ni le français	86
						Connaissance des langues non officielles[7,11]	
0	460	50	0	65	90	Italien	87
0	600	65	15	75	55	Espagnol	88
0	3,380	355	600	180	445	Allemand	89
0	150	0	0	0	0	Chinois, n.d.a.[61]	90
0	15	10	0	0	0	Cantonais	91
0	55	0	0	0	25	Pendjabi	92
0	240	0	15	15	65	Portugais	93
						Première langue officielle parlée[10]	
50	89,855	6,670	6,250	10,395	9,155	Anglais	94
0	720	70	55	20	140	Français	95
0	105	0	0	50	35	Anglais et français	96
0	220	0	25	15	80	Ni l'anglais ni le français	97
0	770	70	55	50	160	Minorité de langue officielle - (nombre)[12]	98
0.0	0.8	1.0	0.9	0.5	1.7	Minorité de langue officielle - (pourcentage)[12]	99
						Origine ethnique[13]	
10	37,060	2,955	2,200	4,345	4,125	Anglais	100
0	29,120	2,045	1,915	3,705	2,955	Canadien	101
0	30,830	2,080	2,005	3,805	3,210	Écossais	102
0	24,750	1,835	1,630	2,950	2,565	Irlandais	103
10	8,030	640	475	760	795	Français	104
0	19,505	810	1,970	1,870	1,450	Allemand	105
0	1,725	315	65	165	215	Italien	106
0	310	10	55	10	20	Chinois	107
0	350	0	30	0	20	Indien de l'Inde	108
0	5,860	335	555	975	500	Hollandais (Néerlandais)	109
0	1,675	105	175	180	155	Polonais	110
0	1,320	145	175	90	225	Ukrainien	111
35	1,875	35	130	140	85	Indien de l'Amérique du Nord	112
0	495	0	10	15	200	Portugais	113
0	145	0	0	10	0	Philippin	114
						Population ayant une identité autochtone et population n'ayant pas d'identité autochtone	
45	1,475	20	90	130	75	Total de la population ayant une identité autochtone[14]	115
10	89,430	6,725	6,235	10,350	9,335	Total de la population n'ayant pas d'identité autochtone	116

Nota : Voir les symboles et les abréviations dans les documents d'introduction et voir les documents de référence à la fin de la publication.

Selected characteristics for census divisions and census subdivisions – 100% data and 20% sample data, Ontario, 2006 Census (continued)

No.	Characteristics	Frontenac Islands, TP ◆◊	Kingston, CY ◆◊	North Frontenac, TP ◆◊◊	South Frontenac, TP ◆◊	**Greater Sudbury / Grand Sudbury CD/DR** ◊	Greater Sudbury / Grand Sudbury, C ◊
	Population characteristics						
	Aboriginal and non-Aboriginal ancestry						
117	Total Aboriginal ancestry population[15]	60	4,795	40	1,160	14,280	14,240
118	Total non-Aboriginal ancestry population	1,805	109,245	1,860	17,055	141,765	141,755
	Registered Indian status						
119	Registered Indian[16]	10	715	10	130	3,455	3,415
120	Not a Registered Indian	1,865	113,330	1,885	18,085	152,590	152,575
	Visible minority groups						
121	Total visible minority population[17]	45	8,150	0	235	3,280	3,280
122	Chinese	40	2,370	0	25	620	620
123	South Asian[18]	0	1,720	0	50	580	580
124	Black	0	1,030	0	85	1,095	1,095
125	Filipino	0	445	0	0	150	150
126	Latin American	0	710	0	15	180	180
127	Southeast Asian[19]	0	310	0	15	145	145
128	Arab	0	365	0	0	120	120
129	West Asian[20]	0	280	0	0	55	60
130	Korean	0	310	0	0	70	70
131	Japanese	0	240	0	10	65	65
132	Visible minority, n.i.e.[21]	0	155	0	20	55	60
133	Multiple visible minority[22]	0	205	0	0	145	145
	Citizenship[23]						
134	Canadian citizens[24]	1,840	110,090	1,875	18,015	154,225	154,175
135	Not Canadian citizens[25]	25	3,955	25	200	1,820	1,820
	Immigrant status and place of birth[26]						
136	Non-immigrants[27]	1,725	96,850	1,710	17,085	145,210	145,160
137	Born in province of residence	1,555	78,690	1,545	15,280	131,085	131,035
138	Immigrants[28]	135	16,210	190	1,100	10,450	10,450
139	United States of America	20	1,250	75	120	630	630
140	Central and South America	0	675	10	10	230	230
141	Caribbean and Bermuda	0	330	0	35	195	200
142	United Kingdom	55	3,670	35	435	1,460	1,465
143	Other Europe	35	5,835	75	420	6,350	6,350
144	Africa	0	660	0	35	445	445
145	Asia and the Middle East	15	3,640	0	40	1,075	1,075
146	Oceania and other[29]	10	135	0	0	50	50
147	Non-permanent residents[30]	10	985	0	25	390	385
148	**Total immigrant population[28]**	**130**	**16,210**	**190**	**1,105**	**10,450**	**10,450**
	Period of immigration						
149	Before 1961	65	4,240	70	330	4,750	4,750
150	1961 to 1970	10	3,110	55	335	2,085	2,085
151	1971 to 1980	25	2,165	25	200	1,275	1,275
152	1981 to 1990	30	2,085	30	115	790	790
153	1991 to 2000	0	2,555	10	70	895	895
154	1991 to 1995	0	1,225	0	0	425	425
155	1996 to 2000	0	1,330	0	65	470	470
156	2001 to 2006[31]	0	2,055	0	45	660	660
	Age at immigration						
157	Under 5 years	20	1,865	20	190	1,235	1,240
158	5 to 19 years	50	4,400	45	380	2,990	2,990
159	20 years and over	60	9,940	120	530	6,220	6,220
160	**Total population 15 years and over**	**1,630**	**95,520**	**1,730**	**14,875**	**129,480**	**129,435**
	Generation status						
161	1st generation[32]	145	16,885	190	1,175	10,655	10,655
162	2nd generation[33]	310	17,400	180	1,960	16,715	16,715
163	3rd generation or more[34]	1,180	61,235	1,355	11,740	102,110	102,065

Note: See symbols and abbreviations in the introductory material and see reference material at the end of the publication.

Certaines caractéristiques des divisions de recensement et des subdivisions de recensement – Données intégrales et données-échantillon (20 %), Ontario, Recensement de 2006 (suite)

Wahnapitei 11, IRI	**Grey CD/DR** ◆	Blue Mountains, T ◆◆◇	Chatsworth, TP	Georgian Bluffs, TP ◇**A**	Grey Highlands, MU ◆◇	**Caractéristiques**	N°
						Caractéristiques de la population	
						Population ayant une ascendance autochtone et population n'ayant pas d'ascendance autochtone	
40	2,830	50	195	215	170	Total de la population ayant une ascendance autochtone[15]	117
10	88,075	6,700	6,130	10,265	9,240	Total de la population n'ayant pas d'ascendance autochtone	118
						Statut d'Indien inscrit	
35	390	10	35	25	10	Indien inscrit[16]	119
15	90,510	6,735	6,290	10,460	9,400	Pas un Indien inscrit	120
						Groupes de minorités visibles	
0	1,435	50	55	60	130	Total de la population des minorités visibles[17]	121
0	230	15	15	0	10	Chinois	122
0	310	0	10	0	25	Sud-Asiatique[18]	123
0	445	20	10	15	65	Noir	124
0	110	0	0	10	0	Philippin	125
0	70	0	0	10	0	Latino-Américain	126
0	20	0	0	0	10	Asiatique du Sud-Est[19]	127
0	35	0	0	15	0	Arabe	128
0	10	0	0	10	0	Asiatique occidental[20]	129
0	80	10	15	0	0	Coréen	130
0	50	10	0	0	15	Japonais	131
0	20	0	0	0	0	Minorité visible, n.i.a.[21]	132
0	50	0	0	0	10	Minorités visibles multiples[22]	133
						Citoyenneté[23]	
X	89,115	6,620	6,165	10,280	9,255	Citoyens canadiens[24]	134
X	1,780	125	160	200	160	Ne sont pas des citoyens canadiens[25]	135
						Statut d'immigrant et le lieu de naissance[26]	
X	82,880	5,820	5,785	9,690	8,480	Non-immigrants[27]	136
X	77,270	5,230	5,445	9,190	7,865	Né dans la province de résidence	137
X	7,830	910	540	790	925	Immigrants[28]	138
X	770	50	130	70	70	États-Unis d'Amérique	139
X	140	0	15	10	10	Amérique centrale et Amérique du Sud	140
X	165	10	0	0	40	Antilles et Bermudes	141
X	2,700	320	145	300	345	Royaume-Uni	142
X	3,295	475	235	360	365	Autre Europe	143
X	165	10	0	20	20	Afrique	144
X	525	45	15	0	60	Asie et Moyen-Orient	145
X	70	10	0	10	0	Océanie et autres[29]	146
X	195	15	0	0	10	Résidents non permanents[30]	147
X	**7,830**	**910**	**540**	**790**	**925**	**Population totale des immigrants[28]**	148
						Période d'immigration	
X	3,215	560	190	300	390	Avant 1961	149
X	1,725	110	175	165	190	1961 à 1970	150
X	1,110	120	55	125	195	1971 à 1980	151
X	700	50	95	55	45	1981 à 1990	152
X	615	30	10	115	70	1991 à 2000	153
X	265	10	0	10	30	1991 à 1995	154
X	345	20	10	105	35	1996 à 2000	155
X	465	40	10	25	40	2001 à 2006[31]	156
						Âge à l'immigration	
X	1,030	75	90	110	90	Moins de 5 ans	157
X	2,425	305	170	235	365	5 à 19 ans	158
X	4,370	525	280	440	470	20 ans et plus	159
45	**75,690**	**5,835**	**5,120**	**8,855**	**7,765**	**Population totale de 15 ans et plus**	160
						Statut des générations	
0	7,975	955	545	760	945	1re génération[32]	161
0	10,315	1,175	755	1,110	995	2e génération[33]	162
45	57,400	3,710	3,825	6,985	5,825	3e génération ou plus[34]	163

Nota : Voir les symboles et les abréviations dans les documents d'introduction et voir les documents de référence à la fin de la publication.

Selected characteristics for census divisions and census subdivisions – 100% data and 20% sample data, Ontario, 2006 Census (continued)

No.	Characteristics	Frontenac Islands, TP ◆◊	Kingston, CY ◆◊	North Frontenac, TP ◆◊◊	South Frontenac, TP ◆◊	**Greater Sudbury / Grand Sudbury CD/DR** ◊	Greater Sudbury / Grand Sudbury, C ◊
	Population characteristics						
164	**Total population 1 year and over[35]**	**1,845**	**112,970**	**1,900**	**18,065**	**154,580**	**154,530**
	Place of residence 1 year ago (mobility)						
165	Non-movers	1,720	93,365	1,795	16,585	135,070	135,025
166	Movers	125	19,605	100	1,480	19,510	19,500
167	Non-migrants	55	12,095	20	355	14,180	14,180
168	Migrants	75	7,510	80	1,125	5,325	5,320
169	Internal migrants	75	6,475	85	1,095	5,060	5,060
170	Intraprovincial migrants	65	4,675	80	960	4,290	4,290
171	Interprovincial migrants	0	1,805	0	135	765	765
172	External migrants	0	1,035	0	25	265	265
173	**Total population 5 years and over[36]**	**1,780**	**108,425**	**1,835**	**17,320**	**148,310**	**148,265**
	Place of residence 5 years ago (mobility)						
174	Non-movers	1,360	58,495	1,340	11,685	95,150	95,115
175	Movers	420	49,925	495	5,630	53,160	53,145
176	Non-migrants	105	26,875	130	1,885	37,545	37,545
177	Migrants	315	23,050	370	3,740	15,615	15,600
178	Internal migrants	295	19,620	360	3,605	14,720	14,705
179	Intraprovincial migrants	255	14,390	335	3,310	12,385	12,375
180	Interprovincial migrants	40	5,230	25	295	2,330	2,330
181	External migrants	15	3,435	10	140	895	895
182	**Total population 15 years and over**	**1,635**	**95,520**	**1,730**	**14,875**	**129,475**	**129,435**
	Highest certificate, diploma or degree[37]						
183	No certificate, diploma or degree	345	17,400	470	3,005	33,300	33,290
184	Certificate, diploma or degree	1,285	78,120	1,255	11,870	96,180	96,145
185	High school certificate or equivalent[38]	460	25,435	535	4,015	32,395	32,385
186	Apprenticeship or trades certificate or diploma	155	7,095	225	1,570	13,865	13,850
187	College, CEGEP or other non-university certificate or diploma[39]	365	19,480	325	3,670	29,895	29,890
188	University certificate or diploma below bachelor level[40]	100	3,070	45	315	2,960	2,960
189	University certificate or degree[41]	205	23,035	120	2,305	17,065	17,060
190	Bachelor's degree	140	12,190	50	1,455	10,500	10,500
191	University certificate or diploma above bachelor level	10	2,380	15	355	2,855	2,855
192	Degree in medicine, dentistry, veterinary medicine or optometry	0	1,230	10	40	500	500
193	Master's degree	45	4,930	40	280	2,530	2,530
194	Earned doctorate	10	2,305	10	175	675	670
195	**Total population 15 years and over with postsecondary qualifications**	**830**	**52,685**	**725**	**7,855**	**63,780**	**63,760**
	Major field of study - Classification of Instructional Programs, 2000[42]						
196	Education	75	4,010	60	705	4,730	4,730
197	Visual and performing arts, and communications technologies	10	1,635	0	175	1,175	1,175
198	Humanities	50	3,630	35	400	2,360	2,360
199	Social and behavioural sciences and law	85	6,655	55	795	5,500	5,500
200	Business, management and public administration	115	8,970	120	1,255	12,530	12,530
201	Physical and life sciences and technologies	35	2,695	10	260	2,200	2,200
202	Mathematics, computer and information sciences	30	2,095	15	315	1,930	1,925
203	Architecture, engineering, and related technologies	175	9,150	250	1,890	17,510	17,500
204	Agriculture, natural resources and conservation	45	575	30	125	880	875
205	Health, parks, recreation and fitness	165	10,025	85	1,390	10,365	10,365
206	Personal, protective and transportation services	35	3,230	55	545	4,585	4,585
207	Other fields of study[43]	0	0	0	0	10	10
	Location of study[44]						
208	Inside Canada	775	46,485	675	7,430	61,005	60,985
209	Outside Canada	50	6,200	50	425	2,775	2,770
210	**Total population 15 years and over**	**1,635**	**95,520**	**1,730**	**14,875**	**129,475**	**129,435**
	Unpaid work						
211	Males 15 years and over	800	44,940	845	7,430	62,380	62,360
212	Reported unpaid work[45]	760	40,610	770	6,760	56,510	56,485
213	Housework and child care and care or assistance to seniors	75	3,230	50	545	5,265	5,265
214	Housework and child care only	200	10,705	140	1,980	15,350	15,340

Note: See symbols and abbreviations in the introductory material and see reference material at the end of the publication.

Wahnapitei 11, IRI	**Grey CD/DR** ◆	Blue Mountains, T ◆◆◊	Chatsworth, TP	Georgian Bluffs, TP ◊A	Grey Highlands, MU ◆◊	**Caractéristiques**	Nº
						Caractéristiques de la population	
55	**90,080**	**6,715**	**6,230**	**10,435**	**9,315**	**Population totale de 1 an et plus[35]**	164
						Lieu de résidence 1 an auparavant (mobilité)	
45	79,440	5,910	5,615	9,485	8,305	Personnes n'ayant pas déménagé	165
0	10,640	805	615	950	1,005	Personnes ayant déménagé	166
0	4,660	320	210	310	240	Non-migrants	167
0	5,975	485	405	645	770	Migrants	168
0	5,710	450	400	625	765	Migrants internes	169
10	5,440	435	395	575	725	Migrants infraprovinciaux	170
0	275	20	10	45	40	Migrants interprovinciaux	171
0	260	35	10	20	10	Migrants externes	172
50	**86,725**	**6,545**	**5,975**	**10,080**	**8,950**	**Population totale de 5 ans et plus[36]**	173
						Lieu de résidence 5 ans auparavant (mobilité)	
35	56,090	4,320	4,295	7,250	6,180	Personnes n'ayant pas déménagé	174
10	30,640	2,225	1,680	2,830	2,765	Personnes ayant déménagé	175
0	13,230	720	600	1,025	895	Non-migrants	176
10	17,405	1,505	1,085	1,805	1,875	Migrants	177
10	16,810	1,420	1,055	1,750	1,865	Migrants internes	178
10	15,720	1,285	995	1,665	1,835	Migrants infraprovinciaux	179
0	1,090	130	60	85	30	Migrants interprovinciaux	180
0	595	85	25	55	10	Migrants externes	181
45	**75,690**	**5,835**	**5,120**	**8,855**	**7,765**	**Population totale de 15 ans et plus**	182
						Plus haut certificat, diplôme ou grade[37]	
15	21,465	955	1,590	2,145	2,265	Aucun certificat, diplôme ou grade	183
30	54,225	4,880	3,530	6,710	5,500	Certificat, diplôme ou grade	184
10	20,930	1,345	1,370	2,660	2,170	Diplôme d'études secondaires ou l'équivalent[38]	185
15	7,955	560	535	1,045	835	Certificat ou diplôme d'apprenti ou d'une école de métiers	186
0	14,905	1,320	1,075	1,840	1,415	Certificat ou diplôme d'un collège, d'un cégep ou d'un autre établissement d'enseignement non universitaire[39]	187
0	1,970	290	90	280	180	Certificat ou diplôme universitaire inférieur au baccalauréat[40]	188
10	8,470	1,365	460	885	905	Certificat ou grade universitaire[41]	189
0	5,255	800	295	490	535	Baccalauréat	190
0	1,315	180	60	195	115	Certificat ou diplôme universitaire supérieur au baccalauréat	191
0	355	60	10	45	45	Diplôme en médecine, en art dentaire, en médecine vétérinaire ou en optométrie	192
0	1,340	275	85	130	180	Maîtrise	193
0	210	55	0	25	25	Doctorat acquis	194
20	**33,295**	**3,535**	**2,165**	**4,050**	**3,330**	**Population totale de 15 ans et plus avec titres du niveau postsecondaire**	195
						Principal domaine d'études - Classification des programmes d'enseignement, 2000[42]	
0	2,755	415	145	240	265	Éducation	196
0	1,320	160	115	160	90	Arts visuels et d'interprétation, et technologie des communications	197
0	1,430	235	40	140	130	Sciences humaines	198
0	2,800	395	170	305	415	Sciences sociales et de comportements, et droit	199
10	5,755	735	395	690	535	Commerce, gestion et administration publique	200
0	775	90	55	90	100	Sciences physiques et de la vie, et technologies	201
0	635	55	40	80	70	Mathématiques, informatique et sciences de l'information	202
10	7,790	595	530	1,145	805	Architecture, génie et services connexes	203
0	1,205	75	125	120	160	Agriculture, ressources naturelles et conservation	204
0	6,470	585	385	805	540	Santé, parcs, récréation et conditionnement physique	205
10	2,335	190	155	275	215	Services personnels, de protection et de transport	206
0	10	10	0	0	0	Autres domaines d'études[43]	207
						Lieu des études[44]	
20	30,370	3,095	2,005	3,760	3,070	À l'intérieur du Canada	208
0	2,925	440	155	295	265	À l'extérieur du Canada	209
45	**75,690**	**5,835**	**5,120**	**8,855**	**7,765**	**Population totale de 15 ans et plus**	210
						Travail non rémunéré	
25	36,985	2,860	2,615	4,475	3,885	Hommes de 15 ans et plus	211
25	33,465	2,595	2,375	4,140	3,470	Travail non rémunéré déclaré[45]	212
0	2,745	205	185	480	245	Travaux ménagers et soins aux enfants et soins ou aide aux personnes âgées	213
10	8,125	540	610	995	855	Travaux ménagers et soins aux enfants seulement	214

Nota : Voir les symboles et les abréviations dans les documents d'introduction et voir les documents de référence à la fin de la publication.

Selected characteristics for census divisions and census subdivisions – 100% data and 20% sample data, Ontario, 2006 Census (continued)

No.	Characteristics	Frontenac Islands, TP ◆◊	Kingston, CY ◆◊	North Frontenac, TP ◆◊◊	South Frontenac, TP ◆◊	**Greater Sudbury / Grand Sudbury CD/DR** ◊	Greater Sudbury / Grand Sudbury, C ◊
	Population characteristics						
	Unpaid work (continued)						
215	Housework and care or assistance to seniors only	90	3,370	85	685	5,730	5,730
216	Child care and care or assistance to seniors only	0	55	0	10	55	55
217	Housework only	390	22,865	500	3,470	29,345	29,330
218	Child care only	10	215	0	35	545	545
219	Care or assistance to seniors only	0	165	0	30	210	210
220	Females 15 years and over	835	50,575	880	7,445	67,095	67,075
221	Reported unpaid work[45]	810	47,170	840	6,985	63,020	63,000
222	Housework and child care and care or assistance to seniors	75	4,620	60	870	8,570	8,570
223	Housework and child care only	190	13,510	170	2,200	18,555	18,545
224	Housework and care or assistance to seniors only	105	4,910	125	760	6,740	6,735
225	Child care and care or assistance to seniors only	0	20	0	0	45	50
226	Housework only	430	23,800	485	3,080	28,650	28,640
227	Child care only	10	160	0	50	275	275
228	Care or assistance to seniors only	0	150	0	30	180	180
	Labour force activity						
229	Males 15 years and over	800	44,940	845	7,425	62,380	62,360
230	In the labour force	555	30,575	500	5,275	42,150	42,130
231	Employed	525	28,360	450	5,030	38,795	38,780
232	Unemployed	35	2,210	50	250	3,355	3,355
233	Not in the labour force	240	14,365	345	2,150	20,235	20,225
234	Participation rate	69.4	68.0	59.2	71.0	67.6	67.6
235	Employment rate	65.6	63.1	53.3	67.7	62.2	62.2
236	Unemployment rate	6.3	7.2	10.0	4.7	8.0	8.0
237	Females 15 years and over	835	50,580	880	7,445	67,095	67,075
238	In the labour force	520	30,665	345	4,900	39,475	39,460
239	Employed	510	28,575	325	4,620	36,425	36,415
240	Unemployed	15	2,090	20	285	3,045	3,045
241	Not in the labour force	315	19,915	535	2,545	27,620	27,615
242	Participation rate	62.3	60.6	39.2	65.8	58.8	58.8
243	Employment rate	61.1	56.5	36.9	62.1	54.3	54.3
244	Unemployment rate	2.9	6.8	5.8	5.8	7.7	7.7
245	Both sexes - Participation rate	66.3	64.1	49.0	68.4	63.0	63.0
246	15 to 24 years	69.2	69.0	68.3	65.8	70.1	70.1
247	25 years and over	65.5	63.1	46.4	68.9	61.7	61.7
248	Both sexes - Employment rate	63.0	59.6	44.5	64.8	58.1	58.1
249	15 to 24 years	59.0	58.6	52.4	54.1	57.7	57.8
250	25 years and over	63.8	59.8	43.6	66.7	58.2	58.2
251	Both sexes - Unemployment rate	4.2	7.0	8.9	5.3	7.9	7.8
252	15 to 24 years	14.3	15.0	21.4	17.7	17.6	17.6
253	25 years and over	3.2	5.1	6.3	3.2	5.7	5.7
254	**Total labour force 15 years and over**	**1,075**	**61,235**	**845**	**10,180**	**81,620**	**81,590**
	Industry - North American Industry Classification System 2002						
255	Industry - Not applicable[46]	0	930	30	90	1,795	1,790
256	All industries[47]	1,075	60,305	815	10,090	79,830	79,795
257	11 Agriculture, forestry, fishing and hunting	85	335	50	230	290	285
258	21 Mining and oil and gas extraction	0	65	0	40	5,725	5,715
259	22 Utilities	10	255	15	105	505	505
260	23 Construction	90	3,055	145	1,010	5,145	5,145
261	31-33 Manufacturing	100	2,845	40	770	4,775	4,775
262	41 Wholesale trade	20	1,210	10	425	3,020	3,020
263	44-45 Retail trade	110	7,325	75	1,160	10,275	10,270
264	48-49 Transportation and warehousing	65	1,730	25	375	3,645	3,645
265	51 Information and cultural industries	25	1,055	0	150	1,225	1,225
266	52 Finance and insurance	20	1,760	10	300	2,195	2,195
267	53 Real estate and rental and leasing	30	1,230	0	185	1,135	1,135
268	54 Professional, scientific and technical services	30	2,870	30	370	3,530	3,525
269	55 Management of companies and enterprises	0	60	0	0	15	15
270	56 Administrative and support, waste management and remediation services	55	2,980	20	455	3,800	3,800
271	61 Educational services	125	8,150	55	1,055	7,040	7,040
272	62 Health care and social assistance	95	8,855	45	1,280	9,920	9,915

Note: See symbols and abbreviations in the introductory material and see reference material at the end of the publication.

Certaines caractéristiques des divisions de recensement et des subdivisions de recensement – Données intégrales et données-échantillon (20 %), Ontario, Recensement de 2006 (suite)

Wahnapitei 11, IRI	**Grey CD/DR** ◆	Blue Mountains, T ◆◆◊	Chatsworth, TP	Georgian Bluffs, TP ◊A	Grey Highlands, MU ◆◊	**Caractéristiques**	N°
						Caractéristiques de la population	
						Travail non rémunéré (suite)	
10	3,360	265	300	280	355	Travaux ménagers et soins ou aide aux personnes âgées seulement	215
0	35	0	0	10	15	Soins aux enfants et soins ou aide aux personnes âgées seulement	216
15	18,890	1,565	1,265	2,355	1,975	Travaux ménagers seulement	217
0	205	15	0	0	25	Soins aux enfants seulement	218
0	100	10	0	20	0	Soins ou aide aux personnes âgées seulement	219
20	38,700	2,975	2,500	4,380	3,875	Femmes de 15 ans et plus	220
20	36,755	2,800	2,425	4,185	3,730	Travail non rémunéré déclaré[45]	221
0	4,560	310	300	685	505	Travaux ménagers et soins aux enfants et soins ou aide aux personnes âgées	222
0	9,755	580	710	1,090	935	Travaux ménagers et soins aux enfants seulement	223
0	4,315	300	255	500	380	Travaux ménagers et soins ou aide aux personnes âgées seulement	224
0	10	0	0	0	0	Soins aux enfants et soins ou aide aux personnes âgées seulement	225
10	17,890	1,565	1,150	1,900	1,880	Travaux ménagers seulement	226
0	110	15	10	0	10	Soins aux enfants seulement	227
0	100	25	0	0	0	Soins ou aide aux personnes âgées seulement	228
						Activité	
25	36,990	2,860	2,615	4,475	3,885	Hommes de 15 ans et plus	229
20	25,825	1,895	1,915	3,180	2,740	Population active	230
15	24,415	1,830	1,795	3,050	2,575	Personnes occupées	231
10	1,405	60	115	130	160	Chômeurs	232
0	11,160	965	705	1,295	1,150	Inactifs	233
80.0	69.8	66.3	73.2	71.1	70.5	Taux d'activité	234
60.0	66.0	64.0	68.6	68.2	66.3	Taux d'emploi	235
50.0	5.4	3.2	6.0	4.1	5.8	Taux de chômage	236
15	38,700	2,980	2,505	4,380	3,875	Femmes de 15 ans et plus	237
10	23,060	1,690	1,620	2,915	2,245	Population active	238
10	21,920	1,600	1,545	2,810	2,125	Personnes occupées	239
0	1,135	85	75	100	115	Chômeuses	240
10	15,640	1,290	885	1,475	1,635	Inactives	241
66.7	59.6	56.7	64.7	66.6	57.9	Taux d'activité	242
66.7	56.6	53.7	61.7	64.2	54.8	Taux d'emploi	243
0.0	4.9	5.0	4.6	3.4	5.1	Taux de chômage	244
77.8	64.6	61.4	69.0	68.8	64.2	Les deux sexes - Taux d'activité	245
100.0	71.1	61.0	65.4	76.5	67.8	15 à 24 ans	246
75.0	63.4	61.3	69.7	67.4	63.6	25 ans et plus	247
55.6	61.2	58.9	65.2	66.1	60.6	Les deux sexes - Taux d'emploi	248
100.0	61.8	52.5	55.6	70.5	58.7	15 à 24 ans	249
50.0	61.1	59.7	66.9	65.4	60.8	25 ans et plus	250
28.6	5.2	4.2	5.4	3.8	5.6	Les deux sexes - Taux de chômage	251
0.0	13.1	14.9	15.0	8.4	12.9	15 à 24 ans	252
33.3	3.6	2.7	4.0	2.9	4.2	25 ans et plus	253
35	**48,880**	**3,585**	**3,535**	**6,090**	**4,985**	**Population active totale de 15 ans et plus**	254
						Industrie - Système de classification des industries de l'Amérique du Nord de 2002	
0	520	10	45	30	70	Industrie - Sans objet[46]	255
30	48,365	3,570	3,485	6,060	4,915	Toutes les industries[47]	256
0	3,065	170	290	245	565	11 Agriculture, foresterie, pêche et chasse	257
10	120	15	10	10	35	21 Extraction minière et extraction de pétrole et de gaz	258
0	560	10	40	95	25	22 Services publics	259
0	4,180	455	385	465	495	23 Construction	260
0	7,700	265	525	830	760	31-33 Fabrication	261
0	1,350	95	110	125	205	41 Commerce de gros	262
0	5,835	285	460	945	435	44-45 Commerce de détail	263
0	1,715	85	130	310	190	48-49 Transport et entreposage	264
0	820	75	20	105	60	51 Industrie de l'information et industrie culturelle	265
0	1,155	135	85	185	75	52 Finance et assurances	266
0	785	175	30	80	70	53 Services immobiliers et services de location et de location à bail	267
0	2,180	360	155	190	270	54 Services professionnels, scientifiques et techniques	268
0	35	10	0	0	0	55 Gestion de sociétés et d'entreprises	269
0	2,090	175	110	275	205	56 Services administratifs, services de soutien, services de gestion des déchets et services d'assainissement	270
0	2,575	255	120	315	240	61 Services d'enseignement	271
0	5,685	325	420	870	475	62 Soins de santé et assistance sociale	272

Nota : Voir les symboles et les abréviations dans les documents d'introduction et voir les documents de référence à la fin de la publication.

Selected characteristics for census divisions and census subdivisions – 100% data and 20% sample data, Ontario, 2006 Census (continued)

No.	Characteristics	Frontenac Islands, TP ◆◊	Kingston, CY ◆◊	North Frontenac, TP ◆◊◊	South Frontenac, TP ◆◊	**Greater Sudbury / Grand Sudbury CD/DR** ◊	Greater Sudbury / Grand Sudbury, C ◊
	Population characteristics						
	Industry - North American Industry Classification System 2002 (continued)						
273	71 Arts, entertainment and recreation	20	1,205	25	160	1,555	1,550
274	72 Accommodation and food services	100	5,190	120	510	5,610	5,610
275	81 Other services (except public administration)	40	2,640	40	395	4,230	4,230
276	91 Public administration	50	7,490	95	1,095	6,185	6,180
	Class of worker						
277	Class of worker - Not applicable[46]	0	930	25	90	1,795	1,790
278	All classes of worker[47]	1,075	60,305	815	10,090	79,830	79,795
279	Paid workers	940	56,230	675	9,055	75,670	75,635
280	Employees	900	54,880	640	8,690	73,695	73,665
281	Self-employed (incorporated)	40	1,350	35	370	1,970	1,970
282	Self-employed (unincorporated)	125	4,035	125	1,010	4,035	4,035
283	Unpaid family workers	10	40	10	25	125	130
	Occupation - National Occupational Classification for Statistics 2006						
284	Male labour force 15 years and over	555	30,575	500	5,275	42,150	42,130
285	Occupation - Not applicable[46]	10	475	20	45	915	915
286	All occupations[47]	550	30,100	475	5,230	41,235	41,210
287	A Management occupations	35	3,505	70	470	4,000	3,995
288	B Business, finance and administrative occupations	40	2,810	0	325	4,035	4,030
289	C Natural and applied sciences and related occupations	55	2,975	15	460	3,375	3,375
290	D Health occupations	15	1,240	0	80	1,040	1,040
291	E Occupations in social science, education, government service and religion	35	3,365	10	425	2,400	2,400
292	F Occupations in art, culture, recreation and sport	0	785	15	75	760	760
293	G Sales and service occupations	120	8,170	90	930	8,235	8,235
294	H Trades, transport and equipment operators and related occupations	160	5,640	200	1,950	12,385	12,380
295	I Occupations unique to primary industry	55	605	45	285	3,525	3,515
296	J Occupations unique to processing, manufacturing and utilities	25	1,015	20	225	1,480	1,480
297	Female labour force 15 years and over	520	30,665	345	4,900	39,470	39,460
298	Occupation - Not applicable[46]	0	455	10	40	875	875
299	All occupations[47]	520	30,205	340	4,860	38,595	38,580
300	A Management occupations	50	2,095	45	350	2,300	2,300
301	B Business, finance and administrative occupations	105	7,625	85	1,360	11,665	11,660
302	C Natural and applied sciences and related occupations	0	775	10	80	615	615
303	D Health occupations	45	3,850	20	595	4,105	4,105
304	E Occupations in social science, education, government service and religion	75	4,805	25	610	5,195	5,190
305	F Occupations in art, culture, recreation and sport	10	1,235	0	160	1,010	1,010
306	G Sales and service occupations	155	9,045	120	1,435	12,500	12,495
307	H Trades, transport and equipment operators and related occupations	25	305	15	110	725	725
308	I Occupations unique to primary industry	35	170	10	90	240	240
309	J Occupations unique to processing, manufacturing and utilities	10	290	0	70	240	235
310	**Total employed labour force 15 years and over**	**1,030**	**56,935**	**770**	**9,650**	**75,215**	**75,190**
	Place of work status						
311	Males	525	28,365	445	5,025	38,795	38,775
312	Usual place of work	360	22,875	300	3,695	31,625	31,615
313	At home	90	1,740	55	440	1,575	1,575
314	Outside Canada	0	210	0	15	85	85
315	No fixed workplace address	65	3,540	85	875	5,505	5,500
316	Females	505	28,570	325	4,620	36,420	36,415
317	Usual place of work	395	25,450	260	3,970	33,120	33,115
318	At home	70	1,765	50	425	1,770	1,770
319	Outside Canada	0	80	0	15	50	45
320	No fixed workplace address	45	1,275	15	210	1,485	1,485

Note: See symbols and abbreviations in the introductory material and see reference material at the end of the publication.

Certaines caractéristiques des divisions de recensement et des subdivisions de recensement – Données intégrales et données-échantillon (20 %), Ontario, Recensement de 2006 (suite)

Wahnapitei 11, IRI	**Grey CD/DR** ◆	Blue Mountains, T ◆◆◊	Chatsworth, TP	Georgian Bluffs, TP ◊A	Grey Highlands, MU ◆◊	Caractéristiques	N°
						Caractéristiques de la population	
						Industrie - Système de classification des industries de l'Amérique du Nord de 2002 (suite)	
0	1,215	150	55	125	155	71 Arts, spectacles et loisirs	273
0	3,220	320	195	295	275	72 Hébergement et services de restauration	274
10	2,360	115	215	360	235	81 Autres services (sauf les administrations publiques)	275
10	1,720	100	130	215	135	91 Administrations publiques	276
						Catégorie de travailleurs	
0	520	10	45	30	70	Catégorie de travailleurs - Sans objet[46]	277
30	48,365	3,570	3,485	6,060	4,915	Toutes les catégories de travailleurs[47]	278
35	40,870	2,755	2,900	5,230	3,775	Travailleurs rémunérés	279
30	39,010	2,460	2,800	4,970	3,560	Employés	280
0	1,855	295	95	255	220	Travailleurs autonomes (entreprise constituée en société)	281
0	7,185	785	565	805	1,105	Travailleurs autonomes (entreprise non constituée en société)	282
0	310	40	20	25	35	Travailleurs familiaux non rémunérés	283
						Profession - Classification nationale des professions pour statistiques de 2006	
20	25,825	1,895	1,915	3,180	2,740	Hommes actifs de 15 ans et plus	284
0	310	0	40	10	45	Profession - Sans objet[46]	285
20	25,515	1,895	1,870	3,165	2,695	Toutes les professions[47]	286
10	2,425	290	155	385	230	A Gestion	287
0	1,460	155	70	230	115	B Affaires, finance et administration	288
0	1,455	85	90	180	185	C Sciences naturelles et appliquées et professions apparentées	289
0	495	40	10	80	30	D Secteur de la santé	290
0	955	100	35	120	95	E Sciences sociales, enseignement, administration publique et religion	291
0	560	100	25	55	45	F Arts, culture, sports et loisirs	292
0	4,295	350	275	520	330	G Ventes et services	293
10	8,395	515	755	1,100	915	H Métiers, transport et machinerie	294
10	2,715	200	245	270	495	I Professions propres au secteur primaire	295
10	2,750	65	215	230	250	J Transformation, fabrication et services d'utilité publique	296
15	23,055	1,685	1,620	2,915	2,245	Femmes actives de 15 ans et plus	297
0	210	10	0	20	25	Profession - Sans objet[46]	298
15	22,855	1,680	1,615	2,890	2,220	Toutes les professions[47]	299
0	1,645	205	130	230	160	A Gestion	300
0	4,755	335	330	720	535	B Affaires, finance et administration	301
0	405	50	20	65	70	C Sciences naturelles et appliquées et professions apparentées	302
0	2,505	125	200	375	220	D Secteur de la santé	303
10	2,330	255	165	245	215	E Sciences sociales, enseignement, administration publique et religion	304
0	710	95	30	75	25	F Arts, culture, sports et loisirs	305
10	7,180	445	480	925	560	G Ventes et services	306
0	620	55	45	75	60	H Métiers, transport et machinerie	307
0	1,080	90	110	60	185	I Professions propres au secteur primaire	308
0	1,615	20	95	120	185	J Transformation, fabrication et services d'utilité publique	309
25	**46,340**	**3,435**	**3,340**	**5,860**	**4,705**	**Population active occupée totale de 15 ans et plus**	310
						Catégorie de lieu de travail	
20	24,420	1,830	1,795	3,050	2,575	Hommes	311
15	16,920	1,025	1,005	2,375	1,515	Lieu habituel de travail	312
0	3,285	400	370	290	525	À domicile	313
0	135	20	10	10	20	En dehors du Canada	314
10	4,080	385	410	370	510	Sans adresse de travail fixe	315
10	21,920	1,600	1,540	2,810	2,125	Femmes	316
10	18,055	1,135	1,180	2,385	1,640	Lieu habituel de travail	317
0	2,610	320	210	275	320	À domicile	318
0	40	10	0	10	0	En dehors du Canada	319
0	1,215	135	145	140	160	Sans adresse de travail fixe	320

Nota : Voir les symboles et les abréviations dans les documents d'introduction et voir les documents de référence à la fin de la publication.

Selected characteristics for census divisions and census subdivisions – 100% data and 20% sample data, Ontario, 2006 Census (continued)

No.	Characteristics	Frontenac Islands, TP ◆◊	Kingston, CY ◆◊	North Frontenac, TP ◆◊◊	South Frontenac, TP ◆◊	**Greater Sudbury / Grand Sudbury CD/DR** ◊	Greater Sudbury / Grand Sudbury, C ◊
	Population characteristics						
321	**Total employed labour force 15 years and over with usual place of work or no fixed workplace address**	**870**	**53,135**	**670**	**8,750**	**71,745**	**71,715**
	Mode of transportation						
322	Males	435	26,415	390	4,570	37,135	37,120
323	Car, truck, van, as driver	320	19,110	290	4,105	30,240	30,230
324	Car, truck, van, as passenger	40	1,815	30	295	2,880	2,880
325	Public transit	10	1,015	0	25	1,215	1,215
326	Walked	40	2,995	50	90	1,950	1,950
327	All other modes	15	1,475	20	50	845	845
328	Females	435	26,720	280	4,180	34,610	34,600
329	Car, truck, van, as driver	305	17,610	210	3,620	25,290	25,285
330	Car, truck, van, as passenger	45	3,310	40	410	3,915	3,915
331	Public transit	15	1,675	0	10	2,495	2,495
332	Walked	70	3,125	25	95	2,470	2,470
333	All other modes	10	1,005	10	45	435	440
334	**Total population 15 years and over who worked since January 1, 2005**	**1,170**	**66,725**	**1,015**	**11,020**	**87,130**	**87,100**
	Language used most often at work						
335	Single responses	1,155	66,340	1,015	10,970	84,805	84,775
336	English	1,155	65,295	1,015	10,915	79,430	79,400
337	French	0	685	0	50	5,315	5,315
338	Non-official languages[7]	0	355	0	0	60	60
339	Chinese, n.o.s.[61]	0	45	0	0	0	0
340	Cantonese	0	30	0	0	0	0
341	Other languages[8]	0	280	0	0	60	60
342	Multiple responses	15	385	0	50	2,325	2,325
343	English and French	15	315	0	45	2,265	2,265
344	English and non-official language	0	65	0	0	40	45
345	French and non-official language	0	0	0	0	10	10
346	English, French and non-official language	0	0	0	0	10	10
	Dwelling and household characteristics						
347	**Total number of occupied private dwellings**	**785**	**48,925**	**870**	**6,770**	**64,960**	**64,940**
	Housing tenure						
348	Owned	715	30,450	780	6,190	43,505	43,490
349	Rented	65	18,475	90	580	21,450	21,450
350	Band housing	0	0	0	0	0	0
	Structural type of dwelling						
351	Single-detached house	750	23,960	840	6,215	39,590	39,570
352	Semi-detached house	20	4,005	0	195	3,085	3,085
353	Row house	0	3,185	0	10	2,770	2,770
354	Apartment, duplex	5	1,870	5	60	3,875	3,875
355	Apartment, building that has five or more storeys	0	7,125	0	0	4,285	4,285
356	Apartment, building that has fewer than five storeys	0	8,365	0	170	10,690	10,690
357	Other single-attached house	0	155	10	40	205	205
358	Movable dwelling[48]	10	190	20	80	460	460
	Condition of dwelling						
359	Regular maintenance only	430	32,465	555	4,205	41,035	41,020
360	Minor repairs	210	13,250	250	2,020	18,845	18,840
361	Major repairs	145	3,205	60	540	5,085	5,085
	Period of construction						
362	Before 1946	265	6,155	175	1,140	7,510	7,515
363	1946 to 1960	75	7,930	90	510	15,990	15,995
364	1961 to 1970	95	7,495	95	730	12,700	12,700
365	1971 to 1980	105	8,985	205	1,175	12,010	12,010
366	1981 to 1985	25	4,595	60	520	3,420	3,420
367	1986 to 1990	55	5,050	55	785	4,975	4,975
368	1991 to 1995	75	2,920	60	715	4,665	4,665
369	1996 to 2000	45	2,510	40	530	1,955	1,945
370	2001 to 2006[49]	45	3,280	80	660	1,725	1,715

Note: See symbols and abbreviations in the introductory material and see reference material at the end of the publication.

Wahnapitei 11, IRI	**Grey CD/DR** ◆	Blue Mountains, T ◆◆◊	Chatsworth, TP	Georgian Bluffs, TP ◊**A**	Grey Highlands, MU ◆◊	**Caractéristiques**	N°
						Caractéristiques de la population	
25	**40,265**	**2,680**	**2,745**	**5,280**	**3,835**	**Population active occupée totale de 15 ans et plus ayant un lieu habituel de travail ou sans adresse de travail fixe**	321
						Mode de transport	
15	20,995	1,405	1,420	2,750	2,030	Hommes	322
15	17,045	1,190	1,200	2,475	1,650	Automobile, camion ou fourgonnette, en tant que conducteur	323
10	1,625	80	130	145	120	Automobile, camion ou fourgonnette, en tant que passager	324
0	235	20	10	0	45	Transport en commun	325
0	1,525	85	50	65	185	À pied	326
0	555	30	25	50	30	Tous les autres modes	327
10	19,270	1,270	1,325	2,530	1,800	Femmes	328
0	14,590	1,090	1,115	2,055	1,440	Automobile, camion ou fourgonnette, en tant que conductrice	329
0	2,080	60	160	315	100	Automobile, camion ou fourgonnette, en tant que passagère	330
0	265	35	10	20	10	Transport en commun	331
0	1,920	80	35	95	230	À pied	332
0	415	10	10	40	25	Tous les autres modes	333
30	**53,355**	**4,050**	**3,845**	**6,610**	**5,510**	**Population totale de 15 ans et plus ayant travaillé depuis le 1er janvier 2005**	334
						Langue utilisée le plus souvent au travail	
35	53,280	4,045	3,835	6,595	5,505	Réponses uniques	335
30	52,700	4,045	3,640	6,585	5,425	Anglais	336
0	70	0	0	10	10	Français	337
0	505	0	195	0	70	Langues non officielles[7]	338
0	35	0	0	0	0	Chinois, n.d.a.[61]	339
0	0	0	0	0	0	Cantonais	340
0	475	0	195	0	70	Autres langues[8]	341
0	75	0	15	15	0	Réponses multiples	342
0	50	10	10	10	10	Anglais et français	343
0	20	0	0	10	0	Anglais et langue non officielle	344
0	0	0	0	0	0	Français et langue non officielle	345
0	0	0	0	0	0	Anglais, français et langue non officielle	346
						Caractéristiques des logements et des ménages	
20	**37,185**	**2,935**	**2,370**	**4,030**	**3,685**	**Nombre total de logements privés occupés**	347
						Mode d'occupation	
15	29,155	2,470	2,195	3,740	3,215	Possédé	348
0	8,025	460	175	290	475	Loué	349
0	0	0	0	0	0	Logement de bande	350
						Type de construction résidentielle	
20	29,095	2,450	2,220	3,840	3,390	Maison individuelle non attenante	351
0	720	15	20	25	20	Maison jumelée	352
0	1,230	225	5	5	75	Maison en rangée	353
0	620	10	30	35	30	Appartement, duplex	354
0	925	0	0	0	10	Appartement, immeuble de cinq étages ou plus	355
0	4,220	220	45	55	140	Appartement, immeuble de moins de cinq étages	356
0	125	5	10	10	10	Autre maison individuelle attenante	357
0	230	10	40	60	15	Logement mobile[48]	358
						État du logement	
15	24,060	2,065	1,480	2,615	2,270	Entretien régulier seulement	359
0	10,255	700	665	1,180	1,095	Réparations mineures	360
0	2,875	170	225	240	320	Réparations majeures	361
						Période de construction	
0	11,920	600	855	890	1,330	Avant 1946	362
0	3,855	265	160	415	255	1946 à 1960	363
0	3,665	310	135	445	315	1961 à 1970	364
0	6,080	520	455	760	505	1971 à 1980	365
0	1,815	240	95	255	190	1981 à 1985	366
0	3,500	250	275	505	295	1986 à 1990	367
0	2,565	255	150	315	295	1991 à 1995	368
10	1,450	205	50	175	185	1996 à 2000	369
0	2,335	290	195	275	315	2001 à 2006[49]	370

Nota : Voir les symboles et les abréviations dans les documents d'introduction et voir les documents de référence à la fin de la publication.

Selected characteristics for census divisions and census subdivisions – 100% data and 20% sample data, Ontario, 2006 Census (continued)

No.	Characteristics	Frontenac Islands, TP ◆◊	Kingston, CY ◆◊	North Frontenac, TP ◆◊◊	South Frontenac, TP ◆◊	**Greater Sudbury / Grand Sudbury CD/DR** ◊	Greater Sudbury / Grand Sudbury, C ◊
	Dwelling and household characteristics						
371	Average number of rooms per dwelling	7.0	6.5	6.3	7.5	6.4	6.4
372	Average number of bedrooms per dwelling	3.1	2.7	2.7	3.1	2.7	2.7
373	Average value of dwelling $	299,635	243,762	176,648	245,600	164,900	164,900
374	**Total number of private households**	**780**	**48,865**	**865**	**6,765**	**64,960**	**64,940**
	Household size						
375	1 person	175	14,840	245	1,085	17,520	17,520
376	2 persons	360	17,330	415	2,635	23,285	23,275
377	3 persons	105	7,235	95	1,165	10,515	10,510
378	4 to 5 persons	125	8,700	105	1,710	12,760	12,760
379	6 or more persons	15	750	10	165	875	870
	Household type						
380	One-family households[50]	600	31,060	635	5,470	45,015	45,000
381	Multiple-family households	0	510	0	95	610	615
382	Non-family households	175	17,360	235	1,205	19,335	19,330
383	Number of persons in private households	1,845	113,050	1,865	18,170	155,230	155,180
384	Average number of persons in private households	2.4	2.3	2.2	2.7	2.4	2.4
385	Tenant-occupied private non-farm, non-reserve dwellings[51]	65	18,465	85	580	21,450	21,450
386	Average gross rent $[51]	651	776	600	776	626	626
387	Tenant-occupied households spending 30% or more of household income on gross rent[52]	15	8,950	55	215	8,665	8,660
388	Tenant-occupied households spending from 30% to 99% of household income on gross rent[52]	0	7,540	35	180	7,685	7,685
389	Owner-occupied private non-farm, non-reserve dwellings[53]	685	30,390	780	6,100	43,460	43,460
390	Average owner's major payments $[53]	851	1,019	620	984	917	917
391	Owner households spending 30% or more of household income on owner's major payments[52]	135	5,005	130	1,000	5,200	5,200
392	Owner households spending from 30% to 99% of household income on owner's major payments[52]	130	4,335	105	895	4,475	4,470
	Census family characteristics						
393	**Total number of census families in private households**	**610**	**32,075**	**640**	**5,655**	**46,245**	**46,230**
	Family structure and number of children						
394	Total couple families	570	26,710	580	5,165	38,450	38,435
395	Total families of married couples	455	22,200	510	4,530	32,060	32,050
396	Without children at home	260	10,390	315	2,045	15,215	15,205
397	With children at home	195	11,805	195	2,480	16,845	16,840
398	1 child	75	4,425	80	910	6,410	6,410
399	2 children	75	5,260	90	1,150	7,890	7,890
400	3 or more children	45	2,115	20	415	2,540	2,540
401	Total families of common-law couples	120	4,515	70	635	6,390	6,385
402	Without children at home	70	2,875	55	405	3,385	3,385
403	With children at home	50	1,645	10	225	3,005	3,000
404	1 child	40	765	0	120	1,590	1,585
405	2 children	10	590	10	85	1,050	1,050
406	3 or more children	0	285	0	20	360	360
407	Total lone-parent families	35	5,360	55	495	7,795	7,795
408	Female parent	30	4,330	45	370	6,350	6,350
409	1 child	30	2,735	35	250	3,820	3,815
410	2 children	0	1,305	10	70	1,910	1,910
411	3 or more children	0	295	0	50	620	620
412	Male parent	0	1,030	0	125	1,445	1,445
413	1 child	0	750	10	90	1,100	1,100
414	2 children	0	225	0	30	300	300
415	3 or more children	0	45	0	0	50	50

Note: See symbols and abbreviations in the introductory material and see reference material at the end of the publication.

Certaines caractéristiques des divisions de recensement et des subdivisions de recensement – Données intégrales et données-échantillon (20 %), Ontario, Recensement de 2006 (suite)

Wahnapitei 11, IRI	**Grey CD/DR** ◆	Blue Mountains, T ◆◆◇	Chatsworth, TP	Georgian Bluffs, TP ◇**A**	Grey Highlands, MU ◆◇	**Caractéristiques**	Nº
						Caractéristiques des logements et des ménages	
6.0	7.0	7.2	7.4	7.8	7.2	Nombre moyen de pièces par logement	371
2.2	2.9	3.1	3.1	3.1	3.1	Nombre moyen de chambres à coucher par logement	372
0	244,305	406,839	213,087	258,625	277,475	Valeur moyenne du logement $	373
20	**37,170**	**2,940**	**2,365**	**4,030**	**3,690**	**Nombre total de ménages privés**	374
						Taille du ménage	
0	9,390	790	445	675	815	1 personne	375
5	14,680	1,280	1,000	1,760	1,470	2 personnes	376
10	5,090	360	335	605	520	3 personnes	377
0	7,100	465	490	880	755	4 à 5 personnes	378
0	900	55	100	105	125	6 personnes ou plus	379
						Genre de ménage	
15	26,720	2,045	1,885	3,195	2,785	Ménages unifamiliaux[50]	380
0	270	10	30	50	35	Ménages multifamiliaux	381
0	10,195	875	460	780	865	Ménages non familiaux	382
50	90,480	6,730	6,315	10,465	9,395	Nombre de personnes dans les ménages privés	383
2.5	2.4	2.3	2.7	2.6	2.5	Nombre moyen de personnes dans les ménages privés	384
0	7,965	455	175	285	460	Ménages locataires dans les logements privés non agricoles hors réserve[51]	385
0	638	854	559	557	633	Loyer brut moyen $[51]	386
0	3,495	175	45	110	230	Ménages locataires consacrant 30 % ou plus du revenu du ménage au loyer brut[52]	387
0	3,145	155	45	95	210	Ménages locataires consacrant de 30 % à 99 % du revenu du ménage au loyer brut[52]	388
0	27,865	2,385	2,030	3,625	2,950	Ménages propriétaires dans les logements privés non agricoles hors réserve[53]	389
0	882	962	801	897	912	Principales dépenses de propriété moyennes $[53]	390
0	5,455	520	435	595	670	Ménages propriétaires consacrant 30 % ou plus du revenu du ménage aux principales dépenses de propriété[52]	391
0	4,790	465	385	510	610	Ménages propriétaires consacrant de 30 % à 99 % du revenu du ménage aux principales dépenses de propriété[52]	392
						Caractéristiques des familles de recensement	
20	**27,265**	**2,065**	**1,940**	**3,300**	**2,855**	**Nombre total de familles de recensement dans les ménages privés**	393
						Structure de la famille et le nombre d'enfants	
15	24,020	1,910	1,730	3,115	2,530	Total des familles avec conjoints	394
10	20,820	1,690	1,515	2,780	2,175	Total des familles avec couples mariés	395
0	11,155	1,035	815	1,475	1,140	Sans enfants à la maison	396
0	9,660	655	700	1,305	1,035	Avec enfants à la maison	397
0	3,135	190	225	455	330	1 enfant	398
0	4,140	300	250	565	430	2 enfants	399
0	2,380	170	225	285	270	3 enfants ou plus	400
0	3,195	215	220	330	355	Total des familles avec couples en union libre	401
10	1,970	145	140	195	230	Sans enfants à la maison	402
0	1,230	75	75	140	120	Avec enfants à la maison	403
0	635	65	30	80	40	1 enfant	404
0	425	10	40	45	45	2 enfants	405
0	165	0	10	10	35	3 enfants ou plus	406
10	3,245	160	210	185	330	Total des familles monoparentales	407
10	2,585	125	135	120	265	Parent de sexe féminin	408
10	1,360	70	80	75	150	1 enfant	409
0	880	40	40	35	80	2 enfants	410
0	345	15	15	10	40	3 enfants ou plus	411
0	660	30	75	65	65	Parent de sexe masculin	412
0	445	25	40	40	45	1 enfant	413
0	170	0	30	10	10	2 enfants	414
0	50	0	10	10	0	3 enfants ou plus	415

Nota : Voir les symboles et les abréviations dans les documents d'introduction et voir les documents de référence à la fin de la publication.

Selected characteristics for census divisions and census subdivisions – 100% data and 20% sample data, Ontario, 2006 Census (continued)

No.	Characteristics	Frontenac Islands, TP ◆◊	Kingston, CY ◆◊	North Frontenac, TP ◆◊◊	South Frontenac, TP ◆◊	**Greater Sudbury / Grand Sudbury CD/DR** ◊	Greater Sudbury / Grand Sudbury, C ◊
	Census family characteristics						
416	**Total number of children at home**	**470**	**32,220**	**410**	**5,655**	**46,710**	**46,700**
	Age group						
417	Under 6 years	90	6,630	65	1,070	9,065	9,060
418	6 to 14 years	140	11,795	105	2,185	17,130	17,120
419	15 to 17 years	60	4,255	65	780	6,485	6,485
420	18 to 24 years	105	6,515	125	1,180	9,300	9,300
421	25 years and over	75	3,015	50	440	4,730	4,730
422	Average number of children at home per census family[54]	0.8	1.0	0.6	1.0	1.0	1.0
423	**Total number of persons in private households**	**1,850**	**113,120**	**1,875**	**18,180**	**155,230**	**155,175**
	Census family status and living arrangements						
424	Number of persons not in census families	190	22,115	245	1,700	23,825	23,815
425	Living with relatives[55]	25	1,660	10	325	2,375	2,375
426	Living with non-relatives only	0	5,555	15	290	3,925	3,925
427	Living alone	165	14,900	225	1,085	17,515	17,515
428	Number of census family persons	1,660	91,005	1,630	16,475	131,410	131,360
429	Average number of persons per census family	2.7	2.8	2.6	2.9	2.8	2.8
430	**Total number of persons aged 65 years and over**	**305**	**17,100**	**485**	**2,130**	**21,585**	**21,580**
431	Number of persons not in census families aged 65 years and over	65	6,040	130	615	7,570	7,570
432	Living with relatives[55]	0	500	0	135	820	825
433	Living with non-relatives only	0	395	0	25	365	365
434	Living alone	65	5,145	120	450	6,380	6,380
435	Number of census family persons aged 65 years and over	240	11,055	355	1,515	14,015	14,010
	Economic family characteristics						
436	**Total number of economic families in private households**	**615**	**31,940**	**640**	**5,600**	**45,990**	**45,970**
	Size of family						
437	2 persons	380	15,985	410	2,620	22,350	22,345
438	3 persons	105	6,800	100	1,140	10,230	10,220
439	4 persons	75	6,260	100	1,285	9,630	9,630
440	5 or more persons	55	2,890	20	555	3,775	3,775
441	Total number of persons in economic families	1,680	92,665	1,635	16,800	133,785	133,735
442	Average number of persons per economic family	3.0	3.0	3.0	3.0	3.0	3.0
443	Total number of persons not in economic families	165	20,455	240	1,375	21,445	21,440
	2005 income characteristics						
444	**Population 15 years and over**	**1,635**	**95,520**	**1,725**	**14,875**	**129,480**	**129,435**
	Sex and total income groups in 2005						
445	Without income	40	4,025	60	665	6,170	6,170
446	With income	1,590	91,495	1,665	14,210	123,305	123,265
447	Under $1,000[56]	20	3,015	70	405	4,415	4,415
448	$1,000 to $2,999	65	3,270	85	545	3,970	3,965
449	$3,000 to $4,999	90	2,795	65	390	4,005	4,005
450	$5,000 to $6,999	55	3,420	70	455	4,410	4,410
451	$7,000 to $9,999	95	5,355	125	665	7,525	7,520
452	$10,000 to $11,999	35	4,070	70	525	5,090	5,090
453	$12,000 to $14,999	95	5,230	170	615	7,175	7,170
454	$15,000 to $19,999	95	9,060	180	1,360	11,685	11,675
455	$20,000 to $24,999	90	6,895	180	930	9,085	9,080
456	$25,000 to $29,999	135	6,185	140	935	8,305	8,300
457	$30,000 to $34,999	115	6,150	135	950	8,120	8,120
458	$35,000 to $39,999	110	5,700	105	1,015	8,395	8,395
459	$40,000 to $44,999	110	4,980	60	1,040	6,825	6,825
460	$45,000 to $49,999	70	3,765	50	780	5,710	5,710
461	$50,000 to $59,999	165	6,355	55	1,305	7,900	7,900
462	$60,000 and over	235	15,255	100	2,280	20,680	20,680
463	Median income $[57]	30,240	26,890	19,747	31,068	27,469	27,476
464	Average income $[57]	36,575	36,344	24,169	35,786	35,970	35,975
465	Standard error of average income $[57]	2,034	280	990	508	245	245

Note: See symbols and abbreviations in the introductory material and see reference material at the end of the publication.

Certaines caractéristiques des divisions de recensement et des subdivisions de recensement – Données intégrales et données-échantillon (20 %), Ontario, Recensement de 2006 (suite)

Wahnapitei 11, IRI	**Grey CD/DR** ◆	Blue Mountains, T ◆◆◇	Chatsworth, TP	Georgian Bluffs, TP ◇**A**	Grey Highlands, MU ◆◇	**Caractéristiques**	N°
						Caractéristiques des familles de recensement	
15	**26,855**	**1,660**	**2,065**	**3,050**	**2,945**	**Nombre total d'enfants à la maison**	416
						Groupes d'âge	
0	5,030	255	425	490	575	Moins de 6 ans	417
0	10,005	645	780	1,105	1,065	6 à 14 ans	418
10	4,030	235	280	450	445	15 à 17 ans	419
10	5,645	360	370	725	590	18 à 24 ans	420
0	2,145	160	205	275	260	25 ans et plus	421
0.5	1.0	0.8	1.1	0.9	1.0	Nombre moyen d'enfants à la maison par famille de recensement[54]	422
50	**90,490**	**6,725**	**6,320**	**10,475**	**9,390**	**Nombre total de personnes dans les ménages privés**	423
						Situation des particuliers dans la famille de recensement et des particuliers dans le ménage	
10	12,355	1,085	585	1,010	1,055	Nombre de personnes hors famille de recensement	424
10	1,070	75	55	200	120	Vivant avec des personnes apparentées[55]	425
0	1,875	225	85	135	115	Vivant avec des personnes non apparentées seulement	426
0	9,405	785	440	675	815	Vivant seules	427
45	78,135	5,635	5,735	9,465	8,335	Nombre de membres d'une famille de recensement	428
2.5	2.9	2.7	3.0	2.9	2.9	Nombre moyen de personnes par famille de recensement	429
0	**15,885**	**1,595**	**950**	**1,560**	**1,650**	**Nombre total de personnes âgées de 65 ans et plus**	430
0	4,875	405	230	385	470	Nombre de personnes hors famille de recensement âgées de 65 ans et plus	431
0	430	30	45	80	55	Vivant avec des personnes apparentées[55]	432
0	185	10	0	15	15	Vivant avec des personnes non apparentées seulement	433
10	4,255	360	185	285	400	Vivant seules	434
0	11,010	1,190	715	1,175	1,180	Nombre de membres d'une famille de recensement âgés de 65 ans et plus	435
						Caractéristiques des familles économiques	
15	**27,200**	**2,065**	**1,925**	**3,300**	**2,845**	**Nombre total de familles économiques dans les ménages privés**	436
						Taille de la famille	
10	14,440	1,220	1,010	1,720	1,485	2 personnes	437
10	4,865	335	345	595	490	3 personnes	438
0	5,035	330	315	630	535	4 personnes	439
0	2,860	180	250	355	340	5 personnes ou plus	440
50	79,205	5,710	5,795	9,665	8,455	Nombre total de personnes dans les familles économiques	441
3.0	3.0	3.0	3.0	3.0	3.0	Nombre moyen de personnes par famille économique	442
0	11,285	1,010	525	805	930	Nombre total de personnes hors famille économique	443
						Caractéristiques du revenu de 2005	
X	**75,695**	**5,835**	**5,125**	**8,855**	**7,765**	**Population de 15 ans et plus**	444
						Sexe et groupes de revenu total en 2005	
X	2,690	145	155	315	280	Sans revenu	445
X	73,000	5,690	4,970	8,540	7,485	Avec un revenu	446
X	2,635	200	210	265	325	Moins de 1 000 $[56]	447
X	2,370	145	250	200	260	1 000 $ à 2 999 $	448
X	2,565	210	185	330	215	3 000 $ à 4 999 $	449
X	2,610	115	180	310	245	5 000 $ à 6 999 $	450
X	4,835	285	320	580	490	7 000 $ à 9 999 $	451
X	3,540	335	250	285	345	10 000 $ à 11 999 $	452
X	4,615	335	300	585	575	12 000 $ à 14 999 $	453
X	7,990	630	555	740	830	15 000 $ à 19 999 $	454
X	6,700	465	460	695	595	20 000 $ à 24 999 $	455
X	5,655	295	440	605	605	25 000 $ à 29 999 $	456
X	5,375	425	300	575	540	30 000 $ à 34 999 $	457
X	4,590	290	275	625	520	35 000 $ à 39 999 $	458
X	3,655	305	265	615	305	40 000 $ à 44 999 $	459
X	2,895	230	225	475	280	45 000 $ à 49 999$	460
X	4,450	365	310	590	485	50 000 $ à 59 999$	461
X	8,525	1,055	430	1,065	875	60 000 $ et plus	462
X	23,914	27,538	22,546	27,258	23,963	Revenu médian $[57]	463
X	31,917	41,088	27,691	35,567	33,835	Revenu moyen $[57]	464
X	301	1,678	689	1,203	1,302	Erreur type de revenu moyen $[57]	465

Nota : Voir les symboles et les abréviations dans les documents d'introduction et voir les documents de référence à la fin de la publication.

Selected characteristics for census divisions and census subdivisions – 100% data and 20% sample data, Ontario, 2006 Census (continued)

No.	Characteristics	Frontenac Islands, TP ◆◇	Kingston, CY ◆◇	North Frontenac, TP ◆◇◇	South Frontenac, TP ◆◇	**Greater Sudbury / Grand Sudbury CD/DR** ◇	Greater Sudbury / Grand Sudbury, C ◇
	2005 income characteristics						
	Sex and total income groups in 2005 (continued)						
466	Total - Males	800	44,940	845	7,430	62,380	62,360
467	Without income	20	1,935	20	315	2,170	2,170
468	With income	780	43,000	825	7,115	60,215	60,190
469	Under $1,000[56]	10	1,685	45	195	2,150	2,145
470	$1,000 to $2,999	20	1,330	30	225	1,280	1,275
471	$3,000 to $4,999	10	935	15	100	1,440	1,445
472	$5,000 to $6,999	15	1,310	25	160	1,330	1,330
473	$7,000 to $9,999	55	1,935	50	240	2,535	2,535
474	$10,000 to $11,999	10	1,680	15	200	1,860	1,860
475	$12,000 to $14,999	35	1,990	50	190	2,335	2,335
476	$15,000 to $19,999	55	3,350	65	605	3,705	3,700
477	$20,000 to $24,999	50	2,825	115	395	3,495	3,495
478	$25,000 to $29,999	75	2,625	85	445	3,765	3,765
479	$30,000 to $34,999	65	2,755	70	440	4,085	4,080
480	$35,000 to $39,999	50	2,675	80	525	4,495	4,495
481	$40,000 to $44,999	60	2,280	50	590	3,950	3,945
482	$45,000 to $49,999	30	1,880	25	420	3,515	3,510
483	$50,000 to $59,999	80	3,700	25	820	5,065	5,060
484	$60,000 and over	140	10,030	70	1,570	15,205	15,200
485	Median income $[57]	32,094	33,387	23,977	38,419	37,091	37,098
486	Average income $[57]	41,451	44,023	28,616	41,557	45,702	45,711
487	Standard error of average income $[57]	3,526	506	1,566	762	435	436
488	Total - Females	835	50,575	880	7,450	67,095	67,075
489	Without income	25	2,085	40	350	4,000	4,000
490	With income	805	48,490	840	7,095	63,095	63,075
491	Under $1,000[56]	10	1,330	20	215	2,270	2,265
492	$1,000 to $2,999	45	1,945	55	320	2,690	2,690
493	$3,000 to $4,999	80	1,865	55	290	2,570	2,565
494	$5,000 to $6,999	40	2,105	45	295	3,080	3,080
495	$7,000 to $9,999	40	3,420	75	430	4,985	4,985
496	$10,000 to $11,999	15	2,385	55	330	3,225	3,230
497	$12,000 to $14,999	55	3,240	125	425	4,840	4,835
498	$15,000 to $19,999	45	5,705	110	755	7,975	7,975
499	$20,000 to $24,999	45	4,065	60	530	5,590	5,585
500	$25,000 to $29,999	60	3,555	60	490	4,540	4,535
501	$30,000 to $34,999	50	3,390	65	515	4,035	4,035
502	$35,000 to $39,999	60	3,020	30	490	3,900	3,900
503	$40,000 to $44,999	50	2,695	10	445	2,875	2,875
504	$45,000 to $49,999	40	1,880	25	360	2,200	2,195
505	$50,000 to $59,999	80	2,660	25	485	2,835	2,840
506	$60,000 and over	90	5,225	25	710	5,480	5,480
507	Median income $[57]	27,552	22,581	15,183	24,600	19,947	19,948
508	Average income $[57]	31,863	29,535	19,809	30,000	26,683	26,685
509	Standard error of average income $[57]	2,106	260	1,116	642	210	210
	Composition of total income						
510	Composition of total income in 2005 %	100.0	100.0	100.0	100.0	100.0	100.0
511	Employment income %	70.9	70.3	51.9	76.2	72.8	72.8
512	Government transfer payments %	10.8	11.4	24.5	9.8	12.6	12.6
513	Other %	18.3	18.2	23.4	14.1	14.7	14.7
514	**Population 15 years and over with employment income in 2005**	**1,175**	**66,640**	**1,040**	**11,070**	**89,215**	**89,185**
	Sex and work activity						
515	Median employment income in 2005 $	29,823	25,357	13,284	30,802	26,809	26,815
516	Average employment income in 2005 $	35,112	35,088	20,145	34,989	36,182	36,188
517	Standard error of average employment income $	2,187	323	1,373	601	309	309
518	Worked full year, full time[59]	640	32,640	385	6,025	43,610	43,595
519	Median employment income in 2005 $	44,371	43,744	34,559	44,895	45,124	45,128
520	Average employment income in 2005 $	46,692	51,571	37,631	48,055	53,880	53,885
521	Standard error of average employment income $	2,165	465	2,462	777	491	492
522	Worked part year or part time[60]	470	28,920	530	4,360	37,680	37,665
523	Median employment income in 2005 $	11,205	11,769	7,716	13,327	12,003	12,004
524	Average employment income in 2005 $	22,861	21,222	11,458	20,958	21,853	21,858
525	Standard error of average employment income $	4,156	422	1,136	782	352	353
526	Males 15 years and over with employment income[58]	615	33,345	570	5,770	47,030	47,010
527	Median employment income in 2005 $	29,009	30,072	14,718	37,580	35,886	35,895
528	Average employment income in 2005 $	36,811	41,293	22,065	39,490	44,348	44,357
529	Standard error of average employment income $	3,764	549	2,047	876	518	518

Note: See symbols and abbreviations in the introductory material and see reference material at the end of the publication.

Certaines caractéristiques des divisions de recensement et des subdivisions de recensement – Données intégrales et données-échantillon (20 %), Ontario, Recensement de 2006 (suite)

Wahnapitei 11, IRI	**Grey CD/DR** ◆	Blue Mountains, T ◆◆◊	Chatsworth, TP	Georgian Bluffs, TP ◊**A**	Grey Highlands, MU ◆◊	**Caractéristiques**	N°
						Caractéristiques du revenu de 2005	
						Sexe et groupes de revenu total en 2005 (suite)	
X	36,990	2,860	2,620	4,475	3,890	Total - Hommes	466
X	1,105	75	80	105	115	Sans revenu	467
X	35,885	2,785	2,535	4,365	3,775	Avec un revenu	468
X	1,395	100	85	145	195	Moins de 1 000 $[56]	469
X	930	80	80	80	105	1 000 $ à 2 999 $	470
X	950	70	70	120	105	3 000 $ à 4 999 $	471
X	1,010	35	70	130	120	5 000 $ à 6 999 $	472
X	1,710	90	145	230	225	7 000 $ à 9 999 $	473
X	1,395	170	90	105	155	10 000 $ à 11 999 $	474
X	1,695	100	115	205	250	12 000 $ à 14 999 $	475
X	3,320	280	270	380	340	15 000 $ à 19 999 $	476
X	2,945	205	245	265	245	20 000 $ à 24 999 $	477
X	2,680	165	210	270	260	25 000 $ à 29 999 $	478
X	2,635	210	145	260	250	30 000 $ à 34 999 $	479
X	2,510	110	150	355	290	35 000 $ à 39 999 $	480
X	2,150	170	180	380	135	40 000 $ à $44 999 $	481
X	1,840	135	155	305	185	45 000 $ à $49 999 $	482
X	2,835	175	235	390	305	50 000 $ à $59 999 $	483
X	5,880	690	295	740	610	60 000 $ et plus	484
X	29,757	32,019	27,409	34,866	27,176	Revenu médian $[57]	485
X	38,186	49,323	32,683	43,938	38,451	Revenu moyen $[57]	486
X	514	3,056	1,065	2,223	1,776	Erreur type de revenu moyen $[57]	487
X	38,700	2,975	2,500	4,380	3,875	Total - Femmes	488
X	1,590	70	65	210	165	Sans revenu	489
X	37,115	2,905	2,435	4,175	3,710	Avec un revenu	490
X	1,245	100	125	120	130	Moins de 1 000 $[56]	491
X	1,440	60	170	125	155	1 000$ à 2 999 $	492
X	1,615	145	105	215	110	3 000 $ à 4 999 $	493
X	1,600	80	105	180	120	5 000 $ à 6 999 $	494
X	3,125	195	175	345	265	7 000 $ à 9 999 $	495
X	2,145	165	160	185	190	10 000 $ à 11 999 $	496
X	2,915	235	185	380	325	12 000 $ à 14 999 $	497
X	4,670	350	290	360	490	15 000 $ à 19 999 $	498
X	3,755	260	220	430	350	20 000 $ à 24 999 $	499
X	2,975	125	235	340	345	25 000 $ à 29 999 $	500
X	2,735	215	155	310	290	30 000 $ à 34 999 $	501
X	2,075	175	130	265	230	35 000 $ à 39 999 $	502
X	1,505	140	90	235	170	40 000 $ à 44 999 $	503
X	1,050	100	75	165	95	45 000 $ à 49 999 $	504
X	1,605	185	75	190	180	50 000 $ à 59 999 $	505
X	2,645	370	135	325	265	60 000 $ et plus	506
X	19,754	22,469	18,458	21,733	20,451	Revenu médian $[57]	507
X	25,857	33,196	22,495	26,810	29,139	Revenu moyen $[57]	508
X	307	1,447	797	793	1,895	Erreur type de revenu moyen $[57]	509
						Composition du revenu total	
X	100.0	100.0	100.0	100.0	100.0	Composition du revenu total en 2005 %	510
X	69.1	61.4	71.6	74.4	69.5	Revenu d'emploi %	511
X	14.2	11.4	15.3	11.0	13.1	Transferts gouvernementaux %	512
X	16.7	27.2	13.0	14.6	17.4	Autres %	513
X	**52,945**	**4,020**	**3,740**	**6,485**	**5,515**	**Population de 15 ans et plus avec un revenu d'emploi en 2005**	514
						Sexe et travail	
X	22,978	20,932	21,328	25,900	22,462	Revenu médian d'emploi en 2005 $	515
X	30,416	35,718	26,393	34,869	31,902	Revenu moyen d'emploi en 2005 $	516
X	361	1,615	849	1,485	1,631	Erreur type de revenu moyen d'emploi $	517
X	26,905	1,735	2,005	3,440	2,730	A travaillé toute l'année à plein temps[59]	518
X	36,035	42,238	35,194	38,254	34,468	Revenu médian d'emploi en 2005 $	519
X	43,108	54,413	36,556	48,384	46,775	Revenu moyen d'emploi en 2005 $	520
X	589	2,732	1,165	2,536	2,963	Erreur type de revenu moyen d'emploi $	521
X	22,625	1,990	1,520	2,705	2,420	A travaillé une partie de l'année ou à temps partiel[60]	522
X	10,879	12,508	11,828	12,521	10,358	Revenu médian d'emploi en 2005 $	523
X	18,887	23,427	16,344	21,212	18,833	Revenu moyen d'emploi en 2005 $	524
X	379	1,898	1,070	1,222	1,299	Erreur type de revenu moyen d'emploi $	525
X	27,665	2,120	1,990	3,360	2,995	Hommes de 15 ans et plus avec un revenu d'emploi[58]	526
X	28,506	23,478	25,901	33,183	24,797	Revenu médian d'emploi en 2005 $	527
X	35,729	39,067	30,934	43,115	34,541	Revenu moyen d'emploi en 2005 $	528
X	568	2,436	1,291	2,721	1,945	Erreur type de revenu moyen d'emploi $	529

Nota : Voir les symboles et les abréviations dans les documents d'introduction et voir les documents de référence à la fin de la publication.

Selected characteristics for census divisions and census subdivisions – 100% data and 20% sample data, Ontario, 2006 Census (continued)

No.	Characteristics	Frontenac Islands, TP ◆◇	Kingston, CY ◆◇	North Frontenac, TP ◆◇◇	South Frontenac, TP ◆◇	**Greater Sudbury / Grand Sudbury CD/DR** ◇	Greater Sudbury / Grand Sudbury, C ◇
	2005 income characteristics						
	Sex and work activity (continued)						
530	Worked full year, full time[59]	330	17,850	220	3,390	25,255	25,250
531	Median employment income in 2005 $	44,310	49,245	35,764	49,069	53,962	53,964
532	Average employment income in 2005 $	47,719	57,901	41,545	52,483	62,810	62,815
533	Standard error of average employment income $	3,644	727	3,379	1,091	767	768
534	Worked part year or part time[60]	240	12,720	275	1,970	16,590	16,580
535	Median employment income in 2005 $	12,877	12,065	7,358	15,004	14,487	14,490
536	Average employment income in 2005 $	27,725	25,258	11,857	23,558	28,225	28,236
537	Standard error of average employment income $	7,826	841	1,810	1,156	686	687
538	Females 15 years and over with employment income[58]	560	33,295	470	5,300	42,185	42,175
539	Median employment income in 2005 $	30,286	22,441	12,392	24,617	20,617	20,618
540	Average employment income in 2005 $	33,247	28,875	17,804	30,088	27,079	27,081
541	Standard error of average employment income $	2,153	320	1,700	792	277	278
542	Worked full year, full time[59]	310	14,790	165	2,635	18,355	18,345
543	Median employment income in 2005 $	45,177	39,110	32,224	39,498	36,686	36,688
544	Average employment income in 2005 $	45,610	43,933	32,459	42,356	41,589	41,594
545	Standard error of average employment income $	2,351	495	3,325	1,045	435	436
546	Worked part year or part time[60]	225	16,205	250	2,385	21,090	21,085
547	Median employment income in 2005 $	8,921	11,427	7,717	12,598	10,578	10,579
548	Average employment income in 2005 $	17,717	18,055	11,023	18,807	16,840	16,842
549	Standard error of average employment income $	2,944	348	1,324	1,053	302	302
550	**Total number of economic families in private households**	**615**	**31,940**	**635**	**5,600**	**45,990**	**45,970**
	Family income groups in 2005						
551	Under $10,000	0	705	10	65	820	825
552	$10,000 to $19,999	30	1,385	40	160	2,165	2,165
553	$20,000 to $29,999	10	2,185	85	290	3,040	3,035
554	$30,000 to $39,999	60	2,755	155	395	4,095	4,095
555	$40,000 to $49,999	70	3,080	65	495	4,705	4,700
556	$50,000 to $59,999	35	3,355	85	530	4,075	4,075
557	$60,000 to $69,999	50	2,585	40	445	4,125	4,120
558	$70,000 to $79,999	60	2,670	40	530	3,585	3,585
559	$80,000 to $89,999	105	2,315	35	610	3,665	3,670
560	$90,000 to $99,999	45	2,010	20	560	2,945	2,945
561	$100,000 and over	140	8,895	55	1,520	12,755	12,755
562	Median family income $	78,014	69,530	43,269	77,545	69,907	69,926
563	Average family income $	84,521	83,163	52,599	81,889	81,709	81,721
564	Standard error of average family income $	6,359	798	2,596	1,303	683	684
	Family after-tax income groups in 2005						
565	Under $10,000	0	720	20	65	830	830
566	$10,000 to $19,999	30	1,425	35	170	2,215	2,215
567	$20,000 to $29,999	25	2,480	115	340	3,425	3,420
568	$30,000 to $39,999	80	3,535	160	515	5,635	5,635
569	$40,000 to $49,999	80	4,240	105	690	5,685	5,680
570	$50,000 to $59,999	60	3,680	30	595	5,280	5,280
571	$60,000 to $69,999	90	3,440	65	770	4,985	4,985
572	$70,000 to $79,999	95	2,950	35	770	4,480	4,480
573	$80,000 to $89,999	45	2,250	40	585	3,645	3,645
574	$90,000 to $99,999	30	1,965	10	255	2,715	2,715
575	$100,000 and over	75	5,255	20	840	7,085	7,085
576	Median after-tax family income $	64,962	59,702	39,256	65,292	59,808	59,819
577	Average after-tax family income $	69,054	68,293	46,085	68,503	67,122	67,131
578	Standard error of average after-tax family income $	4,065	550	2,027	963	450	451
	Income status in 2005						
579	Total population in private households for income status	1,850	113,095	1,875	18,180	155,120	155,120
580	Below low income cut-off before tax in 2005	95	17,415	180	960	19,705	19,705
581	Prevalence of low income before tax in 2005 %	5.1	15.4	9.9	5.3	12.7	12.7
582	Below low income cut-off after tax in 2005	35	12,545	155	645	14,575	14,570
583	Prevalence of low income after tax in 2005 %	1.9	11.1	8.0	3.5	9.4	9.4

Note: See symbols and abbreviations in the introductory material and see reference material at the end of the publication.

Certaines caractéristiques des divisions de recensement et des subdivisions de recensement – Données intégrales et données-échantillon (20 %), Ontario, Recensement de 2006 (suite)

Wahnapitei 11, IRI	**Grey CD/DR** ◆	Blue Mountains, T ◆◆◊	Chatsworth, TP	Georgian Bluffs, TP ◊**A**	Grey Highlands, MU ◆◊	**Caractéristiques**	N°
						Caractéristiques du revenu de 2005	
						Sexe et travail (suite)	
X	15,890	1,025	1,230	2,030	1,665	A travaillé toute l'année à plein temps[59]	530
X	39,676	44,763	39,593	41,686	36,915	Revenu médian d'emploi en 2005 $	531
X	47,412	58,047	38,992	56,773	46,291	Revenu moyen d'emploi en 2005 $	532
X	840	3,710	1,620	4,197	2,878	Erreur type de revenu moyen d'emploi $	533
X	10,095	935	640	1,155	1,170	A travaillé une partie de l'année ou à temps partiel[60]	534
X	12,230	12,365	12,633	13,207	10,049	Revenu médian d'emploi en 2005 $	535
X	22,095	23,539	20,535	24,595	21,145	Revenu moyen d'emploi en 2005 $	536
X	666	3,085	2,019	2,132	2,452	Erreur type de revenu moyen d'emploi $	537
X	25,280	1,900	1,745	3,125	2,520	Femmes de 15 ans et plus avec un revenu d'emploi[58]	538
X	18,589	19,599	17,004	20,761	20,974	Revenu médian d'emploi en 2005 $	539
X	24,603	31,969	21,219	26,005	28,768	Revenu moyen d'emploi en 2005 $	540
X	415	2,064	984	971	2,727	Erreur type de revenu moyen d'emploi $	541
X	11,015	715	775	1,410	1,060	A travaillé toute l'année à plein temps[59]	542
X	31,829	37,860	32,220	34,213	32,004	Revenu médian d'emploi en 2005 $	543
X	36,900	49,200	32,687	36,311	47,532	Revenu moyen d'emploi en 2005 $	544
X	757	3,926	1,515	1,266	6,186	Erreur type de revenu moyen d'emploi $	545
X	12,535	1,055	875	1,545	1,255	A travaillé une partie de l'année ou à temps partiel[60]	546
X	9,910	12,626	10,427	11,896	11,917	Revenu médian d'emploi en 2005 $	547
X	16,304	23,328	13,278	18,684	16,681	Revenu moyen d'emploi en 2005 $	548
X	416	2,338	976	1,419	973	Erreur type de revenu moyen d'emploi $	549
X	**27,205**	**2,065**	**1,925**	**3,300**	**2,850**	**Nombre total des familles économiques dans les ménages privés**	550
						Revenu de la famille économique en 2005	
X	575	45	45	45	50	Moins de 10 000 $	551
X	1,130	50	65	100	140	10 000 $ à 19 999 $	552
X	2,485	150	195	155	290	20 000 $ à 29 999 $	553
X	3,190	165	240	335	325	30 000 $ à 39 999 $	554
X	3,230	160	240	380	315	40 000 $ à 49 999 $	555
X	2,995	205	205	315	270	50 000 $ à 59 999 $	556
X	2,640	170	200	340	290	60 000 $ à 69 999 $	557
X	2,330	170	160	370	220	70 000 $ à 79 999 $	558
X	1,905	170	140	285	170	80 000 $ à 89 999 $	559
X	1,400	160	110	165	115	90 000 $ à 99 999 $	560
X	5,310	610	310	810	650	100 000 $ et plus	561
X	59,978	74,782	58,474	69,634	60,796	Revenu médian des familles $	562
X	73,210	96,343	64,364	84,333	78,987	Revenu moyen des familles $	563
X	846	4,612	1,753	3,247	3,514	Erreur type de revenu moyen des familles $	564
						Revenu après impôt de la famille économique en 2005	
X	605	45	45	45	55	Moins de 10 000 $	565
X	1,190	50	70	100	150	10 000 $ à 19 999 $	566
X	2,830	190	225	210	315	20 000 $ à 29 999 $	567
X	4,055	180	325	420	420	30 000 $ à 39 999 $	568
X	4,030	265	280	470	370	40 000 $ à 49 999 $	569
X	3,475	220	250	415	355	50 000 $ à 59 999 $	570
X	2,935	270	185	395	340	60 000 $ à 69 999 $	571
X	2,235	185	165	385	150	70 000 $ à 79 999 $	572
X	1,685	130	130	270	205	80 000 $ à 89 999 $	573
X	1,125	125	130	120	135	90 000 $ à 99 999 $	574
X	3,030	395	115	465	355	100 000 $ et plus	575
X	52,494	62,148	50,666	59,573	53,366	Revenu médian après impôt des familles $	576
X	61,161	76,642	55,380	68,944	64,730	Revenu moyen après impôt des familles $	577
X	574	3,140	1,352	2,017	2,266	Erreur type de revenu moyen après impôt des familles $	578
						Catégorie de revenu en 2005	
X	90,415	6,720	6,320	10,470	9,385	Population totale dans les ménages privés pour la catégorie de revenu	579
X	9,140	535	500	605	870	Au-dessous du seuil de faible revenu avant impôt en 2005	580
X	10.1	7.9	7.8	5.7	9.3	Fréquence du faible revenu avant impôt en 2005 %	581
X	5,850	390	310	390	455	Au-dessous du seuil de faible revenu après impôt en 2005	582
X	6.5	5.7	4.9	3.8	4.8	Fréquence du faible revenu après impôt en 2005 %	583

Nota : Voir les symboles et les abréviations dans les documents d'introduction et voir les documents de référence à la fin de la publication.

Selected characteristics for census divisions and census subdivisions – 100% data and 20% sample data, Ontario, 2006 Census (continued)

No.	Characteristics	Frontenac Islands, TP ◆◊	Kingston, CY ◆◊	North Frontenac, TP ◆◊◊	South Frontenac, TP ◆◊	**Greater Sudbury / Grand Sudbury CD/DR** ◊	Greater Sudbury / Grand Sudbury, C ◊
	2005 income characteristics						
584	**Total number of private households**	**785**	**48,925**	**870**	**6,770**	**64,960**	**64,940**
	Household income groups in 2005						
585	Under $10,000	25	2,530	60	150	2,965	2,960
586	$10,000 to $19,999	65	5,265	100	400	7,040	7,040
587	$20,000 to $29,999	50	5,005	140	475	6,335	6,330
588	$30,000 to $39,999	80	5,330	185	530	6,825	6,825
589	$40,000 to $49,999	85	4,975	75	650	6,505	6,500
590	$50,000 to $59,999	50	4,410	95	690	5,340	5,340
591	$60,000 to $69,999	60	3,420	60	475	5,035	5,030
592	$70,000 to $79,999	65	3,385	40	570	4,205	4,205
593	$80,000 to $89,999	110	2,670	35	670	4,150	4,155
594	$90,000 to $99,999	50	2,230	30	580	3,200	3,195
595	$100,000 and over	145	9,705	60	1,575	13,350	13,355
596	Median household income $	66,965	53,072	37,035	70,297	55,008	55,019
597	Average household income $	73,582	67,622	45,924	74,988	68,117	68,126
598	Standard error of average household income $	5,245	597	2,166	1,198	530	530
	Household after-tax income groups in 2005						
599	Under $10,000	25	2,560	65	160	3,005	3,005
600	$10,000 to $19,999	70	5,685	110	430	7,635	7,630
601	$20,000 to $29,999	60	6,040	175	560	7,380	7,385
602	$30,000 to $39,999	110	6,495	175	740	8,605	8,600
603	$40,000 to $49,999	95	5,785	120	825	7,540	7,535
604	$50,000 to $59,999	65	4,695	45	695	6,245	6,245
605	$60,000 to $69,999	95	4,155	65	800	5,720	5,720
606	$70,000 to $79,999	110	3,290	40	815	4,850	4,855
607	$80,000 to $89,999	45	2,470	45	600	3,830	3,825
608	$90,000 to $99,999	25	2,125	15	265	2,815	2,820
609	$100,000 and over	80	5,610	20	875	7,330	7,330
610	Median after-tax household income $	55,907	46,351	34,573	59,360	47,588	47,593
611	Average after-tax household income $	60,303	55,791	40,173	62,712	56,245	56,251
612	Standard error of average after-tax household income $	3,450	422	1,712	899	360	361

Note: See symbols and abbreviations in the introductory material and see reference material at the end of the publication.

Certaines caractéristiques des divisions de recensement et des subdivisions de recensement – Données intégrales et données-échantillon (20 %), Ontario, Recensement de 2006 (suite)

Wahnapitei 11, IRI	**Grey CD/DR** ◆	Blue Mountains, T ◆◆◊	Chatsworth, TP	Georgian Bluffs, TP ◊A	Grey Highlands, MU ◆◊	**Caractéristiques**	Nº
						Caractéristiques du revenu de 2005	
X	**37,185**	**2,935**	**2,370**	**4,030**	**3,685**	**Nombre total des ménages privés**	584
						Tranches de revenu des ménages en 2005	
X	1,400	110	80	120	120	Moins de 10 000 $	585
X	4,290	305	225	290	375	10 000 $ à 19 999 $	586
X	4,410	290	300	285	480	20 000 $ à 29 999 $	587
X	4,460	295	280	420	415	30 000 $ à 39 999 $	588
X	4,050	245	270	480	365	40 000 $ à 49 999 $	589
X	3,670	235	225	375	385	50 000 $ à 59 999 $	590
X	3,045	210	225	370	335	60 000 $ à 69 999 $	591
X	2,660	220	185	385	220	70 000 $ à 79 999 $	592
X	2,105	180	160	300	165	80 000 $ à 89 999 $	593
X	1,495	165	105	165	130	90 000 $ à 99 999 $	594
X	5,590	670	310	830	680	100 000 $ et plus	595
X	49,912	59,061	50,647	62,082	51,771	Revenu médian des ménages $	596
X	62,546	79,691	58,008	75,355	68,698	Revenu moyen des ménages $	597
X	662	3,485	1,573	2,767	2,759	Erreur type de revenu moyen des ménages $	598
						Tranches du revenu après impôt des ménages en 2005	
X	1,480	110	80	135	125	Moins de 10 000 $	599
X	4,615	335	230	300	415	10 000 $ à 19 999 $	600
X	5,120	365	355	350	535	20 000 $ à 29 999 $	601
X	5,330	325	340	565	475	30 000 $ à 39 999 $	602
X	4,935	320	320	540	510	40 000 $ à 49 999 $	603
X	3,935	270	285	455	400	50 000 $ à 59 999 $	604
X	3,225	285	210	415	325	60 000 $ à 69 999 $	605
X	2,430	205	175	400	160	70 000 $ à 79 999 $	606
X	1,755	145	130	270	210	80 000 $ à 89 999 $	607
X	1,180	125	130	120	155	90 000 $ à 99 999 $	608
X	3,190	450	120	480	365	100 000 $ et plus	609
X	44,294	51,058	45,269	52,678	45,649	Revenu médian après impôt des ménages $	610
X	52,452	63,863	50,021	61,741	56,579	Revenu moyen après impôt des ménages $	611
X	460	2,406	1,230	1,754	1,811	Erreur type de revenu moyen après impôt des ménages $	612

Nota : Voir les symboles et les abréviations dans les documents d'introduction et voir les documents de référence à la fin de la publication.

Selected characteristics for census divisions and census subdivisions – 100% data and 20% sample data, Ontario, 2006 Census (continued)

No.	Characteristics	Hanover, T	Meaford, MU	Owen Sound, CY ◆A	Southgate, TP ◊	West Grey, MU ◊	**Haldimand-Norfolk CD/DR †**
	Population characteristics						
1	**Population, 2001[1]**	**6,869**	**10,381**	**21,456**	**6,907**	**11,741**	**104,670**
2	**Population, 2006[2]**	**7,147**	**10,948**	**21,753**	**7,167**	**12,193**	**107,812**
3	Population percentage change, 2001 to 2006	4.0	5.5	1.4	3.8	3.8	3.0
4	Land area in square kilometres, 2006	9.81	588.47	24.22	643.95	875.37	2,894.15
5	**Total population – 100% data[3]**	**7,150**	**10,950**	**21,755**	**7,165**	**12,190**	**107,810**
	Sex and age groups						
6	Male	3,320	5,415	10,145	3,680	6,190	53,500
7	0 to 4 years	205	205	565	220	330	2,850
8	5 to 9 years	195	280	575	300	370	3,165
9	10 to 14 years	175	340	670	330	425	3,935
10	15 to 19 years	220	425	770	305	460	4,160
11	20 to 24 years	235	335	690	180	325	3,335
12	25 to 29 years	165	220	560	155	240	2,485
13	30 to 34 years	190	210	525	175	290	2,580
14	35 to 39 years	195	265	555	245	325	3,150
15	40 to 44 years	210	385	750	305	470	4,225
16	45 to 49 years	255	405	800	325	485	4,555
17	50 to 54 years	240	460	765	260	515	4,380
18	55 to 59 years	240	480	670	205	505	3,960
19	60 to 64 years	165	370	535	190	430	3,060
20	65 to 69 years	155	355	415	155	350	2,440
21	70 to 74 years	145	250	435	130	280	1,975
22	75 to 79 years	145	215	395	110	220	1,600
23	80 to 84 years	90	135	240	55	90	1,055
24	85 years and over	95	85	240	30	85	585
25	Female	3,825	5,530	11,605	3,490	6,005	54,315
26	0 to 4 years	180	205	470	205	240	2,550
27	5 to 9 years	175	240	530	225	340	3,100
28	10 to 14 years	205	315	640	285	400	3,765
29	15 to 19 years	235	350	800	315	395	3,970
30	20 to 24 years	220	290	685	180	295	3,090
31	25 to 29 years	195	195	600	160	255	2,385
32	30 to 34 years	180	235	575	165	275	2,700
33	35 to 39 years	210	285	630	245	365	3,315
34	40 to 44 years	235	400	805	340	415	4,335
35	45 to 49 years	310	480	940	260	520	4,555
36	50 to 54 years	270	485	830	255	470	4,360
37	55 to 59 years	220	475	730	230	555	3,765
38	60 to 64 years	205	395	605	200	405	3,110
39	65 to 69 years	195	345	520	140	315	2,415
40	70 to 74 years	195	285	575	120	255	2,150
41	75 to 79 years	200	235	615	95	225	1,845
42	80 to 84 years	170	170	475	55	145	1,515
43	85 years and over	235	145	590	25	120	1,370
44	**Total population 15 years and over[3]**	**6,015**	**9,370**	**18,305**	**5,610**	**10,090**	**88,440**
	Legal marital status						
45	Never legally married (single)	1,545	2,395	5,490	1,565	2,545	23,155
46	Legally married (and not separated)[4,5]	3,080	5,355	8,325	3,195	5,850	49,965
47	Separated, but still legally married	245	305	825	200	345	3,105
48	Divorced	455	680	1,660	375	670	6,155
49	Widowed	690	640	2,010	280	685	6,060
	Common-law status						
50	Not in a common-law relationship	5,570	8,595	16,655	5,110	9,230	81,910
51	In a common-law relationship	440	775	1,650	505	855	6,530
52	**Total population – 20% sample data[6]**	**6,965**	**10,830**	**20,895**	**7,165**	**12,075**	**106,605**
	Mother tongue						
53	Single responses	6,935	10,800	20,785	7,120	12,030	106,055
54	English	6,505	10,135	19,755	6,065	11,270	93,800
55	French	60	130	180	45	30	1,110
56	Non-official languages[7]	360	530	855	1,010	730	11,140
57	Italian	10	15	0	70	50	510
58	Chinese, n.o.s.[61]	35	0	115	0	0	80
59	Cantonese	10	0	0	0	0	60
60	Spanish	0	0	10	15	35	250
61	German	155	195	165	600	345	4,580
62	Other languages[8]	155	315	550	320	295	5,660

Note: See symbols and abbreviations in the introductory material and see reference material at the end of the publication.

Certaines caractéristiques des divisions de recensement et des subdivisions de recensement – Données intégrales et données-échantillon (20 %), Ontario, Recensement de 2006 (suite)

Haldimand County, CY	Norfolk County, CY ◊	**Haliburton CD/DR** ♦◊	Algonquin Highlands, TP ♦♦◊◊	Dysart and Others, TP ♦◊	Highlands East, MU ♦◊◊	**Caractéristiques**	N°
						Caractéristiques de la population	
43,728	**60,847**	**15,085**	**1,827**	**4,924**	**3,022**	**Population, 2001**[1]	1
45,212	**62,563**	**16,147**	**1,976**	**5,526**	**3,089**	**Population, 2006**[2]	2
3.4	2.8	7.0	8.2	12.2	2.2	Variation en pourcentage de la population, 2001 à 2006	3
1,251.58	1,606.91	4,025.27	1,002.12	1,474.07	701.32	Superficie des terres en kilomètres carrés, 2006	4
45,215	**62,560**	**16,145**	**1,980**	**5,525**	**3,085**	**Population totale – Données intégrales**[3]	5
						Sexe et groupes d'âge	
22,535	30,945	8,015	1,000	2,670	1,545	Sexe masculin	6
1,305	1,545	275	20	95	55	0 à 4 ans	7
1,470	1,700	340	40	120	60	5 à 9 ans	8
1,820	2,115	455	50	165	80	10 à 14 ans	9
1,740	2,420	505	55	170	85	15 à 19 ans	10
1,350	1,985	320	30	125	50	20 à 24 ans	11
1,075	1,405	255	30	90	40	25 à 29 ans	12
1,155	1,420	300	35	105	60	30 à 34 ans	13
1,410	1,740	355	45	105	90	35 à 39 ans	14
1,865	2,355	540	55	205	100	40 à 44 ans	15
1,960	2,595	655	80	220	125	45 à 49 ans	16
1,790	2,590	630	55	215	135	50 à 54 ans	17
1,635	2,325	735	100	240	130	55 à 59 ans	18
1,190	1,870	690	120	225	135	60 à 64 ans	19
895	1,550	660	95	205	135	65 à 69 ans	20
700	1,275	545	90	165	105	70 à 74 ans	21
550	1,050	410	70	120	85	75 à 79 ans	22
400	660	220	25	65	50	80 à 84 ans	23
230	355	105	10	40	15	85 ans et plus	24
22,675	31,615	8,135	975	2,860	1,545	Sexe féminin	25
1,130	1,420	245	30	90	40	0 à 4 ans	26
1,400	1,700	305	35	115	60	5 à 9 ans	27
1,690	2,080	400	40	160	70	10 à 14 ans	28
1,725	2,245	515	55	195	100	15 à 19 ans	29
1,310	1,780	330	25	130	60	20 à 24 ans	30
1,045	1,345	240	25	95	35	25 à 29 ans	31
1,240	1,460	315	35	100	60	30 à 34 ans	32
1,505	1,810	370	45	130	85	35 à 39 ans	33
1,960	2,380	555	75	195	95	40 à 44 ans	34
1,920	2,630	665	55	245	130	45 à 49 ans	35
1,790	2,570	675	75	230	140	50 à 54 ans	36
1,450	2,320	745	105	245	145	55 à 59 ans	37
1,205	1,905	735	120	260	140	60 à 64 ans	38
865	1,545	600	80	170	120	65 à 69 ans	39
735	1,415	540	80	180	105	70 à 74 ans	40
650	1,195	395	45	125	85	75 à 79 ans	41
555	960	270	30	100	40	80 à 84 ans	42
510	860	235	20	105	40	85 ans et plus	43
36,400	**52,005**	**14,120**	**1,765**	**4,785**	**2,720**	**Population totale de 15 ans et plus**[3]	44
						État matrimonial légal	
9,545	13,600	3,070	340	1,085	605	Jamais légalement marié(e) (célibataire)	45
21,110	28,845	8,020	1,085	2,685	1,550	Légalement marié(e) (et non séparé[e])[4,5]	46
1,230	1,870	620	80	195	115	Séparé(e), mais toujours légalement marié(e)	47
2,330	3,820	1,205	155	380	220	Divorcé(e)	48
2,185	3,870	1,205	110	440	230	Veuf(ve)	49
						Union libre	
33,905	47,975	12,790	1,615	4,355	2,465	Ne vivant pas en union libre	50
2,500	4,030	1,330	150	435	260	Vivant en union libre	51
44,710	**61,860**	**15,995**	**1,975**	**5,435**	**3,090**	**Population totale – Données-échantillon (20 %)**[6]	52
						Langue maternelle	
44,560	61,455	15,965	1,975	5,425	3,085	Réponses uniques	53
41,110	52,655	14,750	1,820	5,165	2,830	Anglais	54
475	630	250	25	55	60	Français	55
2,970	8,165	970	130	195	200	Langues non officielles[7]	56
360	150	45	0	20	10	Italien	57
10	75	0	0	0	0	Chinois, n.d.a.[61]	58
10	50	0	0	0	0	Cantonais	59
100	145	10	0	0	0	Espagnol	60
425	4,160	360	60	50	100	Allemand	61
2,080	3,585	555	65	130	100	Autres langues[8]	62

Nota : Voir les symboles et les abréviations dans les documents d'introduction et voir les documents de référence à la fin de la publication.

Selected characteristics for census divisions and census subdivisions – 100% data and 20% sample data, Ontario, 2006 Census (continued)

No.	Characteristics	Hanover, T	Meaford, MU	Owen Sound, CY ◆A	Southgate, TP ◊	West Grey, MU ◊	**Haldimand-Norfolk CD/DR †**
	Population characteristics						
	Mother tongue (continued)						
63	Multiple responses	30	35	105	45	45	550
64	English and French	20	35	25	15	20	105
65	English and non-official language	10	0	75	30	20	400
66	French and non-official language	0	0	10	0	0	45
67	English, French and non-official language	0	0	0	0	0	0
	Language spoken most often at home[9]						
68	Single responses	6,945	10,820	20,815	7,155	12,075	106,150
69	English	6,870	10,735	20,545	6,530	11,865	102,065
70	French	0	40	40	10	0	170
71	Non-official languages[7]	70	45	235	615	210	3,910
72	Chinese, n.o.s.[61]	0	0	100	0	0	50
73	Cantonese	0	0	0	0	0	60
74	Panjabi (Punjabi)	0	0	0	0	0	0
75	Italian	0	0	0	15	0	115
76	Spanish	0	0	0	10	10	125
77	Other languages[8]	70	45	135	590	200	3,555
78	Multiple responses	15	10	75	10	0	455
79	English and French	0	10	35	0	0	40
80	English and non-official language	10	0	45	0	0	415
81	French and non-official language	0	0	0	0	0	0
82	English, French and non-official language	0	0	0	0	0	0
	Knowledge of official languages[10]						
83	English only	6,710	9,865	19,485	6,835	11,665	102,375
84	French only	0	10	15	0	0	10
85	English and French	250	955	1,350	280	400	3,705
86	Neither English nor French	0	0	50	50	10	515
	Knowledge of non-official languages[7,11]						
87	Italian	30	60	20	75	55	765
88	Spanish	15	65	170	20	120	910
89	German	155	310	235	660	430	5,075
90	Chinese, n.o.s.[61]	20	0	125	0	0	120
91	Cantonese	10	0	0	0	0	65
92	Panjabi (Punjabi)	15	0	0	10	0	0
93	Portuguese	0	10	45	65	15	900
	First official language spoken[10]						
94	English	6,905	10,710	20,665	7,075	12,035	105,135
95	French	60	120	170	45	35	895
96	English and French	0	0	10	0	10	80
97	Neither English nor French	0	0	50	45	0	495
98	Official language minority - (number)[12]	60	120	175	40	35	940
99	Official language minority - (percentage)[12]	0.9	1.1	0.8	0.6	0.3	0.9
	Ethnic origin[13]						
100	English	2,135	4,890	9,405	2,655	4,335	38,920
101	Canadian	2,010	3,690	6,655	2,545	3,595	32,185
102	Scottish	1,800	3,660	7,835	2,240	4,190	23,680
103	Irish	1,785	2,785	6,275	1,745	3,185	20,205
104	French	550	1,125	2,055	705	915	8,825
105	German	2,950	1,505	3,730	1,315	3,900	21,190
106	Italian	180	165	240	230	150	3,405
107	Chinese	40	20	160	0	0	315
108	East Indian	40	15	190	35	20	175
109	Dutch (Netherlands)	225	650	1,115	460	1,040	10,990
110	Polish	130	135	425	160	205	3,455
111	Ukrainian	110	210	185	85	90	3,940
112	North American Indian	105	135	730	245	260	3,455
113	Portuguese	25	15	80	90	45	1,500
114	Filipino	0	20	45	0	55	55
	Aboriginal and non-Aboriginal identity						
115	Total Aboriginal identity population[14]	0	130	680	160	175	2,020
116	Total non-Aboriginal identity population	6,955	10,700	20,215	7,005	11,900	104,590

Note: See symbols and abbreviations in the introductory material and see reference material at the end of the publication.

Certaines caractéristiques des divisions de recensement et des subdivisions de recensement – Données intégrales et données-échantillon (20 %), Ontario, Recensement de 2006 (suite)

Haldimand County, CY	Norfolk County, CY ◇	**Haliburton CD/DR** ◆◇	Algonquin Highlands, TP ◆◆◇◇	Dysart and Others, TP ◆◇	Highlands East, MU ◆◇◇	**Caractéristiques**	N°
						Caractéristiques de la population	
						Langue maternelle (suite)	
150	405	30	0	15	0	Réponses multiples	63
35	75	10	0	10	0	Anglais et français	64
115	285	20	0	10	0	Anglais et langue non officielle	65
0	45	0	0	0	0	Français et langue non officielle	66
0	0	0	0	0	0	Anglais, français et langue non officielle	67
						Langue parlée le plus souvent à la maison[9]	
44,615	61,500	15,975	1,970	5,415	3,080	Réponses uniques	68
43,805	58,225	15,760	1,960	5,365	3,035	Anglais	69
115	50	20	0	0	20	Français	70
690	3,220	195	10	55	30	Langues non officielles[7]	71
0	55	0	0	0	0	Chinois, n.d.a.[61]	72
10	55	0	0	0	0	Cantonais	73
0	0	20	0	0	0	Pendjabi	74
80	35	0	0	0	0	Italien	75
35	95	10	0	10	0	Espagnol	76
570	2,985	165	10	50	25	Autres langues[8]	77
95	365	30	0	20	10	Réponses multiples	78
15	25	0	0	0	0	Anglais et français	79
80	335	25	0	15	10	Anglais et langue non officielle	80
0	0	0	0	0	0	Français et langue non officielle	81
0	0	0	0	0	0	Anglais, français et langue non officielle	82
						Connaissance des langues officielles[10]	
43,075	59,265	15,110	1,770	5,115	2,960	Anglais seulement	83
0	0	10	10	0	0	Français seulement	84
1,605	2,095	880	195	320	125	Anglais et français	85
15	500	10	0	0	0	Ni l'anglais ni le français	86
						Connaissance des langues non officielles[7,11]	
535	235	55	0	35	0	Italien	87
260	650	110	0	45	10	Espagnol	88
600	4,480	405	85	75	90	Allemand	89
0	115	0	0	0	0	Chinois, n.d.a.[61]	90
20	45	0	0	0	0	Cantonais	91
0	0	20	0	0	0	Pendjabi	92
290	610	15	0	15	0	Portugais	93
						Première langue officielle parlée[10]	
44,210	60,885	15,750	1,945	5,385	3,030	Anglais	94
435	460	230	25	45	60	Français	95
45	35	15	0	0	0	Anglais et français	96
15	480	10	0	0	0	Ni l'anglais ni le français	97
460	475	235	25	45	55	Minorité de langue officielle - (nombre)[12]	98
1.0	0.8	1.5	1.3	0.8	1.8	Minorité de langue officielle - (pourcentage)[12]	99
						Origine ethnique[13]	
16,720	22,200	7,005	1,020	2,550	1,125	Anglais	100
14,630	17,555	5,265	505	2,075	1,095	Canadien	101
11,125	12,560	4,350	510	1,615	690	Écossais	102
8,990	11,210	4,060	460	1,265	745	Irlandais	103
3,835	4,990	1,535	165	620	270	Français	104
8,225	12,965	2,220	300	775	470	Allemand	105
1,985	1,420	395	10	220	50	Italien	106
95	225	10	0	10	0	Chinois	107
80	90	65	0	20	0	Indien de l'Inde	108
5,970	5,015	850	120	300	185	Hollandais (Néerlandais)	109
1,210	2,245	455	110	95	60	Polonais	110
1,215	2,720	350	40	100	30	Ukrainien	111
1,495	1,935	450	10	100	155	Indien de l'Amérique du Nord	112
560	940	70	10	40	15	Portugais	113
10	50	20	0	10	0	Philippin	114
						Population ayant une identité autochtone et population n'ayant pas d'identité autochtone	
835	1,150	460	20	35	200	Total de la population ayant une identité autochtone[14]	115
43,875	60,705	15,535	1,955	5,400	2,890	Total de la population n'ayant pas d'identité autochtone	116

Nota : Voir les symboles et les abréviations dans les documents d'introduction et voir les documents de référence à la fin de la publication.

Selected characteristics for census divisions and census subdivisions – 100% data and 20% sample data, Ontario, 2006 Census (continued)

No.	Characteristics	Hanover, T	Meaford, MU	Owen Sound, CY ◆A	Southgate, TP ◊	West Grey, MU ◊	**Haldimand-Norfolk CD/DR †**
	Population characteristics						
	Aboriginal and non-Aboriginal ancestry						
117	Total Aboriginal ancestry population[15]	120	275	1,100	350	345	3,900
118	Total non-Aboriginal ancestry population	6,845	10,555	19,795	6,815	11,730	102,705
	Registered Indian status						
119	Registered Indian[16]	0	30	160	85	30	1,140
120	Not a Registered Indian	6,960	10,800	20,740	7,085	12,040	105,465
	Visible minority groups						
121	Total visible minority population[17]	135	130	645	125	100	1,605
122	Chinese	50	15	130	0	0	275
123	South Asian[18]	45	10	165	30	20	145
124	Black	15	65	155	55	35	620
125	Filipino	10	15	45	10	40	65
126	Latin American	10	0	20	20	0	160
127	Southeast Asian[19]	0	0	15	0	0	35
128	Arab	10	0	20	0	0	25
129	West Asian[20]	0	0	0	0	0	25
130	Korean	0	10	50	0	0	150
131	Japanese	0	15	0	0	0	35
132	Visible minority, n.i.e.[21]	0	0	10	0	0	30
133	Multiple visible minority[22]	0	10	30	0	0	40
	Citizenship[23]						
134	Canadian citizens[24]	6,865	10,535	20,530	6,975	11,885	104,410
135	Not Canadian citizens[25]	95	300	365	190	195	2,195
	Immigrant status and place of birth[26]						
136	Non-immigrants[27]	6,455	9,650	19,365	6,405	11,230	94,355
137	Born in province of residence	6,110	8,845	18,050	5,885	10,640	88,705
138	Immigrants[28]	505	1,125	1,495	735	800	11,860
139	United States of America	65	100	150	65	55	710
140	Central and South America	10	0	25	50	10	1,795
141	Caribbean and Bermuda	0	45	45	15	10	210
142	United Kingdom	170	465	550	180	220	2,855
143	Other Europe	175	410	440	385	450	5,715
144	Africa	10	35	50	10	10	55
145	Asia and the Middle East	70	55	225	20	35	485
146	Oceania and other[29]	0	15	15	0	0	30
147	Non-permanent residents[30]	0	50	30	30	45	385
148	**Total immigrant population[28]**	**505**	**1,125**	**1,500**	**730**	**800**	**11,860**
	Period of immigration						
149	Before 1961	205	485	480	245	350	4,685
150	1961 to 1970	105	245	300	225	200	1,905
151	1971 to 1980	70	160	205	80	95	1,685
152	1981 to 1990	30	90	205	70	55	1,785
153	1991 to 2000	70	70	105	85	50	1,205
154	1991 to 1995	30	40	50	70	20	640
155	1996 to 2000	40	35	50	15	30	565
156	2001 to 2006[31]	20	75	195	25	40	595
	Age at immigration						
157	Under 5 years	60	135	245	105	115	1,770
158	5 to 19 years	155	360	395	195	240	4,220
159	20 years and over	295	635	855	425	445	5,865
160	**Total population 15 years and over**	**5,825**	**9,240**	**17,445**	**5,635**	**9,965**	**87,285**
	Generation status						
161	1st generation[32]	495	1,195	1,480	760	840	12,065
162	2nd generation[33]	745	1,135	2,370	715	1,320	18,105
163	3rd generation or more[34]	4,590	6,915	13,595	4,155	7,800	57,115

Note: See symbols and abbreviations in the introductory material and see reference material at the end of the publication.

Certaines caractéristiques des divisions de recensement et des subdivisions de recensement – Données intégrales et données-échantillon (20 %), Ontario, Recensement de 2006 (suite)

Haldimand County, CY	Norfolk County, CY ◊	**Haliburton CD/DR** ◆◊	Algonquin Highlands, TP ◆◆◊◊	Dysart and Others, TP ◆◊	Highlands East, MU ◆◊◊	**Caractéristiques**	N°
						Caractéristiques de la population	
						Population ayant une ascendance autochtone et population n'ayant pas d'ascendance autochtone	
1,735	2,130	695	10	125	235	Total de la population ayant une ascendance autochtone[15]	117
42,970	59,730	15,305	1,960	5,310	2,850	Total de la population n'ayant pas d'ascendance autochtone	118
						Statut d'Indien inscrit	
505	600	65	0	15	0	Indien inscrit[16]	119
44,200	61,255	15,935	1,970	5,420	3,085	Pas un Indien inscrit	120
						Groupes de minorités visibles	
580	1,025	165	0	50	45	Total de la population des minorités visibles[17]	121
55	220	0	0	0	0	Chinois	122
60	85	60	0	20	10	Sud-Asiatique[18]	123
215	405	30	0	10	15	Noir	124
20	50	20	0	0	0	Philippin	125
35	125	15	0	0	0	Latino-Américain	126
20	10	0	0	0	0	Asiatique du Sud-Est[19]	127
20	10	0	0	0	0	Arabe	128
0	25	0	0	0	0	Asiatique occidental[20]	129
110	35	0	0	0	0	Coréen	130
0	30	0	0	0	0	Japonais	131
20	15	10	0	10	0	Minorité visible, n.i.a.[21]	132
25	15	30	0	0	20	Minorités visibles multiples[22]	133
						Citoyenneté[23]	
43,910	60,455	15,705	1,960	5,340	3,045	Citoyens canadiens[24]	134
795	1,400	290	10	90	45	Ne sont pas des citoyens canadiens[25]	135
						Statut d'immigrant et le lieu de naissance[26]	
40,585	53,735	14,485	1,765	5,045	2,785	Non-immigrants[27]	136
38,180	50,490	13,340	1,550	4,730	2,520	Né dans la province de résidence	137
4,025	7,830	1,485	210	370	295	Immigrants[28]	138
275	435	110	15	50	35	États-Unis d'Amérique	139
95	1,700	20	0	10	0	Amérique centrale et Amérique du Sud	140
105	110	20	0	0	10	Antilles et Bermudes	141
1,180	1,670	560	70	130	85	Royaume-Uni	142
2,160	3,560	685	115	155	155	Autre Europe	143
10	45	15	0	0	0	Afrique	144
185	300	45	0	10	0	Asie et Moyen-Orient	145
20	10	25	10	0	0	Océanie et autres[29]	146
95	290	25	0	15	0	Résidents non permanents[30]	147
4,025	**7,835**	**1,485**	**210**	**370**	**295**	**Population totale des immigrants[28]**	148
						Période d'immigration	
1,590	3,095	705	140	175	120	Avant 1961	149
745	1,160	385	35	75	95	1961 à 1970	150
720	965	175	15	55	40	1971 à 1980	151
465	1,320	85	10	40	20	1981 à 1990	152
365	835	95	10	25	10	1991 à 2000	153
155	480	60	0	10	0	1991 à 1995	154
210	350	35	0	10	10	1996 à 2000	155
140	460	35	10	0	10	2001 à 2006[31]	156
						Âge à l'immigration	
620	1,145	160	20	20	60	Moins de 5 ans	157
1,370	2,850	470	70	100	50	5 à 19 ans	158
2,035	3,835	855	115	255	190	20 ans et plus	159
35,915	**51,335**	**13,980**	**1,845**	**4,605**	**2,720**	**Population totale de 15 ans et plus**	160
						Statut des générations	
4,090	7,975	1,505	205	395	300	1re génération[32]	161
7,185	10,920	2,470	375	715	620	2e génération[33]	162
24,640	32,440	10,005	1,265	3,495	1,805	3e génération ou plus[34]	163

Nota : Voir les symboles et les abréviations dans les documents d'introduction et voir les documents de référence à la fin de la publication.

Selected characteristics for census divisions and census subdivisions – 100% data and 20% sample data, Ontario, 2006 Census (continued)

No.	Characteristics	Hanover, T	Meaford, MU	Owen Sound, CY ◆A	Southgate, TP ◊	West Grey, MU ◊	Haldimand-Norfolk CD/DR †
	Population characteristics						
164	**Total population 1 year and over[35]**	**6,895**	**10,745**	**20,670**	**7,085**	**11,985**	**105,495**
	Place of residence 1 year ago (mobility)						
165	Non-movers	5,800	9,505	17,340	6,535	10,940	96,480
166	Movers	1,090	1,240	3,325	545	1,050	9,020
167	Non-migrants	490	575	2,075	120	325	4,620
168	Migrants	600	665	1,245	430	715	4,395
169	Internal migrants	595	630	1,115	415	715	4,155
170	Intraprovincial migrants	585	565	1,055	415	695	3,915
171	Interprovincial migrants	10	65	65	0	20	230
172	External migrants	0	40	130	20	10	245
173	**Total population 5 years and over[36]**	**6,580**	**10,430**	**19,885**	**6,755**	**11,525**	**101,175**
	Place of residence 5 years ago (mobility)						
174	Non-movers	3,655	6,570	11,330	4,575	7,920	71,050
175	Movers	2,925	3,860	8,555	2,180	3,605	30,130
176	Non-migrants	1,485	1,615	5,100	670	1,125	15,020
177	Migrants	1,440	2,245	3,460	1,510	2,485	15,105
178	Internal migrants	1,420	2,165	3,245	1,460	2,420	14,330
179	Intraprovincial migrants	1,320	1,960	2,890	1,385	2,380	13,515
180	Interprovincial migrants	90	210	360	80	45	815
181	External migrants	25	80	210	45	60	770
182	**Total population 15 years and over**	**5,825**	**9,245**	**17,445**	**5,630**	**9,965**	**87,285**
	Highest certificate, diploma or degree[37]						
183	No certificate, diploma or degree	2,025	2,330	5,020	1,990	3,145	25,955
184	Certificate, diploma or degree	3,800	6,910	12,425	3,640	6,820	61,335
185	High school certificate or equivalent[38]	1,800	2,495	4,695	1,640	2,750	24,030
186	Apprenticeship or trades certificate or diploma	495	975	1,670	645	1,190	10,295
187	College, CEGEP or other non-university certificate or diploma[39]	965	1,900	3,715	905	1,775	17,940
188	University certificate or diploma below bachelor level[40]	80	345	340	105	250	1,945
189	University certificate or degree[41]	460	1,195	2,005	345	850	7,125
190	Bachelor's degree	330	725	1,300	210	570	4,600
191	University certificate or diploma above bachelor level	50	170	305	70	165	1,220
192	Degree in medicine, dentistry, veterinary medicine or optometry	20	55	80	10	25	185
193	Master's degree	45	215	295	35	75	905
194	Earned doctorate	0	30	30	20	10	215
195	**Total population 15 years and over with postsecondary qualifications**	**2,000**	**4,415**	**7,725**	**2,000**	**4,070**	**37,305**
	Major field of study - Classification of Instructional Programs, 2000[42]						
196	Education	210	355	615	145	355	2,770
197	Visual and performing arts, and communications technologies	65	175	310	70	165	870
198	Humanities	110	225	375	30	140	1,405
199	Social and behavioural sciences and law	135	370	620	130	260	2,810
200	Business, management and public administration	395	625	1,400	285	700	6,605
201	Physical and life sciences and technologies	45	135	150	65	45	600
202	Mathematics, computer and information sciences	45	70	210	25	25	870
203	Architecture, engineering, and related technologies	395	1,010	1,595	660	1,060	10,655
204	Agriculture, natural resources and conservation	65	200	125	130	210	1,385
205	Health, parks, recreation and fitness	385	900	1,730	350	785	6,435
206	Personal, protective and transportation services	140	350	590	105	315	2,890
207	Other fields of study[43]	0	0	0	0	0	0
	Location of study[44]						
208	Inside Canada	1,870	3,980	7,115	1,800	3,675	34,795
209	Outside Canada	135	435	610	200	395	2,510
210	**Total population 15 years and over**	**5,825**	**9,245**	**17,445**	**5,630**	**9,965**	**87,285**
	Unpaid work						
211	Males 15 years and over	2,680	4,550	8,045	2,850	5,020	43,190
212	Reported unpaid work[45]	2,425	4,080	7,165	2,590	4,620	39,490
213	Housework and child care and care or assistance to seniors	205	310	555	195	370	3,530
214	Housework and child care only	580	820	1,880	715	1,135	11,150

Note: See symbols and abbreviations in the introductory material and see reference material at the end of the publication.

Certaines caractéristiques des divisions de recensement et des subdivisions de recensement – Données intégrales et données-échantillon (20 %), Ontario, Recensement de 2006 (suite)

Haldimand County, CY	Norfolk County, CY ◊	**Haliburton CD/DR** ◆◊	Algonquin Highlands, TP ◆◆◊◊	Dysart and Others, TP ◆◊	Highlands East, MU ◆◊◊	**Caractéristiques**	N°
						Caractéristiques de la population	
44,230	**61,230**	**15,910**	**1,970**	**5,410**	**3,050**	**Population totale de 1 an et plus[35]**	164
						Lieu de résidence 1 an auparavant (mobilité)	
40,600	55,845	14,270	1,770	4,950	2,635	Personnes n'ayant pas déménagé	165
3,630	5,385	1,645	200	455	415	Personnes ayant déménagé	166
1,810	2,810	720	25	285	150	Non-migrants	167
1,825	2,570	920	175	165	260	Migrants	168
1,760	2,390	890	180	160	260	Migrants internes	169
1,685	2,235	855	175	135	250	Migrants infraprovinciaux	170
75	155	40	0	20	10	Migrants interprovinciaux	171
60	180	25	0	10	0	Migrants externes	172
42,220	**58,920**	**15,510**	**1,935**	**5,260**	**2,990**	**Population totale de 5 ans et plus[36]**	173
						Lieu de résidence 5 ans auparavant (mobilité)	
29,415	41,605	9,990	1,310	3,395	1,885	Personnes n'ayant pas déménagé	174
12,805	17,310	5,520	625	1,865	1,100	Personnes ayant déménagé	175
5,875	9,145	1,855	35	730	285	Non-migrants	176
6,935	8,165	3,670	585	1,135	810	Migrants	177
6,715	7,615	3,560	560	1,095	805	Migrants internes	178
6,305	7,205	3,420	560	1,020	785	Migrants infraprovinciaux	179
410	405	135	0	70	25	Migrants interprovinciaux	180
220	550	110	30	40	10	Migrants externes	181
35,910	**51,340**	**13,980**	**1,845**	**4,610**	**2,725**	**Population totale de 15 ans et plus**	182
						Plus haut certificat, diplôme ou grade[37]	
9,695	16,240	3,840	485	1,200	945	Aucun certificat, diplôme ou grade	183
26,220	35,095	10,140	1,355	3,410	1,775	Certificat, diplôme ou grade	184
10,170	13,845	3,880	510	1,155	740	Diplôme d'études secondaires ou l'équivalent[38]	185
4,505	5,785	1,695	200	520	295	Certificat ou diplôme d'apprenti ou d'une école de métiers	186
7,930	10,000	2,850	440	1,020	535	Certificat ou diplôme d'un collège, d'un cégep ou d'un autre établissement d'enseignement non universitaire[39]	187
905	1,035	320	35	145	55	Certificat ou diplôme universitaire inférieur au baccalauréat[40]	188
2,705	4,420	1,390	170	570	150	Certificat ou grade universitaire[41]	189
1,820	2,780	840	85	335	90	Baccalauréat	190
380	840	215	25	110	25	Certificat ou diplôme universitaire supérieur au baccalauréat	191
75	110	55	10	20	10	Diplôme en médecine, en art dentaire, en médecine vétérinaire ou en optométrie	192
345	555	220	30	95	20	Maîtrise	193
80	135	55	15	15	0	Doctorat acquis	194
16,045	**21,245**	**6,255**	**845**	**2,255**	**1,035**	**Population totale de 15 ans et plus avec titres du niveau postsecondaire**	195
						Principal domaine d'études - Classification des programmes d'enseignement, 2000[42]	
1,160	1,610	570	60	265	70	Éducation	196
325	540	170	15	90	20	Arts visuels et d'interprétation, et technologie des communications	197
550	855	240	30	120	20	Sciences humaines	198
1,220	1,590	510	50	185	65	Sciences sociales et de comportements, et droit	199
2,705	3,900	1,215	170	430	275	Commerce, gestion et administration publique	200
180	425	105	30	20	0	Sciences physiques et de la vie, et technologies	201
365	500	135	15	80	10	Mathématiques, informatique et sciences de l'information	202
4,970	5,685	1,680	235	460	335	Architecture, génie et services connexes	203
605	780	225	35	90	20	Agriculture, ressources naturelles et conservation	204
2,835	3,595	995	145	355	170	Santé, parcs, récréation et conditionnement physique	205
1,130	1,755	405	50	170	45	Services personnels, de protection et de transport	206
0	0	0	0	0	0	Autres domaines d'études[43]	207
						Lieu des études[44]	
15,025	19,765	5,630	760	2,060	930	À l'intérieur du Canada	208
1,020	1,485	625	85	200	110	À l'extérieur du Canada	209
35,910	**51,340**	**13,980**	**1,845**	**4,610**	**2,725**	**Population totale de 15 ans et plus**	210
						Travail non rémunéré	
17,795	25,380	6,895	955	2,190	1,350	Hommes de 15 ans et plus	211
16,470	23,005	6,275	870	2,055	1,185	Travail non rémunéré déclaré[45]	212
1,550	1,975	430	35	175	75	Travaux ménagers et soins aux enfants et soins ou aide aux personnes âgées	213
5,050	6,095	1,165	110	445	170	Travaux ménagers et soins aux enfants seulement	214

Nota : Voir les symboles et les abréviations dans les documents d'introduction et voir les documents de référence à la fin de la publication.

Selected characteristics for census divisions and census subdivisions – 100% data and 20% sample data, Ontario, 2006 Census (continued)

No.	Characteristics	Hanover, T	Meaford, MU	Owen Sound, CY ◆A	Southgate, TP ◊	West Grey, MU ◊	**Haldimand-Norfolk CD/DR †**
	Population characteristics						
	Unpaid work (continued)						
215	Housework and care or assistance to seniors only	220	500	705	215	520	3,720
216	Child care and care or assistance to seniors only	0	10	0	0	0	20
217	Housework only	1,415	2,410	3,935	1,420	2,540	20,590
218	Child care only	0	15	60	40	35	315
219	Care or assistance to seniors only	0	15	30	10	15	165
220	Females 15 years and over	3,145	4,695	9,400	2,780	4,945	44,095
221	Reported unpaid work[45]	2,900	4,480	8,825	2,665	4,740	41,520
222	Housework and child care and care or assistance to seniors	300	460	1,035	320	645	5,685
223	Housework and child care only	805	1,060	2,485	895	1,185	12,345
224	Housework and care or assistance to seniors only	345	515	1,065	230	725	4,810
225	Child care and care or assistance to seniors only	0	10	0	0	0	35
226	Housework only	1,440	2,395	4,180	1,200	2,170	18,400
227	Child care only	0	30	20	20	10	125
228	Care or assistance to seniors only	0	10	45	0	0	115
	Labour force activity						
229	Males 15 years and over	2,685	4,550	8,045	2,850	5,020	43,190
230	In the labour force	1,800	3,120	5,490	2,080	3,605	31,020
231	Employed	1,710	2,965	4,980	1,990	3,515	29,330
232	Unemployed	90	155	510	90	90	1,685
233	Not in the labour force	880	1,430	2,560	770	1,410	12,175
234	Participation rate	67.0	68.6	68.2	73.0	71.8	71.8
235	Employment rate	63.7	65.2	61.9	69.8	70.0	67.9
236	Unemployment rate	5.0	5.0	9.3	4.3	2.5	5.4
237	Females 15 years and over	3,145	4,695	9,400	2,780	4,945	44,095
238	In the labour force	1,750	2,750	5,290	1,725	3,075	26,800
239	Employed	1,660	2,590	5,005	1,630	2,950	25,045
240	Unemployed	95	160	285	90	120	1,755
241	Not in the labour force	1,390	1,935	4,110	1,055	1,870	17,295
242	Participation rate	55.6	58.6	56.3	62.1	62.2	60.8
243	Employment rate	52.8	55.2	53.2	58.6	59.7	56.8
244	Unemployment rate	5.4	5.8	5.4	5.2	3.9	6.5
245	Both sexes - Participation rate	61.0	63.5	61.8	67.7	67.0	66.2
246	15 to 24 years	80.0	70.6	73.1	68.5	70.2	71.8
247	25 years and over	57.6	62.3	59.5	67.4	66.5	65.1
248	Both sexes - Employment rate	57.8	60.1	57.2	64.4	64.9	62.3
249	15 to 24 years	66.1	63.4	59.6	62.8	64.8	63.0
250	25 years and over	56.2	59.6	56.8	64.6	64.9	62.2
251	Both sexes - Unemployment rate	5.2	5.4	7.4	4.7	3.2	6.0
252	15 to 24 years	16.8	10.6	19.0	8.1	6.9	12.2
253	25 years and over	2.1	4.3	4.6	4.1	2.5	4.6
254	**Total labour force 15 years and over**	**3,555**	**5,875**	**10,780**	**3,805**	**6,675**	**57,820**
	Industry - North American Industry Classification System 2002						
255	Industry - Not applicable[46]	55	45	210	20	30	665
256	All industries[47]	3,495	5,830	10,565	3,780	6,650	57,160
257	11 Agriculture, forestry, fishing and hunting	130	355	45	430	830	5,630
258	21 Mining and oil and gas extraction	0	10	30	0	10	195
259	22 Utilities	85	40	145	15	100	890
260	23 Construction	200	585	620	395	590	3,845
261	31-33 Manufacturing	715	730	1,425	1,010	1,430	11,015
262	41 Wholesale trade	100	85	245	155	225	2,165
263	44-45 Retail trade	495	700	1,560	270	670	6,065
264	48-49 Transportation and warehousing	95	135	325	175	260	3,245
265	51 Information and cultural industries	100	65	285	25	80	690
266	52 Finance and insurance	100	150	255	60	115	1,140
267	53 Real estate and rental and leasing	40	145	180	35	30	525
268	54 Professional, scientific and technical services	150	190	470	135	260	1,715
269	55 Management of companies and enterprises	0	0	15	0	0	15
270	56 Administrative and support, waste management and remediation services	65	255	680	110	205	1,930
271	61 Educational services	220	340	695	130	245	3,030
272	62 Health care and social assistance	410	740	1,540	260	645	6,035

Note: See symbols and abbreviations in the introductory material and see reference material at the end of the publication.

Certaines caractéristiques des divisions de recensement et des subdivisions de recensement – Données intégrales et données-échantillon (20 %), Ontario, Recensement de 2006 (suite)

Haldimand County, CY	Norfolk County, CY ◊	**Haliburton CD/DR** ♦◊	Algonquin Highlands, TP ♦♦◊◊	Dysart and Others, TP ♦◊	Highlands East, MU ♦◊◊	**Caractéristiques**	N°
						Caractéristiques de la population	
						Travail non rémunéré (suite)	
1,505	2,215	545	75	160	135	Travaux ménagers et soins ou aide aux personnes âgées seulement	215
10	0	0	0	0	0	Soins aux enfants et soins ou aide aux personnes âgées seulement	216
8,190	12,390	4,055	635	1,255	795	Travaux ménagers seulement	217
90	225	45	0	10	10	Soins aux enfants seulement	218
70	95	15	0	10	0	Soins ou aide aux personnes âgées seulement	219
18,120	25,955	7,085	885	2,415	1,370	Femmes de 15 ans et plus	220
17,330	24,175	6,655	825	2,280	1,300	Travail non rémunéré déclaré[45]	221
2,590	3,095	585	80	240	125	Travaux ménagers et soins aux enfants et soins ou aide aux personnes âgées	222
5,450	6,895	1,455	105	540	250	Travaux ménagers et soins aux enfants seulement	223
1,905	2,900	805	110	310	140	Travaux ménagers et soins ou aide aux personnes âgées seulement	224
15	25	0	0	0	0	Soins aux enfants et soins ou aide aux personnes âgées seulement	225
7,265	11,135	3,760	510	1,175	785	Travaux ménagers seulement	226
65	55	35	15	10	0	Soins aux enfants seulement	227
45	70	15	0	10	0	Soins ou aide aux personnes âgées seulement	228
						Activité	
17,790	25,380	6,895	960	2,195	1,350	Hommes de 15 ans et plus	229
13,100	17,910	3,980	525	1,370	690	Population active	230
12,500	16,820	3,665	455	1,285	605	Personnes occupées	231
600	1,085	315	70	90	85	Chômeurs	232
4,690	7,475	2,915	430	820	660	Inactifs	233
73.6	70.6	57.7	54.7	62.4	51.1	Taux d'activité	234
70.3	66.3	53.2	47.4	58.5	44.8	Taux d'emploi	235
4.6	6.1	7.9	13.3	6.6	12.3	Taux de chômage	236
18,120	25,955	7,085	885	2,415	1,375	Femmes de 15 ans et plus	237
11,545	15,240	3,640	425	1,320	640	Population active	238
10,960	14,075	3,380	405	1,235	545	Personnes occupées	239
585	1,165	260	20	90	95	Chômeuses	240
6,575	10,710	3,445	460	1,090	735	Inactives	241
63.7	58.7	51.4	48.0	54.7	46.5	Taux d'activité	242
60.5	54.2	47.7	45.8	51.1	39.6	Taux d'emploi	243
5.1	7.6	7.1	4.7	6.8	14.8	Taux de chômage	244
68.6	64.6	54.5	51.6	58.5	48.8	Les deux sexes - Taux d'activité	245
73.5	70.5	60.4	80.5	66.1	44.1	15 à 24 ans	246
67.6	63.4	53.7	47.9	57.4	49.4	25 ans et plus	247
65.3	60.2	50.4	46.6	54.6	42.0	Les deux sexes - Taux d'emploi	248
66.1	60.8	48.6	56.1	52.6	31.0	15 à 24 ans	249
65.2	60.1	50.6	45.1	54.7	43.4	25 ans et plus	250
4.8	6.8	7.5	9.5	6.7	13.5	Les deux sexes - Taux de chômage	251
10.0	13.9	19.4	30.3	21.1	26.9	15 à 24 ans	252
3.7	5.3	5.7	5.7	4.5	12.1	25 ans et plus	253
24,645	**33,150**	**7,620**	**955**	**2,695**	**1,325**	**Population active totale de 15 ans et plus**	254
						Industrie - Système de classification des industries de l'Amérique du Nord de 2002	
230	430	135	0	65	40	Industrie - Sans objet[46]	255
24,415	32,720	7,485	950	2,630	1,290	Toutes les industries[47]	256
1,665	3,970	155	15	40	60	11 Agriculture, foresterie, pêche et chasse	257
75	125	35	0	15	0	21 Extraction minière et extraction de pétrole et de gaz	258
320	570	110	10	25	10	22 Services publics	259
1,770	2,070	1,305	110	500	180	23 Construction	260
4,375	6,635	430	65	130	125	31-33 Fabrication	261
1,090	1,075	195	25	60	35	41 Commerce de gros	262
2,740	3,320	1,095	150	440	130	44-45 Commerce de détail	263
1,520	1,725	305	20	55	90	48-49 Transport et entreposage	264
310	375	150	0	60	25	51 Industrie de l'information et industrie culturelle	265
525	620	125	0	40	20	52 Finance et assurances	266
240	275	310	80	115	30	53 Services immobiliers et services de location et de location à bail	267
665	1,050	310	50	85	50	54 Services professionnels, scientifiques et techniques	268
10	10	10	0	0	0	55 Gestion de sociétés et d'entreprises	269
865	1,065	345	95	75	60	56 Services administratifs, services de soutien, services de gestion des déchets et services d'assainissement	270
1,405	1,625	405	25	225	65	61 Services d'enseignement	271
2,915	3,115	665	75	260	80	62 Soins de santé et assistance sociale	272

Nota : Voir les symboles et les abréviations dans les documents d'introduction et voir les documents de référence à la fin de la publication.

Selected characteristics for census divisions and census subdivisions – 100% data and 20% sample data, Ontario, 2006 Census (continued)

No.	Characteristics	Hanover, T	Meaford, MU	Owen Sound, CY ◆A	Southgate, TP ◇	West Grey, MU ◇	**Haldimand-Norfolk CD/DR †**
	Population characteristics						
	Industry - North American Industry Classification System 2002 (continued)						
273	71 Arts, entertainment and recreation	90	230	215	75	115	1,000
274	72 Accommodation and food services	230	460	940	165	340	3,465
275	81 Other services (except public administration)	175	260	460	200	340	2,675
276	91 Public administration	100	330	430	115	155	1,880
	Class of worker						
277	Class of worker - Not applicable[46]	55	40	210	25	30	665
278	All classes of worker[47]	3,495	5,830	10,565	3,785	6,645	57,155
279	Paid workers	3,200	4,825	9,680	3,125	5,380	51,490
280	Employees	3,095	4,620	9,435	2,975	5,090	49,115
281	Self-employed (incorporated)	105	200	245	145	290	2,380
282	Self-employed (unincorporated)	295	975	880	610	1,165	5,305
283	Unpaid family workers	0	35	10	45	105	360
	Occupation - National Occupational Classification for Statistics 2006						
284	Male labour force 15 years and over	1,800	3,120	5,485	2,080	3,605	31,020
285	Occupation - Not applicable[46]	35	25	120	20	20	330
286	All occupations[47]	1,765	3,095	5,370	2,065	3,585	30,690
287	A Management occupations	180	325	475	100	280	2,410
288	B Business, finance and administrative occupations	90	105	415	105	165	1,380
289	C Natural and applied sciences and related occupations	140	165	385	110	110	1,550
290	D Health occupations	30	95	145	10	50	360
291	E Occupations in social science, education, government service and religion	75	110	300	65	65	865
292	F Occupations in art, culture, recreation and sport	20	100	140	30	35	310
293	G Sales and service occupations	320	560	1,295	190	455	4,365
294	H Trades, transport and equipment operators and related occupations	465	1,005	1,525	815	1,305	11,620
295	I Occupations unique to primary industry	105	340	165	340	555	3,990
296	J Occupations unique to processing, manufacturing and utilities	340	285	520	290	555	3,820
297	Female labour force 15 years and over	1,750	2,755	5,290	1,725	3,075	26,805
298	Occupation - Not applicable[46]	20	15	95	0	10	335
299	All occupations[47]	1,730	2,740	5,200	1,720	3,060	26,465
300	A Management occupations	120	145	415	75	170	1,535
301	B Business, finance and administrative occupations	320	525	965	380	635	5,605
302	C Natural and applied sciences and related occupations	35	45	95	30	10	370
303	D Health occupations	160	350	645	140	290	3,120
304	E Occupations in social science, education, government service and religion	225	280	575	95	265	2,780
305	F Occupations in art, culture, recreation and sport	50	140	150	50	85	690
306	G Sales and service occupations	560	915	1,985	475	830	7,755
307	H Trades, transport and equipment operators and related occupations	25	75	100	100	80	840
308	I Occupations unique to primary industry	65	170	15	110	275	2,115
309	J Occupations unique to processing, manufacturing and utilities	175	90	245	260	420	1,655
310	**Total employed labour force 15 years and over**	**3,370**	**5,560**	**9,985**	**3,625**	**6,465**	**54,375**
	Place of work status						
311	Males	1,710	2,965	4,975	1,995	3,510	29,335
312	Usual place of work	1,370	1,960	4,145	1,350	2,165	21,450
313	At home	80	370	245	335	665	3,260
314	Outside Canada	0	20	20	15	20	180
315	No fixed workplace address	255	620	560	290	665	4,445
316	Females	1,660	2,590	5,005	1,630	2,950	25,045
317	Usual place of work	1,455	2,125	4,460	1,345	2,330	21,005
318	At home	150	305	300	215	505	2,685
319	Outside Canada	0	10	10	0	15	30
320	No fixed workplace address	55	155	245	65	105	1,325

Note: See symbols and abbreviations in the introductory material and see reference material at the end of the publication.

Certaines caractéristiques des divisions de recensement et des subdivisions de recensement – Données intégrales et données-échantillon (20 %), Ontario, Recensement de 2006 (suite)

Haldimand County, CY	Norfolk County, CY ◊	**Haliburton CD/DR** ♦◊	Algonquin Highlands, TP ♦♦◊◊	Dysart and Others, TP ♦◊	Highlands East, MU ♦◊◊	**Caractéristiques**	N°
						Caractéristiques de la population	
						Industrie - Système de classification des industries de l'Amérique du Nord de 2002 (suite)	
510	490	200	35	50	20	71 Arts, spectacles et loisirs	273
1,395	2,065	680	105	225	160	72 Hébergement et services de restauration	274
1,170	1,500	395	40	155	85	81 Autres services (sauf les administrations publiques)	275
845	1,035	235	35	60	55	91 Administrations publiques	276
						Catégorie de travailleurs	
235	430	135	0	70	40	Catégorie de travailleurs - Sans objet[46]	277
24,415	32,725	7,480	950	2,625	1,285	Toutes les catégories de travailleurs[47]	278
22,015	29,460	6,165	785	2,170	1,070	Travailleurs rémunérés	279
21,215	27,885	5,725	735	2,010	990	Employés	280
800	1,575	440	50	160	85	Travailleurs autonomes (entreprise constituée en société)	281
2,255	3,045	1,255	170	435	200	Travailleurs autonomes (entreprise non constituée en société)	282
145	215	60	0	25	15	Travailleurs familiaux non rémunérés	283
						Profession - Classification nationale des professions pour statistiques de 2006	
13,100	17,905	3,980	520	1,375	690	Hommes actifs de 15 ans et plus	284
110	220	60	0	40	0	Profession - Sans objet[46]	285
12,985	17,690	3,920	525	1,330	680	Toutes les professions[47]	286
1,005	1,410	490	50	225	40	A Gestion	287
590	795	235	10	80	30	B Affaires, finance et administration	288
640	915	145	25	50	20	C Sciences naturelles et appliquées et professions apparentées	289
140	220	50	10	25	0	D Secteur de la santé	290
390	475	145	10	85	30	E Sciences sociales, enseignement, administration publique et religion	291
175	140	45	10	15	10	F Arts, culture, sports et loisirs	292
1,910	2,455	655	125	225	95	G Ventes et services	293
5,485	6,125	1,650	175	515	285	H Métiers, transport et machinerie	294
1,255	2,730	315	75	70	105	I Professions propres au secteur primaire	295
1,395	2,425	180	40	40	65	J Transformation, fabrication et services d'utilité publique	296
11,545	15,240	3,640	430	1,325	640	Femmes actives de 15 ans et plus	297
120	215	75	0	30	35	Profession - Sans objet[46]	298
11,430	15,030	3,565	425	1,295	605	Toutes les professions[47]	299
685	845	365	55	165	30	A Gestion	300
2,490	3,110	940	80	335	165	B Affaires, finance et administration	301
125	240	50	15	20	0	C Sciences naturelles et appliquées et professions apparentées	302
1,525	1,590	300	25	130	40	D Secteur de la santé	303
1,215	1,565	255	30	105	25	E Sciences sociales, enseignement, administration publique et religion	304
345	350	150	20	35	30	F Arts, culture, sports et loisirs	305
3,550	4,200	1,310	185	415	260	G Ventes et services	306
375	465	100	15	40	10	H Métiers, transport et machinerie	307
705	1,410	40	0	15	15	I Professions propres au secteur primaire	308
400	1,255	45	0	20	15	J Transformation, fabrication et services d'utilité publique	309
23,460	**30,900**	**7,045**	**855**	**2,515**	**1,150**	**Population active occupée totale de 15 ans et plus**	310
						Catégorie de lieu de travail	
12,500	16,825	3,670	450	1,280	605	Hommes	311
9,350	12,090	2,280	295	895	355	Lieu habituel de travail	312
1,120	2,140	365	35	115	95	À domicile	313
75	100	15	0	0	0	En dehors du Canada	314
1,955	2,485	1,005	120	270	160	Sans adresse de travail fixe	315
10,955	14,075	3,380	405	1,235	545	Femmes	316
9,225	11,770	2,625	310	980	375	Lieu habituel de travail	317
1,090	1,595	475	40	195	95	À domicile	318
10	20	0	0	0	0	En dehors du Canada	319
635	690	275	50	60	65	Sans adresse de travail fixe	320

Nota : Voir les symboles et les abréviations dans les documents d'introduction et voir les documents de référence à la fin de la publication.

Selected characteristics for census divisions and census subdivisions – 100% data and 20% sample data, Ontario, 2006 Census (continued)

No.	Characteristics	Hanover, T	Meaford, MU	Owen Sound, CY ◆A	Southgate, TP ◊	West Grey, MU ◊	**Haldimand-Norfolk CD/DR †**
	Population characteristics						
321	**Total employed labour force 15 years and over with usual place of work or no fixed workplace address**	**3,135**	**4,860**	**9,410**	**3,055**	**5,260**	**48,220**
	Mode of transportation						
322	Males	1,630	2,580	4,710	1,640	2,830	25,890
323	Car, truck, van, as driver	1,160	2,110	3,525	1,390	2,335	22,295
324	Car, truck, van, as passenger	160	150	465	120	265	1,800
325	Public transit	10	15	95	20	15	155
326	Walked	225	220	455	55	180	1,180
327	All other modes	75	90	165	60	30	455
328	Females	1,505	2,280	4,700	1,415	2,430	22,330
329	Car, truck, van, as driver	1,000	1,755	3,100	1,165	1,880	18,170
330	Car, truck, van, as passenger	165	250	675	135	220	1,875
331	Public transit	20	15	120	20	20	85
332	Walked	280	225	605	55	310	1,825
333	All other modes	40	40	200	40	0	365
334	**Total population 15 years and over who worked since January 1, 2005**	**3,830**	**6,450**	**11,545**	**4,245**	**7,265**	**62,805**
	Language used most often at work						
335	Single responses	3,815	6,445	11,540	4,235	7,265	62,640
336	English	3,805	6,435	11,475	4,040	7,250	62,090
337	French	0	10	30	0	0	80
338	Non-official languages[7]	0	0	35	190	20	475
339	Chinese, n.o.s.[61]	0	0	35	0	0	35
340	Cantonese	0	0	0	0	0	20
341	Other languages[8]	0	0	0	190	15	420
342	Multiple responses	15	10	10	0	0	160
343	English and French	15	10	0	0	0	30
344	English and non-official language	0	0	0	10	0	130
345	French and non-official language	0	0	0	0	0	0
346	English, French and non-official language	0	0	0	0	0	0
	Dwelling and household characteristics						
347	**Total number of occupied private dwellings**	**3,045**	**4,445**	**9,380**	**2,565**	**4,725**	**40,580**
	Housing tenure						
348	Owned	1,985	3,695	5,610	2,255	3,985	33,180
349	Rented	1,060	750	3,770	305	740	7,395
350	Band housing	0	0	0	0	0	0
	Structural type of dwelling						
351	Single-detached house	1,965	3,735	4,880	2,385	4,225	34,115
352	Semi-detached house	90	55	420	25	45	1,095
353	Row house	100	170	600	5	55	975
354	Apartment, duplex	115	75	245	10	75	840
355	Apartment, building that has five or more storeys	220	0	695	0	0	420
356	Apartment, building that has fewer than five storeys	530	340	2,510	125	245	2,690
357	Other single-attached house	15	50	10	5	5	250
358	Movable dwelling[48]	0	10	25	10	70	195
	Condition of dwelling						
359	Regular maintenance only	2,085	2,955	6,135	1,490	2,960	26,950
360	Minor repairs	785	1,195	2,485	785	1,360	10,690
361	Major repairs	175	290	760	285	405	2,935
	Period of construction						
362	Before 1946	760	1,495	3,485	850	1,650	11,350
363	1946 to 1960	480	415	1,315	170	380	6,620
364	1961 to 1970	425	320	1,115	215	380	4,950
365	1971 to 1980	575	650	1,670	320	610	5,565
366	1981 to 1985	155	225	335	95	215	1,950
367	1986 to 1990	225	400	745	365	440	3,130
368	1991 to 1995	155	375	335	215	465	2,310
369	1996 to 2000	80	195	185	190	195	2,265
370	2001 to 2006[49]	180	355	190	145	385	2,440

Note: See symbols and abbreviations in the introductory material and see reference material at the end of the publication.

Certaines caractéristiques des divisions de recensement et des subdivisions de recensement – Données intégrales et données-échantillon (20 %), Ontario, Recensement de 2006 (suite)

Haldimand County, CY	Norfolk County, CY ◊	**Haliburton CD/DR** ◆◊	Algonquin Highlands, TP ◆◆◊◊	Dysart and Others, TP ◆◊	Highlands East, MU ◆◊◊	**Caractéristiques**	N°
						Caractéristiques de la population	
21,165	**27,040**	**6,185**	**780**	**2,205**	**955**	**Population active occupée totale de 15 ans et plus ayant un lieu habituel de travail ou sans adresse de travail fixe**	321
						Mode de transport	
11,300	14,585	3,285	415	1,170	510	Hommes	322
9,820	12,465	2,795	315	1,025	445	Automobile, camion ou fourgonnette, en tant que conducteur	323
700	1,100	255	50	50	55	Automobile, camion ou fourgonnette, en tant que passager	324
75	80	0	0	0	0	Transport en commun	325
465	715	165	20	65	10	À pied	326
235	220	70	25	30	0	Tous les autres modes	327
9,865	12,460	2,900	365	1,040	445	Femmes	328
8,115	10,050	2,415	290	850	365	Automobile, camion ou fourgonnette, en tant que conductrice	329
790	1,085	215	20	70	30	Automobile, camion ou fourgonnette, en tant que passagère	330
30	55	40	25	10	0	Transport en commun	331
760	1,065	185	20	75	45	À pied	332
165	200	55	0	30	10	Tous les autres modes	333
26,660	**36,125**	**8,670**	**1,115**	**2,970**	**1,470**	**Population totale de 15 ans et plus ayant travaillé depuis le 1er janvier 2005**	334
						Langue utilisée le plus souvent au travail	
26,625	35,995	8,665	1,110	2,975	1,470	Réponses uniques	335
26,550	35,515	8,650	1,105	2,960	1,470	Anglais	336
25	55	0	0	0	0	Français	337
50	420	0	0	10	0	Langues non officielles[7]	338
0	35	0	0	0	0	Chinois, n.d.a.[61]	339
0	15	0	0	0	0	Cantonais	340
50	370	10	0	10	0	Autres langues[8]	341
30	130	10	0	0	0	Réponses multiples	342
0	25	0	10	0	0	Anglais et français	343
20	105	0	0	0	0	Anglais et langue non officielle	344
0	0	0	0	0	0	Français et langue non officielle	345
10	0	0	0	0	0	Anglais, français et langue non officielle	346
						Caractéristiques des logements et des ménages	
16,315	**24,240**	**6,975**	**865**	**2,345**	**1,370**	**Nombre total de logements privés occupés**	347
						Mode d'occupation	
13,765	19,395	6,065	815	1,990	1,155	Possédé	348
2,550	4,840	910	50	360	215	Loué	349
0	0	0	0	0	0	Logement de bande	350
						Type de construction résidentielle	
14,015	20,075	6,445	850	2,070	1,305	Maison individuelle non attenante	351
475	620	40	5	25	0	Maison jumelée	352
440	535	55	0	5	10	Maison en rangée	353
240	600	40	5	30	0	Appartement, duplex	354
5	415	0	0	0	0	Appartement, immeuble de cinq étages ou plus	355
1,075	1,610	330	5	185	40	Appartement, immeuble de moins de cinq étages	356
45	205	35	0	15	10	Autre maison individuelle attenante	357
20	170	35	0	15	10	Logement mobile[48]	358
						État du logement	
10,550	16,390	4,475	580	1,525	835	Entretien régulier seulement	359
4,455	6,235	1,985	260	670	405	Réparations mineures	360
1,305	1,625	515	30	155	130	Réparations majeures	361
						Période de construction	
4,620	6,725	820	80	340	125	Avant 1946	362
2,135	4,480	940	120	310	285	1946 à 1960	363
1,880	3,070	945	140	340	140	1961 à 1970	364
2,255	3,305	1,315	240	305	300	1971 à 1980	365
780	1,170	710	45	235	165	1981 à 1985	366
1,315	1,810	875	80	335	105	1986 à 1990	367
1,080	1,230	595	65	180	85	1991 à 1995	368
1,130	1,130	330	55	115	75	1996 à 2000	369
1,115	1,325	440	40	190	85	2001 à 2006[49]	370

Nota : Voir les symboles et les abréviations dans les documents d'introduction et voir les documents de référence à la fin de la publication.

Selected characteristics for census divisions and census subdivisions – 100% data and 20% sample data, Ontario, 2006 Census (continued)

No.	Characteristics	Hanover, T	Meaford, MU	Owen Sound, CY ◆A	Southgate, TP ◊	West Grey, MU ◊	**Haldimand-Norfolk CD/DR †**
	Dwelling and household characteristics						
371	Average number of rooms per dwelling	6.7	7.2	6.3	7.0	7.2	7.3
372	Average number of bedrooms per dwelling	2.6	2.9	2.6	3.0	3.0	2.9
373	Average value of dwelling $	180,631	261,355	191,623	226,565	223,459	213,466
374	**Total number of private households**	**3,045**	**4,440**	**9,380**	**2,565**	**4,720**	**40,565**
	Household size						
375	1 person	960	1,010	3,175	510	1,010	8,840
376	2 persons	1,135	1,930	3,275	910	1,920	14,980
377	3 persons	375	590	1,305	355	655	6,145
378	4 to 5 persons	535	840	1,500	645	995	9,260
379	6 or more persons	35	75	125	145	135	1,340
	Household type						
380	One-family households[50]	1,995	3,360	5,940	1,975	3,535	30,520
381	Multiple-family households	15	0	45	35	45	530
382	Non-family households	1,035	1,080	3,400	555	1,145	9,525
383	Number of persons in private households	6,890	10,685	20,845	7,170	11,990	105,960
384	Average number of persons in private households	2.3	2.4	2.2	2.8	2.5	2.6
385	Tenant-occupied private non-farm, non-reserve dwellings[51]	1,060	740	3,770	305	715	7,320
386	Average gross rent $[51]	665	684	616	621	596	688
387	Tenant-occupied households spending 30% or more of household income on gross rent[52]	520	330	1,720	95	265	3,060
388	Tenant-occupied households spending from 30% to 99% of household income on gross rent[52]	465	260	1,610	70	235	2,700
389	Owner-occupied private non-farm, non-reserve dwellings[53]	1,980	3,545	5,605	2,045	3,700	32,010
390	Average owner's major payments $[53]	814	863	865	1,028	836	934
391	Owner households spending 30% or more of household income on owner's major payments[52]	265	715	1,125	445	680	5,540
392	Owner households spending from 30% to 99% of household income on owner's major payments[52]	240	650	1,000	360	575	4,760
	Census family characteristics						
393	**Total number of census families in private households**	**2,030**	**3,365**	**6,030**	**2,045**	**3,630**	**31,615**
	Family structure and number of children						
394	Total couple families	1,735	3,015	4,860	1,845	3,275	27,960
395	Total families of married couples	1,510	2,645	4,030	1,590	2,880	24,645
396	Without children at home	810	1,495	2,115	745	1,530	11,565
397	With children at home	700	1,155	1,915	850	1,350	13,080
398	1 child	230	400	690	205	400	4,355
399	2 children	345	515	840	355	540	5,525
400	3 or more children	120	230	380	280	410	3,205
401	Total families of common-law couples	230	365	830	250	395	3,310
402	Without children at home	150	255	495	130	225	1,935
403	With children at home	75	115	330	120	170	1,375
404	1 child	40	70	170	75	65	635
405	2 children	20	35	120	45	70	520
406	3 or more children	15	10	45	0	35	220
407	Total lone-parent families	290	350	1,165	200	350	3,660
408	Female parent	250	265	965	170	270	2,805
409	1 child	120	130	475	105	165	1,650
410	2 children	110	85	350	55	85	825
411	3 or more children	25	55	140	10	25	330
412	Male parent	40	80	200	25	75	855
413	1 child	35	60	140	20	45	545
414	2 children	10	20	45	10	30	255
415	3 or more children	0	0	10	10	0	50

Note: See symbols and abbreviations in the introductory material and see reference material at the end of the publication.

Certaines caractéristiques des divisions de recensement et des subdivisions de recensement – Données intégrales et données-échantillon (20 %), Ontario, Recensement de 2006 (suite)

Haldimand County, CY	Norfolk County, CY ◊	**Haliburton CD/DR** ◆◊	Algonquin Highlands, TP ◆◆◊◊	Dysart and Others, TP ◆◊	Highlands East, MU ◆◊◊	**Caractéristiques**	N°
						Caractéristiques des logements et des ménages	
7.4	7.3	6.6	6.6	6.8	6.2	Nombre moyen de pièces par logement	371
3.0	2.9	2.8	2.8	2.8	2.7	Nombre moyen de chambres à coucher par logement	372
226,781	203,985	233,387	300,947	250,680	182,279	Valeur moyenne du logement $	373
16,310	**24,240**	**6,980**	**870**	**2,345**	**1,370**	**Nombre total de ménages privés**	374
						Taille du ménage	
3,175	5,650	1,765	210	605	355	1 personne	375
5,755	9,210	3,190	445	1,025	625	2 personnes	376
2,500	3,645	830	80	280	190	3 personnes	377
4,250	5,010	1,080	120	395	180	4 à 5 personnes	378
625	715	110	15	45	20	6 personnes ou plus	379
						Genre de ménage	
12,690	17,815	4,950	675	1,655	945	Ménages unifamiliaux[50]	380
225	305	80	10	15	20	Ménages multifamiliaux	381
3,395	6,120	1,950	185	675	405	Ménages non familiaux	382
44,470	61,445	15,895	1,940	5,415	3,060	Nombre de personnes dans les ménages privés	383
2.7	2.5	2.3	2.2	2.3	2.2	Nombre moyen de personnes dans les ménages privés	384
2,520	4,795	910	50	360	215	Ménages locataires dans les logements privés non agricoles hors réserve[51]	385
721	671	619	777	633	620	Loyer brut moyen $[51]	386
1,100	1,965	390	30	175	85	Ménages locataires consacrant 30 % ou plus du revenu du ménage au loyer brut[52]	387
945	1,760	355	20	160	90	Ménages locataires consacrant de 30 % à 99 % du revenu du ménage au loyer brut[52]	388
13,315	18,695	6,055	815	1,990	1,155	Ménages propriétaires dans les logements privés non agricoles hors réserve[53]	389
1,015	876	712	673	755	735	Principales dépenses de propriété moyennes $[53]	390
2,320	3,220	1,180	140	390	295	Ménages propriétaires consacrant 30 % ou plus du revenu du ménage aux principales dépenses de propriété[52]	391
1,920	2,840	980	125	335	230	Ménages propriétaires consacrant de 30 % à 99 % du revenu du ménage aux principales dépenses de propriété[52]	392
						Caractéristiques des familles de recensement	
13,165	**18,440**	**5,105**	**685**	**1,690**	**985**	**Nombre total de familles de recensement dans les ménages privés**	393
						Structure de la famille et le nombre d'enfants	
11,670	16,280	4,615	625	1,530	880	Total des familles avec conjoints	394
10,405	14,235	3,965	540	1,330	775	Total des familles avec couples mariés	395
4,570	6,990	2,505	365	805	505	Sans enfants à la maison	396
5,835	7,245	1,455	175	525	270	Avec enfants à la maison	397
1,780	2,575	545	75	170	125	1 enfant	398
2,600	2,915	680	90	250	110	2 enfants	399
1,455	1,750	230	10	105	35	3 enfants ou plus	400
1,265	2,045	650	90	205	110	Total des familles avec couples en union libre	401
705	1,230	430	70	115	60	Sans enfants à la maison	402
560	810	225	20	95	45	Avec enfants à la maison	403
255	375	125	20	55	25	1 enfant	404
155	360	55	0	15	20	2 enfants	405
140	75	40	0	25	0	3 enfants ou plus	406
1,495	2,160	490	60	160	100	Total des familles monoparentales	407
1,155	1,650	360	30	140	100	Parent de sexe féminin	408
600	1,050	225	20	90	55	1 enfant	409
365	460	80	10	30	25	2 enfants	410
190	140	60	0	20	15	3 enfants ou plus	411
340	515	130	30	15	0	Parent de sexe masculin	412
210	335	95	10	15	10	1 enfant	413
120	140	10	0	10	0	2 enfants	414
15	30	25	20	0	0	3 enfants ou plus	415

Nota : Voir les symboles et les abréviations dans les documents d'introduction et voir les documents de référence à la fin de la publication.

Selected characteristics for census divisions and census subdivisions – 100% data and 20% sample data, Ontario, 2006 Census (continued)

No.	Characteristics	Hanover, T	Meaford, MU	Owen Sound, CY ◆A	Southgate, TP ◇	West Grey, MU ◇	**Haldimand-Norfolk CD/DR †**
	Census family characteristics						
416	**Total number of children at home**	**1,920**	**2,980**	**6,060**	**2,495**	**3,675**	**34,585**
	Age group						
417	Under 6 years	425	485	1,235	470	665	6,400
418	6 to 14 years	675	1,075	2,165	1,055	1,435	12,710
419	15 to 17 years	235	480	1,000	390	505	4,840
420	18 to 24 years	480	700	1,210	450	755	7,755
421	25 years and over	110	240	440	130	315	2,885
422	Average number of children at home per census family[54]	0.9	0.9	1.0	1.2	1.0	1.1
423	**Total number of persons in private households**	**6,890**	**10,685**	**20,845**	**7,165**	**11,995**	**105,975**
	Census family status and living arrangements						
424	Number of persons not in census families	1,200	1,325	3,895	780	1,415	11,810
425	Living with relatives[55]	60	155	200	80	125	1,260
426	Living with non-relatives only	175	155	520	195	275	1,715
427	Living alone	965	1,015	3,180	510	1,020	8,830
428	Number of census family persons	5,690	9,360	16,950	6,385	10,580	94,165
429	Average number of persons per census family	2.8	2.8	2.8	3.1	2.9	3.0
430	**Total number of persons aged 65 years and over**	**1,400**	**2,080**	**3,775**	**915**	**1,945**	**15,660**
431	Number of persons not in census families aged 65 years and over	515	555	1,510	240	575	4,695
432	Living with relatives[55]	20	60	60	35	50	490
433	Living with non-relatives only	10	15	40	30	40	300
434	Living alone	480	480	1,410	175	480	3,905
435	Number of census family persons aged 65 years and over	885	1,530	2,270	680	1,375	10,965
	Economic family characteristics						
436	**Total number of economic families in private households**	**2,030**	**3,375**	**6,020**	**2,020**	**3,620**	**31,220**
	Size of family						
437	2 persons	1,100	1,890	3,175	930	1,905	14,730
438	3 persons	375	585	1,230	335	575	6,025
439	4 persons	400	625	1,085	435	675	6,475
440	5 or more persons	150	275	530	315	460	3,985
441	Total number of persons in economic families	5,750	9,515	17,145	6,465	10,700	95,425
442	Average number of persons per economic family	3.0	3.0	3.0	3.0	3.0	3.0
443	Total number of persons not in economic families	1,140	1,170	3,695	705	1,295	10,550
	2005 income characteristics						
444	**Population 15 years and over**	**5,825**	**9,245**	**17,445**	**5,630**	**9,965**	**87,285**
	Sex and total income groups in 2005						
445	Without income	160	320	660	285	365	3,560
446	With income	5,665	8,920	16,785	5,345	9,595	83,720
447	Under $1,000[56]	160	320	515	230	410	3,090
448	$1,000 to $2,999	245	255	495	175	345	3,015
449	$3,000 to $4,999	195	335	570	230	290	2,715
450	$5,000 to $6,999	250	385	630	210	280	3,290
451	$7,000 to $9,999	365	520	1,115	430	730	5,205
452	$10,000 to $11,999	215	395	955	255	500	3,475
453	$12,000 to $14,999	285	635	1,110	255	535	5,495
454	$15,000 to $19,999	685	930	2,120	515	980	8,620
455	$20,000 to $24,999	585	820	1,765	460	850	6,835
456	$25,000 to $29,999	535	825	1,270	345	725	6,125
457	$30,000 to $34,999	415	600	1,285	365	885	5,860
458	$35,000 to $39,999	345	480	1,140	285	625	5,165
459	$40,000 to $44,999	245	510	790	190	430	4,220
460	$45,000 to $49,999	215	355	480	235	400	3,375
461	$50,000 to $59,999	295	540	885	405	570	5,160
462	$60,000 and over	630	1,010	1,655	765	1,035	12,065
463	Median income $[57]	23,579	24,175	22,182	24,061	24,155	25,033
464	Average income $[57]	30,086	31,863	29,093	32,248	29,810	32,527
465	Standard error of average income $[57]	815	753	462	914	560	275

Note: See symbols and abbreviations in the introductory material and see reference material at the end of the publication.

Certaines caractéristiques des divisions de recensement et des subdivisions de recensement – Données intégrales et données-échantillon (20 %), Ontario, Recensement de 2006 (suite)

Haldimand County, CY	Norfolk County, CY ◊	**Haliburton CD/DR** ◆◊	Algonquin Highlands, TP ◆◆◊◊	Dysart and Others, TP ◆◊	Highlands East, MU ◆◊◊	**Caractéristiques**	N°
						Caractéristiques des familles de recensement	
15,390	**19,190**	**3,825**	**415**	**1,430**	**700**	**Nombre total d'enfants à la maison**	416
						Groupes d'âge	
2,920	3,475	600	45	205	130	Moins de 6 ans	417
5,815	6,895	1,415	80	620	235	6 à 14 ans	418
2,120	2,715	640	75	205	120	15 à 17 ans	419
3,325	4,430	785	105	290	145	18 à 24 ans	420
1,210	1,675	390	115	110	70	25 ans et plus	421
1.2	1.0	0.7	0.6	0.8	0.7	Nombre moyen d'enfants à la maison par famille de recensement[54]	422
44,480	**61,455**	**15,885**	**1,945**	**5,430**	**3,065**	**Nombre total de personnes dans les ménages privés**	423
						Situation des particuliers dans la famille de recensement et des particuliers dans le ménage	
4,260	7,545	2,335	215	770	500	Nombre de personnes hors famille de recensement	424
510	755	240	10	40	75	Vivant avec des personnes apparentées[55]	425
580	1,140	330	30	95	70	Vivant avec des personnes non apparentées seulement	426
3,165	5,650	1,760	175	630	355	Vivant seules	427
40,225	53,910	13,550	1,730	4,655	2,565	Nombre de membres d'une famille de recensement	428
3.1	2.9	2.7	2.5	2.8	2.6	Nombre moyen de personnes par famille de recensement	429
5,515	**10,140**	**3,830**	**550**	**1,180**	**770**	**Nombre total de personnes âgées de 65 ans et plus**	430
1,630	3,065	1,100	120	365	230	Nombre de personnes hors famille de recensement âgées de 65 ans et plus	431
235	255	120	10	40	30	Vivant avec des personnes apparentées[55]	432
70	230	50	10	0	10	Vivant avec des personnes non apparentées seulement	433
1,325	2,575	935	105	325	190	Vivant seules	434
3,885	7,075	2,725	430	815	545	Nombre de membres d'une famille de recensement âgés de 65 ans et plus	435
						Caractéristiques des familles économiques	
12,980	**18,230**	**5,080**	**680**	**1,675**	**990**	**Nombre total de familles économiques dans les ménages privés**	436
						Taille de la famille	
5,685	9,035	3,110	445	985	605	2 personnes	437
2,480	3,545	810	110	265	185	3 personnes	438
2,955	3,525	820	110	285	135	4 personnes	439
1,855	2,125	345	15	145	60	5 personnes ou plus	440
40,735	54,665	13,790	1,740	4,700	2,640	Nombre total de personnes dans les familles économiques	441
3.0	3.0	3.0	3.0	3.0	3.0	Nombre moyen de personnes par famille économique	442
3,745	6,795	2,095	205	725	420	Nombre total de personnes hors famille économique	443
						Caractéristiques du revenu de 2005	
35,915	**51,335**	**13,980**	**1,845**	**4,610**	**2,720**	**Population de 15 ans et plus**	444
						Sexe et groupes de revenu total en 2005	
1,715	1,845	485	35	135	165	Sans revenu	445
34,200	49,490	13,495	1,810	4,475	2,560	Avec un revenu	446
1,425	1,660	455	60	150	125	Moins de 1 000 $[56]	447
1,245	1,770	430	30	100	90	1 000 $ à 2 999 $	448
1,200	1,510	480	35	180	90	3 000 $ à 4 999 $	449
1,545	1,740	525	75	175	140	5 000 $ à 6 999 $	450
2,130	3,080	950	190	335	175	7 000 $ à 9 999 $	451
1,230	2,240	660	70	185	155	10 000 $ à 11 999 $	452
1,835	3,650	920	110	300	205	12 000 $ à 14 999 $	453
2,955	5,660	1,815	265	480	385	15 000 $ à 19 999 $	454
2,810	4,025	1,310	160	400	290	20 000 $ à 24 999 $	455
2,285	3,840	1,315	200	450	185	25 000 $ à 29 999 $	456
2,295	3,560	1,010	130	425	160	30 000 $ à 34 999 $	457
2,200	2,970	795	135	260	110	35 000 $ à 39 999 $	458
1,700	2,520	625	70	240	110	40 000 $ à 44 999 $	459
1,390	1,985	435	65	120	65	45 000 $ à 49 999$	460
2,365	2,795	620	45	200	140	50 000 $ à 59 999$	461
5,585	6,480	1,150	160	475	120	60 000 $ et plus	462
26,360	24,144	21,579	22,266	23,925	18,314	Revenu médian $[57]	463
33,494	31,867	28,368	27,194	30,959	25,493	Revenu moyen $[57]	464
491	319	528	1,070	1,049	1,338	Erreur type de revenu moyen $[57]	465

Nota : Voir les symboles et les abréviations dans les documents d'introduction et voir les documents de référence à la fin de la publication.

Selected characteristics for census divisions and census subdivisions – 100% data and 20% sample data, Ontario, 2006 Census (continued)

No.	Characteristics	Hanover, T	Meaford, MU	Owen Sound, CY ◆A	Southgate, TP ◊	West Grey, MU ◊	Haldimand-Norfolk CD/DR †
	2005 income characteristics						
	Sex and total income groups in 2005 (continued)						
466	Total - Males	2,680	4,550	8,045	2,850	5,020	43,190
467	Without income	60	135	260	110	160	1,520
468	With income	2,620	4,415	7,785	2,735	4,855	41,670
469	Under $1,000[56]	80	180	250	145	210	1,755
470	$1,000 to $2,999	90	105	215	15	150	990
471	$3,000 to $4,999	60	125	225	55	120	875
472	$5,000 to $6,999	65	175	240	55	105	1,110
473	$7,000 to $9,999	90	175	325	150	280	1,675
474	$10,000 to $11,999	40	125	420	120	170	1,255
475	$12,000 to $14,999	100	245	375	85	225	1,935
476	$15,000 to $19,999	265	395	780	210	400	3,295
477	$20,000 to $24,999	245	375	720	255	385	2,855
478	$25,000 to $29,999	255	380	580	190	370	2,995
479	$30,000 to $34,999	200	320	670	135	445	2,990
480	$35,000 to $39,999	215	240	635	190	325	2,705
481	$40,000 to $44,999	150	270	495	110	260	2,540
482	$45,000 to $49,999	115	235	295	165	245	2,170
483	$50,000 to $59,999	190	365	485	305	385	3,515
484	$60,000 and over	460	685	1,075	545	765	9,010
485	Median income $[57]	30,436	29,172	27,761	34,014	30,037	33,306
486	Average income $[57]	37,504	38,211	34,135	39,662	35,299	40,349
487	Standard error of average income $[57]	1,425	1,296	815	1,441	918	489
488	Total - Females	3,140	4,695	9,400	2,780	4,945	44,095
489	Without income	100	185	400	175	210	2,045
490	With income	3,040	4,505	9,000	2,605	4,735	42,050
491	Under $1,000[56]	75	140	265	80	195	1,335
492	$1,000 to $2,999	155	145	275	160	200	2,025
493	$3,000 to $4,999	140	215	345	170	170	1,840
494	$5,000 to $6,999	190	210	390	155	170	2,180
495	$7,000 to $9,999	275	340	795	280	450	3,535
496	$10,000 to $11,999	175	270	535	130	330	2,220
497	$12,000 to $14,999	190	385	735	170	310	3,565
498	$15,000 to $19,999	420	530	1,340	300	580	5,320
499	$20,000 to $24,999	335	440	1,045	210	460	3,980
500	$25,000 to $29,999	280	445	695	155	355	3,130
501	$30,000 to $34,999	210	280	615	225	440	2,870
502	$35,000 to $39,999	135	235	505	100	300	2,465
503	$40,000 to $44,999	95	240	295	80	170	1,680
504	$45,000 to $49,999	95	125	185	70	150	1,205
505	$50,000 to $59,999	105	175	400	95	190	1,640
506	$60,000 and over	165	325	580	215	265	3,060
507	Median income $[57]	18,277	20,132	19,210	17,390	19,494	18,895
508	Average income $[57]	23,688	25,637	24,731	24,463	24,181	24,776
509	Standard error of average income $[57]	827	706	478	1,028	586	226
	Composition of total income						
510	Composition of total income in 2005 %	100.0	100.0	100.0	100.0	100.0	100.0
511	Employment income %	69.5	67.7	66.5	75.7	69.8	74.0
512	Government transfer payments %	16.3	14.1	17.7	12.8	14.2	13.0
513	Other %	14.0	18.2	15.7	11.6	16.0	13.0
514	**Population 15 years and over with employment income in 2005**	**3,915**	**6,330**	**11,555**	**4,080**	**7,305**	**62,555**
	Sex and work activity						
515	Median employment income in 2005 $	24,519	22,660	21,953	25,082	22,126	25,021
516	Average employment income in 2005 $	30,277	30,389	28,135	31,971	27,322	32,235
517	Standard error of average employment income $	1,085	981	553	979	678	340
518	Worked full year, full time[59]	2,095	3,195	5,585	2,230	3,885	31,725
519	Median employment income in 2005 $	36,700	35,059	35,188	37,331	33,813	41,517
520	Average employment income in 2005 $	43,912	42,290	41,267	42,539	37,395	46,897
521	Standard error of average employment income $	1,493	1,622	779	1,293	1,022	563
522	Worked part year or part time[60]	1,575	2,790	5,110	1,625	2,890	26,400
523	Median employment income in 2005 $	8,225	11,336	10,044	9,973	11,448	10,931
524	Average employment income in 2005 $	16,036	19,889	17,314	20,419	17,478	18,716
525	Standard error of average employment income $	1,359	1,046	710	1,347	764	329
526	Males 15 years and over with employment income[58]	2,005	3,305	5,790	2,220	3,870	33,380
527	Median employment income in 2005 $	31,164	26,794	28,122	35,010	28,896	33,357
528	Average employment income in 2005 $	37,329	35,828	33,107	38,030	32,562	39,226
529	Standard error of average employment income $	1,797	1,627	875	1,447	1,086	572

Note: See symbols and abbreviations in the introductory material and see reference material at the end of the publication.

Certaines caractéristiques des divisions de recensement et des subdivisions de recensement – Données intégrales et données-échantillon (20 %), Ontario, Recensement de 2006 (suite)

Haldimand County, CY	Norfolk County, CY ◇	**Haliburton CD/DR** ◆◇	Algonquin Highlands, TP ◆◆◇◇	Dysart and Others, TP ◆◇	Highlands East, MU ◆◇◇	Caractéristiques	N°
						Caractéristiques du revenu de 2005	
						Sexe et groupes de revenu total en 2005 (suite)	
17,790	25,385	6,895	955	2,190	1,350	Total - Hommes	466
725	800	185	15	75	45	Sans revenu	467
17,070	24,585	6,710	940	2,115	1,300	Avec un revenu	468
875	880	245	45	75	60	Moins de 1 000 $[56]	469
385	605	155	0	25	30	1 000 $ à 2 999 $	470
325	545	170	20	65	15	3 000 $ à 4 999 $	471
495	615	140	35	35	20	5 000 $ à 6 999 $	472
645	1,025	300	40	115	50	7 000 $ à 9 999 $	473
410	840	220	20	65	75	10 000 $ à 11 999 $	474
605	1,325	325	15	95	95	12 000 $ à 14 999 $	475
1,050	2,245	850	160	215	200	15 000 $ à 19 999 $	476
1,140	1,715	620	95	130	155	20 000 $ à 24 999 $	477
1,030	1,965	680	115	200	80	25 000 $ à 29 999 $	478
1,185	1,800	525	65	220	110	30 000 $ à 34 999 $	479
1,065	1,635	490	60	160	80	35 000 $ à 39 999 $	480
1,000	1,535	410	55	140	90	40 000 $ à $44 999 $	481
945	1,225	265	55	65	30	45 000 $ à $49 999 $	482
1,650	1,865	480	30	160	95	50 000 $ à $59 999 $	483
4,255	4,755	825	120	345	100	60 000 $ et plus	484
36,608	31,040	27,414	26,397	31,023	22,735	Revenu médian $[57]	485
42,021	39,198	34,116	32,205	38,239	31,395	Revenu moyen $[57]	486
896	550	873	1,691	1,796	2,234	Erreur type de revenu moyen $[57]	487
18,120	25,955	7,085	885	2,415	1,370	Total - Femmes	488
990	1,050	300	20	60	115	Sans revenu	489
17,130	24,905	6,785	865	2,355	1,255	Avec un revenu	490
550	785	205	15	75	65	Moins de 1 000 $[56]	491
860	1,165	270	25	75	60	1 000$ à 2 999 $	492
875	970	310	25	115	75	3 000 $ à 4 999 $	493
1,055	1,120	390	35	135	120	5 000 $ à 6 999 $	494
1,480	2,055	650	145	220	120	7 000 $ à 9 999 $	495
820	1,395	435	50	125	85	10 000 $ à 11 999 $	496
1,230	2,325	595	90	205	115	12 000 $ à 14 999 $	497
1,905	3,415	965	105	270	185	15 000 $ à 19 999 $	498
1,665	2,310	695	70	275	140	20 000 $ à 24 999 $	499
1,255	1,875	640	85	245	100	25 000 $ à 29 999 $	500
1,110	1,760	485	60	205	45	30 000 $ à 34 999 $	501
1,130	1,330	300	75	100	35	35 000 $ à 39 999 $	502
700	980	210	10	100	20	40 000 $ à 44 999 $	503
445	760	170	10	50	35	45 000 $ à 49 999 $	504
710	930	140	10	40	40	50 000 $ à 59 999 $	505
1,335	1,725	325	35	130	20	60 000 $ et plus	506
19,077	18,783	17,835	16,639	19,078	14,916	Revenu médian $[57]	507
24,997	24,629	22,685	21,724	24,429	19,362	Revenu moyen $[57]	508
362	291	575	1,201	1,121	1,391	Erreur type de revenu moyen $[57]	509
						Composition du revenu total	
100.0	100.0	100.0	100.0	100.0	100.0	Composition du revenu total en 2005 %	510
77.9	71.2	58.2	46.7	62.7	54.0	Revenu d'emploi %	511
11.3	14.2	19.7	19.9	16.7	26.3	Transferts gouvernementaux %	512
10.8	14.5	22.0	33.5	20.6	19.6	Autres %	513
26,140	**36,395**	**8,865**	**1,160**	**3,030**	**1,470**	**Population de 15 ans et plus avec un revenu d'emploi en 2005**	514
						Sexe et travail	
27,961	22,659	17,724	14,883	21,058	15,121	Revenu médian d'emploi en 2005 $	515
34,152	30,861	25,158	19,742	28,617	23,994	Revenu moyen d'emploi en 2005 $	516
623	377	690	1,189	1,257	2,212	Erreur type de revenu moyen d'emploi $	517
13,875	17,840	3,645	395	1,370	535	A travaillé toute l'année à plein temps[59]	518
43,805	40,048	32,709	29,336	34,945	27,779	Revenu médian d'emploi en 2005 $	519
48,314	45,809	39,611	33,659	43,724	35,107	Revenu moyen d'emploi en 2005 $	520
1,033	595	1,148	2,432	2,187	2,617	Erreur type de revenu moyen d'emploi $	521
10,540	15,855	4,330	630	1,395	755	A travaillé une partie de l'année ou à temps partiel[60]	522
10,879	10,969	10,454	9,896	10,897	12,024	Revenu médian d'emploi en 2005 $	523
19,717	18,045	16,948	13,341	18,384	20,564	Revenu moyen d'emploi en 2005 $	524
559	404	834	1,027	1,265	3,629	Erreur type de revenu moyen d'emploi $	525
13,890	19,485	4,675	650	1,540	795	Hommes de 15 ans et plus avec un revenu d'emploi[58]	526
38,797	29,898	20,958	15,038	26,098	18,764	Revenu médian d'emploi en 2005 $	527
42,048	37,214	28,683	20,653	33,200	28,135	Revenu moyen d'emploi en 2005 $	528
1,083	606	1,064	1,853	1,900	3,479	Erreur type de revenu moyen d'emploi $	529

Nota : Voir les symboles et les abréviations dans les documents d'introduction et voir les documents de référence à la fin de la publication.

Selected characteristics for census divisions and census subdivisions – 100% data and 20% sample data, Ontario, 2006 Census (continued)

No.	Characteristics	Hanover, T	Meaford, MU	Owen Sound, CY ◆A	Southgate, TP ◊	West Grey, MU ◊	**Haldimand-Norfolk CD/DR** †
	2005 income characteristics						
	Sex and work activity (continued)						
530	Worked full year, full time[59]	1,285	1,850	3,110	1,335	2,360	19,590
531	Median employment income in 2005 $	39,529	38,838	38,365	46,670	37,091	47,512
532	Average employment income in 2005 $	48,442	47,833	45,304	47,513	41,755	52,787
533	Standard error of average employment income $	2,183	2,616	1,161	1,759	1,484	855
534	Worked part year or part time[60]	580	1,265	2,305	750	1,285	11,460
535	Median employment income in 2005 $	10,029	12,672	11,477	15,836	13,107	11,977
536	Average employment income in 2005 $	20,898	22,682	20,594	26,873	20,295	22,470
537	Standard error of average employment income $	2,967	1,659	1,213	2,408	1,377	624
538	Females 15 years and over with employment income[58]	1,910	3,025	5,760	1,855	3,435	29,170
539	Median employment income in 2005 $	16,995	18,999	17,961	18,389	17,374	18,012
540	Average employment income in 2005 $	22,868	24,445	23,136	24,731	21,414	24,234
541	Standard error of average employment income $	1,083	931	653	1,198	695	288
542	Worked full year, full time[59]	810	1,345	2,475	895	1,525	12,135
543	Median employment income in 2005 $	32,102	29,072	31,718	29,954	30,065	33,976
544	Average employment income in 2005 $	36,734	34,674	36,204	35,102	30,649	37,389
545	Standard error of average employment income $	1,623	1,274	941	1,764	1,113	461
546	Worked part year or part time[60]	990	1,520	2,805	875	1,605	14,935
547	Median employment income in 2005 $	7,819	10,513	9,035	8,709	10,629	10,200
548	Average employment income in 2005 $	13,187	17,563	14,619	14,858	15,223	15,835
549	Standard error of average employment income $	1,175	1,289	821	1,320	792	309
550	**Total number of economic families in private households**	**2,030**	**3,380**	**6,020**	**2,020**	**3,620**	**31,220**
	Family income groups in 2005						
551	Under $10,000	25	90	125	35	120	630
552	$10,000 to $19,999	95	115	365	55	145	1,070
553	$20,000 to $29,999	230	310	660	160	320	2,355
554	$30,000 to $39,999	220	390	900	230	375	2,975
555	$40,000 to $49,999	295	420	775	255	395	3,460
556	$50,000 to $59,999	185	420	700	195	500	3,090
557	$60,000 to $69,999	255	335	550	170	315	2,915
558	$70,000 to $79,999	180	275	430	205	320	2,760
559	$80,000 to $89,999	105	305	335	160	240	2,580
560	$90,000 to $99,999	105	120	255	140	230	1,995
561	$100,000 and over	335	595	920	420	660	7,385
562	Median family income $	58,437	58,915	52,378	65,712	58,748	66,691
563	Average family income $	68,014	72,126	63,531	75,306	68,872	76,411
564	Standard error of average family income $	2,403	2,141	1,371	2,576	1,587	764
	Family after-tax income groups in 2005						
565	Under $10,000	20	90	135	35	130	650
566	$10,000 to $19,999	105	125	375	60	150	1,080
567	$20,000 to $29,999	240	350	740	205	360	2,630
568	$30,000 to $39,999	285	500	1,125	300	495	3,960
569	$40,000 to $49,999	350	495	965	285	540	4,285
570	$50,000 to $59,999	265	540	690	245	490	3,950
571	$60,000 to $69,999	220	330	580	230	380	3,660
572	$70,000 to $79,999	165	285	390	215	290	2,905
573	$80,000 to $89,999	105	175	275	105	295	2,380
574	$90,000 to $99,999	85	105	215	90	115	1,870
575	$100,000 and over	175	380	520	255	370	3,855
576	Median after-tax family income $	50,450	51,623	46,513	56,287	51,671	57,353
577	Average after-tax family income $	57,641	60,418	54,213	63,134	58,608	64,188
578	Standard error of average after-tax family income $	1,690	1,475	973	1,918	1,207	540
	Income status in 2005						
579	Total population in private households for income status	6,855	10,685	20,825	7,155	11,990	105,905
580	Below low income cut-off before tax in 2005	705	1,040	3,280	530	1,070	9,245
581	Prevalence of low income before tax in 2005 %	10.3	9.7	15.8	7.4	9.0	8.7
582	Below low income cut-off after tax in 2005	495	630	1,995	405	765	6,085
583	Prevalence of low income after tax in 2005 %	7.3	5.9	9.6	5.7	6.4	5.8

Note: See symbols and abbreviations in the introductory material and see reference material at the end of the publication.

Certaines caractéristiques des divisions de recensement et des subdivisions de recensement – Données intégrales et données-échantillon (20 %), Ontario, Recensement de 2006 (suite)

Haldimand County, CY	Norfolk County, CY ◊	**Haliburton CD/DR** ♦◊	Algonquin Highlands, TP ♦♦◊◊	Dysart and Others, TP ♦◊	Highlands East, MU ♦◊◊	Caractéristiques	N°
						Caractéristiques du revenu de 2005	
						Sexe et travail (suite)	
8,615	10,970	2,175	235	785	380	A travaillé toute l'année à plein temps[59]	530
50,471	44,681	36,013	30,634	40,539	30,121	Revenu médian d'emploi en 2005 $	531
54,262	51,637	42,307	36,178	46,726	34,795	Revenu moyen d'emploi en 2005 $	532
1,584	880	1,520	3,595	2,810	3,005	Erreur type de revenu moyen d'emploi $	533
4,365	7,095	1,920	315	585	295	A travaillé une partie de l'année ou à temps partiel[60]	534
12,391	11,812	12,470	10,038	12,870	14,411	Revenu médian d'emploi en 2005 $	535
25,102	20,840	20,205	13,136	24,080	27,157	Revenu moyen d'emploi en 2005 $	536
1,180	707	1,584	1,452	2,555	7,694	Erreur type de revenu moyen d'emploi $	537
12,245	16,910	4,190	510	1,495	675	Femmes de 15 ans et plus avec un revenu d'emploi[58]	538
19,713	17,061	14,445	11,980	17,039	11,401	Revenu médian d'emploi en 2005 $	539
25,196	23,540	21,221	18,575	23,890	19,119	Revenu moyen d'emploi en 2005 $	540
453	372	843	1,417	1,617	2,522	Erreur type de revenu moyen d'emploi $	541
5,260	6,865	1,475	160	590	150	A travaillé toute l'année à plein temps[59]	542
34,874	32,779	28,017	25,110	29,784	27,559	Revenu médian d'emploi en 2005 $	543
38,573	36,499	35,632	30,007	39,714	35,899	Revenu moyen d'emploi en 2005 $	544
758	571	1,730	2,784	3,414	5,143	Erreur type de revenu moyen d'emploi $	545
6,180	8,755	2,405	320	810	455	A travaillé une partie de l'année ou à temps partiel[60]	546
10,135	10,332	9,303	9,405	9,754	10,368	Revenu médian d'emploi en 2005 $	547
15,915	15,780	14,345	13,542	14,262	16,261	Revenu moyen d'emploi en 2005 $	548
435	430	803	1,442	1,058	3,137	Erreur type de revenu moyen d'emploi $	549
12,980	**18,230**	**5,080**	**680**	**1,675**	**990**	**Nombre total des familles économiques dans les ménages privés**	550
						Revenu de la famille économique en 2005	
295	340	105	10	0	35	Moins de 10 000 $	551
395	675	240	10	75	90	10 000 $ à 19 999 $	552
820	1,530	615	55	210	175	20 000 $ à 29 999 $	553
1,070	1,900	705	115	220	130	30 000 $ à 39 999 $	554
1,365	2,095	665	105	210	150	40 000 $ à 49 999 $	555
1,100	1,990	605	85	210	95	50 000 $ à 59 999 $	556
1,230	1,685	550	65	165	100	60 000 $ à 69 999 $	557
1,205	1,555	425	80	125	50	70 000 $ à 79 999 $	558
1,210	1,365	305	25	100	35	80 000 $ à 89 999 $	559
885	1,115	200	45	60	30	90 000 $ à 99 999 $	560
3,395	3,985	660	90	285	80	100 000 $ et plus	561
71,974	63,617	53,223	54,265	55,689	43,599	Revenu médian des familles $	562
78,914	74,648	63,620	64,063	70,654	53,634	Revenu moyen des familles $	563
1,322	910	1,528	2,864	3,313	3,424	Erreur type de revenu moyen des familles $	564
						Revenu après impôt de la famille économique en 2005	
300	350	135	10	40	40	Moins de 10 000 $	565
400	680	220	10	55	85	10 000 $ à 19 999 $	566
895	1,725	695	65	235	210	20 000 $ à 29 999 $	567
1,445	2,510	865	155	285	145	30 000 $ à 39 999 $	568
1,650	2,635	855	140	260	170	40 000 $ à 49 999 $	569
1,670	2,275	745	75	250	130	50 000 $ à 59 999 $	570
1,620	2,040	485	70	140	60	60 000 $ à 69 999 $	571
1,305	1,595	365	50	115	60	70 000 $ à 79 999 $	572
1,120	1,260	190	35	50	35	80 000 $ à 89 999 $	573
970	905	170	30	45	20	90 000 $ à 99 999 $	574
1,605	2,250	355	45	200	25	100 000 $ et plus	575
60,927	54,949	46,773	48,147	47,590	40,299	Revenu médian après impôt des familles $	576
66,086	62,850	53,622	54,729	57,592	45,778	Revenu moyen après impôt des familles $	577
900	667	1,033	2,197	2,102	2,281	Erreur type de revenu moyen après impôt des familles $	578
						Catégorie de revenu en 2005	
44,480	61,420	15,885	1,950	5,430	3,065	Population totale dans les ménages privés pour la catégorie de revenu	579
3,560	5,680	1,645	130	495	540	Au-dessous du seuil de faible revenu avant impôt en 2005	580
8.0	9.2	10.4	6.9	9.1	17.6	Fréquence du faible revenu avant impôt en 2005 %	581
2,445	3,645	1,105	60	345	405	Au-dessous du seuil de faible revenu après impôt en 2005	582
5.5	5.9	6.9	2.8	6.4	13.1	Fréquence du faible revenu après impôt en 2005 %	583

Nota : Voir les symboles et les abréviations dans les documents d'introduction et voir les documents de référence à la fin de la publication.

Selected characteristics for census divisions and census subdivisions – 100% data and 20% sample data, Ontario, 2006 Census (continued)

No.	Characteristics	Hanover, T	Meaford, MU	Owen Sound, CY ◆A	Southgate, TP ◊	West Grey, MU ◊	**Haldimand-Norfolk CD/DR †**
	2005 income characteristics						
584	**Total number of private households**	**3,045**	**4,445**	**9,380**	**2,560**	**4,725**	**40,580**
	Household income groups in 2005						
585	Under $10,000	110	170	400	95	190	1,315
586	$10,000 to $19,999	395	445	1,525	190	535	3,760
587	$20,000 to $29,999	445	515	1,335	225	530	4,020
588	$30,000 to $39,999	375	505	1,285	315	560	4,360
589	$40,000 to $49,999	380	530	1,060	275	445	4,340
590	$50,000 to $59,999	245	485	890	250	580	3,670
591	$60,000 to $69,999	285	375	690	210	340	3,460
592	$70,000 to $79,999	210	305	555	230	350	3,160
593	$80,000 to $89,999	130	315	380	195	270	2,755
594	$90,000 to $99,999	110	145	300	140	235	2,135
595	$100,000 and over	350	650	975	430	690	7,600
596	Median household income $	44,771	51,634	40,919	56,710	52,119	56,646
597	Average household income $	55,866	63,478	51,952	67,250	60,366	66,926
598	Standard error of average household income $	1,810	1,761	977	2,227	1,332	632
	Household after-tax income groups in 2005						
599	Under $10,000	110	185	430	95	200	1,350
600	$10,000 to $19,999	445	470	1,650	205	565	4,055
601	$20,000 to $29,999	495	590	1,485	310	635	4,710
602	$30,000 to $39,999	455	630	1,540	380	625	5,410
603	$40,000 to $49,999	430	610	1,260	320	620	5,065
604	$50,000 to $59,999	295	575	825	300	520	4,530
605	$60,000 to $69,999	245	350	680	280	430	4,005
606	$70,000 to $79,999	180	310	460	220	315	3,080
607	$80,000 to $89,999	100	205	275	115	305	2,495
608	$90,000 to $99,999	85	120	230	85	125	1,930
609	$100,000 and over	195	395	545	255	380	3,945
610	Median after-tax household income $	40,318	45,401	37,291	49,617	45,745	49,350
611	Average after-tax household income $	47,599	53,209	44,419	56,617	51,548	56,365
612	Standard error of average after-tax household income $	1,310	1,242	718	1,685	1,028	454

Note: See symbols and abbreviations in the introductory material and see reference material at the end of the publication.

Certaines caractéristiques des divisions de recensement et des subdivisions de recensement – Données intégrales et données-échantillon (20 %), Ontario, Recensement de 2006 (suite)

Haldimand County, CY	Norfolk County, CY ◊	**Haliburton CD/DR** ◆◊	Algonquin Highlands, TP ◆◆◊◊	Dysart and Others, TP ◆◊	Highlands East, MU ◆◊◊	**Caractéristiques**	N°
						Caractéristiques du revenu de 2005	
16,315	**24,245**	**6,970**	**870**	**2,350**	**1,375**	**Nombre total des ménages privés**	584
						Tranches de revenu des ménages en 2005	
580	735	300	35	95	80	Moins de 10 000 $	585
1,175	2,580	815	60	290	200	10 000 $ à 19 999 $	586
1,475	2,535	1,010	100	350	240	20 000 $ à 29 999 $	587
1,550	2,805	950	145	285	200	30 000 $ à 39 999 $	588
1,700	2,640	815	115	280	185	40 000 $ à 49 999 $	589
1,385	2,285	745	95	230	140	50 000 $ à 59 999 $	590
1,410	2,045	650	65	210	110	60 000 $ à 69 999 $	591
1,370	1,785	470	90	135	55	70 000 $ à 79 999 $	592
1,280	1,475	320	25	105	40	80 000 $ à 89 999 $	593
925	1,215	205	40	65	30	90 000 $ à 99 999 $	594
3,460	4,135	690	90	305	80	100 000 $ et plus	595
61,776	53,507	45,198	47,450	45,186	38,491	Revenu médian des ménages $	596
70,030	64,867	54,695	56,309	58,910	47,161	Revenu moyen des ménages $	597
1,102	755	1,212	2,519	2,603	2,583	Erreur type de revenu moyen des ménages $	598
						Tranches du revenu après impôt des ménages en 2005	
595	750	340	35	135	85	Moins de 10 000 $	599
1,290	2,760	870	65	285	215	10 000 $ à 19 999 $	600
1,680	3,030	1,180	120	415	290	20 000 $ à 29 999 $	601
2,000	3,410	1,080	180	330	205	30 000 $ à 39 999 $	602
1,995	3,065	990	150	295	210	40 000 $ à 49 999 $	603
1,895	2,630	890	90	300	150	50 000 $ à 59 999 $	604
1,730	2,270	505	70	150	60	60 000 $ à 69 999 $	605
1,360	1,720	375	50	115	65	70 000 $ à 79 999 $	606
1,145	1,345	190	30	50	35	80 000 $ à 89 999 $	607
990	940	190	30	55	15	90 000 $ à 99 999 $	608
1,630	2,315	370	40	210	30	100 000 $ et plus	609
53,068	46,793	40,321	42,531	40,971	34,855	Revenu médian après impôt des ménages $	610
58,793	54,754	46,270	48,118	48,453	40,382	Revenu moyen après impôt des ménages $	611
764	560	846	1,970	1,719	1,757	Erreur type de revenu moyen après impôt des ménages $	612

Nota : Voir les symboles et les abréviations dans les documents d'introduction et voir les documents de référence à la fin de la publication.

Selected characteristics for census divisions and census subdivisions – 100% data and 20% sample data, Ontario, 2006 Census (continued)

No.	Characteristics	Minden Hills, TP ◆◊	**Halton CD/DR**	Burlington, CY	Halton Hills, T	Milton, T	Oakville, T
	Population characteristics						
1	**Population, 2001[1]**	**5,312**	**375,229**	**150,836**	**48,184**	**31,471**	**144,738**
2	**Population, 2006[2]**	**5,556**	**439,256**	**164,415**	**55,289**	**53,939**	**165,613**
3	Population percentage change, 2001 to 2006	4.6	17.1	9.0	14.7	71.4	14.4
4	Land area in square kilometres, 2006	847.76	967.17	185.74	276.26	366.61	138.56
5	**Total population – 100% data[3]**	**5,555**	**439,255**	**164,415**	**55,290**	**53,940**	**165,615**
	Sex and age groups						
6	Male	2,795	213,650	78,985	27,435	26,925	80,305
7	0 to 4 years	105	14,295	4,765	1,850	2,340	5,335
8	5 to 9 years	125	14,595	4,970	2,130	1,790	5,705
9	10 to 14 years	165	16,165	5,520	2,330	1,825	6,490
10	15 to 19 years	195	15,105	5,285	1,970	1,565	6,295
11	20 to 24 years	125	12,620	4,565	1,435	1,645	4,965
12	25 to 29 years	95	11,235	4,320	1,215	2,040	3,655
13	30 to 34 years	105	14,280	5,180	1,695	2,815	4,595
14	35 to 39 years	115	16,900	6,000	2,280	2,455	6,170
15	40 to 44 years	175	19,245	6,770	2,940	2,230	7,300
16	45 to 49 years	230	17,855	6,390	2,460	1,895	7,110
17	50 to 54 years	220	14,605	5,265	1,875	1,620	5,850
18	55 to 59 years	265	12,850	5,020	1,535	1,605	4,685
19	60 to 64 years	215	9,985	4,080	1,215	1,085	3,610
20	65 to 69 years	225	7,410	3,170	890	705	2,645
21	70 to 74 years	190	6,160	2,770	625	520	2,240
22	75 to 79 years	140	5,115	2,435	530	395	1,765
23	80 to 84 years	75	3,220	1,550	275	245	1,150
24	85 years and over	35	1,995	920	180	150	745
25	Female	2,760	225,600	85,425	27,855	27,010	85,305
26	0 to 4 years	90	13,550	4,540	1,750	2,240	5,025
27	5 to 9 years	100	13,995	4,760	2,115	1,625	5,490
28	10 to 14 years	135	15,270	5,230	2,150	1,690	6,195
29	15 to 19 years	165	14,420	5,220	1,765	1,475	5,970
30	20 to 24 years	115	12,160	4,490	1,375	1,405	4,890
31	25 to 29 years	85	12,340	4,645	1,350	2,375	3,970
32	30 to 34 years	120	15,685	5,625	1,810	2,830	5,420
33	35 to 39 years	110	18,290	6,350	2,530	2,365	7,045
34	40 to 44 years	185	20,330	7,330	2,920	2,210	7,865
35	45 to 49 years	240	18,765	6,740	2,375	1,895	7,750
36	50 to 54 years	235	15,455	5,880	1,755	1,740	6,080
37	55 to 59 years	240	13,885	5,620	1,580	1,645	5,035
38	60 to 64 years	225	10,515	4,480	1,245	1,045	3,740
39	65 to 69 years	230	8,175	3,665	910	710	2,885
40	70 to 74 years	170	7,140	3,345	725	540	2,525
41	75 to 79 years	145	6,230	2,970	645	470	2,150
42	80 to 84 years	100	5,055	2,445	480	395	1,730
43	85 years and over	70	4,350	2,085	360	360	1,535
44	**Total population 15 years and over[3]**	**4,845**	**351,380**	**134,630**	**42,955**	**42,435**	**131,365**
	Legal marital status						
45	Never legally married (single)	1,045	95,780	36,605	11,380	11,535	36,250
46	Legally married (and not separated)[4,5]	2,700	204,150	75,190	25,495	25,505	77,965
47	Separated, but still legally married	235	10,725	4,575	1,400	1,305	3,445
48	Divorced	450	21,740	9,630	2,620	2,375	7,120
49	Widowed	420	18,995	8,630	2,060	1,720	6,590
	Common-law status						
50	Not in a common-law relationship	4,355	330,320	125,745	39,995	39,105	125,470
51	In a common-law relationship	490	21,065	8,880	2,965	3,325	5,890
52	**Total population – 20% sample data[6]**	**5,500**	**435,395**	**162,480**	**55,025**	**53,405**	**164,490**
	Mother tongue						
53	Single responses	5,480	430,535	161,085	54,615	52,725	162,105
54	English	4,935	341,670	133,020	47,765	41,430	119,460
55	French	110	8,110	2,985	1,030	945	3,145
56	Non-official languages[7]	440	80,750	25,080	5,820	10,355	39,500
57	Italian	20	7,125	2,160	615	910	3,440
58	Chinese, n.o.s.[61]	0	2,850	785	45	210	1,805
59	Cantonese	0	1,510	330	80	285	815
60	Spanish	10	4,975	1,530	390	805	2,245
61	German	150	5,110	1,895	565	485	2,160
62	Other languages[8]	265	59,175	18,370	4,120	7,655	29,030

Note: See symbols and abbreviations in the introductory material and see reference material at the end of the publication.

Certaines caractéristiques des divisions de recensement et des subdivisions de recensement – Données intégrales et données-échantillon (20 %), Ontario, Recensement de 2006 (suite)

Hamilton CD/DR	Hamilton, C ■■	**Hastings CD/DR** †◆◊	Bancroft, T ◆	Belleville, CY ◊**A**	Carlow/Mayo, TP ◆◆◊◊	**Caractéristiques**	N°
						Caractéristiques de la population	
490,268	**490,268**	**125,915**	**4,089**	**46,029**	**833**	**Population, 2001**[1]	1
504,559	**504,559**	**130,474**	**3,838**	**48,821**	**950**	**Population, 2006**[2]	2
X	X	3.6	-6.1	6.1	14.0	Variation en pourcentage de la population, 2001 à 2006	3
1,117.21	1,117.21	5,977.64	227.84	246.76	388.36	Superficie des terres en kilomètres carrés, 2006	4
504,560	**504,560**	**130,475**	**3,840**	**48,820**	**950**	**Population totale – Données intégrales**[3]	5
						Sexe et groupes d'âge	
245,685	245,685	63,780	1,785	23,120	480	Sexe masculin	6
13,785	13,785	3,260	90	1,200	20	0 à 4 ans	7
15,140	15,145	3,625	85	1,290	35	5 à 9 ans	8
17,230	17,225	4,550	130	1,535	25	10 à 14 ans	9
17,805	17,805	4,745	120	1,720	30	15 à 19 ans	10
17,340	17,335	3,800	85	1,640	20	20 à 24 ans	11
14,795	14,800	3,285	70	1,450	25	25 à 29 ans	12
14,935	14,940	3,290	70	1,315	20	30 à 34 ans	13
17,020	17,020	3,880	95	1,350	20	35 à 39 ans	14
20,335	20,340	5,365	115	1,800	40	40 à 44 ans	15
20,305	20,310	5,270	145	1,835	40	45 à 49 ans	16
17,570	17,570	4,735	150	1,690	40	50 à 54 ans	17
15,475	15,475	4,610	150	1,515	40	55 à 59 ans	18
11,740	11,740	3,645	115	1,200	40	60 à 64 ans	19
9,390	9,390	3,025	85	985	25	65 à 69 ans	20
8,205	8,205	2,610	85	915	30	70 à 74 ans	21
6,930	6,930	2,055	90	780	25	75 à 79 ans	22
4,860	4,855	1,255	60	535	10	80 à 84 ans	23
2,825	2,825	775	40	360	5	85 ans et plus	24
258,870	258,875	66,695	2,055	25,700	470	Sexe féminin	25
13,160	13,160	3,180	80	1,250	20	0 à 4 ans	26
14,270	14,270	3,465	90	1,250	25	5 à 9 ans	27
16,310	16,310	4,240	110	1,475	30	10 à 14 ans	28
17,090	17,090	4,440	135	1,650	30	15 à 19 ans	29
17,050	17,050	3,695	100	1,715	15	20 à 24 ans	30
15,530	15,530	3,365	85	1,510	25	25 à 29 ans	31
15,680	15,685	3,525	95	1,375	20	30 à 34 ans	32
17,745	17,740	4,040	75	1,450	25	35 à 39 ans	33
20,890	20,890	5,425	160	1,925	30	40 à 44 ans	34
20,530	20,530	5,385	150	1,970	45	45 à 49 ans	35
18,550	18,550	4,970	160	1,845	30	50 à 54 ans	36
16,390	16,390	4,775	155	1,675	40	55 à 59 ans	37
12,490	12,490	3,850	125	1,325	35	60 à 64 ans	38
10,350	10,350	3,280	120	1,135	30	65 à 69 ans	39
9,655	9,655	2,850	115	1,125	35	70 à 74 ans	40
9,275	9,275	2,385	110	1,095	10	75 à 79 ans	41
7,760	7,760	2,020	100	975	5	80 à 84 ans	42
6,150	6,150	1,820	85	970	10	85 ans et plus	43
414,670	**414,670**	**108,155**	**3,245**	**40,820**	**795**	**Population totale de 15 ans et plus**[3]	44
						État matrimonial légal	
132,960	132,960	30,245	830	12,650	185	Jamais légalement marié(e) (célibataire)	45
206,235	206,235	56,080	1,620	19,210	460	Légalement marié(e) (et non séparé[e])[4,5]	46
15,035	15,035	4,555	150	1,795	25	Séparé(e), mais toujours légalement marié(e)	47
31,250	31,250	8,985	250	3,645	65	Divorcé(e)	48
29,190	29,190	8,295	395	3,520	55	Veuf(ve)	49
						Union libre	
386,360	386,360	97,340	2,975	36,680	720	Ne vivant pas en union libre	50
28,310	28,310	10,810	275	4,135	70	Vivant en union libre	51
497,395	**497,400**	**128,790**	**3,720**	**47,875**	**950**	**Population totale – Données-échantillon (20 %)**[6]	52
						Langue maternelle	
491,215	491,215	128,290	3,715	47,670	950	Réponses uniques	53
363,115	363,115	118,570	3,590	43,485	905	Anglais	54
6,415	6,415	3,015	30	715	30	Français	55
121,685	121,685	6,700	90	3,475	15	Langues non officielles[7]	56
18,330	18,325	335	0	200	0	Italien	57
4,820	4,820	440	0	375	0	Chinois, n.d.a.[61]	58
1,385	1,380	100	0	60	0	Cantonais	59
5,855	5,850	445	10	315	0	Espagnol	60
5,335	5,335	970	30	290	0	Allemand	61
85,965	85,960	4,405	50	2,225	0	Autres langues[8]	62

Nota : Voir les symboles et les abréviations dans les documents d'introduction et voir les documents de référence à la fin de la publication.

Selected characteristics for census divisions and census subdivisions – 100% data and 20% sample data, Ontario, 2006 Census (continued)

No.	Characteristics	Minden Hills, TP ◆◊	**Halton CD/DR**	Burlington, CY	Halton Hills, T	Milton, T	Oakville, T
	Population characteristics						
	Mother tongue (continued)						
63	Multiple responses	15	4,865	1,395	405	680	2,380
64	English and French	10	715	280	75	75	285
65	English and non-official language	15	3,920	1,005	300	580	2,025
66	French and non-official language	0	160	90	20	25	30
67	English, French and non-official language	0	70	20	10	0	40
	Language spoken most often at home[9]						
68	Single responses	5,500	428,880	160,790	54,565	52,410	161,115
69	English	5,400	391,255	149,660	52,375	47,190	142,035
70	French	0	3,105	1,080	390	360	1,275
71	Non-official languages[7]	100	34,515	10,050	1,805	4,850	17,805
72	Chinese, n.o.s.[61]	0	1,780	475	25	150	1,130
73	Cantonese	0	970	205	65	150	550
74	Panjabi (Punjabi)	20	2,660	1,075	20	330	1,235
75	Italian	0	1,360	350	120	180	710
76	Spanish	0	2,665	845	145	470	1,205
77	Other languages[8]	80	25,075	7,090	1,430	3,570	12,980
78	Multiple responses	0	6,515	1,690	455	1,000	3,370
79	English and French	0	520	140	75	40	260
80	English and non-official language	0	5,910	1,490	365	955	3,090
81	French and non-official language	0	40	25	10	0	10
82	English, French and non-official language	0	50	35	0	0	15
	Knowledge of official languages[10]						
83	English only	5,260	388,150	145,935	50,230	48,545	143,445
84	French only	0	340	150	10	55	125
85	English and French	235	43,560	15,570	4,565	4,295	19,130
86	Neither English nor French	10	3,340	835	215	510	1,785
	Knowledge of non-official languages[7,11]						
87	Italian	20	10,880	3,185	1,025	1,410	5,260
88	Spanish	50	9,165	2,885	745	1,205	4,335
89	German	160	8,450	3,095	800	775	3,785
90	Chinese, n.o.s.[61]	0	2,830	815	45	210	1,755
91	Cantonese	0	2,020	410	110	330	1,175
92	Panjabi (Punjabi)	20	5,660	2,050	140	850	2,615
93	Portuguese	0	7,315	1,395	820	860	4,245
	First official language spoken[10]						
94	English	5,380	422,125	158,070	53,665	51,820	158,575
95	French	100	8,145	3,005	1,020	970	3,145
96	English and French	15	1,915	590	130	165	1,030
97	Neither English nor French	0	3,215	815	210	455	1,735
98	Official language minority - (number)[12]	105	9,100	3,300	1,085	1,050	3,665
99	Official language minority - (percentage)[12]	1.9	2.1	2.0	2.0	2.0	2.2
	Ethnic origin[13]						
100	English	2,315	144,515	59,330	21,000	16,265	47,920
101	Canadian	1,590	98,720	39,095	15,920	13,030	30,675
102	Scottish	1,525	99,975	39,605	14,925	11,390	34,055
103	Irish	1,585	88,140	33,855	12,525	10,960	30,795
104	French	475	40,010	15,980	5,640	4,475	13,905
105	German	670	43,555	16,640	6,215	5,205	15,490
106	Italian	120	35,525	11,430	4,165	4,730	15,195
107	Chinese	10	10,640	2,640	470	1,180	6,355
108	East Indian	40	15,140	4,230	600	2,065	8,245
109	Dutch (Netherlands)	245	21,185	8,570	3,785	2,850	5,985
110	Polish	185	22,300	8,120	2,620	2,690	8,865
111	Ukrainian	185	16,660	6,990	1,695	1,545	6,435
112	North American Indian	185	5,225	2,035	925	735	1,530
113	Portuguese	10	12,865	2,875	1,510	1,745	6,730
114	Filipino	15	4,845	910	240	1,255	2,435
	Aboriginal and non-Aboriginal identity						
115	Total Aboriginal identity population[14]	205	2,640	1,070	480	425	665
116	Total non-Aboriginal identity population	5,295	432,760	161,415	54,545	52,980	163,820

Note: See symbols and abbreviations in the introductory material and see reference material at the end of the publication.

Certaines caractéristiques des divisions de recensement et des subdivisions de recensement – Données intégrales et données-échantillon (20 %), Ontario, Recensement de 2006 (suite)

Hamilton CD/DR	Hamilton, C ■■	**Hastings CD/DR** †◆◇	Bancroft, T ◆	Belleville, CY ◇**A**	Carlow/Mayo, TP ◆◆◇◇	**Caractéristiques**	N°
						Caractéristiques de la population	
						Langue maternelle (suite)	
6,185	6,180	505	10	205	0	Réponses multiples	63
825	820	215	10	80	0	Anglais et français	64
4,955	4,955	265	10	125	0	Anglais et langue non officielle	65
285	285	10	0	0	0	Français et langue non officielle	66
120	120	20	0	0	0	Anglais, français et langue non officielle	67
						Langue parlée le plus souvent à la maison[9]	
487,370	487,370	128,195	3,720	47,520	950	Réponses uniques	68
423,205	423,205	124,820	3,715	46,025	920	Anglais	69
1,840	1,840	1,370	10	140	25	Français	70
62,325	62,325	2,005	0	1,355	0	Langues non officielles[7]	71
3,625	3,625	255	0	230	0	Chinois, n.d.a.[61]	72
1,110	1,110	70	0	45	0	Cantonais	73
3,480	3,480	90	0	40	0	Pendjabi	74
7,320	7,320	90	0	85	0	Italien	75
3,380	3,380	210	0	180	0	Espagnol	76
43,415	43,410	1,290	0	775	0	Autres langues[8]	77
10,025	10,025	600	0	360	0	Réponses multiples	78
575	575	100	0	30	0	Anglais et français	79
9,275	9,275	460	0	325	0	Anglais et langue non officielle	80
70	70	10	0	0	0	Français et langue non officielle	81
100	100	25	0	0	0	Anglais, français et langue non officielle	82
						Connaissance des langues officielles[10]	
458,580	458,580	120,505	3,550	44,865	915	Anglais seulement	83
370	365	160	0	0	0	Français seulement	84
29,955	29,950	7,885	170	2,820	40	Anglais et français	85
8,495	8,495	245	0	195	0	Ni l'anglais ni le français	86
						Connaissance des langues non officielles[7,11]	
24,805	24,805	515	0	320	0	Italien	87
9,455	9,455	960	20	505	0	Espagnol	88
8,580	8,575	1,505	40	530	0	Allemand	89
4,950	4,950	435	0	365	0	Chinois, n.d.a.[61]	90
1,820	1,825	130	0	70	0	Cantonais	91
5,780	5,785	160	0	95	0	Pendjabi	92
10,125	10,125	200	0	115	0	Portugais	93
						Première langue officielle parlée[10]	
480,360	480,355	125,560	3,690	46,965	915	Anglais	94
6,430	6,430	2,890	30	665	35	Français	95
2,315	2,315	110	0	60	0	Anglais et français	96
8,295	8,295	230	0	185	0	Ni l'anglais ni le français	97
7,590	7,590	2,950	25	695	30	Minorité de langue officielle - (nombre)[12]	98
1.5	1.5	2.3	0.7	1.5	3.2	Minorité de langue officielle - (pourcentage)[12]	99
						Origine ethnique[13]	
138,125	138,125	48,425	1,695	17,485	390	Anglais	100
107,780	107,780	50,170	1,370	18,460	445	Canadien	101
98,370	98,370	31,285	1,150	10,775	315	Écossais	102
80,740	80,740	33,075	1,205	12,000	170	Irlandais	103
42,070	42,070	17,550	385	5,615	115	Français	104
47,960	47,960	14,270	730	4,880	210	Allemand	105
58,805	58,800	3,080	80	1,365	10	Italien	106
10,850	10,850	925	0	645	0	Chinois	107
10,570	10,570	640	0	425	0	Indien de l'Inde	108
25,720	25,720	9,590	185	3,205	25	Hollandais (Néerlandais)	109
27,775	27,775	2,735	115	900	55	Polonais	110
18,735	18,735	2,440	50	745	50	Ukrainien	111
11,970	11,970	6,005	245	1,985	30	Indien de l'Amérique du Nord	112
14,120	14,115	525	0	215	0	Portugais	113
4,660	4,660	245	10	180	0	Philippin	114
						Population ayant une identité autochtone et population n'ayant pas d'identité autochtone	
7,630	7,625	4,840	430	1,385	45	Total de la population ayant une identité autochtone[14]	115
489,770	489,770	123,955	3,290	46,495	905	Total de la population n'ayant pas d'identité autochtone	116

Nota : Voir les symboles et les abréviations dans les documents d'introduction et voir les documents de référence à la fin de la publication.

Selected characteristics for census divisions and census subdivisions – 100% data and 20% sample data, Ontario, 2006 Census (continued)

No.	Characteristics	Minden Hills, TP ◆◊	**Halton CD/DR**	Burlington, CY	Halton Hills, T	Milton, T	Oakville, T
	Population characteristics						
	Aboriginal and non-Aboriginal ancestry						
117	Total Aboriginal ancestry population[15]	325	6,595	2,635	1,120	960	1,875
118	Total non-Aboriginal ancestry population	5,175	428,805	159,845	53,900	52,450	162,605
	Registered Indian status						
119	Registered Indian[16]	40	800	280	130	120	270
120	Not a Registered Indian	5,460	434,600	162,200	54,890	53,290	164,220
	Visible minority groups						
121	Total visible minority population[17]	75	57,360	15,690	2,235	9,115	30,315
122	Chinese	0	8,665	2,255	330	815	5,260
123	South Asian[18]	30	18,570	5,030	490	3,105	9,940
124	Black	10	8,100	2,450	420	1,695	3,535
125	Filipino	15	4,465	815	215	1,165	2,270
126	Latin American	15	3,760	1,135	285	695	1,640
127	Southeast Asian[19]	0	1,840	740	65	180	860
128	Arab	0	3,150	1,090	55	395	1,600
129	West Asian[20]	0	1,860	455	30	225	1,145
130	Korean	0	2,630	635	45	145	1,805
131	Japanese	0	1,115	390	135	75	515
132	Visible minority, n.i.e.[21]	0	1,100	250	50	155	650
133	Multiple visible minority[22]	10	2,105	440	110	460	1,095
	Citizenship[23]						
134	Canadian citizens[24]	5,360	410,195	154,270	53,225	50,495	152,210
135	Not Canadian citizens[25]	140	25,200	8,210	1,800	2,910	12,280
	Immigrant status and place of birth[26]						
136	Non-immigrants[27]	4,890	324,325	125,475	46,385	40,070	112,390
137	Born in province of residence	4,535	274,035	106,630	40,325	34,735	92,340
138	Immigrants[28]	605	107,915	36,275	8,360	13,030	50,250
139	United States of America	10	4,955	1,760	405	545	2,245
140	Central and South America	10	5,235	1,525	270	775	2,660
141	Caribbean and Bermuda	10	4,485	1,245	220	915	2,100
142	United Kingdom	275	25,430	11,090	2,800	2,470	9,075
143	Other Europe	255	35,850	11,695	3,650	3,925	16,575
144	Africa	10	4,880	1,410	170	530	2,770
145	Asia and the Middle East	30	26,385	7,310	775	3,835	14,470
146	Oceania and other[29]	15	695	240	75	30	340
147	Non-permanent residents[30]	10	3,155	725	280	300	1,845
148	**Total immigrant population[28]**	**605**	**107,920**	**36,275**	**8,360**	**13,030**	**50,250**
	Period of immigration						
149	Before 1961	265	18,555	8,080	2,125	1,680	6,670
150	1961 to 1970	175	17,830	6,675	1,810	1,540	7,805
151	1971 to 1980	60	19,145	5,960	1,610	2,345	9,225
152	1981 to 1990	10	15,820	4,745	1,200	1,865	8,010
153	1991 to 2000	65	23,460	6,790	1,155	3,795	11,720
154	1991 to 1995	45	10,685	3,130	665	1,840	5,050
155	1996 to 2000	15	12,770	3,660	490	1,955	6,670
156	2001 to 2006[31]	25	13,105	4,025	450	1,810	6,820
	Age at immigration						
157	Under 5 years	55	11,900	3,925	1,120	1,495	5,360
158	5 to 19 years	250	31,015	9,890	2,800	3,945	14,380
159	20 years and over	295	65,005	22,460	4,440	7,585	30,510
160	**Total population 15 years and over**	**4,805**	**347,505**	**132,695**	**42,695**	**41,910**	**130,200**
	Generation status						
161	1st generation[32]	605	105,535	35,620	8,460	12,600	48,855
162	2nd generation[33]	755	85,680	33,265	10,120	9,805	32,490
163	3rd generation or more[34]	3,445	156,290	63,810	24,115	19,505	48,855

Note: See symbols and abbreviations in the introductory material and see reference material at the end of the publication.

Certaines caractéristiques des divisions de recensement et des subdivisions de recensement – Données intégrales et données-échantillon (20 %), Ontario, Recensement de 2006 (suite)

Hamilton CD/DR	Hamilton, C ■ ■	**Hastings CD/DR** †◆◊	Bancroft, T ◆	Belleville, CY ◊**A**	Carlow/Mayo, TP ◆◆◊◊	**Caractéristiques**	N°
						Caractéristiques de la population	
						Population ayant une ascendance autochtone et population n'ayant pas d'ascendance autochtone	
13,735	13,735	7,995	550	2,430	90	Total de la population ayant une ascendance autochtone[15]	117
483,660	483,665	120,795	3,170	45,445	855	Total de la population n'ayant pas d'ascendance autochtone	118
						Statut d'Indien inscrit	
3,260	3,260	1,735	65	640	0	Indien inscrit[16]	119
494,135	494,140	127,060	3,655	47,240	950	Pas un Indien inscrit	120
						Groupes de minorités visibles	
67,845	67,845	3,750	25	2,560	0	Total de la population des minorités visibles[17]	121
9,300	9,300	790	0	625	0	Chinois	122
14,765	14,765	660	0	510	0	Sud-Asiatique[18]	123
13,900	13,900	775	10	435	0	Noir	124
4,045	4,040	230	10	140	0	Philippin	125
5,585	5,590	330	0	255	0	Latino-Américain	126
5,995	6,000	250	0	190	0	Asiatique du Sud-Est[19]	127
5,390	5,390	45	0	30	0	Arabe	128
3,450	3,450	60	0	55	0	Asiatique occidental[20]	129
1,540	1,545	220	0	85	0	Coréen	130
980	980	115	10	65	0	Japonais	131
1,045	1,045	115	0	95	0	Minorité visible, n.i.a.[21]	132
1,845	1,840	155	0	70	0	Minorités visibles multiples[22]	133
						Citoyenneté[23]	
467,330	467,330	126,615	3,650	46,680	930	Citoyens canadiens[24]	134
30,070	30,070	2,180	75	1,200	20	Ne sont pas des citoyens canadiens[25]	135
						Statut d'immigrant et le lieu de naissance[26]	
366,315	366,315	118,070	3,490	42,860	890	Non-immigrants[27]	136
332,105	332,105	102,525	3,265	38,145	835	Né dans la province de résidence	137
126,485	126,485	10,280	225	4,720	60	Immigrants[28]	138
3,985	3,990	820	35	325	10	États-Unis d'Amérique	139
5,440	5,435	390	0	240	0	Amérique centrale et Amérique du Sud	140
4,685	4,685	275	10	90	0	Antilles et Bermudes	141
17,070	17,070	3,395	95	1,405	20	Royaume-Uni	142
59,440	59,440	3,580	90	1,295	20	Autre Europe	143
4,645	4,645	235	0	165	0	Afrique	144
30,735	30,740	1,505	0	1,170	0	Asie et Moyen-Orient	145
485	485	80	0	25	10	Océanie et autres[29]	146
4,595	4,595	440	0	300	0	Résidents non permanents[30]	147
126,485	**126,485**	**10,285**	**225**	**4,720**	**60**	**Population totale des immigrants[28]**	148
						Période d'immigration	
26,165	26,170	4,120	125	1,460	35	Avant 1961	149
21,140	21,140	1,885	50	715	15	1961 à 1970	150
17,500	17,500	1,170	30	630	10	1971 à 1980	151
18,180	18,185	1,090	15	560	0	1981 à 1990	152
26,935	26,940	1,235	10	820	0	1991 à 2000	153
13,045	13,045	635	10	365	0	1991 à 1995	154
13,890	13,890	600	0	455	0	1996 à 2000	155
16,560	16,560	775	10	535	0	2001 à 2006[31]	156
						Âge à l'immigration	
12,465	12,465	1,335	25	545	10	Moins de 5 ans	157
37,130	37,130	3,115	65	1,315	20	5 à 19 ans	158
76,895	76,890	5,840	135	2,850	30	20 ans et plus	159
407,590	**407,590**	**106,580**	**3,130**	**39,925**	**790**	**Population totale de 15 ans et plus**	160
						Statut des générations	
125,230	125,230	10,680	230	4,870	60	1re génération[32]	161
99,005	99,000	14,230	400	5,270	40	2e génération[33]	162
183,360	183,360	81,670	2,495	29,785	685	3e génération ou plus[34]	163

Nota : Voir les symboles et les abréviations dans les documents d'introduction et voir les documents de référence à la fin de la publication.

Selected characteristics for census divisions and census subdivisions – 100% data and 20% sample data, Ontario, 2006 Census (continued)

No.	Characteristics	Minden Hills, TP ◆◊	**Halton CD/DR**	Burlington, CY	Halton Hills, T	Milton, T	Oakville, T
	Population characteristics						
164	**Total population 1 year and over[35]**	**5,480**	**429,775**	**160,430**	**54,415**	**52,395**	**162,535**
	Place of residence 1 year ago (mobility)						
165	Non-movers	4,910	372,585	139,645	47,660	42,150	143,130
166	Movers	570	57,190	20,785	6,750	10,245	19,405
167	Non-migrants	260	24,410	10,505	2,740	2,820	8,340
168	Migrants	310	32,775	10,280	4,010	7,420	11,065
169	Internal migrants	300	29,110	9,145	3,830	7,045	9,090
170	Intraprovincial migrants	290	26,890	8,470	3,690	6,760	7,970
171	Interprovincial migrants	0	2,220	675	140	285	1,120
172	External migrants	10	3,665	1,130	185	375	1,975
173	**Total population 5 years and over[36]**	**5,325**	**407,405**	**153,105**	**51,420**	**48,815**	**154,065**
	Place of residence 5 years ago (mobility)						
174	Non-movers	3,405	228,860	90,500	30,270	19,910	88,180
175	Movers	1,920	178,545	62,605	21,150	28,905	65,885
176	Non-migrants	790	71,335	29,950	8,480	5,875	27,030
177	Migrants	1,130	107,210	32,660	12,665	23,035	38,850
178	Internal migrants	1,100	91,850	27,960	11,945	21,415	30,525
179	Intraprovincial migrants	1,060	85,130	25,710	11,180	20,555	27,685
180	Interprovincial migrants	40	6,720	2,245	765	865	2,845
181	External migrants	30	15,360	4,700	725	1,615	8,325
182	**Total population 15 years and over**	**4,805**	**347,505**	**132,695**	**42,700**	**41,910**	**130,205**
	Highest certificate, diploma or degree[37]						
183	No certificate, diploma or degree	1,210	54,410	20,930	8,065	6,905	18,515
184	Certificate, diploma or degree	3,600	293,095	111,765	34,635	35,010	111,685
185	High school certificate or equivalent[38]	1,480	90,945	35,845	12,710	11,065	31,325
186	Apprenticeship or trades certificate or diploma	675	22,560	9,090	3,455	3,195	6,820
187	College, CEGEP or other non-university certificate or diploma[39]	855	71,815	29,415	9,445	9,230	23,725
188	University certificate or diploma below bachelor level[40]	85	16,450	5,930	1,295	1,870	7,355
189	University certificate or degree[41]	495	91,320	31,480	7,735	9,645	42,465
190	Bachelor's degree	330	59,100	20,770	5,235	6,360	26,735
191	University certificate or diploma above bachelor level	55	10,855	3,750	1,060	1,260	4,780
192	Degree in medicine, dentistry, veterinary medicine or optometry	25	2,075	825	130	200	925
193	Master's degree	70	16,865	5,165	1,165	1,650	8,885
194	Earned doctorate	20	2,425	960	140	170	1,140
195	**Total population 15 years and over with postsecondary qualifications**	**2,120**	**202,150**	**75,920**	**21,920**	**23,940**	**80,360**
	Major field of study - Classification of Instructional Programs, 2000[42]						
196	Education	175	13,970	5,460	1,500	1,710	5,300
197	Visual and performing arts, and communications technologies	45	8,595	3,090	785	945	3,770
198	Humanities	65	11,845	4,585	1,045	1,195	5,025
199	Social and behavioural sciences and law	210	25,785	9,325	2,550	2,855	11,055
200	Business, management and public administration	340	52,125	19,255	4,930	5,420	22,525
201	Physical and life sciences and technologies	45	8,150	2,905	890	975	3,375
202	Mathematics, computer and information sciences	40	8,830	2,915	850	1,245	3,820
203	Architecture, engineering, and related technologies	650	38,025	14,125	5,310	5,075	13,515
204	Agriculture, natural resources and conservation	80	2,740	975	470	470	820
205	Health, parks, recreation and fitness	325	22,515	9,460	2,320	2,465	8,270
206	Personal, protective and transportation services	140	9,550	3,810	1,275	1,580	2,885
207	Other fields of study[43]	0	15	10	0	0	0
	Location of study[44]						
208	Inside Canada	1,880	162,870	62,835	19,535	19,415	61,080
209	Outside Canada	235	39,275	13,080	2,390	4,525	19,280
210	**Total population 15 years and over**	**4,805**	**347,505**	**132,695**	**42,700**	**41,910**	**130,205**
	Unpaid work						
211	Males 15 years and over	2,395	167,260	63,145	21,050	20,640	62,425
212	Reported unpaid work[45]	2,165	152,050	57,355	19,400	18,975	56,315
213	Housework and child care and care or assistance to seniors	145	13,840	4,940	1,940	1,545	5,410
214	Housework and child care only	430	49,255	17,225	6,745	6,470	18,825

Note: See symbols and abbreviations in the introductory material and see reference material at the end of the publication.

Certaines caractéristiques des divisions de recensement et des subdivisions de recensement – Données intégrales et données-échantillon (20 %), Ontario, Recensement de 2006 (suite)

Hamilton CD/DR	Hamilton, C ■■	**Hastings CD/DR** †◆◊	Bancroft, T ◆	Belleville, CY ◊A	Carlow/Mayo, TP ◆◆◊◊	**Caractéristiques**	N°
						Caractéristiques de la population	
491,935	**491,935**	**127,415**	**3,685**	**47,370**	**945**	**Population totale de 1 an et plus[35]**	164
						Lieu de résidence 1 an auparavant (mobilité)	
429,785	429,785	109,440	3,275	39,255	810	Personnes n'ayant pas déménagé	165
62,145	62,150	17,975	410	8,115	130	Personnes ayant déménagé	166
44,505	44,505	9,125	265	4,565	60	Non-migrants	167
17,640	17,640	8,850	145	3,550	75	Migrants	168
14,145	14,145	8,400	145	3,235	70	Migrants internes	169
12,595	12,595	7,365	135	2,900	75	Migrants infraprovinciaux	170
1,550	1,550	1,030	10	340	0	Migrants interprovinciaux	171
3,495	3,495	450	0	315	0	Migrants externes	172
470,175	**470,180**	**122,150**	**3,540**	**45,370**	**895**	**Population totale de 5 ans et plus[36]**	173
						Lieu de résidence 5 ans auparavant (mobilité)	
294,460	294,460	72,975	2,270	25,730	515	Personnes n'ayant pas déménagé	174
175,715	175,715	49,175	1,270	19,635	380	Personnes ayant déménagé	175
115,820	115,820	22,090	695	10,230	95	Non-migrants	176
59,895	59,900	27,080	580	9,410	285	Migrants	177
43,195	43,195	25,775	565	8,520	285	Migrants internes	178
37,655	37,655	21,800	550	7,480	255	Migrants infraprovinciaux	179
5,545	5,545	3,970	15	1,040	30	Migrants interprovinciaux	180
16,700	16,700	1,310	10	885	0	Migrants externes	181
407,590	**407,590**	**106,575**	**3,130**	**39,930**	**790**	**Population totale de 15 ans et plus**	182
						Plus haut certificat, diplôme ou grade[37]	
102,180	102,180	29,400	1,115	10,120	250	Aucun certificat, diplôme ou grade	183
305,410	305,410	77,180	2,015	29,810	540	Certificat, diplôme ou grade	184
111,225	111,225	30,840	835	11,355	235	Diplôme d'études secondaires ou l'équivalent[38]	185
38,115	38,115	11,155	355	3,045	95	Certificat ou diplôme d'apprenti ou d'une école de métiers	186
79,525	79,530	22,600	530	9,300	125	Certificat ou diplôme d'un collège, d'un cégep ou d'un autre établissement d'enseignement non universitaire[39]	187
13,290	13,285	2,585	70	1,005	40	Certificat ou diplôme universitaire inférieur au baccalauréat[40]	188
63,255	63,255	10,000	225	5,105	45	Certificat ou grade universitaire[41]	189
37,795	37,795	6,350	135	3,060	15	Baccalauréat	190
8,105	8,110	1,555	55	835	15	Certificat ou diplôme universitaire supérieur au baccalauréat	191
2,420	2,420	320	15	185	0	Diplôme en médecine, en art dentaire, en médecine vétérinaire ou en optométrie	192
11,935	11,935	1,570	20	955	10	Maîtrise	193
3,000	3,000	200	0	65	10	Doctorat acquis	194
194,185	**194,185**	**46,340**	**1,185**	**18,455**	**310**	**Population totale de 15 ans et plus avec titres du niveau postsecondaire**	195
						Principal domaine d'études - Classification des programmes d'enseignement, 2000[42]	
12,700	12,700	3,635	170	1,520	25	Éducation	196
6,730	6,725	1,080	15	505	0	Arts visuels et d'interprétation, et technologie des communications	197
10,135	10,130	1,750	25	720	15	Sciences humaines	198
20,030	20,030	4,135	50	1,785	0	Sciences sociales et de comportements, et droit	199
37,140	37,140	9,320	195	4,385	30	Commerce, gestion et administration publique	200
6,265	6,265	955	50	425	10	Sciences physiques et de la vie, et technologies	201
7,420	7,425	1,565	0	785	0	Mathématiques, informatique et sciences de l'information	202
48,780	48,780	11,470	315	3,660	90	Architecture, génie et services connexes	203
2,760	2,765	1,085	40	250	15	Agriculture, ressources naturelles et conservation	204
30,495	30,500	7,525	260	3,030	70	Santé, parcs, récréation et conditionnement physique	205
11,700	11,700	3,805	50	1,380	40	Services personnels, de protection et de transport	206
25	25	10	0	0	0	Autres domaines d'études[43]	207
						Lieu des études[44]	
160,355	160,360	43,255	1,115	16,835	270	À l'intérieur du Canada	208
33,825	33,830	3,080	65	1,615	35	À l'extérieur du Canada	209
407,590	**407,590**	**106,575**	**3,130**	**39,930**	**790**	**Population totale de 15 ans et plus**	210
						Travail non rémunéré	
196,690	196,690	51,825	1,430	18,810	390	Hommes de 15 ans et plus	211
176,040	176,045	46,910	1,215	17,015	350	Travail non rémunéré déclaré[45]	212
15,695	15,690	3,495	90	1,170	45	Travaux ménagers et soins aux enfants et soins ou aide aux personnes âgées	213
49,045	49,045	12,605	340	4,545	110	Travaux ménagers et soins aux enfants seulement	214

Nota : Voir les symboles et les abréviations dans les documents d'introduction et voir les documents de référence à la fin de la publication.

Selected characteristics for census divisions and census subdivisions – 100% data and 20% sample data, Ontario, 2006 Census (continued)

No.	Characteristics	Minden Hills, TP ◆◊	**Halton CD/DR**	Burlington, CY	Halton Hills, T	Milton, T	Oakville, T
	Population characteristics						
	Unpaid work (continued)						
215	Housework and care or assistance to seniors only	175	11,445	4,745	1,275	1,290	4,135
216	Child care and care or assistance to seniors only	10	125	45	15	10	55
217	Housework only	1,370	75,345	29,740	9,175	9,430	27,000
218	Child care only	30	1,365	435	170	180	580
219	Care or assistance to seniors only	0	675	230	85	50	305
220	Females 15 years and over	2,410	180,245	69,550	21,645	21,270	67,780
221	Reported unpaid work[45]	2,255	168,995	65,300	20,530	20,045	63,130
222	Housework and child care and care or assistance to seniors	145	19,995	7,335	2,585	2,185	7,885
223	Housework and child care only	555	57,200	20,315	7,595	7,350	21,940
224	Housework and care or assistance to seniors only	245	15,695	7,085	1,580	1,710	5,320
225	Child care and care or assistance to seniors only	0	125	35	10	0	75
226	Housework only	1,290	74,545	29,870	8,590	8,700	27,385
227	Child care only	10	865	390	80	70	325
228	Care or assistance to seniors only	10	575	265	80	30	195
	Labour force activity						
229	Males 15 years and over	2,395	167,260	63,145	21,050	20,640	62,425
230	In the labour force	1,395	129,720	47,370	16,900	17,390	48,060
231	Employed	1,325	124,210	45,375	16,265	16,850	45,720
232	Unemployed	70	5,505	1,995	635	535	2,335
233	Not in the labour force	1,000	37,540	15,770	4,150	3,250	14,365
234	Participation rate	58.2	77.6	75.0	80.3	84.3	77.0
235	Employment rate	55.3	74.3	71.9	77.3	81.6	73.2
236	Unemployment rate	5.0	4.2	4.2	3.8	3.1	4.9
237	Females 15 years and over	2,410	180,245	69,550	21,645	21,270	67,775
238	In the labour force	1,245	120,040	45,215	15,165	15,435	44,225
239	Employed	1,195	113,830	42,900	14,470	14,785	41,675
240	Unemployed	50	6,215	2,310	700	650	2,555
241	Not in the labour force	1,165	60,200	24,335	6,480	5,835	23,550
242	Participation rate	51.7	66.6	65.0	70.1	72.6	65.3
243	Employment rate	49.6	63.2	61.7	66.9	69.5	61.5
244	Unemployment rate	4.0	5.2	5.1	4.6	4.2	5.8
245	Both sexes - Participation rate	54.9	71.9	69.8	75.1	78.3	70.9
246	15 to 24 years	56.4	70.4	73.3	73.5	73.9	66.1
247	25 years and over	54.7	72.1	69.2	75.4	79.1	71.9
248	Both sexes - Employment rate	52.5	68.5	66.5	72.0	75.5	67.1
249	15 to 24 years	50.8	61.9	65.6	65.1	66.8	56.4
250	25 years and over	52.8	69.7	66.7	73.2	76.9	69.3
251	Both sexes - Unemployment rate	4.4	4.7	4.6	4.1	3.6	5.3
252	15 to 24 years	9.1	12.2	10.5	11.3	9.7	14.8
253	25 years and over	3.7	3.3	3.6	2.9	2.7	3.5
254	**Total labour force 15 years and over**	**2,640**	**249,760**	**92,585**	**32,065**	**32,825**	**92,285**
	Industry - North American Industry Classification System 2002						
255	Industry - Not applicable[46]	25	2,560	855	345	220	1,135
256	All industries[47]	2,620	247,200	91,730	31,715	32,605	91,150
257	11 Agriculture, forestry, fishing and hunting	45	1,745	460	595	525	170
258	21 Mining and oil and gas extraction	10	875	310	125	95	345
259	22 Utilities	65	1,555	445	245	215	650
260	23 Construction	520	12,060	4,120	2,155	2,020	3,765
261	31-33 Manufacturing	110	31,635	11,995	5,490	4,425	9,720
262	41 Wholesale trade	80	18,920	6,860	2,595	2,960	6,505
263	44-45 Retail trade	380	27,240	10,735	3,520	3,360	9,625
264	48-49 Transportation and warehousing	140	12,150	4,125	1,970	2,085	3,965
265	51 Information and cultural industries	55	7,005	2,465	675	695	3,170
266	52 Finance and insurance	65	17,540	6,245	1,230	1,760	8,305
267	53 Real estate and rental and leasing	85	5,480	1,980	555	625	2,330
268	54 Professional, scientific and technical services	125	24,520	7,905	2,400	2,685	11,520
269	55 Management of companies and enterprises	10	645	235	50	70	290
270	56 Administrative and support, waste management and remediation services	105	9,655	3,615	1,195	1,245	3,595
271	61 Educational services	85	17,060	6,680	1,940	2,080	6,355
272	62 Health care and social assistance	250	19,535	8,155	2,080	2,320	6,975

Note: See symbols and abbreviations in the introductory material and see reference material at the end of the publication.

Certaines caractéristiques des divisions de recensement et des subdivisions de recensement – Données intégrales et données-échantillon (20 %), Ontario, Recensement de 2006 (suite)

Hamilton CD/DR	Hamilton, C ■ ■	**Hastings CD/DR** †◆◊	Bancroft, T ◆	Belleville, CY ◊**A**	Carlow/Mayo, TP ◆◆◊◊	**Caractéristiques**	N°
						Caractéristiques de la population	
						Travail non rémunéré (suite)	
15,475	15,475	4,350	140	1,575	35	Travaux ménagers et soins ou aide aux personnes âgées seulement	215
325	325	30	0	0	0	Soins aux enfants et soins ou aide aux personnes âgées seulement	216
92,665	92,665	25,880	645	9,475	155	Travaux ménagers seulement	217
1,890	1,890	355	0	150	0	Soins aux enfants seulement	218
945	945	195	0	90	0	Soins ou aide aux personnes âgées seulement	219
210,900	210,900	54,750	1,700	21,120	400	Femmes de 15 ans et plus	220
196,770	196,770	51,605	1,585	19,870	360	Travail non rémunéré déclaré[45]	221
24,005	24,000	5,475	170	2,110	65	Travaux ménagers et soins aux enfants et soins ou aide aux personnes âgées	222
60,450	60,450	15,220	425	5,765	90	Travaux ménagers et soins aux enfants seulement	223
19,680	19,680	5,850	235	2,170	30	Travaux ménagers et soins ou aide aux personnes âgées seulement	224
185	185	50	0	15	0	Soins aux enfants et soins ou aide aux personnes âgées seulement	225
90,825	90,820	24,725	740	9,690	175	Travaux ménagers seulement	226
1,120	1,120	160	0	65	0	Soins aux enfants seulement	227
510	510	135	15	45	0	Soins ou aide aux personnes âgées seulement	228
						Activité	
196,690	196,690	51,825	1,425	18,810	390	Hommes de 15 ans et plus	229
138,075	138,070	34,640	840	12,985	225	Population active	230
129,305	129,305	32,560	805	12,160	210	Personnes occupées	231
8,770	8,765	2,085	30	830	15	Chômeurs	232
58,620	58,620	17,180	590	5,820	165	Inactifs	233
70.2	70.2	66.8	58.9	69.0	57.7	Taux d'activité	234
65.7	65.7	62.8	56.5	64.6	53.8	Taux d'emploi	235
6.4	6.3	6.0	3.6	6.4	6.7	Taux de chômage	236
210,900	210,900	54,750	1,700	21,120	400	Femmes de 15 ans et plus	237
125,525	125,525	31,345	870	12,350	195	Population active	238
117,040	117,040	29,420	815	11,530	190	Personnes occupées	239
8,485	8,485	1,925	50	815	10	Chômeuses	240
85,375	85,375	23,405	830	8,765	205	Inactives	241
59.5	59.5	57.3	51.2	58.5	48.8	Taux d'activité	242
55.5	55.5	53.7	47.9	54.6	47.5	Taux d'emploi	243
6.8	6.8	6.1	5.7	6.6	5.1	Taux de chômage	244
64.7	64.7	61.9	54.5	63.5	53.2	Les deux sexes - Taux d'activité	245
66.8	66.8	68.5	67.8	69.8	66.7	15 à 24 ans	246
64.2	64.2	60.7	52.5	62.2	51.8	25 ans et plus	247
60.4	60.4	58.2	51.8	59.3	50.0	Les deux sexes - Taux d'emploi	248
57.0	57.0	58.0	62.1	58.9	66.7	15 à 24 ans	249
61.1	61.1	58.2	50.2	59.4	48.2	25 ans et plus	250
6.5	6.5	6.1	5.0	6.5	5.9	Les deux sexes - Taux de chômage	251
14.6	14.6	15.2	8.5	15.5	0.0	15 à 24 ans	252
4.8	4.8	4.2	4.2	4.4	6.8	25 ans et plus	253
263,595	**263,595**	**65,990**	**1,705**	**25,340**	**420**	**Population active totale de 15 ans et plus**	254
						Industrie - Système de classification des industries de l'Amérique du Nord de 2002	
4,840	4,840	870	20	340	0	Industrie - Sans objet[46]	255
258,755	258,755	65,120	1,685	25,000	420	Toutes les industries[47]	256
3,725	3,730	1,825	120	300	25	11 Agriculture, foresterie, pêche et chasse	257
430	430	205	10	45	0	21 Extraction minière et extraction de pétrole et de gaz	258
1,305	1,305	525	15	145	0	22 Services publics	259
17,485	17,490	4,270	195	1,255	95	23 Construction	260
42,530	42,525	9,225	95	3,595	45	31-33 Fabrication	261
12,020	12,020	1,910	30	650	25	41 Commerce de gros	262
29,595	29,595	10,140	300	4,170	60	44-45 Commerce de détail	263
11,740	11,745	3,505	70	1,140	0	48-49 Transport et entreposage	264
5,255	5,250	985	15	385	10	51 Industrie de l'information et industrie culturelle	265
9,745	9,750	1,265	50	640	0	52 Finance et assurances	266
4,510	4,515	1,165	15	535	25	53 Services immobiliers et services de location et de location à bail	267
12,735	12,740	2,615	95	1,270	0	54 Services professionnels, scientifiques et techniques	268
195	195	20	0	10	0	55 Gestion de sociétés et d'entreprises	269
12,435	12,435	3,900	25	1,800	10	56 Services administratifs, services de soutien, services de gestion des déchets et services d'assainissement	270
20,340	20,340	3,620	80	1,655	20	61 Services d'enseignement	271
30,295	30,295	6,415	235	2,890	45	62 Soins de santé et assistance sociale	272

Nota : Voir les symboles et les abréviations dans les documents d'introduction et voir les documents de référence à la fin de la publication.

Selected characteristics for census divisions and census subdivisions – 100% data and 20% sample data, Ontario, 2006 Census (continued)

No.	Characteristics	Minden Hills, TP ◆◊	**Halton CD/DR**	Burlington, CY	Halton Hills, T	Milton, T	Oakville, T
	Population characteristics						
	Industry - North American Industry Classification System 2002 (continued)						
273	71 Arts, entertainment and recreation	90	4,955	1,810	600	735	1,810
274	72 Accommodation and food services	195	13,620	5,850	1,410	1,695	4,670
275	81 Other services (except public administration)	120	10,790	3,985	1,425	1,535	3,850
276	91 Public administration	80	10,190	3,745	1,450	1,475	3,520
	Class of worker						
277	Class of worker - Not applicable[46]	25	2,560	860	345	220	1,140
278	All classes of worker[47]	2,615	247,200	91,730	31,715	32,605	91,150
279	Paid workers	2,145	228,895	85,115	29,450	30,315	84,015
280	Employees	1,995	216,910	81,205	28,040	28,835	78,835
281	Self-employed (incorporated)	145	11,980	3,910	1,405	1,485	5,175
282	Self-employed (unincorporated)	450	17,740	6,450	2,180	2,215	6,890
283	Unpaid family workers	25	570	165	85	70	250
	Occupation - National Occupational Classification for Statistics 2006						
284	Male labour force 15 years and over	1,395	129,720	47,370	16,900	17,390	48,060
285	Occupation - Not applicable[46]	10	1,285	365	210	130	580
286	All occupations[47]	1,380	128,435	47,005	16,690	17,260	47,485
287	A Management occupations	170	27,020	9,380	3,060	3,110	11,470
288	B Business, finance and administrative occupations	110	15,635	5,420	1,700	2,025	6,485
289	C Natural and applied sciences and related occupations	50	14,655	5,080	1,600	1,960	6,015
290	D Health occupations	15	2,180	920	165	225	865
291	E Occupations in social science, education, government service and religion	25	6,020	2,175	585	660	2,605
292	F Occupations in art, culture, recreation and sport	15	3,250	1,180	300	240	1,535
293	G Sales and service occupations	210	25,895	10,405	2,740	3,330	9,425
294	H Trades, transport and equipment operators and related occupations	675	23,885	8,850	4,515	4,160	6,355
295	I Occupations unique to primary industry	65	2,990	895	725	570	800
296	J Occupations unique to processing, manufacturing and utilities	40	6,900	2,700	1,305	985	1,915
297	Female labour force 15 years and over	1,250	120,040	45,215	15,165	15,435	44,230
298	Occupation - Not applicable[46]	15	1,280	490	140	90	565
299	All occupations[47]	1,230	118,760	44,720	15,025	15,350	43,665
300	A Management occupations	110	13,510	4,435	1,685	1,670	5,715
301	B Business, finance and administrative occupations	360	34,560	12,935	4,510	4,740	12,375
302	C Natural and applied sciences and related occupations	10	4,335	1,485	455	590	1,810
303	D Health occupations	100	8,865	3,815	1,010	975	3,060
304	E Occupations in social science, education, government service and religion	90	15,600	5,790	1,785	2,040	5,985
305	F Occupations in art, culture, recreation and sport	60	4,520	1,590	430	550	1,940
306	G Sales and service occupations	450	31,290	12,385	3,930	3,940	11,040
307	H Trades, transport and equipment operators and related occupations	30	1,885	775	370	230	505
308	I Occupations unique to primary industry	10	965	305	185	255	225
309	J Occupations unique to processing, manufacturing and utilities	10	3,225	1,200	655	360	1,005
310	**Total employed labour force 15 years and over**	**2,520**	**238,040**	**88,280**	**30,730**	**31,635**	**87,395**
	Place of work status						
311	Males	1,325	124,210	45,375	16,265	16,850	45,720
312	Usual place of work	730	99,730	36,970	12,935	13,315	36,505
313	At home	125	9,755	3,380	1,055	1,285	4,030
314	Outside Canada	15	870	300	70	105	390
315	No fixed workplace address	450	13,855	4,725	2,195	2,140	4,795
316	Females	1,200	113,830	42,900	14,470	14,785	41,670
317	Usual place of work	955	97,875	37,395	12,505	12,995	34,985
318	At home	145	10,360	3,420	1,280	1,150	4,510
319	Outside Canada	0	295	90	40	30	140
320	No fixed workplace address	95	5,295	2,005	650	610	2,035

Note: See symbols and abbreviations in the introductory material and see reference material at the end of the publication.

Certaines caractéristiques des divisions de recensement et des subdivisions de recensement – Données intégrales et données-échantillon (20 %), Ontario, Recensement de 2006 (suite)

Hamilton CD/DR	Hamilton, C ■ ■	**Hastings CD/DR** †◆◇	Bancroft, T ◆	Belleville, CY ◇**A**	Carlow/Mayo, TP ◆◆◇◇	**Caractéristiques**	N°
						Caractéristiques de la population	
						Industrie - Système de classification des industries de l'Amérique du Nord de 2002 (suite)	
5,140	5,135	970	30	300	20	71 Arts, spectacles et loisirs	273
16,430	16,430	4,400	145	1,980	10	72 Hébergement et services de restauration	274
12,815	12,810	2,825	115	1,020	20	81 Autres services (sauf les administrations publiques)	275
10,025	10,020	5,330	40	1,215	10	91 Administrations publiques	276
						Catégorie de travailleurs	
4,840	4,840	865	20	340	10	Catégorie de travailleurs - Sans objet[46]	277
258,755	258,755	65,120	1,685	25,000	425	Toutes les catégories de travailleurs[47]	278
241,925	241,920	59,335	1,465	23,130	320	Travailleurs rémunérés	279
233,620	233,620	57,825	1,395	22,610	320	Employés	280
8,305	8,300	1,505	70	515	0	Travailleurs autonomes (entreprise constituée en société)	281
16,260	16,255	5,615	205	1,835	100	Travailleurs autonomes (entreprise non constituée en société)	282
575	575	170	20	40	0	Travailleurs familiaux non rémunérés	283
						Profession - Classification nationale des professions pour statistiques de 2006	
138,075	138,070	34,640	840	12,990	230	Hommes actifs de 15 ans et plus	284
2,250	2,250	385	0	145	0	Profession - Sans objet[46]	285
135,825	135,820	34,255	840	12,845	225	Toutes les professions[47]	286
14,425	14,430	3,280	115	1,330	10	A Gestion	287
11,455	11,455	2,825	60	1,490	0	B Affaires, finance et administration	288
11,265	11,260	2,545	80	1,140	0	C Sciences naturelles et appliquées et professions apparentées	289
3,085	3,085	530	20	265	0	D Secteur de la santé	290
7,510	7,510	1,425	15	695	15	E Sciences sociales, enseignement, administration publique et religion	291
3,080	3,080	500	10	235	0	F Arts, culture, sports et loisirs	292
26,055	26,055	7,135	125	2,750	15	G Ventes et services	293
41,340	41,335	10,085	275	2,960	135	H Métiers, transport et machinerie	294
4,375	4,375	1,960	95	380	25	I Professions propres au secteur primaire	295
13,230	13,230	3,965	40	1,590	10	J Transformation, fabrication et services d'utilité publique	296
125,525	125,525	31,345	865	12,350	195	Femmes actives de 15 ans et plus	297
2,590	2,590	480	25	195	0	Profession - Sans objet[46]	298
122,935	122,935	30,870	850	12,155	195	Toutes les professions[47]	299
8,650	8,655	1,980	75	800	15	A Gestion	300
31,155	31,160	7,250	230	2,990	20	B Affaires, finance et administration	301
2,720	2,725	805	10	385	0	C Sciences naturelles et appliquées et professions apparentées	302
13,865	13,865	2,925	110	1,290	20	D Secteur de la santé	303
14,540	14,545	3,065	50	1,350	0	E Sciences sociales, enseignement, administration publique et religion	304
3,455	3,455	755	10	320	10	F Arts, culture, sports et loisirs	305
37,810	37,810	10,440	340	3,840	115	G Ventes et services	306
2,865	2,860	1,070	10	360	0	H Métiers, transport et machinerie	307
1,915	1,920	480	0	120	10	I Professions propres au secteur primaire	308
5,950	5,945	2,095	10	695	0	J Transformation, fabrication et services d'utilité publique	309
246,340	**246,340**	**61,980**	**1,625**	**23,690**	**400**	**Population active occupée totale de 15 ans et plus**	310
						Catégorie de lieu de travail	
129,305	129,300	32,560	810	12,160	210	Hommes	311
103,385	103,380	25,655	520	10,085	110	Lieu habituel de travail	312
6,685	6,685	2,120	75	580	35	À domicile	313
625	630	140	0	55	0	En dehors du Canada	314
18,610	18,610	4,640	210	1,445	65	Sans adresse de travail fixe	315
117,040	117,040	29,420	815	11,530	190	Femmes	316
104,065	104,070	25,790	705	10,340	130	Lieu habituel de travail	317
6,920	6,915	2,120	65	710	40	À domicile	318
270	270	70	0	35	0	En dehors du Canada	319
5,785	5,785	1,440	45	440	20	Sans adresse de travail fixe	320

Nota : Voir les symboles et les abréviations dans les documents d'introduction et voir les documents de référence à la fin de la publication.

Selected characteristics for census divisions and census subdivisions – 100% data and 20% sample data, Ontario, 2006 Census (continued)

No.	Characteristics	Minden Hills, TP ◆◊	**Halton CD/DR**	Burlington, CY	Halton Hills, T	Milton, T	Oakville, T
	Population characteristics						
321	**Total employed labour force 15 years and over with usual place of work or no fixed workplace address**	**2,235**	**216,760**	**81,095**	**28,285**	**29,055**	**78,320**
	Mode of transportation						
322	Males	1,185	113,585	41,695	15,135	15,455	41,295
323	Car, truck, van, as driver	1,005	91,590	34,060	12,885	13,300	31,335
324	Car, truck, van, as passenger	100	6,830	2,520	1,010	925	2,375
325	Public transit	0	9,715	3,025	430	625	5,640
326	Walked	65	3,370	1,310	510	330	1,210
327	All other modes	10	2,080	775	295	270	735
328	Females	1,050	103,170	39,395	13,150	13,600	37,020
329	Car, truck, van, as driver	905	78,490	30,590	10,895	10,850	26,160
330	Car, truck, van, as passenger	95	8,865	3,295	1,050	1,215	3,300
331	Public transit	0	10,240	3,430	480	785	5,540
332	Walked	40	4,275	1,680	540	575	1,475
333	All other modes	10	1,300	400	185	165	545
334	**Total population 15 years and over who worked since January 1, 2005**	**3,115**	**267,560**	**99,355**	**34,000**	**35,105**	**99,095**
	Language used most often at work						
335	Single responses	3,115	266,005	98,975	33,890	34,855	98,285
336	English	3,110	263,765	98,510	33,615	34,405	97,235
337	French	0	870	260	145	110	355
338	Non-official languages[7]	0	1,365	200	130	345	690
339	Chinese, n.o.s.[61]	0	95	15	10	10	65
340	Cantonese	0	55	10	0	35	15
341	Other languages[8]	0	1,210	185	120	300	610
342	Multiple responses	0	1,555	385	110	250	810
343	English and French	0	750	275	55	95	325
344	English and non-official language	0	725	85	55	150	440
345	French and non-official language	0	0	0	0	0	10
346	English, French and non-official language	0	75	20	0	0	45
	Dwelling and household characteristics						
347	**Total number of occupied private dwellings**	**2,385**	**157,085**	**63,255**	**18,785**	**18,465**	**56,580**
	Housing tenure						
348	Owned	2,100	130,330	50,330	16,145	16,260	47,595
349	Rented	285	26,750	12,925	2,640	2,205	8,980
350	Band housing	0	0	0	0	0	0
	Structural type of dwelling						
351	Single-detached house	2,215	96,415	34,090	13,910	11,985	36,430
352	Semi-detached house	10	7,630	2,445	825	1,925	2,435
353	Row house	35	23,620	11,505	1,365	2,780	7,975
354	Apartment, duplex	5	2,485	805	575	245	855
355	Apartment, building that has five or more storeys	0	17,880	9,670	775	995	6,430
356	Apartment, building that has fewer than five storeys	105	8,660	4,580	1,260	470	2,355
357	Other single-attached house	10	215	50	85	30	45
358	Movable dwelling[48]	15	50	15	15	20	5
	Condition of dwelling						
359	Regular maintenance only	1,535	118,725	46,975	13,845	15,110	42,795
360	Minor repairs	645	31,990	13,310	4,090	2,745	11,845
361	Major repairs	200	6,365	2,975	850	615	1,935
	Period of construction						
362	Before 1946	280	7,025	2,560	2,050	1,105	1,305
363	1946 to 1960	225	19,685	9,070	2,680	1,155	6,770
364	1961 to 1970	325	21,470	10,995	2,960	1,210	6,305
365	1971 to 1980	465	27,290	13,030	2,430	4,000	7,825
366	1981 to 1985	260	11,295	3,800	750	1,460	5,290
367	1986 to 1990	360	16,620	6,210	1,065	610	8,725
368	1991 to 1995	265	10,380	3,585	1,835	350	4,615
369	1996 to 2000	75	15,635	6,640	2,000	390	6,600
370	2001 to 2006[49]	130	27,690	7,365	3,005	8,175	9,140

Note: See symbols and abbreviations in the introductory material and see reference material at the end of the publication.

Certaines caractéristiques des divisions de recensement et des subdivisions de recensement – Données intégrales et données-échantillon (20 %), Ontario, Recensement de 2006 (suite)

Hamilton CD/DR	Hamilton, C ■■	**Hastings CD/DR** †◆◊	Bancroft, T ◆	Belleville, CY ◊A	Carlow/Mayo, TP ◆◆◊◊	**Caractéristiques**	N°
						Caractéristiques de la population	
231,845	**231,845**	**57,525**	**1,480**	**22,310**	**325**	**Population active occupée totale de 15 ans et plus ayant un lieu habituel de travail ou sans adresse de travail fixe**	321
						Mode de transport	
121,995	121,995	30,295	730	11,525	180	Hommes	322
96,620	96,620	24,640	590	8,730	155	Automobile, camion ou fourgonnette, en tant que conducteur	323
8,980	8,980	2,590	75	1,190	10	Automobile, camion ou fourgonnette, en tant que passager	324
8,855	8,855	445	0	345	0	Transport en commun	325
4,920	4,915	1,590	50	825	0	À pied	326
2,620	2,615	1,025	0	430	10	Tous les autres modes	327
109,850	109,855	27,230	750	10,785	145	Femmes	328
75,900	75,900	21,035	545	7,850	125	Automobile, camion ou fourgonnette, en tant que conductrice	329
11,990	11,990	3,010	100	1,220	10	Automobile, camion ou fourgonnette, en tant que passagère	330
12,810	12,805	685	10	565	10	Transport en commun	331
7,605	7,610	1,940	90	865	0	À pied	332
1,545	1,550	555	10	285	0	Tous les autres modes	333
281,905	**281,905**	**71,530**	**1,835**	**27,275**	**495**	**Population totale de 15 ans et plus ayant travaillé depuis le 1er janvier 2005**	334
						Langue utilisée le plus souvent au travail	
279,940	279,940	71,275	1,830	27,215	495	Réponses uniques	335
276,765	276,765	70,915	1,825	27,085	495	Anglais	336
555	560	230	0	30	0	Français	337
2,620	2,615	125	0	95	0	Langues non officielles[7]	338
350	350	30	0	25	0	Chinois, n.d.a.[61]	339
60	60	10	0	10	0	Cantonais	340
2,200	2,200	80	0	60	0	Autres langues[8]	341
1,960	1,960	255	10	60	0	Réponses multiples	342
510	510	175	0	25	0	Anglais et français	343
1,325	1,320	85	0	35	0	Anglais et langue non officielle	344
15	15	0	0	0	0	Français et langue non officielle	345
110	110	0	0	0	0	Anglais, français et langue non officielle	346
						Caractéristiques des logements et des ménages	
194,460	**194,455**	**52,645**	**1,655**	**20,490**	**370**	**Nombre total de logements privés occupés**	347
						Mode d'occupation	
132,785	132,785	38,375	1,125	12,870	350	Possédé	348
61,675	61,675	14,270	535	7,620	15	Loué	349
0	0	0	0	0	0	Logement de bande	350
						Type de construction résidentielle	
112,045	112,045	37,845	1,155	11,825	360	Maison individuelle non attenante	351
5,980	5,980	1,760	10	660	0	Maison jumelée	352
18,640	18,640	1,685	55	1,295	0	Maison en rangée	353
6,815	6,810	1,105	30	650	5	Appartement, duplex	354
32,750	32,750	2,465	0	1,950	0	Appartement, immeuble de cinq étages ou plus	355
17,510	17,515	6,995	375	3,970	0	Appartement, immeuble de moins de cinq étages	356
505	505	300	25	115	0	Autre maison individuelle attenante	357
235	235	480	5	20	5	Logement mobile[48]	358
						État du logement	
126,865	126,870	33,140	1,040	13,700	190	Entretien régulier seulement	359
53,160	53,160	15,190	465	5,310	130	Réparations mineures	360
14,430	14,425	4,310	150	1,480	45	Réparations majeures	361
						Période de construction	
36,980	36,985	11,025	225	4,270	55	Avant 1946	362
42,210	42,215	8,410	325	3,880	55	1946 à 1960	363
29,395	29,395	7,400	130	3,300	25	1961 à 1970	364
30,245	30,240	9,795	400	3,330	75	1971 à 1980	365
11,605	11,605	3,360	140	1,450	25	1981 à 1985	366
13,660	13,660	4,435	155	1,650	35	1986 à 1990	367
9,945	9,950	3,005	155	710	25	1991 à 1995	368
10,015	10,015	2,345	60	780	20	1996 à 2000	369
10,390	10,390	2,865	60	1,120	50	2001 à 2006[49]	370

Nota : Voir les symboles et les abréviations dans les documents d'introduction et voir les documents de référence à la fin de la publication.

Selected characteristics for census divisions and census subdivisions – 100% data and 20% sample data, Ontario, 2006 Census (continued)

No.	Characteristics	Minden Hills, TP ◆◊	**Halton CD/DR**	Burlington, CY	Halton Hills, T	Milton, T	Oakville, T
	Dwelling and household characteristics						
371	Average number of rooms per dwelling	6.7	7.3	7.0	7.5	7.3	7.7
372	Average number of bedrooms per dwelling	2.8	3.1	2.9	3.2	3.2	3.2
373	Average value of dwelling $	218,838	398,680	348,041	373,908	364,417	472,244
374	**Total number of private households**	**2,400**	**156,950**	**63,160**	**18,810**	**18,445**	**56,525**
	Household size						
375	1 person	605	29,870	14,600	3,035	2,610	9,620
376	2 persons	1,100	50,010	21,800	5,705	6,005	16,495
377	3 persons	280	27,830	10,260	3,480	3,830	10,255
378	4 to 5 persons	385	44,750	15,155	5,995	5,370	18,220
379	6 or more persons	35	4,490	1,340	590	625	1,925
	Household type						
380	One-family households[50]	1,670	120,365	46,075	14,905	14,985	44,400
381	Multiple-family households	40	3,060	950	435	450	1,225
382	Non-family households	680	33,660	16,240	3,440	3,030	10,950
383	Number of persons in private households	5,475	433,385	162,145	54,330	53,185	163,725
384	Average number of persons in private households	2.3	2.8	2.6	2.9	2.9	2.9
385	Tenant-occupied private non-farm, non-reserve dwellings[51]	285	26,730	12,925	2,630	2,185	8,980
386	Average gross rent $[51]	573	1,019	972	929	1,032	1,111
387	Tenant-occupied households spending 30% or more of household income on gross rent[52]	95	11,465	5,420	1,085	915	4,050
388	Tenant-occupied households spending from 30% to 99% of household income on gross rent[52]	90	10,020	4,830	965	805	3,425
389	Owner-occupied private non-farm, non-reserve dwellings[53]	2,095	130,135	50,310	16,085	16,165	47,575
390	Average owner's major payments $[53]	674	1,416	1,297	1,388	1,463	1,535
391	Owner households spending 30% or more of household income on owner's major payments[52]	350	25,055	9,305	2,970	3,515	9,265
392	Owner households spending from 30% to 99% of household income on owner's major payments[52]	290	21,975	8,175	2,640	3,190	7,965
	Census family characteristics						
393	**Total number of census families in private households**	**1,745**	**126,630**	**48,010**	**15,800**	**15,900**	**46,915**
	Family structure and number of children						
394	Total couple families	1,570	111,410	41,670	13,990	14,305	41,445
395	Total families of married couples	1,325	100,610	37,145	12,470	12,550	38,440
396	Without children at home	830	37,030	15,505	4,285	4,560	12,680
397	With children at home	495	63,575	21,635	8,185	7,990	25,765
398	1 child	170	21,480	7,540	2,635	3,100	8,205
399	2 children	235	29,765	10,120	3,945	3,475	12,230
400	3 or more children	85	12,330	3,975	1,605	1,420	5,325
401	Total families of common-law couples	250	10,800	4,525	1,525	1,750	3,005
402	Without children at home	185	6,800	3,140	845	1,015	1,805
403	With children at home	60	4,000	1,385	675	735	1,200
404	1 child	25	2,115	790	390	355	580
405	2 children	30	1,285	415	215	230	425
406	3 or more children	10	600	175	80	155	195
407	Total lone-parent families	175	15,225	6,340	1,810	1,595	5,470
408	Female parent	90	12,425	5,180	1,385	1,300	4,555
409	1 child	55	7,145	3,170	735	670	2,565
410	2 children	10	4,085	1,530	500	500	1,545
411	3 or more children	20	1,200	475	145	130	450
412	Male parent	80	2,800	1,160	425	295	915
413	1 child	70	1,840	785	255	220	585
414	2 children	0	725	305	125	55	235
415	3 or more children	10	235	70	40	20	95

Note: See symbols and abbreviations in the introductory material and see reference material at the end of the publication.

Certaines caractéristiques des divisions de recensement et des subdivisions de recensement – Données intégrales et données-échantillon (20 %), Ontario, Recensement de 2006 (suite)

Hamilton CD/DR	Hamilton, C ■ ■	**Hastings CD/DR** †◆◊	Bancroft, T ◆	Belleville, CY ◊**A**	Carlow/Mayo, TP ◆◆◊◊	**Caractéristiques**	N°
						Caractéristiques des logements et des ménages	
6.6	6.6	6.7	6.2	6.4	6.8	Nombre moyen de pièces par logement	371
2.7	2.7	2.8	2.5	2.6	2.8	Nombre moyen de chambres à coucher par logement	372
252,248	252,248	181,719	161,706	187,927	215,909	Valeur moyenne du logement $	373
194,475	**194,475**	**52,645**	**1,660**	**20,495**	**370**	**Nombre total de ménages privés**	374
						Taille du ménage	
51,770	51,775	13,220	555	5,965	80	1 personne	375
61,300	61,295	20,075	605	7,600	155	2 personnes	376
31,595	31,595	8,110	205	3,110	55	3 personnes	377
43,960	43,965	10,135	250	3,475	70	4 à 5 personnes	378
5,845	5,845	1,100	40	345	5	6 personnes ou plus	379
						Genre de ménage	
133,585	133,590	37,355	1,065	13,590	290	Ménages unifamiliaux[50]	380
3,520	3,520	615	0	190	10	Ménages multifamiliaux	381
57,345	57,350	14,675	585	6,710	70	Ménages non familiaux	382
495,630	495,630	128,155	3,715	47,520	935	Nombre de personnes dans les ménages privés	383
2.5	2.5	2.4	2.2	2.3	2.5	Nombre moyen de personnes dans les ménages privés	384
61,645	61,645	14,265	535	7,620	15	Ménages locataires dans les logements privés non agricoles hors réserve[51]	385
721	721	684	638	706	626	Loyer brut moyen $[51]	386
27,470	27,470	6,315	310	3,505	0	Ménages locataires consacrant 30 % ou plus du revenu du ménage au loyer brut[52]	387
23,190	23,195	5,680	240	3,170	0	Ménages locataires consacrant de 30 % à 99 % du revenu du ménage au loyer brut[52]	388
132,310	132,310	37,965	1,110	12,830	355	Ménages propriétaires dans les logements privés non agricoles hors réserve[53]	389
1,096	1,096	857	744	927	687	Principales dépenses de propriété moyennes $[53]	390
25,565	25,565	6,555	230	2,240	35	Ménages propriétaires consacrant 30 % ou plus du revenu du ménage aux principales dépenses de propriété[52]	391
22,385	22,385	5,590	205	2,030	25	Ménages propriétaires consacrant de 30 % à 99 % du revenu du ménage aux principales dépenses de propriété[52]	392
						Caractéristiques des familles de recensement	
140,810	**140,810**	**38,595**	**1,075**	**13,975**	**305**	**Nombre total de familles de recensement dans les ménages privés**	393
						Structure de la famille et le nombre d'enfants	
115,720	115,720	33,225	930	11,545	265	Total des familles avec conjoints	394
101,220	101,215	27,700	795	9,450	230	Total des familles avec couples mariés	395
40,390	40,390	14,165	435	4,850	115	Sans enfants à la maison	396
60,825	60,825	13,535	360	4,605	110	Avec enfants à la maison	397
21,635	21,640	5,190	110	1,820	35	1 enfant	398
26,520	26,520	5,850	180	1,990	55	2 enfants	399
12,670	12,665	2,495	65	790	20	3 enfants ou plus	400
14,505	14,500	5,520	135	2,095	40	Total des familles avec couples en union libre	401
8,560	8,565	2,885	70	1,160	25	Sans enfants à la maison	402
5,945	5,940	2,640	60	935	10	Avec enfants à la maison	403
2,800	2,800	1,325	40	510	10	1 enfant	404
2,230	2,230	815	10	290	0	2 enfants	405
910	905	500	10	135	0	3 enfants ou plus	406
25,085	25,085	5,370	140	2,435	35	Total des familles monoparentales	407
20,790	20,795	4,200	115	1,965	20	Parent de sexe féminin	408
12,345	12,345	2,630	85	1,250	20	1 enfant	409
6,080	6,080	1,145	20	530	0	2 enfants	410
2,365	2,365	430	10	180	0	3 enfants ou plus	411
4,290	4,295	1,165	25	465	15	Parent de sexe masculin	412
2,870	2,865	800	0	330	10	1 enfant	413
1,135	1,135	300	20	95	10	2 enfants	414
290	290	70	0	40	0	3 enfants ou plus	415

Nota : Voir les symboles et les abréviations dans les documents d'introduction et voir les documents de référence à la fin de la publication.

Selected characteristics for census divisions and census subdivisions – 100% data and 20% sample data, Ontario, 2006 Census (continued)

No.	Characteristics	Minden Hills, TP ◆◊	**Halton CD/DR**	Burlington, CY	Halton Hills, T	Milton, T	Oakville, T
	Census family characteristics						
416	**Total number of children at home**	**1,280**	**150,610**	**52,185**	**19,625**	**18,485**	**60,320**
	Age group						
417	Under 6 years	220	33,360	11,210	4,505	5,250	12,395
418	6 to 14 years	475	54,255	18,500	7,795	6,205	21,755
419	15 to 17 years	240	18,170	6,455	2,275	1,900	7,535
420	18 to 24 years	250	30,315	10,695	3,565	3,425	12,630
421	25 years and over	100	14,515	5,325	1,485	1,700	6,005
422	Average number of children at home per census family[54]	0.7	1.2	1.1	1.2	1.2	1.3
423	**Total number of persons in private households**	**5,445**	**433,470**	**162,230**	**54,290**	**53,205**	**163,740**
	Census family status and living arrangements						
424	Number of persons not in census families	850	44,820	20,370	4,870	4,520	15,055
425	Living with relatives[55]	115	6,755	2,420	890	945	2,495
426	Living with non-relatives only	135	8,035	3,275	965	955	2,835
427	Living alone	600	30,030	14,670	3,010	2,615	9,725
428	Number of census family persons	4,595	388,655	141,860	49,420	48,690	148,680
429	Average number of persons per census family	2.6	3.1	3.0	3.1	3.1	3.2
430	**Total number of persons aged 65 years and over**	**1,325**	**50,860**	**23,650**	**5,245**	**4,220**	**17,740**
431	Number of persons not in census families aged 65 years and over	385	15,305	7,340	1,560	1,325	5,075
432	Living with relatives[55]	45	2,860	985	305	460	1,115
433	Living with non-relatives only	30	615	300	80	40	200
434	Living alone	310	11,825	6,060	1,175	825	3,765
435	Number of census family persons aged 65 years and over	940	35,560	16,305	3,690	2,895	12,660
	Economic family characteristics						
436	**Total number of economic families in private households**	**1,735**	**124,575**	**47,460**	**15,495**	**15,550**	**46,065**
	Size of family						
437	2 persons	1,070	48,900	21,235	5,610	5,830	16,230
438	3 persons	250	27,275	9,985	3,410	3,865	10,020
439	4 persons	285	32,050	11,000	4,305	3,790	12,950
440	5 or more persons	130	16,340	5,235	2,165	2,075	6,865
441	Total number of persons in economic families	4,710	395,410	144,280	50,315	49,635	151,175
442	Average number of persons per economic family	3.0	3.0	3.0	3.0	3.0	3.0
443	Total number of persons not in economic families	735	38,060	17,945	3,975	3,575	12,560
	2005 income characteristics						
444	**Population 15 years and over**	**4,805**	**347,505**	**132,695**	**42,695**	**41,910**	**130,205**
	Sex and total income groups in 2005						
445	Without income	145	14,760	4,570	1,815	1,360	7,010
446	With income	4,660	332,745	128,125	40,880	40,550	123,190
447	Under $1,000[56]	115	12,210	4,305	1,555	1,350	5,000
448	$1,000 to $2,999	205	11,765	4,180	1,535	1,405	4,645
449	$3,000 to $4,999	175	9,930	3,695	955	1,180	4,100
450	$5,000 to $6,999	145	10,040	3,695	1,120	1,065	4,165
451	$7,000 to $9,999	250	15,540	6,165	1,810	1,670	5,895
452	$10,000 to $11,999	245	10,550	4,370	1,210	1,130	3,845
453	$12,000 to $14,999	305	14,635	5,795	1,685	1,565	5,580
454	$15,000 to $19,999	680	22,925	9,335	2,855	2,705	8,020
455	$20,000 to $24,999	460	19,050	7,550	2,310	2,450	6,735
456	$25,000 to $29,999	485	17,960	7,525	2,115	2,105	6,215
457	$30,000 to $34,999	295	19,570	8,225	2,615	2,335	6,390
458	$35,000 to $39,999	290	19,285	7,740	2,530	2,895	6,125
459	$40,000 to $44,999	210	17,350	6,895	2,330	2,445	5,680
460	$45,000 to $49,999	180	15,905	6,355	2,125	2,265	5,160
461	$50,000 to $59,999	230	26,545	10,475	3,880	3,875	8,315
462	$60,000 and over	395	89,495	31,815	10,265	10,110	37,305
463	Median income $[57]	21,891	35,433	34,379	36,162	37,041	35,650
464	Average income $[57]	27,915	51,098	47,406	47,439	44,738	58,246
465	Standard error of average income $[57]	763	353	510	1,066	515	685

Note: See symbols and abbreviations in the introductory material and see reference material at the end of the publication.

Hamilton CD/DR	Hamilton, C ■ ■	**Hastings CD/DR** †◆◇	Bancroft, T ◆	Belleville, CY ◇**A**	Carlow/Mayo, TP ◆◆◇◇	**Caractéristiques**	N°
						Caractéristiques des familles de recensement	
165,540	**165,540**	**37,595**	**1,015**	**13,430**	**270**	**Nombre total d'enfants à la maison**	416
						Groupes d'âge	
32,325	32,325	7,920	235	2,930	55	Moins de 6 ans	417
56,640	56,645	13,910	355	4,890	100	6 à 14 ans	418
20,275	20,280	5,460	160	1,895	55	15 à 17 ans	419
35,585	35,580	7,105	195	2,545	20	18 à 24 ans	420
20,715	20,710	3,205	65	1,175	35	25 ans et plus	421
1.2	1.2	1.0	0.9	1.0	0.9	Nombre moyen d'enfants à la maison par famille de recensement[54]	422
495,590	**495,590**	**128,185**	**3,715**	**47,525**	**930**	**Nombre total de personnes dans les ménages privés**	423
						Situation des particuliers dans la famille de recensement et des particuliers dans le ménage	
73,515	73,515	18,765	690	8,570	90	Nombre de personnes hors famille de recensement	424
10,340	10,340	2,060	75	740	10	Vivant avec des personnes apparentées[55]	425
11,450	11,445	3,495	65	1,875	20	Vivant avec des personnes non apparentées seulement	426
51,730	51,730	13,215	550	5,955	65	Vivant seules	427
422,075	422,070	109,415	3,025	38,950	840	Nombre de membres d'une famille de recensement	428
3.0	3.0	2.8	2.8	2.8	2.8	Nombre moyen de personnes par famille de recensement	429
69,490	**69,495**	**20,730**	**785**	**8,125**	**175**	**Nombre total de personnes âgées de 65 ans et plus**	430
24,390	24,390	6,910	350	2,955	40	Nombre de personnes hors famille de recensement âgées de 65 ans et plus	431
3,770	3,765	735	35	285	0	Vivant avec des personnes apparentées[55]	432
805	805	350	25	140	10	Vivant avec des personnes non apparentées seulement	433
19,815	19,815	5,825	285	2,520	35	Vivant seules	434
45,100	45,105	13,815	435	5,170	130	Nombre de membres d'une famille de recensement âgés de 65 ans et plus	435
						Caractéristiques des familles économiques	
138,895	**138,895**	**38,270**	**1,070**	**13,905**	**300**	**Nombre total de familles économiques dans les ménages privés**	436
						Taille de la famille	
59,165	59,165	19,395	570	7,235	165	2 personnes	437
30,850	30,845	7,920	200	3,010	50	3 personnes	438
30,875	30,875	7,225	180	2,475	55	4 personnes	439
18,010	18,010	3,730	120	1,185	25	5 personnes ou plus	440
432,415	432,410	111,475	3,100	39,690	850	Nombre total de personnes dans les familles économiques	441
3.0	3.0	3.0	3.0	3.0	3.0	Nombre moyen de personnes par famille économique	442
63,175	63,180	16,705	615	7,830	85	Nombre total de personnes hors famille économique	443
						Caractéristiques du revenu de 2005	
407,590	**407,590**	**106,580**	**3,130**	**39,925**	**790**	**Population de 15 ans et plus**	444
						Sexe et groupes de revenu total en 2005	
19,100	19,105	4,835	135	1,635	40	Sans revenu	445
388,490	388,490	101,740	2,990	38,290	755	Avec un revenu	446
16,145	16,150	3,925	115	1,235	35	Moins de 1 000 $[56]	447
13,105	13,105	3,540	90	1,275	25	1 000 $ à 2 999 $	448
12,565	12,565	3,510	120	1,140	15	3 000 $ à 4 999 $	449
13,475	13,475	3,740	180	1,355	45	5 000 $ à 6 999 $	450
22,815	22,815	6,130	120	2,330	70	7 000 $ à 9 999 $	451
16,975	16,975	4,825	150	1,810	55	10 000 $ à 11 999 $	452
23,835	23,835	6,975	275	2,470	75	12 000 $ à 14 999 $	453
37,145	37,145	10,875	395	4,205	120	15 000 $ à 19 999 $	454
30,550	30,550	9,230	400	3,440	40	20 000 $ à 24 999 $	455
27,165	27,160	7,340	225	2,950	30	25 000 $ à 29 999 $	456
26,530	26,530	7,580	190	2,770	40	30 000 $ à 34 999 $	457
23,675	23,675	6,755	180	2,615	35	35 000 $ à 39 999 $	458
19,955	19,955	5,270	155	2,010	55	40 000 $ à 44 999 $	459
16,850	16,850	4,225	65	1,520	35	45 000 $ à 49 999$	460
26,620	26,620	6,890	135	2,525	30	50 000 $ à 59 999$	461
61,075	61,075	10,935	205	4,630	45	60 000 $ et plus	462
26,353	26,353	23,916	20,612	24,751	16,718	Revenu médian $[57]	463
35,117	35,117	30,243	27,580	31,859	27,900	Revenu moyen $[57]	464
172	172	198	1,905	365	2,522	Erreur type de revenu moyen $[57]	465

Nota : Voir les symboles et les abréviations dans les documents d'introduction et voir les documents de référence à la fin de la publication.

Selected characteristics for census divisions and census subdivisions – 100% data and 20% sample data, Ontario, 2006 Census (continued)

No.	Characteristics	Minden Hills, TP ◆◊	**Halton CD/DR**	Burlington, CY	Halton Hills, T	Milton, T	Oakville, T
	2005 income characteristics						
	Sex and total income groups in 2005 (continued)						
466	Total - Males	2,395	167,260	63,140	21,050	20,635	62,425
467	Without income	45	5,960	1,865	675	595	2,825
468	With income	2,350	161,295	61,275	20,370	20,045	59,600
469	Under $1,000[56]	65	6,035	2,135	770	730	2,400
470	$1,000 to $2,999	100	4,345	1,610	605	435	1,695
471	$3,000 to $4,999	75	3,660	1,300	425	420	1,515
472	$5,000 to $6,999	40	3,485	1,165	400	385	1,535
473	$7,000 to $9,999	90	5,620	2,235	720	540	2,125
474	$10,000 to $11,999	65	3,740	1,525	355	430	1,425
475	$12,000 to $14,999	115	4,840	1,780	590	610	1,855
476	$15,000 to $19,999	280	7,645	2,830	995	925	2,880
477	$20,000 to $24,999	240	7,125	2,760	845	920	2,595
478	$25,000 to $29,999	285	6,980	2,965	820	860	2,330
479	$30,000 to $34,999	125	8,365	3,585	1,035	930	2,810
480	$35,000 to $39,999	190	8,135	3,225	1,200	1,210	2,500
481	$40,000 to $44,999	125	7,950	3,310	1,025	1,215	2,400
482	$45,000 to $49,999	110	7,735	3,070	1,045	1,220	2,395
483	$50,000 to $59,999	185	14,560	5,820	2,265	2,220	4,250
484	$60,000 and over	255	61,080	21,960	7,265	6,990	24,870
485	Median income $[57]	26,523	46,647	45,225	47,022	46,034	48,613
486	Average income $[57]	32,682	67,159	62,100	60,433	55,197	78,683
487	Standard error of average income $[57]	1,225	668	1,002	2,046	905	1,264
488	Total - Females	2,410	180,245	69,550	21,645	21,270	67,775
489	Without income	100	8,795	2,705	1,135	765	4,185
490	With income	2,310	171,450	66,845	20,510	20,510	63,590
491	Under $1,000[56]	55	6,170	2,170	785	615	2,595
492	$1,000 to $2,999	110	7,420	2,570	930	970	2,950
493	$3,000 to $4,999	95	6,275	2,395	525	765	2,590
494	$5,000 to $6,999	100	6,555	2,530	720	680	2,625
495	$7,000 to $9,999	160	9,915	3,930	1,090	1,130	3,765
496	$10,000 to $11,999	180	6,805	2,840	860	700	2,415
497	$12,000 to $14,999	185	9,790	4,020	1,095	960	3,725
498	$15,000 to $19,999	405	15,280	6,505	1,855	1,775	5,140
499	$20,000 to $24,999	220	11,925	4,790	1,465	1,525	4,140
500	$25,000 to $29,999	205	10,980	4,560	1,290	1,245	3,880
501	$30,000 to $34,999	165	11,205	4,640	1,575	1,405	3,580
502	$35,000 to $39,999	100	11,145	4,510	1,325	1,685	3,630
503	$40,000 to $44,999	80	9,395	3,580	1,300	1,230	3,280
504	$45,000 to $49,999	70	8,175	3,285	1,080	1,040	2,765
505	$50,000 to $59,999	50	11,985	4,650	1,610	1,655	4,060
506	$60,000 and over	135	28,420	9,855	3,000	3,125	12,435
507	Median income $[57]	18,519	27,420	26,761	28,432	29,602	27,303
508	Average income $[57]	23,071	35,988	33,934	34,532	34,516	39,090
509	Standard error of average income $[57]	852	249	297	493	458	552
	Composition of total income						
510	Composition of total income in 2005 %	100.0	100.0	100.0	100.0	100.0	100.0
511	Employment income %	59.9	81.8	78.5	85.0	86.2	82.6
512	Government transfer payments %	19.6	5.9	7.3	6.0	5.5	4.8
513	Other %	20.5	12.3	14.2	8.9	8.3	12.6
514	**Population 15 years and over with employment income in 2005**	**3,195**	**266,625**	**99,925**	**33,725**	**34,575**	**98,390**
	Sex and work activity						
515	Median employment income in 2005 $	17,552	36,995	35,113	38,558	38,989	37,702
516	Average employment income in 2005 $	24,380	52,156	47,731	48,905	45,215	60,204
517	Standard error of average employment income $	979	393	564	1,286	538	755
518	Worked full year, full time[59]	1,340	149,455	55,085	20,055	21,170	53,145
519	Median employment income in 2005 $	32,927	53,958	51,645	51,976	50,737	60,013
520	Average employment income in 2005 $	38,961	71,938	65,454	66,396	58,949	85,924
521	Standard error of average employment income $	1,674	569	695	2,108	713	1,140
522	Worked part year or part time[60]	1,550	102,285	38,745	12,050	12,050	39,435
523	Median employment income in 2005 $	9,895	13,633	13,335	13,358	14,744	13,752
524	Average employment income in 2005 $	15,372	28,776	28,395	24,979	24,616	31,583
525	Standard error of average employment income $	940	528	1,013	689	704	896
526	Males 15 years and over with employment income[58]	1,685	137,345	51,055	17,600	17,930	50,765
527	Median employment income in 2005 $	20,613	47,335	44,895	49,115	47,309	49,110
528	Average employment income in 2005 $	27,923	66,829	60,661	61,523	54,678	79,163
529	Standard error of average employment income $	1,522	706	1,037	2,369	916	1,324

Note: See symbols and abbreviations in the introductory material and see reference material at the end of the publication.

Certaines caractéristiques des divisions de recensement et des subdivisions de recensement – Données intégrales et données-échantillon (20 %), Ontario, Recensement de 2006 (suite)

Hamilton CD/DR	Hamilton, C ■ ■	**Hastings CD/DR** †◆◊	Bancroft, T ◆	Belleville, CY ◊**A**	Carlow/Mayo, TP ◆◆◊◊	**Caractéristiques**	N°
						Caractéristiques du revenu de 2005	
						Sexe et groupes de revenu total en 2005 (suite)	
196,690	196,690	51,825	1,430	18,810	390	Total - Hommes	466
8,320	8,320	2,085	50	745	25	Sans revenu	467
188,370	188,375	49,740	1,380	18,070	365	Avec un revenu	468
8,905	8,905	2,370	60	765	15	Moins de 1 000 $[56]	469
4,825	4,820	1,305	40	495	15	1 000 $ à 2 999 $	470
4,335	4,335	1,320	55	465	0	3 000 $ à 4 999 $	471
4,665	4,670	1,250	50	520	10	5 000 $ à 6 999 $	472
8,395	8,395	2,245	50	870	25	7 000 $ à 9 999 $	473
6,455	6,460	1,820	55	690	10	10 000 $ à 11 999 $	474
8,240	8,240	2,395	80	815	30	12 000 $ à 14 999 $	475
12,505	12,505	3,890	155	1,570	35	15 000 $ à 19 999 $	476
12,580	12,580	3,910	195	1,410	15	20 000 $ à 24 999 $	477
11,900	11,905	3,410	95	1,290	20	25 000 $ à 29 999 $	478
12,565	12,565	3,715	120	1,195	25	30 000 $ à 34 999 $	479
11,740	11,740	3,800	100	1,335	30	35 000 $ à 39 999 $	480
10,780	10,780	3,100	90	1,115	55	40 000 $ à $44 999 $	481
9,975	9,975	2,595	30	810	35	45 000 $ à $49 999 $	482
17,210	17,210	4,675	90	1,570	25	50 000 $ à $59 999 $	483
43,290	43,290	7,915	125	3,145	25	60 000 $ et plus	484
34,462	34,462	31,131	24,584	30,657	33,436	Revenu médian $[57]	485
43,217	43,217	36,144	29,956	37,406	34,643	Revenu moyen $[57]	486
301	301	310	1,775	593	3,306	Erreur type de revenu moyen $[57]	487
210,900	210,900	54,750	1,700	21,120	400	Total - Femmes	488
10,785	10,785	2,745	90	890	15	Sans revenu	489
200,115	200,115	52,005	1,610	20,225	385	Avec un revenu	490
7,245	7,245	1,555	55	470	15	Moins de 1 000 $[56]	491
8,280	8,285	2,230	55	780	10	1 000$ à 2 999 $	492
8,225	8,230	2,190	65	680	10	3 000 $ à 4 999 $	493
8,805	8,805	2,485	125	830	35	5 000 $ à 6 999 $	494
14,420	14,420	3,890	65	1,465	45	7 000 $ à 9 999 $	495
10,515	10,520	3,005	100	1,120	40	10 000 $ à 11 999 $	496
15,590	15,595	4,580	195	1,660	45	12 000 $ à 14 999 $	497
24,640	24,640	6,985	240	2,635	85	15 000 $ à 19 999 $	498
17,970	17,970	5,315	205	2,025	25	20 000 $ à 24 999 $	499
15,260	15,260	3,930	130	1,660	10	25 000 $ à 29 999 $	500
13,965	13,965	3,860	70	1,575	15	30 000 $ à 34 999 $	501
11,935	11,935	2,955	80	1,285	0	35 000 $ à 39 999 $	502
9,180	9,175	2,170	60	895	0	40 000 $ à 44 999 $	503
6,875	6,875	1,635	40	710	10	45 000 $ à 49 999 $	504
9,410	9,410	2,215	40	960	0	50 000 $ à 59 999 $	505
17,785	17,780	3,015	85	1,485	25	60 000 $ et plus	506
20,567	20,567	19,340	17,920	21,237	14,417	Revenu médian $[57]	507
27,493	27,493	24,598	25,544	26,904	21,468	Revenu moyen $[57]	508
169	169	239	3,222	430	3,671	Erreur type de revenu moyen $[57]	509
						Composition du revenu total	
100.0	100.0	100.0	100.0	100.0	100.0	Composition du revenu total en 2005 %	510
75.4	75.4	67.9	55.5	68.0	51.5	Revenu d'emploi %	511
12.0	12.0	15.4	21.4	14.3	22.0	Transferts gouvernementaux %	512
12.6	12.6	16.7	23.1	17.7	26.1	Autres %	513
280,930	**280,925**	**71,145**	**1,875**	**27,360**	**460**	**Population de 15 ans et plus avec un revenu d'emploi en 2005**	514
						Sexe et travail	
28,933	28,933	23,466	19,014	23,411	11,735	Revenu médian d'emploi en 2005 $	515
36,610	36,610	29,368	24,410	30,304	23,705	Revenu moyen d'emploi en 2005 $	516
198	198	228	1,479	384	3,171	Erreur type de revenu moyen d'emploi $	517
147,395	147,400	36,885	825	14,275	135	A travaillé toute l'année à plein temps[59]	518
43,970	43,970	37,619	32,790	37,339	33,370	Revenu médian d'emploi en 2005 $	519
51,622	51,622	42,050	36,001	43,235	51,523	Revenu moyen d'emploi en 2005 $	520
274	274	324	2,842	543	8,483	Erreur type de revenu moyen d'emploi $	521
113,690	113,690	28,950	875	11,035	270	A travaillé une partie de l'année ou à temps partiel[60]	522
12,683	12,683	10,820	12,019	10,768	9,688	Revenu médian d'emploi en 2005 $	523
22,081	22,081	17,385	17,186	18,049	14,343	Revenu moyen d'emploi en 2005 $	524
296	296	270	1,274	471	1,567	Erreur type de revenu moyen d'emploi $	525
146,600	146,595	36,940	940	13,775	225	Hommes de 15 ans et plus avec un revenu d'emploi[58]	526
36,857	36,857	30,086	24,077	28,388	28,072	Revenu médian d'emploi en 2005 $	527
43,979	43,979	34,969	28,644	35,696	32,800	Revenu moyen d'emploi en 2005 $	528
315	315	362	2,575	622	5,635	Erreur type de revenu moyen d'emploi $	529

Nota : Voir les symboles et les abréviations dans les documents d'introduction et voir les documents de référence à la fin de la publication.

Selected characteristics for census divisions and census subdivisions – 100% data and 20% sample data, Ontario, 2006 Census (continued)

No.	Characteristics	Minden Hills, TP ◆◊	**Halton CD/DR**	Burlington, CY	Halton Hills, T	Milton, T	Oakville, T
	2005 income characteristics						
	Sex and work activity (continued)						
530	Worked full year, full time[59]	770	86,605	31,525	11,635	12,210	31,230
531	Median employment income in 2005 $	37,732	62,304	60,313	59,994	56,668	69,714
532	Average employment income in 2005 $	43,411	85,441	77,122	78,581	66,773	103,693
533	Standard error of average employment income $	2,473	906	1,116	3,543	1,125	1,739
534	Worked part year or part time[60]	725	43,410	16,275	5,225	5,180	16,735
535	Median employment income in 2005 $	11,485	14,564	13,932	14,529	15,667	14,773
536	Average employment income in 2005 $	17,286	38,221	38,953	30,486	30,498	42,314
537	Standard error of average employment income $	1,514	1,184	2,358	1,356	1,452	1,978
538	Females 15 years and over with employment income[58]	1,510	129,280	48,870	16,130	16,650	47,625
539	Median employment income in 2005 $	14,483	29,257	27,911	30,210	31,455	29,204
540	Average employment income in 2005 $	20,413	36,568	34,223	35,139	35,028	39,997
541	Standard error of average employment income $	1,148	279	350	599	471	611
542	Worked full year, full time[59]	570	62,850	23,560	8,420	8,960	21,915
543	Median employment income in 2005 $	27,643	45,196	43,514	43,213	43,648	49,285
544	Average employment income in 2005 $	32,962	53,330	49,843	49,550	48,279	60,597
545	Standard error of average employment income $	2,004	480	575	934	628	1,138
546	Worked part year or part time[60]	820	58,880	22,470	6,830	6,875	22,700
547	Median employment income in 2005 $	8,678	13,016	13,003	12,409	13,457	13,051
548	Average employment income in 2005 $	13,677	21,813	20,749	20,766	20,187	23,673
549	Standard error of average employment income $	1,141	259	334	582	531	533
550	**Total number of economic families in private households**	**1,735**	**124,575**	**47,460**	**15,495**	**15,550**	**46,065**
	Family income groups in 2005						
551	Under $10,000	55	1,885	695	200	185	810
552	$10,000 to $19,999	65	2,330	900	235	220	980
553	$20,000 to $29,999	165	4,300	1,935	470	415	1,485
554	$30,000 to $39,999	235	6,410	2,870	650	715	2,170
555	$40,000 to $49,999	200	7,170	3,080	830	855	2,405
556	$50,000 to $59,999	215	8,100	3,595	985	1,090	2,430
557	$60,000 to $69,999	220	8,755	3,580	1,170	1,180	2,830
558	$70,000 to $79,999	170	8,985	3,840	1,210	1,245	2,695
559	$80,000 to $89,999	145	9,140	3,500	1,245	1,425	2,970
560	$90,000 to $99,999	65	8,845	3,535	1,305	1,245	2,755
561	$100,000 and over	200	58,645	19,920	7,200	6,985	24,545
562	Median family income $	57,554	95,766	89,209	95,464	92,906	105,563
563	Average family income $	62,336	121,884	110,052	114,711	106,031	141,836
564	Standard error of average family income $	2,018	923	1,319	2,905	1,333	1,775
	Family after-tax income groups in 2005						
565	Under $10,000	50	2,015	735	210	190	880
566	$10,000 to $19,999	65	2,430	940	240	210	1,035
567	$20,000 to $29,999	185	5,025	2,275	525	515	1,710
568	$30,000 to $39,999	285	8,665	3,875	935	990	2,865
569	$40,000 to $49,999	275	9,835	4,235	1,265	1,285	3,050
570	$50,000 to $59,999	290	11,610	5,030	1,405	1,470	3,710
571	$60,000 to $69,999	215	12,125	4,820	1,695	1,730	3,875
572	$70,000 to $79,999	135	11,690	4,565	1,635	1,775	3,705
573	$80,000 to $89,999	70	11,090	4,140	1,660	1,685	3,605
574	$90,000 to $99,999	80	9,570	3,705	1,360	1,400	3,100
575	$100,000 and over	80	40,515	13,135	4,550	4,280	18,540
576	Median after-tax family income $	50,142	78,870	74,033	78,637	77,652	86,054
577	Average after-tax family income $	53,819	94,421	86,361	90,950	85,140	107,026
578	Standard error of average after-tax family income $	1,531	637	826	2,626	883	1,160
	Income status in 2005						
579	Total population in private households for income status	5,445	433,380	162,200	54,290	53,205	163,685
580	Below low income cut-off before tax in 2005	485	36,645	15,345	2,750	2,670	15,880
581	Prevalence of low income before tax in 2005 %	8.9	8.5	9.5	5.1	5.0	9.7
582	Below low income cut-off after tax in 2005	295	28,045	11,555	1,945	1,960	12,585
583	Prevalence of low income after tax in 2005 %	5.4	6.5	7.1	3.6	3.7	7.7

Note: See symbols and abbreviations in the introductory material and see reference material at the end of the publication.

Certaines caractéristiques des divisions de recensement et des subdivisions de recensement – Données intégrales et données-échantillon (20 %), Ontario, Recensement de 2006 (suite)

Hamilton CD/DR	Hamilton, C ■ ■	**Hastings CD/DR** †◆◇	Bancroft, T ◆	Belleville, CY ◇**A**	Carlow/Mayo, TP ◆◆◇◇	**Caractéristiques**	N°
						Caractéristiques du revenu de 2005	
						Sexe et travail (suite)	
85,815	85,815	21,325	495	7,835	95	A travaillé toute l'année à plein temps[59]	530
50,429	50,429	42,893	35,916	41,991	37,496	Revenu médian d'emploi en 2005 $	531
58,573	58,573	47,169	39,325	48,993	54,092	Revenu moyen d'emploi en 2005 $	532
431	431	478	4,514	829	11,263	Erreur type de revenu moyen d'emploi $	533
50,260	50,260	12,675	345	4,880	95	A travaillé une partie de l'année ou à temps partiel[60]	534
14,399	14,399	12,270	14,353	12,066	30,915	Revenu médian d'emploi en 2005 $	535
26,623	26,623	20,945	20,112	20,606	23,255	Revenu moyen d'emploi en 2005 $	536
468	468	491	2,259	830	3,145	Erreur type de revenu moyen d'emploi $	537
134,330	134,330	34,210	930	13,585	235	Femmes de 15 ans et plus avec un revenu d'emploi[58]	538
22,473	22,473	18,511	14,535	19,977	9,666	Revenu médian d'emploi en 2005 $	539
28,568	28,568	23,321	20,132	24,836	14,964	Revenu moyen d'emploi en 2005 $	540
223	223	248	1,325	425	2,699	Erreur type de revenu moyen d'emploi $	541
61,580	61,580	15,555	330	6,445	40	A travaillé toute l'année à plein temps[59]	542
36,969	36,969	31,521	29,474	32,440	26,675	Revenu médian d'emploi en 2005 $	543
41,934	41,934	35,032	31,094	36,232	45,406	Revenu moyen d'emploi en 2005 $	544
247	247	370	2,256	614	10,362	Erreur type de revenu moyen d'emploi $	545
63,425	63,425	16,275	530	6,155	175	A travaillé une partie de l'année ou à temps partiel[60]	546
11,738	11,738	10,039	10,809	10,066	8,909	Revenu médian d'emploi en 2005 $	547
18,481	18,481	14,611	15,277	16,022	9,509	Revenu moyen d'emploi en 2005 $	548
377	377	279	1,458	518	1,198	Erreur type de revenu moyen d'emploi $	549
138,895	**138,895**	**38,275**	**1,070**	**13,905**	**300**	**Nombre total des familles économiques dans les ménages privés**	550
						Revenu de la famille économique en 2005	
3,430	3,430	940	15	285	15	Moins de 10 000 $	551
6,055	6,055	1,775	55	675	0	10 000 $ à 19 999 $	552
9,980	9,980	3,545	165	1,230	35	20 000 $ à 29 999 $	553
12,970	12,970	4,445	140	1,740	60	30 000 $ à 39 999 $	554
12,915	12,910	4,165	145	1,395	60	40 000 $ à 49 999 $	555
12,530	12,530	4,420	170	1,595	40	50 000 $ à 59 999 $	556
12,075	12,075	3,875	55	1,395	20	60 000 $ à 69 999 $	557
11,225	11,230	3,485	130	1,210	15	70 000 $ à 79 999 $	558
10,350	10,345	2,950	40	1,005	0	80 000 $ à 89 999 $	559
8,495	8,490	2,040	60	700	0	90 000 $ à 99 999 $	560
38,870	38,870	6,635	85	2,680	45	100 000 $ et plus	561
69,566	69,566	59,698	50,407	60,262	45,014	Revenu médian des familles $	562
83,352	83,352	67,614	63,039	70,518	60,947	Revenu moyen des familles $	563
506	506	566	5,456	1,146	6,315	Erreur type de revenu moyen des familles $	564
						Revenu après impôt de la famille économique en 2005	
3,520	3,520	980	15	295	15	Moins de 10 000 $	565
6,200	6,200	1,850	65	690	10	10 000 $ à 19 999 $	566
11,225	11,220	3,935	180	1,355	35	20 000 $ à 29 999 $	567
16,540	16,540	5,580	170	2,125	70	30 000 $ à 39 999 $	568
16,795	16,800	5,785	185	2,085	80	40 000 $ à 49 999 $	569
15,565	15,565	5,115	150	1,815	25	50 000 $ à 59 999 $	570
14,625	14,625	4,455	140	1,510	20	60 000 $ à 69 999 $	571
12,675	12,675	3,160	45	1,135	0	70 000 $ à 79 999 $	572
9,995	9,995	2,440	45	810	0	80 000 $ à 89 999 $	573
8,125	8,125	1,665	15	570	0	90 000 $ à 99 999 $	574
23,625	23,620	3,310	60	1,520	45	100 000 $ et plus	575
59,765	59,765	51,847	45,144	52,532	41,843	Revenu médian après impôt des familles $	576
68,631	68,631	56,630	51,210	57,716	51,432	Revenu moyen après impôt des familles $	577
326	326	502	2,203	1,137	4,295	Erreur type de revenu moyen après impôt des familles $	578
						Catégorie de revenu en 2005	
495,455	495,455	128,100	3,715	47,470	935	Population totale dans les ménages privés pour la catégorie de revenu	579
89,785	89,790	16,915	325	7,180	60	Au-dessous du seuil de faible revenu avant impôt en 2005	580
18.1	18.1	13.2	8.7	15.1	6.4	Fréquence du faible revenu avant impôt en 2005 %	581
69,320	69,320	11,295	185	4,875	50	Au-dessous du seuil de faible revenu après impôt en 2005	582
14.0	14.0	8.8	5.0	10.3	4.8	Fréquence du faible revenu après impôt en 2005 %	583

Nota : Voir les symboles et les abréviations dans les documents d'introduction et voir les documents de référence à la fin de la publication.

Selected characteristics for census divisions and census subdivisions – 100% data and 20% sample data, Ontario, 2006 Census (continued)

No.	Characteristics	Minden Hills, TP ◆◇	**Halton CD/DR**	Burlington, CY	Halton Hills, T	Milton, T	Oakville, T
	2005 income characteristics						
584	**Total number of private households**	**2,385**	**157,085**	**63,255**	**18,785**	**18,465**	**56,580**
	Household income groups in 2005						
585	Under $10,000	90	3,540	1,330	380	360	1,470
586	$10,000 to $19,999	260	7,235	3,335	860	605	2,440
587	$20,000 to $29,999	330	8,550	4,110	920	765	2,750
588	$30,000 to $39,999	315	10,705	5,085	1,060	1,070	3,485
589	$40,000 to $49,999	235	11,145	5,135	1,265	1,165	3,575
590	$50,000 to $59,999	275	11,075	5,110	1,250	1,380	3,330
591	$60,000 to $69,999	260	11,310	4,930	1,370	1,420	3,590
592	$70,000 to $79,999	185	11,010	4,720	1,440	1,470	3,380
593	$80,000 to $89,999	145	10,700	4,285	1,365	1,555	3,495
594	$90,000 to $99,999	75	9,870	3,940	1,375	1,395	3,160
595	$100,000 and over	210	61,935	21,270	7,485	7,280	25,895
596	Median household income $	48,739	83,496	74,969	85,520	86,604	92,394
597	Average household income $	54,292	108,126	95,948	102,952	98,025	126,757
598	Standard error of average household income $	1,657	764	1,069	2,424	1,190	1,494
	Household after-tax income groups in 2005						
599	Under $10,000	85	3,745	1,390	410	365	1,575
600	$10,000 to $19,999	300	7,985	3,710	915	655	2,695
601	$20,000 to $29,999	350	10,605	5,130	1,125	990	3,355
602	$30,000 to $39,999	365	14,330	6,765	1,525	1,440	4,600
603	$40,000 to $49,999	330	14,200	6,490	1,690	1,675	4,340
604	$50,000 to $59,999	345	14,565	6,485	1,670	1,800	4,605
605	$60,000 to $69,999	220	14,435	5,965	1,875	1,910	4,680
606	$70,000 to $79,999	145	12,920	5,055	1,710	1,945	4,210
607	$80,000 to $89,999	70	11,980	4,550	1,725	1,790	3,915
608	$90,000 to $99,999	80	10,210	4,020	1,420	1,440	3,330
609	$100,000 and over	85	42,120	13,685	4,715	4,445	19,270
610	Median after-tax household income $	43,602	69,014	62,541	70,951	71,900	75,571
611	Average after-tax household income $	46,835	84,057	75,497	81,875	78,839	96,054
612	Standard error of average after-tax household income $	1,279	527	671	2,181	804	981

Note: See symbols and abbreviations in the introductory material and see reference material at the end of the publication.

Certaines caractéristiques des divisions de recensement et des subdivisions de recensement – Données intégrales et données-échantillon (20 %), Ontario, Recensement de 2006 (suite)

Hamilton CD/DR	Hamilton, C ■ ■	**Hastings CD/DR** †◆◇	Bancroft, T ◆	Belleville, CY ◇**A**	Carlow/Mayo, TP ◆◆◇◇	**Caractéristiques**	Nº
						Caractéristiques du revenu de 2005	
194,455	**194,455**	**52,645**	**1,655**	**20,490**	**370**	**Nombre total des ménages privés**	584
						Tranches de revenu des ménages en 2005	
8,945	8,945	2,300	95	870	20	Moins de 10 000 $	585
20,180	20,180	5,810	300	2,405	30	10 000 $ à 19 999 $	586
19,555	19,555	6,050	285	2,380	30	20 000 $ à 29 999 $	587
20,645	20,645	6,750	180	2,755	60	30 000 $ à 39 999 $	588
18,665	18,660	5,505	175	2,035	95	40 000 $ à 49 999 $	589
16,450	16,450	5,475	195	2,115	45	50 000 $ à 59 999 $	590
15,120	15,120	4,480	70	1,715	25	60 000 $ à 69 999 $	591
13,415	13,415	3,975	150	1,445	10	70 000 $ à 79 999 $	592
11,495	11,495	3,150	45	1,115	0	80 000 $ à 89 999 $	593
9,170	9,170	2,215	55	785	0	90 000 $ à 99 999 $	594
40,820	40,820	6,940	95	2,870	45	100 000 $ et plus	595
55,312	55,312	49,811	38,480	48,567	43,460	Revenu médian des ménages $	596
70,025	70,025	58,285	49,764	59,385	55,914	Revenu moyen des ménages $	597
388	388	451	3,599	851	5,347	Erreur type de revenu moyen des ménages $	598
						Tranches du revenu après impôt des ménages en 2005	
9,145	9,145	2,345	95	875	20	Moins de 10 000 $	599
21,750	21,745	6,250	320	2,585	30	10 000 $ à 19 999 $	600
22,900	22,900	7,165	305	2,755	30	20 000 $ à 29 999 $	601
25,485	25,485	7,925	220	3,295	95	30 000 $ à 39 999 $	602
22,240	22,240	7,210	225	2,785	105	40 000 $ à 49 999 $	603
19,210	19,210	5,725	160	2,115	30	50 000 $ à 59 999 $	604
16,435	16,435	4,950	150	1,745	15	60 000 $ à 69 999 $	605
13,680	13,675	3,305	50	1,225	0	70 000 $ à 79 999 $	606
10,525	10,525	2,600	55	875	0	80 000 $ à 89 999 $	607
8,545	8,545	1,680	10	590	0	90 000 $ à 99 999 $	608
24,540	24,545	3,485	65	1,640	45	100 000 $ et plus	609
48,070	48,070	43,744	34,664	42,535	40,865	Revenu médian après impôt des ménages $	610
57,890	57,890	49,054	41,118	49,045	47,357	Revenu moyen après impôt des ménages $	611
256	256	393	1,619	817	3,682	Erreur type de revenu moyen après impôt des ménages $	612

Nota : Voir les symboles et les abréviations dans les documents d'introduction et voir les documents de référence à la fin de la publication.

Selected characteristics for census divisions and census subdivisions – 100% data and 20% sample data, Ontario, 2006 Census (continued)

No.	Characteristics	Centre Hastings, MU	Deseronto, T ◆◇	Faraday, TP ◆◇◇	Hastings Highlands, MU ◆◇	Limerick, TP ◆◆◇◇	Madoc, TP ◆
	Population characteristics						
1	**Population, 2001**[1]	**4,226**	**1,796**	**1,581**	**3,992**	**362**	**2,044**
2	**Population, 2006**[2]	**4,386**	**1,824**	**1,578**	**4,033**	**364**	**2,069**
3	Population percentage change, 2001 to 2006	3.8	1.6	-0.2	1.0	0.6	1.2
4	Land area in square kilometres, 2006	222.09	2.52	215.23	967.34	200.59	269.98
5	**Total population – 100% data**[3]	**4,385**	**1,825**	**1,575**	**4,030**	**365**	**2,070**
	Sex and age groups						
6	Male	2,225	905	775	2,030	195	1,050
7	0 to 4 years	115	55	30	80	10	35
8	5 to 9 years	135	70	25	95	10	55
9	10 to 14 years	165	60	45	110	10	80
10	15 to 19 years	160	60	50	145	20	85
11	20 to 24 years	105	50	40	85	5	50
12	25 to 29 years	115	55	25	65	5	35
13	30 to 34 years	120	50	30	80	5	45
14	35 to 39 years	120	60	40	100	10	60
15	40 to 44 years	195	80	60	140	15	85
16	45 to 49 years	165	75	55	175	15	100
17	50 to 54 years	170	55	80	165	20	85
18	55 to 59 years	185	80	95	210	25	95
19	60 to 64 years	150	50	60	180	20	70
20	65 to 69 years	120	30	70	150	15	65
21	70 to 74 years	90	25	40	130	15	45
22	75 to 79 years	55	25	30	85	5	30
23	80 to 84 years	40	20	15	40	5	15
24	85 years and over	20	5	5	15	0	10
25	Female	2,160	915	805	2,000	170	1,020
26	0 to 4 years	110	55	20	85	5	35
27	5 to 9 years	120	45	35	90	5	50
28	10 to 14 years	130	70	50	100	10	80
29	15 to 19 years	125	60	60	135	5	75
30	20 to 24 years	95	45	35	70	0	45
31	25 to 29 years	110	65	15	80	5	40
32	30 to 34 years	125	60	30	85	10	50
33	35 to 39 years	115	60	40	85	10	70
34	40 to 44 years	155	80	65	155	10	90
35	45 to 49 years	190	70	75	155	10	85
36	50 to 54 years	190	70	75	195	25	85
37	55 to 59 years	185	70	85	210	20	85
38	60 to 64 years	165	45	70	190	25	75
39	65 to 69 years	85	35	55	140	10	60
40	70 to 74 years	100	30	40	105	5	40
41	75 to 79 years	70	40	30	55	10	30
42	80 to 84 years	50	20	15	35	5	20
43	85 years and over	40	10	5	25	0	10
44	**Total population 15 years and over**[3]	**3,610**	**1,475**	**1,370**	**3,480**	**320**	**1,720**
	Legal marital status						
45	Never legally married (single)	905	440	310	770	65	445
46	Legally married (and not separated)[4,5]	2,035	750	790	2,075	175	1,005
47	Separated, but still legally married	125	65	55	125	15	55
48	Divorced	290	125	115	275	30	120
49	Widowed	255	95	100	230	30	95
	Common-law status						
50	Not in a common-law relationship	3,240	1,300	1,250	3,170	285	1,555
51	In a common-law relationship	370	165	125	310	30	165
52	**Total population – 20% sample data**[6]	**4,355**	**1,800**	**1,580**	**4,025**	**360**	**2,065**
	Mother tongue						
53	Single responses	4,355	1,795	1,575	4,015	360	2,035
54	English	4,160	1,670	1,490	3,785	365	1,910
55	French	40	10	10	45	0	20
56	Non-official languages[7]	150	115	75	190	0	110
57	Italian	15	0	0	0	0	0
58	Chinese, n.o.s.[61]	0	0	0	0	0	0
59	Cantonese	10	0	0	0	0	0
60	Spanish	0	15	0	0	0	0
61	German	45	0	15	60	0	30
62	Other languages[8]	75	100	65	120	0	75

Note: See symbols and abbreviations in the introductory material and see reference material at the end of the publication.

Certaines caractéristiques des divisions de recensement et des subdivisions de recensement – Données intégrales et données-échantillon (20 %), Ontario, Recensement de 2006 (suite)

Marmora and Lake, MU ◆◇	Quinte West, CY ◇A	Stirling-Rawdon, TP	Tudor and Cashel, TP ◆◆◇◇	Tweed, MU ◆◇	Tyendinaga, TP	Caractéristiques	N°
						Caractéristiques de la population	
3,985	**41,366**	**4,887**	**665**	**5,612**	**3,769**	**Population, 2001[1]**	1
3,912	**42,697**	**4,906**	**682**	**5,614**	**4,070**	**Population, 2006[2]**	2
-1.8	3.2	0.4	2.6	0.0	8.0	Variation en pourcentage de la population, 2001 à 2006	3
533.75	493.85	280.63	433.49	896.98	311.94	Superficie des terres en kilomètres carrés, 2006	4
3,915	**42,695**	**4,905**	**680**	**5,615**	**4,070**	**Population totale – Données intégrales[3]**	5
						Sexe et groupes d'âge	
1,935	21,180	2,410	375	2,855	2,080	Sexe masculin	6
90	1,120	135	20	130	120	0 à 4 ans	7
80	1,275	130	20	170	145	5 à 9 ans	8
120	1,635	185	20	210	195	10 à 14 ans	9
125	1,585	195	20	200	200	15 à 19 ans	10
65	1,250	140	20	140	110	20 à 24 ans	11
70	1,020	110	15	120	100	25 à 29 ans	12
95	1,105	115	20	110	110	30 à 34 ans	13
120	1,400	145	25	165	140	35 à 39 ans	14
160	1,995	205	35	220	195	40 à 44 ans	15
155	1,790	225	35	225	195	45 à 49 ans	16
145	1,530	160	20	245	145	50 à 54 ans	17
175	1,415	190	45	240	130	55 à 59 ans	18
135	1,120	145	25	210	100	60 à 64 ans	19
120	950	110	30	170	70	65 à 69 ans	20
115	825	70	25	125	65	70 à 74 ans	21
95	605	75	10	95	35	75 à 79 ans	22
40	350	40	10	50	20	80 à 84 ans	23
40	190	30	5	30	5	85 ans et plus	24
1,975	21,525	2,500	305	2,765	1,995	Sexe féminin	25
80	1,065	125	15	110	115	0 à 4 ans	26
85	1,240	120	15	145	125	5 à 9 ans	27
110	1,510	160	15	180	185	10 à 14 ans	28
100	1,505	185	15	180	170	15 à 19 ans	29
70	1,115	125	10	130	110	20 à 24 ans	30
75	1,015	105	10	105	110	25 à 29 ans	31
85	1,200	135	10	125	110	30 à 34 ans	32
110	1,485	155	25	165	150	35 à 39 ans	33
125	1,925	220	35	230	195	40 à 44 ans	34
140	1,770	215	20	250	210	45 à 49 ans	35
135	1,540	185	35	230	125	50 à 54 ans	36
195	1,460	185	35	240	115	55 à 59 ans	37
140	1,205	120	25	190	75	60 à 64 ans	38
150	1,085	115	30	145	60	65 à 69 ans	39
110	845	90	10	120	55	70 à 74 ans	40
80	645	85	5	95	30	75 à 79 ans	41
70	540	70	5	80	25	80 à 84 ans	42
110	380	100	0	50	20	85 ans et plus	43
3,345	**34,850**	**4,040**	**590**	**4,675**	**3,180**	**Population totale de 15 ans et plus[3]**	44
						État matrimonial légal	
795	9,445	1,040	155	1,155	905	Jamais légalement marié(e) (célibataire)	45
1,820	18,745	2,240	330	2,615	1,860	Légalement marié(e) (et non séparé[e])[4,5]	46
110	1,545	175	20	170	90	Séparé(e), mais toujours légalement marié(e)	47
255	2,825	265	50	410	195	Divorcé(e)	48
365	2,285	320	35	325	130	Veuf(ve)	49
						Union libre	
3,050	31,255	3,670	545	4,220	2,860	Ne vivant pas en union libre	50
295	3,595	370	50	455	320	Vivant en union libre	51
3,765	**42,375**	**4,800**	**680**	**5,600**	**4,095**	**Population totale – Données-échantillon (20 %)[6]**	52
						Langue maternelle	
3,765	42,175	4,790	680	5,570	4,095	Réponses uniques	53
3,485	38,465	4,695	570	5,365	3,930	Anglais	54
60	1,900	30	55	45	30	Français	55
220	1,805	65	60	165	140	Langues non officielles[7]	56
20	90	0	0	0	0	Italien	57
0	55	10	0	0	0	Chinois, n.d.a.[61]	58
0	30	0	0	0	0	Cantonais	59
0	65	0	0	0	15	Espagnol	60
40	335	0	25	35	40	Allemand	61
160	1,220	50	30	130	80	Autres langues[8]	62

Nota : Voir les symboles et les abréviations dans les documents d'introduction et voir les documents de référence à la fin de la publication.

Selected characteristics for census divisions and census subdivisions – 100% data and 20% sample data, Ontario, 2006 Census (continued)

No.	Characteristics	Centre Hastings, MU	Deseronto, T ◆◇	Faraday, TP ◆◇◇	Hastings Highlands, MU ◆◇	Limerick, TP ◆◆◇◇	Madoc, TP ◆
	Population characteristics						
	Mother tongue (continued)						
63	Multiple responses	0	0	0	10	0	30
64	English and French	0	0	0	0	0	10
65	English and non-official language	0	0	0	10	0	30
66	French and non-official language	0	0	0	0	0	0
67	English, French and non-official language	0	0	0	0	0	0
	Language spoken most often at home[9]						
68	Single responses	4,340	1,800	1,570	4,025	365	2,065
69	English	4,340	1,730	1,570	4,025	365	2,015
70	French	0	0	0	0	0	10
71	Non-official languages[7]	0	70	0	0	0	40
72	Chinese, n.o.s.[61]	0	0	0	0	0	0
73	Cantonese	0	0	0	0	0	0
74	Panjabi (Punjabi)	0	0	0	0	0	0
75	Italian	0	0	0	0	0	0
76	Spanish	0	15	0	0	0	0
77	Other languages[8]	0	55	0	0	0	40
78	Multiple responses	10	0	0	0	0	0
79	English and French	0	0	0	0	0	0
80	English and non-official language	10	0	0	0	0	0
81	French and non-official language	0	0	0	0	0	0
82	English, French and non-official language	0	0	0	0	0	0
	Knowledge of official languages[10]						
83	English only	4,190	1,740	1,535	3,815	350	2,000
84	French only	0	0	0	0	0	0
85	English and French	160	55	45	210	10	70
86	Neither English nor French	0	0	0	0	0	0
	Knowledge of non-official languages[7,11]						
87	Italian	20	0	0	0	0	0
88	Spanish	20	20	0	25	0	0
89	German	75	0	15	60	0	45
90	Chinese, n.o.s.[61]	0	0	0	0	0	0
91	Cantonese	0	10	0	0	0	0
92	Panjabi (Punjabi)	0	0	0	0	0	10
93	Portuguese	0	0	10	0	0	10
	First official language spoken[10]						
94	English	4,315	1,785	1,570	3,985	360	2,050
95	French	35	10	0	40	0	20
96	English and French	0	0	0	0	0	0
97	Neither English nor French	0	0	0	0	0	0
98	Official language minority - (number)[12]	40	10	0	40	0	20
99	Official language minority - (percentage)[12]	0.9	0.6	0.0	1.0	0.0	1.0
	Ethnic origin[13]						
100	English	1,630	715	555	1,515	150	845
101	Canadian	1,890	590	590	1,345	95	565
102	Scottish	1,055	375	570	1,055	60	665
103	Irish	1,225	650	440	1,190	120	635
104	French	545	290	145	535	60	200
105	German	650	205	150	720	0	200
106	Italian	85	10	30	25	0	65
107	Chinese	10	0	0	0	0	0
108	East Indian	0	0	0	10	15	0
109	Dutch (Netherlands)	290	80	45	325	15	105
110	Polish	65	0	30	275	0	60
111	Ukrainian	80	10	10	130	0	15
112	North American Indian	150	365	160	180	25	80
113	Portuguese	20	10	15	0	0	15
114	Filipino	10	10	0	15	0	0
	Aboriginal and non-Aboriginal identity						
115	Total Aboriginal identity population[14]	130	250	175	365	50	45
116	Total non-Aboriginal identity population	4,225	1,550	1,405	3,660	310	2,025

Note: See symbols and abbreviations in the introductory material and see reference material at the end of the publication.

Certaines caractéristiques des divisions de recensement et des subdivisions de recensement – Données intégrales et données-échantillon (20 %), Ontario, Recensement de 2006 (suite)

Marmora and Lake, MU ◆◇	Quinte West, CY ◇A	Stirling-Rawdon, TP	Tudor and Cashel, TP ◆◆◇◇	Tweed, MU ◆◇	Tyendinaga, TP	Caractéristiques	N°
						Caractéristiques de la population	
						Langue maternelle (suite)	
0	200	0	0	25	0	Réponses multiples	63
0	95	10	0	20	0	Anglais et français	64
0	85	10	0	10	0	Anglais et langue non officielle	65
0	0	0	0	0	0	Français et langue non officielle	66
0	15	0	0	0	0	Anglais, français et langue non officielle	67
						Langue parlée le plus souvent à la maison[9]	
3,770	42,180	4,800	675	5,600	4,085	Réponses uniques	68
3,720	40,650	4,795	605	5,570	4,040	Anglais	69
0	1,130	0	50	10	0	Français	70
45	395	0	15	20	45	Langues non officielles[7]	71
0	25	0	0	0	0	Chinois, n.d.a.[61]	72
0	25	0	0	0	0	Cantonais	73
0	45	0	0	0	0	Pendjabi	74
0	10	0	0	0	0	Italien	75
0	0	10	0	0	10	Espagnol	76
45	285	0	15	25	40	Autres langues[8]	77
0	200	0	0	0	10	Réponses multiples	78
0	65	0	0	0	0	Anglais et français	79
0	100	0	10	0	10	Anglais et langue non officielle	80
0	0	0	0	0	0	Français et langue non officielle	81
0	25	0	0	0	0	Anglais, français et langue non officielle	82
						Connaissance des langues officielles[10]	
3,665	38,565	4,650	610	5,365	3,990	Anglais seulement	83
0	155	0	0	0	0	Français seulement	84
105	3,605	150	70	235	105	Anglais et français	85
0	55	0	0	0	0	Ni l'anglais ni le français	86
						Connaissance des langues non officielles[7,11]	
25	140	0	10	10	0	Italien	87
25	285	15	0	10	25	Espagnol	88
45	525	10	25	70	45	Allemand	89
0	75	0	0	0	0	Chinois, n.d.a.[61]	90
0	45	0	0	0	0	Cantonais	91
10	55	0	0	0	0	Pendjabi	92
0	60	0	0	0	0	Portugais	93
						Première langue officielle parlée[10]	
3,725	40,435	4,765	630	5,555	4,065	Anglais	94
35	1,850	30	55	40	30	Français	95
0	45	0	0	0	0	Anglais et français	96
0	45	0	0	0	0	Ni l'anglais ni le français	97
35	1,870	35	55	40	25	Minorité de langue officielle - (nombre)[12]	98
0.9	4.4	0.7	8.1	0.7	0.6	Minorité de langue officielle - (pourcentage)[12]	99
						Origine ethnique[13]	
1,395	16,050	1,980	255	1,915	1,535	Anglais	100
1,290	17,210	1,905	105	2,205	1,785	Canadien	101
1,050	9,820	1,345	215	1,705	940	Écossais	102
985	9,710	1,280	165	1,875	1,285	Irlandais	103
530	6,550	595	140	1,325	460	Français	104
365	4,505	400	125	610	385	Allemand	105
140	1,045	95	15	20	60	Italien	106
0	250	0	10	0	0	Chinois	107
10	185	0	0	0	0	Indien de l'Inde	108
195	3,715	390	50	465	435	Hollandais (Néerlandais)	109
90	800	125	15	145	40	Polonais	110
50	1,015	110	0	65	80	Ukrainien	111
170	1,715	170	40	255	395	Indien de l'Amérique du Nord	112
0	170	10	0	60	0	Portugais	113
0	20	0	0	0	0	Philippin	114
						Population ayant une identité autochtone et population n'ayant pas d'identité autochtone	
115	1,140	120	70	170	240	Total de la population ayant une identité autochtone[14]	115
3,650	41,240	4,680	610	5,425	3,855	Total de la population n'ayant pas d'identité autochtone	116

Nota : Voir les symboles et les abréviations dans les documents d'introduction et voir les documents de référence à la fin de la publication.

Selected characteristics for census divisions and census subdivisions – 100% data and 20% sample data, Ontario, 2006 Census (continued)

No.	Characteristics	Centre Hastings, MU	Deseronto, T ◆◇	Faraday, TP ◆◇◇	Hastings Highlands, MU ◆◇	Limerick, TP ◆◆◇◇	Madoc, TP ◆
	Population characteristics						
	Aboriginal and non-Aboriginal ancestry						
117	Total Aboriginal ancestry population[15]	220	395	230	420	55	85
118	Total non-Aboriginal ancestry population	4,130	1,410	1,345	3,605	305	1,985
	Registered Indian status						
119	Registered Indian[16]	40	150	35	75	20	10
120	Not a Registered Indian	4,310	1,650	1,540	3,950	340	2,060
	Visible minority groups						
121	Total visible minority population[17]	40	85	0	15	20	15
122	Chinese	0	0	0	0	0	0
123	South Asian[18]	10	0	0	0	15	10
124	Black	10	10	0	0	10	0
125	Filipino	0	35	0	10	0	0
126	Latin American	0	15	0	0	0	0
127	Southeast Asian[19]	10	25	0	0	0	0
128	Arab	0	0	0	0	0	0
129	West Asian[20]	0	0	0	0	0	0
130	Korean	20	0	0	0	0	0
131	Japanese	0	0	0	0	0	0
132	Visible minority, n.i.e.[21]	0	0	0	0	0	0
133	Multiple visible minority[22]	0	0	0	0	0	0
	Citizenship[23]						
134	Canadian citizens[24]	4,315	1,790	1,570	3,975	365	2,030
135	Not Canadian citizens[25]	35	10	10	55	0	40
	Immigrant status and place of birth[26]						
136	Non-immigrants[27]	4,085	1,690	1,455	3,745	355	1,930
137	Born in province of residence	3,735	1,570	1,360	3,475	320	1,800
138	Immigrants[28]	265	110	125	280	0	130
139	United States of America	35	10	0	30	0	10
140	Central and South America	0	15	10	0	0	0
141	Caribbean and Bermuda	10	10	0	0	0	0
142	United Kingdom	95	10	65	90	0	60
143	Other Europe	115	35	50	155	0	40
144	Africa	0	0	0	0	0	0
145	Asia and the Middle East	20	25	0	10	10	10
146	Oceania and other[29]	0	10	0	0	0	0
147	Non-permanent residents[30]	0	0	0	10	0	10
148	**Total immigrant population[28]**	**270**	**110**	**125**	**280**	**10**	**130**
	Period of immigration						
149	Before 1961	115	15	90	180	0	70
150	1961 to 1970	75	40	10	45	0	25
151	1971 to 1980	50	0	15	15	0	25
152	1981 to 1990	0	10	0	10	10	0
153	1991 to 2000	25	15	0	25	0	10
154	1991 to 1995	15	15	0	10	0	10
155	1996 to 2000	15	0	0	10	0	0
156	2001 to 2006[31]	0	25	10	10	0	0
	Age at immigration						
157	Under 5 years	25	35	15	25	0	15
158	5 to 19 years	90	10	45	95	10	35
159	20 years and over	150	65	65	165	0	75
160	**Total population 15 years and over**	**3,575**	**1,495**	**1,325**	**3,475**	**315**	**1,730**
	Generation status						
161	1st generation[32]	265	95	130	290	15	140
162	2nd generation[33]	405	195	185	535	25	225
163	3rd generation or more[34]	2,905	1,210	1,010	2,655	280	1,365

Note: See symbols and abbreviations in the introductory material and see reference material at the end of the publication.

Certaines caractéristiques des divisions de recensement et des subdivisions de recensement – Données intégrales et données-échantillon (20 %), Ontario, Recensement de 2006 (suite)

Marmora and Lake, MU ◆◊	Quinte West, CY ◊**A**	Stirling-Rawdon, TP	Tudor and Cashel, TP ◆◆◊◊	Tweed, MU ◆◊	Tyendinaga, TP	**Caractéristiques**	N°
						Caractéristiques de la population	
						Population ayant une ascendance autochtone et population n'ayant pas d'ascendance autochtone	
190	2,180	215	70	315	430	Total de la population ayant une ascendance autochtone[15]	117
3,575	40,200	4,590	615	5,280	3,660	Total de la population n'ayant pas d'ascendance autochtone	118
						Statut d'Indien inscrit	
15	400	60	20	25	175	Indien inscrit[16]	119
3,750	41,980	4,740	660	5,570	3,920	Pas un Indien inscrit	120
						Groupes de minorités visibles	
50	880	10	15	25	10	Total de la population des minorités visibles[17]	121
0	160	10	0	0	0	Chinois	122
0	115	10	0	0	0	Sud-Asiatique[18]	123
20	260	0	10	10	0	Noir	124
0	25	0	0	0	10	Philippin	125
0	60	0	0	0	0	Latino-Américain	126
0	35	0	0	0	0	Asiatique du Sud-Est[19]	127
0	15	0	0	0	0	Arabe	128
10	0	0	0	0	0	Asiatique occidental[20]	129
20	90	0	0	0	0	Coréen	130
0	30	0	0	0	0	Japonais	131
0	10	0	0	10	0	Minorité visible, n.i.a.[21]	132
0	85	0	0	0	0	Minorités visibles multiples[22]	133
						Citoyenneté[23]	
3,695	41,865	4,775	655	5,580	4,020	Citoyens canadiens[24]	134
65	510	30	25	15	70	Ne sont pas des citoyens canadiens[25]	135
						Statut d'immigrant et le lieu de naissance[26]	
3,400	39,110	4,555	590	5,345	3,900	Non-immigrants[27]	136
3,075	30,995	4,155	510	4,995	3,645	Né dans la province de résidence	137
350	3,160	240	95	255	200	Immigrants[28]	138
35	225	15	10	15	35	États-Unis d'Amérique	139
15	80	0	0	0	0	Amérique centrale et Amérique du Sud	140
15	115	0	10	10	10	Antilles et Bermudes	141
100	1,085	145	20	105	70	Royaume-Uni	142
150	1,330	65	50	120	70	Autre Europe	143
0	65	0	0	0	0	Afrique	144
30	225	10	0	0	0	Asie et Moyen-Orient	145
0	30	0	0	0	10	Océanie et autres[29]	146
20	105	0	0	0	0	Résidents non permanents[30]	147
350	**3,160**	**245**	**90**	**255**	**195**	**Population totale des immigrants[28]**	148
						Période d'immigration	
135	1,495	140	30	160	65	Avant 1961	149
75	630	45	25	55	65	1961 à 1970	150
50	260	10	20	30	15	1971 à 1980	151
60	355	25	0	15	25	1981 à 1990	152
30	235	20	10	0	30	1991 à 2000	153
30	155	15	10	0	15	1991 à 1995	154
0	80	10	0	0	15	1996 à 2000	155
0	180	0	0	10	0	2001 à 2006[31]	156
						Âge à l'immigration	
65	465	55	0	0	30	Moins de 5 ans	157
100	1,030	100	35	100	50	5 à 19 ans	158
185	1,660	85	60	145	120	20 ans et plus	159
3,190	**34,570**	**3,945**	**655**	**4,655**	**3,175**	**Population totale de 15 ans et plus**	160
						Statut des générations	
375	3,355	245	95	260	200	1re génération[32]	161
470	4,955	435	75	585	310	2e génération[33]	162
2,345	26,255	3,255	490	3,805	2,660	3e génération ou plus[34]	163

Nota : Voir les symboles et les abréviations dans les documents d'introduction et voir les documents de référence à la fin de la publication.

Selected characteristics for census divisions and census subdivisions – 100% data and 20% sample data, Ontario, 2006 Census (continued)

No.	Characteristics	Centre Hastings, MU	Deseronto, T ◆◇	Faraday, TP ◆◇◇	Hastings Highlands, MU ◆◇	Limerick, TP ◆◆◇◇	Madoc, TP ◆
	Population characteristics						
164	**Total population 1 year and over[35]**	**4,325**	**1,785**	**1,570**	**3,995**	**360**	**2,045**
	Place of residence 1 year ago (mobility)						
165	Non-movers	3,755	1,465	1,320	3,660	340	1,770
166	Movers	570	325	250	340	25	275
167	Non-migrants	180	90	105	130	25	125
168	Migrants	390	235	140	205	0	150
169	Internal migrants	390	225	140	200	0	145
170	Intraprovincial migrants	390	225	140	200	0	140
171	Interprovincial migrants	0	0	0	0	0	10
172	External migrants	0	10	0	0	0	10
173	**Total population 5 years and over[36]**	**4,130**	**1,710**	**1,530**	**3,865**	**330**	**1,995**
	Place of residence 5 years ago (mobility)						
174	Non-movers	2,385	1,080	1,070	2,485	240	1,400
175	Movers	1,745	630	460	1,380	90	600
176	Non-migrants	580	210	125	530	40	255
177	Migrants	1,165	420	335	845	50	345
178	Internal migrants	1,160	405	330	845	50	335
179	Intraprovincial migrants	1,160	390	330	815	50	290
180	Interprovincial migrants	0	15	0	30	0	40
181	External migrants	0	10	0	0	0	10
182	**Total population 15 years and over**	**3,575**	**1,495**	**1,325**	**3,480**	**315**	**1,730**
	Highest certificate, diploma or degree[37]						
183	No certificate, diploma or degree	1,060	590	380	1,085	140	450
184	Certificate, diploma or degree	2,520	905	945	2,390	180	1,275
185	High school certificate or equivalent[38]	920	430	345	925	30	545
186	Apprenticeship or trades certificate or diploma	425	95	180	410	45	280
187	College, CEGEP or other non-university certificate or diploma[39]	785	280	230	625	45	280
188	University certificate or diploma below bachelor level[40]	60	35	60	135	25	55
189	University certificate or degree[41]	325	60	125	300	40	115
190	Bachelor's degree	220	30	70	200	10	75
191	University certificate or diploma above bachelor level	60	0	35	35	0	10
192	Degree in medicine, dentistry, veterinary medicine or optometry	10	0	0	0	0	0
193	Master's degree	35	10	15	45	25	35
194	Earned doctorate	10	10	0	10	0	0
195	**Total population 15 years and over with postsecondary qualifications**	**1,600**	**470**	**600**	**1,465**	**150**	**730**
	Major field of study - Classification of Instructional Programs, 2000[42]						
196	Education	155	25	55	165	10	55
197	Visual and performing arts, and communications technologies	35	10	45	30	0	20
198	Humanities	65	10	10	75	0	10
199	Social and behavioural sciences and law	120	75	60	95	35	75
200	Business, management and public administration	320	70	95	275	20	145
201	Physical and life sciences and technologies	40	0	15	30	0	10
202	Mathematics, computer and information sciences	100	10	10	25	0	20
203	Architecture, engineering, and related technologies	405	120	120	435	45	255
204	Agriculture, natural resources and conservation	70	0	35	115	0	15
205	Health, parks, recreation and fitness	160	90	130	155	30	70
206	Personal, protective and transportation services	125	65	35	70	15	50
207	Other fields of study[43]	0	0	0	0	0	0
	Location of study[44]						
208	Inside Canada	1,535	440	560	1,335	135	695
209	Outside Canada	65	30	40	130	10	40
210	**Total population 15 years and over**	**3,575**	**1,495**	**1,325**	**3,480**	**315**	**1,730**
	Unpaid work						
211	Males 15 years and over	1,790	740	655	1,760	175	870
212	Reported unpaid work[45]	1,640	665	570	1,650	170	795
213	Housework and child care and care or assistance to seniors	135	70	45	115	15	90
214	Housework and child care only	485	185	105	310	35	195

Note: See symbols and abbreviations in the introductory material and see reference material at the end of the publication.

Certaines caractéristiques des divisions de recensement et des subdivisions de recensement – Données intégrales et données-échantillon (20 %), Ontario, Recensement de 2006 (suite)

Marmora and Lake, MU ◆◇	Quinte West, CY ◇A	Stirling-Rawdon, TP	Tudor and Cashel, TP ◆◆◇◇	Tweed, MU ◆◇	Tyendinaga, TP	Caractéristiques	N°
						Caractéristiques de la population	
3,745	**41,820**	**4,765**	**680**	**5,565**	**4,025**	**Population totale de 1 an et plus[35]**	164
						Lieu de résidence 1 an auparavant (mobilité)	
3,245	36,240	4,350	615	5,000	3,650	Personnes n'ayant pas déménagé	165
500	5,580	415	70	560	375	Personnes ayant déménagé	166
100	2,915	145	15	305	90	Non-migrants	167
395	2,670	270	55	260	280	Migrants	168
365	2,600	260	55	255	285	Migrants internes	169
360	1,975	245	55	225	280	Migrants infraprovinciaux	170
0	625	15	0	30	0	Migrants interprovinciaux	171
30	70	10	0	0	0	Migrants externes	172
3,605	**40,095**	**4,545**	**665**	**5,355**	**3,850**	**Population totale de 5 ans et plus[36]**	173
						Lieu de résidence 5 ans auparavant (mobilité)	
2,355	23,020	3,120	505	3,640	2,690	Personnes n'ayant pas déménagé	174
1,250	17,075	1,420	155	1,715	1,160	Personnes ayant déménagé	175
440	7,480	450	25	695	225	Non-migrants	176
810	9,590	975	135	1,025	940	Migrants	177
780	9,330	950	135	1,005	895	Migrants internes	178
720	6,775	910	80	940	880	Migrants infraprovinciaux	179
65	2,555	40	55	65	15	Migrants interprovinciaux	180
25	265	25	0	20	40	Migrants externes	181
3,190	**34,570**	**3,945**	**655**	**4,655**	**3,175**	**Population totale de 15 ans et plus**	182
						Plus haut certificat, diplôme ou grade[37]	
1,150	9,090	1,090	245	1,585	865	Aucun certificat, diplôme ou grade	183
2,045	25,475	2,850	405	3,065	2,305	Certificat, diplôme ou grade	184
815	10,395	1,240	140	1,375	1,055	Diplôme d'études secondaires ou l'équivalent[38]	185
420	4,330	415	155	445	365	Certificat ou diplôme d'apprenti ou d'une école de métiers	186
610	7,380	810	90	755	640	Certificat ou diplôme d'un collège, d'un cégep ou d'un autre établissement d'enseignement non universitaire[39]	187
30	795	75	10	120	60	Certificat ou diplôme universitaire inférieur au baccalauréat[40]	188
170	2,575	310	15	370	195	Certificat ou grade universitaire[41]	189
110	1,790	220	10	260	115	Baccalauréat	190
35	365	25	0	50	30	Certificat ou diplôme universitaire supérieur au baccalauréat	191
10	85	10	0	10	0	Diplôme en médecine, en art dentaire, en médecine vétérinaire ou en optométrie	192
0	265	50	0	55	45	Maîtrise	193
15	65	10	0	10	0	Doctorat acquis	194
1,230	**15,080**	**1,615**	**270**	**1,695**	**1,250**	**Population totale de 15 ans et plus avec titres du niveau postsecondaire**	195
						Principal domaine d'études - Classification des programmes d'enseignement, 2000[42]	
90	905	190	15	155	90	Éducation	196
20	280	25	0	45	35	Arts visuels et d'interprétation, et technologie des communications	197
35	565	55	10	90	45	Sciences humaines	198
95	1,365	140	10	110	75	Sciences sociales et de comportements, et droit	199
150	2,815	320	20	280	165	Commerce, gestion et administration publique	200
35	235	20	0	60	35	Sciences physiques et de la vie, et technologies	201
35	470	35	0	25	50	Mathématiques, informatique et sciences de l'information	202
370	4,280	370	110	385	425	Architecture, génie et services connexes	203
45	255	55	20	145	25	Agriculture, ressources naturelles et conservation	204
250	2,400	265	55	310	215	Santé, parcs, récréation et conditionnement physique	205
100	1,510	145	20	80	75	Services personnels, de protection et de transport	206
0	0	0	0	0	0	Autres domaines d'études[43]	207
						Lieu des études[44]	
1,150	14,380	1,565	230	1,595	1,185	À l'intérieur du Canada	208
80	700	45	40	95	60	À l'extérieur du Canada	209
3,190	**34,570**	**3,945**	**655**	**4,655**	**3,175**	**Population totale de 15 ans et plus**	210
						Travail non rémunéré	
1,605	17,030	1,920	365	2,345	1,615	Hommes de 15 ans et plus	211
1,440	15,385	1,775	320	2,110	1,505	Travail non rémunéré déclaré[45]	212
85	1,160	125	10	155	165	Travaux ménagers et soins aux enfants et soins ou aide aux personnes âgées	213
285	4,355	515	80	515	485	Travaux ménagers et soins aux enfants seulement	214

Nota : Voir les symboles et les abréviations dans les documents d'introduction et voir les documents de référence à la fin de la publication.

Selected characteristics for census divisions and census subdivisions – 100% data and 20% sample data, Ontario, 2006 Census (continued)

No.	Characteristics	Centre Hastings, MU	Deseronto, T ◆◇	Faraday, TP ◆◇◇	Hastings Highlands, MU ◆◇	Limerick, TP ◆◆◇◇	Madoc, TP ◆
	Population characteristics						
	Unpaid work (continued)						
215	Housework and care or assistance to seniors only	130	60	35	260	10	85
216	Child care and care or assistance to seniors only	0	0	0	10	0	0
217	Housework only	855	325	375	945	95	415
218	Child care only	15	0	10	0	10	0
219	Care or assistance to seniors only	10	15	0	15	0	0
220	Females 15 years and over	1,790	755	670	1,715	145	855
221	Reported unpaid work[45]	1,680	690	650	1,615	130	810
222	Housework and child care and care or assistance to seniors	155	95	90	145	10	100
223	Housework and child care only	580	190	145	380	50	220
224	Housework and care or assistance to seniors only	175	65	100	270	0	115
225	Child care and care or assistance to seniors only	0	0	0	10	0	0
226	Housework only	760	340	310	790	70	375
227	Child care only	0	0	0	0	0	0
228	Care or assistance to seniors only	0	0	0	0	0	0
	Labour force activity						
229	Males 15 years and over	1,790	740	655	1,755	170	870
230	In the labour force	1,225	490	335	935	110	575
231	Employed	1,125	430	320	855	85	535
232	Unemployed	100	60	15	80	25	35
233	Not in the labour force	560	250	315	825	65	295
234	Participation rate	68.4	66.2	51.1	53.3	64.7	66.1
235	Employment rate	62.8	58.1	48.9	48.7	50.0	61.5
236	Unemployment rate	8.2	12.2	4.5	8.6	22.7	6.1
237	Females 15 years and over	1,790	750	670	1,715	145	860
238	In the labour force	985	470	235	855	70	470
239	Employed	910	435	225	805	50	445
240	Unemployed	75	30	10	50	15	20
241	Not in the labour force	805	285	435	865	75	390
242	Participation rate	55.0	62.7	35.1	49.9	48.3	54.7
243	Employment rate	50.8	58.0	33.6	46.9	34.5	51.7
244	Unemployment rate	7.6	6.4	4.3	5.8	21.4	4.3
245	Both sexes - Participation rate	61.8	64.2	43.4	51.3	54.7	60.4
246	15 to 24 years	65.6	78.7	56.0	63.6	0.0	74.1
247	25 years and over	61.2	61.4	42.1	49.6	59.3	57.8
248	Both sexes - Employment rate	56.8	57.9	41.1	47.8	42.2	57.1
249	15 to 24 years	48.4	61.7	48.0	56.2	0.0	69.0
250	25 years and over	58.2	57.5	40.0	46.5	45.8	55.1
251	Both sexes - Unemployment rate	7.9	9.4	5.2	7.0	22.9	5.7
252	15 to 24 years	27.9	24.3	14.3	12.5	0.0	7.0
253	25 years and over	5.0	5.8	4.0	6.3	22.9	4.8
254	**Total labour force 15 years and over**	**2,210**	**960**	**575**	**1,785**	**175**	**1,045**
	Industry - North American Industry Classification System 2002						
255	Industry - Not applicable[46]	45	25	0	50	0	15
256	All industries[47]	2,160	935	575	1,735	175	1,030
257	11 Agriculture, forestry, fishing and hunting	85	25	30	140	30	85
258	21 Mining and oil and gas extraction	45	0	0	15	0	10
259	22 Utilities	30	0	10	10	0	30
260	23 Construction	200	35	70	215	45	120
261	31-33 Manufacturing	290	175	35	125	10	80
262	41 Wholesale trade	75	25	10	30	0	40
263	44-45 Retail trade	290	170	115	290	10	140
264	48-49 Transportation and warehousing	150	25	35	85	15	100
265	51 Information and cultural industries	30	10	20	30	0	0
266	52 Finance and insurance	30	0	0	50	10	20
267	53 Real estate and rental and leasing	30	0	10	60	0	0
268	54 Professional, scientific and technical services	65	30	20	75	20	0
269	55 Management of companies and enterprises	10	0	0	0	0	0
270	56 Administrative and support, waste management and remediation services	85	65	10	75	0	30
271	61 Educational services	150	30	35	85	0	75
272	62 Health care and social assistance	225	120	70	100	0	85

Note: See symbols and abbreviations in the introductory material and see reference material at the end of the publication.

Certaines caractéristiques des divisions de recensement et des subdivisions de recensement – Données intégrales et données-échantillon (20 %), Ontario, Recensement de 2006 (suite)

Marmora and Lake, MU ◆◇	Quinte West, CY ◇A	Stirling-Rawdon, TP	Tudor and Cashel, TP ◆◆◇◇	Tweed, MU ◆◇	Tyendinaga, TP	Caractéristiques	N°
						Caractéristiques de la population	
						Travail non rémunéré (suite)	
90	1,435	175	35	145	100	Travaux ménagers et soins ou aide aux personnes âgées seulement	215
0	0	0	0	0	0	Soins aux enfants et soins ou aide aux personnes âgées seulement	216
965	8,250	945	190	1,280	735	Travaux ménagers seulement	217
10	130	0	0	10	10	Soins aux enfants seulement	218
0	55	0	0	0	10	Soins ou aide aux personnes âgées seulement	219
1,585	17,540	2,025	290	2,310	1,560	Femmes de 15 ans et plus	220
1,480	16,550	1,890	275	2,220	1,510	Travail non rémunéré déclaré[45]	221
105	1,655	205	15	230	290	Travaux ménagers et soins aux enfants et soins ou aide aux personnes âgées	222
405	5,125	560	85	620	495	Travaux ménagers et soins aux enfants seulement	223
140	1,865	250	55	180	125	Travaux ménagers et soins ou aide aux personnes âgées seulement	224
0	10	0	0	10	0	Soins aux enfants et soins ou aide aux personnes âgées seulement	225
820	7,780	850	120	1,170	595	Travaux ménagers seulement	226
0	70	0	0	10	0	Soins aux enfants seulement	227
10	45	20	0	0	0	Soins ou aide aux personnes âgées seulement	228
						Activité	
1,605	17,030	1,920	365	2,340	1,615	Hommes de 15 ans et plus	229
785	11,630	1,340	210	1,495	1,270	Population active	230
715	11,080	1,320	165	1,355	1,225	Personnes occupées	231
75	560	25	45	135	45	Chômeurs	232
820	5,395	575	155	845	345	Inactifs	233
48.9	68.3	69.8	57.5	63.9	78.6	Taux d'activité	234
44.5	65.1	68.8	45.2	57.9	75.9	Taux d'emploi	235
9.6	4.8	1.9	21.4	9.0	3.5	Taux de chômage	236
1,585	17,540	2,025	285	2,310	1,560	Femmes de 15 ans et plus	237
710	10,340	1,265	135	1,195	1,070	Population active	238
675	9,705	1,215	135	1,140	1,025	Personnes occupées	239
35	635	50	0	50	45	Chômeuses	240
870	7,200	755	155	1,120	490	Inactives	241
44.8	59.0	62.5	47.4	51.7	68.6	Taux d'activité	242
42.6	55.3	60.0	47.4	49.4	65.7	Taux d'emploi	243
4.9	6.1	4.0	0.0	4.2	4.2	Taux de chômage	244
47.0	63.6	66.0	52.7	57.8	73.7	Les deux sexes - Taux d'activité	245
56.6	68.1	67.7	64.3	67.4	73.0	15 à 24 ans	246
45.6	62.7	65.9	48.5	56.1	73.7	25 ans et plus	247
43.5	60.1	64.3	45.8	53.6	70.9	Les deux sexes - Taux d'emploi	248
39.5	58.2	63.1	57.1	53.5	60.9	15 à 24 ans	249
44.0	60.5	64.6	42.7	53.6	73.1	25 ans et plus	250
7.3	5.4	2.9	11.6	7.3	3.8	Les deux sexes - Taux de chômage	251
27.3	14.4	6.8	10.5	20.5	16.7	15 à 24 ans	252
3.5	3.6	2.1	13.7	4.4	0.5	25 ans et plus	253
1,500	**21,975**	**2,610**	**345**	**2,685**	**2,340**	**Population active totale de 15 ans et plus**	254
						Industrie - Système de classification des industries de l'Amérique du Nord de 2002	
20	270	10	10	30	25	Industrie - Sans objet[46]	255
1,485	21,705	2,600	340	2,650	2,315	Toutes les industries[47]	256
55	340	180	25	190	145	11 Agriculture, foresterie, pêche et chasse	257
15	25	0	0	25	10	21 Extraction minière et extraction de pétrole et de gaz	258
15	190	25	10	25	25	22 Services publics	259
145	1,105	180	70	235	265	23 Construction	260
190	3,460	350	25	425	285	31-33 Fabrication	261
40	615	150	0	120	95	41 Commerce de gros	262
205	3,140	455	75	370	340	44-45 Commerce de détail	263
130	1,205	155	25	115	235	48-49 Transport et entreposage	264
35	370	35	0	20	20	51 Industrie de l'information et industrie culturelle	265
20	320	35	0	30	40	52 Finance et assurances	266
60	350	15	0	50	10	53 Services immobiliers et services de location et de location à bail	267
35	685	130	10	100	50	54 Services professionnels, scientifiques et techniques	268
0	0	0	0	0	0	55 Gestion de sociétés et d'entreprises	269
80	1,365	105	40	80	95	56 Services administratifs, services de soutien, services de gestion des déchets et services d'assainissement	270
85	900	180	10	190	100	61 Services d'enseignement	271
135	1,785	195	15	290	185	62 Soins de santé et assistance sociale	272

Nota : Voir les symboles et les abréviations dans les documents d'introduction et voir les documents de référence à la fin de la publication.

Selected characteristics for census divisions and census subdivisions – 100% data and 20% sample data, Ontario, 2006 Census (continued)

No.	Characteristics	Centre Hastings, MU	Deseronto, T ◆◇	Faraday, TP ◆◇◇	Hastings Highlands, MU ◆◇	Limerick, TP ◆◆◇◇	Madoc, TP ◆
	Population characteristics						
	Industry - North American Industry Classification System 2002 (continued)						
273	71 Arts, entertainment and recreation	30	0	10	50	10	20
274	72 Accommodation and food services	100	100	50	115	10	65
275	81 Other services (except public administration)	90	70	35	130	0	50
276	91 Public administration	130	35	15	70	10	55
	Class of worker						
277	Class of worker - Not applicable[46]	50	25	0	50	0	15
278	All classes of worker[47]	2,160	935	580	1,735	175	1,030
279	Paid workers	1,935	850	465	1,415	130	865
280	Employees	1,895	830	430	1,340	115	830
281	Self-employed (incorporated)	45	25	35	75	10	35
282	Self-employed (unincorporated)	225	60	110	320	45	160
283	Unpaid family workers	10	20	0	0	0	0
	Occupation - National Occupational Classification for Statistics 2006						
284	Male labour force 15 years and over	1,225	490	340	935	105	575
285	Occupation - Not applicable[46]	10	0	0	25	0	10
286	All occupations[47]	1,215	490	340	910	105	565
287	A Management occupations	50	40	45	70	20	50
288	B Business, finance and administrative occupations	70	30	15	55	0	20
289	C Natural and applied sciences and related occupations	75	0	15	15	10	30
290	D Health occupations	15	0	15	0	0	0
291	E Occupations in social science, education, government service and religion	40	20	30	65	0	35
292	F Occupations in art, culture, recreation and sport	10	0	15	35	0	10
293	G Sales and service occupations	205	115	35	165	10	90
294	H Trades, transport and equipment operators and related occupations	465	140	115	330	55	220
295	I Occupations unique to primary industry	125	20	25	105	10	75
296	J Occupations unique to processing, manufacturing and utilities	145	110	30	60	0	40
297	Female labour force 15 years and over	985	470	235	855	65	470
298	Occupation - Not applicable[46]	35	25	0	25	0	10
299	All occupations[47]	945	445	235	830	70	465
300	A Management occupations	40	10	20	65	10	35
301	B Business, finance and administrative occupations	205	75	30	200	15	90
302	C Natural and applied sciences and related occupations	15	0	0	0	20	0
303	D Health occupations	95	65	40	45	10	55
304	E Occupations in social science, education, government service and religion	130	40	20	95	0	40
305	F Occupations in art, culture, recreation and sport	35	0	10	15	0	0
306	G Sales and service occupations	285	165	105	305	15	190
307	H Trades, transport and equipment operators and related occupations	35	0	0	25	0	35
308	I Occupations unique to primary industry	30	30	0	40	0	15
309	J Occupations unique to processing, manufacturing and utilities	75	55	0	35	0	0
310	**Total employed labour force 15 years and over**	**2,035**	**865**	**545**	**1,660**	**135**	**985**
	Place of work status						
311	Males	1,125	430	320	855	85	535
312	Usual place of work	810	355	180	555	35	305
313	At home	100	15	45	100	15	75
314	Outside Canada	0	10	0	0	0	0
315	No fixed workplace address	215	55	105	200	35	155
316	Females	910	440	220	805	50	445
317	Usual place of work	760	405	205	645	45	385
318	At home	70	0	15	150	10	30
319	Outside Canada	0	0	0	0	0	0
320	No fixed workplace address	75	35	0	10	0	30

Note: See symbols and abbreviations in the introductory material and see reference material at the end of the publication.

Certaines caractéristiques des divisions de recensement et des subdivisions de recensement – Données intégrales et données-échantillon (20 %), Ontario, Recensement de 2006 (suite)

Marmora and Lake, MU ◆◇	Quinte West, CY ◇**A**	Stirling-Rawdon, TP	Tudor and Cashel, TP ◆◆◇◇	Tweed, MU ◆◇	Tyendinaga, TP	Caractéristiques	N°
						Caractéristiques de la population	
						Industrie - Système de classification des industries de l'Amérique du Nord de 2002 (suite)	
15	360	65	0	45	15	71 Arts, spectacles et loisirs	273
95	1,250	135	20	115	180	72 Hébergement et services de restauration	274
50	935	95	15	90	80	81 Autres services (sauf les administrations publiques)	275
75	3,290	110	0	125	125	91 Administrations publiques	276
						Catégorie de travailleurs	
20	270	10	10	35	25	Catégorie de travailleurs - Sans objet[46]	277
1,485	21,705	2,600	340	2,655	2,315	Toutes les catégories de travailleurs[47]	278
1,345	20,240	2,275	325	2,255	2,080	Travailleurs rémunérés	279
1,330	19,795	2,160	310	2,200	2,030	Employés	280
20	445	110	10	55	45	Travailleurs autonomes (entreprise constituée en société)	281
125	1,410	315	15	390	235	Travailleurs autonomes (entreprise non constituée en société)	282
10	55	10	0	0	0	Travailleurs familiaux non rémunérés	283
						Profession - Classification nationale des professions pour statistiques de 2006	
785	11,630	1,340	210	1,495	1,270	Hommes actifs de 15 ans et plus	284
15	135	0	10	30	10	Profession - Sans objet[46]	285
775	11,495	1,340	205	1,465	1,260	Toutes les professions[47]	286
80	1,200	100	10	70	85	A Gestion	287
60	815	70	0	80	45	B Affaires, finance et administration	288
35	860	90	25	105	55	C Sciences naturelles et appliquées et professions apparentées	289
0	145	20	0	15	20	D Secteur de la santé	290
25	315	60	0	60	30	E Sciences sociales, enseignement, administration publique et religion	291
15	100	35	0	15	15	F Arts, culture, sports et loisirs	292
135	2,745	210	30	260	225	G Ventes et services	293
290	3,475	420	95	495	525	H Métiers, transport et machinerie	294
65	495	165	25	160	120	I Professions propres au secteur primaire	295
60	1,345	170	15	205	130	J Transformation, fabrication et services d'utilité publique	296
710	10,340	1,265	135	1,190	1,070	Femmes actives de 15 ans et plus	297
0	135	10	0	0	20	Profession - Sans objet[46]	298
710	10,205	1,260	130	1,190	1,055	Toutes les professions[47]	299
60	560	135	10	105	50	A Gestion	300
175	2,390	320	45	225	205	B Affaires, finance et administration	301
10	275	15	0	20	35	C Sciences naturelles et appliquées et professions apparentées	302
75	825	65	10	120	85	D Secteur de la santé	303
40	870	125	0	175	100	E Sciences sociales, enseignement, administration publique et religion	304
20	255	30	0	25	0	F Arts, culture, sports et loisirs	305
260	3,515	475	70	335	375	G Ventes et services	306
35	410	10	0	40	95	H Métiers, transport et machinerie	307
25	105	30	0	45	35	I Professions propres au secteur primaire	308
10	990	60	0	90	65	J Transformation, fabrication et services d'utilité publique	309
1,390	**20,780**	**2,535**	**305**	**2,495**	**2,255**	**Population active occupée totale de 15 ans et plus**	310
						Catégorie de lieu de travail	
715	11,075	1,320	170	1,355	1,225	Hommes	311
510	9,155	1,030	95	905	915	Lieu habituel de travail	312
45	480	160	10	230	145	À domicile	313
0	60	0	15	0	0	En dehors du Canada	314
165	1,380	125	45	220	170	Sans adresse de travail fixe	315
680	9,705	1,220	135	1,140	1,025	Femmes	316
560	8,520	1,040	130	930	895	Lieu habituel de travail	317
65	625	150	0	105	80	À domicile	318
0	25	0	0	0	10	En dehors du Canada	319
55	530	30	0	105	45	Sans adresse de travail fixe	320

Nota : Voir les symboles et les abréviations dans les documents d'introduction et voir les documents de référence à la fin de la publication.

Selected characteristics for census divisions and census subdivisions – 100% data and 20% sample data, Ontario, 2006 Census (continued)

No.	Characteristics	Centre Hastings, MU	Deseronto, T ◆◇	Faraday, TP ◆◇◇	Hastings Highlands, MU ◆◇	Limerick, TP ◆◆◇◇	Madoc, TP ◆
	Population characteristics						
321	**Total employed labour force 15 years and over with usual place of work or no fixed workplace address**	**1,860**	**845**	**490**	**1,415**	**110**	**880**
	Mode of transportation						
322	Males	1,025	405	280	755	70	465
323	Car, truck, van, as driver	905	325	245	650	45	385
324	Car, truck, van, as passenger	80	30	15	60	0	45
325	Public transit	0	0	0	0	0	10
326	Walked	20	55	15	10	0	25
327	All other modes	20	0	0	30	15	0
328	Females	835	440	210	655	45	420
329	Car, truck, van, as driver	655	295	155	510	40	340
330	Car, truck, van, as passenger	110	65	40	95	0	50
331	Public transit	0	10	0	30	0	0
332	Walked	60	60	10	15	0	15
333	All other modes	0	15	0	10	0	15
334	**Total population 15 years and over who worked since January 1, 2005**	**2,440**	**995**	**715**	**1,990**	**175**	**1,160**
	Language used most often at work						
335	Single responses	2,440	985	715	1,990	175	1,160
336	English	2,435	980	715	1,980	175	1,155
337	French	0	10	0	10	0	0
338	Non-official languages[7]	0	0	0	0	0	0
339	Chinese, n.o.s.[61]	0	0	0	0	0	0
340	Cantonese	0	0	0	0	0	0
341	Other languages[8]	0	0	0	0	0	0
342	Multiple responses	0	0	0	0	0	0
343	English and French	0	0	0	0	0	0
344	English and non-official language	0	10	0	0	0	0
345	French and non-official language	0	0	0	0	0	0
346	English, French and non-official language	0	0	0	0	0	0
	Dwelling and household characteristics						
347	**Total number of occupied private dwellings**	**1,690**	**710**	**670**	**1,690**	**175**	**775**
	Housing tenure						
348	Owned	1,405	545	595	1,570	160	735
349	Rented	285	165	75	115	20	45
350	Band housing	0	0	0	0	0	0
	Structural type of dwelling						
351	Single-detached house	1,420	515	620	1,625	155	760
352	Semi-detached house	65	25	0	0	5	5
353	Row house	30	30	0	0	0	0
354	Apartment, duplex	25	35	5	15	5	5
355	Apartment, building that has five or more storeys	0	0	0	0	5	0
356	Apartment, building that has fewer than five storeys	135	90	5	20	0	5
357	Other single-attached house	10	5	10	5	0	0
358	Movable dwelling[48]	10	5	20	20	0	5
	Condition of dwelling						
359	Regular maintenance only	965	325	365	1,000	90	450
360	Minor repairs	550	270	225	550	70	230
361	Major repairs	175	115	80	130	20	95
	Period of construction						
362	Before 1946	570	340	55	180	40	325
363	1946 to 1960	110	90	155	235	25	30
364	1961 to 1970	130	60	105	180	0	25
365	1971 to 1980	175	85	155	310	25	85
366	1981 to 1985	105	35	55	95	15	30
367	1986 to 1990	180	35	40	220	25	100
368	1991 to 1995	220	20	40	180	10	105
369	1996 to 2000	100	0	25	155	10	40
370	2001 to 2006[49]	100	35	30	125	30	35

Note: See symbols and abbreviations in the introductory material and see reference material at the end of the publication.

Certaines caractéristiques des divisions de recensement et des subdivisions de recensement – Données intégrales et données-échantillon (20 %), Ontario, Recensement de 2006 (suite)

Marmora and Lake, MU ◆◊	Quinte West, CY ◊A	Stirling-Rawdon, TP	Tudor and Cashel, TP ◆◆◊◊	Tweed, MU ◆◊	Tyendinaga, TP	Caractéristiques	N°
						Caractéristiques de la population	
1,280	**19,585**	**2,230**	**280**	**2,155**	**2,020**	**Population active occupée totale de 15 ans et plus ayant un lieu habituel de travail ou sans adresse de travail fixe**	321
						Mode de transport	
670	10,535	1,160	145	1,125	1,085	Hommes	322
620	8,770	990	125	1,000	970	Automobile, camion ou fourgonnette, en tant que conducteur	323
25	845	65	10	50	85	Automobile, camion ou fourgonnette, en tant que passager	324
0	50	15	10	0	15	Transport en commun	325
15	445	55	0	40	20	À pied	326
15	430	30	0	30	0	Tous les autres modes	327
610	9,050	1,070	135	1,035	940	Femmes	328
530	7,250	895	90	895	775	Automobile, camion ou fourgonnette, en tant que conductrice	329
30	1,030	50	25	65	95	Automobile, camion ou fourgonnette, en tant que passagère	330
0	35	15	10	0	0	Transport en commun	331
50	560	90	10	60	60	À pied	332
10	170	20	0	15	0	Tous les autres modes	333
1,645	**23,810**	**2,805**	**360**	**3,010**	**2,485**	**Population totale de 15 ans et plus ayant travaillé depuis le 1er janvier 2005**	334
						Langue utilisée le plus souvent au travail	
1,650	23,645	2,790	355	3,010	2,485	Réponses uniques	335
1,645	23,455	2,785	355	3,010	2,475	Anglais	336
0	175	0	0	0	0	Français	337
0	15	0	0	0	0	Langues non officielles[7]	338
0	0	0	0	0	0	Chinois, n.d.a.[61]	339
0	0	0	0	0	0	Cantonais	340
0	10	0	0	0	0	Autres langues[8]	341
0	160	20	0	0	0	Réponses multiples	342
0	135	0	0	0	0	Anglais et français	343
0	25	15	0	10	0	Anglais et langue non officielle	344
0	0	0	0	0	0	Français et langue non officielle	345
0	0	0	0	0	0	Anglais, français et langue non officielle	346
						Caractéristiques des logements et des ménages	
1,600	**16,715**	**1,845**	**285**	**2,285**	**1,370**	**Nombre total de logements privés occupés**	347
						Mode d'occupation	
1,315	12,385	1,605	265	1,935	1,220	Possédé	348
280	4,330	235	15	350	145	Loué	349
0	0	0	0	0	0	Logement de bande	350
						Type de construction résidentielle	
1,415	12,470	1,615	270	2,010	1,325	Maison individuelle non attenante	351
50	815	45	5	50	20	Maison jumelée	352
0	275	0	0	0	5	Maison en rangée	353
20	270	10	0	35	0	Appartement, duplex	354
0	510	0	0	0	0	Appartement, immeuble de cinq étages ou plus	355
90	1,945	145	5	175	5	Appartement, immeuble de moins de cinq étages	356
10	75	25	0	0	5	Autre maison individuelle attenante	357
10	355	0	15	5	5	Logement mobile[48]	358
						État du logement	
930	10,540	1,160	130	1,255	860	Entretien régulier seulement	359
470	4,870	550	120	820	385	Réparations mineures	360
195	1,300	130	25	210	125	Réparations majeures	361
						Période de construction	
405	2,595	725	35	750	385	Avant 1946	362
200	2,690	155	35	255	95	1946 à 1960	363
145	2,740	115	55	290	80	1961 à 1970	364
355	3,735	305	60	415	190	1971 à 1980	365
85	1,055	85	25	110	40	1981 à 1985	366
150	1,300	150	25	145	195	1986 à 1990	367
125	1,000	120	20	160	105	1991 à 1995	368
55	730	95	20	80	150	1996 à 2000	369
70	865	90	10	85	130	2001 à 2006[49]	370

Nota : Voir les symboles et les abréviations dans les documents d'introduction et voir les documents de référence à la fin de la publication.

Selected characteristics for census divisions and census subdivisions – 100% data and 20% sample data, Ontario, 2006 Census (continued)

No.	Characteristics	Centre Hastings, MU	Deseronto, T ◆◇	Faraday, TP ◆◇◇	Hastings Highlands, MU ◆◇	Limerick, TP ◆◆◇◇	Madoc, TP ◆
	Dwelling and household characteristics						
371	Average number of rooms per dwelling	7.1	6.7	6.6	6.8	6.2	7.4
372	Average number of bedrooms per dwelling	2.9	2.8	2.8	2.8	2.6	3.2
373	Average value of dwelling $	178,226	120,817	210,140	187,047	146,562	157,232
374	**Total number of private households**	**1,690**	**705**	**670**	**1,685**	**165**	**775**
	Household size						
375	1 person	370	160	140	385	50	130
376	2 persons	670	255	325	755	70	320
377	3 persons	260	115	85	225	25	120
378	4 to 5 persons	355	165	110	280	20	190
379	6 or more persons	40	15	10	35	0	15
	Household type						
380	One-family households[50]	1,280	495	485	1,235	120	600
381	Multiple-family households	15	15	10	25	0	20
382	Non-family households	395	200	170	420	60	155
383	Number of persons in private households	4,285	1,815	1,580	4,005	365	2,070
384	Average number of persons in private households	2.5	2.6	2.4	2.4	2.2	2.7
385	Tenant-occupied private non-farm, non-reserve dwellings[51]	285	165	75	115	20	45
386	Average gross rent $[51]	659	617	603	526	0	642
387	Tenant-occupied households spending 30% or more of household income on gross rent[52]	145	110	30	55	10	10
388	Tenant-occupied households spending from 30% to 99% of household income on gross rent[52]	140	95	30	45	10	10
389	Owner-occupied private non-farm, non-reserve dwellings[53]	1,390	545	595	1,545	155	690
390	Average owner's major payments $[53]	894	916	646	646	682	700
391	Owner households spending 30% or more of household income on owner's major payments[52]	265	170	60	315	55	115
392	Owner households spending from 30% to 99% of household income on owner's major payments[52]	240	150	60	230	25	105
	Census family characteristics						
393	**Total number of census families in private households**	**1,315**	**525**	**505**	**1,295**	**120**	**640**
	Family structure and number of children						
394	Total couple families	1,195	460	445	1,175	110	570
395	Total families of married couples	995	380	385	1,030	100	495
396	Without children at home	525	200	240	625	70	270
397	With children at home	465	180	150	400	35	225
398	1 child	170	65	50	165	20	55
399	2 children	200	85	40	160	15	130
400	3 or more children	100	25	60	70	0	35
401	Total families of common-law couples	200	80	55	145	10	75
402	Without children at home	100	45	45	95	0	25
403	With children at home	105	35	10	55	10	55
404	1 child	45	10	10	25	10	25
405	2 children	40	10	0	25	0	10
406	3 or more children	10	15	0	0	0	25
407	Total lone-parent families	120	65	55	120	10	70
408	Female parent	75	40	55	100	0	40
409	1 child	55	15	50	35	0	35
410	2 children	20	10	10	45	0	0
411	3 or more children	10	20	0	25	0	0
412	Male parent	45	20	0	20	0	30
413	1 child	15	0	0	15	0	20
414	2 children	10	15	0	10	10	10
415	3 or more children	15	0	0	0	0	0

Note: See symbols and abbreviations in the introductory material and see reference material at the end of the publication.

Certaines caractéristiques des divisions de recensement et des subdivisions de recensement – Données intégrales et données-échantillon (20 %), Ontario, Recensement de 2006 (suite)

Marmora and Lake, MU ◆◇	Quinte West, CY ◇**A**	Stirling-Rawdon, TP	Tudor and Cashel, TP ◆◆◇◇	Tweed, MU ◆◇	Tyendinaga, TP	Caractéristiques	N°
						Caractéristiques des logements et des ménages	
6.6	7.0	7.2	6.3	6.8	7.5	Nombre moyen de pièces par logement	371
2.7	2.9	3.0	2.7	2.9	3.3	Nombre moyen de chambres à coucher par logement	372
181,290	181,187	178,804	174,469	176,969	186,760	Valeur moyenne du logement $	373
1,600	**16,715**	**1,845**	**295**	**2,285**	**1,370**	**Nombre total de ménages privés**	374
						Taille du ménage	
415	3,695	365	80	565	180	1 personne	375
670	6,315	715	115	905	465	2 personnes	376
210	2,760	300	50	315	240	3 personnes	377
270	3,555	420	40	450	430	4 à 5 personnes	378
30	390	45	5	55	60	6 personnes ou plus	379
						Genre de ménage	
1,120	12,465	1,380	200	1,655	1,140	Ménages unifamiliaux[50]	380
25	200	60	0	10	20	Ménages multifamiliaux	381
455	4,050	400	75	620	210	Ménages non familiaux	382
3,745	42,265	4,800	675	5,590	4,070	Nombre de personnes dans les ménages privés	383
2.3	2.5	2.6	2.3	2.4	3.0	Nombre moyen de personnes dans les ménages privés	384
280	4,335	235	15	350	145	Ménages locataires dans les logements privés non agricoles hors réserve[51]	385
534	680	572	477	600	896	Loyer brut moyen $[51]	386
175	1,625	115	10	160	40	Ménages locataires consacrant 30 % ou plus du revenu du ménage au loyer brut[52]	387
175	1,455	95	10	150	40	Ménages locataires consacrant de 30 % à 99 % du revenu du ménage au loyer brut[52]	388
1,310	12,325	1,540	265	1,845	1,165	Ménages propriétaires dans les logements privés non agricoles hors réserve[53]	389
697	883	862	609	708	944	Principales dépenses de propriété moyennes $[53]	390
230	1,910	320	55	305	195	Ménages propriétaires consacrant 30 % ou plus du revenu du ménage aux principales dépenses de propriété[52]	391
205	1,545	260	35	240	175	Ménages propriétaires consacrant de 30 % à 99 % du revenu du ménage aux principales dépenses de propriété[52]	392
						Caractéristiques des familles de recensement	
1,170	**12,870**	**1,505**	**210**	**1,680**	**1,185**	**Nombre total de familles de recensement dans les ménages privés**	393
						Structure de la famille et le nombre d'enfants	
1,055	11,155	1,305	190	1,520	1,090	Total des familles avec conjoints	394
900	9,285	1,110	160	1,290	925	Total des familles avec couples mariés	395
575	4,555	535	60	660	330	Sans enfants à la maison	396
325	4,730	580	100	630	595	Avec enfants à la maison	397
150	1,785	235	70	225	210	1 enfant	398
125	2,080	250	15	260	240	2 enfants	399
55	865	95	20	145	145	3 enfants ou plus	400
155	1,870	190	30	225	165	Total des familles avec couples en union libre	401
40	895	115	20	140	85	Sans enfants à la maison	402
120	975	75	10	85	80	Avec enfants à la maison	403
40	455	40	10	35	45	1 enfant	404
50	320	15	0	15	20	2 enfants	405
25	200	15	0	25	10	3 enfants ou plus	406
110	1,710	200	20	160	90	Total des familles monoparentales	407
95	1,325	135	10	120	85	Parent de sexe féminin	408
50	820	80	10	60	65	1 enfant	409
25	405	40	0	30	0	2 enfants	410
20	100	15	0	30	15	3 enfants ou plus	411
20	395	65	10	45	10	Parent de sexe masculin	412
10	275	65	0	30	0	1 enfant	413
0	105	0	0	10	0	2 enfants	414
0	10	0	0	0	0	3 enfants ou plus	415

Nota : Voir les symboles et les abréviations dans les documents d'introduction et voir les documents de référence à la fin de la publication.

Selected characteristics for census divisions and census subdivisions – 100% data and 20% sample data, Ontario, 2006 Census (continued)

No.	Characteristics	Centre Hastings, MU	Deseronto, T ◆◇	Faraday, TP ◆◇◇	Hastings Highlands, MU ◆◇	Limerick, TP ◆◆◇◇	Madoc, TP ◆
	Census family characteristics						
416	**Total number of children at home**	**1,255**	**535**	**425**	**1,040**	**65**	**645**
	Age group						
417	Under 6 years	240	105	55	210	30	80
418	6 to 14 years	520	200	200	335	15	255
419	15 to 17 years	160	70	60	170	10	135
420	18 to 24 years	205	110	50	220	0	120
421	25 years and over	125	50	55	95	10	50
422	Average number of children at home per census family[54]	1.0	1.0	0.8	0.8	0.5	1.0
423	**Total number of persons in private households**	**4,290**	**1,795**	**1,575**	**4,005**	**365**	**2,065**
	Census family status and living arrangements						
424	Number of persons not in census families	520	270	210	495	70	205
425	Living with relatives[55]	100	20	25	40	10	35
426	Living with non-relatives only	55	70	25	70	0	35
427	Living alone	365	175	155	390	55	130
428	Number of census family persons	3,765	1,525	1,365	3,510	295	1,865
429	Average number of persons per census family	2.9	2.9	2.7	2.7	2.5	2.9
430	**Total number of persons aged 65 years and over**	**645**	**245**	**305**	**765**	**50**	**345**
431	Number of persons not in census families aged 65 years and over	210	110	90	195	25	125
432	Living with relatives[55]	20	0	0	20	0	35
433	Living with non-relatives only	10	10	10	0	0	10
434	Living alone	185	100	75	175	30	85
435	Number of census family persons aged 65 years and over	430	135	220	565	25	220
	Economic family characteristics						
436	**Total number of economic families in private households**	**1,315**	**510**	**500**	**1,265**	**120**	**630**
	Size of family						
437	2 persons	680	240	330	725	75	315
438	3 persons	240	100	55	230	20	95
439	4 persons	250	110	55	195	20	140
440	5 or more persons	145	65	65	110	0	75
441	Total number of persons in economic families	3,865	1,545	1,400	3,545	305	1,900
442	Average number of persons per economic family	3.0	3.0	3.0	3.0	3.0	3.0
443	Total number of persons not in economic families	425	245	180	455	60	170
	2005 income characteristics						
444	**Population 15 years and over**	**3,575**	**1,495**	**1,325**	**3,480**	**315**	**1,730**
	Sex and total income groups in 2005						
445	Without income	210	55	50	175	30	125
446	With income	3,365	1,440	1,275	3,305	285	1,605
447	Under $1,000[56]	160	50	45	170	35	50
448	$1,000 to $2,999	90	80	50	115	0	45
449	$3,000 to $4,999	155	85	40	180	25	100
450	$5,000 to $6,999	105	45	50	185	10	50
451	$7,000 to $9,999	155	100	80	320	25	75
452	$10,000 to $11,999	140	90	90	140	25	100
453	$12,000 to $14,999	250	100	105	190	15	105
454	$15,000 to $19,999	340	230	180	400	25	185
455	$20,000 to $24,999	355	165	85	270	10	170
456	$25,000 to $29,999	325	130	60	245	15	130
457	$30,000 to $34,999	240	70	95	250	10	80
458	$35,000 to $39,999	260	80	75	160	20	140
459	$40,000 to $44,999	190	50	100	140	0	60
460	$45,000 to $49,999	150	45	50	110	35	55
461	$50,000 to $59,999	185	55	95	185	20	125
462	$60,000 and over	265	55	75	235	10	135
463	Median income $[57]	24,479	18,205	19,633	18,982	15,431	22,370
464	Average income $[57]	28,625	22,284	26,766	25,618	22,950	27,878
465	Standard error of average income $[57]	820	941	1,147	1,022	2,989	1,199

Note: See symbols and abbreviations in the introductory material and see reference material at the end of the publication.

Certaines caractéristiques des divisions de recensement et des subdivisions de recensement – Données intégrales et données-échantillon (20 %), Ontario, Recensement de 2006 (suite)

Marmora and Lake, MU ◆◊	Quinte West, CY ◊A	Stirling-Rawdon, TP	Tudor and Cashel, TP ◆◆◊◊	Tweed, MU ◆◊	Tyendinaga, TP	Caractéristiques	N°
						Caractéristiques des familles de recensement	
980	**12,955**	**1,460**	**195**	**1,665**	**1,480**	**Nombre total d'enfants à la maison**	416
						Groupes d'âge	
215	2,780	320	20	290	280	Moins de 6 ans	417
335	4,870	510	10	635	615	6 à 14 ans	418
150	1,870	215	50	230	210	15 à 17 ans	419
145	2,415	305	85	350	295	18 à 24 ans	420
135	1,020	110	30	155	85	25 ans et plus	421
0.8	1.0	1.0	0.9	1.0	1.3	Nombre moyen d'enfants à la maison par famille de recensement[54]	422
3,745	**42,265**	**4,800**	**680**	**5,600**	**4,095**	**Nombre total de personnes dans les ménages privés**	423
						Situation des particuliers dans la famille de recensement et des particuliers dans le ménage	
535	5,275	530	85	740	345	Nombre de personnes hors famille de recensement	424
55	715	75	10	60	80	Vivant avec des personnes apparentées[55]	425
70	865	85	15	115	90	Vivant avec des personnes non apparentées seulement	426
415	3,695	365	70	565	170	Vivant seules	427
3,205	36,990	4,270	590	4,860	3,755	Nombre de membres d'une famille de recensement	428
2.7	2.9	2.8	2.8	2.9	3.2	Nombre moyen de personnes par famille de recensement	429
775	**6,200**	**695**	**145**	**950**	**385**	**Nombre total de personnes âgées de 65 ans et plus**	430
285	1,825	215	45	290	80	Nombre de personnes hors famille de recensement âgées de 65 ans et plus	431
10	245	25	0	10	20	Vivant avec des personnes apparentées[55]	432
35	65	10	0	20	0	Vivant avec des personnes non apparentées seulement	433
245	1,510	180	30	260	65	Vivant seules	434
485	4,375	480	105	655	300	Nombre de membres d'une famille de recensement âgés de 65 ans et plus	435
						Caractéristiques des familles économiques	
1,155	**12,760**	**1,455**	**210**	**1,670**	**1,165**	**Nombre total de familles économiques dans les ménages privés**	436
						Taille de la famille	
640	6,175	700	90	870	450	2 personnes	437
225	2,725	295	75	295	245	3 personnes	438
180	2,595	305	20	320	285	4 personnes	439
110	1,270	155	15	185	180	5 personnes ou plus	440
3,260	37,700	4,350	600	4,915	3,830	Nombre total de personnes dans les familles économiques	441
3.0	3.0	3.0	3.0	3.0	3.0	Nombre moyen de personnes par famille économique	442
485	4,560	455	80	680	260	Nombre total de personnes hors famille économique	443
						Caractéristiques du revenu de 2005	
3,190	**34,570**	**3,945**	**650**	**4,655**	**3,175**	**Population de 15 ans et plus**	444
						Sexe et groupes de revenu total en 2005	
185	1,605	175	55	190	140	Sans revenu	445
3,005	32,965	3,765	595	4,465	3,035	Avec un revenu	446
150	1,305	200	30	210	95	Moins de 1 000 $[56]	447
95	1,160	130	30	175	150	1 000 $ à 2 999 $	448
120	1,080	155	15	145	130	3 000 $ à 4 999 $	449
160	1,100	135	35	150	120	5 000 $ à 6 999 $	450
160	1,920	235	40	285	150	7 000 $ à 9 999 $	451
140	1,505	170	45	235	120	10 000 $ à 11 999 $	452
260	2,165	310	75	310	185	12 000 $ à 14 999 $	453
395	3,090	350	40	520	310	15 000 $ à 19 999 $	454
380	2,800	410	60	355	225	20 000 $ à 24 999 $	455
160	2,240	215	30	330	225	25 000 $ à 29 999 $	456
200	2,530	305	85	405	275	30 000 $ à 34 999 $	457
170	2,110	250	15	335	275	35 000 $ à 39 999 $	458
140	1,785	170	30	215	155	40 000 $ à 44 999 $	459
125	1,585	125	10	155	115	45 000 $ à 49 999$	460
155	2,665	215	15	270	190	50 000 $ à 59 999$	461
200	3,915	395	45	360	320	60 000 $ et plus	462
20,357	25,767	22,659	18,452	22,514	25,441	Revenu médian $[57]	463
25,710	31,349	27,574	23,873	27,406	29,453	Revenu moyen $[57]	464
786	319	902	1,788	683	851	Erreur type de revenu moyen $[57]	465

Nota : Voir les symboles et les abréviations dans les documents d'introduction et voir les documents de référence à la fin de la publication.

Selected characteristics for census divisions and census subdivisions – 100% data and 20% sample data, Ontario, 2006 Census (continued)

No.	Characteristics	Centre Hastings, MU	Deseronto, T ◆◇	Faraday, TP ◆◇◇	Hastings Highlands, MU ◆◇	Limerick, TP ◆◆◇◇	Madoc, TP ◆
	2005 income characteristics						
	Sex and total income groups in 2005 (continued)						
466	Total - Males	1,790	740	655	1,760	170	870
467	Without income	80	30	20	70	30	55
468	With income	1,710	710	630	1,690	145	815
469	Under $1,000[56]	75	30	20	100	10	35
470	$1,000 to $2,999	30	45	20	35	0	25
471	$3,000 to $4,999	50	40	15	35	20	10
472	$5,000 to $6,999	40	10	10	55	10	20
473	$7,000 to $9,999	70	10	30	145	15	25
474	$10,000 to $11,999	55	30	60	45	10	50
475	$12,000 to $14,999	90	50	40	75	10	30
476	$15,000 to $19,999	125	85	50	165	25	80
477	$20,000 to $24,999	150	95	30	135	0	75
478	$25,000 to $29,999	185	80	40	125	10	80
479	$30,000 to $34,999	105	40	70	200	0	35
480	$35,000 to $39,999	155	45	40	120	0	110
481	$40,000 to $44,999	120	30	50	90	0	35
482	$45,000 to $49,999	125	20	25	65	25	40
483	$50,000 to $59,999	125	50	70	105	15	80
484	$60,000 and over	220	40	55	185	0	75
485	Median income $[57]	29,236	23,462	30,337	26,865	17,855	27,411
486	Average income $[57]	34,663	25,918	31,761	31,703	23,320	31,993
487	Standard error of average income $[57]	1,336	1,413	1,713	1,725	3,286	1,825
488	Total - Females	1,790	755	670	1,715	145	855
489	Without income	135	20	25	105	10	65
490	With income	1,660	730	640	1,615	135	795
491	Under $1,000[56]	85	25	20	65	25	15
492	$1,000 to $2,999	55	30	30	75	0	25
493	$3,000 to $4,999	105	40	25	145	10	85
494	$5,000 to $6,999	65	30	40	130	10	30
495	$7,000 to $9,999	85	85	45	180	15	50
496	$10,000 to $11,999	85	65	25	100	15	45
497	$12,000 to $14,999	160	50	70	115	10	75
498	$15,000 to $19,999	215	140	130	235	0	100
499	$20,000 to $24,999	200	80	55	135	10	90
500	$25,000 to $29,999	140	50	15	125	0	50
501	$30,000 to $34,999	135	30	30	55	0	45
502	$35,000 to $39,999	110	40	35	40	15	30
503	$40,000 to $44,999	75	20	55	50	0	20
504	$45,000 to $49,999	25	25	20	45	10	20
505	$50,000 to $59,999	60	10	20	75	0	50
506	$60,000 and over	50	10	15	45	0	60
507	Median income $[57]	19,218	16,057	16,828	14,767	11,820	17,876
508	Average income $[57]	22,388	18,755	21,848	19,249	22,566	23,667
509	Standard error of average income $[57]	824	1,161	1,416	938	5,092	1,477
	Composition of total income						
510	Composition of total income in 2005 %	100.0	100.0	100.0	100.0	100.0	100.0
511	Employment income %	68.8	70.1	52.8	54.7	53.3	63.8
512	Government transfer payments %	16.9	23.2	20.3	21.4	25.2	17.9
513	Other %	14.2	6.7	27.2	23.9	21.2	18.1
514	**Population 15 years and over with employment income in 2005**	**2,370**	**980**	**765**	**2,080**	**185**	**1,130**
	Sex and work activity						
515	Median employment income in 2005 $	23,502	20,085	15,752	15,672	9,273	20,036
516	Average employment income in 2005 $	28,052	22,954	23,294	22,222	18,830	25,434
517	Standard error of average employment income $	1,071	1,245	1,723	1,302	4,699	1,590
518	Worked full year, full time[59]	1,185	450	335	840	40	565
519	Median employment income in 2005 $	36,945	32,704	39,601	30,880	45,361	34,569
520	Average employment income in 2005 $	41,068	34,713	41,403	37,033	46,477	37,198
521	Standard error of average employment income $	1,584	1,642	2,683	2,566	11,671	2,078
522	Worked part year or part time[60]	1,045	480	285	955	125	460
523	Median employment income in 2005 $	11,499	9,650	9,764	9,604	7,493	8,767
524	Average employment income in 2005 $	16,350	13,988	11,812	15,186	13,409	14,628
525	Standard error of average employment income $	1,051	1,396	1,111	1,042	4,387	2,114
526	Males 15 years and over with employment income[58]	1,320	545	430	1,105	100	570
527	Median employment income in 2005 $	27,962	22,012	21,300	18,979	9,243	24,963
528	Average employment income in 2005 $	32,828	24,924	27,368	26,652	21,209	28,853
529	Standard error of average employment income $	1,676	1,758	2,394	2,132	4,790	2,423

Note: See symbols and abbreviations in the introductory material and see reference material at the end of the publication.

Certaines caractéristiques des divisions de recensement et des subdivisions de recensement – Données intégrales et données-échantillon (20 %), Ontario, Recensement de 2006 (suite)

Marmora and Lake, MU ◆◇	Quinte West, CY ◇A	Stirling-Rawdon, TP	Tudor and Cashel, TP ◆◆◇◇	Tweed, MU ◆◇	Tyendinaga, TP	Caractéristiques	N°
						Caractéristiques du revenu de 2005	
						Sexe et groupes de revenu total en 2005 (suite)	
1,605	17,025	1,920	365	2,345	1,615	Total - Hommes	466
70	705	55	35	65	45	Sans revenu	467
1,540	16,325	1,865	330	2,280	1,570	Avec un revenu	468
95	805	140	25	115	50	Moins de 1 000 $[56]	469
20	370	45	0	100	55	1 000 $ à 2 999 $	470
20	410	80	10	60	45	3 000 $ à 4 999 $	471
55	305	40	10	65	45	5 000 $ à 6 999 $	472
55	615	80	20	140	75	7 000 $ à 9 999 $	473
60	580	25	15	65	55	10 000 $ à 11 999 $	474
100	650	135	30	150	90	12 000 $ à 14 999 $	475
140	980	95	15	215	110	15 000 $ à 19 999 $	476
185	1,095	180	35	150	110	20 000 $ à 24 999 $	477
100	985	115	30	140	95	25 000 $ à 29 999 $	478
135	1,190	130	55	255	135	30 000 $ à 34 999 $	479
110	1,180	130	0	230	185	35 000 $ à 39 999 $	480
110	1,100	95	25	110	60	40 000 $ à $44 999 $	481
75	1,050	85	10	85	85	45 000 $ à $49 999 $	482
85	1,970	170	15	155	125	50 000 $ à $59 999 $	483
185	3,035	295	30	235	245	60 000 $ et plus	484
26,694	35,943	29,037	26,398	28,115	32,562	Revenu médian $[57]	485
31,855	38,910	33,589	28,515	30,197	34,611	Revenu moyen $[57]	486
1,270	528	1,295	2,398	1,048	1,327	Erreur type de revenu moyen $[57]	487
1,585	17,540	2,020	290	2,310	1,560	Total - Femmes	488
120	900	120	20	125	100	Sans revenu	489
1,470	16,640	1,900	265	2,185	1,460	Avec un revenu	490
50	505	60	10	95	45	Moins de 1 000 $[56]	491
70	785	85	35	75	95	1 000$ à 2 999 $	492
95	670	75	10	85	85	3 000 $ à 4 999 $	493
100	790	95	20	90	75	5 000 $ à 6 999 $	494
110	1,305	155	20	150	75	7 000 $ à 9 999 $	495
75	925	140	25	170	65	10 000 $ à 11 999 $	496
155	1,515	170	40	160	90	12 000 $ à 14 999 $	497
260	2,110	250	25	305	200	15 000 $ à 19 999 $	498
195	1,700	225	25	205	115	20 000 $ à 24 999 $	499
60	1,255	95	0	185	125	25 000 $ à 29 999 $	500
70	1,335	170	25	145	135	30 000 $ à 34 999 $	501
55	930	115	10	105	90	35 000 $ à 39 999 $	502
25	690	75	0	100	95	40 000 $ à 44 999 $	503
50	535	40	0	70	30	45 000 $ à 49 999 $	504
70	695	40	0	110	65	50 000 $ à 59 999 $	505
15	880	100	15	120	75	60 000 $ et plus	506
16,509	19,207	18,304	12,506	19,264	19,951	Revenu médian $[57]	507
19,272	23,933	21,685	18,092	24,491	23,911	Revenu moyen $[57]	508
790	320	1,196	2,448	855	946	Erreur type de revenu moyen $[57]	509
						Composition du revenu total	
100.0	100.0	100.0	100.0	100.0	100.0	Composition du revenu total en 2005 %	510
61.5	70.9	69.1	54.2	64.6	79.6	Revenu d'emploi %	511
24.4	14.0	14.7	24.1	18.5	10.9	Transferts gouvernementaux %	512
14.1	15.0	16.3	21.4	16.8	9.4	Autres %	513
1,650	**23,340**	**2,805**	**335**	**3,010**	**2,455**	**Population de 15 ans et plus avec un revenu d'emploi en 2005**	514
						Sexe et travail	
23,974	26,100	21,153	19,758	22,627	24,957	Revenu médian d'emploi en 2005 $	515
28,786	31,412	25,592	23,326	26,304	28,979	Revenu moyen d'emploi en 2005 $	516
1,238	404	1,126	2,655	959	1,019	Erreur type de revenu moyen d'emploi $	517
815	12,905	1,485	115	1,425	1,340	A travaillé toute l'année à plein temps[59]	518
38,669	39,977	34,958	32,886	35,871	37,695	Revenu médian d'emploi en 2005 $	519
40,410	43,208	38,400	39,937	38,400	39,777	Revenu moyen d'emploi en 2005 $	520
1,700	552	1,325	4,997	1,441	1,247	Erreur type de revenu moyen d'emploi $	521
655	9,025	1,115	145	1,315	995	A travaillé une partie de l'année ou à temps partiel[60]	522
11,794	11,081	9,720	11,432	10,970	11,586	Revenu médian d'emploi en 2005 $	523
19,416	18,220	12,935	16,494	15,708	17,511	Revenu moyen d'emploi en 2005 $	524
1,643	491	1,747	2,585	960	1,418	Erreur type de revenu moyen d'emploi $	525
880	12,220	1,430	175	1,695	1,310	Hommes de 15 ans et plus avec un revenu d'emploi[58]	526
34,044	36,711	28,371	26,180	23,950	33,677	Revenu médian d'emploi en 2005 $	527
35,456	38,696	31,087	28,253	27,125	34,246	Revenu moyen d'emploi en 2005 $	528
1,957	649	1,528	3,352	1,397	1,571	Erreur type de revenu moyen d'emploi $	529

Nota : Voir les symboles et les abréviations dans les documents d'introduction et voir les documents de référence à la fin de la publication.

Selected characteristics for census divisions and census subdivisions – 100% data and 20% sample data, Ontario, 2006 Census (continued)

No.	Characteristics	Centre Hastings, MU	Deseronto, T ◆◇	Faraday, TP ◆◇◇	Hastings Highlands, MU ◆◇	Limerick, TP ◆◆◇◇	Madoc, TP ◆
	2005 income characteristics						
	Sex and work activity (continued)						
530	Worked full year, full time[59]	730	270	220	515	0	355
531	Median employment income in 2005 $	43,775	34,948	43,029	34,588	0	34,910
532	Average employment income in 2005 $	46,695	35,948	44,048	40,710	0	37,513
533	Standard error of average employment income $	2,283	2,134	3,213	3,874	0	2,720
534	Worked part year or part time[60]	505	230	135	435	80	180
535	Median employment income in 2005 $	11,493	9,995	12,277	14,820	4,437	9,036
536	Average employment income in 2005 $	17,831	15,658	12,618	19,094	17,333	15,959
537	Standard error of average employment income $	1,775	2,339	1,356	1,691	5,182	4,340
538	Females 15 years and over with employment income[58]	1,040	435	340	975	85	555
539	Median employment income in 2005 $	20,053	19,340	9,779	9,948	9,805	15,043
540	Average employment income in 2005 $	21,998	20,523	18,111	17,217	16,068	21,934
541	Standard error of average employment income $	1,064	1,688	2,341	1,299	8,564	1,980
542	Worked full year, full time[59]	455	175	115	330	0	210
543	Median employment income in 2005 $	31,213	24,902	33,514	26,644	0	30,436
544	Average employment income in 2005 $	32,104	32,823	36,458	31,269	0	36,676
545	Standard error of average employment income $	1,510	2,540	4,684	2,535	0	3,177
546	Worked part year or part time[60]	535	250	155	525	45	280
547	Median employment income in 2005 $	11,971	9,645	8,270	8,013	7,519	8,494
548	Average employment income in 2005 $	14,946	12,427	11,121	11,970	6,707	13,779
549	Standard error of average employment income $	1,172	1,458	1,714	1,213	7,293	1,920
550	**Total number of economic families in private households**	**1,315**	**510**	**500**	**1,265**	**120**	**630**
	Family income groups in 2005						
551	Under $10,000	10	0	0	55	20	10
552	$10,000 to $19,999	55	30	25	75	25	30
553	$20,000 to $29,999	130	75	70	125	20	55
554	$30,000 to $39,999	155	100	65	185	10	60
555	$40,000 to $49,999	185	70	85	205	0	85
556	$50,000 to $59,999	130	50	65	145	20	115
557	$60,000 to $69,999	105	45	75	115	10	50
558	$70,000 to $79,999	120	50	10	110	0	70
559	$80,000 to $89,999	145	20	30	105	0	35
560	$90,000 to $99,999	85	25	25	10	0	20
561	$100,000 and over	185	35	40	130	10	100
562	Median family income $	58,506	46,150	51,330	49,778	27,298	55,785
563	Average family income $	64,660	54,470	58,023	57,175	40,882	63,822
564	Standard error of average family income $	1,944	2,649	2,853	2,619	7,690	3,028
	Family after-tax income groups in 2005						
565	Under $10,000	20	0	0	60	15	10
566	$10,000 to $19,999	60	30	35	70	30	25
567	$20,000 to $29,999	130	80	65	140	20	60
568	$30,000 to $39,999	205	115	100	255	10	90
569	$40,000 to $49,999	210	80	110	225	20	135
570	$50,000 to $59,999	155	50	70	165	0	80
571	$60,000 to $69,999	205	70	35	170	0	75
572	$70,000 to $79,999	100	25	35	30	0	30
573	$80,000 to $89,999	95	20	20	30	0	50
574	$90,000 to $99,999	60	15	20	30	0	10
575	$100,000 and over	70	20	15	80	0	55
576	Median after-tax family income $	51,286	44,360	45,107	45,964	27,298	49,529
577	Average after-tax family income $	55,392	48,414	49,970	49,536	35,703	54,940
578	Standard error of average after-tax family income $	1,469	2,121	2,173	1,872	5,994	2,368
	Income status in 2005						
579	Total population in private households for income status	4,290	1,795	1,575	4,005	360	2,070
580	Below low income cut-off before tax in 2005	415	340	125	560	130	155
581	Prevalence of low income before tax in 2005 %	9.7	18.9	7.6	14.0	35.6	7.5
582	Below low income cut-off after tax in 2005	280	190	30	385	55	100
583	Prevalence of low income after tax in 2005 %	6.4	10.3	1.9	9.6	15.1	5.1

Note: See symbols and abbreviations in the introductory material and see reference material at the end of the publication.

Certaines caractéristiques des divisions de recensement et des subdivisions de recensement – Données intégrales et données-échantillon (20 %), Ontario, Recensement de 2006 (suite)

Marmora and Lake, MU ◆◇	Quinte West, CY ◇A	Stirling-Rawdon, TP	Tudor and Cashel, TP ◆◆◇◇	Tweed, MU ◆◇	Tyendinaga, TP	Caractéristiques	N°
						Caractéristiques du revenu de 2005	
						Sexe et travail (suite)	
485	7,665	870	70	835	795	A travaillé toute l'année à plein temps[59]	530
44,611	46,957	38,497	33,140	37,754	40,004	Revenu médian d'emploi en 2005 $	531
46,247	49,399	40,844	42,931	38,939	43,943	Revenu moyen d'emploi en 2005 $	532
2,458	797	1,870	5,771	1,968	1,741	Erreur type de revenu moyen d'emploi $	533
270	3,780	440	60	685	455	A travaillé une partie de l'année ou à temps partiel[60]	534
24,463	12,519	11,305	24,091	11,869	11,622	Revenu médian d'emploi en 2005 $	535
28,202	23,520	20,204	26,723	15,369	20,805	Revenu moyen d'emploi en 2005 $	536
3,243	1,004	2,299	3,898	1,470	2,668	Erreur type de revenu moyen d'emploi $	537
775	11,120	1,375	155	1,315	1,150	Femmes de 15 ans et plus avec un revenu d'emploi[58]	538
17,608	19,187	16,198	11,751	21,932	19,136	Revenu médian d'emploi en 2005 $	539
21,231	23,407	19,878	17,622	25,248	22,963	Revenu moyen d'emploi en 2005 $	540
1,231	401	1,599	4,077	1,278	1,135	Erreur type de revenu moyen d'emploi $	541
335	5,245	615	50	585	540	A travaillé toute l'année à plein temps[59]	542
31,023	31,072	33,542	30,081	31,950	33,141	Revenu médian d'emploi en 2005 $	543
31,998	34,164	34,943	35,954	37,630	33,643	Revenu moyen d'emploi en 2005 $	544
1,788	607	1,733	9,122	2,095	1,598	Erreur type de revenu moyen d'emploi $	545
385	5,245	670	85	630	540	A travaillé une partie de l'année ou à temps partiel[60]	546
10,191	10,335	9,112	9,667	10,547	11,262	Revenu médian d'emploi en 2005 $	547
13,179	14,396	8,178	9,228	16,075	14,729	Revenu moyen d'emploi en 2005 $	548
1,226	398	2,392	2,202	1,232	1,171	Erreur type de revenu moyen d'emploi $	549
1,155	**12,765**	**1,455**	**210**	**1,675**	**1,165**	**Nombre total des familles économiques dans les ménages privés**	550
						Revenu de la famille économique en 2005	
15	390	60	15	25	10	Moins de 10 000 $	551
60	485	75	20	100	15	10 000 $ à 19 999 $	552
220	940	125	15	190	115	20 000 $ à 29 999 $	553
150	1,285	135	20	220	95	30 000 $ à 39 999 $	554
135	1,330	115	15	195	110	40 000 $ à 49 999 $	555
135	1,380	140	30	230	145	50 000 $ à 59 999 $	556
90	1,365	195	25	145	155	60 000 $ à 69 999 $	557
75	1,260	160	20	90	135	70 000 $ à 79 999 $	558
60	1,100	145	15	165	80	80 000 $ à 89 999 $	559
70	765	65	25	70	100	90 000 $ à 99 999 $	560
140	2,455	240	10	235	205	100 000 $ et plus	561
49,341	63,694	63,108	54,906	54,391	66,738	Revenu médian des familles $	562
56,742	70,052	63,744	58,273	61,866	69,868	Revenu moyen des familles $	563
2,008	832	2,372	5,128	1,837	2,045	Erreur type de revenu moyen des familles $	564
						Revenu après impôt de la famille économique en 2005	
15	395	70	15	35	10	Moins de 10 000 $	565
70	520	80	20	95	15	10 000 $ à 19 999 $	566
240	1,070	150	15	225	125	20 000 $ à 29 999 $	567
175	1,650	175	30	245	135	30 000 $ à 39 999 $	568
175	1,780	155	20	300	170	40 000 $ à 49 999 $	569
130	1,790	260	20	200	175	50 000 $ à 59 999 $	570
110	1,580	195	40	135	150	60 000 $ à 69 999 $	571
85	1,250	120	15	160	135	70 000 $ à 79 999 $	572
55	965	115	25	105	90	80 000 $ à 89 999 $	573
35	705	65	0	50	70	90 000 $ à 99 999 $	574
65	1,055	75	10	125	85	100 000 $ et plus	575
45,565	54,781	53,565	52,355	48,444	57,153	Revenu médian après impôt des familles $	576
49,304	59,422	51,244	50,861	53,478	59,648	Revenu moyen après impôt des familles $	577
1,570	625	2,656	4,047	1,447	1,566	Erreur type de revenu moyen après impôt des familles $	578
						Catégorie de revenu en 2005	
3,745	42,240	4,800	680	5,600	4,095	Population totale dans les ménages privés pour la catégorie de revenu	579
575	5,070	575	145	805	355	Au-dessous du seuil de faible revenu avant impôt en 2005	580
15.4	12.0	12.0	21.3	14.5	8.8	Fréquence du faible revenu avant impôt en 2005 %	581
270	3,605	460	115	520	105	Au-dessous du seuil de faible revenu après impôt en 2005	582
7.2	8.5	9.5	16.9	9.3	2.6	Fréquence du faible revenu après impôt en 2005 %	583

Nota : Voir les symboles et les abréviations dans les documents d'introduction et voir les documents de référence à la fin de la publication.

Selected characteristics for census divisions and census subdivisions – 100% data and 20% sample data, Ontario, 2006 Census (continued)

No.	Characteristics	Centre Hastings, MU	Deseronto, T ◆◇	Faraday, TP ◆◇◇	Hastings Highlands, MU ◆◇	Limerick, TP ◆◆◇◇	Madoc, TP ◆
	2005 income characteristics						
584	**Total number of private households**	**1,690**	**710**	**670**	**1,685**	**175**	**775**
	Household income groups in 2005						
585	Under $10,000	40	25	10	120	25	20
586	$10,000 to $19,999	185	145	110	190	40	60
587	$20,000 to $29,999	180	75	70	200	30	95
588	$30,000 to $39,999	235	140	90	245	25	95
589	$40,000 to $49,999	220	80	115	255	10	100
590	$50,000 to $59,999	145	55	70	165	30	120
591	$60,000 to $69,999	110	45	80	115	10	65
592	$70,000 to $79,999	140	55	25	130	0	70
593	$80,000 to $89,999	140	25	30	110	0	35
594	$90,000 to $99,999	95	30	30	10	10	20
595	$100,000 and over	190	40	40	135	10	100
596	Median household income $	49,428	36,619	44,365	43,151	27,333	51,826
597	Average household income $	56,923	45,212	50,998	49,957	36,820	57,669
598	Standard error of average household income $	1,784	2,459	2,562	2,227	5,674	2,624
	Household after-tax income groups in 2005						
599	Under $10,000	45	25	10	130	25	20
600	$10,000 to $19,999	185	150	120	205	35	70
601	$20,000 to $29,999	245	90	80	240	35	90
602	$30,000 to $39,999	250	160	135	310	25	135
603	$40,000 to $49,999	245	75	115	265	25	145
604	$50,000 to $59,999	170	50	70	175	10	90
605	$60,000 to $69,999	210	70	50	180	10	75
606	$70,000 to $79,999	105	30	35	30	0	30
607	$80,000 to $89,999	100	20	20	35	10	50
608	$90,000 to $99,999	55	15	10	30	0	15
609	$100,000 and over	80	20	25	85	10	60
610	Median after-tax household income $	43,593	34,361	39,767	38,774	27,333	43,426
611	Average after-tax household income $	48,961	40,410	43,977	43,177	31,976	49,752
612	Standard error of average after-tax household income $	1,379	2,016	1,994	1,633	4,464	2,069

Note: See symbols and abbreviations in the introductory material and see reference material at the end of the publication.

Certaines caractéristiques des divisions de recensement et des subdivisions de recensement – Données intégrales et données-échantillon (20 %), Ontario, Recensement de 2006 (suite)

Marmora and Lake, MU ◆◊	Quinte West, CY ◊**A**	Stirling-Rawdon, TP	Tudor and Cashel, TP ◆◆◊◊	Tweed, MU ◆◊	Tyendinaga, TP	**Caractéristiques**	N°
						Caractéristiques du revenu de 2005	
1,600	**16,715**	**1,845**	**285**	**2,285**	**1,370**	**Nombre total des ménages privés**	584
						Tranches de revenu des ménages en 2005	
50	720	130	30	115	15	Moins de 10 000 $	585
225	1,445	190	45	295	60	10 000 $ à 19 999 $	586
325	1,665	180	25	280	160	20 000 $ à 29 999 $	587
210	1,990	205	25	305	145	30 000 $ à 39 999 $	588
175	1,715	125	20	235	110	40 000 $ à 49 999 $	589
155	1,730	170	30	275	145	50 000 $ à 59 999 $	590
100	1,575	215	25	150	165	60 000 $ à 69 999 $	591
80	1,375	165	25	130	145	70 000 $ à 79 999 $	592
60	1,145	150	25	175	90	80 000 $ à 89 999 $	593
70	820	70	25	90	100	90 000 $ à 99 999 $	594
140	2,530	240	10	240	220	100 000 $ et plus	595
39,743	55,564	56,357	48,925	46,519	63,254	Revenu médian des ménages $	596
48,169	61,582	56,321	50,019	53,554	65,227	Revenu moyen des ménages $	597
1,643	699	2,036	3,989	1,577	1,945	Erreur type de revenu moyen des ménages $	598
						Tranches du revenu après impôt des ménages en 2005	
50	730	135	30	120	15	Moins de 10 000 $	599
245	1,575	200	45	325	70	10 000 $ à 19 999 $	600
365	2,090	230	35	320	190	20 000 $ à 29 999 $	601
235	2,270	230	30	320	170	30 000 $ à 39 999 $	602
210	2,250	170	30	345	180	40 000 $ à 49 999 $	603
135	1,980	290	20	225	180	50 000 $ à 59 999 $	604
120	1,730	205	45	160	160	60 000 $ à 69 999 $	605
85	1,255	120	15	170	145	70 000 $ à 79 999 $	606
55	1,025	110	25	105	105	80 000 $ à 89 999 $	607
40	705	70	0	50	70	90 000 $ à 99 999 $	608
60	1,100	75	10	130	85	100 000 $ et plus	609
35,512	47,539	48,223	39,971	41,732	53,099	Revenu médian après impôt des ménages $	610
42,154	52,341	45,726	43,588	46,360	55,753	Revenu moyen après impôt des ménages $	611
1,303	534	2,173	3,180	1,258	1,508	Erreur type de revenu moyen après impôt des ménages $	612

Nota : Voir les symboles et les abréviations dans les documents d'introduction et voir les documents de référence à la fin de la publication.

Selected characteristics for census divisions and census subdivisions – 100% data and 20% sample data, Ontario, 2006 Census (continued)

No.	Characteristics	Wollaston, TP ◆◆◊	Huron CD/DR	Ashfield-Colborne-Wawanosh, TP ◆	Bluewater, MU ◆◊	Central Huron, MU	Goderich, T
	Population characteristics						
1	**Population, 2001**[1]	**679**	**59,701**	**5,411**	**6,919**	**7,806**	**7,604**
2	**Population, 2006**[2]	**730**	**59,325**	**5,409**	**7,120**	**7,641**	**7,563**
3	Population percentage change, 2001 to 2006	7.5	-0.6	0.0	2.9	-2.1	-0.5
4	Land area in square kilometres, 2006	215.22	3,396.68	587.07	416.99	447.60	7.91
5	**Total population – 100% data**[3]	**730**	**59,325**	**5,410**	**7,120**	**7,645**	**7,565**
	Sex and age groups						
6	Male	390	29,250	2,745	3,530	3,815	3,555
7	0 to 4 years	10	1,585	150	160	190	170
8	5 to 9 years	10	1,885	180	235	230	230
9	10 to 14 years	25	2,125	215	250	255	220
10	15 to 19 years	25	2,210	250	225	295	225
11	20 to 24 years	5	1,755	150	195	230	215
12	25 to 29 years	25	1,410	105	140	175	150
13	30 to 34 years	5	1,450	115	175	170	180
14	35 to 39 years	20	1,635	125	180	190	205
15	40 to 44 years	25	2,090	195	260	255	225
16	45 to 49 years	30	2,275	200	280	300	275
17	50 to 54 years	40	2,195	230	275	295	295
18	55 to 59 years	30	2,180	210	285	310	300
19	60 to 64 years	35	1,685	150	240	270	190
20	65 to 69 years	25	1,445	165	200	205	180
21	70 to 74 years	25	1,205	140	165	165	150
22	75 to 79 years	20	1,035	100	140	145	160
23	80 to 84 years	10	615	35	80	80	105
24	85 years and over	10	465	35	40	50	90
25	Female	340	30,075	2,665	3,585	3,830	4,010
26	0 to 4 years	15	1,555	170	170	170	140
27	5 to 9 years	15	1,740	155	215	195	190
28	10 to 14 years	20	2,135	240	235	240	235
29	15 to 19 years	15	2,095	185	225	275	250
30	20 to 24 years	5	1,735	160	190	220	210
31	25 to 29 years	10	1,380	100	125	185	190
32	30 to 34 years	15	1,425	110	165	175	180
33	35 to 39 years	20	1,665	150	205	200	200
34	40 to 44 years	25	2,190	190	255	270	290
35	45 to 49 years	30	2,245	200	270	300	295
36	50 to 54 years	40	2,215	215	285	305	325
37	55 to 59 years	30	2,105	205	290	310	305
38	60 to 64 years	35	1,755	165	245	270	235
39	65 to 69 years	25	1,490	150	205	210	195
40	70 to 74 years	20	1,215	105	145	160	200
41	75 to 79 years	10	1,255	95	150	145	205
42	80 to 84 years	10	885	45	80	125	170
43	85 years and over	5	1,000	25	140	85	185
44	**Total population 15 years and over**[3]	**630**	**48,310**	**4,295**	**5,855**	**6,365**	**6,375**
	Legal marital status						
45	Never legally married (single)	145	12,510	1,065	1,395	1,635	1,670
46	Legally married (and not separated)[4,5]	345	27,585	2,680	3,485	3,690	3,370
47	Separated, but still legally married	25	1,565	110	175	175	250
48	Divorced	65	2,915	215	350	410	470
49	Widowed	50	3,735	220	445	440	615
	Common-law status						
50	Not in a common-law relationship	560	44,900	4,005	5,445	5,905	5,955
51	In a common-law relationship	75	3,410	290	415	460	420
52	**Total population – 20% sample data**[6]	**730**	**58,590**	**5,405**	**6,970**	**7,610**	**7,450**
	Mother tongue						
53	Single responses	730	58,400	5,375	6,965	7,590	7,405
54	English	715	53,375	4,560	6,400	7,005	7,045
55	French	0	385	35	120	20	80
56	Non-official languages[7]	15	4,635	785	445	565	280
57	Italian	0	65	35	0	0	0
58	Chinese, n.o.s.[61]	0	30	10	0	0	0
59	Cantonese	0	40	0	0	0	10
60	Spanish	0	65	0	0	0	0
61	German	10	2,130	490	205	110	75
62	Other languages[8]	10	2,305	255	240	460	195

Note: See symbols and abbreviations in the introductory material and see reference material at the end of the publication.

Certaines caractéristiques des divisions de recensement et des subdivisions de recensement – Données intégrales et données-échantillon (20 %), Ontario, Recensement de 2006 (suite)

Howick, TP ◆◇	Huron East, MU	Morris-Turnberry, MU ◇◇	North Huron, TP	South Huron, MU	**Kawartha Lakes CD/DR ◆◇**	Caractéristiques	Nº
						Caractéristiques de la population	
3,779	**9,680**	**3,499**	**4,984**	**10,019**	**69,179**	**Population, 2001[1]**	1
3,882	**9,310**	**3,403**	**5,015**	**9,982**	**74,561**	**Population, 2006[2]**	2
2.7	-3.8	-2.7	0.6	-0.4	7.8	Variation en pourcentage de la population, 2001 à 2006	3
287.17	669.16	376.45	178.98	425.35	3,059.47	Superficie des terres en kilomètres carrés, 2006	4
3,880	**9,310**	**3,400**	**5,015**	**9,985**	**74,560**	**Population totale – Données intégrales[3]**	5
						Sexe et groupes d'âge	
1,935	4,615	1,725	2,455	4,885	36,705	Sexe masculin	6
170	265	110	135	230	1,530	0 à 4 ans	7
165	340	105	155	250	1,970	5 à 9 ans	8
180	385	120	175	325	2,570	10 à 14 ans	9
165	365	165	170	345	2,690	15 à 19 ans	10
110	270	100	170	305	2,060	20 à 24 ans	11
105	245	100	170	230	1,525	25 à 29 ans	12
115	230	80	135	255	1,670	30 à 34 ans	13
105	275	95	145	320	1,990	35 à 39 ans	14
145	365	135	140	370	2,780	40 à 44 ans	15
150	360	115	185	410	3,110	45 à 49 ans	16
115	340	115	195	340	2,930	50 à 54 ans	17
110	320	125	180	345	2,795	55 à 59 ans	18
85	250	85	135	275	2,450	60 à 64 ans	19
70	175	75	110	270	1,935	65 à 69 ans	20
60	140	50	100	235	1,780	70 à 74 ans	21
50	135	55	75	180	1,495	75 à 79 ans	22
20	80	45	50	130	920	80 à 84 ans	23
15	75	40	45	80	510	85 ans et plus	24
1,950	4,695	1,680	2,560	5,095	37,855	Sexe féminin	25
150	260	105	150	225	1,560	0 à 4 ans	26
165	305	120	140	255	1,885	5 à 9 ans	27
185	370	120	165	345	2,380	10 à 14 ans	28
175	325	135	190	320	2,375	15 à 19 ans	29
130	310	90	155	280	1,845	20 à 24 ans	30
100	225	75	160	220	1,575	25 à 29 ans	31
100	270	60	125	235	1,690	30 à 34 ans	32
115	290	110	140	255	2,145	35 à 39 ans	33
140	340	140	175	395	2,895	40 à 44 ans	34
140	345	105	190	405	3,140	45 à 49 ans	35
100	325	125	190	360	3,110	50 à 54 ans	36
115	270	105	175	340	2,955	55 à 59 ans	37
80	215	85	135	315	2,425	60 à 64 ans	38
80	185	70	95	300	1,995	65 à 69 ans	39
50	160	45	100	240	1,835	70 à 74 ans	40
55	170	60	100	275	1,630	75 à 79 ans	41
25	135	45	90	180	1,270	80 à 84 ans	42
45	195	95	75	160	1,150	85 ans et plus	43
2,870	**7,380**	**2,720**	**4,095**	**8,355**	**62,680**	**Population totale de 15 ans et plus[3]**	44
						État matrimonial légal	
795	1,960	735	1,140	2,115	16,095	Jamais légalement marié(e) (célibataire)	45
1,735	4,125	1,580	2,245	4,665	34,345	Légalement marié(e) (et non séparé[e])[4,5]	46
75	270	60	125	330	2,395	Séparé(e), mais toujours légalement marié(e)	47
120	430	125	265	520	4,815	Divorcé(e)	48
140	595	220	320	725	5,020	Veuf(ve)	49
						Union libre	
2,695	6,830	2,545	3,775	7,740	56,905	Ne vivant pas en union libre	50
175	545	175	315	620	5,775	Vivant en union libre	51
3,850	**9,075**	**3,335**	**5,010**	**9,885**	**73,360**	**Population totale – Données-échantillon (20 %)[6]**	52
						Langue maternelle	
3,845	9,040	3,325	5,005	9,845	73,090	Réponses uniques	53
3,190	8,305	2,830	4,795	9,250	68,575	Anglais	54
0	50	20	15	45	755	Français	55
650	680	475	195	550	3,760	Langues non officielles[7]	56
0	15	0	10	0	190	Italien	57
0	0	10	0	0	30	Chinois, n.d.a.[61]	58
0	0	0	25	10	15	Cantonais	59
0	40	0	0	25	95	Espagnol	60
430	290	390	45	100	950	Allemand	61
220	325	70	125	410	2,475	Autres langues[8]	62

Nota : Voir les symboles et les abréviations dans les documents d'introduction et voir les documents de référence à la fin de la publication.

Selected characteristics for census divisions and census subdivisions – 100% data and 20% sample data, Ontario, 2006 Census (continued)

No.	Characteristics	Wollaston, TP ◆◆◊	**Huron CD/DR**	Ashfield-Colborne-Wawanosh, TP ◆	Bluewater, MU ◆◊	Central Huron, MU	Goderich, T
	Population characteristics						
	Mother tongue (continued)						
63	Multiple responses	0	195	30	0	25	45
64	English and French	0	85	10	0	10	35
65	English and non-official language	0	110	15	0	10	10
66	French and non-official language	0	0	0	0	0	0
67	English, French and non-official language	0	0	0	0	0	0
	Language spoken most often at home[9]						
68	Single responses	730	58,460	5,370	6,960	7,595	7,445
69	English	730	56,255	4,870	6,825	7,505	7,420
70	French	0	10	0	0	0	0
71	Non-official languages[7]	0	2,195	500	135	90	20
72	Chinese, n.o.s.[61]	0	10	0	0	0	0
73	Cantonese	0	20	0	0	0	0
74	Panjabi (Punjabi)	0	0	0	0	0	0
75	Italian	0	0	0	0	0	0
76	Spanish	0	55	0	0	0	0
77	Other languages[8]	0	2,105	500	135	90	20
78	Multiple responses	0	130	30	10	15	0
79	English and French	0	20	15	0	0	0
80	English and non-official language	0	110	15	10	15	10
81	French and non-official language	0	0	0	0	0	0
82	English, French and non-official language	0	0	0	0	0	0
	Knowledge of official languages[10]						
83	English only	705	56,385	5,170	6,775	7,425	6,955
84	French only	0	0	0	0	0	0
85	English and French	25	1,810	160	190	185	490
86	Neither English nor French	0	395	70	0	0	0
	Knowledge of non-official languages[7,11]						
87	Italian	0	90	35	0	10	0
88	Spanish	0	255	10	0	25	30
89	German	10	2,350	560	220	125	80
90	Chinese, n.o.s.[61]	0	35	10	0	0	0
91	Cantonese	0	40	0	0	0	10
92	Panjabi (Punjabi)	0	0	0	0	0	0
93	Portuguese	0	10	0	0	0	10
	First official language spoken[10]						
94	English	730	57,865	5,300	6,930	7,575	7,365
95	French	0	280	30	40	10	80
96	English and French	0	80	10	0	25	0
97	Neither English nor French	0	365	60	0	0	0
98	Official language minority - (number)[12]	0	320	35	40	20	80
99	Official language minority - (percentage)[12]	0.0	0.5	0.6	0.6	0.3	1.1
	Ethnic origin[13]						
100	English	310	22,295	2,130	2,410	2,665	3,035
101	Canadian	310	18,060	1,460	2,255	2,255	2,505
102	Scottish	170	18,035	1,530	2,060	2,035	2,355
103	Irish	135	15,750	1,525	1,545	1,725	2,320
104	French	55	5,435	280	1,100	475	985
105	German	145	13,220	1,235	2,105	1,325	1,275
106	Italian	40	835	120	110	50	145
107	Chinese	0	170	20	0	0	20
108	East Indian	0	135	0	10	10	30
109	Dutch (Netherlands)	60	8,055	920	900	1,735	580
110	Polish	0	865	65	95	165	115
111	Ukrainian	15	675	55	60	110	80
112	North American Indian	30	1,175	190	110	100	185
113	Portuguese	0	30	0	10	10	10
114	Filipino	0	10	0	0	0	0
	Aboriginal and non-Aboriginal identity						
115	Total Aboriginal identity population[14]	105	320	15	35	25	50
116	Total non-Aboriginal identity population	625	58,275	5,390	6,930	7,585	7,400

Note: See symbols and abbreviations in the introductory material and see reference material at the end of the publication.

Certaines caractéristiques des divisions de recensement et des subdivisions de recensement – Données intégrales et données-échantillon (20 %), Ontario, Recensement de 2006 (suite)

Howick, TP ◆◇	Huron East, MU	Morris-Turnberry, MU ◇◇	North Huron, TP	South Huron, MU	**Kawartha Lakes CD/DR** ◆◇	**Caractéristiques**	N°
						Caractéristiques de la population	
						Langue maternelle (suite)	
0	35	15	10	40	275	Réponses multiples	63
0	10	0	0	20	115	Anglais et français	64
0	25	15	0	20	155	Anglais et langue non officielle	65
0	0	0	0	0	0	Français et langue non officielle	66
0	0	0	0	0	0	Anglais, français et langue non officielle	67
						Langue parlée le plus souvent à la maison[9]	
3,845	9,055	3,340	5,010	9,845	73,225	Réponses uniques	68
3,400	8,650	2,930	4,955	9,705	72,180	Anglais	69
0	0	0	10	0	100	Français	70
445	405	410	50	140	945	Langues non officielles[7]	71
0	0	10	0	0	15	Chinois, n.d.a.[61]	72
0	0	0	20	0	20	Cantonais	73
0	0	0	0	0	25	Pendjabi	74
0	0	0	0	0	15	Italien	75
0	35	0	0	25	0	Espagnol	76
445	375	400	25	115	860	Autres langues[8]	77
0	25	0	0	35	140	Réponses multiples	78
0	0	0	0	0	50	Anglais et français	79
10	25	0	0	35	90	Anglais et langue non officielle	80
0	0	0	0	0	0	Français et langue non officielle	81
0	0	0	0	0	0	Anglais, français et langue non officielle	82
						Connaissance des langues officielles[10]	
3,680	8,770	3,110	4,925	9,570	69,640	Anglais seulement	83
0	0	0	0	0	35	Français seulement	84
75	265	105	80	260	3,610	Anglais et français	85
95	40	120	10	55	75	Ni l'anglais ni le français	86
						Connaissance des langues non officielles[7,11]	
0	30	0	10	0	270	Italien	87
0	80	20	25	45	310	Espagnol	88
455	310	410	35	150	1,130	Allemand	89
0	10	10	0	10	20	Chinois, n.d.a.[61]	90
0	0	0	20	10	35	Cantonais	91
0	0	0	0	0	85	Pendjabi	92
0	0	0	0	0	140	Portugais	93
						Première langue officielle parlée[10]	
3,745	8,965	3,195	4,990	9,790	72,510	Anglais	94
10	45	20	10	45	710	Français	95
0	35	0	0	10	80	Anglais et français	96
95	35	120	10	45	60	Ni l'anglais ni le français	97
0	60	20	15	50	755	Minorité de langue officielle - (nombre)[12]	98
0.0	0.7	0.6	0.3	0.5	1.0	Minorité de langue officielle - (pourcentage)[12]	99
						Origine ethnique[13]	
1,380	3,065	1,005	2,190	4,420	33,195	Anglais	100
915	3,115	1,145	1,280	3,135	26,315	Canadien	101
1,250	2,760	995	2,145	2,895	20,070	Écossais	102
1,100	2,445	840	1,770	2,470	20,255	Irlandais	103
380	635	240	385	955	7,660	Français	104
1,295	2,045	635	1,125	2,180	6,915	Allemand	105
15	180	15	85	110	1,625	Italien	106
10	40	10	35	30	155	Chinois	107
0	0	0	45	40	335	Indien de l'Inde	108
490	1,420	390	595	1,020	4,585	Hollandais (Néerlandais)	109
50	95	95	70	115	1,650	Polonais	110
45	120	50	60	85	1,605	Ukrainien	111
80	195	35	60	215	2,150	Indien de l'Amérique du Nord	112
0	0	10	0	0	415	Portugais	113
0	0	0	0	0	65	Philippin	114
						Population ayant une identité autochtone et population n'ayant pas d'identité autochtone	
0	70	25	20	65	1,255	Total de la population ayant une identité autochtone[14]	115
3,850	9,005	3,310	4,985	9,820	72,110	Total de la population n'ayant pas d'identité autochtone	116

Nota : Voir les symboles et les abréviations dans les documents d'introduction et voir les documents de référence à la fin de la publication.

Selected characteristics for census divisions and census subdivisions – 100% data and 20% sample data, Ontario, 2006 Census (continued)

No.	Characteristics	Wollaston, TP ◆◆◊	**Huron CD/DR**	Ashfield-Colborne-Wawanosh, TP ◆	Bluewater, MU ◆◊	Central Huron, MU	Goderich, T
	Population characteristics						
	Aboriginal and non-Aboriginal ancestry						
117	Total Aboriginal ancestry population[15]	110	1,395	200	135	110	200
118	Total non-Aboriginal ancestry population	620	57,195	5,200	6,835	7,505	7,245
	Registered Indian status						
119	Registered Indian[16]	0	130	10	25	0	35
120	Not a Registered Indian	730	58,460	5,395	6,940	7,605	7,415
	Visible minority groups						
121	Total visible minority population[17]	0	875	35	15	40	85
122	Chinese	0	120	20	0	0	20
123	South Asian[18]	0	145	0	0	0	35
124	Black	0	255	10	10	0	15
125	Filipino	0	10	0	0	0	0
126	Latin American	0	140	0	0	0	10
127	Southeast Asian[19]	0	100	0	0	0	0
128	Arab	0	0	0	0	10	0
129	West Asian[20]	0	0	0	0	0	0
130	Korean	0	40	0	0	15	0
131	Japanese	0	30	0	10	20	0
132	Visible minority, n.i.e.[21]	0	20	0	0	0	10
133	Multiple visible minority[22]	0	25	0	0	10	0
	Citizenship[23]						
134	Canadian citizens[24]	715	57,670	5,275	6,930	7,515	7,380
135	Not Canadian citizens[25]	15	920	125	40	100	65
	Immigrant status and place of birth[26]						
136	Non-immigrants[27]	675	53,690	4,750	6,555	6,875	6,845
137	Born in province of residence	630	50,865	4,510	6,215	6,495	6,375
138	Immigrants[28]	55	4,665	650	410	735	580
139	United States of America	25	320	80	30	45	35
140	Central and South America	0	160	0	0	0	0
141	Caribbean and Bermuda	0	85	0	10	0	10
142	United Kingdom	25	1,310	160	125	155	240
143	Other Europe	10	2,445	385	230	525	230
144	Africa	0	20	10	0	0	15
145	Asia and the Middle East	0	280	10	20	10	40
146	Oceania and other[29]	0	50	0	0	10	0
147	Non-permanent residents[30]	0	235	10	10	0	20
148	**Total immigrant population[28]**	**55**	**4,665**	**650**	**410**	**735**	**585**
	Period of immigration						
149	Before 1961	10	1,880	240	185	360	295
150	1961 to 1970	10	755	95	90	115	100
151	1971 to 1980	15	605	85	45	40	60
152	1981 to 1990	0	590	80	45	30	70
153	1991 to 2000	15	555	105	45	75	45
154	1991 to 1995	0	155	10	10	15	10
155	1996 to 2000	15	395	95	35	60	30
156	2001 to 2006[31]	0	275	35	10	120	0
	Age at immigration						
157	Under 5 years	0	670	55	45	120	75
158	5 to 19 years	10	1,410	215	125	255	155
159	20 years and over	45	2,585	380	240	365	355
160	**Total population 15 years and over**	**620**	**47,580**	**4,290**	**5,705**	**6,335**	**6,265**
	Generation status						
161	1st generation[32]	55	4,640	610	415	680	600
162	2nd generation[33]	100	6,325	715	725	1,125	835
163	3rd generation or more[34]	460	36,615	2,960	4,565	4,530	4,825

Note: See symbols and abbreviations in the introductory material and see reference material at the end of the publication.

Certaines caractéristiques des divisions de recensement et des subdivisions de recensement – Données intégrales et données-échantillon (20 %), Ontario, Recensement de 2006 (suite)

Howick, TP ◆◊	Huron East, MU	Morris-Turnberry, MU ◊◊	North Huron, TP	South Huron, MU	**Kawartha Lakes CD/DR ◆◊**	Caractéristiques	Nº
						Caractéristiques de la population	
						Population ayant une ascendance autochtone et population n'ayant pas d'ascendance autochtone	
130	250	40	70	255	2,785	Total de la population ayant une ascendance autochtone[15]	117
3,720	8,825	3,300	4,940	9,630	70,575	Total de la population n'ayant pas d'ascendance autochtone	118
						Statut d'Indien inscrit	
0	30	0	10	15	310	Indien inscrit[16]	119
3,850	9,045	3,340	5,005	9,870	73,055	Pas un Indien inscrit	120
						Groupes de minorités visibles	
0	210	35	105	350	1,195	Total de la population des minorités visibles[17]	121
0	20	0	35	15	100	Chinois	122
0	0	0	45	60	360	Sud-Asiatique[18]	123
0	50	15	10	145	250	Noir	124
0	0	0	0	0	55	Philippin	125
0	45	20	0	65	70	Latino-Américain	126
0	60	0	0	30	20	Asiatique du Sud-Est[19]	127
0	0	0	0	0	40	Arabe	128
0	0	0	0	0	0	Asiatique occidental[20]	129
0	20	0	0	10	160	Coréen	130
0	0	0	0	10	20	Japonais	131
0	10	0	10	0	50	Minorité visible, n.i.a.[21]	132
0	10	0	10	10	60	Minorités visibles multiples[22]	133
						Citoyenneté[23]	
3,835	8,960	3,320	4,950	9,505	72,505	Citoyens canadiens[24]	134
10	115	15	55	380	855	Ne sont pas des citoyens canadiens[25]	135
						Statut d'immigrant et le lieu de naissance[26]	
3,655	8,340	3,165	4,710	8,790	67,265	Non-immigrants[27]	136
3,485	8,070	3,000	4,535	8,180	62,170	Né dans la province de résidence	137
190	690	175	295	930	6,010	Immigrants[28]	138
0	35	20	15	60	285	États-Unis d'Amérique	139
30	65	20	0	40	130	Amérique centrale et Amérique du Sud	140
0	25	0	30	0	120	Antilles et Bermudes	141
25	140	30	70	360	2,390	Royaume-Uni	142
130	345	80	145	370	2,485	Autre Europe	143
0	0	0	0	0	85	Afrique	144
10	85	0	20	90	460	Asie et Moyen-Orient	145
0	0	15	0	10	50	Océanie et autres[29]	146
0	40	0	0	160	95	Résidents non permanents[30]	147
190	**695**	**170**	**295**	**935**	**6,005**	**Population totale des immigrants[28]**	148
						Période d'immigration	
115	210	60	145	270	2,755	Avant 1961	149
20	80	15	25	215	1,350	1961 à 1970	150
0	90	60	40	175	780	1971 à 1980	151
30	215	10	35	75	460	1981 à 1990	152
20	60	20	30	150	420	1991 à 2000	153
10	15	10	20	50	160	1991 à 1995	154
10	45	10	10	105	260	1996 à 2000	155
0	40	0	20	40	235	2001 à 2006[31]	156
						Âge à l'immigration	
0	125	50	35	155	755	Moins de 5 ans	157
75	220	55	120	185	1,905	5 à 19 ans	158
110	345	65	140	595	3,350	20 ans et plus	159
2,820	**7,140**	**2,655**	**4,095**	**8,260**	**61,460**	**Population totale de 15 ans et plus**	160
						Statut des générations	
205	700	150	300	975	5,985	1re génération[32]	161
240	840	260	540	1,045	10,685	2e génération[33]	162
2,375	5,605	2,245	3,255	6,245	44,790	3e génération ou plus[34]	163

Nota : Voir les symboles et les abréviations dans les documents d'introduction et voir les documents de référence à la fin de la publication.

Selected characteristics for census divisions and census subdivisions – 100% data and 20% sample data, Ontario, 2006 Census (continued)

No.	Characteristics	Wollaston, TP ◆◆◊	Huron CD/DR	Ashfield-Colborne-Wawanosh, TP ◆	Bluewater, MU ◆◊	Central Huron, MU	Goderich, T
	Population characteristics						
164	**Total population 1 year and over[35]**	**730**	**57,945**	**5,330**	**6,900**	**7,555**	**7,385**
	Place of residence 1 year ago (mobility)						
165	Non-movers	700	52,220	4,955	6,295	6,905	6,545
166	Movers	30	5,725	370	605	650	840
167	Non-migrants	0	2,525	95	275	310	515
168	Migrants	25	3,205	270	330	335	325
169	Internal migrants	20	3,110	265	320	325	310
170	Intraprovincial migrants	25	2,895	240	255	310	300
171	Interprovincial migrants	0	215	25	60	20	15
172	External migrants	10	90	0	10	10	10
173	**Total population 5 years and over[36]**	**675**	**55,505**	**5,080**	**6,635**	**7,255**	**7,195**
	Place of residence 5 years ago (mobility)						
174	Non-movers	475	38,520	3,815	4,780	5,270	4,440
175	Movers	200	16,980	1,260	1,855	1,985	2,750
176	Non-migrants	25	7,190	415	715	960	1,350
177	Migrants	170	9,790	850	1,140	1,025	1,400
178	Internal migrants	170	9,305	810	1,115	915	1,360
179	Intraprovincial migrants	165	8,825	795	1,090	885	1,260
180	Interprovincial migrants	10	480	15	25	35	100
181	External migrants	0	485	35	25	110	40
182	**Total population 15 years and over**	**620**	**47,580**	**4,290**	**5,705**	**6,335**	**6,265**
	Highest certificate, diploma or degree[37]						
183	No certificate, diploma or degree	175	14,965	1,260	1,690	1,835	1,555
184	Certificate, diploma or degree	445	32,610	3,030	4,015	4,495	4,705
185	High school certificate or equivalent[38]	210	13,250	1,110	1,645	1,800	1,725
186	Apprenticeship or trades certificate or diploma	85	4,965	495	565	695	725
187	College, CEGEP or other non-university certificate or diploma[39]	110	9,530	905	1,130	1,185	1,370
188	University certificate or diploma below bachelor level[40]	10	1,095	165	125	125	200
189	University certificate or degree[41]	30	3,770	350	545	695	685
190	Bachelor's degree	25	2,395	220	370	420	410
191	University certificate or diploma above bachelor level	0	670	45	100	135	135
192	Degree in medicine, dentistry, veterinary medicine or optometry	0	150	15	10	45	35
193	Master's degree	0	480	65	50	75	80
194	Earned doctorate	0	75	10	10	15	15
195	**Total population 15 years and over with postsecondary qualifications**	**235**	**19,360**	**1,920**	**2,370**	**2,700**	**2,985**
	Major field of study - Classification of Instructional Programs, 2000[42]						
196	Education	0	1,695	185	215	345	250
197	Visual and performing arts, and communications technologies	10	495	45	35	50	105
198	Humanities	15	790	75	105	90	175
199	Social and behavioural sciences and law	25	1,595	135	230	230	265
200	Business, management and public administration	25	3,320	310	470	400	585
201	Physical and life sciences and technologies	0	280	15	20	45	55
202	Mathematics, computer and information sciences	0	390	70	45	50	35
203	Architecture, engineering, and related technologies	80	4,460	460	550	580	680
204	Agriculture, natural resources and conservation	0	1,530	230	150	240	80
205	Health, parks, recreation and fitness	35	3,555	280	430	540	560
206	Personal, protective and transportation services	45	1,255	115	110	130	200
207	Other fields of study[43]	0	0	0	0	0	0
	Location of study[44]						
208	Inside Canada	220	17,855	1,700	2,200	2,465	2,740
209	Outside Canada	15	1,500	220	170	235	245
210	**Total population 15 years and over**	**620**	**47,580**	**4,290**	**5,705**	**6,335**	**6,265**
	Unpaid work						
211	Males 15 years and over	335	23,385	2,180	2,840	3,105	2,895
212	Reported unpaid work[45]	315	21,610	2,010	2,635	2,885	2,585
213	Housework and child care and care or assistance to seniors	15	1,965	195	280	155	220
214	Housework and child care only	50	6,015	470	650	835	775

Note: See symbols and abbreviations in the introductory material and see reference material at the end of the publication.

Certaines caractéristiques des divisions de recensement et des subdivisions de recensement – Données intégrales et données-échantillon (20 %), Ontario, Recensement de 2006 (suite)

Howick, TP ♦◊	Huron East, MU	Morris-Turnberry, MU ◊◊	North Huron, TP	South Huron, MU	**Kawartha Lakes CD/DR ♦◊**	**Caractéristiques**	N°
						Caractéristiques de la population	
3,765	**8,990**	**3,285**	**4,965**	**9,780**	**72,805**	**Population totale de 1 an et plus[35]**	164
						Lieu de résidence 1 an auparavant (mobilité)	
3,490	7,970	3,095	4,315	8,650	65,350	Personnes n'ayant pas déménagé	165
275	1,015	195	650	1,130	7,455	Personnes ayant déménagé	166
105	470	35	240	470	4,180	Non-migrants	167
175	545	155	405	655	3,280	Migrants	168
175	510	155	400	640	3,115	Migrants internes	169
165	450	155	395	630	2,910	Migrants infraprovinciaux	170
10	60	0	10	15	210	Migrants interprovinciaux	171
0	35	0	0	20	160	Migrants externes	172
3,530	**8,545**	**3,115**	**4,725**	**9,425**	**70,350**	**Population totale de 5 ans et plus[36]**	173
						Lieu de résidence 5 ans auparavant (mobilité)	
2,555	5,895	2,390	3,065	6,310	46,440	Personnes n'ayant pas déménagé	174
975	2,645	725	1,655	3,120	23,910	Personnes ayant déménagé	175
370	1,025	195	790	1,365	10,905	Non-migrants	176
600	1,620	530	870	1,750	13,005	Migrants	177
600	1,520	515	865	1,600	12,655	Migrants internes	178
580	1,425	485	820	1,485	11,955	Migrants infraprovinciaux	179
20	95	30	50	115	700	Migrants interprovinciaux	180
0	100	15	10	155	350	Migrants externes	181
2,825	**7,140**	**2,655**	**4,095**	**8,260**	**61,460**	**Population totale de 15 ans et plus**	182
						Plus haut certificat, diplôme ou grade[37]	
1,155	2,565	990	1,325	2,580	16,555	Aucun certificat, diplôme ou grade	183
1,670	4,575	1,660	2,770	5,685	44,905	Certificat, diplôme ou grade	184
690	2,045	665	1,200	2,365	17,925	Diplôme d'études secondaires ou l'équivalent[38]	185
275	620	235	430	930	6,925	Certificat ou diplôme d'apprenti ou d'une école de métiers	186
530	1,370	505	875	1,650	13,025	Certificat ou diplôme d'un collège, d'un cégep ou d'un autre établissement d'enseignement non universitaire[39]	187
70	105	85	60	155	1,600	Certificat ou diplôme universitaire inférieur au baccalauréat[40]	188
100	430	170	200	590	5,430	Certificat ou grade universitaire[41]	189
70	300	85	145	375	3,420	Baccalauréat	190
25	50	55	25	95	1,080	Certificat ou diplôme universitaire supérieur au baccalauréat	191
0	15	10	15	0	140	Diplôme en médecine, en art dentaire, en médecine vétérinaire ou en optométrie	192
10	55	25	20	95	680	Maîtrise	193
0	10	0	0	15	95	Doctorat acquis	194
980	**2,530**	**1,000**	**1,570**	**3,320**	**26,980**	**Population totale de 15 ans et plus avec titres du niveau postsecondaire**	195
						Principal domaine d'études - Classification des programmes d'enseignement, 2000[42]	
80	210	85	70	255	2,300	Éducation	196
10	45	50	85	65	840	Arts visuels et d'interprétation, et technologie des communications	197
30	80	40	70	120	900	Sciences humaines	198
30	205	110	100	290	2,395	Sciences sociales et de comportements, et droit	199
130	395	170	260	605	4,455	Commerce, gestion et administration publique	200
20	35	15	30	40	530	Sciences physiques et de la vie, et technologies	201
20	50	10	35	65	735	Mathématiques, informatique et sciences de l'information	202
250	670	215	310	740	7,240	Architecture, génie et services connexes	203
100	225	105	80	310	915	Agriculture, ressources naturelles et conservation	204
200	485	130	395	530	4,550	Santé, parcs, récréation et conditionnement physique	205
100	120	65	130	290	2,105	Services personnels, de protection et de transport	206
0	0	0	0	0	0	Autres domaines d'études[43]	207
						Lieu des études[44]	
945	2,340	960	1,460	3,045	24,930	À l'intérieur du Canada	208
30	190	40	105	270	2,045	À l'extérieur du Canada	209
2,825	**7,140**	**2,655**	**4,095**	**8,260**	**61,460**	**Population totale de 15 ans et plus**	210
						Travail non rémunéré	
1,405	3,550	1,365	1,995	4,045	30,095	Hommes de 15 ans et plus	211
1,330	3,305	1,280	1,835	3,740	27,345	Travail non rémunéré déclaré[45]	212
100	335	165	170	345	2,140	Travaux ménagers et soins aux enfants et soins ou aide aux personnes âgées	213
475	1,000	355	500	950	6,785	Travaux ménagers et soins aux enfants seulement	214

Nota : Voir les symboles et les abréviations dans les documents d'introduction et voir les documents de référence à la fin de la publication.

Selected characteristics for census divisions and census subdivisions – 100% data and 20% sample data, Ontario, 2006 Census (continued)

No.	Characteristics	Wollaston, TP ◆◆◊	**Huron CD/DR**	Ashfield-Colborne-Wawanosh, TP ◆	Bluewater, MU ◆◊	Central Huron, MU	Goderich, T
	Population characteristics						
	Unpaid work (continued)						
215	Housework and care or assistance to seniors only	25	2,170	215	260	325	255
216	Child care and care or assistance to seniors only	0	20	0	0	0	0
217	Housework only	220	11,115	1,080	1,405	1,530	1,315
218	Child care only	0	180	40	25	15	10
219	Care or assistance to seniors only	0	140	10	15	20	0
220	Females 15 years and over	285	24,190	2,105	2,865	3,230	3,370
221	Reported unpaid work[45]	275	22,875	2,015	2,725	3,040	3,140
222	Housework and child care and care or assistance to seniors	25	3,065	295	450	375	305
223	Housework and child care only	70	6,680	610	675	805	945
224	Housework and care or assistance to seniors only	60	2,680	250	305	395	330
225	Child care and care or assistance to seniors only	0	20	0	0	0	0
226	Housework only	120	10,270	850	1,265	1,445	1,545
227	Child care only	0	70	0	0	15	10
228	Care or assistance to seniors only	0	80	0	20	0	0
	Labour force activity						
229	Males 15 years and over	330	23,385	2,185	2,840	3,105	2,895
230	In the labour force	175	17,380	1,635	2,095	2,300	1,945
231	Employed	170	16,730	1,550	2,050	2,245	1,795
232	Unemployed	10	645	80	45	60	150
233	Not in the labour force	155	6,010	550	745	800	950
234	Participation rate	53.0	74.3	74.8	73.8	74.1	67.2
235	Employment rate	51.5	71.5	70.9	72.2	72.3	62.0
236	Unemployment rate	5.7	3.7	4.9	2.1	2.6	7.7
237	Females 15 years and over	285	24,190	2,105	2,865	3,225	3,370
238	In the labour force	130	14,725	1,225	1,795	1,935	1,840
239	Employed	110	13,955	1,170	1,735	1,840	1,755
240	Unemployed	20	770	55	60	95	90
241	Not in the labour force	155	9,465	885	1,070	1,295	1,530
242	Participation rate	45.6	60.9	58.2	62.7	60.0	54.6
243	Employment rate	38.6	57.7	55.6	60.6	57.1	52.1
244	Unemployment rate	15.4	5.2	4.5	3.3	4.9	4.9
245	Both sexes - Participation rate	50.4	67.5	66.7	68.2	66.9	60.4
246	15 to 24 years	60.0	77.6	76.0	81.4	82.2	77.5
247	25 years and over	49.6	65.5	64.7	66.1	63.9	57.4
248	Both sexes - Employment rate	45.2	64.5	63.5	66.3	64.5	56.6
249	15 to 24 years	60.0	69.7	72.7	77.0	74.6	61.0
250	25 years and over	44.2	63.5	61.6	64.6	62.5	55.7
251	Both sexes - Unemployment rate	8.1	4.4	4.9	2.8	3.5	6.3
252	15 to 24 years	0.0	10.2	5.3	5.3	9.0	21.4
253	25 years and over	8.9	3.1	4.8	2.3	2.2	2.8
254	**Total labour force 15 years and over**	**310**	**32,105**	**2,860**	**3,890**	**4,235**	**3,785**
	Industry - North American Industry Classification System 2002						
255	Industry - Not applicable[46]	10	330	25	30	25	80
256	All industries[47]	300	31,775	2,835	3,860	4,215	3,705
257	11 Agriculture, forestry, fishing and hunting	45	4,570	625	470	675	40
258	21 Mining and oil and gas extraction	0	505	155	10	80	185
259	22 Utilities	0	255	40	20	60	20
260	23 Construction	45	2,420	260	335	330	175
261	31-33 Manufacturing	20	4,935	255	555	470	380
262	41 Wholesale trade	0	1,515	100	235	210	160
263	44-45 Retail trade	0	3,325	285	400	400	560
264	48-49 Transportation and warehousing	20	1,350	100	175	140	150
265	51 Information and cultural industries	0	340	10	35	70	65
266	52 Finance and insurance	0	775	45	105	120	50
267	53 Real estate and rental and leasing	0	325	30	50	35	50
268	54 Professional, scientific and technical services	10	915	80	145	150	165
269	55 Management of companies and enterprises	0	15	0	10	0	0
270	56 Administrative and support, waste management and remediation services	40	855	90	95	65	85
271	61 Educational services	20	1,610	130	170	260	245
272	62 Health care and social assistance	25	3,185	225	425	425	475

Note: See symbols and abbreviations in the introductory material and see reference material at the end of the publication.

Certaines caractéristiques des divisions de recensement et des subdivisions de recensement – Données intégrales et données-échantillon (20 %), Ontario, Recensement de 2006 (suite)

Howick, TP ◆◇	Huron East, MU	Morris-Turnberry, MU ◇◇	North Huron, TP	South Huron, MU	Kawartha Lakes CD/DR ◆◇	Caractéristiques	N°
						Caractéristiques de la population	
						Travail non rémunéré (suite)	
135	250	105	185	430	2,525	Travaux ménagers et soins ou aide aux personnes âgées seulement	215
0	10	0	0	0	20	Soins aux enfants et soins ou aide aux personnes âgées seulement	216
615	1,655	640	940	1,935	15,610	Travaux ménagers seulement	217
0	25	10	15	40	150	Soins aux enfants seulement	218
0	25	0	25	30	110	Soins ou aide aux personnes âgées seulement	219
1,420	3,590	1,290	2,100	4,215	31,360	Femmes de 15 ans et plus	220
1,360	3,395	1,210	1,960	4,020	29,625	Travail non rémunéré déclaré[45]	221
195	525	195	265	460	3,455	Travaux ménagers et soins aux enfants et soins ou aide aux personnes âgées	222
520	1,120	335	610	1,065	7,750	Travaux ménagers et soins aux enfants seulement	223
160	390	150	215	470	3,120	Travaux ménagers et soins ou aide aux personnes âgées seulement	224
0	15	0	0	0	25	Soins aux enfants et soins ou aide aux personnes âgées seulement	225
465	1,315	530	855	1,990	15,095	Travaux ménagers seulement	226
10	10	0	10	20	85	Soins aux enfants seulement	227
10	25	0	10	10	100	Soins ou aide aux personnes âgées seulement	228
						Activité	
1,405	3,555	1,365	1,995	4,045	30,095	Hommes de 15 ans et plus	229
1,145	2,780	1,125	1,450	2,900	20,015	Population active	230
1,135	2,705	1,075	1,405	2,765	18,745	Personnes occupées	231
10	75	45	40	135	1,270	Chômeurs	232
265	770	245	540	1,145	10,080	Inactifs	233
81.5	78.2	82.4	72.7	71.7	66.5	Taux d'activité	234
80.8	76.1	78.8	70.4	68.4	62.3	Taux d'emploi	235
0.9	2.7	4.0	2.8	4.7	6.3	Taux de chômage	236
1,415	3,590	1,290	2,105	4,215	31,365	Femmes de 15 ans et plus	237
905	2,440	795	1,430	2,365	17,760	Population active	238
840	2,350	780	1,300	2,195	16,675	Personnes occupées	239
60	90	15	130	175	1,090	Chômeuses	240
510	1,150	495	675	1,850	13,600	Inactives	241
64.0	68.0	61.6	67.9	56.1	56.6	Taux d'activité	242
59.4	65.5	60.5	61.8	52.1	53.2	Taux d'emploi	243
6.6	3.7	1.9	9.1	7.4	6.1	Taux de chômage	244
72.6	73.1	72.1	70.3	63.7	61.5	Les deux sexes - Taux d'activité	245
69.2	77.3	75.8	78.4	77.2	69.4	15 à 24 ans	246
73.5	72.2	71.3	68.5	61.4	60.1	25 ans et plus	247
70.1	70.7	69.7	66.2	60.0	57.6	Les deux sexes - Taux d'emploi	248
65.8	73.3	69.8	67.9	64.9	58.6	15 à 24 ans	249
71.1	70.2	69.7	65.6	59.1	57.5	25 ans et plus	250
3.4	3.2	3.1	5.9	5.8	6.2	Les deux sexes - Taux de chômage	251
4.9	5.1	6.9	13.8	15.5	15.6	15 à 24 ans	252
2.7	2.6	2.6	4.3	3.6	4.4	25 ans et plus	253
2,045	**5,220**	**1,915**	**2,880**	**5,265**	**37,780**	**Population active totale de 15 ans et plus**	254
						Industrie - Système de classification des industries de l'Amérique du Nord de 2002	
10	30	10	40	85	530	Industrie - Sans objet[46]	255
2,045	5,185	1,910	2,840	5,180	37,250	Toutes les industries[47]	256
435	995	455	245	620	1,430	11 Agriculture, foresterie, pêche et chasse	257
0	25	0	15	25	205	21 Extraction minière et extraction de pétrole et de gaz	258
0	25	30	20	40	495	22 Services publics	259
135	360	125	195	500	3,515	23 Construction	260
375	1,050	395	660	795	4,840	31-33 Fabrication	261
135	235	90	80	270	1,375	41 Commerce de gros	262
160	465	165	345	545	4,865	44-45 Commerce de détail	263
130	220	70	110	245	1,475	48-49 Transport et entreposage	264
25	20	0	25	85	460	51 Industrie de l'information et industrie culturelle	265
45	140	30	80	155	925	52 Finance et assurances	266
20	30	20	20	55	585	53 Services immobiliers et services de location et de location à bail	267
35	135	20	60	115	1,595	54 Services professionnels, scientifiques et techniques	268
0	10	0	0	0	10	55 Gestion de sociétés et d'entreprises	269
60	110	45	95	215	1,835	56 Services administratifs, services de soutien, services de gestion des déchets et services d'assainissement	270
60	255	120	125	245	2,270	61 Services d'enseignement	271
205	515	140	320	440	4,185	62 Soins de santé et assistance sociale	272

Nota : Voir les symboles et les abréviations dans les documents d'introduction et voir les documents de référence à la fin de la publication.

Selected characteristics for census divisions and census subdivisions – 100% data and 20% sample data, Ontario, 2006 Census (continued)

No.	Characteristics	Wollaston, TP ◆◆◇	**Huron CD/DR**	Ashfield-Colborne-Wawanosh, TP ◆	Bluewater, MU ◆◇	Central Huron, MU	Goderich, T
	Population characteristics						
	Industry - North American Industry Classification System 2002 (continued)						
273	71 Arts, entertainment and recreation	0	490	40	95	115	50
274	72 Accommodation and food services	20	2,070	130	290	315	405
275	81 Other services (except public administration)	25	1,485	135	130	180	225
276	91 Public administration	15	840	85	125	110	190
	Class of worker						
277	Class of worker - Not applicable[46]	0	330	25	30	25	80
278	All classes of worker[47]	300	31,775	2,835	3,865	4,210	3,705
279	Paid workers	240	27,435	2,255	3,415	3,655	3,350
280	Employees	235	25,810	2,070	3,185	3,415	3,265
281	Self-employed (incorporated)	0	1,620	190	230	235	90
282	Self-employed (unincorporated)	60	4,105	535	420	530	350
283	Unpaid family workers	0	240	35	30	25	10
	Occupation - National Occupational Classification for Statistics 2006						
284	Male labour force 15 years and over	180	17,380	1,635	2,100	2,300	1,945
285	Occupation - Not applicable[46]	0	160	10	20	10	60
286	All occupations[47]	180	17,220	1,630	2,075	2,300	1,885
287	A Management occupations	20	1,415	135	270	185	245
288	B Business, finance and administrative occupations	0	890	80	140	140	60
289	C Natural and applied sciences and related occupations	10	670	50	90	85	90
290	D Health occupations	0	170	0	0	50	55
291	E Occupations in social science, education, government service and religion	0	460	40	70	80	85
292	F Occupations in art, culture, recreation and sport	0	165	20	25	20	30
293	G Sales and service occupations	10	2,320	180	270	285	400
294	H Trades, transport and equipment operators and related occupations	75	5,620	480	630	765	600
295	I Occupations unique to primary industry	55	3,650	490	375	505	170
296	J Occupations unique to processing, manufacturing and utilities	10	1,850	140	205	190	145
297	Female labour force 15 years and over	130	14,725	1,225	1,795	1,935	1,840
298	Occupation - Not applicable[46]	0	170	20	10	20	20
299	All occupations[47]	120	14,555	1,205	1,785	1,915	1,820
300	A Management occupations	0	850	45	150	150	90
301	B Business, finance and administrative occupations	30	2,950	230	410	395	365
302	C Natural and applied sciences and related occupations	0	300	45	50	15	25
303	D Health occupations	25	1,570	100	220	195	165
304	E Occupations in social science, education, government service and religion	20	1,245	110	110	195	245
305	F Occupations in art, culture, recreation and sport	0	325	40	45	45	40
306	G Sales and service occupations	35	4,755	365	590	580	840
307	H Trades, transport and equipment operators and related occupations	0	430	35	55	40	30
308	I Occupations unique to primary industry	0	1,160	190	90	200	0
309	J Occupations unique to processing, manufacturing and utilities	0	970	30	75	90	10
310	**Total employed labour force 15 years and over**	**280**	**30,685**	**2,725**	**3,785**	**4,080**	**3,545**
	Place of work status						
311	Males	165	16,730	1,550	2,050	2,240	1,795
312	Usual place of work	95	11,405	945	1,360	1,515	1,505
313	At home	25	2,945	425	365	415	55
314	Outside Canada	0	45	0	0	0	10
315	No fixed workplace address	50	2,335	180	320	305	230
316	Females	110	13,955	1,170	1,730	1,840	1,750
317	Usual place of work	95	11,290	785	1,520	1,460	1,570
318	At home	0	1,855	280	130	305	115
319	Outside Canada	0	25	0	0	10	0
320	No fixed workplace address	10	790	100	80	65	65

Note: See symbols and abbreviations in the introductory material and see reference material at the end of the publication.

Certaines caractéristiques des divisions de recensement et des subdivisions de recensement – Données intégrales et données-échantillon (20 %), Ontario, Recensement de 2006 (suite)

Howick, TP ◆◊	Huron East, MU	Morris-Turnberry, MU ◊◊	North Huron, TP	South Huron, MU	**Kawartha Lakes CD/DR ◆◊**	**Caractéristiques**	N°
						Caractéristiques de la population	
						Industrie - Système de classification des industries de l'Amérique du Nord de 2002 (suite)	
0	75	0	45	60	1,050	71 Arts, spectacles et loisirs	273
90	265	45	185	345	2,045	72 Hébergement et services de restauration	274
95	205	70	140	295	2,085	81 Autres services (sauf les administrations publiques)	275
35	50	70	55	105	2,005	91 Administrations publiques	276
						Catégorie de travailleurs	
0	35	10	35	85	530	Catégorie de travailleurs - Sans objet[46]	277
2,040	5,185	1,910	2,845	5,180	37,245	Toutes les catégories de travailleurs[47]	278
1,605	4,455	1,520	2,560	4,600	32,615	Travailleurs rémunérés	279
1,545	4,095	1,430	2,465	4,335	31,275	Employés	280
60	360	90	90	265	1,340	Travailleurs autonomes (entreprise constituée en société)	281
380	695	360	265	565	4,460	Travailleurs autonomes (entreprise non constituée en société)	282
55	35	25	15	10	175	Travailleurs familiaux non rémunérés	283
						Profession - Classification nationale des professions pour statistiques de 2006	
1,140	2,780	1,125	1,450	2,900	20,015	Hommes actifs de 15 ans et plus	284
0	10	0	20	45	285	Profession - Sans objet[46]	285
1,140	2,770	1,120	1,430	2,855	19,730	Toutes les professions[47]	286
50	150	30	145	200	2,160	A Gestion	287
45	85	50	95	195	1,110	B Affaires, finance et administration	288
55	85	55	80	75	960	C Sciences naturelles et appliquées et professions apparentées	289
0	10	10	15	20	240	D Secteur de la santé	290
20	65	20	20	50	800	E Sciences sociales, enseignement, administration publique et religion	291
10	20	10	25	15	235	F Arts, culture, sports et loisirs	292
90	350	105	220	425	3,640	G Ventes et services	293
415	905	365	400	1,050	7,070	H Métiers, transport et machinerie	294
325	715	305	195	570	1,510	I Professions propres au secteur primaire	295
120	380	180	230	260	2,010	J Transformation, fabrication et services d'utilité publique	296
905	2,435	795	1,430	2,365	17,765	Femmes actives de 15 ans et plus	297
10	25	10	15	45	245	Profession - Sans objet[46]	298
900	2,415	790	1,410	2,320	17,515	Toutes les professions[47]	299
55	115	35	90	110	1,110	A Gestion	300
155	515	155	240	490	3,980	B Affaires, finance et administration	301
10	45	0	20	80	165	C Sciences naturelles et appliquées et professions apparentées	302
115	265	80	195	225	2,165	D Secteur de la santé	303
45	130	70	80	260	1,745	E Sciences sociales, enseignement, administration publique et religion	304
10	65	10	30	35	480	F Arts, culture, sports et loisirs	305
255	685	215	505	720	6,090	G Ventes et services	306
45	90	35	10	80	520	H Métiers, transport et machinerie	307
120	250	120	55	130	450	I Professions propres au secteur primaire	308
95	245	55	180	180	800	J Transformation, fabrication et services d'utilité publique	309
1,975	**5,055**	**1,850**	**2,710**	**4,960**	**35,420**	**Population active occupée totale de 15 ans et plus**	310
						Catégorie de lieu de travail	
1,135	2,705	1,075	1,410	2,765	18,745	Hommes	311
690	1,765	640	1,085	1,895	13,160	Lieu habituel de travail	312
325	575	240	140	410	2,155	À domicile	313
10	0	0	0	10	80	En dehors du Canada	314
110	360	195	180	455	3,345	Sans adresse de travail fixe	315
840	2,350	780	1,300	2,190	16,675	Femmes	316
600	1,795	555	1,150	1,850	13,895	Lieu habituel de travail	317
180	360	175	95	210	1,790	À domicile	318
0	0	0	0	10	35	En dehors du Canada	319
55	190	50	50	125	955	Sans adresse de travail fixe	320

Nota : Voir les symboles et les abréviations dans les documents d'introduction et voir les documents de référence à la fin de la publication.

Selected characteristics for census divisions and census subdivisions – 100% data and 20% sample data, Ontario, 2006 Census (continued)

No.	Characteristics	Wollaston, TP ◆◆◊	**Huron CD/DR**	Ashfield-Colborne-Wawanosh, TP ◆	Bluewater, MU ◆◊	Central Huron, MU	Goderich, T
	Population characteristics						
321	**Total employed labour force 15 years and over with usual place of work or no fixed workplace address**	**250**	**25,815**	**2,010**	**3,280**	**3,345**	**3,370**
	Mode of transportation						
322	Males	145	13,740	1,125	1,680	1,820	1,735
323	Car, truck, van, as driver	130	11,300	955	1,365	1,605	1,315
324	Car, truck, van, as passenger	0	855	55	115	85	55
325	Public transit	0	30	10	0	0	0
326	Walked	0	1,085	65	165	105	245
327	All other modes	10	470	45	35	25	110
328	Females	110	12,080	885	1,600	1,520	1,635
329	Car, truck, van, as driver	75	9,435	730	1,250	1,230	1,235
330	Car, truck, van, as passenger	10	960	115	135	100	120
331	Public transit	0	40	0	10	0	0
332	Walked	10	1,450	40	175	170	255
333	All other modes	15	195	10	30	15	30
334	**Total population 15 years and over who worked since January 1, 2005**	**330**	**34,485**	**3,020**	**4,165**	**4,545**	**4,150**
	Language used most often at work						
335	Single responses	330	34,375	2,980	4,165	4,540	4,145
336	English	330	33,895	2,835	4,150	4,525	4,145
337	French	0	0	0	0	0	0
338	Non-official languages[7]	0	475	150	15	20	0
339	Chinese, n.o.s.[61]	0	0	0	0	0	0
340	Cantonese	0	10	0	0	0	0
341	Other languages[8]	0	470	145	15	20	0
342	Multiple responses	0	110	40	0	0	0
343	English and French	0	20	0	0	10	0
344	English and non-official language	0	90	40	0	0	0
345	French and non-official language	0	0	0	0	0	0
346	English, French and non-official language	0	0	0	0	0	0
	Dwelling and household characteristics						
347	**Total number of occupied private dwellings**	**320**	**22,900**	**1,960**	**2,765**	**2,960**	**3,255**
	Housing tenure						
348	Owned	290	17,975	1,665	2,305	2,455	2,295
349	Rented	35	4,925	290	460	505	960
350	Band housing	0	0	0	0	0	0
	Structural type of dwelling						
351	Single-detached house	300	19,280	1,820	2,500	2,595	2,295
352	Semi-detached house	5	595	50	15	65	150
353	Row house	0	415	0	5	20	115
354	Apartment, duplex	0	190	0	10	25	80
355	Apartment, building that has five or more storeys	0	10	0	0	0	0
356	Apartment, building that has fewer than five storeys	15	2,045	15	230	240	600
357	Other single-attached house	5	130	0	5	5	30
358	Movable dwelling[48]	0	250	60	5	10	0
	Condition of dwelling						
359	Regular maintenance only	125	14,445	1,170	1,895	1,815	2,225
360	Minor repairs	160	6,670	625	675	925	785
361	Major repairs	35	1,790	160	195	225	245
	Period of construction						
362	Before 1946	65	9,225	745	985	1,215	1,190
363	1946 to 1960	70	2,665	70	300	420	540
364	1961 to 1970	15	2,265	170	265	225	440
365	1971 to 1980	85	3,450	435	475	455	465
366	1981 to 1985	25	985	120	100	120	160
367	1986 to 1990	30	1,295	120	180	140	105
368	1991 to 1995	10	1,145	105	155	100	135
369	1996 to 2000	0	820	85	125	140	75
370	2001 to 2006[49]	25	1,045	105	170	150	150

Note: See symbols and abbreviations in the introductory material and see reference material at the end of the publication.

Certaines caractéristiques des divisions de recensement et des subdivisions de recensement – Données intégrales et données-échantillon (20 %), Ontario, Recensement de 2006 (suite)

Howick, TP ♦◊	Huron East, MU	Morris-Turnberry, MU ◊◊	North Huron, TP	South Huron, MU	**Kawartha Lakes CD/DR ♦◊**	**Caractéristiques**	N°
						Caractéristiques de la population	
1,465	**4,120**	**1,440**	**2,470**	**4,320**	**31,355**	**Population active occupée totale de 15 ans et plus ayant un lieu habituel de travail ou sans adresse de travail fixe**	321
						Mode de transport	
800	2,130	835	1,270	2,345	16,510	Hommes	322
715	1,755	730	910	1,955	13,895	Automobile, camion ou fourgonnette, en tant que conducteur	323
45	160	50	150	145	1,580	Automobile, camion ou fourgonnette, en tant que passager	324
0	0	10	0	0	80	Transport en commun	325
15	125	35	140	185	615	À pied	326
25	85	15	70	55	340	Tous les autres modes	327
660	1,985	605	1,205	1,975	14,850	Femmes	328
555	1,545	525	835	1,530	12,105	Automobile, camion ou fourgonnette, en tant que conductrice	329
45	210	35	55	155	1,300	Automobile, camion ou fourgonnette, en tant que passagère	330
0	0	0	10	10	145	Transport en commun	331
40	205	30	275	255	1,055	À pied	332
20	30	10	25	25	245	Tous les autres modes	333
2,205	**5,620**	**2,010**	**3,055**	**5,715**	**40,625**	**Population totale de 15 ans et plus ayant travaillé depuis le 1er janvier 2005**	334
						Langue utilisée le plus souvent au travail	
2,190	5,600	1,975	3,055	5,710	40,570	Réponses uniques	335
2,055	5,575	1,885	3,040	5,675	40,460	Anglais	336
0	0	0	0	0	45	Français	337
130	25	95	0	30	65	Langues non officielles[7]	338
0	0	0	0	0	0	Chinois, n.d.a.[61]	339
0	0	0	0	0	0	Cantonais	340
130	20	95	0	35	65	Autres langues[8]	341
15	15	25	0	0	55	Réponses multiples	342
0	10	0	0	0	10	Anglais et français	343
10	10	30	0	0	35	Anglais et langue non officielle	344
0	0	0	0	0	0	Français et langue non officielle	345
0	0	0	0	0	0	Anglais, français et langue non officielle	346
						Caractéristiques des logements et des ménages	
1,245	**3,430**	**1,150**	**2,065**	**4,065**	**29,500**	**Nombre total de logements privés occupés**	347
						Mode d'occupation	
1,050	2,710	995	1,550	2,935	24,515	Possédé	348
190	720	150	515	1,130	4,985	Loué	349
0	0	0	0	0	0	Logement de bande	350
						Type de construction résidentielle	
1,135	3,010	1,040	1,595	3,295	24,725	Maison individuelle non attenante	351
15	60	10	75	150	535	Maison jumelée	352
45	30	0	45	150	445	Maison en rangée	353
5	10	10	25	25	655	Appartement, duplex	354
0	0	0	0	5	630	Appartement, immeuble de cinq étages ou plus	355
20	280	30	275	360	2,245	Appartement, immeuble de moins de cinq étages	356
0	10	5	45	30	135	Autre maison individuelle attenante	357
25	35	60	10	40	140	Logement mobile[48]	358
						État du logement	
720	1,980	655	1,315	2,660	18,715	Entretien régulier seulement	359
420	1,130	405	525	1,180	8,615	Réparations mineures	360
105	320	85	220	225	2,175	Réparations majeures	361
						Période de construction	
670	1,560	475	890	1,485	6,300	Avant 1946	362
50	420	70	270	525	3,295	1946 à 1960	363
85	270	125	265	410	3,550	1961 à 1970	364
160	495	160	200	615	5,525	1971 à 1980	365
25	115	45	90	210	2,145	1981 à 1985	366
80	155	90	100	330	3,360	1986 à 1990	367
80	190	100	95	175	2,035	1991 à 1995	368
45	75	40	85	160	1,500	1996 à 2000	369
50	145	55	75	150	1,785	2001 à 2006[49]	370

Nota : Voir les symboles et les abréviations dans les documents d'introduction et voir les documents de référence à la fin de la publication.

Selected characteristics for census divisions and census subdivisions – 100% data and 20% sample data, Ontario, 2006 Census (continued)

No.	Characteristics	Wollaston, TP ◆◆◇	**Huron CD/DR**	Ashfield-Colborne-Wawanosh, TP ◆	Bluewater, MU ◆◇	Central Huron, MU	Goderich, T
	Dwelling and household characteristics						
371	Average number of rooms per dwelling	7.0	7.3	7.5	7.4	7.5	6.8
372	Average number of bedrooms per dwelling	2.7	2.9	3.1	3.0	3.0	2.7
373	Average value of dwelling $	120,946	200,790	209,043	241,917	209,033	184,746
374	**Total number of private households**	**325**	**22,915**	**1,955**	**2,765**	**2,965**	**3,270**
	Household size						
375	1 person	80	5,745	370	670	705	1,050
376	2 persons	155	8,755	825	1,150	1,180	1,210
377	3 persons	40	2,985	230	315	430	405
378	4 to 5 persons	40	4,560	410	550	540	560
379	6 or more persons	5	865	120	85	110	40
	Household type						
380	One-family households[50]	220	16,685	1,560	2,065	2,215	2,125
381	Multiple-family households	0	125	10	0	10	30
382	Non-family households	105	6,090	390	690	740	1,095
383	Number of persons in private households	730	57,885	5,400	6,865	7,405	7,340
384	Average number of persons in private households	2.2	2.5	2.8	2.5	2.5	2.2
385	Tenant-occupied private non-farm, non-reserve dwellings[51]	35	4,860	280	455	505	960
386	Average gross rent $[51]	549	622	533	607	652	634
387	Tenant-occupied households spending 30% or more of household income on gross rent[52]	20	1,685	55	130	230	355
388	Tenant-occupied households spending from 30% to 99% of household income on gross rent[52]	15	1,545	55	95	205	325
389	Owner-occupied private non-farm, non-reserve dwellings[53]	290	16,590	1,450	2,165	2,265	2,295
390	Average owner's major payments $[53]	547	828	721	843	826	887
391	Owner households spending 30% or more of household income on owner's major payments[52]	55	2,480	205	350	345	330
392	Owner households spending from 30% to 99% of household income on owner's major payments[52]	55	2,240	185	330	300	325
	Census family characteristics						
393	**Total number of census families in private households**	**220**	**16,945**	**1,580**	**2,080**	**2,235**	**2,190**
	Family structure and number of children						
394	Total couple families	205	15,230	1,490	1,905	2,015	1,885
395	Total families of married couples	165	13,480	1,340	1,705	1,780	1,645
396	Without children at home	115	6,670	680	905	920	835
397	With children at home	50	6,810	660	800	855	815
398	1 child	25	2,075	160	225	295	300
399	2 children	15	2,665	275	320	275	370
400	3 or more children	0	2,070	225	250	285	140
401	Total families of common-law couples	45	1,750	145	205	235	240
402	Without children at home	10	1,085	110	140	150	175
403	With children at home	30	670	35	60	85	65
404	1 child	0	320	20	20	35	30
405	2 children	10	255	20	30	40	25
406	3 or more children	15	95	0	15	0	10
407	Total lone-parent families	10	1,715	90	170	220	310
408	Female parent	10	1,280	85	120	150	240
409	1 child	10	780	40	70	85	180
410	2 children	10	375	35	45	40	45
411	3 or more children	0	125	15	0	20	20
412	Male parent	0	435	0	55	70	65
413	1 child	0	255	0	30	40	40
414	2 children	0	145	0	25	20	15
415	3 or more children	0	35	0	0	15	10

Note: See symbols and abbreviations in the introductory material and see reference material at the end of the publication.

Certaines caractéristiques des divisions de recensement et des subdivisions de recensement – Données intégrales et données-échantillon (20 %), Ontario, Recensement de 2006 (suite)

Howick, TP ◆◇	Huron East, MU	Morris-Turnberry, MU ◇◇	North Huron, TP	South Huron, MU	**Kawartha Lakes CD/DR ◆◇**	**Caractéristiques**	N°
						Caractéristiques des logements et des ménages	
8.0	7.3	7.5	7.3	7.0	7.0	Nombre moyen de pièces par logement	371
3.4	3.0	3.2	2.9	2.8	2.9	Nombre moyen de chambres à coucher par logement	372
215,096	176,322	196,153	170,607	205,102	245,161	Valeur moyenne du logement $	373
1,245	**3,430**	**1,155**	**2,065**	**4,060**	**29,510**	**Nombre total de ménages privés**	374
						Taille du ménage	
210	845	220	605	1,075	6,770	1 personne	375
425	1,190	440	710	1,625	11,935	2 personnes	376
195	450	160	280	515	4,195	3 personnes	377
295	800	260	410	740	5,915	4 à 5 personnes	378
120	155	75	55	100	690	6 personnes ou plus	379
						Genre de ménage	
1,010	2,525	900	1,415	2,875	21,715	Ménages unifamiliaux[50]	380
20	15	10	10	25	405	Ménages multifamiliaux	381
215	890	235	650	1,170	7,380	Ménages non familiaux	382
3,850	9,060	3,250	5,000	9,715	73,150	Nombre de personnes dans les ménages privés	383
3.1	2.6	2.8	2.4	2.4	2.5	Nombre moyen de personnes dans les ménages privés	384
190	705	140	515	1,110	4,965	Ménages locataires dans les logements privés non agricoles hors réserve[51]	385
620	572	673	620	654	749	Loyer brut moyen $[51]	386
40	225	45	225	360	2,585	Ménages locataires consacrant 30 % ou plus du revenu du ménage au loyer brut[52]	387
40	225	45	215	335	2,290	Ménages locataires consacrant de 30 % à 99 % du revenu du ménage au loyer brut[52]	388
900	2,430	835	1,475	2,775	23,930	Ménages propriétaires dans les logements privés non agricoles hors réserve[53]	389
806	808	779	872	842	935	Principales dépenses de propriété moyennes $[53]	390
130	345	120	240	415	4,790	Ménages propriétaires consacrant 30 % ou plus du revenu du ménage aux principales dépenses de propriété[52]	391
120	300	105	210	365	4,120	Ménages propriétaires consacrant de 30 % à 99 % du revenu du ménage aux principales dépenses de propriété[52]	392
						Caractéristiques des familles de recensement	
1,050	**2,550**	**920**	**1,425**	**2,920**	**22,530**	**Nombre total de familles de recensement dans les ménages privés**	393
						Structure de la famille et le nombre d'enfants	
960	2,295	820	1,280	2,575	19,875	Total des familles avec conjoints	394
870	2,020	730	1,110	2,270	16,915	Total des familles avec couples mariés	395
330	915	310	560	1,205	9,265	Sans enfants à la maison	396
540	1,105	420	550	1,065	7,650	Avec enfants à la maison	397
165	295	110	175	345	2,690	1 enfant	398
170	400	175	225	455	3,245	2 enfants	399
210	405	135	150	265	1,720	3 enfants ou plus	400
85	275	90	170	305	2,955	Total des familles avec couples en union libre	401
55	125	60	65	200	1,735	Sans enfants à la maison	402
30	150	30	105	105	1,225	Avec enfants à la maison	403
10	75	10	50	70	545	1 enfant	404
15	55	10	50	25	485	2 enfants	405
10	25	10	0	15	200	3 enfants ou plus	406
95	255	95	140	340	2,660	Total des familles monoparentales	407
55	195	60	120	255	2,085	Parent de sexe féminin	408
35	110	40	50	170	1,170	1 enfant	409
20	70	10	40	70	650	2 enfants	410
0	20	0	30	10	270	3 enfants ou plus	411
35	60	35	20	90	570	Parent de sexe masculin	412
15	35	30	15	50	365	1 enfant	413
20	20	10	10	25	135	2 enfants	414
0	0	0	0	15	70	3 enfants ou plus	415

Nota : Voir les symboles et les abréviations dans les documents d'introduction et voir les documents de référence à la fin de la publication.

Selected characteristics for census divisions and census subdivisions – 100% data and 20% sample data, Ontario, 2006 Census (continued)

No.	Characteristics	Wollaston, TP ◆◆◊	Huron CD/DR	Ashfield-Colborne-Wawanosh, TP ◆	Bluewater, MU ◆◊	Central Huron, MU	Goderich, T
	Census family characteristics						
416	**Total number of children at home**	**170**	**18,590**	**1,840**	**2,085**	**2,305**	**2,020**
	Age group						
417	Under 6 years	55	3,730	400	400	460	310
418	6 to 14 years	55	7,155	670	860	820	850
419	15 to 17 years	20	2,690	255	245	385	305
420	18 to 24 years	25	3,800	405	465	455	450
421	25 years and over	10	1,215	110	125	175	110
422	Average number of children at home per census family[54]	0.8	1.1	1.2	1.0	1.0	0.9
423	**Total number of persons in private households**	**730**	**57,875**	**5,400**	**6,865**	**7,410**	**7,330**
	Census family status and living arrangements						
424	Number of persons not in census families	135	7,105	490	795	860	1,230
425	Living with relatives[55]	15	515	90	55	80	25
426	Living with non-relatives only	35	880	30	80	75	185
427	Living alone	80	5,710	365	660	700	1,020
428	Number of census family persons	595	50,770	4,905	6,070	6,555	6,095
429	Average number of persons per census family	2.7	3.0	3.1	2.9	2.9	2.8
430	**Total number of persons aged 65 years and over**	**145**	**9,595**	**890**	**1,150**	**1,250**	**1,480**
431	Number of persons not in census families aged 65 years and over	60	3,015	215	290	355	590
432	Living with relatives[55]	0	185	10	35	60	10
433	Living with non-relatives only	15	65	0	0	0	25
434	Living alone	40	2,760	200	255	295	560
435	Number of census family persons aged 65 years and over	85	6,580	675	860	890	890
	Economic family characteristics						
436	**Total number of economic families in private households**	**225**	**16,895**	**1,575**	**2,080**	**2,235**	**2,160**
	Size of family						
437	2 persons	130	8,605	815	1,140	1,175	1,165
438	3 persons	45	2,920	225	315	400	395
439	4 persons	30	2,975	275	335	355	410
440	5 or more persons	20	2,395	265	290	310	185
441	Total number of persons in economic families	610	51,285	5,000	6,130	6,630	6,125
442	Average number of persons per economic family	3.0	3.0	3.0	3.0	3.0	3.0
443	Total number of persons not in economic families	115	6,585	400	735	775	1,205
	2005 income characteristics						
444	**Population 15 years and over**	**620**	**47,580**	**4,290**	**5,705**	**6,335**	**6,265**
	Sex and total income groups in 2005						
445	Without income	25	1,540	190	70	195	225
446	With income	590	46,040	4,105	5,635	6,140	6,040
447	Under $1,000[56]	45	1,300	165	120	160	140
448	$1,000 to $2,999	25	1,385	125	135	195	205
449	$3,000 to $4,999	10	1,560	140	240	235	215
450	$5,000 to $6,999	15	1,680	190	215	150	215
451	$7,000 to $9,999	60	2,755	275	285	365	305
452	$10,000 to $11,999	10	2,150	245	190	250	315
453	$12,000 to $14,999	70	2,960	255	395	370	335
454	$15,000 to $19,999	85	5,215	455	655	745	735
455	$20,000 to $24,999	65	3,840	350	435	550	440
456	$25,000 to $29,999	25	3,660	260	425	515	490
457	$30,000 to $34,999	40	3,780	305	460	425	495
458	$35,000 to $39,999	35	3,325	240	530	410	375
459	$40,000 to $44,999	15	2,275	200	320	330	260
460	$45,000 to $49,999	30	1,935	130	255	250	185
461	$50,000 to $59,999	20	3,140	265	425	455	440
462	$60,000 and over	40	5,075	495	555	735	880
463	Median income $[57]	18,649	25,192	22,544	26,507	25,300	25,827
464	Average income $[57]	24,193	31,597	34,773	31,320	33,744	33,153
465	Standard error of average income $[57]	1,919	356	2,512	704	1,196	803

Note: See symbols and abbreviations in the introductory material and see reference material at the end of the publication.

Certaines caractéristiques des divisions de recensement et des subdivisions de recensement – Données intégrales et données-échantillon (20 %), Ontario, Recensement de 2006 (suite)

Howick, TP ◆◊	Huron East, MU	Morris-Turnberry, MU ◊◊	North Huron, TP	South Huron, MU	**Kawartha Lakes CD/DR ◆◊**	Caractéristiques	N°
						Caractéristiques des familles de recensement	
1,585	**3,170**	**1,175**	**1,565**	**2,840**	**21,250**	**Nombre total d'enfants à la maison**	416
						Groupes d'âge	
355	675	250	355	520	3,610	Moins de 6 ans	417
660	1,235	425	555	1,080	8,105	6 à 14 ans	418
240	445	190	205	430	3,115	15 à 17 ans	419
210	600	220	375	615	4,555	18 à 24 ans	420
120	210	95	70	195	1,870	25 ans et plus	421
1.5	1.2	1.3	1.1	1.0	0.9	Nombre moyen d'enfants à la maison par famille de recensement[54]	422
3,850	**9,060**	**3,245**	**5,000**	**9,715**	**73,140**	**Nombre total de personnes dans les ménages privés**	423
						Situation des particuliers dans la famille de recensement et des particuliers dans le ménage	
255	1,035	325	730	1,380	9,475	Nombre de personnes hors famille de recensement	424
45	75	45	55	50	1,095	Vivant avec des personnes apparentées[55]	425
10	120	65	65	245	1,605	Vivant avec des personnes non apparentées seulement	426
210	840	215	610	1,090	6,775	Vivant seules	427
3,595	8,020	2,920	4,270	8,335	63,660	Nombre de membres d'une famille de recensement	428
3.4	3.1	3.2	3.0	2.9	2.8	Nombre moyen de personnes par famille de recensement	429
400	**1,220**	**455**	**825**	**1,925**	**13,565**	**Nombre total de personnes âgées de 65 ans et plus**	430
100	425	105	310	620	4,110	Nombre de personnes hors famille de recensement âgées de 65 ans et plus	431
10	20	15	15	15	465	Vivant avec des personnes apparentées[55]	432
0	0	0	0	30	235	Vivant avec des personnes non apparentées seulement	433
95	400	85	295	570	3,410	Vivant seules	434
300	800	350	510	1,310	9,460	Nombre de membres d'une famille de recensement âgés de 65 ans et plus	435
						Caractéristiques des familles économiques	
1,040	**2,550**	**915**	**1,435**	**2,905**	**22,260**	**Nombre total de familles économiques dans les ménages privés**	436
						Taille de la famille	
425	1,165	430	700	1,590	11,705	2 personnes	437
205	450	140	270	525	4,145	3 personnes	438
180	475	180	270	480	4,100	4 personnes	439
230	460	155	190	310	2,310	5 personnes ou plus	440
3,635	8,100	2,960	4,325	8,385	64,755	Nombre total de personnes dans les familles économiques	441
4.0	3.0	3.0	3.0	3.0	3.0	Nombre moyen de personnes par famille économique	442
210	960	280	680	1,330	8,385	Nombre total de personnes hors famille économique	443
						Caractéristiques du revenu de 2005	
2,825	**7,145**	**2,655**	**4,095**	**8,265**	**61,460**	**Population de 15 ans et plus**	444
						Sexe et groupes de revenu total en 2005	
125	245	125	110	255	2,795	Sans revenu	445
2,695	6,900	2,530	3,985	8,005	58,670	Avec un revenu	446
85	150	75	150	260	2,090	Moins de 1 000 $[56]	447
120	170	70	130	220	1,965	1 000 $ à 2 999 $	448
100	225	85	135	190	2,060	3 000 $ à 4 999 $	449
105	305	115	125	260	2,115	5 000 $ à 6 999 $	450
180	405	225	215	510	3,515	7 000 $ à 9 999 $	451
100	310	100	235	390	2,590	10 000 $ à 11 999 $	452
240	490	200	240	435	3,810	12 000 $ à 14 999 $	453
270	735	260	475	885	6,440	15 000 $ à 19 999 $	454
235	550	205	315	760	4,750	20 000 $ à 24 999 $	455
220	605	185	335	620	4,180	25 000 $ à 29 999 $	456
200	735	185	315	665	4,170	30 000 $ à 34 999 $	457
185	550	145	195	685	3,665	35 000 $ à 39 999 $	458
145	310	90	180	445	3,195	40 000 $ à 44 999 $	459
95	355	100	190	360	2,390	45 000 $ à 49 999$	460
210	405	160	315	465	3,675	50 000 $ à 59 999$	461
205	590	315	440	850	8,055	60 000 $ et plus	462
22,664	25,812	22,562	24,723	25,709	25,005	Revenu médian $[57]	463
27,557	29,475	30,744	30,877	31,159	33,022	Revenu moyen $[57]	464
810	592	1,291	932	625	385	Erreur type de revenu moyen $[57]	465

Nota : Voir les symboles et les abréviations dans les documents d'introduction et voir les documents de référence à la fin de la publication.

Selected characteristics for census divisions and census subdivisions – 100% data and 20% sample data, Ontario, 2006 Census (continued)

No.	Characteristics	Wollaston, TP ◆◆◊	Huron CD/DR	Ashfield-Colborne-Wawanosh, TP ◆	Bluewater, MU ◆◊	Central Huron, MU	Goderich, T
	2005 income characteristics						
	Sex and total income groups in 2005 (continued)						
466	Total - Males	335	23,385	2,185	2,840	3,105	2,895
467	Without income	20	555	100	25	60	60
468	With income	315	22,830	2,080	2,815	3,045	2,830
469	Under $1,000[56]	30	615	40	45	110	40
470	$1,000 to $2,999	10	490	50	50	65	55
471	$3,000 to $4,999	10	550	35	90	105	75
472	$5,000 to $6,999	0	555	60	105	65	90
473	$7,000 to $9,999	25	970	130	70	135	90
474	$10,000 to $11,999	10	805	60	40	100	100
475	$12,000 to $14,999	20	1,130	105	135	110	85
476	$15,000 to $19,999	45	2,090	225	305	295	210
477	$20,000 to $24,999	45	1,645	170	150	215	170
478	$25,000 to $29,999	0	1,695	150	195	230	215
479	$30,000 to $34,999	20	1,790	105	215	185	245
480	$35,000 to $39,999	35	1,815	140	310	220	165
481	$40,000 to $44,999	10	1,415	135	215	155	165
482	$45,000 to $49,999	15	1,315	90	180	155	130
483	$50,000 to $59,999	15	2,250	190	310	340	320
484	$60,000 and over	20	3,690	395	390	555	665
485	Median income $[57]	20,787	32,519	30,890	34,938	32,169	35,829
486	Average income $[57]	24,484	38,038	39,044	37,672	41,111	43,121
487	Standard error of average income $[57]	2,523	492	1,776	1,162	1,994	1,386
488	Total - Females	285	24,190	2,110	2,865	3,225	3,370
489	Without income	10	985	85	40	135	160
490	With income	275	23,205	2,020	2,820	3,095	3,210
491	Under $1,000[56]	15	685	125	70	50	100
492	$1,000 to $2,999	15	890	80	85	125	150
493	$3,000 to $4,999	10	1,010	105	145	130	140
494	$5,000 to $6,999	0	1,130	125	105	85	125
495	$7,000 to $9,999	35	1,780	145	215	225	220
496	$10,000 to $11,999	0	1,350	185	145	145	215
497	$12,000 to $14,999	55	1,825	150	255	265	250
498	$15,000 to $19,999	45	3,125	230	350	450	520
499	$20,000 to $24,999	20	2,190	180	280	335	270
500	$25,000 to $29,999	20	1,960	115	230	285	270
501	$30,000 to $34,999	15	1,990	195	245	240	255
502	$35,000 to $39,999	10	1,505	100	220	195	210
503	$40,000 to $44,999	10	855	65	105	180	95
504	$45,000 to $49,999	10	620	40	75	95	60
505	$50,000 to $59,999	10	890	75	120	115	115
506	$60,000 and over	25	1,390	100	170	180	215
507	Median income $[57]	16,359	19,601	16,774	20,676	20,689	18,728
508	Average income $[57]	23,861	25,260	30,369	24,991	26,497	24,376
509	Standard error of average income $[57]	2,937	500	4,766	724	1,266	748
	Composition of total income						
510	Composition of total income in 2005 %	100.0	100.0	100.0	100.0	100.0	100.0
511	Employment income %	53.3	71.4	71.6	68.2	70.0	71.2
512	Government transfer payments %	27.1	13.6	12.8	12.7	13.2	14.0
513	Other %	19.5	15.0	15.7	19.1	16.8	14.8
514	**Population 15 years and over with employment income in 2005**	**345**	**34,505**	**2,975**	**4,295**	**4,540**	**4,285**
	Sex and work activity						
515	Median employment income in 2005 $	16,615	23,610	22,040	21,878	22,998	25,085
516	Average employment income in 2005 $	22,567	30,091	34,332	28,044	31,943	33,278
517	Standard error of average employment income $	2,581	422	2,761	875	1,610	1,057
518	Worked full year, full time[59]	140	17,990	1,610	2,310	2,410	2,055
519	Median employment income in 2005 $	24,116	36,349	34,849	35,576	35,754	44,280
520	Average employment income in 2005 $	31,836	42,510	50,235	39,434	45,998	48,841
521	Standard error of average employment income $	5,192	703	4,849	1,325	2,874	1,406
522	Worked part year or part time[60]	160	14,355	1,190	1,695	1,860	1,815
523	Median employment income in 2005 $	15,586	11,008	10,181	10,663	9,898	10,958
524	Average employment income in 2005 $	18,172	17,737	17,162	16,221	17,833	20,312
525	Standard error of average employment income $	1,720	370	1,248	868	1,023	1,479
526	Males 15 years and over with employment income[58]	210	18,570	1,665	2,285	2,470	2,250
527	Median employment income in 2005 $	15,614	30,174	27,156	30,051	29,506	35,884
528	Average employment income in 2005 $	20,990	35,630	37,031	33,052	38,902	41,277
529	Standard error of average employment income $	3,492	585	2,220	1,397	2,540	1,659

Note: See symbols and abbreviations in the introductory material and see reference material at the end of the publication.

Certaines caractéristiques des divisions de recensement et des subdivisions de recensement – Données intégrales et données-échantillon (20 %), Ontario, Recensement de 2006 (suite)

Howick, TP ◆◊	Huron East, MU	Morris-Turnberry, MU ◊◊	North Huron, TP	South Huron, MU	**Kawartha Lakes CD/DR** ◆◊	**Caractéristiques**	N°
						Caractéristiques du revenu de 2005	
						Sexe et groupes de revenu total en 2005 (suite)	
1,405	3,555	1,365	1,990	4,050	30,095	Total - Hommes	466
30	85	50	50	85	1,280	Sans revenu	467
1,370	3,470	1,315	1,945	3,965	28,815	Avec un revenu	468
25	75	35	85	145	1,010	Moins de 1 000 $[56]	469
40	85	15	50	75	770	1 000 $ à 2 999 $	470
30	65	45	35	60	785	3 000 $ à 4 999 $	471
35	110	20	10	50	730	5 000 $ à 6 999 $	472
65	115	100	85	175	1,170	7 000 $ à 9 999 $	473
40	160	45	75	170	875	10 000 $ à 11 999 $	474
100	225	85	100	185	1,310	12 000 $ à 14 999 $	475
130	265	135	185	335	2,585	15 000 $ à 19 999 $	476
115	245	100	150	325	1,950	20 000 $ à 24 999 $	477
100	265	85	135	310	1,815	25 000 $ à 29 999 $	478
110	335	100	150	350	2,180	30 000 $ à 34 999 $	479
120	320	80	75	385	2,090	35 000 $ à 39 999 $	480
95	225	60	110	260	1,845	40 000 $ à $44 999 $	481
80	230	85	105	260	1,375	45 000 $ à $49 999 $	482
145	325	110	230	290	2,580	50 000 $ à $59 999 $	483
135	415	205	350	575	5,740	60 000 $ et plus	484
29,047	32,628	29,360	31,437	31,296	33,230	Revenu médian $[57]	485
32,751	34,669	35,902	38,605	36,985	40,480	Revenu moyen $[57]	486
1,217	980	1,996	1,604	1,016	672	Erreur type de revenu moyen $[57]	487
1,415	3,590	1,290	2,105	4,215	31,360	Total - Femmes	488
95	160	70	60	175	1,510	Sans revenu	489
1,325	3,430	1,215	2,040	4,040	29,855	Avec un revenu	490
60	70	40	65	115	1,080	Moins de 1 000 $[56]	491
85	90	55	80	145	1,200	1 000$ à 2 999 $	492
70	155	45	90	125	1,280	3 000 $ à 4 999 $	493
70	195	95	110	205	1,385	5 000 $ à 6 999 $	494
105	285	125	125	335	2,345	7 000 $ à 9 999 $	495
60	150	55	160	220	1,710	10 000 $ à 11 999 $	496
135	265	120	135	255	2,505	12 000 $ à 14 999 $	497
140	465	125	290	550	3,860	15 000 $ à 19 999 $	498
120	310	105	165	430	2,800	20 000 $ à 24 999 $	499
115	345	100	195	310	2,360	25 000 $ à 29 999 $	500
95	400	85	165	310	1,985	30 000 $ à 34 999 $	501
65	235	65	115	300	1,575	35 000 $ à 39 999 $	502
45	85	30	70	185	1,350	40 000 $ à 44 999 $	503
15	125	15	90	105	1,015	45 000 $ à 49 999 $	504
65	80	50	85	175	1,095	50 000 $ à 59 999 $	505
70	175	110	90	275	2,315	60 000 $ et plus	506
17,725	20,470	17,572	18,495	20,577	19,334	Revenu médian $[57]	507
22,178	24,227	25,172	23,524	25,443	25,823	Revenu moyen $[57]	508
983	612	1,571	824	649	374	Erreur type de revenu moyen $[57]	509
						Composition du revenu total	
100.0	100.0	100.0	100.0	100.0	100.0	Composition du revenu total en 2005 %	510
76.8	72.7	76.8	73.6	69.3	67.7	Revenu d'emploi %	511
12.6	13.6	12.8	13.9	15.0	14.1	Transferts gouvernementaux %	512
10.5	13.7	10.3	12.6	15.7	18.2	Autres %	513
2,165	**5,530**	**1,975**	**2,960**	**5,770**	**40,885**	**Population de 15 ans et plus avec un revenu d'emploi en 2005**	514
						Sexe et travail	
22,747	23,417	22,463	24,016	25,142	23,761	Revenu médian d'emploi en 2005 $	515
26,336	26,732	30,257	30,556	29,938	32,079	Revenu moyen d'emploi en 2005 $	516
942	603	1,675	1,098	809	496	Erreur type de revenu moyen d'emploi $	517
1,255	2,845	1,145	1,450	2,905	20,610	A travaillé toute l'année à plein temps[59]	518
32,786	35,039	32,342	39,443	37,734	39,933	Revenu médian d'emploi en 2005 $	519
34,747	37,155	39,380	42,960	42,888	45,551	Revenu moyen d'emploi en 2005 $	520
1,275	778	2,446	1,703	1,244	549	Erreur type de revenu moyen d'emploi $	521
820	2,470	735	1,375	2,400	16,785	A travaillé une partie de l'année ou à temps partiel[60]	522
10,344	12,046	12,193	11,352	12,180	11,710	Revenu médian d'emploi en 2005 $	523
15,668	16,475	19,239	19,150	17,810	20,597	Revenu moyen d'emploi en 2005 $	524
1,055	758	1,916	1,158	881	903	Erreur type de revenu moyen d'emploi $	525
1,175	2,950	1,150	1,510	3,110	21,755	Hommes de 15 ans et plus avec un revenu d'emploi[58]	526
29,332	30,568	27,927	34,851	30,009	30,349	Revenu médian d'emploi en 2005 $	527
31,045	31,577	33,871	38,630	34,861	38,215	Revenu moyen d'emploi en 2005 $	528
1,368	906	2,400	1,842	1,242	847	Erreur type de revenu moyen d'emploi $	529

Nota : Voir les symboles et les abréviations dans les documents d'introduction et voir les documents de référence à la fin de la publication.

Selected characteristics for census divisions and census subdivisions – 100% data and 20% sample data, Ontario, 2006 Census (continued)

No.	Characteristics	Wollaston, TP ◆◆◇	**Huron CD/DR**	Ashfield-Colborne-Wawanosh, TP ◆	Bluewater, MU ◆◇	Central Huron, MU	Goderich, T
	2005 income characteristics						
	Sex and work activity (continued)						
530	Worked full year, full time[59]	85	11,485	1,050	1,470	1,485	1,275
531	Median employment income in 2005 $	23,984	40,704	38,753	38,508	42,867	52,122
532	Average employment income in 2005 $	28,257	45,966	47,089	42,555	52,986	55,796
533	Standard error of average employment income $	7,222	819	3,074	1,906	4,014	1,959
534	Worked part year or part time[60]	95	5,945	515	655	840	680
535	Median employment income in 2005 $	15,610	12,134	10,565	12,799	9,494	13,290
536	Average employment income in 2005 $	18,128	20,730	22,573	18,088	20,185	25,904
537	Standard error of average employment income $	1,934	693	2,555	1,442	1,831	3,080
538	Females 15 years and over with employment income[58]	130	15,935	1,310	2,010	2,070	2,035
539	Median employment income in 2005 $	19,339	17,617	14,551	18,229	17,719	18,429
540	Average employment income in 2005 $	25,203	23,639	30,904	22,349	23,643	24,462
541	Standard error of average employment income $	3,634	591	5,615	923	1,716	1,110
542	Worked full year, full time[59]	50	6,500	560	840	925	780
543	Median employment income in 2005 $	24,172	31,471	31,270	32,255	27,564	34,251
544	Average employment income in 2005 $	37,900	36,405	56,153	33,971	34,821	37,486
545	Standard error of average employment income $	6,408	1,286	12,917	1,363	3,620	1,537
546	Worked part year or part time[60]	60	8,405	670	1,035	1,015	1,135
547	Median employment income in 2005 $	14,737	10,643	10,078	9,300	10,785	10,066
548	Average employment income in 2005 $	18,238	15,619	12,978	15,031	15,889	16,961
549	Standard error of average employment income $	3,142	378	902	1,076	1,071	1,402
550	**Total number of economic families in private households**	**225**	**16,895**	**1,575**	**2,080**	**2,235**	**2,160**
	Family income groups in 2005						
551	Under $10,000	0	240	30	10	40	15
552	$10,000 to $19,999	30	385	25	60	50	55
553	$20,000 to $29,999	40	1,455	170	90	240	190
554	$30,000 to $39,999	30	1,935	230	230	255	200
555	$40,000 to $49,999	30	1,985	185	275	155	280
556	$50,000 to $59,999	30	1,860	155	235	205	235
557	$60,000 to $69,999	20	1,855	135	335	240	185
558	$70,000 to $79,999	15	1,645	145	190	210	190
559	$80,000 to $89,999	0	1,310	105	145	200	155
560	$90,000 to $99,999	0	990	75	120	195	130
561	$100,000 and over	30	3,240	315	390	450	515
562	Median family income $	43,178	63,001	59,796	65,001	65,534	65,252
563	Average family income $	53,128	73,855	83,167	72,819	80,202	76,081
564	Standard error of average family income $	5,506	1,101	8,125	1,980	3,728	2,213
	Family after-tax income groups in 2005						
565	Under $10,000	0	250	30	10	45	10
566	$10,000 to $19,999	35	400	35	65	60	60
567	$20,000 to $29,999	45	1,685	190	135	270	220
568	$30,000 to $39,999	25	2,425	280	290	260	270
569	$40,000 to $49,999	45	2,445	200	310	240	320
570	$50,000 to $59,999	30	2,435	185	400	310	325
571	$60,000 to $69,999	15	2,040	190	230	255	240
572	$70,000 to $79,999	0	1,515	120	195	225	165
573	$80,000 to $89,999	0	1,105	65	100	180	170
574	$90,000 to $99,999	15	720	55	130	105	130
575	$100,000 and over	15	1,870	225	205	290	250
576	Median after-tax family income $	42,154	55,109	52,899	56,071	57,450	55,741
577	Average after-tax family income $	46,040	62,114	65,840	61,876	66,739	63,162
578	Standard error of average after-tax family income $	4,107	684	4,139	1,442	2,406	1,566
	Income status in 2005						
579	Total population in private households for income status	730	57,840	5,400	6,865	7,410	7,330
580	Below low income cut-off before tax in 2005	90	4,355	405	305	665	640
581	Prevalence of low income before tax in 2005 %	13.0	7.5	7.4	4.4	9.0	8.7
582	Below low income cut-off after tax in 2005	70	2,805	320	260	455	385
583	Prevalence of low income after tax in 2005 %	10.3	4.8	5.9	3.8	6.1	5.2

Note: See symbols and abbreviations in the introductory material and see reference material at the end of the publication.

Certaines caractéristiques des divisions de recensement et des subdivisions de recensement – Données intégrales et données-échantillon (20 %), Ontario, Recensement de 2006 (suite)

Howick, TP ◆◊	Huron East, MU	Morris-Turnberry, MU ◊◊	North Huron, TP	South Huron, MU	**Kawartha Lakes CD/DR ◆◊**	Caractéristiques	N°
						Caractéristiques du revenu de 2005	
						Sexe et travail (suite)	
795	1,900	790	900	1,815	12,240	A travaillé toute l'année à plein temps[59]	530
35,481	37,652	32,804	47,625	40,208	44,764	Revenu médian d'emploi en 2005 $	531
37,847	39,601	39,949	49,690	46,414	50,686	Revenu moyen d'emploi en 2005 $	532
1,662	1,006	3,098	2,477	1,806	821	Erreur type de revenu moyen d'emploi $	533
345	940	320	545	1,090	7,560	A travaillé une partie de l'année ou à temps partiel[60]	534
12,767	12,156	14,335	11,064	13,280	13,778	Revenu médian d'emploi en 2005 $	535
17,666	18,179	22,207	23,232	20,136	26,200	Revenu moyen d'emploi en 2005 $	536
1,717	1,503	3,410	2,342	1,473	1,929	Erreur type de revenu moyen d'emploi $	537
995	2,580	825	1,450	2,660	19,130	Femmes de 15 ans et plus avec un revenu d'emploi[58]	538
15,934	17,031	18,189	17,139	19,763	18,735	Revenu médian d'emploi en 2005 $	539
20,784	21,190	25,200	22,136	24,179	25,100	Revenu moyen d'emploi en 2005 $	540
1,178	714	2,189	937	869	425	Erreur type de revenu moyen d'emploi $	541
460	945	355	545	1,090	8,370	A travaillé toute l'année à plein temps[59]	542
28,135	30,938	31,179	29,895	34,618	34,121	Revenu médian d'emploi en 2005 $	543
29,350	32,241	38,117	31,816	37,012	38,046	Revenu moyen d'emploi en 2005 $	544
1,850	1,123	3,897	1,455	1,291	586	Erreur type de revenu moyen d'emploi $	545
480	1,525	410	830	1,305	9,225	A travaillé une partie de l'année ou à temps partiel[60]	546
9,008	11,993	9,896	11,702	10,808	10,256	Revenu médian d'emploi en 2005 $	547
14,225	15,420	16,938	16,452	15,864	16,006	Revenu moyen d'emploi en 2005 $	548
1,316	794	2,132	1,074	907	449	Erreur type de revenu moyen d'emploi $	549
1,040	**2,550**	**915**	**1,435**	**2,905**	**22,260**	**Nombre total des familles économiques dans les ménages privés**	550
						Revenu de la famille économique en 2005	
10	55	20	15	45	480	Moins de 10 000 $	551
0	45	30	45	65	845	10 000 $ à 19 999 $	552
95	190	95	145	235	1,920	20 000 $ à 29 999 $	553
120	295	120	115	365	2,385	30 000 $ à 39 999 $	554
140	295	120	175	360	2,325	40 000 $ à 49 999 $	555
160	340	50	160	315	2,335	50 000 $ à 59 999 $	556
125	315	80	140	295	2,155	60 000 $ à 69 999 $	557
125	250	75	180	275	2,045	70 000 $ à 79 999 $	558
75	220	65	120	220	1,695	80 000 $ à 89 999 $	559
30	145	60	75	160	1,205	90 000 $ à 99 999 $	560
145	395	205	260	560	4,860	100 000 $ et plus	561
58,097	61,188	61,968	66,068	62,736	63,782	Revenu médian des familles $	562
64,741	68,385	73,710	70,678	72,694	75,609	Revenu moyen des familles $	563
1,978	1,626	4,433	2,436	1,896	1,083	Erreur type de revenu moyen des familles $	564
						Revenu après impôt de la famille économique en 2005	
15	55	25	15	50	500	Moins de 10 000 $	565
0	45	25	50	70	865	10 000 $ à 19 999 $	566
105	240	100	175	250	2,165	20 000 $ à 29 999 $	567
165	370	170	145	475	3,050	30 000 $ à 39 999 $	568
190	415	80	215	470	3,070	40 000 $ à 49 999 $	569
165	390	115	185	355	2,815	50 000 $ à 59 999 $	570
160	310	80	215	350	2,665	60 000 $ à 69 999 $	571
85	250	95	145	230	1,995	70 000 $ à 79 999 $	572
40	175	50	85	235	1,280	80 000 $ à 89 999 $	573
30	80	65	40	85	1,025	90 000 $ à 99 999 $	574
85	215	110	150	340	2,830	100 000 $ et plus	575
52,068	54,410	52,888	57,170	53,914	55,046	Revenu médian après impôt des familles $	576
56,745	58,978	61,826	60,554	61,464	62,766	Revenu moyen après impôt des familles $	577
1,645	1,251	3,038	1,801	1,377	761	Erreur type de revenu moyen après impôt des familles $	578
						Catégorie de revenu en 2005	
3,850	9,055	3,245	5,000	9,690	73,110	Population totale dans les ménages privés pour la catégorie de revenu	579
185	765	230	495	665	7,520	Au-dessous du seuil de faible revenu avant impôt en 2005	580
4.7	8.5	7.1	9.9	6.9	10.3	Fréquence du faible revenu avant impôt en 2005 %	581
70	460	145	325	380	5,070	Au-dessous du seuil de faible revenu après impôt en 2005	582
1.7	5.1	4.5	6.6	3.9	6.9	Fréquence du faible revenu après impôt en 2005 %	583

Nota : Voir les symboles et les abréviations dans les documents d'introduction et voir les documents de référence à la fin de la publication.

Selected characteristics for census divisions and census subdivisions – 100% data and 20% sample data, Ontario, 2006 Census (continued)

No.	Characteristics	Wollaston, TP ◆◆◊	**Huron CD/DR**	Ashfield-Colborne-Wawanosh, TP ◆	Bluewater, MU ◆◊	Central Huron, MU	Goderich, T
	2005 income characteristics						
584	**Total number of private households**	**325**	**22,900**	**1,955**	**2,765**	**2,960**	**3,255**
	Household income groups in 2005						
585	Under $10,000	0	700	40	85	110	90
586	$10,000 to $19,999	85	2,055	160	205	250	375
587	$20,000 to $29,999	60	2,645	270	205	390	415
588	$30,000 to $39,999	35	2,985	270	365	380	405
589	$40,000 to $49,999	30	2,540	230	335	235	375
590	$50,000 to $59,999	30	2,285	170	305	245	290
591	$60,000 to $69,999	20	2,135	155	405	270	245
592	$70,000 to $79,999	15	1,825	155	195	225	215
593	$80,000 to $89,999	0	1,390	100	145	205	185
594	$90,000 to $99,999	0	1,015	80	120	190	140
595	$100,000 and over	30	3,325	325	390	465	520
596	Median household income $	32,010	51,910	50,350	54,831	54,238	48,904
597	Average household income $	44,460	63,011	72,802	62,988	68,562	61,124
598	Standard error of average household income $	4,213	868	6,424	1,705	2,975	1,694
	Household after-tax income groups in 2005						
599	Under $10,000	0	720	40	80	105	90
600	$10,000 to $19,999	90	2,260	185	250	285	405
601	$20,000 to $29,999	65	3,245	295	290	440	505
602	$30,000 to $39,999	25	3,385	335	395	415	450
603	$40,000 to $49,999	45	3,005	225	440	285	400
604	$50,000 to $59,999	30	2,735	210	425	350	390
605	$60,000 to $69,999	15	2,195	195	240	270	275
606	$70,000 to $79,999	0	1,570	125	190	225	180
607	$80,000 to $89,999	10	1,130	65	100	190	175
608	$90,000 to $99,999	15	740	50	135	100	130
609	$100,000 and over	15	1,905	225	210	300	250
610	Median after-tax household income $	29,036	45,579	43,295	47,865	47,292	43,395
611	Average after-tax household income $	39,085	53,213	58,103	53,566	57,151	51,160
612	Standard error of average after-tax household income $	3,251	559	3,320	1,278	1,958	1,231

Note: See symbols and abbreviations in the introductory material and see reference material at the end of the publication.

Certaines caractéristiques des divisions de recensement et des subdivisions de recensement – Données intégrales et données-échantillon (20 %), Ontario, Recensement de 2006 (suite)

Howick, TP ◆◇	Huron East, MU	Morris-Turnberry, MU ◇◇	North Huron, TP	South Huron, MU	**Kawartha Lakes CD/DR** ◆◇	**Caractéristiques**	N°
						Caractéristiques du revenu de 2005	
1,250	**3,430**	**1,145**	**2,065**	**4,065**	**29,500**	**Nombre total des ménages privés**	584
						Tranches de revenu des ménages en 2005	
20	105	35	90	135	1,125	Moins de 10 000 $	585
50	305	105	245	350	2,830	10 000 $ à 19 999 $	586
125	335	120	250	525	3,285	20 000 $ à 29 999 $	587
195	460	175	160	570	3,405	30 000 $ à 39 999 $	588
160	360	130	245	470	3,040	40 000 $ à 49 999 $	589
170	415	60	220	410	2,875	50 000 $ à 59 999 $	590
125	340	85	175	335	2,390	60 000 $ à 69 999 $	591
135	320	95	190	290	2,290	70 000 $ à 79 999 $	592
75	240	75	135	220	1,840	80 000 $ à 89 999 $	593
40	140	55	80	170	1,335	90 000 $ à 99 999 $	594
145	395	220	280	580	5,075	100 000 $ et plus	595
53,951	52,838	51,469	51,140	49,275	52,955	Revenu médian des ménages $	596
59,616	59,281	66,053	59,587	60,845	65,549	Revenu moyen des ménages $	597
1,833	1,431	3,761	1,979	1,516	861	Erreur type de revenu moyen des ménages $	598
						Tranches du revenu après impôt des ménages en 2005	
15	100	40	90	145	1,165	Moins de 10 000 $	599
60	345	100	250	375	3,085	10 000 $ à 19 999 $	600
185	465	155	275	630	3,695	20 000 $ à 29 999 $	601
205	485	200	245	650	4,325	30 000 $ à 39 999 $	602
200	470	95	300	590	3,675	40 000 $ à 49 999 $	603
165	475	120	220	380	3,150	50 000 $ à 59 999 $	604
170	355	90	235	365	2,895	60 000 $ à 69 999 $	605
90	250	100	155	250	2,140	70 000 $ à 79 999 $	606
40	180	55	90	235	1,375	80 000 $ à 89 999 $	607
30	80	75	40	95	1,075	90 000 $ à 99 999 $	608
80	215	110	165	340	2,915	100 000 $ et plus	609
47,595	46,761	46,909	44,089	43,524	46,881	Revenu médian après impôt des ménages $	610
52,231	51,285	55,694	51,109	51,689	54,625	Revenu moyen après impôt des ménages $	611
1,531	1,122	2,627	1,509	1,132	614	Erreur type de revenu moyen après impôt des ménages $	612

Nota : Voir les symboles et les abréviations dans les documents d'introduction et voir les documents de référence à la fin de la publication.

Selected characteristics for census divisions and census subdivisions – 100% data and 20% sample data, Ontario, 2006 Census (continued)

No.	Characteristics	Kawartha Lakes, CY ◆◇	**Kenora CD/DR** †◆◆◇◇	Bearskin Lake, IRI ◆◆◇◇	Cat Lake 63C, IRI ◆◇	Deer Lake, IRI ◆◆◇◇	Dryden, CY
	Population characteristics						
1	**Population, 2001**[1]	**69,179**	**61,802**	**363**	**428**	**756**	**8,198**
2	**Population, 2006**[2]	**74,561**	**64,419**	**459**	**492**	**681**	**8,195**
3	Population percentage change, 2001 to 2006	7.8	4.2	26.4	15.0	-9.9	0.0
4	Land area in square kilometres, 2006	3,059.47	407,192.66	125.78	17.04	17.85	65.20
5	**Total population – 100% data**[3]	**74,560**	**64,415**	**460**	**490**	**680**	**8,195**
	Sex and age groups						
6	Male	36,700	32,270	245	270	350	3,955
7	0 to 4 years	1,530	2,460	30	50	50	205
8	5 to 9 years	1,970	2,510	30	35	35	250
9	10 to 14 years	2,570	2,765	25	35	40	275
10	15 to 19 years	2,685	2,735	30	20	25	320
11	20 to 24 years	2,060	2,095	10	20	35	220
12	25 to 29 years	1,525	1,890	25	15	30	160
13	30 to 34 years	1,670	1,870	15	15	25	205
14	35 to 39 years	1,990	2,025	20	20	25	270
15	40 to 44 years	2,775	2,465	15	15	15	320
16	45 to 49 years	3,105	2,585	10	15	20	390
17	50 to 54 years	2,930	2,240	5	5	15	320
18	55 to 59 years	2,795	1,960	10	10	10	270
19	60 to 64 years	2,445	1,385	0	5	10	185
20	65 to 69 years	1,935	1,130	5	0	5	175
21	70 to 74 years	1,780	890	5	0	0	160
22	75 to 79 years	1,495	645	5	5	5	110
23	80 to 84 years	925	395	0	0	0	80
24	85 years and over	515	225	0	0	0	50
25	Female	37,860	32,155	215	220	330	4,240
26	0 to 4 years	1,555	2,360	35	30	40	175
27	5 to 9 years	1,880	2,425	20	20	40	255
28	10 to 14 years	2,375	2,645	20	25	55	290
29	15 to 19 years	2,375	2,550	20	20	25	300
30	20 to 24 years	1,840	2,140	25	25	25	250
31	25 to 29 years	1,570	1,965	15	20	35	195
32	30 to 34 years	1,690	1,895	15	20	20	235
33	35 to 39 years	2,150	2,145	5	10	25	295
34	40 to 44 years	2,895	2,535	25	15	20	340
35	45 to 49 years	3,140	2,445	5	10	15	350
36	50 to 54 years	3,110	2,075	0	5	5	300
37	55 to 59 years	2,955	1,830	10	5	15	300
38	60 to 64 years	2,425	1,310	5	5	5	210
39	65 to 69 years	1,995	1,105	0	5	5	210
40	70 to 74 years	1,835	925	5	0	5	150
41	75 to 79 years	1,635	710	0	0	0	135
42	80 to 84 years	1,275	595	5	0	5	120
43	85 years and over	1,150	505	0	0	0	135
44	**Total population 15 years and over**[3]	**62,675**	**49,255**	**295**	**290**	**415**	**6,745**
	Legal marital status						
45	Never legally married (single)	16,100	18,500	150	185	155	1,895
46	Legally married (and not separated)[4,5]	34,350	22,840	115	85	220	3,570
47	Separated, but still legally married	2,395	2,040	25	5	25	250
48	Divorced	4,820	2,955	5	10	5	460
49	Widowed	5,015	2,920	10	5	15	575
	Common-law status						
50	Not in a common-law relationship	56,900	42,460	245	230	335	6,155
51	In a common-law relationship	5,775	6,800	55	65	80	595
52	**Total population – 20% sample data**[6]	**73,360**	**63,995**	**460**	**490**	**680**	**8,080**
	Mother tongue						
53	Single responses	73,090	63,605	460	495	680	8,040
54	English	68,575	46,725	130	95	295	7,380
55	French	755	1,455	0	0	0	195
56	Non-official languages[7]	3,760	15,430	330	400	385	465
57	Italian	190	255	0	0	0	45
58	Chinese, n.o.s.[61]	25	25	0	0	0	0
59	Cantonese	15	20	0	0	0	0
60	Spanish	95	80	0	0	0	20
61	German	955	850	0	0	0	95
62	Other languages[8]	2,475	14,195	330	395	390	295

Note: See symbols and abbreviations in the introductory material and see reference material at the end of the publication.

Certaines caractéristiques des divisions de recensement et des subdivisions de recensement – Données intégrales et données-échantillon (20 %), Ontario, Recensement de 2006 (suite)

Eagle Lake 27, IRI	Ear Falls, TP ◆◊	English River 21, IRI ◆◊	Fort Hope 64, IRI ◆◆◊◊	Ignace, TP ◊	Kasabonika Lake, IRI	Caractéristiques	N°
						Caractéristiques de la population	
211	**1,150**	**454**	**1,001**	**1,709**	**740**	**Population, 2001**[1]	1
232	**1,153**	**633**	**1,144**	**1,431**	**681**	**Population, 2006**[2]	2
10.0	0.3	39.4	14.3	-16.3	-8.0	Variation en pourcentage de la population, 2001 à 2006	3
34.40	330.99	39.61	245.59	72.66	104.71	Superficie des terres en kilomètres carrés, 2006	4
230	**1,150**	**630**	**1,145**	**1,430**	**680**	**Population totale – Données intégrales**[3]	5
						Sexe et groupes d'âge	
125	555	325	575	745	350	Sexe masculin	6
10	30	30	85	30	50	0 à 4 ans	7
10	30	40	85	65	40	5 à 9 ans	8
15	30	35	90	50	50	10 à 14 ans	9
15	30	35	65	45	40	15 à 19 ans	10
5	35	20	35	35	30	20 à 24 ans	11
5	30	35	35	40	20	25 à 29 ans	12
10	40	15	45	50	20	30 à 34 ans	13
10	40	35	45	35	15	35 à 39 ans	14
20	45	25	25	60	15	40 à 44 ans	15
10	40	15	20	65	15	45 à 49 ans	16
15	50	15	5	75	15	50 à 54 ans	17
10	50	15	5	60	5	55 à 59 ans	18
5	30	5	20	50	10	60 à 64 ans	19
0	25	5	5	40	5	65 à 69 ans	20
5	20	5	5	25	5	70 à 74 ans	21
0	25	0	10	15	5	75 à 79 ans	22
0	0	0	0	10	0	80 à 84 ans	23
0	5	0	0	5	0	85 ans et plus	24
105	600	305	565	685	335	Sexe féminin	25
5	45	40	100	35	55	0 à 4 ans	26
15	50	25	80	45	45	5 à 9 ans	27
5	40	40	65	45	45	10 à 14 ans	28
10	45	35	45	40	15	15 à 19 ans	29
10	30	35	45	30	25	20 à 24 ans	30
5	35	30	45	40	30	25 à 29 ans	31
10	40	20	40	45	25	30 à 34 ans	32
15	30	15	35	45	15	35 à 39 ans	33
15	45	15	30	55	25	40 à 44 ans	34
5	50	15	30	60	10	45 à 49 ans	35
5	55	5	10	70	15	50 à 54 ans	36
10	30	10	15	55	10	55 à 59 ans	37
5	25	5	10	45	10	60 à 64 ans	38
5	30	5	5	30	10	65 à 69 ans	39
0	15	0	5	20	0	70 à 74 ans	40
0	5	0	0	10	5	75 à 79 ans	41
0	5	5	0	15	5	80 à 84 ans	42
0	10	0	0	5	5	85 ans et plus	43
175	**935**	**425**	**635**	**1,170**	**400**	**Population totale de 15 ans et plus**[3]	44
						État matrimonial légal	
110	270	340	390	340	210	Jamais légalement marié(e) (célibataire)	45
35	510	35	175	650	165	Légalement marié(e) (et non séparé[e])[4,5]	46
15	40	15	40	50	10	Séparé(e), mais toujours légalement marié(e)	47
10	60	15	10	80	5	Divorcé(e)	48
5	40	20	20	50	15	Veuf(ve)	49
						Union libre	
135	810	270	500	1,030	350	Ne vivant pas en union libre	50
40	120	155	135	145	50	Vivant en union libre	51
230	**1,155**	**630**	**1,145**	**1,430**	**680**	**Population totale – Données-échantillon (20 %)**[6]	52
						Langue maternelle	
235	1,150	630	1,140	1,425	685	Réponses uniques	53
180	1,020	315	845	1,150	60	Anglais	54
0	65	0	0	140	0	Français	55
50	65	320	295	135	625	Langues non officielles[7]	56
0	10	0	0	50	0	Italien	57
0	0	0	0	0	0	Chinois, n.d.a.[61]	58
0	0	0	0	0	0	Cantonais	59
0	0	0	0	0	0	Espagnol	60
0	25	0	0	10	0	Allemand	61
50	35	315	295	70	625	Autres langues[8]	62

Nota : Voir les symboles et les abréviations dans les documents d'introduction et voir les documents de référence à la fin de la publication.

Selected characteristics for census divisions and census subdivisions – 100% data and 20% sample data, Ontario, 2006 Census (continued)

No.	Characteristics	Kawartha Lakes, CY ◆◊	**Kenora CD/DR** †◆◆◊◊	Bearskin Lake, IRI ◆◆◊◊	Cat Lake 63C, IRI ◆◊	Deer Lake, IRI ◆◆◊◊	Dryden, CY
	Population characteristics						
	Mother tongue (continued)						
63	Multiple responses	275	385	0	0	0	40
64	English and French	115	100	0	0	0	15
65	English and non-official language	160	275	0	0	10	20
66	French and non-official language	0	15	0	0	0	10
67	English, French and non-official language	0	0	0	0	0	0
	Language spoken most often at home[9]						
68	Single responses	73,225	63,700	460	495	680	8,075
69	English	72,175	54,240	220	150	615	7,970
70	French	105	335	0	0	0	30
71	Non-official languages[7]	945	9,130	240	335	65	75
72	Chinese, n.o.s.[61]	20	30	0	0	0	0
73	Cantonese	15	0	0	0	0	0
74	Panjabi (Punjabi)	30	0	0	0	0	0
75	Italian	15	25	0	0	0	10
76	Spanish	0	40	0	0	0	10
77	Other languages[8]	860	9,035	235	340	65	65
78	Multiple responses	140	295	0	0	0	10
79	English and French	50	85	0	0	0	0
80	English and non-official language	90	205	0	0	0	10
81	French and non-official language	0	0	0	0	0	0
82	English, French and non-official language	0	0	0	0	0	0
	Knowledge of official languages[10]						
83	English only	69,640	59,500	425	460	665	7,505
84	French only	35	10	0	0	0	0
85	English and French	3,610	3,530	0	0	0	560
86	Neither English nor French	75	955	35	35	20	15
	Knowledge of non-official languages[7,11]						
87	Italian	270	320	0	0	0	75
88	Spanish	315	250	0	0	0	40
89	German	1,125	1,015	0	0	0	125
90	Chinese, n.o.s.[61]	20	30	0	0	0	0
91	Cantonese	30	20	0	0	0	0
92	Panjabi (Punjabi)	85	0	0	0	0	0
93	Portuguese	140	170	0	0	0	55
	First official language spoken[10]						
94	English	72,510	61,720	425	455	665	7,895
95	French	715	1,295	0	0	0	175
96	English and French	80	30	0	0	0	0
97	Neither English nor French	55	950	30	35	20	10
98	Official language minority - (number)[12]	755	1,310	0	0	0	170
99	Official language minority - (percentage)[12]	1.0	2.0	0.0	0.0	0.0	2.1
	Ethnic origin[13]						
100	English	33,195	13,255	0	10	0	2,875
101	Canadian	26,320	11,175	0	0	0	2,265
102	Scottish	20,065	10,215	0	10	0	2,180
103	Irish	20,255	7,915	0	0	0	1,525
104	French	7,660	8,740	0	0	0	1,600
105	German	6,915	7,110	0	0	0	1,350
106	Italian	1,625	1,610	0	0	0	285
107	Chinese	155	105	0	0	0	0
108	East Indian	335	80	0	0	0	50
109	Dutch (Netherlands)	4,585	1,540	0	0	0	305
110	Polish	1,650	2,330	0	0	0	260
111	Ukrainian	1,605	5,015	0	0	0	975
112	North American Indian	2,150	24,725	450	475	680	500
113	Portuguese	415	305	0	0	0	100
114	Filipino	65	75	0	0	0	0
	Aboriginal and non-Aboriginal identity						
115	Total Aboriginal identity population[14]	1,255	26,345	445	485	680	780
116	Total non-Aboriginal identity population	72,110	37,650	15	10	0	7,295

Note: See symbols and abbreviations in the introductory material and see reference material at the end of the publication.

Certaines caractéristiques des divisions de recensement et des subdivisions de recensement – Données intégrales et données-échantillon (20 %), Ontario, Recensement de 2006 (suite)

Eagle Lake 27, IRI	Ear Falls, TP ◆◇	English River 21, IRI ◆◇	Fort Hope 64, IRI ◆◆◇◇	Ignace, TP ◇	Kasabonika Lake, IRI	Caractéristiques	N°
						Caractéristiques de la population	
						Langue maternelle (suite)	
0	0	0	0	0	0	Réponses multiples	63
0	0	0	0	10	0	Anglais et français	64
0	0	0	10	0	0	Anglais et langue non officielle	65
0	0	0	0	0	0	Français et langue non officielle	66
0	0	0	0	0	0	Anglais, français et langue non officielle	67
						Langue parlée le plus souvent à la maison[9]	
230	1,140	635	1,140	1,400	680	Réponses uniques	68
215	1,115	450	1,015	1,365	160	Anglais	69
0	25	0	0	35	0	Français	70
15	0	185	130	10	520	Langues non officielles[7]	71
0	0	0	0	0	0	Chinois, n.d.a.[61]	72
0	0	0	0	0	0	Cantonais	73
0	0	0	0	0	0	Pendjabi	74
0	0	0	0	0	0	Italien	75
0	0	0	0	0	0	Espagnol	76
15	0	180	130	0	520	Autres langues[8]	77
0	15	0	0	30	10	Réponses multiples	78
0	0	0	0	30	0	Anglais et français	79
0	15	0	0	0	0	Anglais et langue non officielle	80
0	0	0	0	0	0	Français et langue non officielle	81
0	0	0	0	0	0	Anglais, français et langue non officielle	82
						Connaissance des langues officielles[10]	
230	1,080	625	1,095	1,235	620	Anglais seulement	83
0	10	0	0	0	0	Français seulement	84
10	70	0	0	190	0	Anglais et français	85
0	0	0	55	0	60	Ni l'anglais ni le français	86
						Connaissance des langues non officielles[7,11]	
0	0	0	0	70	0	Italien	87
0	0	0	0	0	0	Espagnol	88
0	25	0	0	10	0	Allemand	89
0	0	0	0	10	0	Chinois, n.d.a.[61]	90
0	0	0	0	0	0	Cantonais	91
0	0	0	0	0	0	Pendjabi	92
0	0	0	0	0	0	Portugais	93
						Première langue officielle parlée[10]	
230	1,090	630	1,090	1,295	615	Anglais	94
0	60	0	0	135	0	Français	95
0	0	0	0	0	0	Anglais et français	96
0	0	0	50	0	60	Ni l'anglais ni le français	97
0	60	0	0	140	0	Minorité de langue officielle - (nombre)[12]	98
0.0	5.2	0.0	0.0	9.8	0.0	Minorité de langue officielle - (pourcentage)[12]	99
						Origine ethnique[13]	
10	265	10	0	445	0	Anglais	100
0	435	0	0	365	10	Canadien	101
0	200	25	0	360	0	Écossais	102
0	215	10	0	175	0	Irlandais	103
10	250	10	0	250	0	Français	104
10	215	0	0	80	0	Allemand	105
0	15	0	0	225	0	Italien	106
0	0	0	0	0	0	Chinois	107
0	0	0	0	0	0	Indien de l'Inde	108
0	60	0	0	20	0	Hollandais (Néerlandais)	109
0	25	0	0	50	0	Polonais	110
0	80	0	0	150	0	Ukrainien	111
225	150	620	1,140	140	680	Indien de l'Amérique du Nord	112
0	10	0	0	0	0	Portugais	113
0	0	0	0	0	0	Philippin	114
						Population ayant une identité autochtone et population n'ayant pas d'identité autochtone	
225	115	620	1,140	200	680	Total de la population ayant une identité autochtone[14]	115
10	1,035	10	0	1,230	0	Total de la population n'ayant pas d'identité autochtone	116

Nota : Voir les symboles et les abréviations dans les documents d'introduction et voir les documents de référence à la fin de la publication.

Selected characteristics for census divisions and census subdivisions – 100% data and 20% sample data, Ontario, 2006 Census (continued)

No.	Characteristics	Kawartha Lakes, CY ◆◇	**Kenora CD/DR** †◆◆◇◇	Bearskin Lake, IRI ◆◆◇◇	Cat Lake 63C, IRI ◆◇	Deer Lake, IRI ◆◆◇◇	Dryden, CY
	Population characteristics						
	Aboriginal and non-Aboriginal ancestry						
117	Total Aboriginal ancestry population[15]	2,785	27,275	445	480	680	975
118	Total non-Aboriginal ancestry population	70,580	36,720	10	10	10	7,100
	Registered Indian status						
119	Registered Indian[16]	310	22,865	435	475	675	250
120	Not a Registered Indian	73,055	41,130	25	15	10	7,825
	Visible minority groups						
121	Total visible minority population[17]	1,195	595	0	0	0	140
122	Chinese	95	80	0	0	0	0
123	South Asian[18]	365	110	0	0	0	45
124	Black	250	100	0	0	0	10
125	Filipino	60	70	0	0	0	10
126	Latin American	65	80	0	0	0	10
127	Southeast Asian[19]	20	15	0	0	0	15
128	Arab	45	55	0	0	0	10
129	West Asian[20]	0	0	0	0	0	0
130	Korean	160	10	0	0	0	10
131	Japanese	25	50	0	0	0	25
132	Visible minority, n.i.e.[21]	50	10	0	0	0	0
133	Multiple visible minority[22]	60	15	0	0	0	10
	Citizenship[23]						
134	Canadian citizens[24]	72,510	63,180	X	X	X	7,940
135	Not Canadian citizens[25]	860	810	X	X	X	140
	Immigrant status and place of birth[26]						
136	Non-immigrants[27]	67,260	60,935	X	X	X	7,580
137	Born in province of residence	62,170	48,420	X	X	X	5,865
138	Immigrants[28]	6,010	2,835	X	X	X	430
139	United States of America	290	720	X	X	X	40
140	Central and South America	135	80	X	X	X	15
141	Caribbean and Bermuda	120	15	X	X	X	0
142	United Kingdom	2,390	460	X	X	X	110
143	Other Europe	2,485	1,330	X	X	X	230
144	Africa	85	65	X	X	X	10
145	Asia and the Middle East	460	140	X	X	X	20
146	Oceania and other[29]	50	25	X	X	X	0
147	Non-permanent residents[30]	90	220	X	X	X	75
148	**Total immigrant population[28]**	**6,005**	**2,840**	**X**	**X**	**X**	**430**
	Period of immigration						
149	Before 1961	2,755	1,055	X	X	X	195
150	1961 to 1970	1,350	430	X	X	X	95
151	1971 to 1980	785	480	X	X	X	80
152	1981 to 1990	460	345	X	X	X	25
153	1991 to 2000	425	325	X	X	X	25
154	1991 to 1995	165	140	X	X	X	0
155	1996 to 2000	260	180	X	X	X	25
156	2001 to 2006[31]	235	210	X	X	X	15
	Age at immigration						
157	Under 5 years	750	430	X	X	X	50
158	5 to 19 years	1,905	810	X	X	X	140
159	20 years and over	3,345	1,595	X	X	X	240
160	**Total population 15 years and over**	**61,460**	**48,860**	**295**	**290**	**410**	**6,630**
	Generation status						
161	1st generation[32]	5,985	2,990	0	0	0	470
162	2nd generation[33]	10,685	6,405	10	10	0	1,190
163	3rd generation or more[34]	44,790	39,460	295	290	415	4,975

Note: See symbols and abbreviations in the introductory material and see reference material at the end of the publication.

Certaines caractéristiques des divisions de recensement et des subdivisions de recensement – Données intégrales et données-échantillon (20 %), Ontario, Recensement de 2006 (suite)

Eagle Lake 27, IRI	Ear Falls, TP ◆◇	English River 21, IRI ◆◇	Fort Hope 64, IRI ◆◆◇◇	Ignace, TP ◇	Kasabonika Lake, IRI	Caractéristiques	N°
						Caractéristiques de la population	
						Population ayant une ascendance autochtone et population n'ayant pas d'ascendance autochtone	
225	220	625	1,140	230	680	Total de la population ayant une ascendance autochtone[15]	117
0	930	10	10	1,200	0	Total de la population n'ayant pas d'ascendance autochtone	118
						Statut d'Indien inscrit	
220	55	615	1,140	70	660	Indien inscrit[16]	119
15	1,095	15	10	1,355	20	Pas un Indien inscrit	120
						Groupes de minorités visibles	
0	10	0	0	0	0	Total de la population des minorités visibles[17]	121
0	0	0	0	0	0	Chinois	122
0	10	0	0	0	0	Sud-Asiatique[18]	123
0	0	0	0	0	0	Noir	124
0	0	0	0	0	0	Philippin	125
0	0	0	0	0	0	Latino-Américain	126
10	0	0	0	0	0	Asiatique du Sud-Est[19]	127
0	0	0	0	0	0	Arabe	128
0	0	0	0	0	0	Asiatique occidental[20]	129
0	0	0	0	0	0	Coréen	130
0	0	0	0	0	0	Japonais	131
0	0	0	0	0	0	Minorité visible, n.i.a.[21]	132
0	0	0	0	0	0	Minorités visibles multiples[22]	133
						Citoyenneté[23]	
X	1,145	X	X	1,415	X	Citoyens canadiens[24]	134
X	10	X	X	15	X	Ne sont pas des citoyens canadiens[25]	135
						Statut d'immigrant et le lieu de naissance[26]	
X	1,085	X	X	1,285	X	Non-immigrants[27]	136
X	790	X	X	945	X	Né dans la province de résidence	137
X	70	X	X	140	X	Immigrants[28]	138
X	10	X	X	40	X	États-Unis d'Amérique	139
X	0	X	X	0	X	Amérique centrale et Amérique du Sud	140
X	0	X	X	0	X	Antilles et Bermudes	141
X	0	X	X	10	X	Royaume-Uni	142
X	40	X	X	85	X	Autre Europe	143
X	0	X	X	0	X	Afrique	144
X	10	X	X	10	X	Asie et Moyen-Orient	145
X	0	X	X	0	X	Océanie et autres[29]	146
X	0	X	X	0	X	Résidents non permanents[30]	147
X	**65**	**X**	**X**	**145**	**X**	**Population totale des immigrants[28]**	148
						Période d'immigration	
X	30	X	X	65	X	Avant 1961	149
X	10	X	X	25	X	1961 à 1970	150
X	10	X	X	40	X	1971 à 1980	151
X	0	X	X	0	X	1981 à 1990	152
X	10	X	X	10	X	1991 à 2000	153
X	0	X	X	0	X	1991 à 1995	154
X	10	X	X	10	X	1996 à 2000	155
X	0	X	X	0	X	2001 à 2006[31]	156
						Âge à l'immigration	
X	10	X	X	30	X	Moins de 5 ans	157
X	15	X	X	50	X	5 à 19 ans	158
X	40	X	X	60	X	20 ans et plus	159
175	**945**	**430**	**635**	**1,200**	**400**	**Population totale de 15 ans et plus**	160
						Statut des générations	
0	70	0	0	140	0	1re génération[32]	161
0	135	0	0	215	0	2e génération[33]	162
175	740	420	635	835	400	3e génération ou plus[34]	163

Nota : Voir les symboles et les abréviations dans les documents d'introduction et voir les documents de référence à la fin de la publication.

Selected characteristics for census divisions and census subdivisions – 100% data and 20% sample data, Ontario, 2006 Census (continued)

No.	Characteristics	Kawartha Lakes, CY ◆◇	**Kenora CD/DR** †◆◆◇◇	Bearskin Lake, IRI ◆◆◇◇	Cat Lake 63C, IRI ◆◇	Deer Lake, IRI ◆◆◇◇	Dryden, CY
	Population characteristics						
164	**Total population 1 year and over[35]**	**72,805**	**63,090**	**445**	**475**	**670**	**8,035**
	Place of residence 1 year ago (mobility)						
165	Non-movers	65,345	56,660	410	420	655	6,860
166	Movers	7,455	6,430	35	55	15	1,170
167	Non-migrants	4,175	4,010	25	25	0	740
168	Migrants	3,280	2,420	10	25	10	435
169	Internal migrants	3,115	2,295	10	30	10	400
170	Intraprovincial migrants	2,905	1,550	10	25	10	280
171	Interprovincial migrants	210	745	0	0	0	125
172	External migrants	165	130	0	0	0	30
173	**Total population 5 years and over[36]**	**70,350**	**59,350**	**395**	**410**	**590**	**7,765**
	Place of residence 5 years ago (mobility)						
174	Non-movers	46,435	40,605	230	260	515	4,975
175	Movers	23,910	18,750	160	155	70	2,790
176	Non-migrants	10,900	11,100	120	80	40	1,795
177	Migrants	13,005	7,645	40	70	30	995
178	Internal migrants	12,655	7,250	40	70	30	900
179	Intraprovincial migrants	11,955	4,640	25	65	25	555
180	Interprovincial migrants	700	2,610	10	10	0	345
181	External migrants	350	395	10	0	0	90
182	**Total population 15 years and over**	**61,460**	**48,860**	**295**	**290**	**410**	**6,635**
	Highest certificate, diploma or degree[37]						
183	No certificate, diploma or degree	16,555	18,875	175	240	315	1,640
184	Certificate, diploma or degree	44,905	29,985	120	55	100	4,995
185	High school certificate or equivalent[38]	17,930	11,665	70	30	55	2,020
186	Apprenticeship or trades certificate or diploma	6,925	5,040	0	0	15	705
187	College, CEGEP or other non-university certificate or diploma[39]	13,025	7,765	40	10	10	1,375
188	University certificate or diploma below bachelor level[40]	1,600	1,320	0	0	10	235
189	University certificate or degree[41]	5,430	4,195	0	10	10	655
190	Bachelor's degree	3,425	2,725	10	10	10	475
191	University certificate or diploma above bachelor level	1,080	765	0	0	0	120
192	Degree in medicine, dentistry, veterinary medicine or optometry	140	115	0	0	0	10
193	Master's degree	685	525	0	0	0	50
194	Earned doctorate	100	70	0	0	0	0
195	**Total population 15 years and over with postsecondary qualifications**	**26,975**	**18,325**	**55**	**25**	**40**	**2,970**
	Major field of study - Classification of Instructional Programs, 2000[42]						
196	Education	2,305	1,985	10	0	20	315
197	Visual and performing arts, and communications technologies	840	250	0	0	0	10
198	Humanities	905	670	0	0	0	90
199	Social and behavioural sciences and law	2,395	1,150	0	0	0	145
200	Business, management and public administration	4,455	3,310	15	0	0	640
201	Physical and life sciences and technologies	530	390	0	0	0	50
202	Mathematics, computer and information sciences	740	295	0	10	0	45
203	Architecture, engineering, and related technologies	7,240	4,670	10	0	10	835
204	Agriculture, natural resources and conservation	915	760	0	0	0	125
205	Health, parks, recreation and fitness	4,550	2,900	10	10	10	475
206	Personal, protective and transportation services	2,105	1,935	10	0	0	235
207	Other fields of study[43]	0	0	0	0	0	0
	Location of study[44]						
208	Inside Canada	24,930	17,305	55	20	45	2,815
209	Outside Canada	2,045	1,015	0	0	0	155
210	**Total population 15 years and over**	**61,460**	**48,860**	**295**	**290**	**410**	**6,635**
	Unpaid work						
211	Males 15 years and over	30,095	24,385	160	145	220	3,180
212	Reported unpaid work[45]	27,340	22,185	150	115	205	2,920
213	Housework and child care and care or assistance to seniors	2,140	3,235	40	45	45	315
214	Housework and child care only	6,785	6,545	55	30	85	795

Note: See symbols and abbreviations in the introductory material and see reference material at the end of the publication.

Certaines caractéristiques des divisions de recensement et des subdivisions de recensement – Données intégrales et données-échantillon (20 %), Ontario, Recensement de 2006 (suite)

Eagle Lake 27, IRI	Ear Falls, TP ◆◇	English River 21, IRI ◆◇	Fort Hope 64, IRI ◆◆◇◇	Ignace, TP ◇	Kasabonika Lake, IRI	Caractéristiques	N°
						Caractéristiques de la population	
235	**1,150**	**620**	**1,115**	**1,425**	**665**	**Population totale de 1 an et plus[35]**	164
						Lieu de résidence 1 an auparavant (mobilité)	
225	1,030	555	1,035	1,325	635	Personnes n'ayant pas déménagé	165
10	120	60	85	100	25	Personnes ayant déménagé	166
10	65	30	80	60	30	Non-migrants	167
10	60	25	0	40	0	Migrants	168
10	60	30	10	40	0	Migrants internes	169
0	15	20	10	35	0	Migrants infraprovinciaux	170
10	45	0	0	0	0	Migrants interprovinciaux	171
0	0	0	0	0	0	Migrants externes	172
220	**1,105**	**570**	**960**	**1,390**	**580**	**Population totale de 5 ans et plus[36]**	173
						Lieu de résidence 5 ans auparavant (mobilité)	
165	725	420	765	1,100	400	Personnes n'ayant pas déménagé	174
50	375	145	190	290	180	Personnes ayant déménagé	175
20	135	105	140	150	160	Non-migrants	176
30	245	40	50	140	15	Migrants	177
25	240	40	50	145	20	Migrants internes	178
25	155	25	50	115	15	Migrants infraprovinciaux	179
0	80	15	0	25	0	Migrants interprovinciaux	180
0	0	0	0	0	0	Migrants externes	181
175	**945**	**425**	**635**	**1,195**	**400**	**Population totale de 15 ans et plus**	182
						Plus haut certificat, diplôme ou grade[37]	
80	205	275	530	470	325	Aucun certificat, diplôme ou grade	183
95	740	150	105	720	75	Certificat, diplôme ou grade	184
35	310	40	20	335	45	Diplôme d'études secondaires ou l'équivalent[38]	185
15	140	60	40	135	10	Certificat ou diplôme d'apprenti ou d'une école de métiers	186
30	210	35	0	160	25	Certificat ou diplôme d'un collège, d'un cégep ou d'un autre établissement d'enseignement non universitaire[39]	187
0	35	10	30	30	0	Certificat ou diplôme universitaire inférieur au baccalauréat[40]	188
10	50	10	0	60	0	Certificat ou grade universitaire[41]	189
0	35	0	0	35	0	Baccalauréat	190
0	10	0	0	15	0	Certificat ou diplôme universitaire supérieur au baccalauréat	191
0	0	0	0	0	0	Diplôme en médecine, en art dentaire, en médecine vétérinaire ou en optométrie	192
0	10	10	0	10	0	Maîtrise	193
0	0	0	0	0	0	Doctorat acquis	194
60	**430**	**110**	**85**	**385**	**35**	**Population totale de 15 ans et plus avec titres du niveau postsecondaire**	195
						Principal domaine d'études - Classification des programmes d'enseignement, 2000[42]	
0	45	15	20	40	10	Éducation	196
0	10	0	0	10	0	Arts visuels et d'interprétation, et technologie des communications	197
0	10	0	10	0	10	Sciences humaines	198
10	30	10	0	15	0	Sciences sociales et de comportements, et droit	199
15	65	15	10	55	10	Commerce, gestion et administration publique	200
0	0	0	0	0	0	Sciences physiques et de la vie, et technologies	201
10	0	0	10	20	0	Mathématiques, informatique et sciences de l'information	202
10	140	35	10	130	10	Architecture, génie et services connexes	203
10	20	0	0	40	0	Agriculture, ressources naturelles et conservation	204
0	65	0	10	15	10	Santé, parcs, récréation et conditionnement physique	205
10	40	15	15	60	0	Services personnels, de protection et de transport	206
0	0	0	0	0	0	Autres domaines d'études[43]	207
						Lieu des études[44]	
60	420	110	80	385	35	À l'intérieur du Canada	208
0	10	0	0	10	0	À l'extérieur du Canada	209
175	**945**	**425**	**635**	**1,195**	**400**	**Population totale de 15 ans et plus**	210
						Travail non rémunéré	
100	475	225	315	620	210	Hommes de 15 ans et plus	211
90	425	190	260	570	200	Travail non rémunéré déclaré[45]	212
15	20	40	45	30	100	Travaux ménagers et soins aux enfants et soins ou aide aux personnes âgées	213
20	135	65	150	155	70	Travaux ménagers et soins aux enfants seulement	214

Nota : Voir les symboles et les abréviations dans les documents d'introduction et voir les documents de référence à la fin de la publication.

Selected characteristics for census divisions and census subdivisions – 100% data and 20% sample data, Ontario, 2006 Census (continued)

No.	Characteristics	Kawartha Lakes, CY ◆◇	Kenora CD/DR †◆◆◇◇	Bearskin Lake, IRI ◆◆◇◇	Cat Lake 63C, IRI ◆◇	Deer Lake, IRI ◆◆◇◇	Dryden, CY
	Population characteristics						
	Unpaid work (continued)						
215	Housework and care or assistance to seniors only	2,525	1,875	15	15	10	260
216	Child care and care or assistance to seniors only	20	100	0	0	0	0
217	Housework only	15,610	10,010	25	25	30	1,530
218	Child care only	150	285	10	10	35	10
219	Care or assistance to seniors only	115	130	0	0	0	10
220	Females 15 years and over	31,360	24,475	140	145	195	3,445
221	Reported unpaid work[45]	29,630	23,285	135	135	190	3,185
222	Housework and child care and care or assistance to seniors	3,450	4,060	65	45	55	365
223	Housework and child care only	7,750	7,950	45	50	95	970
224	Housework and care or assistance to seniors only	3,120	2,285	0	0	0	485
225	Child care and care or assistance to seniors only	20	45	0	0	0	0
226	Housework only	15,095	8,690	15	15	20	1,345
227	Child care only	90	185	0	10	10	0
228	Care or assistance to seniors only	95	50	0	0	0	10
	Labour force activity						
229	Males 15 years and over	30,095	24,385	155	145	220	3,180
230	In the labour force	20,015	16,515	110	70	120	2,130
231	Employed	18,745	14,915	105	55	95	1,985
232	Unemployed	1,270	1,605	0	15	25	150
233	Not in the labour force	10,085	7,870	50	75	100	1,055
234	Participation rate	66.5	67.7	71.0	48.3	54.5	67.0
235	Employment rate	62.3	61.2	67.7	37.9	43.2	62.4
236	Unemployment rate	6.3	9.7	0.0	21.4	20.8	7.0
237	Females 15 years and over	31,365	24,475	135	145	195	3,450
238	In the labour force	17,760	14,825	85	70	75	2,160
239	Employed	16,675	13,680	65	60	60	2,055
240	Unemployed	1,085	1,140	15	15	15	105
241	Not in the labour force	13,600	9,655	60	75	120	1,285
242	Participation rate	56.6	60.6	63.0	48.3	38.5	62.6
243	Employment rate	53.2	55.9	48.1	41.4	30.8	59.6
244	Unemployment rate	6.1	7.7	17.6	21.4	20.0	4.9
245	Both sexes - Participation rate	61.5	64.1	64.4	48.3	47.0	64.7
246	15 to 24 years	69.4	58.2	47.1	29.4	47.8	71.5
247	25 years and over	60.1	65.6	67.4	53.7	47.5	63.3
248	Both sexes - Employment rate	57.6	58.5	57.6	37.3	39.0	60.9
249	15 to 24 years	58.6	48.2	47.1	17.6	27.3	63.5
250	25 years and over	57.5	61.0	61.9	46.3	43.3	60.4
251	Both sexes - Unemployment rate	6.2	8.8	10.5	21.4	20.0	5.8
252	15 to 24 years	15.6	17.3	22.2	50.0	45.5	10.8
253	25 years and over	4.4	6.9	10.0	17.4	10.3	4.7
254	**Total labour force 15 years and over**	**37,780**	**31,340**	**190**	**140**	**195**	**4,290**
	Industry - North American Industry Classification System 2002						
255	Industry - Not applicable[46]	530	680	0	20	20	50
256	All industries[47]	37,250	30,660	190	120	180	4,240
257	11 Agriculture, forestry, fishing and hunting	1,425	1,255	0	0	0	200
258	21 Mining and oil and gas extraction	205	1,075	0	0	0	10
259	22 Utilities	495	390	10	10	10	60
260	23 Construction	3,515	1,725	10	0	25	145
261	31-33 Manufacturing	4,840	2,285	0	0	0	595
262	41 Wholesale trade	1,370	450	0	0	0	105
263	44-45 Retail trade	4,865	3,985	15	10	10	740
264	48-49 Transportation and warehousing	1,475	1,785	10	0	10	190
265	51 Information and cultural industries	460	335	0	0	10	60
266	52 Finance and insurance	925	610	0	0	0	80
267	53 Real estate and rental and leasing	590	315	0	0	0	40
268	54 Professional, scientific and technical services	1,595	655	0	0	0	115
269	55 Management of companies and enterprises	0	10	0	0	0	0
270	56 Administrative and support, waste management and remediation services	1,830	695	0	10	10	50
271	61 Educational services	2,270	2,590	25	25	25	300
272	62 Health care and social assistance	4,185	4,505	25	30	40	495

Note: See symbols and abbreviations in the introductory material and see reference material at the end of the publication.

Certaines caractéristiques des divisions de recensement et des subdivisions de recensement – Données intégrales et données-échantillon (20 %), Ontario, Recensement de 2006 (suite)

Eagle Lake 27, IRI	Ear Falls, TP ◆◊	English River 21, IRI ◆◊	Fort Hope 64, IRI ◆◆◊◊	Ignace, TP ◊	Kasabonika Lake, IRI	Caractéristiques	N°
						Caractéristiques de la population	
						Travail non rémunéré (suite)	
10	40	15	0	70	20	Travaux ménagers et soins ou aide aux personnes âgées seulement	215
0	0	10	0	10	0	Soins aux enfants et soins ou aide aux personnes âgées seulement	216
40	225	60	45	300	15	Travaux ménagers seulement	217
0	0	0	15	0	0	Soins aux enfants seulement	218
0	0	0	0	0	0	Soins ou aide aux personnes âgées seulement	219
75	470	205	320	575	195	Femmes de 15 ans et plus	220
70	445	185	295	570	195	Travail non rémunéré déclaré[45]	221
15	40	50	55	55	105	Travaux ménagers et soins aux enfants et soins ou aide aux personnes âgées	222
30	150	85	190	175	60	Travaux ménagers et soins aux enfants seulement	223
0	40	10	10	65	20	Travaux ménagers et soins ou aide aux personnes âgées seulement	224
0	0	0	0	10	0	Soins aux enfants et soins ou aide aux personnes âgées seulement	225
20	215	30	40	255	15	Travaux ménagers seulement	226
10	0	10	10	0	0	Soins aux enfants seulement	227
0	0	0	0	10	0	Soins ou aide aux personnes âgées seulement	228
						Activité	
95	475	225	315	620	210	Hommes de 15 ans et plus	229
55	360	130	130	450	140	Population active	230
45	335	80	85	410	125	Personnes occupées	231
15	25	45	45	35	15	Chômeurs	232
40	115	100	185	170	70	Inactifs	233
57.9	75.8	57.8	41.3	72.6	66.7	Taux d'activité	234
47.4	70.5	35.6	27.0	66.1	59.5	Taux d'emploi	235
27.3	6.9	34.6	34.6	7.8	10.7	Taux de chômage	236
80	470	205	320	570	195	Femmes de 15 ans et plus	237
40	355	105	100	350	75	Population active	238
30	360	75	80	305	65	Personnes occupées	239
10	0	30	25	45	10	Chômeuses	240
40	115	95	220	225	125	Inactives	241
50.0	75.5	51.2	31.2	61.4	38.5	Taux d'activité	242
37.5	76.6	36.6	25.0	53.5	33.3	Taux d'emploi	243
25.0	0.0	28.6	25.0	12.9	13.3	Taux de chômage	244
51.4	75.7	55.3	37.0	66.9	53.8	Les deux sexes - Taux d'activité	245
0.0	73.3	34.6	15.8	66.7	50.0	15 à 24 ans	246
64.3	76.2	64.4	45.6	67.5	56.1	25 ans et plus	247
42.9	73.5	36.5	25.0	60.3	47.5	Les deux sexes - Taux d'emploi	248
0.0	66.7	19.2	7.9	43.3	39.1	15 à 24 ans	249
50.0	74.4	44.1	32.6	62.7	50.0	25 ans et plus	250
21.1	2.8	34.0	30.4	10.6	9.5	Les deux sexes - Taux de chômage	251
100.0	9.1	44.4	33.3	36.8	18.2	15 à 24 ans	252
17.6	1.6	30.8	29.3	7.1	9.7	25 ans et plus	253
95	**715**	**235**	**235**	**805**	**210**	**Population active totale de 15 ans et plus**	254
						Industrie - Système de classification des industries de l'Amérique du Nord de 2002	
0	10	30	30	20	10	Industrie - Sans objet[46]	255
90	715	205	205	780	205	Toutes les industries[47]	256
10	115	10	10	165	0	11 Agriculture, foresterie, pêche et chasse	257
0	15	0	0	25	10	21 Extraction minière et extraction de pétrole et de gaz	258
0	15	0	10	0	10	22 Services publics	259
10	10	15	15	35	35	23 Construction	260
0	125	0	0	65	0	31-33 Fabrication	261
0	20	0	0	10	0	41 Commerce de gros	262
10	75	10	35	75	10	44-45 Commerce de détail	263
0	40	10	0	40	0	48-49 Transport et entreposage	264
0	0	0	0	10	0	51 Industrie de l'information et industrie culturelle	265
0	10	0	0	20	0	52 Finance et assurances	266
0	10	0	0	10	0	53 Services immobiliers et services de location et de location à bail	267
0	0	0	0	0	0	54 Services professionnels, scientifiques et techniques	268
0	0	0	0	0	0	55 Gestion de sociétés et d'entreprises	269
0	15	10	0	30	0	56 Services administratifs, services de soutien, services de gestion des déchets et services d'assainissement	270
10	70	50	30	55	25	61 Services d'enseignement	271
15	45	50	40	40	20	62 Soins de santé et assistance sociale	272

Nota : Voir les symboles et les abréviations dans les documents d'introduction et voir les documents de référence à la fin de la publication.

Selected characteristics for census divisions and census subdivisions – 100% data and 20% sample data, Ontario, 2006 Census (continued)

No.	Characteristics	Kawartha Lakes, CY ◆◊	**Kenora CD/DR** †◆◆◊◊	Bearskin Lake, IRI ◆◆◊◊	Cat Lake 63C, IRI ◆◊	Deer Lake, IRI ◆◆◊◊	Dryden, CY
	Population characteristics						
	Industry - North American Industry Classification System 2002 (continued)						
273	71 Arts, entertainment and recreation	1,050	375	0	0	0	15
274	72 Accommodation and food services	2,045	2,660	10	0	0	435
275	81 Other services (except public administration)	2,090	1,295	0	0	0	290
276	91 Public administration	2,005	3,660	85	25	40	295
	Class of worker						
277	Class of worker - Not applicable[46]	530	680	0	20	20	55
278	All classes of worker[47]	37,245	30,660	190	120	180	4,235
279	Paid workers	32,615	29,065	190	120	180	4,055
280	Employees	31,275	28,105	190	120	180	3,925
281	Self-employed (incorporated)	1,340	960	0	0	0	130
282	Self-employed (unincorporated)	4,460	1,525	0	0	0	170
283	Unpaid family workers	175	75	0	0	0	10
	Occupation - National Occupational Classification for Statistics 2006						
284	Male labour force 15 years and over	20,015	16,515	110	70	120	2,130
285	Occupation - Not applicable[46]	285	430	0	10	10	30
286	All occupations[47]	19,730	16,090	110	55	110	2,100
287	A Management occupations	2,155	1,495	15	10	10	225
288	B Business, finance and administrative occupations	1,110	700	10	0	10	130
289	C Natural and applied sciences and related occupations	965	1,145	0	0	0	200
290	D Health occupations	240	340	0	0	0	65
291	E Occupations in social science, education, government service and religion	795	1,025	10	10	15	50
292	F Occupations in art, culture, recreation and sport	235	135	0	0	0	10
293	G Sales and service occupations	3,640	3,350	15	25	25	405
294	H Trades, transport and equipment operators and related occupations	7,070	5,395	50	15	45	695
295	I Occupations unique to primary industry	1,510	1,510	0	10	0	100
296	J Occupations unique to processing, manufacturing and utilities	2,005	990	10	10	0	225
297	Female labour force 15 years and over	17,760	14,825	80	75	75	2,160
298	Occupation - Not applicable[46]	245	250	0	10	0	25
299	All occupations[47]	17,515	14,570	80	65	70	2,140
300	A Management occupations	1,110	1,170	10	10	0	185
301	B Business, finance and administrative occupations	3,980	3,210	10	10	15	510
302	C Natural and applied sciences and related occupations	170	270	0	0	0	40
303	D Health occupations	2,165	1,285	0	0	0	190
304	E Occupations in social science, education, government service and religion	1,745	2,480	25	20	15	275
305	F Occupations in art, culture, recreation and sport	485	155	0	0	0	20
306	G Sales and service occupations	6,095	5,185	25	25	25	815
307	H Trades, transport and equipment operators and related occupations	520	450	10	0	10	55
308	I Occupations unique to primary industry	450	150	0	0	0	15
309	J Occupations unique to processing, manufacturing and utilities	800	205	0	0	0	20
310	**Total employed labour force 15 years and over**	**35,420**	**28,590**	**175**	**110**	**160**	**4,040**
	Place of work status						
311	Males	18,745	14,915	105	55	100	1,985
312	Usual place of work	13,165	11,685	100	50	50	1,730
313	At home	2,160	715	0	0	0	65
314	Outside Canada	80	15	0	0	0	0
315	No fixed workplace address	3,345	2,495	0	0	40	185
316	Females	16,675	13,680	70	55	65	2,055
317	Usual place of work	13,895	12,120	70	55	50	1,895
318	At home	1,790	665	0	0	0	75
319	Outside Canada	35	0	0	0	0	0
320	No fixed workplace address	955	890	0	0	10	90

Note: See symbols and abbreviations in the introductory material and see reference material at the end of the publication.

Certaines caractéristiques des divisions de recensement et des subdivisions de recensement – Données intégrales et données-échantillon (20 %), Ontario, Recensement de 2006 (suite)

Eagle Lake 27, IRI	Ear Falls, TP ◆◇	English River 21, IRI ◆◇	Fort Hope 64, IRI ◆◆◇◇	Ignace, TP ◇	Kasabonika Lake, IRI	Caractéristiques	N°
						Caractéristiques de la population	
						Industrie - Système de classification des industries de l'Amérique du Nord de 2002 (suite)	
10	10	0	0	0	0	71 Arts, spectacles et loisirs	273
10	85	20	0	115	0	72 Hébergement et services de restauration	274
0	15	0	10	30	0	81 Autres services (sauf les administrations publiques)	275
25	35	40	45	40	80	91 Administrations publiques	276
						Catégorie de travailleurs	
0	0	30	25	25	10	Catégorie de travailleurs - Sans objet[46]	277
95	715	205	210	780	200	Toutes les catégories de travailleurs[47]	278
90	690	200	205	680	200	Travailleurs rémunérés	279
90	600	200	205	655	200	Employés	280
0	85	0	0	25	0	Travailleurs autonomes (entreprise constituée en société)	281
0	30	0	0	95	0	Travailleurs autonomes (entreprise non constituée en société)	282
0	0	0	0	10	0	Travailleurs familiaux non rémunérés	283
						Profession - Classification nationale des professions pour statistiques de 2006	
55	360	130	130	455	135	Hommes actifs de 15 ans et plus	284
10	0	15	20	0	0	Profession - Sans objet[46]	285
50	360	110	110	450	130	Toutes les professions[47]	286
10	20	0	15	15	10	A Gestion	287
10	0	0	0	30	10	B Affaires, finance et administration	288
0	30	0	0	10	0	C Sciences naturelles et appliquées et professions apparentées	289
0	10	0	0	0	0	D Secteur de la santé	290
0	10	25	15	10	0	E Sciences sociales, enseignement, administration publique et religion	291
0	0	0	0	0	0	F Arts, culture, sports et loisirs	292
15	45	40	35	65	15	G Ventes et services	293
10	95	20	20	175	80	H Métiers, transport et machinerie	294
10	90	10	25	115	0	I Professions propres au secteur primaire	295
0	55	10	0	30	10	J Transformation, fabrication et services d'utilité publique	296
40	360	110	100	350	75	Femmes actives de 15 ans et plus	297
0	0	20	10	20	0	Profession - Sans objet[46]	298
35	355	90	95	330	70	Toutes les professions[47]	299
0	35	10	10	30	10	A Gestion	300
0	100	10	25	70	10	B Affaires, finance et administration	301
0	0	0	0	0	0	C Sciences naturelles et appliquées et professions apparentées	302
0	15	0	0	0	0	D Secteur de la santé	303
10	40	35	20	25	20	E Sciences sociales, enseignement, administration publique et religion	304
0	0	0	0	0	0	F Arts, culture, sports et loisirs	305
10	110	30	40	175	25	G Ventes et services	306
0	20	10	0	10	10	H Métiers, transport et machinerie	307
0	0	0	0	0	0	I Professions propres au secteur primaire	308
10	25	0	0	10	0	J Transformation, fabrication et services d'utilité publique	309
75	**695**	**155**	**160**	**720**	**190**	**Population active occupée totale de 15 ans et plus**	310
						Catégorie de lieu de travail	
45	335	85	85	415	125	Hommes	311
30	240	75	65	285	110	Lieu habituel de travail	312
0	35	0	10	15	0	À domicile	313
0	0	0	0	0	0	En dehors du Canada	314
10	65	0	20	110	15	Sans adresse de travail fixe	315
30	355	75	75	305	65	Femmes	316
25	310	70	70	280	60	Lieu habituel de travail	317
0	35	0	0	15	0	À domicile	318
0	0	0	0	0	0	En dehors du Canada	319
0	10	0	10	10	0	Sans adresse de travail fixe	320

Nota : Voir les symboles et les abréviations dans les documents d'introduction et voir les documents de référence à la fin de la publication.

Selected characteristics for census divisions and census subdivisions – 100% data and 20% sample data, Ontario, 2006 Census (continued)

No.	Characteristics	Kawartha Lakes, CY ◆◇	**Kenora CD/DR** †◆◆◇◇	Bearskin Lake, IRI ◆◆◇◇	Cat Lake 63C, IRI ◆◇	Deer Lake, IRI ◆◆◇◇	Dryden, CY
	Population characteristics						
321	**Total employed labour force 15 years and over with usual place of work or no fixed workplace address**	**31,355**	**27,195**	**170**	**110**	**160**	**3,900**
	Mode of transportation						
322	Males	16,505	14,185	105	50	100	1,915
323	Car, truck, van, as driver	13,895	10,035	60	15	65	1,440
324	Car, truck, van, as passenger	1,580	1,205	20	10	20	180
325	Public transit	80	70	0	0	0	0
326	Walked	620	2,120	20	30	10	215
327	All other modes	335	745	10	10	0	75
328	Females	14,850	13,015	65	55	60	1,980
329	Car, truck, van, as driver	12,105	8,730	25	0	45	1,460
330	Car, truck, van, as passenger	1,300	1,605	20	0	10	200
331	Public transit	145	35	0	0	0	0
332	Walked	1,055	2,315	20	45	10	245
333	All other modes	245	330	0	10	0	70
334	**Total population 15 years and over who worked since January 1, 2005**	**40,625**	**34,495**	**230**	**150**	**235**	**4,735**
	Language used most often at work						
335	Single responses	40,570	34,340	230	150	235	4,715
336	English	40,460	32,405	120	85	220	4,710
337	French	45	70	0	0	0	10
338	Non-official languages[7]	65	1,865	110	65	20	0
339	Chinese, n.o.s.[61]	10	10	0	0	0	0
340	Cantonese	0	0	0	0	0	0
341	Other languages[8]	60	1,855	110	65	20	0
342	Multiple responses	50	155	0	0	0	15
343	English and French	10	35	0	0	0	10
344	English and non-official language	35	120	0	0	0	10
345	French and non-official language	0	0	0	0	0	0
346	English, French and non-official language	0	0	0	0	0	0
	Dwelling and household characteristics						
347	**Total number of occupied private dwellings**	**29,500**	**23,025**	**130**	**105**	**185**	**3,280**
	Housing tenure						
348	Owned	24,515	14,370	20	10	15	2,515
349	Rented	4,985	4,275	15	0	10	770
350	Band housing	0	4,375	95	95	160	0
	Structural type of dwelling						
351	Single-detached house	24,730	18,865	115	105	170	2,445
352	Semi-detached house	535	605	0	0	0	90
353	Row house	445	395	5	0	5	75
354	Apartment, duplex	655	485	5	0	0	35
355	Apartment, building that has five or more storeys	630	165	0	0	0	0
356	Apartment, building that has fewer than five storeys	2,240	1,455	0	0	0	355
357	Other single-attached house	135	180	0	0	0	80
358	Movable dwelling[48]	135	865	0	0	10	195
	Condition of dwelling						
359	Regular maintenance only	18,710	11,635	30	25	40	1,965
360	Minor repairs	8,615	7,170	55	20	60	1,020
361	Major repairs	2,170	4,220	45	65	85	295
	Period of construction						
362	Before 1946	6,300	2,370	0	0	0	295
363	1946 to 1960	3,290	3,705	0	0	10	695
364	1961 to 1970	3,550	2,775	0	10	10	725
365	1971 to 1980	5,525	4,270	15	15	45	675
366	1981 to 1985	2,145	2,200	30	25	25	235
367	1986 to 1990	3,360	2,270	15	10	30	235
368	1991 to 1995	2,040	2,050	15	10	25	165
369	1996 to 2000	1,495	1,885	30	30	25	175
370	2001 to 2006[49]	1,790	1,500	20	15	30	85

Note: See symbols and abbreviations in the introductory material and see reference material at the end of the publication.

Certaines caractéristiques des divisions de recensement et des subdivisions de recensement – Données intégrales et données-échantillon (20 %), Ontario, Recensement de 2006 (suite)

Eagle Lake 27, IRI	Ear Falls, TP ◆◊	English River 21, IRI ◆◊	Fort Hope 64, IRI ◆◆◊◊	Ignace, TP ◊	Kasabonika Lake, IRI	Caractéristiques	N°
						Caractéristiques de la population	
75	**625**	**150**	**160**	**680**	**190**	**Population active occupée totale de 15 ans et plus ayant un lieu habituel de travail ou sans adresse de travail fixe**	321
						Mode de transport	
40	305	80	80	395	125	Hommes	322
35	215	40	15	265	30	Automobile, camion ou fourgonnette, en tant que conducteur	323
0	45	0	0	55	0	Automobile, camion ou fourgonnette, en tant que passager	324
0	0	0	0	0	0	Transport en commun	325
10	35	25	50	45	80	À pied	326
0	10	0	15	30	0	Tous les autres modes	327
30	325	75	75	285	65	Femmes	328
15	200	35	0	230	0	Automobile, camion ou fourgonnette, en tant que conductrice	329
0	35	15	10	20	10	Automobile, camion ou fourgonnette, en tant que passagère	330
0	0	0	0	0	0	Transport en commun	331
0	75	25	75	35	45	À pied	332
0	10	0	0	0	10	Tous les autres modes	333
120	**780**	**245**	**290**	**855**	**215**	**Population totale de 15 ans et plus ayant travaillé depuis le 1er janvier 2005**	334
						Langue utilisée le plus souvent au travail	
120	780	240	295	850	220	Réponses uniques	335
110	770	210	270	835	60	Anglais	336
0	0	0	0	10	0	Français	337
10	10	30	25	0	155	Langues non officielles[7]	338
0	0	0	0	10	0	Chinois, n.d.a.[61]	339
0	0	0	0	0	0	Cantonais	340
0	10	35	20	0	155	Autres langues[8]	341
0	0	0	0	0	0	Réponses multiples	342
0	0	0	0	0	0	Anglais et français	343
0	0	0	10	0	0	Anglais et langue non officielle	344
0	0	0	0	0	0	Français et langue non officielle	345
0	0	0	0	0	0	Anglais, français et langue non officielle	346
						Caractéristiques des logements et des ménages	
90	**470**	**185**	**265**	**590**	**150**	**Nombre total de logements privés occupés**	347
						Mode d'occupation	
0	365	15	10	485	20	Possédé	348
20	105	10	75	100	0	Loué	349
60	0	165	185	0	130	Logement de bande	350
						Type de construction résidentielle	
85	355	180	255	470	150	Maison individuelle non attenante	351
0	50	0	15	20	0	Maison jumelée	352
0	15	0	0	0	0	Maison en rangée	353
0	0	0	0	5	0	Appartement, duplex	354
0	0	0	0	5	0	Appartement, immeuble de cinq étages ou plus	355
0	25	0	0	20	0	Appartement, immeuble de moins de cinq étages	356
0	10	0	0	5	0	Autre maison individuelle attenante	357
0	0	0	0	70	0	Logement mobile[48]	358
						État du logement	
20	280	30	130	310	50	Entretien régulier seulement	359
35	135	40	50	230	25	Réparations mineures	360
30	55	110	95	45	80	Réparations majeures	361
						Période de construction	
0	10	0	0	10	0	Avant 1946	362
0	60	10	0	85	0	1946 à 1960	363
0	105	0	20	75	10	1961 à 1970	364
10	190	45	45	325	20	1971 à 1980	365
10	25	25	45	45	20	1981 à 1985	366
10	20	25	20	15	25	1986 à 1990	367
25	20	20	35	15	25	1991 à 1995	368
10	25	30	60	0	30	1996 à 2000	369
10	15	10	50	10	25	2001 à 2006[49]	370

Nota : Voir les symboles et les abréviations dans les documents d'introduction et voir les documents de référence à la fin de la publication.

Selected characteristics for census divisions and census subdivisions – 100% data and 20% sample data, Ontario, 2006 Census (continued)

No.	Characteristics	Kawartha Lakes, CY ♦◊	**Kenora CD/DR** †♦♦◊◊	Bearskin Lake, IRI ♦♦◊◊	Cat Lake 63C, IRI ♦◊	Deer Lake, IRI ♦♦◊◊	Dryden, CY
	Dwelling and household characteristics						
371	Average number of rooms per dwelling	7.0	6.2	5.1	5.1	4.9	6.9
372	Average number of bedrooms per dwelling	2.9	2.8	2.9	3.0	2.4	2.8
373	Average value of dwelling $	245,161	171,056	0	0	0	171,993
374	**Total number of private households**	**29,505**	**23,015**	**125**	**110**	**185**	**3,285**
	Household size						
375	1 person	6,775	5,255	20	15	15	860
376	2 persons	11,935	7,435	25	15	35	1,145
377	3 persons	4,195	3,635	20	15	40	500
378	4 to 5 persons	5,915	5,320	35	30	70	725
379	6 or more persons	695	1,370	25	30	25	50
	Household type						
380	One-family households[50]	21,720	16,475	95	70	155	2,335
381	Multiple-family households	405	825	15	20	10	40
382	Non-family households	7,380	5,720	20	20	20	915
383	Number of persons in private households	73,155	63,725	460	495	680	8,025
384	Average number of persons in private households	2.5	2.8	3.7	4.5	3.7	2.4
385	Tenant-occupied private non-farm, non-reserve dwellings[51]	4,965	3,895	0	0	0	770
386	Average gross rent $[51]	749	655	0	0	0	653
387	Tenant-occupied households spending 30% or more of household income on gross rent[52]	2,590	1,345	0	0	0	305
388	Tenant-occupied households spending from 30% to 99% of household income on gross rent[52]	2,290	1,265	0	0	0	280
389	Owner-occupied private non-farm, non-reserve dwellings[53]	23,935	13,985	0	0	0	2,510
390	Average owner's major payments $[53]	935	846	0	0	0	916
391	Owner households spending 30% or more of household income on owner's major payments[52]	4,795	1,625	0	0	0	300
392	Owner households spending from 30% to 99% of household income on owner's major payments[52]	4,120	1,415	0	0	0	260
	Census family characteristics						
393	**Total number of census families in private households**	**22,530**	**18,215**	**115**	**105**	**175**	**2,410**
	Family structure and number of children						
394	Total couple families	19,875	14,660	85	75	145	2,045
395	Total families of married couples	16,920	11,255	55	40	105	1,745
396	Without children at home	9,265	4,945	10	10	15	800
397	With children at home	7,650	6,310	45	30	95	945
398	1 child	2,690	2,195	10	10	25	315
399	2 children	3,245	2,580	20	10	30	515
400	3 or more children	1,715	1,530	15	20	35	115
401	Total families of common-law couples	2,960	3,405	25	35	35	295
402	Without children at home	1,730	1,475	0	0	15	190
403	With children at home	1,225	1,925	25	30	20	110
404	1 child	545	790	10	10	10	50
405	2 children	480	640	10	10	10	25
406	3 or more children	200	500	0	20	0	30
407	Total lone-parent families	2,655	3,555	35	35	30	365
408	Female parent	2,090	2,645	25	30	15	300
409	1 child	1,170	1,390	15	20	10	155
410	2 children	650	810	10	10	10	125
411	3 or more children	270	445	0	10	0	20
412	Male parent	570	910	10	10	10	70
413	1 child	360	535	10	0	10	20
414	2 children	135	250	0	0	10	40
415	3 or more children	70	130	10	0	0	10

Note: See symbols and abbreviations in the introductory material and see reference material at the end of the publication.

Certaines caractéristiques des divisions de recensement et des subdivisions de recensement – Données intégrales et données-échantillon (20 %), Ontario, Recensement de 2006 (suite)

Eagle Lake 27, IRI	Ear Falls, TP ◆◊	English River 21, IRI ◆◊	Fort Hope 64, IRI ◆◆◊◊	Ignace, TP ◊	Kasabonika Lake, IRI	Caractéristiques	Nº
						Caractéristiques des logements et des ménages	
4.9	6.4	5.1	5.2	6.6	5.4	Nombre moyen de pièces par logement	371
2.3	2.8	2.6	2.9	3.0	2.9	Nombre moyen de chambres à coucher par logement	372
0	95,281	0	0	78,455	0	Valeur moyenne du logement $	373
90	**465**	**185**	**265**	**590**	**155**	**Nombre total de ménages privés**	374
						Taille du ménage	
20	100	35	30	130	20	1 personne	375
20	190	35	35	245	10	2 personnes	376
20	75	35	30	95	25	3 personnes	377
15	95	50	110	100	55	4 à 5 personnes	378
5	5	25	65	10	45	6 personnes ou plus	379
						Genre de ménage	
55	355	120	205	435	100	Ménages unifamiliaux[50]	380
0	0	20	30	10	30	Ménages multifamiliaux	381
30	110	45	35	150	25	Ménages non familiaux	382
230	1,145	635	1,145	1,430	680	Nombre de personnes dans les ménages privés	383
2.6	2.5	3.4	4.3	2.4	4.5	Nombre moyen de personnes dans les ménages privés	384
0	105	0	0	100	0	Ménages locataires dans les logements privés non agricoles hors réserve[51]	385
0	707	0	0	579	0	Loyer brut moyen $[51]	386
0	25	0	0	25	0	Ménages locataires consacrant 30 % ou plus du revenu du ménage au loyer brut[52]	387
0	10	0	0	20	0	Ménages locataires consacrant de 30 % à 99 % du revenu du ménage au loyer brut[52]	388
0	365	0	0	485	0	Ménages propriétaires dans les logements privés non agricoles hors réserve[53]	389
0	793	0	0	696	0	Principales dépenses de propriété moyennes $[53]	390
0	25	0	0	40	0	Ménages propriétaires consacrant 30 % ou plus du revenu du ménage aux principales dépenses de propriété[52]	391
0	25	0	0	35	0	Ménages propriétaires consacrant de 30 % à 99 % du revenu du ménage aux principales dépenses de propriété[52]	392
						Caractéristiques des familles de recensement	
60	**360**	**160**	**265**	**440**	**160**	**Nombre total de familles de recensement dans les ménages privés**	393
						Structure de la famille et le nombre d'enfants	
35	320	100	155	380	105	Total des familles avec conjoints	394
20	245	15	85	335	80	Total des familles avec couples mariés	395
10	125	10	20	195	10	Sans enfants à la maison	396
15	120	15	65	140	75	Avec enfants à la maison	397
10	35	0	10	65	20	1 enfant	398
0	60	0	15	50	20	2 enfants	399
0	30	0	45	25	35	3 enfants ou plus	400
20	75	75	70	45	25	Total des familles avec couples en union libre	401
10	25	25	0	10	10	Sans enfants à la maison	402
15	45	55	60	40	20	Avec enfants à la maison	403
10	30	20	0	20	10	1 enfant	404
10	15	10	20	20	10	2 enfants	405
10	0	25	30	0	0	3 enfants ou plus	406
25	35	65	115	60	55	Total des familles monoparentales	407
20	35	45	85	50	45	Parent de sexe féminin	408
10	20	20	30	20	20	1 enfant	409
10	10	15	20	25	10	2 enfants	410
0	0	10	40	0	15	3 enfants ou plus	411
10	10	25	25	10	15	Parent de sexe masculin	412
0	10	15	15	10	10	1 enfant	413
0	0	0	10	0	0	2 enfants	414
0	0	10	0	0	0	3 enfants ou plus	415

Nota : Voir les symboles et les abréviations dans les documents d'introduction et voir les documents de référence à la fin de la publication.

Selected characteristics for census divisions and census subdivisions – 100% data and 20% sample data, Ontario, 2006 Census (continued)

No.	Characteristics	Kawartha Lakes, CY ◆◇	**Kenora CD/DR** †◆◆◇◇	Bearskin Lake, IRI ◆◆◇◇	Cat Lake 63C, IRI ◆◇	Deer Lake, IRI ◆◆◇◇	Dryden, CY
	Census family characteristics						
416	**Total number of children at home**	**21,255**	**22,895**	**220**	**255**	**320**	**2,510**
	Age group						
417	Under 6 years	3,605	5,540	90	95	105	430
418	6 to 14 years	8,105	9,040	70	95	155	1,010
419	15 to 17 years	3,115	2,980	25	20	30	370
420	18 to 24 years	4,555	3,830	25	30	20	555
421	25 years and over	1,875	1,515	15	15	15	145
422	Average number of children at home per census family[54]	0.9	1.3	1.8	2.3	1.9	1.0
423	**Total number of persons in private households**	**73,140**	**63,740**	**455**	**490**	**680**	**8,030**
	Census family status and living arrangements						
424	Number of persons not in census families	9,475	7,960	35	55	40	1,060
425	Living with relatives[55]	1,095	1,805	20	35	15	115
426	Living with non-relatives only	1,605	900	0	0	0	90
427	Living alone	6,780	5,250	20	20	20	860
428	Number of census family persons	63,665	55,775	420	440	640	6,970
429	Average number of persons per census family	2.8	3.1	3.5	4.2	3.7	2.9
430	**Total number of persons aged 65 years and over**	**13,565**	**6,755**	**30**	**15**	**15**	**1,210**
431	Number of persons not in census families aged 65 years and over	4,105	2,325	15	0	10	425
432	Living with relatives[55]	465	265	0	0	0	55
433	Living with non-relatives only	230	85	0	0	0	10
434	Living alone	3,405	1,975	10	0	0	370
435	Number of census family persons aged 65 years and over	9,460	4,425	20	15	10	780
	Economic family characteristics						
436	**Total number of economic families in private households**	**22,255**	**17,535**	**105**	**90**	**165**	**2,395**
	Size of family						
437	2 persons	11,710	7,335	25	15	35	1,130
438	3 persons	4,140	3,635	20	15	35	500
439	4 persons	4,100	3,565	20	15	40	575
440	5 or more persons	2,310	3,000	40	50	50	195
441	Total number of persons in economic families	64,755	57,585	440	470	660	7,085
442	Average number of persons per economic family	3.0	3.0	4.0	5.0	4.0	3.0
443	Total number of persons not in economic families	8,385	6,155	20	20	20	945
	2005 income characteristics						
444	**Population 15 years and over**	**61,460**	**48,860**	**300**	**290**	**415**	**6,635**
	Sex and total income groups in 2005						
445	Without income	2,790	1,975	10	20	15	235
446	With income	58,665	46,890	285	275	395	6,395
447	Under $1,000[56]	2,090	2,910	25	60	80	155
448	$1,000 to $2,999	1,965	2,010	15	20	30	190
449	$3,000 to $4,999	2,065	2,015	15	30	25	230
450	$5,000 to $6,999	2,115	1,940	10	10	20	205
451	$7,000 to $9,999	3,515	2,690	15	25	40	360
452	$10,000 to $11,999	2,585	2,005	10	15	25	195
453	$12,000 to $14,999	3,810	2,975	30	25	40	310
454	$15,000 to $19,999	6,445	4,335	35	25	35	700
455	$20,000 to $24,999	4,750	3,445	35	25	25	495
456	$25,000 to $29,999	4,180	3,145	25	15	15	305
457	$30,000 to $34,999	4,165	2,950	25	10	15	460
458	$35,000 to $39,999	3,665	2,445	10	0	15	330
459	$40,000 to $44,999	3,195	2,510	10	0	15	410
460	$45,000 to $49,999	2,390	2,000	0	0	0	300
461	$50,000 to $59,999	3,675	2,915	10	0	10	385
462	$60,000 and over	8,055	6,590	0	10	10	1,340
463	Median income $[57]	25,005	23,667	15,712	9,248	10,272	30,305
464	Average income $[57]	33,022	31,220	19,091	13,312	14,736	37,246
465	Standard error of average income $[57]	385	159	0	0	0	862

Note: See symbols and abbreviations in the introductory material and see reference material at the end of the publication.

Certaines caractéristiques des divisions de recensement et des subdivisions de recensement – Données intégrales et données-échantillon (20 %), Ontario, Recensement de 2006 (suite)

Eagle Lake 27, IRI	Ear Falls, TP ◆◊	English River 21, IRI ◆◊	Fort Hope 64, IRI ◆◆◊◊	Ignace, TP ◊	Kasabonika Lake, IRI	Caractéristiques	N°
						Caractéristiques des familles de recensement	
90	**345**	**280**	**640**	**405**	**355**	**Nombre total d'enfants à la maison**	416
						Groupes d'âge	
20	70	80	210	70	115	Moins de 6 ans	417
35	135	115	280	160	150	6 à 14 ans	418
15	50	30	60	65	25	15 à 17 ans	419
15	70	35	60	60	40	18 à 24 ans	420
10	20	15	30	50	20	25 ans et plus	421
1.4	1.0	1.7	2.4	0.9	2.1	Nombre moyen d'enfants à la maison par famille de recensement[54]	422
235	**1,150**	**635**	**1,145**	**1,430**	**685**	**Nombre total de personnes dans les ménages privés**	423
						Situation des particuliers dans la famille de recensement et des particuliers dans le ménage	
45	125	95	85	200	60	Nombre de personnes hors famille de recensement	424
20	10	55	45	40	40	Vivant avec des personnes apparentées[55]	425
0	25	0	10	30	0	Vivant avec des personnes non apparentées seulement	426
25	95	35	30	125	15	Vivant seules	427
185	1,025	540	1,060	1,230	620	Nombre de membres d'une famille de recensement	428
3.2	2.9	3.4	4.0	2.8	3.8	Nombre moyen de personnes par famille de recensement	429
10	**115**	**20**	**40**	**185**	**35**	**Nombre total de personnes âgées de 65 ans et plus**	430
10	20	15	10	50	10	Nombre de personnes hors famille de recensement âgées de 65 ans et plus	431
0	0	10	0	10	0	Vivant avec des personnes apparentées[55]	432
0	0	0	0	0	0	Vivant avec des personnes non apparentées seulement	433
0	20	10	0	40	0	Vivant seules	434
10	95	10	30	135	30	Nombre de membres d'une famille de recensement âgés de 65 ans et plus	435
						Caractéristiques des familles économiques	
60	**360**	**150**	**240**	**450**	**135**	**Nombre total de familles économiques dans les ménages privés**	436
						Taille de la famille	
20	185	30	35	235	15	2 personnes	437
25	75	35	30	115	25	3 personnes	438
10	75	25	40	70	35	4 personnes	439
10	25	55	125	30	65	5 personnes ou plus	440
205	1,030	590	1,110	1,270	660	Nombre total de personnes dans les familles économiques	441
3.0	3.0	4.0	5.0	3.0	5.0	Nombre moyen de personnes par famille économique	442
30	120	40	35	160	20	Nombre total de personnes hors famille économique	443
						Caractéristiques du revenu de 2005	
X	**945**	**430**	**635**	**1,195**	**405**	**Population de 15 ans et plus**	444
						Sexe et groupes de revenu total en 2005	
X	25	20	35	40	15	Sans revenu	445
X	920	405	595	1,155	385	Avec un revenu	446
X	20	95	125	50	55	Moins de 1 000 $[56]	447
X	20	50	45	80	50	1 000 $ à 2 999 $	448
X	50	45	40	80	35	3 000 $ à 4 999 $	449
X	25	25	40	25	20	5 000 $ à 6 999 $	450
X	35	25	45	35	35	7 000 $ à 9 999 $	451
X	35	20	35	50	30	10 000 $ à 11 999 $	452
X	70	30	55	85	40	12 000 $ à 14 999 $	453
X	55	25	55	150	30	15 000 $ à 19 999 $	454
X	40	30	45	80	30	20 000 $ à 24 999 $	455
X	50	15	35	60	20	25 000 $ à 29 999 $	456
X	40	15	25	65	20	30 000 $ à 34 999 $	457
X	15	20	25	45	15	35 000 $ à 39 999 $	458
X	80	0	15	35	10	40 000 $ à 44 999 $	459
X	60	0	10	25	0	45 000 $ à 49 999$	460
X	95	0	10	70	0	50 000 $ à 59 999$	461
X	225	0	0	220	10	60 000 $ et plus	462
X	39,149	6,136	10,187	20,602	10,123	Revenu médian $[57]	463
X	39,521	11,599	13,153	30,538	13,150	Revenu moyen $[57]	464
X	1,812	0	0	1,469	0	Erreur type de revenu moyen $[57]	465

Nota : Voir les symboles et les abréviations dans les documents d'introduction et voir les documents de référence à la fin de la publication.

Selected characteristics for census divisions and census subdivisions – 100% data and 20% sample data, Ontario, 2006 Census (continued)

No.	Characteristics	Kawartha Lakes, CY ◆◊	**Kenora CD/DR** †◆◆◊◊	Bearskin Lake, IRI ◆◆◊◊	Cat Lake 63C, IRI ◆◊	Deer Lake, IRI ◆◆◊◊	Dryden, CY
	2005 income characteristics						
	Sex and total income groups in 2005 (continued)						
466	Total - Males	30,095	24,385	155	145	225	3,180
467	Without income	1,280	925	10	0	15	150
468	With income	28,815	23,460	150	140	210	3,035
469	Under $1,000[56]	1,010	1,715	20	35	50	60
470	$1,000 to $2,999	770	985	10	10	20	85
471	$3,000 to $4,999	785	855	10	20	0	105
472	$5,000 to $6,999	730	755	0	0	10	80
473	$7,000 to $9,999	1,170	980	10	15	15	110
474	$10,000 to $11,999	870	860	0	10	10	70
475	$12,000 to $14,999	1,310	1,110	20	10	25	80
476	$15,000 to $19,999	2,585	1,685	25	15	15	155
477	$20,000 to $24,999	1,950	1,320	10	10	20	125
478	$25,000 to $29,999	1,815	1,345	10	0	0	90
479	$30,000 to $34,999	2,180	1,370	15	0	10	210
480	$35,000 to $39,999	2,095	1,150	0	10	10	165
481	$40,000 to $44,999	1,845	1,320	0	0	10	250
482	$45,000 to $49,999	1,380	1,205	0	0	0	195
483	$50,000 to $59,999	2,585	1,935	10	0	0	275
484	$60,000 and over	5,740	4,870	0	0	0	975
485	Median income $[57]	33,230	30,335	15,808	8,080	9,856	43,884
486	Average income $[57]	40,480	37,326	20,012	11,829	13,152	48,407
487	Standard error of average income $[57]	672	262	0	0	0	1,473
488	Total - Females	31,365	24,480	140	145	195	3,450
489	Without income	1,510	1,050	0	10	10	85
490	With income	29,850	23,425	130	135	190	3,365
491	Under $1,000[56]	1,075	1,200	10	25	30	95
492	$1,000 to $2,999	1,200	1,020	10	10	10	105
493	$3,000 to $4,999	1,275	1,155	10	10	20	130
494	$5,000 to $6,999	1,385	1,190	10	0	15	125
495	$7,000 to $9,999	2,345	1,715	10	10	20	255
496	$10,000 to $11,999	1,710	1,145	0	10	10	125
497	$12,000 to $14,999	2,505	1,865	10	15	20	230
498	$15,000 to $19,999	3,860	2,650	10	10	15	545
499	$20,000 to $24,999	2,800	2,130	25	20	10	370
500	$25,000 to $29,999	2,360	1,800	15	10	10	215
501	$30,000 to $34,999	1,985	1,585	10	10	10	255
502	$35,000 to $39,999	1,570	1,295	0	10	10	165
503	$40,000 to $44,999	1,350	1,185	0	0	10	165
504	$45,000 to $49,999	1,015	795	0	0	0	105
505	$50,000 to $59,999	1,095	980	0	10	10	105
506	$60,000 and over	2,310	1,720	10	0	0	365
507	Median income $[57]	19,334	19,541	15,712	12,000	10,416	21,159
508	Average income $[57]	25,823	25,103	18,039	14,840	16,497	27,181
509	Standard error of average income $[57]	374	166	0	0	0	794
	Composition of total income						
510	Composition of total income in 2005 %	100.0	100.0	100.0	100.0	100.0	100.0
511	Employment income %	67.7	75.9	79.6	65.4	77.7	75.6
512	Government transfer payments %	14.1	13.3	20.9	32.5	21.7	10.9
513	Other %	18.2	10.8	0.2	0.8	1.1	13.5
514	**Population 15 years and over with employment income in 2005**	**40,885**	**34,485**	**210**	**160**	**255**	**4,840**
	Sex and work activity						
515	Median employment income in 2005 $	23,761	24,504	17,952	10,848	13,216	29,701
516	Average employment income in 2005 $	32,079	32,231	20,150	15,451	17,384	37,199
517	Standard error of average employment income $	496	208	0	0	0	1,089
518	Worked full year, full time[59]	20,610	16,915	95	60	90	2,505
519	Median employment income in 2005 $	39,933	41,376	26,048	17,888	24,768	50,109
520	Average employment income in 2005 $	45,551	47,304	30,209	21,853	26,464	56,255
521	Standard error of average employment income $	549	331	0	0	0	1,571
522	Worked part year or part time[60]	16,785	14,640	100	55	100	2,040
523	Median employment income in 2005 $	11,710	10,946	11,040	10,976	11,904	11,164
524	Average employment income in 2005 $	20,597	19,704	11,799	15,305	14,206	18,283
525	Standard error of average employment income $	903	244	0	0	0	882
526	Males 15 years and over with employment income[58]	21,755	18,120	115	75	135	2,455
527	Median employment income in 2005 $	30,349	30,061	16,352	10,400	12,576	41,014
528	Average employment income in 2005 $	38,215	38,027	22,018	15,930	16,455	47,068
529	Standard error of average employment income $	847	334	0	0	0	1,801

Note: See symbols and abbreviations in the introductory material and see reference material at the end of the publication.

Certaines caractéristiques des divisions de recensement et des subdivisions de recensement – Données intégrales et données-échantillon (20 %), Ontario, Recensement de 2006 (suite)

Eagle Lake 27, IRI	Ear Falls, TP ◆◇	English River 21, IRI ◆◇	Fort Hope 64, IRI ◆◆◇◇	Ignace, TP ◇	Kasabonika Lake, IRI	Caractéristiques	N°
						Caractéristiques du revenu de 2005	
						Sexe et groupes de revenu total en 2005 (suite)	
X	475	225	315	625	210	Total - Hommes	466
X	0	10	30	10	10	Sans revenu	467
X	475	220	290	620	200	Avec un revenu	468
X	10	55	75	30	35	Moins de 1 000 $[56]	469
X	10	30	30	25	30	1 000 $ à 2 999 $	470
X	0	30	20	35	20	3 000 $ à 4 999 $	471
X	10	10	15	0	10	5 000 $ à 6 999 $	472
X	20	10	15	15	15	7 000 $ à 9 999 $	473
X	10	15	20	20	10	10 000 $ à 11 999 $	474
X	20	25	15	15	20	12 000 $ à 14 999 $	475
X	30	0	25	70	20	15 000 $ à 19 999 $	476
X	25	10	20	30	15	20 000 $ à 24 999 $	477
X	20	0	15	30	10	25 000 $ à 29 999 $	478
X	25	10	10	55	10	30 000 $ à 34 999 $	479
X	10	10	10	35	0	35 000 $ à 39 999 $	480
X	50	10	10	10	0	40 000 $ à $44 999 $	481
X	10	0	10	15	0	45 000 $ à $49 999 $	482
X	50	0	0	60	0	50 000 $ à $59 999 $	483
X	190	0	0	185	0	60 000 $ et plus	484
X	52,622	3,832	6,416	33,598	9,824	Revenu médian $[57]	485
X	49,790	9,863	12,140	39,543	12,376	Revenu moyen $[57]	486
X	2,591	0	0	2,147	0	Erreur type de revenu moyen $[57]	487
X	470	205	320	575	195	Total - Femmes	488
X	25	15	15	35	0	Sans revenu	489
X	450	190	310	535	190	Avec un revenu	490
X	10	40	45	20	25	Moins de 1 000 $[56]	491
X	15	20	10	50	20	1 000$ à 2 999 $	492
X	50	10	20	45	15	3 000 $ à 4 999 $	493
X	15	15	20	30	15	5 000 $ à 6 999 $	494
X	15	10	30	20	15	7 000 $ à 9 999 $	495
X	25	10	20	30	15	10 000 $ à 11 999 $	496
X	55	0	40	70	20	12 000 $ à 14 999 $	497
X	25	15	25	75	15	15 000 $ à 19 999 $	498
X	10	20	30	50	15	20 000 $ à 24 999 $	499
X	35	10	20	25	10	25 000 $ à 29 999 $	500
X	20	0	15	10	10	30 000 $ à 34 999 $	501
X	10	10	10	10	10	35 000 $ à 39 999 $	502
X	30	0	0	30	0	40 000 $ à 44 999 $	503
X	45	0	0	15	0	45 000 $ à 49 999 $	504
X	45	10	0	10	0	50 000 $ à 59 999 $	505
X	30	0	0	35	0	60 000 $ et plus	506
X	23,822	7,840	12,000	14,894	10,384	Revenu médian $[57]	507
X	28,639	13,630	14,104	20,147	13,944	Revenu moyen $[57]	508
X	2,106	0	0	1,548	0	Erreur type de revenu moyen $[57]	509
						Composition du revenu total	
X	100.0	100.0	100.0	100.0	100.0	Composition du revenu total en 2005 %	510
X	82.3	68.1	62.6	73.3	65.0	Revenu d'emploi %	511
X	8.8	30.8	36.7	16.3	34.2	Transferts gouvernementaux %	512
X	8.9	1.0	0.4	10.3	1.0	Autres %	513
X	**770**	**200**	**360**	**825**	**235**	**Population de 15 ans et plus avec un revenu d'emploi en 2005**	514
						Sexe et travail	
X	39,045	12,256	8,373	19,302	10,144	Revenu médian d'emploi en 2005 $	515
X	38,843	16,194	13,799	31,347	14,012	Revenu moyen d'emploi en 2005 $	516
X	2,055	0	0	1,872	0	Erreur type de revenu moyen d'emploi $	517
X	425	80	120	440	75	A travaillé toute l'année à plein temps[59]	518
X	50,157	26,112	24,768	51,349	28,587	Revenu médian d'emploi en 2005 $	519
X	54,116	28,159	24,960	47,279	27,262	Revenu moyen d'emploi en 2005 $	520
X	2,209	0	0	2,495	0	Erreur type de revenu moyen d'emploi $	521
X	295	95	125	345	105	A travaillé une partie de l'année ou à temps partiel[60]	522
X	10,443	5,008	5,888	8,189	5,328	Revenu médian d'emploi en 2005 $	523
X	22,084	8,410	9,291	13,666	8,911	Revenu moyen d'emploi en 2005 $	524
X	2,777	0	0	1,798	0	Erreur type de revenu moyen d'emploi $	525
X	385	110	185	480	135	Hommes de 15 ans et plus avec un revenu d'emploi[58]	526
X	52,680	9,728	8,832	34,573	10,112	Revenu médian d'emploi en 2005 $	527
X	50,220	13,909	14,538	38,791	13,328	Revenu moyen d'emploi en 2005 $	528
X	3,041	0	0	2,610	0	Erreur type de revenu moyen d'emploi $	529

Nota : Voir les symboles et les abréviations dans les documents d'introduction et voir les documents de référence à la fin de la publication.

Selected characteristics for census divisions and census subdivisions – 100% data and 20% sample data, Ontario, 2006 Census (continued)

No.	Characteristics	Kawartha Lakes, CY ◆◇	**Kenora CD/DR** †◆◆◇◇	Bearskin Lake, IRI ◆◆◇◇	Cat Lake 63C, IRI ◆◇	Deer Lake, IRI ◆◆◇◇	Dryden, CY
	2005 income characteristics						
	Sex and work activity (continued)						
530	Worked full year, full time[59]	12,235	9,485	45	30	45	1,480
531	Median employment income in 2005 $	44,764	48,989	33,728	16,032	24,640	64,286
532	Average employment income in 2005 $	50,686	54,498	36,173	21,125	25,388	67,139
533	Standard error of average employment income $	821	514	0	0	0	2,267
534	Worked part year or part time[60]	7,560	7,125	60	25	60	825
535	Median employment income in 2005 $	13,778	11,818	11,147	8,288	11,200	10,662
536	Average employment income in 2005 $	26,200	22,473	11,507	14,787	12,695	18,099
537	Standard error of average employment income $	1,929	390	0	0	0	1,444
538	Females 15 years and over with employment income[58]	19,125	16,365	100	85	120	2,380
539	Median employment income in 2005 $	18,735	20,667	19,104	11,296	16,811	22,170
540	Average employment income in 2005 $	25,100	25,812	17,999	15,007	18,461	27,020
541	Standard error of average employment income $	425	223	0	0	0	1,011
542	Worked full year, full time[59]	8,375	7,430	50	30	45	1,025
543	Median employment income in 2005 $	34,121	34,688	23,968	18,624	27,456	37,110
544	Average employment income in 2005 $	38,046	38,122	24,488	22,660	27,564	40,492
545	Standard error of average employment income $	586	347	0	0	0	1,466
546	Worked part year or part time[60]	9,225	7,515	35	25	40	1,215
547	Median employment income in 2005 $	10,256	10,304	7,360	13,088	15,360	12,428
548	Average employment income in 2005 $	16,006	17,080	12,268	15,862	16,398	18,407
549	Standard error of average employment income $	449	278	0	0	0	1,110
550	**Total number of economic families in private households**	**22,260**	**17,535**	**105**	**90**	**170**	**2,395**
	Family income groups in 2005						
551	Under $10,000	480	670	0	10	30	10
552	$10,000 to $19,999	845	1,065	10	10	25	100
553	$20,000 to $29,999	1,925	1,515	10	20	30	110
554	$30,000 to $39,999	2,385	1,745	25	15	15	130
555	$40,000 to $49,999	2,320	1,735	10	15	25	205
556	$50,000 to $59,999	2,340	1,525	15	10	20	230
557	$60,000 to $69,999	2,150	1,400	10	0	10	190
558	$70,000 to $79,999	2,050	1,420	0	0	10	265
559	$80,000 to $89,999	1,695	1,325	10	0	10	185
560	$90,000 to $99,999	1,205	1,135	0	10	0	165
561	$100,000 and over	4,860	4,005	0	0	0	795
562	Median family income $	63,782	63,969	43,008	30,784	28,096	78,529
563	Average family income $	75,609	71,757	47,778	33,783	33,168	85,207
564	Standard error of average family income $	1,083	428	0	0	0	2,149
	Family after-tax income groups in 2005						
565	Under $10,000	500	690	10	15	35	10
566	$10,000 to $19,999	865	1,075	15	10	25	100
567	$20,000 to $29,999	2,160	1,630	10	25	30	130
568	$30,000 to $39,999	3,050	2,005	25	15	15	210
569	$40,000 to $49,999	3,070	2,240	10	15	25	295
570	$50,000 to $59,999	2,815	1,775	15	10	20	225
571	$60,000 to $69,999	2,670	1,865	10	10	10	320
572	$70,000 to $79,999	1,995	1,790	10	0	0	300
573	$80,000 to $89,999	1,280	1,235	10	0	0	240
574	$90,000 to $99,999	1,025	1,065	0	0	0	155
575	$100,000 and over	2,830	2,150	0	0	0	405
576	Median after-tax family income $	55,046	56,399	43,008	30,784	28,096	65,231
577	Average after-tax family income $	62,766	61,050	47,236	33,262	32,921	69,853
578	Standard error of average after-tax family income $	761	313	0	0	0	1,544
	Income status in 2005						
579	Total population in private households for income status	73,110	44,155	0	0	0	8,030
580	Below low income cut-off before tax in 2005	7,515	3,195	0	0	0	605
581	Prevalence of low income before tax in 2005 %	10.3	7.2	0.0	0.0	0.0	7.6
582	Below low income cut-off after tax in 2005	5,070	1,865	0	0	0	315
583	Prevalence of low income after tax in 2005 %	6.9	4.2	0.0	0.0	0.0	3.9

Note: See symbols and abbreviations in the introductory material and see reference material at the end of the publication.

Certaines caractéristiques des divisions de recensement et des subdivisions de recensement – Données intégrales et données-échantillon (20 %), Ontario, Recensement de 2006 (suite)

Eagle Lake 27, IRI	Ear Falls, TP ◆◇	English River 21, IRI ◆◇	Fort Hope 64, IRI ◆◆◇◇	Ignace, TP ◇	Kasabonika Lake, IRI	Caractéristiques	N°
						Caractéristiques du revenu de 2005	
						Sexe et travail (suite)	
X	250	35	60	290	40	A travaillé toute l'année à plein temps[59]	530
X	64,730	21,824	28,224	59,312	27,328	Revenu médian d'emploi en 2005 $	531
X	61,283	25,931	28,167	54,137	26,723	Revenu moyen d'emploi en 2005 $	532
X	3,007	0	0	3,076	0	Erreur type de revenu moyen d'emploi $	533
X	125	65	70	165	80	A travaillé une partie de l'année ou à temps partiel[60]	534
X	29,828	5,008	5,872	8,465	7,248	Revenu médian d'emploi en 2005 $	535
X	32,823	8,623	10,182	15,727	9,189	Revenu moyen d'emploi en 2005 $	536
X	5,191	0	0	2,789	0	Erreur type de revenu moyen d'emploi $	537
X	390	85	170	345	100	Femmes de 15 ans et plus avec un revenu d'emploi[58]	538
X	23,256	17,024	8,368	12,032	10,592	Revenu médian d'emploi en 2005 $	539
X	27,500	19,103	13,014	20,960	14,965	Revenu moyen d'emploi en 2005 $	540
X	2,269	0	0	2,171	0	Erreur type de revenu moyen d'emploi $	541
X	175	45	65	150	35	A travaillé toute l'année à plein temps[59]	542
X	45,346	27,136	20,704	30,005	28,640	Revenu médian d'emploi en 2005 $	543
X	43,917	29,982	22,148	33,904	27,829	Revenu moyen d'emploi en 2005 $	544
X	2,603	0	0	3,307	0	Erreur type de revenu moyen d'emploi $	545
X	175	30	50	180	25	A travaillé une partie de l'année ou à temps partiel[60]	546
X	8,247	5,008	6,000	7,831	3,496	Revenu médian d'emploi en 2005 $	547
X	14,604	7,976	8,098	11,735	8,031	Revenu moyen d'emploi en 2005 $	548
X	2,436	0	0	2,221	0	Erreur type de revenu moyen d'emploi $	549
X	**365**	**145**	**240**	**450**	**135**	**Nombre total des familles économiques dans les ménages privés**	550
						Revenu de la famille économique en 2005	
X	0	35	40	0	10	Moins de 10 000 $	551
X	10	30	50	30	20	10 000 $ à 19 999 $	552
X	10	15	35	35	25	20 000 $ à 29 999 $	553
X	15	20	45	65	35	30 000 $ à 39 999 $	554
X	35	10	30	20	20	40 000 $ à 49 999 $	555
X	35	20	20	40	10	50 000 $ à 59 999 $	556
X	40	10	15	50	10	60 000 $ à 69 999 $	557
X	10	0	10	65	10	70 000 $ à 79 999 $	558
X	45	0	0	35	0	80 000 $ à 89 999 $	559
X	30	0	0	20	0	90 000 $ à 99 999 $	560
X	135	0	0	85	0	100 000 $ et plus	561
X	86,440	21,568	27,968	67,189	32,704	Revenu médian des familles $	562
X	87,432	28,978	30,845	66,366	35,337	Revenu moyen des familles $	563
X	4,334	0	0	3,209	0	Erreur type de revenu moyen des familles $	564
						Revenu après impôt de la famille économique en 2005	
X	10	40	40	0	10	Moins de 10 000 $	565
X	10	35	50	30	20	10 000 $ à 19 999 $	566
X	10	15	35	40	30	20 000 $ à 29 999 $	567
X	15	20	40	70	30	30 000 $ à 39 999 $	568
X	65	10	25	50	20	40 000 $ à 49 999 $	569
X	35	15	25	60	15	50 000 $ à 59 999 $	570
X	40	10	15	80	10	60 000 $ à 69 999 $	571
X	35	10	10	10	0	70 000 $ à 79 999 $	572
X	40	0	0	40	0	80 000 $ à 89 999 $	573
X	45	0	0	35	0	90 000 $ à 99 999 $	574
X	60	0	0	25	0	100 000 $ et plus	575
X	68,574	21,568	27,968	56,687	32,704	Revenu médian après impôt des familles $	576
X	72,311	28,797	30,788	56,438	35,336	Revenu moyen après impôt des familles $	577
X	3,262	0	0	2,459	0	Erreur type de revenu moyen après impôt des familles $	578
						Catégorie de revenu en 2005	
X	1,150	0	0	1,430	0	Population totale dans les ménages privés pour la catégorie de revenu	579
X	55	0	0	85	0	Au-dessous du seuil de faible revenu avant impôt en 2005	580
X	4.8	0.0	0.0	5.6	0.0	Fréquence du faible revenu avant impôt en 2005 %	581
X	40	0	0	60	0	Au-dessous du seuil de faible revenu après impôt en 2005	582
X	3.5	0.0	0.0	4.2	0.0	Fréquence du faible revenu après impôt en 2005 %	583

Nota : Voir les symboles et les abréviations dans les documents d'introduction et voir les documents de référence à la fin de la publication.

Selected characteristics for census divisions and census subdivisions – 100% data and 20% sample data, Ontario, 2006 Census (continued)

No.	Characteristics	Kawartha Lakes, CY ◆◇	**Kenora CD/DR** †◆◆◇◇	Bearskin Lake, IRI ◆◆◇◇	Cat Lake 63C, IRI ◆◇	Deer Lake, IRI ◆◆◇◇	Dryden, CY
	2005 income characteristics						
584	**Total number of private households**	**29,500**	**23,020**	**125**	**110**	**180**	**3,280**
	Household income groups in 2005						
585	Under $10,000	1,125	1,255	10	20	40	75
586	$10,000 to $19,999	2,830	2,470	20	10	35	305
587	$20,000 to $29,999	3,285	2,380	10	20	35	250
588	$30,000 to $39,999	3,410	2,490	20	20	15	255
589	$40,000 to $49,999	3,040	2,350	10	15	25	340
590	$50,000 to $59,999	2,875	1,930	15	15	20	300
591	$60,000 to $69,999	2,395	1,765	10	10	0	260
592	$70,000 to $79,999	2,290	1,585	10	10	10	290
593	$80,000 to $89,999	1,835	1,420	10	0	0	205
594	$90,000 to $99,999	1,340	1,195	0	10	0	195
595	$100,000 and over	5,075	4,180	0	0	10	810
596	Median household income $	52,955	52,750	36,224	30,784	26,880	64,237
597	Average household income $	65,549	63,297	42,843	33,220	31,634	72,443
598	Standard error of average household income $	861	376	0	0	0	1,790
	Household after-tax income groups in 2005						
599	Under $10,000	1,165	1,290	10	20	40	75
600	$10,000 to $19,999	3,085	2,575	20	15	35	330
601	$20,000 to $29,999	3,690	2,685	15	25	35	290
602	$30,000 to $39,999	4,325	2,920	20	20	15	365
603	$40,000 to $49,999	3,680	2,835	15	15	25	435
604	$50,000 to $59,999	3,145	2,165	15	10	20	290
605	$60,000 to $69,999	2,900	2,060	15	10	10	350
606	$70,000 to $79,999	2,140	1,880	10	10	0	325
607	$80,000 to $89,999	1,380	1,275	0	0	0	245
608	$90,000 to $99,999	1,075	1,060	0	0	0	150
609	$100,000 and over	2,915	2,270	0	0	0	420
610	Median after-tax household income $	46,881	46,890	36,224	30,784	26,880	54,413
611	Average after-tax household income $	54,625	53,872	42,338	32,465	31,410	59,641
612	Standard error of average after-tax household income $	614	279	0	0	0	1,318

Note: See symbols and abbreviations in the introductory material and see reference material at the end of the publication.

Certaines caractéristiques des divisions de recensement et des subdivisions de recensement – Données intégrales et données-échantillon (20 %), Ontario, Recensement de 2006 (suite)

Eagle Lake 27, IRI	Ear Falls, TP ◆◊	English River 21, IRI ◆◊	Fort Hope 64, IRI ◆◆◊◊	Ignace, TP ◊	Kasabonika Lake, IRI	Caractéristiques	N°
						Caractéristiques du revenu de 2005	
X	**470**	**185**	**270**	**590**	**155**	**Nombre total des ménages privés**	584
						Tranches de revenu des ménages en 2005	
X	10	55	55	15	15	Moins de 10 000 $	585
X	30	45	55	75	25	10 000 $ à 19 999 $	586
X	20	20	40	50	30	20 000 $ à 29 999 $	587
X	25	20	50	85	35	30 000 $ à 39 999 $	588
X	55	10	25	20	20	40 000 $ à 49 999 $	589
X	50	15	25	55	10	50 000 $ à 59 999 $	590
X	45	10	20	70	10	60 000 $ à 69 999 $	591
X	15	0	10	70	0	70 000 $ à 79 999 $	592
X	45	10	0	35	0	80 000 $ à 89 999 $	593
X	30	0	10	20	0	90 000 $ à 99 999 $	594
X	140	0	0	90	0	100 000 $ et plus	595
X	70,293	17,824	24,128	57,250	30,080	Revenu médian des ménages $	596
X	77,387	25,580	29,191	59,904	33,046	Revenu moyen des ménages $	597
X	4,007	0	0	2,893	0	Erreur type de revenu moyen des ménages $	598
						Tranches du revenu après impôt des ménages en 2005	
X	15	55	50	10	20	Moins de 10 000 $	599
X	30	45	55	80	25	10 000 $ à 19 999 $	600
X	25	20	40	60	35	20 000 $ à 29 999 $	601
X	30	20	50	80	35	30 000 $ à 39 999 $	602
X	80	15	30	65	25	40 000 $ à 49 999 $	603
X	45	15	25	75	10	50 000 $ à 59 999 $	604
X	50	10	15	90	0	60 000 $ à 69 999 $	605
X	40	0	0	15	0	70 000 $ à 79 999 $	606
X	45	0	0	45	0	80 000 $ à 89 999 $	607
X	45	0	0	35	0	90 000 $ à 99 999 $	608
X	60	0	0	25	0	100 000 $ et plus	609
X	61,016	17,824	24,128	49,610	30,080	Revenu médian après impôt des ménages $	610
X	64,231	25,422	29,141	50,897	32,967	Revenu moyen après impôt des ménages $	611
X	3,068	0	0	2,242	0	Erreur type de revenu moyen après impôt des ménages $	612

Nota : Voir les symboles et les abréviations dans les documents d'introduction et voir les documents de référence à la fin de la publication.

Selected characteristics for census divisions and census subdivisions – 100% data and 20% sample data, Ontario, 2006 Census (continued)

No.	Characteristics	Kee-Way-Win, IRI	Kenora, CY ◆◇	Kenora 38B, IRI ◆◆◇◇	Kenora, Unorganized, NO ◆◇◇A	Kingfisher Lake 1, IRI ◆◇◇	Kitchenuhmaykoosib Aaki 84 (Big Trout Lake), IRI ◆◆◇◇
	Population characteristics						
1	**Population, 2001**[1]	**265**	**15,838**	**119**	**7,631**	**368**	**435**
2	**Population, 2006**[2]	**318**	**15,177**	**350**	**7,041**	**415**	**916**
3	Population percentage change, 2001 to 2006	20.0	-4.2	194.1	-7.7	12.8	110.6
4	Land area in square kilometres, 2006	189.78	210.91	18.88	400,652.34	7.75	319.85
5	**Total population – 100% data**[3]	**320**	**15,180**	**350**	**7,040**	**415**	**920**
	Sex and age groups						
6	Male	155	7,410	180	3,625	205	460
7	0 to 4 years	20	345	15	145	25	75
8	5 to 9 years	20	410	15	200	35	40
9	10 to 14 years	20	585	15	240	20	55
10	15 to 19 years	15	615	20	245	20	45
11	20 to 24 years	5	425	15	185	20	45
12	25 to 29 years	15	360	25	135	15	25
13	30 to 34 years	10	360	10	150	20	30
14	35 to 39 years	15	445	5	225	10	25
15	40 to 44 years	15	595	15	300	10	35
16	45 to 49 years	5	715	10	345	10	20
17	50 to 54 years	5	615	10	355	5	10
18	55 to 59 years	0	545	5	330	5	10
19	60 to 64 years	0	365	5	250	5	10
20	65 to 69 years	0	305	0	215	0	10
21	70 to 74 years	0	255	5	160	5	10
22	75 to 79 years	0	225	0	95	5	5
23	80 to 84 years	0	150	0	40	0	0
24	85 years and over	0	100	5	15	0	0
25	Female	160	7,770	170	3,415	210	460
26	0 to 4 years	20	345	20	150	30	70
27	5 to 9 years	25	375	15	190	25	35
28	10 to 14 years	30	520	20	210	25	45
29	15 to 19 years	20	575	15	230	20	55
30	20 to 24 years	15	435	15	170	10	45
31	25 to 29 years	10	375	15	140	25	30
32	30 to 34 years	10	405	10	155	10	30
33	35 to 39 years	10	455	15	220	20	35
34	40 to 44 years	5	690	10	325	10	30
35	45 to 49 years	5	685	10	340	15	20
36	50 to 54 years	5	615	10	305	5	15
37	55 to 59 years	0	505	5	310	10	20
38	60 to 64 years	0	355	0	220	10	15
39	65 to 69 years	0	340	5	165	5	10
40	70 to 74 years	0	325	5	145	5	10
41	75 to 79 years	0	270	0	85	0	10
42	80 to 84 years	0	255	0	45	0	5
43	85 years and over	0	240	0	10	0	0
44	**Total population 15 years and over**[3]	**190**	**12,600**	**245**	**5,910**	**260**	**600**
	Legal marital status						
45	Never legally married (single)	85	3,985	165	1,545	105	320
46	Legally married (and not separated)[4,5]	90	6,050	55	3,525	130	185
47	Separated, but still legally married	10	520	10	155	10	45
48	Divorced	0	1,015	10	420	0	20
49	Widowed	5	1,030	10	270	10	30
	Common-law status						
50	Not in a common-law relationship	175	11,315	170	5,305	225	480
51	In a common-law relationship	15	1,285	75	605	35	115
52	**Total population – 20% sample data**[6]	**320**	**14,955**	**350**	**7,045**	**415**	**915**
	Mother tongue						
53	Single responses	320	14,840	345	7,005	415	915
54	English	135	13,575	240	6,225	20	250
55	French	0	345	0	190	0	0
56	Non-official languages[7]	180	920	105	595	395	670
57	Italian	0	75	0	30	0	0
58	Chinese, n.o.s.[61]	0	10	0	0	0	0
59	Cantonese	0	0	0	0	0	0
60	Spanish	0	0	0	0	0	0
61	German	0	230	0	260	0	0
62	Other languages[8]	180	600	105	295	395	670

Note: See symbols and abbreviations in the introductory material and see reference material at the end of the publication.

Certaines caractéristiques des divisions de recensement et des subdivisions de recensement – Données intégrales et données-échantillon (20 %), Ontario, Recensement de 2006 (suite)

Lac Seul 28, IRI ◆◆◇◇	Lake Of The Woods 37, IRI ◇	Machin, TP ◆◆◇◇	Marten Falls 65, IRI ◆◇	Muskrat Dam Lake, IRI ◆◇	Neskantaga, IRI ◆◆◇◇	Caractéristiques	N°
						Caractéristiques de la population	
702	**99**	**1,143**	**X**	**61**	**0**	**Population, 2001[1]**	1
821	**58**	**978**	**221**	**252**	**265**	**Population, 2006[2]**	2
17.0	-41.4	-14.4	X	313.1	X	Variation en pourcentage de la population, 2001 à 2006	3
239.09	11.74	288.85	81.43	20.58	8.30	Superficie des terres en kilomètres carrés, 2006	4
820	**60**	**980**	**220**	**255**	**265**	**Population totale – Données intégrales[3]**	5
						Sexe et groupes d'âge	
425	25	510	120	135	140	Sexe masculin	6
45	0	25	20	15	25	0 à 4 ans	7
40	10	30	15	15	10	5 à 9 ans	8
35	5	45	20	15	15	10 à 14 ans	9
55	0	30	10	10	15	15 à 19 ans	10
45	0	15	5	10	10	20 à 24 ans	11
35	0	20	5	15	15	25 à 29 ans	12
15	0	30	5	15	5	30 à 34 ans	13
20	5	25	5	10	10	35 à 39 ans	14
30	0	45	15	10	10	40 à 44 ans	15
30	0	45	0	0	5	45 à 49 ans	16
25	0	45	5	5	10	50 à 54 ans	17
20	0	40	5	0	5	55 à 59 ans	18
15	5	30	0	0	0	60 à 64 ans	19
5	0	25	5	5	5	65 à 69 ans	20
10	0	30	0	0	0	70 à 74 ans	21
0	0	10	0	0	0	75 à 79 ans	22
0	0	15	0	0	5	80 à 84 ans	23
0	0	5	0	5	0	85 ans et plus	24
390	30	470	100	120	125	Sexe féminin	25
45	0	15	15	10	15	0 à 4 ans	26
50	5	30	10	10	15	5 à 9 ans	27
50	10	30	15	15	15	10 à 14 ans	28
35	5	25	10	10	10	15 à 19 ans	29
45	0	25	0	5	20	20 à 24 ans	30
25	0	20	5	15	10	25 à 29 ans	31
15	0	30	15	10	15	30 à 34 ans	32
30	5	30	10	10	5	35 à 39 ans	33
30	0	40	0	5	5	40 à 44 ans	34
20	0	50	0	10	10	45 à 49 ans	35
10	0	35	0	0	5	50 à 54 ans	36
10	5	35	5	5	5	55 à 59 ans	37
15	0	30	5	5	5	60 à 64 ans	38
5	0	20	5	5	0	65 à 69 ans	39
0	0	25	0	0	5	70 à 74 ans	40
0	0	15	0	0	0	75 à 79 ans	41
0	0	10	5	0	0	80 à 84 ans	42
0	0	10	0	0	5	85 ans et plus	43
560	**30**	**810**	**120**	**160**	**165**	**Population totale de 15 ans et plus[3]**	44
						État matrimonial légal	
335	25	200	85	60	85	Jamais légalement marié(e) (célibataire)	45
175	0	450	20	80	65	Légalement marié(e) (et non séparé[e])[4,5]	46
5	0	35	10	15	5	Séparé(e), mais toujours légalement marié(e)	47
20	0	60	0	0	5	Divorcé(e)	48
20	0	55	5	5	5	Veuf(ve)	49
						Union libre	
425	10	710	90	145	125	Ne vivant pas en union libre	50
135	10	95	30	20	40	Vivant en union libre	51
820	**60**	**980**	**220**	**255**	**265**	**Population totale – Données-échantillon (20 %)[6]**	52
						Langue maternelle	
820	60	965	220	255	265	Réponses uniques	53
550	50	835	155	85	40	Anglais	54
0	0	60	0	0	0	Français	55
265	10	70	65	165	225	Langues non officielles[7]	56
0	0	10	0	0	0	Italien	57
0	0	0	0	0	0	Chinois, n.d.a.[61]	58
0	0	0	0	0	0	Cantonais	59
0	0	0	0	0	0	Espagnol	60
0	0	25	0	0	0	Allemand	61
265	10	40	65	170	220	Autres langues[8]	62

Nota : Voir les symboles et les abréviations dans les documents d'introduction et voir les documents de référence à la fin de la publication.

Selected characteristics for census divisions and census subdivisions – 100% data and 20% sample data, Ontario, 2006 Census (continued)

No.	Characteristics	Kee-Way-Win, IRI	Kenora, CY ◆◊	Kenora 38B, IRI ◆◆◊◊	Kenora, Unorganized, NO ◆◊◊A	Kingfisher Lake 1, IRI ◆◊◊	Kitchenuhmaykoosib Aaki 84 (Big Trout Lake), IRI ◆◆◊◊
	Population characteristics						
	Mother tongue (continued)						
63	Multiple responses	0	115	0	40	0	0
64	English and French	0	35	0	10	0	0
65	English and non-official language	0	75	0	25	0	0
66	French and non-official language	0	0	0	0	0	0
67	English, French and non-official language	0	0	0	10	0	0
	Language spoken most often at home[9]						
68	Single responses	320	14,885	345	7,030	415	915
69	English	270	14,655	305	6,765	110	520
70	French	0	50	0	40	0	0
71	Non-official languages[7]	50	180	40	220	305	395
72	Chinese, n.o.s.[61]	0	10	0	0	0	0
73	Cantonese	0	0	0	0	0	0
74	Panjabi (Punjabi)	0	0	0	0	0	0
75	Italian	0	10	0	0	0	0
76	Spanish	0	0	0	0	0	0
77	Other languages[8]	50	165	45	215	300	395
78	Multiple responses	0	70	0	15	0	0
79	English and French	0	25	0	10	0	0
80	English and non-official language	0	40	0	10	0	0
81	French and non-official language	0	0	0	0	0	0
82	English, French and non-official language	0	0	0	0	0	0
	Knowledge of official languages[10]						
83	English only	315	13,735	340	6,515	355	825
84	French only	0	0	0	0	0	0
85	English and French	0	1,175	10	525	0	10
86	Neither English nor French	0	40	0	0	55	90
	Knowledge of non-official languages[7,11]						
87	Italian	0	90	0	35	0	0
88	Spanish	0	55	0	35	0	0
89	German	0	265	0	270	0	10
90	Chinese, n.o.s.[61]	0	10	0	0	0	0
91	Cantonese	0	10	0	0	0	0
92	Panjabi (Punjabi)	0	0	0	0	0	0
93	Portuguese	0	50	0	20	0	0
	First official language spoken[10]						
94	English	310	14,605	350	6,895	355	825
95	French	0	295	0	150	0	0
96	English and French	0	20	0	0	0	0
97	Neither English nor French	10	35	0	0	55	90
98	Official language minority - (number)[12]	0	305	0	150	0	0
99	Official language minority - (percentage)[12]	0.0	2.0	0.0	2.1	0.0	0.0
	Ethnic origin[13]						
100	English	0	4,610	10	2,100	0	0
101	Canadian	0	3,625	0	1,540	0	0
102	Scottish	0	3,515	15	1,640	0	0
103	Irish	0	2,595	10	1,445	0	0
104	French	0	2,750	10	1,315	0	0
105	German	0	2,210	0	1,350	0	0
106	Italian	0	455	0	125	0	0
107	Chinese	0	55	0	10	0	0
108	East Indian	0	0	0	0	0	0
109	Dutch (Netherlands)	0	535	0	240	0	0
110	Polish	0	1,050	0	260	0	0
111	Ukrainian	10	2,120	10	525	0	0
112	North American Indian	315	1,600	330	585	415	910
113	Portuguese	0	60	0	45	0	0
114	Filipino	0	30	0	10	0	0
	Aboriginal and non-Aboriginal identity						
115	Total Aboriginal identity population[14]	315	2,365	335	910	415	910
116	Total non-Aboriginal identity population	0	12,590	15	6,135	0	0

Note: See symbols and abbreviations in the introductory material and see reference material at the end of the publication.

Certaines caractéristiques des divisions de recensement et des subdivisions de recensement – Données intégrales et données-échantillon (20 %), Ontario, Recensement de 2006 (suite)

Lac Seul 28, IRI ◆◆◇◇	Lake Of The Woods 37, IRI ◇	Machin, TP ◆◆◇◇	Marten Falls 65, IRI ◆◇	Muskrat Dam Lake, IRI ◆◇	Neskantaga, IRI ◆◆◇◇	Caractéristiques	N°
						Caractéristiques de la population	
						Langue maternelle (suite)	
0	0	15	0	0	0	Réponses multiples	63
0	0	0	0	0	0	Anglais et français	64
0	0	15	0	0	0	Anglais et langue non officielle	65
0	0	0	0	0	0	Français et langue non officielle	66
0	0	0	0	0	0	Anglais, français et langue non officielle	67
						Langue parlée le plus souvent à la maison[9]	
820	55	965	225	255	265	Réponses uniques	68
730	55	950	190	200	100	Anglais	69
0	0	0	0	0	0	Français	70
90	0	15	35	55	165	Langues non officielles[7]	71
0	0	0	0	0	0	Chinois, n.d.a.[61]	72
0	0	0	0	0	0	Cantonais	73
0	0	0	0	0	0	Pendjabi	74
0	0	0	0	0	0	Italien	75
0	0	0	0	0	0	Espagnol	76
90	0	10	30	55	170	Autres langues[8]	77
0	0	15	0	0	0	Réponses multiples	78
0	0	10	0	0	0	Anglais et français	79
0	0	10	0	0	0	Anglais et langue non officielle	80
0	0	0	0	0	0	Français et langue non officielle	81
0	0	0	0	0	0	Anglais, français et langue non officielle	82
						Connaissance des langues officielles[10]	
815	60	895	220	240	255	Anglais seulement	83
0	0	0	0	0	0	Français seulement	84
10	0	85	0	0	0	Anglais et français	85
0	0	0	0	10	0	Ni l'anglais ni le français	86
						Connaissance des langues non officielles[7,11]	
0	0	0	0	0	0	Italien	87
0	0	0	0	0	0	Espagnol	88
0	0	25	0	0	0	Allemand	89
0	0	0	0	0	0	Chinois, n.d.a.[61]	90
0	0	0	0	0	0	Cantonais	91
0	0	0	0	0	0	Pendjabi	92
0	0	0	0	0	0	Portugais	93
						Première langue officielle parlée[10]	
815	60	925	220	240	260	Anglais	94
0	0	55	0	0	0	Français	95
0	0	0	0	0	0	Anglais et français	96
0	0	0	0	10	10	Ni l'anglais ni le français	97
0	0	55	0	0	0	Minorité de langue officielle - (nombre)[12]	98
0.0	0.0	5.6	0.0	0.0	0.0	Minorité de langue officielle - (pourcentage)[12]	99
						Origine ethnique[13]	
10	0	300	0	0	0	Anglais	100
0	0	120	0	0	10	Canadien	101
40	0	135	0	0	0	Écossais	102
0	0	140	0	0	0	Irlandais	103
10	0	230	0	0	0	Français	104
0	0	235	0	0	0	Allemand	105
0	0	10	0	0	0	Italien	106
0	0	0	0	0	0	Chinois	107
0	0	0	0	0	0	Indien de l'Inde	108
0	0	15	0	0	0	Hollandais (Néerlandais)	109
0	0	30	0	0	0	Polonais	110
0	0	55	0	0	0	Ukrainien	111
815	55	110	225	250	265	Indien de l'Amérique du Nord	112
0	0	0	0	0	0	Portugais	113
0	0	0	0	0	0	Philippin	114
						Population ayant une identité autochtone et population n'ayant pas d'identité autochtone	
820	55	195	220	250	260	Total de la population ayant une identité autochtone[14]	115
0	0	785	0	0	0	Total de la population n'ayant pas d'identité autochtone	116

Nota : Voir les symboles et les abréviations dans les documents d'introduction et voir les documents de référence à la fin de la publication.

Selected characteristics for census divisions and census subdivisions – 100% data and 20% sample data, Ontario, 2006 Census (continued)

No.	Characteristics	Kee-Way-Win, IRI	Kenora, CY ◆◇	Kenora 38B, IRI ◆◆◇◇	Kenora, Unorganized, NO ◆◇◇A	Kingfisher Lake 1, IRI ◆◇◇	Kitchenuhmaykoosib Aaki 84 (Big Trout Lake), IRI ◆◆◇◇
	Population characteristics						
	Aboriginal and non-Aboriginal ancestry						
117	Total Aboriginal ancestry population[15]	315	2,615	340	1,000	415	910
118	Total non-Aboriginal ancestry population	0	12,335	15	6,050	0	0
	Registered Indian status						
119	Registered Indian[16]	315	1,150	330	350	415	885
120	Not a Registered Indian	0	13,800	20	6,695	0	30
	Visible minority groups						
121	Total visible minority population[17]	0	135	0	20	0	0
122	Chinese	0	40	0	0	0	0
123	South Asian[18]	0	20	0	0	0	0
124	Black	0	25	0	0	0	0
125	Filipino	0	35	0	10	0	0
126	Latin American	0	10	0	0	0	0
127	Southeast Asian[19]	0	0	0	0	0	0
128	Arab	0	0	0	10	0	0
129	West Asian[20]	0	0	0	0	0	0
130	Korean	0	0	0	0	0	0
131	Japanese	0	10	0	0	0	0
132	Visible minority, n.i.e.[21]	0	10	0	0	0	0
133	Multiple visible minority[22]	0	0	0	0	0	0
	Citizenship[23]						
134	Canadian citizens[24]	X	14,830	X	6,875	X	X
135	Not Canadian citizens[25]	X	125	X	175	X	X
	Immigrant status and place of birth[26]						
136	Non-immigrants[27]	X	14,190	X	6,465	X	X
137	Born in province of residence	X	10,820	X	4,710	X	X
138	Immigrants[28]	X	745	X	545	X	X
139	United States of America	X	160	X	210	X	X
140	Central and South America	X	0	X	10	X	X
141	Caribbean and Bermuda	X	10	X	0	X	X
142	United Kingdom	X	130	X	95	X	X
143	Other Europe	X	390	X	200	X	X
144	Africa	X	0	X	0	X	X
145	Asia and the Middle East	X	45	X	0	X	X
146	Oceania and other[29]	X	10	X	20	X	X
147	Non-permanent residents[30]	X	20	X	40	X	X
148	**Total immigrant population[28]**	**X**	**745**	**X**	**540**	**X**	**X**
	Period of immigration						
149	Before 1961	X	330	X	155	X	X
150	1961 to 1970	X	90	X	85	X	X
151	1971 to 1980	X	120	X	100	X	X
152	1981 to 1990	X	110	X	70	X	X
153	1991 to 2000	X	80	X	70	X	X
154	1991 to 1995	X	40	X	25	X	X
155	1996 to 2000	X	40	X	45	X	X
156	2001 to 2006[31]	X	15	X	60	X	X
	Age at immigration						
157	Under 5 years	X	145	X	105	X	X
158	5 to 19 years	X	210	X	125	X	X
159	20 years and over	X	390	X	315	X	X
160	**Total population 15 years and over**	**190**	**12,375**	**245**	**5,920**	**260**	**595**
	Generation status						
161	1st generation[32]	0	780	10	540	0	0
162	2nd generation[33]	0	2,280	0	995	0	0
163	3rd generation or more[34]	190	9,310	235	4,380	260	595

Note: See symbols and abbreviations in the introductory material and see reference material at the end of the publication.

Lac Seul 28, IRI ◆◆◇◇	Lake Of The Woods 37, IRI ◇	Machin, TP ◆◆◇◇	Marten Falls 65, IRI ◆◇	Muskrat Dam Lake, IRI ◆◇	Neskantaga, IRI ◆◆◇◇	Caractéristiques	N°
						Caractéristiques de la population	
						Population ayant une ascendance autochtone et population n'ayant pas d'ascendance autochtone	
815	60	170	225	255	265	Total de la population ayant une ascendance autochtone[15]	117
0	0	805	0	0	0	Total de la population n'ayant pas d'ascendance autochtone	118
						Statut d'Indien inscrit	
815	60	45	220	250	260	Indien inscrit[16]	119
10	0	930	0	0	10	Pas un Indien inscrit	120
						Groupes de minorités visibles	
0	0	10	0	0	0	Total de la population des minorités visibles[17]	121
0	0	0	0	0	0	Chinois	122
0	0	10	0	0	0	Sud-Asiatique[18]	123
0	0	0	0	0	0	Noir	124
0	0	0	0	0	0	Philippin	125
0	0	0	0	0	0	Latino-Américain	126
0	0	0	0	0	0	Asiatique du Sud-Est[19]	127
0	0	0	0	0	0	Arabe	128
0	0	0	0	0	0	Asiatique occidental[20]	129
0	0	0	0	0	0	Coréen	130
0	0	0	0	0	0	Japonais	131
0	0	0	0	0	0	Minorité visible, n.i.a.[21]	132
0	0	0	0	0	0	Minorités visibles multiples[22]	133
						Citoyenneté[23]	
X	X	955	X	X	X	Citoyens canadiens[24]	134
X	X	25	X	X	X	Ne sont pas des citoyens canadiens[25]	135
						Statut d'immigrant et le lieu de naissance[26]	
X	X	900	X	X	X	Non-immigrants[27]	136
X	X	670	X	X	X	Né dans la province de résidence	137
X	X	75	X	X	X	Immigrants[28]	138
X	X	35	X	X	X	États-Unis d'Amérique	139
X	X	0	X	X	X	Amérique centrale et Amérique du Sud	140
X	X	0	X	X	X	Antilles et Bermudes	141
X	X	0	X	X	X	Royaume-Uni	142
X	X	25	X	X	X	Autre Europe	143
X	X	0	X	X	X	Afrique	144
X	X	0	X	X	X	Asie et Moyen-Orient	145
X	X	0	X	X	X	Océanie et autres[29]	146
X	X	10	X	X	X	Résidents non permanents[30]	147
X	**X**	**70**	**X**	**X**	**X**	**Population totale des immigrants[28]**	148
						Période d'immigration	
X	X	20	X	X	X	Avant 1961	149
X	X	10	X	X	X	1961 à 1970	150
X	X	15	X	X	X	1971 à 1980	151
X	X	15	X	X	X	1981 à 1990	152
X	X	10	X	X	X	1991 à 2000	153
X	X	0	X	X	X	1991 à 1995	154
X	X	10	X	X	X	1996 à 2000	155
X	X	10	X	X	X	2001 à 2006[31]	156
						Âge à l'immigration	
X	X	10	X	X	X	Moins de 5 ans	157
X	X	20	X	X	X	5 à 19 ans	158
X	X	50	X	X	X	20 ans et plus	159
560	**25**	**805**	**125**	**160**	**165**	**Population totale de 15 ans et plus**	160
						Statut des générations	
0	0	85	0	0	0	1re génération[32]	161
0	0	155	0	0	0	2e génération[33]	162
555	25	570	125	155	165	3e génération ou plus[34]	163

Nota : Voir les symboles et les abréviations dans les documents d'introduction et voir les documents de référence à la fin de la publication.

Selected characteristics for census divisions and census subdivisions – 100% data and 20% sample data, Ontario, 2006 Census (continued)

No.	Characteristics	Kee-Way-Win, IRI	Kenora, CY ◆◇	Kenora 38B, IRI ◆◆◇◇	Kenora, Unorganized, NO ◆◇◇A	Kingfisher Lake 1, IRI ◆◇◇	Kitchenuhmaykoosib Aaki 84 (Big Trout Lake), IRI ◆◆◇◇
	Population characteristics						
164	**Total population 1 year and over[35]**	**310**	**14,865**	**340**	**6,975**	**405**	**875**
	Place of residence 1 year ago (mobility)						
165	Non-movers	295	13,415	335	6,295	380	825
166	Movers	15	1,450	10	675	25	45
167	Non-migrants	10	1,085	0	320	15	20
168	Migrants	0	355	0	360	10	20
169	Internal migrants	0	345	10	320	10	20
170	Intraprovincial migrants	0	205	10	220	10	25
171	Interprovincial migrants	0	135	0	100	0	0
172	External migrants	0	15	0	40	0	0
173	**Total population 5 years and over[36]**	**280**	**14,385**	**310**	**6,760**	**360**	**775**
	Place of residence 5 years ago (mobility)						
174	Non-movers	210	9,720	230	5,160	250	630
175	Movers	70	4,665	80	1,595	105	140
176	Non-migrants	40	3,265	40	640	95	105
177	Migrants	30	1,400	45	955	15	35
178	Internal migrants	30	1,345	45	900	15	35
179	Intraprovincial migrants	25	775	40	510	15	25
180	Interprovincial migrants	10	575	10	390	0	0
181	External migrants	0	50	0	50	0	0
182	**Total population 15 years and over**	**190**	**12,375**	**245**	**5,920**	**260**	**595**
	Highest certificate, diploma or degree[37]						
183	No certificate, diploma or degree	145	3,375	140	1,490	210	495
184	Certificate, diploma or degree	45	8,995	110	4,435	50	100
185	High school certificate or equivalent[38]	15	3,455	30	1,730	40	25
186	Apprenticeship or trades certificate or diploma	0	1,505	35	715	10	20
187	College, CEGEP or other non-university certificate or diploma[39]	20	2,190	30	1,135	10	40
188	University certificate or diploma below bachelor level[40]	0	440	0	170	0	10
189	University certificate or degree[41]	0	1,405	10	680	0	10
190	Bachelor's degree	10	890	10	470	0	0
191	University certificate or diploma above bachelor level	10	255	0	105	10	10
192	Degree in medicine, dentistry, veterinary medicine or optometry	0	35	0	25	0	0
193	Master's degree	0	190	0	65	0	0
194	Earned doctorate	0	30	0	10	0	0
195	**Total population 15 years and over with postsecondary qualifications**	**30**	**5,545**	**75**	**2,700**	**0**	**75**
	Major field of study - Classification of Instructional Programs, 2000[42]						
196	Education	10	625	0	290	0	10
197	Visual and performing arts, and communications technologies	0	80	0	45	0	0
198	Humanities	10	205	10	120	0	0
199	Social and behavioural sciences and law	0	300	10	135	0	0
200	Business, management and public administration	10	945	25	445	10	30
201	Physical and life sciences and technologies	0	115	0	55	0	0
202	Mathematics, computer and information sciences	0	75	0	35	0	10
203	Architecture, engineering, and related technologies	0	1,365	20	805	0	0
204	Agriculture, natural resources and conservation	0	200	0	170	0	0
205	Health, parks, recreation and fitness	10	1,065	10	410	10	15
206	Personal, protective and transportation services	10	560	10	190	0	0
207	Other fields of study[43]	0	0	0	0	0	0
	Location of study[44]						
208	Inside Canada	30	5,325	75	2,505	10	75
209	Outside Canada	0	215	0	195	0	10
210	**Total population 15 years and over**	**190**	**12,375**	**245**	**5,920**	**260**	**595**
	Unpaid work						
211	Males 15 years and over	95	5,980	130	3,060	130	285
212	Reported unpaid work[45]	90	5,390	115	2,815	120	250
213	Housework and child care and care or assistance to seniors	30	610	15	250	50	70
214	Housework and child care only	40	1,410	50	735	50	90

Note: See symbols and abbreviations in the introductory material and see reference material at the end of the publication.

Certaines caractéristiques des divisions de recensement et des subdivisions de recensement – Données intégrales et données-échantillon (20 %), Ontario, Recensement de 2006 (suite)

Lac Seul 28, IRI ◆◆◇◇	Lake Of The Woods 37, IRI ◇	Machin, TP ◆◆◇◇	Marten Falls 65, IRI ◆◇	Muskrat Dam Lake, IRI ◆◇	Neskantaga, IRI ◆◆◇◇	Caractéristiques	Nº
						Caractéristiques de la population	
800	**55**	**975**	**215**	**250**	**255**	**Population totale de 1 an et plus[35]**	164
						Lieu de résidence 1 an auparavant (mobilité)	
750	55	910	185	220	235	Personnes n'ayant pas déménagé	165
50	0	65	30	25	15	Personnes ayant déménagé	166
25	0	20	20	10	10	Non-migrants	167
25	0	45	10	20	0	Migrants	168
20	0	40	10	20	10	Migrants internes	169
20	0	35	10	20	10	Migrants infraprovinciaux	170
10	0	0	0	0	0	Migrants interprovinciaux	171
0	0	0	0	0	0	Migrants externes	172
725	**55**	**945**	**185**	**220**	**225**	**Population totale de 5 ans et plus[36]**	173
						Lieu de résidence 5 ans auparavant (mobilité)	
520	45	735	110	120	160	Personnes n'ayant pas déménagé	174
210	0	210	75	105	60	Personnes ayant déménagé	175
165	0	70	60	70	50	Non-migrants	176
50	0	140	10	30	15	Migrants	177
50	0	135	10	35	15	Migrants internes	178
45	0	95	10	30	15	Migrants infraprovinciaux	179
10	0	40	0	0	0	Migrants interprovinciaux	180
0	0	10	0	0	0	Migrants externes	181
560	**25**	**805**	**125**	**160**	**165**	**Population totale de 15 ans et plus**	182
						Plus haut certificat, diplôme ou grade[37]	
345	15	285	105	105	150	Aucun certificat, diplôme ou grade	183
210	10	520	15	50	15	Certificat, diplôme ou grade	184
90	10	210	10	30	10	Diplôme d'études secondaires ou l'équivalent[38]	185
40	0	115	0	0	0	Certificat ou diplôme d'apprenti ou d'une école de métiers	186
55	0	130	10	20	10	Certificat ou diplôme d'un collège, d'un cégep ou d'un autre établissement d'enseignement non universitaire[39]	187
10	0	10	0	0	0	Certificat ou diplôme universitaire inférieur au baccalauréat[40]	188
10	0	60	0	0	0	Certificat ou grade universitaire[41]	189
10	0	45	0	10	0	Baccalauréat	190
0	0	10	0	0	0	Certificat ou diplôme universitaire supérieur au baccalauréat	191
0	0	0	0	0	0	Diplôme en médecine, en art dentaire, en médecine vétérinaire ou en optométrie	192
0	0	10	0	0	0	Maîtrise	193
0	0	0	0	0	0	Doctorat acquis	194
115	**10**	**315**	**10**	**20**	**10**	**Population totale de 15 ans et plus avec titres du niveau postsecondaire**	195
						Principal domaine d'études - Classification des programmes d'enseignement, 2000[42]	
10	0	35	10	10	0	Éducation	196
10	0	10	0	0	0	Arts visuels et d'interprétation, et technologie des communications	197
10	0	15	0	10	0	Sciences humaines	198
10	0	20	0	10	0	Sciences sociales et de comportements, et droit	199
25	10	50	10	10	0	Commerce, gestion et administration publique	200
0	0	10	0	0	0	Sciences physiques et de la vie, et technologies	201
0	0	10	0	0	0	Mathématiques, informatique et sciences de l'information	202
30	0	85	0	0	0	Architecture, génie et services connexes	203
10	0	20	0	0	0	Agriculture, ressources naturelles et conservation	204
10	0	35	0	0	0	Santé, parcs, récréation et conditionnement physique	205
15	0	35	10	0	0	Services personnels, de protection et de transport	206
0	0	0	0	0	0	Autres domaines d'études[43]	207
						Lieu des études[44]	
115	0	280	10	20	0	À l'intérieur du Canada	208
0	0	30	0	0	0	À l'extérieur du Canada	209
560	**25**	**805**	**125**	**160**	**165**	**Population totale de 15 ans et plus**	210
						Travail non rémunéré	
310	10	410	65	80	85	Hommes de 15 ans et plus	211
280	15	375	55	80	85	Travail non rémunéré déclaré[45]	212
40	10	20	20	35	30	Travaux ménagers et soins aux enfants et soins ou aide aux personnes âgées	213
120	0	100	20	35	25	Travaux ménagers et soins aux enfants seulement	214

Nota : Voir les symboles et les abréviations dans les documents d'introduction et voir les documents de référence à la fin de la publication.

No.	Characteristics	Kee-Way-Win, IRI	Kenora, CY ◆◊	Kenora 38B, IRI ◆◆◊◊	Kenora, Unorganized, NO ◆◊◊A	Kingfisher Lake 1, IRI ◆◊◊	Kitchenuhmaykoosib Aaki 84 (Big Trout Lake), IRI ◆◆◊◊
	Population characteristics						
	Unpaid work (continued)						
215	Housework and care or assistance to seniors only	0	520	15	260	0	25
216	Child care and care or assistance to seniors only	0	15	0	0	0	0
217	Housework only	15	2,790	30	1,530	20	60
218	Child care only	10	15	0	30	0	10
219	Care or assistance to seniors only	0	25	0	10	0	0
220	Females 15 years and over	95	6,395	115	2,855	135	315
221	Reported unpaid work[45]	90	6,095	105	2,725	130	305
222	Housework and child care and care or assistance to seniors	35	795	20	340	55	90
223	Housework and child care only	40	1,890	50	755	60	125
224	Housework and care or assistance to seniors only	0	740	10	305	0	15
225	Child care and care or assistance to seniors only	0	10	0	0	0	0
226	Housework only	10	2,645	25	1,290	10	65
227	Child care only	0	15	0	30	0	10
228	Care or assistance to seniors only	10	0	0	0	0	0
	Labour force activity						
229	Males 15 years and over	95	5,980	130	3,060	125	280
230	In the labour force	55	4,140	75	2,100	75	170
231	Employed	40	3,780	60	1,960	70	145
232	Unemployed	15	360	15	140	10	20
233	Not in the labour force	40	1,840	60	960	50	115
234	Participation rate	57.9	69.2	57.7	68.6	60.0	60.7
235	Employment rate	42.1	63.2	46.2	64.1	56.0	51.8
236	Unemployment rate	27.3	8.7	20.0	6.7	13.3	11.8
237	Females 15 years and over	95	6,400	115	2,860	135	315
238	In the labour force	45	4,085	55	1,795	65	125
239	Employed	35	3,855	50	1,650	60	110
240	Unemployed	10	230	10	140	10	15
241	Not in the labour force	45	2,310	55	1,065	70	190
242	Participation rate	47.4	63.8	47.8	62.8	48.1	39.7
243	Employment rate	36.8	60.2	43.5	57.7	44.4	34.9
244	Unemployment rate	22.2	5.6	18.2	7.8	15.4	12.0
245	Both sexes - Participation rate	52.6	66.5	53.1	65.8	53.8	48.7
246	15 to 24 years	27.3	74.7	25.0	73.2	30.8	36.1
247	25 years and over	65.4	64.8	62.2	64.7	61.5	54.2
248	Both sexes - Employment rate	39.5	61.7	42.0	61.0	50.0	42.9
249	15 to 24 years	16.7	64.9	15.4	61.5	30.8	27.8
250	25 years and over	48.1	61.1	51.4	60.9	56.4	48.2
251	Both sexes - Unemployment rate	25.0	7.2	19.2	7.3	6.9	13.8
252	15 to 24 years	0.0	13.2	66.7	16.4	0.0	23.1
253	25 years and over	23.5	5.8	13.6	5.6	8.3	11.1
254	**Total labour force 15 years and over**	**100**	**8,225**	**125**	**3,900**	**140**	**295**
	Industry - North American Industry Classification System 2002						
255	Industry - Not applicable[46]	10	70	0	30	10	10
256	All industries[47]	95	8,155	125	3,865	145	280
257	11 Agriculture, forestry, fishing and hunting	0	130	10	295	0	0
258	21 Mining and oil and gas extraction	0	45	0	55	0	0
259	22 Utilities	10	105	0	35	0	10
260	23 Construction	0	565	10	235	15	20
261	31-33 Manufacturing	0	560	0	460	0	0
262	41 Wholesale trade	0	110	0	90	0	0
263	44-45 Retail trade	10	1,245	10	535	10	40
264	48-49 Transportation and warehousing	0	480	0	255	10	15
265	51 Information and cultural industries	0	110	0	40	0	10
266	52 Finance and insurance	0	270	0	85	10	0
267	53 Real estate and rental and leasing	0	115	0	35	0	0
268	54 Professional, scientific and technical services	0	215	0	80	0	10
269	55 Management of companies and enterprises	0	0	0	0	0	0
270	56 Administrative and support, waste management and remediation services	0	170	0	70	10	10
271	61 Educational services	15	610	10	250	20	25
272	62 Health care and social assistance	10	1,310	35	435	25	65

Note: See symbols and abbreviations in the introductory material and see reference material at the end of the publication.

Certaines caractéristiques des divisions de recensement et des subdivisions de recensement – Données intégrales et données-échantillon (20 %), Ontario, Recensement de 2006 (suite)

Lac Seul 28, IRI ◆◆◇◇	Lake Of The Woods 37, IRI ◇	Machin, TP ◆◆◇◇	Marten Falls 65, IRI ◆◇	Muskrat Dam Lake, IRI ◆◇	Neskantaga, IRI ◆◆◇◇	Caractéristiques	N°
						Caractéristiques de la population	
						Travail non rémunéré (suite)	
15	0	25	0	0	10	Travaux ménagers et soins ou aide aux personnes âgées seulement	215
10	0	0	0	0	0	Soins aux enfants et soins ou aide aux personnes âgées seulement	216
90	10	230	10	10	20	Travaux ménagers seulement	217
10	0	0	0	0	0	Soins aux enfants seulement	218
10	0	0	0	0	0	Soins ou aide aux personnes âgées seulement	219
250	15	395	60	80	80	Femmes de 15 ans et plus	220
245	15	380	50	75	75	Travail non rémunéré déclaré[45]	221
35	10	35	20	40	30	Travaux ménagers et soins aux enfants et soins ou aide aux personnes âgées	222
130	10	120	25	30	40	Travaux ménagers et soins aux enfants seulement	223
10	0	25	0	0	0	Travaux ménagers et soins ou aide aux personnes âgées seulement	224
0	0	0	0	0	0	Soins aux enfants et soins ou aide aux personnes âgées seulement	225
65	10	200	10	10	10	Travaux ménagers seulement	226
0	0	0	0	0	0	Soins aux enfants seulement	227
0	0	0	0	0	0	Soins ou aide aux personnes âgées seulement	228
						Activité	
310	10	415	65	80	85	Hommes de 15 ans et plus	229
215	0	295	35	65	35	Population active	230
180	10	280	30	65	30	Personnes occupées	231
35	0	15	10	0	0	Chômeurs	232
90	10	120	25	20	55	Inactifs	233
69.4	0.0	71.1	53.8	81.2	41.2	Taux d'activité	234
58.1	100.0	67.5	46.2	81.2	35.3	Taux d'emploi	235
16.3	0.0	5.1	28.6	0.0	0.0	Taux de chômage	236
250	20	395	60	80	80	Femmes de 15 ans et plus	237
155	10	240	25	50	30	Population active	238
135	0	230	15	50	25	Personnes occupées	239
25	0	10	10	0	0	Chômeuses	240
95	10	160	35	25	50	Inactives	241
62.0	50.0	60.8	41.7	62.5	37.5	Taux d'activité	242
54.0	0.0	58.2	25.0	62.5	31.2	Taux d'emploi	243
16.1	0.0	4.2	40.0	0.0	0.0	Taux de chômage	244
66.7	40.0	65.8	52.0	71.9	36.4	Les deux sexes - Taux d'activité	245
54.3	100.0	73.7	28.6	50.0	20.0	15 à 24 ans	246
71.4	0.0	64.8	58.8	79.2	47.8	25 ans et plus	247
55.4	60.0	63.4	41.7	71.9	36.4	Les deux sexes - Taux d'emploi	248
47.1	0.0	68.4	28.6	57.1	18.2	15 à 24 ans	249
59.7	0.0	63.1	44.4	79.2	43.5	25 ans et plus	250
16.2	0.0	4.7	25.0	0.0	0.0	Les deux sexes - Taux de chômage	251
15.8	0.0	14.3	100.0	0.0	0.0	15 à 24 ans	252
16.4	0.0	3.3	18.2	0.0	0.0	25 ans et plus	253
375	**10**	**530**	**60**	**120**	**60**	**Population active totale de 15 ans et plus**	254
						Industrie - Système de classification des industries de l'Amérique du Nord de 2002	
10	0	0	0	0	0	Industrie - Sans objet[46]	255
360	15	530	60	115	60	Toutes les industries[47]	256
15	0	45	0	0	0	11 Agriculture, foresterie, pêche et chasse	257
0	0	15	0	0	0	21 Extraction minière et extraction de pétrole et de gaz	258
0	0	0	0	10	0	22 Services publics	259
60	0	30	0	15	0	23 Construction	260
10	0	65	0	0	0	31-33 Fabrication	261
0	0	10	0	0	0	41 Commerce de gros	262
10	0	70	0	0	10	44-45 Commerce de détail	263
10	0	55	0	0	0	48-49 Transport et entreposage	264
0	0	0	0	0	0	51 Industrie de l'information et industrie culturelle	265
0	0	10	0	0	0	52 Finance et assurances	266
0	0	10	0	0	0	53 Services immobiliers et services de location et de location à bail	267
0	0	0	0	0	0	54 Services professionnels, scientifiques et techniques	268
0	0	0	0	0	0	55 Gestion de sociétés et d'entreprises	269
30	0	0	0	0	0	56 Services administratifs, services de soutien, services de gestion des déchets et services d'assainissement	270
35	0	30	10	10	10	61 Services d'enseignement	271
75	0	40	10	20	10	62 Soins de santé et assistance sociale	272

Nota : Voir les symboles et les abréviations dans les documents d'introduction et voir les documents de référence à la fin de la publication.

Selected characteristics for census divisions and census subdivisions – 100% data and 20% sample data, Ontario, 2006 Census (continued)

No.	Characteristics	Kee-Way-Win, IRI	Kenora, CY ◆◇	Kenora 38B, IRI ◆◆◇◇	Kenora, Unorganized, NO ◆◇◇A	Kingfisher Lake 1, IRI ◆◇◇	Kitchenuhmaykoosib Aaki 84 (Big Trout Lake), IRI ◆◆◇◇
	Population characteristics						
	Industry - North American Industry Classification System 2002 (continued)						
273	71 Arts, entertainment and recreation	0	115	10	95	0	0
274	72 Accommodation and food services	0	715	0	370	0	0
275	81 Other services (except public administration)	0	475	10	175	10	10
276	91 Public administration	45	790	30	275	50	65
	Class of worker						
277	Class of worker - Not applicable[46]	0	65	0	30	0	10
278	All classes of worker[47]	95	8,155	125	3,865	140	285
279	Paid workers	95	7,735	125	3,465	145	275
280	Employees	95	7,570	125	3,225	145	280
281	Self-employed (incorporated)	0	165	0	245	0	0
282	Self-employed (unincorporated)	0	400	0	375	0	0
283	Unpaid family workers	0	15	0	25	0	0
	Occupation - National Occupational Classification for Statistics 2006						
284	Male labour force 15 years and over	55	4,140	70	2,100	80	170
285	Occupation - Not applicable[46]	0	30	0	25	0	10
286	All occupations[47]	50	4,105	70	2,080	80	165
287	A Management occupations	10	265	0	260	10	20
288	B Business, finance and administrative occupations	0	210	0	60	0	10
289	C Natural and applied sciences and related occupations	0	210	0	130	0	0
290	D Health occupations	0	95	10	40	0	0
291	E Occupations in social science, education, government service and religion	0	255	0	75	10	25
292	F Occupations in art, culture, recreation and sport	0	50	0	20	0	0
293	G Sales and service occupations	15	1,065	25	325	20	45
294	H Trades, transport and equipment operators and related occupations	20	1,625	15	775	30	50
295	I Occupations unique to primary industry	0	145	0	205	10	10
296	J Occupations unique to processing, manufacturing and utilities	0	180	0	180	0	0
297	Female labour force 15 years and over	45	4,085	55	1,790	65	125
298	Occupation - Not applicable[46]	0	35	0	0	0	10
299	All occupations[47]	45	4,050	55	1,785	65	120
300	A Management occupations	0	235	10	185	10	10
301	B Business, finance and administrative occupations	0	840	10	435	20	25
302	C Natural and applied sciences and related occupations	0	50	0	50	0	0
303	D Health occupations	0	525	10	145	0	10
304	E Occupations in social science, education, government service and religion	15	590	20	255	0	25
305	F Occupations in art, culture, recreation and sport	0	20	0	25	0	0
306	G Sales and service occupations	15	1,580	20	545	30	45
307	H Trades, transport and equipment operators and related occupations	0	100	10	60	0	0
308	I Occupations unique to primary industry	0	15	0	55	0	0
309	J Occupations unique to processing, manufacturing and utilities	0	85	0	25	0	0
310	**Total employed labour force 15 years and over**	**75**	**7,635**	**105**	**3,610**	**130**	**255**
	Place of work status						
311	Males	40	3,780	55	1,960	70	145
312	Usual place of work	25	3,030	50	1,475	30	125
313	At home	0	210	0	160	0	10
314	Outside Canada	0	0	0	0	0	0
315	No fixed workplace address	15	535	10	320	40	15
316	Females	35	3,855	50	1,650	60	105
317	Usual place of work	25	3,580	45	1,415	35	110
318	At home	0	165	0	165	0	0
319	Outside Canada	0	0	0	0	0	0
320	No fixed workplace address	15	110	0	70	25	0

Note: See symbols and abbreviations in the introductory material and see reference material at the end of the publication.

Certaines caractéristiques des divisions de recensement et des subdivisions de recensement – Données intégrales et données-échantillon (20 %), Ontario, Recensement de 2006 (suite)

Lac Seul 28, IRI ◆◆◊◊	Lake Of The Woods 37, IRI ◊	Machin, TP ◆◆◊◊	Marten Falls 65, IRI ◆◊	Muskrat Dam Lake, IRI ◆◊	Neskantaga, IRI ◆◆◊◊	Caractéristiques	N°
						Caractéristiques de la population	
						Industrie - Système de classification des industries de l'Amérique du Nord de 2002 (suite)	
10	0	0	0	0	0	71 Arts, spectacles et loisirs	273
40	0	90	0	0	0	72 Hébergement et services de restauration	274
0	0	20	0	10	0	81 Autres services (sauf les administrations publiques)	275
55	0	30	35	45	35	91 Administrations publiques	276
						Catégorie de travailleurs	
15	0	0	0	0	0	Catégorie de travailleurs - Sans objet[46]	277
360	10	530	65	120	60	Toutes les catégories de travailleurs[47]	278
360	10	495	60	115	60	Travailleurs rémunérés	279
355	10	475	60	120	60	Employés	280
0	0	25	0	0	0	Travailleurs autonomes (entreprise constituée en société)	281
10	0	35	0	0	0	Travailleurs autonomes (entreprise non constituée en société)	282
0	0	0	0	0	0	Travailleurs familiaux non rémunérés	283
						Profession - Classification nationale des professions pour statistiques de 2006	
215	0	295	35	65	30	Hommes actifs de 15 ans et plus	284
0	0	0	0	0	0	Profession - Sans objet[46]	285
210	0	290	40	65	30	Toutes les professions[47]	286
10	0	20	0	15	10	A Gestion	287
10	0	10	0	0	0	B Affaires, finance et administration	288
10	0	10	0	0	10	C Sciences naturelles et appliquées et professions apparentées	289
0	0	0	0	0	0	D Secteur de la santé	290
15	0	10	10	10	0	E Sciences sociales, enseignement, administration publique et religion	291
10	0	0	0	0	0	F Arts, culture, sports et loisirs	292
35	0	45	20	0	10	G Ventes et services	293
100	0	120	10	30	10	H Métiers, transport et machinerie	294
20	0	40	0	0	0	I Professions propres au secteur primaire	295
15	0	30	0	10	0	J Transformation, fabrication et services d'utilité publique	296
155	10	240	20	55	30	Femmes actives de 15 ans et plus	297
10	0	0	0	0	0	Profession - Sans objet[46]	298
155	10	240	20	55	25	Toutes les professions[47]	299
15	0	25	0	0	0	A Gestion	300
40	0	35	0	15	0	B Affaires, finance et administration	301
0	0	0	0	0	0	C Sciences naturelles et appliquées et professions apparentées	302
0	0	10	0	0	0	D Secteur de la santé	303
40	10	25	0	20	10	E Sciences sociales, enseignement, administration publique et religion	304
0	0	0	0	0	0	F Arts, culture, sports et loisirs	305
50	0	115	0	15	10	G Ventes et services	306
10	0	10	0	0	0	H Métiers, transport et machinerie	307
0	0	10	0	0	0	I Professions propres au secteur primaire	308
0	0	10	0	0	0	J Transformation, fabrication et services d'utilité publique	309
310	**10**	**510**	**50**	**120**	**60**	**Population active occupée totale de 15 ans et plus**	310
						Catégorie de lieu de travail	
175	0	280	30	65	35	Hommes	311
120	0	210	30	0	15	Lieu habituel de travail	312
10	0	15	0	0	0	À domicile	313
0	0	0	0	0	0	En dehors du Canada	314
50	10	55	0	60	20	Sans adresse de travail fixe	315
135	10	230	20	50	25	Femmes	316
120	0	210	20	10	10	Lieu habituel de travail	317
0	0	10	0	0	0	À domicile	318
0	0	0	0	0	0	En dehors du Canada	319
10	0	0	0	40	15	Sans adresse de travail fixe	320

Nota : Voir les symboles et les abréviations dans les documents d'introduction et voir les documents de référence à la fin de la publication.

Selected characteristics for census divisions and census subdivisions – 100% data and 20% sample data, Ontario, 2006 Census (continued)

No.	Characteristics	Kee-Way-Win, IRI	Kenora, CY ◆◇	Kenora 38B, IRI ◆◆◇◇	Kenora, Unorganized, NO ◆◇◇A	Kingfisher Lake 1, IRI ◆◇◇	Kitchenuhmaykoosib Aaki 84 (Big Trout Lake), IRI ◆◆◇◇
	Population characteristics						
321	**Total employed labour force 15 years and over with usual place of work or no fixed workplace address**	**75**	**7,255**	**105**	**3,285**	**130**	**245**
	Mode of transportation						
322	Males	40	3,560	60	1,795	70	135
323	Car, truck, van, as driver	25	2,825	40	1,530	45	75
324	Car, truck, van, as passenger	10	280	0	115	0	30
325	Public transit	0	55	0	0	10	0
326	Walked	10	275	0	90	20	20
327	All other modes	0	130	0	55	0	10
328	Females	35	3,690	45	1,490	60	105
329	Car, truck, van, as driver	20	2,675	35	1,245	25	55
330	Car, truck, van, as passenger	10	535	0	145	15	25
331	Public transit	0	20	0	0	0	0
332	Walked	15	400	10	60	20	25
333	All other modes	0	60	0	30	0	0
334	**Total population 15 years and over who worked since January 1, 2005**	**120**	**9,065**	**155**	**4,310**	**145**	**315**
	Language used most often at work						
335	Single responses	120	9,035	155	4,290	145	320
336	English	105	8,970	145	4,245	55	235
337	French	0	25	0	15	0	0
338	Non-official languages[7]	20	35	10	25	90	85
339	Chinese, n.o.s.[61]	0	0	0	0	0	0
340	Cantonese	0	0	0	0	0	0
341	Other languages[8]	15	30	10	25	90	85
342	Multiple responses	0	30	0	25	0	0
343	English and French	0	10	0	10	0	0
344	English and non-official language	0	20	10	10	0	0
345	French and non-official language	0	0	0	0	0	0
346	English, French and non-official language	0	0	0	0	0	0
	Dwelling and household characteristics						
347	**Total number of occupied private dwellings**	**80**	**6,250**	**100**	**2,800**	**105**	**275**
	Housing tenure						
348	Owned	10	4,830	20	2,510	0	25
349	Rented	0	1,420	0	290	0	35
350	Band housing	65	0	75	0	90	215
	Structural type of dwelling						
351	Single-detached house	70	4,985	75	2,440	95	235
352	Semi-detached house	10	165	0	15	5	0
353	Row house	0	85	20	5	0	0
354	Apartment, duplex	0	275	0	50	0	5
355	Apartment, building that has five or more storeys	0	160	0	0	0	0
356	Apartment, building that has fewer than five storeys	0	530	0	20	5	25
357	Other single-attached house	0	35	0	15	0	0
358	Movable dwelling[48]	0	30	5	255	0	20
	Condition of dwelling						
359	Regular maintenance only	10	3,715	15	1,615	40	55
360	Minor repairs	15	1,955	25	880	25	95
361	Major repairs	60	580	60	305	40	125
	Period of construction						
362	Before 1946	0	1,485	0	145	0	0
363	1946 to 1960	0	1,455	0	355	0	0
364	1961 to 1970	0	720	0	355	0	10
365	1971 to 1980	0	910	15	660	10	40
366	1981 to 1985	0	410	20	295	15	45
367	1986 to 1990	10	395	15	395	25	55
368	1991 to 1995	35	400	15	255	15	40
369	1996 to 2000	10	255	10	200	25	30
370	2001 to 2006[49]	20	215	20	135	15	50

Note: See symbols and abbreviations in the introductory material and see reference material at the end of the publication.

Certaines caractéristiques des divisions de recensement et des subdivisions de recensement – Données intégrales et données-échantillon (20 %), Ontario, Recensement de 2006 (suite)

Lac Seul 28, IRI ◆◆◇◇	Lake Of The Woods 37, IRI ◇	Machin, TP ◆◆◇◇	Marten Falls 65, IRI ◆◇	Muskrat Dam Lake, IRI ◆◇	Neskantaga, IRI ◆◆◇◇	Caractéristiques	N°
						Caractéristiques de la population	
300	**10**	**480**	**50**	**115**	**60**	**Population active occupée totale de 15 ans et plus ayant un lieu habituel de travail ou sans adresse de travail fixe**	321
						Mode de transport	
170	10	265	30	65	35	Hommes	322
55	0	230	10	35	25	Automobile, camion ou fourgonnette, en tant que conducteur	323
0	0	15	0	0	0	Automobile, camion ou fourgonnette, en tant que passager	324
0	0	0	0	0	0	Transport en commun	325
80	10	20	15	20	10	À pied	326
25	0	0	0	0	10	Tous les autres modes	327
130	10	215	20	55	30	Femmes	328
55	0	180	10	20	10	Automobile, camion ou fourgonnette, en tant que conductrice	329
15	0	15	0	0	10	Automobile, camion ou fourgonnette, en tant que passagère	330
0	0	0	0	0	0	Transport en commun	331
50	0	15	15	30	15	À pied	332
10	0	10	0	0	0	Tous les autres modes	333
415	**15**	**585**	**85**	**125**	**65**	**Population totale de 15 ans et plus ayant travaillé depuis le 1er janvier 2005**	334
						Langue utilisée le plus souvent au travail	
415	15	585	85	130	65	Réponses uniques	335
400	15	580	80	110	30	Anglais	336
0	0	0	0	0	0	Français	337
15	0	0	10	20	35	Langues non officielles[7]	338
0	0	0	0	0	0	Chinois, n.d.a.[61]	339
0	0	0	0	0	0	Cantonais	340
15	0	0	0	15	40	Autres langues[8]	341
0	0	0	0	0	0	Réponses multiples	342
0	0	0	0	0	0	Anglais et français	343
0	0	0	0	0	0	Anglais et langue non officielle	344
0	0	0	0	0	0	Français et langue non officielle	345
0	0	0	0	0	0	Anglais, français et langue non officielle	346
						Caractéristiques des logements et des ménages	
225	**10**	**405**	**65**	**75**	**75**	**Nombre total de logements privés occupés**	347
						Mode d'occupation	
20	0	335	0	0	0	Possédé	348
0	0	60	40	0	0	Loué	349
205	10	10	20	75	75	Logement de bande	350
						Type de construction résidentielle	
200	15	360	60	75	75	Maison individuelle non attenante	351
0	0	5	0	0	0	Maison jumelée	352
0	0	5	0	0	0	Maison en rangée	353
0	0	0	5	0	0	Appartement, duplex	354
0	0	0	0	0	0	Appartement, immeuble de cinq étages ou plus	355
0	0	0	10	0	0	Appartement, immeuble de moins de cinq étages	356
0	0	0	0	0	0	Autre maison individuelle attenante	357
25	0	30	0	0	0	Logement mobile[48]	358
						État du logement	
55	10	245	20	20	10	Entretien régulier seulement	359
60	0	115	20	20	20	Réparations mineures	360
115	0	45	20	40	40	Réparations majeures	361
						Période de construction	
0	0	40	0	0	0	Avant 1946	362
0	0	70	0	0	0	1946 à 1960	363
15	0	65	0	0	0	1961 à 1970	364
45	10	80	0	10	0	1971 à 1980	365
35	0	55	0	10	10	1981 à 1985	366
35	10	30	0	10	10	1986 à 1990	367
15	0	25	15	10	30	1991 à 1995	368
35	0	35	25	20	25	1996 à 2000	369
45	0	15	20	15	10	2001 à 2006[49]	370

Nota : Voir les symboles et les abréviations dans les documents d'introduction et voir les documents de référence à la fin de la publication.

Selected characteristics for census divisions and census subdivisions – 100% data and 20% sample data, Ontario, 2006 Census (continued)

No.	Characteristics	Kee-Way-Win, IRI	Kenora, CY ◆◇	Kenora 38B, IRI ◆◆◇◇	Kenora, Unorganized, NO ◆◇◇A	Kingfisher Lake 1, IRI ◆◇◇	Kitchenuhmay koosib Aaki 84 (Big Trout Lake), IRI ◆◆◇◇
	Dwelling and household characteristics						
371	Average number of rooms per dwelling	5.1	6.4	5.5	6.6	5.5	4.6
372	Average number of bedrooms per dwelling	2.6	2.7	2.6	2.8	3.0	2.4
373	Average value of dwelling $	0	172,060	0	199,226	0	0
374	**Total number of private households**	**80**	**6,250**	**100**	**2,795**	**100**	**275**
	Household size						
375	1 person	10	1,785	15	545	10	65
376	2 persons	15	2,205	20	1,205	15	45
377	3 persons	15	900	20	450	20	45
378	4 to 5 persons	25	1,260	35	540	35	80
379	6 or more persons	15	105	15	60	25	45
	Household type						
380	One-family households[50]	60	4,335	70	2,175	75	170
381	Multiple-family households	0	35	0	25	15	35
382	Non-family households	10	1,880	20	595	15	70
383	Number of persons in private households	320	14,930	350	6,985	415	915
384	Average number of persons in private households	3.9	2.4	3.5	2.5	4.2	3.4
385	Tenant-occupied private non-farm, non-reserve dwellings[51]	0	1,420	0	290	0	0
386	Average gross rent $[51]	0	633	0	596	0	0
387	Tenant-occupied households spending 30% or more of household income on gross rent[52]	0	585	0	50	0	0
388	Tenant-occupied households spending from 30% to 99% of household income on gross rent[52]	0	570	0	40	0	0
389	Owner-occupied private non-farm, non-reserve dwellings[53]	0	4,825	0	2,490	0	0
390	Average owner's major payments $[53]	0	877	0	666	0	0
391	Owner households spending 30% or more of household income on owner's major payments[52]	0	680	0	220	0	0
392	Owner households spending from 30% to 99% of household income on owner's major payments[52]	0	595	0	180	0	0
	Census family characteristics						
393	**Total number of census families in private households**	**75**	**4,410**	**95**	**2,230**	**105**	**245**
	Family structure and number of children						
394	Total couple families	55	3,655	65	2,040	85	150
395	Total families of married couples	45	2,995	25	1,755	65	95
396	Without children at home	10	1,420	10	950	15	15
397	With children at home	40	1,575	20	810	50	75
398	1 child	10	555	0	360	15	15
399	2 children	10	735	10	335	15	25
400	3 or more children	20	280	0	115	20	30
401	Total families of common-law couples	10	665	35	285	15	60
402	Without children at home	0	370	10	145	0	15
403	With children at home	0	290	30	140	10	45
404	1 child	10	135	10	50	10	20
405	2 children	10	115	10	80	0	10
406	3 or more children	0	40	10	15	0	10
407	Total lone-parent families	25	750	25	190	25	100
408	Female parent	10	595	20	120	20	80
409	1 child	0	360	10	65	0	55
410	2 children	10	180	10	40	10	15
411	3 or more children	0	55	0	15	10	10
412	Male parent	10	155	10	65	0	15
413	1 child	0	100	0	50	0	10
414	2 children	0	30	0	15	0	10
415	3 or more children	10	20	0	0	0	10

Note: See symbols and abbreviations in the introductory material and see reference material at the end of the publication.

Certaines caractéristiques des divisions de recensement et des subdivisions de recensement – Données intégrales et données-échantillon (20 %), Ontario, Recensement de 2006 (suite)

Lac Seul 28, IRI ◆◆◇◇	Lake Of The Woods 37, IRI ◇	Machin, TP ◆◆◇◇	Marten Falls 65, IRI ◆◇	Muskrat Dam Lake, IRI ◆◇	Neskantaga, IRI ◆◆◇◇	Caractéristiques	N°
						Caractéristiques des logements et des ménages	
5.2	5.3	6.4	5.0	5.9	5.7	Nombre moyen de pièces par logement	371
2.7	2.7	2.7	2.4	3.0	3.0	Nombre moyen de chambres à coucher par logement	372
0	0	145,600	0	0	0	Valeur moyenne du logement $	373
225	**10**	**405**	**70**	**75**	**75**	**Nombre total de ménages privés**	374
						Taille du ménage	
35	0	90	25	15	10	1 personne	375
45	5	175	5	10	10	2 personnes	376
35	0	55	5	15	5	3 personnes	377
70	0	75	15	25	25	4 à 5 personnes	378
40	10	5	15	10	10	6 personnes ou plus	379
						Genre de ménage	
160	10	305	40	60	55	Ménages unifamiliaux[50]	380
20	0	0	0	0	10	Ménages multifamiliaux	381
40	0	90	25	15	15	Ménages non familiaux	382
820	60	970	220	250	265	Nombre de personnes dans les ménages privés	383
3.6	6.0	2.4	3.2	3.4	3.8	Nombre moyen de personnes dans les ménages privés	384
0	0	60	0	0	0	Ménages locataires dans les logements privés non agricoles hors réserve[51]	385
0	0	571	0	0	0	Loyer brut moyen $[51]	386
0	0	20	0	0	0	Ménages locataires consacrant 30 % ou plus du revenu du ménage au loyer brut[52]	387
0	0	20	0	0	0	Ménages locataires consacrant de 30 % à 99 % du revenu du ménage au loyer brut[52]	388
0	0	330	0	0	0	Ménages propriétaires dans les logements privés non agricoles hors réserve[53]	389
0	0	680	0	0	0	Principales dépenses de propriété moyennes $[53]	390
0	0	35	0	0	0	Ménages propriétaires consacrant 30 % ou plus du revenu du ménage aux principales dépenses de propriété[52]	391
0	0	30	0	0	0	Ménages propriétaires consacrant de 30 % à 99 % du revenu du ménage aux principales dépenses de propriété[52]	392
						Caractéristiques des familles de recensement	
215	**10**	**315**	**45**	**65**	**70**	**Nombre total de familles de recensement dans les ménages privés**	393
						Structure de la famille et le nombre d'enfants	
155	10	275	25	45	50	Total des familles avec conjoints	394
85	0	225	10	35	30	Total des familles avec couples mariés	395
15	0	135	10	0	10	Sans enfants à la maison	396
65	0	90	10	35	20	Avec enfants à la maison	397
25	0	40	0	10	10	1 enfant	398
20	0	35	0	15	0	2 enfants	399
20	0	15	10	10	10	3 enfants ou plus	400
65	10	45	15	10	15	Total des familles avec couples en union libre	401
20	0	25	0	0	0	Sans enfants à la maison	402
50	10	25	15	10	15	Avec enfants à la maison	403
20	0	10	0	0	10	1 enfant	404
15	0	15	0	10	10	2 enfants	405
10	0	0	10	0	10	3 enfants ou plus	406
60	0	50	15	15	20	Total des familles monoparentales	407
40	10	35	15	10	15	Parent de sexe féminin	408
20	0	25	0	0	10	1 enfant	409
10	0	10	10	0	0	2 enfants	410
10	0	10	0	0	0	3 enfants ou plus	411
20	0	15	0	10	0	Parent de sexe masculin	412
15	0	10	0	10	10	1 enfant	413
0	0	10	0	0	0	2 enfants	414
0	0	10	0	0	0	3 enfants ou plus	415

Nota : Voir les symboles et les abréviations dans les documents d'introduction et voir les documents de référence à la fin de la publication.

Selected characteristics for census divisions and census subdivisions – 100% data and 20% sample data, Ontario, 2006 Census (continued)

No.	Characteristics	Kee-Way-Win, IRI	Kenora, CY ◆◇	Kenora 38B, IRI ◆◆◇◇	Kenora, Unorganized, NO ◆◇◇A	Kingfisher Lake 1, IRI ◆◇◇	Kitchenuhmaykoosib Aaki 84 (Big Trout Lake), IRI ◆◆◇◇
	Census family characteristics						
416	**Total number of children at home**	**155**	**4,610**	**150**	**1,950**	**195**	**410**
	Age group						
417	Under 6 years	45	795	40	320	65	150
418	6 to 14 years	80	1,725	65	750	90	155
419	15 to 17 years	20	695	20	280	20	50
420	18 to 24 years	10	1,010	15	435	15	40
421	25 years and over	0	380	15	165	10	20
422	Average number of children at home per census family[54]	2.1	1.0	1.7	0.9	1.8	1.7
423	**Total number of persons in private households**	**320**	**14,925**	**350**	**6,990**	**415**	**915**
	Census family status and living arrangements						
424	Number of persons not in census families	35	2,255	40	760	30	110
425	Living with relatives[55]	20	270	10	110	15	35
426	Living with non-relatives only	0	205	15	105	10	10
427	Living alone	10	1,780	15	545	10	65
428	Number of census family persons	285	12,675	310	6,230	385	805
429	Average number of persons per census family	3.8	2.9	3.3	2.8	3.5	3.3
430	**Total number of persons aged 65 years and over**	**0**	**2,275**	**15**	**1,005**	**25**	**65**
431	Number of persons not in census families aged 65 years and over	0	935	10	245	0	25
432	Living with relatives[55]	0	60	0	35	10	0
433	Living with non-relatives only	0	60	0	0	0	0
434	Living alone	0	820	10	200	10	25
435	Number of census family persons aged 65 years and over	10	1,335	10	765	25	40
	Economic family characteristics						
436	**Total number of economic families in private households**	**65**	**4,405**	**90**	**2,220**	**95**	**210**
	Size of family						
437	2 persons	15	2,165	25	1,170	15	50
438	3 persons	15	900	20	440	15	40
439	4 persons	10	930	20	440	15	40
440	5 or more persons	30	405	25	170	45	80
441	Total number of persons in economic families	305	12,940	325	6,340	400	840
442	Average number of persons per economic family	5.0	3.0	4.0	3.0	4.0	4.0
443	Total number of persons not in economic families	10	1,990	25	650	15	75
	2005 income characteristics						
444	**Population 15 years and over**	**190**	**12,375**	**245**	**5,920**	**260**	**600**
	Sex and total income groups in 2005						
445	Without income	15	340	25	200	10	30
446	With income	180	12,035	220	5,720	245	565
447	Under $1,000[56]	25	280	55	195	25	95
448	$1,000 to $2,999	10	385	15	200	15	35
449	$3,000 to $4,999	0	325	10	180	15	45
450	$5,000 to $6,999	10	410	15	225	15	40
451	$7,000 to $9,999	20	655	20	295	15	35
452	$10,000 to $11,999	15	485	10	195	25	40
453	$12,000 to $14,999	15	655	30	295	30	70
454	$15,000 to $19,999	10	1,080	15	535	20	55
455	$20,000 to $24,999	15	900	20	455	30	25
456	$25,000 to $29,999	20	910	15	440	30	30
457	$30,000 to $34,999	20	785	10	385	10	35
458	$35,000 to $39,999	10	740	10	335	10	30
459	$40,000 to $44,999	10	860	0	305	10	10
460	$45,000 to $49,999	0	605	0	305	0	10
461	$50,000 to $59,999	10	1,035	0	430	0	0
462	$60,000 and over	0	1,915	0	935	0	10
463	Median income $[57]	14,304	29,703	9,424	28,041	13,582	11,563
464	Average income $[57]	18,120	35,252	13,709	35,173	16,246	16,322
465	Standard error of average income $[57]	0	552	0	386	0	0

Note: See symbols and abbreviations in the introductory material and see reference material at the end of the publication.

Certaines caractéristiques des divisions de recensement et des subdivisions de recensement – Données intégrales et données-échantillon (20 %), Ontario, Recensement de 2006 (suite)

Lac Seul 28, IRI ◆◆◇◇	Lake Of The Woods 37, IRI ◇	Machin, TP ◆◆◇◇	Marten Falls 65, IRI ◆◇	Muskrat Dam Lake, IRI ◆◇	Neskantaga, IRI ◆◆◇◇	Caractéristiques	N°
						Caractéristiques des familles de recensement	
365	**40**	**270**	**120**	**120**	**130**	**Nombre total d'enfants à la maison**	416
						Groupes d'âge	
105	10	50	40	40	45	Moins de 6 ans	417
140	25	120	60	55	55	6 à 14 ans	418
45	10	35	10	10	15	15 à 17 ans	419
60	0	40	10	10	10	18 à 24 ans	420
15	0	25	0	0	10	25 ans et plus	421
1.7	3.5	0.8	2.7	2.0	1.8	Nombre moyen d'enfants à la maison par famille de recensement[54]	422
820	**55**	**970**	**220**	**250**	**265**	**Nombre total de personnes dans les ménages privés**	423
						Situation des particuliers dans la famille de recensement et des particuliers dans le ménage	
90	0	115	35	20	20	Nombre de personnes hors famille de recensement	424
50	0	15	10	10	0	Vivant avec des personnes apparentées[55]	425
0	0	15	0	10	10	Vivant avec des personnes non apparentées seulement	426
35	0	85	25	15	15	Vivant seules	427
730	60	855	185	230	245	Nombre de membres d'une famille de recensement	428
3.5	4.0	2.7	4.2	3.5	3.5	Nombre moyen de personnes par famille de recensement	429
35	**0**	**155**	**0**	**15**	**15**	**Nombre total de personnes âgées de 65 ans et plus**	430
10	0	50	0	10	0	Nombre de personnes hors famille de recensement âgées de 65 ans et plus	431
0	0	10	0	0	0	Vivant avec des personnes apparentées[55]	432
0	0	0	0	0	0	Vivant avec des personnes non apparentées seulement	433
10	0	45	0	0	10	Vivant seules	434
20	0	105	0	10	0	Nombre de membres d'une famille de recensement âgés de 65 ans et plus	435
						Caractéristiques des familles économiques	
190	**15**	**310**	**40**	**65**	**60**	**Nombre total de familles économiques dans les ménages privés**	436
						Taille de la famille	
45	10	175	10	15	15	2 personnes	437
35	10	55	0	15	10	3 personnes	438
45	0	55	10	20	10	4 personnes	439
65	0	25	20	15	30	5 personnes ou plus	440
785	55	870	195	235	245	Nombre total de personnes dans les familles économiques	441
4.0	4.0	3.0	5.0	4.0	4.0	Nombre moyen de personnes par famille économique	442
40	0	100	25	20	15	Nombre total de personnes hors famille économique	443
						Caractéristiques du revenu de 2005	
555	**X**	**810**	**X**	**160**	**165**	**Population de 15 ans et plus**	444
						Sexe et groupes de revenu total en 2005	
40	X	30	X	0	10	Sans revenu	445
520	X	780	X	155	160	Avec un revenu	446
70	X	10	X	10	25	Moins de 1 000 $[56]	447
35	X	25	X	10	0	1 000 $ à 2 999 $	448
35	X	20	X	10	0	3 000 $ à 4 999 $	449
30	X	40	X	10	10	5 000 $ à 6 999 $	450
40	X	45	X	10	15	7 000 $ à 9 999 $	451
30	X	35	X	10	15	10 000 $ à 11 999 $	452
40	X	50	X	20	10	12 000 $ à 14 999 $	453
45	X	90	X	10	15	15 000 $ à 19 999 $	454
35	X	60	X	15	10	20 000 $ à 24 999 $	455
40	X	70	X	25	15	25 000 $ à 29 999 $	456
25	X	50	X	25	15	30 000 $ à 34 999 $	457
25	X	45	X	10	10	35 000 $ à 39 999 $	458
15	X	50	X	0	10	40 000 $ à 44 999 $	459
20	X	25	X	0	10	45 000 $ à 49 999$	460
15	X	50	X	10	0	50 000 $ à 59 999$	461
10	X	115	X	0	0	60 000 $ et plus	462
13,216	X	25,920	X	20,960	13,600	Revenu médian $[57]	463
17,995	X	32,508	X	20,739	18,442	Revenu moyen $[57]	464
0	X	0	X	0	0	Erreur type de revenu moyen $[57]	465

Nota : Voir les symboles et les abréviations dans les documents d'introduction et voir les documents de référence à la fin de la publication.

Selected characteristics for census divisions and census subdivisions – 100% data and 20% sample data, Ontario, 2006 Census (continued)

No.	Characteristics	Kee-Way-Win, IRI	Kenora, CY ◆◇	Kenora 38B, IRI ◆◆◇◇	Kenora, Unorganized, NO ◆◇◇**A**	Kingfisher Lake 1, IRI ◆◇◇	Kitchenuhmaykoosib Aaki 84 (Big Trout Lake), IRI ◆◆◇◇
	2005 income characteristics						
	Sex and total income groups in 2005 (continued)						
466	Total - Males	100	5,975	130	3,065	130	285
467	Without income	0	115	15	90	10	20
468	With income	95	5,860	120	2,975	120	265
469	Under $1,000[56]	15	115	40	95	10	55
470	$1,000 to $2,999	0	155	10	85	15	15
471	$3,000 to $4,999	0	155	0	50	10	10
472	$5,000 to $6,999	0	190	10	55	10	10
473	$7,000 to $9,999	15	210	10	100	0	15
474	$10,000 to $11,999	10	205	0	45	10	20
475	$12,000 to $14,999	10	255	0	105	10	25
476	$15,000 to $19,999	0	430	10	215	10	30
477	$20,000 to $24,999	0	285	10	205	20	20
478	$25,000 to $29,999	10	345	0	200	15	15
479	$30,000 to $34,999	10	350	0	205	0	15
480	$35,000 to $39,999	0	315	10	200	10	10
481	$40,000 to $44,999	0	410	0	170	0	10
482	$45,000 to $49,999	0	385	0	210	0	10
483	$50,000 to $59,999	0	690	0	280	0	10
484	$60,000 and over	0	1,350	0	750	0	0
485	Median income $[57]	13,056	38,397	7,344	37,476	13,984	11,608
486	Average income $[57]	18,605	42,474	12,175	44,104	16,683	14,818
487	Standard error of average income $[57]	0	970	0	632	0	0
488	Total - Females	90	6,395	115	2,855	130	315
489	Without income	10	220	10	110	0	10
490	With income	85	6,170	105	2,745	125	300
491	Under $1,000[56]	10	165	10	95	10	40
492	$1,000 to $2,999	0	230	10	110	10	15
493	$3,000 to $4,999	10	170	0	130	10	30
494	$5,000 to $6,999	0	220	10	170	10	25
495	$7,000 to $9,999	10	440	10	200	10	25
496	$10,000 to $11,999	0	280	10	145	20	15
497	$12,000 to $14,999	10	400	15	185	20	40
498	$15,000 to $19,999	10	650	10	320	10	30
499	$20,000 to $24,999	10	610	10	250	10	10
500	$25,000 to $29,999	15	565	0	245	15	15
501	$30,000 to $34,999	10	435	0	185	10	20
502	$35,000 to $39,999	0	420	10	130	0	15
503	$40,000 to $44,999	10	450	0	135	0	10
504	$45,000 to $49,999	10	220	0	95	0	0
505	$50,000 to $59,999	10	350	0	150	0	0
506	$60,000 and over	0	565	0	190	0	10
507	Median income $[57]	14,848	23,984	12,672	20,074	13,408	10,928
508	Average income $[57]	17,577	28,395	15,464	25,494	15,839	17,628
509	Standard error of average income $[57]	0	508	0	364	0	0
	Composition of total income						
510	Composition of total income in 2005 %	100.0	100.0	100.0	100.0	100.0	100.0
511	Employment income %	82.1	73.6	66.6	73.7	73.7	70.0
512	Government transfer payments %	21.5	12.1	27.7	11.8	25.4	28.7
513	Other %	0.1	14.2	5.0	14.4	0.6	0.7
514	**Population 15 years and over with employment income in 2005**	**125**	**9,235**	**120**	**4,265**	**185**	**300**
	Sex and work activity						
515	Median employment income in 2005 $	18,176	28,557	10,816	26,992	14,944	15,552
516	Average employment income in 2005 $	20,017	33,809	16,741	34,775	16,295	21,883
517	Standard error of average employment income $	0	664	0	486	0	0
518	Worked full year, full time[59]	55	4,535	50	2,005	90	135
519	Median employment income in 2005 $	28,480	44,123	26,347	44,810	23,744	29,120
520	Average employment income in 2005 $	31,053	48,356	27,053	50,212	23,572	35,440
521	Standard error of average employment income $	0	915	0	745	0	0
522	Worked part year or part time[60]	55	4,120	55	2,010	45	95
523	Median employment income in 2005 $	10,912	10,970	7,848	14,432	9,696	7,531
524	Average employment income in 2005 $	13,396	21,539	11,849	22,932	10,299	12,036
525	Standard error of average employment income $	0	865	0	551	0	0
526	Males 15 years and over with employment income[58]	65	4,775	60	2,305	95	150
527	Median employment income in 2005 $	13,984	33,900	12,736	37,129	15,776	15,584
528	Average employment income in 2005 $	21,926	39,028	17,697	43,144	17,057	19,551
529	Standard error of average employment income $	0	1,110	0	800	0	0

Note: See symbols and abbreviations in the introductory material and see reference material at the end of the publication.

Certaines caractéristiques des divisions de recensement et des subdivisions de recensement – Données intégrales et données-échantillon (20 %), Ontario, Recensement de 2006 (suite)

Lac Seul 28, IRI ◆◆◇◇	Lake Of The Woods 37, IRI ◇	Machin, TP ◆◆◇◇	Marten Falls 65, IRI ◆◇	Muskrat Dam Lake, IRI ◆◇	Neskantaga, IRI ◆◆◇◇	Caractéristiques	N°
						Caractéristiques du revenu de 2005	
						Sexe et groupes de revenu total en 2005 (suite)	
305	X	410	X	80	85	Total - Hommes	466
25	X	15	X	0	0	Sans revenu	467
285	X	400	X	75	80	Avec un revenu	468
45	X	10	X	0	20	Moins de 1 000 $[56]	469
25	X	10	X	10	0	1 000 $ à 2 999 $	470
20	X	10	X	10	0	3 000 $ à 4 999 $	471
10	X	10	X	10	0	5 000 $ à 6 999 $	472
25	X	10	X	10	10	7 000 $ à 9 999 $	473
15	X	15	X	10	10	10 000 $ à 11 999 $	474
15	X	25	X	10	0	12 000 $ à 14 999 $	475
30	X	35	X	10	10	15 000 $ à 19 999 $	476
20	X	30	X	10	0	20 000 $ à 24 999 $	477
20	X	45	X	15	10	25 000 $ à 29 999 $	478
10	X	15	X	0	0	30 000 $ à 34 999 $	479
10	X	15	X	10	10	35 000 $ à 39 999 $	480
10	X	25	X	0	0	40 000 $ à $44 999 $	481
10	X	15	X	0	0	45 000 $ à $49 999 $	482
10	X	30	X	10	0	50 000 $ à $59 999 $	483
0	X	95	X	0	10	60 000 $ et plus	484
11,696	X	33,600	X	20,928	13,216	Revenu médian $[57]	485
17,377	X	40,915	X	20,642	18,233	Revenu moyen $[57]	486
0	X	0	X	0	0	Erreur type de revenu moyen $[57]	487
250	X	395	X	75	75	Total - Femmes	488
15	X	15	X	0	0	Sans revenu	489
235	X	380	X	75	75	Avec un revenu	490
25	X	10	X	10	10	Moins de 1 000 $[56]	491
15	X	20	X	0	0	1 000$ à 2 999 $	492
15	X	10	X	0	0	3 000 $ à 4 999 $	493
20	X	30	X	0	0	5 000 $ à 6 999 $	494
20	X	35	X	0	10	7 000 $ à 9 999 $	495
10	X	25	X	0	10	10 000 $ à 11 999 $	496
20	X	30	X	15	0	12 000 $ à 14 999 $	497
15	X	55	X	0	10	15 000 $ à 19 999 $	498
20	X	30	X	10	0	20 000 $ à 24 999 $	499
20	X	20	X	10	15	25 000 $ à 29 999 $	500
15	X	35	X	20	10	30 000 $ à 34 999 $	501
15	X	20	X	0	0	35 000 $ à 39 999 $	502
10	X	20	X	0	10	40 000 $ à 44 999 $	503
10	X	10	X	0	0	45 000 $ à 49 999 $	504
10	X	20	X	0	0	50 000 $ à 59 999 $	505
0	X	15	X	0	0	60 000 $ et plus	506
13,984	X	18,320	X	21,888	14,304	Revenu médian $[57]	507
18,748	X	23,657	X	20,839	18,668	Revenu moyen $[57]	508
0	X	0	X	0	0	Erreur type de revenu moyen $[57]	509
						Composition du revenu total	
100.0	X	100.0	X	100.0	100.0	Composition du revenu total en 2005 %	510
76.3	X	71.9	X	82.9	68.1	Revenu d'emploi %	511
21.7	X	17.5	X	18.1	30.1	Transferts gouvernementaux %	512
1.3	X	11.0	X	0.2	0.5	Autres %	513
375	**X**	**585**	**X**	**130**	**95**	**Population de 15 ans et plus avec un revenu d'emploi en 2005**	514
						Sexe et travail	
15,456	X	22,848	X	20,288	18,368	Revenu médian d'emploi en 2005 $	515
19,293	X	30,959	X	19,751	21,163	Revenu moyen d'emploi en 2005 $	516
0	X	0	X	0	0	Erreur type de revenu moyen d'emploi $	517
190	X	270	X	80	50	A travaillé toute l'année à plein temps[59]	518
25,952	X	44,608	X	27,712	27,264	Revenu médian d'emploi en 2005 $	519
28,180	X	47,818	X	25,373	29,559	Revenu moyen d'emploi en 2005 $	520
0	X	0	X	0	0	Erreur type de revenu moyen d'emploi $	521
150	X	275	X	40	10	A travaillé une partie de l'année ou à temps partiel[60]	522
6,288	X	12,128	X	6,816	0	Revenu médian d'emploi en 2005 $	523
10,449	X	18,083	X	10,524	0	Revenu moyen d'emploi en 2005 $	524
0	X	0	X	0	0	Erreur type de revenu moyen d'emploi $	525
205	X	320	X	70	50	Hommes de 15 ans et plus avec un revenu d'emploi[58]	526
14,997	X	27,243	X	21,568	19,456	Revenu médian d'emploi en 2005 $	527
19,108	X	37,782	X	20,544	22,918	Revenu moyen d'emploi en 2005 $	528
0	X	0	X	0	0	Erreur type de revenu moyen d'emploi $	529

Nota : Voir les symboles et les abréviations dans les documents d'introduction et voir les documents de référence à la fin de la publication.

Selected characteristics for census divisions and census subdivisions – 100% data and 20% sample data, Ontario, 2006 Census (continued)

No.	Characteristics	Kee-Way-Win, IRI	Kenora, CY ◆◊	Kenora 38B, IRI ◆◆◊◊	Kenora, Unorganized, NO ◆◊◊A	Kingfisher Lake 1, IRI ◆◊◊	Kitchenuhmaykoosib Aaki 84 (Big Trout Lake), IRI ◆◆◊◊
	2005 income characteristics						
	Sex and work activity (continued)						
530	Worked full year, full time[59]	25	2,450	25	1,215	40	65
531	Median employment income in 2005 $	36,480	50,856	29,312	52,497	25,664	28,448
532	Average employment income in 2005 $	35,200	55,167	27,515	58,405	27,772	29,261
533	Standard error of average employment income $	0	1,499	0	1,132	0	0
534	Worked part year or part time[60]	30	1,940	30	955	35	60
535	Median employment income in 2005 $	11,072	11,631	10,784	20,039	10,272	8,384
536	Average employment income in 2005 $	14,296	24,895	14,354	29,540	11,229	11,811
537	Standard error of average employment income $	0	1,557	0	989	0	0
538	Females 15 years and over with employment income[58]	60	4,455	60	1,960	85	150
539	Median employment income in 2005 $	19,648	25,631	8,544	20,228	14,304	14,784
540	Average employment income in 2005 $	17,982	28,214	15,754	24,915	15,387	24,246
541	Standard error of average employment income $	0	656	0	439	0	0
542	Worked full year, full time[59]	25	2,080	25	795	50	70
543	Median employment income in 2005 $	25,472	38,171	26,304	34,185	19,648	30,443
544	Average employment income in 2005 $	27,349	40,344	26,609	37,689	19,984	41,619
545	Standard error of average employment income $	0	802	0	650	0	0
546	Worked part year or part time[60]	20	2,175	25	1,055	15	35
547	Median employment income in 2005 $	10,528	10,298	4,008	10,479	6,752	3,936
548	Average employment income in 2005 $	11,940	18,540	9,252	16,927	8,173	12,445
549	Standard error of average employment income $	0	852	0	525	0	0
550	**Total number of economic families in private households**	**65**	**4,405**	**85**	**2,215**	**90**	**215**
	Family income groups in 2005						
551	Under $10,000	0	45	25	40	0	40
552	$10,000 to $19,999	10	130	10	35	10	30
553	$20,000 to $29,999	15	235	20	160	10	30
554	$30,000 to $39,999	10	360	10	190	20	40
555	$40,000 to $49,999	10	475	0	210	20	30
556	$50,000 to $59,999	10	325	0	280	0	0
557	$60,000 to $69,999	10	380	10	200	0	0
558	$70,000 to $79,999	0	420	0	205	10	10
559	$80,000 to $89,999	0	435	0	175	0	0
560	$90,000 to $99,999	0	370	0	180	0	0
561	$100,000 and over	0	1,215	0	550	0	0
562	Median family income $	40,576	75,708	26,624	69,819	39,296	31,456
563	Average family income $	43,619	80,257	33,331	80,210	42,056	36,465
564	Standard error of average family income $	0	1,337	0	1,011	0	0
	Family after-tax income groups in 2005						
565	Under $10,000	0	45	20	45	0	40
566	$10,000 to $19,999	0	135	15	40	10	35
567	$20,000 to $29,999	15	275	15	175	15	25
568	$30,000 to $39,999	15	485	10	245	25	40
569	$40,000 to $49,999	10	565	10	325	20	35
570	$50,000 to $59,999	10	470	0	290	0	10
571	$60,000 to $69,999	10	540	0	255	0	10
572	$70,000 to $79,999	0	550	0	230	10	15
573	$80,000 to $89,999	10	325	0	145	0	10
574	$90,000 to $99,999	0	370	0	135	0	0
575	$100,000 and over	0	640	10	325	0	10
576	Median after-tax family income $	40,576	64,412	25,984	58,446	39,296	31,456
577	Average after-tax family income $	43,582	67,200	32,359	66,678	42,038	36,439
578	Standard error of average after-tax family income $	0	986	0	734	0	0
	Income status in 2005						
579	Total population in private households for income status	0	14,930	0	6,985	0	0
580	Below low income cut-off before tax in 2005	0	1,290	0	330	0	0
581	Prevalence of low income before tax in 2005 %	0.0	8.6	0.0	4.7	0.0	0.0
582	Below low income cut-off after tax in 2005	0	640	0	255	0	0
583	Prevalence of low income after tax in 2005 %	0.0	4.3	0.0	3.7	0.0	0.0

Note: See symbols and abbreviations in the introductory material and see reference material at the end of the publication.

Certaines caractéristiques des divisions de recensement et des subdivisions de recensement – Données intégrales et données-échantillon (20 %), Ontario, Recensement de 2006 (suite)

Lac Seul 28, IRI ◆◆◇◇	Lake Of The Woods 37, IRI ◇	Machin, TP ◆◆◇◇	Marten Falls 65, IRI ◆◇	Muskrat Dam Lake, IRI ◆◇	Neskantaga, IRI ◆◆◇◇	Caractéristiques	N°
						Caractéristiques du revenu de 2005	
						Sexe et travail (suite)	
100	X	155	X	40	25	A travaillé toute l'année à plein temps[59]	530
25,920	X	53,504	X	27,792	31,168	Revenu médian d'emploi en 2005 $	531
28,582	X	56,765	X	26,412	30,743	Revenu moyen d'emploi en 2005 $	532
0	X	0	X	0	0	Erreur type de revenu moyen d'emploi $	533
95	X	140	X	20	0	A travaillé une partie de l'année ou à temps partiel[60]	534
6,848	X	14,976	X	9,376	0	Revenu médian d'emploi en 2005 $	535
10,830	X	20,649	X	12,612	0	Revenu moyen d'emploi en 2005 $	536
0	X	0	X	0	0	Erreur type de revenu moyen d'emploi $	537
165	X	265	X	65	45	Femmes de 15 ans et plus avec un revenu d'emploi[58]	538
16,960	X	16,640	X	20,096	10,848	Revenu médian d'emploi en 2005 $	539
19,521	X	22,776	X	18,896	19,040	Revenu moyen d'emploi en 2005 $	540
0	X	0	X	0	0	Erreur type de revenu moyen d'emploi $	541
95	X	115	X	40	20	A travaillé toute l'année à plein temps[59]	542
25,984	X	32,320	X	26,304	24,384	Revenu médian d'emploi en 2005 $	543
27,762	X	35,244	X	24,309	28,065	Revenu moyen d'emploi en 2005 $	544
0	X	0	X	0	0	Erreur type de revenu moyen d'emploi $	545
60	X	135	X	15	0	A travaillé une partie de l'année ou à temps partiel[60]	546
5,712	X	10,464	X	5,016	0	Revenu médian d'emploi en 2005 $	547
9,832	X	15,305	X	7,323	0	Revenu moyen d'emploi en 2005 $	548
0	X	0	X	0	0	Erreur type de revenu moyen d'emploi $	549
190	**X**	**315**	**X**	**65**	**60**	**Nombre total des familles économiques dans les ménages privés**	550
						Revenu de la famille économique en 2005	
15	X	10	X	0	0	Moins de 10 000 $	551
30	X	10	X	10	0	10 000 $ à 19 999 $	552
25	X	25	X	10	15	20 000 $ à 29 999 $	553
30	X	30	X	10	10	30 000 $ à 39 999 $	554
20	X	30	X	10	15	40 000 $ à 49 999 $	555
15	X	40	X	10	0	50 000 $ à 59 999 $	556
20	X	25	X	10	10	60 000 $ à 69 999 $	557
15	X	30	X	10	0	70 000 $ à 79 999 $	558
0	X	20	X	0	0	80 000 $ à 89 999 $	559
10	X	20	X	0	0	90 000 $ à 99 999 $	560
15	X	75	X	0	0	100 000 $ et plus	561
39,296	X	66,475	X	44,416	38,912	Revenu médian des familles $	562
45,965	X	72,790	X	45,846	43,944	Revenu moyen des familles $	563
0	X	0	X	0	0	Erreur type de revenu moyen des familles $	564
						Revenu après impôt de la famille économique en 2005	
15	X	0	X	0	0	Moins de 10 000 $	565
30	X	10	X	0	0	10 000 $ à 19 999 $	566
25	X	30	X	10	15	20 000 $ à 29 999 $	567
30	X	35	X	15	15	30 000 $ à 39 999 $	568
25	X	50	X	15	15	40 000 $ à 49 999 $	569
15	X	40	X	0	0	50 000 $ à 59 999 $	570
20	X	35	X	10	10	60 000 $ à 69 999 $	571
15	X	25	X	10	10	70 000 $ à 79 999 $	572
0	X	40	X	10	0	80 000 $ à 89 999 $	573
10	X	25	X	0	0	90 000 $ à 99 999 $	574
10	X	25	X	0	0	100 000 $ et plus	575
38,784	X	57,557	X	44,416	38,912	Revenu médian après impôt des familles $	576
44,745	X	61,367	X	45,608	42,945	Revenu moyen après impôt des familles $	577
0	X	0	X	0	0	Erreur type de revenu moyen après impôt des familles $	578
						Catégorie de revenu en 2005	
0	X	970	X	0	0	Population totale dans les ménages privés pour la catégorie de revenu	579
0	X	70	X	0	0	Au-dessous du seuil de faible revenu avant impôt en 2005	580
0.0	X	7.2	X	0.0	0.0	Fréquence du faible revenu avant impôt en 2005 %	581
0	X	60	X	0	0	Au-dessous du seuil de faible revenu après impôt en 2005	582
0.0	X	6.2	X	0.0	0.0	Fréquence du faible revenu après impôt en 2005 %	583

Nota : Voir les symboles et les abréviations dans les documents d'introduction et voir les documents de référence à la fin de la publication.

Selected characteristics for census divisions and census subdivisions – 100% data and 20% sample data, Ontario, 2006 Census (continued)

No.	Characteristics	Kee-Way-Win, IRI	Kenora, CY ◆◊	Kenora 38B, IRI ◆◆◊◊	Kenora, Unorganized, NO ◆◊◊A	Kingfisher Lake 1, IRI ◆◊◊	Kitchenuhmaykoosib Aaki 84 (Big Trout Lake), IRI ◆◆◊◊
	2005 income characteristics						
584	**Total number of private households**	**80**	**6,250**	**105**	**2,800**	**100**	**275**
	Household income groups in 2005						
585	Under $10,000	0	165	30	80	10	55
586	$10,000 to $19,999	0	605	20	155	10	55
587	$20,000 to $29,999	10	580	20	275	15	35
588	$30,000 to $39,999	15	650	15	275	25	45
589	$40,000 to $49,999	10	680	10	275	20	40
590	$50,000 to $59,999	10	440	0	330	10	15
591	$60,000 to $69,999	10	535	0	225	0	0
592	$70,000 to $79,999	10	480	10	230	10	15
593	$80,000 to $89,999	0	455	0	190	0	0
594	$90,000 to $99,999	10	395	10	185	0	10
595	$100,000 and over	0	1,265	10	570	0	10
596	Median household income $	36,160	59,946	22,592	60,089	35,840	28,000
597	Average household income $	40,828	67,773	29,971	71,560	39,340	33,840
598	Standard error of average household income $	0	1,181	0	892	0	0
	Household after-tax income groups in 2005						
599	Under $10,000	0	175	30	90	10	50
600	$10,000 to $19,999	10	630	20	170	15	55
601	$20,000 to $29,999	15	690	15	325	15	35
602	$30,000 to $39,999	15	855	15	355	25	50
603	$40,000 to $49,999	10	730	0	380	20	35
604	$50,000 to $59,999	10	610	10	335	10	15
605	$60,000 to $69,999	10	605	10	280	0	10
606	$70,000 to $79,999	10	570	0	240	10	10
607	$80,000 to $89,999	0	325	0	160	0	0
608	$90,000 to $99,999	10	370	10	135	10	0
609	$100,000 and over	0	685	10	330	0	10
610	Median after-tax household income $	35,456	50,426	22,592	52,417	35,840	28,000
611	Average after-tax household income $	40,745	56,794	29,140	59,547	39,324	33,432
612	Standard error of average after-tax household income $	0	877	0	658	0	0

Note: See symbols and abbreviations in the introductory material and see reference material at the end of the publication.

Certaines caractéristiques des divisions de recensement et des subdivisions de recensement – Données intégrales et données-échantillon (20 %), Ontario, Recensement de 2006 (suite)

Lac Seul 28, IRI ◆◆◇◇	Lake Of The Woods 37, IRI ◇	Machin, TP ◆◆◇◇	Marten Falls 65, IRI ◆◇	Muskrat Dam Lake, IRI ◆◇	Neskantaga, IRI ◆◆◇◇	Caractéristiques	Nº
						Caractéristiques du revenu de 2005	
225	**X**	**405**	**X**	**80**	**75**	**Nombre total des ménages privés**	584
						Tranches de revenu des ménages en 2005	
30	X	15	X	0	0	Moins de 10 000 $	585
40	X	45	X	10	15	10 000 $ à 19 999 $	586
30	X	40	X	10	15	20 000 $ à 29 999 $	587
25	X	45	X	20	15	30 000 $ à 39 999 $	588
25	X	35	X	10	15	40 000 $ à 49 999 $	589
20	X	45	X	10	0	50 000 $ à 59 999 $	590
20	X	30	X	10	0	60 000 $ à 69 999 $	591
15	X	30	X	10	10	70 000 $ à 79 999 $	592
0	X	20	X	0	0	80 000 $ à 89 999 $	593
10	X	25	X	0	0	90 000 $ à 99 999 $	594
10	X	75	X	0	0	100 000 $ et plus	595
34,176	X	55,616	X	40,064	36,949	Revenu médian des ménages $	596
41,143	X	62,525	X	41,747	39,377	Revenu moyen des ménages $	597
0	X	0	X	0	0	Erreur type de revenu moyen des ménages $	598
						Tranches du revenu après impôt des ménages en 2005	
30	X	15	X	0	10	Moins de 10 000 $	599
40	X	45	X	10	15	10 000 $ à 19 999 $	600
30	X	50	X	10	10	20 000 $ à 29 999 $	601
30	X	50	X	20	15	30 000 $ à 39 999 $	602
25	X	55	X	10	15	40 000 $ à 49 999 $	603
15	X	40	X	10	10	50 000 $ à 59 999 $	604
20	X	40	X	10	0	60 000 $ à 69 999 $	605
15	X	30	X	0	10	70 000 $ à 79 999 $	606
10	X	35	X	0	0	80 000 $ à 89 999 $	607
0	X	25	X	0	0	90 000 $ à 99 999 $	608
10	X	25	X	0	0	100 000 $ et plus	609
34,091	X	48,171	X	40,064	36,949	Revenu médian après impôt des ménages $	610
40,073	X	52,935	X	41,558	38,566	Revenu moyen après impôt des ménages $	611
0	X	0	X	0	0	Erreur type de revenu moyen après impôt des ménages $	612

Nota : Voir les symboles et les abréviations dans les documents d'introduction et voir les documents de référence à la fin de la publication.

Footnotes

1. Based on 2006 area. These figures have not been subjected to random rounding.
2. These figures have not been subjected to random rounding.
3. Includes institutional residents.
4. Since 1996, Aboriginal people married according to traditional customs were instructed to report themselves as legally married.
5. In 2006, legally married same-sex couples are included in this category.
6. Excludes institutional residents. These data are based on weighted sample data (20%). In some instances, due to weighting factors, it is possible for small areas to have an 'estimated population excluding institutional residents' higher than the 'population including institutional residents.'
7. Non-official language categories are based on the most frequently reported responses in the province or territory. When zero values are obtained for most of the non-official languages in some geographic areas, the number of non-official languages shown is less.
8. This is a subtotal of all languages collected by the census that are not displayed separately here. For a full list of languages collected in the census, please refer to Appendix G in the *2006 Census Dictionary*.
9. Refers to the language spoken most often at home by the individual at the time of the census. Other languages spoken at home on a regular basis are also collected.
10. Data on knowledge of official languages - According to studies on data certification, the 2006 Census statistics on knowledge of official languages could underestimate the category 'English and French' and overestimate the category 'French only,' particularly for the francophone population and, therefore, for the whole population. More information on the subject is available in the *Languages Reference Guide, 2006 Census*, Catalogue no. 97-555-GWE2006003.
11. Indicates the number of respondents reporting knowledge of each of these non-official languages.
12. The official language minority is English in Quebec and French in all other provinces and territories.

Renvois

1. Selon la superficie de 2006. Ces chiffres n'ont pas fait l'objet d'un arrondissement aléatoire.
2. Ces chiffres n'ont pas fait l'objet d'un arrondissement aléatoire.
3. Comprend les pensionnaires d'un établissement institutionnel.
4. Depuis 1996, les Autochtones mariés selon les coutumes traditionnelles devaient indiquer qu'ils étaient légalement mariés.
5. En 2006, les couples de même sexe légalement mariés sont inclus dans cette catégorie.
6. Ne comprend pas les pensionnaires d'un établissement institutionnel. Ces données sont basées sur les données-échantillon pondérées (20 %). Dans certains cas, en raison des coefficients de pondération, il est possible que, dans les petites régions, « l'estimation de la population ne comprenant pas les pensionnaires d'un établissement institutionnel » soit plus élevée que « la population comprenant les pensionnaires d'un établissement institutionnel ».
7. Les catégories de langues non officielles sont basées sur les réponses le plus souvent déclarées dans la province ou le territoire. Le nombre de langues non officielles présentées est moindre lorsque des valeurs égales à zéro sont obtenues pour la plupart des langues non officielles dans certaines régions géographiques.
8. Ceci est un sous-total de toutes les langues recueillies par le recensement qui ne sont pas affichées séparément ici. Pour obtenir une liste complète des langues recueillies au recensement, veuillez vous référer à l'annexe G dans le *Dictionnaire du Recensement de 2006*.
9. Langue que le recensé parlait le plus souvent à la maison au moment du recensement. Des données sur les autres langues parlées à la maison de façon régulière ont aussi été recueillies.
10. Données sur la connaissance des langues officielles - D'après des études de certification des données, les statistiques du Recensement de 2006 sur la connaissance des langues officielles pourraient sous-estimer la catégorie « français et anglais » et surestimer la catégorie « français seulement », surtout pour la population francophone et, par conséquent, pour l'ensemble de la population. Plus d'information sur le sujet est présentée dans le *Guide de référence sur les langues, Recensement de 2006*, numéro 97-555-GWF2006003 au catalogue.
11. Indique le nombre de répondants qui ont indiqué avoir une connaissance de chacune de ces langues non officielles.
12. Au Québec, la langue officielle minoritaire est l'anglais; et, dans les autres provinces et territoires, la langue officielle minoritaire est le français.

Footnotes (continued)

13. This table shows total response counts for the 15 most frequently reported ethnic origins in the province or territory. Total responses indicate the number of respondents who reported each ethnic origin, either as their only response or in addition to one or more other ethnic origins. Total responses represent the sum of single ethnic origin responses and multiple ethnic origin responses received in the census.

14. Included in the Aboriginal identity population are those persons who reported identifying with at least one Aboriginal group, that is, North American Indian, Métis or Inuit, and/or those who reported being a Treaty Indian or a Registered Indian, as defined by the *Indian Act* of Canada, and/or those who reported they were members of an Indian band or First Nation.

15. Refers to those persons who reported at least one Aboriginal ancestry (North American Indian, Métis or Inuit) to the ethnic origin question. 'Ethnic origin' refers to the ethnic or cultural origins of a person's ancestors. 'Aboriginal ancestry' was referred to as 'Aboriginal origin' prior to the 2006 Census.

16. Registered or Treaty Indian: 'Registered Indian' refers to those persons who reported they were registered under the *Indian Act* of Canada. Treaty Indians are persons who reported they were registered under the *Indian Act* of Canada and can prove descent from a band that signed a treaty.

    The Registered Indian counts in this table may differ from the administrative counts from the Indian Register maintained by the Department of Indian Affairs and Northern Development, with the most important causes of these differences being the incompletely enumerated Indian reserves and Indian settlements as well as methodological and conceptual differences between the two sources.

17. The *Employment Equity Act* defines visible minorities as 'persons, other than Aboriginal peoples, who are non-Caucasian in race or non-white in colour."

18. For example, 'East Indian,' 'Pakistani,' 'Sri Lankan,' etc.

19. For example, 'Vietnamese,' 'Cambodian,' 'Malaysian,' 'Laotian,' etc.

20. For example, 'Iranian,' 'Afghan,' etc.

Renvois (suite)

13. Ce tableau présente les chiffres des réponses totales des 15 origines ethniques le plus souvent déclarées dans la province ou le territoire. Le total des réponses correspond au nombre de recensés ayant indiqué chaque origine ethnique, soit comme étant leur seule réponse ou comme étant associée à une autre origine ethnique ou plus. Le total des réponses représente la somme des réponses uniques portant sur l'origine ethnique et des réponses multiples portant sur l'origine ethnique déclarées dans le cadre du recensement.

14. Sont incluses dans la population ayant une identité autochtone les personnes ayant déclaré appartenir à au moins un groupe autochtone, c'est-à-dire Indien de l'Amérique du Nord, Métis, ou Inuit, et/ou les personnes ayant déclaré être des Indiens des traités ou des Indiens inscrits tel que défini par la *Loi sur les Indiens* du Canada, et/ou les personnes ayant déclaré appartenir à une bande indienne ou à une Première nation.

15. Personne ayant indiqué au moins une ascendance autochtone (Indien de l'Amérique du Nord, Métis ou Inuit) à la question sur l'origine ethnique. « Origine ethnique » fait référence aux origines ethniques ou culturelles des ancêtres du répondant. « Ascendance autochtone » était « origine autochtone » avant le Recensement de 2006.

16. Indien inscrit ou Indien des traités : Les Indiens inscrits sont des personnes ayant déclaré être inscrites en vertu de la *Loi sur les Indiens* du Canada. Les Indiens des traités sont des personnes ayant déclaré être inscrites en vertu de la *Loi sur les Indiens* du Canada et qui peuvent démontrer qu'elles descendent d'une bande qui a signé un traité.

    Il est possible que les chiffres d'Indiens inscrits qui figurent dans le présent tableau ne concordent pas avec les chiffres du Registre des Indiens du ministère des Affaires indiennes et du Nord canadien, les divergences étant surtout attribuables au dénombrement partiel des réserves indiennes et des établissements indiens et à la diversité des méthodes et concepts adoptés par chaque source.

17. Selon la *Loi sur l'équité en matière d'emploi* font partie des minorités visibles « les personnes, autres que les Autochtones, qui ne sont pas de race blanche ou qui n'ont pas la peau blanche ».

18. Par exemple, « Indien de l'Inde », « Pakistanais », « Sri-Lankais », etc.

19. Par exemple, « Vietnamien », « Cambodgien », « Malaisien », « Laotien », etc.

20. Par exemple, « Iranien », « Afghan », etc.

Footnotes (continued)

21. The abbreviation 'n.i.e.' means 'not included elsewhere.' Includes respondents who reported a write-in response such as 'Guyanese,' 'West Indian,' 'Kurd,' 'Tibetan,' 'Polynesian,' 'Pacific Islander,' etc.

22. Includes respondents who reported more than one visible minority group by checking two or more mark-in circles, e.g., 'Black' and 'South Asian.'

23. Includes persons who are stateless.

24. Includes those who reported dual citizenship including 'Canadian.'

25. Includes persons who are stateless. Prior to the 2006 Census, this category was called 'Citizens of other countries'. The content of the category remains unchanged in 2006 compared with previous censuses.

26. For information on the specific countries included in each regional grouping in this variable, please refer to Appendix J in the *2006 Census Dictionary*.

27. Non-immigrants are persons who are Canadian citizens by birth. Although most Canadian citizens by birth were born in Canada, a small number were born outside Canada to Canadian parents.

28. Immigrants are persons who are, or have ever been, landed immigrants in Canada. A landed immigrant is a person who has been granted the right to live in Canada permanently by immigration authorities. Some immigrants have resided in Canada for a number of years, while others are recent arrivals. Most immigrants are born outside Canada, but a small number were born in Canada. Includes immigrants who landed in Canada prior to Census Day, May 16, 2006.

29. 'Other' includes Greenland, Saint Pierre and Miquelon, the category 'Other country,' as well as immigrants born in Canada.

30. Non-permanent residents are persons from another country who, at the time of the census, held a Work or Study Permit or who were refugee claimants, as well as family members living with them in Canada.

31. Includes immigrants who landed in Canada prior to Census Day, May 16, 2006.

Renvois (suite)

21. L'abréviation « n.i.a. » signifie « non incluses ailleurs ». Comprend les répondants ayant fourni une réponse écrite classifiée comme « Guyanais », « Antillais britannique », « Kurde », « Tibétain », « Polynésien », « Insulaire des îles du Pacifique », etc.

22. Comprend les répondants ayant déclaré plus d'un groupe de minorités visibles en cochant au moins deux cercles, p. ex., « Noir » et « Sud-Asiatique ».

23. Comprend les apatrides.

24. Comprend les personnes qui ont indiqué une double citoyenneté, y compris « Canadien »

25. Comprend les apatrides. Avant le Recensement de 2006, cette catégorie s'appelait « Citoyens d'autres pays ». Toutefois, le contenu de la catégorie demeure inchangé en 2006 par rapport aux recensements précédents.

26. Pour obtenir des renseignements relatifs aux pays spécifiques de chacun des groupes régionaux de cette variable, veuillez vous référer à l'annexe H du *Dictionnaire du Recensement de 2006*.

27. Les non-immigrants sont des personnes qui sont citoyens canadiens de naissance. Bien que la plupart des citoyens canadiens de naissance soient nés au Canada, un petit nombre d'entre eux sont nés à l'extérieur du Canada de parents canadiens.

28. Les immigrants sont des personnes qui sont, ou qui ont déjà été, des immigrants reçus au Canada. Un immigrant reçu est une personne à qui les autorités de l'immigration ont accordé le droit de résider au Canada en permanence. Certains immigrants résident au Canada depuis un certain nombre d'années, alors que d'autres sont arrivés récemment. La plupart des immigrants sont nés à l'extérieur du Canada, mais un petit nombre d'entre eux sont nés au Canada. Comprend les immigrants arrivés au Canada avant le jour du recensement, le 16 mai 2006.

29. La catégorie « Autres » comprend le Groenland, Saint-Pierre-et-Miquelon, la catégorie « Autre pays », ainsi que les immigrants nés au Canada.

30. Les résidents non permanents sont des personnes d'un autre pays qui, au moment du recensement, étaient titulaires d'un permis de travail ou d'un permis d'études, ou qui revendiquaient le statut de réfugié, ainsi que les membres de leur famille vivant avec elles au Canada.

31. Comprend les immigrants arrivés au Canada avant le jour du recensement, le 16 mai 2006.

Footnotes (continued)

32. Persons born outside Canada. For the most part, these are people who are now, or have ever been, landed immigrants in Canada. Also included in the first generation are a small number of people born outside Canada to parents who are Canadian citizens by birth. In addition, the first generation includes people who are non-permanent residents (defined as people from another country living in Canada on Work or Study Permits or as refugee claimants, and any family members living with them in Canada).

33. Persons born inside Canada with at least one parent born outside Canada. This includes (a) persons born in Canada with both parents born outside Canada and (b) persons born in Canada with one parent born in Canada and one parent born outside Canada (these persons may have grandparents born inside or outside Canada as well).

34. Persons born inside Canada with both parents born inside Canada (these persons may have grandparents born inside or outside Canada as well).

35. Population 1 year of age and over residing in Canada, excluding institutional residents and Canadians (military and government personnel) in households outside Canada.

    The concept of 'migrants' is defined at the Census Subdivision (CSD) level. For geographic levels below the CSD, such as census tracts (CTs), the distinction between the migrant and non-migrant population refers to the corresponding CSD of the CT. For example, migrants within a CT are those persons who moved from a different CSD, while non-migrants are those who moved within the same CSD, although they moved in from a different CT in the same CSD or moved within the same CT.

36. Population 5 years of age and over residing in Canada, excluding institutional residents and Canadians (military and government personnel) in households outside Canada.

    The concept of 'migrants' is defined at the Census Subdivision (CSD) level. For geographic levels below the CSD, such as census tracts (CTs), the distinction between the migrant and non-migrant population refers to the corresponding CSD of the CT. For example, migrants within a CT are those persons who moved from a different CSD, while non-migrants are those who moved within the same CSD, although they moved in from a different CT in the same CSD or moved within the same CT.

Renvois (suite)

32. Personnes nées à l'extérieur du Canada. Il s'agit, pour la plupart, de personnes qui sont, ou qui ont déjà été, des immigrants reçus au Canada. Sont également incluses dans la première génération, un petit nombre de personnes nées à l'extérieur du Canada de parents qui sont citoyens canadiens de naissance. En outre, la première génération comprend les résidents non permanents (personnes au Canada venant d'un autre pays qui sont titulaires d'un permis de travail ou d'un permis d'études ou qui revendiquent le statut de réfugié ainsi que les membres de leur famille vivant avec eux au Canada).

33. Personnes nées au Canada dont au moins un des parents est né à l'extérieur du Canada. Sont incluses a) les personnes nées au Canada dont les deux parents sont nés à l'extérieur du Canada et b) les personnes nées au Canada dont un des parents est né au Canada et l'autre est né à l'extérieur du Canada (les grands-parents de ces personnes peuvent être nés au Canada ou à l'extérieur du Canada).

34. Personnes nées au Canada dont les deux parents sont nés au Canada (les grands-parents de ces personnes peuvent être nés au Canada ou à l'extérieur du Canada).

35. Population de 1 an et plus résidant au Canada, à l'exclusion des pensionnaires d'un établissement institutionnel et des Canadiens (militaires et fonctionnaires) appartenant à un ménage à l'extérieur du Canada.

    Le concept de « migrants » est défini au niveau des subdivisions de recensement (SDR). Pour les niveaux géographiques inférieurs aux SDR, comme les secteurs de recensement (SR), la distinction entre la population des migrants et des non-migrants est faite au niveau de la SDR correspondant au SR. Par exemple, les migrants au sein d'un SR sont les personnes qui sont originaires d'une SDR différente, alors que les non-migrants sont celles qui ont déménagé à l'intérieur de la même SDR, même s'ils sont passés d'un SR à un autre à l'intérieur de la même SDR ou ont déménagé à l'intérieur du même SR.

36. Population de 5 ans et plus résidant au Canada, à l'exclusion des pensionnaires d'un établissement institutionnel et des Canadiens (militaires et fonctionnaires) appartenant à un ménage à l'extérieur du Canada.

    Le concept de « migrants » est défini au niveau des subdivisions de recensement (SDR). Pour les niveaux géographiques inférieurs aux SDR, comme les secteurs de recensement (SR), la distinction entre la population des migrants et des non-migrants est faite au niveau de la SDR correspondant au SR. Par exemple, les migrants au sein d'un SR sont les personnes qui sont originaires d'une SDR différente, alors que les non-migrants sont celles qui ont déménagé à l'intérieur de la même SDR, même s'ils sont passés d'un SR à un autre à l'intérieur de la même SDR ou ont déménagé à l'intérieur du même SR.

Footnotes (continued)

37. 'Highest certificate, diploma or degree' refers to the highest certificate, diploma or degree completed based on a hierarchy which is generally related to the amount of time spent 'in-class.' For postsecondary completers, a university education is considered to be a higher level of schooling than a college education, while a college education is considered to be a higher level of education than in the trades. Although some trades requirements may take as long or longer to complete than a given college or university program, the majority of time is spent in on-the-job paid training and less time is spent in the classroom.

38. 'High school certificate or equivalent' includes persons who have graduated from a secondary school or equivalent. Excludes persons with a postsecondary certificate, diploma or degree. Examples of postsecondary institutions include community colleges, institutes of technology, CEGEPs, private trade schools, private business colleges, schools of nursing and universities.

39. 'College, CEGEP or other non-university certificate or diploma' replaces the category 'Other non-university certificate or diploma' in previous censuses. This category includes accreditation by non-degree-granting institutions such as community colleges, CEGEPs, private business colleges and technical institutes.

40. The overall quality of the 'Highest certificate, diploma or degree' variable from the 2006 Census is acceptable. However, users of the 'University certificate or diploma below the bachelor level' category should know that an unexpected growth in this category was noted compared to the 2001 Census.

    In fact, in the 2001 Census, 2.5% of respondents aged 15 years or over declared such a diploma, compared to 4.4% in 2006, representing 89% growth. This phenomenon was not found in other sources like the *Labour Force Survey.*

    We recommend users interpret the 2006 Census results for this category with caution.

    For more information on factors that may explain such variances in census data, such as response errors and processing errors, please refer to the *2006 Census Dictionary*, Appendix B: Data quality, sampling and weighting, confidentiality and random rounding.

Renvois (suite)

37. « Plus haut certificat, diplôme ou grade » renvoie au plus haut certificat, diplôme ou grade obtenu selon une hiérarchie généralement liée au temps passé en classe. Dans le cas des études postsecondaires, on considère qu'un diplôme universitaire est plus élevé qu'un diplôme collégial et qu'un diplôme collégial est plus élevé qu'un diplôme d'une école de métiers. Même si certains programmes d'écoles de métiers peuvent durer aussi longtemps ou plus longtemps que certains programmes collégiaux ou universitaires, la majorité des heures des programmes de métiers sont consacrées à la formation en cours d'emploi et un moins grand nombre d'heures sont consacrées à la formation en classe.

38. « Diplôme d'études secondaires ou l'équivalent » comprend les diplômés des écoles secondaires ou l'équivalent. Ne comprend pas les personnes titulaires d'un certificat, diplôme ou d'un grade postsecondaire. Exemples d'établissements d'enseignement postsecondaire : collèges communautaires, instituts de technologie, cégeps, écoles de métiers privées, collèges commerciaux privés, écoles de sciences infirmières et universités.

39. « Certificat ou diplôme d'un collège, d'un cégep ou autre établissement d'enseignement non universitaire » remplace la catégorie « Autre certificat ou diplôme non universitaire » des recensements précédents. Cette catégorie comprend l'accréditation des établissements ne décernant aucun grade, comme les collèges communautaires, les cégeps, les collèges commerciaux privés et les instituts d'études techniques.

40. La qualité générale de la variable du Recensement de 2006 portant sur le « Plus haut certificat, diplôme ou grade » est acceptable. Toutefois, il importe aux utilisateurs de la catégorie « Certificat ou diplôme universitaire inférieur au baccalauréat » de savoir qu'une croissance inattendue de cette catégorie par rapport au Recensement de 2001 a été notée.

    En effet, lors du Recensement de 2001, 2,5 % des répondants âgés de 15 ans et plus avaient déclaré un tel diplôme alors que cette proportion s'établit à 4,4 % en 2006, une croissance de 89 %. Un tel phénomène n'a pas été observé dans d'autres sources de données comme l'*Enquête sur la population active*.

    Nous recommandons aux utilisateurs de cette catégorie d'interpréter avec prudence les résultats du Recensement de 2006 pour cette catégorie.

    Pour plus de renseignements sur les facteurs susceptibles de fournir une explication relative à de telles variances dans les données du recensement, telles que les erreurs de réponse et les erreurs de traitement, veuillez consulter le *Dictionnaire du recensement de 2006*, Annexe B : Qualité des données, échantillonnage et pondération, confidentialité et arrondissement aléatoire.

Footnotes (continued)

More information is available in the *Education Reference Guide, 2006 Census*.

41. Census questions relating to education changed substantially between 2001 and 2006, principally to reflect developments in Canada's education system.

    These changes improved the quality of data and provided more precise information on the level of educational attainment as well as fields of study.

    However, this means that comparisons with data from previous censuses will be limited. The only data that can be compared to the 2001 Census consist of the number of individuals who have a Bachelor's degree or higher as their highest level of educational attainment.

    This is because categories relating to university degrees attained in 2006 – for example, bachelor's and master's degrees – were similar to those used in 2001. The questions in 2006 concerning certification at other institutions of learning, such as trade schools and colleges, changed substantially from 2001.

    Further analysis of these data is underway with an intention to report on historical comparability of the individual categories of educational attainment and attendance at school later in 2008.

42. Field of study' is defined as the main discipline or subject of learning. It is collected for the highest certificate, diploma or degree above the high school or secondary school level.

    For the first time with the 2006 Census, major field of study data were coded with the Classification of Instructional Programs – (CIP), Canada, 2000.

    Prior to the 2006 Census, the Major Field of Study Classification (MFS) was used to classify major field of study. We recommend users not make historical comparisons between the two classification systems. Even though some entries in the two classifications are similar, direct comparison would be inappropriate given the much more detailed character of the new classification.

Renvois (suite)

Vous pouvez obtenir plus de renseignements en consultant le *Guide de référence sur la scolarité, Recensement de 2006*.

41. Les questions du recensement relatives à la scolarité ont fait l'objet de modifications importantes entre 2001 et 2006, principalement pour tenir compte de l'évolution du système d'éducation du Canada.

    Ces modifications ont permis d'améliorer la qualité des données et de fournir des renseignements plus précis sur le niveau de scolarité de même que sur les domaines d'études.

    Cependant, ces modifications restreignent les comparaisons avec les données des recensements antérieurs. Seules les données se rapportant au nombre de personnes dont le plus haut niveau de scolarité est un baccalauréat ou supérieur peuvent être comparées à celles du Recensement de 2001.

    En effet, les catégories se rapportant aux grades universitaires en 2006 – baccalauréats et maîtrises, par exemple – sont semblables à celles utilisées en 2001. Les questions de 2006 qui touchent les attestations décernées par d'autres établissements d'enseignement, comme les écoles de métiers et les collèges, diffèrent considérablement de celles de 2001.

    Une analyse plus poussée de ces données est en cours, afin de faire un compte rendu de la comparabilité historique des catégories individuelles de niveaux de scolarité et de fréquentation scolaire plus tard en 2008.

42. « Domaine d'études » renvoie à la principale discipline ou au principal sujet d'apprentissage. Cette variable est recueillie pour le plus haut certificat, diplôme ou grade obtenu après le diplôme d'études secondaires.

    Pour la première fois lors du Recensement de 2006, les données sur le principal domaine d'études ont été codées à l'aide de la Classification des programmes d'enseignement – (CPE), Canada, 2000.

    Aux recensements antérieurs à celui de 2006, la Classification du principal domaine d'études (PDÉ) était utilisée pour classifier le principal domaine d'études. Nous recommandons aux utilisateurs de ne pas effectuer de comparaisons historiques entre les deux systèmes de classification. Bien que des entrées dans les deux classifications soient similaires, les comparaisons directes s'avèrent inappropriées étant donné le caractère beaucoup plus détaillé de la nouvelle classification.

Footnotes (continued)

A theoretical concordance table between the Classification of Instructional Programs (CIP) and the Major Field of Study Classification (MFS) showing the definitional relationship between the two classifications was developed. This table is available in the 2006 Census Dictionary (Appendix N). However, users are cautioned that this type of concordance can not be used to convert counts from one classification system to another.

43. Includes Multidisciplinary/interdisciplinary studies, Other.

44. 'Location of study' refers to the province, territory or country where the highest certificate, diploma, or degree above high school level was completed.

45. Refers to persons who reported time spent doing one or more of the following unpaid work activities: (a) unpaid housework; (b) unpaid child care; (c) unpaid care or assistance to seniors. For example, a respondent who reported 5 to 14 hours of housework, 30 to 59 hours of child care and no hours of care or assistance to seniors would fall into the category 'Housework and child care only.'

46. Unemployed persons 15 years and over who have never worked for pay or in self-employment or who had last worked prior to January 1, 2005, only.

47. Refers to the experienced labour force population: includes persons who were employed and persons who were unemployed who worked for pay or in self-employment since January 1, 2005.

48. Includes mobile homes and other movable dwellings such as houseboats and railroad cars.

49. Includes data up to May 16, 2006.

50. Refers to one-family households containing a couple (with or without persons not in census families).

51. Includes households in tenant-occupied, non-farm, non-reserve dwellings with household income greater than $0 in 2005 (i.e. excludes negative or zero household income).

Renvois (suite)

Une table de concordance théorique entre la Classification des programmes d'enseignement (CPE) et la Classification du principal domaine d'études (PDÉ) montrant les relations définitionnelles entre les deux classifications a été développée. Cette table de concordance est disponible dans le Dictionnaire du Recensement de 2006 (annexe N). Toutefois, les utilisateurs doivent être prévenus que ce type de concordance ne permet pas de convertir des chiffres d'un système de classification à un autre.

43. Comprend Études multidisciplinaires/interdisciplinaires (autres).

44. « Lieu des études » renvoie à la province, au territoire ou au pays où le plus haut certificat, diplôme ou grade supérieur au diplôme d'études secondaires a été obtenu.

45. Personnes qui ont déclaré du temps consacré à une ou plusieurs des activités de travail non rémunéré suivantes : a) travaux ménagers, sans paye ou sans salaire; b) soins aux enfants, sans paye ou sans salaire; c) soins ou aide aux personnes âgées, sans paye ou sans salaire. Par exemple, un répondant qui a déclaré 5 à 14 heures de travaux ménagers, 30 à 59 heures de soins aux enfants et aucune heure de soins ou d'aide aux personnes âgées serait classé dans la catégorie « Travaux ménagers et soins aux enfants seulement ».

46. Chômeurs de 15 ans et plus qui n'ont jamais travaillé à un emploi salarié ou à leur compte ou qui ont travaillé la dernière fois avant le 1er janvier 2005 seulement.

47. S'entend de la population active expérimentée : comprend les personnes qui étaient occupées et les personnes en chômage qui avaient travaillé à un emploi salarié ou à leur compte depuis le 1er janvier 2005.

48. Comprend les maisons mobiles et les autres logements mobiles tels que les bateaux-maisons et les wagons de chemin de fer.

49. Comprend les données jusqu'au 16 mai 2006.

50. Se rapporte aux ménages unifamiliaux comptant un couple (avec ou sans autres personnes hors famille de recensement).

51. Comprend les ménages ayant un revenu supérieur à 0 $ en 2005 dans les logements non agricoles hors réserve occupés par un locataire (sont exclus les ménages ayant un revenu négatif ou nul).

Footnotes (continued)

52. Refers to the proportion of average monthly 2005 total household income which is spent on owner's major payments (in the case of owner-occupied dwellings) or on gross rent (in the case of tenant-occupied dwellings). Includes private households in occupied non-farm, non-reserve dwellings with household income greater than $0 in 2005 (i.e., excludes negative or zero household income). It should be noted that not all households spending 30% or more of incomes on shelter costs are necessarily experiencing housing affordability problems. This is particularly true of households with high incomes. There are also other households who choose to spend more on shelter than on other goods. Nevertheless, the allocation of 30% or more of a household's income to housing expenses provides a useful benchmark for assessing trends in housing affordability.

    The relatively high shelter costs to household income ratios for some households may have resulted from the difference in the reference period for shelter costs and household income data.

    The reference period for shelter cost data (gross rent for tenants, and owner's major payments for owners) is 2006, while household income is reported for the year 2005. As well, for some households, the 2005 household income may represent income for only part of a year.

53. Includes households in owner-occupied, non-farm, non-reserve dwellings with household income greater than $0 in 2005 (i.e. excludes negative or zero household income).
54. The average number of children at home per census family is calculated using the total number of children at home and the total number of census families.
55. Non-relatives may be present.
56. Including loss.
57. For persons with income.
58. Includes persons who did not work in 2005 but reported employment income.
59. Worked 49 to 52 weeks in 2005, mostly full time.
60. Worked less than 49 weeks or worked mostly part time in 2005.

Renvois (suite)

52. Proportion du revenu mensuel total moyen du ménage en 2005 consacrée aux principales dépenses de propriété (dans le cas des logements occupés par leur propriétaire) ou au loyer brut (dans le cas des logements occupés par un locataire). Comprend les ménages privés dans les logements non agricoles hors réserve occupés dont le revenu du ménage est supérieur à 0 $ en 2005 (c'est-à-dire ne comprend pas les ménages ayant un revenu négatif ou n'ayant aucun revenu). Il convient de souligner que les ménages qui consacrent 30 % ou plus de leur revenu aux coûts d'habitation n'éprouvent pas nécessairement des problèmes d'abordabilité du logement. C'est notamment le cas des ménages ayant un revenu élevé. D'autres ménages choisissent de consacrer une plus grande part de leur revenu aux coûts d'habitation qu'à d'autres biens. Néanmoins, ce seuil (30 % ou plus du revenu du ménage consacré aux coûts d'habitation) constitue un repère utile pour l'évaluation des tendances en matière d'abordabilité du logement.

    Les rapports entre les coûts d'habitation et le revenu du ménage relativement élevés pour certains ménages s'expliquent du fait que les périodes de référence utilisées pour les données sur les coûts d'habitation et pour les données sur le revenu du ménage ne sont pas les mêmes.

    En effet, la période de référence est l'année 2006 dans le cas des données sur les coûts d'habitation (loyer brut pour les locataires et principales dépenses de propriété pour les propriétaires), et l'année 2005 dans le cas des données sur le revenu du ménage. En outre, pour certains ménages, le revenu du ménage déclaré ne correspond qu'à une partie de l'année 2005.

53. Comprend les ménages ayant un revenu supérieur à 0 $ en 2005 dans les logements non agricoles hors réserve occupés par le propriétaire (sont exclus les ménages ayant un revenu négatif ou nul).
54. Le nombre moyen d'enfants à la maison par famille de recensement est calculé à partir du nombre total d'enfants à la maison et du nombre total de familles de recensement.
55. Il peut y avoir des personnes non apparentées.
56. Comprend les pertes.
57. Pour les personnes avec un revenu.
58. Comprend les personnes qui n'ont pas travaillé pendant l'année 2005, mais ont déclaré un revenu d'emploi.
59. A travaillé de 49 à 52 semaines pendant l'année de référence, surtout à plein temps.
60. A travaillé moins de 49 semaines ou a travaillé à temps partiel en 2005.

Footnotes (continued)

61. The 2006 category 'Chinese, n.o.s.' includes responses of 'Chinese' as well as all Chinese languages other than Cantonese, Mandarin, Taiwanese, Chaochow (Teochow), Fukien, Hakka and Shanghainese. Data for the 'Chinese, n.o.s.' category in 2001 and 2006 are not directly comparable. The 2001 category 'Chinese, n.o.s.' is equivalent to the sum of the 2006 categories 'Chinese, n.o.s.' and 'Chaochow (Teochow),' 'Fukien,' 'Shanghainese' and 'Taiwanese.'

Renvois (suite)

61. La catégorie « Chinois, n.d.a. » de 2006 comprend les réponses « Chinois », de même que toutes les langues chinoises autres que Cantonais, Mandarin, Taïwanais, Chaochow (teochow), Fou-kien, Hakka et Shanghaïen. Les données pour la catégorie « Chinois, n.d.a. » de 2001 et de 2006 ne sont pas directement comparables. La catégorie « Chinois, n.d.a. » de 2001 équivaut à la somme des catégories de 2006 « Chinois, n.d.a. », et « Chaochow (teochow) », « Foukien », « Shanghaïen » et « Taïwanais ».

Definitions

The definitions of geographic terms and census concepts are presented here in a summary form only. Users should refer to the *2006 Census Dictionary* (Catalogue no. 92-566-XWE) for the full definitions and additional remarks related to these concepts and definitions.

Aboriginal ancestry

Refers to those persons who reported at least one Aboriginal ancestry (North American Indian, Métis or Inuit) to the ethnic origin question. 'Ethnic origin' refers to the ethnic or cultural origins of the respondent's ancestors. 'Aboriginal ancestry' was referred to as 'Aboriginal origin' prior to the 2006 Census.

Aboriginal identity

Refers to those persons who reported identifying with at least one Aboriginal group, that is, North American Indian, Métis or Inuit, and/or those who reported being a Treaty Indian or a Registered Indian, as defined by the *Indian Act* of Canada and/or those who reported they were members of an Indian band or First Nation.

Age

Refers to the age at last birthday (as of the census reference date, May 16, 2006). This variable is derived from date of birth.

Age at immigration

Refers to the age at which the respondent first obtained landed immigrant status. A landed immigrant is a person who has been granted the right to live in Canada permanently by immigration authorities.

Bedrooms

Refers to all rooms designed and furnished as bedrooms and used mainly for sleeping purposes, even though the use may be occasional (e.g., spare bedroom).

Census agglomeration (CA)

See the definition of Census Metropolitan Area (CMA) and Census Agglomeration (CA).

Census division (CD)

Census division (CD) is the general term for provincially legislated areas (such as county, *municipalité régionale de comté* and regional district) or their equivalents. Census divisions are intermediate geographic areas between the province/territory level and the municipality (census subdivision).

Census family

Refers to a married couple (with or without children of either or both spouses), a couple living common-law (with or without children of either or both partners) or a lone parent of any marital status, with at least one child living in the same dwelling. A couple may be of opposite or same sex. 'Children' in a census family include grandchildren living with their grandparent(s) but with no parents present.

Census family structure

Refers to the classification of census families into **married couples** (with or without children of either or both spouses), **common-law couples** (with or without children of either or both partners), and **lone-parent families** by sex of parent. A couple may be of opposite or same sex. 'Children' in a census family include grandchildren living with their grandparent(s) but with no parents present.

Census metropolitan area (CMA) and census agglomeration (CA)

A census metropolitan area (CMA) or a census agglomeration (CA) is formed by one or more adjacent municipalities centred on a large urban area (known as the urban core). A CMA must have a total population of at least 100,000 of which 50,000 or more must live in the urban core. A CA must have an urban core population of at least 10,000. To be included in the CMA or CA, other adjacent municipalities must have a high degree of integration with the central urban area, as measured by commuting flows derived from census place of work data.

If the population of the urban core of a CA declines below 10,000, the CA is retired. However, once an area becomes a CMA, it is retained as a CMA even if its total population declines below 100,000 or the population of its urban core falls below 50,000. The urban areas in the CMA or CA that are not contiguous to the urban core are called the urban fringe. Rural areas in the CMA or CA are called the rural fringe.

When a CA has an urban core of at least 50,000, it is subdivided into census tracts. Census tracts are maintained for the CA even if the population of the urban core subsequently falls below 50,000. All CMAs are subdivided into census tracts.

Census subdivision (CSD)

Census subdivision (CSD) is the general term for municipalities (as determined by provincial/territorial legislation) or areas treated as municipal equivalents for statistical purposes (e.g., Indian reserves, Indian settlements and unorganized territories).

Census subdivision type

Census subdivisions (CSDs) are classified into 55 types according to official designations adopted by provincial/territorial or federal authorities. Two exceptions are 'Subdivision of unorganized (SNO)' in Newfoundland and Labrador, and 'Subdivision of county municipality (SC)' in Nova Scotia, which are geographic areas created as equivalents for municipalities by Statistics Canada, in cooperation with those provinces, for the purpose of disseminating statistical data.

The **census subdivision type** accompanies the census subdivision name in order to distinguish CSDs from each other, for example, Granby, V (for the *ville* of Granby) and Granby, CT (for the *municipalité de canton* of Granby).

Census tract (CT)

Census tracts (CTs) are small, relatively stable geographic areas that usually have a population of 2,500 to 8,000. They are located in census metropolitan areas and in census agglomerations with an urban core population of 50,000 or more in the previous census.

A committee of local specialists (for example, planners, health and social workers, and educators) initially delineates census tracts in conjunction with Statistics Canada. Once a census metropolitan area (CMA) or census agglomeration (CA) has been subdivided into census tracts, the census tracts are maintained even if the urban core population subsequently declines below 50,000.

Citizenship

Refers to the legal citizenship status of the respondent. Persons who are citizens of more than one country were instructed to provide the name of the other country(ies).

Class of worker

This variable classifies persons who reported a job into the following categories:

(a) persons who worked mainly for wages, salaries, commissions, tips, piece-rates, or payments 'in kind' (payments in goods or services rather than money);

(b) persons who worked mainly for themselves, with or without paid help, operating a business, farm or professional practice, alone or in partnership;

(c) persons who worked without pay in a family business, farm or professional practice owned or operated by a related household member; unpaid family work does not include unpaid housework, unpaid childcare, unpaid care to seniors and volunteer work.

The job reported was the one held in the week (Sunday to Saturday) prior to enumeration (May 16, 2006) if the person was employed, or the job of longest duration since January 1, 2005, if the person was not employed during the reference week. Persons with two or more jobs in the reference week were asked to provide information for the job at which they worked the most hours.

Common-law status

Refers to two people who live together as a couple, but who are not legally married to each other. These persons can be of the opposite sex or of the same sex.

Condition of dwelling

Refers to whether, in the judgement of the respondent, the dwelling requires any repairs (excluding desirable remodelling or additions).

Dwelling, occupied private

Refers to a private dwelling in which a person or a group of persons is permanently residing. Also included are private dwellings whose usual residents are temporarily absent on Census Day. Unless otherwise specified, all data in housing products are for occupied private dwellings, rather than for unoccupied private dwellings or dwellings occupied solely by foreign and/or temporary residents.

Dwelling, private

Refers to a separate set of living quarters with a private entrance either from outside or from a common hall, lobby, vestibule or stairway inside the building. The entrance to the dwelling must be one that can be used without passing through the living quarters of someone else. The dwelling must meet the two conditions necessary for year-round occupancy:

1. a source of heat or power (as evidenced by chimneys, power lines, oil or gas pipes or meters, generators, woodpiles, electric lights, heating pumps, solar heating panels, etc.);

2. an enclosed space that provides shelter from the elements (as evidenced by complete and enclosed walls and roof, and by doors and windows that provide protection from wind, rain and snow).

The census classifies private dwellings into **regular private dwellings and occupied marginal dwellings**. Regular private dwellings are further classified into three major groups: **occupied dwellings** (occupied by usual residents), **dwellings occupied by foreign and/or temporary residents and unoccupied dwellings**. Marginal dwellings are classified as occupied by usual residents or by foreign and/or temporary residents. Marginal dwellings that were unoccupied on Census Day are not counted in the housing stock.

Earner or employment income recipient

Refers to a person, 15 years of age and over, who received wages and salaries, net income from a non-farm unincorporated business and/or professional practice, and/or net farm self-employment income during calendar year 2005.

Earnings or employment income

Refers to total income received by persons 15 years of age and over during calendar year 2005 as wages and salaries, net income from a non-farm unincorporated business and/or professional practice, and/or net farm self-employment income.

Economic family

Refers to a group of two or more persons who live in the same dwelling and are related to each other by blood, marriage, common-law or adoption.

Economic family total income

The total income of an economic family is the sum of the total incomes of all members of that family.

Ethnic origin

Refers to the ethnic or cultural origins of the respondent's ancestors.

First official language spoken

Refers to a variable specified within the framework of the *Official Languages Act*.

Generation status

Refers to the generational status of a person, that is, 1st generation, 2nd generation or 3rd generation or more.

Highest certificate, diploma or degree

This is a derived variable obtained from the educational qualifications questions, which asked for all certificates, diplomas and degrees to be reported. There is an implied hierarchy in this variable (secondary school graduation, registered apprenticeship and trades, college, university) which is loosely tied to the 'in-class' duration of the various types of education. However, at the detailed level a registered apprenticeship graduate may not have completed a secondary school certificate or diploma, nor does an individual with a master's degree necessarily have a certificate or diploma above the bachelor's degree level. Therefore, although the sequence is more or less hierarchical, it is a general rather than an absolute gradient measure of academic achievement.

Hours spent doing unpaid housework

Refers to the number of hours persons spent doing unpaid housework, yard work or home maintenance in the week (Sunday to Saturday) prior to Census Day (May 16, 2006). It includes hours spent doing unpaid housework for members of one's own household, for other family members outside the household, and for friends or neighbours.

Unpaid housework does not include volunteer work for a non-profit organization, a religious organization, a charity or community group, or work without pay in the operation of a family farm, business or professional practice.

Hours spent looking after children, without pay

Refers to the number of hours persons spent looking after children without pay. It includes hours spent providing unpaid child care for members of one's own household, for other family members outside the household, for friends or neighbours in the week (Sunday to Saturday) prior to Census Day (May 16, 2006).

Unpaid child care does not include volunteer work for a non-profit organization, a religious organization, a charity or community group, or work without pay in the operation of a family farm, business or professional practice.

Hours spent providing unpaid care or assistance to seniors

Refers to the number of hours persons spent providing unpaid care or assistance to seniors of one's own household, to other senior family members outside the household, and to friends or neighbours in the week (Sunday to Saturday) prior to Census Day (May 16, 2006).

Unpaid care or assistance to seniors does not include volunteer work for a non-profit organization, religious organization, charity or community group, or work without pay in the operation of a family farm, business or professional practice.

Household

Refers to a person or a group of persons (other than foreign residents) who occupy the same dwelling and do not have a usual place of residence elsewhere in Canada. It may consist of a family group (census family) with or without other non-family persons, of two or more families sharing a dwelling, of a group of unrelated persons, or of one person living alone. Household members who are temporarily absent on Census Day (e.g., temporary residents elsewhere) are considered as part of their usual household. For census purposes, every person is a member of one and only one household. Unless otherwise specified, all data in household reports are for private households only. Households are classified into three groups: private households, collective households and households outside Canada.

Household living arrangements

Refers to the classification of persons in terms of whether they are members of a family household or of a non-family household, that is, whether or not they are living in a household that contains at least one census family, and whether they are members of a census family or not in a census family. Persons not in census families are further classified as living with relatives, living with non-relatives (only) or living alone.

Household, private

Refers to a person or a group of persons (other than foreign residents) who occupy a private dwelling and do not have a usual place of residence elsewhere in Canada.

Household size

Refers to the number of persons in a private household.

Household type

Refers to the basic division of private households into family and non-family households. Family household refers to a household that contains at least one census family, that is, a married couple with or without children, or a couple living common-law with or without children, or a lone parent living with one or more children (lone-parent family). One-family household refers to a single census family (with or without other non-family persons) that occupies a private dwelling. Multiple-family household refers to a household in which two or more census families (with or without additional non-family persons) occupy the same private dwelling.

Non-family household refers to either one person living alone in a private dwelling or to a group of two or more people who share a private dwelling, but who do not constitute a census family.

Immigrant population

Refers to people who are, or have been, landed immigrants in Canada. A landed immigrant is a person who has been granted the right to live in Canada permanently by immigration authorities. Some immigrants have resided in Canada for a number of years, while others have arrived recently. Most immigrants are born outside Canada, but a small number were born in Canada.

Income status before or after tax

Refers to the position of an economic family or persons not in economic families 15 years of age and over in relation to Statistics Canada's low income before-tax or after-tax cut-offs.

Industry (based on the 2002 *North American Industry Classification System* [*NAICS*])

General nature of the business carried out in the establishment where the person worked. The 2006 Census data on industry (based on the 2002 NAICS) can be compared with data from Canada's NAFTA partners (United States and Mexico).

Knowledge of non-official languages

Refers to languages, other than English or French, in which the respondent can conduct a conversation.

Knowledge of official languages

Refers to the ability to conduct a conversation in English only, in French only, in both English and French, or in neither English nor French.

Labour force activity

Refers to the labour market activity of the population 15 years of age and over in the week (Sunday to Saturday) prior to Census Day (May 16, 2006). Respondents were classified as Employed, Unemployed, or Not in the labour force. The labour force includes the employed and the unemployed.

Employed

Refers to persons who, during the week (Sunday to Saturday) prior to Census Day (May 16, 2006):

(a) did any work at all for pay or in self-employment or without pay in a family farm, business or professional practice

(b) were absent from their job or business, with or without pay, for the entire week because of a vacation, an illness, a labour dispute at their place of work, or any other reasons.

Unemployed

Refers to persons who, during the week (Sunday to Saturday) prior to Census Day (May 16, 2006), were without paid work or without self-employment work and were available for work and either:

(a) had actively looked for paid work in the past four weeks; or

(b) were on temporary lay-off and expected to return to their job; or

(c) had definite arrangements to start a new job in four weeks or less.

Not in the labour force

Refers to persons who, in the week (Sunday to Saturday) prior to Census Day (May 16, 2006), were neither employed nor unemployed. It includes students, homemakers, retired workers, seasonal workers in an 'off' season who were not looking for work, and persons who could not work because of a long term illness or disability.

Labour force

Refers to persons who were either employed or unemployed during the week (Sunday to Saturday) prior to Census Day (May 16, 2006).

Participation rate

Refers to the labour force in the week (Sunday to Saturday) prior to Census Day (May 16, 2006), expressed as a percentage of the population 15 years of age and over.

The participation rate for a particular group (age, sex, marital status, geographic area, etc.) is the total labour force in that group, expressed as a percentage of the total population in that group.

Employment rate

Refers to the number of persons employed in the week (Sunday to Saturday) prior to Census Day (May 16, 2006), expressed as a percentage of the total population 15 years of age and over.

The employment rate for a particular group (age, sex, marital status, geographic area, etc.) is the number of employed persons in that group, expressed as a percentage of the population 15 years of age and over, in that group.

Unemployment rate

Refers to the unemployed expressed as a percentage of the labour force in the week (Sunday to Saturday) prior to Census Day (May 16, 2006).

The unemployment rate for a particular group (age, sex, marital status, geographic area, etc.) is the unemployed in that group, expressed as a percentage of the labour force in that group, in the week prior to enumeration.

Land area

Land area is the area in square kilometres of the land-based portions of standard geographic areas.

The land area data are unofficial, and are provided for the sole purpose of calculating population density.

Landed immigrant status

Refers to whether or not the person is a landed immigrant in Canada. Landed immigrants are people who have been granted the right to live in Canada permanently by immigration authorities.

Language of work

Refers to the language used most often at work by the individual at the time of the census. Other languages used at work on a regular basis are also collected.

Language spoken most often at home

Refers to the language spoken most often at home by the individual at the time of the census.

Legal marital status

Refers to the legal conjugal status of a person.

The various responses are defined as follows:

Never legally married (single) - Persons who have never married (including all persons less than 15 years of age) and persons whose marriage has been annulled and who have not remarried.

Legally married (and not separated) - Persons whose spouse is living, unless the couple is separated or a divorce has been obtained.

Separated, but still legally married - Persons currently married, but who are no longer living with their spouse (for any reason other than illness or work) and have not obtained a divorce.

Divorced - Persons who have obtained a legal divorce and who have not remarried.

Widowed - Persons who have lost their spouse through death and who have not remarried.

Location of study

This variable indicates the province, territory (in Canada) or country (outside Canada) where the highest certificate, diploma or degree was obtained. It is only reported for individuals who had completed a certificate, diploma or degree above the secondary (high) school level.

Low income cut-offs (before or after tax)

Measures of low income known as low income (before-tax or after-tax) cut-offs were first introduced in Canada in 1968 based on 1961 Census income data and 1959 family expenditure patterns. At that time, expenditure patterns indicated that Canadian families spent about 50% of their total income on food, shelter and clothing. It was arbitrarily estimated that families spending 70% or more of their income (20 percentage points more than the average) on these basic necessities would be in 'straitened' circumstances. With this assumption, low income cut-off points were set for five different sizes of families.

Subsequent to these initial cut-offs, revised low income cut-offs were established based on national family expenditure data from 1969, 1978, 1986 and 1992. The initial LICOs were based upon the total income before tax of families and persons 15 years and over, not in economic families.

After a comprehensive review of low income cut-offs completed in 1991, low income cut-offs based upon after-tax income were published for the first time in Income After Tax, Distributions by Size in Canada, 1990 (Catalogue no. 13-210).

In a similar fashion to the derivation of low income cut-offs based upon total income, cut-offs are estimated independently for economic families and persons not in economic families based upon family expenditure and income after tax. Consequently the low income after-tax cut-offs are set at after-tax income levels, differentiated by size of family and area of residence, where families spend 20 percentage points more of their after-tax income than the average family on food, shelter and clothing.

Major field of study (MFS)

Refers to the predominant discipline or area of learning or training of a person's highest postsecondary certificate, diploma or degree. The major field of study classification structure consists of 10 broad or major categories: educational, recreational and counselling services; fine and applied arts; humanities and related fields; social sciences and related fields; commerce, management and business administration; agricultural, biological, nutritional, and food sciences; engineering and applied sciences; applied science technologies and trades; health professions and related technologies; and mathematics, computer and physical sciences. This structure is, in turn, subdivided into over 100 'minor' classification categories and about 980 'unit' groups.

Mode of transportation

Refers to the mode of transportation to work of non-institutional residents 15 years of age and over who worked at some time since January 1, 2005. Persons who indicate in the place of work question that they either had no fixed workplace address, or specified a usual workplace address, are asked to identify the mode of transportation they usually use to commute from home to work. The variable usually relates to the individual's job in the week prior to enumeration. However, if the person did not work during that week but had worked at some time since January 1, 2005, the information relates to the job held longest during that period.

Persons who use more than one mode of transportation are asked to identify the single mode they use for most of the travel distance. As a result, the question provides data on the primary mode of transportation to work. The question does not measure multiple modes of transportation, nor does it measure the seasonal variation in mode of transportation or trips made for purposes other than the commute from home to work.

Mother tongue

Refers to the first language learned at home in childhood and still understood by the individual at the time of the census.

Non-immigrant population

Refers to people who are Canadian citizens by birth. Although most were born in Canada, a small number of them were born outside Canada to Canadian parents.

Occupation (based on the *National Occupational Classification for Statistics 2006 [NOC–S 2006]*)

Kind of work done by persons aged 15 and over. Occupation is based on the type of job the person holds and the description of his or her duties. The 2006 Census data on occupation are classified according to the *National Occupational Classification for Statistics 2006 (NOC–S 2006),* Catalogue no. 12-583-XIE. For comparisons with data from the 1991 and 1996 censuses, the variable Occupation (historical) should be used.

Owner's major payments

Refers to the total average monthly payments made by owner households to secure shelter. The **owner's major payments** include, for example, the mortgage payment and the costs of electricity, heat and municipal services.

Period of construction

Refers to the period in time during which the building or dwelling was originally constructed.

Period of immigration

Refers to ranges of years based on the year of immigration question. Year of immigration refers to the year in which landed immigrant status was first obtained. A landed immigrant is a person who has been granted the right to live in Canada permanently by immigration authorities.

Place of birth of respondent

Refers to the province or territory where the respondent was born, for respondents who were born in Canada, or to the country where the respondent was born, for respondents born outside Canada.

Place of residence 1 year ago – Mobility status

Refers to the relationship between a person's usual place of residence on Census Day and his or her usual place of residence one year earlier. A person is classified as a non-mover if no difference exists. Otherwise, a person is classified as a mover and this categorization is called Mobility status (1 year ago). Within the category of movers, a further distinction is made between non-migrants and migrants; this difference is called migration status.

Non-movers are persons who, on Census Day, were living at the same address as the one at which they resided one year earlier.

Movers are persons who, on Census Day, were living at a different address than the one at which they resided one year earlier.

Non-migrants are movers who, on Census Day, were living at a different address, but in the same census subdivision (CSD) as the one they lived in one year earlier.

Migrants are movers who, on Census Day, were residing in a different CSD one year earlier (internal migrants) or who were living outside Canada one year earlier (external migrants).

Intraprovincial migrants are movers who, on Census Day, were living in a different census subdivision than the one in which they resided one year earlier, in the same province.

Interprovincial migrants are movers who, on Census Day, were living in a different census subdivision than the one in which they resided one year earlier, in a different province.

Place of residence 5 years ago – Mobility status

Refers to the relationship between a person's usual place of residence on Census Day and his or her usual place of residence five years earlier. A person is classified as a non-mover if no difference exists. Otherwise, a person is classified as a mover and this categorization is called mobility status (5 years ago). Within the movers category, a further distinction is made between non-migrants and migrants; this difference is called migration status.

Non-movers are persons who, on Census Day, were living at the same address as the one at which they resided five years earlier.

Movers are persons who, on Census Day, were living at a different address than the one at which they resided five years earlier.

Non-migrants are movers who, on Census Day, were living at a different address, but in the same census subdivision (CSD) as the one they lived in five years earlier.

Migrants are movers who, on Census Day, were residing in a different CSD five years earlier (internal migrants) or who were living outside Canada five years earlier (external migrants).

Intraprovincial migrants are movers who, on Census Day, were living in a different census subdivision than the one in which they resided five years earlier, in the same province.

Interprovincial migrants are movers who, on Census Day, were living in a different census subdivision than the one in which they resided five years earlier, in a different province.

Place of work status

Refers to the place of work of non-institutional residents 15 years of age and over who worked at some time since January 1, 2005. The variable usually relates to the individual's job held in the week prior to enumeration. However, if the person did not work during that week but had worked at some time since January 1, 2005, the information relates to the job held longest during that period.

Worked at home – Persons whose job is located in the same building as their place of residence, persons who live and work on the same farm, building superintendents and teleworkers who spend most of their work week working at home.

Worked outside Canada – Persons who work at a location outside Canada. This can include diplomats, Armed Forces personnel and other persons enumerated abroad. This category also includes recent immigrants who may not currently be employed, but whose job of longest duration since January 1, 2005 was held outside Canada.

No fixed workplace address – Persons who do not go from home to the same workplace location at the beginning of each shift. Such persons include building and landscape contractors, travelling salespersons, independent truck drivers, etc.

Worked at the address specified below – Persons who are not included in the categories described above and who report to the same (usual) workplace location at the beginning of each shift are included here. Respondents are asked to provide the street address, city, town, village, township, municipality or Indian reserve, province/territory and postal code of their workplace. If the full street address was not known, the name of the building or nearest street intersection could be substituted.

Teleworkers who spend less than one-half of their workweek working at their home office are asked to report the full address of their employer. Persons whose workplace location varied, but who reported regularly to an employer's address at the beginning of each shift, are asked to report the full address of the employer.

Population universe

The population universe of the 2006 Census includes the following groups:

- Canadian citizens (by birth or by naturalization) and landed immigrants with a usual place of residence in Canada;
- Canadian citizens (by birth or by naturalization) and landed immigrants who are abroad, either on a military base or attached to a diplomatic mission;
- Canadian citizens (by birth or by naturalization) and landed immigrants at sea or in port aboard merchant vessels under Canadian registry;
- persons with a usual place of residence in Canada who are claiming refugee status and members of their families living with them;
- persons with a usual place of residence in Canada who hold Study Permits and members of their families living with them;
- persons with a usual place of residence in Canada who hold Work Permits and members of their families living with them.

For census purposes, the last three groups in this list are referred to as 'non-permanent residents'.

Province or territory

Province and territory refer to the major political units of Canada. From a statistical point of view, province and territory are basic areas for which data are tabulated. Canada is divided into 10 provinces and three territories.

Rent, gross

Refers to the total average monthly payments paid by tenant households to secure shelter. **Gross rent** includes the monthly rent and the costs of electricity, heat and municipal services.

Registered or Treaty Indian

Refers to those persons who reported they were registered under the *Indian Act* of Canada. Treaty Indians are persons who are registered under the *Indian Act* and can prove descent from a band that signed a treaty.

Prior to 1996, the term 'treaty' was not included in the question. It was added in 1996 at the request of individuals from the Western provinces, where the term is more widely used. The 2006 Census question is the same as the one used in 1996 and 2001.

Rooms

Refers to the number of rooms in a dwelling. A room is an enclosed area within a dwelling which is finished and suitable for year-round living.

Sex

Refers to the gender of the respondent.

Structural type of dwelling

Refers to the structural characteristics and/or dwelling configuration, that is, whether the dwelling is a single-detached house, an apartment in a high-rise building, a row house, a mobile home, etc.

In 2006, improvements to the enumeration process and changes in structural type classification affect the historical comparability of the 'structural type of dwelling' variable. In 2006, 'apartment or flat in a duplex' replaces 'apartment or flat in a detached duplex' and includes duplexes attached to other dwellings or buildings. This is a change from the 2001 Census where duplexes attached to other dwellings or buildings were classified as an 'apartment in a building that has fewer than five storeys'.

Tenure

Refers to whether some member of the household owns or rents the dwelling, or whether the dwelling is Band housing (on an Indian reserve or settlement).

Total income

Refers to the total money income received from the following sources during calendar year 2005 by persons 15 years of age and over:

- wages and salaries (total);
- net farm income;
- net non-farm income from unincorporated business and/or professional practice;
- child benefits;
- Old Age Security pension and Guaranteed Income Supplement;
- benefits from Canada or Quebec Pension Plan;
- benefits from Employment Insurance;
- other income from government sources;

- dividends, interest on bonds, deposits and savings certificates, and other investment income;
- retirement pensions, superannuation and annuities, including those from RRSPs and RRIFs;
- other money income.

'After-tax income' refers to total income from all sources minus federal, provincial and territorial income taxes paid for 2005.

Receipts not counted as income - The income concept excluded gambling gains and losses, lottery prizes, money inherited during the year in a lump sum, capital gains or losses, receipts from the sale of property, income tax refunds, loan payments received, lump sum settlements of insurance policies, rebates received on property taxes, refunds of pension contributions, as well as all income 'in kind,' such as free meals and living accommodations, or agricultural products produced and consumed on the farm.

Average income of individuals - Average income of individuals refers to the weighted mean total income of individuals 15 years of age and over who reported income for 2005. Average income is calculated from unrounded data by dividing the aggregate income of a specified group of individuals (e.g., males 45 to 54 years of age) by the number of individuals with income in that group.

Median income of individuals - The median income of a specified group of income recipients is that amount which divides their income size distribution into two halves, i.e., the incomes of the first half of individuals are below the median, while those of the second half are above the median. Median income is calculated from the unrounded number of individuals (e.g., males 45 to 54 years of age) with income in that group.

Standard error of average income - Refers to the estimated standard error of average income for an income size distribution. If interpreted as shown below, it serves as a rough indicator of the precision of the corresponding estimate of average income. For about 68% of the samples which could be selected from the sample frame, the difference between the sample estimate of average income and the corresponding figure based on complete enumeration would be less than one standard error. For about 95% of the possible samples, the difference would be less than two standard errors and, in about 99% of the samples, the difference would be less than approximately two and one half standard errors. The above concept and procedures also apply in the calculation of these statistics for earnings or any other source of income and after-tax income of persons 15 years of age and over not in families and households.

Average and median incomes and standard errors of average income of individuals will be calculated for those individuals who are at least 15 years of age and who have an income (positive or negative). For all other universes (families [census/economic]), persons 15 years of age and over not in families or private households), these statistics will be calculated over all units, whether or not they reported any income. These statistics can be derived for after-tax income, earnings, wages and salaries, or any other particular source of income in the same manner.

Value of dwelling

Refers to the dollar amount expected by the owner if the dwelling were to be sold.

Visible minority population

Refers to the visible minority group to which the respondent belongs. The *Employment Equity Act* defines visible minorities as 'persons, other than Aboriginal peoples, who are non-Caucasian in race or non-white in colour'.

Work activity in 2005

Refers to the number of weeks in which a person worked for pay or in self-employment in 2005 at all jobs held, even if only for a few hours, and whether these weeks were mostly full time (30 hours or more per week) or mostly part time (1 to 29 hours per week).

The term 'full-year full-time workers' refers to persons 15 years of age and over who worked 49 to 52 weeks (mostly full time) in 2005 for pay or in self-employment.

Data quality

General

The 2006 Census was a large and complex undertaking and, while considerable effort was taken to ensure high standards throughout all collection and processing operations, the resulting estimates are inevitably subject to a certain degree of error. Users of census data should be aware that such error exists, and should have some appreciation of its main components, so that they can assess the usefulness of census data for their purposes and the risks involved in basing conclusions or decisions on these data.

Errors can arise at virtually every stage of the census process, from the preparation of materials through data processing, including the listing of dwellings and the collection of data. Some errors occur at random, and when the individual responses are aggregated for a sufficiently large group, such errors tend to cancel out. For errors of this nature, the larger the group, the more accurate the corresponding estimate. It is for this reason that users are advised to be cautious when using small area estimates. There are some errors, however, which might occur more systematically, and which result in 'biased' estimates. Because the bias from such errors is persistent no matter how large the group for which responses are aggregated, and because bias is particularly difficult to measure, systematic errors are a more serious problem for most data users than the random errors referred to previously.

For census data in general, the principal types of error are as follows:

- **coverage errors**, which occur when dwellings or individuals are missed, incorrectly enumerated or counted more than once

- **non-response errors**, which result when responses cannot be obtained from a certain number of households and/or individuals, because of extended absence or some other reason or when responses cannot be obtained from a certain number of questions in a complete questionnaire

- **response errors**, which occur when the respondent, or sometimes the census representative, misunderstands a census question, and records an incorrect response or simply uses the wrong response box

- **processing errors**, which can occur at various steps including **coding**, when 'write-in' responses are transformed into numerical codes; **data capture**, when responses are transferred from the census questionnaire in an electronic format, by optical character recognition methods or key-entry operators; and **imputation**, when a 'valid', but not necessarily correct, response is inserted into a record by the computer to replace missing or 'invalid' data ('valid' and 'invalid' referring to whether or not the response is consistent with other information on the record)

- **sampling errors**, which apply only to the supplementary questions on the 'long form' asked of a one-fifth sample of households, and which arise from the fact that the responses to these questions, when weighted up to represent the whole population, inevitably differ somewhat from the responses which would have been obtained if these questions had been asked of all households.

The above types of error each have both random and systematic components. Usually, however, the systematic component of sampling error is very small in relation to its random component. For the other non-sampling errors, both random and systematic components may be significant.

Coverage errors

Coverage errors affect the accuracy of the census counts, that is, the sizes of the various census universes: population, families, households and dwellings. While steps have been taken to correct certain identifiable errors, the final counts are still subject to some degree of error because persons or dwellings have been missed, incorrectly enumerated in the census or counted more than once.

Missed dwellings or persons result in **undercoverage**. Dwellings can be missed because of the misunderstanding of collection unit (CU) boundaries, or because either they do not look like dwellings or they appear uninhabitable. Persons can be missed when their dwelling is missed or is classified as vacant, or because the respondent misinterprets the instructions on whom to include on the questionnaire. Some individuals may be missed because they have no usual residence and did not spend census night in a dwelling.

Dwellings or persons incorrectly enumerated or double-counted result in overcoverage. **Overcoverage** of dwellings can occur when structures unfit for habitation are listed as dwellings (incorrectly enumerated), when there is a certain ambiguity regarding the collection unit (CU) boundaries or when units (for example, rooms) are listed separately instead of being treated as part of one dwelling (double-counted). Persons can be counted more than once because their dwelling is double counted or because the guidelines on whom to include on the questionnaire have been misunderstood. Occasionally, someone who is not in the census population universe, such as a foreign resident or a fictitious person, may, incorrectly, be enumerated in the census. On average, overcoverage is less likely to occur than undercoverage and, as a result, counts of dwellings and persons are likely to be slightly underestimated.

For the 2006 Census, three studies are used to measure coverage error. In the Dwelling Classification Study, dwellings listed as vacant were revisited to verify that they were vacant on Census Day, and dwellings whose households were listed as non-respondent were revisited to determine the number of usual residents and their characteristics. Adjustments have been made to the final census counts to account for households and persons missed because their dwelling was incorrectly classified as vacant. The census counts may also have been adjusted for dwellings whose households were classified as non-respondent. Despite these adjustments, the final counts still may be subject to some undercoverage. Undercoverage tends to be higher for certain segments of the population, such as young adults (especially young adult males) and recent immigrants. The Reverse Record Check Study is used to measure the residual undercoverage for Canada, and each province and territory. The Overcoverage Study is designed to investigate overcoverage errors. The results of the Reverse Record Check and the Overcoverage Study, when taken together, furnish an estimate of net undercoverage.

Other non-sampling errors

While coverage errors affect the number of units in the various census universes, other errors affect the characteristics of those units.

Sometimes it is not possible to obtain a complete response from a household, even though the dwelling was identified as occupied and a questionnaire was mailed out or dropped off. The household members may have been away throughout the census period or, in rare instances, the householder may have refused to complete the form. More frequently, the questionnaire is returned but no response is provided to certain questions. Effort is devoted to ensure as complete a questionnaire as possible. Once the questionnaires are captured, edit analysis are performed to detect significant cases of partial non-response and follow-up interviews are attempted to get the missing information. Despite this, at the end of the collection stage, a small number of responses are still missing, i.e., **non-response errors**. Although missing responses are eliminated during processing by replacing each one of them by the corresponding response for a 'similar' record, there remain some potential imputation errors. This is particularly serious if the non-respondents differ in some respects from the respondents; this procedure will then introduce a **non-response bias**.

Even when a response is obtained, it may not be entirely accurate. The respondent may have misinterpreted the question or may have guessed the answer, especially when answering on behalf of another, possibly absent, household member. The respondent may also have entered the answer in the wrong place on the questionnaire. Such errors are referred to as **response errors**. While response errors usually arise from inaccurate information provided by respondents, they can also result from mistakes by the census representative who completed certain parts of the questionnaire, such as the structural type of dwelling, or who followed up to obtain a missing response.

Some of the census questions require a written response. During processing, these 'write-in' entries are given a numeric code. **Coding errors** can occur when the written response is ambiguous, incomplete, and difficult to read or when the code list is extensive (e.g., major field of study, place of work). A formal quality control (QC) operation is used to detect, rectify and reduce coding errors. Within each work unit, a sample of responses is independently coded a second time. The resolution of discrepancies between the first and second codings determines whether recoding of the work unit is necessary. Census coding is now entirely automated, resulting in a reduction of coding errors.

The information on the questionnaires is scanned and captured into a computer file. To monitor and to ensure that the number of **data capture errors** are within tolerable limits, a sample of fields are sampled and reprocessed. Analysis of the two captures is done. Unsatisfactory work is identified, corrected and appropriate feedback is done to the system in order to minimize their occurrence.

Once captured, the data are edited where they undergo a series of computer checks to identify missing or inconsistent responses. These are replaced during the imputation stage of processing where either a response consistent with the other respondents' data is inferred or a response from a similar donor is substituted. Imputation ensures a complete database where the data correspond to the census counts and facilitate multivariate analyses. Although errors may have been introduced during **imputation**, the methods used have been rigorously tested to minimize systematic errors.

Various studies are being carried out to evaluate the quality of the responses obtained in the 2006 Census. For each question, non-response rates and edit failure rates have been calculated. These can be useful in identifying the potential for non-response errors and other types of errors. Also, tabulations from the 2006 Census have been or will be compared with corresponding estimates from previous censuses, from sample surveys (such as the Labour Force Survey) and from various administrative records (such as birth registrations and municipal assessment records). Such comparisons can indicate potential quality problems or at least discrepancies between the sources.

In addition to these aggregate-level comparisons, there are some micro-match studies in progress, in which census responses are compared with another source of information at the individual record level. For certain 'stable' characteristics (such as age, sex, mother tongue and place of birth), the responses obtained in the 2006 Census, for a sample of individuals, are being compared with those for the same individuals in the 2001 Census.

Sampling errors

Estimates obtained by weighting up responses collected on a sample basis are subject to error due to the fact that the distribution of characteristics within the sample will not usually be identical to the distribution of characteristics within the population from which the sample has been selected.

The potential error introduced by sampling will vary according to the relative scarcity of the characteristics in the population. For large cell values, the potential error due to sampling, as a proportion of the cell value, will be relatively small. For small cell values, this potential error, as a proportion of the cell value, will be relatively large.

The potential error due to sampling is usually expressed in terms of the so-called 'standard error'. This is the square root of the average, taken over all possible samples of the same size and design, of the squared deviation of the sample estimate from the value for the total population.

The following table provides approximate measures of the standard error due to sampling for census long form (2B) data. These measures are intended as a general guide only.

Text table 1 Approximate standard error due to sampling for 2006 Census sample data

Cell value	Approximate standard error
50 or less	15
100	20
200	30
500	45
1,000	65
2,000	90
5,000	140
10,000	200
20,000	280
50,000	450
100,000	630
500,000	1,400

Users wishing to determine the approximate error due to sampling for any given cell of data, based upon the 20% sample, should choose the standard error value corresponding to the cell value that is closest to the value of the given cell in the census tabulation. When using the obtained standard error value, the user, in general, can be reasonably certain that, for the enumerated population, the true value (discounting all forms of error other than sampling) lies within plus or minus three times the standard error (e.g., for a cell value of 1,000, the range would be 1,000 ± [3 x 65] or 1,000 ± 195).

The standard errors given in the table above will not apply to population, household, dwelling or family counts for the geographic area under consideration (see Sampling and weighting below). The effect of sampling for these cells can be determined by a comparison with a corresponding 100% data product.

The effect of the particular sample design and weighting procedure used in the 2006 Census will vary, however, from one characteristic to another and from one geographic area to another. The standard error values in the table may, therefore, understate or overstate the error due to sampling.

Sampling and weighting

The 2006 Census data were collected either from 100% of the households or on a sample basis with the data weighted to provide estimates for the entire population. The long form questionnaire (2B) information was collected on a 20% random sample basis of the households and weighted to compensate for sampling. All table headings are noted accordingly. Note that on Indian reserves and in remote areas all data were collected on a 100% basis.

For any given geographic area, the weighted population, household, dwelling or family total or subtotal may differ from that shown in reports containing data collected on a 100% basis. Such variations are due to sampling and to the fact that, unlike sample data, 100% data do not exclude institutional residents.

Confidentiality and random rounding

The figures shown in the tables have been subjected to a confidentiality procedure known as **random rounding** to prevent the possibility of associating statistical data with any identifiable individual. Under this method, all figures, including totals and margins, are randomly rounded either up or down to a multiple of '5', and in some cases '10'. While providing strong protection against disclosure, this technique does not add significant error to the census data. The user should be aware that totals and margins are rounded independently of the cell data so that some differences between these and the sum of rounded cell data may exist. Also, minor differences can be expected in corresponding totals and cell values among various census tabulations. Similarly, percentages, which are calculated on rounded figures, do not necessarily add up to 100%. Order statistics (median, quartiles, percentiles, etc.) and measures of dispersion such as the standard error are computed in the usual manner. When a statistic is defined as the quotient of two numbers (which is the case for averages, percentages, and proportions), the two numbers are rounded before the division is performed. For income, owner's payments, value of dwelling, hours worked, weeks worked and age, the sum is defined as the product of the average and the rounded weighted frequency. Otherwise, it is the weighted sum that is rounded. It should also be noted that small cell counts may suffer a significant distortion as a result of random rounding. Individual data cells containing small numbers may lose their precision as a result. Also, a statistic is suppressed if the number of actual records used in the calculation is less than 4 or if the sum of the weight of these records is less than 10. In addition, for values expressed in dollar units, the statistic is suppressed if the range of the values is too narrow or if all values are less than, in absolute value, a specified threshold. Finally, again for values expressed in dollar units, the statistic is suppressed if there is a dollar value too large compared to all the others.

Users should be aware of possible data distortions when they are aggregating these rounded data. Imprecisions as a result of rounding tend to cancel each other out when data cells are re-aggregated. However, users can minimize these distortions by using, whenever possible, the appropriate subtotals when aggregating.

For those requiring maximum precision, the option exists to use custom tabulations. With custom products, aggregation is done using individual census database records. Random rounding occurs only after the data cells have been aggregated, thus minimizing any distortion.

In addition to random rounding, **area suppression** has been adopted to further protect the confidentiality of individual responses.

Area suppression is the deletion of all characteristic data for geographic areas with populations below a specified size. The extent to which data are suppressed depends upon the following factors:

- if the data are tabulated from the 100% database, they are suppressed if the total population in the area is less than 40

- if the data are tabulated from the 20% sample database, they are suppressed if the total non-institutional population in the area from either the 100% or 20% database is less than 40.

There are some exceptions to these rules:

- income distributions and related statistics are suppressed if the population in the area, excluding institutional residents, is less than 250 from either the 100% or the 20% database, or if the number of private households is less than 40 from the 20% database

- place-of-work distributions and related statistics are suppressed if the total number of employed persons in the area is less than 40, according to the sample database. If the data also include an income distribution, the threshold is raised to 250, again according to the sample database

- tabulations covering both place of work and place of residence along with related statistics are suppressed, if the total number of employed persons in the area is less than 40 according to the sample database, or if the area's total population, excluding institutional residents, according to either the 100% or the sample database, is less than 40. If the tabulations also include an income distribution, the threshold is raised to 250 in all cases and the tabulations are suppressed if the number of private dwellings in the place of residence area is less than 40

- if the data are tabulated from the 100% database and refer to six-character postal codes or to groups of either dissemination blocks or block-faces, they are suppressed if the total population in the area is less than 100

- if the data are tabulated from the 20% sample database and refer to six-character postal codes or to groups of either dissemination blocks or block-faces, they are suppressed if the total non-institutional population in the area from either the 100% or 20% database is less than 100

- if the data refer to groups of either dissemination blocks or block-faces, and cover place of work, they are suppressed if the total number of employed persons in the area is less than 100, according to the sample database

- if the data refer to groups of either dissemination blocks or block-faces, and cover both place of work and place of residence, they are suppressed if the total number of employed persons in the area is less than 100, according to the sample database, or if the area's total population, excluding institutional residents, according to either 100% or the sample database, is less than 100.

In all cases, suppressed data are included in the appropriate higher aggregate subtotals and totals.

The suppression technique is being implemented for all products involving subprovincial data (i.e., Profile series, basic cross-tabulations, semi-custom and custom data products) collected on a 100% or 20% sample basis.

For further information on the quality of census data, contact the Social Survey Methods Division at Statistics Canada, Ottawa, Ontario, Canada K1A 0T6, or by calling 613-951-4783.

Special notes

Aboriginal identity

Users should be aware that the population counts associated with this variable are more affected than most by the incomplete enumeration of certain Indian reserves and Indian settlements. The extent of the impact will depend on the geographical area under study. In 2006, a total of 22 Indian reserves and Indian settlements were incompletely enumerated by the census. The population of these 22 communities are not included in the census counts.

Age at immigration

There was a slight overestimation of age at immigration in the 2006 Census. For more information on the age at immigration variable, please refer to the *Place of Birth, Generation Status, Citizenship and Immigration Reference Guide, 2006 Census*, catalogue number 97-557-GWE2006003.

Broad occupational category A - Management occupations

Census data for occupation groups in Broad occupational category A - Management occupations should be used with caution. Some coding errors were made in assigning the appropriate level of management, e.g., senior manager as opposed to middle manager, and in determining the appropriate area of specialization or activity, e.g., a manager of a health care program in a hospital as opposed to a government manager in health policy administration. Some non-management occupations have also been miscoded to management due to confusion over titles such as program manager and project manager. Data users may wish to use data for management occupations in conjunction with other variables such as Income, Age and Education.

Comparability of 2006 place of work data

Working at home can be measured in different ways. In the census, the 'Worked at home' category includes persons who live and work at the same physical location, such as farmers, teleworkers and work camp workers. In addition, the 2006 Census Guide instructed persons who worked part of the time at home and part of the time at an employer's address to indicate that they 'Worked at home' if most of their time was spent working at home (e.g., three days out of five).

Other Statistics Canada surveys such as the General Social Survey, the Survey of Labour and Income Dynamics, and the Workplace and Employee Survey also collect information on working at home. However, the survey data are not directly comparable to the census data since the surveys ask respondents whether they did some or all of their paid work at home, whereas the census asks them where they usually worked most of the time. Consequently, census estimates on work at home are lower than survey estimates.

The place-of-work question has remained in virtually the same format in each census since 1971. However, in 1996, the category 'No fixed workplace address' replaced 'No usual place of work.' In 1996, the census questionnaire was modified by adding a check box for the 'No fixed workplace' response category. In previous censuses, respondents were asked to write 'No usual place of work' in the address fields. It is believed that previous censuses have undercounted the number of persons with 'No fixed workplace address.'

Annexations, incorporations and amalgamations of municipalities could create some difficulties when comparing spatial units and structures which change over time.

Dwelling universe

The dwelling universe pertains to characteristics of dwellings in Canada. Dwellings are distinct from households. Dwelling characteristics refer to the physical attributes of a set of living quarters, whereas household characteristics pertain to the person or the group of persons (other than temporary or foreign residents) who occupy a dwelling.

Earnings historical variations

Due to improved collection methodology, income and earnings data from the 2006 Census is more complete, precise and less subject to rounding than in prior censuses. Small dollar amounts, which in the past may not have been reported, are now more likely to be captured. Compared to prior censuses, this has resulted in an increased number of earners and lower median and average earnings. Users are advised to exercise caution when interpreting census-to-census changes in statistics and counts of specific cells within an earnings distribution. This comparability issue is less apparent when considering the earnings of full-year, full-time workers.

Empty columns in the table of selected characteristics for census divisions and census subdivisions

In some cases, the table contains empty columns when all census subdivisions have been shown for the province or the territory.

Historical earnings and income data and outliers

Changes in methodology and response modes introduced in the 2006 Census resulted in improved income data. However, these changes also mean that some comparisons with data from previous censuses and some data for the highest earnings and income amounts are affected.

For the 2006 Census, changes to methods for capturing and processing the 2006 Census income data and the introduction of data from tax files may have an impact on the trends analysis for earnings at the individual level in particular (but also total income).

There are more reported small amounts in 2006 and less rounding of the amounts that now come from tax data. To compare from census to census, users are advised to consider full-year full-time earners as the presence of more small amounts tends to lower the mean and median when considering the full population of earners.

As in the past, when considering small populations, one or more outliers may affect the average. In regions with sampling, this makes the estimate of the mean unreliable because of the variance due to sampling for smaller populations. The standard error of the average should help identify these situations. With extremely small populations, the median might also be affected by the presence of outliers. Users are required to interpret data with caution when the sub-population has small or very small counts.

Impact of municipal restructuring

The boundaries and names of municipalities (census subdivisions) can change from one census to the next because of annexations, dissolutions and incorporations. To bridge the impact of these municipal changes on data dissemination, the 2006 Census team produced a profile for dissolved census subdivisions.

Income data for seniors in collective dwellings

In the 2006 Census, individuals who resided in institutions or residences with distinct, separate living quarters, and who were able to complete the census questionnaire, received their own census form to complete. These individuals were excluded from measurements of income in prior censuses. This census, their incomes have been set to zero. This results in a slight overestimation in the count of population 15 years and over, and primarily the age group 65 years and over, without income (or without earnings). Counts and income statistics for families or persons not in families are not affected, as individuals in these types of collective dwellings have always, and continue to be excluded from those populations.

Income reference period

The Canadian census was conducted in 2006. Income data from the census relate to the calendar year prior to the census year, i.e. 2005.

Income suppression

Area suppression is the deletion of all characteristic data for geographic areas with populations below a specified size. Income distributions and related statistics are suppressed if the population in the area, excluding institutional residents, is less than 250 from either the 100% or the 20% database, or if the number of private households is less than 40 from the 20% database.

Tables with income, after-tax income or earnings distributions

Income, after-tax income and earnings distributions have been suppressed where the estimated total number of units (persons, families or households) in the reference year is less than 250. All suppressed cells and associated averages, medians and standard errors of average income, average after-tax income or average earnings have been replaced with zeroes or symbols.

In all cases, suppressed data are included in the appropriate higher aggregate subtotals and totals.

Tables with number and median or average income, after-tax income or earnings

Statistics have been suppressed if the estimated total number of persons (males, females or both sexes) with income, after-tax income or earnings in the reference year is less than 250 persons. All suppressed counts and associated averages and medians have been replaced by zeroes or symbols.

In all cases, suppressed data are included in the appropriate higher aggregate subtotals and totals.

Institutional residents

People in seniors' residences in the 2006 Census are classified as 'not living in an institution'. This is a change from the 2001 Census where they were classified as institutional residents, specifically, 'living in an institution, resident under care or custody'.

Labour force growth for the Northwest Territories

Care should be exercised in comparing the Northwest Territories 2006 Census population counts with those from the 2001 Census. In 2001, the net undercount for the Northwest Territories was estimated at 8.11%, substantially higher than the national level of 2.99%, and almost double its 1996 level. The increase in the labour force, the employed, unemployed and not in the labour force populations between 2001 and 2006 is likely overstated due to improvements in coverage of the Northwest Territories in 2006.

Migration data for small geographic areas

Estimates of internal migration may be less accurate for small geographic areas, areas with a place name that is duplicated elsewhere, and for some census subdivisions (CSDs) where residents may have provided the name of the census metropolitan area or census agglomeration instead of the specific name of the component CSD from which they migrated.

To improve the accuracy of the 2006 Census data, postal codes are used to pinpoint the exact CSD of the previous residence.

Non-permanent residents and the census universe

In the 2006 Census, non-permanent residents are defined as people from another country who, at the time of the census, held a Work or Study Permit, or who were refugee claimants, as well as family members living in Canada with them. In the 1991, 1996 and 2001 censuses, non-permanent residents also included persons who held a Minister's permit; this was discontinued by Citizenship and Immigration Canada prior to the 2006 Census.

From 1991 on, the Census of Population has enumerated both permanent and non-permanent residents of Canada. Prior to 1991, only permanent residents of Canada were included in the census. (The only exception to this occurred in 1941.) Non-permanent residents were considered foreign residents and were not enumerated.

Total population counts, as well as counts for all variables, are affected by this change in the census universe. Users should be especially careful when comparing data from 1991, 1996, 2001 or 2006 with data from previous censuses in geographic areas where there is a concentration of non-permanent residents.

Today in Canada, non-permanent residents make up a significant segment of the population, especially in several census metropolitan areas. Their presence can affect the demand for such government services as health care, schooling, employment programs and language training. The inclusion of non-permanent residents in the census facilitates comparisons with provincial and territorial statistics (marriages, divorces, births and deaths) which include this population. In addition, this inclusion of non-permanent residents brings Canadian practice closer to the United Nations (UN) recommendation that long-term residents (persons living in a country for one year or longer) be enumerated in the census.

Although every attempt has been made to enumerate non-permanent residents, factors such as language difficulties, the reluctance to complete a government form or to understand the need to participate may have affected the enumeration of this population.

For counts of the non-permanent resident population in 1991, 2001 and 2006, please refer to the 2006 Census table 97-557-XCB2006006.

Population 15 years and over who worked since 2005

Refers to those who have worked since January 1, 2005, regardless of whether or not they were in the labour force in the reference week.

Population and dwelling count amendments

After the release of the population and dwelling counts, errors are occasionally uncovered in the data. It is not possible to make changes to the 2006 Census data presented in tables. Users can, however, obtain the population and dwelling count amendments listed by census subdivisions and other levels of geography by visiting the 2006 Census portion of the Statistics Canada Web site at www.statcan.gc.ca/census. In addition, users can contact the nearest Statistics Canada's National Contact Centre by telephone at 1-800-263-1136 or by e-mail at infostats@statcan.gc.ca.

Population counts

The 2006 Census population counts for a particular area represent the number of Canadians whose usual place of residence is in that area, regardless of where they happened to be on Census Day. Also included are any Canadians who were staying in that area on Census Day and who had no usual place of residence elsewhere in Canada, as well as those considered to be 'non-permanent residents' (see the Special notes). For most areas, there is little difference between the number of usual residents and the number of people staying in the area on Census Day. For certain places, however, such as tourist or vacation areas, or those including large work camps, the number of people staying in that area at any particular time could significantly exceed the number of usual residents shown here. The population counts include Canadians living in other countries, but do not include foreign residents living in Canada (the 'foreign residents' category does not include 'non-permanent residents' – see the Special notes). Given these differences, users are advised not to interpret population counts as being the number of people living in the reported dwellings.

Prevalence of low income rates (before- or after-tax)

Prevalence of low income rates (before- or after-tax) are calculated from rounded counts of low income persons or families and the total number of persons or families. These counts have been rounded independently of the rounded counts shown in the table; thus, there may be a small difference between the rate shown and one derived from the counts shown. Users are advised to interpret prevalence of low income rates based upon small counts with caution.

Relationship of census income estimates to the national accounts and Survey of Labour and Income Dynamics

Census income estimates of aggregate income in 2005 were compared to similar personal income estimates from the national accounts. After adjustments to the personal income estimates for differences in concepts and coverage, the census estimate of aggregate income in 2005 from comparable sources was 1.2% lower than the national accounts estimate. As in the past, census estimates for some income components and for some provinces compared more favourably than for others.

Census estimates of aggregate wages and salaries, the largest component of income, were slightly higher (1.0%) than the national accounts estimates. This was partially offset by the difference (-7.8%) between the census estimates of aggregate self-employment income from both farm and non-farm self-employment and the adjusted national accounts figures. Overall, estimates of aggregate employment income or earnings were nearly identical (0.3% difference).

Census estimates of Old Age Security pensions and the Guaranteed Income Supplement were slightly lower (-1.4%), as they were for Canada/Quebec Pension Plan benefits (-0.9%), than adjusted national accounts estimates. Employment Insurance benefits reported in the census were smaller by 6.1%. Census estimates of aggregate child benefits were 2.0% higher than the adjusted national accounts estimates. Census estimates of other government transfer payments, which include such items as social welfare benefits, provincial income supplements to seniors, veterans' pensions and GST/HST/QST refunds, were significantly below (-39.2%) the estimates from the national accounts. Overall, census estimates of aggregate income from all government transfer payments were lower by 12.0%. The census estimate of aggregate investment income in 2005 was slightly lower (-2.7%) than the comparable national accounts estimate. This is a significant improvement when compared to previous census comparisons.

Census income statistics were also compared with similar statistics from the annual Survey of Labour and Income Dynamics (SLID). SLID estimates reflect adjustments made for population undercoverage, while census estimates do not include such an adjustment. This adjustment contributes to census estimates showing fewer income recipients (-2.1%) and earners (-1.4%) than SLID estimates. However, due to higher average amounts, census estimates of aggregate earnings are 2.8% higher than the SLID estimate, while the census estimate of aggregate total income of individuals is 2.3% higher. Most of the observed provincial differences were considered acceptable in the light of sampling errors in the Survey. The all-person low income prevalence rates for Canada (excluding the Territories) were almost identical in both sources for the before-tax measure at 15.3% and only slightly higher (0.6 percentage points) in census than SLID for the after-tax rate.

Suppression of citizenship and immigration data on Indian reserves and settlements

Persons living on Indian reserves and Indian settlements who were enumerated with the 2006 Census Form 2D questionnaire were not asked the questions on citizenship (Question 10), landed immigrant status (Question 11) and year of immigration (Question 12). Consequently, citizenship, landed immigrant status and period of immigration data are suppressed for Indian reserves and Indian settlements at census subdivision and lower levels of geography where the majority of the population was enumerated with the 2D Form. These data are, however, included in the totals for larger geographic areas, such as census divisions and provinces.

For a complete list of Indian reserves and Indian settlements for which citizenship, landed immigrant status and period of immigration data are suppressed, please contact Statistics Canada's National Contact Centre at 1-800-263-1136.

Value of dwelling

Post-censual evaluation of data for Value of dwelling has revealed that for some smaller communities there are a few high values of dwelling that cause substantial differences between the average and median values of dwelling. In most cases, the few high values of dwelling reflect the range of different housing characteristics in the community. However, in some instances, the high values of dwelling may reflect a response error where the value was overreported. Furthermore, in some smaller communities, high non-response rates for the Value of dwelling question resulted in some high values of dwelling being estimated during data processing. Data users should consider both average and median values of dwelling as well as the community housing characteristics when examining data for Value of dwelling in small communities.

Yukon

Geographic name changes may occur after the census and therefore could be reflected in various areas of the Statistics Canada website.

Effective October 20, 2008, the following name change has occurred:

Yukon Territory **changed to** Yukon

There is no change to the abbreviation (Y.T.). The 2006 Census products will maintain the name of the geographic area that was official when the census was taken (May 16, 2006).

Appendix 1 Incompletely enumerated Indian reserves and Indian settlements, 2001 and 1996 population counts

Province	Incompletely enumerated Indian reserves and Indian settlements, 2006	Population	
		2001	1996
Quebec	Gesgapegiag (formerly Gesgapegiag 2) (Avignon CD)	488	442
	Doncaster (formerly Doncaster 17) (Les Laurentides CD)	¶	0
	Kanesatake (Deux-Montagnes CD)	¶	¶
	Kahnawake (formerly Kahnawake 14) (Roussillon CD)	¶	¶
	Akwesasne (formerly Akwesasne (Partie)) (Le Haut-Saint-Laurent CD)	¶	¶
	Lac-Rapide (La Vallée-de-la-Gatineau CD)	¶	228
	Wendake (Quebec CD)	1,555	¶
Ontario	Fort Severn 89 (Kenora CD)	401	362
	Attawapiskat 91A (Kenora CD)	1,293	1,258
	Factory Island 1 (Cochrane CD)	1,430	1,286
	Bear Island 1 (Nipissing CD)	¶	153
	Tyendinaga Mohawk Territory (Hastings CD)	¶	¶
	Wahta Mohawk Territory (Muskoka CD)	¶	¶
	Six Nations (Part) 40 (Brant CD)	¶	¶
	Six Nations (Part) 40 (Haldimand-Norfolk CD)	¶	¶
	Oneida 41 (Middlesex CD)	¶	¶
	Akwesasne (Part) 59 (Stormont, Dundas and Glengarry CD)	¶	¶
Saskatchewan	Big Island Lake Cree Territory (formerly Big Head 124) (Division No. 17 CD)	¶	¶
Alberta	Little Buffalo (Division No. 17 CD)	¶	¶
	Saddle Lake 125 (Division No. 12 CD)	¶	¶
	Tsuu T'ina Nation 145 (Sarcee 145) (Division No. 6 CD)	1,982	1,509
British Columbia	Esquimalt (Capital CD)	¶	¶

Appendix 2 Suppressed census subdivisions, 2006 Census

Newfoundland and Labrador

Division No. 1, Subd. V, SNO ◆◆◆◇◇◇A
Division No. 1, Subd. J, SNO
Division No. 1, Subd. K, SNO ◆◆◆◇◇◇
Division No. 1, Subd. D, SNO ◆◆◆◇◇◇
Division No. 2, Subd. G, SNO ◆◆◆
Division No. 2, Subd. J, SNO
Division No. 2, Subd. L, SNO ◆◆◆
Division No. 3, Subd. A, SNO
Division No. 3, Subd. B, SNO
Division No. 3, Subd. C, SNO ◆◆◆◇◇◇
Division No. 5, Subd. D, SNO ◆◆◆
Division No. 6, Subd. E, SNO ◆◆◆◇◇◇
Division No. 7, Subd. D, SNO ◆◆◆◇◇◇
Division No. 7, Subd. N, SNO ◆◆◆◇◇◇
Division No. 7, Subd. B, SNO ◆◆◆◇◇◇
Division No. 8, Subd. D, SNO
Tilt Cove, T
Sally's Cove, T ◆◆◆◇◇◇
Division No. 10, Subd. E, SNO
Division No. 11, Subd. C, SNO A
Division No. 11, Subd. E, SNO A

Prince Edward Island

Morell 2, IRI ◆◇

Nova Scotia

Ponhook Lake 10, IRI ◆◆◇◇A
Wildcat 12, IRI
Bear River (Part) 6, IRI ◆◆◆◇◇◇
Bear River 6B, IRI ◆◆◆◇◇◇
Pennal 19, IRI ■■■A
New Ross 20, IRI ■■■A
Shubenacadie 13, IRI
Beaver Lake 17, IRI A
Sheet Harbour 36, IRI
Merigomish Harbour 31, IRI
Summerside 38, IRI

New Brunswick

Alma, P ◆◆
Red Bank 7, IRI
Tabusintac 9, IRI ◆◆◆◇◇◇
St. Mary's 24, IRI
Woodstock 23, IRI ◆◆◆◇◇◇
Madawaska, P ◆◆◆◇◇◇

Quebec

Mont-Alexandre, NO
Rivière-Saint-Jean, NO ◆◆◆■
Collines-du-Basque, NO
Coulée-des-Adolphe, NO
Rivière-Bonaventure, NO ◆◆◆◇◇
Gesgapegiag, IRI ¶
Rivière-Nouvelle, NO
Ruisseau-Ferguson, NO
Routhierville, NO ◆◆◆
Rivière-Vaseuse, NO
Rivière-Patapédia-Est, NO
Lac-Casault, NO ◆◆◆
Ruisseau-des-Mineurs, NO ◆◆◆
Lac-Alfred, NO
Lac-Matapédia, NO ◆◇◇◇
Rivière-Bonjour, NO ◆◆◆◇◇◇
Lac-des-Eaux-Mortes, NO ◆◆◆■◇◇◇
Lac-à-la-Croix, NO
Lac-Huron, NO ◆◆◆◇◇◇
Lac-Boisbouscache, NO
Whitworth, IRI
Cacouna, IRI
Picard, NO
Petit-Lac-Sainte-Anne, NO
Lac-Pikauba, NO ◆◆◇◇
Saint-Louis-de-Gonzague-du-Cap-Tourmente, PE
Sault-au-Cochon, NO
Lac-Jacques-Cartier, NO
Saint-Gabriel-de-Valcartier, MÉ ◆◆◆◇◇◇
Lac-Croche, NO
Wendake, IRI ¶
Lac-Blanc, NO ◆◆◆
Linton, NO ◆◆◆
Lac-Lapeyrère, NO
Lac-Masketsi, NO ◆◆◆
Lac-Normand, NO
Rivière-de-la-Savane, NO ◆◆
Lac-Boulé, NO
Lingwick, CT ◆◆◆■◇◇◇
Lac-Minaki, NO
Lac-Devenyns, NO ◆◇◇◇
Baie-de-la-Bouteille, NO ◆◆◆
Lac-Matawin, NO ◆◆◇◇
Lac-Legendre, NO
Lac-des-Dix-Milles, NO
Lac-Santé, NO
Baie-Obaoca, NO
Lac-Cabasta, NO
Baie-Atibenne, NO
Lac-du-Taureau, NO
L'Île-Dorval, V ◆◆◆A
Kahnawake, IRI ¶
Akwesasne, IRI ¶
Kanesatake, S-É ¶
Lac-Tremblant-Nord, MÉ ◆◆◆◇◇◇A
Doncaster, IRI ¶
Lac-de-la-Pomme, NO
Lac-Akonapwehikan, NO
Lac-Wagwabika, NO
Lac-Bazinet, NO
Lac-De La Bidière, NO
Lac-Oscar, NO
Lac-de-la-Maison-de-Pierre, NO
Baie-des-Chaloupes, NO
Lac-Douaire, NO
Lac-Ernest, NO
Lac-Marguerite, NO
Lac-Rapide, IRI ¶
Lac-Pythonga, NO ◆
Cascades-Malignes, NO
Lac-Lenôtre, NO
Lac-Moselle, NO
Dépôt-Échouani, NO
Lac-Nilgaut, NO ◆◆◆◇◇◇
Hunter's Point, S-É ◆◆◆◇◇◇
Laniel, NO ◆◆◆◇◇◇A
Les Lacs-du-Témiscamingue, NO ◆◆◆A
Lac-Duparquet, NO
Lac-Despinassy, NO ◆
Matchi-Manitou, NO
Lac-Metei, NO
Réservoir-Dozois, NO
Coucoucache, IRI
Lac-Ashuapmushuan, NO ◆◆◆
Rivière-Mistassini, NO ◆◆
Mont-Apica, NO
Lac-Moncouche, NO
Lac-Achouakan, NO
Belle-Rivière, NO
Lalemant, NO
Lac-Ministuk, NO
Mont-Valin, NO ◆◆◆
Lac-au-Brochet, NO
Rivière-aux-Outardes, NO ◆◆◆◇◇◇
Lac-John, IRI
Rivière-Nipissis, NO
Rivière-Mouchalagane, NO
Caniapiscau, NO
Lac-Juillet, NO
Lac-Vacher, NO
Petit-Mécatina, NO
Lac-Jérôme, NO
Waswanipi, VC
Mistissini, VC
Waskaganish, VC
Nemiscau, VC
Eastmain, VC
Wemindji, VC
Chisasibi, VC
Kawawachikamach, VK
Whapmagoostui, VC
Kuujjuarapik, TI A
Umiujaq, TI A
Inukjuak, TI
Akulivik, TI
Salluit, TI
Kangiqsujuaq, TI
Quaqtaq, TI
Kangirsuk, TI
Aupaluk, TI
Tasiujaq, TI
Kuujjuaq, TI
Kangiqsualujjuaq, TI
Rivière-Koksoak, NO ◆◆◆
Baie-d'Hudson, NO ◆◆◆

Ontario

Akwesasne (Part) 59, IRI ¶
Tyendinaga Mohawk Territory, IRI ¶
Hiawatha First Nation, IRI ◆◆◆◇◇◇
Chippewas of Georgina Island First Nation, IRI ◆◆◆◇◇◇
New Credit (Part) 40A, IRI
Six Nations (Part) 40, IRI ¶
Six Nations (Part) 40, IRI ¶
New Credit (Part) 40A, IRI ◆◆◆◇◇◇
Sarnia 45, IRI ◆◆◆◇◇◇
Oneida 41, IRI ¶
Christian Island 30A, IRI
Wahta Mohawk Territory, IRI ¶
Bear Island 1, IRI ¶
Nipissing, Unorganized, South Part, NO ◆◆◆■◇◇◇
Henvey Inlet 2, IRI

Ontario (continued)

Naiscoutaing 17A, IRI
Cockburn Island, TP ◆◆◆
Zhiibaahaasing 19 (Cockburn Island 19), IRI
Manitoulin, Unorganized, Mainland, NO ◆◆◆
Whitefish River (Part) 4, IRI
Chapleau 74A, IRI ◆◆◇◇
Mountbatten 76A, IRI
Matachewan, TP ◆◆◆◇◇◇
Timiskaming, Unorganized, East Part, NO ◆◆◆
Cochrane, Unorganized, South West Part, NO
Fort Albany (Part) 67, IRI ◆◆◆◇◇◇
Factory Island 1, IRI ¶◆◆◇◇
Moose Factory 68, IRI
Cochrane, Unorganized, South East Part, NO
Flying Post 73, IRI ◆◆◆◇◇◇
New Post 69, IRI
Moosonee, TV ◆◆◆■■◇◇◇
Missanabie 62, IRI
Algoma, Unorganized, South East Part, NO
Gull River 55, IRI ◆◆◆◇◇◇
Ojibway Nation of Saugeen (Savant Lake), IRI ◆◆◆◇◇◇
Seine River 22A2, IRI
Lac des Mille Lacs 22A1, IRI ◆◆◆◇◇◇
Sabaskong Bay (Part) 35C, IRI **A**
Big Island Mainland 93, IRI
Agency 1, IRI
Seine River 23B, IRI
Rainy Lake 17B, IRI
Long Sault 12, IRI ◆◆◇◇◇
Sabaskong Bay (Part) 35C, IRI **A**
Fort Albany (Part) 67, IRI
Attawapiskat 91A, IRI ¶◆◆◆◇◇◇
Northwest Angle 33B, IRI ◆◆◆◇◇◇
Lake Of The Woods 31G, IRI
Rat Portage 38A, IRI ◆◆◆■◇◇◇
Wunnumin 2, IRI
Wapekeka 1, IRI
Pikangikum 14, IRI ◆◆◆◇◇◇
Fort Severn 89, IRI ¶◆◆◆◇◇◇
Lansdowne House, S-É
Sachigo Lake 2, IRI
Wawakapewin (Long Dog Lake), IRI ◆◆◆◇◇◇
MacDowell Lake, S-É

Manitoba

Shoal Lake (Part) 40, IRI
Shoal Lake (Part) 39A, IRI **A**
Reed River 36A, IRI
Long Plain (Part) 6, IRI
Gambler 63 (Part), IRI **A**
Division No. 17, Unorganized, NO ◆◆◆◇◇◇
Division No. 18, Unorganized, West Part, NO
Fairford (Part) 50, IRI **A**
Chemawawin 3, IRI ◇
Division No. 20, Unorganized, South Part, NO ◆◆◆◇◇◇
Division No. 20, Unorganized, North Part, NO ◆
Opaskwayak Cree Nation 21B, IRI ◇
Opaskwayak Cree Nation 21C, IRI
Cross Lake 19B, IRI ■■
Cross Lake 19C, IRI ■■
Nelson House 170A, IRI
Nelson House 170B, IRI
Nelson House 170C, IRI
Gillam, S-É
Split Lake (Part) 171, IRI **A**
Highrock 199, IRI

Saskatchewan

Heward, VL ◆◆◇◇◇
Ocean Man 69A, IRI
Ocean Man 69B, IRI
Ocean Man 69C, IRI
Ocean Man 69E, IRI ◆◆◆◇◇◇
Ocean Man 69F, IRI
Ocean Man 69G, IRI ◆◆◇◇◇**A**
Ocean Man 69I, IRI **A**
Ocean Man 69H, IRI ◆◆◆◇◇◇**A**
Ocean Man 69D, IRI **A**
Tribune, VL
Lake Alma, VL ◆◇◇
Goodwater, VL
Osage, VL
Piapot Cree First Nation 75H, IRI
Wood Mountain, VL ◆
Meyronne, VL ◆◆
Wood Mountain 160, IRI ◆◆◇◇
Bracken, VL
Admiral, VL ◆◆
Carmichael, VL
Nekaneet Cree Nation, IRI ◆◆◆◇◇◇
West End, RV ◆◆◆◇◇◇
Atwater, VL
Melville Beach, RV ◆◆◆◇◇◇
Waldron, VL
Duff, VL ◇
Fenwood, VL ◆
Shesheep 74A, IRI ◆◆◆◇◇◇
Little Bone 74B, IRI ◆◆◇◇◇
Ochapowace 71-10, IRI
Ochapowace 71-54, IRI
Ochapowace 71-26, IRI
Ochapowace 71-70, IRI
Ochapowace 71-7, IRI
Ochapowace 71-18, IRI
Ochapowace 71-51, IRI
Ochapowace 71-44, IRI
Lumsden Beach, RV ◆◆◆◇◇◇
Penzance, VL
Grandview Beach, RV ◆◆◆◇◇◇
Sunset Cove, RV ◆◆◇◇◇
Pelican Pointe, RV ◆◆◆
Star Blanket 83C, IRI
Treaty Four Reserve Grounds 77, IRI
Shamrock, VL
Ernfold, VL ◆◆
Keeler, VL ◆◆◇◇◇
Coteau Beach, RV ◆◆◆
Golden Prairie, VL ◆◇
Shackleton, VL
Mendham, VL
Mantario, VL
Stornoway, VL
Keeseekoose 66A, IRI
Keeseekoose 66-CA-04, IRI
Keeseekoose 66-CA-05, IRI
Keeseekoose 66-CA-06, IRI
Keeseekoose 66-KE-04, IRI
Keeseekoose 66-KE-05, IRI
Chorney Beach, RV ◆◆■◇◇◇
Leslie Beach, RV ◆
Leslie, VL
Dafoe, VL ◆
Beardy's and Okemasis 96 and 97A, IRI
Muskowekwan 85-17, IRI
Muskowekwan 85-26, IRI ◆◆
Muskowekwan 85-33, IRI
Muskowekwan 85-28, IRI
Muskowekwan 85-29, IRI
Muskowekwan 85-23, IRI
Muskowekwan 85-12, IRI
Muskowekwan 85-24, IRI
Muskowekwan 85-22, IRI
Muskowekwan 85-27, IRI
Muskowekwan 85-10, IRI
Muskowekwan 85-1, IRI
Muskowekwan 85-8, IRI
Muskowekwan 85-15, IRI
Muskowekwan 85-2A, IRI
Muskowekwan 85-31, IRI
Fishing Lake 89A, IRI **A**
Etters Beach, RV ◆◆◆
Zelma, VL
Tessier, VL
Herschel, VL ◆◆◇◇
Springwater, VL ◇◇
Kinley, VL ◆
Sweet Grass 113-M16, IRI
Netherhill, VL ◆◆◇
Ruthilda, VL
Handel, VL ◆◇
Rockhaven, VL
Valparaiso, VL
Opaskwayak Cree Nation 27A (Carrot River), IRI **A**
Wakaw Lake, RV ◆◆◇◇◇
Opawakoscikan, IRI
One Arrow 95-1C, IRI
Beardy's and Okemasis 96 and 97B, IRI ◆◆◇◇
One Arrow 95-1D, IRI
One Arrow 95-1A, IRI
Ruddell, VL ◇◇
Krydor, VL ◆
Richard, VL ◆◆
Pebble Baye, RV ◆◆◆
Big Shell, RV ◆◆◆◇◇
Little Red River 106D, IRI
Saulteaux 159A, IRI ◆◆◆◇◇◇
Lucky Man, IRI ◆◆◇◇◇
Muskeg Lake 102B, IRI ◆◇◇◇
Pelican Lake 191B, IRI ◆◆◇◇◇
Muskeg Lake 102E, IRI
Muskeg Lake 102F, IRI
Muskeg Lake 102G, IRI
Muskeg Lake 102D, IRI ◇◇
Sweet Grass 113-L6, IRI
Pelican Lake 191A, IRI
Greig Lake, RV ◆◆
Thunderchild First Nation 115C, IRI
Makwa Lake 129, IRI
Big Island Lake Cree Territory, IRI ¶
Makwa Lake 129A, IRI

Saskatchewan (continued)

Makwa Lake 129C, IRI
Thunderchild First Nation 115D, IRI
Meadow Lake 105A, IRI
Onion Lake 119-1, IRI A
Min-A-He-Quo-Sis 116C, IRI
Timber Bay, NH ◆◆◆◇◇◇
Dore Lake, NH ◆◆
Missinipe, NH
St. George's Hill, NH
Stanley 157A, IRI
Île-à-la-Crosse 192E, IRI
Potato River 156A, IRI
Four Portages 157C, IRI
Dipper Rapids 192C, IRI
Clearwater River Dene Band 223, IRI
Primeau Lake 192F, IRI
Fond du Lac 229, IRI
Turnor Lake 194, IRI
Clearwater River Dene Band 221, IRI
Elak Dase 192A, IRI
Little Hills 158, IRI
Fond du Lac 232, IRI
Fond du Lac 231, IRI
Fond du Lac 233, IRI
Little Hills 158B, IRI ◇

Alberta

Blood 148A, IRI
Tsuu T'ina Nation 145 (Sarcee 145), IRI ¶
Gadsby, VL ◆
White Sands, SV ◆◆◆◇◇◇
Half Moon Bay, SV ◆
Sunbreaker Cove, SV ◆◆◆◇◇◇
Samson 137A, IRI ◆◇◇
Burnstick Lake, SV ◆◆◆◇◇◇
Improvement District No. 13, ID
Argentia Beach, SV ◆◆◆◇◇◇
Crystal Springs, SV ◆◆◆◇◇◇
Norris Beach, SV ◆◆◆◇◇◇
Sundance Beach, SV ◆◆◆◇◇◇
Itaska Beach, SV ◆◆◆
Betula Beach, SV ◆◆
Point Alison, SV
Lakeview, SV ◆◆◆◇◇
Kapasiwin, SV ◆◆◆■
Stony Plain 135, IRI ◆◆◆◇◇◇
Wabamun 133B, IRI A
Saddle Lake 125, IRI ¶
Heart Lake 167, IRI ◆◆◆◇◇◇
Nakamun Park, SV ◆◆◆◇◇◇
Castle Island, SV ◆◆◆◇◇◇
Birch Cove, SV ◆
Larkspur, SV ◆◆◆◇◇◇
West Baptiste, SV ◆◆◆◇◇◇
Improvement District No. 25, ID
Improvement District No. 12, ID ◆◆◇
Clearwater 175, IRI
Devil's Gate 220, IRI
Chipewyan 201, IRI
Chipewyan 201A, IRI
Chipewyan 201B, IRI
Chipewyan 201C, IRI
Chipewyan 201D, IRI
Chipewyan 201E, IRI
Chipewyan 201F, IRI
Chipewyan 201G, IRI
Old Fort 217, IRI
Allison Bay 219, IRI ◆◆◆◇◇◇
Sandy Point 221, IRI
Cornwall Lake 224, IRI
Collin Lake 223, IRI
Charles Lake 225, IRI
Fort McKay 174, IRI
Namur River 174A, IRI
Namur Lake 174B, IRI
Thebathi 196, IRI ◆◆◇◇◇A
Thabacha Náre 196A, IRI A
Clear Hills 152C, IRI
Kapawe'no First Nation (Pakashan 150D), IRI
Sawridge 150H, IRI
Kapawe'no First Nation (Freeman 150B), IRI ◆◆◆◇◇◇
Beaver Ranch 163, IRI ◇◇
Kapawe'no First Nation (Halcro 150C), IRI
Little Buffalo, S-É ¶
Carcajou 187, S-É
Desmarais, S-É ◆◆◆◇◇◇
Kapawe'no First Nation (Grouard 230), IRI
Sturgeon Lake 154A, IRI

British Columbia

Isidore's Ranch 4, IRI
Cassimayooks (Mayook) 5, IRI
Bummers Flat 6, IRI
Blind Creek 6, IRI ◆◇
Alexis 9, IRI
Ashnola 10, IRI ◆◆◆◇◇◇
Aywawwis 15, IRI
Boothroyd 5A, IRI
Boothroyd 8A (Part), IRI
Inkahtsaph 6, IRI ◆◆◆◇◇◇
Kopchitchin 2, IRI ◆◆◇◇
Puckatholetchin 11, IRI
Saddle Rock 9, IRI ◆
Lukseetsissum 9, IRI
Ruby Creek 2, IRI
Sho-ook 5, IRI
Skawahlook 1, IRI ◆◆◆◇◇◇
Speyum 3, IRI
Spuzzum 1, IRI ◆◇
Tuckkwiowhum 1, IRI ◆
Yale Town 1, IRI
Chaumox 11, IRI
Skwali 3, IRI
Squiaala 8, IRI
Yakweakwioose 12, IRI ◇
Scowlitz 1, IRI ◆◇◇◇
Tseatah 2, IRI ◇◇
Aitchelitch 9, IRI
Boston Bar 1A, IRI
Schelowat 1, IRI
Swahliseah 14, IRI
Stullawheets 8, IRI ◆◆◆◇◇◇
Douglas 8, IRI
Popkum 1, IRI ◆◆◆◇◇◇
Franks 10, IRI
Bucktum 4, IRI ◆◆◇◇◇
Tipella 7, IRI
Skwahla 2, IRI
Baptiste Smith 1A, IRI
Sachteen 2, IRI
Sachteen 2A, IRI
Samahquam 1, IRI
Kuthlalth 3, IRI
Albert Flat 5, IRI
Coquitlam 2, IRI ◇◇
Coquitlam 1, IRI ◆◇◇
Musqueam 4, IRI ◆
Katzie 2, IRI
Langley 5, IRI
Whonnock 1, IRI
Union Bay 4, IRI ◆◆◆◇◇◇
South Saanich 1, IRI ◆◆◆◇◇◇
Galiano Island 9, IRI
Mayne Island 6, IRI
Esquimalt, IRI ¶
Pacheena 1, IRI
Squaw-hay-one 11, IRI ◆◆◆◇◇◇
Claoose 4, IRI
Cowichan 9, IRI ◆◆◆◇◇◇
Kil-pah-las 3, IRI ◆◆◇
Kuper Island 7, IRI ◆◆◆◇◇◇
Lyacksun 3, IRI
Shingle Point 4, IRI
Cowichan Lake, IRI ◆◆◇◇◇
Portier Pass 5, IRI
Wyah 3, IRI
Est-Patrolas 4, IRI A
Tzart-Lam 5, IRI ◆A
Nanaimo River 2, IRI ◆◆◇◇
Nanaimo Town 1, IRI ◆◆◆◇◇◇
Qualicum, IRI ◆◆◆◇◇◇
Alberni 2, IRI ◆◆◆◇◇◇
Anacla 12, IRI ◆◆◆◇◇◇
Clakamucus 2, IRI
Elhlateese 2, IRI ◆◆◆◇◇◇
Hesquiat 1, IRI ◆◆◆◇◇◇
Numukamis 1, IRI
Macoah 1, IRI ◆◆◆◇◇◇
Openit 27, IRI
Sachsa 4, IRI ◆◇
Stuart Bay 6, IRI
Keeshan 9, IRI
Klehkoot 2, IRI
Tin Wis 11, IRI ◆◆◆◇◇◇A
Pentledge 2, IRI
Ahaminaquus 12, IRI
Chenahkint 12, IRI
Houpsitas 6, IRI ◆◆◆◇◇◇
Nuchatl 2, IRI
Nuchatl 1, IRI
Village Island 1, IRI
Yuquot 1, IRI
Aupe 6, IRI
Aupe 6A, IRI
Squirrel Cove 8, IRI ◆◇
Tatpo-oose 10, IRI
Matsayno 5, IRI
Saaiyouck 6, IRI
Oclucje 7, IRI ◆◆◆◇◇◇
Tsa Xana 18, IRI ◆◆◆◇◇◇
Harwood Island 2, IRI
Sechelt (Part), IGD

British Columbia (continued)

Chekwelp 26, IRI ◆◆◆◇◇◇
Chekwelp 26A, IRI
Schaltuuch 27, IRI
Kowtain 17, IRI ◇◇
Mount Currie 1, IRI ◆◆◆◇◇◇
Nequatque 1, IRI ◆◆◆◇◇◇
Yekwaupsum 18, IRI
Nequatque 3A, IRI ◆◆◆◇◇◇
Mount Currie 2, IRI ◆◆
Cayoosh Creek 1, IRI ◆◆◆◇◇◇
Fountain 3, IRI
Fountain 10, IRI
Fountain 11, IRI ◇
Fountain 12, IRI ◆
Fountain Creek 8, IRI ◇◇
McCartney's Flat 4, IRI ◆◆◆◇◇◇
Seton Lake 5, IRI ◆◆◆◇◇◇A
Necait 6, IRI ◆◇◇
Nesikep 6, IRI
Pashilqua 2, IRI ◆◆◆◇◇◇
Pavilion 1, IRI ◆◆◆◇◇◇
Seton Lake 5A, IRI
Slosh 1, IRI ◆◆◆◇◇◇
Towinock 2, IRI
Mission 5, IRI ◆◆◆◇◇◇
Mount Currie 8, IRI ◆◆◆◇◇◇
Slosh 1A, IRI
Nequatque 2, IRI ◆◆◆◇◇◇
Fountain 1B, IRI A
Douglas Lake 3, IRI ◆◆◆◇◇◇
Hamilton Creek 2, IRI ◆◆◇◇
Hamilton Creek 7, IRI
Nicola Lake 1, IRI ◆◆◆◇◇◇
Paul's Basin 2, IRI ◆◆◆◇◇◇
Zoht 4, IRI ◆
Halhalaeden 14A, IRI
Chuchhriaschin 5, IRI ◇
Skeetchestn, IRI ◆◆◆◇◇◇
Halhalaeden 14, IRI ◆◆◆◇◇◇
High Bar 1, IRI
Inkluckcheen 21, IRI ◆◆◆◇◇◇
Canoe Creek 2, IRI
Chuchhriaschin 5A, IRI
Kitzowit 20, IRI ◆◆◇◇
Skuppah 2A, IRI
Kanaka Bar 2, IRI ◆◆◇◇
Basque 18, IRI ◆◆
Klahkowit 5, IRI
Kleetlekut 22, IRI ◆◆◇◇
Kumcheen 1, IRI ◆◆◆◇◇◇
Leon Creek 2, IRI
Lytton 4A, IRI ◆◆◇
Lytton 4E, IRI
Lytton 9A, IRI ◆◆◆◇◇◇
Lytton 9B, IRI ◆◆◆◇◇◇
105 Mile Post 2, IRI ◆◆◆◇◇◇
Oregon Jack Creek 5, IRI
Spatsum 11, IRI
Nickel Palm 4, IRI ◇
Nickeyeah 25, IRI ◆◇
Nohomeen 23, IRI
Paska Island 3, IRI
Papyum 27, IRI
Papyum 27A, IRI
Pemynoos 9, IRI
Seah 5, IRI ◆◆◇
Kloklowuck 7, IRI
Siska Flat 5A, IRI
Siska Flat 5B, IRI
Siska Flat 8, IRI ◆◇◇
Skuppah 4, IRI
Skwayaynope 26, IRI ◆◇◇◇
Spences Bridge 4, IRI
Spintlum Flat 3, IRI
Staiyahanny 8, IRI
Nkaih 10, IRI
Spences Bridge 4C, IRI
Stryen 9, IRI ◆◆◆◇◇◇
Tsaukan 12, IRI ◆◆◆◇◇◇
Upper Nepa 6, IRI ◆◆◆◇◇◇
Yawaucht 11, IRI ◆
Zacht 5, IRI
Sahhaltkum 4, IRI ◆◆◆◇◇◇
Neskonlith 2, IRI ◆◆◆◇◇◇
Nekalliston 2, IRI ◆◆◆◇◇◇
Louis Creek 4, IRI ◆◆◆◇◇◇
Squaam 2, IRI ◆◆◆◇◇◇
Cameron Bar 13, IRI
Inkluckcheen 21B, IRI A
Shawniken 4B, IRI A
Nekliptum 1, IRI A
Boothroyd 8A (Part), IRI A
Harris 3, IRI ◆◆◆◇◇◇
Chum Creek 2, IRI ◆◆◆◇◇◇
Hustalen 1, IRI ◆◆◆◇◇◇
Scotch Creek 4, IRI ◆◆◆◇◇◇
Switsemalph 6, IRI ◆◆◆◇◇◇
Switsemalph 7, IRI ◆◆◆◇◇◇
Canim Lake 4, IRI
Deep Creek 2, IRI ◆◆◆◇◇◇
Quesnel 1, IRI ◆◆◆◇◇◇
Johny Sticks 2, IRI ◆◆◆◇◇◇
Williams Lake 1, IRI ◆◆◆◇◇◇
Canim Lake 2, IRI ◆◆◆◇◇◇
Alexandria 3A, IRI ◆◆◆◇◇◇
Alexandria 1, IRI ◆◆◆◇◇◇
Alexandria 3, IRI
Alexis Creek 14, IRI
Alexis Creek 16, IRI
Alexis Creek 24, IRI
Alexis Creek 25, IRI
Anahim's Meadow 2, IRI
Anahim's Meadow 2A, IRI
Andy Cahoose Meadow 16, IRI
Baezaeko River 25, IRI
Cahoose 8, IRI
Charley Boy's Meadow 3, IRI
Chilco Lake 1, IRI
Garden 2, IRI
Tanakut 4, IRI ◆◆◇◇◇
Garden 2A, IRI
Kluskus 1, IRI ◆◆◆◇◇◇
Louis Squinas Ranch 14, IRI
Coglistiko River 29, IRI
Baezaeko River 26, IRI
Puntzi Lake 2, IRI
Redstone Flat 1, IRI ◆◆◆◇◇◇
Stone 1, IRI ◆◆◆◇◇◇
Alexis Creek 17, IRI
Seymour Meadows 19, IRI
Agats Meadow 8, IRI
Thomas Squinas Ranch 2A, IRI ◆◆◇◇
Toby's Meadow 4, IRI
Alexis Creek 6, IRI
Alexis Creek 21, IRI
Baptiste Meadow 2, IRI
Toosey 1, IRI ◆◆◆◇◇◇
Towdystan Lake 3, IRI
Trout Lake Alec 16, IRI
Tsunnia Lake 5, IRI
Ulkatcho 13, IRI
Windy Mouth 7, IRI
Alexis Creek 34, IRI
Casimiel Meadows 15A, IRI
Cahoose 10, IRI
Blackwater Meadow 11, IRI
Cahoose 12, IRI
Betty Creek 18, IRI
Salmon River Meadow 7, IRI
Tzetzi Lake 11, IRI
Sundayman's Meadow 3, IRI
Tatelkus Lake 28, IRI
Euchinico Creek 17, IRI ◆◆◆◇◇◇
Kushya Creek 7, IRI
Sandy Harry 4, IRI
Alexandria 1A, IRI ◆◆◆◇◇◇
Fishtrap 19, IRI ◆◆◇◇
Swan Lake 3, IRI
Alkali Lake 4A, IRI ◇
Little Springs 8, IRI ◇
Little Springs 18, IRI ◆◆
Lezbye 6, IRI ◆◆◆◇◇◇A
Michel Gardens 36, IRI A
Baezaeko River 27, IRI A
Alert Bay 1, IRI ◆◆◆■◇◇◇
Alert Bay 1A, IRI ◆◆◆◇◇◇
Fort Rupert 1, IRI ◆◆◆
Quattishe 1, IRI
Dead Point 5, IRI
Gwayasdums 1, IRI ◆◆◆◇◇◇
Hopetown 10A, IRI
Karlukwees 1, IRI
Quaee 7, IRI ◆◆◆◇◇◇
Thomas Point 5, IRI
Apsagayu 1A, IRI
Compton Island 6, IRI
Mahmalillikullah 1, IRI
Glen-Gla-Ouch 5, IRI
Hope Island 1, IRI
Bella Coola 1, IRI ◆◆◆◇◇◇
Skeena-Queen Charlotte C, RDA ◆◆◇◇
Lax Kw'alaams 1, IRI ◆◆◆◇◇◇A
Kitimat-Stikine C (Part 2), RDA
Nisga'a, NL ◆◆◆◇◇◇
Kitimat-Stikine A, RDA ◆◆◆◇◇◇
Kitimat-Stikine D, RDA ◆◆◆◇◇◇
Kshish 4, IRI ◆◆◇◇
Bulkley River 19, IRI ◆
Telegraph Creek 6, IRI ◆◆◆◇◇◇
Telegraph Creek 6A, IRI ◇
Kluachon Lake 1, IRI
Gitzault 24, IRI
Aiyansh (Kitladamas) 1, NVL
Laxgalts'ap, NVL ◆◆◆◇◇◇

British Columbia (continued)

Kitselas 1, IRI ◆◆◆◊◊◊A
Ye Koo Che 3, IRI ◆◆◆◊◊◊
Sowchea 3, IRI ◆◆◆◊◊◊
Seaspunkut 4, IRI
Tsay Cho 4, IRI
Tacla Lake (Ferry Landing) 9, IRI
Laketown 3, IRI ◆◆◊◊
Dzitline Lee 9, IRI ◆
Kuz Che 5, IRI
Bihl' k'a 18, IRI
Omineca 1, IRI
Duncan Lake 2, IRI ◆◆◆◊◊◊
Francois Lake 7, IRI ◆◆
Skins Lake 16A, IRI ◆◆
Skins Lake 16B, IRI
Tatla West 11, IRI ◆◆◆◊◊◊
Uncha Lake 13A, IRI ◆◆◆◊
Jean Baptiste 28, IRI
Tatla't East 2, IRI
Isaac (Gale Lake) 8, IRI
Maxan Lake 4, IRI
Williams Prairie Meadow 1A, IRI ◆◆◆◊◊◊
North Tacla Lake 7A, IRI ◆
Bihlk'a 6, IRI
Poison Creek 17A, IRI ◆◆◆A
Tadinlay 15, IRI A
Nedoats 11, IRI ◆◆◆◊◊◊A
Babine Lake 21B, IRI A
Parsnip 5, IRI
Halfway River 168, IRI ◆◆◆◊◊◊
Ingenika Point, S-É
Good Hope Lake, S-É ◊
Tahltan 1, IRI
Liard River 3, IRI
Fontas 1, IRI
Kahntah 3, IRI
Prophet River 4, IRI ◆◆◆◊◊◊

Yukon Territory

Carcross 4, IRI ■
Lake Laberge 1, IRI
Klukshu, S-É
Kloo Lake, S-É
Moosehide Creek 2, IRI
Champagne Landing 10, S-É ◊
Swift River, SÉ ◆◆◊◊
Johnsons Crossing, SÉ ◆◊
Stewart Crossing, SÉ ◆◊
Keno Hill, SÉ ◆◆◊◊
Teslin, TL

Northwest Territories

Salt Plains 195, IRI
Reliance, SET ◆◆◆◊◊◊
Inuvik, Unorganized, NO ◆

Nunavut

Nanisivik, SET
Baffin, Unorganized, NO ◆◆◆◊◊◊
Keewatin, Unorganized, NO
Bathurst Inlet, SET
Umingmaktok, SET
Kitikmeot, Unorganized, NO ◆◆◆◊◊◊

Notes: For more information on the 2006 suppression rules, please see the Data quality section in the Reference material of this publication.
For population characteristics of these suppressed census subdivisions, please see *A National Overview: Population and Dwelling Counts, 2006 Census*, Catalogue no. 92-200-XPB.

Définitions

Seul un résumé des définitions des termes géographiques et des concepts du recensement est présenté ici. Les utilisateurs doivent consulter le Dictionnaire du recensement de 2006 (n° 92-566-XWF au catalogue) pour les définitions complètes et des observations additionnelles pertinentes.

Activité

Activité sur le marché du travail des personnes âgées de 15 ans et plus au cours de la semaine (du dimanche au samedi) ayant précédé le jour du recensement (le 16 mai 2006). Les recensés sont classés dans les catégories Personnes occupées, Chômeurs ou Inactifs. La population active comprend les personnes occupées et les chômeurs.

Personnes occupées

Personnes qui, au cours de la semaine (du dimanche au samedi) ayant précédé le jour du recensement (le 16 mai 2006) :

(a) avaient fait un travail quelconque à un emploi salarié ou à leur compte ou sans rémunération dans une ferme ou une entreprise familiale ou dans l'exercice d'une profession;

(b) étaient absentes de leur travail ou de l'entreprise, avec ou sans rémunération, toute la semaine à cause de vacances, d'une maladie, d'un conflit de travail à leur lieu de travail, ou encore pour d'autres raisons.

Chômeurs

Personnes qui, pendant la semaine (du dimanche au samedi) ayant précédé le jour du recensement (le 16 mai 2006), étaient sans emploi salarié et sans travail à leur compte, étaient prêtes à travailler et :

(a) avaient activement cherché un emploi salarié au cours des quatre semaines précédentes; ou

(b) avaient été mises à pied mais prévoyaient reprendre leur emploi; ou

(c) avaient pris des arrangements définis en vue de se présenter à un nouvel emploi dans les quatre semaines suivantes.

Inactifs

Personnes qui, pendant la semaine (du dimanche au samedi) ayant précédé le jour du recensement (le 16 mai 2006), n'étaient ni occupées ni en chômage. Les inactifs comprennent les étudiants, les personnes au foyer, les retraités, les travailleurs saisonniers en période de relâche qui ne cherchaient pas un travail et les personnes qui ne pouvaient travailler en raison d'une maladie chronique ou d'une incapacité à long terme.

Population active

Personnes qui étaient soit occupées, soit en chômage pendant la semaine (du dimanche au samedi) ayant précédé le jour du recensement (le 16 mai 2006).

Taux d'activité

Pourcentage de la population active pendant la semaine (du dimanche au samedi) ayant précédé le jour du recensement (le 16 mai 2006) par rapport aux personnes âgées de 15 ans et plus.

Le taux d'activité d'un groupe donné (âge, sexe, état matrimonial, région géographique, etc.) correspond au nombre total d'actifs dans ce groupe, exprimé en pourcentage de la population totale de ce groupe.

Taux d'emploi

Pourcentage de la population occupée au cours de la semaine (du dimanche au samedi) ayant précédé le jour du recensement (le 16 mai 2006), par rapport au pourcentage de la population âgée de 15 ans et plus.

Le taux d'emploi pour un groupe donné (âge, sexe, état matrimonial, région géographique, etc.) correspond au nombre de personnes occupées dans ce groupe, exprimé en pourcentage des personnes âgée de 15 ans et plus, de ce groupe.

Taux de chômage

Pourcentage de la population en chômage par rapport à la population active pendant la semaine (du dimanche au samedi) ayant précédé le jour du recensement (le 16 mai 2006).

Le taux de chômage d'un groupe donné (âge, sexe, état matrimonial, région géographique, etc.) correspond au nombre de chômeurs dans ce groupe exprimé en pourcentage de la population active dans ce groupe pendant la semaine ayant précédé le recensement.

Âge

Âge au dernier anniversaire de naissance (à la date de référence du recensement, soit le 16 mai 2006). Cette variable est établie d'après la réponse à la question sur la date de naissance.

Âge à l'immigration

Âge du recensé lorsqu'il a obtenu pour la première fois le statut d'immigrant reçu. Un immigrant reçu est une personne à qui les autorités de l'immigration ont accordé le droit de résider au Canada en permanence.

Agglomération de recensement (AR)

Se reporter à la définition de Région métropolitaine de recensement (RMR) et agglomération de recensement (AR).

Ascendance autochtone

Personne ayant indiqué au moins une ascendance autochtone (Indien de l'Amérique du Nord, Métis ou Inuit) à la question sur l'origine ethnique. « Origine ethnique » fait référence aux origines ethniques ou culturelles des ancêtres du répondant. « Ascendance autochtone » était « Origine autochtone » avant le Recensement de 2006.

Catégorie de lieu de travail

Lieu de travail des personnes âgées de 15 ans et plus, à l'exclusion des pensionnaires d'un établissement institutionnel, qui ont travaillé depuis le 1er janvier 2005. La variable se rapporte habituellement à l'emploi occupé par les recensés au cours de la semaine ayant précédé le recensement. Toutefois, dans le cas des personnes qui n'ont pas travaillé cette semaine-là, mais qui avaient travaillé à un moment quelconque depuis le 1er janvier 2005, les données portent sur l'emploi occupé le plus longtemps au cours de cette période.

À domicile - Personnes dont le lieu de travail et la résidence se trouvaient dans le même immeuble, celles qui habitaient la ferme où elles travaillaient, les concierges d'immeuble et les télétravailleurs qui travaillaient à domicile pendant la plus grande partie de leur semaine de travail.

En dehors du Canada - Personnes dont le lieu de travail est à l'extérieur du Canada. Les diplomates, les membres des Forces armées et les autres personnes dénombrées à l'étranger, de même que les nouveaux immigrants ne travaillant pas en ce moment, mais dont l'emploi de plus longue durée depuis le 1er janvier 2005 avait été exercé à l'extérieur du Canada.

Sans adresse de travail fixe - Personnes qui ne se rendaient pas au même lieu de travail au début de chaque quart, notamment les entrepreneurs en bâtiments, les entrepreneurs paysagistes, les représentants de commerce, les chauffeurs de camion indépendants, etc.

À l'adresse précisée ci-dessous - Les personnes qui ne sont pas incluses dans les catégories ci-dessus et qui se rendent au même lieu de travail (habituel) au début de chaque quart sont incluses ici. Les recensés devaient inscrire le numéro de voirie, la ville, le village, le canton, la municipalité ou la réserve indienne, la province ou le territoire et le code postal de leur lieu de travail. Ceux qui ne connaissaient pas l'adresse complète pouvaient donner uniquement le nom de l'immeuble ou de l'intersection la plus proche.

Les télétravailleurs qui passaient moins que la moitié de la semaine de travail à leur bureau à domicile devaient donner l'adresse complète de leur employeur. Les personnes qui travaillaient à des endroits différents, mais se présentaient à un siège social au début de chaque quart devaient donner l'adresse complète du siège social.

Catégorie de revenu avant ou après impôt

Situation de la famille économique ou de la personne hors famille économique de 15 ans et plus par rapport aux seuils de faible revenu avant ou après impôt de Statistique Canada.

Catégorie de travailleurs

Variable permettant de classer les personnes qui ont déclaré un emploi selon les catégories suivantes :

(a) personnes qui ont travaillé principalement pour un salaire, pour un traitement, à commission, pour des pourboires, à la pièce ou contre rémunération « en nature » (paiements sous forme de biens ou de services, plutôt qu'en espèces);

(b) personnes qui ont travaillé surtout à leur compte, avec ou sans aide rémunérée dans une entreprise, une ferme ou à exercer une profession, seules ou avec des associés;

(c) personnes qui ont travaillé sans rémunération à exercer une profession ou dans une entreprise ou une ferme familiale appartenant à un parent du même ménage ou exploitée par celui-ci; le travail familial non rémunéré ne comprend pas les travaux ménagers non rémunérés, les soins aux enfants non rémunérés, les soins ou l'aide aux personnes âgées non rémunérés, ni le travail bénévole.

L'emploi déclaré désigne l'emploi que la personne occupait au cours de la semaine (du dimanche au samedi) ayant précédé le recensement (le 16 mai 2006) si elle avait travaillé, ou l'emploi qu'elle a occupé le plus longtemps depuis le 1er janvier 2005, si la personne n'avait pas travaillé au cours de la semaine de référence. Les personnes ayant occupé deux emplois ou plus cette semaine-là devaient donner des renseignements sur celui auquel elles avaient consacré le plus grand nombre d'heures.

Chambres à coucher

Pièces conçues et meublées pour servir de chambres à coucher et utilisées principalement pour y dormir, même si ce n'est qu'à l'occasion (une chambre d'ami par exemple).

Citoyenneté

Statut légal de citoyenneté du recensé. Les personnes ayant plus d'une citoyenneté devaient indiquer le nom du ou des autres pays dont ils sont citoyens.

Connaissance des langues non officielles

Langues autres que le français ou l'anglais dans lesquelles le recensé peut soutenir une conversation.

Connaissance des langues officielles

Indique si le recensé peut soutenir une conversation en français seulement, en anglais seulement, en français et en anglais, ou dans aucune des deux langues officielles du Canada.

Division de recensement (DR)

Division de recensement (DR) est le terme général de régions créées en vertu des lois provinciales (comme les comtés, les municipalités régionales de comté et les *regional districts*) ou des régions équivalentes. Les divisions de recensement sont des régions géographiques intermédiaires entre la municipalité (subdivision de recensement) et la province/territoire.

État du logement

Variable indiquant si, selon le répondant, le logement nécessite des réparations (à l'exception des rénovations ou ajouts souhaités).

État matrimonial légal
Situation conjugale légale d'une personne.

Voici la définition des diverses catégories de réponse :

Jamais légalement marié (célibataire) - Personne qui n'a jamais été mariée (y compris toute personne de moins de 15 ans) ou personne dont le mariage a été annulé et qui ne s'est pas remariée.

Légalement marié (et non séparé) - Personne mariée dont le conjoint est vivant, à moins que le couple ne soit séparé ou divorcé.

Séparé, mais toujours légalement marié - Personne actuellement mariée, mais qui ne vit plus avec son conjoint (pour quelque raison que ce soit autre que la maladie ou le travail) et qui n'a pas obtenu de divorce.

Divorcé - Personne qui a obtenu un divorce officiel et qui ne s'est pas remariée.

Veuf ou veuve - Personne dont le conjoint est décédé et qui ne s'est pas remariée.

Famille économique
Groupe de deux personnes ou plus qui vivent dans le même logement et qui sont apparentées par le sang, par alliance, par union libre ou par adoption.

Famille de recensement
Couple marié (avec ou sans enfants des deux conjoints ou de l'un d'eux), couple vivant en union libre (avec ou sans enfants des deux partenaires ou de l'un d'eux) ou parent seul (peu importe son état matrimonial) demeurant avec au moins un enfant dans le même logement. Un couple peut être de sexe opposé ou de même sexe. Les « enfants » dans une famille de recensement incluent les petits-enfants vivant dans le ménage d'au moins un de leurs grands-parents, en l'absence des parents.

Gains ou revenu d'emploi
Revenu total reçu au cours de l'année civile 2005 par les personnes âgées de 15 ans et plus sous forme de salaires et traitements, de revenu net de l'exploitation d'une entreprise non agricole non constituée en société et/ou de l'exercice d'une profession, et de revenu net provenant d'un travail autonome agricole.

Genre de ménage
Répartition fondamentale des ménages privés en ménages familiaux et en ménages non familiaux. Un ménage familial est un ménage qui comprend au moins une famille de recensement, c'est-à-dire un couple marié avec ou sans enfants, ou un couple vivant en union libre avec ou sans enfants, ou un parent seul avec un ou plusieurs enfants (famille monoparentale). Un ménage unifamilial se compose d'une seule famille de recensement (avec ou sans autres personnes) qui occupe un logement privé. Un ménage multifamilial se compose de deux familles de recensement ou plus (avec ou sans autres personnes) qui occupent le même logement privé.

Un ménage non familial est constitué soit d'une personne vivant seule dans un logement privé, soit d'un groupe de deux personnes ou plus qui partagent un logement privé, mais qui ne forment pas une famille de recensement.

Genre de subdivision de recensement
Les subdivisions de recensement (SDR) sont classées en 55 genres, selon les appellations officielles adoptées par les autorités provinciales/territoriales ou fédérales. Il y a toutefois deux exceptions, soit la subdivision non organisée à Terre-Neuve-et-Labrador et la subdivision de municipalité en Nouvelle-Écosse, qui sont des régions géographiques équivalant aux municipalités et ayant été créées par Statistique Canada de concert avec ces provinces, aux fins de la diffusion des données statistiques.

Afin de mieux distinguer les SDR les unes des autres, le nom de chaque subdivision de recensement est accompagné d'une indication du **genre de subdivision de recensement**, par exemple, Granby, V (pour la « ville » de Granby) et Granby, CT (pour la « municipalité de canton » de Granby).

Heures consacrées à offrir des soins ou de l'aide aux personnes âgées, sans paye ou sans salaire
Nombre d'heures que la personne a consacrées à offrir des soins ou de l'aide aux personnes âgées, sans salaire, pour des membres du ménage du recensé, pour d'autres membres âgés de la famille ne faisant pas partie du ménage, pour des amis ou des voisins pendant la semaine (du dimanche au samedi) ayant précédé le jour du recensement (le 16 mai 2006).

Les soins ou l'aide aux personnes âgées sans paye ou sans salaire ne comprennent pas le travail bénévole pour un organisme à but non lucratif, un organisme religieux, une oeuvre de charité ou un groupe communautaire, ni le travail sans paye dans une ferme ou une entreprise familiale ou dans l'exercice d'une profession.

Heures consacrées aux soins des enfants, sans rémunération
Nombre d'heures que la personne a consacrées à donner des soins aux enfants, sans paye ou sans salaire. Sont incluses les heures consacrées à donner des soins aux enfants, sans paye ou sans salaire, pour des membres du ménage du recensé, pour d'autres membres de la famille ne faisant pas partie du ménage, pour des amis ou des voisins pendant la semaine (du dimanche au samedi) ayant précédé le jour du recensement (le 16 mai 2006).

Les soins aux enfants sans paye ou sans salaire ne comprennent pas le travail bénévole pour un organisme à but non lucratif, un organisme religieux, une oeuvre de charité ou un groupe communautaire, ni le travail sans paye dans une ferme ou une entreprise familiale ou dans l'exercice d'une profession.

Heures consacrées aux travaux ménagers, sans paye ou sans salaire

Nombre d'heures que la personne a consacrées aux travaux ménagers, à l'entretien de la maison ou du jardin, sans paye ou sans salaire, pendant la semaine (du dimanche au samedi) ayant précédé le jour du recensement (le 16 mai 2006). Sont incluses les heures consacrées aux travaux ménagers, sans paye ou sans salaire, pour des membres du ménage du recensé, pour d'autres membres de la famille ne faisant pas partie du ménage, pour des amis ou des voisins.

Les travaux ménagers sans paye ou sans salaire ne comprennent pas le travail bénévole pour un organisme à but non lucratif, un organisme religieux, une oeuvre de charité ou un groupe communautaire ni le travail sans paye dans une ferme ou une entreprise familiale ou dans l'exercice d'une profession.

Identité autochtone

Personne ayant déclaré appartenir à au moins un groupe autochtone, c'est-à-dire Indien de l'Amérique du Nord, Métis ou Inuit, et/ou personne ayant déclaré être un Indien des traités ou un Indien inscrit tel que défini par la *Loi sur les Indiens* du Canada, et/ou personne ayant déclaré appartenir à une bande indienne ou à une Première nation.

Indien inscrit ou Indien des traités

Personnes ayant déclaré être inscrites en vertu de la *Loi sur les Indiens* du Canada. Les Indiens des traités sont des personnes qui sont inscrites en vertu de la *Loi sur les Indiens* et qui peuvent démontrer qu'elles descendent d'une bande qui a signé un traité.

Avant 1996, le terme « Indien des traités » n'était pas utilisé dans la question. Il a été ajouté en 1996 à la demande des personnes des provinces de l'Ouest où ce terme est davantage utilisé. La question du Recensement de 2006 est identique à celle utilisée en 1996 et en 2001.

Industrie (selon le *Système de classification des industries de l'Amérique du Nord [SCIAN]* de 2002)

Nature générale de l'activité de l'établissement où travaille la personne. Les données du Recensement de 2006 sur l'industrie (selon le SCIAN de 2002) sont comparables à celles des autres partenaires de l'ALENA (États-Unis et Mexique).

Langue de travail

Langue le plus souvent utilisée au travail par le recensé au moment du recensement. Des données sur les autres langues utilisées au travail de façon régulière ont aussi été recueillies.

Langue maternelle

Première langue apprise à la maison dans l'enfance et encore comprise par le recensé au moment du recensement.

Langue parlée le plus souvent à la maison

Langue que le recensé parlait le plus souvent à la maison au moment du recensement.

Lieu de naissance du répondant

Province ou territoire où est né le répondant, s'il est né au Canada, ou pays où il est né, s'il est né à l'extérieur du Canada.

Lieu de résidence 1 an auparavant - Mobilité

La mobilité est déterminée d'après le lien entre le domicile habituel d'une personne le jour du recensement et son domicile habituel un an plus tôt. Il s'agit d'une personne n'ayant pas déménagé si son domicile n'a pas changé dans l'intervalle; sinon, il s'agit d'une personne ayant déménagé. Cette catégorisation correspond à la mobilité (1 an auparavant). Dans la catégorie des personnes ayant déménagé, on peut également distinguer les non-migrants et les migrants; cette distinction correspond au statut migratoire.

Les **personnes n'ayant pas déménagé** sont celles qui, le jour du recensement, demeuraient à la même adresse que celle où elles résidaient un an plus tôt.

Les **personnes ayant déménagé** sont celles qui, le jour du recensement, demeuraient à une autre adresse que celle où elles résidaient un an plus tôt.

Les **non-migrants** sont des personnes ayant déménagé qui, le jour du recensement, demeuraient à une autre adresse mais dans la même subdivision de recensement (SDR) que celle où elles résidaient un an plus tôt.

Les **migrants** sont des personnes ayant déménagé qui, le jour du recensement, demeuraient dans une SDR autre que celle où elles résidaient un an plus tôt (migrants internes) ou qui résidaient à l'extérieur du Canada un an plus tôt (migrants externes).

Les **migrants infraprovinciaux** sont des personnes ayant déménagé qui, le jour du recensement, demeuraient dans une subdivision de recensement autre que celle où elles résidaient un an plus tôt, dans la même province.

Les **migrants interprovinciaux** sont des personnes ayant déménagé qui, le jour du recensement, demeuraient dans une subdivision de recensement autre que celle où elles résidaient un an plus tôt, dans une province différente.

Lieu de résidence 5 ans auparavant - Mobilité

La mobilité est déterminée d'après le lien entre le domicile habituel d'une personne le jour du recensement et son domicile habituel cinq ans plus tôt. Il s'agit d'une personne n'ayant pas déménagé si son domicile n'a pas changé dans l'intervalle; sinon, il s'agit d'une personne ayant déménagé. Cette catégorisation correspond à la mobilité (5 ans auparavant). Dans la catégorie des personnes ayant déménagé, on peut également distinguer les non-migrants et les migrants; cette distinction correspond au statut migratoire.

Les **personnes n'ayant pas déménagé** sont celles qui, le jour du recensement, demeuraient à la même adresse que celle où elles résidaient cinq ans plus tôt.

Les **personnes ayant déménagé** sont celles qui, le jour du recensement, demeuraient à une autre adresse que celle où elles résidaient cinq ans plus tôt.

Les **non-migrants** sont des personnes ayant déménagé qui, le jour du recensement, demeuraient à une autre adresse, mais dans la même subdivision de recensement (SDR) que celle où elles résidaient cinq ans plus tôt.

Les **migrants** sont des personnes ayant déménagé qui, le jour du recensement, demeuraient dans une SDR autre que celle où elles résidaient cinq ans plus tôt (migrants internes) ou qui résidaient à l'extérieur du Canada cinq ans plus tôt (migrants externes).

Les **migrants infraprovinciaux** sont des personnes ayant déménagé qui, le jour du recensement, demeuraient dans une subdivision de recensement autre que celle où elles résidaient cinq ans plus tôt, dans la même province.

Les **migrants interprovinciaux** sont des personnes ayant déménagé qui, le jour du recensement, demeuraient dans une subdivision de recensement autre que celle où elles résidaient cinq ans plus tôt, dans une province différente.

Lieu des études

Province, territoire (au Canada) ou pays (à l'extérieur du Canada) où le plus haut certificat, diplôme ou grade a été obtenu. Seules les personnes ayant obtenu un certificat, diplôme ou grade postsecondaire sont incluses dans la population visée.

Logement privé

Ensemble distinct de pièces d'habitation ayant une entrée privée donnant sur l'extérieur ou sur un corridor, un hall, un vestibule ou un escalier commun à l'intérieur. L'entrée doit donner accès au logement sans que l'on ait à passer par les pièces d'habitation de quelqu'un d'autre. Le logement doit répondre aux deux conditions qui le rendent propre à l'habitation durant toute l'année :

1. avoir une source de chauffage ou d'énergie (comme en atteste la présence d'une cheminée, de fils électriques, de tuyaux ou compteurs pour l'huile [mazout] ou le gaz, d'une génératrice, de bois de chauffage, d'ampoules électriques, d'une thermopompe, de panneaux solaires, etc.);

2. fournir un espace clos permettant de s'abriter des intempéries (comme en atteste la présence de murs d'enceinte et d'un toit ainsi que de portes et fenêtres offrant une protection contre le vent, la pluie et la neige).

Pour les besoins du recensement, on classe les logements privés comme **logements privés ordinaires et logements marginaux occupés**. Les logements privés ordinaires se subdivisent en trois grandes catégories : les **logements occupés** (par des résidents habituels), les **logements occupés par des résidents étrangers et/ou temporaires** et **les logements inoccupés**. Les logements marginaux sont classés comme logements occupés par des résidents habituels ou comme logements occupés par des résidents étrangers et/ou temporaires. Les logements marginaux inoccupés le jour du recensement ne font pas partie du parc immobilier.

Logement privé occupé

Logement privé occupé de façon permanente par une personne ou un groupe de personnes. Sont également inclus dans cette catégorie les logements privés dont les résidents habituels sont temporairement absents le jour du recensement. Sauf indication contraire, toutes les données présentées dans les produits sur le logement ont trait aux logements privés occupés et non aux logements privés inoccupés ou aux logements occupés par des résidents étrangers et/ou temporaires uniquement.

Loyer brut

Total des montants mensuels moyens versés par les ménages locataires au titre de l'habitation. Le **loyer brut** comprend le prix du loyer, ainsi que les frais d'électricité, de chauffage et des services municipaux.

Ménage

Personne ou groupe de personnes (autres que des résidents étrangers) occupant un même logement et n'ayant pas de domicile habituel ailleurs au Canada. Il peut se composer d'un groupe familial (famille de recensement) avec ou sans autres personnes, de deux familles ou plus partageant le même logement, d'un groupe de personnes non apparentées ou d'une personne seule. Les membres d'un ménage qui sont temporairement absents le jour du recensement (par exemple, qui résident temporairement ailleurs) sont considérés comme faisant partie de leur ménage habituel. Pour les besoins du recensement, chaque personne est membre d'un seul et unique ménage. À moins d'indications contraires, toutes les données contenues dans les rapports sur les ménages se rapportent aux ménages privés seulement. Les ménages sont classés en trois catégories : les ménages privés, les ménages collectifs et les ménages à l'extérieur du Canada.

Ménage privé

Personne ou groupe de personnes (autres que des résidents étrangers) occupant un logement privé et n'ayant pas de domicile habituel ailleurs au Canada.

Mode de transport

Mode de transport utilisé pour se rendre au travail par les personnes âgées de 15 ans et plus, à l'exclusion des pensionnaires d'un établissement institutionnel, qui ont travaillé depuis le 1er janvier 2005. Les personnes qui ont indiqué qu'elles n'avaient pas d'adresse de travail fixe, ou ont précisé l'adresse d'un lieu habituel de travail, devaient inscrire le moyen de transport utilisé habituellement pour faire la navette entre le domicile et le travail. La variable se rapporte habituellement à l'emploi occupé par les recensés au cours de la semaine ayant précédé le recensement. Toutefois, dans le cas des personnes qui n'ont pas travaillé cette semaine-là, mais qui avaient travaillé à un moment quelconque depuis le 1er janvier 2005, les données portent sur l'emploi occupé le plus longtemps au cours de cette période.

Les personnes qui utilisaient plus d'un moyen de transport devaient indiquer seulement celui qu'elles utilisaient pour faire la plus grande partie du trajet. En conséquence, la question a permis de recueillir des données sur le principal mode de transport utilisé pour se rendre au travail. Elle ne permet toutefois pas d'obtenir des données sur l'utilisation de plusieurs modes de transport, la variation saisonnière dans le choix du mode de transport, ni sur les déplacements faits à d'autres fins que pour faire la navette entre le domicile et le travail.

Mode d'occupation

Indique si le logement est possédé ou loué par un membre du ménage, ou s'il s'agit d'un logement de bande (dans une réserve ou un établissement indien).

Origine ethnique

Origines ethniques ou culturelles des ancêtres du répondant.

Période de construction

Période au cours de laquelle l'immeuble ou le logement a été construit.

Période d'immigration

Tranches d'années établies d'après les réponses à la question sur l'année d'immigration. Par année d'immigration, on entend l'année au cours de laquelle la personne a obtenu le statut d'immigrant reçu pour la première fois. Un immigrant reçu est une personne à qui les autorités de l'immigration ont accordé le droit de résider au Canada en permanence.

Pièces

Nombre de pièces dans un logement. Une pièce est un espace fermé à l'intérieur d'un logement, fini et habitable toute l'année.

Plus haut certificat, diplôme ou grade

Il s'agit d'une variable dérivée obtenue à partir des réponses aux questions sur les titres scolaires où l'on demandait de déclarer tous les certificats, diplômes ou grades obtenus. Cette variable comporte une hiérarchie implicite (diplôme d'études secondaires, certificat d'apprenti inscrit ou d'une école de métiers, diplôme collégial, certificat, diplôme ou grade universitaire) qui est plus ou moins reliée à la durée des divers programmes d'études « en classe » menant aux titres scolaires en question. Toutefois, au niveau détaillé de la hiérarchie, un apprenti inscrit n'a pas toujours obtenu de diplôme d'études secondaires, de même qu'une personne possédant une maîtrise n'a pas nécessairement un certificat ou un diplôme supérieur au baccalauréat. Par conséquent, même si la liste des catégories n'est pas nécessairement hiérarchique, elle donne quand même une mesure générale de la réussite scolaire.

Population des immigrants

Personnes ayant le statut d'immigrant reçu au Canada, ou l'ayant déjà eu. Un immigrant reçu est une personne à qui les autorités de l'immigration ont accordé le droit de résider au Canada en permanence. Certains immigrants résident au Canada depuis un certain nombre d'années, alors que d'autres sont arrivés récemment. La plupart des immigrants sont nés à l'extérieur du Canada, mais un petit nombre d'entre eux sont nés au Canada.

Population des minorités visibles

Groupe de minorités visibles auquel le recensé appartient. Selon la *Loi sur l'équité en matière d'emploi*, font partie des minorités visibles « les personnes, autres que les Autochtones, qui ne sont pas de race blanche ou qui n'ont pas la peau blanche ».

Population des non-immigrants

Personnes qui sont des citoyens canadiens de naissance. Bien que la plupart de ces personnes soient nées au Canada, un petit nombre d'entre elles sont nées à l'étranger de parents canadiens.

Première langue officielle parlée

Variable élaborée pour l'application de la *Loi sur les langues officielles*.

Principal domaine d'études (PDE)

Principale discipline ou principal domaine dans lequel le recensé a fait ses études ou reçu sa formation et obtenu son plus haut certificat, diplôme ou grade postsecondaire. La classification du principal domaine d'études comporte 10 grandes catégories : enseignement, loisirs et orientation; beaux-arts et arts appliqués; lettres, sciences humaines et disciplines connexes; sciences sociales et disciplines connexes; commerce, gestion et administration des affaires; sciences agricoles et biologiques et services de la nutrition et de l'alimentation; génie et sciences appliquées; techniques et métiers des sciences appliquées; professions de la santé et technologies connexes; mathématiques, informatique et sciences physiques. Ces catégories sont elles-mêmes subdivisées en plus de 100 « sous-catégories » et environ 980 groupes de « base ».

Principales dépenses de propriété

Total des paiements mensuels moyens versés par les ménages propriétaires au titre de l'habitation. Les **principales dépenses de propriété** comprennent, par exemple, le paiement de l'hypothèque, ainsi que les frais d'électricité, de chauffage et des services municipaux.

Profession (selon la *Classification nationale des professions pour statistiques de 2006 [CNP–S 2006]*)

Nature du métier des personnes âgées de 15 ans et plus. La profession est déterminée à partir du type d'emploi occupé et de la description des tâches effectuées par la personne recensée. Les données du Recensement de 2006 sur la profession sont classées selon la *Classification nationale des professions pour statistiques de 2006 (CNP–S 2006)*, n° 12-583-XIF au catalogue. Pour faire des comparaisons avec les données des recensements de 1991 et 1996, il faut utiliser la variable Profession (historique).

Province ou territoire

Les termes « province » et « territoire » désignent les principales unités politiques du Canada. Du point de vue statistique, les provinces et les territoires sont des régions de base selon lesquelles les données du recensement sont totalisées. Le Canada est divisé en 10 provinces et trois territoires.

Région métropolitaine de recensement (RMR) et agglomération de recensement (AR)

Une région métropolitaine de recensement (RMR) ou une agglomération de recensement (AR) est formée d'une ou de plusieurs municipalités adjacentes situées autour d'une grande région urbaine (appelée noyau urbain). Une RMR doit avoir une population d'au moins 100 000 habitants et le noyau urbain doit compter au moins 50 000 habitants. L'agglomération de recensement doit avoir un noyau urbain d'au moins 10 000 habitants. Pour être incluses dans une RMR ou une AR, les autres municipalités adjacentes doivent avoir un degré d'intégration élevé avec la région urbaine centrale, lequel est déterminé par le pourcentage de navetteurs établi d'après les données du recensement sur le lieu de travail.

Si la population du noyau urbain d'une AR devient inférieure à 10 000 habitants, l'AR est retirée du programme. Cependant, une RMR restera une RMR même si la population totale devient inférieure à 100 000 habitants ou si la population de son noyau urbain devient inférieure à 50 000 habitants. Les régions urbaines comprises dans une RMR ou une AR qui ne sont pas contiguës à un noyau urbain sont appelées banlieues urbaines, tandis que les régions rurales sont appelées banlieues rurales.

Lorsque le noyau urbain d'une AR compte au moins 50 000 habitants, elle est subdivisée en secteurs de recensement. Les secteurs de recensement de l'AR sont maintenus même si, ultérieurement, la population de son noyau urbain devient inférieure à 50 000 habitants. Toutes les RMR sont subdivisées en secteurs de recensement.

Revenu total

Revenu total en espèces, reçu par les personnes âgées de 15 ans et plus durant l'année civile 2005, provenant des sources suivantes :

- salaires et traitements (total);
- revenu agricole net;
- revenu non agricole net de l'exploitation d'une entreprise non constituée en société et/ou de l'exercice d'une profession;
- prestations pour enfants;
- pension de sécurité de la vieillesse et supplément de revenu garanti;
- prestations du Régime de rentes du Québec ou du Régime de pensions du Canada;
- prestations d'assurance-emploi;
- autre revenu provenant de sources publiques;
- dividendes, intérêts d'obligations, de dépôts et de certificats d'épargne, et autre revenu de placements;
- pensions de retraite et rentes, y compris les rentes de REER et de FERR;
- autre revenu en espèces.

Le revenu après impôt est le revenu total de toutes les sources moins les impôts fédéral, provinciaux et territoriaux sur le revenu payés pour l'année civile 2005.

Recettes non comptées comme revenu - Le concept du revenu excluait les gains et les pertes au jeu, les prix gagnés à la loterie, les sommes forfaitaires reçues en héritage au cours de l'année, les gains et les pertes en capital, le produit de la vente d'une propriété, les remboursements d'impôt sur le revenu, les remboursements de prêts reçus, les règlements monétaires forfaitaires d'assurance, les remboursements d'impôt foncier, les remboursements de cotisations à un régime de pensions ainsi que les revenus en nature tels que les repas et l'hébergement gratuits ou les produits agricoles cultivés et consommés à la ferme.

Revenu moyen des particuliers - Revenu total moyen pondéré des personnes âgées de 15 ans et plus qui ont déclaré un revenu en 2005. Pour établir le revenu moyen à partir des données non arrondies, il faut diviser le revenu agrégé d'un groupe de particuliers (par exemple, les hommes de 45 à 54 ans) par le nombre de personnes qui ont déclaré un revenu dans ce groupe.

Revenu médian des particuliers - Valeur centrale séparant en deux parties égales la répartition par tranches de revenu d'un groupe donné de personnes ayant un revenu; la première partie regroupe les personnes ayant un revenu inférieur à la médiane, et la seconde, les personnes ayant un revenu supérieur à la médiane. Le revenu médian pour un groupe de personnes est calculé à partir des données non arrondies pour les membres de ce groupe (par exemple, les hommes de 45 à 54 ans) qui ont déclaré un revenu.

Erreur type de revenu moyen - Estimation de l'erreur type de revenu moyen pour une répartition par tranches de revenu. Si elle est interprétée de la façon décrite ci-après, elle sert d'indicateur brut de la précision avec laquelle le revenu moyen a été estimé. Pour environ 68 % des échantillons qui peuvent être tirés de la base de sondage, la différence entre l'estimation du revenu moyen calculée pour un échantillon et le chiffre correspondant obtenu par un dénombrement exhaustif est inférieure à une erreur type. Pour près de 95 % des échantillons possibles, la différence est de moins de deux erreurs types et, dans environ 99 % des échantillons, elle est inférieure à environ deux erreurs types et demie. Les revenus moyen et médian des particuliers, ainsi que les erreurs types de revenu moyen correspondantes, sont calculés pour les personnes qui sont âgées d'au moins 15 ans et qui ont un revenu (positif ou négatif).

En ce qui concerne tous les autres univers (familles [de recensement/économiques], personnes hors famille de 15 ans et plus ou ménages privés) ces statistiques sont calculées pour toutes les unités, qu'un revenu ait été déclaré ou non. Ces statistiques peuvent être calculées pour le revenu après impôt, les gains, les salaires et traitements, ou toute autre source particulière de revenu de la même façon.

Revenu total de la famille économique

Somme des revenus totaux de tous les membres d'une famille économique donnée.

Salarié ou bénéficiaire d'un revenu d'emploi

Personnes âgées de 15 ans et plus ayant reçu un revenu au cours de l'année civile 2005 sous forme de salaires et traitements, de revenu net de l'exploitation d'une entreprise non agricole non constituée en société et/ou dans l'exercice d'une profession, et de revenu net provenant d'un travail autonome agricole.

Secteur de recensement (SR)

Les secteurs de recensement (SR) sont de petites régions géographiques relativement stables qui comptent habituellement entre 2 500 et 8 000 habitants. Ils sont créés au sein de régions métropolitaines de recensement et d'agglomérations de recensement dont le noyau urbain compte 50 000 habitants ou plus d'après le recensement précédent.

Un comité de spécialistes locaux (par exemple, des planificateurs, des travailleurs sociaux, des travailleurs du secteur de la santé et des éducateurs) délimite initialement les secteurs de recensement de concert avec Statistique Canada. Une fois qu'une région métropolitaine de recensement (RMR) ou qu'une agglomération de recensement (AR) a été divisée en secteurs de recensement, les secteurs de recensement sont maintenus même si, ultérieurement, la population du noyau urbain de la RMR ou de l'AR devient inférieure à 50 000 habitants.

Seuils de faible revenu (SFR) (avant ou après impôt)

Les mesures du faible revenu appelées seuils de faible revenu (avant ou après impôt) ont été établies pour la première fois au Canada en 1968, d'après les données sur le revenu du Recensement de 1961 et les régimes de dépenses des familles en 1959. À cette époque, les régimes de dépenses indiquaient que les familles canadiennes consacraient environ 50 % de leur revenu total à la nourriture, au logement et à l'habillement. On a arbitrairement estimé que les familles consacrant 70 % ou plus de leur revenu (soit 20 points de pourcentage de plus que la moyenne) à ces biens de première nécessité se trouvent dans une « situation difficile ». À partir de cette hypothèse, des seuils de faible revenu ont été établis pour cinq différentes tailles de famille.

Par la suite, les seuils de faible revenu ont été révisés d'après les données nationales sur les dépenses des familles pour 1969, 1978, 1986 et 1992. Initialement, les SFR étaient établis en fonction du revenu total avant impôt des familles et des personnes hors famille économique âgées de 15 ans et plus.

À la suite d'une examen approfondi des seuils de faible revenu réalisé en 1991, des SFR établis à partir du revenu après impôt ont été publiés pour la première fois dans la publication Revenu après impôt, répartition selon la taille du revenu au Canada, 1990, n° 13-210 au catalogue.

Tout comme les seuils de faible revenu établis à partir du revenu total, les SFR après impôt sont établis séparément pour les familles économiques et les personnes hors famille économique d'après les données sur les dépenses des familles et le revenu après impôt. En conséquence, les seuils de faible revenu après impôt sont fixés en ajoutant 20 points de pourcentage au revenu après impôt consacré par la famille moyenne à la nourriture, au logement et à l'habillement, et en tenant compte de la taille de la famille et de la taille du secteur de résidence.

Sexe

Qualité d'homme ou de femme.

Situation des particuliers dans le ménage

Classement des personnes selon qu'elles sont membres d'un ménage familial ou d'un ménage non familial, c'est-à-dire que leur ménage est composé d'au moins une famille de recensement, et selon qu'elles sont membres d'une famille de recensement ou hors famille de recensement. Les personnes hors famille de recensement sont encore classifiées selon qu'elles vivent avec des personnes apparentées, des personnes non apparentées (seulement) ou seules.

Statut des générations

Fait référence au statut générationnel d'une personne, c'est-à-dire, 1re génération, 2e génération ou 3e génération ou plus.

Statut d'immigrant reçu

Indique si la personne est un immigrant reçu au Canada ou non. Les immigrants reçus sont les personnes à qui les autorités de l'immigration ont accordé le droit de résider au Canada en permanence.

Structure de la famille de recensement

Classement des familles de recensement en **couples mariés** (avec ou sans enfants des deux conjoints ou de l'un d'eux), en **couples en union libre** (avec ou sans enfants des deux partenaires ou de l'un deux) et en **familles monoparentales** selon le sexe du parent. Un couple peut être de sexe opposé ou de même sexe. Les « enfants » dans une famille de recensement incluent les petits-enfants vivant dans le ménage d'au moins un de leurs grands-parents, en l'absence des parents.

Subdivision de recensement (SDR)

Subdivision de recensement (SDR) est un terme générique qui désigne les municipalités (telles que définies par les lois provinciales/territoriales) ou les territoires considérés comme étant des équivalents municipaux à des fins statistiques (p. ex., les réserves indiennes, les établissements indiens et les territoires non organisés).

Superficie des terres

La superficie des terres correspond à la surface en kilomètres carrés des parties terrestres des régions géographiques normalisées.

Les données sur les superficies des terres ne sont pas officielles et servent uniquement à calculer la densité de la population.

Taille du ménage

Nombre de personnes dans un ménage privé.

Travail en 2005

Variable indiquant le nombre de semaines au cours desquelles les personnes ont travaillé à un emploi salarié ou à leur compte, en 2005, pour l'ensemble des emplois occupés, ne serait-ce que pour quelques heures, et si ces semaines étaient travaillées surtout à plein temps (30 heures ou plus par semaine) ou à temps partiel (de 1 à 29 heures par semaine).

L'expression « personnes ayant travaillé toute l'année à plein temps » désigne les personnes âgées de 15 ans et plus qui ont travaillé, à un emploi salarié ou à leur compte, de 49 à 52 semaines surtout à plein temps en 2005.

Type de construction résidentielle

Type de construction et/ou caractéristiques du logement (maison individuelle non attenante, appartement dans une tour d'habitation, maison en rangée, habitation mobile, etc.).

En 2006, les améliorations apportées au processus de dénombrement et les modifications apportées à la classification du type de construction ont une incidence sur la comparabilité dans le temps de la variable « type de construction résidentielle ». En 2006, « appartement ou plain-pied dans un duplex » a remplacé « appartement ou plain-pied dans un duplex non attenant » et comprend les duplex attenant à d'autres logements ou immeubles, alors qu'en 2001, un duplex attenant à d'autres logements ou immeubles était classé dans la catégorie « appartement dans un immeuble de moins de cinq étages ».

Union libre

Par union libre, on entend des personnes qui vivent ensemble en tant que couple sans être légalement mariées l'une à l'autre. Ces personnes peuvent être de sexe opposé ou de même sexe.

Univers de la population

L'univers de la population du Recensement de 2006 comprend les groupes suivants :

- les citoyens canadiens (par naissance ou par naturalisation) et les immigrants reçus ayant un lieu habituel de résidence au Canada;
- les citoyens canadiens (par naissance ou par naturalisation) et les immigrants reçus qui sont à l'étranger, dans une base militaire ou en mission diplomatique;
- les citoyens canadiens (par naissance ou par naturalisation) et les immigrants reçus qui sont en mer ou dans des ports à bord de navires marchands battant pavillon canadien;
- les personnes ayant un lieu habituel de résidence au Canada, qui demandent le statut de réfugié et les membres de leur famille vivant avec elles;
- les personnes ayant un lieu habituel de résidence au Canada, qui sont titulaires d'un permis d'études et les membres de leur famille vivant avec elles;
- les personnes ayant un lieu habituel de résidence au Canada, qui sont titulaires d'un permis de travail et les membres de leur famille vivant avec elles.

Aux fins du recensement, les personnes des trois derniers groupes de la liste sont des « résidents non permanents ».

Valeur du logement

Montant en dollars que s'attendrait à recevoir le propriétaire s'il vendait son logement.

Qualité des données

Généralités

Le Recensement de 2006 a été une entreprise complexe et de grande envergure. Bien que l'on ait déployé des efforts considérables pour assurer le respect de normes élevées au cours des opérations de la collecte et du traitement, il est inévitable que les estimations résultantes soient entachées d'erreurs. Les utilisateurs des données du recensement doivent savoir que ces erreurs existent et doivent avoir une idée générale de leurs principales composantes afin d'être en mesure de déterminer l'utilité des données produites et d'évaluer les risques qu'ils courent en tirant des conclusions ou en prenant des décisions à partir de ces données.

Des erreurs peuvent se produire pratiquement à toutes les étapes du recensement, depuis la préparation du matériel d'enquête jusqu'au traitement des données, en passant par l'établissement des listes de logements et la collecte des données. Certaines erreurs, qui surviennent par hasard, ont tendance à s'annuler lorsque les réponses fournies par les divers répondants sont agrégées pour un groupe assez important. Dans le cas d'erreurs de cette nature, l'estimation correspondante sera d'autant plus précise que le groupe visé sera grand. C'est pourquoi on conseille aux utilisateurs de faire preuve de prudence lorsqu'ils utilisent des estimations relatives à de petits groupes. Toutefois, certaines erreurs peuvent survenir de façon plus systématique et introduire un « biais » dans les estimations. Comme ce biais persiste quelle que soit la taille du groupe pour lequel les réponses sont agrégées et comme il est particulièrement difficile d'en mesurer l'importance, les erreurs systématiques posent pour la plupart des utilisateurs de données des problèmes plus graves que les erreurs aléatoires mentionnées plus haut.

En ce qui concerne les données du recensement en général, les principaux types d'erreurs sont les suivants :

- les **erreurs de couverture** qui se produisent lorsqu'on oublie des logements ou des personnes, qu'on les dénombre à tort ou qu'on les compte plus d'une fois;
- les **erreurs dues à la non-réponse** qui surviennent lorsqu'on n'a pu obtenir de réponses d'un certain nombre de ménages ou de personnes en raison d'une absence prolongée ou pour toute autre raison ou bien lorsqu'on n'a pu obtenir de réponses pour un certain nombre de questions dans un questionnaire rempli;

- les **erreurs de réponse** qui surviennent lorsque le répondant, ou parfois le recenseur, a mal interprété une question du recensement et a inscrit une mauvaise réponse ou s'est tout simplement trompé de case de réponse;
- les **erreurs de traitement** qui peuvent se produire à diverses étapes, notamment lors du **codage**, lorsque les réponses en lettres sont converties en codes numériques; lors de la **saisie des données**, lorsque les réponses figurant au questionnaire du recensement sont transférées dans un format électronique par un système de reconnaissance optique de caractères ou par des préposés à l'entrée de données; lors de l'**imputation**, lorsqu'une réponse « valide », mais pas nécessairement exacte, est insérée dans un enregistrement par l'ordinateur pour remplacer une réponse manquante ou « invalide » (« valide » et « invalide » renvoient à la cohérence de la réponse, compte tenu des autres renseignements compris dans l'enregistrement);
- les **erreurs d'échantillonnage** qui s'appliquent uniquement aux questions supplémentaires figurant dans le questionnaire complet distribué à un échantillon de un cinquième des ménages. Ces erreurs résultent du fait que les réponses à ces questions supplémentaires, une fois pondérées pour représenter l'ensemble de la population, diffèrent inévitablement des réponses qu'on aurait obtenues si l'on avait posé ces questions à tous les ménages.

Les types d'erreur mentionnés plus haut ont tous une composante aléatoire et une composante systématique. Toutefois, la composante systématique de l'erreur d'échantillonnage est d'ordinaire très petite comparativement à sa composante aléatoire. Dans le cas des autres erreurs non dues à l'échantillonnage, tant la composante aléatoire que la composante systématique peuvent être importantes.

Erreurs de couverture

Les erreurs de couverture ont une incidence directe sur la précision des chiffres du recensement, c'est-à-dire sur la taille des divers univers du recensement : la population, les familles, les ménages et les logements. Bien que des mesures aient été prises pour corriger certaines erreurs identifiables, les chiffres définitifs sont toujours entachés d'une certaine erreur parce que des personnes ou des logements ont été omis, dénombrés à tort ou comptés plus d'une fois.

L'omission de logements ou de personnes se traduit par un **sous-dénombrement.** Des logements peuvent être oubliés en raison soit d'une mauvaise interprétation des limites des unités de collecte (UC), soit qu'ils n'ont pas l'apparence de logements ou soit qu'ils semblent inhabitables. Des personnes peuvent être omises parce que leur logement est omis ou classé comme inoccupé, ou parce que le répondant a mal interprété les instructions concernant les personnes à inclure sur le questionnaire. Enfin, certaines personnes peuvent être omises parce qu'elles n'ont pas de domicile habituel et qu'elles n'ont pas passé la nuit du recensement dans un logement.

Le dénombrement erroné ou le double compte de logements ou de personnes se traduit par un **surdénombrement**. Il peut y avoir surdénombrement de logements lorsque des constructions impropres à l'habitation sont classées comme logements (dénombrement erroné), lorsqu'il existe une certaine ambiguïté au sujet des limites des unités de collecte (UC) ou lorsque des unités d'habitation (par exemple, des chambres) sont comptées séparément plutôt que d'être considérées comme faisant partie d'un seul logement (double compte). Les personnes peuvent être comptées plus d'une fois parce que leur logement a été compté deux fois ou parce que les lignes directrices concernant les personnes à inscrire dans le questionnaire ont été mal interprétées. À l'occasion, il arrive qu'une personne ne faisant pas partie de l'univers de la population du recensement, comme un résident étranger ou une personne fictive, soit dénombrée à tort. En moyenne, le surdénombrement est moins susceptible de se produire que le sous-dénombrement; les chiffres des logements et des personnes sont donc probablement légèrement sous-estimés.

Pour le Recensement de 2006, trois études permettent de mesurer l'erreur de couverture. Au cours de l'Enquête sur la classification des logements, les logements initialement listés comme inoccupés étaient revisités pour vérifier qu'ils étaient effectivement inoccupés le jour de recensement. Parallèlement, les logements classés comme non répondants au recensement étaient revisités pour déterminer le nombre de résidents habituels et leurs caractéristiques. Les chiffres définitifs du recensement des logements et des particuliers ont été ajustés pour compenser les logements qui étaient classés inoccupés par erreur. Il se peut aussi que les chiffres du recensement étaient ajustés pour les logements classés comme non répondants. En dépit de ces ajustements, les chiffres définitifs peuvent tout de même être entachés d'un certain sous-dénombrement. Le sous-dénombrement tend à être plus élevé pour certains segments de la population comme les jeunes adultes (plus particulièrement ceux de sexe masculin) et les personnes récemment immigrées. L'Étude de la contre-vérification des dossiers permet de mesurer le sous-dénombrement résiduel pour le Canada, de même que pour chaque province et chaque territoire. L'Étude sur le surdénombrement a pour objet d'étudier les erreurs de surdénombrement. Ensemble, les résultats de l'Étude de la contre-vérification des dossiers et de l'Étude sur le surdénombrement fournissent une estimation du sous-dénombrement net.

Autres erreurs non dues à l'échantillonnage

Alors que les erreurs de couverture ont une incidence sur le nombre d'unités comprises dans les divers univers du recensement, d'autres erreurs influent sur les caractéristiques de ces unités.

Il est parfois impossible d'obtenir une réponse complète d'un ménage, même si le logement a été classé comme étant occupé et un questionnaire y a été posté ou livré. Il se peut que les membres du ménage aient été absents pendant toute la période du recensement ou, en de rares occasions, que le membre responsable du ménage ait refusé de remplir le questionnaire. Il arrive plus souvent que le questionnaire soit retourné, mais qu'il y ait des questions laissées sans réponse. Des efforts sont déployés afin d'obtenir un questionnaire le plus complet possible. Une fois les questionnaires saisis, une analyse est faite pour détecter les cas spécifiques de non-réponses partielles et des suivis par interview sont tentés afin d'obtenir l'information manquante. Malgré tout, il existe toujours un petit nombre de réponses manquantes à la fin de l'étape de la collecte, c'est-à-dire d'**erreurs dues à la non-réponse**. Bien que les réponses manquantes soient éliminées en cours de traitement en remplaçant chacune d'elles par la réponse correspondante figurant dans un enregistrement « similaire », il est possible que certaines erreurs d'imputation s'y glissent. Cela est particulièrement grave lorsque les personnes non répondantes diffèrent des répondants sous certains aspects; en effet, cette procédure introduit un **biais dû à la non-réponse**.

Même lorsqu'une réponse est obtenue, il se peut qu'elle ne soit pas tout à fait exacte. Il est possible que le répondant ait mal interprété la question ou ait donné une réponse au jugé, surtout lorsqu'il répondait pour le compte d'un autre membre du ménage, qui était peut-être absent. Il est aussi possible que le répondant ait inscrit sa réponse au mauvais endroit sur le questionnaire. Ces erreurs sont désignées sous le nom d'**erreurs de réponse**. Bien que ces erreurs surviennent d'ordinaire parce que les répondants ont fourni des renseignements inexacts, elles peuvent aussi résulter d'erreurs commises par les recenseurs qui ont rempli certaines parties du questionnaire, comme le type de construction résidentielle, ou qui ont effectué le suivi pour obtenir une réponse manquante.

Certaines questions du recensement nécessitent une réponse en toutes lettres. Pendant le traitement, on attribue un code numérique à ces réponses. Il est possible que des **erreurs de codage** se produisent lorsque la réponse écrite est ambiguë, incomplète ou difficile à lire, ou lorsque la liste des codes est longue (p. ex., principal domaine d'études, lieu de travail). L'étape formelle du contrôle qualitatif (CQ) permet de cerner et de rectifier les erreurs de codage et d'en réduire le nombre. Un échantillon continu des réponses est codé indépendamment une deuxième fois. La résolution des incohérences entre les premier et deuxième codages détermine la nécessité, s'il y a lieu, de coder de nouveau l'unité de travail. Les tâches de codage du recensement sont maintenant automatisées, ce qui a pour conséquence de réduire le nombre d'erreurs de codage.

Les renseignements figurant dans les questionnaires sont balayés et saisis dans un fichier informatique. Afin de s'assurer que le nombre d'**erreurs de saisies de données** se retrouve en deçà des seuils admissibles, un échantillon des champs est prélevé et ressaisi. Une analyse des deux saisies est faite. Les résultats insatisfaisants sont identifiés, corrigés et des mesures correctives sont faites au système afin de minimiser leur occurrence.

Une fois saisies, les données font l'objet de vérifications qui consistent à les soumettre à une série de contrôles informatiques visant à relever les réponses manquantes ou incohérentes. À l'étape de l'imputation, on substitue à ces dernières des réponses déduites à partir des autres données de l'enregistrement ou des réponses tirées d'un enregistrement donneur similaire. L'imputation permet d'obtenir une base de données complète dont les données correspondent aux chiffres du recensement et facilitent les analyses multidimensionnelles. Même si des erreurs peuvent être introduites à l'**étape de l'imputation**, les méthodes utilisées ont fait l'objet de tests rigoureux visant à réduire au minimum les erreurs systématiques.

Diverses études sont réalisées afin d'évaluer la qualité des réponses obtenues dans le cadre du Recensement de 2006. Ainsi, on a calculé les taux de non-réponse et les taux de rejet au contrôle pour chaque question. Ces taux peuvent permettre de déterminer le potentiel d'erreurs dues à la non-réponse et d'autres types d'erreurs. De même, les totalisations établies à partir des données du Recensement de 2006 ont été ou seront comparées avec les estimations correspondantes obtenues à partir des données des recensements précédents, des enquêtes-échantillon (comme l'Enquête sur la population active) et de divers dossiers administratifs (comme les registres des naissances et le cadastre municipal). Ces comparaisons peuvent permettre de cerner les problèmes de qualité éventuels ou, à tout le moins, de relever les divergences entre les sources.

Outre ces comparaisons entre données agrégées, certaines études de couplage de microdonnées sont actuellement menées afin de comparer les réponses de certains particuliers obtenues au recensement à celles d'une autre source de renseignements. Pour un certain nombre de caractéristiques « stables » (comme l'âge, le sexe, la langue maternelle et le lieu de naissance), on compare les réponses obtenues auprès d'un échantillon de personnes à l'occasion du Recensement de 2006 aux réponses obtenues des mêmes personnes à l'occasion du Recensement de 2001.

Erreurs d'échantillonnage

Les estimations obtenues en pondérant les réponses recueillies auprès d'un échantillon sont susceptibles d'être entachées d'erreurs en raison de la répartition des caractéristiques au sein de l'échantillon, qui n'est généralement pas identique à la répartition correspondante au sein de la population dans laquelle l'échantillon a été prélevé.

L'erreur susceptible d'être introduite par l'échantillonnage variera en fonction de la rareté relative de la caractéristique étudiée au sein de la population. Lorsque la valeur contenue dans la case est élevée, cette erreur sera relativement faible proportionnellement à cette valeur. Lorsque la valeur contenue dans la case est faible, cette erreur sera relativement importante proportionnellement à cette valeur.

L'erreur susceptible d'être introduite par l'échantillonnage est d'ordinaire exprimée sous forme d'« erreur type ». Il s'agit de la racine carrée de la moyenne, calculée pour l'ensemble des échantillons de même taille prélevés selon le même plan d'échantillonnage, des carrés de l'écart de l'estimation obtenue à partir de l'échantillon par rapport à la valeur pour l'ensemble de la population.

Le tableau ci-dessous fournit des mesures approximatives de l'erreur type due à l'échantillonnage des données obtenues à partir du questionnaire complet (2B). Ces mesures sont données uniquement à titre indicatif.

Tableau explicatif 1 Erreur type approximative due à l'échantillonnage pour les données-échantillon du Recensement de 2006

Valeur contenue dans la case	Erreur type approximative
50 ou moins	15
100	20
200	30
500	45
1 000	65
2 000	90
5 000	140
10 000	200
20 000	280
50 000	450
100 000	630
500 000	1 400

Les utilisateurs souhaitant déterminer l'erreur d'échantillonnage approximative pour une case de données dont la valeur a été obtenue à partir de l'échantillon de 20 % doivent choisir l'erreur type correspondant à l'entrée dans la colonne « Valeur contenue dans la case » ci-dessus qui se rapproche le plus du chiffre de personnes, de ménages ou de familles qui figure dans la case de données de la totalisation en cause. En utilisant la valeur ainsi obtenue pour l'erreur type, l'utilisateur peut, en général et à juste titre, être certain que la valeur réelle pour la population dénombrée (ne tenant pas compte des formes d'erreurs autres que l'erreur d'échantillonnage) ne s'écarte pas de la valeur contenue dans la case dans une proportion supérieure ou inférieure à trois fois l'erreur type (p. ex., si la valeur contenue dans la case est 1 000, la fourchette à l'intérieur de laquelle se situe la valeur réelle serait de 1 000 ± [3 x 65] ou de 1 000 ± 195).

Les erreurs types données dans le tableau ci-dessus ne s'appliquent pas aux totaux de population, de logements, de ménages ou de familles pour les régions géographiques en discussion (voir Échantillonnage et pondération ci-dessous). On peut déterminer l'effet de l'échantillonnage pour ces valeurs en les comparant à celles des produits correspondants contenant des données intégrales.

Il est à noter que l'effet du plan d'échantillonnage et de la méthode de pondération utilisés dans le cadre du Recensement de 2006 variera d'une caractéristique à l'autre et d'une région géographique à l'autre. Il est donc possible que les valeurs de l'erreur type données dans le tableau ci-dessus sous-estiment ou surestiment l'erreur attribuable à l'échantillonnage.

Échantillonnage et pondération

Les données du Recensement de 2006 sont soit des données intégrales (c'est-à-dire recueillies auprès de l'ensemble des ménages), soit des données-échantillon que l'on a pondérées pour obtenir des estimations pour l'ensemble de la population.

Les données obtenues à partir du questionnaire complet (2B) étaient recueillies auprès d'un échantillon aléatoire de 20 % des ménages. Tous les en-têtes de tableaux sont annotés en conséquence. On notera que, dans les réserves indiennes et les régions éloignées, toutes les données ont été recueillies auprès de l'ensemble de la population.

Il est possible que, pour une région géographique donnée, le total ou le total partiel pondéré de la population, des ménages, des logements ou des familles diffère du chiffre correspondant figurant dans les publications contenant des données intégrales. Ces variations sont attribuables à l'échantillonnage et au fait que les données intégrales n'excluent pas les pensionnaires d'établissements institutionnels, contrairement aux données-échantillon.

Confidentialité et arrondissement aléatoire

Afin de protéger le caractère confidentiel des renseignements fournis, les chiffres indiqués aux tableaux ont fait l'objet d'un **arrondissement aléatoire** qui supprime toute possibilité d'associer des données statistiques à une personne facilement reconnaissable. Selon cette méthode, tous les chiffres, y compris les totaux et les marges, sont arrondis de façon aléatoire (vers le haut ou vers le bas) jusqu'à un multiple de « 5 » et, dans certains cas, de « 10 ». Cette technique assure une protection efficace contre la divulgation sans ajouter d'erreur significative dans les données du recensement. Les utilisateurs doivent savoir que les totaux et les marges sont arrondis séparément et qu'ils ne correspondent pas nécessairement à la somme des chiffres arrondis séparément dans les répartitions. De plus, il faut s'attendre à ce que les totaux et les autres chiffres correspondants dans diverses totalisations du recensement présentent quelques légères différences. De même, la somme des pourcentages, qui sont calculés à partir de chiffres arrondis, ne correspond pas forcément à 100 %. Les statistiques d'ordre (médiane, quartiles, percentiles, etc.) ainsi que les mesures de dispersion comme l'erreur type sont calculées de la façon habituelle. Lorsqu'une statistique est définie comme le quotient de deux nombres (c'est le cas pour des moyennes, des pourcentages et des proportions), les deux nombres sont arrondis avant d'effectuer la division. S'il s'agit de revenu, de dépenses de propriété, de valeur du logement, d'heures travaillées, de semaines travaillées ou d'âge, la somme est définie comme le produit de la moyenne par la fréquence pondérée arrondie. Sinon, c'est la somme pondérée qui est arrondie. Il faut noter que la distorsion importante peut résulter de l'arrondissement aléatoire dans le cas des cases de faible valeur. Cette distorsion peut entraîner une perte de précision pour les cases de données renfermant des chiffres peu élevés. De plus, une statistique est supprimée si le nombre actuel d'enregistrements ayant servi au calcul est inférieur à 4 ou si la somme du poids de ces enregistrements est inférieure à 10. En outre, dans le cas de valeurs exprimées en dollars, la statistique est supprimée si l'étendue des valeurs est trop petite ou si toutes les valeurs sont inférieures, en valeur absolue, à un certain seuil. De plus, toujours dans le contexte des valeurs exprimées en dollars, la statistique est supprimée si une valeur exprimée en dollars est trop grande comparée aux autres.

Les utilisateurs devraient, lors de l'agrégation des données arrondies, être conscients de cette distorsion. Les erreurs dues à l'arrondissement ont tendance à s'annuler lorsque les chiffres contenus dans les cases sont agrégés de nouveau. Cependant, il est possible de réduire les distorsions en intégrant dans la mesure du possible les totaux partiels appropriés dans les totalisations.

Les utilisateurs désirant obtenir un maximum de précision peuvent aussi choisir de demander des totalisations personnalisées. Dans le cas de produits personnalisés, l'agrégation se fait à partir des enregistrements dans la base de données du recensement se rapportant aux particuliers. L'arrondissement aléatoire a lieu uniquement après que les cases de données ont été agrégées, ce qui réduit la distorsion au minimum.

Outre l'arrondissement aléatoire, on a adopté la technique de la **suppression des régions**, afin d'assurer encore mieux la confidentialité des réponses des particuliers.

Dans le cadre de la **suppression des régions**, toutes les données caractéristiques se rapportant aux régions géographiques dont la population est inférieure à une taille donnée sont supprimées. L'importance de la suppression est fonction des facteurs suivants :

- si les données sont totalisées à partir de la base de données intégrales, elles sont supprimées si la population totale de la région est inférieure à 40 personnes;

- si les données sont totalisées à partir de la base de données-échantillon, elles sont supprimées si la population totale de la région, à l'exclusion des pensionnaires d'un établissement institutionnel, est inférieure à 40 personnes, selon la base de données intégrales ou la base de données-échantillon.

Il y a quelques exceptions à ces règles :

- les données renfermant une répartition du revenu et les statistiques connexes sont supprimées si la population de la région, à l'exclusion des pensionnaires d'un établissement institutionnel, est inférieure à 250 personnes selon la base de données intégrales ou la base de données-échantillon, ou encore si le nombre de ménages privés est inférieur à 40, selon la base de données-échantillon;

- les données renfermant une répartition du lieu du travail et les statistiques connexes sont supprimées si le nombre de personnes occupées dans la région est inférieur à 40, selon la base de données-échantillon. Si ces données incluent, en plus, une répartition du revenu, le seuil est changé à 250 personnes, toujours selon la base de données-échantillon;

- les totalisations traitant à la fois du lieu de travail et du lieu de résidence ainsi que les statistiques connexes sont supprimées si le nombre de personnes occupées dans la région est inférieur à 40 selon la base de données-échantillon ou si la population totale de la région, à l'exclusion des pensionnaires d'un établissement institutionnel, selon la base de données intégrales ou la base de données-échantillon est inférieure à 40 personnes. Si ces totalisations incluent, en plus, une répartition du revenu, le seuil est changé à 250 personnes dans tous les cas et les totalisations sont supprimées si le nombre de ménages privés dans la région du lieu de résidence est inférieur à 40;

- si les données sont totalisées à partir de la base de données intégrales et se réfèrent aux codes postaux de six caractères ou encore à des regroupements d'îlots de diffusion ou de côtés d'îlots, elles sont supprimées si la population totale de la région est inférieure à 100 personnes;

- si les données sont totalisées à partir de la base de données-échantillon et se réfèrent aux codes postaux de six caractères ou encore à des regroupements d'îlots de diffusion ou de côtés d'îlots, elles sont supprimées si la population totale de la région, à l'exclusion des pensionnaires d'un établissement institutionnel, et selon la base de données intégrales ou la base de données-échantillon, est inférieure à 100 personnes;

- si les données se réfèrent à des regroupements d'îlots de diffusion ou de côtés d'îlots, et renferment le lieu de travail, elles sont supprimées si le nombre de personnes occupées dans la région est inférieur à 100 selon la base de données-échantillon;

- si les données se réfèrent à des regroupements d'îlots de diffusion ou de côtés d'îlots, et renferment, à la fois, le lieu de travail et le lieu de résidence, elles sont supprimées si le nombre total de personnes occupées dans la région est inférieur à 100 selon la base de données-échantillon ou si la population totale de la région, à l'exclusion des pensionnaires d'un établissement institutionnel, selon la base de données intégrales ou la base de données-échantillon, est inférieure à 100 personnes.

Dans tous les cas, les données supprimées sont incluses dans les totaux ou totaux partiels du niveau d'agrégation supérieur approprié.

La technique de suppression est appliquée à tous les produits renfermant des données infraprovinciales (c'est-à-dire la série des Profils, les tableaux croisés de base, les produits personnalisés et semi-personnalisés), qu'il s'agisse de données intégrales ou de données-échantillon.

Pour obtenir de plus amples renseignements sur la qualité des données du recensement, veuillez communiquer avec la Division des méthodes d'enquêtes sociales, Statistique Canada, Ottawa (Ontario), Canada K1A 0T6, ou en composant le 613-951-4783.

Notes spéciales

Âge à l'immigration

Il y a eu une légère surestimation de l'âge à l'immigration dans le cadre du Recensement de 2006. Pour de plus amples renseignements sur la variable Âge à l'immigration, veuillez consulter le *Guide de référence sur le lieu de naissance, le statut des générations, la citoyenneté et l'immigration, Recensement de 2006*, numéro 97-557-GWF2006003 au catalogue.

Chiffres de population

Les chiffres de population du Recensement de 2006 pour une région particulière représentent le nombre de Canadiens dont le domicile habituel est dans cette région, quel que soit l'endroit où ils se trouvent le jour du recensement. Sont également compris dans ces chiffres tous les Canadiens qui demeurent dans un logement de cette région le jour du recensement qui n'ont pas de domicile habituel ailleurs au Canada, de même que ceux qui sont considérés comme des « résidents non permanents » (voir les Notes spéciales). Dans la plupart des régions, la différence entre le nombre de résidents habituels et le nombre de résidents qui demeurent dans cette région le jour du recensement est minime. Toutefois, à certains endroits, notamment dans des régions touristiques ou de villégiature, ou dans celles où l'on trouve d'importants camps de travail, le nombre de personnes qui demeurent dans la région à n'importe quel moment pourrait être bien supérieur au nombre de résidents habituels dont il est ici fait mention. Les chiffres de population tiennent compte des Canadiens qui habitent dans d'autres pays, mais non pas des résidents étrangers qui habitent au Canada (la catégorie des « résidents étrangers » ne comprend pas les « résidents non permanents » [voir les Notes spéciales]). Compte tenu de ces divergences, les utilisateurs ne doivent pas déduire que les chiffres de population correspondent au nombre de personnes qui habitent dans les logements déclarés.

Colonnes vides dans le tableau de certaines caractéristiques des divisions de recensement et des subdivisions de recensement

Dans certains cas, le tableau contient des colonnes vides lorsqu'il ne reste aucune subdivision de recensement à présenter pour la province ou le territoire.

Comparabilité des données de 2006 sur le lieu de travail

Le travail à domicile peut être mesuré de différentes façons. Dans le cadre du recensement, la catégorie des personnes travaillant à domicile comprend les personnes qui résident et travaillent au même endroit, comme les agriculteurs, les télétravailleurs et les travailleurs d'un camp de chantier. Par ailleurs, selon les instructions données dans le Guide du Recensement de 2006, les personnes ayant travaillé à domicile une partie du temps et à l'adresse d'un employeur le reste du temps devaient indiquer qu'elles avaient travaillé à domicile si elles avaient travaillé la majeure partie du temps chez elles (par exemple trois jours sur cinq).

D'autres enquêtes de Statistique Canada, telles que l'Enquête sociale générale, l'Enquête sur la dynamique du travail et du revenu et l'Enquête sur le milieu de travail et les employés, recueillent également des données sur les personnes travaillant à domicile. Toutefois, les données de ces enquêtes ne sont pas directement comparables à celles du recensement, étant donné que dans le cadre des enquêtes, les répondants doivent indiquer s'ils font une partie ou la totalité de leur travail rémunéré à domicile, alors qu'au recensement, ils doivent indiquer où ils travaillent habituellement la plupart du temps. Par conséquent, les estimations du travail à domicile tirées du recensement sont inférieures à celles tirées des enquêtes.

La présentation de la question sur le lieu de travail est demeurée à peu près la même pour chaque recensement depuis 1971. Cependant, en 1996, la catégorie « Sans adresse de travail fixe » a remplacé la catégorie « Sans lieu habituel de travail ». En 1996, le questionnaire du recensement a été modifié par l'ajout d'une case à cocher pour la catégorie de réponse « Sans adresse de travail fixe ». Lors des recensements antérieurs, les répondants devaient inscrire « Sans lieu habituel de travail » dans les zones réservées à l'adresse. Il semble y avoir eu un sous-dénombrement des personnes sans lieu de travail fixe lors des recensements antérieurs.

Les annexions, les incorporations et les fusions de municipalités pourraient rendre difficile l'établissement de comparaisons entre des unités et des structures spatiales qui changent dans le temps.

Comparaison des estimations du revenu tirées du recensement avec des estimations établies à partir des comptes nationaux et de l'Enquête sur la dynamique du travail et du revenu

Les estimations du revenu agrégé en 2005 qui ont été tirées du recensement ont été comparées à des estimations semblables du revenu des particuliers établies à partir des comptes nationaux. Une fois que les estimations du revenu des particuliers ont été ajustées pour tenir compte des différences touchant les concepts et la couverture, on a observé que les estimations du revenu agrégé en 2005 qui sont tirées du recensement sont inférieures de 1,2 % à celles qui sont établies à partir des comptes nationaux. Comme par le passé, les estimations tirées du recensement soutiennent davantage la comparaison pour certaines composantes du revenu et pour certaines provinces que pour d'autres.

Dans le cas des salaires et traitements agrégés, qui constituent la plus grande composante du revenu, les estimations ont été légèrement supérieures (1,0 %) aux estimations des comptes nationaux. La différence a en partie été compensée par l'écart (-7,8 %) entre les estimations du recensement et les chiffres corrigés des comptes nationaux dans le cas du revenu agrégé provenant d'un travail autonome agricole et non agricole. Dans l'ensemble, les estimations des gains ou du revenu d'emploi agrégés étaient presque identiques (écart de 0,3 %).

Les estimations des prestations de la sécurité de la vieillesse et du supplément de revenu garanti ont été légèrement inférieures (-1,4 %) aux estimations corrigées des comptes nationaux, comme d'ailleurs celles des prestations du Régime de pensions du Canada/Régime des rentes du Québec (-0,9 %). Les prestations d'assurance-emploi déclarées au recensement ont été inférieures de 6,1 %. Les estimations agrégées des prestations pour enfants tirées du recensement ont été supérieures de 2,0 % aux estimations corrigées des comptes nationaux. Les estimations des autres transferts gouvernementaux tirées du recensement, qui incluent notamment les allocations sociales, les prestations provinciales de supplément du revenu aux personnes âgées, les pensions d'ancien combattant et les remboursements de la TPS/TVH/TVQ, sont plus faibles (-39,2 %) que les estimations tirées des comptes nationaux. Dans l'ensemble, les estimations du revenu agrégé tirées du recensement, qui proviennent de tous les transferts gouvernementaux, sont inférieures d'environ 12,0 %. Les estimations du revenu de placement agrégé en 2005 tirées du recensement sont légèrement plus faibles (-2,7 %) que l'estimation comparable des comptes nationaux. Il s'agit là d'une amélioration marquée par rapport aux comparaisons des recensements précédents.

Les statistiques du recensement sur le revenu ont également été comparées à des statistiques similaires tirées de l'Enquête sur la dynamique du travail et du revenu (EDTR), qui est tenue chaque année. Les estimations tirées de l'EDTR ont été ajustées pour tenir compte du sous-dénombrement de la population, alors que ce n'est pas le cas pour les estimations du recensement. Cet ajustement explique en partie pourquoi les estimations du recensement sont inférieures aux estimations de l'EDTR pour ce qui est du nombre de bénéficiaires d'un revenu (-2,1 %) et de bénéficiaires d'un revenu d'emploi (-1,4 %). Toutefois, parce que les montants moyens sont plus élevés, les estimations des gains agrégés tirées du recensement sont supérieures de 2,8 % à l'estimation de l'EDTR, alors que l'estimation du recensement pour le revenu total agrégé des particuliers dépasse de 2,3 % celle de l'EDTR. La plupart des écarts observés entre les provinces ont été jugés acceptables compte tenu des erreurs d'échantillonnage de l'enquête. Les taux de prévalence du faible revenu pour l'ensemble de la population du Canada (à l'exclusion des Territoires) ont été presque identiques dans les deux sources pour la mesure avant impôt (15,3 %), et seulement légèrement supérieurs après impôt (0,6 point de pourcentage) dans le recensement par rapport à l'EDTR.

Croissance de la population active pour les Territoires du Nord-Ouest

Il importe de faire preuve de circonspection lorsqu'on compare les chiffres de population des Territoires du Nord-Ouest du Recensement de 2006 avec ceux du Recensement de 2001. En effet, en 2001, le sous-dénombrement net pour les Territoires du Nord-Ouest a été estimé à 8,11 %, ce qui est beaucoup plus élevé que le taux national de 2,99 %, et représente presque le double du sous-dénombrement estimé en 1996. L'accroissement de la population active, des personnes occupées, des chômeurs et des inactifs entre 2001 et 2006 est probablement surévalué en raison de l'amélioration de la couverture dans les Territoires du Nord-Ouest en 2006.

Données historiques sur les gains et le revenu et valeurs aberrantes

Les modifications apportées à la méthodologie et aux modes de déclaration dans le cadre du Recensement de 2006 ont permis d'améliorer les données sur le revenu. Toutefois, ces changements ont également une incidence sur certaines comparaisons avec les données des recensements antérieurs et sur certaines données relatives aux montants les plus élevés au chapitre des gains et du revenu.

Les modifications aux méthodes de saisie et de traitement des données du Recensement de 2006 se rapportant au revenu et le recours aux données tirées des déclaration de revenus peuvent avoir une incidence sur l'analyse des tendances pour les gains des particuliers, notamment (mais aussi pour le revenu total).

On observe, en 2006, une déclaration plus importante de petits montants et une diminution de l'arrondissement des montants provenant maintenant des données fiscales. Pour établir des comparaisons d'un recensement à l'autre, les utilisateurs devraient examiner la population des personnes qui travaillent à temps plein toute l'année, car la présence accrue de petits montants tend à réduire la moyenne et la médiane lorsqu'on prend en considération la population de l'ensemble des travailleurs.

Comme par le passé, dans l'analyse de petites populations, la présence d'une ou de plusieurs valeurs aberrantes peut avoir un effet sur la moyenne. Dans les régions faisant l'objet d'un échantillonnage, les estimations de la moyenne ne seront pas fiables, en raison de la variance attribuable à l'échantillonnage dans le cas de petites populations. L'erreur type de la moyenne devrait permettre de détecter de telles situations. Dans le cas de populations extrêmement petites, la présence de valeurs aberrantes peut aussi avoir une incidence sur la médiane. Les utilisateurs doivent faire preuve de prudence lorsqu'ils interprètent des données visant des sous-populations ayant des effectifs peu nombreux ou très peu nombreux.

Données sur la migration pour les petites régions géographiques

Les chiffres estimatifs sur la migration interne peuvent manquer d'exactitude pour les petites régions géographiques, pour les localités ayant le même nom que d'autres localités situées ailleurs et pour certaines subdivisions de recensement (SDR) dans les cas où des résidents, au lieu d'indiquer le nom de la composante SDR dans laquelle ils résidaient auparavant, ont fourni le nom de la région métropolitaine de recensement ou de l'agglomération de recensement.

Pour améliorer la qualité des données du Recensement de 2006, les codes postaux sont utilisés afin d'identifier la SDR précise de la résidence antérieure.

Données sur le revenu des personnes âgées vivant dans des logements collectifs

Dans le cadre du Recensement de 2006, les personnes qui vivent dans des établissements institutionnels ou des résidences, qui disposent d'un ensemble distinct et séparé de pièces d'habitation et qui sont capables de remplir le questionnaire du recensement ont reçu leur propre questionnaire à remplir. Dans les recensements antérieurs, les mesures du revenu ne tenaient pas compte de ces personnes. Lors du Recensement de 2006, le revenu de ces personnes a été fixé à zéro, ce qui s'est traduit par une légèrement surestimation des chiffres de la population âgée de 15 ans et plus, et tout particulièrement de la population âgée de 65 ans et plus, sans revenu (ou sans gains). Cette modification n'a pas d'incidence sur les chiffres et les statistiques sur le revenu s'appliquant aux familles ou aux personnes hors famille puisque les personnes vivant dans ces types de logements collectifs ont toujours été exclues de la population des familles et des personnes hors famille et continueront de l'être.

Grande catégorie professionnelle A - Gestion

Les données du recensement présentées pour les groupes de professions de la Grande catégorie professionnelle A - Gestion doivent être utilisées avec circonspection. Des erreurs de codage sont survenues au moment de déterminer le niveau de gestion, p. ex., cadre supérieur par opposition à cadre intermédiaire, ainsi que le champ de spécialisation ou d'activité, p. ex., directeur d'un programme de soins de santé dans un hôpital par opposition à gestionnaire de la fonction publique œuvrant dans le domaine de l'administration de politiques de la santé. Certaines professions non comprises dans la catégorie de la gestion y ont été assignées incorrectement en raison de la confusion entourant les titres tels que gestionnaire de programme et gestionnaire de projet. Les utilisateurs de données voudront peut-être utiliser les données relatives aux professions de la catégorie de la gestion conjointement avec d'autres variables telles que le Revenu, l'Âge ou la Scolarité.

Identité autochtone

Les utilisateurs doivent prendre note du fait que le dénombrement partiel de certaines réserves indiennes ou de certains établissements indiens a une plus grande incidence sur les chiffres de population associés à la présente variable que sur la plupart des autres chiffres. L'ampleur de cette incidence sera fonction de la région géographique à l'étude. En 2006, un total de 22 réserves indiennes et établissements indiens ont été partiellement dénombrés dans le contexte du recensement. Les chiffres du recensement ne tiennent pas compte des populations de ces 22 collectivités.

Incidence de la restructuration municipale

Il est possible que les limites et les noms des municipalités (subdivisions de recensement) soient modifiés d'un recensement à un autre par suite d'annexions, de dissolutions et d'incorporations. Afin d'atténuer l'impact de ces modifications sur la diffusion des données, l'équipe du Recensement de 2006 a produit un profil pour les subdivisions de recensement abolies.

Modifications aux chiffres de population et des logements

Suite à la diffusion des chiffres de population et des logements, des erreurs sont occasionnellement relevées dans les données. Il est impossible d'apporter des changements aux données du Recensement de 2006 présentées dans les tableaux. Toutefois, les utilisateurs peuvent obtenir les modifications aux chiffres de population et des logements touchant les subdivisions de recensement et d'autres niveaux géographiques en visitant la section consacrée au Recensement de 2006 dans le site Web de Statistique Canada à l'adresse suivante : www.statcan.gc.ca/recensement. Ils peuvent également communiquer avec le Centre de contact national de Statistique Canada le plus près au numéro 1-800-263-1136 ou par courriel à infostats@statcan.gc.ca.

Pensionnaires d'un établissement institutionnel

Dans le cadre du Recensement de 2006, les personnes vivant dans des foyers pour personnes âgées sont classées comme « ne vivant pas dans un établissement institutionnel ». Il s'agit d'un changement depuis le Recensement de 2001 alors qu'elles faisaient partie des pensionnaires d'un établissement institutionnel, plus précisément, « vivant dans un établissement institutionnel, pensionnaire d'un établissement de soins ou de détention ».

Période de référence du revenu

Le recensement canadien a eu lieu en 2006. Les données du recensement portant sur le revenu correspondent à l'année civile précédant l'année du recensement, c.-à-d. 2005.

Population de 15 ans et plus ayant travaillé depuis 2005

Ce sont les personnes ayant travaillé depuis le 1er janvier 2005, qu'elles aient fait partie ou non de la population active pendant la semaine de référence.

Résidents non permanents et l'univers du recensement

Au Recensement de 2006, les résidents non permanents sont les personnes d'un autre pays qui, au moment du recensement, étaient titulaires d'un permis de travail ou d'un permis d'études, ou qui revendiquaient le statut de réfugié, ainsi que les membres de leur famille vivant avec elles au Canada. Aux recensements de 1991, 1996 et 2001, les résidents non permanents incluaient aussi les titulaires d'un permis ministériel; ce permis a été supprimé par Citoyenneté et Immigration Canada avant le Recensement de 2006.

À partir de 1991, le Recensement de la population a énuméré les résidents permanents et les résidents non permanents du Canada. Avant 1991, seuls les résidents permanents du Canada étaient inclus dans le recensement (exception faite pour 1941). Les résidents non permanents étaient considérés comme des résidents étrangers et n'étaient pas dénombrés.

Le total des chiffres de population, de même que ceux de toutes les variables, sont touchés par ce changement apporté à l'univers du recensement. Les utilisateurs doivent faire preuve d'une très grande prudence lorsqu'ils comparent des données de 1991, de 1996, de 2001 ou de 2006 avec celles de recensements antérieurs pour des régions géographiques où la concentration de résidents non permanents est importante.

Présentement au Canada, les résidents non permanents forment un segment important de la population, en particulier dans plusieurs régions métropolitaines de recensement. Leur présence peut influer sur la demande de services gouvernementaux tels que les soins de santé, l'éducation, les programmes d'emploi et la formation linguistique. L'inclusion des résidents non permanents au recensement facilite la comparaison avec les statistiques provinciales et territoriales (mariages, divorces, naissances et décès) qui incluent cette population. En outre, l'inclusion des résidents non permanents permet au Canada de mieux refléter la recommandation de l'ONU, à savoir que les résidents à long terme (personnes demeurant dans un pays pour un an ou plus) soient dénombrés au recensement.

Même si tous les efforts possibles ont été déployés pour dénombrer les résidents non permanents, des facteurs tels que les problèmes linguistiques, la réticence à remplir un formulaire du gouvernement ou à comprendre l'importance de participer peuvent avoir influé sur le dénombrement de cette population.

Pour obtenir les chiffres des résidents non permanents pour 1991, 2001 et 2006, veuillez vous référer au tableau 97-557-XCB2006006 du Recensement de 2006.

Suppression des données sur la citoyenneté et l'immigration dans les réserves et les établissements indiens

Les questions sur la citoyenneté (question 10), le statut d'immigrant reçu (question 11) et l'année d'immigration (question 12) n'ont pas été posées aux personnes qui vivent dans des réserves indiennes et dans des établissements indiens et qui ont été dénombrées à l'aide du questionnaire 2D du Recensement de 2006. Par conséquent, les données sur la citoyenneté, le statut d'immigrant reçu et la période d'immigration ont été supprimées pour les réserves indiennes et les établissements indiens au niveau de la subdivision de recensement et aux niveaux géographiques inférieurs où la majorité de la population a été dénombrée à l'aide du questionnaire 2D. Toutefois, ces données sont comprises dans les totaux pour les plus grandes régions géographiques, telles que les divisions de recensement et les provinces.

Pour obtenir la liste complète des réserves indiennes et des établissements indiens pour lesquels les données portant sur la citoyenneté, le statut d'immigrant reçu et la période d'immigration ont été supprimées, veuillez communiquer avec le Centre de contact national de Statistique Canada au 1-800-263-1136.

Suppression des données sur le revenu

La suppression des données sur des régions consiste à éliminer les données relatives aux caractéristiques des populations dont la taille se situe en deçà d'un chiffre donné. Les données renfermant une répartition du revenu et les statistiques connexes sont supprimées si la population de la région, à l'exclusion des pensionnaires d'un établissement institutionnel, est inférieure à 250 personnes selon la base de données intégrales ou la base de données-échantillon, ou encore si le nombre de ménages privés est inférieur à 40, selon la base de données-échantillon.

Tableaux présentant des répartitions du revenu, du revenu après impôt et des gains

Les répartitions du revenu, du revenu après impôt et des gains ont été supprimées lorsque le nombre estimatif total d'unités (personnes, familles ou ménages) pendant l'année de référence est inférieur à 250. Toutes les données supprimées ainsi que les données connexes, c'est-à-dire les moyennes, les médianes et les erreurs types du revenu moyen, du revenu après impôt moyen ou des gains moyens, ont été remplacées par des zéros ou des signes conventionnels.

Dans tous les cas, les données supprimées sont comprises dans les totaux et les totaux partiels aux niveaux d'agrégation supérieurs appropriés.

Tableaux présentant le nombre et la médiane ou la moyenne du revenu, du revenu après impôt ou des gains

Les statistiques ont été supprimées si le nombre estimatif total de personnes (hommes, femmes ou les deux sexes) ayant touché un revenu, un revenu après impôt ou un revenu d'emploi au cours de l'année de référence est inférieur à 250 personnes. Tous les nombres supprimés ainsi que les moyennes et les médianes connexes ont été remplacés par des zéros ou des signes conventionnels.

Dans tous les cas, les données supprimées sont comprises dans les totaux et les totaux partiels aux niveaux d'agrégation supérieurs appropriés.

Taux de fréquence des unités à faible revenu (avant ou après impôt)

Les taux de fréquence des unités à faible revenu (avant ou après impôt) sont calculés à partir des chiffres arrondis des personnes ou des familles à faible revenu et du nombre total de personnes ou de familles. Ces chiffres ont été arrondis séparément des chiffres arrondis figurant dans le tableau; par conséquent, il peut y avoir une légère différence entre la fréquence indiquée et une fréquence calculée à partir des chiffres figurant dans le tableau. Les utilisateurs doivent faire preuve de circonspection lorsqu'ils interprètent les taux de fréquence des unités à faible revenu fondées sur des chiffres peu élevés.

Univers des logements

L'univers des logements a trait aux caractéristiques des logements au Canada. Les logements se distinguent des ménages. Les caractéristiques d'un logement sont les attributs physiques d'un ensemble de pièces d'habitation, alors que les caractéristiques d'un ménage ont trait à la personne ou au groupe de personnes (autres que des résidents temporaires ou étrangers) qui occupe un logement.

Valeur du logement

L'évaluation postcensitaire des données portant sur la valeur du logement a révélé que dans certaines petites communautés, certaines valeurs élevées du logement entraînent des écarts importants entre les valeurs moyennes et médianes du logement. Dans la plupart des cas, les quelques valeurs élevées du logement sont attribuables aux différentes caractéristiques des logements de la communauté. Cependant, dans certains cas, les valeurs élevées du logement pourraient être attribuables à une erreur de réponse, lorsque la valeur a été surdénombrée. En outre, dans certaines petites communautés, le taux de non-réponse élevé à la question sur la valeur du logement a entraîné l'estimation de certaines valeurs élevées du logement pendant le traitement des données. Les utilisateurs des données devraient tenir compte des valeurs moyennes et médianes du logement, ainsi que des caractéristiques des logements de la communauté lorsqu'ils examinent les données sur la valeur du logement dans les petites communautés.

Variations des gains au fil des ans

Grâce à l'amélioration des méthodes de collecte, les données du Recensement de 2006 portant sur le revenu et les gains sont plus complètes, plus précises et moins sujettes à l'arrondissement que celles des recensements antérieurs. Les petites sommes, qui par le passé, n'étaient pas toujours déclarées, sont maintenant plus susceptibles d'être saisies. Ces modifications se sont traduites, comparativement aux recensements antérieurs, par un nombre plus élevé de personnes gagnant un revenu et par des gains médians et moyens inférieurs. Les utilisateurs sont priés de faire preuve de prudence lorsqu'ils interprètent les variations, d'un recensement à l'autre, des statistiques et des chiffres de cellules particulières dans le cadre d'une répartition des gains. La comparabilité de ces données pose moins de problèmes lorsqu'il s'agit des gains des travailleurs ayant travaillé toute l'année à plein temps.

Yukon

Il est possible qu'après le recensement, des modifications soient apportées aux noms géographiques, ce qui pourrait avoir des répercussions sur certaines sections du site Web de Statistique Canada.

Depuis le 20 octobre 2008, le nom suivant a été modifié :

Territoire du Yukon **devient** Yukon.

Aucun changement n'a été apporté à l'abréviation (Yn). Les produits du Recensement de 2006 conserveront le nom de la région géographique qui était officiel au moment du recensement, soit le 16 mai 2006.

Annexe 1 Réserves indiennes et établissements indiens partiellement dénombrés, chiffres de population de 2001 et 1996

Province	Réserves indiennes et établissements indiens partiellement dénombrés, 2006	Population	
		2001	1996
Québec	Gesgapegiag (anciennement Gesgapegiag 2) (Avignon DR)	488	442
	Doncaster (anciennement Doncaster 17) (Les Laurentides DR)	¶	0
	Kanesatake (Deux-Montagnes DR)	¶	¶
	Kahnawake (anciennement Kahnawake 14) (Roussillon DR)	¶	¶
	Akwesasne (anciennement Akwesasne (Partie)) (Le Haut-Saint-Laurent DR)	¶	¶
	Lac-Rapide (La Vallée-de-la-Gatineau DR)	¶	228
	Wendake (Québec DR)	1 555	¶
Ontario	Fort Severn 89 (Kenora DR)	401	362
	Attawapiskat 91A (Kenora DR)	1 293	1 258
	Factory Island 1 (Cochrane DR)	1 430	1 286
	Bear Island 1 (Nipissing DR)	¶	153
	Tyendinaga Mohawk Territory (Hastings DR)	¶	¶
	Wahta Mohawk Territory (Muskoka DR)	¶	¶
	Six Nations (Part) 40 (Brant DR)	¶	¶
	Six Nations (Part) 40 (Haldimand-Norfolk DR)	¶	¶
	Oneida 41 (Middlesex DR)	¶	¶
	Akwesasne (Part) 59 (Stormont, Dundas and Glengarry DR)	¶	¶
Saskatchewan	Big Island Lake Cree Territory (anciennement Big Head 124) (Division No. 17 DR)	¶	¶
Alberta	Little Buffalo (Division No. 17 DR)	¶	¶
	Saddle Lake 125 (Division No. 12 DR)	¶	¶
	Tsuu T'ina Nation 145 (Sarcee 145) (Division No. 6 DR)	1 982	1 509
Colombie-Britannique	Esquimalt (Capital DR)	¶	¶

Terre-Neuve-et-Labrador

Division No. 1, Subd. V, SNO ♦♦♦◊◊◊A
Division No. 1, Subd. J, SNO
Division No. 1, Subd. K, SNO ♦♦♦◊◊◊
Division No. 1, Subd. D, SNO ♦♦♦◊◊◊
Division No. 2, Subd. G, SNO ♦♦♦
Division No. 2, Subd. J, SNO
Division No. 2, Subd. L, SNO ♦♦♦
Division No. 3, Subd. A, SNO
Division No. 3, Subd. B, SNO
Division No. 3, Subd. C, SNO ♦♦♦◊◊◊
Division No. 5, Subd. D, SNO ♦♦♦
Division No. 6, Subd. E, SNO ♦♦♦◊◊◊
Division No. 7, Subd. D, SNO ♦♦♦◊◊◊
Division No. 7, Subd. N, SNO ♦♦♦◊◊◊
Division No. 7, Subd. B, SNO ♦♦♦◊◊◊
Division No. 8, Subd. D, SNO
Tilt Cove, T
Sally's Cove, T ♦♦♦◊◊◊
Division No. 10, Subd. E, SNO
Division No. 11, Subd. C, SNO A
Division No. 11, Subd. E, SNO A

Île-du-Prince-Édouard

Morell 2, IRI ♦◊

Nouvelle-Écosse

Ponhook Lake 10, IRI ♦♦◊◊A
Wildcat 12, IRI
Bear River (Part) 6, IRI ♦♦♦◊◊◊
Bear River 6B, IRI ♦♦♦◊◊◊
Pennal 19, IRI ■■■A
New Ross 20, IRI ■■■A
Shubenacadie 13, IRI
Beaver Lake 17, IRI A
Sheet Harbour 36, IRI
Merigomish Harbour 31, IRI
Summerside 38, IRI

Nouveau-Brunswick

Alma, P ♦♦
Red Bank 7, IRI
Tabusintac 9, IRI ♦♦♦◊◊◊
St. Mary's 24, IRI
Woodstock 23, IRI ♦♦♦◊◊◊
Madawaska, P ♦♦♦◊◊◊

Québec

Mont-Alexandre, NO
Rivière-Saint-Jean, NO ♦♦♦■
Collines-du-Basque, NO
Coulée-des-Adolphe, NO
Rivière-Bonaventure, NO ♦♦♦◊◊
Gesgapegiag, IRI ¶
Rivière-Nouvelle, NO
Ruisseau-Ferguson, NO
Routhierville, NO ♦♦♦
Rivière-Vaseuse, NO
Rivière-Patapédia-Est, NO
Lac-Casault, NO ♦♦♦
Ruisseau-des-Mineurs, NO ♦♦♦
Lac-Alfred, NO
Lac-Matapédia, NO ♦◊◊◊
Rivière-Bonjour, NO ♦♦♦◊◊◊
Lac-des-Eaux-Mortes, NO ♦♦♦■◊◊◊
Lac-à-la-Croix, NO
Lac-Huron, NO ♦♦♦◊◊◊
Lac-Boisbouscache, NO
Whitworth, IRI
Cacouna, IRI
Picard, NO
Petit-Lac-Sainte-Anne, NO
Lac-Pikauba, NO ♦♦◊◊
Saint-Louis-de-Gonzague-du-Cap-Tourmente, PE
Sault-au-Cochon, NO
Lac-Jacques-Cartier, NO
Saint-Gabriel-de-Valcartier, MÉ ♦♦♦◊◊◊
Lac-Croche, NO
Wendake, IRI ¶
Lac-Blanc, NO ♦♦♦
Linton, NO ♦♦♦
Lac-Lapeyrère, NO
Lac-Masketsi, NO ♦♦♦
Lac-Normand, NO
Rivière-de-la-Savane, NO ♦♦
Lac-Boulé, NO
Lingwick, CT ♦♦♦■◊◊◊
Lac-Minaki, NO
Lac-Devenyns, NO ♦◊◊◊
Baie-de-la-Bouteille, NO ♦♦♦
Lac-Matawin, NO ♦♦◊◊
Lac-Legendre, NO
Lac-des-Dix-Milles, NO
Lac-Santé, NO
Baie-Obaoca, NO
Lac-Cabasta, NO
Baie-Atibenne, NO
Lac-du-Taureau, NO
L'Île-Dorval, V ♦♦♦A
Kahnawake, IRI ¶
Akwesasne, IRI ¶
Kanesatake, S-É ¶
Lac-Tremblant-Nord, MÉ ♦♦♦◊◊◊A
Doncaster, IRI ¶
Lac-de-la-Pomme, NO
Lac-Akonapwehikan, NO
Lac-Wagwabika, NO
Lac-Bazinet, NO
Lac-De La Bidière, NO
Lac-Oscar, NO
Lac-de-la-Maison-de-Pierre, NO
Baie-des-Chaloupes, NO
Lac-Douaire, NO
Lac-Ernest, NO
Lac-Marguerite, NO
Lac-Rapide, IRI ¶
Lac-Pythonga, NO ♦
Cascades-Malignes, NO
Lac-Lenôtre, NO
Lac-Moselle, NO
Dépôt-Échouani, NO
Lac-Nilgaut, NO ♦♦♦◊◊◊
Hunter's Point, S-É ♦♦♦◊◊◊
Laniel, NO ♦♦♦◊◊◊A
Les Lacs-du-Témiscamingue, NO ♦♦♦A
Lac-Duparquet, NO
Lac-Despinassy, NO ♦
Matchi-Manitou, NO
Lac-Metei, NO
Réservoir-Dozois, NO
Coucoucache, IRI
Lac-Ashuapmushuan, NO ♦♦♦
Rivière-Mistassini, NO ♦♦
Mont-Apica, NO
Lac-Moncouche, NO
Lac-Achouakan, NO
Belle-Rivière, NO
Lalemant, NO
Lac-Ministuk, NO
Mont-Valin, NO ♦♦♦
Lac-au-Brochet, NO
Rivière-aux-Outardes, NO ♦♦♦◊◊◊
Lac-John, IRI
Rivière-Nipissis, NO
Rivière-Mouchalagane, NO
Caniapiscau, NO
Lac-Juillet, NO
Lac-Vacher, NO
Petit-Mécatina, NO
Lac-Jérôme, NO
Waswanipi, VC
Mistissini, VC
Waskaganish, VC
Nemiscau, VC
Eastmain, VC
Wemindji, VC
Chisasibi, VC
Kawawachikamach, VK
Whapmagoostui, VC
Kuujjuarapik, TI A
Umiujaq, TI A
Inukjuak, TI
Akulivik, TI
Salluit, TI
Kangiqsujuaq, TI
Quaqtaq, TI
Kangirsuk, TI
Aupaluk, TI
Tasiujaq, TI
Kuujjuaq, TI
Kangiqsualujjuaq, TI
Rivière-Koksoak, NO ♦♦♦
Baie-d'Hudson, NO ♦♦♦

Ontario

Akwesasne (Part) 59, IRI ¶
Tyendinaga Mohawk Territory, IRI ¶
Hiawatha First Nation, IRI ♦♦♦◊◊◊
Chippewas of Georgina Island First Nation, IRI ♦♦♦◊◊◊
New Credit (Part) 40A, IRI
Six Nations (Part) 40, IRI ¶
Six Nations (Part) 40, IRI ¶
New Credit (Part) 40A, IRI ♦♦♦◊◊◊
Sarnia 45, IRI ♦♦♦◊◊◊
Oneida 41, IRI ¶
Christian Island 30A, IRI
Wahta Mohawk Territory, IRI ¶
Bear Island 1, IRI ¶
Nipissing, Unorganized, South Part, NO ♦♦♦■◊◊◊
Henvey Inlet 2, IRI

Ontario (suite)

Naiscoutaing 17A, IRI
Cockburn Island, TP ◆◆◆
Zhiibaahaasing 19 (Cockburn Island 19), IRI
Manitoulin, Unorganized, Mainland, NO ◆◆◆
Whitefish River (Part) 4, IRI
Chapleau 74A, IRI ◆◆◇◇
Mountbatten 76A, IRI
Matachewan, TP ◆◆◆◇◇◇
Timiskaming, Unorganized, East Part, NO ◆◆◆
Cochrane, Unorganized, South West Part, NO
Fort Albany (Part) 67, IRI ◆◆◆◇◇◇
Factory Island 1, IRI ¶◆◆◇◇
Moose Factory 68, IRI
Cochrane, Unorganized, South East Part, NO
Flying Post 73, IRI ◆◆◆◇◇◇
New Post 69, IRI
Moosonee, TV ◆◆◆■■◇◇◇
Missanabie 62, IRI
Algoma, Unorganized, South East Part, NO
Gull River 55, IRI ◆◆◆◇◇◇
Ojibway Nation of Saugeen (Savant Lake), IRI ◆◆◆◇◇◇
Seine River 22A2, IRI
Lac des Mille Lacs 22A1, IRI ◆◆◆◇◇◇
Sabaskong Bay (Part) 35C, IRI **A**
Big Island Mainland 93, IRI
Agency 1, IRI
Seine River 23B, IRI
Rainy Lake 17B, IRI
Long Sault 12, IRI ◆◆◇◇◇
Sabaskong Bay (Part) 35C, IRI **A**
Fort Albany (Part) 67, IRI
Attawapiskat 91A, IRI ¶◆◆◆◇◇◇
Northwest Angle 33B, IRI ◆◆◆◇◇◇
Lake Of The Woods 31G, IRI
Rat Portage 38A, IRI ◆◆◆■◇◇◇
Wunnumin 2, IRI
Wapekeka 1, IRI
Pikangikum 14, IRI ◆◆◆◇◇◇
Fort Severn 89, IRI ¶◆◆◆◇◇◇
Lansdowne House, S-É
Sachigo Lake 2, IRI
Wawakapewin (Long Dog Lake), IRI ◆◆◆◇◇◇
MacDowell Lake, S-É

Manitoba

Shoal Lake (Part) 40, IRI
Shoal Lake (Part) 39A, IRI **A**
Reed River 36A, IRI
Long Plain (Part) 6, IRI
Gambler 63 (Part), IRI **A**
Division No. 17, Unorganized, NO ◆◆◆◇◇◇
Division No. 18, Unorganized, West Part, NO
Fairford (Part) 50, IRI **A**
Chemawawin 3, IRI ◇
Division No. 20, Unorganized, South Part, NO ◆◆◆◇◇◇
Division No. 20, Unorganized, North Part, NO ◆
Opaskwayak Cree Nation 21B, IRI ◇
Opaskwayak Cree Nation 21C, IRI
Cross Lake 19B, IRI ■■
Cross Lake 19C, IRI ■■
Nelson House 170A, IRI
Nelson House 170B, IRI
Nelson House 170C, IRI
Gillam, S-É
Split Lake (Part) 171, IRI **A**
Highrock 199, IRI

Saskatchewan

Heward, VL ◆◆◇◇◇
Ocean Man 69A, IRI
Ocean Man 69B, IRI
Ocean Man 69C, IRI
Ocean Man 69E, IRI ◆◆◆◇◇◇
Ocean Man 69F, IRI
Ocean Man 69G, IRI ◆◆◇◇◇**A**
Ocean Man 69I, IRI **A**
Ocean Man 69H, IRI ◆◆◆◇◇◇**A**
Ocean Man 69D, IRI **A**
Tribune, VL
Lake Alma, VL ◆◇◇
Goodwater, VL
Osage, VL
Piapot Cree First Nation 75H, IRI
Wood Mountain, VL ◆
Meyronne, VL ◆◆
Wood Mountain 160, IRI ◆◆◇◇
Bracken, VL
Admiral, VL ◆◆
Carmichael, VL
Nekaneet Cree Nation, IRI ◆◆◆◇◇◇
West End, RV ◆◆◆◇◇◇
Atwater, VL
Melville Beach, RV ◆◆◆◇◇◇
Waldron, VL
Duff, VL ◇
Fenwood, VL ◆
Shesheep 74A, IRI ◆◆◆◇◇◇
Little Bone 74B, IRI ◆◆◇◇◇
Ochapowace 71-10, IRI
Ochapowace 71-54, IRI
Ochapowace 71-26, IRI
Ochapowace 71-70, IRI
Ochapowace 71-7, IRI
Ochapowace 71-18, IRI
Ochapowace 71-51, IRI
Ochapowace 71-44, IRI
Lumsden Beach, RV ◆◆◆◇◇◇
Penzance, VL
Grandview Beach, RV ◆◆◆◇◇◇
Sunset Cove, RV ◆◆◇◇◇
Pelican Pointe, RV ◆◆◆
Star Blanket 83C, IRI
Treaty Four Reserve Grounds 77, IRI
Shamrock, VL
Ernfold, VL ◆◆
Keeler, VL ◆◆◇◇◇
Coteau Beach, RV ◆◆◆
Golden Prairie, VL ◆◇
Shackleton, VL
Mendham, VL
Mantario, VL
Stornoway, VL
Keeseekoose 66A, IRI
Keeseekoose 66-CA-04, IRI
Keeseekoose 66-CA-05, IRI
Keeseekoose 66-CA-06, IRI
Keeseekoose 66-KE-04, IRI
Keeseekoose 66-KE-05, IRI
Chorney Beach, RV ◆◆■◇◇◇
Leslie Beach, RV ◆
Leslie, VL
Dafoe, VL ◆
Beardy's and Okemasis 96 and 97A, IRI
Muskowekwan 85-17, IRI
Muskowekwan 85-26, IRI ◆◆
Muskowekwan 85-33, IRI
Muskowekwan 85-28, IRI
Muskowekwan 85-29, IRI
Muskowekwan 85-23, IRI
Muskowekwan 85-12, IRI
Muskowekwan 85-24, IRI
Muskowekwan 85-22, IRI
Muskowekwan 85-27, IRI
Muskowekwan 85-10, IRI
Muskowekwan 85-1, IRI
Muskowekwan 85-8, IRI
Muskowekwan 85-15, IRI
Muskowekwan 85-2A, IRI
Muskowekwan 85-31, IRI
Fishing Lake 89A, IRI **A**
Etters Beach, RV ◆◆◆
Zelma, VL
Tessier, VL
Herschel, VL ◆◆◇◇
Springwater, VL ◇◇
Kinley, VL ◆
Sweet Grass 113-M16, IRI
Netherhill, VL ◆◆◇
Ruthilda, VL
Handel, VL ◆◇
Rockhaven, VL
Valparaiso, VL
Opaskwayak Cree Nation 27A (Carrot River), IRI **A**
Wakaw Lake, RV ◆◆◇◇◇
Opawakoscikan, IRI
One Arrow 95-1C, IRI
Beardy's and Okemasis 96 and 97B, IRI ◆◆◇◇
One Arrow 95-1D, IRI
One Arrow 95-1A, IRI
Ruddell, VL ◇◇
Krydor, VL ◆
Richard, VL ◆◆
Pebble Baye, RV ◆◆◆
Big Shell, RV ◆◆◆◇◇
Little Red River 106D, IRI
Saulteaux 159A, IRI ◆◆◆◇◇◇
Lucky Man, IRI ◆◆◇◇◇
Muskeg Lake 102B, IRI ◆◇◇◇
Pelican Lake 191B, IRI ◆◆◇◇◇
Muskeg Lake 102E, IRI
Muskeg Lake 102F, IRI
Muskeg Lake 102G, IRI
Muskeg Lake 102D, IRI ◇◇
Sweet Grass 113-L6, IRI
Pelican Lake 191A, IRI
Greig Lake, RV ◆◆
Thunderchild First Nation 115C, IRI
Makwa Lake 129, IRI
Big Island Lake Cree Territory, IRI ¶
Makwa Lake 129A, IRI

Saskatchewan (suite)

Makwa Lake 129C, IRI
Thunderchild First Nation 115D, IRI
Meadow Lake 105A, IRI
Onion Lake 119-1, IRI A
Min-A-He-Quo-Sis 116C, IRI
Timber Bay, NH ◆◆◆◊◊◊
Dore Lake, NH ◆◆
Missinipe, NH
St. George's Hill, NH
Stanley 157A, IRI
Île-à-la-Crosse 192E, IRI
Potato River 156A, IRI
Four Portages 157C, IRI
Dipper Rapids 192C, IRI
Clearwater River Dene Band 223, IRI
Primeau Lake 192F, IRI
Fond du Lac 229, IRI
Turnor Lake 194, IRI
Clearwater River Dene Band 221, IRI
Elak Dase 192A, IRI
Little Hills 158, IRI
Fond du Lac 232, IRI
Fond du Lac 231, IRI
Fond du Lac 233, IRI
Little Hills 158B, IRI ◊

Alberta

Blood 148A, IRI
Tsuu T'ina Nation 145 (Sarcee 145), IRI ¶
Gadsby, VL ◆
White Sands, SV ◆◆◆◊◊◊
Half Moon Bay, SV ◆
Sunbreaker Cove, SV ◆◆◆◊◊◊
Samson 137A, IRI ◆◊◊
Burnstick Lake, SV ◆◆◆◊◊◊
Improvement District No. 13, ID
Argentia Beach, SV ◆◆◆◊◊◊
Crystal Springs, SV ◆◆◆◊◊◊
Norris Beach, SV ◆◆◆◊◊◊
Sundance Beach, SV ◆◆◆◊◊◊
Itaska Beach, SV ◆◆◆
Betula Beach, SV ◆◆
Point Alison, SV
Lakeview, SV ◆◆◆◊◊
Kapasiwin, SV ◆◆◆■
Stony Plain 135, IRI ◆◆◆◊◊◊
Wabamun 133B, IRI A
Saddle Lake 125, IRI ¶
Heart Lake 167, IRI ◆◆◆◊◊◊
Nakamun Park, SV ◆◆◆◊◊◊
Castle Island, SV ◆◆◆◊◊◊
Birch Cove, SV ◆
Larkspur, SV ◆◆◆◊◊◊
West Baptiste, SV ◆◆◆◊◊◊
Improvement District No. 25, ID
Improvement District No. 12, ID ◆◆◊
Clearwater 175, IRI
Devil's Gate 220, IRI
Chipewyan 201, IRI
Chipewyan 201A, IRI
Chipewyan 201B, IRI
Chipewyan 201C, IRI
Chipewyan 201D, IRI
Chipewyan 201E, IRI
Chipewyan 201F, IRI
Chipewyan 201G, IRI
Old Fort 217, IRI
Allison Bay 219, IRI ◆◆◆◊◊◊
Sandy Point 221, IRI
Cornwall Lake 224, IRI
Collin Lake 223, IRI
Charles Lake 225, IRI
Fort McKay 174, IRI
Namur River 174A, IRI
Namur Lake 174B, IRI
Thebathi 196, IRI ◆◆◊◊◊A
Thabacha Náre 196A, IRI A
Clear Hills 152C, IRI
Kapawe'no First Nation (Pakashan 150D), IRI
Sawridge 150H, IRI
Kapawe'no First Nation (Freeman 150B), IRI ◆◆◆◊◊◊
Beaver Ranch 163, IRI ◊◊
Kapawe'no First Nation (Halcro 150C), IRI
Little Buffalo, S-É ¶
Carcajou 187, S-É
Desmarais, S-É ◆◆◆◊◊◊
Kapawe'no First Nation (Grouard 230), IRI
Sturgeon Lake 154A, IRI

Colombie-Britannique

Isidore's Ranch 4, IRI
Cassimayooks (Mayook) 5, IRI
Bummers Flat 6, IRI
Blind Creek 6, IRI ◆◊
Alexis 9, IRI
Ashnola 10, IRI ◆◆◆◊◊◊
Aywawwis 15, IRI
Boothroyd 5A, IRI
Boothroyd 8A (Part), IRI
Inkahtsaph 6, IRI ◆◆◆◊◊◊
Kopchitchin 2, IRI ◆◆◊◊
Puckatholetchin 11, IRI
Saddle Rock 9, IRI ◆
Lukseetsissum 9, IRI
Ruby Creek 2, IRI
Sho-ook 5, IRI
Skawahlook 1, IRI ◆◆◆◊◊◊
Speyum 3, IRI
Spuzzum 1, IRI ◆◊
Tuckkwiowhum 1, IRI ◆
Yale Town 1, IRI
Chaumox 11, IRI
Skwali 3, IRI
Squiaala 8, IRI
Yakweakwioose 12, IRI ◊
Scowlitz 1, IRI ◆◊◊◊
Tseatah 2, IRI ◊◊
Aitchelitch 9, IRI
Boston Bar 1A, IRI
Schelowat 1, IRI
Swahliseah 14, IRI
Stullawheets 8, IRI ◆◆◆◊◊◊
Douglas 8, IRI
Popkum 1, IRI ◆◆◆◊◊◊
Franks 10, IRI
Bucktum 4, IRI ◆◆◊◊◊
Tipella 7, IRI
Skwahla 2, IRI
Baptiste Smith 1A, IRI
Sachteen 2, IRI
Sachteen 2A, IRI
Samahquam 1, IRI
Kuthlalth 3, IRI
Albert Flat 5, IRI
Coquitlam 2, IRI ◊◊
Coquitlam 1, IRI ◆◊◊
Musqueam 4, IRI ◆
Katzie 2, IRI
Langley 5, IRI
Whonnock 1, IRI
Union Bay 4, IRI ◆◆◆◊◊◊
South Saanich 1, IRI ◆◆◆◊◊◊
Galiano Island 9, IRI
Mayne Island 6, IRI
Esquimalt, IRI ¶
Pacheena 1, IRI
Squaw-hay-one 11, IRI ◆◆◆◊◊◊
Claoose 4, IRI
Cowichan 9, IRI ◆◆◆◊◊◊
Kil-pah-las 3, IRI ◆◆◊
Kuper Island 7, IRI ◆◆◆◊◊◊
Lyacksun 3, IRI
Shingle Point 4, IRI
Cowichan Lake, IRI ◆◆◊◊◊
Portier Pass 5, IRI
Wyah 3, IRI
Est-Patrolas 4, IRI A
Tzart-Lam 5, IRI ◆A
Nanaimo River 2, IRI ◆◆◊◊
Nanaimo Town 1, IRI ◆◆◆◊◊◊
Qualicum, IRI ◆◆◆◊◊◊
Alberni 2, IRI ◆◆◆◊◊◊
Anacla 12, IRI ◆◆◆◊◊◊
Clakamucus 2, IRI
Elhlateese 2, IRI ◆◆◆◊◊◊
Hesquiat 1, IRI ◆◆◆◊◊◊
Numukamis 1, IRI
Macoah 1, IRI ◆◆◆◊◊◊
Openit 27, IRI
Sachsa 4, IRI ◆◊
Stuart Bay 6, IRI
Keeshan 9, IRI
Klehkoot 2, IRI
Tin Wis 11, IRI ◆◆◆◊◊◊A
Pentledge 2, IRI
Ahaminaquus 12, IRI
Chenahkint 12, IRI
Houpsitas 6, IRI ◆◆◆◊◊◊
Nuchatl 2, IRI
Nuchatl 1, IRI
Village Island 1, IRI
Yuquot 1, IRI
Aupe 6, IRI
Aupe 6A, IRI
Squirrel Cove 8, IRI ◆◊
Tatpo-oose 10, IRI
Matsayno 5, IRI
Saaiyouck 6, IRI
Oclucje 7, IRI ◆◆◆◊◊◊
Tsa Xana 18, IRI ◆◆◆◊◊◊
Harwood Island 2, IRI
Sechelt (Part), IGD

Colombie-Britannique (suite)

Chekwelp 26, IRI ◆◆◆◇◇◇
Chekwelp 26A, IRI
Schaltuuch 27, IRI
Kowtain 17, IRI ◇◇
Mount Currie 1, IRI ◆◆◆◇◇◇
Nequatque 1, IRI ◆◆◆◇◇◇
Yekwaupsum 18, IRI
Nequatque 3A, IRI ◆◆◆◇◇◇
Mount Currie 2, IRI ◆◆
Cayoosh Creek 1, IRI ◆◆◆◇◇◇
Fountain 3, IRI
Fountain 10, IRI
Fountain 11, IRI ◇
Fountain 12, IRI ◆
Fountain Creek 8, IRI ◇◇
McCartney's Flat 4, IRI ◆◆◆◇◇◇
Seton Lake 5, IRI ◆◆◆◇◇◇A
Necait 6, IRI ◆◇◇
Nesikep 6, IRI
Pashilqua 2, IRI ◆◆◆◇◇◇
Pavilion 1, IRI ◆◆◆◇◇◇
Seton Lake 5A, IRI
Slosh 1, IRI ◆◆◆◇◇◇
Towinock 2, IRI
Mission 5, IRI ◆◆◆◇◇◇
Mount Currie 8, IRI ◆◆◆◇◇◇
Slosh 1A, IRI
Nequatque 2, IRI ◆◆◆◇◇◇
Fountain 1B, IRI A
Douglas Lake 3, IRI ◆◆◆◇◇◇
Hamilton Creek 2, IRI ◆◆◇◇
Hamilton Creek 7, IRI
Nicola Lake 1, IRI ◆◆◆◇◇◇
Paul's Basin 2, IRI ◆◆◆◇◇◇
Zoht 4, IRI ◆
Halhalaeden 14A, IRI
Chuchhriaschin 5, IRI ◇
Skeetchestn, IRI ◆◆◆◇◇◇
Halhalaeden 14, IRI ◆◆◆◇◇◇
High Bar 1, IRI
Inkluckcheen 21, IRI ◆◆◆◇◇◇
Canoe Creek 2, IRI
Chuchhriaschin 5A, IRI
Kitzowit 20, IRI ◆◆◇◇
Skuppah 2A, IRI
Kanaka Bar 2, IRI ◆◆◇◇
Basque 18, IRI ◆◆
Klahkowit 5, IRI
Kleetlekut 22, IRI ◆◆◇◇
Kumcheen 1, IRI ◆◆◆◇◇◇
Leon Creek 2, IRI
Lytton 4A, IRI ◆◆◇
Lytton 4E, IRI
Lytton 9A, IRI ◆◆◆◇◇◇
Lytton 9B, IRI ◆◆◆◇◇◇
105 Mile Post 2, IRI ◆◆◆◇◇◇
Oregon Jack Creek 5, IRI
Spatsum 11, IRI
Nickel Palm 4, IRI ◇
Nickeyeah 25, IRI ◆◇
Nohomeen 23, IRI
Paska Island 3, IRI
Papyum 27, IRI
Papyum 27A, IRI
Pemynoos 9, IRI
Seah 5, IRI ◆◆◇
Kloklowuck 7, IRI
Siska Flat 5A, IRI
Siska Flat 5B, IRI
Siska Flat 8, IRI ◆◇◇
Skuppah 4, IRI
Skwayaynope 26, IRI ◆◇◇◇
Spences Bridge 4, IRI
Spintlum Flat 3, IRI
Staiyahanny 8, IRI
Nkaih 10, IRI
Spences Bridge 4C, IRI
Stryen 9, IRI ◆◆◆◇◇◇
Tsaukan 12, IRI ◆◆◆◇◇◇
Upper Nepa 6, IRI ◆◆◆◇◇◇
Yawaucht 11, IRI ◆
Zacht 5, IRI
Sahhaltkum 4, IRI ◆◆◆◇◇◇
Neskonlith 2, IRI ◆◆◆◇◇◇
Nekalliston 2, IRI ◆◆◆◇◇◇
Louis Creek 4, IRI ◆◆◆◇◇◇
Squaam 2, IRI ◆◆◆◇◇◇
Cameron Bar 13, IRI
Inkluckcheen 21B, IRI A
Shawniken 4B, IRI A
Nekliptum 1, IRI A
Boothroyd 8A (Part), IRI A
Harris 3, IRI ◆◆◆◇◇◇
Chum Creek 2, IRI ◆◆◆◇◇◇
Hustalen 1, IRI ◆◆◆◇◇◇
Scotch Creek 4, IRI ◆◆◆◇◇◇
Switsemalph 6, IRI ◆◆◆◇◇◇
Switsemalph 7, IRI ◆◆◆◇◇◇
Canim Lake 4, IRI
Deep Creek 2, IRI ◆◆◆◇◇◇
Quesnel 1, IRI ◆◆◆◇◇◇
Johny Sticks 2, IRI ◆◆◆◇◇◇
Williams Lake 1, IRI ◆◆◆◇◇◇
Canim Lake 2, IRI ◆◆◆◇◇◇
Alexandria 3A, IRI ◆◆◆◇◇◇
Alexandria 1, IRI ◆◆◆◇◇◇
Alexandria 3, IRI
Alexis Creek 14, IRI
Alexis Creek 16, IRI
Alexis Creek 24, IRI
Alexis Creek 25, IRI
Anahim's Meadow 2, IRI
Anahim's Meadow 2A, IRI
Andy Cahoose Meadow 16, IRI
Baezaeko River 25, IRI
Cahoose 8, IRI
Charley Boy's Meadow 3, IRI
Chilco Lake 1, IRI
Garden 2, IRI
Tanakut 4, IRI ◆◆◇◇◇
Garden 2A, IRI
Kluskus 1, IRI ◆◆◆◇◇◇
Louis Squinas Ranch 14, IRI
Coglistiko River 29, IRI
Baezaeko River 26, IRI
Puntzi Lake 2, IRI
Redstone Flat 1, IRI ◆◆◆◇◇◇
Stone 1, IRI ◆◆◆◇◇◇
Alexis Creek 17, IRI
Seymour Meadows 19, IRI
Agats Meadow 8, IRI
Thomas Squinas Ranch 2A, IRI ◆◆◇◇
Toby's Meadow 4, IRI
Alexis Creek 6, IRI
Alexis Creek 21, IRI
Baptiste Meadow 2, IRI
Toosey 1, IRI ◆◆◆◇◇◇
Towdystan Lake 3, IRI
Trout Lake Alec 16, IRI
Tsunnia Lake 5, IRI
Ulkatcho 13, IRI
Windy Mouth 7, IRI
Alexis Creek 34, IRI
Casimiel Meadows 15A, IRI
Cahoose 10, IRI
Blackwater Meadow 11, IRI
Cahoose 12, IRI
Betty Creek 18, IRI
Salmon River Meadow 7, IRI
Tzetzi Lake 11, IRI
Sundayman's Meadow 3, IRI
Tatelkus Lake 28, IRI
Euchinico Creek 17, IRI ◆◆◆◇◇◇
Kushya Creek 7, IRI
Sandy Harry 4, IRI
Alexandria 1A, IRI ◆◆◆◇◇◇
Fishtrap 19, IRI ◆◆◇◇
Swan Lake 3, IRI
Alkali Lake 4A, IRI ◇
Little Springs 8, IRI ◇
Little Springs 18, IRI ◆◆
Lezbye 6, IRI ◆◆◆◇◇◇A
Michel Gardens 36, IRI A
Baezaeko River 27, IRI A
Alert Bay 1, IRI ◆◆◆■◇◇◇
Alert Bay 1A, IRI ◆◆◆◇◇◇
Fort Rupert 1, IRI ◆◆◆
Quattishe 1, IRI
Dead Point 5, IRI
Gwayasdums 1, IRI ◆◆◆◇◇◇
Hopetown 10A, IRI
Karlukwees 1, IRI
Quaee 7, IRI ◆◆◆◇◇◇
Thomas Point 5, IRI
Apsagayu 1A, IRI
Compton Island 6, IRI
Mahmalillikullah 1, IRI
Glen-Gla-Ouch 5, IRI
Hope Island 1, IRI
Bella Coola 1, IRI ◆◆◆◇◇◇
Skeena-Queen Charlotte C, RDA ◆◆◇◇
Lax Kw'alaams 1, IRI ◆◆◆◇◇◇A
Kitimat-Stikine C (Part 2), RDA
Nisga'a, NL ◆◆◆◇◇◇
Kitimat-Stikine A, RDA ◆◆◆◇◇◇
Kitimat-Stikine D, RDA ◆◆◆◇◇◇
Kshish 4, IRI ◆◆◇◇
Bulkley River 19, IRI ◆
Telegraph Creek 6, IRI ◆◆◆◇◇◇
Telegraph Creek 6A, IRI ◇
Kluachon Lake 1, IRI
Gitzault 24, IRI
Aiyansh (Kitladamas) 1, NVL
Laxgalts'ap, NVL ◆◆◆◇◇◇

Annexe 2 Subdivisions de recensement supprimées, Recensement de 2006 (suite)

Colombie-Britannique (suite)

Kitselas 1, IRI ◆◆◆◇◇◇A
Ye Koo Che 3, IRI ◆◆◆◇◇◇
Sowchea 3, IRI ◆◆◆◇◇◇
Seaspunkut 4, IRI
Tsay Cho 4, IRI
Tacla Lake (Ferry Landing) 9, IRI
Laketown 3, IRI ◆◆◇◇
Dzitline Lee 9, IRI ◆
Kuz Che 5, IRI
Bihl' k'a 18, IRI
Omineca 1, IRI
Duncan Lake 2, IRI ◆◆◆◇◇◇
Francois Lake 7, IRI ◆◆
Skins Lake 16A, IRI ◆◆
Skins Lake 16B, IRI
Tatla West 11, IRI ◆◆◆◇◇◇
Uncha Lake 13A, IRI ◆◆◆◇
Jean Baptiste 28, IRI
Tatla't East 2, IRI
Isaac (Gale Lake) 8, IRI
Maxan Lake 4, IRI
Williams Prairie Meadow 1A, IRI ◆◆◆◇◇◇
North Tacla Lake 7A, IRI ◆
Bihlk'a 6, IRI
Poison Creek 17A, IRI ◆◆◆A
Tadinlay 15, IRI A
Nedoats 11, IRI ◆◆◆◇◇◇A
Babine Lake 21B, IRI A
Parsnip 5, IRI
Halfway River 168, IRI ◆◆◆◇◇◇
Ingenika Point, S-É
Good Hope Lake, S-É ◇
Tahltan 1, IRI
Liard River 3, IRI
Fontas 1, IRI
Kahntah 3, IRI
Prophet River 4, IRI ◆◆◆◇◇◇

Territoire du Yukon

Carcross 4, IRI ■
Lake Laberge 1, IRI
Klukshu, S-É
Kloo Lake, S-É
Moosehide Creek 2, IRI
Champagne Landing 10, S-É ◇
Swift River, SÉ ◆◆◇◇
Johnsons Crossing, SÉ ◆◇
Stewart Crossing, SÉ ◆◇
Keno Hill, SÉ ◆◆◇◇
Teslin, TL

Territoires du Nord-Ouest

Salt Plains 195, IRI
Reliance, SET ◆◆◆◇◇◇
Inuvik, Unorganized, NO ◆

Nunavut

Nanisivik, SET
Baffin, Unorganized, NO ◆◆◆◇◇◇
Keewatin, Unorganized, NO
Bathurst Inlet, SET
Umingmaktok, SET
Kitikmeot, Unorganized, NO ◆◆◆◇◇◇

Notes : Pour obtenir de plus amples renseignements sur les règles de suppression du recensement de 2006, se reporter à « Qualité des données » de la section « Documents de référence » de cette publication.
Pour les caractéristiques de la population des subdivisions de recensement supprimées, se reporter à la publication *Un aperçu national : chiffres de population et des logements, Recensement de 2006*, n° 92-200-XPB au catalogue.

Order Form
Statistics Canada

To order

Mail:
Statistics Canada
Finance
R.H. Coats Bldg., 6-H
150 Tunney's Pasture Driveway
Ottawa, Ontario
K1A 0T6

(Please print)

Phone: 1-800-267-6677

Fax: 1-877-287-4369

E-mail: infostats@statcan.gc.ca

Telecommunication device for the hearing impaired: 1-800-363-7629

Company

Department

Attention

Address

City　　Province

Postal code　　Telephone - -　　Fax - -

E-mail address

Your personal information is protected by the *Privacy Act*.**

Method of payment

(Check only one)

Please charge my: ❑ VISA ❑ MasterCard ❑ American Express

Card number

Expiry date

Cardholder *(please print)*

Signature

❑ **Payment enclosed $**

(Payable to the Receiver General for Canada)

Authorized signature

Catalogue number	Title	Date of issue(s) or indicate an "S" for subscription(s)	Price (all prices exclude sales tax)	*Shipping charges (applicable to shipments sent outside Canada)	Quantity	Total $

* Shipping charges: no shipping charges for delivery in Canada. For shipments to the United States, please add $6 per issue or item ordered. For shipments to other countries, please add $10 per issue or item ordered. Annual frequency = 1. Quarterly frequency = 4. Monthly frequency = 12.	**Subtotal**	
Canadian clients add **either** 5% GST and applicable PST **or** HST (GST Registration No. R121491807).	**GST (5%)**	
Clients outside Canada pay in Canadian dollars drawn on a Canadian bank **or** pay in equivalent US dollars, converted at the prevailing daily exchange rate, drawn on a US bank.	**Applicable PST**	
Canadian federal government departments and agencies must include with all orders their IS organization code ________ IS reference code ________ and Department No. ________ .	**Applicable HST (N.S., N.B., N.L.)**	
**** Statistics Canada will only use your information to complete this sales transaction, deliver your product(s), announce product updates and administer your account. From time to time, we may also offer you other Statistics Canada products and services or ask you to participate in our market research. If you do not wish to be contacted again for** promotional purposes ❑ and /or market research ❑, check as appropriate and fax or mail this page to us, call **1-800-267-6677** or e-mail **infostats@statcan.gc.ca**.	**Grand total**	
	PF028135	

Thank you for your order

7-2900-C23: 2008-11-25

www.statcan.gc.ca

Bon de commande
Statistique Canada

Pour commander

Courrier :
Statistique Canada
Finances
Immeuble R.-H.-Coats, 6-H
150, promenade Tunney's Pasture
Ottawa (Ontario)
K1A 0T6

(Veuillez écrire en majuscules)

Téléphone : 1-800-267-6677

Télécopieur : 1-877-287-4369

Courriel : infostats@statcan.gc.ca

Appareils de télécommunications pour les malentendants : 1-800-363-7629

Compagnie

Service

À l'attention de

Adresse

Ville	Province

Code postal	Téléphone - -	Télécopieur - -

Courriel

Vos renseignements personnels sont protégés par la *Loi sur la protection des renseignements personnels* **.

Modalités de paiement

(Cochez une seule case)

Veuillez débiter mon compte : ❑ VISA ❑ MasterCard ❑ American Express

Nº de carte

Date d'expiration

Détenteur de carte *(en majuscules s.v.p.)*

Signature

❑ **Paiement inclus $**

(À l'ordre du Receveur général du Canada)

Signature de la personne autorisée

Numéro au catalogue	Titre	Édition(s) demandée(s) ou inscrire « A » pour les abonnements	Prix (les prix n'incluent pas la taxe de vente)	*Frais de port (pour les envois à l'extérieur du Canada)	Quantité	Total $

* Frais de port : aucuns frais pour les envois au Canada. Pour les envois à destination des États-Unis, veuillez ajouter 6 $ pour chaque numéro ou article commandé. Pour les envois à destination des autres pays, veuillez ajouter 10 $ pour chaque numéro ou article commandé. Fréquence des parutions : publication annuelle = 1; publication trimestrielle = 4; publication mensuelle = 12.	**Total**	
Les clients canadiens ajoutent **soit** la TPS de 5 % et la TVP en vigueur **ou** la TVH (TPS numéro R121491807).	**TPS (5 %)**	
Les clients de l'étranger paient en dollars canadiens tirés sur une banque canadienne **ou** en dollars US tirés sur une banque américaine selon le taux de change quotidien en vigueur.	**TVP en vigueur**	
Les ministères et les organismes du gouvernement fédéral canadien doivent indiquer sur toutes les commandes leur code d'organisme RI ___________ ,leur code de référence RI ___________ et leur no. de ministère ___________.	**TVH en vigueur (N.-É., N.-B., T.-N.-L.)**	
**** Statistique Canada utilisera les renseignements qui vous concernent seulement pour effectuer la présente transaction, livrer votre (vos) produit(s), annoncer les mises à jour de ce(s) produit(s) et gérer votre compte. Nous pourrions de temps à autre vous informer au sujet d'autres produits et services de Statistique Canada ou vous demander de participer à nos études de marché. Si vous ne voulez pas qu'on communique avec vous de nouveau pour** des promotions ❑ ou des études de marché ❑, cochez la case correspondante et faites-nous parvenir cette page par télécopieur ou par la poste, téléphonez-nous au **1-800-267-6677** ou envoyez un courriel à **infostats@statcan.gc.ca**.	**Total général**	
	PF028135	

Merci de votre commande

7-2900-C23: 2008-11-25

www.statcan.gc.ca

Statistique Canada	Statistics Canada

Canada